Your guide to touring in France

Touring France is your essential companion to independent touring in a caravan, motorhome or tent. This comprehensive handbook contains everything you need to know before you go, while you're away and for your return to the UK.

The guide includes over 2000 sites - all of which have been visited, recommended and reviewed by Caravan and Motorhome Club members and other users of this book. You can even contribute yourself by reviewing the sites you visit.

Cap Ferret, Arcachon Bay

£10.99

ISBN 978-0-9932781-9-8

Also available:

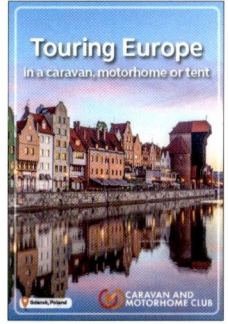

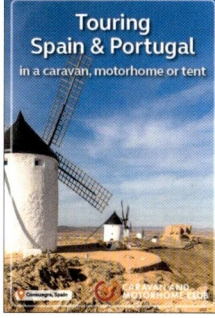

Discover our Worldwide Holidays for a once in a lifetime experience

11 NEW TOURS FOR 2019

Twelve Apostles, Australia

Experience unforgettable sights and create everlasting memories by choosing from our wide range of escorted and independent Worldwide Holidays. Covering USA, Canada, New Zealand and new for 2019 Southern Africa and Australia.

Visit **camc.com/worldwide** for more information

Club members call: **01342 779 349**

Explanation of a Campsite Entry

The town under which the campsite is listed, as shown on the relevant Sites Location Map at the end of each country's site entry pages

Distance and direction of the site from the centre of the town the site is listed under in kilometres (or metres), together with site's aspect

Site Location Map grid reference

GPS co-ordinates – latitude and longitude

Campsite name

Campsite address, including postcode

Telephone and fax numbers including national code where applicable

Description of the campsite and its facilities

Comments and opinions of visitors to the site

Unspecified facilities for disabled guests

⊞ **ABBEVILLE** *3B3* (10km SW Rural) *50.08586, 1.71519* Camping Le Clos Cacheleux, Rue des Sources, Route de Bouillancourt, 80132 Miannay [03 22 19 17 47; fax 03 22 31 35 33; raphael@ camping-lecloscacheleux.fr;www.camping-lecloscacheleux.fr] Fr A28 exit junc 2 onto D925 sp Cambron. In 5km at Miannay turn S onto D86 sp Bouillancourt. Med, hdg/mkd pitch, pt sl pt shd; wc; chem disp; baby facs; fam bthrm; shwrs inc; el pnts (10A) inc; gas; lndtte; shop; tradsmn; rest & 1km; snacks; bar; BBQ (charcoal/gas); playgrnd; htd pool adj; games area; games rm; wifi; entmnt; TV rm; dogs €2.10; some Eng spkn; adv bkg; quiet; ccard acc; red low ssn; CKE/CCI. "Pleasant, peaceful, wooded site; lge pitches; charming, helpful owner; excel facs; gd walking, cycling; gd for dogs." ♦ € 31.55 2016*

Contact email address and website address

Directions to the campsite

Charge per night in high season for car, caravan + 2 adults (in local currency) as at year of last report

The year in which the site was last reported on by a visitor

Popular Abbreviations (for a full list see page 10)

Site Description
sm: max 50 pitches   med: 51–150 pitches   lge: 151–500 pitches   v lge: 501+ pitches
hdg: hedged   mkd: marked   sl: sloping site   pt sl: part sloping
terr: terraced   unshd: no shade   shd: plenty of shade   pt shd: part shaded
hdstg: some hard standing or gravel pitches

Popular Abbreviations for Site Facilities

Adv bkg:	advanced booking accepted	lndtte:	washing machine(s) with or without tumble dryers
CCI:	Camping Card International accepted	NH:	suitable as a night halt;
chem disp:	dedicated chemical toilet disposal facilities	quiet:	peaceful, tranquil site
		rest:	restaurant
chem disp (wc):	no dedicated point, disposal via wc	shwrs:	hot showers available at a fee
CL-type:	very small, privately-owned, informal and usually basic, farm or country site	shwrs inc:	cost included in the site fee
		tradsmn:	tradesmen call at the site, e.g. baker
El pnts:	mains electric hook-ups	SBS	Site Booking Reference - Ref for a site in the Caravan Club's network i.e. bookable through the Club.
Eng spkn:	English spoken		
entmnt:	entertainment (facilities or organised)	ssn	season

Popular Generic Abbreviations

Adj: adjacent, nearby; app: approach, on approaching; arr: arrival, arriving; bef: before; bet: between; c'van: caravan; ccard acc: Credit and/or debit cards accepted; CChq acc: Camping cheques accepted; clsd: closed; E: East; ent: entrance/entry to; excel: excellent; facs: facilities; foll: follow; fr: from; gd: good; inc: included/inclusive; L: left; M'van: motorhome/motorcaravan; narr: narrow; N: North; o'fits: outfits; R: right; rec: recommend/ed; red: reduced/reduction; rte: route; S: South; sp: sign post/signposted; strt: straight, straight ahead; sw: swimming; vg: very good; W: West

Cover from £60*

Red Pennant Overseas Holiday, Breakdown and Emergency Insurance

For you, your vehicle and your holiday

- ✓ Breakdown cover, personal travel cover or combined

- ✓ Cover for single-trips (up to 122 days), long stays (up to one year**) and annual multi-trip policies

- ✓ Friendly emergency services team

  Based at our Head Office, our multi-lingual team and ready to help when you need us.

- ✓ Holiday cancellation cover

  From the point you purchase Red Pennant personal travel cover.

For full details of cover offered, including limitations and exclusions that apply, a sample of the policy wording is available upon request.

Call 01342 336 633 or visit camc.com/insurance/redpennant

Terms and conditions:
*Price is based on two travellers under the age of 50 on a 5 day single trip policy with motoring and personal cover. Additional premiums may apply on larger and/or vehicles over 15 years old.
** Age limits apply

Touring France

Also available:

© The Caravan Club Limited 2019 Published by The Caravan and Motorhome Club Limited
East Grinstead House, East Grinstead
West Sussex RH19 1UA

General Enquiries: 01342 326944
Travel Service Reservations: 01342 316101
Red Pennant Overseas Holiday Insurance: 01342 336633
Website: camc.com

Editor: Kate Walters
Publishing service provided by Fyooz Ltd
Printed by Stephens & George Ltd
Merthyr Tydfil

ISBN 978-0-9932781-9-8

Maps and distance charts generated from Collins Bartholomew Digital Database
Maps ©Collins Bartholomew Ltd 2019, reproduced by permission of HarperCollins Publishers.

Except as otherwise permitted under Copyright, Design and Patents Act, 1998, this publication may only be reproduced, stored or transmitted in any form, or by any means, with the prior permission in writing of the publisher.

The contents of this publication are believed to be correct at the time of printing. Nevertheless, the publisher and copyright owner(s) can accept no responsibility for errors or omissions, changes in the detail given, or for any expense or loss thereby caused.

DO YOU ? SANDAYA

CAMPING INSPIRED BY FREEDOM

SANDAYA
★★★★ & ★★★★★

YES I DO !

Because with Sandaya, you are free to choose from our 18 campsites, all either 4 or 5 star and set in the most beautiful regions of France or on the Costa Brava in Catalonia. You are free to sleep in places others only dream of, to get-up-and-go all day long or kick back and relax just the way you want to. And, above all, you have the freedom to be yourself.

Because camping inspired by freedom, that's Sandaya!

18 CAMPSITES IN FRANCE & SPAIN

SANDAYA.CO.UK

Welcome...

...to another year of touring across Europe!

Wherever and however you travel, people who camp (whether in a caravan, motorhome, campervan or tent) share a sense of adventure and freedom that you don't get from other types of holidays.

However as we enter 2019 we must be aware that there is a great period of change ahead for the UK which may affect the way we travel to the continent. While it is unlikely that Brexit will stop us from touring the EU, you might need to plan further ahead and do more research before you travel.

At the time of this book going to press much of what will change once the UK leaves the EU is unknown, and therefore it is very difficult to advise on issues such as border controls, customs, visa requirements and pet passports. Therefore you're strongly advised to check this information before you travel, especially if the UK has already left or will leave the EU while you're travelling. Check camc.com/overseas for our most up-to-date advice.

So as you start another year of touring adventures, I would like to thank you for continuing to buy and contribute to these guides. If you can, please spare five minutes to fill in one of the site report forms at the back of this book or visit camc.com/europereport to let us know what you think about the sites you've stayed on this year. Happy touring!

Kate Walters

Kate Walters, Editor

Contents

How To Use This Guide
The Handbook 6
Regional Introductions 6
Campsite Entries 6
Campsite Fees 7
Sites Maps & Satellite Navigation 7
Site Report Forms 8
Acknowledgements 9

Explanation of a Campsite Entry 10
Site description abbreviations 11

Planning your trip
Documents 14
Camping card schemes 14
Driving Licence 14
MOT Certificate 15
Passport 15
Pet Travel Scheme (PETS) 16
Travelling with Children 17
Vehicle Tax 17
Vehicle Registration Certificate 17
CRIS Document 17
Hired or borrowed vehicles 17
Visas 17

Insurance 18
Car, Motorhome and Caravan Insurance 18
European Accident Statement 18
Vehicles Left Behind Abroad 19
Legal Costs Abroad 19
Holiday Travel Insurance 19
Holiday Insurance for Pets 20
Home Insurance 20

Customs Regulations 21
Caravans and Vehicles 21
Currency 21
Customs Allowances 21
Medicines 23
Personal Possessions 23
Plants & Foods 23

Money 24
Local Currency 24
Foreign Currency Bank Accounts 24
Prepaid Travel Cards 25
Credit & Debit Cards 25
Emergency Cash 25

Ferries & the Channel Tunnel 26
Booking Your Ferry 26
On the Ferry 26
Channel Tunnel 27
Pets 27
Gas 27
Club Sites near Ports 28
Ferry Routes and Operators 29

Motoring advice
Motoring – Advice 30
Preparing for Your Journey 30
Weight Limits 30
Some Final Checks 30
Driving in France 31
Fuel 33
Low Emission Zones 33
Motorhomes Towing Cars 33
Motorways 33
Overtaking and Passing 34
Parking 34
Priority 35
Public Transport 35
Pedestrian Crossings 36
Roads 36
Road Signs and Markings 36
Recently Qualified Drivers 37
Roundabouts 37
Speed Limits 37
Traffic Jams 38
Traffic Lights 39
Violation of Traffic Regulations 39

Motoring – Equipment 40
Essential Equipment 40
Child Restraint Systems 40
Fire Extinguisher 40
Lights 40
Nationality Plate (GB/IRL) 41
Reflective Jackets 41
Route Planning 42
Satellite Navigation/GPS 42
Seat Belts 42
Spares 42
Towbar 43
Tyres 43
Winter Driving 44
Warning Triangles 44
Essential Equipment Table 44-45

Route Planning Maps 46-47

Mountain Passes & Tunnels 48
Advice for Drivers 48
Mountain Pass Information 49
Table and Map Information 49
Major Mountain Passes – Alpine 50
Major Road Tunnels – Alpine 53
Alpine Passes & Tunnels Maps 54
Major Mountain Passes - Pyrenees 58
Major Road Tunnels – Pyrenees 59
Pyrenean Passes & Tunnels Maps 60

During your stay

Keeping in Touch 62
Telephones and Calling 62
Accessing the Internet 63
Radio & Television 64

Medical Matters 66
European Health Insurance Card (EHIC) 66
Holiday Travel Insurance 67
First Aid 67
Accidents & Emergencies 67
Sun Protection 68
Tick-Bourne Encephalitis and Lyme Disease 68
Water & Food 69
Returning Home 69

Electricity & Gas 70
Electricity – General Advice 70
Electrical Connections – CEE17 70
Hooking up to the Mains 71
Reversed Polarity 72
Shaver Sockets 72
Gas – General Advice 73

Safety & Security 74
Beaches, Lakes & Rivers 74
Campsite Safety 74
On The Road 76
Overnight Stops 77
Personal Security 77
Money Security 77
Winter Sports 78
British Consular Services Abroad 78

Continental Campsites

Camping in France 80
Booking a Campsite 80
Overseas Travel Service 80
Overseas Site Night Vouchers 81
Caravan Storage Abroad 81
Facilities & Site Description 81
Finding a Campsite 82
Overnight Stops 82
Municipal Campsites 82
Naturist Campsites 82
Opening Dates 83
Pets on Campsites 83
Prices 84
Registering on Arrival 84
General Advice 85
Complaints 85
Campsite Groups 85

Introduction to France 86
Opening Hours 86
Touring in France 87
Channel Islands 87
Medical advice 88
Ferries 88
Cycling 88

Site Listings

France 89

Corsica 427
Ile de Re 428
Ile D'oleron 430
Andorra 432
Distance Chart 433
Site Location Maps 434
Map of Regions and Departments in France 444

Report forms   445

Subject Index   455

How to use this guide

The Handbook

This includes general information about touring in France and Andorra, such as legal requirements, advice and regulations. The Handbook chapters are at the front of the guide and are separated as follows:

Planning Your Trip	Information you'll need before you travel including information on documents and insurance, advice on money, customs regulations and planning your channel crossings.
Motoring Advice	Advice on motoring overseas, essential equipment and roads in Europe including mountain passes and tunnels.
During Your Stay	Information for while you're away including telephone, internet and TV advice, medical information and advice on staying safe.

Campsite Entries

After the country introduction you will find the campsite entries listed alphabetically under their nearest town or village. Where there are several campsites shown in and around the same town they will be listed in clockwise order from the north.

To find a campsite all you need to do is look for the town or village of where you would like to stay, or use the maps at the back of the book to find a town where sites are listed. Where there are no sites listed in a relatively large or popular town you may find a cross reference, directing you to the closest town which does have sites.

In order to provide you with the details of as many site as possible in Touring France we use abbreviations in the site entries.

For a full and detailed list of these abbreviations please see the following pages of this section.

We have also included some of the most regularly used abbreviations, as well as an explanation of a campsite entry, on the fold-out on the back cover.

Campsite Fees

Campsite entries show high season fees per night for an outfit plus two adults, as at the year of the last report. Prices given may not include electricity or showers, unless indicated. Outside of the main holiday season many sites offer discounts on the prices shown and some sites may also offer a reduction for longer stays.

Campsite fees may vary to the prices stated in the site entries, especially if the site has not been reported on for a few years. You are advised to always check fees when booking, or at least before pitching, as those shown in site entries should be used as a guide only.

Site Maps

Each town and village listed alphabetically in the site entry pages has a map grid reference number, e.g. 3B4. The map grid reference number is shown on each site entry.

The maps can be found at the end of the book. The reference number will show you where each town or village is located, and the site entry will tell you how far the site is from that town. Place names are shown on the maps in two colours:
Red where we list a site which is open all year (or for at least eleven months of the year)

Black where we only list seasonal sites which close in winter.

These maps are intended for general campsite location purposes only; a detailed road map or atlas is essential for route planning and touring.

Town names in capital letters (RED, BLACK or in ITALICS) correspond with towns listed on the Distance Chart.

The scale of the map means that it isn't possible to show every town or village where a campsite is listed, so some sites in small villages may be listed under a nearby larger town instead.

Satellite Navigation

Most campsite entries now show a GPS (sat nav) reference. There are several different formats of writing co-ordinates, and in this guide we use decimal degrees, for example 48.85661 (latitude north) and 2.35222 (longitude east).

Minus readings, shown as -1.23456, indicate that the longitude is west of the Greenwich meridian. This will only apply to sites in the west of France, most of Spain and all of Portugal as the majority of Europe is east of the Greenwich meridian.

Manufacturers of sat navs all use different formats of co-ordinates so you may need to convert the co-ordinates before using them with your device. There are plenty of online conversion tools which enable you to do this quickly and easily - just type 'co-ordinate converter' into your search engine.

Please be aware if you are using a sat nav device some routes may take you on roads that are narrow and/or are not suitable for caravans or large outfits.

The GPS co-ordinates given in this guide are provided by members and checked wherever possible, however we cannot guarantee their accuracy due to the rural nature of most of the sites. The Caravan and Motorhome Club cannot accept responsibility for any inaccuracies, errors or omissions or for their effects.

Site Report Forms

With the exception of campsites in The Club's Overseas Site Booking Service (SBS) network, The Caravan and Motorhome Club does not inspect sites listed in this guide. Virtually all of the sites listed in Touring France are from site reports submitted by users of these guides. You can use the forms at the back of the book or visit camc.com/europereport tell us about great sites you have found or update the details of sites already within the books.

Sites which are not reported on for five years are deleted from the guide, so even if you visit a site and find nothing different from the site listing we'd appreciate an update to tell us as much.

You will find site report forms towards the back of this guide which we hope you will complete and return to us. Use the abbreviated site report form if you are reporting no changes, or only minor changes, to a site entry. The full report form should be used for new sites or sites which have changed a lot since the last report.

You can complete both the full and abbreviated versions of the site report forms by visiting camc.com/europereport.

Please submit reports as soon as possible. Information received by mid August 2017 will be used wherever possible in the next edition of Touring France. Reports received after that date are still very welcome and will appear in the following edition. The editor is unable to respond individually to site reports submitted due to the large quantity that we receive.

Tips for Completing Site Reports

- If possible fill in a site report form while at the campsite. Once back at home it can be difficult to remember details of individual sites, especially if you visited several during your trip.
- When giving directions to a site, remember to include the direction of travel, e.g. 'from north on D137, turn left onto D794 signposted Combourg' or 'on N83 from Poligny turn right at petrol station in village'. Wherever possible give road numbers, junction numbers and/or kilometre post numbers, where you exit from motorways or main roads. It is also helpful to mention useful landmarks such as bridges, roundabouts, traffic lights or prominent buildings.

We very much appreciate the time and trouble you take submitting reports on campsites that you have visited; without your valuable contributions it would be impossible to update this guide.

Acknowledgements

Thanks go to the AIT/FIA Information Centre (OTA), the Alliance Internationale de Tourisme (AIT), the Fédération International de Camping et de Caravaning (FICC) and to the national clubs and tourist offices of those countries who have assisted with this publication.

Every effort is made to ensure that information provided in this publication is accurate. The Caravan and Motorhome Club Ltd has not checked these details by inspection or other investigation and cannot accept responsibility for the accuracy of these reports as provided by members and non-members, or for errors, omissions or their effects. In addition The Caravan and Motorhome Club Ltd cannot be held accountable for the quality, safety or operation of the sites concerned, or for the fact that conditions, facilities, management or prices may have changed since the last recorded visit. Any recommendations, additional comments or opinions have been contributed by people staying on the site and are not those of The Caravan and Motorhome Club.

The inclusion of advertisements or other inserted material does not imply any form of approval or recognition, nor can The Caravan and Motorhome Club Ltd undertake any responsibility for checking the accuracy of advertising material.

Explanation of a Campsite Entry

The town under which the campsite is listed, as shown on the relevant Sites Location Map at the end of each country's site entry pages

Distance and direction of the site from the centre of the town the site is listed under in kilometres (or metres), together with site's aspect

Site Location Map grid reference

Indicates that the site is open all year

Campsite name

Telephone and fax numbers including national code where applicable

Description of the campsite and its facilities

Unspecified facilities for disabled guests.

⊞ABBEVILLE *3B3* (10km SW Rural) *50.08586, 1.71519* Camping Le Clos Cacheleux, Rue des Sources, Route de Bouillancourt, 80132 Miannay [03 22 19 17 47; fax 03 22 31 35 33; raphael@camping-lecloscacheleux.fr; www.camping-lecloscacheleux.fr] Fr A28 exit junc 2 onto D925 sp Cambron. In 5km at Miannay turn S onto D86 sp Bouillancourt. Site thro vill of R opp sister site Camping Le Val de Trie which is sp fr A28. Med, hdg/mkd pitch, pt sl pt shd; wc; chem disp; baby facs; fam bthrm; shwrs inc; el pnts (10A) inc; gas; lndtte (inc dryer); shop; rest & 1km; snacks; bar; playgrnd; htd, covrd pool adj; jacuzzi; fishing pond; tennis 3km; games area; games rm; farm animals; wifi; dogs €2.10; adv bkg; quiet; ccard acc; red low ssn; CKE/CCI. "Pleasant, peaceful, wooded site; lge pitches; charming, helpful owner; excel facs; all services (inc shop, rest & pool) are on sister site 'Le Val de Trie' on opp side of rd, accessed via steep track 50m fr site ent; gd walking, cycling; gd for dogs." ♦ € 31.55 2011*

Contact email and website address

Directions to the campsite

Charge per night in high season for car, caravan + 2 adults as at year of last report

The year in which the site was last reported on by a visitor

GPS co-ordinates – latitude and longitude in decimal degrees. Minus figures indicate that the site is west of the Greenwich meridian

Comments and opinions of caravanners who have visited the site (within inverted commas)

Opening dates

ST PALAIS SUR MER *7B1* (2km E Coastal) *45.64396,-1.06425* Camping Le Val Vert, 108 Ave Frédéric Garnier,17640 Vaux-sur-Mer [05 46 38 25 51; fax 05 46 38 06 15;camping-val-vert@wanadoo.fr; www.val-vert.com] Fr Saintes on N150 dir Royan; join D25 dir St Palais-sur-Mer; turn L at rndabt sp Vaux-sur-Mer & Centre Hospitaliers; at traff lts ahead; at 2nd rndabt take 3rd exit & then turn immed R. Site on R in 500m. Med, hdg pitch; wc; chem disp; mv service pnt; baby facs; shwrs inc; el pnts (6A) €5.50 or (10A) €6.00; gas; lndtte; shop; rest, snacks; playgrnd; htd pool; fishing; cycle hire; tennis 400m; horseriding & golf 5km; games area; games rm; some wifi; entmnt; dogs €3.40; no c'vans/m'vans over 6.50m high ssn; adv bkg; ccard acc; red low ssn; "Well kept, family-run site; gd sized pitches; unisex san facs; no twinaxles; a stream runs alongside site; sh walk to pleasant vill; daily mkt in Royan; excel" ♦ ltd 6 Apr-30 Sep. € 31.30 (CChq acc) SBS - A25 2013*

Campsite address

The site accepts Camping Cheques, see the Continental Campsites chapter for details

Booking reference for a site the Club's Overseas Travel Service work with, i.e. bookable via The Club.

10 How to use this Guide

Site Description Abbreviations

Each site entry assumes the following unless stated otherwise:

Level ground, open grass pitches, drinking water on site, clean wc unless otherwise stated (own sanitation required if wc not listed), site is suitable for any length of stay within the dates shown.

aspect
    urban – within a city or town, or on its outskirts
    rural – within or on edge of a village or in open countryside
    coastal – within one kilometre of the coast

size of site
    sm – max 50 pitches
    med – 51 to 150 pitches
    lge – 151 to 500 pitches
    v lge – 501+ pitches

pitches
    hdg pitch – hedged pitches
    mkd pitch – marked or numbered pitches
    hdstg – some hard standing or gravel

levels
    sl – sloping site
    pt sl – sloping in parts
    terr – terraced site

shade
    shd – plenty of shade
    pt shd – part shaded
    unshd – no shade

Site Facilities

adv bkg
    Advance booking accepted;
    adv bkg rec – advance booking recommended

baby facs
    Nursing room/bathroom for babies/children

beach
    Beach for swimming nearby;
    1km – distance to beach
    sand beach – sandy beach
    shgl beach – shingle beach

bus/metro/tram
    Public transport within an easy walk of the site

chem disp
    Dedicated chemical toilet disposal facilities;
    chem disp (wc) – no dedicated point; disposal via wc only

CKE/CCI
    Camping Key Europe and/or Camping Card International accepted

CL-type
    Very small, privately-owned, informal and usually basic, farm or country site similar to those in the Caravan and Motorhome Club's network of Certificated Locations

dogs
    Dogs allowed on site with appropriate certification (a daily fee may be quoted and conditions may apply)

el pnts
    Mains electric hook-ups available for a fee;
    inc – cost included in site fee quoted
    10A – amperage provided
    conn fee – one-off charge for connection to metered electricity supply
    rev pol – reversed polarity may be present
    (see Electricity and Gas in the section DURING YOUR STAY)

Eng spkn
    English spoken by campsite reception staff

entmnt
    Entertainment facilities or organised entertainment for adults and/or children

fam bthrm
    Bathroom for use by families with small children

gas
    Supplies of bottled gas available on site or nearby

wifi
    Wireless local area network available

lndry
    Washing machine(s) with or without tumble dryers, sometimes other equipment available, eg ironing boards

Mairie
    Town hall (France); will usually make municipal campsite reservations

mv service pnt
    Special low level waste discharge point for motor caravans; fresh water tap and rinse facilities should also be available

NH
    Suitable as a night halt

noisy
    Noisy site with reasons given;
    quiet – peaceful, tranquil site

open 1 Apr-15 Oct
    Where no specific dates are given, opening dates are assumed to be inclusive, ie Apr-Oct – beginning April to end October
    (NB: opening dates may vary from those shown; check before travelling, particularly when travelling out of the main holiday season)

phone
    Public payphone on or adjacent to site

playgrnd
    Children's playground

pool
    Swimming pool (may be open high season only);
    htd – heated pool
    covrd – indoor pool or one with retractable cover

poss cr
    During high season site may be crowded or overcrowded and pitches cramped

red CCI/CCS
    Reduction in fees on production of a Camping Card International or Camping Card Scandinavia

rest
    Restaurant;
    bar – bar
    BBQ – barbecues allowed (may be restricted to a separate, designated area)
    cooking facs – communal kitchen area
    snacks – snack bar, cafeteria or takeaway

SBS
    Site Booking Service (pitch reservation can be made through the Club's Travel Service)

serviced pitch
    Electric hook-ups and mains water inlet and grey water waste outlet to pitch;
    all – to all pitches
    50% – percentage of pitches

shop(s)
    Shop on site;
    adj – shops next to site
    500m – nearest shops
    supmkt – supermarket
    hypmkt – hypermarket

shwrs
    Hot showers available for a fee;
    inc – cost included in site fee quoted

ssn
    Season;
    high ssn – peak holiday season
    low ssn – out of peak season

50% statics
    Percentage of static caravans/mobile homes/chalets/fixed tents/cabins or long term seasonal pitches on site, including those run by tour operators

sw
    Swimming nearby;
    1km – nearest swimming
    lake – in lake
    rv – in river

TV
    TV available for viewing by visitors (often in the bar);
    TV rm – separate TV room (often also a games room)
    cab/sat – cable or satellite connections to pitches

wc
    Clean flushing toilets on site;
    (cont) – continental type with floor-level hole
    htd – sanitary block centrally heated in winter
    own san – use of own sanitation facilities recommended

Other Abbreviations

AIT	Alliance Internationale de Tourisme
a'bahn	Autobahn
a'pista	Autopista
a'route	Autoroute
a'strada	Autostrada
adj	Adjacent, nearby
alt	Alternative
app	Approach, on approaching
arr	Arrival, arriving
avail	Available
Ave	Avenue
bdge	Bridge
bef	Before
bet	Between
Blvd	Boulevard
C	Century, eg 16thC
c'van	Caravan
CC	Caravan and Motorhome Club
ccard acc	Credit and/or debit cards accepted (check with site for specific details)
CChq acc	Camping Cheques accepted

cent	Centre or central	o'night	Overnight
clsd	Closed	o'skts	Outskirts
conn	Connection	PO	Post office
cont	Continue or continental (wc)	poss	Possible, possibly
conv	Convenient	pt	Part
covrd	Covered	R	Right
dep	Departure	rd	Road or street
diff	Difficult, with difficulty	rec	Recommend/ed
dir	Direction	recep	Reception
dist	Distance	red	Reduced, reduction (for)
dual c'way	Dual carriageway	reg	Regular
E	East	req	Required
ent	Entrance/entry to	RH	Right-hand
espec	Especially	rlwy	Railway line
ess	Essential	rm	Room
excel	Excellent	rndabt	Roundabout
facs	Facilities	rte	Route
FIA	Fédération Internationale de l'Automobile	RV	Recreational vehicle, ie large motor caravan
FICC	Fédération Internationale de Camping & de Caravaning	rv/rvside	River/riverside
		S	South
FFCC	Fédération Française de Camping et de Caravaning	san facs	Sanitary facilities ie wc, showers, etc
		snr citizens	Senior citizens
FKK/FNF	Naturist federation, ie naturist site	sep	Separate
foll	Follow	sh	Short
fr	From	sp	Sign post, signposted
g'ge	Garage	sq	Square
gd	Good	ssn	Season
grnd(s)	Ground(s)	stn	Station
hr(s)	Hour(s)	strt	Straight, straight ahead
immac	Immaculate	sw	Swimming
immed	Immediate(ly)	thro	Through
inc	Included/inclusive	TO	Tourist Office
indus est	Industrial estate	tour ops	Tour operators
INF	Naturist federation, ie naturist site	traff lts	Traffic lights
int'l	International	twd	Toward(s)
irreg	Irregular	unrel	Unreliable
junc	Junction	vg	Very good
km	Kilometre	vill	Village
L	Left	W	West
LH	Left-hand	w/end	Weekend
LS	Low season	x-ing	Crossing
ltd	Limited	x-rds	Cross roads
mkd	Marked		
mkt	Market		
mob	Mobile (phone)		
m'van	Motor caravan		
m'way	Motorway		
N	North		
narr	Narrow		
nr, nrby	Near, nearby		
opp	Opposite		
o'fits	Outfits		
o'look(ing)	Overlook(ing)		

Symbols Used

◆   Unspecified facilities for disabled guests check before arrival

⊞   Open all year

★   Last year site report received (see Campsite Entries in Introduction)

Documents

Camping Card Schemes

Camping Key Europe (CKE) is a useful touring companion. Not only does it serve as ID at campsites, meaning that you don't have to leave your passport at reception, it also entitles you to discounts at over 2200 sites.

CKE also offers third-party liability insurance for families including up to three children, which provides cover for loss or damage that occurs while on site. For more information on the scheme and all its benefits visit www.campingkey.com.

You can purchase the CKE from the Club by calling 01342 336633, or it is provided free for Red Pennant Overseas Holiday Insurance customers taking out 'Motoring' cover.

An alternative scheme is Camping Card International (CCI) - to find out more visit www.campingcardinternational.com.

If you are using a CKE or CCI card as ID at a site, make sure that you collect your card when checking out. Also check that you have been given your own card instead of someone else's.

Driving Licence

A full (not provisional), valid driving licence should be carried at all times when driving abroad. You must produce it when asked to do so by the police and other authorities, or you may be liable for an immediate fine and confiscation of your vehicle(s).

If your driving licence is due to expire while you are away it can be renewed up to three months before expiry - contact the DVLA if you need to renew more than three months ahead.

All EU countries recognise the photocard driving licence introduced in the UK in 1990, subject to the minimum age requirements (normally 18 years for a vehicle with a maximum weight of 3,500 kg carrying no more than 8 people).

Old-style green paper licences or Northern Irish licences issued before 1991 should be updated before travelling as they may not be recognised by local authorities.

Selected post offices and DVLA local offices offer a premium checking service for photocard applications but the service is not available for online applications.

MOT Certificate

Carry your vehicle's MOT certificate (if applicable) when driving on the Continent. You may need to show it to the authorities if your vehicle is involved in an accident, or in the event of random vehicle checks. If your MOT certificate is due to expire while you are away you should have the vehicle tested before you leave home.

Passport

In many EU countries everyone is required to carry photographic ID at all times. Enter next-of-kin details in the back of your passport and keep a separate photocopy. It's also a good idea to leave a photocopy of it with a relative or friend at home.

The following information applies to British passport holders only. For information on passports issued by other countries you should contact the local embassy.

Applying for a Passport

Each person travelling out of the UK (including babies) must hold a valid passport - it is no longer possible to include children on a parent's passport. A standard British passport is valid for ten years, or 5 years for under 16s.

All newly issued UK passports are now biometric, also known as e-passports, which contain a microchip with information which can be used to authenticate the holder's identity.

Full information and application forms are available from main post offices or from the Identity & Passport Service's website, www.gov.uk where you can complete an online application. Allow at least six weeks for first-time passport applications, for which you may need to attend an interview at your nearest Identity and Passport Service (IPS) regional office. Allow three weeks for a renewal application or replacement of a lost, stolen or damaged passport.

Post offices offer a 'Check & Send' service for passport applications which can prevent delays due to errors on your application form. To find your nearest 'Check & Send' post office call 0345 611 2970 or see www.postoffice.co.uk.

Passport Validity

Most countries in the EU only require your passport to be valid for the duration of your stay. However, in case your return home is delayed it is a good idea make sure you have six month's validity remaining. Any time left on a passport (up to a maximum of nine months) will be added to the validity of your new passport on renewal.

Schengen Agreement

The Schengen Agreement allows people and vehicles to pass freely without border checks from country to country within the Schengen area (a total of 26 countries). Where there are no longer any border checks you should still not attempt to cross land borders without a full, valid passport. It is likely that random identity checks will continue to be made for the foreseeable future in areas surrounding land borders. The United Kingdom and Republic of Ireland do not fully participate in the Schengen Agreement.

Regulations for Pets

Some campsites do not accept dogs at all and some have restrictions on the number and breed of dogs allowed. Visit camc.com/overseasadvice for more information and country specific advice.

In popular tourist areas local regulations may ban dogs from beaches during the summer months.

Pet Travel Scheme (PETS)

The Pet Travel Scheme (PETS) allows owners of dogs, cats and ferrets from qualifying European countries, to bring their pets into the UK (up to a limit of five per person) without quarantine. The animal must have an EU pet passport, be microchipped and be vaccinated against rabies. Dogs must also have been treated for tapeworm. It also allows pets to travel from the UK to other EU qualifying countries.

There are country specific regulations regarding certain breeds of dogs. You can't import breeds classed as dangerous dogs to many countries, and other breeds will require additional documentation. For more information or to find out which breeds are banned or restricted visit camc.com/pets or call us on 01342 336766.

Pets resident anywhere in the British Isles (excluding the Republic of Ireland) are able to travel freely within the British Isles and are not subject to PETS rules.

For details of how to obtain a Pet Passport visit www.defra.gov.uk of call 0370 241 1710.

Returning to the UK

On your return to the UK with your pet you will need to visit a vet between 24 and 120 hours prior to your return journey in order for your pet to be treated for tapeworm. The vet will need to sign your pet passport - ensure that they put the correct date against their signature or you may not fall within the correct time range for travel. Ask your campsite to recommend a local vet, or research vets near to the port you will be returning from before you travel.

Travelling with Children

Some countries require evidence of parental responsibility for people travelling alone with children, especially those who have a different surname to them (including lone parents and grandparent). The authorities may want to see a birth certificate, a letter of consent from the child's parent (or other parent if you are travelling alone with your own child) and some evidence as to your responsibility for the child.

For further information on exactly what will be required at immigration contact the Embassy or Consulate of the countries you intend to visit.

Vehicle Tax

While driving abroad you still need to have current UK vehicle tax. If your vehicle's tax is due to expire while you are abroad you may apply to re-license the vehicle at a post office, by post, or in person at a DVLA local office, up to two months in advance.

Since October 2014 the DVLA have no longer issued paper tax discs - EU Authorities are aware of this change.

Vehicle Registration Certificate (V5C)

You must always carry your Vehicle Registration Certificate (V5C) and MOT Certificate (if applicable) when taking your vehicle abroad. If yours has been lost, stolen or destroyed you should apply to a DVLA local office on form V62. Call DVLA Customer Enquiries on 0300 790 6802 for more information.

Caravan – Proof of Ownership (CRIS)

In Britain and Ireland, unlike most other European countries, caravans are not formally registered in the same way as cars. This may not be fully understood by police and other authorities on the Continent. You are strongly advised, therefore, to carry a copy of your Caravan Registration Identification Scheme (CRIS) document.

Hired or Borrowed Vehicles

If using a borrowed vehicle you must obtain a letter of authority to use the vehicle from the registered owner. You should also carry the Vehicle Registration Certificate (V5C).

In the case of hired or leased vehicles, including company cars, when the user does not normally possess the V5C, ask the company which owns the vehicle to supply a Vehicle On Hire Certificate, form VE103, which is the only legal substitute for a V5C. The BVRLA, the trade body for the vehicle rental and leasing sector, provide advice on hired or leased vehicles - see www.bvrla.co.uk or call them on 01494 434747 for more information.

If you are caught driving a hired vehicle abroad without this certificate you may be fined and/or the vehicle impounded.

Visas

British citizens holding a full UK passport do not require a visa for entry into any EU countries, although you may require a permit for stays of more than three months. Contact the relevant country's UK embassy before you travel for information.

British subjects, British overseas citizens, British dependent territories citizens and citizens of other countries may need visas that are not required by British citizens. Again check with the authorities of the country you are due to visit at their UK embassy or consulate. Citizens of other countries should apply to their own embassy, consulate or High Commission.

Insurance

Car, Motorhome and Caravan Insurance

It is important to make sure your outfit is covered whilst you are travelling abroad. Your car or motorhome insurance should cover you for driving in the EU, but check what you are covered for before you travel. If you are travelling outside the EU or associated countries you'll need to inform your insurer and may have to pay an additional premium.

Make sure your caravan insurance includes travel outside of the UK, speak to your provider to check this. You may need to notify them of your dates of travel and may be charged an extra premium dependent on your level of cover.

The Caravan and Motorhome Club's Car, Caravan Cover and Motorhome Insurance schemes extend to provide policy cover for travel within the EU free of charge, provided the total period of foreign travel in any one year does not exceed 270 days for Car and Motorhome Insurance and 182 for Caravan Insurance. It may be possible to extend this period, although a charge may apply.

Should you be delayed beyond these limits notify your broker or insurer immediately in order to maintain your cover until you can return to the UK.

If your outfit is damaged during ferry travel (including while loading or unloading) it must be reported to the carrier at the time of the incident. Most insurance policies will cover short sea crossings (up to 65 hours) but check with your insurer before travelling.

Visit camc.com/insurance or call 01342 336610 for full details of our Caravan Cover or for Car or Motorhome Insurance call 0345 504 0334.

European Accident Statement

Your car or motorhome insurer may provide you with a European Accident Statement form (EAS), or you may be given one if you are involved in an accident abroad. The EAS is a standard form, available in different languages, which gives all parties involved in an accident the opportunity to agree on the facts. Signing the form doesn't mean that you are accepting liability, just that you agree

with what has been stated on the form. Only sign an EAS if you are completely sure that you understand what has been written and always make sure that you take a copy of the completed EAS.

Vehicles Left Behind Abroad

If you are involved in an accident or breakdown abroad which prevents you taking your vehicle home, you must ensure that your normal insurance will cover your vehicle if left overseas while you return home. Also check if you're covered for the cost of recovering it to your home address.

In this event you should remove all items of baggage and personal belongings from your vehicles before leaving them unattended. If this isn't possible you should check with your insurer if extended cover can be provided. In all circumstances, you must remove any valuables and items liable for customs duty, including wine, beer, spirits and cigarettes.

Legal Costs Abroad

If an accident abroad leads to you being taken to court you may find yourself liable for legal costs – even if you are not found to be at fault. Most UK vehicle insurance policies include cover for legal costs or have the option to add cover for a small additional cost – check if you are covered before you travel.

Holiday Travel Insurance

A standard motor insurance policy won't cover you for all eventualities, for example vehicle breakdown, medical expenses or accommodation so it's important to also take out adequate travel insurance. Make sure that the travel insurance you take out is suitable for a caravan or motorhome holiday.

Remember to check exemptions and exclusions, especially those relating to pre-existing medical conditions or the use of alcohol. Be sure to declare any pre-existing medical conditions to your insurer.

The Club's Red Pennant Overseas Holiday Insurance is designed specifically for touring holidays and can cover both motoring and personal use. Depending on the level of cover chosen the policy will cover you for vehicle recovery and repair, holiday continuation, medical expenses and accommodation.

Visit camc.com/redpennant for full details or call us on 01342 336633.

Holiday Insurance for Pets

Taking your pet with you? Make sure they're covered too. Some holiday insurance policies, including The Club's Red Pennant, can be extended to cover pet expenses relating to an incident normally covered under the policy – such as pet repatriation in the event that your vehicle is written off.

However in order to provide cover for pet injury or illness you will need a separate pet insurance policy which covers your pet while out of the UK. For details of The Club's Pet Insurance scheme visit camc.com/petins or call 0345 504 0336.

Home Insurance

Your home insurer may require advance notification if you are leaving your home unoccupied for 30 days or more. There may be specific requirements, such as turning off mains services (except electricity), draining water down and having somebody check your home periodically. Read your policy documents or speak to your provider.

The Club's Home Insurance policy provides full cover for up to 90 days when you are away from home (for instance when touring) and requires only common sense precautions for longer periods of unoccupancy. See camc.com/homeins or call 0345 504 0335 for details.

Personal Belongings

The majority of travellers are able to cover their valuables such as jewellery, watches, cameras, laptops, and bikes under a home insurance policy. This includes the Club's Home Insurance scheme.

Specialist gadget insurance is now commonly available and can provide valuable benefits if you are taking smart phones, tablets, laptops or other gadets on holiday with you. The Club offers a Gadget Insurance policy - visit camc.com/gadget or call 01342 779413 to find out more.

Customs Regulations

Caravans and Vehicles

A caravan, motorhome or trailer tent imported into France from an EU country can stay there indefinitely, although you must have a purchase invoice showing that tax (VAT) has been paid in the country of purchase.

Although a permit is not required for vehicles being imported on a permanent basis, they must be covered by an EU certificate of conformity. This can be issued by the manufacturer, their representative in France or by the "Direction Régionale de l'Environnement, de l'Aménagement et du Logement" (DREAL). Vehicles that do not conform to EU standards, and vehicles over 4 years old, must be presented to the DREAL for an inspection.

Borrowed Vehicles

If you are borrowing a vehicle from a friend or relative, or loaning yours to someone, you should be aware of the following:

- The total time the vehicle spends abroad must not exceed six months.
- The owner of the caravan must provide the other person with a letter of authority.
- The owner cannot accept a hire fee or reward.
- The number plate on the caravan must match the number plate on the tow car.
- Both drivers' insurers must be informed if a caravan is being towed and any additional premium must be paid.

Currency

You must declare cash of €10,000 (or equivalent in other currencies) or more when travelling between the UK and a non-EU country. The term 'cash' includes cheques, travellers' cheques, bankers' drafts, notes and coins. You don't need to declare cash when travelling within the EU.

For further information contact HMRC Excise & Customs Helpline on 0300 200 3700.

Customs Allowances

Travelling within the European Union

If you are travelling to the UK from within the EU you can bring an unlimited amount of most goods without being liable for any duty or tax, but certain rules apply. The goods must be for

your own personal use, which can include use as a gift (if the person you are gifting the goods to reimburses you in any way this is not classed as a gift), and you must have paid duty and tax in the country where you purchased the goods. If a customs official suspects that any goods are not for your own personal use they can question you, make further checks and ultimately seize both the goods and the vehicle used to transport them. Although no limits are in place, customs officials are less likely to question you regarding your goods if they are under the following limits:

- 800 cigarettes
- 400 cigarillos
- 200 cigars
- 1kg tobacco
- 10 litres of spirits
- 20 litres of fortified wine (e.g. port or sherry)
- 90 litres of wine
- 110 litres of beer

The same rules and recommended limits apply for travel between other EU countries.

Travelling outside the EU

There are limits to the amount of goods you can bring back into the UK from countries outside the EU. All goods must be for your own personal use. Each person aged 17 and over is entitled to the following allowance:

- 200 cigarettes, or 100 cigarillos, or 50 cigars, or 250gms tobacco
- 1 litre of spirits or strong liqueurs over 22% volume, or 2 litres of fortified wine, sparkling wine or any other alcoholic drink that's less than 22% volume
- 4 litres of still wine
- 16 litres of beer
- £390 worth of all other goods including perfume, gifts and souvenirs without having to pay tax and/or duty

For further information contact HMRC National Advice Service on 0300 200 3700.

Duty-Free Imports from Andorra

Duty-free shopping is permitted in Andorra, which is not a member of the EU, but there are strict limits on the amount of goods which can be exported. Each person aged 17 years or over is permitted to export the following items from Andorra free of duty or tax:

- 1.5 litre of spirits over 22 % vol or 3 litres spirits under 22 % vol or sparkling wine
- 5 litres of still wine
- 300 cigarettes or 150 cigarillos or 75 cigars or 400g of tobacco
- 75g perfume + 375 ml eau de cologne

There are also limits on other items such as coffee, tea and other food products, so if in any doubt check before you travel. There are no Customs formalities when entering Andorra from France or Spain.

Medicines

There is no limit to the amount of medicines you can take abroad if they are obtained without prescription (i.e. over the counter medicines). Medicines prescribed by your doctor may contain controlled drugs (e.g. morphine), for which you will need a licence if you're leaving the UK for 3 months or more. Visit www.gov.uk/travelling-controlled-drugs or call 020 7035 0771 for a list of controlled drugs and to apply for a licence.

You don't need a licence if you carry less than 3 months' supply or your medication doesn't contain controlled drugs, but you should carry a letter from your doctor stating your name, a list of your prescribed drugs and dosages for each drug. You may have to show this letter when going through customs.

Personal Possessions

Visitors to countries within the EU are free to carry reasonable quantities of any personal possessions such as jewellery, cameras, and electrical equipment required for the duration of their stay. It is sensible to carry sales receipts for new items in case you need to prove that tax has already been paid.

Prohibited and Restricted Goods

Regardless of where you are travelling from the importation of some goods into the UK is restricted or banned, mainly to protect health and the environment. These include:

- Endangered animals or plants including live animals, birds and plants, ivory, skins, coral, hides, shells and goods made from them such as jewellery, shoes, bags and belts.
- Controlled, unlicensed or dangerous drugs.
- Counterfeit or pirated goods such as watches, CDs and clothes; goods bearing a false indication of their place of manufacture or in breach of UK copyright.
- Offensive weapons such as firearms, flick knives, knuckledusters, push daggers, self-defence sprays and stun guns.
- Pornographic material depicting extreme violence or featuring children

This list is not exhaustive; if in doubt contact HMRC on 0300 200 3700 (+44 2920 501 261 from outside the UK) or go through the red Customs channel and ask a Customs officer when returning to the UK.

Plants and Food

Travellers from within the EU may bring into the UK any fruit, vegetable or plant products without restriction as long as they are grown in the EU, are free from pests or disease and are for your own consumption. For food products Andorra, the Channel Islands, the Isle of Man, San Marino and Switzerland are treated as part of the EU. From most countries outside the EU you are not allowed to bring into the UK any meat or dairy products. Other animal products may be severely restricted or banned and it is important that you declare any such products on entering the UK. For up to date information contact the Department for Environment, Food and Rural Affairs (Defra) on 0345 33 55 77 or +44 20 7238 6951 from outside the UK. You can also visit www.defra.gov.uk to find out more.

Money

Being able to safely access your money while you're away is a necessity for you to enjoy your break. It isn't a good idea to rely on one method of payment, so always have a backup plan. A mixture of a small amount of cash plus one or two electronic means of payment are a good idea.

Traveller's cheques have become less popular in recent years as fewer banks and hotels are willing or able to cash them. There are alternative options which offer the same level of security but are easier to use, such as prepaid credit cards.

Local Currency

It is a good idea to take enough foreign currency for your journey and immediate needs on arrival, don't forget you may need change for tolls or parking on your journey. Currency exchange facilities will be available at ports and on ferries but rates offered may not be as good as you would find elsewhere.

The Post Office, banks, exchange offices and travel agents offer foreign exchange. All should stock Euros but during peak holiday times or if you need a large amount it may be sensible to pre-order your currency. You should also pre-order any less common currencies. Shop around and compare commission and exchange rates, together with minimum charges.

Banks and money exchanges in central and eastern Europe won't usually accept Scottish and Northern Irish bank notes and may be reluctant to change any sterling which has been written on or is creased or worn.

Foreign Currency Bank Accounts

Frequent travellers or those who spend long periods abroad may find a Euro bank account useful. Most such accounts impose no currency conversion charges for debit or credit card use and allow fee-free cash withdrawals at ATMs. Some banks may also allow you to spread your account across different currencies, depending on your circumstances. Speak to your bank about the services they offer.

Prepaid Travel Cards

Prepaid travel money cards are issued by various providers including the Post Office, Travelex, Lloyds Bank and American Express.

They are increasingly popular as the PIN protected travel money card offers the security of Traveller's Cheques, with the convenience of paying by card. You load the card with the amount you need before leaving home, and then use cash machines to make withdrawals or use the card to pay for goods and services as you would a credit or debit card. You can top the card up over the telephone or online while you are abroad. However there can be issues with using them with some automated payment systems, such as pay-at-pump petrol stations and toll booths, so you should always have an alternative payment method available.

These cards can be cheaper to use than credit or debit cards for both cash withdrawals and purchases as there are usually no loading or transaction fees to pay. In addition, because they are separate from your bank account, if the card is lost or stolen you bank account will still be secure.

Credit and Debit Cards

Credit and debit cards offer a convenient way of spending abroad. For the use of cards abroad most banks impose a foreign currency conversion charge of up to 3% per transaction. If you use your card to withdraw cash there will be a further commission charge of up to 3% and you will be charged interest (possibly at a higher rate than normal) as soon as you withdraw the money.

There are credit cards available which are specifically designed for spending overseas and will give you the best available rates. However they often have high interest rates so are only economical if you're able to pay them off in full each month.

If you have several cards, take at least two in case you encounter problems. Credit and debit 'Chip and PIN' cards issued by UK banks may not be universally accepted abroad so check that your card will be accepted if using it in restaurants or other situations where you pay after you have received goods or services

Contact your credit or debit card issuer before you leave home to let them know that you will be travelling abroad. In the battle against card fraud, card issuers frequently query transactions which they regard as unusual or suspicious, causing your card to be declined or temporarily stopped. You should always carry your card issuer's helpline number with you so that you can contact them if this happens. You will also need this number should you need to report the loss or theft of your card.

Dynamic Currency Conversion

When you pay with a credit or debit card, retailers may offer you the choice of currency for payment, e.g. a euro amount will be converted into sterling and then charged to your card account. This is known as a 'Dynamic Currency Conversion' but the exchange rate used is likely to be worse than the rate offered by your card issuer, so will work out more expensive than paying in the local currency.

Emergency Cash

If an emergency or theft means that you need cash in a hurry, then friends or relatives at home can send you emergency cash via money transfer services. The Post Office, MoneyGram and Western Union all offer services which, allows the transfer of money to over 233,000 money transfer agents around the world. Transfers take approximately ten minutes and charges are levied on a sliding scale.

Ferries & the Channel Tunnel

Booking Your Ferry

If travelling at peak times, such as Easter or school holidays, make reservations as early as possible. Each ferry will have limited room for caravans and large vehicles so spaces can fill up quickly, especially on cheaper crossings. If you need any special assistance or arrangements request this at the time of booking.

When booking any ferry crossing, make sure you give the correct measurements for your outfit including bikes, roof boxes or anything which may add to the length or height of your vehicle - if you underestimate your vehicle's size you may be turned away or charged an additional fee.

The Caravan and Motorhome Club is an agent for most major ferry companies operating services. Call The Club's Travel Service on 01342 316 101 or see camc.com/ferries to book.

The table at the end of this section shows ferry routes from the UK to the Continent and Ireland. Some ferry routes may not be operational all year, and during peak periods there may be a limit to the number of caravans or motorhomes accepted. For the most up-to-date information visit camc.com/ferries or call the Club's Travel Services team.

On the Ferry

Arrive at the port with plenty of time before your boarding time. Motorhomes and car/caravan outfits will usually either be the first or last vehicles boarded onto the ferry. Almost all ferries are now 'drive on – drive off' so you won't be required to do any complicated manoeuvres. You may be required to show ferry staff that your gas is switched off before boarding the ferry.

Be careful using the ferry access ramps, as they are often very steep which can mean there is a risk of grounding the tow bar or caravan hitch. Drive slowly and, if your ground clearance is low, consider whether removing your jockey wheel and any stabilising devices would help.

Vehicles are often parked close together on ferries, meaning that if you have towing extension mirrors they could get knocked or damaged by people trying to get past your

vehicle. If you leave them attached during the ferry crossing then make sure you check their position on returning to your vehicle.

Channel Tunnel

The Channel Tunnel operator, Eurotunnel, accepts cars, caravans and motorhomes (except those running on LPG) on their service between Folkestone and Calais. You can just turn up and see if there is availability on the day, however prices increase as it gets closer to the departure time so if you know your plans in advance it is best to book as early as possible.

On the Journey

You will be asked to open your roof vents prior to travel and you will also need to apply the caravan brake once you have parked your vehicle on the train. You will not be able to use your caravan until arrival.

Pets

It is possible to transport your pet on a number of ferry routes to the Continent and Ireland, as well as on Eurotunnel services from Folkestone to Calais. Advance booking is essential as restrictions apply to the number of animals allowed on any one crossing. Make sure you understand the carrier's terms and conditions for transporting pets. Brittany Ferries ask for all dogs to be muzzled when out of the vehicle but this varies for other operators so please check at the time of booking.

Once on board pets are normally required to remain in their owner's vehicle or in kennels on the car deck and you won't be able to access your vehicle to check on your pet while the ferry is at sea. On longer crossings you should make arrangements at the on-board information desk for permission to visit your pet in order to check its well-being. You should always make sure that ferry staff know your vehicle has a pet on board.

Information and advice on the welfare of animals before and during a journey is available on the website of the Department for Environment, Food and Rural Affairs (Defra), www.defra.gov.uk.

Gas

UK based ferry companies usually allow up to three gas cylinders per caravan, including the cylinder currently in use, however some may restrict this to a maximum of two cylinders. Some operators may ask you to hand over your gas cylinders to a member of the crew so that they can be safely stored during the crossing. Check that you know the rules of your ferry operator before you travel.

Cylinder valves should be fully closed and covered with a cap, if provided, and should remain closed during the crossing. Cylinders should be fixed securely in or on the caravan in the position specified by the manufacturer.

Gas cylinders must be declared at check-in and the crew may ask to inspect each cylinder for leakage before travel.

The carriage of spare petrol cans, whether full or empty, is not permitted on ferries or through the Channel Tunnel.

LPG Vehicles

Vehicles fully or partially powered by LPG can't be carried through the Channel Tunnel. Gas for domestic use (e.g. heating, lighting or cooking) can be carried, but the maximum limit is 47kg for a single bottle or 50kg in multiple bottles. Tanks must be switched off before boarding and must be less than 80% full; you will be asked to demonstrate this before you travel.

Most ferry companies will accept LPG-powered vehicles but you must let them know at the time of booking. During the crossing the tank must be no more than 75% full and it must be turned off. In the case of vehicles converted to use LPG, some ferry companies also require a certificate showing that the conversion has been carried out by a professional - before you book speak to the ferry company to see what their requirements are.

Club Sites Near Ports

If you've got a long drive to the ferry port, or want to catch an early ferry then an overnight stop near to the port gives you a relaxing start to your holiday. The following table lists Club sites which are close to ports.

Club Members can book online at camc.com or call 01342 327490. Non-members can book by calling the sites directly on the telephone numbers below when the sites are open.

Please note that Commons Wood, Fairlight Wood, Hunter's Moon, Mildenhall and Old Hartley are open to Club members only. Non-members are welcome at all other sites listed below.

Port	Nearest Club Site	Tel No.
Cairnryan	New England Bay	01776 860275
Dover, Folkestone, Channel Tunnel	Bearsted	01622 730018
	Black Horse Farm*	01303 892665
	Daleacres	01303 267679
	Fairlight Wood	01424 812333
Fishguard, Pembroke	Freshwater East	01646 672341
Harwich	Cambridge Cherry Hinton*	01223 244088
	Commons Wood*	01707 260786
	Mildenhall	01638 713089
Holyhead	Penrhos	01248 852617
Hull	York Beechwood Grange*	01904 424637
	York Rowntree Park*	01904 658997
Newcastle upon Tyne	Old Hartley	0191 237 0256
Newhaven	Brighton*	01273 626546
Plymouth	Plymouth Sound	01752 862325
Poole	Hunter's Moon*	01929 556605
Portsmouth	Rookesbury Park	01329 834085
Rosslare	River Valley	00353 (0)404 41647
Weymouth	Crossways	01305 852032

*Site open all year

Ferry Routes and Operators

Route	Operator	Approximate Crossing Time	Maximum Frequency
Belgium			
Hull – Zeebrugge	P & O Ferries	12-14 hrs	1 daily
France			
Dover – Calais	P & O Ferries	1½ hrs	22 daily
Dover – Calais	DFDS Seaways	1½ hrs	10 daily
Dover – Dunkerque	DFDS Seaways	2 hrs	12 daily
Folkestone – Calais	Eurotunnel	35 mins	3 per hour
Newhaven – Dieppe	DFDS Seaways	4 hrs	2 daily
Plymouth – Roscoff	Brittany Ferries	6 hrs	2 daily
Poole – St Malo (via Channel Islands)*	Condor Ferries	5 hrs	1 daily (May to Sep)
Portsmouth – Caen	Brittany Ferries	6 / 7 hrs	3 daily (maximum)
Portsmouth – Cherbourg	Brittany Ferries	3 hrs	2 daily (maximum)
Portsmouth – Le Havre	Brittany Ferries	3¼ / 8 hrs	1 daily (minimum)
Portsmouth – St Malo	Brittany Ferries	9 hrs	1 daily
Ireland – Northern			
Cairnryan – Larne	P & O Irish Sea	1 / 2 hrs	7 daily
Liverpool (Birkenhead) – Belfast	Stena Line	8 hrs	2 daily
Cairnryan – Belfast	Stena Line	2 / 3 hrs	7 daily
Ireland – Republic			
Cork – Roscoff*	Brittany Ferries	14 hrs	1 per week
Dublin – Cherbourg	Irish Ferries	19 hrs	1 per week
Fishguard – Rosslare	Stena Line	3½ hrs	2 daily
Holyhead – Dublin	Irish Ferries	2-4 hrs	Max 4 daily
Holyhead – Dublin	Stena Line	2-4 hrs	Max 4 daily
Liverpool – Dublin	P & O Irish Sea	8 hrs	2 daily
Pembroke – Rosslare	Irish Ferries	4 hrs	2 daily
Rosslare – Cherbourg*	Irish Ferries	19½ hrs	3 per week
Rosslare – Cherbourg	Stena Line	19 hrs	3 per week
Rosslare – Roscoff*	Irish Ferries	19½ hrs	4 per week
Netherlands			
Harwich – Hook of Holland	Stena Line	7 hrs	2 daily
Hull – Rotterdam	P & O Ferries	11-12 hrs	1 daily
Newcastle – Ijmuiden (Amsterdam)	DFDS Seaways	15½ hrs	1 daily
Spain			
Portsmouth – Bilbao	Brittany Ferries	24 / 32 hrs	1 - 3 per week
Portsmouth or Plymouth – Santander	Brittany Ferries	20 / 32 hrs	4 per week

*Not bookable through The Club's Travel Service.
Note: Services and routes correct at time of publication but subject to change.

Motoring Advice

Preparing for Your Journey

The first priority in preparing your outfit for your journey should be to make sure it has a full service. Make sure that you have a fully equipped spares kit, and a spare wheel and tyre for your caravan – it is easier to get hold of them from your local dealer than to have to spend time searching for spares where you don't know the local area.

Club members should carry their UK Sites Directory & Handbook with them, as it contains a section of technical advice which may be useful when travelling. The Club also has a free advice service covering a wide range of technical topics – download free information leaflets at camc.com/advice or contact the team - call 01342 336611 or email technical@caravanclub.co.uk.

For advice on issues specific to countries other than the UK, Club members can contact the Travel Service Information Officer; email travelserviceinfo@caravanclub.co.uk or call 01342 336766.

Weight Limits

From both a legal and a safety point of view, it is essential not to exceed vehicle weight limits. It is advisable to carry documentation confirming your vehicle's maximum permitted laden weight - if your Vehicle Registration Certificate (V5C) does not state this, you will need to produce alternative certification, e.g. from a weighbridge.

If you are pulled over by the police and don't have certification you will be taken to a weighbridge. If your vehicle(s) are then found to be overweight you will be liable to a fine and may have to discard items to lower the weight before you can continue on your journey.

Some Final Checks

Before you start any journey make sure you complete the following checks:

- All car and caravan or motorhome lights are working and sets of spare bulbs are packed.
- The coupling is correctly seated on the towball and the breakaway cable is attached.
- Windows, vents and hatches are shut.

- On-board water systems are drained.
- Mirrors are adjusted for maximum visibility.
- Corner steadies are fully wound up and the brace is handy for your arrival on site.
- Any fires or flames are extinguished and the gas cylinder tap is turned off. Fire extinguishers are fully charged and close at hand.
- The over-run brake is working correctly.
- The jockey wheel is raised and secured, the handbrake is released.

Driving in France

Driving abroad for the first time can be a daunting prospect, especially when towing a caravan. Here are a few tips to make the transition easier:

- Remember that sat navs may take you on unsuitable roads, so have a map or atlas to hand to help you find an alternative route.
- It can be tempting to try and get to your destination as quickly as possible but we recommend travelling a maximum of 250 miles a day when towing.
- Share the driving if possible, and on long journeys plan an overnight stop.
- Remember that if you need to overtake or pull out around an obstruction you will not be able to see clearly from the driver's seat. If possible, always have a responsible adult in the passenger seat who can advise you when it is clear to pull out. If that is not possible then stay well back to get a better view and pull out slowly.
- If traffic builds up behind you, pull over safely and let it pass.
- Driving on the right should become second nature after a while, but pay particular attention when turning left, after leaving a rest area, petrol station or site or after a one-way system.
- Stop at least every two hours to stretch your legs and take a break.

Accidents

Drivers involved in an accident or those who commit a traffic offence may be required to take a saliva or urine drugs test as well as a breathalyser test. In the event of an accident where people are injured or if emergency assistance is required, dial 17 (police) or 112 from any phone.

Alcohol

In both France and Andorra the maximum legal level of alcohol is 50 milligrams in 100 millilitres of blood, i.e. less than permitted in the UK (80 milligrams). To ensure you stay under the limit it is best to avoid drinking at all if you plan to drive. For novice drivers who have less than 3 years' experience the limit has been reduced to 20 milligrams, which effectively means you cannot drink any alcohol at all. The police carry out random breath tests and penalties are severe.

There is a legal requirement to carry a breathalyser, however there is currently no punishment for non-compliance. Check camc.com/overseasadvice for the most up-to-date advice before you travel.

Breakdown Service

If you break down on a motorway or in a motorway service area you must call the police directly. They can be called from one of the orange emergency telephones placed every 2km along motorways. If you are in a service area, ask service station staff to contact the police for you, or dial 112 from a public phone and the police will be able to pinpoint your exact whereabouts. The police will arrange breakdown and towing assistance. No breakdown vehicle will enter a motorway without police authority.

Charges for motorway assistance are fixed by the government. The basic cost (2015) of repairing a vehicle up to 1,800 kg in weight, on the spot from Monday Friday, from 8am to 6pm is €122.84 or €151.90 for vehicles over 1800kg. After 6pm and over weekends and public holidays a 50% supplement applies.

If you have taken out breakdown insurance you should contact your insurance provider once the breakdown service has arrived in order to establish a means of payment. Your insurance provider cannot summon the police on your behalf if you breakdown on a motorway.

Headphones

From June 2015 it is illegal to drive any vehicle or cycle while wearing headphones or headsets. This includes listening to music or using headphones to make phone calls.

Fuel

Unleaded petrol pumps are marked 'Essence Sans Plomb'. Diesel pumps are marked Gas Oil or Gazole.

Petrol stations may close on Sundays and those at supermarkets, where petrol is generally cheaper, may close for lunch. At supermarkets it is advisable to check the height and width clearance before towing past the pumps. Credit cards are generally accepted. Some automatic pumps at unmanned petrol stations are operated by credit cards and some may not accept credit or debit cards issued outside France. Away from major roads and towns try not to let your fuel tank run too low as you may have difficulty finding an open petrol station, especially at night or on Sundays.

Fuel containing 10% bioethanol is on sale at many petrol stations in France alongside the regular Euro 95 unleaded fuel, which it will eventually replace. Pumps are labelled SP95-E10. This fuel can be used in most modern vehicles manufactured since 2000 but if you are in any doubt about using it then regular Euro 95 or 98 Super Plus unleaded fuel is still available at most petrol stations. Check your vehicle handbook or visit www.acea.be and search for 'E10' to find the publication 'Vehicle compatibility with new fuel standards'.

To find the cheapest fuel in any area log on to www.zagaz.com and simply click on the map of France to find the locations of petrol stations, together with prices charged. Alternatively view the French government website, www.prix-carburants.gouv.fr which gives fuel prices all over the country.

Members of the Caravan and Motorhome Club can check current average fuel prices by country at camc.com/overseasadvice.

Automotive Liquefied Petroleum Gas (LPG)

LPG (also called Gepel or GPL) is available in petrol stations across France, especially on motorways. However LPG may not be available in more rural areas so you are advised to fill up at the first opportunity. Maps showing their company's outlets are issued free by most LPG suppliers, e.g. Shell, Elf, etc. A list of locations is available at the website stations.gpl.online.fr. LPG is not available in Andorra.

Low Emission Zones

A low emission zone was introduced in Paris from July 2015, initially only affecting vehicles over 3500kg. From 1st July 2016 vehicles under 3500kg which are rated Euro 1 for emissions standards will also be included, and then Euro 2-4 will also be regulated at different stages. You are advised to check the most up-to-date information at www.lowemissionzones.eu before you travel.

Motorhomes Towing Cars

If you are towing a car behind a motorhome, our advice would be to use a trailer with all four wheels of the car off the ground. Although France doesn't have a specific law banning A-frames, they do have a law which prohibits a motor vehicle towing another motor vehicle.

Motorways

France has 11,500 kilometres of excellent motorways. Tolls are payable on most routes according to distance travelled and category of vehicle(s) and, because motorways are privately financed, prices per km vary in different parts of the country. Emergency telephones connected to the police are located every 2km.

Motorway Service Areas

Stopping is allowed for a few hours at the service areas of motorways, called 'aires', and some have sections specially laid out for caravans. Most have toilet facilities and a water supply but at 'aires' with only basic facilities, water may not be suitable for drinking, indicated by a sign 'eau non potable'.

In addition there are 'aires de repos' which have picnic and play areas, whereas 'aires de services' resemble UK motorway service areas with fuel, shop, restaurant and parking facilities for all types of vehicle.

Motorway Tolls

Motorways tolls are common throughout France by a number of different operating companies, although there are numerous stretches, particularly around large cities, where no tolls are levied. Vehicles are classified as follows:

Category 1: (Light Vehicles) Vehicle with overall height under 2m and gross vehicle weight not exceeding 3,500kg. Train with overall height under 2m and gross vehicle weight of towing vehicle not exceeding 3,500kg.

Category 2: (Intermediate Vehicles) Vehicle with overall height from 2m to 3m and gross vehicle weight up to 3,500kg. Train with overall height from 2m to 3m and gross vehicle weight up to 3,500kg.

Category 3: (HGV or bus with two axles) Vehicle with overall height of 3m or more. Vehicle with gross vehicle weight of more than 3,500kg. On the A14 all twin-axle buses are in category 4.

Category 4: (HGV or bus with three or more axles) Vehicle with more than two axles and height of 3m or more, or gross vehicle weight of more than 3,500kg. Train with overall height of 3m or more. Train with towing vehicle having gross vehicle weight of more than 3,500kg.

Motorists driving Category 2 vehicles adapted for the transport of disabled persons pay the toll specified for Category 1 vehicles. Holding a disabled person's Blue Badge does not automatically entitle foreign motorists to pay Category 1 charges, and the decision whether to downgrade from Category 2 to 1 will be made by the person at the toll booth, based on experience of similar vehicles registered in France.

To calculate the tolls payable on your planned route see www.viamichelin.com and tick the box marked 'Caravan' (ticking this box will also give the toll for a motorhome) and select the 'Michelin recommended' route. For more detailed information, consult the websites of the individual motorway operating companies, a list of which can be found on www.autoroutes.fr/en/asfa/french-motorway-companies (English option). Alternatively calculate tolls payable on your chosen route on www.autoroutes.fr.

Payment

Toll payments may be made in cash or by credit card, but be aware that when paying with a credit card you may not be asked for a signature or required to key in a PIN. Pre-paid credit cards, Maestro and Electron are not accepted.

On less frequently-used motorways, toll collection is increasingly by automatic machines equipped with height detectors. It is simplest to pay with a credit card but there should be a cash/change machine adjacent. There are lanes at nearly all toll plazas specifically for drivers who have a Liber-t toll tag which allows them to pay for tolls directly from their bank account. Club members can benefit from a free Liber-t tag application (normally €10) - visit camc.com/sanef for details.

Overtaking and Passing

Crossing a solid single or double centre line is heavily penalised. Outside built-up areas, outfits weighing more than 3,500 kg, or more than 7m in length, are required by law to leave at least 50m between themselves and the vehicle in front. They are only permitted to use the two right-hand lanes on roads with three or more lanes and, where overtaking is difficult, should slow down or stop to allow other smaller vehicles to pass.

Parking

As a general rule, all prohibitions are indicated by road signs or by yellow road markings. Stopping or parking on the left-hand side of the road is prohibited except in one-way streets.

In most French cities parking meters have largely been replaced by 'pay and display' machines which take coins and credit or debit cards. Where parking signs show 'Horodateur' or 'Stationnement Payant' you must obtain a ticket from a nearby machine.

In Paris two red routes ('axe rouge') have been created on which stopping and parking are prohibited. Elsewhere, drivers must observe parking restrictions indicated by signs. Car parks are expensive and the best advice is to use public transport, which is cheap and efficient.

In many cities and towns there are blue zones (indicated by blue street markings) where you can sometimes park for free, usually for one hour between 9am and 12pm and between 2pm and 7pm from Monday to Saturday. You must display a parking disc ('disque de contrôle/stationnement') in your windscreen; these are available free, or for a small fee, from garages, travel agencies, motoring organisations, tourist offices, police stations, tobacconists and some shops.

Priority

In built up areas, give way to traffic coming from the right, unless otherwise indicated. Outside built-up areas traffic on all main roads of any importance has right of way, indicated by the following signs:

Priority road

Priority road

On entering towns, the same sign will often have a line through it, warning that vehicles may pull out from a side road on the right and will have priority.

End of priority road

On steep gradients, vehicles travelling downhill must give way to vehicles travelling uphill.

Public Transport

In built-up areas you must stop to allow a bus to pull out from a bus stop. Take particular care when school buses have stopped and passengers are getting on and off.

Overtaking trams in motion is normally only allowed on the right, unless on a one way street where you can overtake on the left if there is not enough space on the right. Do not overtake a tram near a tram stop, which can be in the centre of the road. When a tram or bus stops to allow passengers on and off, you should stop to allow them to cross to the pavement. Give way to trams which are turning across your carriageway.

Pedestrian Crossings

Stopping to allow pedestrians to cross at zebra crossings is not always common practice on the Continent. Pedestrians expect to wait until the road is clear before crossing, while motorists behind may be taken by surprise by your stopping. The result may be a rear-end shunt or vehicles overtaking you at the crossing and putting pedestrians at risk.

Roads

French roads fall into three categories: autoroutes (A) i.e. motorways; national (N) roads; and departmental (D) roads. There are over 10,500 kilometres of motorways, on most of which tolls are levied. British motorists will find French roads relatively uncongested.

Andorra

Travellers to Andorra from France should be aware that conditions on the road from Toulouse to Andorra, the N20/E9, can quickly become difficult in severe winter weather and you should be prepared for delays. Stick to main roads in Andorra when towing and don't attempt the many unsurfaced roads.

Road Signs and Markings

Directional signposting on major roads is generally good. Signs may be placed on walls pointing across the road they indicate and this may be confusing at first. Generally a sign on the right pointing left means that you go straight ahead. The same sign on the right pointing right means 'turn right' at the first opportunity. The words 'tout droit' mean 'go straight ahead' or 'straight on'.

Road signs on approach to roundabouts and at junctions usually do not show road numbers, just the destination, with numbers being displayed once you are on the road itself. Make sure you know the names of places along your proposed route, and not just the road numbers. Once you have seen your destination town signposted continue along the road until directed otherwise. Intermediate junctions or roundabouts where you do not have to turn usually omit the destination name if the route to it is straight on.

Lines on the carriageway are generally white. A yellow zigzag line indicates a bus stop, blue markings indicate that parking is restricted and yellow lines on the edge of the roadway also indicate that stopping and/or parking is

Andorra

prohibited. A solid single or double white line in the centre of the road indicates that overtaking is not permitted. STOP signs mean stop - you must come to a complete halt otherwise you may be liable to a fine if caught.

Whilst road signs conform to international standards, some other commonly used signs you may see include:

French	English translation
Allumez vos feux	Switch on lights
Attention	Caution
Bouchon	Traffic jam
Chausée deformée	Uneven road
Chemin sans issue	No through road
Col	Mountain pass
Créneau de dépassement	2-lane passing zone, dual carriageway
Déviation	Diversion
Fin d'interdiction de stationner	End of parking restrictions
Gravillons	Loose chippings
Interdit aux piétons	No pedestrians
Itineraire bis	Alternative route
Péage	Toll
Ralentissez	Slow down
Rappel	Continued restriction
Rétrécissement	Narrow lane
Route barrée	Road closed
Sens interdit	No entry
Sens unique	One-way street
Serrez à gauche/droite	Keep left/right
Stationnement interdit	No parking
Tout droit	Straight on
Toutes directions	All directions
Travaux	Road works
Virages	Bends

Andorra

Main roads are prefixed 'CG' (Carretera General) and side roads are prefixed 'CS' (Carretera Secundaria). CG road signs are white on red and CS signs are white on green.

Recently-Qualified Drivers

The minimum age to drive in France is 18 years and this also applies to foreign drivers. Driving without professionally qualified supervision/instruction on a provisional licence is not allowed.

Roundabouts

At roundabouts drivers must give way to traffic already on the roundabout, i.e. on the left, if indicated by a red-bordered triangular sign showing a roundabout symbol with the words 'Vous n'avez pas la priorité' or 'Cédez le passage' underneath.

Traffic on the roundabout has priority

In the absence of these signs traffic entering the roundabout has priority, however it is always very important to be watchful and to take extra care at roundabouts and junctions to avoid accidents.

Speed Limits

Police are strict about speeding - motorists caught driving more than 40 km/h (25mph) over the speed limit face immediate confiscation of their driving licence. Speed limits on motorways (in dry weather) are higher than in the UK – although they are lower on ordinary roads.

Fixed speed cameras are common on both motorways and major roads. The use of mobile speed cameras and radar traps is frequent, even on remote country roads, and may be operated from parked vans or motor bikes, or they may be hand-held. They may also be in use on exit slip roads from motorways or major roads where there is a posted speed limit. Motorway toll booths will also calculate your speed from the distance you have travelled and the time it has taken.

Motoring Advice

Radar Detectors

Radar detectors, laser detectors or speed camera jammers are illegal in France. If caught carrying one – even if it is not in use – you are liable to both a fine of up to €1,500 and confiscation of the device, and possibly confiscation of your vehicle if you're unable to pay the fine. GPS or sat nav devices which pinpoint the position of fixed speed cameras are also illegal in France. You can still use the device, but you must disable the function which pinpoints speed cameras.

Inside Built-up Areas

The general speed limit is 50 km/h (31 mph) which may be raised to 70 km/h (44 mph) on important through roads, indicated by signs. The beginning of a built-up area is marked by a road sign giving the name of the town or village in blue or black letters on a light background with a red border. The end of the built-up area is indicated by the same sign with a red diagonal line through it. See examples below:

Therefore, when you enter a town or village, even if there is no actual speed limit warning sign, the place name sign itself indicates that you are entering a 50 km/h zone. The end of the 50 km/h zone is indicated by the place name sign crossed out. The word 'rappel' on a speed limit sign is a reminder of that limit.

The speed limit on stretches of motorway in built-up areas is 110 km/h (68 mph), except on the Paris ring road where the limit is 80 km/h (50 mph).

Outside Built-up Areas

General speed limits are as follows:

- On single carriageway roads 90 km/h (56 mph)
- On dual-carriageways separated by a central reservation 110 km/h (68 mph)
- On motorways 130 km/h (81 mph)

These general speed limits also apply to private cars towing a trailer tent or caravan, provided the gross train mass (fully laden weight of the car, plus the cars towing limit) of the vehicle does not exceed 3,500 kg. If the gross train mass of the towing vehicle is over 3,500 kg the speed limits are 90 km/h (56 mph) on motorways, 80-90 km/h (50 mph) on dual carriageways and 80 km/h (50 mph) on single carriageways.

Large motorhomes over 3,500 kg have a speed limit of 110 km/h (68 mph) on motorways, 100 km/h (62 mph) on dual carriageways and 80 km/h (50 mph) on single carriageway roads.

For full details of speed regulations see camc.com/overseasadvice.

Adverse Weather Conditions

In case of rain or adverse weather conditions, general speed limits are lowered as follows:

- On motorways 110 km/h (68 mph)
- On urban motorways and dual carriageways 100 km/h (62 mph)
- Outside built-up areas 80 km/h (50 mph)

A speed limit of 50 km/h (31 mph) applies on all roads (including motorways) in foggy conditions when visibility is less than 50 metres.

Traffic Jams

The A6/A7 (the Autoroute du Soleil) from Paris via Lyon to the south are busy motorways prone to traffic jams. Travelling from the north, bottlenecks are often encountered at Auxerre, Chalon-sur-Saône, Lyon, Valence and Orange. An alternative route to the south is the A20, which is largely toll-free, or the toll-free A75 via Clermont-Ferrand.

During periods of severe congestion on the A6, A7 and A10 Paris-Bordeaux motorways, traffic police close off junctions and divert holiday traffic onto alternative routes or 'Itinéraires Bis' which run parallel to main roads.

The signs above indicate these routes. For a traffic calendar, indicating when certain areas are most prone to traffic jams, together with a real-time congestion map and regional phone numbers to call for traffic/travel information, see www.bison-fute.equipement.gouv.fr.

Realtime traffic information on traffic conditions on motorways can be found on www.autoroutes.fr.

In general, Friday afternoons and Saturday mornings are busiest on roads leading south, and on Saturday and Sunday afternoons roads leading north may well be congested. Many French people drop everything for lunch and, therefore, between noon and 2pm roads are quieter.

At the start of the school holidays in early July, at the end of July and during the first and last few days of August, roads are particularly busy. Avoid the changeover weekend at the end of July/beginning of August when traffic both north and south bound can be virtually at a standstill. Traffic can also be very heavy around the Christmas/New Year period and on the weekend of any public holiday.

Andorra

There is heavy traffic in Andorra-la-Vella town centre on most days of the year. During the peak summer holiday period you are likely to encounter queues of traffic on the Envalira pass from France on the N22. Traffic is at its worst in the morning from France and in the afternoon and evening from Andorra and you are recommended to use the Envalira Tunnel to avoid some of the congestion and reduce travel time.

Traffic Lights

There is no amber light after the red light in the traffic light sequence.

A flashing amber light indicates caution, slow down, proceed but give way to vehicles coming from the right. A flashing red light indicates no entry; it may also be used to mark level crossings, obstacles, etc.

A yellow arrow at the same time as a red light indicates that drivers may turn in the direction of the arrow, traffic permitting, and providing they give way to pedestrians.

Watch out for traffic lights which may be mounted high above the road and hard to spot.

Violation of Traffic Regulations

Severe fines and penalties are in force for motoring offences and the police are authorised to impose and collect fines on the spot. Violations include minor infringements such as not wearing a seat belt, not carrying a set of spare bulbs or not respecting a STOP sign. More serious infringements such as dangerous overtaking, crossing a continuous central white line and driving at very high speeds, can result in confiscation of your driving licence.

If the offence committed is serious and likely to entail a heavy fine and the suspension of your driving licence or a prison sentence, a motorist who is not resident in France and has no employment there must deposit a guarantee. The police may hold a vehicle until payment is made.

Drivers who are deemed to have deliberately put the lives of others in danger face a maximum fine of €15,000 and a jail sentence. Failure to pay may result in your car being impounded. Your driving licence may also be suspended for up to five years.

By paying fines on the spot (request a receipt) or within three days, motorists can avoid court action and even reduce the fine. Standard fines can now be paid electronically in post offices and newsagents equipped with a dedicated terminal or by visiting www.amendes.gouv.fr.

Motoring Equipment

Essential Equipment

The equipment that you legally have to carry differs by country. For a full list see the Essential Equipment table at the end of this chapter. Please note equipment requirements and regulations can change frequently. To keep up to date with the latest equipment information visit camc.com/overseasadvice.

Child Restraint Systems

Children under 10 years of age are not permitted to travel in front seats of vehicles, unless there are no rear seats in the vehicle, the rear seats are already occupied with other children, or there are no seat belts in the rear. In these situations a child must not be placed in the front seats in a rear-facing child seat, unless any airbag is deactivated. Children up to 10 must travel in an approved child seat or restraint system, adapted to their size. A baby up to 13kg in weight must be carried in a rear facing baby seat. A child between 9kg and 18kg in weight must be seated in a child seat. A child from 15kg in weight up to the age of 10 can use a booster seat with a seat belt.

Children must not travel in the front of a vehicle if there are rear seats available. If they travel in the front the airbag must be deactivated and again they must use an EU approved restraint system adapted to their size.

Fire Extinguisher

As a safety precaution, an approved fire extinguisher should be carried in all vehicles. This is a legal requirement in several countries in Europe.

Lights

When driving in on the right headlights should be adjusted if they are likely to dazzle other road users. You can do this by applying beam deflectors, or some newer vehicles have a built-in adjustment system. Some high-density discharge (HID), xenon or halogen lights, may need to be taken to a dealer to make the necessary adjustment.

Remember also to adjust headlights according to the load being carried and to compensate for the weight of the caravan on the back of

your car. Even if you do not intend to drive at night, it is important to ensure that your headlights are correctly adjusted as you may need to use them in heavy rain, fog or in tunnels. If using tape or a pre-cut adhesive mask remember to remove it on your return home.

All vehicle lights must be in working condition. If your lights are not in working order you may be liable for a fine of up to €450 and confiscation of your vehicle is a possibility in some European countries.

Headlight-Flashing

On the Continent headlight-flashing is used as a warning of approach or as an overtaking signal at night, and not, as is commonly the case in the UK, an indication that you are giving way. Be more cautious with both flashing your headlights and when another driver flashes you. If a driver flashes his headlights they are generally indicating that he has priority and you should give way, contrary to standard practice in the UK.

Hazard Warning Lights

Hazard warning lights should not be used in place of a warning triangle, but should be used in addition to it.

Nationality Plate (GB/IRL)

A nationality plate must be fixed to the rear of both your car or motorhome and caravan. Checks are made and a fine may be imposed for failure to display a nationality plate correctly. If your number plates have the Euro-Symbol on them there is no requirement to display an additional GB sticker within the EU and Switzerland. If your number plate doesn't have the EU symbol or you are planning to travel outside of the EU you will need a GB sticker.

GB is the only national identification code allowed for cars registered in the UK.

Reflective Jackets/ Waistcoats

If you break down outside of a built-up area it is normally a legal requirement that anyone leaving the vehicle must be wearing a reflective jacket or waistcoat. Make sure that your jacket is accessible from inside the car as you will need to put it on before exiting the vehicle. Carry one for each passenger as well as the driver.

Route Planning

It is always a good idea to carry a road atlas or map of the countries you plan to visit, even if you have Satellite Navigation. You can find information on UK roads from Keep Moving – www.keepmoving.co.uk or call 09003 401100. Websites offering a European route mapping service include www.google.co.uk/maps, www.mappy.com or www.viamichelin.com.

Satellite Navigation/GPS

European postcodes don't cover just one street or part of a street in the same way as UK postcodes, they can cover a very large area. GPS co-ordinates and full addresses are given for site entries in this guide wherever possible, so that you can programme your device as accurately as possible.

It is important to remember that sat nav devices don't usually allow for towing or driving a large motorhome and may try to send you down unsuitable roads. Always use your common sense, and if a road looks unsuitable find an alternative route.

Use your sat nav in conjunction with the directions given in the site entries, which have been provided by members who have actually visited. Please note that directions given in site entries have not been checked by the Caravan and Motorhome Club.

In nearly all European countries it is illegal to use car navigation systems which actively search for mobile speed cameras or interfere with police equipment (laser or radar detection).

Car navigation systems which give a warning of fixed speed camera locations are legal in most countries with the exception of France, Germany, and Switzerland where this function must be de-activated.

Seat Belts

The wearing of seat belts is compulsory throughout Europe. On-the-spot fines will be incurred for failure to wear them and, in the event of an accident failure to wear a seat belt may reduce any claim for injury. See the country introductions for specific regulations on both seat belts and car seats.

Caravan Spares

It will generally be much harder to get hold of spare parts for caravans on the continent, especially for UK manufactured caravans. It is therefore advisable to carry any commonly required spares (such as light bulbs) with you.

Take contact details of your UK dealer or manufacturer with you, as they may be able to assist in getting spares delivered to you in an emergency.

Car Spares

Some car manufacturers produce spares kits; contact your dealer for details. The choice of spares will depend on the vehicle and how long you are away, but the following is a list of basic items which should cover the most common causes of breakdown:

- Radiator top hose
- Fan belt
- Fuses and bulbs
- Windscreen wiper blade
- Length of 12V electrical cable
- Tools, torch and WD40 or equivalent water repellent/ dispersant spray

Spare Wheel

Your local caravan dealer should be able to supply an appropriate spare wheel. If you have any difficulty in obtaining one, the Club's Technical Department can provide Club members with a list of suppliers on request.

Tyre legislation across Europe is more or less consistent and, while the Club has no specific knowledge of laws on the Continent regarding the use of space-saver spare wheels, there should be no problems in using such a wheel provided its use is in accordance with the manufacturer's instructions. Space-saver spare wheels are designed for short journeys to get to a place where it can be repaired and there will usually be restrictions on the distance and speed at which the vehicle should be driven.

Towbar

The vast majority of cars registered after 1 August 1998 are legally required to have a European Type approved towbar (complying with European Directive 94/20) carrying a plate giving its approval number and various technical details, including the maximum noseweight. Your car dealer or specialist towbar fitter will be able to give further advice.

All new motorhomes will need some form of type approval before they can be registered in the UK and as such can only be fitted with a type approved towbar. Older vehicles can continue to be fitted with non-approved towing brackets.

Tyres

Tyre condition has a major effect on the safe handling of your outfit. Caravan tyres must be suitable for the highest speed at which you can legally tow, even if you choose to drive slower.

Most countries require a minimum tread depth of 1.6mm but motoring organisations recommend at least 3mm. If you are planning a long journey, consider if they will still be above the legal minimum by the end of your journey.

Tyre Pressure

Tyre pressure should be checked and adjusted when the tyres are cold; checking warm tyres will result in a higher pressure reading. The correct pressures will be found in your car handbook, but unless it states otherwise to add an extra 4 - 6 pounds per square inch to the rear tyres of a car when towing to improve handling. Make sure you know what pressure your caravan tyres should be. Some require a pressure much higher than that normally used for cars. Check your caravan handbook for details.

Tyre Sizes

It is worth noting that some sizes of radial tyre to fit the 13" wheels commonly used on older UK caravans are virtually impossible to find in stock at retailers abroad, e.g. 175R13C.

After a Puncture

A lot of cars now have a liquid sealant puncture repair kit instead of a spare wheel. These should not be considered a permanent repair, and in some cases have been known to make repair of the tyre impossible. If you need to use a liquid sealant you should get the tyre repaired or replaced as soon as possible.

Following a caravan tyre puncture, especially on a single-axle caravan, it is advisable to have the non-punctured tyre removed from its wheel and checked inside and out for signs of damage resulting from overloading during the deflation of the punctured tyre.

Winter Driving

Snow chains must be fitted to vehicles using snow-covered roads in compliance with the relevant road signs. Fines may be imposed for non-compliance. Vehicles fitted with chains must not exceed 50 km/h (31mph).

They are not difficult to fit but it's a good idea to carry sturdy gloves to protect your hands when handling the chains in freezing conditions. Polar Automotive Ltd sells and hires out snow chains, contact them on 01892 519933, www.snowchains.com, or email: polar@snowchains.com.

In Andorra winter tyres are recommended. Snow chains must be used when road conditions necessitate their use and/or when road signs indicate.

Warning Triangles

In almost all European countries it is compulsory to carry a warning triangle which, in the event of vehicle breakdown or accident, must be placed (providing it is safe to do so) on the carriageway at least 30 metres from the vehicle. In some instances it is not compulsory to use the triangle but only when this action would endanger the driver.

A warning triangle should be placed on the road approximately 30 metres (100 metres on motorways) behind the broken down vehicle on the same side of the road. Always assemble the triangle before leaving your vehicle and walk with it so that the red, reflective surface is facing oncoming traffic. If a breakdown occurs round a blind corner, place the triangle in advance of the corner. Hazard warning lights may be used in conjunction with the triangle but they do not replace it.

Essential Equipment Table

The table below shows the essential equipment required for each country. Please note that this information was correct at the time of going to print but is subject to change.

For up to date information on equipment requirements for countries in Europe visit camc.com/overseasadvice.

Country	Warning Triangle	Spare Bulbs	First Aid Kit	Reflective Jacket	Additional Equipment to be Carried/Used
Andorra	Yes (2)	Yes	Rec	Yes	Dipped headlights in poor daytime visibility. Winter tyres recommended; snow chains when road conditions or signs dictate.
Austria	Yes	Rec	Yes	Yes	Winter tyres from 1 Nov to 15 April.*
Belgium	Yes	Rec	Rec	Yes	Dipped headlights in poor daytime visibility.
Croatia	Yes (2 for vehicle with trailer)	Yes	Yes	Yes	Dipped headlights at all times from last Sunday in Oct - last Sunday in Mar. Spare bulbs compulsory if lights are xenon, neon or LED. Snow chains compulsory in winter in certain regions.*
Czech Rep	Yes	Yes	Yes	Yes	Dipped headlights at all times. Replacement fuses. Winter tyres or snow chains from 1 Nov - 31st March.*
Denmark	Yes	Rec	Rec	Rec	Dipped headlights at all times. On motorways use hazard warning lights when queues or danger ahead.
Finland	Yes	Rec	Rec	Yes	Dipped headlights at all times. Winter tyres Dec - Feb.*
France	Yes	Rec	Rec	Yes	Dipped headlights recommended at all times. Legal requirement to carry a breathalyser, but no penalty for non-compliance.

Country	Warning Triangle	Spare Bulbs	First Aid Kit	Reflective Jacket	Additional Equipment to be Carried/Used
Germany	Rec	Rec	Rec	Rec	Dipped headlights recommended at all times. Winter tyres to be used in winter weather conditions.*
Greece	Yes	Rec	Yes	Rec	Fire extinguisher compulsory. Dipped headlights in towns at night and in poor daytime visibility.
Hungary	Yes	Rec	Yes	Yes	Dipped headlights at all times outside built-up areas and in built-up areas at night. Snow chains compulsory on some roads in winter conditions.*
Italy	Yes	Rec	Rec	Yes	Dipped headlights at all times outside built-up areas and in poor visibility. Snow chains from 15 Oct - 15 April.*
Luxembourg	Yes	Rec	Rec	Yes	Dipped headlights at night and daytime in bad weather.
Netherlands	Yes	Rec	Rec	Rec	Dipped headlights at night and in bad weather and recommended during the day.
Norway	Yes	Rec	Rec	Rec	Dipped headlights at all times. Winter tyres compulsory when snow or ice on the roads.*
Poland	Yes	Rec	Rec	Rec	Dipped headlights at all times. Fire extinguisher compulsory.
Portugal	Yes	Rec	Rec	Rec	Dipped headlights in poor daytime visibility, in tunnels and in lanes where traffic flow is reversible.
Slovakia	Yes	Rec	Yes	Yes	Dipped headlights at all times. Winter tyres compulsory when compact snow or ice on the road.*
Slovenia	Yes (2 for vehicle with trailer)	Yes	Rec	Yes	Dipped headlights at all times. Hazard warning lights when reversing. Use winter tyres or carry snow chains 15 Nov - 15 Mar.
Spain	Yes (2 Rec)	Rec	Rec	Yes	Dipped headlights at night, in tunnels and on 'special' roads (roadworks).
Sweden	Yes	Rec	Rec	Rec	Dipped headlights at all times. Winter tyres 1 Dec to 31 March.
Switzerland (inc Liechtenstein)	Yes	Rec	Rec	Rec	Dipped headlights recommended at all times, compulsory in tunnels. Snow chains where indicated by signs.

NOTES:
1) All countries: seat belts (if fitted) must be worn by all passengers.
2) Rec: not compulsory for foreign-registered vehicles, but strongly recommended
3) Headlamp converters, spare bulbs, fire extinguisher, first aid kit and reflective waistcoat are strongly recommended for all countries.
4) In some countries drivers who wear prescription glasses must carry a spare pair.
5) Please check information for any country before you travel. This information is to be used as a guide only and it is your responsibility to make sure you have the correct equipment.

* For more information and regulations on winter driving please see the Country Introduction.

Route Planning

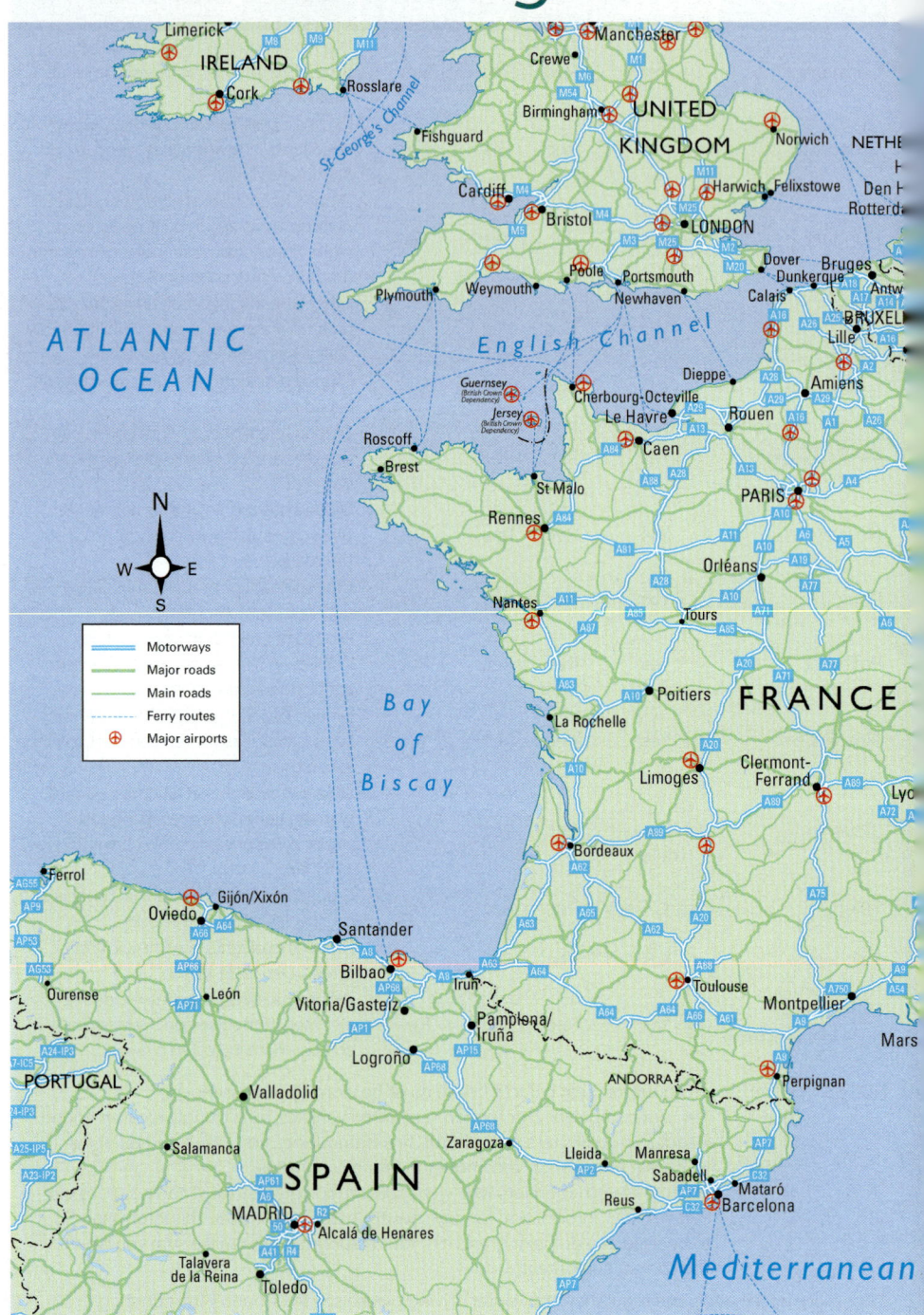

Mountain Passes & Tunnels

Mountain Passes

Mountain passes can create difficult driving conditions, especially when towing or driving a large vehicle. You should only use them if you have a good power to weight ratio and in good driving conditions. If in any doubt as to your outfit's suitability or the weather then stick to motorway routes across mountain ranges if possible.

The tables on the following pages show which passes are not suitable for caravans, and those where caravans are not permitted. Motorhomes aren't usually included in these restrictions, but relatively low powered or very large vehicles should find an alternative route. Road signs at the foot of a pass may restrict access or offer advice, especially for heavy vehicles. Warning notices are usually posted at the foot of a pass if it is closed, or if chains or winter tyres must be used.

Caravanners are particularly sensitive to gradients and traffic/road conditions on passes. The maximum gradient is usually on the inside of bends but exercise caution if it is necessary to pull out. Always engage a lower gear before taking a hairpin bend and give priority to vehicles ascending. On mountain roads it is not the gradient which puts strain on your car but the duration of the climb and the loss of power at high altitudes: approximately 10% at 915 metres (3,000 feet) and even more as you get higher. To minimise the risk of the engine overheating, take high passes in the cool part of the day, don't climb any faster than necessary and keep the engine pulling steadily. To prevent a radiator boiling, pull off the road safely, turn the heater and blower full on and switch off air conditioning. Keep an eye on water and oil levels. Never put cold water into a boiling radiator or it may crack. Check that the radiator is not obstructed by debris sucked up during the journey.

A long descent may result in overheating brakes; select the correct gear for the gradient and avoid excessive use of brakes. Even if you are using engine braking to control speed, caravan brakes may activate due to the overrun mechanism, which may cause them to overheat.

Travelling at altitude can cause a pressure build up in tanks and water pipes. You can prevent this by slightly opening the blade valve of your portable toilet and opening a tap a fraction.

Tunnels

Long tunnels are a much more commonly seen feature in Europe than in the UK, especially in mountainous regions. Tolls are usually charged for the use of major tunnels.

Dipped headlights are usually required by law even in well-lit tunnels, so switch them on before you enter. Snow chains, if used, must be removed before entering a tunnel in lay-bys provided for this purpose.

'No overtaking' signs must be strictly observed. Never cross central single or double lines. If overtaking is permitted in twin-tube tunnels, bear in mind that it is very easy to underestimate distances and speed once inside. In order to minimise the effects of exhaust fumes close all car windows and set the ventilator to circulate air, or operate the air conditioning system coupled with the recycled air option.

If you break down, try to reach the next lay-by and call for help from an emergency phone. If you cannot reach a lay-by, place your warning triangle at least 100 metres behind your vehicle. Modern tunnels have video surveillance systems to ensure prompt assistance in an emergency. Some tunnels can extend for miles and a high number of breakdowns are due to running out of fuel so make sure you have enough before entering the tunnel.

Mountain Pass Information

The dates of opening and closing given in the following tables are approximate. Before attempting late afternoon or early morning journeys across borders, check their opening times as some borders close at night.

Gradients listed are the maximum which may be encountered on the pass and may be steeper at the inside of curves, particularly on older roads.

Gravel surfaces (such as dirt and stone chips) vary considerably; they can be dusty when dry and slippery when wet. Where known to exist, this type of surface has been noted.

In fine weather winter tyres or snow chains will only be required on very high passes, or for short periods in early or late summer. In winter conditions you will probably need to use them at altitudes exceeding 600 metres (approximately 2,000 feet).

Converting Gradients

20% = 1 in 5	11% = 1 in 9
16% = 1 in 6	10% = 1 in 8
14% = 1 in 7	8% = 1 in 12
12% = 1 in 8	6% = 1 in 16

Tables and Maps

Much of the information contained in the following tables was originally supplied by The Automobile Association and other motoring and tourist organisations. The Caravan and Motorhome Club haven't checked this information and cannot accept responsibility for the accuracy or for errors or omissions to these tables.

The mountain passes, rail and road tunnels listed in the tables are shown on the following maps. Numbers and letters against each pass or tunnel in the tables correspond with the numbers and letters on the maps.

Abbreviations

MHV	Maximum height of vehicle
MLV	Maximum length of vehicle
MWV	Maximum width of vehicle
MWR	Minimum width of road
OC	Occasionally closed between dates
UC	Usually closed between dates
UO	Usually open between dates, although a fall of snow may obstruct the road for 24-48 hours.

Major Alpine Mountain Passes

Before using any of these passes, please read the advice at the beginning of this chapter.

	Pass Height In Metres (Feet)	From To	Max Gradient	Conditions and Comments
1	**Allos** (France) 2250 (7382)	Colmars Barcelonette	10%	UC early Nov-early Jun. MWR 4m (13'1") Very winding, single track, mostly unguarded pass on D908; passing bays on southern slope; poor surface, MWV 1.8m (5'11"). **Not recommended for caravans.**
2	**Aravis** (France) 1498 (4915)	La Clusaz Flumet	9%	OC Dec-Mar. MWR 4m (13'1"). Fine scenery; D909, fairly easy road. Poor surface in parts on Chamonix side. Some single-line traffic.
3	**Ballon d'Alsace** (France) 1178 (3865)	Giromagny St Maurice-sur-Moselle	11%	OC Dec-Mar. MWR 4m (13'1") Fairly straightforward ascent/descent; narrow in places; numerous bends. On road D465.
4	**Bayard** (France) 1248 (4094)	Chauffayer Gap	14%	UO. MWR 6m (19'8") Part of the Route Napoléon N85. Fairly easy, steepest on the S side with several hairpin bends. Negotiable by caravans from N-to-S via D1075 (N75) and Col-de-la-Croix Haute, avoiding Gap.
5	**Brouis** (France) 1279 (4196)	Nice Col-de-Tende	12.50%	UO. MWR 6m (19'8") Good surface but many hairpins on D6204 (N204)/S20. Steep gradients on approaches. Height of tunnel at Col-de-Tende at the Italian border is 3.8m (12'4") **Not recommended for caravans.**
6	**Bussang** (France) 721 (2365)	Thann St Maurice-sur-Moselle	7%	UO. MWR 4m (13'1") A very easy road (N66) over the Vosges; beautiful scenery.
7	**Cabre** (France) 1180 (3871)	Luc-en-Diois Aspres-sur-Buëch	9%	UO. MWR 5.5m (18') An easy pleasant road (D93/D993), winding at Col-de-Cabre.
8	**Cayolle** (France) 2326 (7631)	Barcelonnette Guillaumes	10%	UC early Nov-early Jun. MWR 4m (13'1") Narrow, winding road (D902) with hairpin bends; poor surface, broken edges with steep drops. Long stretches of single-track road with passing places. **Caravans prohibited.**
9	**Croix Haute** (France) 1179 (3868)	Monestier-de-Clermont Aspres-sur-Buëch	7%	UO on N75. MWR 5.5m (18') Well-engineered road (D1075/N75); several hairpin bends on N side.
10	**Faucille** (France) 1323 (4341)	Gex Morez	10%	UO. MWR 5m (16'5") Fairly wide, winding road (N5) across the Jura mountains; negotiable by caravans but probably better to follow route via La Cure-St Cergue-Nyon.

Before using any of these passes, please read the advice at the beginning of this chapter.

	Pass Height In Metres (Feet)	From To	Max Gradient	Conditions and Comments
11	**Forclaz** (Switzerland – France) 1527 (5010)	Martigny Argentière	8.50%	UO Forclaz; OC Montets Dec-early Apr. MWR 5m (16'5") MWV 2.5m (8'2") Good road over the pass and to the French border; long, hard climb out of Martigny; narrow and rough over Col-des-Montets on D1506 (N506).
12	**Galibier** (France) 2645 (8678)	La Grave St Michel-de-Maurienne	12.50%	UC Oct-Jun. MWR 3m (9'10") Mainly wide, well-surfaced road (D902) but unprotected and narrow over summit. From Col-du-Lautaret it rises over the Col-du-Telegraphe then 11 more hairpin bends on descent then 5km (3.1 miles) narrow and rough; easier in N to S direction. Limited parking at summit. **Not recommended for caravans.** (There is a single-track tunnel under the Galibier summit, controlled by traffic lights; caravans are not permitted).
13	**Gorges-du-Verdon** (France) 1032 (3386)	Castellane Moustiers-Ste Marie	9%	UO. MWR probably 5m (16'5") On road D952 over Col-d'Ayen and Col-d'Olivier. Moderate gradients but slow, narrow and winding. Poss heavy traffic.
14	**Iseran** (France) 2770 (9088)	Bourg-St Maurice Lanslebourg	11%	UC mid Oct-late Jun. MWR 4m (13'1") Second highest pass in the Alps on road D902. Well-graded with reasonable bends, average surface. Several unlit tunnels on N approach. **Not recommended for caravans.**
15	**Izoard** (France) 2360 (7743)	Guillestre Briançon	12.50%	UC late Oct-mid Jun. MWR 5m (16'5") Fine scenery. Winding, sometimes narrow road (D902) with many hairpin bends; care required at several unlit tunnels near Guillestre. **Not recommended for caravans.**
16	**Larche (della Maddalena)** (France – Italy) 1994 (6542)	La Condamine-Châtelard Vinadio	8.50%	OC Dec-Mar. MWR 3.5m (11'6") An easy, well-graded road (D900); long, steady ascent on French side, many hairpins on Italian side (S21). Fine scenery; ample parking at summit.
17	**Lautaret** (France) 2058 (6752)	Le Bourg-d'Oisans Briançon	12.50%	OC Dec-Mar. MWR 4m (13'1") Modern, evenly graded but winding road (D1091), and unguarded in places; very fine scenery; suitable for caravans but with care through narrow tunnels.
18	**Leques** (France) 1146 (3760)	Barrême Castellane	8%	UO. MWR 4m (13'1") On Route Napoléon (D4085). Light traffic; excellent surface; narrow in places on N ascent. S ascent has many hairpins.
19	**Mont Cenis** (France – Italy) 2083 (6834)	Lanslebourg Susa	12.50%	UC Nov-May. MWR 5m (16'5") Approach by industrial valley. An easy highway (D1006/S25) with mostly good surface; spectacular scenery; long descent into Italy with few stopping places. Alternative Fréjus road tunnel available.
20	**Montgenèvre** (France – Italy) 1850 (6070)	Briançon Cesana-Torinese	9%	UO. MWR 5m (16'5") An easy, modern road (N94/S24) with some tight hairpin bends on French side; road widened & tunnels improved on Italian side. Much used by lorries; may be necessary to travel at their speed and give way to oncoming large vehicles on hairpins.

Major Alpine Mountain Passes

Before using any of these passes, please read the advice at the beginning of this chapter.

Pass Height In Metres (Feet)	From To	Max Gradient	Conditions and Comments
Montets (See Forclaz)			
21 Morgins (France – Switzerland) 1369 (4491)	Abondance Monthey	14%	UO. MWR 4m (13'1") A lesser used route (D22) through pleasant, forested countryside crossing French/Swiss border. **Not recommended for caravans.**
22 Petit St Bernard (France – Italy) 2188 (7178)	Bourg-St Maurice Pré-St Didier	8.50%	UC mid Oct-Jun. MWR 5m (16'5") Outstanding scenery, but poor surface and unguarded broken edges near summit. Easiest from France (D1090); sharp hairpins on climb from Italy (S26). **Vehicles towing another vehicle prohibited.**
23 Restefond (La Bonette) (France) 2802 (9193)	Barcelonnette St Etienne-de-Tinée	16%	UC Oct-Jun. MWR 3m (9'10") The highest pass in the Alps. Rebuilt, resurfaced road (D64) with rest area at summit – top loop narrow and unguarded. Winding with hairpin bends. **Not recommended for caravans.**
24 Schlucht (France) 1139 (3737)	Gérardmer Munster	7%	UO. MWR 5m (16'5") An extremely picturesque route (D417) crossing the Vosges mountains, with easy, wide bends on the descent. Good surface.
25 Tenda (Tende) Italy – France 1321 (4334)	Borgo-San Dalmazzo Tende	9%	UO. MWR 6m (19'8") Well-guarded, modern road (S20/ND6204) with several hairpin bends; road tunnel (height 3.8m) at summit narrow with poor road surface. Less steep on Italian side. **Caravans prohibited during winter.**
26 Vars (France) 2109 (6919)	St Paul-sur-Ubaye Guillestre	9%	OC Dec-Mar. MWR 5m (16'5") Easy winding ascent and descent on D902 with 14 hairpin bends; good surface.

Technical information by courtesy of the Automobile Association. Additional update and amendments supplied by caravanners and tourers who have themselves used the passes and tunnels.
The Caravan and Motorhome Club has not checked the information contained in these tables and cannot accept responsibility for their accuracy, or for any errors, omissions, or their effects.

The Alpine maps only show the major Alpine mountain passes for France. For other countries please refer to the Touring Europe guide.

Major Alpine Road Tunnels - France

Before using any of these tunnels, please read the advice at the beginning of this chapter.

	Tunnel	Route and Height above Sea Level	General Information and Comments
A	**Frejus** (France – Italy) 12.8 km (8 miles)	Modane to Bardonecchia 1220m (4000')	MWR 9m (29'6"), tunnel height 4.3m (14'). Min/max speed 60/70 km/h (37/44 mph). Return tickets valid until midnight on 7th day after day of issue. Season tickets are available. Approach via A43 and D1006; heavy use by freight vehicles. Good surface on approach roads. **Tolls charged.** www.sftrf.fr
B	**Mont Blanc** (France – Italy) 11.6 km (7.2 miles)	Chamonix to Courmayeur 1381m (4530')	MHV 4.7m (15'5"), MWV 6m (19'6") On N205 France, S26 (Italy). Max speed in tunnel 70 km/h (44 mph) – lower limits when exiting; min speed 50 km/h. Leave 150m between vehicles; ensure enough fuel for 30km. Return tickets valid until midnight on 7th day after issue. Season tickets are available. **Tolls charged.** www.tunnelmb.net
-	**Ste Marie-aux-Mines** (France) 6.8 km (4.25 miles)	St Dié to Ste-Marie-aux-Mines 772m (2533')	At 7km, this is the longest road tunnel situated entirely in France. Also known as Maurice Lemaire Tunnel, through the Vosges in north-east France from Lusse on N159 to N59. **Tolls charged.** Alternate route via Col-de-Ste Marie on D459.

NOTES: *Dipped headlights should be used (unless stated otherwise) when travelling through road tunnels, even when the road appears to be well lit. In some countries police make spot checks and impose on-the-spot fines.*

During the winter wheel chains may be required on the approaches to some tunnels. These must not be used in tunnels and lay-bys are available for the removal and refitting of wheel chains.

Major Alpine Mountain Passes & Tunnels

Alpine Passes and Tunnel Maps   55

Major Pyrenees Mountain Passes

Before using any of these passes, please read the advice at the beginning of this chapter.

	Pass Height In Metres (Feet)	From To	Max Gradient	Conditions and Comments
27	**Aubisque** (France) 1710 (5610)	Eaux Bonnes *Argelés-Gazost*	10%	UC mid Oct-Jun. MWR 3.5m (11'6") Very winding; continuous on D918 but easy ascent; descent including Col-d'Aubisque 1709m (5607 feet) and Col-du-Soulor 1450m (4757 feet); 8km (5 miles) of very narrow, rough, unguarded road with steep drop. **Not recommended for caravans.**
28	**Col d'Haltza and Col-de-Burdincurutcheta** (France) 782 (2565) and 1135 (3724)	St Jean-Pied-de-Port *Larrau*	11%	UO. A narrow road (D18/D19) leading to Iraty skiing area. Narrow with some tight hairpin bends; rarely has central white line and stretches are unguarded. Not for the faint-hearted. **Not recommended for caravans.**
29	**Envalira** (France – Andorra) 2407 (7897)	Pas-de-la-Casa *Andorra*	12.5%	OC Nov-Apr. MWR 6m (19'8") Good road (N22/CG2) with wide bends on ascent and descent; fine views. MHV 3.5m (11'6") on N approach near l'Hospitalet. Early start rec in summer to avoid border delays. Envalira Tunnel (toll) reduces congestion and avoids highest part of pass. See *Pyrenean Road Tunnels* in this section.
30	**Ibañeta (Roncevalles)** (France – Spain) 1057 (3468)	St Jean-Pied-de-Port *Pamplona*	10%	UO. MWR 4m (13'1") Slow and winding, scenic route on N135.
31	**Peyresourde** (France) 1563 (5128)	Arreau *Bagnères-de-Luchon*	10%	UO. MWR 4m (13'1") D618 somewhat narrow with several hairpin bends, though not difficult. **Not recommended for caravans.**
32	**Port** (France) 1249 (4098)	Tarascon-sur-Ariège *Massat*	10%	OC Nov-Mar. MWR 4m (13'1") A fairly easy, scenic road (D618), but narrow on some bends.
33	**Portet-d'Aspet** (France) 1069 (3507)	Audressein *Fronsac*	14%	UO. MWR 3.5m (11'6") Approached from W by the easy Col-des-Ares and Col-de-Buret; well-engineered but narrow road (D618); care needed on hairpin bends. **Not recommended for caravans.**
34	**Pourtalet** (France – Spain) 1792 (5879)	Laruns *Biescas*	10%	UC late Oct-early Jun. MWR 3.5m (11'6") A fairly easy, unguarded road, but narrow in places. Easier from Spain (A136), steeper in France (D934). **Not recommended for caravans.**
35	**Puymorens** (France) 1915 (6283)	Ax-les-Thermes *Bourg-Madame*	10%	OC Nov-Apr. MWR 5.5m (18') MHV 3.5m (11'6") A generally easy, modern tarmac road (N20). Parallel toll road tunnel available. See *Pyrenean Road Tunnels* in this section.
36	**Quillane** (France) 1714 (5623)	Axat *Mont-Louis*	8.5%	OC Nov-Mar. MWR 5m (16'5") An easy, straightforward ascent and descent on D118.

Before using any of these passes, please read the advice at the beginning of this chapter.

Pass Height In Metres (Feet)	From To	Max Gradient	Conditions and Comments
㊲ **Somport** (France – Spain) 1632 (5354)	Accous Jaca	10%	UO. MWR 3.5m (11'6"). A favoured, old-established route; not particularly easy and narrow in places with many unguarded bends on French side (N134); excellent road on Spanish side (N330). Use of road tunnel advised – see *Pyrenean Road Tunnels* in this section. NB Visitors advise re-fuelling no later than Sabiñánigo when travelling south to north.
㊳ **Tourmalet** (France) 2114 (6936)	Ste Marie-de-Campan Luz-St Sauveur	12.5%	UC Oct-mid Jun. MWR 4m (13'1"). The highest French Pyrenean route (D918); approaches good, though winding, narrow in places and exacting over summit; sufficiently guarded. Rough surface & uneven edges on west side. **Not recommended for caravans.**

Major Pyrenean Road Tunnels

Before using any of these tunnels, please read the advice at the beginning of this chapter.

Tunnel	Route and Height Above Sea Level	General Information and Comments
Ⓐ **Bielsa** (France – Spain) 3.2 km (2 miles)	Aragnouet to Bielsa 1830m (6000')	Open 24 hours but possibly closed October-Easter. On French side (D173) generally good road surface but narrow with steep hairpin bends and steep gradients near summit. Often no middle white line. Spanish side (A138) has good width and is less steep and winding. Used by heavy vehicles. No tolls. Please note the tunnel may be undergoing repair works and as a result may be closed at certain times and on certain days.
Ⓑ **Envalira** (France – Spain via Andorra) 2.8 km (1.75 miles)	Pas de la Casa to El Grau Roig 2000m (6562')	Tunnel width 8.25m. On N22/CG2 France to Andorra. **Tolls charged.**
Ⓒ **Puymorens** (France – Spain) 4.8 km (2.9 miles)	Ax-les-Thermes to Puigcerda 1515m (4970')	MHV 3.5m (11'6"). Part of Puymorens pass on N20/E9. **Tolls charged.**
Ⓓ **Somport** (France – Spain) 8.6 km (5.3 miles)	Urdos to Canfranc 1116m (3661')	Tunnel height 4.55m (14'9"), width 10.5m (34'). Max speed 90 km/h (56 mph); leave 100m between vehicles. On N134 (France), N330 (Spain). No tolls.

Keeping in Touch

Telephones and Calling

Most people need to use a telephone at some point while they're away, whether to keep in touch with family and friends back home or call ahead to sites. Even if you don't plan to use a phone while you're away, it is best to make sure you have access to one in case of emergencies.

International Direct Dial Calls

Each country has a unique dialing code you must use if phoning from outside that country. You can find the international dialing code for any country by visiting www.thephonebook.bt.com. First dial the code then the local number. If the area code starts with a zero this should be omitted.

The international access code to dial the UK from anywhere in the world is 0044.

Ringing Tones

Ringing tones vary from country to country, so may sound very different to UK tones. Some ringing tones sound similar to error or engaged tones that you would hear on a UK line.

Using Mobile Phones

Mobile phones have an international calling option called 'roaming' which will automatically search for a local network when you switch your phone on. The EU abolished roaming charges in 2017, but you should contact your service provider to check if there are any chardges for your tariff.

Storing telephone numbers in your phone's contact list in international format (i.e. use the prefix of +44 and omit the initial '0') will mean that your contacts will automatically work abroad as well as in the UK.

Global SIM Cards

If you're planning on travelling to more than one country consider buying a global SIM card. This will mean your mobile phone can operate on foreign mobile networks, which will be more cost effective than your service provider's roaming charges. For details of SIM cards available, speak to your service provider or visit www.0044.co.uk or www.globalsimcard.co.uk.

You may find it simpler to buy a SIM card or cheap 'pay-as-you-go' phone abroad if you plan to make a lot for local calls, e.g. to book campsites or restaurants. This may mean

that you still have higher call charges for international calls (such as calling the UK). Before buying a different SIM card, check with you provider whether your phone is locked against use on other networks.

Hands-Free

Legislation in Europe forbids the use of mobile or car phones while driving except when using hands-free equipment. In some European countries it is now also illegal to drive while wearing headphones or a headset - including hands-free kits.

If you are involved in an accident whilst driving and using a hand-held mobile phone, your insurance company may refuse to honour the claim.

Accessing the internet

Accessing the internet via your mobile (data roaming) while outside of the UK can be very expensive. It is recommended that you disable your internet access by switching 'data roaming' off to avoid a large mobile phone bill.

Internet Access

Wi-Fi is available on lots of campsites in Europe, the cost may be an additional charge or included in your pitch fee. Most larger towns may have internet cafés or libraries where you can access the internet, however lots of fast food restaurants and coffee chains now offer free Wi-Fi for customers so you can get access for the price of a coffee or bite to eat.

Many people now use their smartphones for internet access. Another option is a dongle – a device which connects to your laptop to give internet access using a mobile phone network. While these methods are economical in the UK, overseas you will be charged data roaming charges which can run into hundreds or thousands of pounds depending on how much data you use. If you plan on using your smartphone or a dongle abroad speak to your service provider before you leave the UK to make sure you understand the costs or add an overseas data roaming package to your phone contract.

Making Calls from your Laptop

If you download Skype to your laptop you can make free calls to other Skype users anywhere in the world using a Wi-Fi connection. Rates for calls to non-Skype users (landline or mobile phone) are also very competitively-priced. You will need a computer with a microphone and speakers, and a webcam is handy too. It is also possible to download Skype to an internet-enabled mobile phone to take advantage of the same low-cost calls – see www.skype.com.

Club Together

If you want to chat to other members either at home or while you're away, you can do so on The Club's online community Club Together. You can ask questions and gather opinions on the forums at camc.com/together.

Radio and Television

The BBC World Service broadcasts radio programmes 24 hours a day worldwide and you can listen on a number of platforms: online, via satellite or cable, DRM digital radio, internet radio or mobile phone. You can find detailed information and programme schedules at www.bbc.co.uk/worldservice.

Whereas analogue television signals were switched off in the UK during 2012, no date has yet been fixed for the switch off of analogue radio signals.

Digital Terrestrial Television

As in the UK, television transmissions in most of Europe have been converted to digital. The UK's high definition transmission technology may be more advanced than any currently implemented or planned in Europe. This means that digital televisions intended for use in the UK might not be able to receive HD terrestrial signals in some countries.

Satellite Television

For English-language TV programmes the only realistic option is satellite, and satellite dishes are a common sight on campsites all over Europe. A satellite dish mounted on the caravan roof or clamped to a pole fixed to the drawbar, or one mounted on a foldable free-standing tripod, will provide good reception and minimal interference. Remember however that obstructions to the south east (such as tall trees or even mountains) or heavy rain, can interrupt the signals. A specialist dealer will be able to advise you on the best way of mounting your dish. You will also need a satellite receiver and ideally a satellite-finding meter.

The main entertainment channels such as BBC1, ITV1 and Channel 4 can be difficult to pick up in mainland Europe as they are now being transmitted by new narrow-beam satellites. A 60cm dish should pick up these channels in most of France, Belgium and the Netherlands but as you travel further afield, you'll need a progressively larger dish. See www.satelliteforcaravans.co.uk (created and operated by a Club member) for the latest changes and developments, and for information on how to set up your equipment.

Medical Matters

Before You Travel

You can find country specific medical advice, including any vaccinations you may need, from www.nhs.uk/healthcareabroad, or speak to your GP surgery. For general enquiries about medical care abroad contact NHS England on 0300 311 22 33 or email england.contactus@nhs.uk.

If you have any pre-existing medical conditions you should check with your GP that you are fit to travel. Ask your doctor for a written summary of any medical problems and a list of medications , which is especially imporant for those who use controlled drugs or hypodermic syringes.

Always make sure that you have enough medication for the duration of your holiday and some extra in case your return is delayed. Take details of the generic name of any drugs you use, as brand names may be different abroad, your blood group and details of any allergies (translations may be useful for restaurants).

An emergency dental kit is available from High Street chemists which will allow you temporarily to restore a crown, bridge or filling or to dress a broken tooth until you can get to a dentist.

A good website to check before you travel is www.nathnac.org/travel which gives general health and safety advice, as well as highlighting potential health risks by country.

European Heath Insurance Card (EHIC)

Before leaving home apply for a European Health Insurance Card (EHIC). British residents temporarily visiting another EU country are entitled to receive state-provided emergency treatment during their stay on the same terms as residents of those countries, but you must have a valid EHIC to claim these services.

To apply for your EHIC visit www.ehic.org.uk, call 0300 330 1350 or pick up an application form from a post office. An EHIC is required by each family member, with children under 16 included in a parent or guardian's application. The EHIC is free of charge, is valid for up to five years and can be renewed up to six months before its expiry date. Before you travel remember to check that your EHIC is still valid.

An EHIC is not a substitute for travel insurance and it is strongly recommended that you arrange full travel insurance before leaving home regardless of the cover provided by your EHIC. Some insurance companies require you to have an EHIC and some will waive the policy excess if an EHIC has been used.

If your EHIC is stolen or lost while you are abroad contact 0044 191 2127500 for help. If you experience difficulties in getting your EHIC accepted, telephone the Department for Work & Pensions for assistance on the overseas healthcare team line 0044 (0)191 218 1999 between 8am to 5pm Monday to Friday. Residents of the Republic of Ireland, the Isle of Man and Channel Islands, should check with their own health authorities about reciprocal arrangements with other countries.

Holiday Travel Insurance

Despite having an EHIC you may incur high medical costs if you fall ill or have an accident. The cost of bringing a person back to the UK in the event of illness or death is never covered by the EHIC.

Separate additional travel insurance adequate for your destination is essential, such as the Club's Red Pennant Overseas Holiday Insurance – see camc.com/redpennant.

First Aid

A first aid kit containing at least the basic requirements is an essential item, and in some countries it is compulsory to carry one in your vehicle (see the Essential Equipment Table in the chapter Motoring – Equipment). Kits should contain items such as sterile pads, assorted dressings, bandages and plasters, antiseptic wipes or cream, cotton wool, scissors, eye bath and tweezers. Also make sure you carry something for upset stomachs, painkillers and an antihistamine in case of hay fever or mild allergic reactions.

If you're travelling to remote areas then you may find it useful to carry a good first aid manual. The British Red Cross publishes a comprehensive First Aid Manual in conjunction with St John Ambulance and St Andrew's Ambulance Association.

Accidents and Emergencies

If you are involved in or witness a road accident the police may want to question you about it. If possible take photographs or make sketches of the scene, and write a few notes about what happened as it may be more difficult to remember the details at a later date.

For sports activities such as skiing and mountaineering, travel insurance must include provision for covering the cost of mountain and helicopter rescue. Visitors to the Savoie and Haute-Savoie areas should be aware that an accident or illness may result in a transfer to Switzerland for hospital treatment. There is a reciprocal healthcare agreement for British citizens visiting Switzerland but you will be required to pay the full costs of treatment and afterwards apply for a refund.

Sun Protection

Never under-estimate how ill exposure to the sun can make you. If you are not used to the heat it is very easy to fall victim to heat exhaustion or heat stroke. Avoid sitting in the sun between 11am and 3pm and cover your head if sitting or walking in the sun. Use a high sun protection factor (SPF) and re-apply frequently. Make sure you drink plenty of fluids.

Tick-Borne Encephalitis (TBE) and Lyme Disease

Hikers and outdoor sports enthusiasts planning trips to forested, rural areas should be aware of tick-borne encephalitis, which is transmitted by the bite of an infected tick. If you think you may be at risk, seek medical advice on prevention and immunisation before you leave the UK.

There is no vaccine against Lyme disease, an equally serious tick-borne infection, which, if left untreated, can attack the nervous system and joints. You can minimise the risk by using an insect repellent containing DEET, wearing long sleeves and long trousers, and checking for ticks after outdoor activity.

Avoid unpasteurised dairy products in risk areas. See www.tickalert.org or telephone 01943 468010 for more information.

Water and food

Water from mains supplies throughout Europe is generally safe, but may be treated with chemicals which make it taste different to tap water in the UK. If in any doubt, always drink bottled water or boil it before drinking.

Food poisoning is potential anywhere, and a complete change of diet may upset your stomach as well. In hot conditions avoid any food that hasn't been refrigerated or hot food that has been left to cool. Be sensible about the food that you eat – don't eat unpasteurised or undercooked food and if you aren't sure about the freshness of meat or seafood then it is best avoided.

Returning Home

If you become ill on your return home tell your doctor that you have been abroad and which countries you have visited. Even if you have received medical treatment in another country, always consult your doctor if you have been bitten or scratched by an animal while on holiday. If you were given any medicines in another country, it may be illegal to bring them back into the UK. If in doubt, declare them at Customs when you return.

Electricity and Gas

Electricity – General Advice

The voltage for mains electricity is 230V across the EU, but varying degrees of 'acceptable tolerance' mean you may find variations in the actual voltage. Most appliances sold in the UK are 220-240V so should work correctly. However, some high-powered equipment, such as microwave ovens, may not function well – check your instruction manual for any specific instructions. Appliances marked with 'CE' have been designed to meet the requirements of relevant European directives.

The table below gives an approximate idea of which appliances can be used based on the amperage which is being supplied (although not all appliances should be used at the same time). You can work it out more accurately by making a note of the wattage of each appliance in your caravan. The wattages given are based on appliances designed for use in caravans and motorhomes. Household kettles, for example, have at least a 2000W element. Each caravan circuit will also have a maximum amp rating which should not be exceeded.

Electrical Connections – EN60309-2 (CEE17)

EN60309-2 (formerly known as CEE17) is the European Standard for all newly fitted connectors. Most sites should now have these connectors, however there is no requirement

Amps	Wattage (Approx)	Fridge	Battery Charger	Air Conditioning	LCD TV	Water Heater	Kettle (750W)	Heater (1kW)
2	400	✓	✓					
4	900	✓	✓		✓	✓		
6	1300	✓	✓	-*	✓	✓	✓	
8	1800	✓	✓	✓**	✓	✓	✓	✓**
10	2300	✓	✓	✓**	✓	✓	✓	✓**
16	3600	✓	✓	✓	✓	✓	✓	✓**

*   Usage possible, depending on wattage of appliance in question
** Not to be used at the same time as other high-wattage equipment

to replace connectors which were installed before this was standardised so you may still find some sites where your UK 3 pin connector doesn't fit. For this reason it is a good idea to carry a 2-pin adapter. If you are already on site and find your connector doesn't fit, ask campsite staff to borrow or hire an adaptor. You may still encounter a poor electrical supply on site even with an EN60309-2 connection.

If the campsite does not have a modern EN60309-2 (CEE17) supply, ask to see the electrical protection for the socket outlet. If there is a device marked with IDn = 30mA, then the risk is minimised.

Hooking Up to the Mains

Connection should always be made in the following order:

- Check your outfit isolating switch is at 'off'.
- Uncoil the connecting cable from the drum. A coiled cable with current flowing through it may overheat. Take your cable and insert the connector (female end) into your outfit inlet.
- Insert the plug (male end) into the site outlet socket.
- Switch outfit isolating switch to 'on'.
- Use a polarity tester in one of the 13A sockets in the outfit to check all connections are correctly wired. Never leave it in the socket.

Some caravans have these devices built in as standard.

It is recommended that the supply is not used if the polarity is incorrect (see Reversed Polarity overleaf).

Warnings:

If you are in any doubt of the safety of the system, if you don't receive electricity once connected or if the supply stops then contact the site staff.

If the fault is found to be with your outfit then call a qualified electrician rather than trying to fix the problem yourself.

To ensure your safety you should never use an electrical system which you can't confirm to be safe. Use a mains tester such as the one shown below to test the electrical supply.

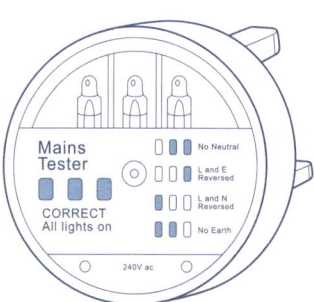

Electricity and Gas 71

Always check that a proper earth connection exists before using the electrics. Please note that these testers may not pick up all earth faults so if there is any doubt as to the integrity of the earth system do not use the electrical supply.

Disconnection

- Switch your outfit isolating switch to 'off'.
- At the site supply socket withdraw the plug.
- Disconnect the cable from your outfit.

Motorhomes – if leaving your pitch during the day, don't leave your mains cable plugged into the site supply, as this creates a hazard if the exposed live connections in the plug are touched or if the cable is not seen during grass-cutting.

Reversed Polarity

Even if the site connector meets European Standard EN60309-2 (CEE17), British caravanners are still likely to encounter the problem known as reversed polarity. This is where the site supply 'live' line connects to the outfit's 'neutral' and vice versa. You should always check the polarity immediately on connection, using a polarity tester available from caravan accessory shops. If polarity is reversed the caravan mains electricity should not be used. Try using another nearby socket instead. Frequent travellers to the Continent can make up an adaptor themselves, or ask an electrician to make one for you, with the live and neutral wires reversed. Using a reversed polarity socket will probably not affect how an electrical appliance works, however your

protection is greatly reduced. For example, a lamp socket may still be live as you touch it while replacing a blown bulb, even if the light switch is turned off.

Shaver Sockets

Most campsites provide shaver sockets with a voltage of 220V or 110V. Using an incorrect voltage may cause the shaver to become hot or break. The 2-pin adaptor available in the UK may not fit Continental sockets so it is advisable to buy 2-pin adaptors on the Continent. Many modern shavers will work on a range of voltages which make them suitable for travelling abroad. Check you instruction manual to see if this is the case.

Gas – General Advice

Gas usage can be difficult to predict as so many factors, such as temperature and how often you eat out, can affect the amount you need. As a rough guide allow 0.45kg of gas a day for normal summer usage.

With the exception of Campingaz, LPG cylinders normally available in the UK cannot be exchanged abroad. If possible, take enough gas with you and bring back the empty cylinders. Always check how many you can take with you as ferry and tunnel operators may restrict the number of cylinders you are permitted to carry for safety reasons.

The full range of Campingaz cylinders is widely available from large supermarkets and hypermarkets, although at the end of the holiday season stocks may be low. Other popular brands of gas are Primagaz, Butagaz,

Site Hooking Up Adaptor
ADAPTATEUR DE PRISE AU SITE (SECTEUR)
CAMPINGPLATZ-ANSCHLUSS (NETZ)

EXTENSION LEAD TO CARAVAN
Câble de rallonge à la caravane
Verlâengerungskabel zum wohnwagen

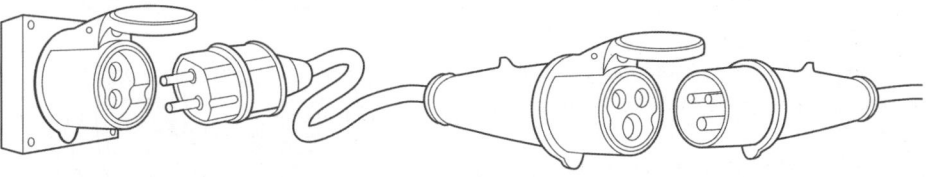

SITE OUTLET
Prise du site
Campingplatz-Steckdose

MAINS ADAPTOR
Adaptateur Secteur
Netzanschlußstacker

16A 230V AC

Totalgaz and Le Cube. A loan deposit is required and if you are buying a cylinder for the first time you may also need to buy the appropriate regulator or adaptor hose.

If you are touring in cold weather conditions use propane gas instead of butane. Many other brands of gas are available in different countries and, as long as you have the correct regulator, adaptor and hose and the cylinders fit in your gas locker these local brands can also be used.

Gas cylinders are now standardised with a pressure of 30mbar for both butane and propane within the EU. On UK-specification caravans and motorhomes (2004 models and later) a 30mbar regulator suited to both propane and butane use is fitted to the bulkhead of the gas locker. This is connected to the cylinder with a connecting hose (and sometimes an adaptor) to suit different brands or types of gas. Older outfits and some foreign-built ones may use a cylinder-mounted regulator, which may need to be changed to suit different brands or types of gas.

Warnings:

- Refilling gas cylinders intended to be exchanged is against the law in most countries, however you may still find that some sites and dealers will offer to refill cylinders for you. Never take them up on this service as it can be dangerous; the cylinders haven't been designed for user-refilling and it is possible to overfill them with catastrophic consequences.

- Regular servicing of gas appliances is important as a faulty appliance can emit carbon monoxide, which could prove fatal. Check your vehicle or appliance handbook for service recommendations.

- Never use a hob or oven as a space heater.

The Caravan and Motorhome Club publishes a range of technical leaflets for its members including detailed advice on the use of electricity and gas – you can request copies or see camc.com/advice-and-training.

Safety and Security

EU countries have good legislation in place to protect your safety wherever possible. However accidents and crime will still occur and taking sensible precautions can help to minimise your risk of being involved.

Beaches, Lakes and Rivers

Check for any warning signs or flags before you swim and ensure that you know what they mean. Check the depth of water before diving and avoid diving or jumping into murky water as submerged objects may not be visible. Familiarise yourself with the location of safety apparatus and/or lifeguards.

Use only the designated areas for swimming, watersports and boating and always use life jackets where appropriate. Watch out for tides, undertows, currents and wind strength and direction before swimming in the sea. This applies in particular when using inflatables, windsurfing equipment, body boards, kayaks or sailing boats. Sudden changes of wave and weather conditions combined with fast tides and currents are particularly dangerous.

Campsite Safety

Once you've settled in, take a walk around the site to familiarise yourself with its layout and locate the nearest safety equipment. Ensure that children know their way around and where your pitch is.

Natural disasters are rare, but always think about what could happen. A combination of heavy rain and a riverside pitch could lead to flash flooding, for example, so make yourself aware of site evacuation procedures.

Be aware of sources of electricity and cabling on and around your pitch – electrical safety might not be up to the same standards as in the UK.

Poison for rodent control is sometimes used on sites or surrounding farmland. Warning notices are not always posted and you are strongly advised to check if staying on a rural site with dogs or children.

Incidents of theft on campsites are rare but when leaving your caravan unattended make sure you lock all doors and shut windows. Conceal valuables from sight and lock up any bicycles.

Children

Watch out for children as you drive around the site and don't exceed walking pace.

Children's play areas are generally unsupervised, so check which are suitable for your children's ages and abilities. Read and respect the displayed rules. Remember it is your responsibility to supervise your children at all times.

Be aware of any campsite rules concerning ball games or use of play equipment, such as roller blades and skateboards. When your children attend organised activities, arrange when and where to meet afterwards. You should never leave children alone inside a caravan.

Fire

Fire prevention is important on sites, as fire can spread quickly between outfits. Certain areas of southern Europe experience severe water shortages in summer months leading to an increased fire risk. This may result in some local authorities imposing restrictions at short notice on the use of barbecues and open flames.

Fires can be a regular occurrence in forested areas, especially along the Mediterranean coast during summer months. They are generally extinguished quickly and efficiently but short term evacuations are sometimes necessary. If visiting forested areas familiarise yourself with local emergency procedures in the event of fire. Never use paraffin or gas heaters inside your caravan. Gas heaters should only be fitted when air is taken from outside the caravan. Don't change your gas cylinder inside the caravan. If you smell gas turn off the cylinder immediately, extinguish all naked flames and seek professional help.

Make sure you know where the fire points and telephones are on site and know the site fire drill. Make sure everyone in your party knows how to call the emergency services.

Where site rules permit the use of barbecues, take the following precautions to prevent fire:

- Never locate a barbecue near trees or hedges.
- Have a bucket of water to hand in case of sparks.
- Only use recommended fire-lighting materials.
- Don't leave a barbecue unattended when lit and dispose of hot ash safely.
- Never take a barbecue into an enclosed area or awning – even when cooling they continue to release carbon monoxide which can lead to fatal poisoning.

Swimming Pools

Familiarize yourself with the pool area before you venture in for a swim - check the pool layout and identify shallow and deep ends and the location of safety equipment. Check the gradient of the pool bottom as pools which shelve off sharply can catch weak or non-swimmers unawares.

Never dive or jump into a pool without knowing the depth – if there is a no diving rule it usually means the pool isn't deep enough for safe diving.

For pools with a supervisor or lifeguard, note any times or dates when the pool is not supervised. Read safety notices and rules posted around the pool.

On the Road

Don't leave valuables on view in cars or caravans, even if they are locked. Make sure items on roof racks or cycle carriers are locked securely.

Near to ports British owned cars have been targeted by thieves, both while parked and on the move, e.g. by flagging drivers down or indicating that a vehicle has a flat tyre. If you stop in such circumstances be wary of anyone offering help, ensure that car keys are not left in the ignition and that vehicle doors are locked while you investigate.

Always keep car doors locked and windows closed when driving in populated areas. Beware of a 'snatch' through open car windows at traffic lights, filling stations or in traffic jams. When driving through towns and cities keep your doors locked. Keep handbags, valuables and documents out of sight at all times.

If flagged down by another motorist for whatever reason, take care that your own car is locked and windows closed while you check outside, even if someone is left inside.

Be particularly careful on long, empty stretches of motorway and when you stop for fuel. Even if the people flagging you down appear to be officials (e.g. wearing yellow reflective jackets or dark, 'uniform-type' clothing) lock your vehicle doors. They may appear to be friendly and helpful, but could be opportunistic thieves. Have a mobile phone to hand and, if necessary, be seen to use it.

Road accidents are a increased risk in some countries where traffic laws may be inadequately enforced, roads may be poorly maintained, road signs and lighting inadequate, and driving standards poor. It's a good idea to keep a fully-charged mobile phone with you in your car with the number of your breakdown organisation saved into it. On your return to the UK there are increasing issues with migrants attempting to stowaway in vehicles, especially if you're travelling through Calais. The UK government have issued the following instructions to prevent people entering the UK illegally:

- Where possible all access to vehicles or storage compartments should be fitted with locks.
- All locks must be engaged when the vehicle is stationary or unattended.
- Immediately before boarding your ferry or train check that the locks on your vehicle haven't been compromised.
- If you have any reason to suspect someone may have accessed your outfit speak to border control staff or call the police. Do not board the ferry or train or you may be liable for a fine of up to £2000.

Overnight Stops

Overnight stops should always be at campsites and not at motorway service areas, ferry terminal car parks, petrol station forecourts or isolated 'aires de services' on motorways where robberies are occasionally reported. If you decide to use these areas for a rest then take appropriate precautions, for example, shutting all windows, securing locks and making a thorough external check of your vehicle(s) before departing. Safeguard your property, e.g. handbags, while out of the caravan and beware of approaches by strangers.

For a safer place to take a break, there is a wide network of 'Aires de Services' in cities, towns and villages across Europe, many specifically for motorhomes with good security and overnight facilities. They are often less isolated and therefore safer than the motorway aires. It is rare that you will be the only vehicle staying on such areas, but take sensible precautions and trust your instincts.

Personal Security

Petty crime happens all over the world, including in the UK; however as a tourist you are more vulnerable to it. This shouldn't stop you from exploring new horizons, but there are a few sensible precautions you can take to minimise the risk.

- Leave valuables and jewellery at home. If you do take them, fit a small safe in your caravan or lock them in the boot of your car. Don't leave money or valuables in a car glovebox or on view. Don't leave bags in full view when sitting outside at cafés or restaurants, or leave valuables unattended on the beach.
- When walking be security-conscious. Avoid unlit streets at night, walk away from the kerb edge and carry handbags or shoulder bags on the side away from the kerb. The less of a tourist you appear, the less of a target you are.
- Keep a note of your holiday insurance details and emergency telephone numbers in more than one place, in case the bag or vehicle containing them is stolen.
- Beware of pickpockets in crowded areas, at tourist attractions and in cities. Be especially aware when using public transport in cities.
- Be cautious of bogus plain-clothes policemen who may ask to see your foreign currency or credit cards and passport. If approached, decline to show your money or to hand over your passport but ask for credentials and offer instead to go to the nearest police station.
- Laws and punishment vary from country to country so make yourself aware of anything which may affect you before you travel. Be especially careful on laws involving alcohol consumption (such as drinking in public areas), and never buy or use illegal drugs abroad.
- Respect customs regulations - smuggling is a serious offence and can carry heavy penalties. Do not carry parcels or luggage through customs for other people and never cross borders with people you do not know in your vehicle, such as hitchhikers.

The Foreign & Commonwealth Office produces a range of material to advise and inform British citizens travelling abroad about issues affecting their safety - www.gov.uk/foreign-travel-advice has country specific guides.

Money Security

We would rarely walk around at home carrying large amounts of cash, but as you may not have the usual access to bank accounts and credit cards you are more likely to do so on holiday. You are also less likely to have the same degree of security when online banking as you would in your own home. Take the following precautions to keep your money safe:

- Carry only the minimum amount of cash and don't rely on one person to carry everything. Never carry a wallet in your back pocket. Concealed money belts are the most secure way to carry cash and passports.
- Keep a separate note of bank account and credit/debit card numbers. Carry your credit card issuer/bank's 24-hour UK contact number with you.
- Be careful when using cash machines (ATMs) – try to use a machine in an area with high footfall and don't allow yourself to be distracted. Put your cash away before moving away from the cash machine.
- Always guard your PIN number, both at cash machines and when using your card to pay in shops and restaurants. Never let your card out of your sight while paying.
- If using internet banking do not leave the PC or mobile device unattended and make sure you log out fully at the end of the session.

Winter Sports

If you are planning a skiing holiday in Andorra you should contact the Andorran Embassy in London (tel 020 8874 4806) for advice on safety and weather conditions before travelling. All safety instructions should be followed meticulously given the dangers of avalanches in some areas. See www.ski.andorra.com or www.avalanches.org for more information.

British Consular Services Abroad

British Embassy and Consular staff offer practical advice, assistance and support to British travellers abroad. They can, for example, issue replacement passports, help Britons who have been the victims of crime, contact relatives and friends in the event of an

accident, illness or death, provide information about transferring funds and provide details of local lawyers, doctors and interpreters. But there are limits to their powers and a British Consul cannot, for example, give legal advice, intervene in court proceedings, put up bail, pay for legal or medical bills, or for funerals or the repatriation of bodies, or undertake work more properly done by banks, motoring organisations and travel insurers. If you are charged with a serious offence, insist on the British Consul being informed. You will be contacted as soon as possible by a Consular Officer who can advise on local procedures, provide access to lawyers and insist that you are treated as well as nationals of the country which is holding you. However, they cannot get you released as a matter of course.

British Embassy in France

35 RUE DU FAUBOURG ST HONORE
75363 PARIS CEDEX 08 PARIS
Tel: 01 44 51 31 00
www.ukinfrance.fco.gov.uk

There are also Consulates in Bordeaux, Lille, Lyon and Marseilles.

Irish Embassy in France

12 AVENUE FOCH, 75116 PARIS
Tel: 01 44 17 67 00
www.embassyofireland.fr

There are also Irish Consulates-General/ Consulates in Cannes, Cherbourg, Lyon and Monaco.

For Consular help while in Andorra contact the British Consulate-General in Barcelona:

AVDA DIAGNOL 477-13, 08036 BARCELONA

Tel: 00 34 902 109 356

www.ukinspain.fco.gov.uk

Safety and Security   79

Continental Campsites

The quantity and variety of sites across France means you're sure to find one that suits your needs – from full facilities and entertainment to quiet rural retreats. If you haven't previously toured outside of the UK you may notice some differences, such as pitches being smaller or closer together.

Camping in France

There are approximately 10,400 campsites throughout France classified from 1 to 5 stars, including many small farm sites. Higher rated sites often have a wider range of facilities available. All classified sites must display their classification, current charges, capacity and site regulations at the site entrance.

Casual/wild camping is prohibited in many state forests, national parks and nature reserves, and in all public or private forests in the départements of Landes and Gironde, along the Mediterranean coast including the Camargue, parts of the Atlantic and Brittany coasts, Versailles and Paris, and along areas of coast that are covered by spring tides.

Booking a Campsite

At peak times it's best to book in advance, or a quick call ahead while you're travelling to the site will save you a lot of hassle if the site is already full. If you don't book ahead aim to arrive early, no later than 4pm to secure a pitch, after this time sites fill up quickly. You also need to allow time to find another campsite if your first choice is fully booked.

You can often book directly via a campsite's website using a credit or debit card to pay any deposit - just be aware that some sites regard the deposit as a booking fee, which won't be deducted from your final bill.

Overseas Travel Service

The Club's Overseas Travel Service offers members an overseas site booking service to over 300 campsites in Europe. Full details of these sites plus special offers on channel crossings and Red Pennant Overseas Holiday Insurance can be found in the Club's Venture Abroad brochure – call 01342 327 410 to request a copy or visit camc.com/overseas.

Overseas Site Booking Service sites are marked 'SBS' in the site listings. Many of them can be booked at camc.com/overseas. We can't make

advance reservations for any other campsites listed in this guide. Only those sites marked SBS have been inspected by Caravan and Motorhome Club staff.

Overseas Site Night Vouchers

The Club offers Overseas Site Night Vouchers which can be used at over 300 Club inspected sites in Europe. The vouchers cost £21.95 each (2019 cost) and you'll need one voucher per night to stay on a site in low season and two per night in high season. You'll also be eligible for the Club's special packaged ferry rates when you're buying vouchers. For more information and the view the voucher terms and conditions visit www.camc.com/overseasoffers or call 01342 327 410.

Caravan Storage Abroad

Storing your caravan on a site in France can be a great way to avoid a long tow and to save on ferry and fuel costs. Even sites which don't offer a specific long-term storage facility may be willing to negotiate a price to store your caravan for you. You can download a list of sites which offer storage facilities in France from camc.com. Before you leave your caravan in storage abroad always check whether your insurance covers this, as many policies don't. If you aren't covered then look for a specialist policy. Towergate Insurance (tel: 01242 538431 or www.towergateinsurance.co.uk) offer insurance policies for caravans stored abroad.

Facilities and Site Description

All of the site facilities shown in the site listings of this guide have been taken from member reports, as have the comments at the end of each site entry. Please remember that opinions and expectations can differ significantly from one person to the next.

The year of report is shown at the end of each site listing – sites which haven't been reported on for a few years may have had changes to their prices, facilities, opening dates and standards. It is always best to check any specific details before travelling by contacting the site or looking at their website.

Many French campsites ban the wearing of loose or swimming shorts in pools on grounds of hygiene. Sites may also require swimmers to wear swimming caps.

Sanitary Facilities

Facilities normally include toilet and shower blocks with shower cubicles, wash basins and razor sockets. In site listings the abbreviation 'wc' indicates that the site has the kind of toilets we are used to in the UK (pedestal style). Some sites have footplate style toilets and, where this is known, you will see the abbreviation 'cont', i.e. continental. Sites do not always provide sink plugs, toilet paper or soap so it is best to carry these items with you.

In low season some sites will only have a few toilet and shower cubicles in use to be shared by ladies and gents.

Waste Disposal

Site entries show (when known) where a campsite has a chemical disposal and/or a motorhome service point, which is assumed to include a waste (grey) water dump station and toilet cassette-emptying point. You may find fewer waste water disposal facilities as use of the site sanitary blocks is more common in France.

Chemical disposal points may be fixed at a high level requiring lifting of cassettes in order to empty them. Disposal may simply be down a toilet. Wastemaster-style emptying points are not very common in Europe.

Finding a Campsite

Directions are given for all campsites listed in this guide and most listings also include GPS co-ordinates. Where known full street addresses are also given. The directions have been supplied by member reports and haven't been checked in detail by The Club.

For information about using satellite navigation to find a site see the Motoring Equipment section.

Overnight Stops

Many towns and villages in France provide dedicated overnight or short stay areas specifically for motorhomes, usually with security, electricity, water and waste facilities. These are known as 'Aires de Services' and are usually well signposted with a motorhome icon. Aires vary from region to region. Some are free of charge while others charge a small fee. Facilities also vary - some will have electrics available as well as other facilities, whilst others will just provide a basic parking area.

There are guidebooks available which list just these overnight stops, Vicarious Books publish an English guide to Aires including directions and GPS co-ordinates. Contact 0131 208 3333 or visit their website www.vicarious-shop.com.

Many campsites in popular tourist resorts have separate overnight areas of hardstanding with appropriate facilities, often adjacent to, or just outside, the main campsite area. Look for the 'Stop Accueil Camping-Car' sign.

Motorhomes are also welcome to park overnight free of charge at approximately 1,500 vineyards and farms throughout France through an organisation called France Passion. Membership is open to motorhomes only - write to France Passion, BP 57, 84202 Carpentras. Alternatively join online at www.france-passion.com. It is illegal to spend the night at the roadside.

For security reasons you shouldn't spend the night on petrol station service areas, ferry terminal car parks or isolated 'Aires de Repos' or 'Aires de Services' along motorways.

Municipal Campsites

Municipal sites are found in towns and villages all over France. Once very basic, many have been improved in recent years and now offer a wider range of facilities. They can usually be booked in advance through the local town hall or tourism office. When approaching a town you may find that municipal sites are not always named and signposts may simply state 'Camping' or show a tent or caravan symbol. Most municipal sites are clean, well-run and very reasonably prices but security may be basic.

These sites may be used by seasonal workers, market traders and travellers in low season and as a result there may be restrictions or very high charges for some types of outfits (such as twin axles) in order to discourage this. If you may be affected check for any restrictions when you book.

Naturist Campsites

Some naturist sites are included in this guide and are shown with the word 'naturist' after their site name. Those marked 'part naturist' have separate areas for naturists.

Visitors to naturist sites aged 16 and over usually require an INF card or Naturist Licence covered by membership of British Naturism (tel 01604 620361, visit www.british-naturism.org.uk or email headoffice@british-naturism.org.uk) or you can apply for a licence on arrival at any recognised naturist site (a passport-size photograph is required). For further details contact the French Federation of Naturism, email contact@ffn-naturisme.com, or visit www.ffn-naturisme.com.

Opening Dates and Times

Opening dates should always be taken with a pinch of salt - including those given in this guide. Sites may close without notice due to refurbishment work, a lack of visitors or bad weather. Outside the high season it is always best to contact campsites in advance, even if the site advertises itself as open all year.

Following incidents in recent years some authorities in southern France have introduced tighter regulations concerning sites liable to flooding, including limiting opening dates from April/May until August/September in some areas.

Most sites will close their gates or barriers overnight – if you are planning to arrive late or are delayed on your journey you should call ahead to make sure you will be able to gain access to the site. There may be a late arrivals area outside of the barriers where you can pitch overnight. Motorhomers should also consider barrier closing times if leaving site in your vehicle for the evening.

Check out time is usually between 10am and 12 noon – speak to the site staff if you need to leave very early to make sure you can check out on departure. Sites may also close for an extended lunch break, so if you're planning to arrive or check out around lunchtime check that the office will be open.

Pets on Campsites

Dogs are welcome on many sites, although you may have to prove that all of their vaccinations are up to date before they are allowed onto the site. Certain breeds of dogs are banned in some countries and other breeds will need to be muzzled and kept on a lead at all times. A list of breeds with restrictions by country can be found at camc.com/pets.

Sites usually charge for dogs and may limit the number allowed per pitch. On arrival make yourself aware of site rules regarding dogs, such as keeping them on a lead, muzzling them or not leaving them unattended in your outfit. In popular tourist areas local regulations may ban dogs from beaches during the summer. Some dogs may find it difficult to cope with changes in climate. Also watch out for diseases transmitted by ticks, caterpillars, mosquitoes or sandflies - dogs from the UK will have no natural resistance. Consult your vet about preventative treatment before you travel.

Visitors to parts of central France should be aware of the danger of Pine Processionary Caterpillars from mid-winter to late spring. Dogs should be kept away from pine trees if possible or fitted with a muzzle that prevents the nose and mouth from touching the ground. This will also protect against poisoned bait sometimes used by farmers and hunters.

In the event that your pet is taken ill abroad a campsite should have information about local vets.

Dogs are required to wear a collar identifying their owners at all times. If your dog goes missing, report the matter to the local police and the local animal welfare organisation.

See the Documents section of this book for more information about the Pet Travel Scheme.

Prices and Payment

Prices per night (for an outfit and two adults) are shown in the site entries. If you stay on site after midday you may be charged for an extra day. Many campsites have a minimum amount for credit card transactions, meaning they can't be used to pay for overnight or short stays. Check which payment methods are accepted when you check in.

Sites with automatic barriers may ask for a deposit for a swipe card or fob to operate it.

Extra charges may apply for the use of facilities such as swimming pools, showers or laundry rooms. You may also be charged extra for dogs, Wi-Fi, tents and extra cars. Visitors are usually required to pay a tourism tax (taxe de séjour) that is imposed by local authorities. This tax is collected by campsite owners and will be included in your bill.

Registering on Arrival

Local authority requirements mean you will usually have to produce an identity document on arrival, which will be retained by the site until you check out. If you don't want to leave your passport with reception then most sites will accept a camping document such as the Camping Key Europe (CKE) or Camping Card International (CCI) - if this is known site entries are marked CKE/CCI.

CKE are available for Club members to purchase by calling 01342 336633 or are free to members if you take out the 'motoring' level of cover from the Club's Red Pennant Overseas Holiday Insurance.

General Advice

If you've visiting a new site see if it is possible to take a look around the site and facilities before booking in. If your pitch is allocated at check in ask to see it first to check the condition and access, as marked or hedged pitches can sometimes be difficult for large outfits. Riverside pitches can be very scenic but keep an eye on the water level; in periods of heavy rain this may rise rapidly.

A tourist tax, eco tax and/or rubbish tax may be imposed by local authorities. VAT may also be payable on top of your campsite fees.

Speed limits on campsites are usually restricted to 10 km/h (6 mph). You may be asked to park your car in a separate area away from your caravan, particularly in the high season.

The use of the term 'statics' in the campsite reports in this guide may refer to long-term seasonal pitches, chalets, cottages, tour operators' fixed tents and cabins, as well as mobile homes.

Complaints

If a situation arises where you want to make a complaint, take it up with site staff or owners at the time. It is much better to make staff aware of a problem while something could be done to rectify the situation for the rest of your stay than to complain once you are home.

The Club has no control or influence over day to day campsite operations or administration of the sites listed in this guide. Therefore we aren't able to intervene in any dispute you should have with a campsite, unless the booking has been made through our Site Booking Service - see listings marked 'SBS' for sites we are able to book for you.

Campsite Groups

Across Europe there are many 'groups' of campsites with sites in various locations. While you may find that sites within a group can be slightly more expensive than independent sites, there are also many benefits to choosing a group campsite.

You will generally find that group sites will be consistent in their format and the quality and variety of facilities they offer. If you liked one site you can be fairly confident that you will like other sites within the same group.

If you're looking for a full facility site, with swimming pools, play areas, bars and restaurants on site you're likely to find these on sites which are part of a group. You might even find organised excursions and activities such as archery on site.

Crozon Peninsula, Brittany

Welcome to France

Population (approx): 67 million

Capital: Paris

Area: 549,970 sq km

Bordered by: Andorra, Belgium, Germany, Italy, Luxembourg, Monaco, Spain, Switzerland

Terrain: Mostly flat plains or gently rolling hills in north and west; mountain ranges in south and east

Climate: Temperate climate with regional variations; generally warm summers and cool winters; harsh winters in mountainous areas; hot summers in central and Mediterranean areas

Coastline: 3,427km

Highest Point: Mont Blanc 4,807m

Language: French

Local Time: GMT or BST + 1, i.e. 1 hour ahead of the UK all year

Currency: Euros divided into 100 cents; €1.13, €1 = £0.89 (November 2018)

Telephoning: From the UK dial 0033 for France and omit the initial 0 of the 10-digit number you are calling. Mobile phone numbers start 06. For Monaco the code is 00377.

Emergency Numbers: Police 112; Fire brigade 112; Ambulance 112.

Public Holidays 2019

France: Jan 1; Apr 22; May 1, 8 (VE Day), 30; Jun 10; Jul 14 (Bastille Day); Aug 15; Nov 1, 11 (Armistice Day); Dec 25.

Find out more

French Government Tourist Board
Maison de la France
Lincoln House
300 High Holborn
London
WC1V 7JH
Tel: 09068 244123
Website: www.franceguide.com
Email: info.uk@atout-france.fr

Opening Hours

Banks – Mon-Fri 9am-noon & 2pm-4pm/5pm/6pm; in Paris Mon-Fri 10am-5pm; some open Sat & close on Mon. Early closing the day before a public holiday.

Museums – 10am-5pm; closed Mon or Tues. In Paris many open late once a week.

Post Offices – Mon-Fri 8am/9am-6pm/7pm; Sat 8am/9am-noon.

Shops: Food shops - Tues-Sat 7am/9am-6.30pm/7.30pm; some food shops i.e. bakers, grocers, etc, are open sun morning. Other shops - Tues-Sat 9am/10am-7.30pm. Shops generally close all or half day on Mon; in small towns shops close for lunch from noon to 2pm. Major Shops - Mon-Sat 9am/10am-7pm. Supermarkets may stay open until 9pm/10pm. Shops in tourist areas may open on Sunday.

Touring in France

France is divided administratively into 'régions', each of which consists of several 'départements'. There are 96 départements in total including Corsica, and these are approximately equivalent to our counties.

Paris, the capital and hub of the region known as the Ile-de-France, remains the political, economic, artistic, cultural and tourist centre of France. Visit www.parisinfo.com for a wealth of information on what to see and do in the city. A Paris Pass, valid for 2 to 6 days, entitles you to free entrance (ahead of the queues) to over 60 Paris attractions and free unlimited public transport plus discounts and free offers – see www.parispass.com.

Visitors under the age of 26 are admitted free to permanent collections in national museums; show your passport as proof of age. National museums, including the Louvre, are closed on Tuesday, with the exception of Versailles and the Musée d'Orsay which are closed on Monday. Entrance to national museums is free on the first Sunday of every month. Municipal museums are usually closed on Monday and public holidays.

Restaurants must display priced menus outside and most offer a set menu 'plat du jour' or 'table d'hôte' which usually represents good value. A service charge of 15% is included in restaurant bills but it is also expected to leave a small tip if you have received good service. Smoking is not allowed in bars and restaurants.

France has a large network of well-marked, long-distance footpaths and hiking trails – Les Sentiers de Grande Randonnée – which generally follow ancient tracks formerly used by pilgrims, merchants and soldiers. In addition to these 'GR' paths there are also 'PR' paths (Chemins de Petite Randonnée) which are most suited for local hiking. For a list of GR routes see www.gr-infos.com or contact the French Tourist Board or local tourist offices in France for more information.

Channel Islands

Ferry services operate for cars and passengers between Poole and Portsmouth and St Malo via Jersey and Guernsey. Caravans and motorhomes are permitted to enter Jersey, subject to certain conditions, including pre-booking direct with a registered campsite and the acquisition of a permit. For further information and details of the campsites on Jersey where caravans are permitted, see www.jersey.com or contact The Club's Travel Service Information Officer, email: travelserviceinfo@camc.com.

There are three campsites on Guernsey but, for the moment, the authorities in Guernsey do not permit entry to trailer caravans. Motorhomes can only be taken onto the island if they are stored under cover and not used for human habitation. Trailer tents can be taken onto the island without restrictions.

Local Travel

Several large cities have metro or tram systems and all have a comprehensive bus network. The Paris metro network comprises 16 lines and around 300 stations, and has many connections to the RER (regional suburban rail network) and the SNCF national railway system. Tickets for the metro, also valid on RATP buses, can be bought singly from vending machines at the turnstiles or from ticket offices, but a 'carnet' of 10 tickets is a more economical option. Your ticket is valid for an hour and a half from the time it is validated at the machines, on buses or at metro stations.

For tourists Paris Visite travel passes are available allowing unlimited travel for one to five days across some or all of the travel zones and a range of discounts at attractions. For further information see www.ratp.fr.

Senior citizens aged 60 and over are entitled to a discount of up to 25% when using French railways. Show your passport as proof of age.

Medical advice

In France an EHIC will allow you to claim reimbursement of around 70% of standard doctors' and dentists' fees, and between 35% and 65% of the cost of most prescribed medicines.

For the address of a doctor 'conventionné', i.e. working within the French state healthcare system, ask at a pharmacy. After treatment make sure you are given a signed statement of treatment ('feuille de soins') showing the amount paid as you will need this for a refund.

Pharmacies dispense prescriptions and first aid. Your prescription will be returned to you and you should attach this, together with the stickers (vignettes) attached to the packaging of any medication or drugs, to the 'feuille de soins' in order to obtain a refund.

If you are admitted to hospital make sure you present your EHIC on admission. This will save you from paying any refundable costs up front and ensure that you only pay the patient contribution. You may have to pay a co-payment towards your treatment and if you are an inpatient you will have to pay a daily hospital charge. These charges are not refundable in France but you may be able to seek reimbursement when back in the UK. Applications for refunds should be sent to a local sickness insurance office (Caisse Primaire d'Assurance-Maladie) and you should receive payment at your home address within about two months.

Andorra is not a member of the EU and there are no reciprocal emergency healthcare arrangements with Britain. You will be required to pay the full cost of medical treatment so make sure that you have comprehensive travel insurance which includes cover for travel to non-EU countries.

Ferries

Car ferry services operate all year across the Gironde estuary between Royan and Le Verdon eliminating a 155km detour. 2015 prices are €41.30 single journey for car, caravan under 3m and 2 adults or €54.10 for car, caravan over 3m and 2 adults. A motorhome and 2 adults costs €47.90. Between Blaye and Lamarque north of Bordeaux approximate 2015 prices are €28.20 single journey for car, caravan under 3m and 2 adults or for a motorhome and 2 adults, and €33.60 for car, caravan over 3m.

See www.bernezac.com for more details.

Ferry services operate from Marseille, Nice and Toulon to Corsica. For information contact:

Southern Ferries
30 Churton Street
London
SW1V 2LP
www.southernferries.co.uk
mail@southernferries.com

Cycling

A number of French towns are actively promoting the use of bicycles. Initiatives include increasing the number of cycle paths, providing parking space for bicycles and constructing shelters and cycle hire points in car parks. You may hire bicycles at many local tourist offices and from some railway stations.

Recent initiatives have included the improvement of cycle tracks along rivers and canals and many former gravel tracks have been replaced with tarmac along the Rivers Rhône, Loire and Yonne/Canal de Nivernais. It is understood that similar improvements will take place along the Canal de Bourgogne.

In and around Paris there are 370 kilometres of cycle lanes, and bicycles, known as 'Les Vélibs', are available for hire at very reasonable rates at more than 1,600 self-service stations – roughly one every 300 metres.

The French Tourist Board has information on cycle routes and tours throughout France.

Place names used in the Site Entry listings which follow can be found in Michelin's France Atlas, scale 1:200,000 (1 cm = 2 km).

Sites in France

ABBEVILLE *3B3* (14km SE Rural) *50.03416, 1.98383*
Camp Municipal La Peupleraie, 80510 Long [03 22 31 84 27 or 03 22 31 80 21; fax 03 22 31 82 39; bacquet.lionel@free.fr; www.long.fr]
Exit A16 at junc 21 for D1001 N then turn L at Ailly-le-Haut Clocher onto D32 for Long & foll sp. Med, mkd, pt shd, wc; chem disp; shwrs inc; EHU (6A) inc (caution - poss rev pol & poss other elec concerns) (long lead req); lndry; shop nr; rest nr; bar nr; bbq; playgrnd; red long stay; 90% statics; dogs; adv bkg acc; fishing adj; CKE/CCI. "Pretty, busy site beside Rv Somme; gd san facs; gd walking/cycling by rv; site busy 1st week Sep - flea mkt in town; interesting area; old power stn museum; warden lives on site; conv en rte Calais; san facs v clean; quiet peaceful site; highly rec." 15 Mar-15 Nov. € 9.00   2018*

ABBEVILLE *3B3* (5km S Urban) *50.07826, 1.82378*
Camp Municipal du Marais-Talsac/Le Marais Communal, 62 Rue du Marais-Talsac, 80132 Mareuil-Caubert [03 22 31 62 37 or 03 22 24 11 46 (Mairie); fax 03 22 31 34 28; mairie.mareuilcaubert@wanadoo.fr] Leave A28 at junc 3; at T-junc turn L onto D928; foll camping sp; in 4km turn sharp R onto D3 into Mareuil-Caubert; in 1km turn L thro housing est to site by stadium. Well sp. Med, hdstg, mkd, pt shd, wc; chem disp; mv service pnt; shwrs inc; EHU (6A) €2.90 (poss rev pol); shop; rest nr; playgrnd; 25% statics; Eng spkn; quiet; CKE/CCI. "Well-kept, friendly site; sm pitches; helpful staff; clean dated facs, poss tired LS; no twin axles or o'fits over 8m; hdstgs stony/loose gravel; gates clsd 2000-0800; interesting area; poss travellers LS (2010); vg NH Calais." 1 Apr-30 Sep. € 15.00   2014*

ABBEVILLE *3B3* (10km SW Rural) *50.08586, 1.71519*
Camping Le Clos Cacheleux, Rue des Sources, Route de Bouillancourt, 80132 Miannay [03 22 19 17 47; fax 03 22 31 35 33; raphael@camping-lecloscacheleux.fr; www.camping-lecloscacheleux.fr]
Fr A28 exit junc 2 onto D925 sp Cambron. In 5km at Miannay turn S onto D86 sp Bouillancourt. Site thro vill of R opp sister site Camping Le Val de Trie which is sp fr A28. Med, mkd, hdg, pt shd, pt sl, wc; chem disp; fam bthrm; shwrs inc; EHU (10A) inc (poss long lead req); gas; lndry; shop; rest; snacks; bar; bbq (charcoal, gas); playgrnd; entmnt; wifi; TV; dogs €2.10; Eng spkn; adv bkg acc; quiet; ccard acc; tennis 3km; games area; games rm; CKE/CCI. "Pleasant, peaceful, wooded site; lge pitches; charming, helpful owner; farm animals; fishing pond; excel facs; all services (inc shop, rest & pool) are on sister site 'Le Val de Trie' on opp side of rd, accessed via steep track 500m fr site ent; no o'fits over18m; htd covrd pool, paddling pool adj; jacuzzi; gd walking, cycling; gd for dogs." ♦ 15 Mar-14 Oct. € 26.00   2014*

ABBEVILLE *3B3* (10km SW Rural) *50.08570, 1.71480*
Camping Le Val de Trie, 1 Rue des Sources, Bouillancourt-sous-Miannay, 80870 Moyenneville [03 22 31 48 88; fax 03 22 31 35 33; raphael@camping-levaldetrie.fr; www.camping-levaldetrie.fr]
Fr A28 exit junc 2 onto D925 sp Cambron. In 5km at Miannay turn S onto D86 sp Bouillancourt. Site thro vill on L. Site sp fr A28. NB Last pt of app narr with bends. Med, mkd, hdg, hdstg, shd, pt sl, wc (htd); chem disp; mv service pnt; fam bthrm; shwrs inc; EHU (6-10A) inc; gas; lndry; shop; rest; snacks; bar; bbq; playgrnd; pool (covrd, htd); paddling pool; red long stay; entmnt; wifi; TV; 1% statics; dogs €2.10; phone; Eng spkn; adv bkg acc; ccard acc; lake fishing; games rm; CKE/CCI. "Beautiful, well-run site; well-shd; welcoming, helpful, conscientious owner; excel, clean, modern, san facs; ltd LS; gd family site; woodland walks; interesting area; conv Calais; great location for visiting the Somme area." ♦ 1 Apr-4 Oct. € 28.00   2014*

> **"There aren't many sites open at this time of year"**
>
> If you're travelling outside peak season remember to call ahead to check site opening dates – even if the entry says 'open all year'.

ABBEVILLE *3B3* (7km NW Rural) *50.14166, 1.76237*
Camping Le Château des Tilleuls, Rue de la Baie, 80132 Port-le-Grand [03 22 24 07 75; fax 03 22 24 23 80; contact@chateaudestilleuls.com; www.chateaudestilleuls.com] Fr N on A16 join A28 dir Rouen. At junc 1 take D40 dir St Valery-sur-Somme, site on R in approx 3km. Med, hdstg, hdg, mkd, pt shd, sl, terr, wc (htd); chem disp; mv service pnt; fam bthrm; shwrs inc; EHU (10-16A) €4; lndry; shop; rest; snacks; bar; bbq; playgrnd; pool (htd); red long stay; wifi; TV; dogs free; Eng spkn; adv bkg acc; quiet; ccard acc; games rm; bike hire; tennis; CKE/CCI. "Pleasant site; improvements in progress (2011); lge, v sl pitches; find suitable pitch bef booking in; long uphill walk fr recep; unisex san facs; new pitches far fr ent; site being updated; new san facs (2015); well run; v clean; excel." ♦ 1 Mar-30 Dec. € 26.50   2015*

ABRETS, LES

ABRETS, LES 9B3 (2km E Rural) 45.54065, 5.60834
Kawan Village Le Coin Tranquille, 6 Chemin des Vignes, 38490 Les Abrets [04 76 32 13 48; fax 04 76 37 40 67; contact@coin-tranquille.com; www.coin-tranquille.com] Fr N exit A43 at junc 10 Les Abrets & foll D592 to town cent. At rndbt at monument take D1006 twd Chambéry/Campings; cont for 500m then turn L sp Le Coin Tranquille; cross level x-ing & cont for 500m to site. Or fr S on A48 exit junc 10 at Voiron onto D1075 to Les Abrets; turn R at rndabt onto D1006 twd Le Pont-de-Beauvoisin, then as above. Lge, hdg, mkd, pt shd, wc; chem disp; mv service pnt; fam bthrm; shwrs inc; EHU (6A) inc (poss rev pol & long lead poss req); gas; lndry; shop; rest; snacks; bar; bbq; playgrnd; pool; paddling pool; entmnt; wifi; TV; dogs €1.50; Eng spkn; adv bkg req; ccard acc; bike hire; archery; games area; games rm; CKE/CCI. "Well-kept, well-run site in gd location; no o'fits over 8m unless bkd in adv; lge narr pitches; busy/noisy site, but some quiet pitches avail; helpful & friendly staff; horseriding 7km; fishing 7km; golf 15km; well-kept, clean san facs; ltd LS; lovely pool; vg activities for children; poss flooding in wet weather; excel." ♦ 1 Apr-31 Oct. € 33.50   2012*

ABRETS, LES 9B3 (3km S Rural) 45.47079, 5.54688
Camping Le Calatrin (formerly Municipal), 799 Rue de la Morgerie, 38850 Paladru [04 76 32 37 48; fax 04 76 32 42 02; camping.le.calatrin@gmail.com; www.camping-paladru.fr] S fr Les Abrets on D1075; turn R onto D50 to Paladru; site 1km beyond vill on L, on brow of hill. Or exit A48 junc 9 & foll sp 'Lac de Paladru'; 3km after rndabt junc of D50 & D17, site on R (by another rndabt). Med, hdg, mkd, shd, terr, wc; chem disp; mv service pnt; fam bthrm; shwrs inc; EHU (10A) €4 (long lead poss req); gas; lndry; shop; snacks; bar; bbq; playgrnd; sw nr; red long stay; entmnt; wifi; TV; 30% statics; dogs €3.5; bus 200m; Eng spkn; adv bkg acc; quiet; fishing; games area; watersports; games rm; tennis 500m; bike hire; CKE/CCI. "Attractive site; direct access to lake; lge pitches; welcoming & helpful owners; gd recreational facs; nice walks; excel." ♦ 1 Apr-30 Sep. € 17.00   2017*

ABRETS, LES 9B3 (11km SW Rural) 45.44621, 5.53183
Camp Municipal le Bord du Lac, 687 route du Bord du Lac, 38850 Bilieu [04 76 06 67 00 or 04 76 06 62 41 (Mairie); fax 04 76 06 67 15; camping.bilieu@live.fr; www.camping-bilieu.com]
S on D1075 fr Les Abrets. Turn R onto D50. Just bef Paladru, turn L to Charavines. site on R on ent Bilieu, by lakeside. Med, mkd, pt shd, pt sl, terr, wc (htd); chem disp; shwrs inc; EHU (10A) €3; lndry; playgrnd; wifi; 10% statics, quiet; ccard acc; CKE/CCI. "Nice site by lake; san facs vg; staff helpful; no sw in lake fr site, only boat launch; pitch access poss diff; gd."
1 Apr-30 Sep. € 23.00   2013*

ACCOUS 8G2 (1km NW Rural) 42.97717, -0.60592
Camping Despourrins, Route du Somport, D'Arrechau, 64490 Accous [05 59 34 71 16]
On N134 rte to & fr Spain via Somport Pass. Site sp on main rd. Sm, pt shd, wc; chem disp; shwrs inc; EHU (6A) €2.70; lndry; shop nr; rest nr; bar nr; bbq; 10% statics; dogs free; quiet; fishing. "Clean, tidy NH; conv Col de Somport." 1 Mar-31 Oct.
€ 10.50   2014*

> **"That's changed – Should I let the Club know?"**
>
> If you find something on site that's different from the site entry, fill in a report and let us know. See camc.com/europereport.

AGAY 10F4 (2km S Coastal) 43.41995, 6.85696
Royal Camping, Plage de Camp-Long, 83530 Agay [04 94 82 00 20; contact@royalcamping.net; www.royalcamping.net] On D559 twd St Raphaël. Turn at sp Tiki Plage & site. Stop in ent rd at recep bef ent site. Sm, mkd, hdstg, pt shd, wc; chem disp; shwrs inc; EHU (6A) €3.50; gas; lndry; shop; rest nr; bar nr; beach sand adj; wifi; 10% statics; dogs; phone; bus 200m; Eng spkn; adv bkg acc; CKE/CCI. "Gd walks; lovely site; some pitches adj to beach in sep area; vg." ♦
10 Feb-4 Nov. € 25.00   2018*

AGAY 10F4 (1km W Coastal) 43.43376, 6.85245
Camping des Rives de l'Agay, Ave de Gratadis, 83530 Agay [04 94 82 02 74; fax 04 94 82 74 14; reception@lesrivesdelagay.fr; www.lesrivesdelagay.fr]
Fr Agay take D100 dir Valescure, site in 400m on L. NB Dangerous bend & steep ent. Med, hdg, mkd, shd, wc (htd); chem disp; fam bthrm; shwrs inc; EHU (6A) €3.60; gas; lndry; shop; rest; snacks; bar; pool (htd); paddling pool; beach sand 500m; entmnt; 10% statics; dogs €3; Eng spkn; adv bkg acc; CKE/CCI. "San facs & pool v clean; gd pool with shd; excel site." ♦
9 Mar-7 Nov. € 28.00   2016*

AGDE 10F1 (3km SE Coastal) 43.27949, 3.48114
Camping Le Rochelongue, Chemin des Ronciers, Route de Rochelongue, 34300 Le Cap d'Agde [04 67 21 25 51; fax 04 67 94 04 23; le.rochelongue@wanadoo.fr; www.camping-le-rochelongue.fr]
Exit A9 junc 34 sp Agde. Foll D612 to Le Cap d'Agde then thro Rochelongue. Site on L just bef rndabt. Med, mkd, hdstg, pt shd, wc cont; chem disp; mv service pnt; fam bthrm; shwrs inc; EHU (6A) inc; gas; lndry; shop; rest; snacks; bar; bbq; playgrnd; pool (htd); beach sand 500m; entmnt; wifi; 50% statics; dogs €4; phone; Eng spkn; adv bkg acc; bike hire; table tennis; golf 1.5km; CKE/CCI. "Friendly, well-kept site; takeaway; sh walk to vill & beach." ♦ 29 Mar-28 Oct.
€ 47.00   2013*

AGDE 10F1 (7km SE Coastal) 43.29645, 3.52255
Centre Hélio-Marin René Oltra (Naturist), 1 Rue des Néréïdes, 34307 Le Cap-d'Agde [04 67 01 06 36 or 04 67 01 06 37; fax 04 67 01 22 38; contact@ centrenaturiste-oltra.fr; www.centrenaturiste-oltra.fr] S fr m'way A9 Agde-Pézenas junc on N312/D612 for 14km to Cap d'Agde turn-off; foll Camping Naturist sp to site on E side of Le Cap-d'Agde. V lge, hdg, mkd, pt shd, serviced pitches; wc; chem disp; mv service pnt; shwrs inc; EHU (6A) inc; lndry; shop; rest; bar; pool; beach sand adj; 50% statics; dogs €3.40; bus adj; Eng spkn; adv bkg rec; quiet; ccard acc; INF card. "Naturist area in Cap-d'Agde has all facs; lovely beach; gd size pitches; friendly atmosphere; modern san facs; gd family facs; excel; great location; gd public transport & walking; facs upgraded (2015); v busy but mostly quiet." ♦ 15 Mar-14 Oct. € 42.00   2018*

AGDE 10F1 (2km SW Rural) 43.29806, 3.45639
Camping Le Neptune, 46 Boulevard du St Christ, 34300 Agde [04 67 94 23 94; fax 04 67 94 48 77; info@ campingleneptune.com; www.campingleneptune.com] Fr A9 exit junc 34 onto N312, then E on D612. Foll sp Grau d'Agde after x-ing bdge. Site on D32E on E bank of Rv Hérault on 1-way system. Lge, mkd, hdg, pt shd, wc; chem disp; fam bthrm; shwrs inc; EHU (6-10A) inc; gas; lndry; shop; rest nr; bar; bbq; playgrnd; pool (htd); paddling pool; beach sand 2km; entmnt; wifi; TV; 40% statics; dogs €3 (no Pitbulls or Rottweillers); phone; Eng spkn; adv bkg rec; quiet; ccard acc; games area; tennis; CKE/CCI. "Peaceful, pleasant, clean site; helpful owners; modern facs, ltd LS; liable to flood after heavy rain; easy rvside walk/ cycle to vill; gd cycleways; rv cruises; boat launch/ slipway 500m; v popular site; gd facs; excel." ♦ 1 Apr-30 Sep. € 41.00   2018*

> "I like to fill in the reports as I travel from site to site"
>
> You'll find report forms at the back of this guide, or you can fill them in online at camc.com/europereport.

AGDE 10F1 (3km SW Coastal) 43.29440, 3.45010
Camping Les Romarins, Le Grau d'Agde, 34300 Agde [04 67 94 18 59; fax 04 67 26 58 80; contact@ romarins.com; www.romarins.com] Fr Agde take rd to Grau d'Agde, site at ent to Grau d'Agde adj Rv Hérault. Med, hdstg, mkd, pt shd, wc; chem disp; mv service pnt; fam bthrm; shwrs inc; EHU (10A) inc; lndry; shop nr; rest; snacks; bar; bbq; playgrnd; pool (htd); beach sand 1km; twin axles; entmnt; wifi; 25% statics; dogs €3.30; bus; Eng spkn; adv bkg rec; quiet; bike hire; games area; CKE/CCI. "Pleasant town with many bars, rests; shop; helpful owner; excel site; v.busy; small pitches; crowded; gd location; nr rv & cycling to beach." ♦ 26 May-1 Oct. € 39.00   2014*

AGEN 8E3 (8km NW Rural) 44.24368, 0.54290
Camping Le Moulin de Mellet, Route de Prayssas, 47450 St Hilaire-de-Lusignan [05 53 87 50 89; fax 05 53 47 13 41; moulin.mellet@wanadoo.fr; www.camping-moulin-mellet.com] NW fr Agen on N113 twd Bordeaux for 5km. At traff lts just bef Colayrac-St Cirq take D107 N twd Prayssas for 3km. Site on R. Sm, mkd, shd, wc; chem disp; fam bthrm; shwrs inc; EHU (10A) €3.80 (poss rev pol); gas; lndry; shop nr; rest; snacks; bbq; playgrnd; pool; dogs €2.85; phone; Eng spkn; adv bkg acc; quiet; games rm; CKE/CCI. "Delightful, well-run site; helpful, friendly new owners; sm children's farm; RVs & twin axles phone ahead; excel; spotless facs; rest & bar open in LS; pretty location; gd for long stay." ♦ 1 Apr-15 Oct. € 29.60   2017*

AGON COUTAINVILLE 1D4 (0km NE Urban/Coastal) 49.05105, -1.59112 Camp Municipal Le Martinet, Blvd Lebel-Jéhenne, 50230 Agon-Coutainville [02 33 47 05 20; martinetmarais@wanadoo.fr; www.agoncoutainville.fr or www.coutainville.com] Fr Coutances take D44 to Agon-Coutainville; site sp nr Hippodrome. Med, hdg, mkd, pt shd, wc; mv service pnt; shwrs inc; EHU (6A); lndry; shop nr; bbq; playgrnd; beach sand 600m; 55% statics; dogs €3.20; bus; Eng spkn; adv bkg acc; ccard acc; CKE/CCI. "V pleasant site; ltd facs LS; horse racecourse adj; vg." ♦ 1 Apr-30 Oct. € 18.00   2018*

AIGLE, L' 4E2 (14km W Rural) 48.78841, 0.46533
Camp Municipal des Saints-Pères, 61550 St Evroult-Notre-Dame-du-Bois [06 78 33 04 94 (mob) or 02 33 34 93 12 (Mairie); mairiestevroultndubois@ wanadoo.fr] Fr L'Aigle on D13, on ent vill site on L by lake. Sm, hdstg, pt shd, terr, wc; chem disp; mv service pnt; shwrs inc; EHU (4-10A) €1.50-2.50; shop nr; rest nr; bar nr; playgrnd; sw nr; dogs €0.20; watersports; fishing; CKE/CCI. "Pleasant lakeside vill; facs gd & clean with hot water, ltd LS; quiet; walks; on edge of sm vill opp ruins of ancient abbey; friendly, helpful staff, but no Eng spkn." ♦ 1 Apr-30 Sep. € 14.00   2016*

⊞ **AIGNAN** 8E2 (1km S Rural) 43.69290, 0.07528
Camping Le Domaine du Castex, 32290 Aignan [05 62 09 25 13; fax 05 62 09 24 79; info@domaine-castex.com; www.gers-vacances.com] Fr N on D924/ N124 turn S on D20 thro Aignan onto D48; in 500m g'ge on R, immed after turn L; site sp. Fr S on D935 turn E at Monplaisir onto D3/D48 to Aignan; site on R bef vill. Sm, mkd, hdstg, hdg, pt shd, wc; chem disp; mv service pnt; shwrs inc; EHU (10A) €3; lndry; shop nr; rest; snacks; bar; bbq; playgrnd; pool; sw nr; TV; 4% statics; dogs €4; phone; Eng spkn; adv bkg acc; quiet; ccard acc; tennis adj; games area; CKE/CCI. "Lovely site in grnds of medieval farmhouse; helpful Dutch owners; modern san facs; excel pool & rest; squash adj; gd touring cent for Bastide vills; mkt Mon; phone ahead LS; vg." ♦ € 20.00   2016*

AIGREFEUILLE D'AUNIS

AIGREFEUILLE D'AUNIS *7A1* (2km N Rural) 46.14621, -0.94571 **Camp Municipal de la Garenne, Route de la Mazurie, 17220 St Christophe [05 46 35 51 79 or 05 46 35 16 15 (LS); fax 05 46 35 64 29; saintchristophe@mairie17.com]** Fr Aigrefeuille-d'Aunis take D112 2.5km N to vill of St Christophe, site sp. Sm, mkd, hdg, pt shd, wc; chem disp; mv service pnt; shwrs inc; EHU (4A) €2.50; lndry; shop nr; playgrnd; dogs €0.85; quiet; lake fishing 3km; horseriding; tennis; CKE/CCI. "V clean site in sm vill; unrel opening dates, phone ahead LS." ♦ 15 Mar-15 Oct. € 23.00   2012*

AIGUES MORTES *10F2* (3km NE Rural) 43.57314, 4.21836 **Camping à la Ferme (Loup), Le Mas de Plaisance, 30220 Aigues-Mortes [04 66 53 92 84 or 06 22 20 92 37 (mob); info@ot-aiguesmortes.fr; www.ot-aiguesmortes.fr]** Site sp in Aigues-Mortes or foll D58 E dir Stes Maries-de-la-Mer, then sharp R along farm rd (v narr & potholed) at end of rv bdge. NB Fr town narr rd with much traff calming & sharp bends. Either way for v sm o'fits only. Sm, pt shd, wc; chem disp; mv service pnt; shwrs inc; EHU inc; lndry; bbq; quiet; CKE/CCI. "Excel sm site; superb san facs; helpful owners; rec not to use water at m'van service point as off irrigation system - other water points avail; video security at gate." 1 Apr-30 Sep. € 22.00   2014*

AIGUES MORTES *10F2* (4km W Rural) 43.56300, 4.15910 **Yelloh! Village La Petite Camargue, 30220 Aigues-Mortes [04 66 53 98 98; fax 04 66 53 98 80; info@yellohvillage-petite-camargue.fr; www.yellohvillage-petite-camargue.com or www.yellohvillage.co.uk]** Heading S on N979 turn L onto D62 bef Aigues-Mortes & go over canal bdge twd Montpellier; site on R in 3km; sp. V lge, mkd, pt shd, wc; chem disp; mv service pnt; fam bthrm; shwrs inc; EHU (10A) inc; lndry; shop; rest; snacks; bar; bbq (charcoal, gas); playgrnd; pool; paddling pool; beach sand 3km; entmnt; wifi; TV; 50% statics; dogs €4; Eng spkn; adv bkg acc; ccard acc; games rm; serviced; horseriding; bike hire; tennis; games area; jacuzzi; CKE/CCI. "Lively, busy, well-run, youth-oriented commercial site with many sports facs; no o'fits over 7m; clean san facs, poss stretched high ssn; excel pool complex; bus to beach high ssn; some sm pitches; take care o'head branches; gd cycling; mkt Wed & Sun." ♦ 26 Apr-15 Sep. € 44.00   2017*

AIGUILLES *9D4* (1km NE Rural) 44.78783, 6.88849 **Camp Municipal Le Gouret, 05470 Aiguilles-en-Queyras [04 92 46 74 61 or 04 92 46 70 34; fax 04 92 46 79 05; www.aiguilles.com]** Fr Aiguilles on D947 dir Abriès, sp to site on R across rv bdge. Lge, shd, wc; chem disp; mv service pnt; fam bthrm; shwrs inc; EHU (3-10A) €2.20-3.20; lndry; shop nr; rest nr; bar nr; bbq; playgrnd; 10% statics; dogs €1; phone; bus 100m; quiet; games area. "Site on bank of Rv Guil; random pitching in lge area of larch forest; excel cent for Queyras National Park; vg." 1 Jun-15 Sep. € 12.00   2013*

AIGUILLON *7D2* (1km NE Rural) 44.30467, 0.34491 **Camp Municipal du Vieux Moulin, Route de Villeneuve, 47190 Aiguillon [05 53 79 61 43; fax 05 53 79 82 01; mairie@ville-aiguillon.fr; www.ville-aiguillon.eu]** On ent town on D813, turn E onto D666 to site on bank of Rv Lot. Clearly sp. Or exit A62 junc 6 at Damazan onto D8 to Aiguillon. Med, mkd, shd, wc; chem disp; shwrs; EHU (10A) inc; shop nr; rest nr; bar nr; playgrnd. "Gd site adj old mill house by rv; gd san facs; conv A62; NH only." 1 Jul-31 Aug. € 10.00   2014*

AIGUILLON SUR MER, L' *7A1* (1km W Coastal) 46.34349, -1.32006 **Camp'Atlantique Bel Air, 2 Route de Bel Air, 85460 L'Aiguillon-sur-Mer [02 51 20 41 94; belair.camp-atlantique.co.uk]** Fr La Roche-sur-Yon take D747 to La Tranche-sur-Mer via coast rd D46 to La Faute-sur-Mer. Cross bdge to L'Aiguillon-sur-Mer. Site 1km W of town on D44. Sp fr all dir. Lge, pt shd, wc; fam bthrm; shwrs; EHU (3A) €3.50; lndry; shop; rest; snacks; bar; bbq; playgrnd; pool; beach sand 800m; entmnt; 10% statics; dogs €3.50; adv bkg acc; waterslide; archery; bike hire. "Excel, clean, friendly site; pony trekking." 1 Apr-30 Sep. € 42.00   2015*

> **"We must tell the Club about that great site we found"**
>
> Get your site reports in by mid-August and we'll do our best to get your updates into the next edition.

AINHOA *8F1* (3km SW Rural) 43.29143, -1.50394 **Camping Xokoan, Quartier Dancharia, 64250 Ainhoa [05 59 29 90 26; fax 05 59 29 73 82; etchartenea@orange.fr; www.camping-xokoan.com]** S fr Ainhoa on D20, site on L in 2km. Narr ent & app. Fr Spain on N121B, pass Frontier site 250m on R. Sm, mkd, hdstg, pt shd, pt sl, wc; chem disp; mv service pnt; shwrs inc; EHU (6A) €3.50; lndry; shop nr; rest; bar; bbq; playgrnd; dogs; adv bkg acc; quiet; games rm; CKE/CCI. "Conv for N Spain & Pyrenees; gd walks; v interesting & scenic site in grnds of sm hotel; gd." ♦ € 17.50   2017*

AINHOA *8F1* (0km NW Urban) 43.30913, -1.50178 **Aire Naturelle Harazpy (Zaldua), 64250 Ainhoa [05 59 29 89 38 or 05 59 29 90 26 (LS); etchartenea@orange.fr; www.camping-harazpy.com]** Take D918 E fr St Jean-de-Luz sp Espelette: in approx 20km turn R on D20 sp Ainhoa. App church in Ainhoa turn R thro open car park to rd at rear; site on R in 250m. Site sp. Sm, mkd, pt shd, pt sl, terr, wc; chem disp; mv service pnt; shwrs; EHU (10A) inc; lndry; shop; dogs; phone; adv bkg acc; quiet; CKE/CCI. "Beautiful location; conv Spanish border; helpful staff; excel walking area." ♦ 1 Apr-30 Sep. € 17.50   2016*

AIRE SUR LA LYS 3A3 (2km NE Urban) 50.64390, 2.40630 Camp Municipal de la Lys, Bassin des Quatre Faces, Rue de Fort Gassion, 62120 Aire-sur-la-Lys [03 21 95 40 40; fax 03 21 95 40 41; camping@ville-airesurlalys.fr; www.ville-airesurlalys.fr]
Fr town cent, find main sq & exit to R of town hall. Thro traff lts turn R into narr lane just bef rv bdge dir of Hazebrouck. Site poorly sp. High vehicles beware low bdge at site ent. Sm, hdstg, mkd, hdg, pt shd, wc (htd); chem disp; shwrs inc; EHU (6A) €2.10; 95% statics; quiet. "Ltd touring pitches; ltd but clean san facs; not suitable lge o'fits; rec for NH only; v welcoming; waterside pitches; vg NH; easy walk to town." 1 Apr-31 Oct. € 12.00   2016*

AIRE SUR L'ADOUR 8E2 (1km NE Urban) 43.70259, -0.25792 Camping Les Ombrages de l'Adour, Rue des Graviers, 40800 Aire-sur-l'Adour [05 58 71 75 10; hetapsarl@yahoo.fr; www.camping-adour-landes.com] Turn E on S side of bdge over Rv Adour in town. Site close to bdge & sp, past La Arena off rd to Bourdeaux. Med, pt shd, wc; chem disp; mv service pnt; shwrs inc; EHU (10A) inc; lndry; shop; snacks; bbq; playgrnd; wifi; dogs €1.80; adv bkg acc; ccard acc; fishing 500m; tennis 500m; games area. "Vg; htd pool 500m; canoeing 500m; v clean facs but dated." 16 Apr-15 Oct. € 19.00   2016*

"I need an on-site restaurant"
We do our best to make sure site information is correct, but it is always best to check any must-have facilities are still available or will be open during your visit.

AIRVAULT 4H1 (1km N Rural) 46.83200, -0.14690 Camping de Courte Vallée, 8 Rue de Courte Vallée, 79600 Airvault [05 49 64 70 65; info@caravanningfrance.com; www.caravanningfrance.com] Fr N, S or W leave D938 sp Parthenay to Thouars rd at La Maucarrière twd Airvault & foll lge sp to site. Site on D121 twd Availles-Thouarsais. NB If app fr NE or E c'vans not permitted thro Airvault - watch carefully for sp R at Gendarmerie. Well sp fr all dirs. Sm, mkd, hdstg, hdg, pt shd, pt sl, wc; chem disp; mv service pnt; shwrs inc; EHU (13A) inc (poss long lead req); gas; lndry; shop; rest; snacks; bar; bbq; playgrnd; pool (htd); red long stay; twin axles; wifi; TV; 8% statics; dogs €1.50; adv bkg acc; quiet; ccard acc; games rm; bike hire; fishing; CKE/CCI. "Peaceful, popular; pleasant, helpful British owners; excel, clean & vg facs, poss stretched high ssn; conv Futuroscope & Puy du Fou theme park; mkt Sat; not as well kept & expensive compared to similar sites; c'van storage; town dissapointing, empty shops; new rest & bar(2018)." ♦ 1 Mar-15 Nov. € 33.00   2018*

AIX EN PROVENCE 10F3 (9km E Rural) 43.51771, 5.54128 FFCC Camping Ste Victoire, Quartier La Paradou, 13100 Beaurecueil [04 42 66 91 31; fax 04 42 66 96 43; campingvictoire@orange.fr; www.campingsaintevictoire.com] Exit A8/E80 junc 32 onto D7n dir Aix, then R onto D58 & foll sp for 3km. Sm, hdg, mkd, hdstg, shd, wc (htd); chem disp; mv service pnt; fam bthrm; shwrs inc; EHU (6A)(some rev pol & poss no neutral); lndry; shop nr; playgrnd; red long stay; wifi; TV; dogs €1.10; phone; bus; adv bkg acc; quiet; archery; bike hire; CKE/CCI. "Well-run site in attractive hilly, wooded area; friendly, helpful owners; clean, basic, dated & small san facs, ltd LS, but clean; various pitch sizes; lge o'fits poss diff manoeuvring; pool 9km; some pitches too soft for lge o'fits when wet; no twin axles; no lighting at night; gd walking & climbing; lovely location; shady; frequent cheap bus to Aix; narr rds; site can be diff to find." ♦ 5 Mar-30 Nov. € 21.50   2018*

"Satellite navigation makes touring much easier"
Remember most sat navs don't know if you're towing or in a larger vehicle – always use yours alongside maps and site directions.

⊞ AIX EN PROVENCE 10F3 (3km SE Urban) 43.51556, 5.47431 Airotel Camping Chantecler, Val-St André, 13100 Aix-en-Provence [04 42 26 12 98; fax 04 42 27 33 53; info@campingchantecler.com; www.campingchantecler.com]
Fr town inner ring rd foll sps Nice-Toulon, after 1km look for sp Chantecler to L of dual c'way. Foll camp sp past blocks of flats. Well sp in Val-St André. If on A8 exit at junc 31 sp Val-St André; R at rndabt; R at Rndabt; L at 2nd traff lts onto Ave Andre Magnan; R ar rndabt; site sp. If app fr SE on D7n turn R immed after passing under A8. Lge, hdg, hdstg, pt shd, sl, terr, wc (htd); chem disp; mv service pnt; shwrs inc; EHU (5A) €4.10 (long lead poss req); gas; lndry; shop; rest; snacks; bar; bbq (elec, gas); playgrnd; pool; red long stay; entmnt; TV; dogs €3.60; bus; adv bkg acc; ccard acc; site clsd 1 & 2 Jan; CKE/CCI. "Lovely, well-kept, wooded site; facs ltd LS; some site rds steep - gd power/weight ratio rec; access poss diff some pitches; rec request low level pitch & walk to pitch bef driving to it; ent narr; recep clsd 12.30-13.30; gd pool; conv city; vg touring base; access diff to some pitches, refurb san facs now htd & excel (2014)." ♦ € 36.00   2014*

AIX EN PROVENCE

AIX EN PROVENCE *10F3* (9km SE Urban) *43.51250, 5.47196* Camping L'Arc-en-Ciel, 45 Ave Henri Malacrida, Pont des 3 Sautets, 13100 Aix-en-Provence [04 42 26 14 28; camping-arcenciel@neuf.fr; www.campingarcenciel.com] Fr E or W exit A8 at junc 31 for D7n dir SE; (turn N for 300m to 1st rndabt where turn R; in 200m at 2nd rndabt turn R again onto D7n dir SE); pass under m'way; site ent immed on R; sp. Take care at ent. NB Access easier if go past site for 1km to rndabt, turn round & app fr S. Sm, hdg, mkd, shd, terr, wc (htd); chem disp; shwrs; EHU (6A) €3.60 (poss rev pol); gas; lndry; shop nr; rest nr; bar nr; bbq; playgrnd; pool; TV; dogs; phone; bus adj; Eng spkn; adv bkg acc; fishing; canoeing; golf 1km; games area; CKE/CCI. "Delightful, well-kept, well-run, great site; friendly, helpful owner; some pitches sm; some steep site rds, tow avail; vg immac facs; superb pool; if recep clsd use intercom in door; gd dog walk adj; bus to Marseille; conv NH nr a'route; highly rec; v secure; easy access to Aix town; bank cards not acc."
1 Apr-30 Sep. € 24.00   2014*

AIX LES BAINS *9B3* (7km SW Rural) *45.65511, 5.86142* Camp Municipal L'Ile aux Cygnes, La Croix Verte, 501 Blvd Ernest Coudurier, 73370 Le Bourget-du-Lac [04 79 25 01 76; fax 04 79 25 32 94; camping@lebourgetdulac.fr; www.lebourgetdulac.fr] Fr N foll Bourget-du-Lac & Lac sp soon after Tunnel Le Chat. Fr Chambéry take D1504 dir Aix-les-Bains; foll sp to Le Bourget-du-Lac & Le Lac, bear R at Camping/Plage sp to site at end of rd. Lge, shd, wc; mv service pnt; fam bthrm; shwrs inc; EHU (6A) inc; gas; lndry; shop; rest; snacks; bar; playgrnd; TV; 10% statics; dogs €1.50; phone; bus; adv bkg acc; quiet; watersports; boating; waterslide; CKE/CCI. "On beautiful lake; mountain scenery; grnd stoney; tight pitches; poss cr; reasonable facs; site badly sp." ♦
1 Apr-1 Oct. € 25.50   2013*

AIX LES BAINS *9B3* (3km W Rural) *45.70005, 5.88666* Camp Municipal International du Sierroz, Blvd Robert Barrier, Route du Lac, 73100 Aix-les-Bains [04 79 61 21 43; fax 04 79 63 35 08; info@camping-sierroz.com; www.camping-sierroz.com] Fr Annecy S on D1201, thro Aix-les-Bains, turn R at site sp. Keep to lakeside rd, site on R. Nr Grand Port. Lge, hdg, mkd, shd, wc (htd); chem disp; mv service pnt; fam bthrm; shwrs inc; EHU (6A) inc; gas; lndry; shop; rest; snacks; bar; playgrnd; TV; 5% statics; dogs €1.60; bus (ask at recep for free pass); adv bkg acc; quiet; ccard acc; golf 4km; games area; CKE/CCI. "Pleasant location; lake adj for watersports; lge pitches; poss travellers & v unclean facs LS (June 2010)." ♦ 15 Mar-15 Nov. € 28.00   2014*

AIXE SUR VIENNE *7B3* (1km NE Rural) *45.79887, 1.13928* Camp Municipal Les Grèves, Ave des Grèves, 87700 Aixe-sur-Vienne [06 73 67 23 48; fax 05 55 70 43 00; camping@mairie-aixesurvienne.fr; www.mairie-aixesurvienne.fr] SW fr Limoges for approx 13km, on N21 twds Périgueux, cross bdge over Rv Vienne & in about 600m turn to R (site sp) by rv. Steep down hill app & U-turn into site - take care gate posts! Med, shd, wc; chem disp; mv service pnt; shwrs inc; EHU (10A) €2.50 (poss rev pol); lndry; shop nr; rest nr; bar nr; playgrnd; red long stay; dogs free; adv bkg acc; quiet; fishing. "Pleasant, clean site by rv; spacious pitches; friendly, helpful warden; gd san facs, but ltd LS; conv Limoges area & Vienne valley; several chateaux in easy reach; pool adj; no twin axles; vg." ♦
1 Jun-30 Sep. € 19.00   2013*

AIZELLES *3C4* (0km NW Rural) *49.49076, 3.80817* Camping du Moulin (Merlo), 16 Rue du Moulin, 02820 Aizelles [03 23 22 41 18 or 06 14 20 47 43 (mob); magali.merlo@orange.fr; www.camping-du-Moulin.fr] Fr Laon take D1044 dir Reims; in 13km turn L on D88 to Aizelles; site sp in vill 'Camping à la Ferme'. Fr Reims on A26 exit junc 14 onto D925 then D1044 N. Turn R to Aizelles on D889 past Corbeny. Turn onto Rue du Moulin & site on R in 250m. Camping sp at church says 100m but allow 300m to see ent. NB Lge o'fits take care sharp R turn at ent to site. Sm, pt shd, pt sl, wc; chem disp; shwrs; EHU (10A) inc (poss rev pol, poss long lead req); shop nr; playgrnd; Eng spkn; quiet; ccard acc; fishing 800m; CKE/CCI. "Attractive, well-kept CL-type farm site; v friendly, helpful owners; basic san facs need update; gates clsd 2200-0700; wonderful well maintained site in a sm pretty vil; conv Calais 3 hrs; vg site; conv for Zeebrugge; few statics." 1 Apr-15 Oct. € 16.00   2018*

> **"There aren't many sites open at this time of year"**
>
> If you're travelling outside peak season remember to call ahead to check site opening dates – even if the entry says 'open all year'.

AIZENAY *2H4* (2km SE Rural) *46.73410, -1.58950* FFCC Camping La Forêt, 1 Rue de la Clairière, 85190 Aizenay [02 51 34 78 12; info@camping-laforet.com; www.camping-laforet.com] Exit Aizenay on D948 twd La Roche-sur-Yon. Site 1.5km on L. Med, mkd, hdg, pt shd, wc; chem disp; mv service pnt; shwrs inc; EHU (6A) €2.70; gas; lndry; shop; rest nr; snacks; bar; bbq; playgrnd; pool (htd); sw nr; wifi; 10% statics; dogs €1.30; phone; adv bkg acc; quiet; ccard acc; tennis; bike hire; CKE/CCI. "Undergoing refurbishment 2013; new bar & ent; v pleasant site; gd size pitches."
♦ Easter-30 Sep. € 18.00   2015*

ALBERTVILLE

AIZENAY 2H4 (8km NW Rural) *46.75282, -1.68645*
Camping Val de Vie, Rue du Stade, 85190 Maché [02 51 60 21 02; campingvaldevie@bbox.fr; www.campingvaldevie.fr] Fr Aizenay on D948 dir Challans. After 5km turn L onto D40 to Maché. Fr vill cent cont twd Apremont. Sm, blue site sp 100m on L. Med, hdg, mkd, pt shd, pt sl, serviced pitches; wc; chem disp; fam bthrm; shwrs inc; EHU (6-10A) €3.50-4; gas; lndry; shop nr; bbq; playgrnd; pool (htd); red long stay; twin axles; wifi; 20% statics; dogs €3; Eng spkn; adv bkg acc; quiet; fishing; bike hire; tennis adj; boat hire. "Lovely, peaceful, well-run site in pretty vill; new young owners upgrading facs & rds (2011); warm welcome; clean san facs; steel pegs useful; gd touring base, gd cycling; excel." ♦ 1 Apr-1 Oct. € 25.60   2016*

AJACCIO 10H2 (26km N Coastal) *42.04791, 8.74919*
Camping A Marina, Golfe de la Liscia, 20111 Calcatoggio [95 52 21 84 or 72 83 62 34; fax 95 52 30 76; fabiani.famille@wanadoo.fr; www.camping-amarina.com] Take D81 N fr Ajaccio for 20km; site ent on L 3km fr turn off to Calcatoggio. Foll sp to end of lane. Sm, hdg, pt shd, wc (htd); chem disp; mv service pnt; fam bthrm; shwrs inc; EHU (16A) €4; lndry; shop; snacks; bar; bbq; playgrnd; beach sandy adj; wifi; 50% statics; dogs; Eng spkn; quiet; ccard acc; games area. "Sm garden site adj to beautiful sandy bay; excell san facs, bar; friendly, family run; an oasis; excel." ♦ 1 Apr-31 Oct. € 35.00   2015*

ALBAN 8E4 (1km NW Rural) *43.89386, 2.45416* **Camp Municipal La Franquèze, 81250 Alban [05 63 55 91 87 or 05 63 55 82 09 (Mairie); fax 05 63 55 01 97; mairie.alban@wanadoo.fr]** W of Albi on D999 turn L at ent to Alban. Site 300m on R, sp. Sm, hdg, pt shd, pt sl, terr, wc; shwrs; EHU (6A) €2.10; lndry; playgrnd; adv bkg acc; quiet; rv fishing; CKE/CCI. "Beautiful area, conv Tarn Valley; vg; water taps scarce; gd hilltop site with views." 1 Jun-30 Sep. € 14.00   2014*

ALBERT 3B3 (2km N Urban) *50.01136, 2.65556*
Camp Municipal du Vélodrome, Ave Henri Dunant, 80300 Albert [03 64 62 22 53 or 06 42 58 71 64; fax 03 22 74 38 30; campingalbert@laposte.net; www.camping-albert.com] Fr town cent take Rue Godin E adj to Basilica & foll sp for site. Easiest access fr Bapaume (N) twds Albert; turn R at camping sp on edge of town. Med, mkd, unshd, wc; chem disp; mv service pnt; shwrs inc; EHU (4-10A) €2.20-4.40 (rev pol); shop nr; red long stay; wifi; 40% statics; dogs; Eng spkn; adv bkg acc; fishing adj; CKE/CCI. "Pleasant, well-run, well maintained, clean site; nr lake; friendly, helpful warden; poss security prob; conv for Lille, Arras & Amien by train & for WW1 battlefields etc; poss rlwy noise; facs basic but rates reasonable; if office close find pitch and inform warden later; gates clsd fairly early, will need ent code if late; easy walk into Albert." ♦ 1 Apr-11 Oct. € 18.00   2016*

ALBERT 3B3 (5km NE Rural) *50.04141, 2.66868*
International Camping Bellevue, 25 Rue d'Albert, 80300 Authuille [03 22 74 59 29 or 06 71 96 88 78 (mob); fax 03 22 74 05 14; camping.bellevue0767@orange.fr; campingbellevue.pagesperso-orange.fr] Take D929 Albert to Bapaume rd; in 3km turn L at La Boiselle, foll sp to Aveluy cont to Authuille. Site on R in vill cent. Med, hdg, pt shd, pt sl, wc; chem disp; shwrs; EHU (6A) inc (rev pol); rest; playgrnd; 80% statics; dogs €1; other stay; rv fishing 500m; CKE/CCI. "Helpful owner; basic site, well maintained; useful touring Somme WW1 battlefields; walking dist of Thiepval Ridge; gd NH; lovely site; excel rest in vill; san facs old fashioned but clean; church clock chiming thro night." 15 Mar-31 Oct. € 17.00   2017*

ALBERT 3B3 (14km SW Rural) *49.91930, 2.57985*
FFCC Camping Les Puits Tournants, 6 Rue du Marais, 80800 Sailly-le-Sec [03 22 76 65 56; camping.puitstournants@wanadoo.fr; www.camping-les-puits-tournants.com] Fr N exit A1 junc 14 onto D929 dir Amiens, at Albert take D42 S to Sailly-Laurette then turn R onto D233 to Sailly-le-Sec & foll sp. Or fr S exit junc 13 twd Albert onto D1029. At Lamotte-Warfusée R onto D42 to Sailly-Laurette, turn L to Sailley-le-Sec. Med, hdstg, mkd, pt shd, wc (htd); chem disp; mv service pnt; shwrs inc; EHU (4A) €3; gas; lndry; shop; bbq; playgrnd; pool (htd); paddling pool; sw; wifi; TV; 60% statics; dogs; Eng spkn; adv bkg acc; quiet; ccard acc; games area; bike hire; canoe hire; fishing; horseriding 5km; tennis 2km. "Lovely, pleasant family-run site; amiable staff; gd clean san facs, need updating; grass pitches muddy when wet; tight ent, lge o'fits poss diff; gd pool; walks by rv; excel; picturesque site nr rv Somme; nice dog walks by rv; facs poss stretched in HS; new pools & rest under construction (2017)." ♦ 1 Apr-31 Oct. € 25.00   2017*

ALBERTVILLE 9B3 (1km NNE Urban) *45.67922, 6.39636* **Camp Municipal Les Adoubes, Ave du Camping, 73200 Albertville [04 79 32 06 62 or 06 85 84 02 56; hello@camping-albertville.fr; www.camping-albertville.fr]** Site is 200m fr town cent; over bdge on banks of Rv Arly. Med, mkd, pt shd, pt sl, wc (htd); chem disp; mv service pnt; shwrs inc; EHU (10A) €3.50; gas; lndry; shop nr; rest nr; bar nr; bbq; twin axles; wifi; TV; 5% statics; dogs; Eng spkn; adv bkg acc; ccard acc; CKE/CCI. "Excel site in excel location; plenty of rm, even high ssn; v helpful staff; site yourself if recep clsd; well kept; 10% red for CC memb; under new management; site being upgraded for 2015; rallies acc." 1 Jan-30 Oct & 1 Dec-31 Dec. € 20.50   2015*

ALBI

ALBI *8E4* (2km NE Urban) *43.93485, 2.16213*
Albirondack Park, Camping Lodge & Spa (formerly Camping Caussels), 31 Allée de la Piscine, 81000 Albi [05 63 60 37 06 or 06 84 04 23 13 (mob); fax 05 31 60 51 86; albirondack@orange.fr; www.albirondack.fr] Fr Albi ring rd/bypass exit sp Lacause/St Juéry (do not turn twd Millau). Strt over & foll sp Géant-Casino hypmkt & 'Centre Ville', then foll camping/piscine sp. Med, mkd, pt shd, pt sl, wc (htd); chem disp; mv service pnt; shwrs inc; EHU (10A) €5.70; lndry; shop nr; rest; snacks; bbq; playgrnd; pool (htd); 10% statics; dogs €5; bus; adv bkg acc; quiet; CKE/CCI. "Vg, popular site in conv position; pitches unlevelled - soft in wet & some poss diff lge o'fits due trees; gd walk (40 min) by rv to town cent; Albi Cathedral; spa; Toulouse Lautrec exhibitions; spa & pool inc; excel rest; excel clean modern san facs; beware of low lying wooden & concrete posts; v cramped site; rec arr early." ♦ 20 Jan-10 Nov & 2 Dec-31 Dec. € 36.50   2018*

ALBINE *8F4* (1km SW Rural) *43.45406, 2.52706*
Camping L'Estap Albine, Le Suc, 81240 Albine [05 63 98 34 74; campinglestap@orange.fr; www.campinglestap.com] Fr Mazamet on D612 dir Béziers for approx 12km; turn R onto D88 sp Albine. On app to vill turn R at sp 'Camping du Lac'. Site in 1km. Sm, hdg, mkd, hdstg, pt shd, terr, wc; chem disp; fam bthrm; shwrs inc; EHU (6A) €4; gas; lndry; shop nr; snacks; bar; bbq (gas); playgrnd; pool; dogs €2; Eng spkn; adv bkg acc; quiet; ccard acc; fishing; games area; CKE/CCI. "Well-kept, clean site; superb views; facs adequate; excel touring base; poss diff lge o'fits due sm pitches & steep access; vg; new friendly French owners." ♦ 30 Mar-31 Nov. € 32.40   2013*

ALENCON *4E1* (3km SW Rural) *48.42566, 0.07421*
Camp Municipal de Guérame, 65 Rue de Guérame, 61000 Alençon [02 33 26 34 95; camping.guerame@orange.fr; www.ville-alencon.fr] Located nr town cent. Fr N on D38 take N12 W (Carrefour sp). In 5km take D1 L sp Condé-sur-Sarthe. At rndabt turn L sp Alençon then R immed after Carrefour supmkt, foll site sp. Site is sp fr D112 inner ring rd. Med, hdg, hdstg, pt shd, wc (htd); chem disp; mv service pnt; fam bthrm; shwrs inc; EHU (5A) €3.10 (check EHU carefully) (poss long lead req); lndry; shop nr; bar nr; bbq; playgrnd; entmnt; wifi; TV; dogs €1.90; Eng spkn; adv bkg acc; bike hire; horseriding; rv fishing; tennis; canoeing; CKE/CCI. "Helpful warden; clean san facs; o'night m'vans area; pool complex 700m; barrier/recep clsd 1800 LS; LS phone ahead to check site open; some pitches poss flood in heavy rain; rvside walk to town thro arboretum; peaceful site." ♦ 1 Apr-30 Sep. € 15.00   2015*

ALERIA *10H2* (7km N Coastal) *42.16155, 9.55269*
Camping-Village Riva-Bella (Part Naturist), 20270 Aléria [04 95 38 81 10; fax 04 95 38 91 29; riva-bella@orange.fr; www.naturisme-rivabella.com] Fr Bastia S on N198 for 60km, site sp to L. Poor rd access (2011). Med, pt shd, wc; mv service pnt; shwrs; EHU €4.30; lndry; shop; rest; snacks; bar; playgrnd; beach sand adj; red long stay; entmnt; wifi; TV; 10% statics; dogs €3.50; adv bkg acc; quiet; fishing; games area; watersports; bike hire; tennis; INF card. "Site untidy early ssn (2011); fitness rm; steam rm; sauna; spa treatments; poss insect problem; naturist site 15 May-20 Sep, non-naturist rest of year - but always sm end beach avail for naturists." ♦ € 36.00   2016*

ALET LES BAINS *8G4* (0km W Rural) *42.99490, 2.25525* Camping Val d'Aleth, Ave Nicolas Pavillon, 11580 Alet-les-Bains [04 68 69 90 40; fax 04 68 69 94 60; info@valdaleth.com; www.valdaleth.com] Fr Limoux S on D118 twd Quillan; in approx 8km ignore 1st L turn over Aude bdge into vill but take alt rte for heavy vehicles. Immed after x-ing rv, turn L in front of casino & ent town fr S; site sp on L. Sm, mkd, hdg, hdstg, shd, pt sl, wc (htd); chem disp; mv service pnt; fam bthrm; shwrs inc; EHU (10A) €2.75-4; gas; lndry; shop; rest nr; bbq (gas); playgrnd; red long stay; wifi; 25% statics; dogs €1.55; phone; Eng spkn; adv bkg acc; ccard acc; bike hire; CKE/CCI. "Rvside (no sw) site in attractive, medieval vill; sm pitches (lge o'fits need to book); friendly, helpful British owner; gd clean san facs; v few facs in vill; poss unkempt early ssn; conv Carcassonne & Cathar country - scenic; ACSI acc." ♦ € 20.00   2016*

ALLEGRE LES FUMADES *10E2* (2km NE Rural) *44.2089, 4.25665* Camping Le Château de Boisson, 30500 Allègre-les-Fumades [04 66 24 85 61 or 04 66 24 82 21; fax 04 66 24 80 14; reception@chateaudeboisson.com; www.chateaudeboisson.com or www.les-castels.com] Fr Alès NE on D904, turn R after Les Mages onto D132, then L onto D16 for Boisson. Fr A7 take exit 19 Pont l'Esprit, turn S on N86 to Bagnols-sur-Cèze & then D6 W. Bef Vallérargues turn R onto D979 Lussan, then D37 & D16 to Boisson. Lge, mkd, hdg, shd, pt sl, wc; chem disp; mv service pnt; fam bthrm; shwrs inc; EHU (6A) inc; gas; lndry; shop; rest; snacks; bar; bbq (elec, gas); playgrnd; pool (covrd, htd); paddling pool; red long stay; entmnt; wifi; 80% statics; dogs €5 (no dogs 9 Jul-20 Aug); phone; Eng spkn; adv bkg acc; quiet; ccard acc; games rm; tennis; bike hire. "Vg, well-run, peaceful site; no o'fits over 7m high ssn; gd sized pitches, poss some v sm; helpful staff; excel san facs; excel rest & facs; superb pool complex." ♦ 12 Apr-27 Sep. € 39.00   2016*

⊞ **ALTKIRCH** 6F3 (1km SE Rural) 47.61275, 7.23336
Camp Municipal Les Acacias, Route de Hirtzbach, 68130 Altkirch [03 89 40 69 40 or 03 89 40 00 04 (Mairie); camping.les.acacias@gmail.com; www.sundgau-sudalsace.com] Sp on D419 on app to town fr W. Sp in town. Sm, mkd, shd, wc (htd); chem disp; fam bthrm; shwrs inc; EHU (10A) €3; shop; rest; snacks; bar; playgrnd; 20% statics; dogs; Eng spkn; adv bkg rec; CKE/CCI. "Lovely quiet site; gd, clean facs; office clsd until 1700 - site yourself & pay later; gd NH." € 13.50   2013*

AMBAZAC 7B3 (3km NE Rural) 45.97158, 1.41315
Camping L'Ecrin Nature, 87240 Ambazac [06 52 92 71 65 or 05 55 56 60 25; contact@campinglecrinature.com; www.campinglecrinature.com] Fr A20 foll sp to Ambazac; site on D914. Med, hdg, mkd, pt shd, pt sl, terr, wc; chem disp; mv service pnt; fam bthrm; shwrs inc; EHU (6A) €3.50; lndry; shop; bbq; playgrnd; pool (htd); wifi; 15% statics; dogs; Eng spkn; adv bkg acc; quiet; ccard acc; lake fishing. "Excel waterside site with lovely views, o'looking lake; v friendly new owners, who cont to improve this eco site; san facs clean; ctr for mountain biking & walking; much improved site; gd pool; hg rec; use barrier intercom to contact bureau on arr (bureau clsd midday-3pm); shgl beach adj (sw not allowed); excel site; peaceful; use intercom to gain access." ♦ 8 Apr-2 Oct. € 21.00   2017*

AMBERT 9B1 (1km S Urban) 45.53951, 3.72867
Camping Les Trois Chênes, Rue de la Chaise-Dieu, 63600 Ambert [04 73 82 34 68 or 04 73 82 23 95 (LS); fax 04 73 82 44 00; tourisme@ville-ambert.fr; www.camping-ambert.com] On main rd D906 S twd Le Puy on L bet Leisure Park & Aquacentre. Med, mkd, hdg, pt shd, serviced pitches; wc; chem disp; shwrs inc; EHU (10A) €3.25; lndry; shop nr; rest nr; snacks; playgrnd; 80% statics; dogs €1; adv bkg acc; quiet; waterslide; CKE/CCI. "Excel, well-kept site; gd, clean san facs; rvside walk to town; htd pool adj; rec arrive bef noon peak ssn; recep & barrier clsd 1900 LS; steam museum & working paper mill nr; steam train 1.5km; vg." ♦ 8 May-30 Sep. € 27.00   2014*

AMBIALET 8E4 (1km ESE Rural) 43.94181, 2.38686
Camping La Mise à l'Eau, Fédusse, 81430 Ambialet [05 63 79 58 29; fax 05 63 79 58 09; contact@camping-ambialet.com; www.camping-ambialet.fr] Fr Albi E on D999; in 15km, after Villefranche-d'Albigeois, turn L onto D74 to Ambialet; turn R at junc; in 100m bear L; site on L. Sharp turn, turning pnt avail down rd. NB App via D74 as v narr tunnels on D172/D700 to E & W of Ambialet. Sm, mkd, pt shd, wc; shwrs; EHU (6-10A) €2.15; lndry; shop nr; rest nr; snacks; bar nr; playgrnd; pool; dogs €1.50; adv bkg acc; kayaking; CKE/CCI. "Easy walk to pretty vil; bar 500ml; clean facs; excel; pretty rvside site; no chem disp facs on site, use public toilet in vill." ♦ 1 May-31 Oct. € 17.00   2016*

AMBOISE 4G2 (1km N Rural) 47.41763, 0.98717 **Camp Municipal L'Ile d'Or, 37400 Amboise [02 47 57 23 37 or 02 47 23 47 38 (Mairie); fax 02 47 23 19 80; camping@ville-amboise.fr; www.camping-amboise.com]** Fr N exit A10 exit junc 18 onto D31/D431 to Amboise; at turn R onto D751 dir Blois & get in L lane to cross bdge on D431; site a turning L off bdge, on lge wooded island in Rv Loire. Fr S exit A85 junc 11 onto D31 dir Amboise; foll Centre Ville sp to rv on D431; get in L/H lane to cross bdge (dir Nazelles); turn R off bdge to site on island. Lge, mkd, pt shd, wc; chem disp; mv service pnt; fam bthrm; shwrs inc; EHU (6A) inc (poss rev pol); lndry; shop nr; rest; snacks; bar; red long stay; entmnt; wifi; TV; dogs €1.15; phone; Eng spkn; adv bkg acc; ccard acc; fishing; games area; tennis; CKE/CCI. "Lovely, spacious, secure site in gd location adj Rv Loire & park; well-kept; lge pitches; htd pool & waterslide 500m (high ssn); nice rest & bar; easy walk to interesting old town; vg dog walking; conv Parc Léonardo Da Vinci (last place he lived) & Château d'Amboise; midsummer week music festival in adj park - check date; no twin axles; m'van o'night area open all year, excel stop out of ssn; gd value; vg; excel san facs, stretched in high ssn; v busy." ♦ 31 Mar-9 Oct. € 16.00   2017*

AMBOISE 4G2 (4km N Rural) 47.43113, 0.95430
Camp Municipal des Patis, 37530 Nazelles-Négron [02 47 57 71 07 or 02 47 23 71 71; mairie.nazelles-negron@wanadoo.fr; www.ville-amboise.fr] Fr Amboise, take D952 on N bank of rv twd Tours & turn R (N) onto D5 to Nazelles-Négron. Foll sp to vill. Site N of bdge over Rv Cisse, on R immed after x-ing bdge. Sm, mkd, pt shd, wc; chem disp; shwrs inc; EHU (3-5A) inc (long lead poss req); shop nr; playgrnd; dogs €0.90; quiet; CKE/CCI. "Peaceful, clean, well-kept site; some lge pitches; no lge c'vans or twin axles; boggy in wet weather; excel." 12 Apr-15 Sep. € 11.00   2014*

⊞ **AMBOISE** 4G2 (7km NE Rural) 47.44580, 1.04669
Camping Le Jardin Botanique, 9 bis, Rue de la Rivière, 37530 Limeray [02 47 30 13 50; fax 02 47 30 17 32; campingjardinbotanique@wanadoo.fr; www.camping-jardinbotanique.com] NE fr Amboise on D952 on N side of Rv Loire dir Blois; in approx 6km turn L for Limeray & then immed turn L onto Rue de la Rivière; site on L in 500m. NB Rec not to app fr Limeray, narr rds & diff for lge o'fits. Med, hdg, mkd, hdstg, pt shd, wc (htd); chem disp; mv service pnt; fam bthrm; shwrs inc; EHU (10A) €5 (poss rev pol); gas; lndry; shop nr; rest; snacks; bar; bbq; playgrnd; pool; red long stay; TV; 20% statics; dogs €1.50; Eng spkn; adv bkg acc; bike hire; tennis; games area; CKE/CCI. "Gd for Loire chateaux; 500m fr rv; friendly & helpful owner; gd for children; gd gourmet rest adj; poss muddy when wet; gd cycle rtes; poorly maintained facs (2014)." ♦ € 20.50   2015*

AMBRIERES LES VALLEES

L'Ile des Trois Rois

The park Ile des Trois Rois is situated in the most beautiful bend of the Seine nearby Castle Gaillard in Normandy and is a haven of peace. Paris is situated of less than than an hour and Rouen is half an hour driving from the camp site. Facilities: two heated swimming pools, ping pong, camper service, bar and restaurant (high season) and play area

1, Rue Gilles Nicole - F-27700 Les Andelys - France - Tel. 0033 (0) 2 32 54 23 79
Fax 0033 (0) 2 32 51 14 54 - Email campingtroisrois@aol.com - www.camping-troisrois.com

AMBRIERES LES VALLEES *4E1* (2km SW Rural) 48.39121, -0.61680 **Camping Le Parc de Vaux, 35 Rue des Colverts, 53300 Ambrières-les-Vallées [02 43 04 90 25; parcdevaux@camp-in-ouest.com; www.parcdevaux.com]** Fr S on D23 turn R at sp 'Parc de Loisirs de Vaux'. Site in approx 100m on bank Rv Varenne. Check in at Office de Tourisme bef site recep. Med, mkd, hdstg, hdg, pt shd, terr, wc; shwrs inc; EHU (10A) €3.20 (poss long lead req) (poss rev pol); lndry; shop nr; rest; bar; bbq; playgrnd; pool (htd); red long stay; entmnt; wifi; TV; 40% statics; dogs €1.80; Eng spkn; adv bkg acc; quiet; tennis; canoe hire; fishing; games area; bike hire; waterslide; CKE/CCI. "Excel site in beautiful surroundings; lake adj; helpful recep; nice rvside site adj to leisure pool; vill 20 mins along rv." ♦ 9 Apr-30 Oct. € 15.00   2014*

AMIENS *3C3* (10km N Rural) 49.97240, 2.30150 **FFCC Camping du Château, Rue du Château, 80280 Bertangles [09 51 66 32 60; camping@chateaubertangles.com; www.chateaubertangles.com]** Foll N25 N of Amiens; after 8km turn W on D97 to Bertangles. Well sp in vill. Sm, hdg, pt shd, wc; chem disp; shwrs inc; EHU (5A) €3.70 (poss rev pol); bar nr; red long stay; bus; quiet; CKE/CCI. "Pleasant, peaceful, well-kept site by chateau wall; busy high ssn, early arr rec (bef 1600); pleasant welcome; clean, old san facs; ltd recep hrs, pitch yourself; grnd soft when wet; Amiens attractive city; gd walks; conv a'routes & NH; excel; gd value; basic site, needs updating; lovely location; gd dogs walk adj." ♦ 21 Apr-11 Sep. € 21.00   2017*

AMIENS *3B3* (32km N Rural) 50.13813, 2.36842 **Camping Familial Au Bord De l'Authie, Route d'Albert 80600 Authieule [03 22 32 56 13 or 06 74 59 92 65 (mob); contact@campingauborddelauthie.com; www.campingauborddelauthie.com]** Fr Amiens N25 twd Rue de Longpré, turn R at Doullens onto D938. After 2.6 km site on R. Sm, mkd, shd, pt sl, terr, wc; chem disp; mv service pnt; fam bthrm; shwrs inc; EHU (6A); lndry; shop; rest; snacks; bbq; entmnt; wifi; 80% statics; dogs; Eng spkn; adv bkg acc; quiet; CCI♦ 1 Feb-1 Dec. € 13.00   2014*

AMIENS *3C3* (5km NW Urban) 49.92091, 2.25883 **Camping Parc des Cygnes, 111 Ave des Cygnes, 80080 Amiens-Longpré [03 22 43 29 28; fax 03 22 43 59 42; alban@parcdescygnes.com; www.parcdescygnes.com]** Exit A16 junc 20 twds Amiens onto ring rd Rocade Nord exit junc 40. At 1st rndabt foll sp Amiens, Longpré D412; foll sp Parc de Loisirs & site. Med, mkd, pt shd, wc (htd); chem disp; mv service pnt; fam bthrm; shwrs inc; EHU (10A) inc on most pitches (poss long lead req); gas; lndry; shop; rest; snacks; bar; bbq; playgrnd; twin axles; wifi; TV; dogs €2.40; phone; bus to city adj; adv bkg rec; quiet; ccard acc; fishing nr; bike hire; games rm; kayaking; CKE/CCI. "Peaceful, well-kept, secure site in parkland; leisure park adj; lge pitches; helpful, welcoming staff; gd, clean san facs, ltd LS; ring bell by recep if office clsd; no o'fits over 11m high ssn; access to grass pitches off hard areas - m'vans can keep driving wheels on in wet weather; gd canal-side cycling/walk to city; Amiens cathedral worth visit; longer leads req for some pitches; conv Somme battlefields; gd; rec; 50% of pitches have EHU; san facs adequate but need updating (2018)." ♦ 1 Apr-14 Oct. € 29.00   2018*

ANCENIS *2G4* (12km E Rural) 47.36702, -1.01275 **Camping de l'Ile Batailleuse, St Florent-le-Vieil, 44370 Varades [02 40 96 70 20; contact@campingilebatailleuse.fr; http://ilebatailleuse.onlycamp.fr/en]** On Ancenis-Angers rd D723 turn S in Varades onto D752 to St Florent-le-Vieil. After x-ing 1st bdge over Rv Loire site on L on island immed bef 2nd bdge. Med, pt shd, wc; chem disp; shwrs inc; EHU (10A) €2; shop nr; rest nr; playgrnd; wifi; dogs €1.20; Eng spkn; quiet; bike hire; games area; tennis 1km; CKE/CCI. "Basic, clean site; main shwr facs up stone staircase; panoramic views of Rv Loire in town; gd cycle rtes along rv; new san facs (2014); v pleasant sites." ♦ 30 May-14 Sep. € 18.00   2014*

ANDERNOS LES BAINS

ANCENIS *2G4* (5km SW Rural) *47.34400, -1.20693*
Camp Municipal Beauregret, 49530 Drain [02 40 98 20 30 or 02 40 98 20 16 (Mairie); fax 02 40 98 23 29; mairie-sg.drain@wanadoo.fr] Fr Ancenis take D763 S for 2km, turn R onto D751 & cont for 3km. Site on R bef vill of Drain on L. Sm, hdg, pt shd, wc; chem disp; mv service pnt; shwrs inc; EHU (6A) inc (poss rev pol); lndry; shop nr; bbq; playgrnd; entmnt; TV; adv bkg acc; quiet; games area. "Secluded, tranquil site; immac san facs up steps - ltd number; poss not suitable lge o'fits; warden calls am & pm; gd fishing; lake nrby; nice quiet site." ♦ 1 May-30 Sep. € 11.50   2013*

"That's changed – Should I let the Club know?"

If you find something on site that's different from the site entry, fill in a report and let us know. See camc.com/europereport.

ANCENIS *2G4* (2km W Rural) *47.36201, -1.18721*
FFCC Camping de l'Ile Mouchet, 44156 Ancenis Cedex [02 40 83 08 43 or 06 62 54 24 73 (mob); fax 02 40 83 16 19; camping-ile-mouchet@orange.fr; www.camping-estivance.com] Fr S, exit N249 at Vallet onto D763 to Ancenis; turn L immed after x-ing Rv Loire & foll sp; site on banks of rv. Or fr N, exit A11 junc 20 onto D923 to Ancenis; cont on D923 over rndabt; foll D923 along rv; in 400m, at next rndabt, do not cross rv but cont strt on onto D23; site sp to L in 700m. Med, mkd, pt shd, wc (htd); chem disp; mv service pnt; shwrs inc; EHU (6-10A) €4 (rev pol); gas; lndry; shop nr; rest; snacks; bar; playgrnd; pool; TV; 12% statics; dogs; Eng spkn; adv bkg acc; quiet; ccard acc; waterslide; tennis 50m; games rm; CKE/CCI. "Excel touring base; ltd facs LS; some steps; rvside walks; gd site with modern facs; worth a couple of nights; recep clsd 1200-1430." 2 Apr-23 Oct. € 11.00   2016*

ANDELYS, LES *3D2* (3km SW Rural) *49.23582, 1.40016* **FFCC Camping de L'Ile des Trois Rois, 1 rue Gilles Nicolle, 27700 Les Andelys [02 32 54 23 79; fax 02 32 51 14 54; campingtroisrois@aol.com; www.camping-troisrois.com]** Fr Rouen S on A13, exit junc 18 onto D135 & foll sp Les Andelys. Cross bdge over Rv Seine & turn immed R at rndabt, site on R on rvside. Site sp fr town cent. Med, hdstg, hdg, mkd, pt shd, wc (htd); chem disp; mv service pnt; shwrs inc; EHU (10A) inc; gas; lndry; rest; snacks; bar; bbq; playgrnd; pool (htd); paddling pool; red long stay; entmnt; wifi; TV; 20% statics; dogs €2.50; phone; Eng spkn; adv bkg acc; quiet; ccard acc; fishing; bike hire; games rm; CKE/CCI. "Well-kept site on Rv Seine; extra lge pitches avail; friendly, helpful staff; gd security; conv Rouen, Evreux, Giverny; bowling alley; view ruins of Château Gaillard; nice place, nice people; excel; refurbished san facs, sw pool, vg bar & rest; easy walk to old town; hugh site; gd dog walk adj." ♦ 15 Mar-15 Nov. € 27.70   2017*

See advertisement opposite

ANDERNOS LES BAINS *7D1* (6km W Coastal) *44.73443, -1.1960* **Camping Les Viviers, Ave Léon Lesca, Claouey, 33950 Lège-Cap-Ferret [05 56 60 70 04; fax 05 57 70 37 77; reception@lesviviers.com; www.lesviviers.com]** Fr N exit A10/A630 W of Bordeaux onto D106 sp Cap-Ferret. Foll D106 thro Arès & vill of Claouey on W side of Bassin d'Arcachon, site on L after LH bend (approx 1.5km after Claouey). V lge, mkd, hdg, pt shd, wc (htd); chem disp; mv service pnt; fam bthrm; shwrs inc; EHU (10A) inc; gas; lndry; shop; rest; snacks; bar; bbq (elec, gas); playgrnd; pool (covrd, htd); paddling pool; beach sand adj; red long stay; entmnt; wifi; TV; 27% statics; dogs €5; bus; Eng spkn; adv bkg req; quiet; ccard acc; games rm; sauna; windsurfing; fishing; tennis; waterslide; games area; bike hire; sailing; CKE/CCI. "Sand pitches, various positions & prices; clean san facs; sea water lagoon with private sand beach adj; cinema; vg leisure facs; free night bus along peninsular; vg site." ♦ 01 Apr-17 Sep. € 50.00   2016*

See advertisement above

ANDERNOS LES BAINS 7D1 (5km NW Coastal) 44.77287, -1.14144 Camping La Cigale, Route de Lège, 33740 Arès [05 56 60 22 59; fax 05 56 77 70 41 66; contact@camping-lacigale-ares.com; www.camping-lacigale-ares.com] Fr Andernos proceed NW on D3 to Arès. Take Cap-Ferret rd D106. Site on L in 1km. Sm, mkd, pt shd, wc; chem disp; mv service pnt; fam bthrm; shwrs inc; EHU (6-10A); gas; lndry; shop nr; rest; snacks; bar; bbq; playgrnd; pool (htd); paddling pool; beach 900m; twin axles; wifi; 50% statics; dogs €1; bus 1km; Eng spkn; adv bkg rec; quiet; games rm. "Excel family-run site; v clean; gd sized pitches; bike hire adj; cycle rtes; supmkt 2km." ♦ 27 Apr-25 Sep. € 42.00 2017*

ANDERNOS LES BAINS 7D1 (5km NW Coastal) 44.77792, -1.14280 FLOWER Camping La Canadienne, 82 Rue du Général de Gaulle, 33740 Arès [05 56 60 24 91; fax 05 57 70 40 85; info@lacanadienne.com; www.lacanadienne.com or www.flowercampings.com] N fr town sq at Arès on D3 (Rue du Général de Gaulle) dir Cap Ferret. Site on R after 1km. Med, shd, wc; fam bthrm; shwrs inc; EHU (15A) inc; gas; lndry; shop; rest; snacks; bar; playgrnd; pool; paddling pool; beach sand 2km; entmnt; TV; dogs €2.50; adv bkg rec; quiet; bike hire; archery; tennis; windsurfing 1km; fishing 1km; canoe hire; games rm; sailing 1km. ♦ 1 Feb-30 Nov. € 31.00 2012*

> "There aren't many sites open at this time of year"
>
> If you're travelling outside peak season remember to call ahead to check site opening dates – even if the entry says 'open all year'.

ANDUZE 10E1 (2km SE Rural) 44.03824, 3.99454 Camping Le Bel Eté, 1870 Route de Nîmes, 30140 Anduze [04 66 61 76 04; contact@camping-bel-ete.com; www.camping-bel-ete.com] S fr Alès on D6110; W on D910A to Anduze. In Anduze take D907 SE twds Nîmes. Site on L, 200m after rlwy bdge. Med, mkd, pt shd, serviced pitches; wc; chem disp; shwrs inc; EHU (6A) €4.50; gas; lndry; shop nr; rest; playgrnd; pool; 10% statics; dogs €1.50; phone; adv bkg req; quiet; ccard acc; CKE/CCI. "Delightful, well-kept site in superb location; vg facs but ltd LS; helpful owner; rv adj; gd base for Cévennes area; Thurs mkt." ♦ 8 May-17 Sep. € 33.50 2012*

ANDUZE 10E1 (14km W Rural) 44.04364, 3.88109 Camping La Pommeraie, Route de Lassalle, 30140 Thoiras [04 66 85 20 52; fax 04 66 85 20 53; info@la-pommeraie.fr; www.la-pommeraie.fr] Fr Alès take D6110, & D910A to Anduze, over bdge, R onto D907. In 6km L under rlwy onto D57, site on L 2.5km bef Lasalle. Med, shd, wc; fam bthrm; shwrs; EHU (6A) €4.50; gas; lndry; shop; rest; snacks; bar; cooking facs; playgrnd; pool; entmnt; TV; 10% statics; dogs €2-5.50 (high ssn); adv bkg acc; quiet; tennis; games area. 13 Apr-29 Sep. € 39.00 2014*

ANDUZE 10E1 (1km NW Rural) 44.06430, 3.97694 Camping Castel Rose, 30140 Anduze [04 66 61 80 15; castelrose@wanadoo.fr; www.castelrose.com] Fr Alès S on D6110 & W on N910A to Anduze. Foll sp Camping L'Arche. Lge, shd, wc; shwrs inc; EHU (6-10A) €3.20-4; gas; lndry; shop; rest; snacks; bar; pool; entmnt; wifi; TV; dogs €2; Eng spkn; adv bkg rec; fishing; boating. "Excel site by rv; friendly, helpful owners; attractive countryside; gd cent touring Cévennes." 1 Apr-28 Sep. € 43.00 2014*

ANDUZE 10E1 (2km NW Rural) 44.06785, 3.97336 Camping L'Arche, Quartier de Labahou, 30140 Anduze [04 66 61 74 08; fax 04 66 61 88 94; contact@camping-arche.fr; www.camping-arche.fr] Fr Alès S on D6110/D910A to Anduze. On D907, sp on R. Access poss dff lge o'fits/m'vans. Lge, mkd, shd, wc (htd); chem disp; mv service pnt; fam bthrm; shwrs inc; EHU (10A) €2; gas; lndry; shop; rest; snacks; bar; bbq; playgrnd; pool (covrd, htd); red long stay; entmnt; wifi; TV; 10% statics; dogs €3.80; Eng spkn; adv bkg acc; quiet; waterslide; CKE/CCI. "Well-run site; gd san facs; beautiful area; bamboo gardens worth visit; 24hr security patrols; excel rest; outstanding site; vg value." ♦ 3 Apr-30 Sep. € 48.00 2017*

See advertisement opposite

ANET 3D2 (1km N Urban) 48.86183, 1.44166 Camp Municipal Les Eaux Vives, 1 Route des Cordeliers, 28260 Anet [02 37 41 42 67 or 06 09 74 16 90 (mob); fax 02 37 62 20 99; martine.desrues@cegetel.net; www.camping-anet.fr] Take D928 NE fr Dreux; in Anet thro town & take 1st L after chateau; turn L on rd to Ezy & Ivry (camp sp on corner), site in 150m N of rv. Lge, pt shd, serviced pitches; wc (htd); chem disp; mv service pnt; shwrs; EHU (10A) €3; lndry; shop nr; playgrnd; sw nr; 95% statics; dogs €1.10; Eng spkn; tennis; fishing 2km; CKE/CCI. "Rvside pitches; helpful warden; clean, v basic san facs, poss stretched high ssn; rv adj; grnd soft in wet - site poss clsd early; gd walks in forest; chateau in vill; easy drive to Paris; untidy statics (2010); conv NH." 1 Mar-31 Oct. € 14.00 2013*

ANGERS

France

ANET *3D2* (1km N Urban) *48.86278, 1.41552* **Camp Municipal Les Trillots, Chemin des Trillots, 27530 Ezy-sur-Eure [02 37 64 73 21 or 02 37 64 73 48 (Mairie)]** N fr Dreux on D928/D143. Site on N side of Rv Eure. Med, pt shd, wc (htd); shwrs inc; EHU (4A) inc; lndry; shop nr; rest nr; bar nr; bbq; 95% statics; dogs; quiet. "Quiet site adj rvside walks; gd san facs; helpful warden; poss not suited to tourers; not rec."
1 Mar-15 Nov. € 13.00   2012*

ANGERS *4G1* (15km SE Rural) *47.44332, -0.40881* **Camping du Port Caroline, Rue du Pont Caroline, 49800 Brain-sur-l'Authion [02 41 80 42 18; info@campingduportcaroline.fr; www.campingduportcaroline.fr]** E fr Angers on D347 turn onto D113, site sp at ent to vill. Med, hdstg, hdg, mkd, pt shd, wc (htd); chem disp; shwrs inc; EHU (10A) inc; lndry; shop nr; snacks; bbq; playgrnd; pool (htd); paddling pool; entmnt; TV; 5% statics; dogs €3; adv bkg acc; ccard acc; games rm; tennis nr; fishing nr. "Gd touring base; games area adj; skateboarding; site clsd Feb; lge pitches." ♦ 1 Apr-31 Oct. € 15.00   2017*

ANGERS *4G1* (7km SE Urban) *47.42442, -0.52701* **Camping L'Ile du Château, Ave de la Boire Salée, 49130 Les Ponts-de-Cé [02 41 44 62 05; camping.ileduchateau@gmail.com; www.camping-ileduchateau.fr]** Fr Angers take D160 (sp Cholet) to Les Ponts-de-Cé. Foll sp 'Centre Ville' & turn R at rndabt in town opp Hôtel de Ville, & site on R in 200m on banks of Rv Loire. Med, hdg, shd, wc; chem disp; mv service pnt; fam bthrm; shwrs inc; EHU (10A) inc (poss rev pol); lndry; shop; rest; snacks; bbq; playgrnd; beach sand 500m; entmnt; wifi; TV; 4% statics; dogs €2; phone; Eng spkn; tennis; games rm; golf 5km; waterslide adj; games area; CKE/CCI. "Well-kept, scenic site; excel pool adj; gd touring base for chateaux, vineyards; htd pool adj; gd dog walking; highly rec; v shd, few sunny pitches; v busy area; organised entmnt."
♦ 1 Apr-30 Oct. € 21.00   2015*

⊞ **ANGERS** *4G1* (6km SW Urban) *47.41878, -0.61160* **Camping Aire d'Accueil de Camping Cars, 25 Rue Chevrière, 49080 Bouchemaine [02 41 77 11 04 or 02 41 22 20 00 (Mairie); adm.generale@ville-bouchemaine.fr; www.ville-bouchemaine.fr]** Fr Angers take D160 S, at intersection with D112 W sp Bouchemaine. Cross Rv Maine via suspension bdge. At rndabt on W bank turn L, site on L in 100m dir La Pointe adj rv. Fr Château-Gontier take N162, then D106, then D102E. Bouchemaine well sp. Sm, hdstg, pt shd, wc; chem disp; mv service pnt; shwrs; EHU (16A) €2.55 (poss rev pol); lndry; shop nr; rest nr; dogs; phone; bus; adv bkg acc; quiet; games area; CKE/CCI. "M'vans & tents only; warden calls am & pm; free Oct-Apr but no EHU; san facs upstairs; poss flooding nr rv; vg NH; automated access; pool 500m; excel cycling, track into Angers." € 11.00   2014*

ANGERS *4G1* (6km SW Urban) *47.45387, -0.59463* **Camping du Lac de Maine, Ave du Lac de Maine, 49000 Angers [02 41 73 05 03; fax 02 41 73 02 20; camping@lacdemaine.fr; www.camping-angers.fr]** W fr Angers on D723, exit at 'Quartier du Lac de Maine' then foll sp to site & Bouchemaine. After 4 rndabts site on L; sp W of Rv Maine. Fr S on D160 or A87, turn onto D4 at Les Ponts-de-Cé. In 6km, cross Rv Maine to Bouchemaine & turn R to Pruniers dir Angers. Site on R at Pruniers town exit sp. Med, hdstg, mkd, hdg, pt shd, serviced pitches; wc (htd); chem disp; mv service pnt; fam bthrm; shwrs inc; EHU (10A) €4.20 (rev pol); gas; lndry; shop nr; rest; snacks; bar; bbq; playgrnd; pool (htd); paddling pool; sw nr; red long stay; twin axles; wifi; TV; 10% statics; dogs €2.30; phone; bus adj; Eng spkn; adv bkg rec; quiet; ccard acc; boating; fishing; tennis 800m; games area; windsurfing 500m; jacuzzi; bike hire; CKE/CCI. "Excel, lge, well-run site in leisure park; pitches narr, some suitable v l'ge o'fits; height barrier at ent 3.2m; conv Loire chateaux; pay 6 nights, stay 7; hypmkt 2km; facs ltd in LS; solar shwrs; few lights on site; gd cycling & walking rte; canoeing; gd bus svrs; excel san facs; v helpful recep; bread avail." ♦ 23 Mar-28 Oct. € 30.00   2018*

ANGOULEME

ANGOULEME 7B2 (7km N Rural) 45.68573, 0.14994
Camping du Plan d'Eau, 1 rue du Camping, 16710 St Yrieix-sur-Charante [05 45 92 14 64; camping@grandangouleme.fr; www.camping-angouleme.fr]
Fr N or S on N10/E606 turn NW & foll sp St Yrieix-sur-Charante, 'Plan d'Eau' & 'Nautilis - Centre Nautique'. Site sp. Med, mkd, hdg, pt shd, wc (htd); chem disp; mv service pnt; shwrs inc; EHU (10A) €3.50; gas; lndry; shop; rest; snacks; bar; bbq; playgrnd; pool; sw nr; wifi; TV; 10% statics; dogs; Eng spkn; adv bkg acc; quiet; ccard acc; games area; watersports. "Superb location; gd; rather bare site; notices warn of poss flooding" ♦
1 Apr-31 Oct. € 16.50   2015*

> "I like to fill in the reports as I travel from site to site"
>
> You'll find report forms at the back of this guide, or you can fill them in online at camc.com/europereport.

ANGOULEME 7B2 (23km NW Rural) 45.79769, 000.63639 Camping Marco de Bignac (formerly Les Sablons), Chemin de la Résistance, 16170 Bignac [05 45 21 78 41; fax 05 45 21 52 37; info@marcodebignac.com; www.marcodebignac.com]
Fr N10 approx 14km N Angoulême take exit La Touche & foll D11 W thro Vars; at Basse turn R onto D117 & foll sp in Bignac. Med, mkd, pt shd, wc (htd); chem disp; fam bthrm; shwrs inc; EHU (3-6A) €3-4; lndry; shop; rest; snacks; bar; bbq; playgrnd; pool; red long stay; entmnt; wifi; 2% statics; dogs free; phone; bus adj; Eng spkn; adv bkg acc; quiet; ccard acc; games area; tennis; fishing; watersports CKE/CCI. "Attractive, peaceful, tidy, lakeside site; worth long drive; scenic area; lge pitches; welcoming, helpful British owners; clean san facs; gd rest; pleasant walk round lake; lake adj; ideal for Angoulême Circuit des Remparts; excel; improvements being done (2016); pets corner." ♦
1 Feb-30 Nov. € 29.00   2017*

ANNECY 9B3 (10km SE Rural) 45.84370, 6.16450
Camping Le Solitaire du Lac, 615 Route de Sales, 74410 St Jorioz [04 50 68 59 30 or 06 88 58 94 24 (mob); contact@campinglesolitaire.com or campinglesolitaire@wanadoo.fr; www.campinglesolitaire.com] Exit Annecy on D1508 twd Albertville. Site sp on N o'skts of St Jorioz. Med, mkd, pt shd, wc; chem disp; mv service pnt; shwrs inc; EHU (5A) €3.50; gas; lndry; shop nr; rest; snacks; bar; bbq; playgrnd; sw; red long stay; wifi; TV; 10% statics; dogs €2.60; Eng spkn; adv bkg acc; quiet; ccard acc; boat launch; games area; bike hire; CKE/CCI. "Nice, well-run site in excel location; water to MH's charge €0.20 per 60l; popular but quiet; cycle track; sm pitches; clean, modern san facs; direct access to Lake Annecy; sh walk to public beach & water bus; cycle path nr; gd touring base; excel; perfect for boating & cycling; v helpful staff." 8 Apr-23 Sep. € 29.00   2017*

ANNECY 9B3 (11km SE Rural) 45.82423, 6.18523
Camping Le Familial, 400 Route de Magnonnet, 74410 Duingt [04 50 68 69 91; contact@annecy-camping-familial.com; www.annecy-camping-familial.com] Fr Annecy on D1508 twd Albertville. 5km after St Jorioz turn R at site sp Entrevernes onto D8, foll sp past Camping Champs Fleuris. Sm, mkd, hdstg, pt shd, pt sl, wc; chem disp; shwrs inc; EHU (6A) €4.30; lndry; snacks; bbq; playgrnd; twin axles; wifi; TV; dogs €1.70; Eng spkn; adv bkg rec; quiet; ccard acc; games area; CKE/CCI. "Gd site in scenic area; gd atmosphere; generous pitches; friendly, helpful owner; communal meals & fondu evenings; conv lakeside cycle track; mobile homes for rent, sleeps 6; excel." ♦
1 Apr-30 Sep. € 22.50   2018*

ANNECY 9B3 (12km SE Rural) 45.88990, 6.22367
Camping La Ferme de Ferrières, 74290 Alex [04 50 02 87 09; fax 04 50 02 80 54; campingfermedesferrieres@voila.fr; www.camping-des-ferrieres.com]
Take D909 on E side of lake out of Annecy twds Thônes; look out for sp on L after turn off to Château de Menthon. Site off D909 approx 1km W of Alex. Med, pt shd, pt sl, terr, wc cont; chem disp; fam bthrm; shwrs inc; EHU (5A) €2.80; lndry; shop; snacks; bbq; playgrnd; dogs €1; phone; Eng spkn; adv bkg acc; quiet; ccard acc; games rm; CKE/CCI. "Spectacular views; peaceful, clean site away fr crowds; friendly & accommodating owner; high standard san facs; pitches muddy when wet; gd NH; basic facs; fair." ♦
1 Jun-30 Sep. € 16.50   2015*

ANNECY 9B3 (8km SE Rural) 45.86305, 6.19690
Camping Le Clos Don Jean, Route du Clos Don Jean, 74290 Menthon-St-Bernard [04 50 60 18 66; donjean74@wanadoo.fr; www.clos-don-jean.com]
Fr N site clearly sp fr vill of Menthon. L uphill for 400m. Med, mkd, pt shd, pt sl, wc; chem disp; mv service pnt; shwrs inc; EHU (3-6A) €2.60-3; gas; lndry; shop; playgrnd; sw nr; dogs €1; Eng spkn; quiet; CKE/CCI. "Excel site in orchard; clean san facs, ltd LS; fine views chateau & lake; walk to lake." ♦ 1 Jun-15 Sep. € 21.00   2012*

ANNECY 9B3 (10km S Rural) 45.82995, 6.18215 Village Camping Europa, 1444 Route d'Albertville, 74410 St Jorioz [04 50 68 51 01; fax 04 50 68 55 20; info@camping-europa.com; www.camping-europa.com]
Fr Annecy take D1508 sp Albertville. Site on R 800m S of St Jorioz dir Albertville. Look for yellow sp on o'skirts of St Jorioz. Med, hdg, pt shd, serviced pitches; wc; chem disp; mv service pnt; fam bthrm; shwrs inc; EHU (6A) €3.80; lndry; shop nr; rest; snacks; bar; bbq (elec, gas); playgrnd; pool (htd); red long stay; twin axles; entmnt; wifi; TV; 20% statics; dogs €3; Eng spkn; adv bkg acc; quiet; ccard acc; bike hire; jacuzzi; boat hire; fishing; waterslide; games rm; tennis 700m; windsurfing; CKE/CCI. "Peaceful site; friendly staff; facs stretched high ssn; vg rest; excel for m'vans; conv Chamonix & Mont Blanc; variable pitch prices; cycle track adj; some pitches tight lge o'fits; gd tourist base; excel; no water points around site, collect fr toilet block; brilliant pool complex; no hot water in sinks; gd cycling area." ♦ 30 Apr-17 Sep. € 40.00   2016*

ANNECY 9B3 (2km S Rural) 45.89100, 6.13236
Camp Municipal Le Belvédère, 8 Route du Semnoz, 74000 Annecy [04 50 45 48 30; fax 04 50 51 81 62; camping@ville-annecy.fr; www.annecy.fr] Exit A41 junc 16; initially foll sp 'Albertville' into town; then foll sp 'Le Lac' and 'Le Semnoz'; site is on R off Route du Semnoz (Route du Semnoz is A41). 'Le Semnoz is a main running S fr Annecy. Lge, mkd, pt shd, pt sl, terr, wc (htd); chem disp; shwrs inc; EHU (16A) €3.20 (poss rev pol); gas; lndry; shop; rest; snacks; playgrnd; wifi; TV; dogs free; phone; Eng spkn; adv bkg rec; ccard acc; fishing; bike hire; excursions; sailing; CKE/CCI. "Lovely, tidy site in beautiful setting; well lit at night; sm pitches; staff helpful; san facs OK; steep footpath to old town; sep statics area; excel; v friendly helpful staff, forest walks." ♦ 25 Mar-16 Oct. € 27.00   2016*

ANNECY 9B3 (6km S Urban) 45.85482, 6.14395
Camping au Coeur du Lac, Les Choseaux, 74320 Sévrier [04 50 52 46 45; fax 04 50 19 01 45; info@ aucoeurdulac.com; www.campingaucoeurdulac.com] S fr Annecy on D1508 sp Albertville. Pass thro Sévrier cent. Site on L at lakeside 1km S of Sévrier. 300m after McDonald's. Med, mkd, hdstg, pt shd, pt sl, terr, wc; chem disp; mv service pnt; shwrs inc; EHU (4A) €3.60, long cable rec; lndry; shop; snacks; playgrnd; beach; sw; entmnt; dogs free LS (not acc high ssn); bus nrby; Eng spkn; adv bkg req; quiet; ccard acc; boat hire; bike hire; CKE/CCI. "Busy, nice site in lovely location; gd views of lake fr upper terr; tight for lge o'fits - sm, sl pitches; ok san facs; gd access to lake beach & cycle path; excel, espec LS; v popular site." ♦ 1 Apr-30 Sep. € 28.00   2016*

> "We must tell the Club about that great site we found"
>
> Get your site reports in by mid-August and we'll do our best to get your updates into the next edition.

ANNECY 9B3 (6km S Rural) 45.84333, 6.14175
Camping Le Panoramic, 22 Chemin des Bernets, Route de Cessenaz, 74320 Sévrier [04 50 52 43 09; info@camping-le-panoramic.com; www.camping-le-panoramic.com] Exit A41 junc 16 Annecy Sud onto D1508 sp Albertville. Thro Sévrier to rndabt at Cessenaz (ignore all prior sp to site) & take 1st R onto D10. In 200m turn R up hill to site in 2km. Lge, mkd, pt shd, pt sl, terr, wc (htd); chem disp; shwrs inc; EHU (4-6A) €3.20-4.20 (some rev pol); lndry; shop; rest; snacks; bar; playgrnd; pool; beach 2km; sw; wifi; TV; dogs €1.60; Eng spkn; quiet; ccard acc; games rm; CKE/CCI. "Fantastic views fr many pitches; blocks/wedges ess for sl pitches; excel pool/bar area; rec for families; new san facs (2012); excel views of lake; v friendly staff; high rec." ♦ 18 Apr-30 Sep. € 36.50   2014*

ANNECY 9B3 (7km S Urban) 45.84412, 6.15354
Camping de l'Aloua, 492 Route de Piron, 74320 Sévrier [04 50 52 60 06; fax 04 50 52 64 54; camping.aloua@wanadoo.fr; www.camping-aloua-lac-annecy.com] Foll sp for Albertville D1508 S fr Annecy. Site on E side, approx 1.4km S of Sevrier vill. Turn L at Champion supmkt rndabt & foll sp twd lake. Lge, hdg, mkd, shd, wc; chem disp; mv service pnt; shwrs inc; EHU (2-10A) €2.50-4.80; lndry; shop; rest; snacks; bar; playgrnd; beach shgl 300m; sw nr; entmnt; TV; dogs €2; phone; Eng spkn; adv bkg acc; fishing adj; watersports adj; archery; boating adj; CKE/CCI. "Gd base for lake (no dir access fr site); cycle track around lake; night security; poss noisy at night with youths & some rd noise; basic san facs; pleasant owners; well run & maintained site; nr lac Annecy, Carrefour & g'ge; bike track or bus to Annecy; vg." ♦ 18 Apr-19 Sep. € 23.00   2015*

> "I need an on-site restaurant"
>
> We do our best to make sure site information is correct, but it is always best to check any must-have facilities are still available or will be open during your visit.

ANNECY 9B3 (7km S Rural) 45.84806, 6.15129
FFCC Camping Les Rives du Lac, 331 Chemin du Communaux, 74320 Sévrier [04 50 52 40 14; lesrivesdulac-annecy@ffcc.fr; www.lesrivesdulac-annecy.com] Take D1508 S fr Annecy sp Albertville, thro Sévrier sp FFCC. Turn L 100m past (S) Lidl supmkt, cross cycle path & turn R & foll sp FFCC keeping parallel with cycle path. Site on L in 400m. Med, mkd, pt shd, wc; chem disp; mv service pnt; fam bthrm; shwrs inc; EHU (10A) €4; lndry; shop nr; bbq; playgrnd; beach shgl; sw; entmnt; wifi; dogs €1.20; bus nr; Eng spkn; adv bkg acc; quiet; sailing; fishing; CKE/CCI. "Beautiful situation; generous pitches; helpful staff; excel new toilet block; water bus to Annecy nr; gd touring base; walking; red CC members (check first); walking, sailing & cycling; cycle rte adj." ♦ 1 Apr-30 Sep. € 23.00   2014*

ANNECY 9B3 (9km S Rural) 45.49484, 6.1055
Camping International du Lac d'Annecy, 1184 Route d'Albertville, 74410 St Jorioz [04 50 68 67 93; contact@camping-lac-annecy.com; www.camping-lac-annecy.com] Fr Annecy take D1508 sp Albertville. Site on R just after St Jorioz. Med, hdstg, hdg, mkd, pt shd, wc; chem disp; mv service pnt; fam bthrm; shwrs inc; EHU (6-10A) €4-5.60; gas; lndry; shop; rest; snacks; bar; bbq (elec, gas); playgrnd; pool (htd); sw nr; TV; 30% statics; dogs €2.50; phone; bus 500m; Eng spkn; adv bkg acc; quiet; ccard acc; bike hire; games area; CKE/CCI. "Lovely site; gd san facs; excel for touring lake area; site ent tight for med/lge o'fits (2009); vg cycling; gd rest nrby." 8 May-18 Sep. € 36.00   2012*

ANNECY

ANNECY 9B3 (7km SW Rural) 45.86131, 6.05214
Aire Naturelle La Vidome (Lyonnaz), 74600 Montagny-les-Lanches [04 50 46 61 31; j.lyonnaz@ wanadoo.fr; www.lavidome.fr] Exit Annecy on D1201 sp Aix-les-Bains/Chambéry; after 6km at Le Treige turn R sp Montagny-les-Lanches. In 1km turn R in Avulliens; site on R in 100m. Sm, pt shd, pt sl, wc; chem disp; shwrs; EHU (3-10A) €2.10-4; lndry; shop nr; playgrnd; dogs €0.80; adv bkg acc; quiet; horseriding 1km; fishing 1km; CKE/CCI. "Excel site; gd views; meals avail; friendly owners; vg san facs; access poss tight for lge o'fits; beach & mini golf 10km; pool 3km; gd touring base." 1 May-30 Sep. € 15.00   2014*

ANNONAY 9C2 (4km N Urban) 45.25799, 4.67426
Camp Municipal de Vaure, Rue Mathieu Duret, 07100 Annonay [04 75 33 73 73 or 04 75 33 46 54; fax 04 75 34 62 36; www.mairie-annonay.fr] Sp fr o'skts of town & foll sp St Etienne. Fr St Etienne & NW on D1082 & D820 twd Annonay. For R onto D206 S & foll camping/piscine sp to site. Sm, hdg, mkd, pt shd, wc; shwrs inc; EHU (6-10A) €2.50-3.50; lndry; shop nr; snacks; bar; pool (covrd, htd); paddling pool; 10% statics; dogs €1.50; quiet; tennis; games area. "Helpful staff; gd; basic facs; site not v secure." 1 Apr-31 Oct. € 10.00   2016*

ANTIBES 10E4 (2km N Urban/Coastal) 43.60536, 7.11255
Camping Caravaning Le Rossignol, Ave Jean Michard-Pelissier, Juan-les-Pins, 06600 Antibes [04 93 33 56 98; fax 04 92 91 98 99; campinglerossignol@ wanadoo.fr; www.campingrossignol.com] Turn W off N7 Antibes-Nice at sp to Hospitalier de la Fontonne then bear L along Chemin des Quatres past hospital & traff lts junc. In 400m turn R at rndabt into Ave Jean Michard Pelissier, site 200m on R. NB Narr ent off busy rd. Med, hdg, hdstg, mkd, shd, terr, wc; chem disp; mv service pnt; fam bthrm; shwrs inc; EHU (10A) €5; gas; lndry; shop nr; bar; bbq (elec, gas); playgrnd; pool (htd); paddling pool; beach shgl 1.2km; red long stay; entmnt; wifi; TV; dogs €2.50; Eng spkn; adv bkg acc; quiet; ccard acc; games area; games rm; tennis 2km; CKE/CCI. "Conv Antibes & surrounding area; peaceful site; sm pitches." ♦ 31 Mar-29 Sep. € 32.00   2014*

APREMONT 2H4 (2km N Rural) 46.77848, -1.73394
Camping Les Charmes, Route de la Roussière, 85220 Apremont [02 51 54 48 08 or 06 86 03 96 93 (mob); fax 02 51 55 98 85; contact@campingslescharmes.com; www.campingslescharmes.com] Fr D948 Challans to Aizenay turn W onto D94 sp Commequiers; after 2km L, sp Les Charmes. Med, mkd, pt shd, wc; chem disp; fam bthrm; shwrs inc; EHU (6-10A) €3.30-4 (poss rev pol); gas; lndry; shop; playgrnd; pool; sw nr; red long stay; TV; 60% statics; dogs €2.80; Eng spkn; adv bkg acc; quiet; ccard acc; CKE/CCI. "Beautiful, well-kept site; generous pitches but soft when wet; welcoming, friendly, helpful owners; excel, clean san facs; a great find." ♦ 1 Apr-12 Sep. € 19.00   2013*

APT 10E3 (8km N Rural) 43.92050, 5.34120
Domaine des Chenes Blancs, Route de Gargas, 84490 St Saturnin-lès-Apt [04 90 74 09 20 or 06 63 90 37 66; contact@leschenesblancs.com; www.vauclusecamping.com] Fr W on D900 twd Apt, at NW o'skts of Apt turn N on D101, cont approx 2km turn R on D83 into Gargas; thro Gargas & in 4km turn L at camp sp; site on R in 300m. Narr rd. Lge, hdg, shd, wc; mv service pnt; shwrs inc; EHU (6A) inc; lndry; shop; rest; snacks; bar; bbq; playgrnd; pool (htd); paddling pool; entmnt; TV; dogs €4; Eng spkn; adv bkg rec; quiet; ccard acc; lake fishing 5km; games area. "Well-run, popular site in gd location; pitches amongst oaks poss diff lge o'fits; steel pegs req due stony grnd; friendly staff; vg, modern san facs; nice pool; excel touring base; lots of facs; dated san facs (2015); dusty." ♦ 28 Mar-17 Oct. € 32.60   2015*

> **"Satellite navigation makes touring much easier"**
>
> Remember most sat navs don't know if you're towing or in a larger vehicle – always use yours alongside maps and site directions.

APT 10E3 (1km NE Urban) 43.87753, 5.40302
Camp Municipal Les Cèdres, 63 Impasse de la Fantaisie, 84400 Apt [04 90 74 14 61 or 04 90 74 14 61 (mob); lucie.bouillet@yahoo.fr; www.camping-les-cedres.fr] In town turn N off D900 onto D22 twd Rustrel, site sp. Site on R in 200m immed after going under old rlwy bdge. Med, mkd, pt shd, wc (htd); chem disp; mv service pnt; shwrs inc; EHU (6-10A) €3.50; gas; lndry; shop; snacks; cooking facs; playgrnd; entmnt; wifi; dogs €1; adv bkg acc; ccard acc; CKE/CCI. "Excel site in lovely location; sm pitches; pitching poss haphazard LS; friendly staff; clean san facs; some pitches muddy when wet; cycle tracks; conv Luberon vills & ochre mines; phone ahead to check open LS; v lge mkt Sat; gd NH; site in 2 parts; popular; gd touring cent." ♦ 15 Feb-15 Nov. € 18.00   2014*

ARAMITS 8F1 (0km W Rural) 43.12135, -0.73215
Camping Barétous-Pyrénées, Quartier Ripaude, 64570 Aramits [05 59 34 12 21; contact@campingpyrenees.com; www.camping-pyrenees.com] SW fr Oloron-Ste Marie take D919 sp Aramits, Arette. Fr Aramits cont on D919 sp Lanne; site on R; well sp. Sm, mkd, pt shd, serviced pitches; wc; chem disp; mv service pnt; shwrs inc; EHU (10A) €4.90; lndry; shop nr; rest nr; snacks; bar; playgrnd; pool (htd); paddling pool; twin axles; TV; 50% statics; dogs €2.80; Eng spkn; adv bkg acc; quiet; games rm; bike hire; CKE/CCI. "Friendly, helpful owner; well-kept, clean, lovely site but muddy when wet; ltd facs LS; dated but v clean; gd base for Pyrenees; poss unrel opening dates - phone ahead LS; excel bistro 400m; vg." ♦ 1 Apr-17 Oct. € 28.00   2015*

ARBOIS *6H2* (2km E Urban) *46.90331, 5.78691*
Camp Municipal Les Vignes, 5 Rue de la Piscine, 39600 Arbois [03 84 66 14 12 or 03 84 25 26 19; fax 03 84 25 14 12; campinglesvignes@hotmail.fr; http://alexandrachti.wix.com/camping-les-vignes]
Fr N or S, ent town & at rndabt in cent foll camp sp on D107 dir Mesnay. Site adj stadium & pool. NB Steep slopes to terr & narr ent unsuitable lge o'fits. Med, hdstg, hdg, mkd, pt shd, pt sl, terr, wc; chem disp; mv service pnt; shwrs inc; EHU (10A) inc; gas; lndry; shop; rest; snacks; bar; playgrnd; twin axles; entmnt; wifi; TV; dogs €2.50; Eng spkn; adv bkg acc; quiet; ccard acc; tennis, fishing 1km; CKE/CCI. "Beautiful setting; clean san facs but poss stretched high ssn; site clsd 2200-0800 LS; ltd facs LS; pitches on lower tier mostly sl; pleasant sm town, home of Louis Pasteur; htd pool adj; Roman salt works, grottoes nr; lge fair 1st w/end in Sep; excel." ♦ 16 Apr-2 Oct. € 20.00   2013*

ARC EN BARROIS *6F1* (1km W Urban) *47.95052, 5.00523* Camp Municipal Le Vieux Moulin, 52210 Arc-en-Barrois [03 25 02 51 33 (Mairie); fax 03 25 03 82 89; mairie.arc.en.barrois@wanadoo.fr]
Exit A5 junc 24 onto D10 S to Arc-en-Barrois; turn R onto D3 thro vill; site on L on o'skirts. Or fr D65 turn L onto D6 about 4km S of Châteauvillain; site on R on D3 at ent to vill, adj rv. Med, pt shd, wc (htd); chem disp; mv service pnt; shwrs inc; EHU (6A) inc; shop nr; bbq; playgrnd; wifi; TV; dogs €2.18; quiet; tennis adj; CKE/CCI. "Attractive, peaceful, lovely, well-kept site by sm rv; adj vill sports field; basic, clean san facs but need update - excel hot shwrs; warden calls early eve, poss not on Sundays; gd wildlife; beautiful vill; conv NH fr A5 or longer." 1 May-30 Sep. € 17.00   2017*

> "There aren't many sites open at this time of year"
>
> If you're travelling outside peak season remember to call ahead to check site opening dates – even if the entry says 'open all year'.

ARCACHON *7D1* (1km E Coastal) *44.65089, -1.17381*
Camping Club d'Arcachon, 5 Allée de la Galaxie, 33312 Arcachon [05 56 83 24 15; fax 05 57 52 28 51; info@camping-arcachon.com; www.camping-arcachon.com]
Exit A63 ont A660 dir Arcachon. Foll sp 'Hôpital Jean Hameau' & site sp. Lge, hdg, mkd, hdstg, pt shd, terr, wc (htd); chem disp; mv service pnt; fam bthrm; shwrs inc; EHU (10A) €4; gas; lndry; shop; rest; snacks; bar; bbq; playgrnd; pool; beach sand 1.5km; entmnt; wifi; TV; 40% statics; dogs €4; Eng spkn; adv bkg acc; quiet; ccard acc; bike hire; site clsd mid-Nov to mid-Dec; CKE/CCI. "Vg site in pine trees; excel touring base; gd facs; access rds narr - poss diff manoeuvring into pitches; gd network cycle tracks; private san facs avail; easy walk to town." ♦ 1 Jan-14 Nov, 15 Dec-31 Dec. € 44.00   2017*

ARCACHON *7D1* (9km E Coastal) *44.64400, -1.11167*
Camping de Verdalle, 2 Allée de l'Infante, La Hume, 33470 Gujan-Mestras [05 56 66 12 62; camping.verdalle@wanadoo.fr; www.campingdeverdalle.com]
Fr A63 take A660 twd Arcachon. Turn R at rndabt junc with D652 sp La Hume. In vill at junc with D650 turn L, then R at rndabt; then 3rd turning on R after rlwy line. Med, hdg, pt shd, wc; chem disp; mv service pnt; shwrs inc; EHU (10A) inc; lndry; shop nr; snacks; bbq (sep area); beach sand adj; wifi; dogs €1.50; phone; bus adj; Eng spkn; adv bkg acc; ccard acc; CKE/CCI. "Lovely, well-kept site in excel position in Arcachon bay; friendly, helpful owner; cycling/walking; conv local attractions; vg." ♦ 1 Apr-3 Oct. € 26.00   2016*

ARCIS SUR AUBE *4E4* (1km N Urban) *48.53907, 4.14270* Camping de l'Ile Cherlieu, Rue de Châlons, 10700 Arcis-sur-Aube [03 25 37 98 79; fax 03 25 37 91 29; camping-arcis@hermans.cx] Fr A26 junc 21 foll sp to Arcis. Fr town cent take D677/N77 dir Châlons-en-Champagne. Turn R after rv bdge, site sp. Med, mkd, shd, wc; chem disp; shwrs inc; EHU (10-16A) inc (poss rev pol); lndry; shop nr; rest nr; bar nr; bbq; playgrnd; wifi; dogs €1.60; Eng spkn; rv fishing adj; CKE/CCI. "Pleasant, well-kept site on island surrounded by rv; friendly, helpful Dutch owners; gd, clean san facs; popular NH, rec arr early; bar 500m; vg site; quiet by 10pm; muddy in wet weather; gd site, improves each year; excel facs." ♦ 10 Apr-1 Oct. € 22.00   2018*

⊞ **ARCIS SUR AUBE** *4E4* (8km S Rural) *48.46696, 4.12633* FFCC Camping La Barbuise, 10700 St Remy-sous-Barbuise [03 25 37 50 95 or 03 25 37 41 11; www.camping-ffcc.com] Fr Arcis-sur-Aube, take D677 twd Voué; site on L bef vill of Voué, sp. Fr S exit A26 junc 21 onto D441 W; then onto D677 S twd Voué & as bef. Sm, pt shd, pt sl, wc; chem disp; mv service pnt; shwrs inc; EHU (4A) inc (poss rev pol); bar; bbq; dogs (if on lead); phone; adv bkg acc; CKE/CCI. "Lovely, peaceful, spacious CL-type site; early arr rec; site yourself, owner calls eves (cash only); easy access & pitching for lge o'fits; charming owners; san facs basic but clean; elec poss unrel (2010); elec heaters not allowed; pool 8km; conv NH off A26 or sh stay; 2 pin adapter ess." ♦ € 9.00   2015*

ARDRES *3A3* (1km N Urban) *50.85726, 1.97551*
Camping Ardresien, 64 Rue Basse, 62610 Ardres [03 21 82 82 32] Fr St Omer on D943 to Ardres, strt on at lights in town onto D231; site 500m on R - easy to o'shoot; v narr ent, not suitable twin-axles. Sm, hdg, pt shd, wc; shwrs; EHU (16A) inc; 95% statics; dogs free; CKE/CCI. "Basic site; friendly staff; walk to lakes at rear of site; ltd touring pitches; conv Calais & local vet; NH only." 1 May-30 Sep. € 15.00   2018*

ARDRES

ARDRES *3A3 (9km NE Rural)* *50.88147, 2.08618*
Camp Municipal Les Pyramides, Rue Nord Boutillier, 62370 Audruicq [03 21 35 59 17 or 03 21 46 06 60 (Mairie)] Fr Calais take A16 dir Dunkerque, after 8km exit S at junc 21 onto D219 to Audruicq; foll camp sp. Fr Ardres NE on D224 to Audruicq. Site on NE side of Audruicq nr canal. Med, hdg, unshd, wc; chem disp; shwrs inc; EHU (6A); gas; lndry; playgrnd; 80% statics; dogs; quiet; CKE/CCI. "Conv Calais; few sm pitches for tourers; rec phone ahead." ♦ 1 Apr-30 Sep.   2013*

ARDRES *3A3 (10km SE Rural)* *50.83865, 1.97612*
Camping St Louis, 223 Rue Leulène, 62610 Autingues [03 21 35 46 83; fax 03 21 00 19 78; camping-saint-louis@sfr.fr; www.campingstlouis.com] Fr Calais S on D943 to Ardres; fr Ardres take D224 S twd Licques, after 2km turn L on D227; site well sp in 100m. Or fr junc 2 off A26 onto D943 dir Ardres. Turn L just after Total g'ge on R on app to Ardres. Well sp. If app fr S via Boulogne avoid Nabringhen & Licques as narr, steep hill with bends. NB Mkt Thurs am - avoid R turn when leaving site. Med, hdg, mkd, pt shd, wc; chem disp; mv service pnt; fam bthrm; shwrs inc; EHU (10A) inc (long lead poss req, poss rev pol); gas; lndry; shop; rest; snacks; bar; bbq; playgrnd; entmnt; wifi; 70% statics; dogs free; phone; Eng spkn; adv bkg req; ccard acc; games rm; CKE/CCI. "Peaceful, well-kept, well-run, busy site; conv Dunkerque, Calais ferries; some gd sized pitches; gd welcome & friendly; clean san facs poss stretched high ssn; ltd touring pitches, phone ahead to check avail high ssn; early dep/late arr area; automatic exit barrier; barrier opens 0600 high ssn; gd rest; vg vet in Ardres; vg, conv NH; lovely clean, improved site; newly refurb san facs, excel (2015); well maintained; can be booked thro Pitchup. com." ♦ 1 Apr-18 Oct. € 25.00   2018*

ARDRES *3A3 (10km SE Rural)* *50.80867, 2.05569*
Hôtel Bal Caravaning, 500 Rue du Vieux Château, 62890 Tournehem-sur-la-Hem [03 21 35 65 90; fax 03 21 35 18 57; contact@hotel-bal.com; www.hotel-bal.com] Fr S on A26 leave at exit 2; turn R onto D217 then R onto D943 dir St Omer. Turn R in Nordausques onto D218 (approx 1km), pass under A26, site is 1km on L - ent thro Bal Parc Hotel gates. Fr N or S on D943, turn R or L in Nordausques, then as above. Med, mkd, hdg, hdstg, pt shd, pt sl, chem disp; shwrs inc; EHU (10A) inc (poss rev pol); gas; rest nr; bar nr; playgrnd; entmnt; wifi; 80% statics; Eng spkn; adv bkg acc; quiet; ccard acc; tennis; CKE/CCI. "Tidy area for tourers, but few touring pitches; sports grnd & leisure cent adj; htd wc (in hotel in winter); gd rest & bar; 25km Cité Europe mall; gd NH; ltd facs in LS." ♦ 1 Apr-31 Oct. € 20.00   2016*

ARDRES *3A3 (9km SE Rural)* *50.82193, 2.07577*
Camping Le Relax, 318 Route de Gravelines, 62890 Nordausques [03 21 35 63 77; camping.le.relax@cegetel.net] Fr N on D943 in vill 25km S of Calais at beginning of vill, turn L at sp. Site 200m on R. Or fr S on A26, leave at junc 2 & take D943 S for 1km into Nordausques, then as above. NB Ent diff, beware low o'hanging roof on recep. Med, hdg, pt shd, wc; chem disp; shwrs; EHU (6A) €2.20 (poss rev pol); lndry; shop nr; snacks; playgrnd; 90% statics; adv bkg req; CKE/CCI. "Obliging owner; sm pitches & sharp access, not suitable lge o'fits; basic san facs, poss tired high ssn; conv A26, Calais & war sites; NH only." 1 Apr-30 Sep. € 13.00   2016*

ARGELES GAZOST *8G2 (1km N Rural)* *43.01218, -0.09709* **Camping Sunêlia Les Trois Vallées, Ave des Pyrénées, 65400 Argelès-Gazost [05 62 90 35 47; fax 05 62 90 35 48; 3-vallees@wanadoo.fr; www.l3v.fr]** S fr Lourdes on D821, turn R at rndabt sp Argelès-Gazost on D821A. Site off next rndabt on R. Lge, mkd, pt shd, wc (htd); chem disp; shwrs inc; EHU (6A) inc (poss rev pol); lndry; shop nr; bar; playgrnd; pool (htd); entmnt; wifi; TV; 30% statics; dogs €2; adv bkg req; ccard acc; sauna; games area; bike hire; waterslide; games rm; golf 11km. "Excel touring base; views of Pyrenees; conv Lourdes; interesting area; red facs LS; excel san facs; v helpful staff." ♦ 11 Apr-18 Oct. € 46.00   2015*

ARGELES GAZOST *8G2 (4km NE Rural)* *43.01124, -0.07748* **Camping Deth Potz, 40 route de Silhen, 65400 Boô-Silhen [05 62 90 37 23; fax 08 11 48 68 28; contact@deth-potz.fr; www.deth-potz.fr]** Fr Lourdes on D821 to Argeles Gazost. At 2nd rndabt foll Luz-St-Sauveur sp for 100m over rv and turn L sp Boo-Silhen. Site on L in 1km. Med, mkd, pt shd, pt sl, terr, wc; chem disp; mv service pnt; fam bthrm; shwrs; EHU (3-10A) €3-6; lndry; bbq; pool; twin axles; entmnt; wifi; TV; 20% statics; dogs €1; Eng spkn; adv bkg acc; quiet; games rm; games area; CKE/CCI. "Family run site, o'looking woodland; site has upper (terr) and lower (flat) area; gd for walking, climbing, stunning scenery; vg site." ♦ 1 Jan-10 Oct & 10 Dec-31 Dec. € 17.00   2015*

ARGELES GAZOST *8G2 (7km SE Rural)* *42.98120, -0.06535* **Camping Le Viscos, 16 Route de Préchac, 65400 Beaucens [05 62 97 05 45; domaineviscos@orange.fr]** Fr Lourdes S twd Argelès-Gasost on D821. Cont twd Luz & Gavarnie to L of Argelès town, & turn L within 500m, sp Beaucens. Turn R to D13, site 2.5km on L. Med, shd, pt sl, wc; chem disp; shwrs inc; EHU (2-10A) €2-4.50 (rev pol); gas; lndry; shop nr; snacks; bbq; playgrnd; red long stay; dogs €1; adv bkg req; quiet; lake fishing 500m; CKE/CCI. "Delightful site; landscaped grnds; excel, clean san facs; pool 4km; gd rests in area." 1 May-15 Oct. € 17.50   2015*

ARGELES GAZOST *8G2* (1km S Rural) *42.98670, -0.08854* Camping Les Frênes, 46 Route des Vallées, 65400 Lau-Balagnas [05 62 97 25 12; fax 05 62 97 01 41; campinglesfrenes.fr] Site on R of D821 twd S. Med, hdg, shd, wc (htd); chem disp; shwrs inc; EHU (10A)€4.40; gas; lndry; shop nr; bbq; playgrnd; pool; red long stay; entmnt; TV; 10% statics; adv bkg rec; quiet; games rm; rv fishing 1km. "Gd site." ♦ 15 Dec-15 Oct. € 18.40   2017*

"That's changed – Should I let the Club know?"

If you find something on site that's different from the site entry, fill in a report and let us know. See camc.com/europereport.

ARGELES GAZOST *8G2* (2km S Rural) *42.98826, -0.08923* Kawan Village Le Lavedan, 44 Route des Vallées, 65400 Lau-Balagnas [05 62 97 18 84; fax 05 62 97 20 68; contact@lavedan.com; www.lavedan.com] Fr Lourdes S on D821 dir Argelès-Gazost/Cauterets; 2km after Argelès on D921 site on R after vill of Lau-Balagnas. Med, mkd, shd, wc (htd); chem disp; fam bthrm; shwrs inc; EHU (3A) €3 (poss rev pol, extra for 10A); gas; lndry; shop nr; rest; snacks; bar; bbq; playgrnd; pool (covrd, htd); paddling pool; entmnt; wifi; TV; 80% statics; dogs €2.50; phone; Eng spkn; adv bkg acc; ccard acc; games rm; CKE/CCI. "In beautiful valley; friendly, relaxed staff; clean modern san facs; rd noise if pitched adj to rd & poss noise fr entmnt in café; excel cycle rte to Lourdes; vg; quiet pleasant site." ♦ 15 Mar-30 Oct. € 37.00   2017*

ARGELES GAZOST *8G2* (3km S Rural) *42.9871, -0.1061* Camping du Lac, 29 Chemin d'Azun, 65400 Arcizans-Avant [05 62 97 01 88; campinglac@campinglac65.fr; www.campinglac65.fr] Fr Lourdes S thro Argelès-Gazost on D821 & D921. At 3rd rndabt take exit for St Savin/Arcizans-Avant. Cont thro St Savin vill & foll camp sp; site on L just thro Arcizans-Avant vill. NB: Dir rte to Arcizans-Avant prohibited to c'vans. Med, mkd, hdg, pt shd, pt sl, wc; chem disp; fam bthrm; shwrs inc; EHU (5-10A) €4.30-5; gas; lndry; rest nr; snacks; playgrnd; pool (htd); wifi; TV; dogs €2.50; Eng spkn; adv bkg acc; quiet; bike hire; games rm; CKE/CCI. "Excel, beautiful, peaceful, scenic & attractive site; mountain views; gd size pitches; clean san facs; gd for touring; excel rest." ♦ 20 May-20 Sep. € 34.00   2015*

ARGELES SUR MER

ARGELES GAZOST *8G2* (11km SW Rural) *42.94139, -0.17714* Camping Pyrénées Natura, Route du Lac, 65400 Estaing [05 62 97 45 44; fax 05 62 97 45 81; info@camping-pyrenees-natura.com; www.camping-pyrenees-natura.com] Fr Lourdes take D821 to Argelès Gazost; fr Argelès foll sp Col d'Aubisque & Val d'Azun onto D918; after approx 7.5km turn L onto D13 to Bun; after Bun cross rv & turn R onto D103 twd Estaing; site in 3km - rd narr. NB Rd fr Col d'Aubisque steep, narr & not suitable c'vans or lge m'vans. Med, mkd, hdg, pt shd, terr, wc (htd); chem disp; mv service pnt; fam bthrm; shwrs inc; EHU (3-10A) €2-5 (poss rev pol); gas; lndry; shop; snacks; bar; bbq; wifi; TV; 20% statics; dogs €3; Eng spkn; adv bkg acc; quiet; ccard acc; sauna; games area; solarium; games rm; CKE/CCI. "Superb, peaceful, well-kept, scenic site; friendly, helpful owners; clean unisex san facs; vg takeaway; gd for young families; no plastic grnd-sheets allowed; adj National Park; birdwatching area; excel; home cooked food at bar; no o'fits over 7.5m high ssn; pool 4km; vg site, one of the best ever visited." ♦ 18 Apr-10 Oct. € 30.00   2015*

ARGELES SUR MER *10G1* (1km N Coastal) *42.56320, 3.03498* Camping Les Marsouins, Ave de la Retirada, 66702 Argelès-sur-Mer [04 68 81 14 81; fax 04 68 95 93 58; lesmarsouins@cielavillage.com; www.campsud.com] Fr Perpignan take exit 10 fr D914 & foll sp for Argelès until Shell petrol stn on R. Take next L just bef rv into Allée Ferdinand Buisson to T-junc, turn L at next rndabt dir Plage-Nord. Take 2nd R at next rndabt, site on L opp Spanish war memorial. V lge, hdg, mkd, shd, wc; chem disp; mv service pnt; shwrs inc; EHU (5A) inc; gas; lndry; shop; rest; snacks; bar; bbq (elec, gas); playgrnd; pool (htd); beach sand 800m; entmnt; wifi; 20% statics; dogs €3; Eng spkn; adv bkg acc; ccard acc; games area; windsurfing 1km; games rm; bike hire; sailing 1km. "Lovely, well-kept, well-run site; clean san facs; busy rd to beach, but worth it; many sm coves; gd area for cycling; TO on site; excel; gd pool/slides; v conv for town/beach." ♦ 14 Apr-8 Oct. € 47.00   2017*

ARGELES SUR MER *10G1* (3km NE Coastal) *42.55583, 3.04222* Camping Les Pins, Ave du Tech, Zone des Pins, 66700 Argelès-sur-Mer [04 68 81 10 46; fax 04 68 81 35 06; camping@les-pins.com; www.les-pins.com] Exit D914 junc 10, foll sp Pujols & Plage-Nord, site sp. Lge, mkd, hdg, pt shd, wc; chem disp; mv service pnt; fam bthrm; shwrs inc; EHU (6A) inc; gas; lndry; shop; snacks; playgrnd; pool; beach sand 200m; entmnt; wifi; dogs €4; Eng spkn; adv bkg rec; quiet; ccard acc; games area; CCI. "Cent for beach & town; pleasant, helpful staff; clean, modern san facs; quiet peaceful site; supmkt nrby." ♦ 4 Apr-4 Oct. € 48.00   2015*

See advertisement on next page

ARGELES SUR MER

Sunêlia LES PINS ★★★★
Open from 06/04/2019 to 06/10/2019

- Shady areas, Relaxing Nature
- Seaside enjoyments, Sandy beach at 300m
- Playground, Family holidays
- Tent, Caravan, Mobilhome, Camping-car

Avenue du Tech - Plage des Pins
66700 Argelès-sur-mer
Tel : +33 (0)4 68 81 10 46 - Fax : +33 (0)4 68 81 35 06
camping@les-pins.com - www.les-pins.com

ARGELES SUR MER 10G1 (3km NE Coastal) 42.55147, 3.04444 **Campsite Comanges, Avenue du Général de Gaulle,** 66701 Argelés-sur-Mer [04 68 81 15 62; fax 04 68 95 87 74; infos@campingcomanges.com; www.campingcomanges.com] A9 exit Perpignan-sud, D914 dir Argeles to exit 10. At 2nd rndabt foll Argeles, les plages then foll signs to Cent Plage. Med, hdg, pt shd, wc; chem disp; mv service pnt; fam bthrm; shwrs; EHU (10A); lndry; playgrnd; beach 0.5km; wifi; 20% statics; Eng spkn. "Gd cycling nrby; vg site." 14 Apr-1 Oct. € 46.00 **2014***

ARGELES SUR MER 10G1 (4km NE Coastal) 42.57245, 3.04115 **Camping La Marende, Avenue du Littoral,** 66702 Argelès-sur-Mer [04 68 81 03 88; info@marende.com; www.marende.com] Fr Perpignan S on D914 exit junc 10 Argelès-sur-Mer; foll sp Plage Nord; after 2km at rndabt turn L sp St Cyprian; at next rndabt turn R sp Plages Nord & Sud; site on L in 800m. L onto unmade rd. V lge, mkd, hdg, shd, serviced pitches; wc; chem disp; mv service pnt; fam bthrm; shwrs inc; EHU (6-10A) inc; gas; lndry; shop; rest; snacks; bar; bbq (elec, gas); playgrnd; pool; paddling pool; beach sand adj; wifi; TV; 12% statics; dogs €2.50; phone; Eng spkn; adv bkg acc; quiet; ccard acc; jacuzzi; games area; CKE/CCI. "Beautiful site; lge pitches; friendly, helpful family owners; 1st class facs; excel pool; many static tents high ssn; gd area for cycling & walking; aquarobics, scuba diving lessons Jul & Aug; v quiet Sept; shared facs." ♦ 29 Apr-24 Sep. € 38.00 **2016***

ARGELES SUR MER 10G1 (4km NE Coastal) 42.57543, 3.0431 **Camping Le Soleil, Route du Littoral, Plage-Nord,** 66700 Argelès-sur-Mer [04 68 81 14 48; fax 04 68 81 44 34; camping.lesoleil@wanadoo.fr; www.camping-le-soleil.fr] Exit D914 junc 10 & foll sp Argelès Plage-Nord. Turn L onto D81 to site. Site sp among others. V lge, mkd, pt shd, wc; chem disp; mv service pnt; fam bthrm; shwrs inc; EHU (6A) €3.70; gas; lndry; shop; rest; snacks; bar; playgrnd; pool; paddling pool; beach sand adj; entmnt; wifi; TV; 50% statics; phone; Eng spkn; adv bkg req; ccard acc; bike hire; rv fishing adj; horseriding; tennis; games area. "Lovely views; excel site for partially-sighted & handicapped; rec visit to Collioure; vg." ♦ 16 May-30 Sep. € 32.50 **2016***

ARGELES SUR MER 10G1 (5km SE Coastal) 42.53147, 3.07167 **Camping Les Amandiers, Route des Campings,** 66190 Collioure [04 68 81 14 69; fax 04 68 81 09 95; contact@camping-les-amandiers.com; www.camping-les-amandiers.com] On D914 SE fr Perpignan, leave at junc 13 sp Collioure. After rndabt foll rd to Collioure. Climb coastal rd; site on L, steep descent, not rec lge o'fits. Med, mkd, shd, pt sl, terr, wc (htd); chem disp; mv service pnt; shwrs inc; EHU (10A) inc; gas; lndry; shop; rest; bar; playgrnd; beach shgl 200m; 10% statics; dogs €3; Eng spkn; adv bkg rec; CKE/CCI. "Site access v diff, espec for lge/med o'fits, manhandling prob req - rec investigation bef ent; sm pitches; facs stretched high ssn; many trees - dusty site; steep site rds; friendly, helpful owners; Collioure historic port; gd." ♦ 1 Apr-30 Sep. € 45.40 **2013***

ARGELES SUR MER 10G1 (5km SE Coastal) 42.53413, 3.06826 **Camping Les Criques de Porteils, Corniche de Collioure,** 66701 Argelès-sur-Mer [04 68 81 12 73; fax 04 68 95 85 76; contactcdp@lescriques.com; www.lescriques.com] Fr N on A9/E15 take exit junc 42 onto D914 Argelès-sur-Mer. Fr S exit junc 43 onto D618. In abt 16km R onto D914. At exit 13 leave D914 sp Collioure & foll site sp. Site by Hôtel du Golfe 1.5km fr Collioure. Lge, hdg, mkd, pt shd, pt sl, terr, wc (htd); chem disp; mv service pnt; fam bthrm; shwrs inc; EHU (5A) €6; gas; lndry; shop; rest; snacks; bar; playgrnd; pool (htd); beach shgl adj; wifi; TV; 15% statics; dogs €4; phone; Eng spkn; adv bkg acc; fishing; tennis; games area; games rm; watersports; CKE/CCI. "Excel, well-run site; variable size pitches, some uneven - not all suitable for lge o'fits; splendid views fr many terr pitches; steps to beach; scuba diving; clean, modern, well kept san facs; exposed, poss v windy; gd walks; v challenging (30 min) walk to Collioure but stunning; some narr site rds; gd rest; site shop fully stocked." ♦ 24 Mar-27 Oct. € 58.70 **2018***

ARGENTIERE LA BESSEE, L'

ARGELES SUR MER *10G1* (8km W Urban) *42.52667, 2.93515* **Camp Municipal Le Vivier, 31 Rue du Stade, 66740 Laroque-des-Albères [04 68 89 00 93 or 04 68 95 49 97; fax 04 68 95 42 58; tourisme@laroque-des-alberes.fr; www.laroque-des-alberes.fr]**
D2 fr Argelès-sur-Mer to Laroque-des-Albères; foll sp in cent of vill. Site on rvside. Lge, mkd, pt shd, pt sl, wc; chem disp; shwrs inc; EHU (6A) €3; lndry; shop nr; bbq; playgrnd; 5% statics; dogs €4; bus 300m; adv bkg acc; quiet; CKE/CCI. "Peaceful, simple site on edge Pyrenees, pleasant vill; vg." ♦ 15 Jun-15 Sep. € 24.00   2016*

ARGENTAN *4E1* (1km SE Urban) *48.73991, -0.01668* **Camp Municipal du Parc de la Noé, 34 Rue de la Noé, 61200 Argentan [02 33 36 05 69; fax 02 33 39 96 61; camping@argentan.info; www.argentan.fr]**
S fr Caen on D958 foll camping sp fr by-pass. At rndabt in town cent foll sp to Alencon (Blvd Carnot). In 300m turn L and foll camping signs. NB. Site ent immed on R on entering Rue de la Noe. Sm, shd, wc (htd); chem disp; mv service pnt; shwrs; EHU (12A) inc; lndry; shop nr; playgrnd; wifi; TV; 10% statics; adv bkg req; quiet; games area; rv. "Superb, clean, tidy site adj town park; excel, clean san facs; gd touring base; lovely town; park adj; lake adj; immac site run by efficient, helpful warden; busy even mid Sept, rec arr early; gates close at 8pm, use adj aire." ♦ 2 Apr-1 Oct. € 12.00   2018*

ARGENTAN *4E1* (4km S Rural) *48.71841, -0.01077* **FFCC Aire Naturelle du Val de Baize (Huet des Aunay), 18 Rue de Mauvaisville, 61200 Argentan [02 33 67 27 11; fax 02 33 35 39 16; mhuetdesaunay@orange.fr; www.normandiealaferme.com]** Take D958 fr Argentan twd Sées & Alençon; site clearly sp on D958 - turn R just bef leaving Argentan boundary. Site adj T-junc N of farm buildings. Sm, hdstg, pt shd, wc; chem disp; mv service pnt; shwrs inc; EHU (6A); shop nr; snacks; playgrnd; 10% statics; dogs; Eng spkn; adv bkg acc; quiet; CKE/CCI. "Charming, well-kept site; pool 2.5km; B&B; lge pitches in orchard; clean but dated facs, ltd LS; friendly welcome; NH only; ring in advance to check opening dates." Unknown-30 Sep. € 13.00   2016*

ARGENTAT *7C4* (1km NE Urban) *45.10205, 1.94390* **Camp Municipal Le Longour, Route d'Egletons, 19400 Argentat [05 55 28 13 84; fax 05 55 28 81 26; camping@argentat.fr; www.argentat.fr]**
Fr cent of Argentat head N dir Egletons on D18. Med, pt shd, wc; chem disp; shwrs inc; EHU (10A) €3.20; lndry; shop nr; playgrnd; wifi; dogs €1.30; phone; quiet; ccard acc; tennis; fishing. "Efficiently run, clean site; pleasant rvside walk to old quay & cafés; htd pool adj; sports complex adj; gd touring base; excel; beautiful town." 1 Jun-31 Aug. € 19.70   2014*

ARGENTAT *7C4* (4km NE Rural) *45.11151, 1.95908* **Camping Château de Gibanel, 19400 Argentat (Correza) [05 55 28 10 11; fax 05 55 28 81 62; contact@camping-gibanel.com; www.camping-gibanel.com]** Exit Argentat on D18 twd Egletons & fork R on lakeside past hydro-elec dam. Sp fr all dir. Site in grnds of sm castle on N bank of Rv Dordogne. App rd narr but satisfactory. Lge, mkd, pt shd, pt sl, wc; chem disp; fam bthrm; shwrs inc; EHU (10A) €3.70; gas; lndry; shop; rest; snacks; bar; bbq; playgrnd; pool; paddling pool; sw; entmnt; TV; 15% statics; dogs €2 (free LS); Eng spkn; adv bkg acc; quiet; ccard acc; boating; fishing; games area; games rm; CKE/CCI. "Excel, well-managed site in idyllic location; helpful owner; gd san facs; various pitch sizes; lovely sm town; excel." ♦ 31 May-7 Sep. € 24.00   2013*

ARGENTAT *7C4* (4km SW Rural) *45.07531, 1.91689* **Camping Sunêlia au Soleil d'Oc, 19400 Monceaux-sur-Dordogne [05 55 28 84 84; fax 05 55 28 12 12; info@campingsoleildoc.com; www.campingsoleildoc.com]** Fr N exit A20 junc 46a dir Tulle, then D1120 to Argentat. Fr Argentat take D12 sp Beaulieu. In 4km in Laygues turn L over bdge x-ing Rv Dordogne, site in 300m. Med, mkd, hdg, pt shd, terr, wc; chem disp; mv service pnt; fam bthrm; shwrs inc; EHU (6A) €4.10; gas; lndry; shop; rest; snacks; bar; bbq; playgrnd; pool; paddling pool; red long stay; entmnt; wifi; TV; 10% statics; dogs €3 (free LS); phone; Eng spkn; adv bkg acc; quiet; ccard acc; canoeing; games area; games rm; bike hire; rv; archery; CKE/CCI. "Ideal family site high ssn & peaceful LS; some pitches on rv bank; ltd water points; gd walking & other activities; many beautiful vills in area; tours arranged." ♦ 16 Apr-30 Oct. € 20.70   2016*

ARGENTIERE LA BESSEE, L' *9C3* (3km S Rural) *44.77775, 6.55798* **Camp Municipal Les Ecrins, 05120 L'Argentière-la-Bessée [04 92 23 03 38; fax 04 92 23 09 89; contact@camping-les-ecrins.com; www.camping-les-ecrins.com]** Fr L'Argentière on N94, turn R onto D104, site sp. Med, mkd, pt shd, wc (htd); shwrs inc; EHU (10A) €2.40; lndry; shop; snacks; playgrnd; dogs €2.10; phone; adv bkg acc; tennis 300m; games area. "Mountain scenery; pool 300m." ♦ 20 Apr-15 Sep. € 14.00   2013*

⊞ **ARGENTIERE LA BESSEE, L'** *9C3* (5km S Rural) *44.75765, 6.57995* **FFCC Camping Le Verger, 05310 La Roche-de-Rame [04 92 20 92 23; info@campingleverger.com; www.campingleverger.com]**
S fr Briançon on N94; site 500m L of rd bef vill; sp. Sm, hdg, shd, terr, wc; chem disp; mv service pnt; shwrs inc; EHU (3-10A) €3.50; lndry; shop nr; rest nr; bar nr; sw nr; TV; 25% statics; dogs free; phone; Eng spkn; adv bkg acc; quiet. "Grass pitches in orchard; excel, well-maintained facs; beautiful; ideal loc for visiting Ecrins area; fantastic value; hg rec." € 16.00   2018*

ARGENTIERE LA BESSEE, L'

ARGENTIERE LA BESSEE, L' 9C3 (4km NW Rural) 44.82455, 6.52575 **Campéole Camping Le Courounba, Le Village, 05120 Les Vigneaux [04 92 23 02 09; fax 04 92 23 04 69; courounba@campeole.com; www.campeole.com]** Take N94 S fr Briançon to L'Argentiere-la-Bessée, turn R onto D994E dir Vallouise. Site on L over rv bdge. Lge, hdstg, pt shd, wc (htd); chem disp; mv service pnt; fam bthrm; shwrs inc; EHU (6A) €4.10 (poss long lead req); lndry; shop nr; rest; snacks; bar; bbq; playgrnd; pool (htd); paddling pool; entmnt; wifi; TV; 20% statics; dogs; phone; Eng spkn; adv bkg acc; quiet; ccard acc; tennis; horseriding nr; bike hire; fishing; waterslide; CKE/CCI. "Gd site, beautifully situated in woods by rv in mountains; gd clean san facs; no site lighting." ♦ 16 May-23 Sep. € 39.60   2013*

ARGENTIERE LA BESSEE, L' 9C3 (8km NW Rural) 44.84354, 6.48989 **Camping Indigo Vallouise (formerly Les Chambonnettes), 05290 Vallouise [04 92 23 30 26 or 06 82 23 65 09 (mob); fax 04 92 22 34 03; vallouise@camping-indigo.com; www.camping-indigo.com]** Take N94 Briançon-Gap, on N o'skts of L'Argentière-la-Bessée take D994 W dir Vallouise. In cent of Vallouise turn L over bdge & immed L, site in 200m on rvside. Med, mkd, pt shd, pt sl, wc (htd); chem disp; mv service pnt; shwrs inc; EHU (10A) €5.30; lndry; shop nr; rest nr; snacks; bar; bbq; playgrnd; twin axles; wifi; TV; 25% statics; dogs €1.80; phone; Eng spkn; adv bkg acc; quiet; ccard acc; games area; games rm; tennis; CKE/CCI. "Mountain scenery; gd facs; bar 500m; gd cent for walking, skiing, canoeing; pool 3km; white-water rafting at nrby rv; interesting vill; gd." ♦ 1 Jun-15 Sep. € 32.00   2014*

> "I like to fill in the reports as I travel from site to site"
>
> You'll find report forms at the back of this guide, or you can fill them in online at camc.com/europereport.

ARGENTON LES VALLEES 4H1 (1km N Rural) 46.9877, -0.4504 **Camp Municipal du Lac d'Hautibus, Rue de la Sablière, 79150 Argenton-les-Vallées [05 49 65 95 08 or 05 49 65 70 22 (Mairie); fax 05 49 65 70 84; mairie-argenton-chateau@cegetel.net; www.campings-poitou-charentes.com]** Fr E or W on D759, site well sp in town, on lakeside. Med, hdg, pt sl, wc; chem disp; mv service pnt; shwrs inc; EHU (6A) €2.50; lndry; shop nr; playgrnd; sw nr; 10% statics; Eng spkn; quiet; games rm; tennis 100m; CKE/CCI. "Beautifully-situated, well-kept site; pool 100m; interesting, quiet town; excl." ♦ 1 Apr-30 Sep. € 14.00   2016*

ARGENTON SUR CREUSE 7A3 (13km SW Rural) 46.54192, 1.40328 **Camping La Petite Brenne (Naturist), La Grande Metairie, 36800 Luzeret [02 54 25 05 78; fax 02 54 25 05 97; info@lapetitebrenne.com; www.lapetitebrenne.com]** Fr A20 exit junc 18 sp Luzeret/Prissac; foll D55 to Luzeret vill. After bdge in vill turn L, then next L to site. Med, pt shd, pt sl, wc; chem disp; mv service pnt; fam bthrm; shwrs inc; EHU (10A) €5 (long leads poss req); lndry; rest; snacks; bar; bbq; playgrnd; pool (covrd, htd); paddling pool; red long stay; twin axles; entmnt; wifi; 10% statics; phone; Eng spkn; adv bkg rec; quiet; ccard acc; games rm; sauna; horseriding; games area; CKE/CCI. "Excel family site; friendly Dutch owners; lge pitches; excel san facs; ideal for children; pools excel; gd rest; gd walking in National Park; great facs." ♦ 22 Apr-1 Oct. € 32.00   2017*

ARGENTON SUR CREUSE 7A3 (2km NW Rural) 46.59636, 1.50619 **Camp Municipal Les Chambons, 37 Rue des Chambons, 36200 Argenton-sur-Creuse [02 54 24 15 26; camping-les-chambons@orange.fr; www.entreprisefrery.com]** Fr A20 exit junc 17 onto D937 dir Argenton; turn R at rndabt, then L at mini rndabt nr supmkt sp St Marcel; foll rd downhill over rlwy bdge; then 1st R in 100m. But best app fr N on D927 to avoid traff calming rd humps; at town sp cross rlwy bdge & turn R immed past LH turn for Roman archaeological museum; foll camping sp on narr, busy app rd. Med, hdstg, mkd, shd, pt sl, wc; chem disp; shwrs inc; EHU (5A) €3.60 (poss long lead req); gas; shop nr; rest nr; bar; playgrnd; wifi; quiet. "Beautiful, peaceful, well-kept site by rv; helpful warden; v muddy after heavy rain & poss uneven pitches by rv; rvside walk into interesting old town; no need to unhitch so useful for early start; quiet in day, busy in evening as popular NH high ssn; excel." 1 May-30 Sep. € 20.00   2014*

ARGENTON SUR CREUSE 7A3 (6km NW Rural) 46.62965, 1.47882 **Camp Municipal Les Rives de la Bouzanne, 36800 Le Pont Chrétien-Chabenet [02 54 25 80 53 or 02 54 25 81 40 (Mairie); fax 02 54 25 87 50; commune.pontchretien@wanadoo.fr]** Exit A20 junc 17 onto D927; site well sp over rv bdge. Or fr St Gaultier on D927 dir Argenton-sur-Creuse; turn R in Le Pont Chrétien-Chabenet, bef rv bdge, site 50m on L. Med, pt shd, wc; chem disp; shwrs inc; EHU (6A) inc; lndry; shop nr; bar nr; bbq; playgrnd; dogs €0.50; phone; Eng spkn; adv bkg rec; quiet; CKE/CCI. "Picturesque, quiet, rvside site; site yourself, warden calls; gd, drained pitches; immac san facs; conv A20; excel NH." 15 Jun-10 Sep. € 13.00   2016*

ARRAS

ARLES *10E2 (8km NE Rural) 43.72336, 4.71861*
Huttopia Fontvieille (foremerly Municipal des Pins), Rue Michelet, 13990 Fontvieille [04 90 54 78 69; fontvieille@huttopia.com; www.huttopia.com] Take D570 fr Arles to Avignon, in 2km turn R on D17 to Fontvieille, at far end of vill turn R at rndabt, foll sp. Med, hdg, mkd, pt shd, pt sl, wc; chem disp; shwrs inc; EHU (6A) €3; lndry; shop nr; playgrnd; red long stay; TV; dogs €1.50; bus; Eng spkn; adv bkg acc; games area; games rm; CKE/CCI. "Delightful, pleasant quiet site in pines; friendly staff; vg san facs; 15-20 mins walk to lively vill with rests & 2 supmkts; quiet forest walks; tennis in vill; nr Arles; lots of attractions locally; vg." 30 Mar-14 Oct. € 35.00   2018*

> **"We must tell the Club about that great site we found"**
>
> Get your site reports in by mid-August and we'll do our best to get your updates into the next edition.

ARLES *10E2 (7km E Rural) 43.64799, 4.70625*
Camping La Bienheureuse, 13280 Raphèle-les-Arles [04 90 98 48 06; fax 04 90 98 37 62; contact@labienheureuse.com; www.labienheureuse.com] Fr Arles E on D453, site on L 5km after Pont-de-Crau. W fr Salon-de-Provence on A54/N113; exit N113 junc 12 onto N1435 to St Martin-de-Crau; cont past St Martin-de-Crau on N1435; in 2km rd becomes D435 to Raphèle-les-Arles; site on R 900m after Raphèle-les-Arles. Med, hdg, pt shd, wc; chem disp; shwrs inc; EHU (10A); lndry; snacks; bar; playgrnd; pool; paddling pool; twin axles; entmnt; wifi; 50% statics; dogs €2.50; phone; bus adj; Eng spkn; adv bkg acc; quiet; horseriding nr; CKE/CCI. "Pleasant site; obliging British owners; 700m to shops/bar in vill; gd facs; gd dog walk along nrby lanes and canal." ♦ 1 Mar-31 Oct. € 20.00   2014*

ARLES *10E2 (5km SE Urban) 43.65942, 4.65416*
Camping L'arlesienne, 149 Draille Marseillaise, Pont de Crau, 13631, Arles [04 90 96 02 12; fax 04 90 93 36 72; contact@larlesienne.com; www.larlesienne.com] Exit Arles E by D453 sp Pont-de-Crau or junc 7 fr N113 dir Raphèle-les-Arles; 200m after exit vill take 1st exit at rndabt then R at Flor Hotel sp on D83E. Site in 50m on R adj hotel. Med, pt shd, wc (htd); chem disp; mv service pnt; shwrs inc; EHU (6A) €4; lndry; shop nr; rest; bar; playgrnd; pool; entmnt; TV; 80% statics; dogs €1.50; bus fr rndabt; Eng spkn; games area. "Many mosquitoes; red facs LS; v muddy after rain; visit Les Baux citadel early morning bef coach parties arr; no o'fits over 5.5m allowed (but poss not enforced); gd birdwatching; poss no site lighting LS; conv Arles." 1 Apr-1 Nov. € 27.00   2016*

⊞ **ARMENTIERES** *3A3 (3km E Rural) 50.68774, 2.93279*
Camping L'Image, 140 Rue Brune, 59116 Houplines [03 20 35 69 42 or 06 81 61 56 82 (mob); fax 03 20 87 21 53; campimage@wanadoo.fr; www.campingimage.com] Exit A25 junc 8 sp Armentières, onto D945 N twd Houplines; pass on R Chemin du Pilori in 1.8km; then pass on R Hameau de L'Hépinette in 2.2km; turn R into Rue Brune in 3km; site in 1km on R. Ent not v clearly sp. Med, hdg, shd, serviced pitches; wc (htd); chem disp; mv service pnt; shwrs inc; EHU (6-10A) inc (take care electrics, poss prob 2011); lndry; shop; snacks; playgrnd; entmnt; wifi; 90% statics; Eng spkn; adv bkg acc; quiet; tennis; games area; CKE/CCI. "Mainly statics, adv bkg rec; friendly, helpful staff; dated san facs, poss unclean & unkempt (2011); pitches exposed & poss v windy; gd NH prior to ferry." € 28.00   2017*

ARNAY LE DUC *6H1 (1km E Rural) 47.13388, 4.49835*
Camping L'Etang de Fouché, Rue du 8 Mai 1945, 21230 Arnay-le-Duc [03 80 90 02 23; fax 03 80 90 11 91; info@campingfouche.com; www.campingfouche.com] App by D906 to Arnay (site sp); turn E onto D17, site on R in 2km. Lge, mkd, hdg, hdstg, pt shd, wc (htd); chem disp; fam bthrm; shwrs inc; EHU (6A) €4; lndry; shop; rest; snacks; bar; bbq; playgrnd; pool (htd); paddling pool; sw nr; entmnt; wifi; TV; TV (pitch); dogs €2; Eng spkn; adv bkg acc; quiet; ccard acc; bike hire; waterslide; fishing; tennis; games rm; CKE/CCI. "Excel lakeside site with pleasant views; lge pitches; friendly staff; gd san facs; attractive sm town; gd touring base S Burgundy; gd for young families." ♦ 15 Apr-15 Oct. € 39.60   2014*

ARRAS *3B3 (14km E Rural) 50.27347, 2.94852*
Camping La Paille Haute, 145 Rue de Seilly, 62156 Boiry-Notre-Dame [03 21 48 15 40; fax 03 21 22 07 24; lapaillehaute@wanadoo.fr; www.la-paille-haute.com] Fr Calais take A26/A1 twd Paris, exit junc 15 onto D939 twd Cambrai; in 3km take D34 NE to Boiry-Notre-Dame & foll camp sp. Fr D950 Douai-Arras rd, at Fresnes turn S onto D43, foll sp to Boiry in 7km, site well sp in vill. Med, hdstg, hdg, pt shd, terr, wc; chem disp; mv service pnt; fam bthrm; shwrs inc; EHU (6A) €4 (poss rev pol); lndry; rest; snacks; bar; bbq; playgrnd; pool (htd); paddling pool; red long stay; entmnt; wifi; 60% statics; dogs; Eng spkn; quiet; ccard acc; tennis; games rm; site open w/ends in winter; lake fishing; CKE/CCI. "Popular NH; useful & reliable; pretty site with views; rec arr early; lge pitches; friendly, helpful owner; gd for children; Calais over 1hr; conv WW1 sites & A26; gd reg used site; gd for long stay; peaceful vill; pitches muddy in wet weather; san facs updated and excel; gd dogs walk adj." ♦ 1 Apr-31 Oct. € 30.00   2018*

ARRENS MARSOUS

ARRENS MARSOUS *8G2* (1km E Rural) *42.9613, -0.2034* **Camping La Hèche, 54 Route d'Azun, 65400 Arrens-Marsous [05 62 97 02 64; laheche@free.fr; www.campinglaheche.com]** Fr Argelès-Gazost foll D918. Site on L immed bef Arrens. If towing c'van do not app fr Col d'Aubisque. Lge, mkd, pt shd, wc (htd); fam bthrm; shwrs inc; EHU (3A) €2.70; gas; lndry; shop; playgrnd; TV; 10% statics; dogs €0.50; phone; quiet; games area; waterslide; tennis; CKE/CCI. "Beautiful location; pool in vill high ssn; gd san facs." ♦ 1 Jun-30 Sep. € 12.50   2013*

ARRENS-MARSOUS *8G2* (1km NE Rural) *42.95991, -0.20645* **Camping Mialanne, 63 route du Val d'Azun, 65400 Arrens-Marous [05 62 92 67 14 or 05 62 37 96 08; mialanne@orange.fr; www.campingmialanne.fr]** Sp on D918 bet Arrens-Marsous, 10km WSW of Argeles-Gazost. (Opp ent of Camping La Heche). Med, mkd, pt shd, terr, wc; chem disp; mv service pnt; shwrs inc; EHU (10A) €3.10; lndry; shop nr; rest nr; bar nr; bbq (charcoal, gas); playgrnd; twin axles; wifi; dogs (€0.50); phone; bus 300m; Eng spkn; adv bkg acc; quiet; ccard acc; games rm; CKE/CCI. "Friendly fam site; htd pool 300m; 300m to vill, conv Arrens & Estaing; san facs extended (2015); vg." 1 Jun-30 Sep. € 17.00   2016*

ARROMANCHES LES BAINS *3D1* (3km E Coastal) *49.33963, -0.58188* **Camp Municipal Quintefeuille, Ave Maurice Schumann, 14960 Asnelles [02 31 22 35 50; fax 02 31 21 99 45; campingquintefeuille@wanadoo.fr; www.arromanches.com/uk/camping_accueil.htm]** Site sp on D514, but visible fr vill sq in Asnelles. Med, mkd, unshd, wc; chem disp; shwrs; EHU; lndry; shop nr; rest nr; bar nr; playgrnd; beach sand 300m; quiet; fishing; tennis; games area. ♦ 1 Apr-2 Nov. € 14.50   2014*

"I need an on-site restaurant"

We do our best to make sure site information is correct, but it is always best to check any must-have facilities are still available or will be open during your visit.

ARROMANCHES LES BAINS *3D1* (0km W Urban/Coastal) *49.33793, -0.62647* **Camp Municipal, Ave de Verdun, 14117 Arromanches-les-Bains [02 31 22 36 78; fax 02 31 21 80 22; campingarromanches@wanadoo.fr]** App fr Bayeux on D516. Turn R onto D65 on app to Arromanches to site on L. Med, pt shd, pt sl, terr, wc; shwrs inc; EHU (10A) €3; gas; beach sand 500m."Conv Mulberry Harbour exhibition & invasion beaches; friendly warden; gd san facs; levelling blocks req most pitches; grnd soft when wet; sh stay pitches stony; water access diff for m'vans (2010); gd." 1 Apr-2 Nov. € 16.00   2014*

ARROU *4F2* (1km NW Rural) *48.10189, 1.11556* **Camp Municipal du Pont de Pierre, 28290 Arrou [02 37 97 02 13 (Mairie); fax 02 37 97 10 28; mairie.arrou@wanadoo.fr; www.loirevalleytourism.com]** Take D15 fr Cloyes. Site sp in vill of Arrou. Med, hdg, mkd, unshd, pt sl, wc; chem disp; mv service pnt; shwrs inc; EHU (6-10A) €2-3; lndry; shop nr; rest nr; bar nr; bbq; playgrnd; beach sand adj; 10% statics; phone; adv bkg acc; quiet; horseriding; lake fishing; bike hire; tennis; CKE/CCI. "Lovely, peaceful, well-kept site in park-like setting; lge pitches; excel, clean san facs; gd security; htd pool, paddling pool adj; phone warden (or call at hse) if off & barrier clsd; gd rvside walks/cycle rides; excel value; rec." ♦ 1 May-30 Sep. € 8.00   2017*

ARTIGAT *8F3* (1km NE Urban) *43.13776, 1.44407* **Camping Les Eychecadous, 09130 Artigat [(033) 05 61 68 98 24; campingartigat@hotmail.fr; www.camping-artigat.com]** Fr Toulouse take A64 S, take exit 28 twrds Capens. Marquefave, St. Sulpice. Turn L onto D10, at rndabt take 2nd exit onto D622, turn L sp Av. Antonin Triqué, cont twrds Lombardi on D622, go thro 1 rndabt, turn R sp Rue de la République/D622 cont on D622, to Av. Des Pyrénées/D4 cont onto D919 cont thro 3 rndabts then L onto Chemin du Comté then L twrds Les Eychecadous, then R, then L to site. Sm, mkd, pt shd, wc; chem disp; mv service pnt; fam bthrm; shwrs; EHU (10A); rest; snacks; bar; bbq; playgrnd; pool; twin axles; entmnt; wifi; TV; 10% statics; dogs; adv bkg acc; CKE/CCI. "Vg site on edge of Lèze; warm welcome; fishing, boating, & horseriding." ♦ € 12.00   2012*

ARZON *2G3* (1km NE Coastal) *47.55303, -28.8294* **Camp Municipal Le Tindio, Kerners, 56640 Arzon [02 97 41 25 59; fax 02 97 53 91 23; www.camping-arzon.fr]** Fr Vannes or Muzillac on D780 turn R at rndabt on o'skts of Arzon. Site clearly sp. Lge, pt shd, pt sl, wc; chem disp; mv service pnt; shwrs; EHU (6-10A) €2.50; lndry; playgrnd; beach sand 1km; 3% statics; dogs €1.20; adv bkg acc; golf nr. "Site o'looks Gulf of Morbihan; direct access to sea; excel san facs; gd value; sm boat launching fr site." ♦ 1 Apr-3 Nov. € 13.00   2016*

ARZON *2G3* (2km NE Coastal) *47.56031, -2.87854* **Camping de Bilouris, Route de Kerners, 56640 Arzon [02 97 53 70 55; campingbilouris@gmail.com; www.campingdebilouris.com]** Fr Vannes foll D780 for abt 23km. On app Arzon foll sp for site. Sm, hdg, pt shd, pt sl, wc; chem disp; shwrs; EHU (6A) €3; lndry; bar; bbq; beach; wifi; 60% statics; dogs €2.50; Eng spkn; adv bkg rec. "Coastal walks, boating & kayaking; miles of off-rd cycling; vg." ♦ 1 Apr-1 Nov. € 23.00   2017*

AUBENAS

ARZON 2G3 (2km W Coastal) 47.54403, -2.90945
**Camp Municipal de Port-Sable, Port Navalo,
56640 Arzon [02 97 53 71 98; fax 02 97 53 89
32; portsable@arzon.fr; www.camping-arzon.fr]**
Fr N165/E60 take D780 to Sarzeau, cont to Arzon.
Site sp fr last rndabt bef fort. Med, pt shd, pt sl, wc;
chem disp; mv service pnt; shwrs inc; EHU (6A) €2.30;
gas; lndry; shop nr; playgrnd; beach sand adj; wifi;
dogs €1.40; Eng spkn; quiet; ccard acc; fishing; sailing
school. "Vg, spacious site; beautiful position nr beach
with views; gd beach for children; walk into marina;
boat excursions; gd facs; gd for m'vans - rests nrby." ♦
1 Apr-15 Oct. € 18.50   2016*

ASPET 8G3 (1km SW Rural) 43.00969, 0.79665 **Camp
Municipal Le Cagire, 31160 Aspet [05 61 88 51 55;
fax 05 61 88 44 03; camping.aspet@wanadoo.fr;
www.mairie-aspet.fr/rubrique/afficher/21]**
Exit A64 at junc 18 St Gaudens & take D5 S. In 14km,
site sp on R in vill of Aspet. Sp 'Camping, Stade.' Sm,
mkd, shd, wc; chem disp; shwrs; EHU (6A) €2.50;
lndry; shop nr; rest nr; bar nr; 30% statics; dogs €0.50;
adv bkg acc; quiet; games area; tennis 300m; CKE/
CCI. "Pleasant, gd, clean, well kept site nr lively, sm
town; rec arr bef 1800 hrs high ssn; pool 300m; basic
facs; some pitches muddy when wet; some hdstg."
1 Apr-30 Sep. € 11.00   2015*

ASPRES SUR BUECH 9D3 (1km S Rural) 44.51497,
5.74347 **Camping L'Adrech, Route de Sisteron,
05140 Aspres-sur-Buëch [04 92 58 60 45; fax 04
92 58 78 63; ladrech.camping@wanadoo.fr; www.
campingladrech.fr]** Site on L of D1075 fr Aspres.
Med, hdg, hdstg, pt shd, pt sl, wc; chem disp; shwrs;
EHU (6-10A) €4-6.50; gas; lndry; shop; snacks; bbq;
playgrnd; entmnt; 50% statics; dogs €1; phone; Eng
spkn; adv bkg acc; quiet; ccard acc; fishing; games
area; CKE/CCI. "Wooded site; lovely views; lge pitches;
helpful, friendly owner; remote location; ltd facs LS;
useful NH." ♦ 1 Apr-1 Nov. € 10.00   2014*

ASPRES SUR BUECH 9D3 (7km W Rural) 44.53048,
5.68371 **FFCC Aire Naturelle La Source (Pardoe),
05140 St Pierre-d'Argençon [04 92 58 67 81 or 06 78
32 30 40 (mob); info@lasource-hautesalpes.com;
www.lasource-hautesalpes.com]** Fr S on D1075
at Aspres-sur-Buëch turn onto D993 dir Valence
to St Pierre-d'Argençon; after 6km site sp. Fr N on
D93, cont onto D993 over Col de Cabre; site sp on L
bef St Pierre-d'Argençon. Sm, mkd, pt shd, pt sl, wc;
chem disp; mv service pnt; shwrs inc; EHU (6/10A) €4;
lndry; rest; snacks; bar; bbq; playgrnd; twin axles; red
long stay; wifi; dogs €1.50; phone; Eng spkn; adv bkg
acc; quiet; ccard acc; CKE/CCI. "Peaceful, well-kept
CL-type site in woodland/open field; friendly, helpful
British owners; clean san facs; takeaway; chambre
d'hôte on site; htd pool (4km); highly rec; ideally
located for all mountain sports, walking, climbing,
watersports, gliding, flying & cycling; 3 luxury Teepees
for hire; major improvements planned(2014); excel." ♦
15 Apr-15 Oct. € 18.00   2017*

ASSERAC 2G3 (5km NW Coastal) 47.44533, -2.44766
**Camping Le Moulin de l'Eclis, Pont Mahé, 44410 Assérac
[02 40 01 76 69; fax 02 40 01 77 75; info@camping-
leclis.com; www.camping-moulin-de-leclis.fr]**
Fr D774 turn N onto D83 to Assérac. Take D82 two
coast to Pont Mahé, site sp. Lge, hdg, mkd, pt shd, wc;
chem disp; mv service pnt; fam bthrm; shwrs inc; EHU
(6-10A) €3.60-4; lndry; shop; rest nr; snacks; bar; bbq
(elec, gas); playgrnd; pool (covrd, htd); paddling pool;
beach sand adj; entmnt; wifi; TV; 60% statics; dogs €3;
phone; Eng spkn; adv bkg acc; quiet; ccard acc; games
area; bike hire; waterslide; sailing school; watersports.
"Excel family site; conv Guérande; vg touring base;
superb new (2013) san facs." ♦ 1 Apr-11 Nov.
€ 34.00   2014*

ATTICHY 3C4 (1km SSE Rural) 49.40664, 3.05295
**Camping De l'Aigrette (Formaly Camp municipal
Fleury), 22 Rue Fontaine-Aubier, 60350 Attichy
[03 44 42 15 97 or 06 62 83 79 35 (mob); fax 09 72
42 38 20; contact@campingdelaigrette.com; www.
campingdelaigrette.com]** Fr Compiègne E on N31.
After 16km turn L at traff lts sp Attichy & site. Over
iron bdge & turn R to site on lakeside. Sm, hdg, pt
shd, wc (htd); chem disp; mv service pnt; shwrs inc;
EHU (10A) €2; lndry; shop nr; rest nr; bbq; playgrnd;
pool; wifi; 30% statics; dogs €0.50; quiet; fishing;
site clsd 25 Dec - 31 Jan; CKE/CCI. "Attractive, clean
site in pleasant vill; many w/end statics, few touring
pitches; helpful wardens live on site; modern san facs,
stretched high ssn; gd security; excel NH LS; excel
site." ♦ 1 Mar-30 Nov. € 16.00   2015*

AUBENAS 9D2 (2km E Rural) 44.61885, 4.43220
**Camping Le Plan d'Eau, Route de Lussas, 07200 St
Privat [04 75 35 44 98; info@campingleplandeau.fr;
www.campingleplandeau.fr]** Exit A7 at Montélimar
dir Aubenas. Bef Aubenas turn R at rndabt onto D104
dir St Privat. In approx 1km turn R twd Lussas & foll
site sp. Site on R on rvside. Med, mkd, pt shd, wc; chem
disp; fam bthrm; shwrs inc; EHU (8A) €4.20; lndry;
shop nr; rest; snacks; bar; bbq (gas); cooking facs;
playgrnd; pool (htd); red long stay; entmnt; wifi; TV;
25% statics; dogs €2.70; phone; Eng spkn; adv bkg acc;
quiet; games rm; CKE/CCI. "Vg, peaceful site; gd san &
sports facs." 26 Apr-13 Sep. € 43.00   2012*

AUBENAS 9D2 (10km S Rural) 44.53693, 4.41039
**Camping Les Peupliers, 07200 Vogüé [04 75 37
71 47; fax 04 75 37 70 83; girard.jean-jacques@
club-internet.fr; www.campingpeupliers.com]**
Fr Aubenas take D104 S twd Alès. In 2km, turn L onto
D579 dir Vogüé/Vallon Pont d'Arc. In 9km, pass L
turn to Vogüé. Immed after x-ing rv, turn R at rndabt.
Site on R in 300m, (2nd site of 3 on rd). Lge, mkd, pt
shd, wc; chem disp; mv service pnt; fam bthrm; shwrs
inc; EHU (6A) €4.10; gas; lndry; shop; rest; snacks;
bar; bbq; playgrnd; pool; entmnt; 10% statics; dogs
€2.30; phone; adv bkg acc; quiet; ccard acc; CKE/
CCI. "Gd touring base; access to rv for canoeing &
fishing; sm shop on site with ltd stock." 5 Apr-30 Sep.
€ 24.00   2015*

France

AUBENAS

AUBENAS *9D2* (7km NW Rural) *44.65157, 4.32384*
Camp Municipal le Pont des Issoux, Allée de Vals, 07380 Lalevade-d'Ardèche [06 20 03 09 41 or 04 27 52 96 64; familyscampinglesissoux@gmail.com; www.sud-ardeche-camping.fr] Fr Aubenas, N102 sp Mende & Le Puy-en-Velay; Lalevade in 10km; R in vill; well sp. Med, mkd, pt shd, wc; chem disp; shwrs inc; EHU (10A) €3.10 (poss rev pol); gas; lndry; shop nr; rest nr; bar nr; playgrnd; sw nr; wifi; dogs €1.20; bus 220m; Eng spkn; adv bkg acc; quiet; tennis nr; CKE/CCI. "Pleasant, shady site beside Rv Ardèche; friendly, helpful warden; san facs dated but clean, poss scruffy LS; children's park nrby; no twin axles; close to vill; conv touring base; vg." ♦ 1 Apr-15 Oct. € 11.50   2013*

> **"Satellite navigation makes touring much easier"**
>
> Remember most sat navs don't know if you're towing or in a larger vehicle – always use yours alongside maps and site directions.

AUBERIVES SUR VAREZE *9B2* (8km E Rural) *45.42830, 4.92823* **Kawan Village Camping Le Bontemps, 5 Impasse du Bontemps, 38150 Vernioz** [04 74 57 83 52; fax 04 74 57 83 70; info@campinglebontemps.com; www.camping-lebontemps.com] Take N7 S fr Vienne. At Le Clos turn L onto D37 thro Cheyssieu & Vernioz, site approx 9km E of Vernioz. Fr S, on N7 N of vill of Auberives R onto D37, site on R in 8km. Tight ent - rec swing wide. NB Also sp Hotel de Plein Air. Lge, mkd, pt shd, terr, wc; mv service pnt; fam bthrm; shwrs inc; EHU (6A) inc (poss long lead req); lndry; shop; rest; snacks; bar; bbq; playgrnd; pool; paddling pool; entmnt; wifi; TV; 30% statics; dogs €3; adv bkg acc; ccard acc; games rm; tennis; lake fishing; games area; CKE/CCI. "Attractive, well-kept site; popular NH high ssn; wildlife sanctuary; helpful staff; no o'fits over 10m high ssn; excel sports facs; vg NH/long stay; new san facs (2014)." ♦ 1 Apr-30 Sep. € 31.00   2014*

AUBERIVES SUR VAREZE *9B2* (2km S Rural) *45.41284, 4.81358* **Camping des Nations, 38550 Clonas-sur-Varèze** [04 74 84 95 13 or 04 14 42 42 84; contact@campingdesnations.com; www.campingdesnations.com] Fr Vienne S on N7; site sp on R in 12km. Or fr S exit A7 junc 12 onto N7 dir Vienne; do not go into Clonas vill; site on L adj Hotel des Nations. Med, mkd, hdg, shd, wc (htd); chem disp; shwrs inc; EHU (9A) inc; rest nr; snacks; bbq; pool; dogs €1; adv bkg req; quiet; CKE/CCI. "Pleasant, well-kept, well-laid out site; gd sized pitches; gd, v clean san facs; site muddy when wet; poss under-used; ltd facs LS; poss irreg cleaning end of ssn; useful NH/touring base for Spain & the Med; vg site; friendly, helpful staff." ♦ 1 Mar-31 Oct. € 22.00   2016*

AUBETERRE SUR DRONNE *7C2* (1km SE Rural) *45.26786, 0.17474* **Camping Base de Loisirs d'Aubeterre Sur Dronne (formerly Camp Municipal), Route de Ribérac, 16390 Aubeterre-sur-Dronne** [05 45 78 29 36 or 06 87 29 18 36 (mob); camping.aubeterre-sur-dronne@orange.fr; www.camping-aubeterre.fr] On D2 fr Chalais, take D17 around S end of town. Turn R over rv & site on R adj sports grnd. Med, pt shd, wc cont; chem disp; mv service pnt; shwrs inc; EHU (10A) €2.50; shop nr; rest nr; snacks; bar; playgrnd; wifi; 10% statics; dogs €1; Eng spkn; quiet; rv fishing adj; bike hire; tennis adj; boating adj. "Excel site; gd for children; friendly staff; picturesque town; conv touring Périgord." 1 May-30 Sep. € 20.00   2014*

AUBIGNY SUR NERE *4G3* (2km E Rural) *47.48435, 2.45561* **FLOWER Camping des Etangs, Route de Sancerre, 18700 Aubigny-sur-Nère** [02 48 58 02 37; camping.aubigny@orange.fr; www.camping-aubigny.com or www.flowercampings.com] D940 fr Gien, turn E in vill of Aubigny onto D923, foll sp fr vill; site 1km on R by lake, after Camp des Sports & just bef end of vill sp. Avoid town cent due congestion. Med, mkd, hdstg, pt shd, wc (htd); chem disp; shwrs inc; EHU (6-10A) inc; lndry; shop; rest nr; snacks; bbq; playgrnd; pool (covrd, htd); paddling pool; wifi; TV; 10% statics; dogs €2; phone; Eng spkn; adv bkg acc; quiet; bike hire; fishing; games rm; CKE/CCI. "Vg site with lake views; pretty medieval vill with historical links to Scotland; mkt Sat; 2nd w/e July Scottish Son & Lumière event adj site!" ♦ 1 Apr-30 Sep. € 30.00   2014*

⊞ **AUBUSSON** *7B4* (10km N Rural) *46.02133, 2.17052* **Camping La Perle, Fourneaux, 23200 St Médard-la-Rochette** [05 55 83 01 25; fax 05 55 83 34 18; info@camping-laperle.nl; www.camping-laperle.nl] On D942 N fr Aubusson dir Guéret; site on R bef Fourneaux. Sm, hdg, hdstg, mkd, pt shd, terr, wc; shwrs inc; EHU (10A) poss rev pol €3.50; lndry; rest; bar; bbq; playgrnd; pool (htd); wifi; TV; 10% statics; dogs; Eng spkn; adv bkg acc; quiet; bike hire; CKE/CCI. "Site ever improving (2011); various sized pitches; Dutch owners; tapestry museum in Aubusson & other historical attractions; vg site." € 18.50   2013*

AUBUSSON *7B4* (5km S Rural) *45.91939, 2.17044* **Camping des Combes, Les Combes, 23500 Felletin** [05 55 66 77 29 or 07799 138014 (UK); info@campingdescombes-creuse-france.co.uk; www.campingdescombes-creuse-france.co.uk] Fr Aubusson on D982 to Felletin, when in Felletin & immed bef rlwy line, turn R at cemetery. Foll camping sp approx 4km. Sm, mkd, hdg, pt shd, wc; chem disp; mv service pnt; shwrs inc; EHU (10A) €2 (long lead poss req); lndry; shop; playgrnd; phone; adv bkg acc; quiet; fishing; boating. "Peaceful, British-owned site on edge Lake Combes; ideal touring base; vg; spotless." ♦ 1 Mar-30 Sep. € 20.00   2013*

AUCH *8F3* (8km N Rural) *43.7128, 0.5646* **Kawan Village Le Talouch, Au Cassou, 32810 Roquelaure [05 62 65 52 43; fax 05 62 65 53 68; info@camping-talouch.com; www.camping-talouch.com]** Head W on N124 fr Auch, then N on D148 for 7km to site. Med, mkd, pt shd, wc; chem disp; mv service pnt; fam bthrm; shwrs; EHU (6A) inc; gas; lndry; shop; rest; snacks; bar; bbq; playgrnd; pool (covrd, htd); paddling pool; entmnt; wifi; TV; 15% statics; dogs €2.40; Eng spkn; adv bkg acc; quiet; golf driving range; tennis; games area; CKE/CCI. "Well-kept site; set in lovely countryside with lge grassed pitches, maintained to high standard; friendly Dutch owners who spk excel Eng; steam rm; sauna; recreational facs superb for all age groups; gd walking & nature trails; poss liable to flooding." ♦ 1 Apr-30 Sep. € 33.40   2012*

AUCUN *8F2* (1km E Rural) *42.97338, -0.18496* **Camping Azun Nature, 1 Route des Poueyes, 65400 [05 62 97 45 05; azun.nature@wanadoo.fr; www.camping-azun-nature.com]** Fr Toulouse- A64 exit Tarbes W. Fr Bordeaux or Bayonne- A64 Exit Soumoulou. Fr Lourdes- drive twd Argeles-Gazost, take exit Aubisque col-Val d'Azun; Fr town cent of Argeles-Gazost go twd Aubisque col, Soulor col; Cross Arras-en-Lavedan, go on twd Aucun vill, turn L sp Las Poueyes, site ent 100m on R bet barns. Sm, mkd, pt shd, wc; chem disp; fam bthrm; shwrs inc; EHU (3-6A) €2.50-3.50; lndry; shop; bbq; playgrnd; wifi; TV; 50% statics; dogs free; adv bkg acc; games area; games rm; CKE/CCI. "Stunning setting; ideal walking & cycling area; gd for exploring the Pyrenees, visits to Lourdes; well maintained; pool 3km; friendly, helpful owner." ♦ 1 May-30 Sep. € 15.00   2013*

> **"There aren't many sites open at this time of year"**
>
> If you're travelling outside peak season remember to call ahead to check site opening dates – even if the entry says 'open all year'.

AUDIERNE *2F1* (3km SE Coastal) *48.00723, -4.50923* **Camping de Kersiny-Plage, 1 Rue Nominoé, 29780 Plouhinec [02 98 70 82 44; fax 09 55 54 80 22; info@kersinyplage.com; www.kersinyplage.com]** Fr Audierne on D784 turn R at 2nd traff lts in Plouhinec, cont for 1km; turn L into Rue Nominoé (sp diff to see) for 100m. Or fr Quimper on D784 to Plouhinec, turn L at 1st traff lts & as bef. Med, hdg, pt shd, terr, wc; chem disp; fam bthrm; shwrs inc; EHU (8A) €3; lndry; bbq (gas); playgrnd; beach sand; wifi; dogs €2; Eng spkn; quiet; CKE/CCI. "Quiet, peaceful site; beautiful location & beach; most pitches superb sea views; welcoming, friendly owner; clean san facs; barrier clsd 2300-0730; not much in area for children except beach; gd coastal walks; vg, rec." 14 May-17 Sep. € 15.00   2016*

⊞ **AULUS LES BAINS** *8G3* (1km NW Rural) *42.79402, 1.33197* **Camp Municipal Le Coulédous, 09140 Aulus-les-Bains [05 61 66 43 56; campinglecouledous@orange.fr; www.camping-aulus-couledous.com]** Take D618 fr St Girons. After 13km cross rv; turn R onto D3 sp Aulus-les-Bains. On app to Oust turn L onto D32, site approx 17km on R at ent to vill on rvside. Med, hdstg, mkd, pt shd, sl, wc (htd); chem disp; mv service pnt; shwrs inc; EHU (10A) €4.50-6.50; lndry; shop nr; playgrnd; wifi; 10% statics; dogs €1; Eng spkn; adv bkg acc; quiet; site clsd mid-Nov to mid-Dec; CKE/CCI. "Gd walking & skiing (16km); sm spa in vill; bar 300m; excel; san facs clean but tired; church clock chimes thro night." ♦ € 19.00   2017*

AUMALE *3C3* (1km W Rural) *49.76618, 1.74618* **Camp Municipal Le Grand Mail, Chemin du Grand Mail, 76390 Aumale [02 35 93 40 50 (Mairie); fax 02 35 93 86 79; communeaumale@wanadoo.fr; www.aumale.com]** Clearly sp in town; long steep climb to ent. Med, pt shd, wc; mv service pnt; shwrs; EHU (6A) €2.40; lndry; shop nr; playgrnd; dogs €2; bike hire; fishing 1km. "Gd site; clean, modern san facs; conv Channel ports; steep slope fr town to site; gd NH." ♦ 1 Apr-30 Sep. € 18.00   2014*

AUNAY SUR ODON *3D1* (1km NE Urban) *49.02530, -0.62515* **Camp Municipal La Closerie, Rue de Caen, 14260 Aunay-sur-Odon [02 31 77 32 46 or 07850 511893; fax 02 31 77 70 07; mairieaunaysurodon@orange.fr; www.aunaysurodon.fr]** Exit A84 junc 43 sp Villers-Bocage/Aunay & take D6 twd Aunay. In approx 3km bef Aunay town sp, turn L sp 'Zone Industrielle', in 200m turn R at rndabt. Site on R in 100m nr sports stadium. Sm, mkd, pt shd, pt sl, wc; chem disp; mv service pnt; shwrs inc; EHU €2.80; shop nr; dogs €1.55; Eng spkn; quiet; games area; CKE/CCI. "Delightful, attractive vill; Sat mkt; vet avail; conv NH for Caen ferry & gd touring base; helpful, welcoming warden." ♦ 6 Jul-31 Aug. € 7.50   2017*

AUPS *10E3* (1km SE Rural) *43.62378, 6.22903* **Camping Les Prés, 181 Route de Tourtour, 83630 Aups [04 94 70 00 93; fax 04 94 70 14 41; lespres.camping@wanadoo.fr; www.campinglespres.com]** Fr cent of Aups on rd to Tourtour, site on R. Rough rd. Med, hdg, mkd, pt shd, wc (htd); fam bthrm; shwrs inc; EHU (10A); gas; lndry; shop nr; rest; snacks; bar; playgrnd; pool; entmnt; TV; 10% statics; adv bkg acc; quiet. "Peaceful, friendly site; recep clsd 1200 to 1500; ent not rec for lge o'fits." 1 Mar-31 Oct. € 27.00   2015*

AUPS *10E3* (1km W Rural) *43.62455, 6.21760* **International Camping, Route de Fox-Amphoux, 83630 Aups [04 94 70 06 80; fax 04 94 70 10 51; camping-aups@internationalcamping-aups.com; www.internationalcamping-aups.com]** Site on L on D60 nr vill cent. Lge, mkd, hdg, pt shd, wc; chem disp; shwrs inc; EHU (16A) €5.30; lndry; shop; rest; snacks; bar; pool; entmnt; 80% statics; dogs €1; Eng spkn; adv bkg rec; quiet; ccard acc; tennis; games rm. "Vg site in beautiful area; lge pitches; gd rest." 1 Apr-30 Sep. € 19.00   2016*

AURAY

AURAY *2F3 (7km SE Rural) 47.64320, -2.89890* **Aire Naturelle La Fontaine du Hallate (Le Gloanic), 8 Chemin du Poul Fétan, La Hallate, 56400 Plougoumelen [09 64 04 90 16 or 06 16 30 08 33 (mob); clegloanic@orange. fr; www.camping-hallate.fr]** Fr N165 Vannes-Lorient, turn S onto D101E to Plougoumelen; watch for sp after Plougoumelen, site in La Hallate. Narr, bumpy app rd. Sm, mkd, hdg, pt shd, pt sl, shwrs inc; EHU (6A) €3.40 (poss rev pol); lndry; shop nr; playgrnd; 2% statics; dogs €2.88; phone; adv bkg req; tennis adj; golf adj; CKE/CCI. "Gd alt to lge/noisier sites; gd coast paths; conv local boat trips & Ste Anne-d'Auray; vg." 29 Mar-24 Oct. € 16.00 2013*

AURAY *2F3 (7km S Rural) 47.64402, -2.93774* **FFCC Camping du Parc-Lann, 52 Rue Thiers, Le Varquez, 56400 Le Bono [02 97 57 93 93 or 07 88 00 79 47; campingduparclann@wanadoo.fr; www.campingduparclann.fr]** S fr Auray on D101 sp Le Bono. Site well sp in Le Bono. Med, hdg, mkd, pt shd, wc; chem disp; mv service pnt; fam bthrm; shwrs inc; EHU (6A) €2.30 (long lead req); lndry; shop nr; bbq; playgrnd; dogs €0.70; phone; bus; games area; ice; CKE/CCI. "Lovely quiet site in pretty area; gd, clean san facs poss stretched high ssn & ltd LS; pool 5km; warden on site 1800-1900 only LS; gd walking." ♦ 1 May-30 Sep. € 14.00 2016*

AURAY *2F3 (8km SW Rural) 47.64256, -3.05406* **FFCC Camping de Kergo, Route de Carnac, 56400 Ploemel [02 97 56 80 66; contact@campingkergo.com; www.campingkergo.com]** Fr Auray take D768 SW sp Carnac. After 4km turn NW on D186 twd Ploemel & foll sp. Med, mkd, pt shd, wc; chem disp; shwrs inc; EHU (6-10A) inc; lndry; shop nr; playgrnd; beach sand 5km; 10% statics; dogs €0.70; adv bkg rec; CKE/CCI. "Lovely, peaceful site, lots of trees; gd, clean san facs but dated (2015), ltd LS; welcoming, friendly, helpful owners; gd size pitches; ideal for cycling into Carnac." ♦ 1 May-30 Sep. € 16.00 2017*

⊞ **AURAY** *2F3 (8km W Rural) 47.66406, -3.09985* **FFCC Camp Municipal Le St Laurent, Kergonvo, 56400 Ploemel [02 97 56 85 90; info@campingdesaintlaurent.com; www.campingdesaintlaurent.com]** Fr Auray on D22 twd Belz/ Etel; after 8km turn L on D186 to Ploemel & site on L in 200m. Med, hdstg, shd, wc (htd); chem disp; mv service pnt; fam bthrm; shwrs inc; EHU (10A) €4; lndry; shop; rest; bar; bbq; playgrnd; pool (htd); paddling pool; 10% statics; dogs €1.40; adv bkg acc; quiet; games area. "Peaceful site; friendly staff; red facs LS." ♦ € 27.00 2014*

AURILLAC *7C4 (1km NE Urban) 44.93551, 2.45596* **Camp Municipal de l'Ombrade, Chemin du Gué Bouliaga, 15000 Aurillac [04 71 48 28 87]** Take D17 N fr Aurillac twd Puy-Mary; site on banks of Rv Jordanne. Well sp fr town. Lge, mkd, shd, pt sl, wc; shwrs inc; EHU (10A) €2.10; lndry; shop nr; bbq; entmnt; TV; dogs; quiet; games rm. "Well-managed, spacious site; lge pitches; interesting, lge mkt town; vg; excel new san fac (2014)." ♦ 15 Jun-15 Sep. € 16.00 2015*

AUTRANS *9C3 (1km E Rural) 45.17520, 5.54770* **Kawan Village au Joyeux Réveil, Le Château, 38880 Autrans [04 76 95 33 44; fax 04 76 95 72 98; camping-au-joyeux-reveil@wanadoo.fr; www.camping-au-joyeux-reveil.fr]** Fr Villard-de-Lans take D531 to Lans-en-Vercors & turn L onto D106 to Autrans. On E side of vill site sp at 1st rndabt. NB App on D531 fr W fr Pont-en-Royans not rec - v narr rd & low tunnels. Med, mkd, pt shd, pt sl, wc (htd); chem disp; mv service pnt; fam bthrm; shwrs inc; EHU (2-10A) €2-8; gas; lndry; shop nr; rest nr; snacks; bar; bbq; playgrnd; pool (htd); paddling pool; wifi; TV; TV (pitch); 60% statics; dogs; phone; bus 300m; Eng spkn; adv bkg acc; quiet; ccard acc; golf 20km; games area; tennis 300m; bike hire; rv fishing; waterslide; CKE/CCI. "Site in Vercors National Park with excel views; winter sport facs, 1050m altitude; modern san facs; excel; well run site; friendly staff." ♦ 1 May-30 Sep. € 44.00 2014*

AUTUN *6H1 (2km N Rural) 46.96478, 4.29381* **Camp de la Porte d'Arroux (formerly Municipal), Les Chaumottes, 71400 Autun [03 85 52 10 82; fax 03 86 37 79 20; www.aquadis-loisirs.com]** Fr Autun foll dir for Saulieu on D980; site on L 500m after passing thro Roman Arch; only site in Autun. Sm, hdg, hdstg, pt shd, wc; chem disp; mv service pnt; fam bthrm; shwrs inc; EHU (10A) €3.30 (poss rev pol); lndry; shop; rest; snacks; bar; bbq; playgrnd; sw; twin axles; wifi; TV; dogs €1.35; phone; Eng spkn; adv bkg acc; ccard acc; bike hire; fishing; canoeing; games area; CKE/CCI. "Lovely, quiet, clean site; busy NH high ssn; sm pitches, views fr some pitches; friendly, helpful staff; gd san facs, poss stretched high ssn; no twin axles; v muddy when wet (tow avail); vg, lively rest & bar; medieval architecture & Roman walls around town; m'van Aire de Service nr lake in town; mkt Wed/Fri; poss overpriced for nature of site." ♦ 6 Mar-5 Nov. € 21.00 2016*

> **"That's changed – Should I let the Club know?"**
> If you find something on site that's different from the site entry, fill in a report and let us know. See camc.com/europereport

AUTUN *6H1 (12km NW Rural) 47.01227, 4.19150* **Camping Les Deux Rivières, Le Pré Bouché, 71400 La Celle-en-Morvan [03 45 74 01 38; info@les2rivieres. com; www.les2rivieres.com]** Fr Autun take D978 sp to Chateau-Chinon for approx 12km. Site on R as entering vill. 300m fr main rd. Med, mkd, hdg, pt shd, wc; chem disp; mv service pnt; fam bthrm; shwrs inc; lndry; snacks; bbq; playgrnd; pool (htd); twin axles; wifi; dogs; Eng spkn; adv bkg acc; quiet; games area; CKE/CCI. "V friendly Dutch owners; well kept clean site; supmkt in Autun; excel." ♦ 1 May-20 Sep. € 26.00 2015*

AVALLON

AUXERRE *4F4* (2km SE Urban) *47.78378, 3.58721* **Camp Municipal, 8 Rue de Vaux, 89000 Auxerre [03 86 52 11 15 or 03 86 72 43 00 (Mairie); fax 03 86 51 17 54; camping.mairie@auxerre.com; www.auxerre.com]** Exit A6 at Auxerre; at junc N6 ring rd foll sp Vaux & 'Stade'; site sp by Rv Yonne. Or fr N6 (N) take ring rd, site/stadium sp. Site also well sp fr town cent as 'L'Arbre Sec'. Lge, mkd, pt shd, wc; chem disp; mv service pnt; shwrs inc; EHU (6A) inc (long lead poss req); lndry; shop; bar; playgrnd; TV; dogs; adv bkg acc; fishing 300m; CKE/CCI. "Lovely, peaceful, well-kept site; lge pitches; friendly staff; gd clean san facs, tight access to sinks; pool 250m; poss cr & noisy during football ssn; site poss flooded stormy weather; ltd EHU for site size, pnts locked & unlocked by warden; no vehicles 2200-0700; pretty town; popular NH; few water taps." 15 Apr-15 Sep. € 13.00   2015*

AUXERRE *4F4* (10km S Rural) *47.70704, 3.63593* **FFCC Camping Les Ceriselles, Route de Vincelottes, 89290 Vincelles [03 86 42 50 47; www.campingceriselles.com]** Leave A6 at Auxerre Sud. Fr Auxerre, take D606 S twd Avallon. 10km fr Auxerre turn L into Vincelles. In 400m immed after 'Atac Marche', turn L into site access rd, sp as Camping Les Ceriselles. Site is approx 16km fr a'route exit. Med, hdstg, mkd, pt shd, wc (htd); chem disp; mv service pnt; fam bthrm; shwrs inc; EHU (10A) inc (poss rev pol); lndry; shop nr; rest nr; snacks; bar; bbq; playgrnd; pool; red long stay; wifi; TV; 10% statics; dogs free (2nd €1.50); phone; Eng spkn; adv bkg acc; quiet; ccard acc; bike hire; CKE/CCI. "Excel, busy site by canal, poss full late Jun; friendly, helpful owner; gd san facs, poss insufficient high ssn & ltd LS; lovely walks to vill & along canal; cycle track to Auxerre & Clamecy; highly rec; high ssn overflow area; secure o'night area; gas adj; v popular." ♦ 1 Apr-1 Oct. € 21.00   2018*

AUXI LE CHATEAU *3B3* (1km NW Rural) *50.2341, 2.1058* **Camp Municipal des Peupliers, 22 Rue du Cheval, 62390 Auxi-le-Château [03 21 41 10 79; fax 03 21 04 10 22]** Fr S on D925, turn N onto D933 at Bernaville to Auxi-le-Château; turn W onto D941; then turn R in 300m into Rue du Cheval; site sp on R in 500m by football stadium. Or take D928 S fr Hesdin; in 11km take D119 to Auxi-le-Château. Med, hdg, unshd, wc; chem disp; shwrs inc; EHU (3-6A) €1.85; lndry; shop nr; rest nr; bar nr; playgrnd; 5% statics; adv bkg acc; quiet; fishing; sailing. "Easy walk into town; dir access to rv; supmkt 300m; excel NH or short stay." 1 Apr-30 Sep. € 14.00   2018*

AUXONNE *6G1* (1km NW Rural) *47.19838, 5.38120* **Camping L'Arquebuse, Route d'Athée, 21130 Auxonne [03 80 31 06 89; fax 03 80 31 13 62; camping.arquebuse@wanadoo.fr; www.campingarquebuse.com]** On D905 Dijon-Geneva, site sp on L bef bdge at ent to Auxonne. Med, pt shd, wc (htd); chem disp; mv service pnt; shwrs inc; EHU (10A) €3.70 (poss rev pol); gas; lndry; shop nr; rest; snacks; bar; bbq; playgrnd; twin axles; entmnt; wifi; TV; 40% statics; dogs €1.80; Eng spkn; adv bkg acc; ccard acc; waterskiing; fishing; clsd 2200-0700; windsurfing; sailing; CKE/CCI. "Pleasant rvside site; friendly staff; san facs tatty & dated; htd pool adj; poss busy w/ends as NH; interesting town; child friendly site." 4 Mar-16 Dec. € 21.00   2017*

> **"I like to fill in the reports as I travel from site to site"**
>
> You'll find report forms at the back of this guide, or you can fill them in online at camc.com/europereport.

AVAILLES LIMOUZINE *7A3* (7km E Rural) *46.12342, 0.65975* **FFCC Camp Municipal Le Parc, 86400 Availles-Limouzine [05 49 48 51 22; fax 05 49 48 66 76; camping.leparc@wanadoo.fr; www.campingleparc.monsite-orange.fr]** Fr Confolens N on D948 & turn R on D34 to Availles-Limouzine. Site on Rv Vienne by town bdge. Med, pt shd, wc; chem disp; mv service pnt; shwrs inc; EHU (10A) inc; gas; shop nr; playgrnd; paddling pool; wifi; dogs €2.65; Eng spkn; adv bkg acc; quiet; CKE/CCI. "Attractive, well-run site in beautiful position; rv views; vg playgrnd; barrier clsd 2200-0800; poss scruffy LS; vg value; permanent warden." ♦ 1 Apr-30 Sep. € 16.50   2017*

AVALLON *4G4* (2km SE Rural) *47.48030, 3.91246* **Camp Municipal Sous Roches, Rue Sous Roche; 89200 Avallon [03 86 34 10 39; campingsousroche@ville-avallon.fr; www.campingsousroche.com]** App town fr a'route or fr SE on N6. Turn sharp L at 2nd traff lts in town cent, L in 2km at sp Vallée du Cousin (bef bdge), site 250m on L. If app fr S care needed when turning R after bdge. Med, hdstg, pt shd, terr, wc; mv service pnt; shwrs inc; EHU (6A) €3.80; lndry; shop; rest nr; bbq; playgrnd; wifi; dogs free; rv fishing adj; CKE/CCI. "Popular, well-kept site in lovely location nr rv; friendly, helpful staff; excel immac san facs; conv Morvan National Park; poss flood warning after heavy rain; no twin axles or o'fits over 2,500kg; attractive town; steep walk to town; excel." ♦ 1 Apr-15 Oct. € 18.00   2016*

France

AVIGNON

AVIGNON *10E2* (4km N Rural) 43.97063, 4.79928
Viva Camp la Laune (formerly Municipal), Chemin St Honoré, 30400 Villeneuve-lès-Avignon [04 90 25 76 06 or 04 90 25 61 33; campingdelalaune@wanadoo.fr; www.camping-villeneuvelezavignon.com]
Fr Avignon, take N100 twd Nîmes over rv bdge. At W end of 2nd pt of rv bdge, turn R onto N980 sp Villeneuve-lès-Avignon. Site is 3km on R just past town battlements on L. Adj sports complex. NB Do not foll sat nav rote thro Pujaut. Med, mkd, hdstg, hdg, shd, wc; chem disp; mv service pnt; shwrs inc; EHU (6A) €3.10 (poss rev pol); lndry; shop; snacks; bar; bbq; playgrnd; twin axles; entmnt; wifi; TV; 10% statics; dogs €1.50; phone; bus; Eng spkn; adv bkg acc; quiet; ccard acc; games area; CKE/CCI. "Lovely, peaceful, helpful staff; excel security; sports facs adj; gd walks/cycle rides; htd pool adj; in walking dist of Villeneuve-lès-Avignon with fort & abbey; gd bus to Avignon; sports complex adj (free to campers, but ltd acc); vg local mkt; poss rlwy noise at night; floods in heavy rain; new owners, site deteriorated; scruffy out of ssn."
♦ 1 Apr-15 Oct. € 26.00   2016*

AVIGNON *10E2* (9km NE Rural) 43.99057, 4.91340
Camping Avignon Parc (formerly Camping Flory), 385 Route d'Entraigues, 84270 Vedène [04 90 31 00 51]
Fr A7 exit 23 dir Carpentras for 3km then Vedene. Lge, mkd, pt shd, pt sl, wc; chem disp; mv service pnt; fam bthrm; shwrs inc; EHU (10A) €4 (poss rev pol); gas; lndry; shop; rest; snacks; bar; bbq; playgrnd; pool (htd); twin axles; entmnt; wifi; 15% statics; dogs €2.50; phone; bus; Eng spkn; adv bkg acc; quiet; games area; games rm; CKE/CCI. "Conv touring base Vaucluse; uneven pitches & paths; facs poss stretched high ssn & ltd LS; lovely pool; vg." ♦ 24 May-24 Sep. € 29.00   2017*

> ## "We must tell the Club about that great site we found"
> Get your site reports in by mid-August and we'll do our best to get your updates into the next edition.

AVIGNON *10E2* (8km S Urban) 43.88361, 4.87010
Camping de la Roquette, 746 Ave Jean Mermoz, 13160 Châteaurenard [04 90 94 46 81; fax 09 72 14 01 53; contact@camping-la-roquette.com; www.camping-la-roquette.com] Exit A7/D907 Avignon S to Noves; take D28 to Châteaurenard 4km; foll sp to site & Piscine Olympic/Complex Sportiv. Med, hdg, mkd, pt shd, serviced pitches; wc; chem disp; mv service pnt; fam bthrm; shwrs inc; EHU (10A) €4; lndry; shop nr; rest; snacks; bar; playgrnd; pool; paddling pool; wifi; TV; dogs €2; phone; Eng spkn; adv bkg rec; quiet; ccard acc; tennis; CKE/CCI. "Gd touring cent; sm pitches; owners friendly, helpful; clean facs; gd walks." ♦ 1 Apr-31 Oct. € 37.00   2013*

AVIGNON *10E2* (12km W Rural) 43.95155, 4.66451
Camping Le Bois des Ecureuils, 947 Chemin De La Beaume, 30390 Domazan [04 66 57 10 03; infos@boisdesecureuils.com; www.boisdesecureuils.com]
Exit A9/E15 at Remoulins junc 23 twd Avignon on N100. Site on R in 6km. Fr S on N7 foll sp for Nîmes onto N100. Go over 2 lge rndabts, site about 6km on L at rndabt. Sm, mkd, hdstg, shd, wc; chem disp; fam bthrm; shwrs inc; EHU (6A) inc; gas; lndry; shop; rest nr; snacks; bar; bbq; playgrnd; pool (htd); entmnt; TV; 5% statics; dogs €1.70; phone; Eng spkn; adv bkg rec; quiet; CKE/CCI. "Ideal for touring Avignon & Pont du Gard; friendly owners; clean facs; steel awning pegs ess; many long-stay residents LS; v shd; tired site; mostly residential in LS." € 20.00   2018*

AVIGNON *10E2* (1km NW Urban) 43.95670, 4.80222
Camping du Pont d'Avignon, 10 Chemin de la Barthelasse, 84000 Avignon [04 90 80 63 50; fax 04 90 85 22 12; camping.lepontdavignon@orange.fr; www.camping-avignon.com] Exit A7 junc 23 Avignon Nord dir Avignon Centre (D225) then Villeneuve-les-Avignon. Go round wall & under Pont d'Avignon; then cross rv dir Villeneuve, Ile de la Barthelasse. Turn R onto Ile de la Barthelasse. Lge, hdg, mkd, shd, wc; chem disp; mv service pnt; fam bthrm; shwrs inc; EHU (6-10A); gas; lndry; shop; rest; snacks; bar; bbq; cooking facs; playgrnd; pool; paddling pool; red long stay; entmnt; wifi; TV; dogs €2.70; phone; Eng spkn; adv bkg req; ccard acc; games rm; car wash; games area; tennis; CKE/CCI. "Superb, well-run, busy site; welcoming, helpful staff; lovely pool; gd sized pitches but most with high kerbs; poss flooded LS; extra for c'vans over 5.5m; Avignon festival Jul/Aug; best site for Avignon - 20 mins walk or free ferry; rec arr early even LS; san facs ltd but recently refurbished (2014)."
♦ 2 Mar-23 Nov. € 40.00   2014*

AVIGNON *10E2* (1km NW Urban) 43.95216, 4.79946 **FFCC Camping Bagatelle, 25 allée Antoine Pinay - Ile de la Barthelasse, 84000 Avignon [04 90 86 30 39; fax 04 90 27 16 23; camping.bagatelle@wanadoo.fr; www.campingbagatelle.com]**
Exit D907 at Avignon Nord. After passing end of old bdge bear L, then onto new Daladier bdge & take immed R turn over bdge foll sp to Barthelasse & Villeneuve-lès-Avignon. Caution - do not foll Nîmes sp at more southerly bdge (Pont d'Europe). Lge, mkd, pt shd, wc (htd); mv service pnt; fam bthrm; shwrs inc; EHU (6-10A) €3.50-4.50; gas; lndry; shop; rest; playgrnd; entmnt; dogs €2.40; ccard acc; fishing; games area; boating; tennis 2km; CKE/CCI. "Busy site on rv bank; sm pitches; helpful staff; facs dated but clean, ltd LS & poss stretched high ssn; narr site rds, suggest find pitch bef driving in; pool 100m; if recep unmanned, go to bar or supmkt to check in; free ferry to town; site low lying & poss damp; highly rec; ideal location, sh walk into Avignon Cent." ♦ € 30.00   2016*

AVIGNON *10E2* (5km NW Rural) *43.99573, 4.81843* Campéole Camping L'Ile des Papes, Quartier l'Islon, 30400 Villeneuve-lès-Avignon [04 90 15 15 90; fax 04 90 15 15 91; ile-des-papes@campeole.com; www. avignon-camping.com or www.campeole.com] Fr A9 exit sp Roquemaure; head S on D980. Site adj to rv 2km NW of city. Fr D907 (A7) exit Avignon Nord, twds Avignon cent & cross bdge twds Villeneuve. Turn off after x-ing rv bef x-ing canal. Site bet rv & canal. Lge, pt shd, wc; shwrs; EHU (6A) €4; lndry; shop; rest; cooking facs; playgrnd; pool; red long stay; entmnt; TV; 35% statics; dogs €3.50; Eng spkn; adv bkg acc; ccard acc; archery; lake fishing adj; CKE/CCI. "Lovely area; hiking; well-run site; pleasant staff; lge pitches; gd site rest." ♦ 27 Mar-6 Nov. € 25.00 2012*

AVRANCHES *2E4* (10km W Rural) *48.69663, -1.47434* FFCC Camping La Pérame, 50530 Genêts [02 33 70 82 49] Fr Avranches on N175; in 1km turn L on D911 thro Genêts. Turn R onto D35 immed after passing thro Genêts, site on R in 1km. Sm, pt shd, wc; shwrs inc; EHU (10A) €3 (rev pol); playgrnd; 60% statics; dogs €0.90; phone; quiet; CKE/CCI. "CL-type site in apple orchard nr sm vill; pleasant owner; gd views of Mont-St Michel fr vill; poss ltd & unkempt LS; poss boggy after heavy rain; guided walks to Mont St Michel; rec; farm produce; excel, quiet, simple site; all grass; pricey but special." 1 May-30 Sep. € 15.00 2017*

AVRILLE *7A1* (1km N Rural) *46.47641, -1.49373* Camping Le Domaine des Forges, Rue des Forges, 85440 Avrillé [02 51 22 38 85; fax 02 51 90 98 70; contact@campingdomainedesforges.com; www.campingdomainedesforges.com or www.les-castels.com] Fr N on D747 turn R at Moutiers-les-Mauxfaits onto D19 to Avrillé. In town cent cont strt & after sm rndabt foll yellow/white site sp. Turn R into Rue des Forges, site on R in 600m. Med, mkd, pt shd, wc; chem disp; mv service pnt; fam bthrm; shwrs; EHU (16A) inc; gas; lndry; shop; snacks; bar; bbq; playgrnd; pool (covrd, htd); paddling pool; entmnt; wifi; TV; dogs €4; Eng spkn; adv bkg acc; ccard acc; lake fishing; games area; bike hire; games rm; tennis. "Attractive site in lovely location; no o'fits over 10m Apr-Oct; spacious, well-kept pitches; fitness rm; helpful, friendly owner; gd, clean, modern san facs; lots of fish in lake; highly rec." ♦ 18 Apr-27 Sep. € 43.00 2013*

⊞ **AX LES THERMES** *8G4* (1km NW Rural) *42.72870, 1.82541* Camping Sunêlia Le Malazéou, 09110 Ax-les-Thermes [05 61 64 69 14; fax 05 61 64 05 60; camping.malazeou@wanadoo.fr; www.campingmalazeou.com] Sp on N20 to Foix. Lge, hdg, shd, pt sl, wc (htd); chem disp; mv service pnt; fam bthrm; shwrs inc; EHU (6A) inc; gas; lndry; shop; playgrnd; 70% statics; dogs €3; train 500m; Eng spkn; adv bkg acc; quiet; CKE/CCI. "Pleasant site by rv; lovely scenery; gd fishing; gd htd san facs; site poss clsd Nov, rvside walk to town; gd." ♦ € 37.00 2013*

AXAT *8G4* (2km E Rural) *42.80775, 2.25408* Camping de la Crémade, 11140 Axat [04 68 20 50 64; www.lacremade.com] S fr Quillan on D117, cont 1km beyond junc with D118 twd Perpignan. Turn R into site, sp, narr access. Med, hdg, pt shd, pt sl, wc; chem disp; shwrs inc; EHU (6A) €2.50; lndry; shop; bbq; playgrnd; 5% statics; dogs €1; Eng spkn; adv bkg acc; quiet; games rm; CKE/CCI. "Pleasant, well-maintained site in beautiful location; few level pitches; gd san facs; conv for gorges in Aude Valley." ♦ 1 May-24 Sep. € 15.50 2014*

AYDAT *9B1* (2km NE Rural) *45.66777, 2.98943* Camping du Lac d'Aydat, Forêt du Lot, 63970 Aydat [04 73 79 38 09; fax 04 73 79 34 12; info@camping-lac-aydat.com; www.camping-lac-aydat.com] Exit A75 S fr Clermont-Ferrand at junc 5 onto D13 W. Foll sp Lake Aydat. At x-rds at end of Rouillas-Bas, turn L at rndabt & foll site sp. Med, hdstg, mkd, shd, terr, serviced pitches; wc; chem disp; mv service pnt; shwrs inc; EHU (10A) €4; lndry; shop nr; rest nr; snacks; bar nr; playgrnd; sw nr; entmnt; 30% statics; dogs €1.50; phone; adv bkg acc; quiet; fishing; CKE/CCI. "On shore of Lake Aydat; gd for m'vans; bar 500m; charming woodland pitches, facs tired." ♦ 1 Apr-30 Sep. € 24.00 2012*

AYDAT *9B1* (3km W Rural) *45.66195, 2.94857* Camping Les Volcans, La Garandie, 63970 Aydat [04 73 79 33 90; campinglesvolcans@akeonet.com; www.campinglesvolcans.com] Fr N exit A75 junc 2 onto D2089 dir Bourboule; in 18km turn S onto D213 to Verneuge; in 1km fork R onto D5 dir Murol; in 1.5km turn R onto D788 sp La Grandie; turn R into vill; turn R again & site on L in 100m. Fr S exit A73 junc 5 onto D213 W; in 16km turn S in Verneuge onto D5; after 1.5km turn W onto D788 sp La Garandie; in vill turn R just after phone box, site on L in 100m. Sm, mkd, pt shd, wc; chem disp; mv service pnt; shwrs inc; EHU (6A) €5; lndry; shop; rest nr; snacks; bar; playgrnd; pool (htd); beach sand 3km; sw nr; wifi; 2% statics; dogs €2; Eng spkn; adv bkg acc; quiet; games area; horseriding 3km; watersports 3km. "Relaxing site; friendly, helpful new owners improving (2011); lge pitches; no twin axles; excel walking & cycle rtes nr; beautiful area; gd touring base; excel clean & well stocked facs; loads of hot water always on supply." 1 May-30 Sep. € 18.00 2014*

⊞ **AZAY LE FERRON** *4H2* (8km N Rural) *46.91949, 1.03679* Camping Le Cormier, Route de St Flovier, 36290 Obterre [02 54 39 27 95 or 0844 232 7271 (UK); mike@loireholidays.biz; www.loireholidays.biz] Fr Azay-le-Ferron N on D14, site on R just N of Obterre. Or fr Loches S on D943 for 3.5km, turn onto D41 to St Flovier then turn L onto D21 sp Obterre. In 1km turn R onto D14, site on L in 4km. Sm, hdstg, mkd, hdg, pt shd, wc (htd); chem disp; shwrs inc; EHU (10A) €4; lndry; rest nr; bbq; pool; twin axles; wifi; TV; dogs free; Eng spkn; adv bkg acc; quiet; ice; games area; games rm. "Friendly, helpful British owners (CC members); spacious pitches; gd san facs; excel touring/walking base; nr Brenne National Park; excel birdwatching; vg." € 19.00 2014*

AZAY LE RIDEAU

AZAY LE RIDEAU *4G1* (1km SE Urban) *47.25919, 0.46992* **FFCC Camp Municipal Le Sabot, Rue du Stade, 37190 Azay-le-Rideau [02 47 45 42 72 or 02 47 45 42 11 (Mairie); fax 02 47 45 49 11; camping. lesabot@wanadoo.fr; www.azaylerideau.fr]** Best app is fr D751 by-pass to avoid narr town - ignore Azay-le-Rideau sps until Carrefour rndabt. Strt ahead for 1km, site visible at 2nd rndabt. V lge, mkd, pt shd, wc; chem disp; mv service pnt; shwrs inc; EHU (10A) €4.50 (poss rev pol); lndry; shop nr; rest nr; bbq; playgrnd; red long stay; wifi; TV; dogs; phone; Eng spkn; adv bkg rec; quiet; ccard acc; games area; fishing; CKE/CCI. "Pleasant, spacious, scenic site by rv & chateau; friendly, helpful recep; poss long dist to san facs fr some pitches - cent facs have steps; san facs stretched high ssn, ltd LS; htd pool adj; site prone to flooding; recep open 0800-1200 & 1400-1700; when site clsd m'vans can stay on car park by rv o'night - no facs but well lit (enq at TO); gd loc nr to town and rests; excel." ♦ 1 Apr-31 Oct. € 19.00   2017*

BADEN *2F3* (1km SW Rural) *47.61410, -2.92540* **Camping Mané Guernehué, 52 Rue Mané er Groëz, 56870 Baden [02 97 57 02 06; fax 02 97 57 15 43; info@camping-baden.com; www.camping-baden.com]** Exit N165 sp Arradon/L'Ile aux Moines onto D101 to Baden (10km); in Baden vill turn R at camp sp immed after sharp L-hand bend; in 200m bear R at junc; site on R. Sp at both ends of vill. Lge, mkd, hdg, pt shd, terr, serviced pitches; wc (htd); chem disp; mv service pnt; fam bthrm; shwrs inc; EHU (10A) €4.70; lndry; shop; rest; snacks; bar; bbq; playgrnd; pool (covrd, htd); paddling pool; beach sand 3km; red long stay; entmnt; wifi; TV; 35% statics; dogs €3.90; phone; Eng spkn; quiet; ccard acc; sauna; jacuzzi; games rm; golf 1.5km; waterslide; fishing; bike hire; games area; tennis 600m. "Mature, pleasant site; fitness rm; gd views; excel san facs; some narr site rds; excel." ♦ 12 Apr-2 Nov. € 58.00   2014*

BAERENTHAL *5D3* (2km N Rural) *48.98170, 7.51230* **Camp Municipal Ramstein-Plage, Rue de Ramstein, 57230 Baerenthal [03 87 06 50 73; camping. ramstein@wanadoo.fr; www.baerenthal.eu]** Fr N62 turn onto D36 sp Baerenthal, site sp on lakeside. Lge, hdg, mkd, pt shd, pt sl, wc (htd); chem disp; mv service pnt; fam bthrm; shwrs inc; EHU (12A) €3.50; lndry; shop nr; rest; snacks; bar; playgrnd; pool (htd); sw nr; entmnt; 80% statics; dogs €1.90; Eng spkn; adv bkg acc; quiet; tennis; games area. "Attractive location in important ecological area; generous pitches; modern san facs; m'van o'night area; gd walks; birdwatching; conv Maginot Line; excel." ♦ 1 Apr-30 Sep. € 22.60   2015*

BAGNERES DE BIGORRE *8F2* (3km E Rural) *43.08180, 0.15139* **Camping Le Monlôo, 6 Route de la Plaine, 65200 Bagnères-de-Bigorre [05 62 95 19 65; campingmonloo@yahoo.com; www.lemonloo.com]** Fr A64 exit junc 14 onto D20/D938 to Bagnères-de-Bigorre. At traff lts on ent turn R onto D8, site on R in 1km, sp at ent. Fr Tarbes (N) on D935 turn L at 1st rndabt, L again over old rlwy line, site on R. Med, pt shd, sl, wc; chem disp; mv service pnt; shwrs inc; EHU (10A) €5.20; lndry; shop nr; playgrnd; pool; entmnt; wifi; TV; 30% statics; dogs €1.50; phone; Eng spkn; adv bkg acc; quiet; ccard acc; waterslide; tennis; CKE/CCI. "Pleasant, peaceful, scenic site; spacious & well-kept site; friendly, welcoming, helpful owners; ltd water points; gd facs, poss stretched high ssn; pleasant town; conv Pyrenean mountain passes; nice views of Pyrenees." ♦ 1 Jan-19 Oct & 10 Nov-31 Dec. € 30.70   2013*

⊞ **BAGNERES DE BIGORRE** *8F2* (2km SE Rural) *43.05566, 0.16510* **Camping La Pommeraie, 2 Ave Philadelphe, 65200 Gerde [05 62 91 32 24; fax 05 62 95 16 42; campinglapommeraie@gmail.com; www.campinglapommeraie.com]** App fr E, exit A64 junc 14 (Tournay) onto D20/D938 to Bagnères-de-Bigorre; on ent town turn L at traff lts & foll sp to site. App fr W, exit A64 junc 12 (Tarbes); leave ring rd at junc with D935 & cont to Bagnères-de-Bigorre; foll site sps fr town. Sm, hdstg, mkd, shd, pt sl, wc (htd); chem disp; mv service pnt; shwrs inc; EHU (6A); lndry; shop nr; rest nr; bbq; playgrnd; wifi; 10% statics; dogs (€1.30); phone; Eng spkn; adv bkg acc; quiet; games rm; CKE/CCI. "Mountain views; htd covrd pool 2km; friendly owners; bike hire in Bagnères; excel walking, mountain biking & touring base; gd, clean, well mainteined site; ideal tourist area." ♦ € 9.00   2017*

⊞ **BAGNERES DE BIGORRE** *8F2* (2km SE Urban) *43.07485, 0.16869* **Camping Les Palomieres, 20 Route Palomieres, 65200 Bagnères-de-Bigorre [05 62 95 59 79; fax 05 62 95 18 06; camping-les-palomieres@wanadoo.fr; www.camping-les-palomieres.com]** Take D938 fr Bagnères dir Toulouse, after 2km turn R at Haut de la Côte. Site sp. Sm, pt shd, pt sl, wc; chem disp; shwrs inc; EHU (A-6A) €1.50-4.25; lndry; shop; playgrnd; sw nr; 50% statics; dogs; adv bkg rec; quiet. "Gd views of Pyrenees; simple site; local specialities." € 8.50   2018*

BAGNERES DE BIGORRE *8F2* (13km NW Rural) *43.11196, 0.04931* **Aire Naturelle Le Cerf Volant (Dhom), 7 Cami de la Géline, 65380 Orincles [05 62 42 99 32; lecerfvolant1@yahoo.fr]** Fr Bagnères-de-Bigorre on D935; turn L onto D937 dir Lourdes; site on L opp D407. Single track app rd for 150m. Sm, pt shd, wc; chem disp; shwrs inc; EHU (15A) €2.30; lndry; playgrnd; dogs free; CKE/CCI. "Farm site - produce sold Jul-Aug; conv Lourdes & touring Pyrenees; gd, clean site; lovely site; quiet." ♦ 15 May-15 Oct. € 11.00   2015*

BAIGNES STE RADEGONDE

CAMPING DE LA VÉE ★★★
250 pitches on offer
F-61140 Bagnoles de l'Orne Normandie
Tel : 0033(0) 233 378 745 – Fax : 0033(0) 233 301 432
camping@bagnolesdelorne.com – www.campingbagnolesdelorne.com

BAGNOLES DE L'ORNE *4E1* (2km SW Urban) 48.54783, -0.41995 **Camp Municipal de la Vée,** Avenue du President Coty, 61140 Bagnoles-de-l'Orne [02 33 37 87 45; fax 02 33 30 14 32; info@campingbagnolesdelorne.com; www.campingbagnolesdelorne.com] Access fr D335 in vill of Bagnoles-Château. Or fr La Ferté-Macé on D916 for 6km sp Couterne. Well sp fr all dirs. Lge, hdg, mkd, pt shd, pt sl, wc (htd); chem disp; mv service pnt; fam bthrm; shwrs inc; EHU (10A) €3.50 (poss rev pol); gas; lndry; shop nr; rest; snacks; bar; bbq; playgrnd; wifi; TV; dogs €1.70; phone; bus adj; Eng spkn; quiet; ccard acc; golf nr; tennis nr; CKE/CCI. "Excel, well-kept, well-run site in vg location; vg, spotless facs; htd pool 1.5km; mini golf nr; easy walk to beautiful thermal spa town & lake; free bus to town cent at site ent; forest walks; archery nrby; gd for dogs; gd value; town bus €1 per day." ♦ 3 Mar-11 Nov. € 18.00   2018*

See advertisement

"I need an on-site restaurant"
We do our best to make sure site information is correct, but it is always best to check any must-have facilities are still available or will be open during your visit.

BAGNOLS SUR CEZE *10E2* (2km N Rural) 44.17585, 4.63540 **Camping La Coquille,** Route de Carmignan, 30200 Bagnols-sur-Cèze [04 66 89 03 05; fax 04 66 89 59 86; jose.gimeno@free.fr; www.campinglacoquille.com] Head N fr Bagnols-sur-Cèze over rv bdge turn R at Total stn, site 2km on RH side. Sm, pt shd, wc cont; chem disp; shwrs inc; EHU (4-6A) €4-4.50; lndry; shop nr; rest; pool; dogs; adv bkg rec; ccard acc; canoe hire; fishing; CKE/CCI. "Site under military aircraft flightpath, otherwise gd, friendly, family-run site." 24 Apr-15 Sep. € 34.00   2013*

BAGNOLS SUR CEZE *10E2* (3km NE Rural) 44.17358, 4.63694 **Camping Les Genêts d'Or,** Chemin de Carmigan, 30200 Bagnols-sur-Cèze [04 66 89 58 67; info@camping-genets-dor.com; www.camping-genets-dor.com] N fr Bagnols on N86 over rv bdge, turn R into D360 immed after Total stn. Foll sp to site on rv. Med, hdstg, mkd, pt shd, pt sl, wc (htd); chem disp; fam bthrm; shwrs inc; EHU (6A) €5.50 (poss rev pol); gas; lndry; shop; rest; snacks; bar; playgrnd; pool (htd); paddling pool; entmnt; wifi; 10% statics; dogs (except Jul/Aug); Eng spkn; adv bkg req; quiet; ccard acc; games rm; fishing 2km; games area. "Excel, clean site; welcoming Dutch owners; gd pool; canoeing 2km; wildlife in rv; gd rest; highly rec." ♦ 20 Apr-20 Sep. € 33.00   2016*

BAGNOLS SUR CEZE *10E2* (8km NW Rural) 44.18865, 4.52448 **Camping Les Cascades,** Route de Donnat, 30200 La Roque-sur-Cèze [04 66 82 72 97; fax 04 66 82 68 51; infos@campinglescascades.com; www.campinglescascades.com] Fr Bagnols take D6 W twd Alès. After 4km turn N on D143 & foll sp to La Roque-sur-Cèze. Site on R in 7km. App fr N not rec. Long narr bdge (2.3m). Med, pt shd, pt sl, wc (htd); chem disp; mv service pnt; fam bthrm; shwrs inc; EHU (6-10A) €4.10-4.30; gas; lndry; shop; rest; snacks; bar; bbq; playgrnd; pool (htd); entmnt; wifi; TV; dogs €1.85; adv bkg acc; quiet; boating; rv fishing adj; tennis. "Tranquil site; modern san facs." 19 Apr-13 Oct. € 44.00   2013*

BAIGNES STE RADEGONDE *7B2* (1km SW Rural) 45.38187, -0.23862 **FFCC Camp Municipal, Le Plein,** 16360 Baignes-Ste-Radegonde [05 45 78 79 95 or 05 45 78 40 04 (Mairie); point.i@live.fr; www.baignes-sainte-radegonde.fr] Fr N10 turn W onto D2 to Baignes; site well sp on rvside. Sm, pt shd, wc; fam bthrm; shwrs inc; EHU (6A) €3; lndry; shop nr; adv bkg acc; quiet; ccard acc; tennis nr; CKE/CCI. "Warden calls pm; excel new san facs (2018); chem disp in vill; attractive sm town nr cycle track; excel." 1 Apr-31 Oct. € 27.00   2018*

BAILLEUL

BAILLEUL *3A3* (4km N Rural) *50.76160, 2.74956*
Camping Les Saules (Notteau), 453 Route du Mont Noir, 59270 Bailleul [03 28 49 13 75; www.ferme-des-saules.com] N fr Lille on A25 exit junc 10 & head N into Bailleul cent; in town cent at traff lts turn R onto D23/N375; after 400m turn L on D23; in 2km just bef Belgian border turn L onto D223. Site on L in 300m. Sm, hdstg, pt shd, wc; chem disp; shwrs inc; EHU (6A) €3.35; shop; bbq; playgrnd; 90% statics; dogs; Eng spkn; quiet; CKE/CCI. "Farm site; friendly owner; conv Calais, Dunkerque & WW1 sites; lovely, excel site, highly rec well kept and comfortable site; 1st class farm shop; unkempt in LS; 2 pin adapter ess; new san facs (2017)." 1 Apr-31 Oct. € 11.50 2017*

BAIN DE BRETAGNE *2F4* (1km SE Rural) *47.83000, -1.67083* **Camping du Lac, Route de Launay, 35470 Bain-de-Bretagne [02 99 43 85 67; info@campinglac.fr; www.campinglac.fr]** Fr Bain-de-Bretagne take N772 SE dir Châteaubriant, foll sp. Up hill & turn R into narr lane & foll site sp; narr ent. Not rec to tow thro Bain-de-Bretagne. Med, hdg, mkd, pt shd, wc; chem disp; mv service pnt; shwrs inc; EHU (10A) €2.50; shop nr; rest; snacks; bar; playgrnd; pool (covrd, htd); sw nr; 10% statics; dogs €2; phone; Eng spkn; quiet; sauna; CKE/CCI. "Pretty site with lake views; friendly, helpful new owners (2010) - much improved site; attractive sm town; many leisure facs in walking dist; conv NH; sailing school nr; lovely location, conv for a'route, Vitre & Fougeres; modern & clean facs, but stretched in high ssn." ♦ 15 Mar-15 Oct. € 24.00 2014*

BAIN DE BRETAGNE *2F4* (13km W Rural) *47.8200, -1.8299* **Camp Municipal Le Port, Rue de Camping, 35480 Guipry [02 99 34 72 90 (Mairie) or 02 99 34 28 26; fax 02 99 34 28 06]** W fr Bain-de-Bretagne on D772, cross rv at Messac; cont on D772 sharp L at Leader supmkt into Ave du Port; site sp bef ent Guipry. NB Do not app after dark as rv is at end of app rd. V sharp turn at Leader supmkt into Ave du Camping. Med, mkd, hdg, pt shd, wc; mv service pnt; shwrs; EHU (10A) €3 (poss long lead req); shop nr; rest nr; playgrnd; rv fishing; CKE/CCI. "Excel, pretty site; friendly; warden on duty am & late pm; barrier 1.9m locked at times but phone for help or go to pitch 30; delightful rv walks & cycle paths; cruising & hire boats avail; nr classic cars museum; phone Mairie for warden's number, who calls early PM." ♦ Easter-15 Oct. € 10.00 2018*

BALARUC LES BAINS *10F1* (0km NE Coastal) *43.44084, 3.68320* **Camp Municipal du Pech d'Ay, Ave de la Gare, 34540 Balaruc-les-Bains [04 67 48 50 34; pechday@mairie-balaruc-les-bains.fr; www.herault-tourisme.com]** Exit N113 to Balaruc-les-Bains; foll sp Centre Commercial & then head for prom. Site on prom. Lge, mkd, pt shd, pt sl, wc (htd); chem disp; mv service pnt; shwrs; EHU (10A) €3.40; shop nr; rest nr; bar nr; playgrnd; beach shgl nr; bus; Eng spkn; adv bkg rec; CKE/CCI. "Delightful holiday resort; busy site all ssn, rec arr early; vg, clean san facs poss stretched peak timesshops adj; many gd rests adj; thermal baths in vill; bus to Sète." ♦ 20 Apr-14 Dec. € 16.00 2013*

BALAZUC *9D2* (1km NE Rural) *44.51199, 4.38667*
FFCC Camping La Falaise, Hameau Les Salles, 07120 Balazuc [04 75 37 74 27; www.camping-balazuc.com] Sp on D579 on rvside. Sm, hdg, shd, pt sl, wc; chem disp; fam bthrm; shwrs inc; EHU (6A) €3.80; gas; lndry; shop; snacks; bar; playgrnd; dogs €1.50; phone; Eng spkn; adv bkg acc; rv; canoe hire; CKE/CCI. "Site beside Rv Ardèche; helpful and friendly owners; vg." ♦ 1 Apr-30 Sep. € 21.00 2013*

BALAZUC *9D2* (2km E Rural) *44.50778, 4.40333*
Camping Le Chamadou, Mas de Chaussy, 07120 Balazuc [08 20 36 61 97 or 07 87 64 34 77 (mob); fax 04 75 37 08 04; infos@camping-le-chamadou.com; www.camping-le-chamadou.com] Fr Ruoms foll D579 dir Aubenas. After approx 9km turn R under viaduct, site sp. Keep R up narr rd to site. App recep on foot fr car pk. Med, hdg, hdstg, pt shd, pt sl, wc (htd); chem disp; fam bthrm; shwrs inc; EHU (10A) €4.20 (some rev pol); lndry; shop; snacks; bar; bbq (elec); playgrnd; pool; paddling pool; entmnt; wifi; TV; 10% statics; dogs €2.60; phone; Eng spkn; adv bkg rec; quiet; ccard acc; canoe hire; kayak hire; waterslide; CKE/CCI. "Excel, well-run, family site; panoramic views; most pitches spacious." 1 Apr-31 Oct. € 24.00 2017*

BALBIGNY *9B1* (3km NW Rural) *45.82558, 4.16996*
Camping La Route Bleue, Route D56 du Lac de Villerest, Pralery, 42510 Balbigny [04 77 27 24 97 or 06 85 52 98 66 (mob); camping.balbigny@wanadoo.fr; camping-de-la-route-bleue.fr] Fr N on D1082, take 1st R after a'route (A89/72) junc N of Balbigny onto D56. Fr S on D1082, turn L at RH bend on N o'skirts of Balbigny, D56, sp Lac de Villerest & St Georges-de-Baroille. Well sp. Med, hdg, mkd, pt shd, pt sl, wc; chem disp; mv service pnt; fam bthrm; shwrs inc; EHU (10A) (poss long lead req); lndry; shop nr; rest; snacks; bar; bbq; playgrnd; pool; paddling pool; red long stay; adv bkg acc; quiet; ccard acc; fishing; games rm; CKE/CCI. "Nice site on rv bank; views over rv some pitches; helpful, friendly & welcoming staff; san facs updated (2017); sports complex adj; ltd EHU; extra for twin axles; conv A72; excel; lovely area; lge pitches; gd NH; ok long stay; fishing." ♦ 15 Mar-31 Oct. € 22.00 2017*

BALLEROY *1D4* (1km NE Rural) *49.18680, -0.82463*
Camping Le Clos De Balleroy, Route de Castillon, 14490 Balleroy [02 31 21 41 48; info@camping-leclos deballeroy.fr; www.camping-leclosdeballeroy.fr] Fr N13 junc 37 turn S onto D572. After 6.8km in Le Tronquay turn L onto D73, sp Castillon. Site on R in 5km bef Balleroy. Sm, pt shd, wc; chem disp; mv service pnt; shwrs; EHU (16A); lndry; shop; bar; pool; games area. "Conv for Normandy coast and Bayeux; gd." 15 Mar-15 Nov. € 24.00 2016*

BANDOL *10F3* (3km NW Rural) *43.15980, 5.72905*
Camping Le Clos Ste Thérèse, Route de Bandol, 83270 St Cyr-sur-Mer [04 94 32 12 21; fax 04 94 32 29 62; camping@clos-therese.com; www.clos-therese.com] Fr Bandol take D559 twd St Cyr & Marseilles. Site on R after 3km. Caution - site ent sharp U turn fr rd. Site service rds steep & narr; not suitable lge vans. Med, shd, terr, wc (htd); chem disp; shwrs; EHU (6-10A) €4-5.20; gas; lndry; shop nr; rest; snacks; bar; playgrnd; pool (htd); paddling pool; beach sand 4km; entmnt; TV; 30% statics; dogs €2.30; adv bkg rec; golf nr; tennis nr; horseriding nr. "Many beaches & beauty spots in area; tractor will site c'vans." ♦
5 Apr-30 Sep. € 22.50   2013*

BANON *10E3* (2km S Rural) *44.02607, 5.63088*
Camping L'Epi Bleu, Les Gravières, 04150 Banon [04 92 73 30 30 or 06 15 61 68 63 (mob); campingepibleu@aol.com; www.campingepibleu.com] Fr D4100 8km S of Forcalquier turn R onto D5 N thro St Michel-L'Observatoire & Revest twd Banon (approx 25km). Turn L on D51 twds Simiane-la-Rotunde. Site on R in 500m immed bef town, sp at junc. Med, shd, wc; mv service pnt; fam bthrm; shwrs inc; EHU (10A) €5; lndry; shop; rest; snacks; bar; bbq; playgrnd; pool (htd); paddling pool; entmnt; TV; 70% statics; dogs €4; Eng spkn; adv bkg acc; quiet; games area; CKE/CCI. "Vg, wooded site; pleasant owners; gd walking & cycling tours; access to some pitches diff for lge o'fits; san fac tired but clean (2015); uphill 30m walk to vill with sm supmkt." ♦ 4 Apr-30 Sep. € 30.00   2015*

BANYULS SUR MER *10H1* (2km SW Rural) *42.47665, 3.11904* Camp Municipal La Pinède, Ave Guy Malé, 66650 Banyuls-sur-Mer [04 68 88 32 13; fax 04 68 88 32 48; camp.banyuls@banyuls-sur-mer.com; www.banyuls-sur-mer.com] On D914 foll sp to Banyuls-sur-Mer; turn R at camping sp at cent of sea-front by town hall; foll sp to site. Lge, hdg, mkd, pt shd, pt sl, terr, wc; chem disp; mv service pnt; shwrs; EHU (4-13A) €2-3; lndry; shop nr; snacks; playgrnd; beach shgl 1km; dogs; Eng spkn; quiet; ccard acc; CKE/CCI. "Busy, friendly site; spacious pitches, some with sea view; narr site rds; vg, clean facs." ♦ 23 Feb-12 Nov.
€ 17.50   2018*

BAR LE DUC *6E1* (2km E Urban) *48.77340, 5.17415*
FFCC Camp Municipal du Château de Marbeaumont, Rue du Stade, off Rue de St Mihiel, 55000 Bar-le-Duc [03 29 79 17 33 (TO) or 03 29 79 11 13 (LS); fax 03 29 79 21 95; barleduc.tourisme@wanadoo.fr; www.tourisme-barleduc.com] Fr town cent foll Camping sps. Rue de St Mihiel is pt of D1916 dir Verdun. Fr NW on D994/D694 or fr SE on N1135, at rndabt turn E onto D1916 sp Metz, Verdun & St Mihiel. In 200m turn L into Rue du Stade sp Camping. Site on L in 100m. Sm, pt shd, wc; chem disp; shwrs; EHU (16A) €3 (poss long lead req); lndry; shop nr. "Barrier clsd 1100-1500; delightful site in grnds of chateau; friendly & helpful warden; clean, modern san facs; no twin axles; check gate opening times; lovely walk into historic town; gd NH; vg site; nice open plan site."
1 May-15 Oct. € 13.00   2018*

BARCELONNETTE

BARBIERES *9C2* (1km SE Rural) *44.94470, 5.15100*
Camping Le Gallo-Romain, 1090 Route de Col de Tourniol, 26300 Barbières [04 75 47 44 07; info@legalloromain.net; www.legalloromain.net]
Exit A49 junc 7 onto D149 dir Marches & Barbières. Go thro vill & ascend Rte du Col de Tourniol for 2km, site on R, well sp. Med, mkd, pt shd, pt sl, terr, wc; chem disp; fam bthrm; shwrs inc; EHU (6A) €3.75; lndry; shop; rest; snacks; bar; bbq; playgrnd; pool; entmnt; wifi; TV; 15% statics; dogs €5.50; phone; Eng spkn; adv bkg acc; quiet; CKE/CCI. "Mountain setting; welcoming, friendly, helpful Dutch owners; ltd facs LS; gd; nice location." ♦
22 Apr-30 Sep. € 46.00   2013*

⊞ **BARCARES, LE** *10G1* (1km SW Coastal) *42.77462, 3.02207* Camping L'Europe, Route de St Laurent, 66420 Le Barcarès [04 68 86 15 36; fax 04 68 86 47 88; reception@europe-camping.com; www.europe-camping.com] Exit A9 at Perpignan N & take D83 sp Le Barcarès. After 9km turn R on D81 sp Canet Plage, L on D90 sp Le Barcarès. Site on R. Lge, mkd, hdg, shd, wc; shwrs inc; EHU (16A) inc; gas; lndry; shop; rest; snacks; bar; playgrnd; pool; red long stay; entmnt; 50% statics; dogs €8; Eng spkn; adv bkg acc; tennis; archery; waterslide; CKE/CCI. "Gd location; tidy pitches, all have individual san facs (tired early ssn 2010); ltd facs LS; gd cycle rte to beach & shops; disco; gd winter NH." ♦ € 21.00   2017*

BARCARES, LE *10G1* (1km SW Coastal) *42.78094, 3.02267* Yelloh! Village Le Pré Catalan, Route de St Laurent, 66420 Le Barcarès [04 68 86 12 60; fax 04 68 86 40 17; info@precatalan.com; www.precatalan.com or www.yellohvillage.co.uk]
Exit A9 junc 41 onto D83; app Le Barcarès turn R onto D81, then L onto D90 to Le Barcarès, site sp. Lge, shd, wc; shwrs inc; EHU (6A) €4; gas; shop; rest; snacks; bar; playgrnd; pool (htd); paddling pool; beach sand 1km; entmnt; wifi; TV; dogs €3; phone; adv bkg rec; quiet; tennis; games area; games rm. 14 May-17 Sep.
€ 32.00   2012*

BARCELONNETTE *9D4* (1km W Rural) *44.38393, 6.64281* Camping du Plan, 52 Ave Emile Aubert, 04400 Barcelonnette [04 92 81 08 11; legaudissart@orange.fr; www.campingduplan.fr]
Exit town on D902 sp Col d'Allos & Col de la Cayolle. Site on R. Sm, mkd, pt shd, wc; shwrs inc; EHU (3-10A) €2.95-4.25 gas; lndry; shop; rest; dogs €1; adv bkg acc; quiet. "Garden site; helpful owners; unisex san facs; lovely views & walks; pleasant vill; excel."
25 May-30 Sep. € 13.00   2013*

BARCELONNETTE *9D4* (9km W Rural) *44.39686, 6.54605* Domaine Loisirs de l'Ubaye, Vallée de l'Ubaye, 04340 Barcelonnette [04 92 81 01 96; fax 04 92 81 92 53; info@loisirsubaye.com; www.loisirsubaye.com] Site on S side of D900. Lge, mkd, shd, terr, wc; shwrs inc; EHU (6A) €3.50; gas; lndry; shop; rest; snacks; bar; playgrnd; pool (htd); red long stay; entmnt; TV; dogs €3.50; phone; watersports; bike hire; CKE/CCI. "Magnificent scenery; gd site; friendly."
♦ 15 May-15 Oct. € 29.50   2016*

BARFLEUR

BARFLEUR *1C4* **(1km NW Urban/Coastal) 49.67564, -1.26645 Camp Municipal La Blanche Nef, 12 Chemin de la Masse, 50760 Gatteville-le-Phare [02 33 23 15 40; fax 02 33 23 95 14; www.camping-barfleur.fr]** Foll main rd to harbour; half-way on L side of harbour & turn L at mkd gap in car pk; cross sm side-rd & foll site sp on sea wall; site visible on L in 300m. Site accessible only fr S (Barfleur). Med, unshd, pt sl, wc (htd); chem disp; mv service pnt; shwrs inc; EHU (6-10A); lndry; shop nr; snacks; bar; playgrnd; beach sand adj; wifi; 45% statics; dogs €2.04; Eng spkn; adv bkg acc; quiet; ccard acc; CKE/CCI. "Gd sized pitches; vg facs; lovely site; sea views; gd beach; gd birdwatching, walking, cycling; m'vans all year; walking dist to fishing vill; clean washing facs; bread van at 9am." ♦ 15 Feb-15 Nov. € 21.40   2018*

⊞ BARFLEUR *1C4* **(1km NW Coastal) 49.67971, -1.27364 Camping La Ferme du Bord de Mer, 43 Route du Val de Saire, 50760 Gatteville-Phare [060 895 2434; fax 02 33 54 78 99; camping.gatteville@gmail.com; www.camping-gatteville.fr]** On D901 fr Cherbourg; on o'skts of Barfleur turn L onto D116 for Gatteville-Phare. Site on R in 1km. Sm, mkd, hdg, pt shd, pt sl, serviced pitches; wc; chem disp; shwrs inc; EHU (3-10A) €3.40-5.30; gas; lndry; shop nr; rest; snacks; bar; playgrnd; beach sand adj; entmnt; 25% statics; dogs €1.45; phone; quiet; games rm. "CL-type site; sheltered beach; coastal path to vill & lighthouse; conv ferries (30 mins); Sep 2002 member reported high-strength poison against rodents in field adj site - no warning notices displayed, beware children or dogs; gd." ♦ € 15.00   2016*

BARNEVILLE CARTERET *1C4* **(4km SE Coastal) 49.35952, -1.74879 Camping du Golf, Saint Jean de la Rivière, 50270 Barneville-Cartere [02 33 04 78 90; fax 09 70 63 21 92; contact@camping-du-golf.fr; www.camping-du-golf.co.uk]** Fr Barneville-Carteret, turn W on D130, after 1.5km turn L. Site on R after 1.5km. Site well sp fr Barneville-Carteret. Lge, hdg, mkd, unshd, wc; chem disp; shwrs inc; EHU (6A) inc; gas; lndry; shop; rest nr; snacks; bar; playgrnd; pool (covrd, htd); beach sandy 1km; twin axles; entmnt; wifi; dogs (€4); Eng spkn; adv bkg req; quiet; ccard acc; games rm; CKE/CCI. "Gd quiet site with clean facs; 18 hole course; horse ridding nrby." ♦ 1 Apr-1 Nov. € 37.00   2017*

BARROU *4H2* **(0km S Rural) 46.86500, 0.77100 FFCC Camping Les Rioms, Les Rioms, 37350 Barrou [02 47 94 53 07; campinglesrioms@orange.fr; www.lesrioms.com]** Fr D750 Descartes to La Roche-Posay rd turn R at sp Camping at ent to Barrou vill. Site sp. NB Site has barriers, phone if clsd. Sm, mkd, hdg, pt shd, wc; chem disp; shwrs inc; EHU (16A) €4; lndry; shop nr; rest nr; bbq; playgrnd; pool (htd); 35% statics; dogs free; Eng spkn; adv bkg acc; quiet; CKE/CCI. "Pleasant, peaceful site on bank of Rv Creuse; clean san facs; friendly owners; gd pool; excel." ♦ 30 Mar-26 Oct. € 10.50   2013*

BASTIA *10G2* **(5km N Coastal) 42.74039, 9.45982 Camping Les Orangers, Licciola, 20200 Miomo [06 12 53 73 33; fax 04 95 33 23 65; www.camping-lesorangers.com]** Foll main coast rd D80 N 4km fr ferry. Site well sp on L of rd. Sm, shd, wc; shwrs; EHU; shop; rest; snacks; bar; beach shgl adj; TV; quiet; CKE/CCI. "Poss run down LS; friendly owners; vg rest; site ent tight for lge o'fits; no m'vans (2011); poss unrel opening dates." 1 Apr-30 Sep. € 19.00   2012*

> ### "Satellite navigation makes touring much easier"
>
> Remember most sat navs don't know if you're towing or in a larger vehicle – always use yours alongside maps and site directions.

BASTIA *10G2* **(11km S Coastal) 42.62922, 9.46835 Camping San Damiano, Lido de la Marana, 20620 Biguglia [04 95 33 68 02; fax 04 95 30 84 10; san.damiano@wanadoo.fr; www.campingsandamiano.com]** S fr Bastia on N193 for 4km. Turn SE onto Lagoon Rd (sp Lido de Marana). Site on L in 7km. Lge, pt shd, wc; chem disp; fam bthrm; shwrs inc; EHU (6A) €3.40; lndry; shop; rest; playgrnd; pool; beach sandy adj; red long stay; dogs €0.90; Eng spkn; ccard acc; games area; games rm; CKE/CCI. "San facs basic but clean; cycle path." ♦ 1 Apr-31 Oct. € 22.00   2013*

BASTIDE DE SEROU, LA *8G3* **(1km S Rural) 43.00150, 1.44472 Camping L'Arize, Route de Nescus, 09240 La Bastide-de-Sérou [05 61 65 81 51; fax 05 61 65 83 34; mail@camping-arize.com; www.camping-arize.com]** Fr Foix on D117 on ent La Bastide-de-Sérou turn L at TO/Gendarmerie on D15 sp Nescus, site 1km on R. Med, mkd, hdg, pt shd, serviced pitches; wc; chem disp; mv service pnt; fam bthrm; shwrs inc; EHU (6A) inc (poss rev pol); gas; lndry; shop; rest nr; snacks; playgrnd; pool; sw nr; entmnt; wifi; 10% statics; dogs €2; Eng spkn; adv bkg acc; ccard acc; golf nr; fishing; horseriding adj; golf 5km; bike hire; CKE/CCI. "Pleasant, scenic site on bank Rv Arize; modern facs; gd mkd walking/cycle rtes." ♦ 8 Mar-12 Nov. € 35.00   2013*

BAUD *2F3* **(7km W Rural) 47.88239, 3.10818 Camp Municipal de Pont Augan, Pont Augan, 56150 Baud [02 97 51 04 74; camping.p.augan@live.fr; camping-pontaugan.com]** Fr Baud, W on D6. Site on R on ent vill. Sm, mkd, hdg, pt shd, wc (htd); chem disp; mv service pnt; fam bthrm; shwrs inc; EHU (10A) €3; lndry; shop; rest nr; bar nr; bbq; playgrnd; wifi; dogs; Eng spkn; adv bkg acc; quiet; canoeing adj; fishing adj; games area; bike hire; CKE/CCI. "Peaceful site; barrier & office ltd opening hrs but parking area avail; warden calls morning & teatime; ltd groceries; 4 gites on site; vg." ♦ 1 Apr-30 Sep. € 15.00   2018*

BAUGE *4G1* (1km E Rural) *47.53889, -0.09637* **Camp Municipal du Pont des Fées, Chemin du Pont des Fées, 49150 Baugé [02 41 89 14 79 or 02 41 89 18 07 (Mairie); fax 02 41 84 12 19; camping@ville-bauge.fr; www.ville-bauge.fr]** Fr Saumur traveling N D347/D938 turn 1st R in Baugé onto D766. Foll camping sp to site by sm rv; ent bef rv bdge. Sm, mkd, hdg, pt shd, wc; chem disp; mv service pnt; shwrs inc; EHU (4A) €2.70; lndry; shop nr; bbq; phone; adv bkg acc; quiet; ccard acc; fishing; tennis 150m. "Excel countryside; pleasant, well-kept site; pools 150m; obliging wardens; Aldi within walking dist; camping car site adj; excel municipal well kept site." 15 May-15 Sep. € 13.50   2015*

BAULE, LA *2G3* (2km NE Rural) *47.29833, -2.35722* **Airotel Camping La Roseraie, 20 Ave Jean Sohier, Route du Golf, 44500 La Baule-Escoublac [02 40 60 46 66; fax 02 40 60 11 84; camping@laroseraie.com; www.laroseraie.com]** Take N171 fr St Nazaire to La Baule. In La Baule-Escoublac turn R at x-rds by church, site in 300m on R; sp fr La Baule cent. Lge, mkd, hdg, hdstg, pt shd, wc; chem disp; mv service pnt; fam bthrm; shwrs inc; EHU (6-10A) €5.50-€7.50; gas; lndry; shop nr; rest; snacks; bar; bbq; playgrnd; pool (covrd, htd); paddling pool; beach sand 2km; red long stay; entmnt; wifi; TV; 80% statics; dogs €5; phone; Eng spkn; adv bkg acc; quiet; ccard acc; games rm; waterslide; watersports; tennis; fishing; games area; CKE/CCI. "Gd site & facs; sm pitches; fitness rm; clean unisex san facs; ltd facs LS; easy walk into La Baule-Escoublac; excel beach nrby; vg." ♦ 1 Apr-25 Sep. € 40.00   2012*

BAUME LES DAMES *6G2* (1km S Rural) *47.34050, 6.35752* **Comping du Complex Touristique (Domaine d'Aucroix), Quai du Canal, 25110 Baume-les-Dames [03 81 84 38 89; fax 03 81 80 29 53; www.domainedaucroix.fr]** Fr D683 in Baume-les-Dames turn S onto D50, cross canal & turn W. Site sp. Sm, hdstg, pt shd, wc; chem disp; shwrs; EHU (16A) inc; lndry; 10% statics; dogs €3; quiet. "Peaceful site; gd NH/long stay, v conv fr m/way." 1 May-30 Sep. € 17.00   2013*

BAUME LES DAMES *6G2* (6km S Rural) *47.32506, 6.36127* **Camping L'Ile, 1 Rue de Pontarlier, 25110 Pont-les-Moulins [03 81 84 15 23; info@campingdelile.fr; www.campingdelile.fr]** S fr Baume-les-Dames on D50, site on L on ent Pont-les-Moulins. Sm, pt shd, wc; chem disp; mv service pnt; shwrs inc; EHU (6A) €2.50; gas; lndry; shop nr; rest nr; bar nr; playgrnd; red long stay; 10% statics; dogs free; Eng spkn; adv bkg acc; CKE/CCI. "Tidy, basic site in pleasant setting by Rv Cusancin; helpful, friendly owner; bread 100m; bar 500m; pool 6km; clean, basic facs; gd." 1 May-7 Sep. € 11.50   2016*

BAYEUX *3D1* (1km N Urban) *49.28392, -0.69760* **Camp Municipal des Bords de L'Aure, Blvd d'Eindhoven, 14400 Bayeux [02 31 92 08 43; campingmunicipal@mairie-bayeux.fr; www.mairie-bayeux.fr]** Site sp off Périphérique d'Eindhoven (Bayeux by-pass, D613). Fr W (Cherbourg) exit N13 junc 38, turn L over N13, then R onto D613 thro Vaucelles. At rndabt cont on D613 (3rd exit) Blvd d'Eindhoven. Site on R immed after traff lts, almost opp Briconaute DIY store. Fr E (Caen) on N13 exit junc 36 onto D613 N; foll ring rd across 2 rndabts, 4 traff lts, site on L opp Bayeux town sp. Lge, hdstg, hdg, pt shd, wc; chem disp; mv service pnt; shwrs inc; EHU (6A) €3.66 (poss rev pol); gas; lndry; shop; playgrnd; red long stay; wifi; dogs; phone; Eng spkn; adv bkg req; CKE/CCI. "Excel, well-kept site; indoor pool adj; avoid perimeter pitches (narr hdstgs & rd noise); no twin axles; office open LS; gd footpath to town along stream; Bayeux festival 1st w/end July; conv ferries; lge mkt Sat; new san facs & lndry facs (2018)." ♦ 30 Mar-4 Nov. € 21.00   2018*

BAYEUX *3D1* (18km SE Rural) *49.15722, -0.76018* **Camping Caravaning Escapade, Rue de l'église, 14490 CAHAGNOLLES [02 31 21 63 59; escapadecamping@orange.fr; www.campingescapade.net]** Fr Saint Paul du Varnay take D99 Cahagnolles on the L; foll rd for aprrox 2.5km; turn L & aft church campsite on R. Med, mkd, pt shd, wc; chem disp; shwrs inc; EHU (10A) €3.90; lndry; bar; bbq; pool (htd); wifi; dogs €2.70; adv bkg acc; ccard acc. "Lovely site; well looked after & cared for; clean san facs; friendly owners & staff; recep rm for events; pt of Flower Campings chain." 1 Apr-15 Oct. € 35.00   2014*

BAYEUX *3D1* (7km SE Rural) *49.24840, -0.60245* **Camping Le Château de Martragny, 52 Hameau Saint-Léger, 14740 Martragny [02 31 80 21 40; fax 02 31 08 14 91; chateau.martragny@wanadoo.fr; www.chateau-martragny.com or www.chateau-martragny.fr]** Fr Caen going NW on N13 dir Bayeux/Cherbourg, leave at Martragny/Carcagny exit. Strt on & take 2nd R (past turn for Martragny/Creully) into site & chateau grnds. Fr Bayeux after leaving N13 (Martragny/Carcagny), go L over bdge to end of rd, turn L then take 2nd R into Chateau grnds. Lge, mkd, pt shd, pt sl, wc; chem disp; mv service pnt; fam bthrm; shwrs inc; EHU (15A) €5 (long lead poss req, poss rev pol); gas; lndry; shop; snacks; bar; bbq; playgrnd; pool (htd); paddling pool; entmnt; wifi; TV; dogs €0.50; Eng spkn; adv bkg acc; quiet; ccard acc; games rm; tennis; fishing; horseriding 500m; CKE/CCI. "Popular, attractive, 1st class site on lawns of chateau; attractive area; relaxed atmosphere; friendly, helpful staff; new superb, modern san facs (2013); gd rest; no o'fits over 8m; poss muddy when wet; conv cemetaries; D-Day beaches 15km; Sat mkt in Bayeux; conv Caen ferry; excel." ♦ 2 May-12 Sep. € 36.00   2014*

BAYEUX

⊞ **BAYEUX** *3D1* (8km SE Rural) *49.25041, -0.59251*
Camping Le Manoir de l'Abbaye (Godfroy), 15 Rue de Creully, 14740 Martragny [02 31 80 25 95; yvette. godfroy@libertysurf.fr; http://godfroy.pagesperso-orange.fr] Take N13 Bayeux, Caen dual c'way for 7km, fork R sp Martagny. Over dual c'way L at T-junc, then 1st R sp D82 Martragny & Creully site on R 500m. Sharp L steep turn into site. Sm, pt shd, wc; chem disp; shwrs inc; EHU (15A) €4.(poss rev pol); lndry; dogs €2.30; Eng spkn; adv bkg acc; CKE/CCI. "Peaceful, relaxing, well-kept site; lovely grnds; helpful, welcoming owners; steps to ltd san facs; meals & wine avail on request; winter storage; conv Ouistreham ferries; highly rec; wc, shwr, kitchen fac's in same rm; v restful; some elec hookups rev polarity."
♦ € 16.00   2014*

BAYEUX *3D1* (9km NW Rural) *49.33120, -0.80240*
Camping Reine Mathilde, 14400 Etréham [02 31 21 76 55; fax 02 31 22 18 33; campingreinemathilde@gmail.com; www.camping-normandie-rm.fr] NW fr Bayeux on D6 turn L to Etréham (D100); site 3km (sp). Or W fr Bayeux on N13 for 8km, exist junc 38. At x-rds 1.5km after vill of Tour-en-Bessin turn R on D206 to Etréham & bear L at church. Med, mkd, hdg, pt shd, wc (htd); chem disp; fam bthrm; shwrs inc; EHU (6A) €4.70; lndry; shop; rest; snacks; bar; playgrnd; pool (htd); paddling pool; beach sand 5km; entmnt; wifi; TV; 15% statics; dogs €2.50; phone; Eng spkn; adv bkg acc; quiet; fishing 1km; bike hire; CKE/CCI. "Well-kept, attractive site; lge, well spaced hdg pitches; mv service pnt nr; app rds quite narr; friendly, helpful warden; gd, clean san facs; conv D-Day beaches etc; excel."
♦ 1 Apr-30 Sep. € 26.50   2014*

BAYONNE *8F1* (11km NE Rural) *43.52820, -1.39157*
Camping Lou P'tit Poun, 110 Ave du Quartier Neuf, 40390 St Martin-de-Seignanx [05 59 56 55 79; fax 05 59 56 53 71; contact@louptitpoun.com; www.louptitpoun.com] Fr Bordeaux exit A63 junc 6 dir Bayonne Nord; then take D817 dir Pau & St Martin-de-Seignanx; site sp on R in 7km. Lge, mkd, hdg, pt shd, terr, serviced pitches; wc; chem disp; mv service pnt; fam bthrm; shwrs inc; EHU (10A) inc; gas; lndry; shop nr; rest; snacks; bar; bbq (elec, gas); playgrnd; pool; paddling pool; red long stay; entmnt; TV; 17% statics; dogs €5.90; phone; Eng spkn; adv bkg acc; ccard acc; games area; games rm; tennis; CKE/CCI. "Charming, spacious, family-run site; gd sized pitches; friendly staff; gd clean san facs; ltd facs LS; conv Biarritz, St Jean-de-Luz & a'route; excel." ♦ 9 Jun-15 Sep. € 40.00   2017*

BAYONNE *8F1* (8km NE Rural) *43.54858, -1.40381*
Aire Naturelle L'Arrayade (Barret), 280 Chemin Pradillan, 40390 St Martin-de-Seignanx [05 59 56 10 60; www.seignanx-tourisme.com] On D26 midway bet D810 & D817, 3km W of St Martin. (Opp tall crenellated building). Sm, pt shd, pt sl, wc; shwrs; EHU €2.50 (long lead rec); lndry; bbq; playgrnd; dogs; quiet. "Delightful little site; warm welcome; helpful owner; simple facs poss stretched high ssn; gd base for exploring Basque country." 1 Jun-30 Sep. € 12.00   2013*

BAZAS *7D2* (2km SE Rural) *44.43139, -0.20167*
Campsite Le Paradis de Bazas, Route de Casteljaloux, 33430 Bazas [05 56 65 13 17; fax 05 56 25 90 52; paradis@franceloc.fr; www.camping-paradis-bazas.fr] Exit A62 junc 3 onto N524 twd Bazas, then D655. Cont thro town cent & foll sp Casteljaloux/Grignols. Site sp on R. Sm, hdg, mkd, pt shd, pt sl, wc; chem disp; mv service pnt; fam bthrm; shwrs inc; EHU (6-16A) €3.25-4.90; gas; lndry; shop nr; bar; playgrnd; pool (htd); red long stay; TV; 6% statics; dogs €3 (free LS); Eng spkn; adv bkg acc; quiet; CKE/CCI. "Pleasant, relaxed, well-kept site in picturesque location; views of chateau & town; friendly, helpful staff; san facs v smart but poss stretched high ssn; pleasant walk/cycle track to interesting, walled town; vineyards nr." ♦ 1 Apr-29 Sep. € 25.00   2017*

BEAUGENCY *4F2* (1km E Rural) *47.77628, 1.64294*
Camp Municipal du Val de Flux, Route de Lailly-en-Val, 45190 Beaugency [02 38 44 50 39 or 02 38 44 83 12; fax 02 38 46 49 10; camping@ville-beaugency.fr; www.camping-beaugency.fr] Exit A10 junc 15 onto D2152. In Beaugency turn L at traff lts nr water tower onto D925 & again over rd bdge. Site sp on S bank of Rv Loire. Lge, mkd, pt shd, wc (htd); chem disp; mv service pnt; shwrs inc; EHU (10A) inc (rev pol); lndry; shop; rest nr; snacks; bar; playgrnd; beach sand; red long stay; entmnt; 10% statics; dogs €2; Eng spkn; quiet; ccard acc; fishing; watersports; CKE/CCI. "Beautiful, welcoming, well-kept site; views over Loire; helpful, friendly staff; free 1 night site for m'vans over rv on other side of town; poss unrel opening dates LS, rec phone ahead; vg location close to town; coded ent barrier; next to rv and bdge to town; some rd noise at busy times; facs gd but far away fr pitches; scruffy & unkempt; town dilapidated; free WiFi around shop; gd cycling." ♦ 1 Apr-11 Sep. € 20.40   2018*

⊞ **BEAUGENCY** *4F2* (8km S Rural) *47.68679, 1.55802*
Camp Municipal L'Amitié, 17 Rue du Camping, Nouan-sur-Loire, 41220 St Laurent-Nouan [02 54 87 01 52; fax 02 54 87 09 93; campingdelamitie@stlaurentnouan.fr; www.campingdelamitie.fr] On D951 SW fr Orléans cont past power stn into Nouan-sur-Loire. Site on R sp. Med, hdg, mkd, pt shd, wc (htd); mv service pnt; shwrs; EHU (6A) €4.60; lndry; shop nr; rest nr; 50% statics; dogs €1; adv bkg acc; quiet; CKE/CCI. "Interesting area; view of Rv Loire; workers poss resident on site; friendly, helpful staff; well-maintained site; poor condition portacabins, better san facs nr ent; phone ahead LS to check open; dir access to rv; being redeveloped; excel facs; sports activities nrby; site clsd Xmas & New Year; conv for Chateau Chambord; supmkt 100m fr ent."
€ 8.00   2014*

BEAUMONT SUR OISE

BEAULIEU SUR DORDOGNE 7C4 (3km N Rural) 45.00911, 1.85059 **Aire Naturelle La Berge Ombragée (Lissajoux), Valeyran, 19120 Brivezac [05 55 91 01 17 or 06 08 40 78 69 (mob); contact@berge-ombragee.com; www.berge-ombragee.com]**
N fr Beaulieu-sur-Dordogne on D940; in 500m turn R onto D12; site on R in 2km. Office down on rv bank. NB Front wheel drive tow cars may find diff on gravel hill leading up fr office. Sm, pt shd, pt sl, wc; chem disp; mv service pnt; shwrs inc; EHU (6A) €3; shop; snacks; bbq; playgrnd; sw nr; wifi; dogs €0.30; canoeing; CKE/CCI. "CL-type site; friendly; canoeing fr site; gd." 1 May-15 Sep. € 22.40   2012*

BEAULIEU SUR DORDOGNE 7C4 (5km N Rural) 45.02167, 1.83960 **Camping la Champagne, La Champagne, 19120 Brivezac [05 87 06 01 21 or 06 70 78 65 63 (mob); info@campinglachampagne.com; www.campinglachampagne.com]**
Fr Beaulieu-sur-Dordogne take D940, sp Tulle. R onto D12, sp Argentat. R onto D136. R again after bdge. Site 600m on R. Sm, mkd, pt shd, terr, wc; chem disp; mv service pnt; shwrs; EHU (6A) €3; lndry; snacks; bbq; sw nr; twin axles; wifi; dogs €2.50; phone; Eng spkn; adv bkg acc; quiet; CCI. "Aire Naturella (max 25 vans); fishing; canoeing; horseriding nr; peaceful, spacious rvside location; Dutch owners." ♦ 1 May-15 Sep. € 22.00   2014*

"There aren't many sites open at this time of year"

If you're travelling outside peak season remember to call ahead to check site opening dates – even if the entry says 'open all year'.

BEAULIEU SUR DORDOGNE 7C4 (0km E Urban) 44.97950, 1.84040 **Huttopia Beaulieu Sur Dordogne (formerly Camping des Iles), Blvd Rodolphe-de-Turenne, 19120 Beaulieu-sur-Dordogne [05 55 91 02 65; fax 05 55 91 05 19; www.huttopia.com]**
Exit A20 junc 52 ont D158/D38 dir Collonges-la-Rouge; cont on D38 & turn R onto D940 to Beaulieu-sur-Dordogne; site sp fr o'skts of town. Or on D940 N fr Bretenoux, turn R in Beaulieu town sq, site about 200m on island in Rv Dordogne. NB 3m height limit at ent. Med, mkd, shd, wc (htd); chem disp; fam bthrm; shwrs inc; EHU (10A) inc (poss long lead req); lndry; shop nr; rest; snacks; bar; bbq (gas); playgrnd; pool; red long stay; entmnt; wifi; 15% statics; dogs €2; Eng spkn; adv bkg rec; quiet; games rm; rv; fishing; bike hire; games area; canoeing. "Delightful, wooded site; pitches by rv excel (extra charge); plenty shd; friendly staff; gd clean san facs; ltd LS; attractive medieval town; gd value; highly rec." 20 Apr-30 Sep. € 30.70   2018*

BEAULIEU SUR LOIRE 4G3 (0km E Rural) 47.54407, 2.82167 **FFCC Camp Municipal du Canal, Route de Bonny, 45630 Beaulieu-sur-Loire [02 38 35 89 56 or 02 38 35 32 16 (LS); fax 02 38 35 86 57; renault.campingbeaulieu@orange.fr; www.beaulieu-sur-loire.fr]**
Exit A77 junc 21 Bonny-sur-Loire, cross rv to Beaulieu-sur-Loire on D296. On E o'skirts of vill on D926, nr canal. Sm, mkd, hdstg, hdg, pt shd, wc; chem disp; mv service pnt; shwrs inc; EHU (10A) €4; shop nr; rest nr; bar nr; Eng spkn; adv bkg acc; CKE/CCI. "Well-kept site in pleasant area; direct access to canal; some sm pitches diff lge o'fits; site yourself, warden calls 0800-0900 & 1830-1930; no security; clean modern san facs; gd walking along canal & Rv Loire; boat trips; poss workers' statics LS; mkt Wed; lovely hdg pitches; conv Aqueduct at Briare." ♦ 4 Apr-1 Nov. € 10.40   2017*

BEAUMONT DE LOMAGNE 8E3 (1km E Urban) 43.88406, 0.99800 **Village de Loisirs Le Lomagnol, Ave du Lac, 82500 Beaumont-de-Lomagne [05 63 26 12 00; fax 05 63 65 60 22; villagedeloisirslelomagnol@wanadoo.fr; www.villagelelomagnol.fr]**
On SE of D928 at E end of vill. Sp 'Centre de Loisirs, Plan d'Eau'. Med, mkd, pt shd, wc; chem disp; fam bthrm; shwrs inc; EHU (10A) inc (poss long lead req); lndry; shop; rest; snacks; bar; playgrnd; pool; sw; 25% statics; dogs €2; canoe hire; golf; tennis; jacuzzi; sauna; waterslide; bike hire; fishing. "Gd quality, modern site; interesting old town; mkt Sat; facs tired LS." ♦ 1 Apr-30 Oct. € 18.00   2016*

BEAUMONT DU PERIGORD 7D3 (7km SW Rural) 44.75603, 0.70216 **Centre Naturiste de Vacances Le Couderc (Naturist), 24440 Naussannes [05 53 22 40 40; fax 05 53 23 90 98; info@lecouderc.com; www.lecouderc.com]**
Fr D660 at D25 W thro Naussannes & hamlet of Leydou. Just beyond Leydou turn R into site, well sp. Lge, mkd, pt shd, pt sl, wc; chem disp; shwrs inc; EHU (5A) €4.50; shop; rest; snacks; bar; playgrnd; pool (htd); paddling pool; red long stay; entmnt; wifi; 10% statics; dogs €4.65; adv bkg req; quiet; ccard acc; jacuzzi; sauna; bike hire. "Beautiful site with relaxed atmosphere; friendly, helpful Dutch owners; gd san facs; superb pool; naturist walks on site; gd walking/cycling area; Bastide towns nrby; new sauna,steam rm/spa (2015); new camping field; pond cleaned & enlarged; vg entmnt & activity prog for kids & adults." ♦ 1 Apr-15 Oct. € 41.00   2017*

BEAUMONT SUR OISE 3D3 (8km SW Rural) 49.12805, 2.18318 **Parc de Séjour de l'Etang, 10 Chemin des Belles Vues, 95690 Nesles-la-Vallée [01 34 70 62 89; campinparis@gmail.com; www.campinparis.com]**
Fr D927 Méru-Pontoise rd, turn L onto D64 at sp L'Isle Adam. After passing thro Nesles-la-Vallée camp sp on L. Med, hdg, pt shd, serviced pitches; wc (htd); chem disp; shwrs inc; EHU (3A) inc (rev pol); lndry; shop nr; playgrnd; dogs €2; Eng spkn; quiet; lake fishing adj; CKE/CCI. "Lovely, peaceful, out-of-the way setting; spacious pitches; friendly, helpful staff; gd facs; conv day trips to Paris & Versailles; excel." 1 Apr-30 Sep. € 22.00   2016*

BEAUMONT SUR SARTHE

BEAUMONT SUR SARTHE *4F1* (1km E Rural) *48.22382, 0.13651* FFCC Camp Municipal du Val de Sarthe, Rue de l'Abreuvoir, 72170 Beaumont-sur-Sarthe [02 43 97 01 93; camping-beaumontssarthe@orange.fr; www.beaumontsursarthe.com] Fr D338 Alençon-Le Mans, turn sharp L at 2nd set of traff lts in cent of Beaumont & foll site sp twd E of town. Fr Le Mans on A28 exit 21 onto D6, R onto D338 & R at traff lts & foll sp. NB Narr, sloping app thro town rds with blind corners. Narr site access. Med, hdg, mkd, pt shd, wc; chem disp; mv service pnt; shwrs inc; EHU (10A) inc (long cable poss req & poss rev pol); lndry; shop nr; rest nr; playgrnd; wifi; TV; dogs €0.50; Eng spkn; adv bkg rec; ccard acc; fishing adj; rv boating adj; CKE/CCI. "Beautiful, peaceful, well-run rvside site; lge pitches, some by rv; no twin axles & poss no c'vans over 2,000 kg; barrier clsd 2200; easy walk to interesting, pretty town; mkt Tues; rec; nice clean site; pleasant & friendly; well maintained site; recep open 1000-1200, 1600-1900 (May, Jun & Sep), 900-1200, 1500-2000 (Jul & Aug); barrier unattended bet 1200-1400; pool 500m; admission only aft 4pm; popular NH." ♦ 1 May-30 Sep. € 15.50 2018*

> **"That's changed – Should I let the Club know?"**
>
> If you find something on site that's different from the site entry, fill in a report and let us know. See camc.com/europereport.

BEAUNE *6H1* (1km N Urban) *47.03304, 4.83911* Camp Municipal Les Cent Vignes, 10 Rue Auguste Dubois, 21200 Beaune [03 80 22 03 91; fax 03 80 20 15 51; campinglescentvignes@mairie-beaune.fr; www.beaune.fr] Fr N on A31 & fr S on A6 at junc with m'ways A6/A31 take A6 sp Auxerre-Paris; after 1km leave at junc 24 to join D974 twd Beaune; after approx 1.5km, turn R at 2nd traff lts fr a'route to site (sp) in 200m. If app fr S on D974 site well sp fr inner ring rd & foll sp to Dijon (not a'route sps). Also sp fr Mersault/L'Hôpital x-rds. Med, hdstg, hdg, mkd, pt shd, wc (htd); chem disp; mv service pnt; shwrs inc; EHU (16A) €3.80 (some rev pol); gas; lndry; shop; rest; snacks; bar; bbq; playgrnd; wifi; TV; dogs; phone; Eng spkn; ccard acc; bike hire; games area; tennis; CKE/CCI. "Popular, well-run site; rec arr early even LS; gd modern san facs; vg rest; most pitches gd size but narr site rds makes access some pitches diff, a mover useful; tight turns & low trees poss diff lge o'fits; twin axles; in walking dist of Beaune; v conv site; hypmkt 2km; superb new san facs 2013; excel site; adv bkg in writing only bef 30 May; pool 800m; many pitches with own service pnts." ♦ 15 Mar-31 Oct. € 25.00 2017*

BEAUNE *6H1* (4km NE Rural) *47.02668, 4.88294* Camping Les Bouleaux, 11 Rue Jaune, 21200 Vignoles [03 80 22 26 88] Exit A6 at junc 24.1; 500m after toll turn R at rndabt, in 1.5km turn R sp Dole rndabt. Immed after x-ing m'way turn L sp Vignoles. L again at next junc then R & foll camping sp. Site in approx 1.5km in cent Chevignerot; fr town cent take D973 (E) sp Dole. In 2km cross a'route & 1st L (N) sp Vignoles. Well sp. Sm, hdg, mkd, pt shd, wc (htd); chem disp; shwrs inc; EHU (6A) inc (rev pol altered on request); shop; dogs; adv bkg rec; quiet; CKE/CCI. "Attractive, well-kept, busy site, even in LS; rec arr early high ssn; some gd sized pitches, most sm; superb clean new san facs, poss stretched high ssn & ltd LS; poss muddy after rain - park on rdways; conv NH fr a'route; basic site; long lead may be req'd; excel site; excel walking in area; helpful owner." ♦ € 19.00 2018*

BEAUNE *6H1* (8km SW Rural) *46.98573, 4.76855* La Grappe d'Or (formally Kawan Village), 2 Route de Volnay, 21190 Meursault [03 80 21 22 48; fax 03 80 21 65 74; info@camping-meursault.com; www.camping-meursault.com] Fr N-S, Exit A6 Junc 24.1 SP Beaune Centre Hospices, at rndabt foll sp to Chalon sur Saône RN 74, after 7km foll sp to Meursault, turn r, foll sp for site. Med, mkd, pt shd, terr, wc (htd); chem disp; mv service pnt; fam bthrm; shwrs inc; EHU (10A) inc; gas; lndry; shop; rest; snacks; bar; playgrnd; paddling pool; sw; wifi; dogs €1.40; phone; Eng spkn; adv bkg req; waterslide; bike hire; tennis; games area; CKE/CCI. "Lovely family site; busy high ssn - arr early; all pitches views over vineyards; friendly, helpful owners; basic facs stretched; ltd water pnts & poss steep climb fr lower pitches; some pitches uneven, sm or obstructed by trees - poss diff access lge o'fits; poss muddy when wet; barrier clsd 2200-0730; rambling; sh walk to lovely vill; gd cycle paths; vg; popular site; well run; if full use site at Santenay." ♦ 1 Apr-15 Oct. € 28.50 2014*

BEAUNE *6H1* (7km NW Rural) *47.06861, 4.8029* Camping de Savigny-les-Beaune, Route de Bouilland, 21420 Savigny-lès-Beaune [03 80 26 15 06 or 06 83 23 93 37 (mob); contact@camping-savigny-les-beaune.fr; www.camping-savigny-les-beaune.fr] Fr Beaune ring rd turn N on D974 sp Dijon; in 200m turn L sp Savigny; in 100m ignore camping sp & bear R to Savigny (3km); site 1km thro vill on L. Med, mkd, pt shd, pt sl, wc; chem disp; mv service pnt; shwrs inc; EHU (6A) €3.50 (some rev pol); shop nr; snacks; bbq; playgrnd; wifi; dogs €1.20; adv bkg acc; quiet; bike hire; CKE/CCI. "Pleasant, busy NH in beautiful area; pleasant staff; modern basic san facs; no twin axles; gd touring base; conv A6, A31, A36 & Beaune; easy walk to vill; excel quiet site." ♦ 15 Mar-15 Oct. € 14.00 2016*

BEAUREPAIRE 9C2 (10km S Rural) 45.25332, 5.02803 **Camping du Château, Route de Romans, 26390 Hauterives [04 75 68 80 19; fax 04 75 68 90 94; contact@camping-hauterives.com; www.camping-hauterives.com]** Take D538 S to Hauterives, site sp in vill adj Rv Galaure. Med, mkd, pt shd, wc; mv service pnt; shwrs; EHU (6-10A) €2.50-3; lndry; shop nr; snacks; playgrnd; pool (htd); paddling pool; 10% statics; dogs €2.20; adv bkg acc; quiet; rv fishing adj; games area; tennis. "Gd NH; friendly; gd pool; Do not use sat nav, inaccurate." ♦ 1 Apr-30 Sep. € 26.50   2012*

⊞ **BEAUVAIS** 3C3 (16km E Rural) 49.40506, 2.25803 **Camping de la Trye, Rue de Trye, 60510 Bresles [03 44 07 80 95 or 06 10 40 30 29 (mob); www.camping-de-la-trye.com]** Exit N31 (Beauvais to Clermont) at Bresles; foll site sp. Med, mkd, hdg, pt shd, sl, wc; chem disp; mv service pnt; fam bthrm; shwrs inc; EHU (6A) inc; lndry; bbq; playgrnd; pool; entmnt; wifi; 75% statics; dogs; adv bkg acc; ccard acc; bike hire; CKE/CCI. "Helpful Dutch owners; cycle & walking rtes; theme parks nrby; trampoline; largely a holiday chalet/static site with ltd no of touring pitches; pony rides; fair NH/sh stay." ♦ € 20.00   2016*

BEAUVILLE 7D3 (1km SE Rural) 44.27210, 0.88850 **Camping Les Deux Lacs, 47470 Beauville [05 53 95 45 41; camping-les-2-lacs@wanadoo.fr; www.les2lacs.info]** Fr D656 S to Beauville, site sp on D122. NB Steep descent to site - owners help when leaving if necessary. Med, hdg, mkd, shd, terr, wc; chem disp; mv service pnt; shwrs inc; EHU (6A) €2.45; lndry; shop nr; rest; snacks; bar; playgrnd; sw nr; red long stay; wifi; 10% statics; dogs €2.15; Eng spkn; adv bkg acc; quiet; ccard acc; fishing; games area; watersports; CKE/CCI. "Peaceful; gd fishing; pleasant walk to vill; vg; Dutch owners; facs inadequate when site full." ♦ 1 Apr-31 Oct. € 28.00   2017*

BEAUVOIR SUR MER 2H3 (5km E Rural) 46.92298, -1.99036 **Camping Le Fief d'Angibaud, 85230 St Gervais [02 51 68 43 08; camping.fief.angibaud@orange.fr; www.campinglefiefangibaud.com]** Fr Beauvoir-sur-Mer E on D948 to St Gervais turn L after PO/Mairie onto D59 twd Bouin (narr ent easy to miss); in 2km pass sm chapel; take 2nd rd on L; site on R after 500m. Sm, mkd, pt shd, wc; chem disp; mv service pnt; shwrs inc; EHU (6-13A) €3.50; lndry; shop nr; bbq; beach sand 5km; red long stay; twin axles; wifi; dogs €1.50; Eng spkn; adv bkg rec; quiet; golf nr; fishing nr; CKE/CCI. "Excel, simple site adj farm; lge pitches; pleasant, helpful British owners; clean san facs but need update (2010); conv Ile de Noirmoutier, ferry to Ile d'Yeu, coastal resorts; free parking close to beach (blue flag); gd cycling area; vg value; gd for rallies; gite on site; bike hire." ♦ 16 Apr-24 Sep. € 19.50   2016*

BEDOIN 10E2 (2km NE Rural) 44.13363, 5.18738 **Camping Domaine de Bélézy (Naturist), 84410 Bédoin [04 90 65 60 18; fax 04 90 65 94 45; info@belezy.com; www.belezy.com]** Fr Carpentras D974 to Bédoin. Go thro vill & turn R at rndabt sp Mont Ventoux. In 300m turn L & foll sp to site. Lge, shd, pt sl, wc (htd); chem disp; mv service pnt; fam bthrm; shwrs inc; EHU (12A) €5.60; gas; lndry; shop; rest; snacks; bar; cooking facs; playgrnd; pool (htd); paddling pool; red long stay; entmnt; wifi; TV; 20% statics; phone; Eng spkn; adv bkg acc; quiet; ccard acc; tennis; golf 20km; INF card; horseriding 2km; games area. "Delightful, peaceful, well-kept site in lovely location; warm welcome, helpful staff; sep car park high ssn; extensive facs; sauna; steam rm; many acitivies; some sm & awkward pitches; gd base for Mt Ventoux, Côtes du Rhône; excel; no pets; pitches v close together." ♦ 2 Apr-2 Oct. € 41.00   2013*

BEDOIN 10E2 (1km W Rural) 44.12468, 5.17249 **Camp Municipal de la Pinède, Chemin des Sablières, 84410 Bédoin [04 90 65 61 03; fax 04 90 65 95 22; campingmunicipal@bedoin.fr; www.bedoin.fr]** Take D938 S fr Malaucène for 3km, L onto D19 for 9km to Bédoin. Site adj vill & sp. Med, hdstg, mkd, shd, sl, terr, wc (htd); chem disp; mv service pnt; shwrs inc; EHU (16A) inc; lndry; shop nr; snacks; playgrnd; pool (htd); dogs €1.50; bus; Eng spkn; adv bkg acc; quiet; ccard acc; CKE/CCI. "Pool clsd Mon; 5 min walk to vill; mkt Mon; steep terr site; vans towed to pitch if req; steep climb to some san facs; v clean; v friendly; excel pool; v popular; MH site adj; easy walk to town." ♦ 15 Mar-31 Oct. € 18.50   2017*

BELCAIRE 8G4 (4km SW Rural) 42.79207, 1.92477 **Camping Les Sapins, Ternairols, 11340 Camurac [04 68 20 38 11; info@lessapins-camurac.com; www.lessapins-camurac.com]** Easiest app fr N - at Bélesta on D117 turn S onto D16/D29/D613 to Belcaire then cont to Camurac, site 1km SE of vill. Or take D613 fr Ax-les-Thermes (1st 10km over Col de Chioula diff climb - gd power/weight ratio). Site sp in vill of Camurac & visible fr rd. App rd fairly steep for sh dist. Med, mkd, pt shd, pt sl, wc (htd); chem disp; shwrs inc; EHU (10A) €3; lndry; shop nr; rest; snacks; bar; bbq (elec, gas); playgrnd; pool; paddling pool; entmnt; wifi; TV; 33% statics; dogs €2; Eng spkn; adv bkg acc; quiet; ccard acc; horseriding; games area; site clsd 1 Nov-15 Dec; CKE/CCI. "Lovely, peaceful site in beautiful surroundings; welcoming, friendly, helpful Dutch owners; excel walking; in Cathar region; vg; highly rec; winter sports; mountain biking; ltd facs LS."
♦ 1 Jan-1 Nov, 15 Dec-31 Dec. € 24.50   2017*

BELCAIRE

BELCAIRE *8G4* (0km W Rural) *42.81598, 1.95098*
Les Chalets Du Lac (formerly Camp Municipal La Mousquière/Le Lac), 4 Chemin Lac, 11340 Belcaire [04 68 20 39 47; fax 04 68 20 39 48; chaletsdulac@gmail.com; www.camping-pyrenees-cathare.fr] Site on D613 bet Ax-les-Thermes & Quillan. Sm, mkd, shd, pt sl, wc; chem disp; shwrs inc; EHU (10A) €2; lndry; sw nr; dogs; phone; quiet; tennis nr; horseriding nr; CKE/CCI. "Site by lake; site yourself, warden calls; gd cent for walking; historic vill of Montaillou nr; excel; conv for Georges de la Frau." ♦ 1 Jun-30 Sep. € 14.00   2014*

BELFORT *6G3* (2km N Urban) *47.65335, 6.86445*
FFCC Camping de l'Etang des Forges, 11 Rue du Général Béthouart, 90000 Belfort [03 84 22 54 92; fax 03 84 22 76 55; contact@camping-belfort.com; www.camping-belfort.com] Exit A36 junc 13; go thro cent of Belfort; then foll sp Offemont on D13, then site sp. Or fr W on N19 site well sp. Med, hdg, mkd, pt shd, wc (htd); chem disp; mv service pnt; fam bthrm; shwrs inc; EHU (6A) €3.50; lndry; shop nr; rest nr; snacks; bar; bbq; playgrnd; pool; red long stay; twin axles; entmnt; wifi; TV; 5% statics; dogs €2; bus; Eng spkn; adv bkg acc; quiet; ccard acc; fishing adj; watersports adj; archery; CKE/CCI. "Pleasant, well-kept, basic site; some lovely pitches; friendly; modern, unisex san facs with third cont wc, but needs updating (2014); lovely walk around lake fr site ent; cycle paths; conv for Corbusier's chapel at Ronchamp." ♦ 7 Apr-30 Sep. € 21.00   2016*

🏕 **BELLAC** *7A3* (11km SW Rural) *46.05718, 0.97766*
Camping Fonclaire, 87300 Blond [05 55 60 88 26; fontclair@neuf.fr; www.limousin-gites.com] Fr Bellac take D675 S dir St Junien. Site on L in approx 7km, 2km bef Mortemart. Sm, hdstg, pt shd, wc; own san rec; chem disp; shwrs inc; EHU (6A) €4 (poss long lead req); lndry; shop nr; rest nr; bar nr; pool (htd); sw; dogs; Eng spkn; adv bkg acc; quiet; horseriding 3km; fishing; golf 2km; CKE/CCI. "Lovely & peaceful, spacious CL-type site in lovely location; welcoming, helpful British owners; gd facs; gd hdstg in wet; nr Oradour-sur-Glane martyr vill; conv Futuroscope; gd cycling; gd; v quiet rural location; no night lighting; gd NH/longer; excel; poss boggy when wet." ♦ € 18.00   2018*

BELLEME *4E2* (1km SW Urban) *48.37420, 0.55370*
Camp Municipal Le Val, Route de Mamers, 61130 Bellême [02 33 85 31 00 (Mairie) 06 07 11 27 39 (After 7pm); fax 02 33 83 58 85; mairie.bellame@wanadoo.fr; www.lepaysbellemois.com] Fr Mortagne, take D938 S to Bellême; turn R ent town on D955 Alençon rd; site sp on L half-way down hill. Sm, hdg, pt sl, wc; chem disp; shwrs inc; EHU (8A) €2.65 (poss long lead req); shop nr; playgrnd; pool; dogs €0.50; adv bkg rec; tennis adj; fishing. "Pretty, well-kept site; some pitches v sl; warden visits twice daily; gd san facs; poss long water hoses req; pitches poss soft when wet; steep walk to town." 15 Apr-15 Oct. € 14.50   2014*

BELLENTRE *9B4* (2km E Rural) *45.57576, 6.73553*
Camping L'Eden, 73210 Landry [04 79 07 61 81; fax 04 79 07 62 17; info@camping-eden.net; www.camping-eden.net] Fr N90 Moûtiers to Bourg-St Maurice at 20km turn R sp Landry; site on L after 500m adj Rv Isère. Med, mkd, hdstg, hdg, pt shd, wc (htd); chem disp; shwrs inc; EHU (10A) €4-6; gas; lndry; shop; snacks; bar; playgrnd; pool (htd); wifi; TV; dogs €1.50; phone; Eng spkn; adv bkg acc; quiet; ccard acc; games rm. "Gd cent mountain sports; helpful, friendly owner; red facs LS; ltd site lighting; ski bus; poss unkempt end of ssn; gd cycle track to town." 15 Dec-5 May & 25 May-15 Sep. € 26.00   2016*

BELLEY *9B3* (8km E Rural) *45.76860, 5.76885*
Camping Du Lac du Lit du Roi, La Tuilière, 01300 Massignieu-de-Rives [04 79 42 12 03; fax 04 79 42 19 94; info@camping-savoie.com; www.camping-savoie.com] Fr D1504 turn E onto D992 to Massignieu-de-Rives, site sp. Site on NE of lake nr Les Mures. Med, hdg, mkd, pt shd, terr, wc (htd); chem disp; mv service pnt; shwrs inc; EHU (10A) inc (long lead req); gas; lndry; rest; snacks; bar; bbq; playgrnd; pool; sw; red long stay; wifi; TV; 20% statics; dogs €4; phone; Eng spkn; adv bkg req; ccard acc; boating; tennis; bike hire; CKE/CCI. "Superb location; many pitches on lake with lovely views; some lge pitches, others v sm; lack of site maintenance (2010); few water pnts (2009); bkg fee; v friendly site, idyllic location; recep clsd 1200-1330." ♦ 16 Apr-17 Sep. € 28.60   2016*

BELMONT SUR RANCE *8E4* (1km W Rural) *43.81777, 2.75108* **Camping Val Fleuri du Rance**, Route de Lacaune, 12370 Belmont-sur-Rance [05 65 99 04 76 or 06 88 42 28 78 (mob); marjandejong@wanadoo.fr; www.campinglevalfleuri.com] On D32 on ent vill fr SW; on L side of rd on sh unmade service rd. NB diff ent/exit to/fr S. Sm, mkd, hdg, pt shd, wc; chem disp; shwrs inc; EHU (6A) €3.50; gas; lndry; shop nr; rest; wifi; 10% statics; dogs €1.50; Eng spkn; adv bkg acc; quiet; rv fishing; tennis; CKE/CCI. "Attractive valley setting; helpful Dutch owners; attractive sm town; pool 500m; v welcoming." ♦ 1 Apr-30 Sep. € 14.00   2014*

BELVES *7D3* (12km SW Rural) *44.75813, 0.90222*
Camping Terme d'Astor (Naturist), 24540, St Avit-Rivière [05 53 63 24 52; fax 05 53 63 25 43; camping@termedastor.com; www.termedastor.com] Leave D710 at Belvès onto D53; in 4km turn R onto D26 to Bouillac; pass thro vill; then turn 2nd L. Well sp. Med, mkd, shd, pt sl, wc; chem disp; shwrs inc; EHU (6A) €5.20; gas; lndry; shop; rest; snacks; bar; bbq; playgrnd; pool; paddling pool; entmnt; wifi; TV; 10% statics; dogs free; phone; Eng spkn; adv bkg acc; quiet; ccard acc; INF; rafting; games rm; jacuzzi; archery; canoeing nr; tennis nr; excursions. "Gd cent for Dordogne rv & chateaux; vg; horserding nrby; poss low ampage & rev pol on some pitches." ♦ 1 May-30 Sep. € 37.00   2016*

BELVES *7D3 (5km SW Rural) 44.75258, 0.98330*
FLOWER Caming Les Nauves, Le Bos-Rouge, 24170 Belvès [05 53 29 12 64; campinglesnauves@hotmail. com; www.lesnauves.com or www.flowercampings. com] On D53 fr Belvès. Site on L just after junc to Larzac. Avoid Belves cent - use lorry rte dir Monpazier. Med, hdg, pt shd, pt sl, wc; chem disp; mv service pnt; fam bthrm; shwrs inc; EHU (6A) inc; lndry; shop nr; rest; snacks; bar; bbq; playgrnd; pool; paddling pool; twin axles; entmnt; wifi; TV; 10% statics; dogs €4; Eng spkn; adv bkg acc; ccard acc; bike hire; games area; games rm; horseriding; CCI. "Excel site; gd views fr some pitches; sl site; interesting towns nrby; sm pool."
♦ 11 Apr-26 Sep. € 28.00   2015*

> "I like to fill in the reports as I travel from site to site"
>
> You'll find report forms at the back of this guide, or you can fill them in online at camc.com/europereport.

BELZ *2F3 (3km NW Coastal) 47.68268, -3.18796*
Camping St Cado, Port de St Cado, 56550 Belz [02 97 55 31 98; fax 02 97 55 27 52; info@camping-saintcado.com; www.camping-saintcado.com] W fr Auray on D22 then D16. Well sp fr Belz. Med, hdg, pt shd, wc; EHU (3-6A) €2.60-3.60; lndry; shop nr; rest nr; playgrnd; 10% statics; dogs €1.60; Eng spkn; adv bkg acc; quiet; games rm; fishing 300m; tennis; games area. "Popular site in beautiful location; boat hire 300m; seas views fr some pitches; helpful owner; volleyball; boules; rec phone ahead high ssn; vg; rec."
1 Apr-30 Sep. € 15.00   2013*

BENODET *2F2 (2km E Coastal) 47.86670, -4.09080*
Camping Du Letty, Rue du Canvez, 29950 Bénodet [02 98 57 04 69; fax 02 98 66 22 56; reception@ campingduletty.com; www.campingduletty.com] Fr N ent town on D34, foll sp Fouesnant D44. Le Letty sp R at rndabt. Fr E on N165 take D44 sp Fouesnant & foll rd to o'skirts Bénodet. After town sp, site is sp. Lge, mkd, hdstg, hdg, pt shd, pt sl, wc; chem disp; mv service pnt; fam bthrm; shwrs; EHU (10A) €4; gas; lndry; shop; snacks; bar; bbq (gas); playgrnd; pool (covrd, htd); paddling pool; beach sand adj; entmnt; wifi; TV; dogs €2.30; phone; Eng spkn; adv bkg acc; quiet; ccard acc; golf nr; tennis; games area; kayak hire; sauna; games rm; gym; squash; horseriding nr; waterslide; CKE/CCI. "Excel, well-run, beautifully laid-out site; clean & well-equipped; lovely beach adj; excel playgrnd; many activities; aqua park; library; friendly, helpful staff; highly rec." ♦ 11 Jun-5 Sep. € 33.00   2017*

BENODET *2F2 (1km SE Coastal) 47.86780, -4.09750*
Camping du Poulquer, 23 rue du Poulquer, 29950 Bénodet [02 98 57 04 19; fax 02 98 66 20 30; contact@ campingdupoulquer.com; www.campingdupoulquer. com] Fr N ent town on D34. At rndabt after junc with D44 strt onto Rue Penfoul. At next rndabt (tourist info office on R after rndabt) go strt dir La Plage until reach seafront; turn L at seafront then L at end of prom at camping sp; site in 100m on R. Fr E on N165 take D44 sp Fouesnant & foll rd to o'skirts Bénodet. After town sp, site is sp. Lge, mkd, hdg, pt shd, pt sl, wc; chem disp; fam bthrm; shwrs inc; EHU (6-10A) inc (long lead poss req, poss rev pol); lndry; shop; rest nr; snacks; bar; bbq; playgrnd; pool (covrd, htd); paddling pool; beach sand adj; entmnt; wifi; TV; 5% statics; dogs €2; Eng spkn; adv bkg acc; quiet; jacuzzi; games rm; waterslide; golf nr; tennis; CKE/CCI. "Lovely, well-kept, family-run site; bike hire 1km; boat trips nrby; friendly, helpful owner; aqua park; no o'fits over 7.5m high ssn; gd, clean san facs, poss tired end of ssn; quiet site LS; mkt Mon; rec; vg; gd cafe/bar & shop; indoor pool open LS." ♦ 1 May-30 Sep. € 30.80   2018*

BENODET *2F2 (5km W Coastal) 47.86903, -4.12848*
Camping Le Helles, 55 Rue du Petit-Bourg, 29120 Combrit-Ste Marine [02 98 56 31 46; contact@ le-helles.com; www.le-helles.com] Exit D44 S dir Ste Marine, site sp. Med, mkd, pt shd, pt sl, wc (htd); chem disp; fam bthrm; shwrs inc; EHU (6-10A); lndry; shop; snacks; bbq; playgrnd; pool (htd); paddling pool; beach sand 300m; wifi; 10% statics; dogs €2.60; Eng spkn; adv bkg acc; quiet; ccard acc; CKE/CCI. "Vg site with lge pitches, some shd; gd, clean modern san facs; friendly, helpful owners; excel beach within 5 min walk; vg long stay; 2 pools indoor and out." ♦
1 Apr-23 Oct. € 14.00   2016*

BERCK *3B2 (4km E Rural) 50.41861, 1.60556* **Camping L'Orée du Bois, 251 Chemin Blanc, 62180 Rang-du-Fliers [03 21 84 28 51; fax 03 21 84 28 56; oree. du.bois@wanadoo.fr; www.oreedubois.fr]** Exit A6 junc 25 onto D140 & D917. Thro Rang-du-Fliers, turn R bef pharmacy into Chemin Blanc, site sp. V lge, hdg, mkd, pt shd, serviced pitches; wc; chem disp; mv service pnt; shwrs inc; EHU (6A) inc; gas; lndry; shop nr; rest; snacks; bar; playgrnd; pool (covrd, htd); paddling pool; beach sand 4km; red long stay; entmnt; wifi; 80% statics; dogs €4; phone; Eng spkn; adv bkg acc; quiet; ccard acc; games area; bike hire; tennis; lake fishing; CKE/CCI. "Conv Le Touquet, Boulogne, Montreuil & Calais; peaceful site in woodland; ltd space for tourers; tropical waterpark; vg pools; pleasant, helpful owners; m'van pitches cramped." ♦ 30 Mar-31 Oct. € 47.00   2013*

BERGERAC

BERGERAC 7C3 (2km S Urban) 44.84902, 0.47635
Camping La Pelouse (formerly Municipal), 8 bis Rue Jean-Jacques Rousseau, 24100 Bergerac [05 53 57 06 67; campinglapelouse@orange.fr; www.entreprisefrery.com] On S bank of Rv Dordogne 300m W of old bdge opp town cent. Do not ent town, foll camping sp fr bdge, ent on R after L turn opp block of flats. Well sp, on Rv Dordogne. Med, mkd, pt shd, pt sl, wc (htd); chem disp; mv service pnt; shwrs inc; EHU (6A); gas; lndry; shop nr; playgrnd; dogs €1.25; Eng spkn; adv bkg acc; quiet; rv fishing adj; CKE/CCI. "Peaceful, spacious site on rv bank; friendly warden; san facs ltd LS; easy walk by rv into attractive old town; no twin axles & c'vans over 6m; site poss clsd earlier if weather bad; pitches poss muddy when wet; rec arr bef 1400 high ssn site has lots of trees so not all pitches in sun; facs updated 2012." ♦ 1 Apr-31 Oct. € 20.00 2017*

BERGERAC 7C3 (14km W Rural) 44.83849, 0.33052
FFCC Camping Parc Servois, 11 Rue du Bac, 24680 Gardonne [06 84 38 24 33; mfounaud24@orange.fr; www.parcservois.com] Fr D936 Bergerac to Bordeaux, in vill of Gardonne turn R into sm rd 100m after traff lts; site at end of rd by rv. Well sp in vill. Sm, pt shd, wc; chem disp; mv service pnt; shwrs inc; EHU (10A) €2.60 (poss rev pol); shop nr; rest nr; dogs €0.70; Eng spkn; quiet; CKE/CCI. "Pretty, CL-type site on bank of Rv Dordogne; lge pitches; helpful warden; facs immac but dated & poss stretched when site full; gates clsd 2200-0800 with pedestrian access; sm mkt Wed & Sun; excel, well run site." 30 Apr-30 Sep. € 14.00 2016*

> **"We must tell the Club about that great site we found"**
>
> Get your site reports in by mid-August and we'll do our best to get your updates into the next edition.

BERGUES 3A3 (1km N Urban) 50.97248, 2.43420
Camping Le Vauban, Blvd Vauban, 59380 Bergues [03 28 68 65 25; fax 03 28 63 52 60; cassiopee.tourisme@wanadoo.fr] Exit A16 junc 60 twd Bergues on D916. In 2km turn R at rndabt onto D72 to Bergues thro Couderkerque vill, then turn R immed after canal. Site on R as rd bends to L. Med, hdg, mkd, pt shd, terr, wc cont; chem disp; mv service pnt; fam bthrm; shwrs; EHU (6A) inc (poss rev pol); lndry; shop nr; rest nr; bar nr; playgrnd; 60% statics; dogs €1.05; adv bkg acc; quiet; CKE/CCI. "Pleasant site; sm pitches poss diff lge o'fits; ltd manoeuvring in site rds; friendly & helpful; gates clsd 2130-0700 & poss clsd 1230-1730; lovely fortified town; conv Dunkerque & Calais; NH only; san facs updated (2015)." ♦ 1 Apr-31 Oct. € 16.00 2015*

BERNAY 3D2 (2km S Urban) 49.08020, 0.58703
Camp Municipal, Rue des Canadiens, 27300 Bernay [02 32 43 30 47; camping@bernay27.fr; www.ville-bernay27.fr] Site sp fr S'most (Alençon) rndabt off Bernay by-pass D438; twd France Parc Exposition then 1st L & on R. Well sp. Sm, mkd, hdg, pt shd, wc; chem disp; mv service pnt; shwrs inc; EHU (10A) €3.65 (poss rev pol); lndry; shop nr; rest nr; bar nr; playgrnd; wifi; TV; dogs; phone; adv bkg acc; quiet; CKE/CCI. "Well-kept site; well set-out pitches, diff sizes; helpful & friendly staff; gd clean facs, but dated; barrier clsd 2200-0700; excel, conv NH A28; excel, lovely site; pool 300m; debit card acc; Bernay worth a visit." ♦ 1 May-30 Sep. € 16.00 2016*

⊞ BERNY RIVIERE 3C4 (2km S Rural) 49.40603, 3.12860
Camping La Croix du Vieux Pont, Rue de la Fabrique, 02290 Berny-Rivière [03 23 55 50 02; fax 03 23 55 05 13; info@la-croix-du-vieux-pont.com; www.la-croix-du-vieux-pont.com] On N31 bet Soissons & Compiègne. At site sp turn onto D13, then at Vic-sur-Aisne take next R, R again then L onto D91. Foll sp to site on o'skts of Berny. V lge, hdg, hdstg, pt shd, serviced pitches; wc (htd); chem disp; mv service pnt; fam bthrm; shwrs inc; EHU (6A) €2.50 (poss rev pol, no earth & ltd supply); gas; lndry; shop; rest; snacks; bar; playgrnd; pool (covrd, htd); sw; entmnt; wifi; TV; dogs; Eng spkn; adv bkg rec; quiet; ccard acc; games rm; waterslide; gym; tennis; bike hire; horseriding; boating; archery; fishing; golf; CKE/CCI. "Pleasant, v lge, well-run, clean site; busy LS; lge pitches, some rvside; excel for families or older couples; friendly, helpful staff; vg san facs, ltd LS; some sh stay pitches up steep bank; beauty cent; some pitches worn/uneven end of ssn (2010); some pitches liable to flood; many tour op statics high ssn; site open all yr but no services Nov-Mar; excel; tourers pitch on open area." ♦ € 37.00 2015*

BERNY RIVIERE 3C4 (6km S Rural) 49.39280, 3.15161
Camping La Halte de Mainville, 18 Chemin du Routy, 02290 Ressons-le-Long [03 23 74 26 69; fax 03 23 74 03 60; lahaltedemainville@wanadoo.fr; www.lahaltedemainville.com.planete-moto.com] Fr Soissons W on N31 dir Compiègne, in approx 8km look for site sp on L. Clearly sp. Lge, mkd, hdg, pt shd, wc (htd); chem disp; mv service pnt; fam bthrm; shwrs inc; EHU (10A) €3 (poss rev pol); lndry; shop nr; bbq; playgrnd; pool (htd); paddling pool; wifi; 60% statics; dogs; phone; Eng spkn; adv bkg rec; quiet; games area; tennis; fishing; CKE/CCI. "Pleasant, clean, conv NH; friendly, helpful staff; 1 hr fr Disneyland; vg; lovely area." 8 Jan-8 Dec. € 21.50 2015*

BESANCON *6G2 (6km NE Rural) 47.26472, 6.07255* **Camping de Besancon - La Plage, 12 Route de Belfort, 25220 Chalezeule [03 81 88 04 26; fax 03 81 50 54 62; contact@campingdebesancon.com; www.campingdebesancon.com]** Exit A36 junc 4 S; foll sp Montbéliard & Roulons onto D683; site in 1.5km on R, 200m after rlwy bdge; well sp fr D683. Fr Belfort 2.65m height restriction; foll sp to Chalezeule & 300m after supmkt turn L to rejoin D683, site in 200m on rvside. Med, mkd, pt shd, terr, wc (htd); chem disp; mv service pnt; fam bthrm; shwrs inc; EHU (16A) (poss rev pol); lndry; shop nr; rest nr; snacks; bbq; playgrnd; twin axles; 50% statics; dogs €1.35; bus to city; Eng spkn; ccard acc; kayaking; CKE/CCI. "Helpful staff; htd pool adj; excel modern san facs; access to opp side of dual c'way under sm tunnel, suggest going to rndabt to make the turn; tram to city 1.5km uphill." ♦ 15 Mar-31 Oct. € 25.00 2018*

BESSINES SUR GARTEMPE *7A3 (2km SW Urban) 46.10013, 1.35423* **Camp Municipal Lac de Sagnat, Route de St Pardoux, 87250 Bessines-sur-Gartempe [05 55 76 17 69 or 05 55 76 05 09 (Mairie); fax 05 55 76 01 24; ot.bessines@wanadoo.fr; www.tourisme-bessines87.fr]** Exit A20 junc 24 sp Bessines-sur-Gartempe onto D220; then D27 sp lake. Foll sp to Bellevue Restaurant. At rest, turn R foll site sp. Well sp fr junc 24. Med, mkd, hdg, pt shd, pt sl, terr, wc; chem disp; shwrs inc; EHU (6A) inc; lndry; shop nr; rest nr; snacks; playgrnd; sw nr; TV; Eng spkn; quiet. "Pretty site with lake views; peaceful location; friendly staff; gd, clean san facs; poss unkempt LS (Jun 2009); hotel for meals nrby; conv NH A20." ♦ 15 Jun-15 Sep. € 18.70 2012*

BEZIERS *10F1 (10km NE Rural) 43.39849, 3.37338* **Camping Le Rebau, 34290 Montblanc [04 67 98 50 78; fax 04 67 98 68 63; gilbert@camping-lerebau.fr; www.camping-lerebau.fr]** NE on N9 fr Béziers-Montpellier, turn R onto D18. Site sp, narr ent 2.50m. Lge, hdg, hdstg, mkd, pt shd, wc; chem disp; fam bthrm; shwrs inc; EHU (5A) €4.50; lndry; shop nr; bar nr; playgrnd; pool; entmnt; wifi; TV; 10% statics; dogs €2.80; phone; bus 1km; Eng spkn; adv bkg acc; quiet; CKE/CCI. "Gd site; tight ent & manoeuvring onto pitches; some facs old, but modern shwrs; ltd facs LS, but clean; helpful owner; gd pool; gd touring base; LS phone ahead to check open." 1 May-31 Aug. € 19.30 2012*

BEZIERS *10F1 (7km SE Urban) 43.3169, 3.2842* **Camping Les Berges du Canal, Promenade des Vernets, 34420 Villeneuve-les-Béziers [04 67 39 36 09; fax 04 67 39 82 07; contact@lesbergesducanal.com; www.lesbergesducanal.fr]** Fr A9 exit junc 35 & foll sp for Agde. Exit 1st rndabt fr D612 dir Béziers then 1st L onto D37 sp Villneuve-les-Béziers. Foll site sp to site adj canal. Med, hdg, mkd, shd, wc; chem disp; mv service pnt; fam bthrm; shwrs inc; EHU (16A) €2.50 (poss rev pol); lndry; shop; rest; snacks; playgrnd; pool (htd); wifi; 45% statics; dogs €3; Eng spkn; adv bkg acc; bike hire; CKE/CCI. "Pleasant site; facs clean & modern but poss stretched in ssn; noisy, fr rlwy yard; some pitches tight lge o'fits; pleasant stroll along canal." 12 Mar-15 Oct. € 28.50 2016*

⊞ **BEZIERS** *10F1 (12km SW Rural) 43.31864, 3.14276* **Camping Les Peupliers, 7 Promenade de l'Ancien Stade, 34440 Colombiers [04 67 37 05 26; contact@camping-colombiers.com; www.camping-colombiers.com]** SW fr Béziers on D609 (N9) turn R on D162E & foll sp to site using heavy vehicle rte. Cross canal bdge & fork R; turn R & site on L. Easier ent fr D11 (Béziers-Capestang) avoiding narr vill rds, turn L at rndabt at end of dual c'way sp Colombiers; in 1km at rlwy bdge, go strt on; in 100m turn L (bef canal bdge) where rd turns sharp R. Med, mkd, pt shd, wc; chem disp; mv service pnt; fam bthrm; shwrs inc; EHU (10A) €3.50 (inc in high ssn) (poss rev pol); gas; lndry; shop nr; rest nr; snacks; bar; bbq; playgrnd; pool; red long stay; wifi; 25% statics; dogs €3; adv bkg acc; CKE/CCI. "Nr Canal du Midi away fr busy beach sites; modern san facs; no twin axles; excel walking & cycling; pleasant sm vill, conv NH; gd rest in vill; diff for lge o'fits; touring pitches among statics." ♦ € 28.50 2018*

BIARRITZ *8F1 (5km S Coastal) 43.43371, -1.59040* **Camping Ur-Onéa, Rue de la Chapelle, 64210 Bidart [05 59 26 53 61; fax 05 59 26 53 94; contact@uronea.com; www.uronea.com]** Exit A63 junc 4 dir Bidart, fr Bidart on D810 sp St Jean de Luz, L at traff lts in town where site sp, then 2nd R, L at motel, site is 300m on L. Access fr main rd a bit tricky, 2nd access further S is easier for lge o'fits. Lge, hdstg, mkd, pt shd, terr, serviced pitches; wc; chem disp; fam bthrm; shwrs inc; EHU (10A) inc; gas; lndry; shop; rest; snacks; bar; bbq; playgrnd; pool; paddling pool; beach sand 600m; entmnt; wifi; TV; 20% statics; dogs €2.50; phone; Eng spkn; adv bkg acc; quiet; ccard acc; CKE/CCI. "Well-kept site 600m fr Bidart; various pitch sizes, most not terr; suitable for o'fits up to 8m; staff friendly & helpful; excel, clean san facs; conv Pays Basque vills; new covrd/open pool (2014)." ♦ 12 Apr-19 Sep. € 45.60 2014*

BIARRITZ *8F1 (5km S Coastal) 43.45305, -1.57277* **Yelloh! Village Ilbarritz, Ave de Biarritz, 64210 Bidart [05 59 23 00 29; fax 05 59 41 24 59; contact@camping-ilbarritz.com; www.camping-ilbarritz.com]** S fr Bayonne on D810, by-pass Biarritz. 1km after A63 junc turn R at rndabt immed after Intermarché on R; sp to Pavillon Royal. Site 1km on R sp. Lge, mkd, shd, pt sl, terr, wc; chem disp; fam bthrm; shwrs inc; EHU (10A) inc; gas; lndry; shop; rest; snacks; bar; playgrnd; pool (htd); beach sand 600m; wifi; TV; 80% statics; dogs €4; phone; Eng spkn; adv bkg req; ccard acc; games area; horseriding; bike hire; tennis; golf nr; CKE/CCI. "Attractive, mature site; lge pitches, need blocks as v sl; narr access rds poss diff long o'fits; excel pool; gd beaches nrby; gd." ♦ 27 Mar-5 Oct. € 50.00 2015*

BIARRITZ

A stone's throw from the Ocean
Biarritz Côte Basque
The only campsite in Biarritz
28 Rue d'Harcet. F-64200 Biarritz.
Tél. : +33.(0)5.59.23.00.12
biarritz.camping@gmail.com • www.biarritz-camping.fr

BIARRITZ *8F1 (9km S Coastal) 43.43838, -1.58184*
Village Camping Sunêlia Berrua, Rue Berrua, 64210 Bidart [05 59 54 96 66; fax 05 59 54 78 30; contact@berrua.com; www.berrua.com] Exit A63 junc 4 dir Bidart, fr Bidart on D810 sp St Jean de Luz, L at 1st traff lts, site sp. Lge, pt shd, pt sl, wc; chem disp; mv service pnt; fam bthrm; shwrs inc; EHU (6A) €6.20 (poss long lead req); gas; lndry; shop; rest; snacks; bar; bbq; playgrnd; pool (htd); paddling pool; beach 1km; wifi; TV; 50% statics; dogs €4.20; phone; bus 1km; Eng spkn; adv bkg acc; ccard acc; tennis; bike hire; waterslide; golf 2km; archery; CKE/CCI. "Busy, well-kept site in attractive location; steam rm; excel, clean facs; pitches tight lge o'fits; site rds narr, low trees, some high kerbs; muddy after rain; gd rest; sh walk to vill; gd; pleasant staff." ♦ 1 Apr-27 Sep. € 46.00   2015*

BIARRITZ *8F1 (2km SW Coastal) 43.4625, -1.5672*
Camping Biarritz, 28 Rue Harcet, 64200 Biarritz [05 59 23 00 12; fax 05 59 43 74 67; info@biarritz-camping.fr; www.biarritz-camping.fr] S fr Bayonne on D810, by-pass Biarritz & cont to junc of D810 coast rd sp Bidart & Biarritz; double back on this rd, take 1st exit at next rndabt, 1st L dir Biarritz Cent, foll sp to site in 2km. Lge, mkd, pt shd, pt sl, terr, wc; chem disp; shwrs inc; EHU (10A) €4; gas; lndry; shop; rest; snacks; bar; playgrnd; pool (htd); paddling pool; beach sand 1km; entmnt; 10% statics; bus at gate; adv bkg acc; ccard acc; tennis 4km; CKE/CCI. "One of better sites in area, espec LS." ♦ 12 May-14 Sep. € 24.00   2016*

See advertisement above

BIARRITZ *8F1 (4km SW Coastal) 43.44431, -1.58166*
Camping Erreka, Ave de Cumba, 64210 Bidart [05 59 54 93 64; fax 05 59 47 70 46; erreka@seagreen.fr; www.seagreen-campingerreka.com] Site at junc of D810 Biarritz by-pass & main rd into town cent; well sp. Lge, pt shd, pt sl, terr, wc; chem disp; mv service pnt; fam bthrm; shwrs; EHU (6A) €4; gas; lndry; shop; snacks; playgrnd; pool; paddling pool; beach sand 800m; entmnt; wifi; TV; 75% statics; adv bkg acc; quiet; ccard acc; CKE/CCI. "Some pitches sl & poss v diff to get into, rec adv bkg to ensure suitable pitch; access rds v steep." 16 Jun-16 Sep. € 22.00   2016*

BIARRITZ *8F1 (4km SW Coastal) 43.45525, -1.58119*
Camping Pavillon Royal, Ave du Prince de Galles, 64210 Bidart [05 59 23 00 54; fax 05 59 23 44 47; info@pavillon-royal.com; www.pavillon-royal.com] Exit A63/E4 junc 4; then take D810 S dir Bidart. At rndabt after Intermarché supmkt turn R (sp Biarritz). After 600m turn L at site sp. Lge, hdg, mkd, pt shd, pt sl, serviced pitches; wc; chem disp; mv service pnt; fam bthrm; shwrs inc; EHU (10A) inc (long lead poss req); gas; lndry; shop; rest; snacks; bar; bbq; playgrnd; pool (htd); paddling pool; beach sand adj; entmnt; wifi; TV; Eng spkn; adv bkg rec; ccard acc; tennis nr; golf 500m; games rm; horseriding 2km. "Lovely, well-kept, busy site in beautiful location beside beach; various pitch sizes, some with sea views, some sm & diff lge o'fits; direct access via steps to excel beach; fitness rm; san facs poss irreg cleaning LS; mkt Sat; excel; adv bkg rec as ess; no o'fits over 8m; avoid pitches on perimeter fence as damage to vehicles fr stray golf balls; vg, helpful, friendly staff; excel shwrs, wc, shop, bar & rest." ♦ 15 May-29 Sep. € 60.00   2014*

See advertisement opposite

BINIC *2E3 (1km S Coastal) 48.59216, -2.8238*
Camping Le Panoramic, Rue Gasselin, 22520 Binic [02 96 73 60 43; fax 02 96 69 27 66; lepanoramic22@gmail.com; www.lepanoramic.net] D786 St Brieuc-Paimpol. 1st slip rd for Binic & 1st R up hill 100m, site sp. Med, mkd, pt shd, pt sl, terr, wc (htd); chem disp; shwrs; EHU (10A) €5 (poss rev pol); gas; lndry; shop; snacks; bar; bbq; pool (htd); paddling pool; beach sand 500m; entmnt; wifi; 75% statics; dogs €2.50; quiet; golf adj. "Pleasant site; coastal path nr; clean, excel facs, easy walk to beach & town." 2 Apr-30 Sep. € 30.00   2016*

BINIC *2E3* (3km S Coastal) *48.58269, -2.80477*
Camping Les Madières, Rue du Vau Madec, 22590 Pordic [02 96 79 02 48; fax 02 96 79 46 67; campinglesmadieres@wanadoo.fr; www.campinglesmadieres.com] Site at E end of Pordic vill, sp. Med, pt shd, pt sl, wc (htd); shwrs inc; EHU (10A) €4; gas; lndry; shop; rest; snacks; bar; pool (htd); beach shgl 800m; entmnt; 10% statics; dogs €2.50; adv bkg acc; quiet; watersports 3km; CKE/CCI. "Pleasant, clean, child-friendly site; helpful, friendly owners; immac facs; poss diff access to shgl beach, Binic beach OK; highly rec; beach sand 3km; quiet site." ♦ 30 Mar-2 Nov. € 32.00   2013*

BINIC *2E3* (4km S Coastal) *48.57875, -2.78498* Camping Le Roc de l'Hervieu, 19 Rue d'Estienne d'Orves, 22590 Pordic [02 96 79 30 12; le.roc.de.lherviu@wanadoo.fr; www.campinglerocdelhervieu.fr] Site on E side of vill off N786, Binic-St Brieuc rd. Turn E in cent of vill, sp to Les Madières then sp Le Roc de l'Hervieu. Med, hdg, pt shd, wc; chem disp; mv service pnt; shwrs inc; EHU (10A) €3.60; lndry; shop; bar; bbq; playgrnd; beach sand 600m; 10% statics; quiet; fishing. "Gd walking; pleasant, gd site." ♦ 1 May-30 Sep. € 21.00   2017*

BISCARROSSE *7D1* (3km N Coastal) *44.42955, -1.16792* Campéole Camping Navarrosse, 712 Chemin de Navarrosse, 40600 Biscarrosse [05 58 09 84 32; fax 05 58 09 86 22; navarrosse@campeole.com; www.camping-navarrosse.com or www.campeole.com] Fr Biscarrosse N on D652 dir Sanguinet; 1km beyond turning to L to Biscarrosse-Plage, turn L onto D305 & foll sp to Navarrosse. V lge, mkd, pt shd, wc (htd); mv service pnt; fam bthrm; shwrs inc; EHU (10A) inc (poss rev pol); lndry; shop nr; rest nr; snacks; bar; bbq; playgrnd; sw nr; red long stay; entmnt; wifi; TV; 40% statics; dogs; Eng spkn; quiet; ccard acc; games area; sailing; games rm; fishing; bike hire; tennis; CKE/CCI. "Pleasant site; vg for children; helpful staff; late arr area; gd walking; sailing lessons; cycle rtes; gd value." ♦ 30 Apr-12 Sep. € 33.00   2012*

BISCARROSSE *7D1* (5km N Rural) *44.43996, -1.14068* Aire Naturelle Le Frézat (Dubourg), 2583 Chemin de Mayotte, 40600 Biscarrosse [06 22 65 57 37; www.biscarrosse.com] Fr Biscarrosse on D652 dir Sanguinet; after 5km turn L at water tower onto D333; site 2nd on R in 1km. Med, shd, wc; chem disp; shwrs; EHU (6A) inc; shop nr; bbq; playgrnd; dogs; Eng spkn; adv bkg acc; quiet; CKE/CCI. "Lovely site; friendly owners; clean facs; cycle paths." 15 Apr-15 Oct. € 15.00   2014*

BISCARROSSE *7D1* (5km N Rural) *44.42715, -1.16078* Camping Bimbo, 176 Chemin de Bimbo, 40600 Biscarrosse [05 58 09 85 33; info@campingbimbo.fr; www.campingbimbo.fr] Fr Biscarrosse take D652 N. At rndabt take 2nd exit (D305) sp Biscarrosse Lac. After 1.5km turn R twds Chemin de Bimbo, site on R in 500m. Med, shd, wc; chem disp; fam bthrm; shwrs; EHU (3-10A) inc (poss rev pol); shop; rest; bar; pool (htd); paddling pool; wifi; 80% statics; adv bkg acc; games area; watersports 1km. "Excel full facs site; beach 10km excel for surfing; bakery, pizzeria & creperie on site." 1 Apr-30 Sep. € 50.00   2014*

BISCARROSSE *7D1* (5km N Rural) *44.43535, -1.15496* Camping Village Mayotte Vacances, 368 Chemin des Roseaux, 40600 Biscarrosse [05 58 78 00 00; fax 05 58 78 83 91; camping@mayottevacances.com; www.mayottevacances.com] Twd NE fr Biscarrosse on D652 L sp Navarrosse & at 1st fork R to Mayotte, foll camping sp. V lge, mkd, pt shd, wc; chem disp; mv service pnt; shwrs inc; EHU (10A) inc (poss rev pol); gas; lndry; shop; rest; snacks; bar; bbq; playgrnd; pool; sw nr; entmnt; TV; 95% statics; dogs €5; Eng spkn; adv bkg rec; quiet; ccard acc; tennis; waterslide; games rm; sailing school; bike hire; jacuzzi; CKE/CCI. "Excel leisure facs; vg for families; suitable o'fits up to 8m; rec." ♦ 3 Apr-3 Oct. € 43.00   2016*

BISCARROSSE

BISCARROSSE *7D1* (8km NE Rural) *44.46230, -1.12900* Camping de la Rive, Route de Bordeaux, 40600 Biscarrosse [05 58 78 12 33; fax 05 58 78 12 92; info@larive.fr; www.larive.fr] Fr Bordeaux on A63 dir Bayonne/San Sebastian; at junc 22 turn off onto A660; cont until 1st junc where turn L onto D216; cont for 17km to Sanguinet; cont on A652 for 3km; site sp on R nr Lake Cazaux. V lge, mkd, hdg, pt shd, wc (htd); chem disp; mv service pnt; fam bthrm; shwrs inc; EHU (6A) inc; gas; lndry; shop; rest; snacks; bar; bbq (gas); playgrnd; pool (covrd, htd); paddling pool; sw nr; entmnt; wifi; TV; 30% statics; dogs €8.20; phone; Eng spkn; adv bkg acc; ccard acc; games rm; jacuzzi; tennis; waterslide; bike hire; watersports; games area; CKE/CCI. "On banks of Lake Cazaux-Sanguinet in delightful area; bustling, noisy site high ssn; many acitivies for all ages; no c'van/m'van over 9m; some pitches diff lge o'fits due trees; gd beaches; gd cycling; lovely rest, pleasant staff." ♦ 12 Apr-30 Aug. € 68.00 2013*

See advertisement opposite

BISCARROSSE *7D1* (8km NW Coastal) *44.45804, -1.23968* Campéole Camping Le Vivier, 681 Rue du Tit, 40600 Biscarrosse-Plage [05 58 78 25 76; fax 05 58 78 35 23; contact@andretriganogroupe.com; www.campeole.co.uk] Fr Arcachon & Pyla-sur-Mer, take D218, D83 to Biscarrosse Plage. Town o'skts site sp to R. Foll sps. Lge, pt shd, wc; chem disp; fam bthrm; shwrs; EHU (10A) inc (poss rev pol); lndry; shop; rest; snacks; bar; playgrnd; pool (htd); paddling pool; beach sand 800m; entmnt; wifi; 25% statics; dogs €2.50; quiet; ccard acc; fishing; bike hire; games rm; boating; tennis; horseriding nr. "Sandy site in pine forest; access to beach via path thro dunes." 28 Apr-17 Sep. € 41.20 2017*

BISCARROSSE *7D1* (9km NW Coastal) *44.44133, -1.24558* Campéole Camping Plage Sud, 230 Rue des Bécasses, 40600 Biscarrosse-Plage [05 58 78 21 24; fax 05 58 78 34 23; plage-sud@campeole.com; www.landes-camping.net or www.campeole.com] Clearly sp on D146 on ent to Biscarrosse-Plage in pine forest. V lge, mkd, pt shd, pt sl, wc; chem disp; fam bthrm; shwrs inc; EHU (6A) inc; lndry; shop nr; snacks; bar; bbq; playgrnd; pool (htd); paddling pool; beach sand 800m; entmnt; wifi; 50% statics; dogs €3.50; Eng spkn; adv bkg rec; ccard acc; bike hire; CKE/CCI. "Gd site, lively high ssn; helpful staff; facs stretched high ssn; gd beach, inc surfing; some pitches on soft sand; sm, modern town, lots of rests; new entmnt, pool and san facs (2013); excel for sh or long stay." 27 Apr-15 Sep. € 54.40 2013*

BIZE MINERVOIS *8F4* (0km SW Urban) *43.31584, 2.87070* Camping De La Cesse, Esplanade Champs de Foire, 11120 Bize-Minervois [04 68 46 14 40; marieange.lurqui@gmail.com; www.audetourisme.com] Exit N fr D5/D11 Béziers-Carcassonne rd onto D26 to Bize-Minervois (D26 is 800m to E of D607); site in 1.8km on L, just bef rv bdge in S of vill. Sm, mkd, pt shd, wc; chem disp; shwrs inc; EHU (5A) €2.30; lndry; shop nr; rest nr; bbq; dogs €1.20; phone; adv bkg acc; quiet; CKE/CCI. "Peaceful, relaxing site; in need of TLC (2015)." 1 May-30 Sep. € 12.00 2015*

BLANC, LE *4H2* (2km E Rural) *46.63202, 1.09389* Camping L'Ile d'Avant, Route de Châteauroux, 36300 Le Blanc [02 54 37 88 22; fax 02 54 36 35 42; info@tourisme-leblanc.fr; www.tourisme-leblanc.fr] Fr town cent take D951 twd St Gaultier/Argenton; site on R 1km after supmkt. Med, hdg, mkd, pt shd, wc; mv service pnt; shwrs inc; EHU (6A) inc; lndry; shop nr; rest nr; bar nr; bbq; playgrnd; adv bkg acc; quiet; fishing; tennis adj. "Gd pitches; htd pool adj inc; adj sports field & club house; open Apr with adv bkg only, otherwise May." 1 Apr-30 Sep. € 14.00 2012*

BLANGY LE CHATEAU *3D1* (1km N Rural) *49.24670, 0.27370* Camping Le Domaine du Lac, 14130 Blangy-le-Château [02 31 64 62 00; fax 02 31 65 03 46; info@domaine-du-lac.fr; www.domaine-du-lac.fr] Fr Pont-l'Evêque & A13 S on D579 twd Lisieux. In 5km turn L onto D51 to Blangy where at fountain (rndabt) turn L, taking care. In 200m at end of vill turn L onto D140 Rte de Mesnil & site 200m on R. Site is 5km SE of Pont-l'Evêque. Med, mkd, pt shd, pt sl, wc; chem disp; fam bthrm; shwrs inc; EHU (6A) inc (long lead poss req); gas; lndry; shop; rest; snacks; bar; bbq; wifi; 70% statics; dogs; adv bkg acc; ccard acc; games rm; tennis; lake fishing; CKE/CCI. "Peaceful NH in lovely area; friendly British owner; poss uneven pitches; tired, access to pitches diff when wet; pretty vill; gd walks; conv Honfleur; 1hr to Le Havre ferry; NH only; mainly statics." 1 Apr-31 Oct. € 24.00 2013*

BLANGY LE CHATEAU *3D1* (3km SE Rural) *49.22525, 0.30438* Camping Le Brévedent, 14130 Le Brévedent [02 31 64 72 88 or 02 31 64 21 50 (LS); contact@campinglebrevedent.com; www.campinglebrevedent.com] Fr Pont l'Evêque & A13 go S on D579 twd Lisieux; after 5km turn L onto D51 twd Blangy-le-Château. In Blangy bear R at rndabt to stay on D51 & foll sp to Le Brévedent & Moyaux; site on L in just after le Breveden vill. Med, mkd, pt shd, pt sl, wc (htd); chem disp; mv service pnt; fam bthrm; shwrs inc; EHU (10A) (poss long leads req, poss rev pol); lndry; shop; rest; snacks; bar; bbq; playgrnd; pool (htd); paddling pool; entmnt; wifi; TV; 10% statics; phone; Eng spkn; adv bkg acc; quiet; ccard acc; horseriding 2km; games area; bike hire; tennis; games rm; golf 11km; lake fishing; CKE/CCI. "Pleasant, busy site with all amenities, aruonet lake in grnds of chateau; welcoming, helpful staff; no o'fits over 8m; some modern san facs, ltd LS; gd pool; rallies welcome; excel." ♦ 3 May-12 Sep. € 44.00 2014*

LA RIVE
RESORT & SPA
★★★★★

In the heart of Les Landes and with direct access to the lake of Biscarrosse-Sanguinet. La Rive Resort & Spa has the pleasure to welcome you for the new season in its new and modern reception. You will discover a gigantic aquatic zone of 6500 M2, of which 3300 M2 covered and heated, with a wave pool and Jacuzzi. Outside there is a new 30 meter long swimming pool, 200 meters of water slides and a wild river, our great success. The children can enjoy the kid´s club while parents can relax at the Spa. The entire family can enjoy a nice meal in the Bar-Restaurant or enjoy one of the activities and animations. The innovative concept of our new accommodations ensures comfort and satisfaction.

40600 BISCARROSSE (France)
+33 (0)5 58 78 12 33
info@larive.fr

www.larive.fr

BLANGY SUR BRESLE

BLANGY SUR BRESLE *3C2 (2km SE Rural) 49.92378, 1.65693* **Camping Aux Cygnes d'Opale (formerly Municipal), Zone de Loisirs, 76340 Blangy-sur-Bresle [02 35 94 55 65 or 09 72 32 88 40; fax 09 72 32 88 41; contact@auxcygnesdopale.fr; www.auxcygnesdopale.fr]** Leave A28 at junc 5, R at T-junc onto D49, site on L in 800m. Med, mkd, unshd, wc; chem disp; mv service pnt; fam bthrm; shwrs inc; EHU (5-16A) €3 (poss rev pol); lndry; shop nr; rest nr; bar nr; bbq; playgrnd; wifi; 20% statics; dogs €2; phone; adv bkg rec; tennis nr; CKE/CCI. "Attractive, well-kept site adj lakes; conv Calais, A28 & D928; gd san facs; adv bkg rec lge o'fits high ssn; no twin axles; pleasant & helpful warden; rec wait for warden for pitching; mini golf nr; poss waterlogged in wet (& ent refused); avoid during Int'l Petanque Competition 3rd w/end June on adj leisure cent; excel NH; new owners (2013), many improvements; new pool." ♦ 1 Apr-31 Oct. € 21.00 2016*

BLANGY SUR BRESLE *3C2 (8km W Rural) 49.95430, 1.55098* **Camp Municipal La Forêt, 76340 Bazinval [02 32 97 04 01; bazinval2@wanadoo.fr]** NW fr Blangy on D49 for 6km, then D149 to Bazinval. Site sp. Sm, hdg, pt shd, pt sl, wc; chem disp; shwrs inc; EHU (10A) €4 (poss rev pol); shop nr; playgrnd; twin axles; Eng spkn; quiet; games area; games rm; CKE/CCI. "Gd san facs, poss inadequate; site yourself, warden calls early eve; poss travellers on site; NH only; lovely, peaceful site; conv Dieppe; vg." 1 Apr-30 Oct. € 10.40 2018*

BLAYE *7C2 (5km NE Rural) 45.16708, -0.61666* **Aire Naturelle Les Tilleuls (Paille), Domaine Les Alberts, 33390 Mazion [05 57 42 18 13; fax 05 57 42 13 01; chateau-alberts@hotmail.com]** Fr Blaye on D937 N, sp to site on L. Sm, pt shd, pt sl, own san req; EHU (3-10A) €2.50; bbq; dogs; Eng spkn; CKE/CCI. "Lovely, family-run site in vineyards; charming owners; clean basic san facs; wine-tasting; easy cycling nrby, cycle track to Blaye." 1 May-15 Oct. € 12.50 2013*

⊞ **BLENEAU** *4G3 (12km NE Rural) 47.75833, 3.09960* **Camping Le Bois Guillaume, 89350 Villeneuve-les-Genêts [03 86 45 45 41; fax 03 86 45 49 20; camping@bois-guillaume.com; www.bois-guillaume.com]** Fr W on D965 dir St Fargeau. At Mézilles take D7 thro Tannerre-en-Puisaye; stay on D7 & after 3.5km foll sp for site. Or fr A6 exit junc 18 onto D16 thro Charny, then turn L onto D119 to Champignelles; take D7 dir Tannere for approx 2km; turn R & foll sp to site. Med, hdstg, mkd, hdg, shd, wc (htd); chem disp; mv service pnt; shwrs inc; EHU (5-10A) €3.10-4.60; gas; rest; bar; playgrnd; pool (htd); wifi; dogs €1.40; Eng spkn; tennis; bike hire; games area; CKE/CCI. "Friendly staff; clean, tidy site; facs ltd LS; vg rest." € 14.00 2016*

BLERE *4G2 (1km E Urban) 47.32791, 0.99685* **Camping La Gâtine (Formaly Municipal), Rue de Cdt Le Maître, 37150 Bléré [02 47 57 92 60; info@campingblereplage.com]** Exit A10 S of Tours onto A85 E. Exit A85 junc 11 dir Bléré. Site in 5km adj sports cent on S side of Rv Cher. Lge, mkd, pt shd, wc; chem disp; mv service pnt; fam bthrm; shwrs inc; EHU (10A) €4 (poss rev pol & long lead poss req); lndry; shop nr; snacks; bar nr; bbq; twin axles; wifi; dogs €1.20; adv bkg acc; quiet; ccard acc; rv fishing adj; CKE/CCI. "Excel, well-kept, peaceful, pleasant site; clean san facs, some dated & stretched when site full, some modernised; some dated EHU poss unrel in wet; gd cent for wine rtes & chateaux; htd pool adj high ssn; unrel opening dates LS; new management; looking a bit neglected (2017); excel cycle routes adj." ♦ 1 Apr-10 Oct. € 18.00 2017*

BLOIS *4G2 (12km NE Rural) 47.68666, 1.48583* **Camping Le Château de la Grenouillère, 41500 Suèvres [02 54 87 80 37; fax 02 54 87 84 21; la.grenouillere@wanadoo.fr; www.camping-loire.com or www.les-castels.com]** Exit A10 junc 16 sp Chambord, Mer; take rd to Mer; go thro Mer on D2152 dir Blois; site in 5km, 2km NE of Suèvres. Lge, mkd, pt shd, wc; chem disp; mv service pnt; fam bthrm; shwrs inc; EHU (10A) inc; gas; lndry; shop; rest; snacks; bar; bbq (charcoal, gas); playgrnd; pool (covrd); paddling pool; entmnt; wifi; TV; adv bkg req; ccard acc; bike hire; sauna; waterslide; gym; fishing; tennis; boating; games rm; CKE/CCI. "Ideal for Loire area; clean modern san facs, poss ltd LS; no o'fits over 15m; statics (tour ops); some superb leisure facs; mkt Wed & Sat Blois." ♦ 18 Apr-12 Sep. € 34.00 2014*

BLOIS *4G2 (10km E Rural) 47.59149, 1.45894* **Camping de Chatillon (formerly Aire Naturelle), 6 Rue de Châtillon, 41350 Huisseau-sur-Cosson [02 54 20 35 26]** Fr Blois cross Rv Loire on D765 dir Vineuil. 1km S turn L onto D33. Site at E end of vill of Huisseau on R. Sm, mkd, hdg, pt shd, pt sl, wc; chem disp; mv service pnt; shwrs inc; EHU (10A) €4.20 (poss rev pol); gas; shop nr; dogs €1.50; adv bkg acc; quiet; CKE/CCI. "Pretty, peaceful, garden site; lovely, even LS; beautiful area; friendly owner; gd clean san facs, but ltd; conv Loire Valley chateaux; cycle rte thro Chambord forest; Son et Lumière show in town; rec; delightful, spacious and spotless site." ♦ 1 May-20 Sep. € 18.00 2014*

BLOIS *4G2 (8km S Rural) 47.52539, 1.38675* **Camp Municipal, Rue du Conon, 41120 Cellettes [02 54 70 48 41 or 02 54 70 47 54 (Mairie)]** On D956, Blois to Châteauroux rd, pass almost thro Cellettes, site 120m fr D956 down 1st L after rv bdge, site on L in 100m, well sp. NB Turn-in narr fr v busy main rd. Med, pt shd, wc; chem disp; shwrs inc; EHU (5A) €2.80; shop; snacks; pool; phone; quiet; ccard acc; tennis adj; games area; fishing; CKE/CCI. "Lovely, peaceful site in pleasant rvside location; lge pitches; friendly, helpful warden; Eng spkn; gd san facs; don't checkout late without telling warden - she locks EHU boxes; poss boggy after rain; playgrnd adj; excel for Loire châteaux; rec." ♦ 1 Jun-30 Sep. € 9.30 2014*

BLOIS *4G2* **(6km SW Rural) 47.54379, 1.31114**
FFCC Camping Le Cosson, 1 Rue de la Forêt, 41120 Chailles [02 54 79 46 49] Fr Blois foll sp dir Montrichard (D751); after x-ing rv bdge at rndabt take 1st exit sp Montrichard/Chailles (D751); after x-ing sm rv bdge in Chailles take 1st L onto Rue de la Forêt; site in 50m; sm sp easily missed. Sm, hdg, pt shd, wc cont; chem disp; fam bthrm; shwrs inc; EHU (6A) €3.50; shop nr; playgrnd; dogs; phone; adv bkg acc; games area; CKE/CCI. "Well-maintained, quiet site nr chateaux; pleasant, helpful owners; walks & cycle paths in local forest; poss tired pitches & facs end of ssn; tel no at gate for warden to come and unlock toilet block if site is empty." 1 Apr-15 Oct. € 13.00   2014*

BLOIS *4G2* **(18km W Rural) 47.54277, 1.15712 Ferme de Prunay, 41150 SEILLAC [09 53 86 02 01 or 06 98 99 09 86; contact@prunay.com; www.prunay.fr]** Take exit Blois on the A10; foll dir for Angers Chateau Renault until Molineuf, then Chambon sur Cisse and Seillac, rd D131. Med, mkd, pt shd, wc; chem disp; fam bthrm; shwrs inc; EHU (12A); lndry; shop; rest; snacks; bar; bbq; playgrnd; pool; paddling pool; entmnt; wifi; TV; dogs; Eng spkn; ccard acc; bike hire; games area; fishing. "In the heart of the Loire Valley; spacious pitches; v nice site; san facs tired." 31 Mar-3 Nov. € 37.00   2018*

BOEN SUR LIGNON *9B1* **(1km S Urban) 45.73688, 4.00777 Camping Municipal Domaine De Giraud, Rue de Camping, 42130 Boen Sur Lignon [04 77 24 08 91; camping.boen@orange.fr; www.boen.fr]** Fr Clermont Ferrand head E on D2089. Cont onto D1089. Site well sp immed on exiting Boen sur Lignon. Med, mkd, pt shd, pt sl, wc; chem disp; fam bthrm; shwrs; EHU (10A); bbq; playgrnd; twin axles; TV; 4% statics; dogs; Eng spkn; games area; games rm; CCI. "Peaceful, well run site, 10 mins stroll fr town cent with rest, bars, shops, supmkt & lndry; sports facs nrby; vg." ♦ 20 Mar-20 Oct. € 15.60   2014*

BOIS DE CENE *2H4* **(1km S Rural) 46.93385, -1.88728 Camping Le Bois Joli, 2 Rue de Châteauneuf, 85710 Bois-de-Céné [02 51 68 20 05; fax 02 51 68 46 40; contact@camping-leboisjoli.com; www.camping-leboisjoli.com]** Fr D21 turn R at church in cent of vill, site on R in 500m on rd D28. Med, hdg, pt shd, wc; chem disp; mv service pnt; shwrs inc; EHU (10A); gas; lndry; shop nr; snacks; bar; bbq; playgrnd; pool (covrd, htd); paddling pool; entmnt; wifi; 10% statics; dogs €3.50; phone; bus in vill; Eng spkn; adv bkg acc; fishing; bike hire; games area; tennis; CKE/CCI. "Friendly, helpful owner; clean san facs; gd walks; lovely pool; great site; ltd facs LS; rec; excel." 1 Apr-10 Oct. € 24.50   2016*

BOLLENE *9D2* **(6km E Rural) 44.29811, 4.78645**
FFCC Camping et Centre Equestre La Simioune, Quartier Guffiage, 84500 Bollène [04 90 30 44 62; fax 04 90 30 44 77; la-simioune@wanadoo.fr; www.la-simioune.fr] Exit A7 junc 19 onto D994/D8 dir Carpentras (Ave Salvatore Allende D8). At 3rd x-rd turn L into Ave Alphonse Daudet dir Lambique & foll rd 3km to sp for camping on L, then site 1km. Sm, shd, pt sl, wc; chem disp; fam bthrm; shwrs; EHU (6A) €3; lndry; shop nr; rest; bar; bbq; playgrnd; pool; paddling pool; entmnt; 10% statics; dogs €2; adv bkg rec; quiet; horseriding; CKE/CCI. "In pine forest; facs ltd in winter; pony club for children & adults; NH only; lovely site." 1 Mar-31 Oct. € 24.00   2017*

BOLLENE *9D2* **(7km E Rural) 44.29124, 4.83837**
FFCC Camping Le Pont du Lez, Ave es Côtes du Rhône, 26790 Suze-la-Rousse [04 75 98 82 83; camping-lepontdulez@wanadoo.fr] E fr Bollène on D94 to Suze-la-Rousse; L in vill sq; R immed bef rv bdge. Sm, pt shd, wc; shwrs inc; EHU (6-10A) €3.40 (long lead poss req); lndry; shop nr; snacks; bar; playgrnd; TV; dogs €1.40; fishing; games area; CKE/CCI. "Lovely but decrepit (2009); basic, clean facs - hot water to shwrs only; lovely area." 1 Apr-30 Sep. € 13.00   2017*

BOLLENE *9D2* **(6km SW Rural) 44.24335, 4.72931**
FFCC Camping La Pinède en Provence, Quartier des Massanes, 84430 Mondragon [04 90 40 82 98; fax 09 59 92 16 56; contact@camping-pinede-provence.com; www.camping-pinede-provence.com] Exit A7 junc 19 dir Bollène & take D26 S, site 1.5km N of Mondragon. Steep access. Med, mkd, pt shd, pt sl, terr, wc (htd); chem disp; mv service pnt; fam bthrm; shwrs inc; EHU (8-13A) €4.40-4.85; lndry; shop; bbq; playgrnd; pool; 10% statics; dogs €2; adv bkg acc; quiet; CKE/CCI. "Gd, clean site; gd touring base; conv Ardèche Gorge." 14 Feb-14 Nov. € 20.00   2013*

BONIFACIO *10H2* **(15km N Coastal) 41.47326, 9.26318 Camping Rondinara, Suartone, 20169 Bonifacio [04 95 70 43 15; fax 04 95 70 56 79; reception@rondinara.fr; www.rondinara.fr]** Fr Bonifacio take N198 dir Porte-Vecchio for 10km, then turn R onto D158 dir Suartone (lge camp sp at turning). Site in 5km. NB D158 single track, many bends & hills. Med, pt shd, pt sl, wc; mv service pnt; shwrs inc; EHU (6A) €3.60; lndry; shop; rest; snacks; bar; bbq; playgrnd; pool; beach sand 400m; 10% statics; dogs €2.60; Eng spkn; quiet; ccard acc; games area; watersports; games rm; CKE/CCI. "Excel rest; idyllic location by bay; excel new san facs 2013; rd to campsite steep and narr in places; adv bkg for mkd pitches fr May." 15 May-30 Sep. € 41.00   2014*

BONIFACIO

BONIFACIO *10H2* (4km NE Rural) *41.39986, 9.20141*
Camping Pian del Fosse, Route de Sant' Amanza, 20169 Bonifacio [04 95 73 16 34; camping@piandelfosse.com; www.piandelfosse.com] Leave Bonifacio on D58 dir Sant' Amanza, site on L in 4km. Sm, mkd, hdg, shd, terr, wc; chem disp; mv service pnt; fam bthrm; shwrs inc; EHU (4A) €3.80; lndry; shop; snacks; bbq; playgrnd; beach shgl 3km; red long stay; 20% statics; dogs €2.50; Eng spkn; quiet. "Pitches poss diff lge m'vans due o'hanging trees, vg; ccard acc." ♦ Easter-15 Oct. € 41.50   2013*

"I need an on-site restaurant"

We do our best to make sure site information is correct, but it is always best to check any must-have facilities are still available or will be open during your visit.

BONNAC LA COTE *7B3* (1km S Rural) *45.93238, 1.28977* Camping Le Château de Leychoisier, 1 Route de Leychoisier, 87270 Bonnac-la-Côte [05 55 39 93 43; contact@leychoisier.com; chateau-de-leychoisier.pagesperso-orange.fr] Fr S on A20 exit junc 27 & L at T-junc onto D220. At rndabt take 3rd exit then 1st L onto D97. At mini-rndabt in Bonnac take 2nd exit, site on L in 1km. Fr N exit A20 junc 27, turn R at T-junc onto D97, then as above. Med, mkd, hdg, pt shd, sl, wc; chem disp; mv service pnt; fam bthrm; shwrs inc; EHU (10A) inc; lndry; shop; rest; snacks; bar; bbq (charcoal, gas); playgrnd; pool; twin axles; wifi; TV; dogs €3; phone; Eng spkn; adv bkg acc; ccard acc; games rm; fishing; tennis; CKE/CCI. "Peaceful site in grnds of chateau; lge pitches; welcoming, friendly & helpful staff; no o'fits over 20m; clean san facs but dated, unisex; excel rest; extra for m'vans; blocks req some pitches; rallies welcome; conv NH nr m'way; excel; ccard not acc for 1 night stay; access for lge o'fits diff; gd rest/pool area; less commercial then other Les Castels sites." ♦ 15 Apr-20 Sep. € 34.00   2017*

BONNAL *6G2* (4km N Rural) *47.50777, 6.35583* Camping Le Val de Bonnal, 1 Chemin du Moulin, 25680 Bonnal [03 81 86 90 87; fax 03 81 86 03 92; www.camping-valdebonnal.com or www.les-castels.com] Fr N on D9 fr Vesoul or Villersexel to Esprels, turn S onto D49 sp 'Val de Bonnal'. Fr S exit A36 junc 5 & turn N onto D50 sp Rougemont, site sp to N of Rougemont. Lge, mkd, pt shd, wc; chem disp; mv service pnt; fam bthrm; shwrs inc; EHU (5-10A) inc (poss rev pol); gas; lndry; shop; rest; snacks; bar; bbq; playgrnd; pool; paddling pool; sw nr; twin axles; entmnt; wifi; TV; 40% statics; dogs €2; Eng spkn; adv bkg acc; quiet; ccard acc; fishing; golf 6km; games rm; gym; bike hire; waterslide; canoe hire; watersports; CKE/CCI. "Attractive, busy site; lge accessible pitches; excel welcome; modern, clean san facs; gd child activities; ltd facs LS; tour ops." ♦ 7 May-6 Sep. € 48.40   2016*

BONNEVAL *4F2* (1km SE Rural) *48.17080, 1.38640* Camping Le Bois Chièvre, Route de Vouvray, St Maurice, 28800 Bonneval [02 37 47 54 01; fax 02 37 96 26 79] Rec app fr N (Chartres), or SE (D27 fr Patay/Orléans) as app fr S thro town is narr & diff. Fr Chartres take N10 into Bonneval & foll camp sp (mainly to L). Med, hdg, hdstg, mkd, shd, pt sl, wc (htd); chem disp; mv service pnt; shwrs inc; EHU (6A) inc (rev pol); lndry; shop nr; rest; snacks; bar; bbq; playgrnd; 10% statics; dogs €1.20; Eng spkn; adv bkg acc; quiet; CKE/CCI. "Well-run, well-kept site in woodland; gd, lge pitches; htd pool adj inc; friendly, helpful staff; vg facs but poss stretched in ssn; vg NH for Le Havre or Dieppe." ♦ 1 Apr-20 Oct. € 17.00   2018*

BONNEVILLE *9A3* (1km NE Rural) *46.08206, 6.41288* Camp Municipal Le Bois des Tours, 314 Rue des Bairiers, 74130 Bonneville [04 50 97 04 31 or 04 50 25 22 00 (Mairie)] Fr A40 junc 16 take D1203, or fr Cluses take D1205 to Bonneville. Cross rv bdge into town cent; site sp. Med, pt shd, wc; chem disp; shwrs; EHU (5A) €2.50; shop nr; bbq; playgrnd; adv bkg acc; quiet. "Well-maintained, immac site; gd san facs." 1 Jul-6 Sep. € 8.00   2012*

BONNIERES SUR SEINE *3D2* (7km E Rural) *49.04646, 1.66256* Camping Loisirs des Groux, 1 Chemin de L'ile, 78270 Mousseaux-sur-Seine [01 34 79 33 86; www.campingdesgroux.com] Fr W exit A13 junc 15 onto D113 dir Bonnières. Cont thro Bonnières, turn L onto D37 Mousseaux/Base de Loisirs. Cont strt on D37/D124/D125 & then turn R & foll site sp. Fr E exit A13 junc 14 sp Bonnières & foll sp Zone Industrielle. At rndabt take D113 Bonnières, then as above. Med, mkd, hdg, pt shd, wc; mv service pnt; shwrs inc; EHU (6A) €3.18; lndry; bbq; sw nr; wifi; 90% statics; dogs; Eng spkn; adv bkg rec; quiet; ccard acc; games area; CKE/CCI. "Conv Paris (65km); Versailles, Rouen, Giverny; lge pitches; friendly, helpful staff; basic, dated san facs; leisure cent inc pool 2km; poss clsd earlier than published dates - phone ahead to check in LS; long winding track fr main rd; poor quality." ♦ 15 Mar-30 Nov. € 20.00   2016*

BONNIEUX *10E2* (2km W Rural) *43.81893, 5.31170* Camp Municipal du Vallon, Route de Ménerbes, 84480 Bonnieux [04 90 75 86 14 or 06 48 08 46 79 (mob); contact@campinglevallon.com; www.campinglevallon.com] Fr Bonnieux take D3 twd Ménerbes, site sp on L on leaving vill. Med, mkd, pt shd, terr, wc; chem disp; shwrs inc; EHU (6-10A) €3.80; lndry; shop; snacks; bar; playgrnd; wifi; dogs €2; Eng spkn; quiet; CKE/CCI. "Beautiful, quaint, 'olde worlde' site in wooded area; friendly warden; basic facs but clean; gd walking & mountain biking; attractive hilltop vill; gd touring base; gd rest in walking dist." 15 Mar-15 Oct. € 19.50   2015*

BONZEE *5D1* (2km E Rural) *49.09539, 5.61173*
Base de Loisirs du Colvert Les Eglantines, 55160 Bonzée [03 29 87 31 98; fax 03 29 87 30 60; campingscolvert@free.fr; http://base-de-loisirs-du-colvert.fr] Fr Verdun take D903 twd Metz for 18km; in Manheulles, turn R to Bonzée in 1km; at Bonzée turn L for Fresnes; site on R, adj Camping Marguerites. Or fr A4 exit junc 32 to Fresnes; then foll sp Bonzée. Med, hdg, mkd, pt shd, wc; chem disp; mv service pnt; shwrs inc; EHU (4-6A) €3.71-5.30; gas; lndry; shop; rest; snacks; bar; bbq; playgrnd; sw nr; twin axles; 80% statics; dogs €1.26; phone; Eng spkn; adv bkg acc; ccard acc; boating adj; waterslide; fishing; tennis 1.5km; CKE/CCI. "Spacious pitches in well-planned sites (2 sites together); facs ltd LS; v friendly staff." ♦ 1 Apr-27 Sep. € 15.50   2016*

⊞ **BORDEAUX** *7C2* (7km N Rural) *44.89701, -0.58317*
Camping Le Village du Lac Bordeaux, Blvd Jacques Chaban Delmas, 33520 Bordeaux-Bruges [05 57 87 70 60; fax 05 57 87 70 61; contact@village-du-lac.com; www.camping-bordeaux.com] On ring rd A630 take exit 5 twd lake; site sp on N side of lake, 500m N of Parc des Expositions. Lge, hdstg, mkd, pt shd, wc (htd); chem disp; mv service pnt; fam bthrm; shwrs inc; EHU (10A) inc; lndry; shop; rest; snacks; bar; bbq; playgrnd; pool; paddling pool; sw; wifi; TV; 50% statics; dogs €5; bus/tram to city; Eng spkn; adv bkg acc; quiet; ccard acc; fishing adj; games rm; bike hire; CKE/CCI. "Busy, poorly laid out, modern site; friendly staff; san facs poss streched high ssn; plenty elec & water pnts; excel rest; conv Bordeaux; easy access fr ring rd; pitches poss soft and muddy after rain; bus/tram conn to city; vg rest; gd unisex facs." ♦ € 34.00   2017*

⊞ **BORDEAUX** *7C2* (4km S Urban) *44.75529, -0.62772* **Camping Beausoleil, 371 Cours du Général de Gaulle, 33170 Gradignan [05 56 89 17 66; campingbeausoleil@wanadoo.fr; www.camping-beausoleil-gradignan.fr]** Fr N take exit 16 fr Bordeaux ring rd onto D1010 sp Gradignan. Fr S exit A63 junc 24 onto D211 to Jauge then D1010 to Gradignan. Site S of Gradignan on R after Beau Soleil complex, sp. Sm, mkd, hdstg, hdg, pt shd, pt sl, wc (htd); chem disp; shwrs inc; EHU (6-10A) €1.50 -3 (poss rev pol); lndry; shop nr; rest nr; bar nr; bbq (elec, gas); sw nr; wifi; 70% statics; dogs €1; bus/tram 250m; Eng spkn; adv bkg rec; quiet; CKE/CCI. "Pleasant, family-run site; helpful owners; vg, modern, clean san facs; ltd touring pitches; sm pitches not suitable lge o'fits; adv bkg rec; excel; gd sm site; booking necessary; htd pool & waterslides 5km; highly rec; excel & cheap park & ride tram sys 6km away; lovely quiet gdn site; easy bus rte to city." ♦ € 20.00   2017*

⊞ **BOULOGNE SUR MER** *3A2* (17km E Rural) *50.73337, 1.82440* **Camping à la Ferme Le Bois Groult (Leclercq), 120 impasse du Bois Groult, 62142 Henneveux Le Plouy [03 21 33 32 16; leclercq.gilbert0643@orange.fr; www.leboisgroult.fr]** Take N42 fr Boulogne twd St Omer, take exit S dir Desvres (D127). Immed at rndabt foll sp Colembert. On ent Le Plouy turn R at the calvary & foll sp to site in 1km. Sm, hdstg, pt shd, pt sl, wc; shwrs; EHU (6-10A) €5; shop nr; wifi; dogs €1; adv bkg acc; quiet. "Charming, well-kept, peaceful CL-type site; pleasant & helpful owner; no barrier; WWI places of interest; easy access fr N42; ideal NH to/fr ferry/tunnel; excel; v clean & tidy site; vg; shwrs €2." ♦ € 15.00   2018*

BOULOGNE SUR MER *3A2* (8km E Rural) *50.73111, 1.71582* **Camp Municipal Les Sapins, Route de Crémarest, 62360 La Capelle-lès-Boulogne [03 21 83 16 61]** Exit A16 junc 31 E onto N42 to La Capelle vill; cont to next rndabt & take sp Crémarest; site on L opp horse riding school. Sm, pt shd, wc; shwrs inc; EHU (4-6A) €2.35-4.60 (poss rev pol); lndry; shop nr; rest nr; bar nr; bbq; playgrnd; beach sand 4km; bus 1km; adv bkg acc; CKE/CCI. "Helpful warden; gd modern san facs but insufficient amount; office 0800-0900 & 1600-1700; gd NH for Calais; poss travellers." 15 Apr-15 Sep. € 17.00   2014*

BOULOGNE SUR MER *3A2* (7km S Urban) *50.67752, 1.64335* **Camping Les Cytises, Chemin Georges Ducrocq, 62360 Isques [03 21 31 11 10 or 06 62 91 72 71 (LS); campcytises@orange.fr; www.lescytises.fr]** S fr Boulogne on D901 to Isques; site 150m fr D901. Or on A16 exit junc 28 & foll sp Isques & camp sp. Med, hdg, hdstg, pt shd, terr, wc (htd); chem disp; mv service pnt; fam bthrm; shwrs inc; EHU (6A) inc (poss rev pol); gas; lndry; shop nr; snacks; playgrnd; pool; beach sand 4km; 50% statics; dogs €1; Eng spkn; adv bkg acc; ccard acc; games area; games rm; CKE/CCI. "Pleasant site; poss sm pitches; friendly staff; clean, modern san facs, ltd LS; barrier clsd 2300-0700; conv Channel Tunnel & 5 mins fr Nausicaá; poss unkempt LS; conv NH nr m'way; gd." ♦ 29 Mar-19 Oct. € 19.50   2014*

BOULOGNE SUR MER *3A2* (8km SSW Coastal) *50.67128, 1.57079* **FFCC Camp Municipal La Falaise, Rue Charles Cazin, 62224 Equihen-Plage [03 21 31 22 61; fax 03 21 80 54 01; camping.equihen.plage@orange.fr; www.camping-equihen-plage.fr]** Exit A16 junc 28 onto D901 dir Boulogne, then D940 S. Turn R to Condette then foll sp Equihen-Plage, site sp in vill. Access fr D901 via narr rds. Med, hdg, pt shd, sl, terr, wc; chem disp; mv service pnt; shwrs inc; EHU (10-16A) €4.90-5.40 (poss rev pol); lndry; playgrnd; beach sand 200m; 85% statics; dogs €2.40; phone; adv bkg acc; ccard acc; games rm; watersports; CKE/CCI. "Pleasant, well-run site in excel location, but poss windy; excel clean facs; sl pitches poss diff long o'fits; steep rd to beach." 28 Mar-12 Nov. € 24.00   2015*

BOULOU, LE

BOULOU, LE *8G4* (4km N Rural) *42.54157, 2.83431* Camping Le Mas Llinas, 66165 Le Boulou [04 68 83 25 46; info@camping-mas-llinas.com; www.camping-mas-llinas.com] Fr Perpignan, take D900 S; 1km N of Le Boulou turn R at Intermarché supmkt 100m to mini rndabt, turn L & foll sp to Mas-Llinas to site in 2km. Or fr A9 exit 43 & foll sp Perpignan thro Le Boulou. L at rndabt adj Leclerc supmkt, site well sp. Med, pt shd, terr, wc (htd); chem disp; shwrs inc; EHU (5-10A) €4.10-5.20; gas; lndry; snacks; bbq; playgrnd; pool; paddling pool; TV; 10% statics; dogs €2.20; phone; Eng spkn; adv bkg acc; bike hire; games area; games rm; CKE/CCI. "Friendly, welcoming owners; peaceful, scenic site, mountain views; v peaceful; beware poss high winds on high pitches; ltd water points at top levels; ltd facs LS; facs clean; gd sized pitches; golden orioles on site." ♦ 1 Feb-30 Nov. € 27.00 2017*

BOULOU, LE *8G4* (5km S Rural) *42.49083, 2.79477* Camping Les Pins/Le Congo, Route de Céret, 66480 Maureillas-las-Illas [04 68 83 23 21; fax 04 68 83 45 64; lespinslecongo@hotmail.fr; www.camping-lespinslecongo.com] Fr Le Boulou take D900 S, fork R after 2km onto D618 dir Céret. Site on L 500m after Maureillas. Med, hdg, hdstg, wc (htd); chem disp; shwrs inc; EHU (10A) €3.50; gas; lndry; shop nr; rest; snacks; bbq; playgrnd; pool; 10% statics; dogs; phone; Eng spkn; adv bkg acc; ccard acc. "Shabby and expensive, shwrs OK (2010)." ♦ 1 Feb-30 Nov. € 23.00 2012*

BOULOU, LE *8G4* (4km SW Rural) *42.50664, 2.79502* Camping de la Vallée, Route de Maureillas, 66490 St Jean-Pla-de-Corts [04 68 83 23 20; fax 04 68 83 07 94; campingdelavallee@yahoo.fr; www.campingdelavallee.com] Exit A9 at Le Boulou. Turn W on D115. Turn L after 3km at rndabt, into St Jean-Pla-de-Corts, thro vill, over bdge, site on L. Med, mkd, pt shd, wc (htd); chem disp; mv service pnt; fam bthrm; shwrs inc; EHU (5A) €4; lndry; shop nr; rest; snacks; bar; playgrnd; pool; sw nr; red long stay; entmnt; wifi; TV; 50% statics; dogs €2.50; phone; bus adj; Eng spkn; adv bkg acc; quiet; ccard acc; fishing 1km; archery; CKE/CCI. "Lovely well-kept site; easy access lge, well mkd pitches; friendly, helpful owners with gd local info; excel san facs; conv NH fr A9 or longer; highly rec." ♦ 1 Apr-31 Oct. € 24.60 2018*

⊞ **BOULOU, LE** *8G4* (4km W Rural) *42.50908, 2.78429* FFCC Camping Les Casteillets, 66490 St Jean Pla-de-Corts [04 68 83 26 83; fax 04 68 83 39 67; jc@campinglescasteillets.com; www.campinglescasteillets.com] Exit A9 at Le Boulou; turn W on D115; after 3km turn L immed after St Jean-Pla-de-Corts; site sp on R in 400m. NB Narr app last 200m. Med, mkd, pt shd, serviced pitches; wc; chem disp; shwrs inc; EHU (6A) €3.50 (poss rev pol); gas; lndry; shop; rest; snacks; bar; playgrnd; pool; red long stay; entmnt; wifi; TV; 10% statics; Eng spkn; adv bkg rec; quiet; tennis; games area. "Lovely, friendly, scenic, well run site; lge pitches; conv for touring & en rte NE Spain; low lying; gd food in rest; gd." ♦ € 28.00 2018*

BOURBON LANCY *9A1* (1km S Rural) *46.61949, 3.75506* Camping Le Plan d'Eau du Breuil, 71140 Bourbon Lancy [03 86 37 95 83 or 03 85 89 20 98; fax 03 86 37 79 20; contact@aquadis-loisirs.com; www.aquadis-loisirs.com] Site sp fr town, on lakeside. Sm, pt shd, pt sl, wc; chem disp; shwrs inc; EHU (6A); lndry; snacks; bbq; pool; paddling pool; wifi; TV; dogs €1.50; adv bkg acc; quiet; CKE/CCI. "Excel; 2km to town; lake adj; bike rec." 1 Jun-15 Sep. € 16.00 2017*

BOURBON LANCY *4H4* (0km WNW Urban) *46.62098, 3.76557* Camping St Prix, Rue de St Prix, 71140 Bourbon-Lancy [03 85 89 20 98 or 03 86 37 95 83; aquadis1@wanadoo.fr; www.aquadis-loisirs.com] Fr N turn L fr D979 on D973 & foll into Bourbon-Lancy. Turn R at traff lts after Attac Sup'mkt, keep L, site on R after mini-rndabt. Med, hdstg, hdg, shd, pt sl, terr, wc (htd); chem disp; shwrs inc; EHU (10A) €2; lndry; shop; snacks; playgrnd; pool (htd); sw; 25% statics; dogs €3.10; Eng spkn; quiet; fishing; CKE/CCI. "Tidy, well-run site; helpful staff; new san facs; lovely old town 10 min uphill walk; rec." ♦ Easter-1 Nov. € 14.50 2012*

BOURBON L'ARCHAMBAULT *9A1* (1km W Rural) *46.58058, 3.04804* Camp Municipal de Bignon, 03160 Bourbon-l'Archambault [04 70 67 08 83; fax 04 70 67 35 35; mairie-bourbon-archambault@wanadoo.fr] Exit D953 at Bourbon-l'Archambault onto D1 northwards; in 400m turn L into Blvd Jean Bignon. Site sp. Lge, pt shd, sl, wc; shwrs inc; EHU (6-10A) €2-2.20; lndry; shop nr; wifi; 75% statics; quiet; tennis nr. "Beautifully laid-out in park surroundings; htd pool 300m; waterslide 300m; gd pitches; excel updated san facs (2013); charming town; excel." 1 Mar-12 Nov. € 6.40 2014*

BOURBOULE, LA *7B4* (3km NE Rural) *45.59680, 2.75130* FFCC Camping Le Panoramique, Le Pessy, 63150 Murat-le-Quaire [04 73 81 18 79; fax 04 73 65 57 34; info@campingpanoramique.fr; www.campingpanoramique.fr] Exit A89 junc 25; cont strt until junc with D922; turn R; in 3km turn R onto D219 dir Mont-Dore; in 5km pass thro Murat-le-Quaire; in 1km turn L in Le Pessy; site on L in 300m. Site well sp fr D922. Med, mkd, pt shd, terr, wc (htd); chem disp; mv service pnt; fam bthrm; shwrs inc; EHU (6-10A) €4.30-5.60; gas; lndry; shop nr; rest nr; bar; playgrnd; pool; 50% statics; dogs €1.70; phone; adv bkg acc; quiet; games rm; CKE/CCI. "Site well set-out; mountain views; friendly, helpful recep; clean but dated facs; vg." 15 Feb-15 Mar & 12 Apr-30 Sep. € 24.00 2016*

BOURBOULE, LA *7B4* (1km E Rural) *45.58980, 2.75257* Camp Municipal des Vernières, Ave de Lattre de Tassigny, 63150 La Bourboule [04 73 81 10 20 or 04 73 81 31 00 (Mairie); fax 04 73 65 54 98] Fr N on N89 or S on D922 turn E onto D130 dir Le Mont-Dore, site sp. Lge, hdg, pt shd, terr, wc (htd); chem disp; shwrs inc; EHU (10A) €3.50; lndry; shop nr; playgrnd; dogs €1; fishing nr. "Lovely setting in mountains; gd clean facs; sh walk to fine spa town; gd family site; rec." ♦ Easter-30 Sep. € 10.00 2012*

BOURBOULE, LA 7B4 (4km E Rural) 45.59456, 2.76347 Camping Les Clarines, 1424 Ave Maréchal Leclerc, 63150 La Bourboule [04 73 81 02 30; fax 04 73 81 09 34; clarines.les@wanadoo.fr; www.camping-les-clarines.com] Fr La Bourboule take D996/D88 on N bank of rv (old rd sp Piscine & Gare); fork L at exit fr town. Site sp on R, nr junc with D219. Lge, pt shd, terr, wc (htd); fam bthrm; shwrs inc; EHU (6-10A) €3.50-€5.80; gas; lndry; shop; bar; bbq; playgrnd; pool (htd); paddling pool; entmnt; wifi; TV; dogs €2; adv bkg rec; quiet; games area. "Gd winter sports cent; excel htd facs." ♦ 19 Dec-17 Oct. € 16.00 2012*

BOURDEAUX 9D2 (1km SE Rural) 44.57854, 5.12791 Camping Les Bois du Châtelas, Route de Dieulefit, 26460 Bourdeaux [04 75 00 60 80; fax 04 75 00 60 81; contact@chatelas.com; www.chatelas.com] Fr N exit A7 m'way junc 16 onto D104, head twd Crest. Shortly bef Crest turn R onto D538 S thro Bourdeaux & cont dir Dienlefit (still on D538), site in 1km on L, well sp. Med, mkd, pt shd, terr, wc (htd); chem disp; mv service pnt; fam bthrm; shwrs inc; EHU (10A) inc; gas; lndry; shop; rest; snacks; bar; bbq (elec, gas); cooking facs; playgrnd; pool (covrd, htd); paddling pool; entmnt; wifi; TV; 30% statics; dogs €5; phone; Eng spkn; adv bkg req; ccard acc; games area; horseriding 5km; bike hire; games rm; waterslide; sauna; fitness rm; CKE/CCI. "In lovely, scenic area; site on steep slope; no o'fits over 8m high ssn; gd walking." ♦ 11 Apr-13 Sep. € 34.70 2016*

BOURG ACHARD 3D2 (1km W Rural) 49.35330, 0.80814 Camping Le Clos Normand, 235 Route de Pont Audemer, 27310 Bourg-Achard [02 32 56 34 84 or 06 40 25 53 14 (mob); contact@leclosnormand-camping.com; leclosnormand-camping.fr] 1km W of vill of Bourg-Achard, D675 Rouen-Pont Audemer or exit A13 at Bourg-Achard junc. Med, mkd, hdg, pt shd, pt sl, wc; shwrs inc; EHU (6A) €3.40 (poss rev pol & poss long lead req); gas; shop; playgrnd; pool; paddling pool; 10% statics; dogs free; adv bkg acc; ccard acc; CKE/CCI. "Vg, clean san facs; plenty hot water; many pitches uneven; gd; muddy when wet." ♦ 15 Apr-30 Sep. € 21.00 2016*

⊞ **BOURG ARGENTAL** 9C2 (2km E Rural) 45.29910, 4.58183 Camping Domaine de l'Astrée, L'Allier, 42220 Bourg-Argental [04 77 39 72 97 or 04 77 39 63 49 (TO); prl@bourgargental.fr] S fr St Etienne on D1082 to Bourg-Argental, thro town, site well sp on R soon after rndabt & opp filling stn. Fr Annonay or Andance site on L of D1082 at start of Bourg-Argental, adj rv. Sm, mkd, hdstg, pt shd, wc; chem disp; shwrs inc; EHU (4-6A) inc (long cable poss req); gas; lndry; shop nr; snacks; bbq; playgrnd; paddling pool; 60% statics; dogs €1.60; phone; ccard acc; waterslide; games rm; tennis; fishing; bike hire; CKE/CCI. "Pleasant site with modern facs; htd pool 600m; vg." ♦ € 19.50 2017*

BOURG D'OISANS, LE

BOURG D'OISANS, LE 9C3 (2km NE Rural) 45.06557, 6.03980 Camping à la Rencontre du Soleil, Route de l'Alpe-d'Huez, La Sarenne, 38520 Le Bourg-d'Oisans [04 76 79 12 22; fax 04 76 80 26 37; rencontre.soleil@wanadoo.fr; www.alarencontredusoleil.com] Fr D1091 approx 800m E of town turn N onto D211, sp 'Alpe d'Huez'. In approx 500m cross sm bdge over Rv Sarennes, then turn immed L to site. (Take care not to overshoot ent, as poss diff to turn back). Med, hdg, mkd, pt shd, wc (htd); chem disp; mv service pnt; fam bthrm; shwrs inc; EHU (10A) inc; lndry; shop nr; rest; snacks; bar; bbq; playgrnd; pool (htd); entmnt; wifi; TV; 45% statics; dogs €1; adv bkg req; ccard acc; games rm; tennis; fishing; horseriding 1.5km; games area; CKE/CCI. "Busy site with lovely views; various pitch sizes/shapes; excel, spotless san facs, some unisex; helpful owner; excel rest; La Marmotte cycle race (early Jul) & Tour de France usually pass thro area & access poss restricted; no o'fits over 7m high ssn; pitches poss flooded after heavy rain, but staff excel at responding; mkt Sat; highly rec." 1 May-30 Sep. € 38.00 2012*

BOURG D'OISANS, LE 9C3 (2km NE Rural) 45.06401, 6.03895 Camping La Cascade, Route de l'Alpe d'Huez, 38520 Le Bourg-d'Oisans [04 76 80 02 42; fax 04 76 80 22 63; lacascade@wanadoo.fr; www.lacascadesarenne.com] Fr W drive thro Le Bourg-d'Oisans & cross bdge over Rv Romanche. Approx 800m E of town turn onto D211, sp Alpe-d'Huez. Site on R in 600m. Med, mkd, pt shd, wc (htd); chem disp; fam bthrm; shwrs; EHU (16A) €4.30; lndry; shop nr; snacks; bar; playgrnd; pool (htd); wifi; 10% statics; dogs free; Eng spkn; adv bkg acc; quiet; ccard acc; CKE/CCI. "V friendly, helpful staff; discounts for ski passes fr recep; modern san block; superb high pressure shwrs." 1 Jan-30 Sep & 15 Dec-31 Dec. € 37.00 2015*

BOURG D'OISANS, LE 9C3 (13km SE Rural) 44.98611, 6.12027 Camping Le Champ du Moulin, Bourg d'Arud, 38520 Vénosc [04 76 80 07 38; fax 04 76 80 24 44; info@champ-du-moulin.com; www.champ-du-moulin.com] On D1091 SE fr Le Bourg-d'Oisans sp Briançon for about 6km; turn R onto D530 twd La Bérarde & after 8km site sp. Turn R to site 350m after cable car stn beside Rv Vénéon. NB Site sp bef vill; do not cross rv on D530. Med, mkd, pt shd, wc; chem disp; mv service pnt; fam bthrm; shwrs inc; EHU (6-10A) €4.60-5.60 (extra charge in winter, poss rev pol); gas; lndry; shop; rest; snacks; bar; bbq; playgrnd; red long stay; wifi; TV; 20% statics; dogs €1.70; Eng spkn; adv bkg req; quiet; ccard acc; fishing nr; rafting nr; horseriding nr; sauna; games rm; tennis nr; CKE/CCI. "Lovely, well-run site by alpine torrent (unguarded); friendly, helpful owners; ltd facs LS; htd pool adj; access to pitches poss diff lge o'fits; ideal for walking, climbing & relaxing; no o'fits over 10m; lots of outdoor activities to enjoy; cable car to Les Deux Alpes adj (closes end Aug); mkt Tue Vénosc (high ssn); highly rec." ♦ 1 Jan-30 Apr, 1Jun-15 Sep, 15 Dec-31 Dec. € 35.00 2014*

BOURG D'OISANS, LE

BOURG D'OISANS, LE 9C3 (4km NW Rural) 45.09000, 6.00750 **Camping Ferme Noémie, Chemin Pierre Polycarpe, Les Sables, 38520 Le Bourg-d'Oisans [04 76 11 06 14 or 04 87 45 08 75 (mob); ferme. noemie@orange.fr; www.fermenoemie.fr]** On D1091 Grenoble to Briançon; Les Sables is 4km bef Le Bourg-d'Oisans; turn L next to church, site in 400m. Sm, mkd, unshd, wc (htd); chem disp; mv service pnt; shwrs inc; EHU (16A) €3.50; lndry; shop nr; rest nr; bbq (gas); playgrnd; red long stay; wifi; 25% statics; dogs free; phone; bus 500m; adv bkg acc; quiet; ccard acc; cycling; fishing; games area; CKE/CCI. "Simple site in superb location with excel facs; helpful British owners; lots of sports; skiing; walking; gd touring base lakes & Ecrins National Park; pool 3km; excel site." ♦ 1 May-30 Oct. € 29.00 2017*

BOURG D'OISANS, LE 9C3 (7km NW Rural) 45.11388, 6.00785 **RCN Camping Belledonne, Rochetaillée, 38520 Le Bourg-d'Oisans [04 76 80 07 18; fax 04 76 79 12 95; belledonne@rcn.fr; www.rcn-campings.fr]** Fr S of Grenoble take N85 to Vizille then D1091 twd Le Bourg-d'Oisans; in approx 25km in Rochetaillée turn L onto D526 sp Allemont. Site 100m on R. Med, hdg, shd, wc; chem disp; mv service pnt; fam bthrm; shwrs inc; EHU (10A) inc; lndry; shop; rest; snacks; bar; bbq; playgrnd; pool (htd); paddling pool; entmnt; wifi; TV; dogs €7; Eng spkn; quiet; ccard acc; sauna; games area; tennis; games rm; fishing 500m; horseriding; windsurfing; CKE/CCI. "Beautiful, well-run site in lovely location; no o'fits over 7.5m high ssn; friendly Dutch owners; access to many pitches tight; no twin axles; gd for teenagers; excel pool with views; many walks; gd touring base; La Marmotte cycle race (early Jun) & Tour de France usually pass thro area & access poss restricted; mkt Sat; excel new san facs (2018), gd rest; v helpful staff." ♦ 11 May-2 Oct. € 41.60 2018*

> **"Satellite navigation makes touring much easier"**
>
> Remember most sat navs don't know if you're towing or in a larger vehicle – always use yours alongside maps and site directions.

BOURG EN BRESSE 9A2 (11km NE Rural) 46.29078, 5.29078 **Camp Municipal du Sevron, Chemin du Moulin, 01370 St Etienne-du-Bois [04 74 24 05 47 or 06 47 97 50 73 (mob); campingdusevron@gmail. com; www.campingdusevron.fr]** On D1083 at S end of vill of St Etienne-du-Bois on E side of rd. Sm, hdg, pt shd, wc; chem disp; shwrs inc; EHU (10A) €2.05; shop nr; 50% statics; dogs €1.06; Eng spkn; ccard acc; rv fishing; tennis. "Gd NH; dated but clean facs; friendly; sm pitches; late arr get v sm pitches; poss rd & rlwy noise; gd shwrs & plenty hot water; gd facs." 1 Mar-25 Oct. € 17.00 2018*

BOURG ET COMIN 3D4 (1km NE Rural) 49.39871, 3.66072 **Camping de la Pointe, 5 Rue de Moulins, 02160 Bourg-et-Comin [03 23 25 87 52; fax 03 23 25 06 02; michel.pennec@9online.fr; www.tourisme-paysdelaon.com]** Leave A26/E17 at junc 14 & turn W along D925 dir Soissons for 15km. Site on R on ent vill. Sm, hdg, pt shd, wc (htd); chem disp; mv service pnt; shwrs inc; EHU (6A) €3.20; lndry; rest; bar nr; bbq; playgrnd; pool (covrd, htd); wifi; dogs €2; phone; bus 500m; Eng spkn; adv bkg acc; quiet; CKE/CCI. "CL-type site in orchard; narr ent & access to pitches poss diff lge o'fits; most pitches sm & not suitable lge o'fits; EHU is only 2 pin; gd rest; gd walking area; 10 mins fr Parc Nautique de l'Ailette with watersports; conv Aisne Valley; bar 500m; v accommodating owner; htd pool OAY; wifi not reliable." € 20.80 2018*

BOURG MADAME 8H4 (6km NW Rural) 42.45979, 1.91075 **Camping Le Robinson, 25 Ave Gare Internationale, 66760 Enveitg [04 68 04 80 38 or 06 11 81 25 46 (mob); lerobinson-cerdagne@wanadoo. fr; www.robinson-cerdagne.com]** Fr Bourg-Madame, take N20 N twd Foix. Thro vill of Enveitg & turn L down Chemin de la Gare & L at camping sp. Lge, mkd, shd, pt sl, wc; chem disp; fam bthrm; shwrs inc; EHU (4-13A) €3-9; gas; lndry; shop nr; rest nr; snacks; bbq; playgrnd; pool; entmnt; TV; 10% statics; dogs €1.50; phone; adv bkg acc; quiet; games rm. "Beautiful setting; winter sports cent; conv Barcelona, Andorra; conv scenic rte train (Train Jaune); new management; new shwr block (excel)." ♦ € 20.00 2015*

BOURG ST ANDEOL 9D2 (2km N Rural) 44.38131, 4.64840 **Camping du Lion, Quartier Ile Chenevrier, 07700 Bourg-St Andéol [04 75 54 53 20; fax 09 74 44 55 70; contact@campingdulion.com; www. campingdulion.com]** Exit A7 at junc 18 or 19 onto N7. At Pierrelatte turn W on D59 to Bourg-St Andéol. Site sp fr cent near town ctr Viviers. Med, mkd, shd, wc; shwrs inc; EHU (6A) €3; lndry; shop; snacks; bar; playgrnd; pool; wifi; 10% statics; dogs €3; adv bkg acc; quiet; games rm; games area. "Peaceful site in woodland setting; muddy when wet; dir access to rv; highly rec; new san facs (2015)." 1 Apr-30 Sep. € 35.00 2016*

BOURG ST MAURICE 9B4 (1km E Rural) 45.62241, 6.78503 **Camping Le Versoyen, Route des Arcs, 73700 Bourg-St Maurice [04 79 07 03 45; fax 04 79 07 25 41; versoyen@camping-indigo.com; www. camping-bourgsaintmaurice.com]** Fr SW on N90 thro town turn R to Les Arcs. Site on R in 1km. Do not app fr any other dir. Lge, hdstg, pt shd, wc; chem disp; mv service pnt; shwrs inc; EHU (4-10A) €4.60-5.20; lndry; shop nr; playgrnd; entmnt; dogs €1; Eng spkn; quiet; fishing; sauna; games area; tennis adj; canoeing; CKE/CCI. "Excel for winter sports; mountain views; mkd walks fr site; 2 pools adj; rvside walk to town; well-organised site; dated but clean facs." ♦ 1 Jan-24 Apr, 25 May-3 Nov, 14 Dec-31 Dec. € 32.00 2013*

BOUSSAC

Grand Confort ★★★★ Le Château de Poinsouze

B.P. 12 Route de la Châtre
F-23600 BOUSSAC-BOURG
Tel.: 05 55 65 02 21
campingpoinsouze@gmail.com
www.camping-de-poinsouze.com
- Camping & accomodations
- Nature · Peace · Lake
- Swimming pool · Water slide
- Restaurant · Take away
- Bar · Animation 4-12 years
- Payable Wifi
- On-line reservation

France

BOURG SUR GIRONDE 7C2 (1km S Urban) 45.03880, -0.56065 **Camp Municipal La Citadelle, 33710 Bourg-sur-Gironde** [05 56 68 40 04; fax 05 57 68 39 84; commune-de-bourg@wanadoo.fr] Take D669 fr St André-de-Cubzac (off A10) to Bourg. Foll sp Halte Nautique & Le Port into Rue Franklin on L twd town cent & foll sp to site. Or fr Blaye, foll Camping sp on app Bourg, cont round by-pass to other end of town to Rue Franklin. NB Do not attempt to take c'van thro town. Sm, mkd, pt shd, wc; chem disp; mv service pnt; shwrs inc; EHU (3-10A) €3-6 (poss long lead req); shop nr; bbq; playgrnd; dogs; adv bkg acc; quiet; CKE/CCI. "Scenic, CL-type rvside site; well-maintained but basic facs; poss variable opening dates; pool adj; excel." ♦ 15 May-30 Sep. € 13.00   2013*

> **"There aren't many sites open at this time of year"**
>
> If you're travelling outside peak season remember to call ahead to check site opening dates – even if the entry says 'open all year'.

BOURGES 4H3 (2km S Urban) 47.07228, 2.39497 **Camp Municipal Robinson, 26 Blvd de l'Industrie, 18000 Bourges** [02 48 20 16 85; fax 02 48 50 32 39; camping@ville-bourges.fr; www.ville-bourges.fr] Exit A71/E11 at junc 7, foll sp Bourges Centre & bear R at 'Autres Directions' sp; foll site sp; site at traff lts on N side of S section of inner ring rd half-way bet junc with D2144 & D2076. NB: site access is via a loop - no L turn at traff lts, but rndabt just past site if turning missed. If on outer ring rd D400, app city on D2144 & then as above. Sp on app rds to site gd. Med, mkd, hdg, hdstg, pt shd, serviced pitches; wc (htd); chem disp; mv service pnt; shwrs inc; EHU (10-16A) €3.40-8 (poss rev pol); lndry; rest nr; bar nr; bbq (elec, gas); playgrnd; red long stay; twin axles; wifi; dogs €2.15; bus adj; Eng spkn; quiet; ccard acc; CKE/CCI. "Attractive, well-kept, well-organised, busy, rvside site in gd location; helpful, friendly staff; pool 300m inc; excel, immac san facs; some v lge pitches, some sm & poss diff ent; most pitches hdstg; excel NH or longer; 20 min walk to historic town." ♦ 30 Mar-28 Oct. € 24.00   2018*

BOURGUEIL 4G1 (1km S Rural) 47.26991, 0.16873 **Camp Municipal Parc Capitaine, 37140 Bourgueil** [02 47 97 85 62 or 02 47 97 25 00 LS; camping@bourgueil.fr; www.bourgueil.fr] N on D749 fr junc 5 of A85, site 1km on R. Fr W (Longue) via D10 & by-pass, S at rndabt on D749 to site on L in 200m. Do not app fr N via D749 thro town cent. Med, hdg, mkd, pt shd, wc; chem disp; mv service pnt; shwrs inc; EHU (10A) €2.50 (poss long lead req); gas; lndry; shop nr; playgrnd; sw; dogs €1.38; quiet; ccard acc; CKE/CCI. "Ideal cent Loire châteaux; 2 sites - one on R for tourers; excel; barrier ent & exit by code; office clsd 1230-1500 but warden lives upstairs; conv fr A85 & Loire valley; vg; san facs need refurb." ♦ 15 May-15 Sep. € 15.00   2017*

BOUSSAC 7A4 (2km NE Rural) 46.37192, 2.20036 **Camping du Château de Poinsouze, Route de la Châtre, 23600 Boussac-Bourg** [05 55 65 02 21; fax 05 55 65 86 49; camping-de-poinsouze@gmail.com; www.camping-de-poinsouze.com] Fr junc 10 on A71/E11 by-pass Montluçon via N145 dir Guéret; in 22km turn L onto D917 to Boussac; cont on D917 dir La Châtre; site 3km on L. Or fr Guéret on N145, exit Gouzon, at rndabt take D997 to Boussac, then as above. Med, mkd, unshd, pt sl, serviced pitches; wc; chem disp; mv service pnt; fam bthrm; shwrs inc; EHU (6-20A) inc (poss rev pol); lndry; shop; rest; snacks; bar; bbq; playgrnd; pool; paddling pool; entmnt; wifi; TV; 10% statics; dogs €3 (not acc mid-July to mid Aug; Eng spkn; adv bkg req; quiet; ccard acc; horseriding 5km; games area; games rm; waterslide; lake fishing; golf 20km; bike hire; CKE/CCI. "Peaceful, relaxed site by lake in chateau grnds; well-kept & well-run; lge pitches, some sl; no o'fits over 15m; welcoming, helpful owners; superb san facs; excel rest & snacks; gd for young children; gd walking." ♦ 15 May-15 Sep. € 41.00   2013*

See advertisement

BOUSSAC

BOUSSAC 7A4 (2km W Rural) 46.34938, 2.18462
Camping Creuse-Nature (Naturist), Route de Bétête, 23600 Boussac [05 55 65 18 01; fax 05 55 65 81 40; creuse-nature@wanadoo.fr; www.creuse-nature.com] Fr Boussac take D917 N twd La Châtre. In 500m turn L (W) on D15 sp Bétête. Site on R in 2.5km, clearly sp. Med, mkd, hdg, pt shd, pt sl, wc; shwrs; EHU (10A) €4.50 (poss long lead req); lndry; shop; rest; snacks; bar; playgrnd; pool (covrd, htd); paddling pool; entmnt; 10% statics; dogs €5.50; Eng spkn; adv bkg acc; quiet; ccard acc; fishing; games area. "Excel site in lovely area; great pitches; charming & helpful owners; clean facs; easy walk to town & interesting château; great location." ♦ 5 Apr-31 Oct. € 41.30   2014*

BRACIEUX 4G2 (1km N Urban) 47.55060, 1.53743
Camping Indigo les Châteaux, 11 Rue Roger Brun, 41250 Bracieux [02 54 46 41 84; fax 02 54 46 41 21; chateaux@camping-indigo.com; www.camping-indigo.com] Fr S take D102 to Bracieux fr Cour-Cheverny. Fr N exit Blois on D765 dir Romorantin; after 5km take D923 to Bracieux & site on R on N o'skts of town opp church, sp. Lge, hdg, mkd, hdstg, pt shd, wc; chem disp; shwrs inc; EHU (10A) €2.75 (poss long lead req); lndry; shop nr; rest nr; playgrnd; pool (covrd); paddling pool; red long stay; TV; 10% statics; dogs €2.80; Eng spkn; adv bkg acc; quiet; ccard acc; tennis; games rm; bike hire; CKE/CCI. "Peaceful spot; attractive forest area; busy high ssn; gd security; gd touring base; gas 300m; bike tracks; well run site; all san blocks replaced (2013); superb; excel, well run site." ♦ 30 Mar-4 Nov. € 32.00   2018*

BRANTOME 7C3 (1km E Rural) 45.36074, 0.66035
Camping Brantôme Peyrelevade, Ave André Maurois, 24310 Brantôme [05 53 05 75 24; fax 05 53 05 87 30; info@camping-dordogne.net; www.camping-dordogne.net] Fr N on D675 foll sp Centre Ville; ent vill & turn L onto D78 Thiviers rd, site sp at turn; in 1km on R past stadium opp g'ge. Fr S D939 foll sp 'Centre Ville' fr rndabt N of town. Then L onto D78 Thiviers rd & foll sp. Do not foll 'Centre Ville' sp fr rndabt S of town, use by-pass. Football stadium best ref point for ent. Lge, mkd, hdg, pt shd, wc (htd); chem disp; mv service pnt; fam bthrm; shwrs inc; EHU (10A) inc; lndry; shop nr; snacks; bar; bbq; playgrnd; pool; paddling pool; beach sand adj; sw nr; entmnt; wifi; 7% statics; dogs €2; Eng spkn; adv bkg acc; quiet; ccard acc; tennis nr; CKE/CCI. "Spacious, well-kept rvside site; attractive courtyard layout; friendly, helpful owners; excel, modern, gd san facs; facs stretched in high ssn; grnd poss soft after heavy rain; 10 min walk to lovely town (the Venice of Périgord); mkt Wed; games area adj; beautiful countryside; gd walking & cycling; excel; some pitches heavily shd; excel family camping." ♦ 1 May-30 Sep. € 26.00   2017*

BRANTOME 7C3 (4km SW Rural) 45.32931, 0.63690
Camping du Bas Meygnaud, 24310 Valeuil [05 53 05 58 44; camping-du-bas-meygnaud@wanadoo.fr; www.basmeygnaud.fr] Fr Brantôme, take D939 twd Périgueux; in 4.5km turn R at sp La Serre. In 1km turn L to in 500m, well sp. Winding, narr app thro lanes; poss diff lge o'fits. Sm, pt shd, pt sl, wc; chem disp; shwrs inc; EHU (6A) €3.50; lndry; shop; rest nr; snacks; bar; bbq; playgrnd; pool; entmnt; wifi; dogs €2.50; phone; Eng spkn; quiet; CKE/CCI. "Most pitches shd by pine trees; helpful & friendly owner; dated san facs; unspoilt countryside." 1 Apr-30 Sep. € 15.30   2013*

BRASSAC 8F4 (11km SE Rural) 43.59700, 2.60732
Camping Le Rouquié, Lac de la Raviège, 81260 Lamontélarie [05 63 70 98 06; fax 05 63 50 49 58; camping.rouquie@wanadoo.fr; www.campingrouquie.fr] Fr Brassac take D62 to N side of Lac de la Raviège; site on lakeside. Med, mkd, pt shd, terr, wc; chem disp; fam bthrm; shwrs; EHU (3-6A) €4; lndry; shop; snacks; bar; bbq; playgrnd; sw; entmnt; TV; 50% statics; dogs; adv bkg acc; quiet; ccard acc; bike hire; watersports adj; games area; fishing; sailing; CKE/CCI. "Ltd facs LS; gd lake views; site needs TLC." 15 Apr-31 Oct. € 25.00   2014*

BRASSAC 8F4 (5km S Rural) 43.60835, 2.47148 FFCC
Camping Le Plô, Le Bourg, 81260 Le Bez [05 63 74 00 82; info@leplo.com; www.leplo.com] Fr Castres on D622 to Brassac; then D53 S to Le Bez, site sp W of Le Bez. Med, mkd, pt shd, terr, wc; chem disp; fam bthrm; shwrs inc; EHU (6A) €3; lndry; shop nr; snacks; bbq; playgrnd; pool; wifi; dogs €1.50; Eng spkn; adv bkg acc; quiet; games area; games rm; bike hire; CKE/CCI. "Lovely location; well-equipped site; excel, clean san facs; friendly, helpful Dutch owners; beautiful, historical area with National Park; much wildlife; cafés & gd rest nrby; vg." ♦ 1 May-30 Sep. € 25.50   2014*

BRAUCOURT 6E1 (5km SW Rural) 48.55425, 4.79235
FLOWER Camping Presqu'île de Champaubert, Lac du Der, 52290 Braucourt [03 25 04 13 20; fax 03 25 94 33 51; camping-de-braucourt@wanadoo.fr; www.lescampingsduder.com or www.flowercampings.com] Fr St Dizier take D384 SW twd Montier-en-Der & Troyes. In Braucourt R onto D153 sp Presq'ile de Champaubert, site on L in 2km. Site situated on Lac du Der-Chantecoq. Lge, mkd, hdg, shd, serviced pitches; wc; chem disp; mv service pnt; shwrs inc; EHU (10A) €4 (rev pol); gas, lndry; shop; rest; snacks; bar; playgrnd; sw nr; TV; 60% statics; dogs €1; phone; quiet; ccard acc; boating; fishing; watersports; CKE/CCI. "Beautiful lge beach; birdwatching; lge pitches; improved san facs; gates clsd 2230; ltd spaces." ♦ 15 Apr-25 Nov. € 26.00   2016*

⊞ **BRAUCOURT** *6E1* (9km W Rural) *48.55754, 4.70629* **Camping Le Clos du Vieux Moulin, 33 Rue du Lac, 51290 Châtillon-sur-Broué [03 26 41 30 43; leclosduvieuxmoulin@wanadoo.fr; www.leclosduvieuxmoulin.fr]** Fr N take D13 fr Vitry-le-François. Turn R at sp for Châtillon-sur-Broué; site 100m on R. Fr S 2nd L fr Giffaumont (1km); site 100m on R. Med, hdstg, hdg, mkd, pt shd, pt sl, wc (htd); chem disp; fam bthrm; shwrs inc; EHU (5A) €3.70; gas; lndry; shop; rest nr; snacks; bar; playgrnd; pool; 80% statics; dogs; phone; quiet; ccard acc; watersports; CKE/CCI. "Busy high ssn; birdwatching; san facs need refurb (2010) & ltd LS; site poss unkempt (2010); grnd soft after rain." ♦ € 17.00   2013*

BRENGUES *7D4* (1km S Rural) *44.57509, 1.83261* **Camp Municipal de Brengues, 46320 Brengues [05 81 48 06 99]** W fr Figeac on D13. After 6km turn L onto D41. After 17km, turn L at x-rds with D38, site ent 100m on R bef bdge over Rv Célé. Sm, mkd, pt shd, wc; shwrs inc; EHU (10A) inc (rev pol); lndry; shop nr; rest; bar; playgrnd; sw; tennis; CKE/CCI. "Warden now onsite." 1 Jun-30 Sep. € 15.00   2018*

⊞ **BRESSE, LA** *6F3* (3km E Rural) *47.99893, 6.91801* **FFCC Camp Municipal Le Haut des Bluches, 5 Route des Planches, 88250 La Bresse [03 29 25 64 80; www.hautdesbluches.com]** Leave La Bresse on D34 Rte de la Schlucht. Site on R in 3km. Med, mkd, pt shd, terr, wc (htd); chem disp; mv service pnt; fam bthrm; shwrs inc; EHU (4-13A) €2-4.80; lndry; shop; rest; snacks; bar; bbq; playgrnd; wifi; TV; 10% statics; dogs free; Eng spkn; adv bkg acc; ccard acc; games rm; site clsd early Nov-mid Dec; games area; CKE/CCI. "Excel site in attractive setting; NH area for m'vans; excel san facs; pool in vill; gd walks fr site; conv winter sports." ♦ € 20.00   2017*

BRESSUIRE *4H1* (3km S Rural) *46.82923, -0.50223* **Camping Le Puy Rond, Allee du Puy Rond, Cornet, 79300 Bressuire [05 49 72 43 22 or 06 85 60 37 26 (mob); puyrondcamping@gmail.com; www.puyrondcamping.com]** Fr N149 foll site sp on rte 'Poids Lourds' to site on D38. Fr 'Centre Ville' foll sp for Fontenay-Le-Comte; turn R 100m after overhead bdge & go across junc to site. Well sp. Sm, mkd, pt shd, pt sl, terr, wc (htd); chem disp; mv service pnt; fam bthrm; shwrs inc; EHU (6-10A) €3.50; lndry; shop; rest nr; snacks; bar nr; bbq; playgrnd; pool; twin axles; red long stay; wifi; 15% statics; dogs €1.50; Eng spkn; adv bkg acc; quiet; ccard acc; fishing 1km; CKE/CCI. "Gd touring base, poss tired early ssn; friendly British owners; san facs updated & v gd (2016); adv bkg ess for twin axles; winter storage avail; vg." ♦ 15 Mar-30 Sep. € 25.00   2017*

⊞ **BREST** *2E2* (7km SW Coastal) *48.36544, -4.54163* **Camping du Goulet, Ste Anne-du-Porzic, 29200 Brest [02 98 45 86 84; campingdugoulet@wanadoo.fr; www.campingdugoulet.com]** On D789 turn L at site sp. Approx 4km fr Brest after R bend at T junc, turn L & L again at site sp; down hill to site. Med, unshd, pt sl, terr, wc (htd); chem disp; fam bthrm; shwrs inc; EHU (6-10A) €3-3.50; lndry; shop; snacks; playgrnd; pool; beach sand 1km; 15% statics; dogs €1.50; adv bkg acc; quiet; games area; games rm; waterslide; CKE/CCI. "Excel site; great location; but to Centerville; P&R to city." ♦ € 26.00   2015*

BRETENOUX *7C4* (0km N Urban) *44.91650, 1.83816* **Camping La Bourgnatelle, 46130 Bretenoux [05 65 10 89 04; fax 05 65 10 89 18; contact@dordogne_vacances.fr; www.dordogne-vacances.fr]** In town 100m fr D940. Lge, pt shd, wc; mv service pnt; shwrs inc; EHU (5-10A) €3; lndry; shop nr; rest; snacks; playgrnd; pool; entmnt; dogs €1.50; adv bkg acc; quiet; canoe hire; rv; fishing. "Lovely site along banks of Rv Cère; clean site; gd fishing; lovely town MD Tues." 19 Apr-31 Nov. € 33.40   2014*

BRETEUIL SUR L'ITON *4E2* (0km SSE Urban) *48.83175, 0.91258* **Camping Les Berges de l'Iton, 53 rue du Fourneau, 27160 Breteuil-sur-Iton [02 32 62 70 35 or 06 84 75 70 32 (mob); campinglesberges-de-liton@orange.fr; www.campinglesbergesdeliton.com]** Fr Evreux take D830 twd Conches-en-Ouche. L onto D840 to Breteuil, then foll sp for site. Med, mkd, hdstg, hdg, pt shd, pt sl, wc (htd); chem disp; mv service pnt; shwrs inc; EHU (6A) inc; gas; lndry; snacks; bar; bbq; playgrnd; wifi; 66% statics; dogs; adv bkg acc; INF; CCI. "Well kept, landscaped site; gd NH; mkt on Wednesdays; helpful staff; vg." 1 Apr-30 Sep. € 12.00   2014*

BRETIGNOLLES SUR MER *2H3* (1km E Urban) *46.63583, -1.85861* **Chadotel Camping La Trévillière, Route de Bellevue, 85470 Bretignolles-sur-Mer [02 51 90 09 65 or 02 51 33 05 05; fax 02 51 33 94 04; info@chadotel.com; www.chadotel.com]** S along D38 fr St Gilles Croix-de-Vie twd Olonne-sur-Mer, site is sp to L in Bretignolles-sur-Mer. Site 1km fr town cent nr football stadium. Sp fr town cent. Lge, hdg, mkd, pt shd, serviced pitches; wc; chem disp; mv service pnt; fam bthrm; shwrs inc; EHU (6A) inc; gas; lndry; shop; snacks; bar; bbq (gas); playgrnd; pool (covrd, htd); paddling pool; beach sand 1.5km; red long stay; entmnt; wifi; TV; 70% statics; dogs €3.20; phone; Eng spkn; adv bkg acc; ccard acc; bike hire; waterslide; fishing; horseriding 5km; watersports 3km; games rm; CKE/CCI. "Friendly, family site; lge pitches; no c'van/m'van over 8m high ssn; quiet; gd cycling area; salt marshes worth a visit; mkt Thu & Sun." ♦ 5 Apr-20 Sep. € 30.50   2012*

BRETIGNOLLES SUR MER

BRETIGNOLLES SUR MER 2H3 (5km E Rural) 46.64021, -1.80708 Camping L'Oree de l'Océan, Rue Capitaine de Mazenod, 85220 Landevieille [02 51 22 96 36; fax 02 51 22 29 09; info@camping-oreedelocean.com; www.camping-oreedelocean.com]
Take D12 fr La Mothe-Achard to St Julien-des-Landes & cont to x-rds bef La Chaize-Giraud. Turn L onto D32, take 1st R in Landevieille to site on L in 50m. Adj Mairie. Med, mkd, hdg, pt shd, pt sl, wc; chem disp; shwrs inc; EHU (10A) €4; lndry; shop nr; bar; playgrnd; pool (htd); beach sand 5km; red long stay; TV; 95% statics; dogs €3; phone; Eng spkn; adv bkg acc; quiet; ccard acc; tennis; CKE/CCI. "Gd, friendly, family site; many gd beaches & mkd cycle tracks nr; gd for NH." ♦ 1 Apr-30 Sep. € 23.00   2014*

BRETIGNOLLES SUR MER 2H3 (4km S Coastal) 46.60413, -1.83231 Camping Le Chaponnet, 16 Rue du Chaponnet, 85470 Brem-sur-Mer [02 51 90 55 56; fax 02 51 90 91 67; campingchaponnet@wanadoo.fr; www.le-chaponnet.com]
Fr La Roche-sur-Yon on N160 dir Les Sables-d'Olonne. Turn R onto D87 thro St Mathurin vill & take 1st R (just after church) D38 dir L'Ile d'Olonne. Foll sp Brem-sur-Mer, go thro vill & foll sp 'Océan' (nr bakery & bar); turn L opp hairdresser, site in 50m along 1-way rd. Lge, hdg, pt shd, wc; chem disp; fam bthrm; shwrs inc; EHU (10A) inc; gas; lndry; shop; rest; snacks; bar; bbq; playgrnd; pool (covrd, htd); beach sand 1km; entmnt; TV; 75% statics; dogs; phone; adv bkg acc; quiet; ccard acc; gym; games area; sauna; bike hire; waterslide; games rm; jacuzzi; tennis; CKE/CCI. "Gd beaches adj; vg." ♦ 14 Apr-15 Sep. € 34.00   2017*

⊞ BRIANCON 9C4 (6km NE Rural) 44.93034, 6.68129 Camp Municipal du Bois des Alberts, 05100 Montgenèvre [04 92 21 16 11 or 04 92 21 52 52; fax 04 92 21 98 15; www.montgenevre.com]
Take N94 fr Briançon sp Italie. In 4km turn L onto D994, site 200m past Les Alberts vill on L. Lge, hdstg, shd, wc (htd); chem disp; mv service pnt; fam bthrm; shwrs inc; EHU (6-10A) €4.25 (rev pol); lndry; shop; rest; snacks; bar; playgrnd; 30% statics; adv bkg acc; quiet; ccard acc; fishing; tennis; games area; CKE/CCI. "Pleasant, friendly site in pine trees; cycle & walking paths; x-country skiing; random pitching; facs dated but clean, ltd LS; lge pine cones can fall fr trees - park away fr tall ones; kayak tuition; gd touring base; nice site." ♦ € 13.00   2013*

BRIANCON 9C4 (4km SW Rural) 44.87737, 6.61634 Camping Les Cinq Vallées, St Blaise, 05100 Briançon [04 92 21 06 27; fax 04 92 20 41 69; infos@camping5vallees.com; www.camping5vallees.com]
S of Briançon by N94 to vill St Blaise. Ent on L. Med, pt shd, pt sl, wc; chem disp; mv service pnt; fam bthrm; shwrs inc; EHU (10A) inc; lndry; shop; rest; snacks; bar; playgrnd; pool (htd); wifi; TV; 80% statics; games rm. "Vg site; traff noise barely noticeable; gd shop on site with takeaway food; lge supmkt 2km." ♦ 1 Jun-30 Sep. € 23.60   2015*

BRIARE 4G3 (6km S Rural) 47.60018, 2.76101 Camping Municipal L'ecluse des Combles, Chemin de Loire, 45360 Châtillon-sur-Loire [02 38 36 34 39 or 06 32 07 83 45; camping.chatillonsurloire@orange.fr; www.camping.chatillon-sur-loire.com]
SE fr Briare on N7, in 4km turn SW onto D50. Site immed bef rv bdge on R. Care needed over bdge after ent. Med, pt shd, terr, wc (htd); chem disp; mv service pnt; shwrs inc; EHU (6A) inc; gas; lndry; shop nr; rest nr; bar nr; bbq; playgrnd; dogs €1.20; Eng spkn; quiet; fishing; games rm; CKE/CCI. "Basic site with some nice pitches by Rv Loire & historic canal; pleasant staff; right of way along rv bank passes thro site; mkt 2nd Thurs of month; vg; canal viaduct at Briare worth visit; site neglected; pitch yourself; warden in off late afternoon." ♦ 1 Apr-31 Oct. € 16.50   2017*

> **"That's changed – Should I let the Club know?"**
>
> If you find something on site that's different from the site entry, fill in a report and let us know. See camc.com/europereport.

BRIARE 4G3 (1km W Rural) 47.64137, 2.72560 Camping Le Martinet, Quai Tchékof, 45250 Briare [02 38 31 24 50 or 02 38 31 24 51; fax 02 38 31 39 10; campingbriare@recrea.fr; www.campinglemartinet.fr]
Exit N7 into Briare. Fr N immed R after canal bdge; fr S L bef 2nd canal bdge; sp. Lge, mkd, unshd, wc; shwrs inc; EHU (10A) €3.60; lndry; shop nr; rest nr; bar nr; dogs €1; adv bkg acc; quiet; fishing adj. "Gd views some pitches; pretty bars & rests along canal; gd walking & cycling; interesting town; gates close 2200; slightly neglected (2009); OK sh stay; san facs old style but clean." ♦ 30 Mar-30 Sep. € 22.00   2018*

BRIENNE LE CHATEAU 6E1 (6km S Rural) 48.34876, 4.52726 Camping Le Tertre, Route de Radonvilliers, 10500 Dienville [03 25 92 26 50; campingdutertre@wanadoo.fr; www.campingdutertre.fr]
On D443 S fr Brienne-le-Château; at Dienville turn R at rndabt onto D11; site on R in 200m, sp. NB Site opp Lake Amance harbour, foll sp 'Le Port'. Med, hdstg, hdg, mkd, pt shd, serviced pitches; wc; chem disp; mv service pnt; fam bthrm; shwrs inc; EHU (6-10A) €4 (poss long lead req); gas; lndry; shop; rest; snacks; bar; bbq; playgrnd; pool (htd); paddling pool; entmnt; wifi; TV; 10% statics; dogs €1; phone; bus 500m; Eng spkn; adv bkg acc; quiet; ccard acc; games rm; fishing; games area; gym; CKE/CCI. "Pleasant site 2 mins fr vill; man-made lake with sailing; excel site for all watersports & other activities; cycle tracks; vg; excel rest." ♦ 20 Mar-12 Oct. € 25.00   2016*

BRIONNE

BRIGNOGAN PLAGES *1D2 (1km NW Coastal) 48.67278, -4.32916* **Camping de la Côte des Légendes, Keravezan, 29890 Brignogan-Plages [02 98 83 41 65; fax 02 98 83 59 94; contact@campingcotedeslegendes.com; www.campingcotedeslegendes.com]** Fr Roscoff on D10, fr Brest on D788/770 or fr N12 exit dir Lesneven. In Brignogan foll sp Brignogan-Plages & 'Centre Nautique'. Lge, hdg, hdstg, mkd, pt shd, wc; chem disp; mv service pnt; fam bthrm; shwrs inc; EHU (5-10A) €3.15-4.05 (poss rev pol); lndry; shop; snacks; bar; bbq; playgrnd; beach sand adj; red long stay; entmnt; TV; 30% statics; dogs €1.40; phone; Eng spkn; adv bkg acc; quiet; ccard acc; sailing; watersports; CKE/CCI. "On beautiful sandy cove; friendly, helpful staff; site guarded 24 hrs; ltd facs LS; vg touring base in interesting area; vg." ♦ 29 Mar-12 Nov. € 20.00   2015*

BRIGNOGAN PLAGES *1D2 (2km NW Coastal) 48.67535, -4.34534* **Camping du Phare, Plage du Phare, 29890 Brignogan-Plages [02 98 83 45 06; fax 02 98 83 52 19; camping.du.phare@orange.fr; www.camping-du-phare.com]** Take D770 N fr Lesneven to Brignogan-Plages; take L fork in town cent & foll site sp dir Kerverven. Med, hdstg, hdg, pt shd, wc; chem disp; mv service pnt; shwrs; EHU (6A) €3; gas; lndry; shop nr; snacks; playgrnd; beach sand adj; wifi; 10% statics; dogs €2; Eng spkn; adv bkg acc; quiet; CKE/CCI. "Next to pretty bay & gd beach; helpful owner; vg site nr walking rte GR34." 1 Apr-30 Sep. € 22.00   2014*

BRIGNOLES *10F3 (9km SE Rural) 43.33919, 6.12579* **Camping La Vidaresse, 83136 Ste Anastasie-sur-Issole [04 94 72 21 75; fax 04 98 05 01 21; contact@campinglavidaresse.com; www.campinglavidaresse.com]** On DN7 2km W of Brignoles at rndabt take D43 dir Toulon. In about 10km turn L at rndabt to D15. Do not ent vill, go strt & site is approx 250m on R. Med, hdg, mkd, pt shd, terr, wc; chem disp; mv service pnt; shwrs inc; EHU (10A) €5 (poss rev pol); gas; lndry; shop nr; rest; snacks; bar; bbq (elec, gas); playgrnd; pool (covrd, htd); paddling pool; wifi; 40% statics; dogs €3; adv bkg acc; ccard acc; tennis; fishing 200m; games area; CKE/CCI. "Well-managed, family site in lovely area; peaceful; friendly & helpful; facs adequate; excel pool; gd touring base Haute Provence, Gorges du Verdon & Riviera; vineyard adj; gd." ♦ 20 Mar-30 Sep. € 25.00   2014*

⊞ **BRILLANE, LA** *10E3 (5km E Rural) 43.92282, 5.92369* **Camping les Oliviers, Chemin St Sauveur, 04700 Oraison [04 92 78 20 00; camping-oraison@wanadoo.fr; www.camping-oraison.fr]** Exit A51 junc 19; take rd E to Oraison in 2km; site sp in vill. Med, mkd, pt shd, pt sl, terr, wc; chem disp; mv service pnt; fam bthrm; shwrs inc; EHU (16A) €4.50; gas; lndry; shop; snacks; bar; playgrnd; pool; TV; 10% statics; dogs €2.50; Eng spkn; adv bkg acc; quiet; ccard acc; games area; bike hire; games rm; CKE/CCI. "Pleasant, family-run site among olive trees; friendly, helpful owners; walks fr site; conv Verdon gorge; adj elec sub-stn, elec cables run over small pt of site, not obtrusive; gd." € 25.50   2015*

BRILLANE, LA *10E3 (3km W Rural) 43.93305, 5.86977* **Camping Le Moulin de Ventre, 04300 Niozelles [04 92 78 63 31 or 06 63 51 53 55 (mob); fax 04 92 79 86 92; moulindeventre@gmail.com; www.moulin-de-ventre.com]** Exit A51 junc 19 at La Brillane; turn R onto D4096, then L onto D4100 sp Niozelles & Forcalquier. Site in 3km on L just after bdge, adj Rv Lauzon. Med, mkd, hdg, pt shd, pt sl, serviced pitches; wc (htd); chem disp; mv service pnt; fam bthrm; shwrs inc; EHU (10A) inc; gas; lndry; shop; rest; snacks; bar; bbq (gas); playgrnd; pool; paddling pool; twin axles; red long stay; entmnt; wifi; TV; 10% statics; dogs €3; phone; Eng spkn; adv bkg acc; quiet; ccard acc; rv fishing adj; games rm; CKE/CCI. "Pleasant, peaceful, wooded site by lake & rv; rvside pitches have drop to rv; excel touring base; boat hire adj; lavendar fields in flower Jun/Jul; site neglected; poor san facs." ♦ 9 Apr-30 Sep. € 38.50   2016*

BRIONNE *3D2 (1km N Urban) 49.20256, 0.71554* **Camp Municipal La Vallée, Rue Marcel Nogrette, 27800 Brionne [02 32 44 80 35; fax 02 32 46 25 61; www.ville-brionne.fr]** Fr D438 N or S on by-pass, turn N at D46 junc, pass Carrefour supmkt on L & take 1st R, site on L. Sm, hdg, pt shd, wc; chem disp; mv service pnt; shwrs inc; EHU (8A) €3.45; gas; lndry; shop nr; rest nr; bbq; playgrnd; 10% statics; dogs; quiet; CKE/CCI. "Excel, well maintained site in lovely vill; gd san facs, poss ltd LS; sh walk to supmkt; clean facs but ltd." 30 Apr-30 Sep. € 15.00   2017*

> "I like to fill in the reports as I travel from site to site"
>
> You'll find report forms at the back of this guide, or you can fill them in online at camc.com/europereport.

⊞ **BRIONNE** *3D2 (6km N Rural) 49.24174, 0.70339* **Camp Municipal Les Marronniers, Rue Louise Givon, 27290 Pont-Authou [02 32 42 75 06 or 06 27 25 21 45 (mob); fax 02 32 56 34 51; lesmarronniers27@orange.fr or campingmunicipaldesmarronniers@orange.fr; www.normandie-accueil.fr]** Heading S on D438 take D130 just bef Brionne sp Pont-Audemer (care req at bdge & rndabts). Site on L in approx 5km, well sp on o'skts of Pont-Authou; foll sp in vill. Med, mkd, hdstg, pt shd, wc (htd); chem disp; mv service pnt; shwrs; EHU (10A) €3.40 (poss rev pol); lndry; shop nr; rest nr; bbq; playgrnd; 50% statics; dogs €1.35; adv bkg acc; quiet; fishing; bike hire; CKE/CCI. "Useful, clean stop nr Rouen & m'way; friendly recep; clean san facs; best pitches far side of lake; few hdstg; adv bkg rec; some statics unsightly; stream runs thro site; beautiful valley with many historic towns & vills; excel walking; gd NH; pretty but basic site; recep & security gate cls 1800 in LS." € 13.00   2018*

BRIONNE

BRIONNE *3D2* (9km N Rural) *49.23648, 0.72465*
FFCC Camping Saint Nicolas (formerly Municipal), 15 Rue St Nicolas, 27800 Le Bec-Hellouin [02 32 44 83 55 or 06 84 75 70 32 (Mob); campingstnicolas@ orange.fr; www.campingsaintnicolas.fr]
Exit A28 junc 13 onto D438 then take D581 to Malleville-sur-le-Bec; site on R 1km after Malleville. Well sp. Med, pt shd, wc (htd); chem disp; mv service pnt; shwrs inc; EHU (10A) €3.50; lndry; rest nr; bar nr; bbq; playgrnd; pool (htd, indoor); wifi; 10% statics; dogs €1.50; quiet; tennis nr; horseriding nr; CKE/ CCI. "Attractive, peaceful, well-kept site in pleasant location; spacious pitches; friendly, helpful warden; vg, clean san facs; gate clsd 2200-0700; gd dog walks; vg cycling; attractive countryside; conv NH nr Calais; rec; delightful vill; rec dir in book; vist to Abbey at Bec Hellouin a must." ♦ 15 Mar-15 Oct. € 20.40   2017*

BRIOUDE *9C1* (2km S Rural) *45.2813, 3.4045*
Camping La Bageasse, Ave de la Bageasse, 43100 Brioude [04 71 50 07 70; fax 04 73 34 70 94; labageasse@orange.fr; www.aquadis-loisirs.com]
Turn off N102 & foll sp for Brioude town cent; then foll site sp. Narr app rd. Site on Rv Allier. Med, mkd, pt shd, terr, wc; chem disp; fam bthrm; shwrs inc; EHU (6A) €2 (some rev pol); lndry; shop; snacks; bar; bbq; playgrnd; pool (htd); red long stay; 8% statics; dogs €1.50; phone; Eng spkn; adv bkg acc; quiet; ccard acc; canoe hire; boating adj; fishing adj; CKE/CCI. "Well-kept site; lge pitches; helpful warden; gd, clean san facs; phone ahead to check open LS; interesting basilica; easy cycle to Brioude." ♦ Easter-15 Oct. € 14.50   2014*

BRISSAC QUINCE *4G1* (2km NE Rural) *47.35944, -0.43388* **Le Domaine de L'Etang, Route de St Mathurin, 49320 Brissac-Quincé [02 41 91 70 61; fax 02 41 91 72 65; info@campingetang.com; www. campingetang.com]** Fr N on A11, exit junc 14 onto N260 passing E of Angers, following sp for Cholet/ Poitiers. After x-ing Rv Loire, foll sp to Brissac-Quincé on D748. Foll sp for St Mathurin/Domaine de l'Etang on D55 to site. Med, hdstg, mkd, hdg, pt shd, serviced pitches; wc (htd); chem disp; mv service pnt; fam bthrm; shwrs inc; EHU (10A) inc; gas; lndry; shop; rest; snacks; bar; bbq (charcoal, gas); playgrnd; pool (covrd, htd); paddling pool; red long stay; twin axles; entmnt; wifi; TV; dogs €2.10-9.10; Eng spkn; adv bkg acc; quiet; ccard acc; bike hire; waterslide; games rm; lake fishing; golf 8km; CKE/CCI. "Excel, well-cared for site amongst vineyards; lge pitches; staff pleasant & helpful; clean, modern facs; leisure facs gd for children; pleasant 15 min rvside walk to Brissac-Quincé; wine tasting; gd touring base Loire valley; mkt Thu; rec Apocalypse Tapestry at Chateau d'Angers; gd for walks & sightseeing." ♦ 21 Apr-16 Sep. € 35.00   2018*

BRISSAC QUINCE *4G1* (4km S Rural) *47.33317, -0.43664* **Camping à la Ferme Domaine de la Belle Etoile, La Belle Etoile, 49320 Brissac-Quincé [06 62 32 99 40 (mob); vincent_esnou74@hotmail.com; www.domaine-belle-etoile.fr]**
Take D748 S fr Angers dir Poitiers. At D761 rndabt cont on D748 sp N-D-d'Allençon. Site sp at 2nd turn on L in 500m. Sm, pt shd, wc; chem disp; shwrs; EHU (5A) €3; lndry; bbq; playgrnd; Eng spkn; quiet. "Excel CL-type site in vineyard with wine-tasting & farm produce; clean, modern facs; troglodyte caves, mushroom farms & château nrby; v friendly owners." 1 Apr-1 Nov. € 10.50   2015*

⊞ **BRIVE LA GAILLARDE** *7C3* (8km S Rural) *45.10049, 1.52423* **FFCC Camping à la Ferme (Delmas), Malfarges, 19600 Noailles [05 55 85 81 33]**
Fr A20/E9 take exit 52 sp Noailles; in vill take 1st R across yellow paving at vill café/shop (to avoid steep dangerous hill); turn R at T-junc, site on L. Sp fr m'way. NB All vill rds have 3,500kg limit. Sm, mkd, pt shd, terr, wc; chem disp; mv service pnt; shwrs inc; EHU (5A) €2.70-5.30 (poss rev pol); shop nr; 10% statics; dogs €2.60; adv bkg acc; quiet; fishing 200m; CKE/CCI. "Conv NH/sh stay adj A20; friendly, helpful farmer; if owner not around choose a pitch; farm meals & produce; basic san facs; parking on terr poss awkward; fly problem in hot weather; strict silence after 2200; excel." € 16.00   2014*

BRIVE LA GAILLARDE *7C3* (19km SW Rural) *45.06942, 1.43060* **Camping La Magaudie, La Magaudie Ouest, 19600 Chartrier-Ferrière [05 55 85 26 06 or 06 85 22 54 78; camping@lamagaudie. com; www.lamagaudie.com]** Exit A20 junc 53 onto D920/D19 dir Chasteaux. After rlwy bdge take 2nd L to Chartrier & foll blue sps to site. NB Diff app climbing up narr lane with no passing spaces for 1km. Sm, mkd, pt shd, sl, wc (htd); chem disp; shwrs inc; EHU (10A) €3.50; lndry; shop nr; rest; snacks; bar; bbq (gas); playgrnd; pool; sw nr; 5% statics; dogs €1.25; Eng spkn; adv bkg acc; quiet; CKE/CCI. "Helpful Dutch owners; vg site & facs but v ltd LS; rec arr early high ssn; excel; superb rest; tranquil & relaxing." ♦ 15 Apr-15 Apr. € 23.00   2016*

⊞ **BRIVE LA GAILLARDE** *7C3* (6km SW Rural) *45.09975, 1.45115* **Camping Intercommunal La Prairie, 19600 Lissac-sur-Couze [05 55 85 37 97; fax 05 55 85 37 11; lecausse.correzien@wanadoo. fr; www.caussecorrezien.fr]** A20 exit 51; D1089 to Larche; L onto D19 sp Lissac; take 1st L after St Cernin-de-Larche onto D59 round N side of Lac de Causse, sharp R down hill then bear L over dam; R to site in 2km. Site sp as 'Camping Nautica'. Med, mkd, hdstg, pt shd, terr, serviced pitches; wc; shwrs inc; EHU (16A) €2; lndry; shop; snacks; bar; playgrnd; pool; sw; 5% statics; dogs €3; Eng spkn; adv bkg acc; quiet; boating; windsurfing; CKE/CCI. "Beautiful site in idyllic setting o'looking lake; friendly recep; clean san facs; recep poss clsd Tues & Sun - site inaccessible when recep clsd, phone ahead rec; many outdoor activities." ♦ € 18.60   2014*

BROGLIE *3D2* (0km S Rural) *49.00684, 0.53067*
Aire de Camping-Car Broglie, Route de la Barre-en-Ouche, 27270 Broglie [02 32 44 60 58; mairie-broglie@wanadoo.fr] Exit A28 junc 15 onto D49 E dir Broglie. Turn R in vill onto D6138 Rue des Canadiens, then L into Rue de la Victoire over rv, site on R in former rlwy yard, nr municipal library. Sm, mkd, hdstg, pt shd, chem disp; mv service pnt; shop nr; rest nr; quiet. "M'vans only; gate secured at night; lndry 200m; ideal NH." € 5.00   2013*

BROMMAT *7D4* (0km E Rural) *44.83083, 2.68638*
Camping Municipale, Le Bourg, 12600 Brommat [05 65 66 00 96; fax 05 65 66 22 84; mairie-de.brommat@wanadoo.fr; www.brommat.fr] Fr D98, cross rv bdge, cont uphill to Mairie. Turn R in front of Mairie and cont strt on. Campsite on R. Sm, hdg, pt shd, chem disp; shwrs; EHU (6A); sw nr; TV; dogs; bus 50m; adv bkg acc; quiet; tennis 2km; fishing; CCI. " Beautiful adj walk; vg." ♦ 15 May-15 Sep.
€ 13.00   2014*

BROUSSES ET VILLARET *8F4* (1km S Rural) *43.33932, 2.25201* **Camping Le Martinet Rouge, 11390 Brousses-et-Villaret [04 68 26 51 98 or 06 91 34 41 60 (mob); camping.lemartinetrouge@orange.fr; www.camping-martinet.co.uk]** Fr D118 Mazamet-Carcassonne, turn R 3km after Cuxac-Carbades onto D103; turn L in Brousses & foll sp. Med, hdg, pt shd, pt sl, wc; chem disp; mv service pnt; fam bthrm; shwrs; EHU (6-10A); lndry; shop; rest; snacks; bar; playgrnd; pool; paddling pool; entmnt; wifi; TV; 20% statics; dogs €2; phone; bus; Eng spkn; adv bkg acc; quiet; horseriding; waterslide; trout fishing; games area; canoeing; CKE/CCI. "Helpful owners, great for walking or mountain biking; cather castles, abbeys & churchs, Canal du Midi; forest, lakes, rv & caverns; excel site." ♦ 27 Apr-15 Sep. € 38.00   2014*

BRULON *4F1* (1km SE Rural) *47.96275, -0.22773*
Camping Le Septentrion, Le Bord du Lac, 72350 Brûlon [02 43 95 68 96; fax 02 43 92 60 36; le.septentrion@wanadoo.fr; www.campinglesseptentrion.com] Exit A81 junc 1; foll D4 S to Brûlon; site sp on ent to town to L; turn on L down narr rd (Rue de Buet); then turn R in 300m. Site well sp. Sm, shd, pt sl, wc (htd); mv service pnt; fam bthrm; shwrs inc; EHU (6A) €3; lndry; shop nr; rest; snacks; bar; bbq; playgrnd; pool (htd); sw; red long stay; wifi; TV; 50% statics; dogs €1.20; phone; adv bkg acc; quiet; fishing; bike hire; games rm; boating. "Attractive, well-kept site; spacious pitches; welcoming staff; gd, clean san facs - unisex LS; poss a bit unkempt early ssn; gd cycling & walking area; excel." ♦ 3 Apr-30 Oct. € 13.50   2013*

BUGUE, LE *7C3* (1km SE Urban) *44.90980, 0.93160*
FFCC Camping Les Trois Caupain, Le Port, 24260 Le Bugue Dordogne [05 53 07 24 60 or 06 85 48 44 25 (mob); fax 05 53 08 72 66; info@camping-bugue.com; www.camping-des-trois-caupain.com] Exit Le Bugue town cent on D703 twd Campagne. Turn R at sp after 400m to site in 600m on rvside. Med, mkd, pt shd, wc; chem disp; mv service pnt; fam bthrm; shwrs inc; EHU (6-16A) €4-4.30 (rev pol); gas; shop nr; rest; snacks; bar; playgrnd; pool (covrd, htd); wifi; 25% statics; dogs €2; adv bkg acc; quiet. "Beautiful, lovely, well run site; pleasant, helpful owners; cycle along rv to pretty town; excel; new pool; mkt in Le Bugue well worth a visit; rv adj; games area adj; ideal cent for touring the Dordogne region; lots of attractions; gd rest."
1 Apr-30 Oct. € 21.00   2017*

BUGUE, LE *7C3* (3km SE Rural) *44.90663, 0.97419*
Camping Le Val de la Marquise, Le Petit Moulin, 24260 Campagne [05 53 54 74 10; contact@levaldelamarquise.com; www.camping-dordogne-marquise.com] Fr D703 bet Le Bugue & Les Eyzies take D35 at Campagne dir St Cyprien, site sp. Med, mkd, pt shd, terr, wc; chem disp; mv service pnt; fam bthrm; shwrs inc; EHU (10-15A); lndry; shop nr; rest; snacks; bar; bbq; playgrnd; pool; paddling pool; 5% statics; dogs €2; phone; Eng spkn; adv bkg acc; quiet; lake fishing; games area; CKE/CCI. "Peaceful, attractive site; poss diff access to pitches for lge c'vans due narr rds & low terrs; clean san facs; beautiful pool; Michelin starred rest nrby; brilliant site; great loc; excel fam facs; warm welcome fr new owner; pleasant town, great mkt; high rec." 28 Apr-30 Sep.
€ 30.00   2018*

BUGUE, LE *7C3* (5km SW Rural) *44.89323, 0.87955*
Camping La Ferme des Poutiroux, 24510 Limeuil [05 53 63 31 62; fax 05 53 58 30 84; infos@poutiroux.com; www.poutiroux.com] W fr Le Bugue on D703 twd Bergerac; in 2km take D31 S for 4km; bef bdge take R fork twd Trémolat/Lalinde; in 300m fork R (sp), site well sp. Sm, mkd, pt shd, pt sl, terr, wc; chem disp; mv service pnt; fam bthrm; shwrs; EHU (6A) €4; lndry; shop; snacks; playgrnd; pool (htd); paddling pool; sw nr; wifi; 50% statics; dogs €1; phone; Eng spkn; adv bkg acc; quiet; CKE/CCI. "Peaceful, well-kept, well-positioned, family-run site; friendly, canoeing nr; helpful farmer; facs clean; vg value LS; highly rec." ♦ 1 Apr-2 Oct. € 17.40   2013*

BUGUE, LE *7C3* (6km SW Rural) *44.87990, 0.88576*
Camping du Port de Limeuil, 24480 Alles-sur-Dordogne [05 53 63 29 76; fax 05 53 63 04 19; didierbonvallet@aol.com; www.leportdelimeuil.com] Exit Le Bugue on D31 sp Le Buisson; in 4km turn R on D51 sp Limeuil; at 2km turn L over rv bdge; site on R after bdge. Med, mkd, hdg, pt shd, pt sl, serviced pitches; wc; chem disp; shwrs inc; EHU (5A) €3.50; gas; lndry; shop; snacks; bar; bbq; playgrnd; pool (htd); 40% statics; dogs €2; Eng spkn; adv bkg acc; quiet; bike hire; canoe hire; games rm; CKE/CCI. "Superb location & site for all ages; rv adj; lge pitches; clean san facs, ltd LS; tour ops." ♦ 1 May-30 Sep. € 25.00   2012*

BUGUE, LE *7C3* (9km NW Rural) *44.95130, 0.85070*
Camping St Avit Loisirs, 24260 St Avit-de-Vialard [05 53 02 64 00; fax 05 53 02 64 39; contact@saint-avit-loisirs.com; www.saint-avit-loisirs.com or www.les-castels.com] Leave N89/E70 SE of Périgueux & turn S onto D710 for approx 32km; about 3km N of Le Bugue turn R sp St Avit-de-Vialard. Turn R in vill & cont for approx 1.5km, site on R. NB Narr, twisting app rd. Lge, hdg, pt shd, pt sl, wc; chem disp; mv service pnt; fam bthrm; shwrs inc; EHU (6A) inc; gas; lndry; shop; rest; snacks; bar; bbq; playgrnd; pool (covrd, htd); paddling pool; entmnt; wifi; TV; dogs €2-5.10; adv bkg acc; quiet; ccard acc; games area; golf nr; bike hire; games rm; waterslide; horseriding nr; tennis; watersports nr; CKE/CCI. "Excel, well-kept, well-run, busy site; gd sized pitches; friendly welcome; no o'fits over 7m; gd, clean san facs; archery nrby; gd touring base; conv for Lascaux; many static tents; amazing array of watersport facs." ♦ 26 Mar-24 Sep. € 49.00 2015*

> **"We must tell the Club about that great site we found"**
>
> Get your site reports in by mid-August and we'll do our best to get your updates into the next edition.

BUIS LES BARONNIES *9D2* (1km N Urban) *44.27558, 5.27830* Camp Municipal, Quartier du Jalinier, 26170 Buis-les-Baronnies [04 75 28 04 96 or 06 60 80 44 53 (mob)] Fr Vaison-la-Romaine S on D938; turn L onto D54/D13/D5 to Buis-les-Baronnies; cont N onto D546; at bend turn R over rv bdge; turn L along rv, then 1st R. Site split into 2 either side of sw pool; recep in upper site. Med, hdg, mkd, pt shd, pt sl, wc; chem disp; shwrs inc; EHU (6A) €3; lndry; wifi; 5% statics; dogs €1.20; phone; bus 300m; quiet; CKE/CCI. "Lovely views; san facs dated but clean; not suitable lge o'fits but lger, more accessible pitches on lower level; attractive town; gd mkt Wed & Sat; fair; warden in off 1900-2000 only." 1 Mar-11 Nov. € 11.50 2015*

BUIS LES BARONNIES *9D2* (5km SW Rural) *44.25190, 5.24370* Camping La Gautière, La Penne-sur-l'Ouvèze, 26170 Buis-les-Baronnies [04 75 28 02 68; fax 04 75 28 24 11; accueil@camping-lagautiere.com; www.camping-lagautiere.com] On D5 Vaison-la-Romaine to Buis-les-Baronnies rd, on L. Sm, mkd, pt shd, wc (htd); shwrs inc; EHU (3-10A) €3-4.30; gas; lndry; shop; snacks; bar; bbq; playgrnd; pool; 5% statics; dogs €2.50; phone; bus adj; Eng spkn; adv bkg acc; quiet; ccard acc; games rm; fishing nr; horseriding nr; games area; CKE/CCI. "Beautiful situation; haphazard pitch size; diff for o'fits over 6m; climbing at Rocher St Julien & Gorges d'Ubrieux; helpful owners; ACSI acc; excel cycling." 26 Mar-31 Oct. € 24.50 2016*

BURTONCOURT *5D2* (1km W Rural) *49.22485, 6.39929* FFCC Camping La Croix du Bois Sacker, 57220 Burtoncourt [03 87 35 74 08; camping.croixsacker@wanadoo.fr; www.campingcroixsacker.com] Exit A4 junc 37 sp Argancy; at rndabt foll sp Malroy; at 2nd rndabt foll sp Chieuilles & cont to Vany; then take D3 for 12km dir Bouzonville; turn R onto D53A to Burtoncourt. Lge, hdstg, mkd, hdg, pt shd, terr, wc; mv service pnt; shwrs; EHU (6A) inc; gas; lndry; shop; rest nr; bar; playgrnd; entmnt; wifi; TV; 10% statics; dogs €1.70; phone; bus 300m; Eng spkn; adv bkg acc; quiet; fishing; tennis; games area; CKE/CCI. "Lovely, wooded site in beautiful location; lge pitches; pleasant, friendly owners; clean san facs; forest walks; gd security; gd NH or sh stay en rte Alsace/Germany; conv Maginot Line; excel; Hachenberg Ouvrage tour highly rec (30km)." ♦ 1 Apr-20 Oct. € 20.00 2016*

BUXIERES-SOUS-MONTAIGUT *7A4* (4km SW Rural) *46.19271, 2.81994* Camping Les Suchères, Les Sucheres, 63700 Buxierères-sous-Montaigut [33 04 73 85 92 66; sucheres@gmail.com; www.campinglessucheres.com] Head SE on D92, cont on Buxières. Take Les Gouttes to Les Sucheres; 1st R onto Buxières; cont onto Les Gouttes after 7m turn R twd Les Sucheres, L twd Les Sucheres, 1st R onto Les Sucheres, turn L to stay on Les Sucheres, take the 1st L to stay on Les Sucheres; site on R. Sm, pt sl, wc; chem disp; shwrs; EHU (6A) €3; lndry; rest; bar; bbq; playgrnd; pool; wifi; TV; dogs €1.50; Eng spkn; CCI. "Helpful Dutch owners; lovely peaceful site; gd walking area; Montaigut within walking dist; shop; access to the site could be diff for lge o'fits as rd narr for last km; quiet." 1 Apr-30 Sep. € 20.40 2014*

BUZANCAIS *4H2* (1km N Urban) *46.89309, 1.41801* Camp Municipal La Tête Noire, Allée des Sports, 36500 Buzançais [02 54 84 17 27 or 06 15 85 53 04 (mob); fax 02 54 02 13 45; buzancais@wanadoo.fr] D943 fr Châteauroux thro town cent, cross rv, immed turn R into sports complex. Lge, hdstg, pt shd, wc; mv service pnt; shwrs inc; EHU (16A) inc; lndry; shop nr; rest nr; bar nr; playgrnd; red long stay; entmnt; 10% statics; dogs €1.50; adv bkg acc; quiet; CKE/CCI. "Pleasant, peaceful, well-kept site on rv; clean facs; no access when office clsd but ample parking; no twin axles; pool 500m; gd fishing." ♦ 1 May-30 Sep. € 15.00 2014*

CABANNES, LES *8G3* (2km SW Rural) *42.77269, 1.67172* FFCC Camping Le Pas de l'Ours, Les Gesquis, 09310 Aston [05 61 64 90 33; fax 05 61 64 90 32; contact@lepasdelours.fr; www.campingariege.fr] S on N20, after Tarascon-sur-Ariège turn R sp Plateau de Beille/Les Cabannes. Pass thro Aulos, site well sp. Sm, hdg, mkd, pt shd, pt sl, wc (htd); chem disp; fam bthrm; shwrs inc; EHU (6A) €4; lndry; shop nr; rest nr; snacks; bar; bbq; playgrnd; entmnt; wifi; TV; 50% statics; dogs €2; phone; Eng spkn; adv bkg acc; quiet; ccard acc; games area; bike hire; tennis; CKE/CCI. "Attractive site surrounded by mountains; v clean san facs; not suitable lge o'fits; helpful owners; pool adj; gd touring base; access poss diff for lge o'fits." ♦ 26 May-15 Sep. € 32.00 2013*

CADENET

CABOURG 3D1 (8km SW Rural) 49.25210, -0.18823
Camping Le Clos Tranquille, 17 Route de Troarn, 14810 Gonneville-en-Auge [02 31 24 21 36; fax 02 31 24 28 80; le.clos.tranquille@wanadoo.fr; www.campingleclostranquille.fr] Fr Cabourg, take D513 twd Caen. 2km after Varaville turn R to Gonneville-en-Auge (by garden cent) D95A. Foll sp to vill, site ent on R after LH bend. Med, pt shd, wc; chem disp; shwrs inc; EHU (6-10A) €3.50-€5 (poss rev pol & long lead req); gas; lndry; shop; snacks; playgrnd; beach sand 5km; 12% statics; dogs €2; Eng spkn; adv bkg acc; quiet; ccard acc; bike hire; CKE/CCI. "Excel, quiet site, no bar and nothing within walking dist." 2 Apr-1 Oct. € 27.00   2013*

CABOURG 3D1 (2km W Coastal) 49.28326, -0.17053 **Camping Les Peupliers, Allée des Pins, 14810 Merville-Franceville-Plage [02 31 24 05 07; contact@camping-peupliers.com; www.camping-peupliers.com]** Exit A13 to Cabourg onto D400, take D513 W, turn R sp Le Hôme, site sp, 2km E of Merville-Franceville. Med, unshd, pt sl, wc (htd); chem disp; fam bthrm; shwrs inc; EHU (10A) (rev pol) €5.50; lndry; shop nr; rest; snacks; bar; bbq; playgrnd; pool (htd); beach sand 300m; entmnt; TV; 50% statics; dogs €3.10; phone; Eng spkn; adv bkg acc; ccard acc; tennis 2km; games area; CKE/CCI. "Pleasant, friendly, well-run, busy site; some lge pitches; clean, modern san facs; vg facs for children; conv ferries." ♦ 1 Apr-31 Oct. € 31.00   2014*

> **"I need an on-site restaurant"**
> We do our best to make sure site information is correct, but it is always best to check any must-have facilities are still available or will be open during your visit.

CABOURG 3D1 (6km W Coastal) 49.28319, -0.19098
Camping Le Point du Jour, Route de Cabourg, 14810 Merville-Franceville-Plage [02 31 24 23 34; fax 02 31 24 15 54; contact@camping-lepointdujour.com; www.camping-lepointdujour.com]
Fr Ouistreham on D514 turn E at Bénouville onto D224, cross bdge onto D514, site on L dir Cabourg, 8km beyond Pegasus Bdge at far end of Merville. Or fr A13/D675 exit Dozulé dir Cabourg, then D514 to site. Med, hdg, pt shd, wc (htd); chem disp; mv service pnt; fam bthrm; shwrs inc; EHU (10A) €5 (poss rev pol); gas; lndry; shop; rest; snacks; bar; bbq; playgrnd; pool (covrd, htd); beach sand adj; red long stay; entmnt; wifi; TV; 40% statics; dogs €3; bus; adv bkg acc; quiet; ccard acc; games rm; CKE/CCI. "Site with sea views; direct access to Sword Beach (D-Day) & sand dunes; conv Pegasus Bdge; some pitches might be diff for lge o'fits; open till 2300 for late ferry arr, v obliging; ent & exit diff; sm-med pitches, many sl; facs tired." ♦ 31 Mar-30 Oct. € 37.00   2017*

CABOURG 3D1 (6km W Coastal) 49.28296, -0.19072
Camping Village Ariane, 100 Route de Cabourg, 14810 Merville-Franceville-Plage [02 31 24 52 52; fax 02 31 24 52 41; info@loisirs-ariane.com; www.camping-ariane.com] Fr Ouistreham on D514 turn E at Bénouville onto D224, cross bdge onto D514 to site dir Cabourg. Or fr A13/D675 exit Dozulé dir Cabourg, then D514 to site. Lge, mkd, pt shd, wc (htd); chem disp; fam bthrm; shwrs inc; EHU (6-10A) €4; gas; lndry; shop nr; snacks; playgrnd; beach sand 300m; red long stay; entmnt; wifi; TV; 10% statics; dogs €3; Eng spkn; adv bkg acc; quiet; games area; tennis nr; games rm; watersports nr; CKE/CCI♦ 1 Apr-5 Nov. € 12.00   2018*

CABRERETS 7D3 (1km NE Rural) 44.50771, 1.66234
Camping Cantal, 46330 Cabrerets [05 65 31 26 61; fax 05 65 31 20 47] Fr Cahors take D653 E for approx 15km bef turning R onto D662 E thro Vers & St Géry. Turn L onto D41 to Cabrerets. Site 1km after vill on R. Sm, pt shd, pt sl, serviced pitches; wc; chem disp; shwrs inc; EHU €2.50; quiet; rv canoeing nr; CKE/CCI. "Superb situation; v interesting vill; peaceful site; warden calls; grnd slightly bumpy; excel san facs; not suitable lge o'fits; conv Pech Merle; gd cycling rte; quiet; friendly; overhanging trees, care when pitching; unisex san facs; vg." 1 Apr-15 Oct. € 12.00   2017*

CADENET 10E3 (10km NE Rural) 43.76871, 5.44970
Camping Lou Badareu, La Rasparine, 84160 Cucuron [04 90 77 21 46; fax 04 90 77 27 68; contact@loubadareu.com; www.loubadareu.com]
In Cadenet foll sp for church (église) onto D45 dir Cucuron; S of Cucuron turn onto D27 (do not go into town); site is E 1km. Well sp fr D27. Sm, mkd, pt shd, pt sl, wc; own san rec; chem disp; shwrs inc; EHU (10A) €4.50 (long lead poss req); lndry; shop; playgrnd; pool; 10% statics; dogs €1.80; phone; quiet; CKE/CCI. "Pretty farm site in cherry orchard, vineyard and olive grove adj; basic but adequate san facs; natural spring-fed pool; friendly, helpful owner; sep access for high vans; lge shd camping field." ♦ 1 Apr-15 Oct. € 16.70   2017*

CADENET 10E3 (2km SW Rural) 43.71968, 5.35479
Camping Val de Durance, Les Routes, 84160 Cadenet [04 90 68 37 75 or 04 42 20 47 25 (LS); fax 04 90 68 16 34; info@homair.com; www.homair.com]
Exit A7 at Cavaillon onto D973 dir Cadenet. In Cadenet take D59, site sp. Lge, hdg, pt shd, wc; chem disp; shwrs inc; EHU (4-10A) inc (long lead req); gas; lndry; shop; rest; snacks; bar; bbq; playgrnd; pool; paddling pool; sw; entmnt; wifi; TV; 70% statics; dogs €5; adv bkg acc; ccard acc; games area; canoeing; archery; cycling; CKE/CCI. "Dir access to lake; adj Luberon Park; noisy entmnt till late most evenings high ssn." ♦ 6 Apr-29 Sep. € 32.00   2013*

CAEN

CAEN *3D1* (20km N Coastal) *49.32551, -0.39010*
Camping La Côte de Nacre, 17 Rue du Général Moulton, 14750 St Aubin-sur-Mer [02 31 97 14 45; fax 02 31 97 22 11; camping-cote-de-nacre@wanadoo.fr; www.sandaya.fr/cdn] Fr Caen on D7 dir Douvres-la-Délivrande, Langrune-sur-Mer & St Aubin. Site in St Aubin-sur-Mer on S side of D514; clearly sp on o'skts. Lge, mkd, hdg, hdstg, unshd, wc (htd); chem disp; mv service pnt; fam bthrm; shwrs inc; EHU (10A) inc; lndry; shop; rest; snacks; bar; bbq; playgrnd; pool (covrd, htd); paddling pool; beach sand 500m; entmnt; wifi; TV; 60% statics; dogs €5; phone; Eng spkn; adv bkg rec; quiet; ccard acc; sauna; waterslide; bike hire; games rm; tennis 200m; CKE/CCI. "Ideal for families; lge pitches; conv Caen ferry, Normandy beaches, WW2 sites; helpful staff; excel modern san facs; poss waterlogging; gd cycle tracks along sea front LS; easy walk into quiet vill; vg; payment on arr, no refund for early dep; vg site." ♦ 3 Apr-14 Sep. € 48.00 2017*

CAGNES SUR MER *10E4* (4km N Rural) *43.68717, 7.15589* **Camping Le Val Fleuri, 139 Vallon-des-Vaux, 06800 Cagnes-sur-Mer [04 93 31 21 74; valfleur2@wanadoo.fr; www.campingvalfleuri.fr]** Fr Nice take D6007 W twd Cannes. On app Cagnes turn R & foll sp Camping; site on R after 3km, well sp. NB 3.3m height restriction on this rte. Sm, pt shd, terr, wc; shwrs; EHU (3-10A) €4; shop nr; rest; playgrnd; pool (htd); beach shgl 4km; entmnt; wifi; dogs €1.50; Eng spkn; adv bkg acc. "Gd, clean, improving site, efficient NH; divided by rd (not busy); some sm pitches; helpful, friendly owners; gd; bus to Nice; dated facs (2014)." 5 Apr-27 Sep. € 30.00 2014*

> **"Satellite navigation makes touring much easier"**
>
> Remember most sat navs don't know if you're towing or in a larger vehicle – always use yours alongside maps and site directions.

CAGNES SUR MER *10E4* (5km S Coastal) *43.63128, 7.12993* **Camping Parc des Maurettes, 730 Ave du Docteur Lefebvre, 06270 Villeneuve-Loubet [04 93 20 91 91; fax 04 93 73 77 20; info@parcdesmaurettes.com; www.parcdesmaurettes.com]** Fr Nice exit A8 junc 47, turn L onto D6007 dir Antibes; foll sp Intermarché, then R into Rue des Maurettes; site in 250m. N fr Cannes on A8 exit Villeneuve-Loubet-Plage junc 46; foll D241 over D6007 & rwly line, U-turn back over rwly line, then R onto D6007 dir Antibes as above. NB Site on steep cliff with narr winding rds packed with trees; diff ent. Med, mkd, pt shd, terr, serviced pitches; wc (htd); chem disp; mv service pnt; shwrs inc; EHU (3-10A) €5.30; gas; lndry; shop nr; snacks; playgrnd; beach shgl 500m; red long stay; wifi; TV (pitch); dogs €4; train Nice 400m; Eng spkn; adv bkg rec; quiet; ccard acc; jacuzzi; CKE/CCI. "Well-kept site; variable pitch size/price." ♦ 10 Jan-15 Nov. € 36.00 2016*

CAGNES SUR MER *10E4* (7km S Rural) *43.62027, 7.12583* **Camping La Vieille Ferme, 296 Blvd des Groules, 06270 Villeneuve-Loubet-Plage [04 93 33 41 44; fax 04 93 33 37 28; info@vieilleferme.com; www.vieilleferme.com]** Fr W (Cannes) take Antibes exit 44 fr A8, foll D35 dir Antibes 'Centre Ville'. At lge junc turn onto D6007, Ave de Nice, twd Biot & Villeneuve-Loubet sp Nice (rlwy line on R). Just after Marineland turn L onto Blvd des Groules. Fr E (Nice) leave A8 at junc 47 to join D6007 twd Antibes, take 3rd turning after Intermarché supmkt; site well sp fr D6007. Med, mkd, hdg, pt shd, pt sl, terr, serviced pitches; wc (htd); chem disp; mv service pnt; fam bthrm; shwrs inc; EHU (2A-10A) €3 - €7; gas; lndry; shop nr; snacks; bbq (elec, gas); playgrnd; pool (covrd, htd); paddling pool; beach shgl 1km; red long stay; wifi; TV; 40% statics; dogs €2.50; bus, train nr; Eng spkn; adv bkg acc; ccard acc; games rm. "Peaceful, well-kept family-run site; well-drained pitches, some lge; san facs need refurb (2010); beach not suitable children & non-swimmers; no o'fits over 8m; excel pool; gd walking, cycling & dog walking as lge park adj; some aircraft & rd noise; vg value LS; excel; be wary of bike thieves; nice bar/rest; friendly staff; v quiet at night; bus & train nrby." ♦ € 41.00 2018*

CAGNES SUR MER *10E4* (4km SW Rural) *43.66001, 7.1000* **Parc Saint James Le Sourire, Route de Grasse, 06270 Villeneuve-Loubet [04 93 20 96 11; fax 04 93 22 07 52; lesourire@camping-parcsaintjames.com; www.camping-parcsaintjames.com]** Exit A8 at junc 47; take D2 to Villeneuve; at rndbt take D2085 sp Grasse. Site on L in 2km. Sp Le Sourire. Med, hdg, hdstg, pt shd, wc (htd); shwrs inc; EHU (6A) inc; lndry; rest; bar; playgrnd; pool (htd); beach shgl 5km; red long stay; entmnt; 70% statics; dogs €5; Eng spkn; adv bkg acc; ccard acc; horseriding nr; tennis nr; games area; golf nr. "Site shabby & poorly maintained; park in visitors' car park bef registering; conv Nice, Cannes & beaches." ♦ 7 Apr-29 Sep. € 40.00 2013*

CAGNES SUR MER *10E4* (1km NW Urban) *43.67159, 7.13845* **Camping Le Colombier, 35 Chemin de Ste Colombe, 06800 Cagnes-sur-Mer [04 93 73 12 77; campinglecolombier06@gmail.com; www.campinglecolombier.com]** N fr Cagnes cent foll 1-way system dir Vence. Half way up hill turn R at rndabt dir Cagnes-sur-Mer & R at next island. Site on L 300m, sp fr town cent. Sm, hdg, mkd, pt shd, wc (htd); chem disp; mv service pnt; shwrs inc; EHU (2-16A) (poss rev pol) €2-8; lndry; shop nr; rest nr; snacks; bar; playgrnd; beach 2.5km; red long stay; TV; 10% statics; dogs (except Jul/Aug, €2.50); phone; Eng spkn; quiet; bike hire; CKE/CCI. "Friendly, family-run site; sm pool adj." 1 Apr-30 Sep. € 29.60 2014*

CAHORS *7D3* (2km N Urban) *44.46318, 1.44226*
Camping Rivière de Cabessut, Rue de la Rivière, 46000 Cahors [05 65 30 06 30; fax 05 65 23 99 46; contact@cabessut.com; www.cabessut.com] Fr N or S on D820, at S end Cahors by-pass take D911 sp Rodez. At traff lts by bdge do not cross rv but bear R on D911. In 1km at site sp turn L. Site on E bank of Rv Lot, well sp fr town. Site at end of long lane. 1.8km to site fr bdge (Pont Cabessut). Med, hdg, mkd, pt shd, serviced pitches; wc; chem disp; mv service pnt; fam bthrm; shwrs inc; EHU (10A) inc (poss rev pol); gas; lndry; shop; snacks; bar; bbq (gas); playgrnd; pool; wifi; 5% statics; dogs €2; phone; bus to Cahors 600m; adv bkg req; quiet; CKE/CCI. "Lovely, well-run site by rv; beautiful area; pleasant, mostly lge pitches, sm pitches diff access when site full; gd for children; walk to town by rv 1.8km; food mkt Wed, full mkt Sat; hypmkt 1.5km; excel san facs; well maintained site, helpful, commited owners; rv adj; great site with lge sunny or shd pitches; pre-ordered bread delivered daily; lge o'fits turned away if grnd is damp." ♦
1 Apr-30 Sep. € 26.00   2017*

CAGNES SUR MER *10E4* (4km NW Rural) *43.68272, 7.08391* **Camping Les Pinèdes, Route de Pont de Pierre, 06480 La Colle-sur-Loup [04 93 32 98 94; fax 04 93 32 50 20; info@lespinedes.com; www.lespinedes.com]** Exit A8 junc 47; take D6007 dir Nice, then D2 sp Villeneuve-Loubet; turn R at rndabt sp Villeneuve-Loubet & cross rv bdge; go thro sh tunnel, other side is Cagnes-sur-Mer & rndabt; turn L onto D6 to Colle-sur-Loup; site on R sh dist after Colle-sur-Loup. NB Take 2nd turning into site (1st leads to rest). Lge, hdg, hdstg, mkd, pt shd, pt sl, terr, serviced pitches; wc; chem disp; mv service pnt; shwrs inc; EHU (6-10A) €4.60-5.90 (poss rev pol); lndry; shop; rest; snacks; bar; bbq (elec, gas); playgrnd; pool (htd); paddling pool; sw nr; red long stay; entmnt; wifi; TV; 20% statics; dogs €3.60; Eng spkn; adv bkg acc; quiet; ccard acc; rv fishing adj; games rm; archery; tennis adj; horseriding adj; games area; solarium; CKE/CCI. "Excel, family-run site set in pine & oak trees; no c'vans over 6m (excluding towbar) & m'vans over 8m high ssn; helpful & friendly; spacious pitches; steep access to pitches - poss diff lge o'fits, help avail; adequate san facs; gd rest at site ent; highly rec; vg site has everything you need; spacious pitches; excel pool." 22 Mar-29 Sep. € 53.00   2014*

See advertisement

CAHORS *7D3* (8km N Rural) *44.52585, 1.46048*
Camping Les Graves, 46090 St Pierre-Lafeuille [05 65 36 83 12; infos@camping-lesgraves.com; www.camping-lesgraves.com] Leave A20 at junc 57 Cahors Nord onto D820. Foll sp St Pierre-Lafeuille; at N end of vill, site is opp L'Atrium wine cave. Med, hdg, pt shd, sl, wc; chem disp; mv service pnt; shwrs inc; EHU (6-10A) €2.50-3.50 (poss rev pol); lndry; rest; snacks; bar; playgrnd; pool; 5% statics; dogs €1.50; Eng spkn; adv bkg rec; ccard acc; bike hire; CKE/CCI. "Scenic site; lge pitches; poss clsd during/after wet weather due boggy grnd; disabled facs over stony rd & grass; ltd facs LS; conv A20; nice, quiet, clean site." ♦
1 Apr-31 Oct. € 20.00   2018*

CAHORS

CAHORS *7D3* **(8km N Rural)** *44.53136, 1.45926*
Camping Quercy-Vacances, Mas de la Combe, 46090 St Pierre-Lafeuille [05 65 36 87 15; fax 05 65 36 02 39; quercyvacances@wanadoo.fr; www.quercy-vacances.com] Heading N on D820, turn L at N end of St Pierre-Lafeuille turn W at site sp N of vill, site in 700m down lane. Site sp fr main rd. Fr A20 exit junc 57 & foll sp N20. Med, mkd, pt shd, pt sl, wc; chem disp; mv service pnt; fam bthrm; shwrs; EHU (10A) €3.30-5.30; gas; lndry; shop; rest; snacks; bar; playgrnd; pool; paddling pool; twin axles; entmnt; wifi; TV; 50% statics; dogs €1.50; phone; Eng spkn; adv bkg acc; quiet; ccard acc; games area; CKE/CCI. "Pretty site; most pitches slightly sl; clean, modern san facs; poss unkempt LS; helpful owner; vg; tennis & horse riding nrby; gd for Cahors & Lot Valley." ♦
1 Apr-30 Sep. € 23.00   2017*

⊞ **CAHORS** *7D3* **(13km W Rural)** *44.47968, 1.35906*
Camping de L'écluse, Lieu dit Le Payras, 46140 Douelle [09 84 45 33 78; antinea.loisirs@orange.fr; www.tourisme-lot.com/en] Fr N foll D820 past D811 junc, over rv lot bdge, immed take D8 on R, sp Pradines Douelle. In Douelle cont thro vill, take R sp Antinea Campings. Take R sp Camping, park outside barrier, walk to Antinea (by rv). Sm, mkd, pt shd, wc; shwrs inc; EHU (6A) €1.50; bbq; sw nr; twin axles; dogs; quiet. "Quiet rvside site by disused lock; basic but clean facs; level pitches but uneven & long grass; check in at Antinea Bar; barrier open on req; gd rvside walk into Douelle; attractive vill; fair." € 13.50   2014*

CAJARC *7D4* **(6km NE Rural)** *44.50612, 1.89667*
Camping Les Cournoulises, 46160 Montbrun [06 15 53 00 58 (mob); lescournoulises@sfr.fr; http://lescournoulises.perso.sfr.fr] Fr Cahors foll D662 or fr Figeac foll D19. Foll D622 along N bank of R Lot for 6km. Site well sp on app. Sm, mkd, pt shd, wc; chem disp; shwrs inc; EHU (6A) €3; lndry; shop; rest; snacks; bbq (charcoal, sep area); playgrnd; twin axles; red long stay; dogs €0.50; bus adj; Eng spkn; adv bkg acc; quiet; games area; canoe hire; tennis nr; fishing; CKE/CCI. "Lge pitches; teepee & trapper tents on site (for hire); many attractions within 30km radius; dir access to rv; fishing rods avail; friendly, helpful owner; excel; paragliding, trekking, htd pool 6km; beautiful site; spotless facs; wonderful; highly rec." ♦ 1 Apr-10 Oct. € 14.00   2017*

CAJARC *7D4* **(0km SW Urban)** *44.48374, 1.83928*
Camp Municipal Le Terriol, Rue Le Terriol, 46160 Cajarc [05 65 40 72 74 or 05 65 40 65 20 (Mairie); fax 05 65 40 39 05; mairie.cajarc@wanadoo.fr; www.cajarc.fr] Fr Cahors dir Cajarc on D662 on L foll sp to site. Sm, hdstg, hdg, mkd, pt shd, wc cont; chem disp; fam bthrm; shwrs inc; EHU (10A) inc (poss rev pol); lndry; shop nr; rest nr; bar nr; bbq; playgrnd; dogs; phone; Eng spkn; adv bkg acc; tennis 500m; CKE/CCI. "Gd sized pitches; clean, basic facs; lovely sm town on Rv Lot; pool 500m; vg." 1 May-30 Sep. € 15.40   2017*

CAJARC *7D4* **(6km SW Rural)** *44.46630, 1.75077*
Camp Municipal Le Grand Pré, 46330 Cénevières [05 65 30 22 65 or 05 65 31 28 16 (Marie); fax 05 65 31 37 00; mairie.cenevieres@wanadoo.fr] Fr Villefranche on D911 twd Cahors turn R onto D24 at Limogne for Cénevières. Foll sp. Fr St Cirq-Lapopie on D24 thro vill & over rlwy. Sm, hdg, mkd, pt shd, wc; chem disp; mv service pnt; shwrs inc; EHU (10A) inc; lndry; shop nr; rest nr; bar nr; bbq; sw; dogs; phone; bus; quiet. "Peaceful site by rv; wonderful views of cliffs; vg san facs; site self & warden calls am & pm; excel highly rec." 1 Jun-30 Sep. € 12.50   2014*

CAJARC *7D4* **(6km W Rural)** *44.4735, 1.7835*
Camping Ruisseau du Treil, 46160 Larnagol [05 65 31 23 39; fax 05 65 31 23 27; contact@lotcamping.com; www.lotcamping.com] Exit A20 junc 57 onto D49 sp St Michel; in 4km turn R onto D653; after 5.5km in Vers at mini-rndabt turn L onto D662; site on L immed after leaving Larnagol. Or fr Figeac foll D19 thro Cajarc. At top of hill leaving Cajarc turn R onto D662 sp Cahors & Larnagol. Site sp on R 300m bef Larnagol on blind bend. Sm, mkd, pt shd, pt sl, wc; chem disp; fam bthrm; shwrs inc; EHU (6A) €4; lndry; snacks; bar; bbq; playgrnd; pool; sw nr; TV; 4% statics; dogs €3.90; adv bkg acc; quiet; canoeing adj; fishing adj; games rm; bike hire; horseriding; CKE/CCI. "Beautiful, spacious, peaceful site in lovely area; well-run; friendly, helpful British owners; clean san facs but ltd when site full; lge pitches poss uneven; many long-stay/returning campers; library; guided walks; vg touring base; excel."
♦ 9 May-12 Sep. € 24.60   2014*

CALAIS *3A3* **(12km NE Coastal)** *50.98907, 1.98545*
Les Argousiers, 766 rue des hemmes, 62215 Oye-Plage [03 21 35 32 78; lesargousiers@wanadoo.fr; www.lesargousiers.com] Take D940 fr A16 (exit 49) or Calais. In Oye-Plage, turn L & foll sp for Les Argousiers Camping. Sm, hdg, unshd, wc; chem disp; mv service pnt; shwrs; EHU; lndry; bbq; beach sand 2km; twin axles; 95% statics; dogs €2; bus 100m; quiet; CKE/CCI. "Few touring pitches; gd NH; friendly & helpful owners." ♦ 1 Mar-31 Jan. € 13.70   2015*

⊞ **CALAIS** *3A3* **(12km E Coastal)** *50.99657, 2.05062*
Camping Clairette, 525 Route des Dunes, 62215 Oye-Plage [03 21 35 83 51 or 06 14 22 92 71 (mob); www.campingclairette62.com] Exit A16 junc 50 & foll sp Oye-Plage. At traff lts at D940 cont strt. At junc with D119 turn R then L, site on L in 2km. Foll sp 'Réserve Naturelle'. Med, hdg, mkd, unshd, pt sl, wc (htd); chem disp; mv service pnt; shwrs inc; EHU (10A) €4; lndry; shop nr; bbq; playgrnd; beach 500m; 95% statics; dogs €1.40; Eng spkn; adv bkg acc; quiet; ccard acc; clsd 16 Dec-14 Jan; CKE/CCI. "Ltd touring pitches, rec phone/email in adv; warm welcome; helpful owners; security barrier; nature reserve nrby; conv ferries; fair; san facs OK (2013)." € 15.00   2013*

CALVI

⊞ **CALAIS** *3A3* (12km E Rural) *50.96613, 2.05270*
Camping Le Pont d'Oye, 308 Rue de la Rivière, 62215 Oye-Plage [06 21 85 65 25; ch.lavallee@ laposte.net; www.campingdupontdoye.fr]
Exit A16 at junc 50 onto D219 to Oye-Plage; cross rv & immed turn R sp camping; foll rv; site on L. Sm, hdg, unshd, wc; chem disp; fam bthrm; shwrs; EHU (6A) €2.50; gas; lndry; shop nr; snacks; bar; bbq; playgrnd; beach sandy 5km; wifi; 85% statics; dogs; Eng spkn; adv bkg acc; CKE/CCI. "Basic CL-type site; few touring pitches; grassed field for c'vans; friendly, helpful owners; san facs adj statics park - v dated but clean; conv ferries; NH only; new owner (2012); site improved." ♦ € 13.00   2013*

CALAIS *3A3* (13km SW Rural) *50.91160, 1.75127*
Camping Les Epinettes, Impasse de Mont Pinet, 62231 Peuplingues [03 21 85 21 39; lesepinettes@ aol.com; www.lesepinettes.fr] A16 fr Calais to Boulogne, exit junc 40 W on D243 sp Peuplingues, go thro vill & foll sp; site on L in 3km. Lge, hdg, pt shd, pt sl, wc; chem disp; shwrs; EHU (4-10A) €1.60-3.80; lndry; shop; rest nr; playgrnd; beach sand 3km; wifi; 80% statics; dogs €1.50; phone; adv bkg acc; quiet; ccard acc; CKE/CCI. "Pleasant, easy-going, quiet site; conv NH for m'way, ferries & tunnel; some pitches sm; san facs clean; when bureau clsd, site yourself - warden calls eve or call at cottage to pay; library; if arr late, park on grass verge outside main gate - use facs excel elec, pay half price; few touring pitches." 1 Apr-31 Oct. € 15.50   2017*

CALAIS *3A3* (4km SW Coastal) *50.95677, 1.81101* **Camp du Fort Lapin, Route Provincial 940, 62231 Sangatte-Blériot Plage [03 21 97 67 77; campingdufortlapin@orange.fr; www. campingdufortlapin.fr]** Fr E exit junc 43 fr A16 Calais cent, dir beach (Blériot-Plage). Turn L along coast onto D940 dir Sangatte; site on R in dunes shortly after water tower, opp sports cent; site sp fr D940. Fr S exit A16 junc 41 to Sangatte; at T-junc turn R onto D940; site on L just bef water tower. Med, mkd, unshd, pt sl, wc; chem disp; fam bthrm; shwrs inc; EHU (10A) inc (poss rev pol); lndry; shop nr; rest; snacks; bar; bbq; playgrnd; beach sand adj; 50% statics; dogs; phone; bus; adv bkg acc; quiet; CKE/CCI. "Conv ferry; warden lives on site; rec arr bef 1700 high ssn; gates clsd 2300-0700; recep 0900-1200 & 1600-2000, barrier clsd when recep clsd; ltd parking outside espec w/end - phone ahead for access code; gd bus service; basic, clean, adequate san facs (shwrs and lndry clsd after 2100); conv Auchan & Cité Europe shops; poss youth groups high ssn; conv NH; close to beach; clean tidy site; adequate facs; grnd v well drained; easy cycle into Calais or walk along the promenade to the harbour ent." ♦ 1 Apr-31 Oct. € 18.40   2018*

CALAIS *3A3* (5km W Coastal) *50.94610, 1.75798* **Camping des Noires Mottes, Rue Pierre Dupuy, 62231 Sangatte [03 21 82 04 75; campingdesnoiresmottes@orange.fr; www. ville-sangatte.fr]** Fr A16 exit junc 41 sp Sangatte onto D243, at T-junc in vill turn R then R again bef monument. Lge, hdg, mkd, pt shd, pt sl, wc; chem disp; mv service pnt; shwrs inc; EHU (10A) €4.10; lndry; shop nr; playgrnd; beach sand 500m; 90% statics; dogs €1.30; bus 500m; Eng spkn; adv bkg rec; CKE/CCI. "Conv ferries & Eurotunnel; lge pitches; san facs clean; barrier - no arr bef office opens 1500 (1600 LS); san facs clsd o'night & poss 1200-1600; some pitches boggy when wet; windy spot; OK NH; well maintained site." ♦ 1 Apr-31 Oct. € 23.60   2018*

⊞ **CALAIS** *3A3* (3km NW Coastal) *50.96603, 1.84370* **Aire Communale, Plage de Calais, Ave Raymond Poincaré, 62100 Calais [03 21 97 89 79, 03 21 46 66 41 or 06 79 62 93 22 (mob); camping@marie-calais.fr]** A16 exit junc 43 dir Blériot-Plage/Calais cent & foll sp for beach (plage). Site nr harbour wall & Fort Risban. Well sp fr town cent. Med, wc; shop nr; rest nr. "M'vans only; well-kept, busy site; gd NH to/fr ferries; obtain token/pass fr Camp Municipal adj; warden calls to collect fee pm or pay at Camp Municipal." € 8.00   2016*

CALAIS *3A3* (3km NW Coastal) *50.959323, 1.831833* **Camping Municipal Le Grande Gravelot, 62100 Calais [03 91 91 52 34; camping@mairie-calais.fr]** Head for Calais beach. Site at end of Port de Plaisance dock on rd behind hses & flats o'look beach. Med, mkd, hdg, unshd, wc; chem disp; mv service pnt; fam bthrm; shwrs inc; EHU (16A) inc; lndry; beach 250m; twin axles; wifi; TV; dogs; phone; bus; Eng spkn; adv bkg acc; quiet; sauna; games rm; bike hire; CCI. "Excel; aire de svr adj to site all year round; site patrolled at night; local cafes nrby; short walk to town." ♦ 1 Apr-31 Oct. € 17.00   2018*

> **"I like to fill in the reports as I travel from site to site"**
>
> You'll find report forms at the back of this guide, or you can fill them in online at camc.com/europereport.

CALVI *10G2* (2km SE Coastal) *42.55228, 8.76423* **Camping Paduella, Route de Bastia, 20260 Calvi [04 95 65 06 16 or 04 95 65 13 20; fax 04 95 31 43 99; camping.paduella@wanadoo.fr; www. campingpaduella.com]** On N197 fr Calvi; on R 200m after rndabt by Casino supmkt. Med, mkd, pt shd, pt sl, terr, wc; chem disp; fam bthrm; shwrs inc; EHU (6A) €3.65; lndry; shop; snacks; bar; playgrnd; beach sand 300m; 25% statics; dogs; Eng spkn; quiet; CKE/CCI. "Poss best site in Calvi; immac san facs but slippery when wet, espec ramp; vg." ♦ 15 May-15 Oct. € 21.00   2013*

CALVI

CALVI *10G2* (23km SW Urban) *42.46451, 8.68012*
La Morsetta Camping, Route Calvi-Porta, 20260 Calvi [04 95 65 25 28; fax 04 95 65 25 29; info@lamorsetta.net; www.lamorsetta.net] Drive via the D81 fr Calvi to Galeria. Then about 12 km via the D81b coastal rd dir Calvi. Take the direct rte D81b fr Calvi, 20 km. Med, pt shd, wc; shwrs; EHU €3.20; rest; bar; wifi; dogs €1.70; ♦ 1 May-15 Oct. € 46.60   2013*

CAMARET SUR MER *2E1* (3km NE Coastal) *48.28070, -4.56490* **Camping Le Grand Large, Lambézen, 29570 Camaret-sur-Mer** [02 98 27 91 41; fax 02 98 27 93 72; contact@campinglegrandlarge.com; www.campinglegrandlarge.com] On D8 bet Crozen & Camaret, turn R at ent to Camaret onto D355, sp Roscanvel. Foll sps to site in 3km. Med, hdg, mkd, pt shd, pt sl, wc; chem disp; mv service pnt; fam bthrm; shwrs inc; EHU (10A) inc; gas; lndry; shop; snacks; bar; bbq; playgrnd; pool (htd); paddling pool; beach shgl 500m; wifi; TV; dogs €3; adv bkg acc; quiet; ccard acc; tennis; boating. "Coastal views fr some pitches, lovely beach; pleasant, helpful owners; 45 min cliff top walk to town; excel; excel location; do not arr bef 2pm if not prebooked;." ♦ 30 Mar-30 Sep. € 28.00   2018*

CAMARET SUR MER *2E1* (4km NE Coastal) *48.28788, -4.56540* **Camping Plage de Trez-Rouz, Route de Camaret à Roscanvel, 29160 Crozon** [02 98 27 93 96; contact@trezrouz.com; www.trezrouz.com] Foll D8 to Camaret-sur-Mer & at rndabt turn N sp Roscanvel/D355. Site on R in 3km. Med, mkd, hdg, pt shd, pt sl, wc; chem disp; mv service pnt; fam bthrm; shwrs inc; EHU (16A) €3.50; lndry; shop; rest; snacks; playgrnd; pool (htd); beach sand; wifi; 10% statics; dogs €1.50; adv bkg acc; quiet; horseriding 2km; tennis 500m; CKE/CCI. "Great position opp beach; conv for Presqu'île de Crozon; gd facs but stretched high ssn; site scruffy LS; friendly helpful owner; gd hot shwrs." ♦ 15 Mar-15 Oct. € 19.00   2016*

⊞ **CAMBO LES BAINS** *8F1* (3km SW Rural) *43.33863, -1.40129* **Camping L'Hiriberria, 64250 Itxassou** [05 59 29 98 09; fax 05 59 29 20 88; hiriberria@wanadoo.fr; www.hiriberria.com] Fr Cambo-les-Bains on D932 to Itxassou. Site on L 200m fr D918. Lge, mkd, hdstg, hdg, pt shd, pt sl, wc (htd); chem disp; mv service pnt; fam bthrm; shwrs inc; EHU (5A) €3.25; gas; lndry; shop nr; rest nr; bar nr; bbq; playgrnd; pool (covrd, htd); red long stay; wifi; TV; 20% statics; dogs €1; phone; Eng spkn; quiet; games area; CKE/CCI. "Popular site, phone ahead rec; gd views Pyrenees; pretty vill in 1km; vg walks; friendly owners." ♦ € 35.00   2013*

CAMBO LES BAINS *8F1* (5km W Rural) *43.33969, -1.47000* **Camping Alegera, 64250 Souraïde** [05 59 93 91 80 or 06 13 76 66 87 (mob); www.camping-alegera.com] Fr St Jean-de-Luz take D918 to Souraïde, site sp on L on rvside. Lge, hdg, mkd, pt shd, wc cont; chem disp; mv service pnt; fam bthrm; shwrs inc; EHU (4-10A) €3.40-4 (poss rev pol); gas; lndry; shop; snacks; bbq (elec, gas); playgrnd; pool; 10% statics; dogs €1.30; adv bkg acc; quiet; fishing 4km; golf; games rm; tennis. "Excel for coast & Pyrenees; spacious pitches; red facs LS; pretty vill; v quiet, clean, lovely site." ♦ 1 Apr-31 Oct. € 18.00   2013*

CAMBRAI *3B4* (3km W Urban) *50.17533, 3.21534* **FFCC Camp Municipal Les Trois Clochers, 77 Rue Jean Goudé, 59400 Cambrai** [03 27 70 91 64] Exit A2 junc 14; at rndabt after slip rd (with 6 exits) take D630 dir Cambrai; in 1km (by Buffalo Grill) turn L onto D630; in 200m turn L onto D939; in 100m turn L into Rue Jean Goudé. Or fr Cambrai W on D939; after x-ing rv bdge cont on D939 until traff lts in 300m; go strt over traff lts, then in 100m turn L into Rue Jean Goudé. Site sp fr all dirs on ent town. Sm, hdg, unshd, wc (htd); chem disp; mv service pnt; fam bthrm; shwrs inc; EHU (5-8A) €2.50; shop nr; rest nr; Eng spkn. "Beautiful, well-kept site; gd, spacious pitches; v conv Calais; early arr rec high ssn; v helpful, friendly manager; gd san facs, ltd & stretched when site full; interesting town; excel; 5 min walk to Aldi supmkt; hg rec." ♦ 15 Apr-15 Oct. € 14.50   2017*

> **"We must tell the Club about that great site we found"**
>
> Get your site reports in by mid-August and we'll do our best to get your updates into the next edition.

CANCALE *2E4* (3km N Coastal) *48.70369, -1.84829* **Camp Municipal La Pointe du Grouin, 35260 Cancale** [02 99 89 63 79 or 02 99 89 60 15; fax 02 99 89 54 25; campingcancale@orange.fr; www.ville-cancale.fr] Take D76 twd Cancale & cont on D201 sp Pointe de Grouin; site on R in 3km on cliffs above sea, on N side of Cancale (diff to see, on RH bend mkd with chevrons); sp 'Camp Municipal'. Care req at ent. Med, pt sl, wc; mv service pnt; shwrs inc; EHU (8-13A) €3.40-445 (poss long lead req); lndry; shop; rest nr; bbq; playgrnd; beach shgl adj; dogs €1.75; Eng spkn; quiet; ccard acc; fishing; watersports. "Lovely, well-kept site in gd location; sea views; some pitches uneven; excel san facs; gates clsd 2300-0700; conv Dinan, Mont-St Michel, St Malo; gd walking." 9 Mar-25 Oct. € 17.00   2014*

CANDE SUR BEUVRON

LA GRANDE TORTUE
★★★★★

Well equipped family camp site. Large pitches. Shop, restaurant with terrace and bar. Entertainment in the high season. Swimming pools with slides and games, big pool is covered and a separate toddler pool. Sauna, Whirpool. Pitches with private sanitary. Trampolines, Sportfield, fenced playground for toddlers. Renting of mobile homes and chalets. Cycling and walking routes in the surrounding.

41120 Candé-sur-Beuvron Tel. 00 33 (0)2 54441520
E-mail : camping@grandetortue.com
Internet : www.grandetortue.com

France

CANCALE *2E4* (10km S Coastal) *48.61592, -1.85151*
Camping de l'Ile Verte, 42 Rue de l'Ile Verte, 35114 St Benoît-des-Ondes [02 99 58 62 55; camping-ile-verte@sfr.fr; www.campingdelileverte.com] Site on S side of vill. Fr Cancale, take D76 SW for approx 4km, then turn L onto D155 into St Benoît. Foll site sp. Sm, hdg, pt shd, wc (htd); chem disp; mv service pnt; shwrs inc; EHU (6A) €4 (poss rev pol); gas; lndry; shop; rest nr; bar nr; playgrnd; beach sand adj; 3% statics; dogs €2.50; phone; adv bkg acc; quiet; CKE/CCI. "Well-kept, tidy site on edge of vill; facs poss stretched high ssn; big pitches but narr access rds." 30 Mar-31 Oct. € 28.00   2018*

CANCALE *2E4* (2km NW Coastal) *48.68995, -1.86130*
Camping Les Close Fleuris, La Ville es Poulains et Les, Clos Fleuris, La Ville es Polains, 35260 Cancale [02 99 89 97 68; fax 09 58 18 10 82; campingdosfleuris@free.fr; www.canale-camping.fr] Foll D76 to D355, foll D355 to Blvd d'Armor, cont on Boulrvard D'Armor. Drive on to La Ville Es Poulains, exit the rndbt onto Blvd d'Armor, go over rdbt, bear L twrds Rue du Saussaye, cont onto Rue du Saussaye, turn L onto La Ville Es Poulains, take 1st R to stay on La Ville Es Poulains and the site will be on your L. Med, mkd, pt shd, wc; chem disp; shwrs; EHU (16A) €4.40; lndry; playgrnd; pool; wifi; dogs (€2); Eng spkn; games rm. "Lots of walking trails and coastal walks." 15 Mar-15 Nov. € 20.00   2014*

CANCALE *2E4* (7km NW Coastal) *48.68861, -1.86833*
Camping Le Bois Pastel, 13 Rue de la Corgnais, 35260 Cancale [02 99 89 66 10; fax 02 99 89 60 11; camping.bois-pastel@wanadoo.fr; www.campingboispastel.fr] Fr Cancale take D201 dir Pointe du Grouin & St Malo by Rte Touristique. Site sp on L 2.5km after Pointe du Grouin. Med, mkd, pt shd, wc; chem disp; mv service pnt; shwrs inc; EHU (6A) €4; lndry; shop; snacks; bar; bbq; playgrnd; pool (covrd, htd); paddling pool; beach sand 800m; red long stay; 25% statics; dogs €2.50; adv bkg acc; quiet; games area; games rm; fishing. "Conv Mont-St Michel, St Malo; gd touring base." 1 Apr-30 Sep. € 22.00   2012*

CANCON *7D3* (12km W Rural) *44.53461, 0.50555*
Camping Le Moulin, Lassalle, 47290 Monbahus [05 53 01 68 87; info@lemoulin-monbahus.com; www.lemoulin-monbahus.com] Fr N21 turn W at Cancon on D124 sp Miramont. In 7.5km at Monbahus pass thro vill cent take L turn, still on D124 sp Tombeboeuf. In 3km lge grain silos on L, site next on R. Sm, hdstg, mkd, pt shd, wc; chem disp; fam bthrm; shwrs inc; EHU (5-10A) €3 (most pitches 5A only avail); lndry; shop nr; rest; snacks; bbq; playgrnd; pool (htd); entmnt; wifi; dogs; Eng spkn; adv bkg acc; bike hire; CKE/CCI. "CL-type site in garden; friendly British owners; bistro; clean, basic san facs; vg pool; B & B avail; extra for twin axles over 5m; excel." € 17.00   2016*

CANDE SUR BEUVRON *4G2* (1km S Rural) *47.48952, 1.25834* **La Grande Tortue (Part Naturist), 3 Route de Pontlevoy, 41120 Candé-sur-Beuvron [02 54 44 15 20; fax 02 54 44 19 45; camping@grandetortue.com; www.grandetortue.com]** Exit A10 junc 17 (Blois) & foll 'Autres/Toutes Directions' or 'Vierzon' to cross Rv Loire; immed after bdge R onto D951/D971 dir Chaumont; ignore D173 R fork & foll D751 thro Chailles & Villelouet; R at rndabt to go thro Cande; fork L after Cande; site on L in abt 100m. Lge, hdg, mkd, hdstg, pt shd, pt sl, wc (htd); chem disp; mv service pnt; fam bthrm; shwrs inc; EHU (10A) €3.50; gas; lndry; shop; rest; snacks; bar; bbq; playgrnd; pool (covrd, htd); paddling pool; entmnt; wifi; TV; 50% statics; dogs €3.70; Eng spkn; adv bkg acc; quiet; ccard acc; horseriding; bike hire; games area; CKE/CCI. "Excel, rustic site amongst trees; poss diff access due trees; helpful staff; vg, clean san facs; gd pool; gd for children; gd cycling; gourmet rest by rv bdge in vill; conv Loire chateaux; gd rest." ♦
11 Apr-20 Sep. € 42.00   2015*

See advertisement

CANET PLAGE

Le Brasilia has chosen as its home port a beautiful, peaceful beach located at the far end of Canet-en-Roussillon. There, between the river and the port, in the hollow of a deep pine forest with its Mediterranean scents. The delightful Seychellois atmosphere of the "Archipel" water park will immediately transport you to the Tropics. 2 extra pools: one pool perfect for swimming, a second designed for sports and a 250m^2 well-being centre, the Papillon SPA. Our village is a garden of nature where you can get away from it all, and yet so much closer to your dream holidays. All our shops and services are open throughout the whole time that the site is open.

2, avenue des Anneaux du Roussillon - 66140 Canet-en-Roussillon - France
Tél. : +33 (0)4 68 80 23 82 - Fax : +33 (0)4 68 73 32 97
info@lebrasilia.fr - www.brasilia.fr

The Leading Campings of Europe

CANET PLAGE 10G1 (3km N Coastal) 42.70808, 3.03332 **Camping Le Brasilia, 2 Ave des Anneaux du Roussillon, 66140 Canet-en-Roussillon [04 68 80 23 82; fax 04 68 73 32 97; info@lebrasilia.fr; www.brasilia.fr]** Exit A9 junc 41 sp Perpignan Nord & Rivesaltes onto D83 dir Le Barcarès & Canet for 10km; then take D81 dir Canet for 10km until lge rndabt which goes under D617 (do not foll sp to Canet to R) - cont round rndabt & foll sp Ste Marie-le-Mer (to go back the way you came). Then take 1st R sp Le Brasilia. V lge, mkd, hdg, pt shd, serviced pitches; wc; chem disp; mv service pnt; fam bthrm; shwrs inc; EHU (10A) inc; gas; lndry; shop; rest; snacks; bar; bbq (elec, gas); playgrnd; pool (htd); paddling pool; beach sand 150m; twin axles; entmnt; wifi; TV; 35% statics; dogs €4; bus to Canet; Eng spkn; quiet; ccard acc; bike hire; tennis; fishing; archery; games rm; CKE/CCI. "Excel, well-run, well laid-out site; gd sized pitches; friendly staff; immac san facs; excel facs, espec for families/children/teenagers; rvside walk adj; conv day trips to Barcelona,Carcassonne etc; daily mkt in Canet except Mon." ♦ 12 Apr-4 Oct. € 54.00 2017*

See advertisement

CANET PLAGE 10G1 (4km N Coastal) 42.70905, 3.03285 **Camping Le Bosquet, Ave des Anneaux du Roussillon, 66140 Canet-Plage [04 68 80 23 80; campinglebosquet@club-internet.fr; www.campinglebosquet.com]** Exit A9 junc 41 onto D83 dir Le Barcarès; then turn R onto D81 dir Canet; in Canet at lge rndabt go R round until exit dir Torreilles & Ste Marie; then immed after rndabt take sm rd on R; site sp. Or E on D617 fr Perpignan, turn L on D11 in Canet & foll sp. Med, mkd, hdg, pt shd, wc; chem disp; fam bthrm; shwrs inc; EHU (5A) €3.50; gas; lndry; shop; rest; snacks; bar; bbq; playgrnd; pool; beach sand 400m; entmnt; TV; dogs €3; phone; bus adj; Eng spkn; adv bkg acc; quiet; ccard acc; games rm; games area; CKE/CCI. "Family-run site nr excel sand beach, shops 2km - plenty of choice; gd touring base; vg." 12 Apr-5 Oct. € 38.00 2014*

CANET PLAGE 10G1 (4km NE Coastal) 42.72724, 3.03377 **Camping La Pergola, 66470 Ste Marie la Mer [02 51 20 41 94; contact@camp-atlantique.com; www.campinglapergola.com]** S fr Narbonne, exit N9 at Salses & foll D11 to St Marie-sur-Mer. St Marie-Plage beach for St Marie-sur-Mer. Site not sp but on D12 to coast. Lge, pt shd, wc cont; shwrs inc; EHU; gas; shop; beach sand 500m; adv bkg acc; quiet. "No lge o'fits; v tricky maneuvering as too many trees." 3 Apr-20 Sep. € 39.00 2015*

CANOURGUE, LA

CANET PLAGE *10G1* (1km S Coastal) *42.67540, 3.03120* **Camping Club Mar Estang, Route de St Cyprien, 66140 Canet-Plage [04 68 80 35 53; fax 04 68 73 32 94; contact@marestang.com; www.marestang.com]** Exit A9 junc 41 Perpignan Nord dir Canet, then foll sp St Cyprien, site sp. Site on D81A bet Canet-Plage & St Cyprien-Plage. V lge, mkd, hdstg, pt shd, wc; chem disp; mv service pnt; fam bthrm; shwrs inc; EHU (6A) €7; gas; lndry; shop; rest; snacks; bar; playgrnd; pool (htd); paddling pool; beach sand adj; red long stay; TV; 50% statics; dogs €4; Eng spkn; adv bkg acc; quiet; ccard acc; tennis; waterslide; bike hire; CKE/CCI. "Conv Spanish border & Pyrenees; fitness rm; gd birdwatching." ♦ 26 Apr-14 Sep. € 51.40   2014*

CANET PLAGE *10G1* (4km W Rural) *42.68914, 2.99857* **FFCC Camping Les Fontaines, Route de St Nazaire, 66140 Canet-en-Roussillon [04 68 80 22 57 or 06 77 90 14 91 (mob); campinglesfontaines@wanadoo.fr; www.camping-les-fontaines.com]** Take D11 fr Canet dir St Nazaire; site sp on L in 1.5km. Easy access. Lge, mkd, hdg, unshd, wc; chem disp; mv service pnt; fam bthrm; shwrs inc; EHU (10A) €3.50; lndry; shop; snacks; bar; bbq (elec, gas); playgrnd; pool; paddling pool; beach sand 2.5km; entmnt; wifi; 30% statics; dogs €3.50; phone; bus; Eng spkn; adv bkg acc; quiet; games area. "Pitches lge; conv Etang de Canet et St Nazaire nature reserve with flamingos; excel; relaxed atmosphere; friendly staff." 1 May-30 Sep. € 30.00   2013*

> **"That's changed – Should I let the Club know?"**
>
> If you find something on site that's different from the site entry, fill in a report and let us know. See camc.com/europereport.

CANET PLAGE *10G1* (4km W Urban) *42.70114, 2.99850* **Kawan Village Ma Prairie, 1 Ave des Coteaux, 66140 Canet-en-Roussillon [04 68 73 26 17; fax 04 68 73 28 82; ma.prairie@wanadoo.fr; www.maprairie.com]** Leave A9/E15 at junc 41, sp Perpignan Centre/Canet-en-Roussillon. Take D83, then D81 until Canet-en-Roussillon. At rndabt, take D617 dir Perpignan & in about 500m leave at exit 5. Take D11 dir St Nazaire, pass under bdge & at rndabt turn R. Site on L. Lge, hdg, shd, serviced pitches; wc; chem disp; mv service pnt; fam bthrm; shwrs inc; EHU (10A) inc; gas; lndry; shop nr; rest; snacks; bar; bbq (elec, gas); playgrnd; pool; paddling pool; beach sand 3km; entmnt; wifi; TV; 20% statics; dogs €5; bus to town nr; Eng spkn; adv bkg req; quiet; ccard acc; waterslide; games rm; sailing; waterskiing; canoeing; CKE/CCI. "Peaceful, popular site; friendly, helpful owners; o'fits 7.5m & over by request; reg bus to beach (Jul/Aug); daily mkt Perpignan; gd." ♦ 12 Apr-19 Sep. € 50.00   2014*

CANNES *10F4* (3km NE Urban) *43.55610, 6.96060* **Camping Parc Bellevue, 67 Ave Maurice Chevalier, 06150 Cannes [04 93 47 28 97; fax 04 93 48 66 25; contact@parcbellevue.com; www.parcbellevue.com]** A8 exit junc 41 twd Cannes. Foll N7 & at junc controlled by traff lts, get in L lane. Turn L & in 100m turn L across dual c'way, foll sp for site. Site in 400m on L after sports complex - steep ramp at ent. Lge, mkd, pt shd, wc; chem disp; fam bthrm; shwrs; EHU (6A) €4; gas; lndry; shop; rest; snacks; bar; pool (htd); beach sand 1.5km; entmnt; wifi; TV (pitch); 80% statics; dogs; phone; bus/train nr; Eng spkn; adv bkg acc; CKE/CCI. "Site on 2 levels; gd security; gd san facs; some pitches long way fr facs; many steps to gd pool; helpful; conv beaches & A8; green oasis in busy area; gd bus to prom; no m'van facs; rec use sat nav; not rec in wet weather; no hdstg; o'fits have to be towed off pitches in bad weather." ♦ 1 Apr-30 Sep. € 17.50   2013*

CANNET DES MAURES, LE *10F3* (4km N Rural) *43.42140, 6.33655* **FFCC Camping Domaine de la Cigalière, Route du Thoronet, 83340 Le Cannet-des-Maures [04 94 73 81 06; campinglacigaliere@wanadoo.fr; www.campings-var.com]** Exit A8 at Le Cannet-des-Maures onto D17 N dir Le Thoronet; site in 4km on R, sp. Med, hdg, mkd, hdstg, pt shd, pt sl, wc; chem disp; mv service pnt; fam bthrm; shwrs inc; EHU (6A) €4; lndry; snacks; bar; bbq (elec, gas); playgrnd; pool (htd); 20% statics; dogs €2; quiet; CKE/CCI. "Peaceful site; lge pitches; St Tropez 44km; vg site." ♦ 1 Apr-30 Sep. € 20.00   2014*

CANOURGUE, LA *9D1* (2km E Rural) *44.40789, 3.24178* **Camping Le Val d'Urugne, Route des Gorges-du-Tarn, 48500 La Canourgue [04 66 32 84 00; fax 04 66 32 88 14; lozereleisure@wanadoo.fr; www.lozereleisure.com]** Exit A75 junc 40 dir La Canourgue; thro vill dir Gorges-du-Tarn. In 2km site on R 600m after golf clubhouse. Sm, hdg, pt shd, pt sl, wc; chem disp; mv service pnt; shwrs inc; EHU (6A) €3.50; lndry; shop; rest nr; bar nr; TV; dogs €2; Eng spkn; adv bkg acc; quiet; ccard acc; CKE/CCI. "Vg site; golf adj; conv A75 & Gorges-du-Tarn; some statics adj; LS stop at golf club for key to site; site poss tired end of ssn." ♦ 1 May-30 Sep. € 16.40   2014*

CANOURGUE, LA *9D1* (7km W Rural) *44.43638, 3.1475* **Municipal la Vallèe, Miége Rivière 48500 Canilhac [04 66 32 91 14 or 04 66 32 80 05; commune.canilhac@wanadoo.fr]** Leave A75 at junc 40. Take D988 W, sp St Laurent d'Olt. Site on L at level x-ing after 10 mins. Sm, hdg, pt shd, wc; chem disp; mv service pnt; fam bthrm; shwrs; EHU (16A) €3; lndry; shop; snacks; bar; bbq; playgrnd; pool (htd); paddling pool; wifi; TV; 10% statics; dogs €1; phone; adv bkg acc; quiet; games rm; fishing; CCI. "Sm shop; supmkt 5km; next to rv (sw not allowed); horseriding nr; golf nr; canoeing nr; paint-balling & quad biking nrby; conv for Gorges du Tarn & Aubrac; St laurent d'Olt worth a visit." ♦ 15 Jun-15 Sep. € 15.50   2014*

CANY BARVILLE

CANY BARVILLE *3C2* (3km N Rural) *49.80375, 0.64960* **Camping Maupassant, 12 Route de la Folie, 76450 Vittefleur [02 35 97 97 14; campingmaupassant@orange.fr; www.camping-maupassant.com]** S fr St Valery-en-Caux on D925 dir Cany-Barville; site sp turning to R 700m bef Cany-Barville. Med, hdg, mkd, hdstg, pt shd, wc (htd); chem disp; mv service pnt; fam bthrm; shwrs; EHU (6A) €3.30; gas; lndry; bbq (charcoal); 10% statics; dogs; phone; adv bkg acc; quiet; CKE/CCI. "Friendly staff; gd NH; gd, clean site; 10 touring pitches." 9 Mar-14 Dec. € 20.00 2016*

CANY BARVILLE *3C2* (1km S Urban) *49.78335, 0.64214* **Camp Municipal, Route de Barville, 76450 Cany-Barville [02 35 97 70 37; fax 02 35 97 72 32; camping@cany-barville.fr; www.cany-barville.fr]** Sp fr town cent, off D268 to S of town, adj stadium. Med, mkd, hdg, pt shd, pt shd, wc (htd); chem disp; mv service pnt; shwrs inc; EHU (10A) €3.25 (poss rev pol); lndry; shop nr; playgrnd; red long stay; 25% statics; dogs €1.35; adv bkg acc; ccard acc; CKE/CCI. "Vg facs but poss stretched at high ssn; poss no check-in on Sun; within reach of Dieppe & Fécamp chateau; gd cycling; poss mkt traders on site." ♦ 1 Apr-30 Sep. € 14.00 2014*

CAPESTANG *10F1* (1km W Urban) *43.32759, 3.03865* **Camp Municipal de Tounel, 1 Rue Georges Brassens, Ave de la République, 34310 Capestang [04 67 93 34 23 (TO) or 06 07 97 52 09 (mob); oacinfocapestang@orange.fr; www.ville-capestang.fr]** Fr Béziers on D11, turn R twd vill of Capestang, approx 1km after passing supmkt. Site on L in leisure park opp Gendamarie. Med, hdg, pt shd, wc cont; chem disp; shwrs; EHU (6A) €3; lndry; shop nr; rest nr; playgrnd; wifi; dogs free; tennis; bike hire; fishing. "300m fr Canal de Midi; excel walks or bike rides; lovely rest in vill; LS site yourself, fees collected; facs poss tired LS; poss diff access to pitches for long o'fits; ltd EHU; poss resident workers; NH only." ♦ 1 May-30 Sep. € 15.00 2014*

CARCASSONNE *8F4* (9km N Rural) *43.25999, 2.36509* **FFCC Camping Das Pinhiers, Chemin du Pont Neuf, 11620 Villemoustaussou [04 68 47 81 90; fax 04 68 71 43 49; campingdaspinhiers@wanadoo.fr; www.camping-carcassonne.net]** Exit A6 junc 23 Carcassonne Ouest & foll sp Mazamet on D118; R at rndabt with filling stn; turn R & foll camping sp. Med, hdg, shd, pt sl, wc; chem disp; mv service pnt; shwrs inc; EHU (10A) inc; shop; rest; snacks; bar; playgrnd; pool; 10% statics; dogs €3; bus 1 km; Eng spkn; adv bkg acc; quiet; ccard acc; CKE/CCI. "Diff to pitch lge vans due hdg pitches & sl; san facs basic & stretched high ssn; general area rather run down (2009); office clsd noon-2pm." ♦ 1 Apr-31 Oct. € 18.00 2015*

CARCASSONNE *8F4* (10km E Rural) *43.21498, 2.47031* **Camping La Commanderie, 6 Chemin Eglise,11800 Rustiques [04 68 78 67 63 or 06 25 28 35 80 (mob); contact@campinglacommanderie.com; www.campinglacommanderie.com]** Fr Carcassonne take D6113/D610 E to Trèbes (approx 8km); at Trèbes take D610 & after 2km L onto D906, then L onto D206; site on R; foll sp 'Rustiques'. Or fr A61 ext junc 24 onto D6113 to Trèbes & then as bef. Sm, mkd, pt shd, pt sl, wc (htd); chem disp; shwrs inc; EHU (6A) inc; lndry; shop nr; rest; snacks; bar; playgrnd; pool; wifi; 10% statics; dogs €2; phone; Eng spkn; adv bkg acc; quiet; ccard acc; CKE/CCI. "Pleasant, helpful owner & staff; modern san facs; patron sells own wines; gd cycling along canal fr Trèbes; conv A61; gd NH en rte Spain; superb refurbished pool; excel; quiet relaxing site; excel site improving year on year, running track and 12 fitness machines added this year." 1 Apr-15 Oct. € 25.00 2018*

> **"I need an on-site restaurant"**
>
> We do our best to make sure site information is correct, but it is always best to check any must-have facilities are still available or will be open during your visit.

CARCASSONNE *8F4* (8km E Rural) *43.20700, 2.44258* **FFCC Camping à l'Ombre des Micocouliers, Chemin de la Lande, 11800 Trèbes [04 68 78 61 75; fax 04 68 78 88 77; infos@campingmicocouliers.com; www.audecamping.com]** Fr Carcassonne, take D6113 E for 6km to Trèbes; go under rlway bdge; fork L onto D610; turn R immed bef rv bdge; site on L in 200m. Fr W foll D6113 thro Trebes; at rndabt at E of town take last exit to L sp Sports Centre, site on R. Med, mkd, shd, wc; chem disp; mv service pnt; shwrs; EHU (6A), lndry; shop; rest; snacks; bbq; entmnt; TV; dogs €1.50; phone; Eng spkn; rv fishing; CKE/CCI. "Pleasant, sandy site by rv; well shd; friendly & helpful staff; gd, clean but dated san facs, 1 block up 15 steps; ltd EHU; Trèbes in walking dist; vg cycling, 13 km cycle to Carcassonne along cana, bus for €1; gd base Canal du Midi; can be noisy fr local youths on mbikes; walk into town needs care with busy rd; lovely site; adv to arr early as popular site, site improved, new tiling & paint in toilet block (2015); v.busy." ♦ 1 Apr-30 Sep. € 26.00 2015*

CARNAC

CARCASSONNE *8F4* (2km SE Rural) *43.19994, 2.35271* **Camping d la Cité, Route de St Hilaire, 11000 Carcassonne [04 68 10 01 00; fax 04 68 47 33 13; campingdelacite@carcassonne.fr; www.camping-delacite-carcassonne.com]** Fr N & W exit Carcassonne by D6113 twd Narbonne; cross rv & turn S on D104; foll sp. Fr S (D118) take D104 to E & foll sp. Fr E (D6113) take D342 S to D104; foll sp. Or exit A61 junc 23; at rndabt in 900m turn R onto D6161 sp Limoux; at traff lts in 1km turn L onto D118 sp La Cité; at rndabt in 700m turn R over rv for D104; in 600m turn L at rndabt onto D104 sp Camping La Cité; site on L in 1.4km. Or exit A61 junc 24 to D6113 sp Carcassonne; stay on rd until sp La Cité; cont to sp Camping La Cité. NB Site (La Cité) well sp fr all dirs & easy access fr A61 junc 23. Lge, mkd, hdg, pt shd, wc; chem disp; mv service pnt; shwrs inc; EHU (10A) inc (poss rev pol); lndry; shop nr; rest; snacks; bar; playgrnd; pool; entmnt; wifi; 10% statics; dogs €3.50; Eng spkn; adv bkg rec; quiet; ccard acc; tennis; CKE/CCI. "Delightful, well-kept site in gd location adj woods; popular - rec arr bef 1600; mixed pitch sizes & types; friendly, helpful staff; san facs need refurb & stretched high ssn, poss irreg cleaning LS (2009); ltd water & waste water pnts; many leisure facs; parking area for waiting if office clsd, 1200-1400 LS; pleasant, well-lit walk along rv to La Cité; muddy after rain; no twin axles; gd facs; high ssn o'spill area without EHU; excel site for visiting Carcassonne; excel location for old & new city." ♦ 2 Apr-13 Oct. € 30.50   2014*

⊞ **CARCASSONNE** *8F4* (6km S Rural) *43.17938, 2.37024* **Camping à l'Ombre des Oliviers, Ave du Stade, 11570 Cazilhac [04 68 79 65 08 or 06 81 54 96 00 (mob); florian.romo@wanadoo.fr; www.alombredesoliviers.com]** Fr N & W exit Carcassonne by D6113 dir Narbonne. Cross rv & turn S onto D104, then D142/D56 to Cazilhac, site sp. Sm, pt shd, wc; fam bthrm; shwrs inc; EHU (6-10A) €3 (poss rev pol); lndry; shop nr; bar; bbq; playgrnd; pool; TV; 10% statics; dogs €2; adv bkg acc; quiet; games area; tennis; site clsd 1st week Jan. "Site in pleasant position; if office clsd phone owner on mob, or site yourself; helpful owners; v ltd facs LS; insufficient san facs when site full & ltd other facs; few water pnts; pitches poss muddy/soft when wet; bus to old city nrby; site very shabby (2014); san facs need maintenance (2015)." € 23.00   2015*

CARCASSONNE *8F4* (15km NW Rural) *43.29861, 2.22277* **Camping de Montolieu, L'Olivier, 11170 Montolieu [04 68 76 95 01 or 06 31 90 31 92 (mob); nicole@camping-de-montolieu.com; www.camping-de-montolieu.com]** Fr D6113 4km W Carcassonne, take D629 twd Montolieu; site on R in 2.5km after Moussoulens. Sp fr D6113, approx 5km dist. App thro Montolieu not rec. Sm, hdg, mkd, pt shd, wc; chem disp; shwrs inc; EHU (5A) inc; gas; lndry; shop nr; rest nr; bar nr; bbq; wifi; 10% statics; dogs €2.50; phone; adv bkg acc; games area; games rm; CKE/CCI. "Well-run site in lovely countryside; pool 100m; manoeuvring tight; excel facs; conv Carcassonne; highly rec." ♦ 15 Mar-31 Oct. € 18.00   2014*

CARCES *10F3* (1km SE Urban) *43.47350, 6.18826* **Camping Les Fouguières, 165 chemin des Fouguières, 83570 Carcès [34 94 59 96 28 or 06 74 29 69 02 (mob); info@camping-les-fouguieres.com; www.camping-les-fouguieres.com]** Exit A8 junc 35 at Brignoles onto D554 to Le Val; then take D562 to Carcès. Site sp off D13. Narr app rd, diff entry & exit for long o'fits. Med, pt shd, wc; mv service pnt; shwrs inc; EHU (14A) €3; gas; lndry; snacks; playgrnd; pool (htd); sw nr; wifi; TV; 80% statics; dogs €2; phone; bus; Eng spkn; quiet; canoeing nr; fishing nr. "Pleasant, clean, well-shd site; friendly, helpful owner; Rv Caramy runs thro site; interesting, medieval town; Lake Carcès 2km; don't miss Entrecasteaux chateau; mkt Sat; excel." ♦ 10 Mar-30 Nov. € 29.00   2014*

CARENTAN *1D4* (1km NE Urban) *49.30988, -1.2388* **Camping Le Haut Dick, 30 Chemin du Grand-Bas Pays, 50500 Carentan [02 33 42 16 89; contact@camping-lehautdick.com; www.camping-lehautdick.com]** Exit N13 at Carentan; clearly sp in town cent, nr pool, on L bank of canal, close to marina. Foll sp to Port de Plaisance. Med, hdg, mkd, pt shd, wc; chem disp; mv service pnt; shwrs inc; EHU (6A) €4 (rev pol); gas; shop nr; rest nr; snacks; bar nr; bbq; playgrnd; 5% statics; dogs €1.50; phone; adv bkg acc; quiet; games rm; bike hire; CKE/CCI. "Some pitches poss tight for lge o'fits; gd security; eve meals avail; gates locked 2200-0700; conv Cherbourg ferry & D-Day beaches; crazy golf; gd birdwatching & cycling; htd pool adj; mkt Mon." ♦ 1 Apr-30 Sep. € 25.50   2012*

CARGESE *10H2* (4km N Coastal) *42.1625, 8.59791* **Camping Le Torraccia, Bagghiuccia, 20130 Cargèse [04 95 26 42 39; contact@camping-torraccia.com; www.camping-torraccia.com]** N fr Cargèse twd Porto on D81 for 3km. Site on L. Med, pt shd, terr, wc; fam bthrm; shwrs inc; EHU ltd (6A) €3.10; lndry; shop; rest nr; snacks; bar; playgrnd; pool; beach sand 1km; wifi; games area. "Nearest site to Porto without diff traff conditions." 21 Apr-30 Sep. € 20.00   2013*

CARNAC *2G3* (1km N Rural) *47.59683, -3.06035* **Camping La Grande Métairie, Route des Alignements de Kermario, 56342 Carnac [02 97 52 24 01; fax 02 97 52 83 58; info@lagrandemetairie.com; www.lagrandemetairie.com]** Fr Auray take N768 twd Quiberon. In 8km turn L onto D119 twd Carnac. La Métairie site sp 1km bef Carnac (at traff lts) turn L onto D196 to site on R in 1km. V lge, mkd, hdg, pt shd, wc (htd); chem disp; mv service pnt; fam bthrm; shwrs inc; EHU (6A) €3; gas; lndry; shop; rest; snacks; bar; bbq; playgrnd; pool (covrd, htd); paddling pool; beach sand 2.5km; entmnt; wifi; TV; 80% statics; dogs €4; Eng spkn; adv bkg acc; quiet; ccard acc; games rm; watersports 2.5km; sailing 2.5km; tennis; waterslide. "Excel facs; vg pool complex; friendly, helpful staff; rec." ♦ 2 Apr-10 Sep. € 42.00   2017*

See advertisement on next page

CARNAC

LA GRANDE MÉTAIRIE
★★★★★

Tél. +33 (0)2 30 26 02 29
www.lagrandemetairie.com

Water park with heated indoor pool
Children's club, sports activities, entertainment

CARNAC 2G3 (3km N Rural) 47.60801, -3.09049
Camping Les Bruyères, Kerogile, 56340 Plouharnel [02 97 52 30 57; fax 09 71 70 46 47; contact@camping-lesbruyeres.com; www.camping-lesbruyeres.com]
Fr Vannes W on E60/N165, at Auray take D768 dir Quiberon. At rndabt approx 2km fr Plouharnel turn L into Rte du Hahon, site in 500m, sp. Med, mkd, hdg, hdstg, pt shd, wc (htd); chem disp; mv service pnt; fam bthrm; shwrs inc; EHU (6A) €3.70; lndry; shop; rest; snacks; bar; bbq; playgrnd; beach sand 3km; entmnt; wifi; TV; 30% statics; dogs €2; Eng spkn; adv bkg acc; quiet; ccard acc; tennis; games area; CKE/CCI. "V pleasant, well-run, peaceful site; library; bicycles; pony rides; vg." ♦ 5 Apr-30 Sep. € 33.50   2014*

> **"Satellite navigation makes touring much easier"**
>
> Remember most sat navs don't know if you're towing or in a larger vehicle – always use yours alongside maps and site directions.

CARNAC 2G3 (2km NE Rural) 47.5964, -3.0617
Camping Le Moulin de Kermaux, Route de Kerlescan, 56340 Carnac [02 97 52 15 90; fax 02 97 52 83 85; moulin-de-kermaux@wanadoo.fr; www.camping-moulinkermaux.com] Fr Auray take D768 S sp Carnac, Quiberon. In 8km turn L onto D119 twds Carnac. 1km bef Carnac take D196 (Rte de Kerlescan) L to site in approx 500m opp round, stone observation tower for alignments. Fr St Trinite Sur Mer, take D781, cont to rndabt nr St Michel Tumulus on o'skirts of Carnac. Exit R onto D119. In 1km fork R onto D196, site on R in 1km. Med, hdg, mkd, pt shd, wc (htd); chem disp; mv service pnt; fam bthrm; shwrs inc; EHU (6A) €4 (poss rev pol); gas; lndry; shop; snacks; bar; bbq; playgrnd; pool (covrd, htd); paddling pool; beach sand 3km; entmnt; wifi; TV; 50% statics; dogs €2.50; phone; bus adj; Eng spkn; adv bkg acc; quiet; ccard acc; sauna; waterslide; games area; jacuzzi; CKE/CCI. "Well-kept, friendly, attractive site nr standing stones; many repeat visitors; excel." ♦ 19 Apr-13 Sep. € 38.00   2015*

CARNAC 2G3 (2km NE Rural) 47.60820, -3.06605
Camping Le Moustoir, 71 Route du Moustoir, 56340 Carnac [02 97 52 16 18; fax 02 97 52 88 37; info@lemoustoir.com; www.lemoustoir.com]
Fr N165 take D768 at Auray dir Carnac & Quiberon. In 5km take D119 dir Carnac, site on L at ent to Carnac. Lge, mkd, hdg, pt shd, pt sl, wc; chem disp; mv service pnt; fam bthrm; shwrs inc; EHU (10A) inc; lndry; shop; rest; snacks; bar; bbq; playgrnd; pool (covrd, htd); paddling pool; beach sand 4km; wifi; TV; 60% statics; dogs €1; phone; Eng spkn; adv bkg acc; ccard acc; games area; waterslide; bike hire; tennis; CKE/CCI. "Attractive, friendly, well-run site; facs clean but stretched; megaliths nrby; Sun mkt." ♦ 14 Apr-9 Sep. € 43.00   2017*

CARNAC 2G3 (4km NE Rural) 47.60198, -3.03672
Camping de Kervilor, Route du Latz, 56470 La Trinité-sur-Mer [02 97 55 76 75; infos@camping-kervilor.com; www.camping-kervilor.com]
Sp fr island in cent of Trinité-sur-Mer. Lge, hdstg, mkd, hdg, pt shd, wc; chem disp; mv service pnt; fam bthrm; shwrs inc; EHU (6-10A) €3.85-4.35; gas; lndry; shop; snacks; bar; bbq; playgrnd; pool (covrd, htd); paddling pool; beach sand 4km; entmnt; wifi; 5% statics; dogs €2.90; Eng spkn; adv bkg acc; ccard acc; waterslide; solarium; bike hire; games area; tennis; CKE/CCI. "Busy, well-kept family site; lge pitches; clean dated unisex san facs; 20 min walk into La Trinité-sur-Mer (1.5km); gd cycling to Carnac & megaliths; great site; excel loc; easy walk to lovely town." ♦ 1 Apr-18 Sep. € 29.00   2018*

CARNAC 2G3 (2km E Rural/Coastal) 47.5810, -3.0576
Camping Les Druides, 55 Chemin de Beaumer, 56340 Carnac [02 97 52 08 18; fax 02 97 52 96 13; contact@camping-les-druides.com; www.camping-les-druides.com] Go E on seafront Carnac Plage to end; turn N onto Ave d'Orient; at junc with Rte de la Trinité-sur-Mer, turn L, then 1st R; site 1st on L in 300m. Med, hdg, pt shd, pt sl, wc; chem disp; mv service pnt; fam bthrm; shwrs inc; EHU (6A) €3.70; lndry; shop nr; rest nr; playgrnd; pool (htd); beach sand 500m; entmnt; TV; 5% statics; dogs €2.50; Eng spkn; adv bkg acc; quiet; ccard acc; games rm; CKE/CCI. "Friendly welcome." ♦ 12 Apr-6 Sep. € 49.00   2014*

CARPENTRAS

CARNAC *2G3 (3km E Rural) 47.61122, -3.02908*
Camping du Lac, 56340 Carnac [02 97 55 78 78; fax 02 97 52 88 37; info@lelac-carnac.com; www.lelac-carnac.com] Fr Auray (by-pass) take D768 sp Carnac; in 4km turn L on D186; after 4km look for C105 on L & foll sp to site. Fr E end of quay-side in La Trinité-sur-Mer take main Carnac rd & in 100m turn R onto D186; in 2km R on C105, R on C131; sp. Med, hdg, pt shd, pt sl, serviced pitches; wc; chem disp; mv service pnt; fam bthrm; shwrs inc; EHU (10A) €3.60; gas; lndry; shop; rest nr; bbq; playgrnd; pool (htd); beach sand 3km; entmnt; TV; 50% statics; dogs €2; phone; Eng spkn; adv bkg acc; quiet; ccard acc; bike hire; CKE/CCI. "Excel, beautiful, woodland site o'looking tidal lake; helpful owner; clean, well-cared for; multi-sport court; fitness rm; superb pool; gd cycling & walking; vg; lovely sunsets & sunrises." 1 Apr-30 Sep. € 36.00   2017*

CARNAC *2G3 (2km SE Coastal) 47.58116, -3.05804*
Camping Le Dolmen, Chemin de Beaumer, 56340 Carnac [02 97 52 12 35; fax 02 97 52 63 91; contact@campingledolmen.com; www.campingledolmen.com] Fr N on D768 twd Quiberon; turn L onto D781 twd La Trinité-sur-Mer. At Montauban turn R at rndabt dir Kerfraval & Beaumer, site in 700m, sp. Med, hdstg, mkd, hdg, pt shd, pt sl, wc (htd); chem disp; mv service pnt; fam bthrm; shwrs; EHU (10A) €4.70; lndry; shop nr; rest; snacks; bbq; playgrnd; pool (htd); paddling pool; beach sand 500m; entmnt; wifi; 2% statics; dogs €3; adv bkg acc; quiet; ccard acc; games area; games rm; CKE/CCI. "Excel, v friendly, clean, pleasant site; v well maintained; generous size pitches; modern, clean san facs; highly rec." ♦ 2 Apr-23 Sep. € 38.00   2018*

CARNAC *2G3 (1km S Coastal) 47.57667, -3.06817*
Camping Les Menhirs, Allé saint michel, 56343 Carnac [02 97 52 94 67; fax 02 97 52 25 38; contact@lesmenhirs.com; www.lesmenhirs.com] Fr Auray foll sps to Carnac, Carnac Plage. Site past shopping cent rd on L, sp by camping sps. Lge, pt shd, pt sl, wc; chem disp; shwrs inc; EHU (6A) €4.80; gas; lndry; shop; pool (htd); beach sand 350m; 50% statics; adv bkg acc; quiet; sauna; jacuzzi; games rm. "Extra charge for larger pitches; excel san facs; excel location, nr rest, shops & beach." ♦ 1 Apr-30 Sep. € 56.00   2017*

CARNAC *2G3 (4km NW Rural) 47.59468, -3.09659*
Camping Les Goélands, Kerbachic, 56340 Plouharnel [02 97 52 31 92; contact@camping-lesgoelands.com; www.camping-lesgoelands.com] Take D768 fr Auray twd Quiberon. In Plouharnel turn L at rndabt by supmkt onto D781 to Carnac. Site sp to L in 500m. Med, pt shd, wc; chem disp; shwrs inc; EHU (3-6A) €3.50; gas; lndry; shop nr; playgrnd; pool; beach sand 3km; dogs €1; adv bkg rec. "Good facs; gd-sized pitches; gate clsd at 2200; nr beaches with bathing & gd yachting; bells fr adj abbey not too intrusive; conv for megalithic sites; high standard, pleasant, quiet site; facs basic; clean and tidy; new owners (2015)." 1 Apr-31 Oct. € 20.00   2016*

CARNAC *2G3 (8km NW Rural) 47.62882, -3.14511* **Camping Les Mégalithes, Kerfélicité, 56410 Erdeven [02 97 55 68 76 or 02 97 55 68 09; campingdesmegalithes@orange.fr; www.campingdesmegalithes.fr]** Fr Carnac take D781 thro Plouharnel after further 4km; site on L in 500m. Med, hdg, mkd, pt shd, pt sl, wc (htd); chem disp; mv service pnt; shwrs inc; EHU (10A); lndry; shop; rest nr; bar nr; playgrnd; pool; beach shgl 2km; twin axles; wifi; 40% statics; dogs €1; Eng spkn; adv bkg acc; quiet; games area. "Excel, peaceful, well maintained site with lge pitches but poorly lit; poss diff to manoeuvre lge c'vans; conv for megalithic alignments; v clean facs; helpful & welcoming staff; family run site; pool area beautiful but busy." ♦ 1 May-21 Sep. € 30.00   2015*

CARPENTRAS *10E2 (7km N Rural) 44.12246, 5.03437*
Camp Municipal de Roquefiguier, 84190 Beaumes-de-Venise [04 90 62 95 07 or 04 90 62 94 34 (Mairie); camping.roquefiguier@orange.fr; www.beaumes-de-venise.fr] Leave A7 exit 22, take N7 S then L onto D950 sp Carpentras. At rndabt after Sarrians sp turn L onto D21 to Beaumes-de-Venise. Cross Beaumes & foll site sp. Turn L bef Crédit Agricole to site on R. Med, hdg, mkd, pt shd, pt sl, terr, wc; chem disp; mv service pnt; fam bthrm; shwrs inc; EHU (6A) €3; lndry; bbq; playgrnd; wifi; dogs €1.45; phone; quiet; ccard acc; CKE/CCI. "Gd site; gd views; facs clean; steel pegs req for pitches; poss diff access lge o'fits; steep access some pitches; gate clsd 1900-0830; 5 mins walk to Beaumes-de-Venise; pool in vill; wine caves adj; mini golf; mkd walks & cycle ways; conv for Mt Ventoux, Orange & Avignon MD Tues, excel hot shwrs." ♦ 1 Mar-31 Oct. € 13.60   2014*

> **"There aren't many sites open at this time of year"**
>
> If you're travelling outside peak season remember to call ahead to check site opening dates – even if the entry says 'open all year'.

CARPENTRAS *10E2 (7km N Rural) 44.09723, 5.03682*
Camping Le Brégoux, Chemin du Vas, 84810 Aubignan [04 90 62 62 50 or 04 90 67 10 13 (LS); camping-lebregoux@wanadoo.fr; www.camping-lebregoux.fr] Exit Carpentras on D7 sp Bollène. In Aubignan turn R immed after x-ing bdge, 1st R again in approx 250m at Club de Badminton & foll site sp at fork. Lge, hdstg, mkd, hdg, pt shd, wc; chem disp; mv service pnt; fam bthrm; shwrs inc; EHU (10A) €3.80 (poss long lead req); lndry; shop nr; rest nr; bar nr; bbq; playgrnd; entmnt; wifi; TV; 2% statics; dogs €1.90; phone; Eng spkn; adv bkg acc; ccard acc; games rm; golf nr; tennis; CKE/CCI. "Popular site in beautiful area; lge pitches & gd access; helpful, friendly staff; gates clsd 2200-0700; go-karting nrby; poss flooding in heavy rain; pool 5km in ssn; excel walking & cycling nrby; gd value; gd; san facs upgraded, modern & clean (2015)." ♦ 1 Mar-31 Oct. € 11.40   2015*

CARPENTRAS

CARPENTRAS 10E2 (6km S Urban) 43.99917, 5.06591
Camp Municipal Coucourelle, Ave René Char, 84210 Pernes-les-Fontaines [04 90 66 45 55 or 04 90 61 31 67 (Mairie); fax 04 90 61 32 46; camping@perneslesfontaines.fr; www.tourisme-pernes.fr] Take D938 fr Carpentras to Pernes-les-Fontaines; then take D28 dir St Didier (Ave René Char pt of D28). Site sp (some sps easily missed). Foll sp sports complex, site at rear of sw pool. Sm, hdg, mkd, shd, wc; chem disp; mv service pnt; shwrs inc; EHU (10A) €3.50; lndry; shop nr; rest nr; bbq; playgrnd; dogs €0.50; adv bkg acc; quiet; ccard acc; tennis adj; fishing 2.5km; CKE/CCI. "Pleasant, well-run site; views of Mont Ventoux; most pitches lge but some sm & narr; excel clean facs; m'vans can park adj to mv point free when site clsd; pool 2.5km; gates close 1930; no twin axles; free use of adj pool; attractive old town, easy parking; adv bkg rec LS; vg." ♦ 1 Apr-30 Sep. € 15.50   2016*

CARPENTRAS 10E2 (4km SW Rural) 44.0398, 5.0009
Camp Municipal de Bellerive, 54 Chemin de la Ribière, 84170 Monteux [04 90 66 81 88 or 04 90 66 97 52 (TO); camping.bellerive@orange.fr; www.provenceguide.com] Site on N edge of Monteux cent, sp off ring rd Monteux N, immed after rlwy x-ing. Sm, hdg, mkd, hdstg, pt shd, serviced pitches; wc; chem disp; shwrs inc; EHU (6-10A) €2.50; lndry; shop nr; rest nr; bar nr; playgrnd; red long stay; wifi; 10% statics; dogs €1; phone; bus; quiet; CKE/CCI. "Gd, busy, lovely site; rec arr early high ssn; helpful, friendly, v helpful warden lives adj; gd security; vg, clean, modern san facs; trees a problem for sat TV - choose pitch carefully; park adj gd for children; 5 min walk to vill; poss muddy when wet; poss some workers' statics LS; Mistral blows early & late ssn; pool 4km; gd touring base; free WiFi; no grey water drainage." ♦ 1 Apr-15 Oct. € 14.40   2018*

CASSIS 10F3 (2km N Coastal) 43.22417, 5.54126
Camping Les Cigales, 43 Ave de la Marne, 13260 Cassis [04 42 01 07 34; www.campingcassis.com] App Cassis on D41E, then at 2nd rndabt exit D559 sp Cassis, then turn 1st R sp Les Calanques into Ave de la Marne, site immed on R. Avoid town cent as rds narr. Lge, hdstg, hdg, mkd, pt shd, pt sl, wc; chem disp; mv service pnt; shwrs inc; EHU (3A) €2.60 (poss rev pol & poss long lead req); gas; lndry; shop; rest; snacks; bar; playgrnd; beach shgl 1.5km; 30% statics; dogs €1.10; phone; Eng spkn; ccard acc; CKE/CCI. "Gd base for Calanques; v busy w/ends; popular attractive resort, but steep walk to camp site; poss tired san facs end ssn; poss diff lge o'fits due trees; v strong pegs req to penetrate hardcore; bus to Marseille cent fr campsite." 15 Mar-15 Nov. € 20.00   2014*

CASTELJALOUX 7D2 (10km SE Rural) 44.27262, 0.18969
Camping Moulin de Campech, 47160 Villefranche-du-Queyran [05 53 88 72 43; fax 05 53 88 06 52; camping@moulindecampech.co.uk; www.moulindecampech.co.uk] Fr A62 exit junc 6 (sp Damazan & Aiguillon). Fr toll booth take D8 SW sp Mont-de-Marsan. In 3km turn R in Cap-du-Bosc onto D11 twd Casteljaloux. Site on R in 4km. Or fr Casteljaloux S on D655 then SW on D11 after 1.5km. Site on L after 9.5km. Sm, mkd, hdg, pt shd, wc; chem disp; shwrs inc; EHU (6A) €4; lndry; shop; rest; snacks; bar; bbq; pool (htd); entmnt; wifi; dogs €2.40; phone; adv bkg acc; quiet; ccard acc; lake fishing; games rm; golf nr; CKE/CCI. "Superb, peaceful rvside site in wooded valley; well-run; lge pitches; friendly, helpful & welcoming British owners; clean, dated san facs, needs refurb (2014); gd pool; excel, gd value rest; BBQ suppers; gd cycling; no o'fits over 8.2m; interesting area ideal for nature lovers; excel site; many social events." ♦ 1 Apr-7 Oct. € 32.00   2017*

CASTELLANE 10E3 (3km SE Rural) 43.83833, 6.54194
Camping La Ferme de Castellane, Quartier La Lagne, 04120 Castellane [04 92 83 67 77; fax 04 92 83 75 92; accueil@camping-la-ferme.com; www.camping-la-ferme.com] Fr Castellane take D6085 dir Grasse. In 1km turn R (at Rest L'Escapade) then site in 1km, sp. Narr app rd with passing places. Sm, mkd, pt shd, terr, wc; chem disp; mv service pnt; bar bthrm; shwrs inc; EHU €3.50; lndry; shop nr; rest nr; bar nr; playgrnd; wifi; TV; 25% statics; dogs €1; Eng spkn; adv bkg acc; quiet; ccard acc; games rm; CKE/CCI. "Vg, clean, friendly site; gd touring base; breakfast and BBQ evenings at rest." ♦ 27 Mar-20 Sep. € 17.00   2016*

CASTELLANE 10E3 (0km SW Urban) 43.84623, 6.50995
Camping Frédéric Mistral, 12 Ave Frédéric Mistral, 04120 Castellane [04 92 83 62 27; www.camping-frederic-mistral.fr] In town cent onto D952 sp Gorges-du-Verdon, site on L in 100m. Med, mkd, pt shd, serviced pitches; wc (htd); chem disp; shwrs inc; EHU (6A) €3 (poss rev pol); shop nr; rest; snacks; bar; wifi; 2% statics; adv bkg acc; quiet; CKE/CCI. "Friendly owners; pool 200m; gd san facs but poss stretched in ssn; gd base for gorges etc; gd." ♦ 1 Mar-11 Nov. € 21.00   2017*

CASTELLANE 10E3 (1km SW Rural) 43.84570, 6.50447
Camping Notre Dame, Route des Gorges du Verdon, 04120 Castellane [04 92 83 63 02; camping-notredame@wanadoo.fr; www.camping-notredame.com] N fr Grasse on D6085, turn L in Castellane at sq onto D952 to site on R in 500m. Sm, pt shd, wc; chem disp; mv service pnt; shwrs inc; EHU (6A) €3.50; gas; lndry; shop; rest nr; playgrnd; wifi; 20% statics; dogs free; phone; Eng spkn; adv bkg acc; CKE/CCI. "Ideal touring base; helpful owners; poss a bit unkempt early ssn; excel." ♦ 1 Apr-10 Oct. € 24.50   2014*

CASTELLANE 10E3 (12km SW Rural) 43.79596, 6.43733 Camp Municipal de Carajuan, 04120 Rougon [04 92 83 70 94; fax 04 92 83 66 49; campingverdon.carajuan@gmail.com; www.rougon.fr] Fr N on D4085 turn R on D952 & foll sps for 16km to rv bank of Gorges du Verdon nr Carajuan bdge; site on L. Fr E on D952 ignore turning to Rougon; site sp in 5km. Med, mkd, pt shd, wc; chem disp; shwrs inc; EHU (6A) €2.70; lndry; snacks; playgrnd; red long stay; 10% statics; dogs €1.20; phone; bus Jul/Aug; Eng spkn; adv bkg acc; quiet; CKE/CCI. "Natural, unspoilt site nr rvside with shingle beach (no sw); friendly staff; basic, dated facs, poss unclean LS; gd walking; fair; gd morning sun despite valley." 21 Mar-30 Sep. € 11.40   2014*

CASTELLANE 10E3 (9km W Rural) 43.82276, 6.43143 Camping Indigo Gorges du Verdon, Clos d'Aremus, 04120 Castellane [04 92 83 63 64; fax 04 92 83 74 72; gorgesduverdon@camping-indigo.com; www.camping-indigo.com] On D6085 fr Grasse turn L on D952 in Castellane. Camp in 9km on L. Look for sp Chasteuil on R of rd; site in 500m. Lge, mkd, shd, wc; chem disp; mv service pnt; shwrs inc; EHU (6A) inc; gas; lndry; shop; rest; snacks; bar; playgrnd; pool (htd); paddling pool; entmnt; wifi; TV; 10% statics; dogs free; Eng spkn; adv bkg req; games rm; fishing; boating; games area; canoeing; CKE/CCI. "Some sm pitches; rd along Gorges du Verdon poss diff for lge o'fits; pool & san facs renovated 2015." ♦ 26 Apr-15 Sep. € 28.50   2013*

CASTELLANE 10E3 (2km NW Rural) 43.85861, 6.49795 Kawan Village Camping International, Route Napoléon, La Palud, 04120 Castellane [04 92 83 66 67; fax 04 92 83 77 67; info@camping-international.fr; www.camping-international.fr] Site sp fr D4085 & D602. Lge, hdg, pt shd, pt sl, serviced pitches; wc (htd); chem disp; mv service pnt; fam bthrm; shwrs inc; EHU (6A) €4.50; gas; lndry; shop; rest; snacks; bar; playgrnd; pool; sw nr; entmnt; wifi; TV; 50% statics; dogs €2; Eng spkn; adv bkg acc; ccard acc; golf; horseriding; games area; CKE/CCI. "Busy site; friendly, helpful owners; main san facs vg, some dated, but clean; most pitches on gentle slope; conv Gorges de Verdon; gd walking; gd." ♦ 31 Mar-1 Oct. € 22.50   2013*

CASTELNAUDARY 8F4 (7km E Rural) 43.31723, 2.01582 FFCC Camping à la Ferme Domaine de la Capelle (Sabatte), St Papoul, 11400 St Martin-Lalande [04 68 94 91 90; www.domaine-la-capelle.fr/en] Fr D6113 Castelnaudary/Carcasonne, take D103 E & foll sp to St Papoul & site in 2km. Well sp. NB Ent poss awkward lge o'fits. Sm, hdg, mkd, pt shd, pt sl, wc (htd); chem disp; shwrs inc; EHU (4A) €2.50; lndry; shop nr; bbq; dogs €1; phone; Eng spkn; quiet; CKE/CCI. "Delightful, peaceful, spacious CL-type site; friendly, helpful owner; vg san facs, poss stretched when site full; ltd EHU; gd walking; nr St Papoul Cathar vill with abbey; ideal NH for Spain; excel; close to ind site, gd cycling." 1 Apr-30 Sep. € 14.50   2016*

CASTETS 8E1 (1km E Urban) 43.88069, -1.13768 Flower Camping Le Galan (formerly Municipal), 73 Rue du Stade, 40260 Castets [05 58 89 43 52 or 05 58 89 40 09; fax 05 58 55 00 07; contact@camping-legalan.com; www.camping-legalan.com] Exit N10 junc 12 onto D947; foll sp Castets cent; turn R onto D42; in 500m (after passing over rndabt) turn R onto Rue de Galan; in 200m turn R into Rue du State. Site on L at end of wide cul-de-sac. Site sp in Castets. Lge, shd, pt sl, wc; shwrs inc; EHU (10A) inc; gas; lndry; shop; rest nr; playgrnd; paddling pool; twin axles; 10% statics; dogs €1.70; bus to Dax; adv bkg acc; quiet; tennis; CKE/CCI. "Peaceful, clean site in pleasant vill; NH area poss cr; rv walks; excel; conv for N-S rte." ♦ 1 Mar-30 Nov. € 21.40   2016*

CASTIES LABRANDE 8F3 (2km W Rural) 43.32502, 0.99054 Camping Le Casties, Le Bas de Lebrande, 31430 Casties-Labrande [05 61 90 81 11; fax 05 61 90 81 10; lecasties@wanadoo.fr; www.camping-lecasties.com] S fr Toulouse, exit A64 junc 26 onto D626; after Pouy-de-Touges turn L onto & foll camping sp. Med, hdg, pt shd, wc; chem disp; shwrs inc; EHU (5A) €1; lndry; snacks; bar; bbq; playgrnd; pool; paddling pool; 10% statics; dogs €1; phone; Eng spkn; adv bkg acc; quiet; ccard acc; tennis; fishing; CKE/CCI. "Remote; lge hdg pitches; staff friendly & helpful; value for money; lovely pool; excel; new vg san facs (2013); v peaceful; sm farm for children." ♦ 1 May-30 Sep. € 12.50   2014*

CASTILLON LA BATAILLE 7C2 (1km E Urban) 44.85350, -0.03550 Camp Municipal La Pelouse, Chemin de Halage, 33350 Castillon-la-Bataille [05 57 40 04 22 or 05 56 40 00 06 (Mairie)] Site in town on N bank of Rv Dordogne. After x-ing rv on D17 fr S to N, take 1st avail rd on R to rv. Sm, shd, wc; shwrs inc; EHU (15A) inc; shop; adv bkg acc; quiet; CKE/CCI. "Peaceful, lovely site by rv; busy high ssn; pitches poss rough & muddy when wet; helpful warden; facs dated but clean; conv town; trans, St Emillion & wine area; gd NH." 1 May-15 Oct. € 17.00   2018*

CASTRES 8F4 (2km NE Urban) 43.62054, 2.25401 Camping de Gourjade, Ave de Roquecourbe, 81100 Castres [05 63 59 33 51; contact@camping degourjade.net; www.campingdegourjade.net] Leave Castres NE on D89 sp Rocquecourbe; site on R in 2km. Well sp. Ave de Roquecourbe is pt of D89. Med, hdg, pt shd, terr, wc; chem disp; mv service pnt; shwrs; EHU (6-16A) inc (poss rev pol); gas; lndry; shop; rest nr; bbq; playgrnd; pool; wifi; 5% statics; dogs €2; bus; quiet; ccard acc; cycling; golf adj; CKE/CCI. "Lovely site in beautiful park on Rv Agout; lge pitches; helpful staff; gd, tired clean san facs; 9 hole golf course adj; some lower pitches sl & poss soft; boat fr site to town; extra charge twin axles; gd security; poss groups workers LS; leisure cent & golf adj; vg cycling; highly rec; rest open evenings only; well run; excel for long or sh stay." ♦ 1 Apr-30 Sep. € 22.80   2017*

CASTRIES

CASTRIES *10E1* (3km NE Rural) *43.69406, 3.99585*
Camping Domaine de Fondespierre, 277 Route de Fontmarie, 34160 Castries [04 67 91 20 03; fax 04 67 16 41 48; accueil@campingfondespierre.com; www.campingfondespierre.com] Fr A9 exit junc 28 sp Vendargues, foll sp for Castries on D610. Cont thro Castries in dir of Sommieres. Aprox 1.5km past Castries turn L and foll camp sp. Med, hdstg, mkd, hdg, pt shd, terr, wc (htd); chem disp; mv service pnt; fam bthrm; shwrs inc; EHU (10A) inc (poss long lead req); lndry; shop; rest; snacks; bar; bbq (sep area); playgrnd; pool; sw nr; wifi; 40% statics; dogs €3; phone; Eng spkn; adv bkg acc; quiet; ccard acc; games area; tennis adj; bike hire; golf 2.5km; CKE/CCI. "Gd walking area; poss travellers & site poss unkempt LS; site rds narr with sharp, tree-lined bends - poss diff access to pitches for lge o'fits; NH; superb vill." ♦ 4 Jan-19 Dec. € 34.00   2016*

CAUDEBEC EN CAUX *3C2* (10km SE Urban) *49.48373, 0.77247* **Camp Municipal du Parc, Rue Victor Hugo, 76940 La Mailleraye-sur-Seine [02 35 37 12 04; mairie-sg.lamaillerayesurseine@wanadoo.fr]** Fr N on D131/D490 turn E onto D65. Or fr S on D913. Site sp in cent of town close to rv bank. Sm, hdg, pt shd, pt sl, wc; chem disp; shwrs; EHU (6A) inc; shop nr; rest nr; bar nr; playgrnd; quiet. "Pleasant, tidy site; site yourself, warden calls; adequate, clean san facs; gd walking area; vg NH." 1 Apr-30 Sep. € 12.50   2015*

CAUNES MINERVOIS *8F4* (1km S Rural) *43.32380, 2.52592* **Camp Municipal Les Courtals, Ave du Stade, 11160 Caunes-Minervois [04 68 78 46 58; mairie.de.caunes@wanadoo.fr; www.caunesminervois.com]** Sp fr D620 at stadium & adj rv. Sm, pt shd, wc; mv service pnt; shwrs; EHU (4A) inc; shop nr; playgrnd; phone; quiet; games area. "Pleasantly situated site; office opens 1800; gate locked 2100; site self, warden calls; pool 6km; rv adj; interesting town." 15 Jan-15 Dec. € 12.00   2014*

CAUSSADE *8E3* (2km N Urban) *44.16582, 1.54446* **Camp Municipal de la Piboulette, Rue de la Piboulette, 82300 Caussade [05 63 93 09 07; secretariat@mairie-caussade.com; www.mairie-caussade.fr]** S on D820 fr Cahors (40km), turn L off D820 on ent Caussade onto D17 (Rte de Puylaroque). About 750m turn L (sp), site on R in 100m; lge grass stadium. Med, mkd, pt shd, serviced pitches; wc; chem disp; shwrs inc; EHU (3A/8A) €1.90; lndry; shop nr; playgrnd; wifi; dogs €1.25; adv bkg acc; quiet; CKE/CCI. "Pleasant site adj lake; spacious, mostly shd pitches; pleasant warden; excel, clean san facs, poss tired LS; sports cent adj; gates locked 2100 LS; easy 15 min walk to town; gd walks; pool on far side of stadium; gd cycling round lake; conv A20 & Gorges de l'Aveyron; vg mkt Mon; excel value; vg." ♦ 1 May-30 Sep. € 10.00   2015*

CAUSSADE *8E3* (9km NE Rural) *44.18273, 1.60305* **Camping de Bois Redon, 10 Chemin de Bonnet, 82240 Septfonds [05 63 64 92 49 or 06 78 35 79 97 (Mob); info@campingdeboisredon.com; www.campingdeboisredon.com]** Exit A20 junc 59 to Caussade, then onto D926 to Septfonds (narr rds); after rndabt turn 3rd L; site sp. Site in 2km. One-way system when leaving site. Sm, mkd, pt shd, pt sl, wc; chem disp; fam bthrm; shwrs inc; EHU (10A) €3.50; lndry; shop; snacks; bar; playgrnd; pool; 10% statics; dogs €2; Eng spkn; adv bkg req; quiet; bike hire; CKE/CCI. "Well-shd, spacious site in ancient oak forest with walks; charming Dutch owners; Septfonds nr with all facs; new shwrs (2013/14); enthusiastic owners continually making improvements; excel site; immac new san fac block." ♦ € 24.50   2016*

CAUSSADE *8E3* (10km NW Rural) *44.24323, 1.47573* **Camping Le Faillal, 46 Blvd Pasteur, 82270 Montpezat-de-Quercy [05 63 02 07 08 or 07 68 59 25 32; fax 04 73 93 71 00; contact@parcdufaillal.com; www.parcdufaillal.com]** N on D820, turn L onto D20, site clearly sp on R in 2km. (Do not take D38 bef D20 fr S). Med, hdg, pt shd, pt sl, terr, wc; chem disp; shwrs inc; EHU (10A) €3.70; lndry; shop nr; snacks; bar; bbq; playgrnd; pool; entmnt; wifi; TV; dogs €1.50; phone; Eng spkn; adv bkg acc; quiet; games rm; tennis adj; games area; CKE/CCI. "Pretty, well-kept site; friendly, helpful staff; gd, clean san facs, poss ltd) super pool; many pitches unavail after heavy rain; access to some pitches diff; old town a 'must'; rec pay night bef dep; excel; horse drawn carriage rides, pony rides, kayaking, rafting, paintball." ♦ € 22.00   2017*

CAUTERETS *8G2* (3km NE Rural) *42.91092, -0.09934* **Camping GR10, Route de Pierrefitte, 65110 Cauterets [06 70 72 05 02 or 06 20 30 25 85 (LS); contact@gr10camping.com; www.gr10camping.com]** N fr Cauterets on D920; site in 2.5km on R. Med, mkd, shd, terr, wc (htd); chem disp; shwrs inc; EHU €4; lndry; shop nr; playgrnd; pool (htd); TV; 25% statics; dogs €1.30; Eng spkn; quiet; games rm; tennis; games area. "Pretty site; canyoning (guide on site); excel." 25 Jun-1 Sep. € 20.00   2014*

CAVAILLON *10E2* (8km E Rural) *43.84220, 5.13284* **Camp Municipal Les Royères du Prieuré, La Combe-St Pierre, 84660 Maubec [04 90 76 50 34; fax 04 32 52 91 57; camping.maubec@c-lmv.fr; www.campingmaubec-luberon.com]** Heading E fr Cavaillon on D2, thro vill of Robion, in 400m at end vill sp turn R to Maubec. Site on R in 1km bef old vill. (Avoid any other rte with c'van). Diff access at ent, steep slope. Sm, pt shd, terr, wc; shwrs inc; EHU (6-10A) €5; lndry; shop nr; playgrnd; wifi; 10% statics; dogs €2; quiet; CKE/CCI. "Awkward site for lge o'fits, otherwise vg; san facs stretched high ssn; conv A7; san facs refurbed; restful site; wine tasting on Tue eve." 1 Apr-15 Oct. € 13.00   2018*

CAVALAIRE SUR MER

CAVAILLON *10E2* (1km S Rural) *43.82107, 5.03723*
Camp Municipal de la Durance, 495 Ave Boscodomini, 84300 Cavaillon [04 90 71 11 78; fax 04 90 71 98 77; contact@camping-durance.com; www.camping-durance.com] S of Cavaillon, nr Rv Durance. Fr A7 junc 25 foll sp to town cent. In 200m R immed after x-ing rv. Site sp (Municipal Camping) on L. Lge, pt shd, wc (htd); chem disp; fam bthrm; shwrs; EHU (4A-10A) €2.50- 6.50; shop nr; snacks; paddling pool; TV; 30% statics; dogs €1.50; adv bkg acc; tennis; fishing; games area. "Site OK; gd NH only; close to town; decent facs; reasonably priced." 1 Apr-30 Sep. € 18.60   2018*

CAVAILLON *10E2* (9km S Rural) *43.78182, 5.04040*
Camping de la Vallée Heureuse, Quartier Lavau, 13660 Orgon [04 84 80 01 71; camping.valleeheureuse@gmail.com; www.valleeheureuse.com] Sp in Organ town cent. Lge, mkd, shd, terr, wc; chem disp; mv service pnt; fam bthrm; shwrs inc; EHU (16A); lndry; rest nr; bar; bbq; playgrnd; pool; sw nr; wifi; TV; dogs €1.70; Eng spkn; adv bkg acc; quiet; CKE/CCI. "Site adj to old quarry in beautiful position; friendly, helpful staff; superb san facs; gd pool; gd walking; café; interesting area; conv m'way; isolated site; vill 1.5km." 25 Mar-31 Oct. € 25.00   2016*

CAVAILLON *10E2* (12km SW Rural) *43.76058, 4.95154* **FFCC Camping Les Oliviers**, Ave Jean Jaurès, 13810 Eygalières [tel/fax 04 90 95 91 86; campinglesoliviers13@gmail.com; www.camping-les-oliviers.com] Exit A7 junc 25; D99 dir St Rémy-de-Provence; in 8km camping sp on L; in vill well sp. Sm, hdg, pt shd, wc (htd); EHU (6A) inc; shop nr; rest nr; bar nr; bbq (elec, gas); playgrnd; wifi; dogs €1; adv bkg acc; quiet. "Lovely, friendly site in olive grove nr scenic vill; quiet site; facs rustic but v clean; pitches cramped for lge o'fits; simple site; diff acc for lge o'fits; free WiFi." 30 Mar-30 Sep. € 19.00   2018*

CAVALAIRE SUR MER *10F4* (2km NE Rural) *43.18220, 6.51610* **Kawan Village Cros de Mouton**, Chemin de Cros de Mouton, 83240 Cavalaire-sur-Mer [04 94 64 10 87 or 04 94 05 46 38; fax 04 94 64 63 12; campingcrosdemouton@wanadoo.fr; www.crosdemouton.com] Exit A8 junc 36 dir Ste Maxime on D125/D25, foll sp on D559 to Cavalaire-sur-Mer. Site sp on coast app fr Grimaud/St Tropez & Le Lavandou; diff access. Lge, mkd, shd, terr, serviced pitches; wc; chem disp; mv service pnt; fam bthrm; shwrs inc; EHU (10A); gas; lndry; shop; rest; snacks; bar; playgrnd; pool (htd); paddling pool; beach sand 1.8km; wifi; TV; 10% statics; dogs €2; phone; Eng spkn; adv bkg rec; quiet; ccard acc; bike hire; CKE/CCI. "Attractive, well-run, popular site in hills behind town - rec adv bkg even LS; lge pitches avail; poss diff access to pitches due steep site rds - help avail; pleasant, welcoming & efficient staff; gd san facs; gd pool; vg rest & bar; buses to St Tropez; excel; lovely views; steep walk fr town." ♦ 21 Mar-31 Oct. € 36.00   2015*

CAVALAIRE SUR MER *10F4* (3km NE Coastal) *43.19450, 6.55495* **Sélection Camping**, 12 Blvd de la Mer, 83420 La Croix-Valmer [04 94 55 10 30; fax 04 94 55 10 39; camping-selection@wanadoo.fr; www.selectioncamping.com] Off N559 bet Cavalaire & La Croix-Valmer, 2km past La Croix at rndabt turn R sp Barbigoua, site in 200m. Lge, mkd, hdg, shd, terr, wc (htd); chem disp; mv service pnt; fam bthrm; shwrs inc; EHU (10A) €5; gas; lndry; shop; rest; snacks; bar; playgrnd; pool (htd); paddling pool; beach sand 400m; entmnt; wifi; TV; 20% statics; dogs (not acc Jul/Aug) €4; phone; bus; Eng spkn; adv bkg req; quiet; games area. "Excel location; sm pitches; private bthrms avail; vg san facs; excel pool; excel site." ♦ 15 Mar-15 Oct. € 35.00   2018*

See advertisement

CAVALAIRE SUR MER

CAVALAIRE SUR MER *10F4* (1km S Urban) *43.16956, 6.53005* Camping de La Baie, Blvd Pasteur, 83240 Cavalaire-sur-Mer [04 94 64 08 15 or 04 94 64 08 10; contact@camping-baie.com; www.camping-baie.com] Exit A8 sp Ste Maxime/St Tropez & foll D25 & D559 to Cavalaire. Site sp fr seafront. Lge, mkd, pt shd, pt sl, wc (htd); fam bthrm; shwrs inc; EHU (10A) €5; lndry; shop; rest; snacks; bar; bbq; playgrnd; pool (htd); paddling pool; beach sand 400m; wifi; 10% statics; dogs €4; Eng spkn; adv bkg acc; quiet; ccard acc; sailing; games area; jacuzzi; watersports; games rm. "Well-run, busy site; pleasant staff; excel pool & facs; nr shops, beach, marina & cafes; cycle paths; gd location; diving 500m; sm pitches; narr rd." ♦ 15 Mar-15 Nov. € 66.50   2014*

CAVALAIRE SUR MER *10F4* (1km SW Coastal) *43.17203, 6.52451* Camping La Pinède, Chemin des Mannes, 83240 Cavalaire-sur-Mer [04 94 64 11 14; camping.lapinede83@orange.fr; www.la-pinede.com] Sp on R (N) of N559 on S o'skts of Cavalaire. Lge, mkd, shd, pt sl, wc; shwrs inc; EHU (5A) €3; gas; lndry; shop; snacks; playgrnd; beach sand 500m; adv bkg req. "Cavalaire pleasant, lively resort." ♦ 15 Mar-15 Oct. € 27.00   2014*

CAYEUX SUR MER *3B2* (4km NE Coastal) *50.20291, 1.52641* Camping Les Galets de la Mollière, Rue Faidherbe, 80410 La Mollière-d'Aval [03 22 26 61 85; fax 03 22 26 65 68; info@campinglesgaletsdelamolliere.com; www.campinglesgaletsdelamolliere.com] Fr Cayeux-sur-Mer take D102 N along coast for 3km. Site on R. Lge, mkd, pt shd, wc; chem disp; mv service pnt; fam bthrm; shwrs inc; EHU (6A) inc; gas; lndry; shop; snacks; bar; bbq; playgrnd; pool (htd); paddling pool; beach sand 500m; wifi; 25% statics; dogs €3; quiet; games area; games rm; CKE/CCI. "Spacious, much improved, wooded site with lge pitches; barrier clsd 2300-0700; pleasant staff; dirty pitches; unhelpful staff; poor." 3 Apr-1 Nov. € 33.00   2015*

CAYLAR, LE *10E1* (4km SW Rural) *43.83629, 3.29045* Camping Mas de Messier, St Félix-de-l'Héras, 34520 Le Caylar [04 67 44 52 63; info@masdemessier.com; www.masdemessier.com] Fr N exit A75 junc 49 onto D9 thro Le Caylar. Turn R sp St Félix & foll sp St Félix-de-l'Héras; at x-rds in St Félix turn R, site in 1km on L. Fr S exit A75 junc 50; foll sp to St Félix-de-l'Héras; at x rds turn R & as bef. Sm, hdg, pt shd, pt sl, wc; chem disp; mv service pnt; shwrs; EHU (10A) €3; lndry; shop nr; playgrnd; pool; wifi; dogs free; Eng spkn; adv bkg req; quiet; CKE/CCI. "Excel views fr some pitches; friendly, helpful Dutch owner; facs excel; access unsuitable lge o'fits; meals avail some eves; gd walking; excel long or sh stay; low rates in LS." ♦ 15 Apr-1 Oct. € 23.00   2018*

CAYLUS *8E4* (1km E Rural) *44.23368, 1.77616* FFCC Camping de la Bonnette, 672 route de la Bonnette, 82160 Caylus [05 63 65 70 20; info@campingbonnette.com; www.campingbonnette.com] Fr A20 exit junc 59 dir Caylus; thro Caylus to g'ge on L. Turn R in 1km over next crossrds & foll site sps to site on R in 1km. Med, hdg, mkd, pt shd, wc; chem disp; mv service pnt; fam bthrm; shwrs inc; EHU (10A) €3.50; lndry; shop nr; rest; bar; bbq; playgrnd; pool; red long stay; entmnt; wifi; 10% statics; dogs €1.50; Eng spkn; adv bkg rec; quiet; games area. "Nice, tidy, scenic site on edge of medieval vill - worth a visit; friendly owner; pitches in groups of 4, not v private." ♦ 29 Mar-4 Oct. € 19.00   2014*

CEAUCE *4E1* (1km N Rural) *48.49812, -0.62481* Camp Municipal de la Veillotière, Chemin de la Veillotière, 61330 Ceaucé [02 33 38 31 19; mairie-ceauce@wanadoo.fr] S fr Domfront on D962 dir Mayenne, at rndabt in Ceaucé turn L. Site in 200m on R adj sm lake. Sm, hdg, pt shd, pt sl, wc; chem disp; mv service pnt; shwrs inc; EHU (6A) inc; shop; rest; playgrnd; quiet; fishing adj. "Well-kept site on edge vill; gd; nice as always; bar 200m; quiet cycle rte to Ambrieves Les Vallees; warden calls eves." ♦ 1 May-30 Sep. € 11.00   2018*

CERCY LA TOUR *4H4* (1km S Urban) *46.86680, 3.64328* Camp Municipal Le Port, 58360 Cercy-la-Tour [03 86 50 55 27 or 03 86 50 07 11 (Mairie)] At Decize take D981 E; in 12km L onto D37, then L onto D10 to Cercy-la-Tour; site sp in vill. Adj municipal pool, Rv Aron & canal. Med, hdstg, pt shd, wc; chem disp; shwrs inc; EHU inc; dogs; phone; Eng spkn; quiet; CKE/CCI. "Clean & tidy site; immac san facs; gd cycling/walking along canal; excel value; excel." 25 Apr-25 Oct. € 9.00   2017*

CERESTE *10E3* (3km SW Rural) *43.84564, 5.56394* Camping Bois de Sibourg (Vial-Ménard), 04280 Céreste [04 92 79 02 22 or (mobs) 06 30 88 63 29 or 06 70 64 62 01; campingsibourg@orange.fr; www.sibourg.com] W fr Céreste on D900/D4100; turn L in 2km (site sp); site on L in 1km. Sm, pt shd, wc cont; shwrs inc; EHU (6A) €2.80; dogs free; phone; Eng spkn; CKE/CCI. "Delightful 'green' farm site; St Michel l'Observatoire 15km; gd NH or longer; excel." 15 Apr-15 Oct. € 9.60   2014*

CERESTE *10E3* (9km W Rural) *43.84361, 5.49666* Camping à la Ferme (Bouscarle), Les Monguets, 84400 Castellet-en-Luberon [04 90 75 28 62] Fr W on D900 (Apt) ignore Camping à la Ferme sp to R nr St Martin-de-Castillon (v narr rd). Cont 2km to La Bègude & turn R onto D223 dir Le Boisset. Site 3km on R, well sp. Sm, shd, pt sl, wc; chem disp; shwrs inc; EHU (4A) €3 (long lead req); dogs €1; Eng spkn; adv bkg acc; CKE/CCI. "Excel, scenic CL-type site on fruit farm; friendly owners; excel walking, cycling." Easter-1 Nov. € 13.00   2015*

⊞ **CERET** *8H4* (1km E Rural) *42.48941, 2.76405*
Camping Les Cerisiers, Mas de la Toure, 66400 Céret [04 68 87 00 08 or 06 78 04 60 32 (mob); fax 04 68 88 14 87; camping.lescerisiers@club-internet.fr; www.campingcerisiers.com] Exit A9 junc 43 onto D115, turn off for cent of Céret. Site is on D618 approx 800m E of Céret twd Maureillas, sp. Tight ascent for lge o'fits. Med, mkd, shd, wc; chem disp; fam bthrm; shwrs inc; EHU (4A); gas; lndry; shop nr; rest nr; bar nr; playgrnd; sw nr; entmnt; TV; 60% statics; dogs; phone; quiet; site clsd Jan; CKE/CCI. "Site in cherry orchard; gd size pitches; facs dated & ltd LS; footpath to attractive vill with modern art gallery; pool 600m; conv Andorra, Perpignan, Collioure." ♦ € 18.00   2014*

CERILLY *4H3* (10km N Rural) *46.68210, 2.78630*
Camping des Ecossais, La Salle, 03360 Isle-et-Bardais [04 70 66 62 57 or 04 70 67 50 96; fax 04 70 66 63 99; ecossais@campingstroncais.com; www.campingstroncais.com] Fr Lurcy-Lévis take D978A SW, turn R onto D111 N twd Isle-et-Bardais & foll camp sp. Ent tight. Med, hdg, pt shd, pt sl, wc; chem disp; mv service pnt; fam bthrm; shwrs inc; EHU (10A) inc; lndry; shop; rest nr; snacks; bar; bbq; playgrnd; sw; twin axles; wifi; 10% statics; dogs €1.50; adv bkg acc; quiet; games area; games rm; fishing; CKE/CCI. "Excel; v busy high ssn; ltd facs LS; gd cycling; site in oak forest; rec; mountain bike nec on forest tracks."
1 Apr-30 Sep. € 12.00   2016*

CERNAY *6F3* (6km S Rural) *47.74684, 7.12423*
Camping Les Castors, 4 Route de Guewenheim, 68520 Burnhaupt-le-Haut [03 89 48 78 58; fax 03 89 62 74 66; camping.les.castors@wanadoo.fr; www.camping-les-castors.fr] Exit A36 junc 15 sp Burnhaupt-le-Haut onto D83, then D466 sp Masevaux. Site on R. Med, mkd, pt shd, wc (htd); chem disp; fam bthrm; shwrs inc; EHU (5-10A) €4-5; gas; lndry; shop nr; rest; snacks; bar; bbq; playgrnd; wifi; 40% statics; dogs €15; phone; Eng spkn; adv bkg acc; quiet; games rm; CKE/CCI. "Conv German & Swiss borders, Black Forest; wine rte; Mulhouse motor museum; gd san facs; vg; excel site, nice area; friendly owner; gd cycle path." ♦
1 Apr-31 Oct. € 13.00   2013*

CERNAY *6F3* (1km SW Urban) *47.80448, 7.16999*
Camping Les Cigognes (formerly Camping Les Acacias), 16 Rue René Guibert, 68700 Cernay [03 89 75 56 97; campinglescigognes@orange.fr; www.camping-les-cigognes.com] Fr N on D83 by-pass, exit Cernay Est. Turn R into town at traff lts, immed L bef rv bdge, site sp on L; well sp. Lge, mkd, pt shd, wc; chem disp; mv service pnt; shwrs inc; EHU (5A) €3.50 (poss rev pol); lndry; shop; rest; bar; pool; red long stay; entmnt; wifi; 25% statics; dogs €1.20; quiet; CKE/CCI. "Friendly staff; clean, tidy site; storks nesting over some pitches; sh walk to town." ♦ 1 Apr-30 Sep.
€ 18.00   2015*

⊞ **CERNAY LA VILLE** *4E3* (1km NW Rural) *48.67630, 1.97208* **Cernay Vacances, 37 Rue de la Ferme, 78720 Cernay-la-Ville [33 13 48 52 123; albert.koning@free.fr; www.cernayvacances.com]** Fr Rouen take A13 twrds Paris, then A12 twrds Rambouillet. Aft Leon de Bruxelles rest & metro take exit Mesnil - St. Denis. At rndabt pass by D58 twrds le-Mesnil, dir Dampierre. In Dampierre turn R onto D91 then L onto D149 twrds Senlisse. At top of this rd turn onto D906, aft 500mtrs at Peugeot g'ge turn R on Rue des Moulins strt to fm. Sm, pt shd, wc; chem disp; shwrs; EHU €4; cooking facs; wifi; dogs; Eng spkn; adv bkg acc; quiet; games area. "Vg." € 16.00   2017*

CERVIONE *10G2* (6km SE Coastal) *42.32155, 9.54546*
Camping Calamar, Prunete, 20221 Cervione [04 95 38 03 54 or 04 95 34 08 44 (LS); fax 04 95 31 17 09; contact@campingcalamar.eu; www.campingcalamar.eu] On N198 S fr Prunete for 6km. Turn L at x-rds, site in 500m beside beach, sp. Sm, pt shd, wc; shwrs inc; EHU €2.50; lndry; shop nr; snacks; bar; bbq; beach sand adj; dogs free; Eng spkn; adv bkg acc; quiet; watersports; games area; sailing. "Friendly owner; pleasant site with trees & shrubs; excel."
1 Apr-19 Oct. € 19.00   2013*

CHABLIS *4F4* (1km SE Rural) *47.81376, 3.80563*
Camp Municipal Le Serein, Quai Paul Louis Courier, 89800 Chablis [03 86 42 44 39 or 03 86 42 80 80 (Mairie); fax 03 86 42 49 71; mairie-chablis@chablis.net; www.chablis.net] W fr Tonnere on D965; in approx 16km exit D965 for Chabilis; in 300m, just bef x-ing Rv Serein, turn L at camping sp onto Quai Paul Louis Courier; site in 300m on R. Med, hdg, mkd, shd, wc; shwrs inc; EHU (5A) €2; lndry; shop nr; rest nr; playgrnd; dogs €1.50; Eng spkn; adv bkg acc; quiet; CKE/CCI. "Attractive, tidy site; facs poss stretched high ssn; friendly & helpful warden, calls 0800-1200 & 1600-2000; easy walk to attractive town; vineyards & wine cellars nrby; excel Sun mkt; warden attaches elec supply to locked post." ♦ 2 Jun-15 Sep.
€ 12.00   2016*

CHAGNY *6H1* (1km W Urban) *46.91187, 4.74567*
FFCC Camp Municipal du Pâquier Fané, 20 Rue du Pâquier Fané, 71150 Chagny [03 85 87 21 42 or 06 18 27 21 99 (mob); camping-chagny@orange.fr; www.campingchagny.com] Clearly sp in town. Med, mkd, hdg, pt shd, wc; chem disp; mv service pnt; shwrs inc; EHU (16A) inc; gas; lndry; shop nr; rest nr; bar nr; playgrnd; wifi; dogs €1; Eng spkn; fishing; tennis adj; CKE/CCI. "Well laid-out, well-lit vg site; friendly, helpful resident wardens; clean san facs; htd pool adj; many pitches sm & diff med/lge o'fits; on wine rte; gd cycling nrby (voie verte)." ♦ 1 Apr-31 Oct.
€ 22.50   2014*

CHAILLAC

⊞ CHAILLAC 7A3 (1km SW Rural) 46.43260, 1.29602
Camp Municipal Les Vieux Chênes, 36310 Chaillac
[02 54 25 61 39 or 02 54 25 74 26 (Mairie); fax 02 54 25 65 41; chaillac-mairie@wanadoo.fr] Exit N20 S of Argenton-sur-Creuse at junc 20 onto D36 to Chaillac. Thro vill, site 1st L after sq by 'Mairie', adj Lac du Rochegaudon. Fr S exit J21, take D10 sp St Benoit du Sault. Fr there turn L onto D36 and foll instructions above. Sm, hdg, mkd, pt shd, pt sl, wc (htd); chem disp; shwrs inc; EHU (16A) inc (poss rev pol); lndry; shop nr; rest nr; bar nr; bbq; playgrnd; sw nr; dogs; Eng spkn; adv bkg acc; quiet; waterslide; fishing adj; tennis adj; CKE/CCI. "Excel site, beautiful location, friendly wardens, well kept san facs, gd local supmkt 2 mins walk (clsd Mon); lake nrby." ♦ € 11.40   2018*

CHALAIS 7C2 (10km NW Rural) 45.32758, -0.02385
Chez Sarrazin, 16480 Brossac [05 45 78 21 57 or 07 80 52 27 32; chezsarrazin@yahoo.co.uk; www.chezsarrazin.net] N10 S fr Angouleme, leave exit for Barbezieux to Brossac & Chalais on D731, 700m after rndabt at Brossac Gare, L twd Brie Sous Chalais. After 1.4km R at 4 wheelie bins sp Chez Sarrazin Camping. Sm, shd, pt sl, wc; chem disp; shwrs; EHU (10A); lndry; bbq; playgrnd; pool; wifi; dogs €2; Eng spkn; adv bkg acc; quiet; games area. "Natural site in beautiful setting; many historical vills; walks; san facs & pool excel; charming & peaceful; excel; steep path to shwrs; helpful owners; well equipped." ♦ Easter-31 Oct. € 28.00   2017*

CHALANDRAY 4H1 (1km N Rural) 46.66728, -0.00214
Camping du Bois de St Hilaire, Rue de la Gare, 86190 Chalandray [05 49 60 20 84 or 01246 852823 (UK); acceuil@camping-st-hilaire.com; www.camping-st-hilaire.com] Foll N149 bet Parthenay & Vouille; at xrds in vill, turn N into Rue de la Gare (D24); site 750m on R over rlwy line. Sm, mkd, pt shd, wc; chem disp; shwrs inc; EHU (10A) €3.95; lndry; shop; rest nr; bar nr; bbq; playgrnd; pool; TV; dogs free; bus 750m; adv bkg acc; ccard acc; tennis; games rm; CKE/CCI. "Friendly, helpful British owners; situated in mature forest area, sh walk fr vill; 20 mins fr Futuroscope; lge pitches; excel, clean site & pool; c'van storage; poss muddy in wet weather." ♦ 1 May-30 Sep. € 23.00   2013*

⊞ CHALLANS 2H4 (10km SE Rural) 46.81522, -1.77472 **Camping Domaine de Bellevue, Bellevue Du Ligneron, 85670 Saint Christophe du Ligneron [02 51 93 30 66 or 06 21 55 54 29 (mob); contact@vendee-camping-bellevue.com; www.vendee-camping-bellevue.com]** Fr S: On Route National D948 exit Saint Christophe du Lingeron; turn W in dir Saint Gilles Croix de Vie/Commequirers; at rndbt cont strt on; take 2nd R at Bellevue du Ligneron. Med, hdg, wc; fam bthrm; shwrs inc; EHU (16) €4; lndry; bar; bbq; pool (htd); wifi; 50% statics; dogs €3; Eng spkn; adv bkg acc, ccard acc; fishing; games rm; bike hire; CKE/CCI. "Gd value for money; in lovely Vendee region; gd fishing on site; new site with friendly owners, takeaway; v lge pitches." ♦ € 14.00   2016*

CHALLANS 2H4 (4km S Rural) 46.81869, -1.88874
FFCC Camping Le Ragis, Chemin de la Fradinière, 85300 Challans [02 51 68 08 49; info@camping-leragis.com; www.camping-leragis.com] Fr Challans go S on D32 Rte Les Sables, turn R onto Chemin de la Fradinière & foll sp. Lge, hdg, mkd, pt shd, wc (htd); chem disp; mv service pnt; fam bthrm; shwrs inc; EHU (10A) €4; gas; lndry; shop; rest nr; snacks; bar; bbq; playgrnd; pool (htd); twin axles; entmnt; wifi; TV; 50% statics; dogs €4; bus 1km; Eng spkn; adv bkg acc; quiet; ccard acc; waterslide; games area. "Vg; homegrown veg; tickets for Puy Du Fou; night car park; conv Vendee coast; lake fishing; petanque; traditional French site; kids club 4-10; v friendly staff."
♦ 1 Apr-31 Oct. € 25.00   2016*

CHALON SUR SAONE 6H1 (3km E Rural) 46.78411, 4.87136 **Camping du Pont de Bourgogne, Rue Julien Leneveu, 71380 St Marcel [03 85 48 26 86 or 03 85 94 16 90 (LS); fax 03 85 48 50 63 or 03 85 94 16 97 (LS); campingchalon71@wanadoo.fr; www.camping-chalon.com]** Fr A6 exit junc 26 (sp Chalon Sud) onto N80 E; foll sp Chalon-sur-Saône; at 1st rndabt go strt over (sp Louhans & St Marcel) & over flyover; take 4th exit on 2nd rndbt; immed after this rndabt fork R thro Les Chavannes (still on N80). Turn R at traff lts bef bdge. (DO NOT CROSS BDGE). Site in 500m. Med, hdstg, hdg, mkd, pt shd, terr, wc (htd); chem disp; mv service pnt; shwrs inc; EHU (10A) inc (rev pol); gas; lndry; shop; rest; snacks; bar; bbq; playgrnd; wifi; TV; 2% statics; dogs €2.60; Eng spkn; adv bkg acc; ccard acc; games rm; bike hire; canoeing nr; rv fishing; CKE/CCI. "Peaceful, well-run rvside site in gd location; lge pitches, some by rv; helpful, friendly staff; excel clean san facs, poss stretched high ssn; vg rest/bar; pool 500m; no o'fits over 12m; rvside walks; lovely town, 20 min walk; conv NH fr A6; vg; gd cycling; shopping ctr nrby." ♦ 1 Apr-30 Sep. € 30.70   2018*

CHALON SUR SAONE 6H1 (12km SE Rural) 46.69813, 4.92751 **Mini-Camping Les Tantes, 29 Route de Grigny, 71240 Marnay [03 85 44 23 88 or 06 19 22 09 73 (mob)]** On D978 SE fr Chalon-sur-Saône, turn R in vill of Ouroux-sur-Saône onto D6 twd Marnay. Over bdge, foll site sp. Sm, hdg, pt shd, wc; chem disp; shwrs inc; EHU (5-10A) €2.90-4.20; lndry; snacks; bbq; playgrnd; pool; 30% statics; dogs; phone; quiet; games area. "Gd; o'night area." ♦ 1 Apr-30 Sept. € 9.00   2012*

CHALONNES SUR LOIRE 2G4 (2km E Rural) 47.35164, -0.74679 **Camping Les Portes de la Loire, Le Candais, 49290 Chalonnes-sur-Loire [41 78 02 27; contact@lesportesdelaloire.fr]** Fr D723 cross bdge to Challones. In town turn L sp Rochefort-Sur-Loire. Site on L of this rd in abt 1km. Lge, mkd, pt shd, wc; mv service pnt; fam bthrm; shwrs inc; EHU (10A) €3; bbq; playgrnd; twin axles; wifi; dogs; adv bkg acc. "Close to rv & town; peaceful setting; lge pitches; gd touring base; vg; excel san facs." 1 May-30 Sep. € 20.00   2016*

CHALONNES SUR LOIRE *2G4* (8km SE Rural) *47.32285, -0.71428* **Camp Municipal Les Patisseaux, Route de Chalonnes, 49290 Chaudefonds-sur-Layon [02 41 78 04 10 (Mairie); fax 02 41 78 66 89; mairie. chaudefondsurlayon@wanadoo.fr]** Fr Chalonnes on D961 S dir Cholet; Turn L onto D125 after 3km at narr rlwy bdge. Foll sp to site vill by Rv Layon. Sm, hdg, mkd, pt shd, wc; mv service pnt; shwrs; EHU; shop nr; bar nr; quiet. "V basic, clean, delightful site nr rv; lots of interest in area; reverse polarity; ltd san facs; lovely peaceful site; warden calls." ♦ 1 May-31 Aug. € 6.00   2014*

CHALONNES SUR LOIRE *2G4* (10km NW Urban) *47.39211, -0.87082* **Camping La Promenade, Quai des Mariniers, 49570 Montjean-sur-Loire [02 41 39 02 68 or 06 26 32 60 28 (mob); contact@campinglapromenade.com; www.campinglapromenade.com]** Exit Angers on N23 twd Nantes. Exit 1km beyond St Germain-des-Prés dir Montjean-sur-Loire. Cross rv then R on D210 to site in 500m. Lge, hdg, mkd, pt shd, wc; chem disp; mv service pnt; fam bthrm; shwrs inc; EHU (10A) €4; gas; lndry; shop nr; rest; snacks; bar; bbq; playgrnd; pool (htd); paddling pool; beach sand 600m; twin axles; entmnt; wifi; TV; 30% statics; dogs €2; Eng spkn; adv bkg acc; quiet; ccard acc; games area; CKE/CCI. "Friendly, young owners; interesting sculptures in vill & at Ecomusée; gd for Loire cycling; new san facs (2014) diff exit to R for lge vehicles; fishing nr; vg." 1 Apr-30 Sep. € 20.00   2015*

CHALONS EN CHAMPAGNE *5D1* (3km S Urban) *48.93579, 4.38299* **Camping de Châlons en Champagne, 11-15 Rue de Plaisance, 51000 Châlons-en-Champagne [03 26 68 38 00; camping.chalons@orange.fr; www.aquadis-loisirs.com]** Fr N on A26 exit junc 17, on D3 foll sp to Chalons en Champagne, then to Fagnières. Strt on at traff lts, then L at 1s rndabt. Turn R, sp Vitry le François, site sp. Fr S exit junc 18 onto D977, then D5 over rv & canal nr town cent; then foll site sp to R. Fr N44 S of Châlons sp St Memmie; foll site sp. D977 fr N into Châlons, cont on main rd to traff lts at 6 x-rds & turn R, site well sp. Or exit A4 junc 27 onto N44; turn R at St Memmie; site sp. NB some sps in area still show old town name 'Châlons-sur-Marne'. Do not use SatNav. Med, hdg, mkd, hdstg, pt shd, wc (htd); chem disp; mv service pnt; fam bthrm; shwrs inc; EHU (6-10A) (poss long lead req & rev pol, 2 pin adapter req); lndry; shop nr; snacks; bar; bbq; playgrnd; twin axles; red long stay; wifi; TV; dogs €1.50; bus; Eng spkn; adv bkg acc; quiet; ccard acc; tennis; games area; CKE/CCI. "Popular site adj park; generous pitches, inc hdstg; rec arr early or phone ahead; check barrier arrangements if need early dep; gates shut 2130 LS & 2300 high ssn; ltd bus service; poss noisy high ssn - pop concerts in adj area; hypmkt 1km; flat walk to lovely, interesting town; conv touring base & NH; friendly helpful recep; seasonal workers in Sep; san facs neglected but clean." ♦ 5 Mar-24 Aug. € 24.00   2018*

⊞ **CHALUS** *7B3* (10km NW Rural) *45.71540, 0.91956* **Camping Parc Verger, Le Halte, 87150 Champagnac-la-Rivière, Limousin [0844 232 8500 (Fr UK) or 05 55 01 22 83 or 06 04 09 05 20 (mob); pvbureau@parcverger.com; www.parcverger.com]** N fr Châlus on D901; in 9km turn L onto D75 sp Champagnac-la-Rivière; site on L in 150m. Sm, hdstg, mkd, unshd, wc (htd); chem disp; mv service pnt; fam bthrm; shwrs inc; EHU (16A) inc; lndry; shop; rest nr; bar nr; bbq; pool; sw; red long stay; twin axles; wifi; dogs; bus 150m; Eng spkn; adv bkg acc; quiet; ccard acc; CKE/CCI. "Lovely site; welcoming, friendly, helpful British owners; lge pitches suitable for RVs; gd clean san facs, poss stretched high ssn; gd mkd walks nrby; 15km-long walk/cycle path adj (old rwly track); red grass pitch; excel local vet; excel area for walking; bike hire." ♦ € 18.00   2016*

> **"That's changed – Should I let the Club know?"**
>
> If you find something on site that's different from the site entry, fill in a report and let us know. See camc.com/europereport.

CHAMBERY *9B3* (5km E Rural) *45.55151, 5.98416* **Camp Municipal Le Savoy, Parc des Loisirs, Chemin des Fleurs, 73190 Challes-les-Eaux [04 79 72 97 31; www.camping-challesleseaux.com]** On o'skts of town app fr Chambéry on D1006. Pass airfield, lake & tennis courts on L, L at traff lts just bef cent of Challes-les-Eaux sp Parc de Loisirs, at Hôtel Les Neiges de France foll camp sp to site in 100m. Fr A41 exit junc 20, foll sp Challes-les-Eaux, then 'Centre Ville', then D1006 N. Med, hdstg, mkd, shd, serviced pitches; wc; chem disp; shwrs; EHU (6-10A) €2.90; gas; lndry; shop nr; rest nr; snacks; sw nr; red long stay; dogs €1.40; bus; adv bkg acc; quiet; ccard acc; fishing adj; tennis adj. "Well-designed, well-run, clean site in beautiful setting; diff sized pitches; level (suitable wheelchairs); friendly, helpful staff; excel modern san facs; excel walking; well run site, rec hotel school rest in term time." ♦ 1 Apr-8 Oct. € 18.00   2017*

CHAMBERY *9B3* (25km SW Rural) *45.53804, 5.79973* **Camping Les Peupliers, Lac d'Aiguebelette, 73610 Lépin-le-Lac [04 79 36 00 48 or 06 66 10 09 99 (mob); fax 04 79 44 12 48; info@camping-lespeupliers.net; www.camping-lespeupliers.net]** Exit A43 junc 12 & foll sp Lac d'Aiguebelette (D921). Turn L at rndabt & foll rd on L of lake. Site on R after sm vill. Lge, hdg, mkd, pt shd, wc; chem disp; shwrs inc; EHU (6A) €3.50; lndry; shop nr; rest nr; snacks; bar; playgrnd; sw nr; wifi; dogs €1.20 (NO SW); quiet; ccard acc; fishing; CKE/CCI. "Pleasant site in beautiful setting, espec lakeside pitches; friendly, helpful owner; busy w/ends." 1 Apr-31 Oct. € 19.00   2015*

⊞ **CHAMBON LA FORET** *4F3* (1km N Rural) *48.06381, 2.28192* **Camping Domaine La Rive du Bois, Route de la Forêt, 45340 Chambon-la-Forêt [02 38 32 29 73 or 06 79 95 26 53 (mob); rive.bois@wanadoo. fr; www.larivedubois.com]** Fr Pithiviers take D921 S. Immed after x-ing over A19 turn L onto D30 sp Chambon-la-Forêt, Sully-sur-Loire. At La Rive-du-Bois traff lts foll sp to site on R. Sm, pt shd, wc (htd); chem disp; shwrs inc; EHU (10A) inc; lndry; bbq; playgrnd; pool; 70% statics; dogs free; Eng spkn; adv bkg acc; quiet; bike hire; fishing; tennis; games area; CKE/CCI. "Helpful, friendly manager; gd walking & cycling fr site; deer & red squirrels in woods around; gd; lovely woodland setting." ♦ € 15.00   2013*

CHAMBON SUR LAC *7B4* (2km W Rural) *45.57127, 2.89067* **Camping de Serrette, Serrette, 63790 Chambon-sur-La [04 73 88 67 67; camping. de.serrette@wanadoo.fr; campingdeserrette.com]** Fr A75, exit 6, foll D996 dir Mont Dore. Foll site sp after Lac Chambo. After 1.5km turn L onto D636. Site on R. Sharp turn at ent. Sm, hdg, mkd, pt shd, pt sl, terr, wc; chem disp; mv service pnt; fam bthrm; shwrs; EHU (10A) €4.80; lndry; shop; rest; snacks; bar; bbq; playgrnd; pool; paddling pool; sw nr; twin axles; wifi; TV; 50% statics; dogs €2.50; phone; Eng spkn; adv bkg acc; table tennis; games rm; CKE/CCI. "Excel walking area; watersports on Lac Chambon; gd site." ♦ 28 Apr-17 Sep. € 26.70   2016*

CHAMONIX MONT BLANC *9B4* (3km NE Rural) *45.9378, 6.8925* **Camping La Mer de Glace, 200 Chemin de la Bagna, Praz de Chamonix, 74400 Chamonix [04 50 53 44 03; fax 04 50 53 60 83; info@ chamonix-camp.com; www.chamonix-camping.com]** Foll sp on D1506 thro Chamonix dir Argentière & Swiss Frontier; site well sp on R in 3km but ent under bdge 2.4m. Rec, to avoid low bdge cont to 1st rndabt in Praz-de-Chamonix & foll sp to site (R at rndabt). Med, mkd, hdg, hdstg, pt shd, pt sl, wc (htd); chem disp; mv service pnt; fam bthrm; shwrs inc; EHU (10A) €3; lndry; shop nr; rest nr; snacks; bar nr; bbq; playgrnd; wifi; dogs free; bus & train 500m; Eng spkn; quiet; CKE/CCI. "Well-run, wooded site with superb views; sm pitches; helpful staff; vg facs; bar 500m; v conv trains/buses; close to Flégère lift; sports cent nr; htd pool 2km; path to town via woods & rv; excel." ♦ 4 May-9 Oct. € 25.00   2016*

CHAMONIX MONT BLANC *9B4* (7km NE Rural) *45.97552, 6.92224* **Camping Le Glacier d'Argentière, 161 Chemin des Chosalets, 74400 Argentière [04 50 54 17 36; fax 04 50 54 03 73; info@campingchamonix. com; www.campingchamonix.com]** On Chamonix-Argentière D1506 rd bef Argentière take R fork twd Argentière cable car stn. Site immed on R. Med, pt shd, pt sl, wc; chem disp; shwrs inc; EHU (2-10A) €2.60+.03 per extra amp; lndry; shop nr; bbq; wifi; dogs €0.50; Eng spkn; adv bkg acc; quiet; games area; CKE/CCI. "Alpine excursions; cable cars adj; mountain views; friendly, helpful owners; gd friendly site; Alpine views; quiet relaxed site; bus stop 1 min; 10 min walk to Argentiere Vill', train stn & cable car; mkd paths fr site." ♦ 15 May-30 Sep. € 18.00   2014*

CHAMONIX MONT BLANC *9B4* (2km SW Rural) *45.91466, 6.86138* **Camping Iles des Barrats, 185 Chemin de l'Ile des Barrats, 74400 Chamonix [04 50 53 51 44; campingiledesbarrats74@orange.fr; www.campingdesbarrats.com]** Fr Mont Blanc tunnel take 1st L on app Chamonix, foll sp to hospital, site opp hospital. Do not go into town. Sm, mkd, unshd, pt sl, wc; chem disp; mv service pnt; shwrs inc; EHU (5-10A) €3.30-4.30; gas; lndry; shop nr; sw nr; dogs €1; Eng spkn; adv bkg acc; quiet; CKE/CCI. "Great little site; superb mountain views; friendly family owners; immac facs; 10 mins level walk to town; 10 mins cable car Mont Blanc; excel; bus & train pass fr recep." 1 Jun-23 Sep. € 31.00   2017*

> "I like to fill in the reports as I travel from site to site"
>
> You'll find report forms at the back of this guide, or you can fill them in online at camc.com/europereport.

CHAMONIX MONT BLANC *9B4* (4km SW Rural) *45.90203, 6.83716* **Camping Les Deux Glaciers, 80 Route des Tissières, Les Bossons, 74400 Chamonix [04 50 53 15 84; fax 04 50 55 90 81; info@ les2glaciers.com; www.les2glaciers.com]** Exit Mont Blanc tunnel foll sps Geneva turn L on D1506 (Chamonix-Geneva rd), in 2km turn R for Les Bossons & L under bdge. Fr W foll sps Chamonix & Mont Blanc tunnel. On dual c/way turn R at sp `Les Bossons' & site after Mercure Hotel; adj Les Cimes site; site clearly sp fr D1205. Med, pt shd, sl, wc (htd); chem disp; fam bthrm; shwrs inc; EHU (6-10A) €2.50- 7; lndry; shop; rest; snacks; bar; playgrnd; wifi; dogs free; bus; Eng spkn; games rm; table tennis; CKE/ CCI. "Pleasant, well-kept site in wonderful location just under Mont Blanc; roomy pitches; clean facs; poss diff site for lge o'fits over 6m; if recep clsd pitch & wait until 1730; ideal for walking; skating rink 4km; funicular adj to Glacier des Bossons; rec arr early high ssn; pool 4km; highly rec; vg." ♦ 1 Jan-15 Nov & 15 Dec-31 Dec. € 22.50   2017*

CHANAC *9D1* (1km S Urban) *44.46519, 3.34670* **Camp Municipal La Vignogue, Rue de Plaisance, 48230 Chanac [04 66 48 24 09 or 06 82 93 60 68 (mob); fax 04 13 33 28 43; gites-camping-chanac@ orange.fr; www.chanac.fr]** Exit A75 junc 39.1 onto N88 to Chanac; site well sp in vill. Sm, mkd, pt shd, pt sl, wc (htd); chem disp; shwrs inc; EHU (6A) inc; lndry; shop nr; rest nr; bar nr; bbq; wifi; 10% statics; dogs €1; Eng spkn; adv bkg acc; quiet. "Excel; bar 500m; pool adj; rec arr early (bef 1800)." ♦ 15 Apr-30 Sep. € 15.50   2017*

CHANTILLY *3D3* (5km NW Rural) *49.22571, 2.42862*
Camping Campix, 60340 St Leu d'Esserent [03 44 56 08 48; fax 03 44 56 28 75; campix@orange.fr; www.campingcampix.com] Exit A1 junc 8 to Senlis; cont W fr Senlis on D924 thro Chantilly, x-ing Rv Oise to St Leu-d'Esserent; leave town on D12 NW twd Cramoisy thro housing est; foll site sp for 1km, winding app. Med, hdstg, mkd, shd, terr, wc (htd); chem disp; mv service pnt; fam bthrm; shwrs inc; EHU (6-10A) €3.50 (min 25m cable poss req); gas; lndry; shop; rest; snacks; bbq; playgrnd; pool; sw nr; red long stay; wifi; dogs €2; phone; Eng spkn; adv bkg acc; quiet; ccard acc; fishing; games rm; CKE/CCI. "Beautiful, peaceful site in former quarry - poss unguarded, vertical drops; helpful owner & friendly staff; wide variety of pitches - narr, steep access & o'hanging trees on some; conv Paris Parc Astérix & Disneyland (Astérix tickets fr recep); sh walk to vill; rec; gd facs; long elec leads maybe needed;." ♦ 7 Mar-30 Nov. € 27.00   2018*

⊞ **CHANTILLY** *3D3* (7km NW Rural) *49.21225, 2.40270* Camping L'Abbatiale, 39 Rue Salvador Allendé, 60340 St Leu-d'Esserent [03 44 56 38 76; contact@camping-abbatiale.fr; http://campingabbatiale.wix.com/campingabbatiale] S twds Paris on A1 exit Senlis; cont W fr Senlis on D924/D44 thro Chantilly x-ing Rv Oise to St Leu-d'Esserent; cont on D44, x-ing D603 which becomes Rue Salvador Allendé in 700m; foll site sps; avoid rv x-ing on D17 fr SW; v narr bdge. Sm, mkd, hdg, hdstg, pt shd, wc (htd); chem disp; mv service pnt; shwrs; EHU (3A) €2.50 (some rev pol); lndry; shop nr; rest nr; bbq (sep area); playgrnd; beach sandy 1km; twin axles; red long stay; wifi; dogs; phone; bus adj; Eng spkn; adv bkg acc; quiet; ccard acc; games rm; games area. "Chantilly & chateau interesting; conv for Chantilly, Paris & L'oise Valley; gd walks nrby (woodland & rvside); v friendly family owned & managed; lge nbr of statics on site but does not detract fr touring pitches nor impact on facs; best site in area." € 18.00   2015*

⊞ **CHANTONNAY** *2H4* (12km NE Rural) *46.75168, -0.94568* Camping La Baudonnière, Route des Salinières, 85110 Monsireigne [02 51 66 43 79; tombann1962@gmail.com; www.labaudonniere.com] Fr Chantonnay take D960B NE dir St Prouant & Pouzauges. In St Prouant take D23 to Monsireigne. Foll rd downhill, cross sm rv & as rd starts to climb take 2nd L sp Reaumur; in 400m L onto Rue des Salinières. Site on L in 800m. Sm, pt shd, pt sl, wc; chem disp; shwrs inc; EHU (10A) €4; lndry; shop; rest; snacks; bbq; playgrnd; dogs; Eng spkn; adv bkg acc; quiet; games rm; tennis 2km. "V relaxing, peaceful, pretty CL-type site; welcoming, friendly, helpful Irish owners; excel san facs; conv Puy de Fou theme park; vg; v well kept site." ♦ € 22.00   2014*

CHAPELLE D'ANGILLON, LA *4G3* (1km SE Rural) *47.36044, 2.44261* Camping Paradis Nature (formerly Municipal Les Murailles), Route d'Henrichemont, 18380 La Chapelle-d'Angillon [06 70 29 52 00; christelle@camping-paradis-nature.com; www.camping-paradis-nature.com] Fr Bourges or Aubigny-sur-Nère on D940, turn E onto D926; turn onto D12 in vill, site on R, sp. Sm, pt shd, pt sl, wc; chem disp; shwrs inc; EHU (6A) €3.20; shop nr; rest nr; bar nr; bbq; playgrnd; 10% statics; dogs; ccard acc; lake fishing adj; CKE/CCI. "Lake adj with castle o'looking; quiet; vg; red for 3 nights or more." ♦ 1 Apr-24 Oct. € 17.00   2015*

CHAPELLE EN VERCORS, LA *9C3* (0km S Urban) *44.9695, 5.4156* Camp Municipal Les Bruyères, Ave des Bruyères, 26420 La Chapelle-en-Vercors [04 75 48 21 46] Take D518 N fr Die over Col de Rousset. Fr N on A49 exit 8 to N532 St Nazaire-en-Royans, then D76 thro St Thomas-en-Royans, then D216 to St Laurent-en-Royans. Take D2 round E flank of Combe Laval (2 sh 2-lane tunnels). Fr Col de la Machine foll D76 S 1km, then D199 E over Col de Carri to La Chapelle. (D531 fr Villard de Lons, D76 over Combe Laval & D518 Grandes Goulet not suitable for c'vans & diff lge m'vans due narr rds & tunnels & 5km of o'hanging ledges.) Med, hdstg, pt shd, pt sl, wc (htd); chem disp; mv service pnt; shwrs inc; EHU (6A); lndry; shop nr; rest nr; bar nr; playgrnd; TV; 10% statics; dogs €1; adv bkg acc; quiet; cycling; fishing; horseriding; CKE/CCI. "Excel base for beautiful Vercors plateau; friendly welcome; climbing; pool 300m; excel value; choose own pitch; clean & immac san facs; excel cycling; vg." ♦ 1 May-1 Oct. € 13.50   2016*

CHAPELLE HERMIER, LA *2H4* (4km SW Rural) *46.66652, -1.75543* Camping Le Pin Parasol, Châteaulong, 85220 La Chapelle-Hermier [02 51 34 64 72; fax 02 51 34 64 62; contact@campingpinparasol.fr; www.campingpinparasol.fr] Exit A83 junc 4 onto D763/D937 dir La Roche-sur-Yon; turn R onto D948; at Aizenay turn R onto D6 twd St Gilles Croix-de-Vie; after 10km at x-rds turn L onto D21; in La Chapelle-Hermier foll D42 twds L'Aiguillon-sur-Vie; site sp in 4km. Lge, hdg, mkd, unshd, pt sl, terr, wc; chem disp; mv service pnt; fam bthrm; shwrs inc; EHU (16A) €4.50; gas; lndry; shop; rest nr; snacks; bar; bbq; playgrnd; pool (htd); paddling pool; sw nr; entmnt; wifi; TV; 70% statics; dogs €4.20; Eng spkn; adv bkg acc; quiet; ccard acc; games rm; fishing 200m; excursions; fitness rm; archery; bike hire; games area; waterslide; tennis; CKE/CCI. "On banks of Lake Jaunay; access to lake down sm path; lge pitches; friendly staff; no o'fits over 11m; boating 200m; canoeing 200m; excel facs; adventure zone; lovely pools; away fr crowds but close to beaches; pleasant walks & cycle tracks around lake; beautiful site; v well kept." ♦ 21 Apr-17 Sep. € 42.00   2017*

CHARITE SUR LOIRE, LA

CHARITE SUR LOIRE, LA *4G4* (1km W Urban) *47.17683, 3.01058* FFCC Camp Municipal La Saulaie, Quai de la Saulaie, 58400 La Charité-sur-Loire [03 86 70 00 83 or 03 86 70 15 06 (LS); camping@lacharitesurloire.fr; www.campinglacharitesurloire.fr] Exit A77 junc 30 & foll sp 'Centre Ville'. Turn L over Rv Loire sp Bourges; take 2nd R bef next bdge. Fr Bourges on N151, turn L immed after x-ing 1st bdge over Rv Loire. Foll sp. NB Take care when turn R over narr rv bdge when leaving site - v high kerb. Med, mkd, pt shd, wc; chem disp; shwrs inc; EHU (10A); lndry; shop nr; snacks; sw nr; red long stay; dogs €2; quiet; CKE/CCI. "Lovely, well-kept site on rv island; warm welcome, helpful staff; gd security; poss school groups high ssn; LS phone to check open; beautiful town; playgrnd & htd pool, paddling pool adj inc (pool opens 1 Jul); welcoming staff; new san facs (2016); site v well maintained." ♦ 1 Apr-28 Sep. € 21.00   2017*

CHARLEVILLE MEZIERES *5C1* (12km N Urban) *49.87757, 4.74187* Camp Municipal au Port à Diseur, Rue André Compain, 08800 Monthermé [03 24 53 01 21 or 03 24 53 00 09; fax 03 24 53 01 15] Fr D988 at Revin turn E onto D1 TO Monthermé. Site is on D1 S of town. Site on R, 100m past supmkt on L. Med, mkd, hdg, pt shd, pt sl, wc; chem disp; shwrs inc; EHU (4-10A) inc; lndry; shop nr; rest nr; bar nr; 10% statics; dogs; phone; quiet; CKE/CCI. "Pleasant, rvside site in conv location; lge pitches; excel, clean san facs, poss stretched if site full; gd rvside walks; 20 min easy walk to Monthermé; gd cycling & walking; popular with fishermen & canoeists; excel site; some pitches adj rv; gas 100m; picturesque hilly wooded countryside." ♦ 13 Apr-30 Sep. € 15.30   2014*

CHARLEVILLE MEZIERES *5C1* (4km N Urban) *49.77813, 4.72245* Camp Municipal Mont Olympe, Rue des Pâquis, 08000 Charleville-Mézières [03 24 33 23 60 or 03 24 32 44 80; fax 03 24 33 37 76; camping-charlevillemezieres@wandadoo.fr] Fr N43/E44 head for Hôtel de Ville, with Hôtel de Ville on R, cont N along Ave des Arches, turn R at 'Gare' sp & cross rv bdge. At 'Gare' turn sharp L immed along Rue des Pâquis, site on L in 500m, visible fr rd. Well sp fr town cent. Med, hdg, mkd, hdstg, pt shd, serviced pitches; wc (htd); chem disp; mv service pnt; fam bthrm; shwrs inc; EHU (10A) €3.95; gas; lndry; shop nr; rest nr; bar; bbq; playgrnd; wifi; TV; 10% statics; dogs €1.60; Eng spkn; adv bkg; ccard acc; fishing; boating; games rm; CKE/CCI. "Lovely, spacious, well-kept site on Rv Meuse; v lge pitches extra; helpful staff; htd covrd pool adj; san facs clean, new (2018); useful snack bar; easy walk to charming town; excel; NH for m'van's." 1 Apr-30 Sep. € 20.00   2018*

CHARLIEU *9A1* (1km E Urban) *46.15851, 4.18088* FFCC Camp Municipal de la Douze, chemin du Camping, 42190 Charlieu [04 77 72 86 01; camp-charlieu@voila.fr] N fr Roanne on D482 to Pouilly-sous-Charlieu, then E on D487 to Charlieu town cent, site sp in town, by sw pool. NB Do not confuse with Camp Municipal Pouilly-sous-Charlieu which is sp fr main rd. Med, hdg, pt shd, wc (htd); chem disp; mv service pnt; shwrs inc; EHU (6A) inc; lndry; shop nr; snacks; bar; playgrnd; sw nr; twin axles; entmnt; 5% statics; dogs; Eng spkn; adv bkg acc; boating adj; fishing adj; games area; CKE/CCI. "Gd clean new san facs (2018); vg value; quiet; new cycle rte to Loire; canal cycle paths; sw & tennis adj; historical town." ♦ 1 Apr-30 Sep. € 16.00   2018*

CHARLY SUR MARNE *3D4* (1km S Urban) *48.97363, 3.28210* Camp Municipal Les Illettes, Route de Pavant, 02310 Charly-sur-Marne [03 28 82 12 11 or 03 23 82 00 32 (Mairie); fax 03 23 82 13 99; mairie.charly@wanadoo.fr; www.charly-sur-marne.fr] Exit A4 junc 18 onto D603 dir La Ferté; then take D402/D969 NE to Charly. Site sp in town. Sm, hdg, pt shd, wc; chem disp; shwrs; EHU (5-10A) €2-3; lndry; shop nr; red long stay; dogs €2.50. "Lovely, well-kept site; pleasant warden; 10 min walk to rv & rvside walks; conv for touring Champagne rte; rec arr early to secure pitch during grape harvest; excel." ♦ 1 Apr-30 Sep. € 14.70   2012*

CHARMES *6E2* (1km N Rural) *48.37706, 6.28974* Camp Municipal Les Iles, 20 Rue de l'Ecluse, 88130 Charmes [03 29 38 87 71 or 03 29 38 85 85; andre.michel63@wanadoo.fr; www.ville-charmes.fr] Exit N57 for Charmes, site well sp on Rv Moselle. Do not confuse with sp for 'Camping Cars'. Med, mkd, pt shd, wc; chem disp; mv service pnt; shwrs inc; EHU (10A) €3.55; gas; lndry; shop nr; rest; snacks; bar; bbq; playgrnd; red long stay; wifi; dogs; phone; Eng spkn; adv bkg acc; quiet; kayak hire; fishing; CKE/CCI. "Lovely site bet rv & canal; lge pitches; friendly staff; footpath to town; m'van o'night area in town; vg value; gd; v lge pitches." ♦ 1 Apr-30 Sep. € 16.50   2017*

CHARNY *4F3* (1km N Rural) *47.89078, 3.09419* FFCC Camping des Platanes, 41 Route de la Mothe, 89120 Charny [03 86 91 83 60; info@campinglesplatanes.fr; www.campinglesplatanes.fr] Exit A6 junc 18 onto D943 to Montargis. Turn S onto D950 to Charny, site on R as ent vill; sp. Med, hdg, mkd, pt shd, serviced pitches; wc (htd); chem disp; mv service pnt; shwrs inc; EHU (10A) inc; gas; lndry; shop nr; snacks; bbq; playgrnd; pool; red long stay; wifi; TV; 60% statics; dogs €3; Eng spkn; adv bkg acc; quiet; bike hire; tennis 500m; rv fishing 150m; CKE/CCI. "Pleasant, peaceful site; gd sized pitches; friendly, helpful owners; excel, clean san facs; sh walk to vill; gd walking; gd touring base." ♦ 1 Apr-30 Oct. € 22.50   2016*

CHATEAU ARNOUX

CHAROLLES *9A2 (1km E Rural) 46.43972, 4.28208* **FFCC Camp Municipal, Route de Viry, 71120 Charolles [03 85 24 04 90 or 32 17 10 10 62; fax 03 85 24 08 20; camping.charolles@orange.fr]** Exit N79 at E end of by-pass sp Vendenesse-lès-Charolles; at rndabt foll camping sp; then sharp R bottom hill bef town; site on L, next to Municipal pool. Med, hdstg, hdg, mkd, pt shd, pt sl, wc (htd); chem disp; mv service pnt; fam bthrm; shwrs inc; EHU (6A) €2; lndry; shop nr; snacks; bbq; playgrnd; pool (htd); paddling pool; twin axles; wifi; 2% statics; dogs €1.50; adv bkg rec; quiet; ccard acc; games rm; CKE/CCI. "Well-kept site; sm pitches; friendly, helpful warden; gd, modern san facs; pool adj high ssn (proper sw trunks req); m'van area outside site; negligible security; canoes avail, launching stn to rv on site; excel." ♦ 1 Apr-5 Oct. € 14.00   2018*

CHARTRE SUR LE LOIR, LA *4F2 (1km W Rural) 47.73220, 0.57451* **Camping Le Vieux Moulin, Chemin des Bergivaux, 72340 La Chartre-sur-le Loir [02 43 44 41 18; bordduloir@orange.fr]** Sp fr D305 in town. Fr S exit A28 junc 27 onto D766 dir Beaumont-la-Ronce; then take D29 to La Chartre-sur-le Loir; go over rv, turn L immed after bdge. Fr N leave A20 at junc 24 & foll D304 to Chartre, site well sp on R bef bdge. Med, hdg, mkd, pt shd, wc (htd); chem disp; mv service pnt; fam bthrm; shwrs inc; EHU (5-10A) €4-5 (poss rev pol); lndry; shop nr; bar; bbq; playgrnd; pool (htd); wifi; TV; 20% statics; dogs €1.50; Eng spkn; adv bkg rec; quiet; 15% red CC members; rv fishing; bike hire; CKE/CCI. "Beautiful, well-kept rvside site; helpful, friendly staff; excel pool; gd for dogs; v lge MH's acc; gd base for chateaux, forest & Loir Valley; excel; pleasant walk to town." ♦ 1 Mar-30 Nov. € 24.00   2018*

CHARTRES *4E2 (3km SE Urban) 48.43433, 1.49914* **Camping Les Bords de l'Eure, 9 Rue de Launay, 28000 Chartres [02 37 28 79 43; ets-ya-roussel-montigny@orange.fr; www.camping-de-chartres.fr]** Exit N123 ring rd at D935, R at T-junc dir Chartres; then R at 2nd traff lts dir Chartres immed after rlwy bdge; site on L in 400m; inside of ring rd. Also sp fr town cent on N154 fr N, foll sp town cent under 2 rlwy bdges, L at traff lts sp Orléans, after 1km site sp. Fr SE on N154 cross ring rd, foll site sp & turn L at 2nd traff lts; site on R. Med, hdg, mkd, shd, wc (htd); chem disp; mv service pnt; fam bthrm; shwrs inc; EHU (6A) €4 (poss rev pol); lndry; shop; bbq; playgrnd; wifi; 10% statics; dogs €1.08; Eng spkn; adv bkg acc; quiet; ccard acc; fishing; CKE/CCI. "Popular, spacious, pleasant, well laid-out, dir access to rv; unisex san facs clean but tired, stretched when busy; some pitches diff lge o'fits; gates clsd 2200-0700; poss ssn workers; poss unkempt early ssn; when wet grnd soft & muddy in places; easy walk or cycle along rv to Chartres, well lit at night; rec Son et Lumière; ideal NH & longer; vg; attractive site, bottom of hill, some awkward pitches; friendly helpful staff; excel situation." ♦ 1 Mar-31 Oct. € 23.00   2017*

⊞ **CHASSENEUIL SUR BONNIEURE** *7B3 (10km E Rural) 45.83283, 0.55811* **Camping Le Paradis, Mareuil, 16270 Mazières [05 45 84 92 06 or 078 66 49 67 41 (mob); info@le-paradis-camping.com; www.le-paradis-camping.com]** Fr Limoges W on N141 twd Angoulême, turn L at 1st traff lts in Roumazières-Loubert D161. Site sp in 2km at t-junc. Sm, hdstg, mkd, hdg, pt shd, wc; chem disp; mv service pnt; fam bthrm; shwrs inc; EHU (10-16A) €5.50-8.50; lndry; shop; rest nr; bar nr; bbq; playgrnd; sw nr; 20% statics; dogs free; phone; bus 1km; adv bkg rec; quiet; fishing nr; tennis nr; games area; watersports 5km; CKE/CCI. "Clean, tranquil site; gd sized pitches; vg, immac san facs; welcoming, helpful British owners, helpful & friendly; gd touring base; adv bkg rec lge o'fits; excel; min €30 for 1 night stays; storage avail; highly rec." ♦ € 19.50   2016*

⊞ **CHATAIGNERAIE, LA** *2H4 (8km N Rural) 46.7325, -0.7425* **Camping Le Grand Fraigneau, Le Grand Fraigneau, 85700 Menomblet Vendée [02 51 51 68 21 or 06 42 68 48 12 (mob); info@legrandfraigneau.com; www.legrandfraigneau.com]** NE fr La Châtaigneraie on D938T to St Pierre-du-Chemin; turn L onto D49 to Menomblet; in 500m turn L to Le Grand Fraigneau. Site sp. Sm, pt shd, wc; fam bthrm; shwrs; EHU (10A) €3; bbq; pool; sw; twin axles; wifi; dogs free; Eng spkn; adv bkg acc; quiet. "CL-type site; friendly, helpful British owners; fenced pond; walks in lovely countryside; boating 9km; excel." ♦ € 9.00   2013*

CHATAIGNERAIE, LA *2H4 (6km E Rural) 46.64854, -0.66580* **Camping La Viollière, 85120 Breuil-Barret [02 51 87 44 82; vendeevacances@gmail.com; http://vendeevacances.googlepages.com/]** Take D949B E thro La Châtaigneraie for 5km. Cont thro Breuil-Barret & site 2nd R after passing under rlwy bdge. Sm, pt shd, pt sl, wc; chem disp; shwrs inc; EHU (6A) inc (poss long lead req); shop nr; rest nr; bar nr; bbq; wifi; dogs €1; Eng spkn; adv bkg acc; quiet. "Peaceful, relaxing CL-type site; v lge pitches with views; helpful British owners; excel." Apr-Oct. € 16.00   2016*

CHATEAU ARNOUX *10E3 (3km NE Rural) 44.10476, 6.01680* **Camping Sunêlia L'Hippocampe, Route Napoléon, 04290 Volonne [04 92 33 50 00; fax 04 92 33 50 49; camping@l-hippocampe.com; www.l-hippocampe.com]** Exit A51 junc 21 onto D4085 12km S of Sisteron twd Volonne vill over rv. Turn R on D4 on ent vill & foll camp sp 1km. Lge, hdg, hdstg, mkd, pt shd, serviced pitches; wc; chem disp; mv service pnt; fam bthrm; shwrs inc; EHU (10A) inc (poss rev pol); lndry; shop; rest; bar; bbq (elec, gas); playgrnd; pool (htd); paddling pool; red long stay; entmnt; wifi; TV; 10% statics; dogs €2; Eng spkn; adv bkg acc; quiet; ccard acc; canoeing; fishing; games area; waterslide; bike hire; rafting; tennis; games rm; CKE/CCI. "Pleasant, busy, well-run site; spacious, well-screened pitches; various pitch sizes/prices, some by lake; some pitches poss diff due trees; scruffy." ♦ 25 Apr-30 Sep. € 42.00   2015*

CHATEAU DU LOIR

CHATEAU DU LOIR *4G1* (8km E Rural) *47.71250, 0.49930* **Camping du Lac des Varennes, Route de Port Gauthier, 72340 Marçon** [02 43 44 13 72; fax 02 43 44 54 31; contact@lacdesvarennes.com; www.lacdesvarennes.com] Fr N on D338 fr Château-du-Loir dir Vendôme for 3km. Turn L onto D305 sp Marçon. In vill turn L onto D61 over bdge. Site on R by lake. Lge, hdg, hdstg, mkd, pt shd, wc (htd); chem disp; mv service pnt; fam bthrm; shwrs inc; EHU (10A) €3.40 (poss rev pol, poss long lead req); lndry; shop; rest; snacks; bar; bbq; playgrnd; sw nr; red long stay; entmnt; wifi; 11% statics; dogs €1.80; Eng spkn; adv bkg rec; quiet; ccard acc; boat hire; watersports; horseriding; tennis; bike hire; CKE/CCI. "Pretty site in lovely situation bet lake & rv; friendly, helpful staff; gd security; gd walks & cycling; san facs basic & unisex; LS off clsd 1200-1600; new owners (2016)." ♦ 1 Apr-30 Oct. € 20.00 2016*

⊞ **CHATEAU GONTIER** *4F1* (11km N Rural) *47.92109, -0.68334* **Camping Village Vacances et Pêche, Rue des Haies, 53170 Villiers-Charlemagne** [02 43 07 71 68; fax 02 43 07 72 77; vvp.villiers.charlemagne@wanadoo.fr; www.villiers-charlemagne.mairie53.fr] N fr Château-Gontier on N162; turn R onto D20 to Villiers-Charlemagne; site on R. Sm, pt shd, wc; chem disp; shwrs inc; EHU (6A) inc; lndry; bbq; cooking facs; playgrnd; twin axles; entmnt; wifi; 10% statics; dogs; Eng spkn; fishing; tennis; bike hire; games rm; CKE/CCI. "Sm wooded site in rural surroundings; each pitch has own san facs & kitchenette; site is amazing; helpful, friendly staff; v peaceful; well maintained." € 17.00 2013*

> **"We must tell the Club about that great site we found"**
>
> Get your site reports in by mid-August and we'll do our best to get your updates into the next edition.

⊞ **CHATEAU GONTIER** *4F1* (2km N Urban) *47.83851, -0.69965* **Camping Le Parc, 15 Route de Laval, 53200 Château-Gontier** [02 43 07 35 60; fax 02 43 70 38 94; camping.parc@cc-chateau-gontier.fr; www.sudmayenne.com] App Château-Gontier fr N on N162, at 1st rndabt on bypass take 1st exit. Site on R in 250m. Sm, mkd, pt shd, sl, wc (htd); chem disp; mv service pnt; shwrs inc; EHU (6-10A) inc (rev pol); lndry; shop nr; bar; playgrnd; entmnt; TV; 20% statics; dogs; quiet; ccard acc; tennis; fishing; games rm; CKE/CCI. "V pleasant, beautiful site; most pitches sl, some o'look rv; superb clean unisex san facs; rvside path to attractive town; mkt Thurs; excel site, gd pitches; superb clean san facs; helpful staff; pool 800m; lots of activity on rv to watch." ♦ € 18.00 2018*

CHATEAU GONTIER *4F1* (12km SE Rural) *47.74985, -0.64258* **Camping des Rivières, Rue du Port, 53200 Daon** [02 43 06 94 78; www.campingdaon.fr] On town side of rv bdge, turn down lane & site ent on R at bottom of hill. Med, pt shd, wc; chem disp; shwrs inc; EHU (10A) €3; lndry; shop nr; sw nr; adv bkg acc; quiet; tennis nr; CKE/CCI. "Vg clean & well-cared for site; some pitches diff to access; mini golf nr; boating on adj Rv Mayenne; great san facs." ♦ 1 Apr-30 Sep. € 13.00 2016*

CHATEAU RENAULT *4G2* (7km S Urban) *47.54471, 0.88786* **Camp Municipal du Moulin, Rue du Lavoir, 37110 Villedômer** [02 47 55 05 50 or 02 47 55 00 04 (Mairie); fax 02 47 55 06 27; mairie.villedomer@wanadoo.fr] Fr A10 exit junc 18 onto D31 dir Château-Renault. Turn W onto D73 sp to Auzouer & Villedômer. Fr Château-Renault S on D910, site sp dir Villedômer. Sm, hdg, shd, wc; chem disp; shwrs inc; EHU (10A) €3; shop nr; rest nr; bar nr; dogs €1; adv bkg rec; rv fishing; fishing 2km. "Gd, clean facs but old-fashioned; pitch yourself if warden not present; does not accept twin axles." 15 Jun-15 Sep. € 14.00 2016*

CHATEAU RENAULT *4G2* (1km W Urban) *47.59283, 0.90687* **Camp Municipal du Parc de Vauchevrier, Rue Paul-Louis-Courier, 37110 Château-Renault** [02 47 29 54 43 or 02 47 29 85 50 (LS); fax 02 47 56 87 50; camping.vauchevrier@orange.fr; www.ville-chateau-renault.fr] At Château-Renault foll sp to site 800m fr D910. If app fr a'route turn L on ent town & site on R of main rd adj Rv Brenne. Med, mkd, hdg, pt shd, wc; chem disp; mv service pnt; shwrs inc; EHU (6A) €2.20 (long lead poss req); shop nr; rest nr; bar nr; playgrnd; pool (htd); tennis; fishing; CKE/CCI. "Pleasant site by rv in park; lge pitches; friendly, helpful warden; clean, modern san facs, ltd LS; bar 300m; gd NH nr D910; no twin axles." ♦ 1 May-15 Sep. € 14.00 2016*

CHATEAUBRIANT *2F4* (2km S Urban) *47.70305, -1.37789* **Camp Municipal Les Briotais, Rue de Tugny, 44110 Châteaubriant** [02 40 81 14 38 or 02 40 81 02 32; h.menet@ville-chateaubriant.fr; www.tourisme-chateaubriant.fr/camping-municipal-des-briotais] App fr Nantes (D178) site sp on S end of town. Or fr Angers on D963/D163 foll sp at 1st rndabt; fr town cent, foll sps thro town. Sm, hdg, pt shd, wc; mv service pnt; shwrs; EHU €2.70; shop nr; rest nr; bar nr; dogs €0.35; quiet; games area. "11thC chateau in town; site locked o'night; site on municipal playing field; gd NH; pool in town." ♦ 1 May-30 Sep. € 6.00 2016*

CHATEAUDUN *4F2* (2km N Urban) *48.08008, 1.33141* **Camp Municipal Le Moulin à Tan, Rue de Chollet, 28200 Châteaudun [02 37 45 05 34 or 02 37 45 22 46 (LS); fax 02 37 45 54 46; tourisme-chateaudun@wanadoo.fr]** App Châteaudun fr N on N10; turn R onto D3955 at 2nd rndabt (supmkt & Buffalo Grill on L); L at next rndabt onto D955; in 800m turn L into Rue de Chollet. App Châateaudun fr S on N10, turn L onto D3955 & then as bef. Site adj Rv Loir & well sp fr D955. Med, mkd, pt shd, wc; chem disp; mv service pnt; shwrs inc; EHU (6A) inc; lndry; shop nr; rest nr; playgrnd; TV; 5% statics; fishing; games area; canoeing; CKE/CCI. "Gd touring base, quiet/under-used LS; helpful warden; some night flying fr nrby military airfield; htd covrd pool 2km; security gate 2.1m height; no twin axles; gd; rec open fr 0700 - 2200; walks fr site; OK NH." 1 Apr-30 Sep. € 13.00 2017*

CHATEAULIN *2E2* (2km S Rural) *48.18754, -4.08515* **Camping La Pointe, Route de St Coulitz, 29150 Châteaulin [02 98 86 51 53; lapointecamping@aol.com; www.lapointesuperbecamping.com]** Exit N165 onto D887 to Châteaulin; in town cent, cross bdge & turn L along rv on D770; after approx 750m, turn L at sp for St Coulitz; in 100m turn R into site. NB if app fr S to Châteaulin on D770, do not attempt to turn R at sp for St Coulitz (tight turn); go into town & turn round. Med, hdstg, mkd, hdg, pt shd, pt sl, wc; chem disp; mv service pnt; fam bthrm; shwrs inc; EHU (10A) €3 (poss rev pol); lndry; shop; rest nr; bar nr; bbq; playgrnd; wifi; dogs €1; phone; Eng spkn; adv bkg acc; quiet; rv fishing nrby; games rm; bike hire; CKE/CCI. "Charming, peaceful, spacious site in wooded setting; well-run; helpful & friendly British owners; immac san facs; rvside path to town; gd cycling, walking & fishing; gd touring base; gd." ♦ 15 Mar-15 Oct. € 21.00 2015*

CHATEAULIN *2E2* (1km SW Urban) *48.19099, -4.08597* **Camping de Rodaven (formerly Municipal), Rocade de Prat Bihan 29150 Châteaulin [02 98 86 32 93; fax 02 98 86 31 03; contact@campingderodaven.fr; www.campingderodaven.fr]** Fr canal/rv bdge in town cent take Quai Moulin (SE side of rv) for about 350m; site down track on R opp sw pool. Med, pt shd, wc; chem disp; mv service pnt; shwrs inc; EHU (10A) €2.90; shop nr; snacks; playgrnd; beach sand 5km; entmnt; wifi; dogs free 2nd dog €1; phone; Eng spkn; adv bkg acc; quiet; fishing; rv; CKE/CCI. "Well-kept site; pleasant, helpful owner; htd covrd pool 300m; vg clean facs; walk along rv bank to town; gd touring base; Locronan vill well worth the visit." ♦ 7 Apr-30 Sep. € 18.60 2013*

CHATEAUMEILLANT *7A4* (1km NW Rural) *46.56807, 2.18823* **Camp Municipal L'Etang Merlin, 18370 Châteaumeillant [02 48 61 31 38; fax 02 48 61 39 89; www.camping-etangmerlin.e-monsite.com]** Rec app fr W to avoid narr town rds. Site sp fr rndabt at W end of town on D80 N of Châteaumeillant on lakeside. Fr Culan by pass town on D943, then as above. Sm, mkd, hdg, pt shd, serviced pitches; wc; chem disp; shwrs inc; EHU (5A) inc; lndry; shop nr; playgrnd; pool; dogs €1; Eng spkn; adv bkg acc; quiet; fishing; tennis adj; CKE/CCI. "Superb, well-kept site; lge pitches; friendly & helpful staff; basketball at sports complex adj; lake adj (no sw); rec arr early high ssn to secure pitch; easy walk to town." ♦ 1 May-30 Sep. € 11.50 2012*

CHATEAUNEUF DU FAOU *2E2* (1km S Urban) *48.18306, -3.80986* **Gites & Camping de Penn ar Pont, Rue de la Liberation, 29520 Chateauneuf du Faou [02 98 81 81 25 or 06 60 24 75 42; gites.pennarpont@orange.fr; www.pennarpont.com]** Take D36 S, go over bdge, site at 1st R turn. Sm, hdg, mkd, pt shd, terr, wc; chem disp; mv service pnt; shwrs inc; EHU (16A) €3.50; shop nr; snacks; bar nr; bbq; dogs €2; Eng spkn; adv bkg acc; quiet. "Steep rd on site, diff for lge o'fits; jazz fest last w/end of July; gd; san facs clean but needs upgrade; typical sm municipal site in beautiful setting." 1 Apr-31 Oct. € 15.00 2018*

CHATEAUNEUF SUR ISERE *9C2* (5km W Rural) *44.99710, 4.89333* **Le Soleil Fruité, Les Pèches, 26300 Châteauneuf-sur Isère [04 75 84 19 70; fax 04 75 78 05 85; contact@lesoleifruite.com; www.lesoleilfruite.com]** Fr Valence, take A7 dir Lyon. Take exit 14 Valence Nord twd Bourg les Valence. At rndabt take 1st exit onto N7. Turn R onto D877 and foll sp. Med, hdg, mkd, pt shd, wc; fam bthrm; shwrs; EHU (6A); lndry; rest; snacks; bar; bbq; playgrnd; pool (covrd, htd); paddling pool; entmnt; wifi; TV; Eng spkn; adv bkg acc; bike hire; games area; waterslide; CCI. "Immac site; lovely pool; gd rest; sh drive to vill." ♦ 26 Apr-15 Sep. € 44.00 2014*

CHATEAUNEUF SUR LOIRE *4F3* (1km S Rural) *47.85643, 2.22426* **FFCC Camping de la Maltournée, Route de Châteauneuf, 45110 Châteauneuf-sur-Loire [02 38 58 42 46 or 06 32 11 41 13 (mob); contact@camping-chateauneufsurloire.fr; www.camping-chateauneufsurloire.com]** S fr Chateauneuf cent, cross rv on D11; take 1st L, site in 300m on S bank of Rv Loire. Lge, pt shd, wc (htd); chem disp; mv service pnt; shwrs inc; EHU (10A) €4.20; lndry; shop nr; snacks; playgrnd; wifi; 75% statics; dogs €1.35; adv bkg acc; quiet; canoeing; CKE/CCI. "Well-kept, busy site; helpful, pleasant staff; clean, modern san facs; chem disp v basic via narr pipe; some m'van pitches beside rv; conv Orléans; security barrier; poss ssn workers; gd cycling base for Evro Velo." ♦ 15 Apr-31 Oct. € 18.00 2018*

CHATEAUNEUF SUR LOIRE

CHATEAUNEUF SUR LOIRE *4F3* (9km W Urban) 47.86884, 2.11597 **Camping de l'Isle aux Moulins, Rue du 44ème Régiment d'Infanterie,** 45150 Jargeau [02 38 59 70 04 or 02 54 22 26 61 (LS); camping.jargeau@orange.fr; www.jargeau.fr] Exit Châteauneuf W on D960 dir Orléans; at St Denis-de l'Hôtel turn sharp L onto D921 to Jargeau over Loire bdge; immed after x-ing bdge turn R into Blvd Jeanne d'Arc sp Camping; in 200m cont strt on into Rue du 44ème Régiment d'Infanterie; site on R in 300m. Site clearly visible on R of bdge on W bank of rv. NB App rd & turning to site is v narr; do not arr 1200-1330 (lunch time) as parking diff. Lge, mkd, pt shd, pt sl, wc (htd); chem disp; mv service pnt; fam bthrm; shwrs inc; EHU (5A) €3.50; lndry; shop nr; rest nr; bar nr; bbq; playgrnd; twin axles; red long stay; entmnt; wifi; 2% statics; dogs €1.20; bus 500m; Eng spkn; adv bkg acc; quiet; ccard acc; bike hire; games area; rv fishing adj; CKE/CCI. "V pleasant rvside site; lge pitches amongst trees; friendly farming family; modern san facs; poss muddy when wet; pool adj; sh walk to sm town; conv for Orleans." ♦ 1 Apr-31 Oct. € 19.00   2015*

CHATEAUNEUF SUR SARTHE *4G1* (0km S Rural) 47.67745, -0.48673 **Camp Municipal du Port, Rue de la Gare,** 49330 Châteauneuf-sur-Sarthe [02 41 69 82 02 or 02 41 96 15 20; fax 02 41 96 15 29; tourismechateauneufsursarthe@wanadoo.fr; www.chateauneufsursarthe.fr] Site clearly sp in vill, 18km E of Le Lion-d'Angers. Access to site fr bdge. Sm, pt shd, wc; chem disp; shwrs inc; EHU (10A) €2.70 (long lead poss req); lndry; shop nr; rest nr; playgrnd; quiet; rv fishing adj; sailing; CKE/CCI. "Attractive area; lge pitches; clean facs but poss stretched high ssn; warden on site am & pm; v few elec points." 1 May-30 Sep. € 7.00   2013*

⊞ **CHATEAUPONSAC** *7A3* (0km SW Rural) 46.13163, 1.27083 **Camping De La Gartempe, Ave de Ventenat,** 87290 Chateauponsac [05 55 76 55 33; campingdelagartempe@gmail.com; www.campingdelagartempe.fr] Fr N exit A20 junc 23.1 sp Châteauponsac; go thro vill, well sp on L on rvside. Fr S exit A20 junc 24 sp Châteauponsac & then as above. Sm, hdg, mkd, pt shd, terr, wc (htd); chem disp; shwrs inc; EHU (6A) €3 (poss rev pol); lndry; shop nr; rest; snacks; bar; playgrnd; pool; dogs €1; Eng spkn; adv bkg acc; kayaking; archery; CKE/CCI. "Pleasant site; gd san facs; pitches muddy in wet; not suitable lge m'vans; activities down steep hill by rv; poss noise fr parties in rest; children's activites; adj to holiday bungalows/gites; helpful owners; nice vill." € 16.00   2018*

CHATEAUROUX *4H2* (2km N Rural) 46.82368, 1.69496 **Camp Municipal Le Rochat-Belle Isle, Rue du Rochat,** 36000 Châteauroux [06 02 71 14 55 or 02 54 08 96 29; campinglerochat@gmail.com; www.camping-lerochat.fr] Exit A20 junc 13 onto D943/N143 S; foll sp Châteauroux; site sp bef town. Site on banks of Rv Indre, just S of Lac de Belle-Isle. Sp in town. Med, pt shd, wc; chem disp; mv service pnt; fam bthrm; shwrs inc; EHU (5-10A) inc; gas; lndry; shop nr; rest nr; bar nr; playgrnd; wifi; dogs €1.50; Eng spkn. "Leisure park adj with pool & windsurfing on lake; friendly welcome & helpful; gd, modern, clean san facs; poss music till late w/end high ssn; poss travellers; pleasant walk into town along rv; lge brocante mkt 1st Sun of month Oct-Jul; vg; nice site; excel family site." ♦ 25 Mar-23 Oct. € 20.00   2017*

CHATEAUROUX *4H2* (9km SW Rural) 46.74214, 1.61983 **Camping Les Grands Pins, Les Maisons-Neuves,** 36330 Velles [02 54 36 61 93; contact@les-grands-pins.fr; www.les-grands-pins.fr] Fr N exit A20 junc 14 dir Châteauroux; in 500m turn R onto D920 parallel with m'way. Foll sp Maisons-Neuves & site. Fr S exit A20 junc 15, turn R then L onto D920, site on R. Med, pt shd, pt sl, serviced pitches; wc; chem disp; shwrs inc; EHU (10A) €4.50 (poss rev pol, long lead req if in open field); rest; bar; playgrnd; pool; entmnt; wifi; dogs €1.50; Eng spkn; adv bkg acc; quiet; ccard acc; site clsd w/end 1 Nov-14 Dec; tennis; CKE/CCI. "Gd, tidy site in pine forest; clean facs; gd rest; LS recep in rest; max weight m'van 3,500kg Oct-Apr - heavier acc in summer; vet in Châteauroux; excel NH nr m'way, some noise; nice site, pitches in the woods; san facs need attention; pleasant helpful staff; popular NH." ♦ 22 Mar-23 Oct. € 28.00   2014*

> **"I need an on-site restaurant"**
>
> We do our best to make sure site information is correct, but it is always best to check any must-have facilities are still available or will be open during your visit.

CHATEL DE NEUVRE *9A1* (1km NE Rural) 46.4131, 3.31884 **Camping Deneuvre, Route De Moulins,** 03500 Châtel-de-Neuvre [04 70 42 04 51; fax 09 72 25 62 63; campingdeneuvre@wanadoo.fr; www.camping-deneuvre.fr] S fr Moulins on D2009; sp N of vill on E side of D2009. Med, mkd, hdstg, pt shd, wc; chem disp; mv service pnt; fam bthrm; shwrs inc; EHU (4A) inc; gas; lndry; rest; snacks; bar; playgrnd; wifi; dogs €1; Eng spkn; adv bkg acc; quiet; canoe hire; CKE/CCI. "Site by Rv Allier in nature reserve; clean but not smart; useful NH without unhitching; friendly welcome; excel clean san facs; ltd facs LS; meals avail; splendid place for walking, fishing, cycling & birdwatching; diff ent/exit for lge o'fits; no twin axles." ♦ 1 Apr-30 Sep. € 20.00   2016*

CAMPING AU PORT PUNAY ★★★★

Cosy family campsite for 55 years now ! Partly under large trees at 300m from the sea. Luxurious sanitary block maintained to a high standard. An ideal choice for families with small children. Charming fisherman's village, good starting point to visit the islands of Ré and Aix and located in between the historical and tourist cities of La Rochelle and Rochefort. Châtelaillon and its surroundings can be easily discovered by bicycle. Wireless internet available. French, English, Dutch and German spoken.

Camping Au Port-Punay • Les Boucholeurs • 17340 CHATELAILLON-PLAGE
FRANCE • Tel. +33 (0)5 17 81 00 00 • Fax +33 (0)5 46 56 86 44
www.camping-port-punay.com • Email contact@camping-port-punay.com

⊞ **CHATEL DE NEUVRE** 9A1 (0km W Rural) 46.40320, 3.31350 Canoe Camping la Courtine, 7 Rue de St Laurant, 03500 Châtel-de-Neuvre [04 70 42 06 21; fax 04 70 42 82 89; mail@camping-lacourtine.com; www.camping-lacourtine.com] Fr N on D2009 to cent of vill, turn L at x-rds onto D32; site in 500m. Sm, mkd, hdstg, pt shd, wc (htd); chem disp; mv service pnt; fam bthrm; shwrs inc; EHU (6-10A) €3-5 (poss rev pol); lndry; shop nr; rest nr; snacks; bar; playgrnd; wifi; TV; dogs free; Eng spkn; adv bkg acc; quiet; CKE/CCI. "Friendly welcome; untidy ent masks v nice site; German family-owned site; access to Rv Allier for canoeing, fishing; walking in nature reserve; liable to flood & poss clsd LS, phone ahead to check; conv LS NH; lovely woodland setting." ♦
€ 17.00 2018*

CHATEL MONTAGNE 9A1 (1km W Rural) 46.11526, 3.67700 Camping Retro Passion, La Croix Cognat, 03250 Chatel Montagne [04 70 59 31 38; campingretropassion@gmail.com; www.camping-retro-passion.fr] SW fr Lapalisse on D7, in 15km L on D25 to Chatel Montagne. Site on L bef vill. Sm, mkd, pt shd, pt sl, terr, wc; chem disp; mv service pnt; fam bthrm; shwrs; EHU (6A); lndry; snacks; bar; bbq; pool; paddling pool; twin axles; wifi; TV; 5% statics; dogs; Eng spkn; adv bkg acc; quiet; games area; games rm; tennis 100m; bike hire; CKE/CCI. "Vg." ♦
15 Apr-31 Oct. € 18.00 2015*

CHATELAILLON PLAGE 7A1 (2km N Urban) 46.08632, -1.09489 Camping L'Océan, Ave d'Angoulins, 17340 Châtelaillon-Plage [05 46 56 87 97; reception@oceancamping.fr; www.oceancamping.fr] Fr La Rochelle take D602 to Châtelaillon-Plage, site sp on L in 300m (after passing g'ge & L'Abbaye camp site). Med, mkd, hdg, wc; chem disp; fam bthrm; shwrs inc; EHU (10A) €5; lndry; shop nr; rest nr; bar nr; bbq; pool; beach sand 500m; dogs €2; phone; bus; Eng spkn; ccard acc; waterslide; ice. "Very nice, excel site; gd cycle rtes; top class facs; occasional noise fr rlwy & clay pigeon range; park & ride 400m; beautiful man made lake/beach; new owner (2017)." ♦
20 May-23 Sep. € 33.00 2017*

CHATELAILLON PLAGE 7A1 (3km SE Coastal) 46.05491, -1.08331 Camping Au Port Punay, Les Boucholeurs, Allée Bernard Moreau, 17340 Châtelaillon-Plage [05 17 81 00 00; fax 05 46 56 86 44; contact@camping-port-punay.com; www.camping-port-punay.com] Fr N exit D137 La Rochell-Rochefort rd onto D109; strt on at 1st rndabt, L at 2nd rndabt; then cont for 2.8km to end (harbour); turn L, keep R along narr one-way st; at next junc to L, site sp. Fr S exit D137 onto D203 sp Les Boucholeurs; at rndabt in 1km foll site sp to edge of Châtelaillon & turn R, foll sp. Site in 500m. Lge, pt shd, wc; fam bthrm; shwrs inc; EHU (10A) €5; gas; lndry; shop nr; rest; snacks; bar; playgrnd; pool; beach sand 500m; entmnt; wifi; TV; 25% statics; dogs €2.50; Eng spkn; adv bkg acc; quiet; bike hire; games area. "Busy but quiet site; immac san facs; friendly, energetic, helpful owners; steel pegs req; sm pitches; excel; lovely area & location."
28 Apr-24 Sep. € 37.00 2017*

See advertisement

CHATILLON COLIGNY 4F3 (1km S Rural) 47.81717, 2.84447 Camp Municipal La Lancière, Rue de la Lancière, 45230 Châtillon-Coligny [02 38 92 54 73 or 06 16 09 30 26 (mob); lalanciere@wanadoo.fr] N fr Briare twd Montargis on N7; E fr Les Bézards on D56 twd Châtillon-Coligny; site sp on ent town on R immed bef canal bdge. Fr town cross Canal de Briare on D93 twd Bléneau; immed turn S along canal rd sp Camping & Marina. Med, mkd, pt shd, wc; chem disp; shwrs inc; EHU (3-6A) €2-3.10 (poss long lead req & rev pol); lndry; shop nr; rest nr; bar nr; playgrnd; pool; 25% statics; dogs; quiet; games area; rv fishing; CKE/CCI. "Attractive, peaceful, tidy site; many lge pitches; clean, dated facs; site yourself, warden calls; gd walking/cycling along canal & historic vill; superb site for simple caravaning, excel value." 1 Apr-30 Sep.
€ 10.00 2013*

CHATILLON EN DIOIS

CHATILLON EN DIOIS 9D3 (1km E Urban) 44.69450, 5.48817 **Camp Municipal Les Chaussières, 26410 Châtillon-en-Diois [04 75 21 10 30 or 04 75 21 14 44 (Mairie); fax 04 75 21 18 78; camping.chatillonendiois@wanadoo.fr; www.camping-chatillonendiois.com]** Fr Die take D93 S for 6km then L on D539 to Châtillon (8km) site sp on R on ent to town. Med, mkd, pt shd, wc; chem disp; mv service pnt; shwrs inc; EHU (10A) €3.60; shop nr; bar nr; bbq; playgrnd; entmnt; 30% statics; dogs €2.10; phone; Eng spkn; adv bkg acc; quiet; ccard acc; ice; canoeing; fishing; cycling; horseriding; tennis; CKE/CCI. "Wardens off site 1130- 1630; pool adj; pleasant sweet site, wardens friendly and helpful." 1 Apr-1 Nov. € 25.70   2014*

> **"Satellite navigation makes touring much easier"**
>
> Remember most sat navs don't know if you're towing or in a larger vehicle – always use yours alongside maps and site directions.

CHATILLON SUR CHALARONNE 9A2 (1km SE Urban) 46.11622, 4.96172 **FFCC Camp Municipal du Vieux Moulin, Ave Jean Jaurès, 01400 Châtillon-sur-Chalaronne [04 74 55 04 79; fax 04 74 55 13 11; campingvieuxmoulin@orange.fr; www.camping-vieuxmoulin.com]** Exit A6 junc 30 to Châtillon-sur-Chalaronne; pick up D7 on S side of vill; site on R in 400m. Ave Jean Jaurès is pt of D7. Site sp in town. Med, hdg, hdstg, shd, wc; chem disp; fam bthrm; shwrs inc; EHU (10A) €4 (long lead req on some pitches); lndry; shop nr; rest nr; snacks; bar nr; playgrnd; 50% statics; dogs €2; phone; adv bkg acc; quiet; ccard acc; fishing; CKE/CCI. "Lovely site in picturesque area; helpful warden; immac facs, ltd LS; check office opening hrs for early dep; leisure cent adj; if office clsd ring bell, warden will open barrier; lovely medieval town cent; pool adj inc; excel model rlwy; bar adj; mkt Sat; site remains excel, new municipal pool under construction next door." ♦ 1 May-30 Sep. € 23.00   2014*

CHATILLON SUR INDRE 4H2 (1km N Rural) 46.99116, 1.17382 **Les Rives de L'Indre (formerly municipal), Rue de Moulin de la Grange, 36700 Châtillon-sur-Indre [07 61 39 81 62 or 02 54 38 17 86; camping-chatillon-sur-indre@orange.fr; www.chatillon-sur-indre.fr]** Site well sp in vill. N twd Loches then foll sp. Med, mkd, hdg, pt shd, wc; shwrs inc; EHU (6A) €3; shop nr; rest nr; bbq; playgrnd; wifi; dogs; quiet; CKE/CCI. "Lovely, relaxed, well-kept site; friendly, helpful warden; 4 chalets; gd, clean san facs; conv Loire chateaux; gd birdwatching area; interesting old town; htd pool 400m (proper sw trunks only); lge mkt Fri; excel value; call warden if barrier clsd; warden onsite 0800-1100/1630-2000." ♦ 1 Apr-31 Oct. € 12.00   2017*

CHATILLON SUR SEINE 6F1 (1km E Urban) 47.85955, 4.57975 **Camp Municipal Louis Rigoly, Esplanade Saint Vorles, 21400 Châtillon-sur-Seine [03 80 91 03 05 or 03 80 91 13 19 (LS); fax 03 80 91 21 46; contact@camping-chatillonsurseine.com; camping-chatillonsurseine.com]** Fr N, cross rv bdge (Seine); cont approx 400m twd town cent; at lge metal fountain forming rndabt turn L, foll sp to site. Fr S turn R & foll camping sp. Rec lge o'fits proceed thro town to metal fountain. Turn R & foll sp to site. Med, mkd, hdg, pt shd, pt sl, wc; chem disp; mv service pnt; shwrs inc; EHU (6A) €2.30-4.65; gas; lndry; shop nr; playgrnd; pool; wifi; dogs; Eng spkn; adv bkg acc; quiet; jacuzzi; tennis; fishing; CKE/CCI. "Pretty site adj park; clean, tidy, well-spaced pitches; helpful, welcoming warden; htd pool adj; excel, clean new san facs; easy walk to old town & famous museum housing Celtic Vix treasures; vg; excel disabled san facs." ♦ 1 Apr-30 Sep. € 17.30   2017*

CHATRE, LA 7A4 (3km N Rural) 46.60131, 1.97808 **Camp Municipal Solange-Sand, Rue du Pont, 36400 Montgivray [02 54 06 10 34 or 02 54 06 10 36; fax 02 54 06 10 39; mairie.montgivray@wanadoo.fr]** Fr La Châtre take rd to Montgivray, foll camping sp. Fr Châteauroux on D943 SE twd La Châtre turn R 2km S of Nohant on D72. Site behind church. Med, mkd, pt shd, wc; chem disp; shwrs inc; EHU (10A) inc (poss rev pol); lndry; bbq; dogs; quiet; CKE/CCI. "Pleasant site in chateau grnds; new san facs (2016); gd access; warden calls am & pm; gd rest adj; gd walks; quiet but occ noise fr nrby hall; excel; v gd for stop over or sh stay; welcoming staff." ♦ 15 Mar-15 Oct. € 12.40   2017*

CHAUMONT 6F1 (1km NW Urban) 48.11790, 5.13334 **Camp Municipal Parc Ste Marie, Rue des Tanneries, 52000 Chaumont [03 25 32 11 98 or 03 25 30 60 27 (Mairie); fax 03 25 30 59 50; sports@ville-chaumont.fr]** Site on Chaumont W by-pass joining N19 Troyes rd to N67 St Dizier rd. Do not try to app fr town cent. Exit A5 at exit 24, foll sp to town cent, bef town foll sp to site. Sm, hdg, mkd, pt shd, pt sl, wc cont; chem disp; shwrs inc; EHU (10A) inc (poss long lead req); shop nr; snacks; playgrnd; 20% statics; dogs €1.50; CKE/CCI. "Rec arr early; care needed with steep access to some sl pitches; friendly warden; ent barrier under warden control at all times; gd NH; doesn't acc m'vans." 2 May-30 Sep. € 14.00   2015*

CHAUMONT SUR LOIRE 4G2 (1km NE Rural) 47.48444, 1.19417 **Camp Municipal Grosse Grève, Ave des Trouillas, 41150 Chaumont-sur-Loire [02 54 20 95 22 or 02 54 20 98 41 (Mairie); fax 02 54 20 99 61; mairie.chaumontsloire@wanadoo.fr; www.camping-chaumont-sur-loire.com]** Fr N side of rv on D952 cross bdge to Chaumont on D1, turn R immed & R under bdge. Site sp in vill on D751. Med, pt shd, wc (htd); chem disp; shwrs inc; EHU (6-16A) €2-3.50 (poss long lead req); lndry; rest nr; bar nr; bbq; playgrnd; canoeing; tennis; fishing; bike hire; horseriding; CKE/CCI. "Pleasant site by rv; gd, clean san facs; no twin axles; interesting chateau; cycle track along Loire; gd value; excel." ♦ 29 Apr-30 Sep. € 12.00   2016*

CHAUVIGNY *7A3* (1km E Urban) *46.57072, 0.65326* **Camp Municipal de la Fontaine, Rue de la Fontaine, 86300 Chauvigny [05 49 45 99 10; fax 05 49 46 40 60; camping-chauvigny@cg86.fr; www.chauvigny.fr]** N151 fr Poitiers to Chauvigny. Turn L in cent Chauvigny just bef gate. Site well sp fr Chauvigny. Med, pt shd, wc (htd); chem disp; mv service pnt; fam bthrm; shwrs; EHU (15A) inc; lndry; shop nr; bbq; playgrnd; dogs €1.80; adv bkg acc; tennis 1km; bike hire; CKE/CCI. "Popular; well-kept; well-run site adj park & lake; views of castle; lge pitches; helpful, friendly staff; excel immac san facs; o'night m'vans area; delightful walk to cent; mkts Tue, Thur & Sat; a real find; gd value; rec; vg; interesting town; gd touring base; €20 for barrier key; new ehu pnts & new barrier(2018)." ♦ 1 Apr-30 Sep. € 16.40 2018*

⊞ **CHEF BOUTONNE** *7A2* (2km W Rural) *46.10767, -0.09342* **Camping Le Moulin, 1 Route de Niort, 79110 Chef-Boutonne [05 49 29 73 46 or 06 89 60 00 49 (mob); info@campingchef.com; www.campingchef.com]** Fr D950 to or fr Poitiers, turn E onto D740 to Chef-Boutonne, site on R. Fr N10 turn onto D948 to Sauzé-Vaussais then L onto D1 to Chef-Boutonne; then take D740 dir Brioux-sur-Boutonne; site on L. Sm, hdstg, mkd, hdg, pt shd, wc (htd); chem disp; fam bthrm; shwrs inc; EHU (10A) inc; lndry; shop nr; rest; snacks; bar; bbq (charcoal, elec, gas); playgrnd; pool (htd); red long stay; twin axles; entmnt; wifi; 10% statics; dogs €1.50; Eng spkn; adv bkg acc; quiet; ccard acc; ice; CKE/CCI. "Well-kept site; lge pitches; friendly, helpful British owners; v gd rest; much bird life; conv Futuroscope & La Rochelle; vg; clean san facs refurbed with disabled facs (2018); peaceful; mv service pnt 1km; rest & bar refurb (2018); site acc rallies; excel; chge for wifi." ♦ € 21.60 2018*

CHEMILLE *2G4* (2km SW Rural) *47.20182, -0.73486* **FFCC Camping Coulvée, Route de Cholet, 49120 Chemillé [02 41 30 42 42 or 02 41 30 39 97 (Mairie); fax 02 41 30 39 00; camping-chemille-49@wanadoo.fr; www.camping-coulvee-chemille.com]** Fr Chemillé dir Cholet on D160, turn R in 1km. Sm, hdg, pt shd, terr, wc; chem disp; mv service pnt; shwrs inc; EHU (10A) €3.60; lndry; bar; bbq; playgrnd; beach sand; sw; red long stay; dogs €1.70; Eng spkn; adv bkg acc; quiet; CKE/CCI. "Clean facs; helpful staff; gd pitches, soft when wet; poss unrel opening dates; pedalos; mkt Thurs; mkd cycling and walking rtes fr site." ♦ 1 May-15 Sep. € 23.60 2016*

CHENONCEAUX *4G2* (2km E Rural) *47.32905, 1.08816* **Camping de l'Ecluse, Route de la Plage, 37150 Chisseaux [02 47 23 87 10 or 06 15 83 21 20 (mob); sandrine@campingdelecluse-37.fr; www.campingdelecluse-37.fr]** E fr Chenonceaux on D176; cross bdge; immed hard R & foll rv bank; site in 300m. Med, mkd, pt shd, wc; chem disp; mv service pnt; shwrs inc; EHU (16A) €3.90 (rev pol); lndry; shop nr; snacks; bar; playgrnd; dogs €1.50; phone; Eng spkn; adv bkg acc; quiet; ccard acc; canoeing; watersports; fishing; CKE/CCI. "Rv trips; fishing; gd walking; some rd/rlwy noise; gd." ♦ 1 Mar-31 Oct. € 12.50 2014*

CHENONCEAUX *4G2* (2km S Rural) *47.32765, 1.08936* **Camping Le Moulin Fort, Pont de Chisseaux, 37150 Francueil [02 47 23 86 22; fax 02 47 23 90 83; lemoulinfort@wanadoo.fr; www.lemoulinfort.com]** Exit A85 junc 11 N, then take D976 E dir Montrichard; site on S bank of Rv Cher just off D976. Fr Tours take D976 sp Vierzon; keep on D976 by-passing Bléré until sm rndabt (5km) where site sp to L twd rv. Take sm rd on R to site, bef actually x-ing bdge. Site well sp. Med, hdg, mkd, pt shd, wc; chem disp; fam bthrm; shwrs inc; EHU (6A) €4 (long lead poss req); gas; lndry; shop; rest; snacks; bar; bbq (charcoal, gas); playgrnd; pool; paddling pool; entmnt; wifi; TV; dogs €3; Eng spkn; adv bkg rec; ccard acc; games rm; bike hire; fishing; CKE/CCI. "Lovely, well-kept site on rv bank; beautiful area; friendly, helpful British owners; gd san facs; easy access most pitches; many sm & v shady pitches; no o'fits over 8m high ssn; lge o'fits check in adv; some pitches suitable for lge o'fits; footpath by rv with view of chateau; gd cycle rtes; poss security probs due access to site fr rv bank; Fri mkt Montrichard & Sun mkt Amboise; excel; well laid site to rv view for many pitches." ♦ 12 Apr-25 Sep. € 36.00 2014*

CHERBOURG *1C4* (18km NE Coastal) *49.6928, -1.4387* **Camping De La Plage, 2 Village de Fréval, 50840 Fermanville [02 33 54 38 84; campingdelaplage.fermanville@wanadoo.fr; www.campingdelaplage-fermanville.com]** Fr Cherbourg on D116 dir Barfleur, site in 12km on L. Med, hdg, unshd, wc; chem disp; shwrs inc; EHU (10A); snacks; bar; playgrnd; beach 300m, sand; 70% statics; dogs €2.50; Eng spkn; adv bkg req; quiet. "Friendly owner; conv for ferry & D-Day landing beaches; poss unrel opening dates; vg." 1 Apr-15 Oct. € 20.50 2018*

CHERBOURG *1C4* (10km E Coastal) *49.66720, -1.48772* **Camping L'Anse du Brick, 18 L'Anse du Brick, 50330 Maupertus-sur-Mer [02 33 54 33 57; fax 02 33 54 49 66; contact@adbcamping.com; www.anse-du-brick.com or www.les-castels.com]** At rndabt at port take 2nd exit sp Caen, Rennes & Mont St Michel; at 2nd rndabt take 3rd exit sp Caen & Mont St Michel (N13); at 3rd rndabt take 2nd exit onto dual c'way sp St Lô, Caen (N13), Bretteville-sur-Mer; exit on D116 & foll sp thro Bretteville-en-Saire (take care lge speed hump in Le Becquet); turn R for site just after R-hand blind bend & turning for Maupertus; up v steep incline. Med, mkd, hdg, shd, sl, terr, serviced pitches; wc; chem disp; mv service pnt; fam bthrm; shwrs inc; EHU (10A) inc (poss rev pol); gas; lndry; shop; rest; snacks; bar; bbq; playgrnd; pool (htd); paddling pool; beach sand adj; wifi; TV; dogs €6; adv bkg rec; quiet; ccard acc; archery; waterslide; bike hire; tennis; games rm; CKE/CCI. "Attractive, well-kept site in beautiful setting; conv ferry; gd clean san facs; some pitches for lge o'fits; no o'fits over 8m; conv Landing Beaches, Barfleur, coastal nature reserve." ♦ 1 Apr-29 Sep. € 52.50 2013*

CHERBOURG

CAMPING LES SAULES

In the heart of the Loire Valley, you will discover our family campsite and enjoy unforgettable holidays in a preserved and protected environment. Close to the castle of Cheverny, the castle of Chambord, The domaine of Chaumont sur Loire, the zoopark of Beauval...You will appreciate our services and enjoy the 550 km of cycling tracks of the " Châteaux à vélo ".

Les Saules F. 41700 CHEVERNY
Tel. 33 (0)254 799 001
www.camping-cheverny.com
contact@camping-cheverny.com

Sites & Paysages
LES SAULES
CONNECTÉS À LA NATURE

⊞ **CHERBOURG** *1C4* (4km NW Urban/Coastal) *49.65576, -1.65257* Camp Municipal de la Saline, Rue Jean Bart, 50120 Equeurdreville-Hainneville [02 33 93 88 33 or 02 33 53 96 00 (Mairie); fax 02 33 93 12 70; mairie-equeurdreville@dialoleane.com; www.equeurdreville.com] Fr ferry terminal foll D901 & sp Beaumont-Hague. On dual c'way beside sea look out for site sp to L at traff lts. Med, mkd, hdg, hdstg, pt shd, pt sl, terr, wc (htd); chem disp; shwrs inc; EHU (10A) €4.56; lndry; shop nr; rest nr; bar nr; beach sand adj; 50% statics; dogs €0.50; phone; adv bkg acc; fishing; CKE/CCI. "Sea views; boules & skateboard park adj; aquatic cent 500m; mv service pnt nr; cycle path to town; secured at night; excel NH for ferry." ♦ € 17.50   2016*

CHEVERNY *4G2* (3km S Rural) *47.47798, 1.45070* Camping Les Saules, 102 Route de Contres, 41700 Cheverny [02 54 79 90 01; fax 02 54 79 28 34; contact@camping-cheverny.com; www.camping-cheverny.com] Exit A10 junc 17 dir Blois Sud onto D765 to Romorantin. At Cour-Cheverny foll sp Cheverny & chateau. Fr S on D956 turn R onto D102 just N of Contres, site on L just bef Cheverny. Well sp fr all dirs. Lge, mkd, shd, wc (htd); chem disp; mv service pnt; fam bthrm; shwrs inc; EHU (10A) €3.50 (poss long lead req); gas; lndry; shop; rest; snacks; bar; bbq; playgrnd; pool (htd); paddling pool; red long stay; wifi; TV; 2% statics; dogs €2; phone; Eng spkn; adv bkg rec; quiet; ccard acc; fishing; golf nr; games rm; tennis; excursions; bike hire; CKE/CCI. "Beautiful, well-run site; friendly, welcoming, helpful owners; excel san facs; castle adj; excel pool; all pitches under trees; muddy after heavy rain; many excel cycle & walking rtes nr; Cheverny chateau worth visit; little train & boat rides; excel; gd rest." ♦ 1 Apr-17 Sep. € 36.00   2016*

See advertisement

CHINON *4G1* (1km SW Rural) *47.16397, 0.23377* Camping de L'Ile Auger, Quai Danton, 37500 Chinon [02 47 93 08 35; fax 02 47 93 91 15; camping-chinon@cc-cvl.fr; www.camping-chinon.com] On S side of rv at bdge. Fr S foll sp Chinon St Jacques; when app 2nd bdge on 1-way 'loop', avoid R lane indicated for x-ing bdge & cont strt past S end of main bdge to site on R. Fr N foll sp 'Centre Ville' round castle, cross bdge, site on R. Well sp in town & opp castle. Lge, hdg, mkd, pt shd, wc; chem disp; mv service pnt; fam bthrm; shwrs inc; EHU (12A) inc (poss rev pol); lndry; shop nr; playgrnd; red long stay; wifi; TV (pitch); dogs €1.20; phone; quiet; ccard acc; canoe hire; CKE/CCI. "Excel, well-kept site in gd location; twin axles discretionary; poss midge prob; poss travellers; gd cycle rtes; gd views of chateau; rec; automatic ent barrier; htd pool 300m; well laid out; new san facs (2017); 5min walk to town; exc value; hg rec boat trip on Rv Vienne." ♦ 1 Apr-3 Oct. € 18.50   2018*

CHINON *4G1* (14km NW Rural) *47.20693, 0.08127* Camping Belle Rive, 2 Route de Chinon, 37500 Candes-St Martin [02 47 97 46 03; fax 02 47 95 80 95; contact@camping-candes.fr; www.camping-candes.fr] Fr Chinon take D751. Site on R bef junc with D7, on S bank of Rv Vienne. Med, mkd, pt shd, wc; shwrs; EHU (16A) €3.10; lndry; shop nr; snacks; bar; playgrnd; sw nr; wifi; dogs €1.30; adv bkg acc; quiet; fishing adj; CKE/CCI. "Pleasant rvside site; san facs on 2 floors, need update & poss stretched if site busy; conv Saumur & chateaux; excel location; scruffy & ill kempt site." ♦ 15 Apr-30 Sep. € 16.00   2016*

CIOTAT, LA *10F3* (4km NE Coastal) *43.18733, 5.65810* Campsite La Baie des Anges (formerly Les Oliviers), Chemin des Plaines Baronnes, 13600 La Ciotat [04 42 83 15 04; fax 04 42 83 94 43; info@homair.com; www.camping-laciotat.fr or www.homair.com] Fr La Ciotat, foll D559 coast rd sp Bandol & Toulon. Site in 4km, look for lge sp on L. Caution x-ing dual c'way. V lge, shd, pt sl, terr, wc; chem disp; shwrs inc; EHU (6A) (poss rev pol); gas; lndry; shop nr; rest nr; bar nr; playgrnd; pool; beach shgl 800m; 80% statics; dogs; bus 300m; Eng spkn; adv bkg acc; ccard acc; tennis; CKE/CCI. "Sea views many pitches; friendly staff; gd touring base; v nice." ♦ 12 Apr-1 Oct. € 35.00   2014*

CLAMECY

Camping ★★★ JURA
Domaine du Surchauffant
www.camping-surchauffant.fr
Le Pont de la Pyle
39270 LA TOUR DU MEIX
Tél. : +33(0)3 84 25 41 08

France

CIVRAY *7A2 (1km NE Urban) 46.15835, 0.30169*
Camping de Civray, Route de Roche, 86400 Civray [05 17 34 50 02 or 06 08 51 88 80; campingdecivray@ gmail.com; www.camping-de-civray.com] Civray 9km E of N10 halfway bet Poitiers & Angoulême. Site outside town SE of junc of D1 & D148. Sp on D148 & on S by-pass. Avoid town cent narr rds. Med, pt shd, pt sl, wc; chem disp; mv service pnt; shwrs; EHU (6-10A) €3 (poss long lead req); lndry; shop nr; rest; snacks; bar; bbq; playgrnd; pool (htd); sw nr; wifi; 50% statics; dogs; Eng spkn; quiet; ccard acc; golf; bike hire; fishing adj; CKE/CCI. "Pleasant rvside site, walk to town; pitches soft when wet; vg rest; conv town cent; mkt Wed; vg; new owners; ltd san facs." 10 Apr-2 Nov. € 15.00   2017*

CLAIRVAUX LES LACS *6H2 (1km S Rural) 46.56761, 5.75480* **Camping La Grisière et Europe Vacances, Chemin Langard, 39130 Clairvaux-les-Lacs [03 84 25 80 48; fax 03 84 25 22 34; bailly@la-grisiere.com; www.la-grisiere.com]** Turn S off D678 in Clairvaux opp church onto D118; fork R in 500m & foll site sps to lake. Sp in vill. Camping La Grisière ent after Camping Les Lacs. V lge, mkd, pt shd, pt sl, wc (htd); chem disp; mv service pnt; fam bthrm; shwrs inc; EHU (6-10A) €2.60; lndry; shop; snacks; bar; bbq; playgrnd; sw nr; wifi; TV; 5% statics; dogs €1; phone; bus 700m; Eng spkn; quiet; ccard acc; bike hire; watersports; tennis 1km; fishing; canoe hire; CKE/CCI. "Lovely views in beautiful area; lge pitches; excel site; quiet; few facs." ♦ 1 May-30 Sep. € 25.00   2016*

CLAIRVAUX LES LACS *6H2 (10km SW Rural) 46.52311, 5.67350* **Camping de Surchauffant, Pont de la Pyle, 39270 La Tour-du-Meix [03 84 25 41 08; fax 03 84 25 55 68; info@camping-surchauffant. fr; www.camping-surchauffant.fr]** Fr Clairvaux S on D27 or D49 to D470. Foll sp Lac de Vouglans, site sp. Med, mkd, pt shd, pt sl, wc; chem disp; mv service pnt; shwrs inc; EHU (6A) €3; lndry; shop nr; rest; snacks; bar; bbq; playgrnd; pool; paddling pool; entmnt; TV; 10% statics; dogs €1.60; Eng spkn; adv bkg acc; quiet; ccard acc; watersports; sailing. "Vg facs; lovely location; dir access to lake; hiiking trails." ♦ 22 Apr-19 Sep. € 19.00   2016*

See advertisement

CLAIRVAUX LES LACS *6H2 (7km W Rural) 46.59976, 5.68824* **Camping Beauregard, 2 Grande Rue, 39130 Mesnois [03 84 48 32 51; reception@juracampingbeauregard.com; www. juracampingbeauregard.com]** S fr Lons-le-Saunier on D52/D678, about 1km bef Pont-de-Poitte turn L on D151. Site 1km on L opp rd junc to Pont-de-Poitte. Lge, mkd, hdg, hdstg, pt shd, pt sl, terr, wc (htd); chem disp; fam bthrm; shwrs inc; EHU (6A) €4 (poss long lead req); gas; lndry; shop nr; rest nr; bar nr; playgrnd; pool (htd); beach sand 800m; 10% statics; dogs €2.20; Eng spkn; adv bkg acc; quiet; tennis; bike hire; games rm. "Super site, clean & well-run; different sized pitches; excel san facs, ltd LS; excel rest; kayaking nr; poss muddy when wet; new indoor pool with jacuzzi and sauna (2012), extremely gd quality." ♦ 1 Apr-30 Sep. € 25.50   2012*

CLAMECY *4G4 (5km NE Rural) 47.51665, 3.48001* **Camping Le Bois Joli, 2 Route de Villeprenoy, 89480 Andryes [03 86 81 70 48; info@campingauboisjoli. com; www.campingauboisjoli.com]** S on N151 fr Auxerre to Coulanges-sur-Yonne; W on D39 to Andryes. Foll sps 'Camping Andryes'; site in 500m after vill. Med, mkd, shd, terr, wc (htd); chem disp; fam bthrm; shwrs inc; EHU (10A) €4.80 (poss rev pol); gas; lndry; shop; bbq; playgrnd; pool; sw nr; wifi; TV; 10% statics; dogs €3.50; phone; Eng spkn; quiet; ccard acc; fishing 2km; bike hire; tennis; CKE/CCI. "Dutch owners; beautiful countryside; boat hire 2km; gd pitches; muddy in rain; excel facs & site; quiet; nice site in wooded area." ♦ 1 Apr-31 Oct. € 25.00   2014*

CLAMECY *4G4 (1km SE Urban) 47.45133, 3.52770* **Camp Municipal du Pont-Picot, Rue de Chevroche, 58500 Clamecy [07 86 86 14 31; clamecycamping@ orange.fr; www.clamecy.fr]** On N151 fr S, exit N151 at rndabt 3km SW of town cent, cross level x-ing then R at rndabt on D23, take 1st L, site sp in 2.4km. Narr app rd. App fr N or E thro town not rec. Do not use sat nav thro town. Med, pt shd, pt sl, wc; chem disp; shwrs inc; EHU (6A) inc; lndry; shop nr; playgrnd; sw; Eng spkn; quiet; CKE/CCI. "Pleasant, peaceful site bet rv & canal in beautiful location; friendly, helpful staff; facs poss inadequate when busy; town 10 min walk on towpath; gd cycling; gd NH; narr bdge just bef ent." ♦ 1 Apr-30 Sep. € 18.00   2018*

CLAMECY

CLAMECY *4G4* (8km SE Rural) *47.41390, 3.60828* Camp Municipal Les Fontaines, 58530 Brèves [03 86 24 25 26; mairie-breves@wanadoo.fr; www.vaux-yonne.com] On D985 (Clamecy-Corbigny) at Brèves. Both app clearly sp. Med, unshd, pt sl, wc; chem disp; shwrs inc; EHU (6A) €2; lndry; shop; bbq; playgrnd; 4% statics; dogs; phone; adv bkg rec; CKE/CCI. "Quiet site in pretty area nr Rv Yonne & canal; friendly staff; grnd soft after heavy rain; ltd level sites for m'van vg."
♦ 1 Jun-30 Sep. € 8.60   2014*

CLAYETTE, LA *9A2* (1km E Urban) *46.29159, 4.32020* Camping des Bruyères, 9 Route de Gibles, 71800 La Clayette [03 85 28 09 15 or 03 86 37 95 83 (LS); contact@campingbruyeres.com; http://campingbruyeres.com] Site on D79, 100m fr D987 & lake. Med, mkd, hdg, hdstg, shd, sl, wc (htd); chem disp; mv service pnt; shwrs inc; EHU (6A) inc; gas; lndry; shop nr; bar nr; bbq; playgrnd; entmnt; wifi; 10% statics; dogs €1.60; phone; adv bkg acc; quiet; boating; games area; tennis; CKE/CCI. "Pleasant, well-kept site o'looking lake & chateau; friendly, helpful staff; gd-sized pitches; htd pool adj Jun-Aug inc; excel; 20 min walk to town; supmkt 10 min walk." ♦ 18 Apr-30 Sep. € 25.00   2014*

CLAYETTE, LA *9A2* (13km S Rural) *46.2011, 4.3391* FFCC Camping Les Feuilles, 18 Rue de Châtillon, 71170 Chauffailles [03 85 26 48 12; fax 03 85 26 55 02; campingchauffailles@gmail.com or chalets@chalets-decouverte.com; www.chauffailles.fr or www.chalets-decouverte.com] S fr La Clayette on D985 (dir Les Echarmeaux), turn R at camp sp down hill & cross Rv Botoret to site. Med, hdstg, mkd, pt shd, wc (htd); chem disp; mv service pnt; shwrs; EHU (5A) inc; lndry; shop nr; playgrnd; wifi; TV; Eng spkn; adv bkg req; quiet; games rm; tennis; fishing; CKE/CCI. "Attractive site; poss rallies May/June & Sep (poss noisy); gd san facs but hot water to shwrs & dishwashing only; easy walk to interesting town; pool adj; sep m'van Aire de Service adj rear ent."
1 May-30 Sep. € 19.00   2013*

CLECY *3D1* (1km E Rural) *48.91491, -0.47374* FFCC Camping Les Rochers Des Parcs, La Cour, 14570 Clécy [02 31 69 70 36; camping.normandie@gmail.com; www.camping-normandie-clecy.fr] Fr Condé take D562 dir Caen; turn R onto D133a sp Clécy & Le Vey; do not take turning to Clécy cent but cont downhill, past museum on L & then over bdge; turn R in 150m at campsite sp; site on R. Med, hdstg, mkd, pt shd, pt sl, wc (htd); mv service pnt; fam bthrm; shwrs inc; EHU (6A) €3.50; lndry; shop nr; rest nr; snacks; bar; bbq; playgrnd; red long stay; wifi; 10% statics; dogs €1.60; phone; Eng spkn; quiet; games area; bike hire; rv fishing. "Lovely rvside situation; friendly, helpful owner; facs poss stretched high ssn & ltd LS; excel cent for walking." ♦
1 Apr-30 Sep. € 23.00   2018*

CLERMONT FERRAND *9B1* (16km SE Rural) *45.70027, 3.16953* Camping Le Clos Auroy, Rue de la Narse, 63670 Orcet [04 73 84 26 97; www.camping-le-clos-auroy.com] S on A75 take exit 5 sp Orcet; foll D213 to Orcet for 2km, at rndabt onto D52, take 1st L, site on R. Do not foll SatNav to site. Med, mkd, hdstg, hdg, pt shd, terr, wc (htd); chem disp; mv service pnt; shwrs; EHU (10A) €5 (poss rev pol); gas; lndry; shop nr; snacks; bar; playgrnd; pool (htd); paddling pool; red long stay; entmnt; wifi; 10% statics; dogs €2.25; phone; Eng spkn; adv bkg acc; quiet; ccard acc; tennis; rv fishing 500m; CKE/CCI. "Excel, well-kept; site poss open all year; easy access; lge pitches, poss v high hedges; superb htd san facs; pitches by rv poss liable to flood; extra charge for sh stay m'vans; ltd fresh water points & diff to use for refill; vg winter site; interesting town; gd dog walks adj; snack & bar only open high ssn; vg value; helpful staff; gd site." ♦
€ 33.80   2017*

CLERMONT FERRAND *9B1* (9km SE Urban) *45.74015, 3.22247* Camp Municipal Le Pré des Laveuses, Rue des Laveuses, 63800 Cournon-d'Auvergne [04 73 84 81 30; fax 04 73 84 65 90; camping@cournon-auvergne.fr; www.cournon-auvergne.fr/camping] Fr S o'skts Clermont-Ferrand take D212 E to Cournon & foll sp in town; by Rv Allier, 1km E of Cournon. Lge, mkd, pt shd, wc; chem disp; fam bthrm; shwrs inc; EHU (5-10A) €3.30; lndry; shop; snacks; bar; playgrnd; pool (htd); paddling pool; sw nr; 40% statics; dogs €2.70; Eng spkn; quiet; ccard acc; fishing; boating; CKE/CCI. "Well-kept site - even LS; lge pitches; helpful manager; sports grnd adj; excel; clean new facs." ♦ 1 Apr-25 Oct. € 33.00   2014*

> **"There aren't many sites open at this time of year"**
>
> If you're travelling outside peak season remember to call ahead to check site opening dates – even if the entry says 'open all year'.

CLERMONT FERRAND *9B1* (6km SW Urban) *45.73866, 3.06168* Camp Municipal Le Chanset, Ave Jean-Baptiste Marrou, 63122 Ceyrat [04 73 61 30 73; camping.lechanset@wanadoo.fr; www.campingdeceyrat63.com] Exit A75 junc 2 onto D2089 dir Aubière/Beaumont. Foll sp Beaumont then in approx 7km at rndabt junc foll sp Ceyrat. Uphill into Ceyrat; curve R to traff lts; cross main rd & take L fork up hill. Site at top on R - turn poss diff so cont 50m for U-turn back to site. Lge, mkd, hdg, pt shd, pt sl, terr, wc (htd); chem disp; mv service pnt; fam bthrm; shwrs inc; EHU (10A) €4.50 (poss rev pol); gas; lndry; shop; rest; snacks; bar; bbq; playgrnd; pool (htd); red long stay; TV; 25% statics; dogs €1.80; phone; bus; Eng spkn; adv bkg acc; ccard acc; games rm; CKE/CCI. "Gd base for Clermont Ferrand - gd bus service; friendly, helpful staff; security barrier; shops & supmkt in Vill; late arr can park nr recep." ♦ € 17.00   2013*

CLERMONT FERRAND *9B1* (5km W Rural) *45.75845, 3.05453* **Camping Indigo Royat, Route de Gravenoire, 63130 Royat [04 73 35 97 05; fax 04 73 35 67 69; royat@camping-indigo.com; www.camping-indigo.com]** Site diff to find fr Clermont-Ferrand cent. Fr N, leave A71 at Clermont-Ferrand. Foll sp Chamalières/Royat, then sp Royat. Go under rlwy bdge & pass thermal park on L. At mini-rndabt go L & up hill. At statue, turn L & go up long hill. Look for site sp & turn R. Site on R. NB Do not go down steep rd with traff calming. NB sat nav directs up v narr rds & steep hills. Lge, hdstg, mkd, pt shd, terr, serviced pitches; wc (htd); chem disp; mv service pnt; fam bthrm; shwrs inc; EHU (10A) €5.20; gas; lndry; shop; rest; snacks; bar; bbq; playgrnd; pool (htd); paddling pool; entmnt; wifi; TV; 10% statics; dogs €4; phone; Eng spkn; adv bkg acc; quiet; ccard acc; bike hire; tennis; CKE/CCI. "Excel, clean, spacious, lovely site; set on hillside in trees; gd size earth pitches; views at top levels over Clermont; clean san facs; facs ltd in LS; conv touring base; new recep; vg." ♦ 24 Mar-2 Nov. € 40.00 2016*

⊞ **CLERMONT L'HERAULT** *10F1* (5km NW Rural) *43.64491, 3.38982* **Camp Municipal du Lac du Salagou, 34800 Clermont-l'Hérault [04 67 96 13 13; fax 04 67 96 32 12; contact@le-salagou.fr; www.le-salagou.fr]** Fr N9 S take D909 to Clermont-l'Hérault, foll sp to Lac du Salagou 1.5km after town sp. Fr by-pass foll sp Bédarieux. Well sp. Lge, mkd, pt shd, pt sl, wc (htd); chem disp; mv service pnt; shwrs inc; EHU (5-10A) €2.90-3.40; lndry; shop nr; rest; snacks; bbq; playgrnd; entmnt; TV; 80% statics; dogs €1.70; phone; Eng spkn; adv bkg acc; fishing; watersports; CKE/CCI. "Unique location; poss muddy LS & poss windy; facs dated; gd undeveloped beaches around lake; beautiful scenery." ♦ € 16.00 2013*

CLISSON *2H4* (1km N Urban) *47.09582, -1.28216* **Camp Municipal du Vieux Moulin, Rue de la Fontaine Câlin, Route de Nantes, 44190 Clisson [02 40 54 44 48 or 06 20 29 08 42 (mob); camping.clissonsevremaine.fr]** 1km NW of Clisson cent on main rd to Nantes, at rndabt. Look for old windmill nr ent on L of rd. Leclerc hypmkt on opp side of rd; site sp fr town cent. Narr ent. Sm, hdg, pt shd, pt sl, wc; chem disp; shwrs inc; EHU 10A inc; shop nr; rest nr; TV; dogs €1.12; Eng spkn; adv bkg acc; quiet; fishing adj; boating; horseriding adj; tennis adj; game rm. "Gd municipal site; lge pitches; gd clean san facs; if office clsd pitch self, book in later; picturesque town 15 min walk; bar 500m; hypmkt 500m; mkd walks; interesting old town with castle ruins; next to retail park; excel rest in town." ♦ 1 Mar-30 Nov. € 24.50 2018*

CLOYES SUR LE LOIR *4F2* (1km N Rural) *48.00240, 1.23304* **Parc de Loisirs Le Val Fleuri, Route de Montigny, 28220 Cloyes-sur-le-Loir [02 37 98 50 53; fax 02 37 98 33 84; info@val-fleuri.fr; www.val-fleuri.fr]** Located on L bank of Rv Loir off N10; site sp. Lge, hdg, pt shd, wc (htd); chem disp; fam bthrm; shwrs inc; EHU (5A) inc; lndry; shop; rest; snacks; bar; bbq; playgrnd; pool; twin axles; wifi; 50% statics; dogs €2; phone; Eng spkn; adv bkg acc; quiet; ccard acc; waterslide; bike hire; €3; CKE/CCI. "Facs gd for children but ltd LS; well-run, pleasant site in wooded valley; site fees inc use of sm leisure park, pedalos & rowing boats on Rv Loir; vg san facs." 15 Mar-15 Nov. € 38.00 2017*

> **"That's changed – Should I let the Club know?"**
>
> If you find something on site that's different from the site entry, fill in a report and let us know. See camc.com/europereport.

CLUNY *9A2* (1km E Urban) *46.43086, 4.66756* **Camp Municipal St Vital, 30 Rue de Griottons, 71250 Cluny [03 85 59 08 34; camping.st.vital@orange.fr; www.camping-cluny.blogspot.com]** E fr Cluny on D15 (sp Azé & Camping) across narr rv bdge; in 200m turn R into Rue de Griottonste; site on L in 100m. Site adj sw pool. To avoid bdge app fr S on D15. Lge, mkd, hdstg, pt shd, sl, wc (htd); chem disp; shwrs inc; EHU (6A) €4.50 (poss rev pol); gas; lndry; shop; bbq; playgrnd; twin axles; wifi; dogs; adv bkg rec; ccard acc; fishing; horseriding nr; bike hire; games rm; tennis. "Well-run, tidy site; helpful staff; gd clean san facs; cycle & walking rte adj (Voie Verte); frequent rlwy noise daytime; interesting town; htd pool adj inc; excel, reliable site; well organised and pleasant; busy site." ♦ 26 Apr-5 Oct. € 19.00 2017*

CLUNY *9A2* (12km S Rural) *46.33744, 4.61123* **Camping du Lac, 8 Rue du Port, 71520 St Point [03 85 50 52 31; reservation@campingsaintpoint.com; www.campingsaintpoint.com]** Turn S off N79, Mâcon/Paray-le-Monial rd, turn L bef Ste Cécile on D22; site sp at junc; site 100m on R after St Point vill. Med, hdg, mkd, pt shd, pt sl, terr, wc (htd); chem disp; mv service pnt; shwrs inc; EHU (16A) inc; lndry; shop nr; rest; snacks; bar; bbq; playgrnd; sw nr; wifi; TV; 30% statics; dogs €2; phone; adv bkg acc; quiet; fishing; boat hire; tennis 4km; CKE/CCI. "Cluny attractive town & abbey; lge pitches; clean & basic san facs & ltd LS; lovely scenery & pleasant lake; on edge of Beaujolais; sp walks fr site; peaceful area with wooded hills & valleys." 15 Apr-15 Oct. € 17.60 2018*

CLUSAZ, LA 9B3 (6km N Rural) 45.93972, 6.42777
Camping L'Escale, Route de la Patinoire, 74450 Le Grand-Bornand [04 50 02 20 69; fax 04 50 02 36 04; contact@campinglescale.com; www.campinglescale.com] Exit A41 junc 17 onto D16/D909 E dir La Clusaz. At St Jean-de-Sixt turn L at rndabt sp Le Grand Bornand. After 1.5km foll camping sp on main rd & at junc turn R sp for site & 'Vallée du Bouchet'. Site is 1st exit R at rndabt at end of this rd. D4 S fr Cluses not rec while towing as v steep & winding. Med, mkd, pt shd, pt sl, terr, wc (htd); chem disp; mv service pnt; fam bthrm; shwrs inc; EHU (10A) inc poss rev pol); gas; lndry; shop nr; rest; snacks; bar; bbq; playgrnd; pool (covrd, htd); paddling pool; wifi; TV; 20% statics; dogs €2.30; adv bkg req; ccard acc; archery; tennis; fishing; games rm; CKE/CCI. "Family-run site in scenic area; bike hire 250m; gd san facs; no c'vans over 8.5m or m'vans over 8m high ssn, Feb & wk of New Year; serviced pitch in summer; vg rest; sh walk to attractive vill; winter sports; free use htd ski/boot rm in winter; boggy in wet weather; vg mkt Wed; excel site; ski bus; gd sports facs."
♦ 1 Jan-12 Apr, 22 May-27 Sep & 19 Dec-31 Dec. € 32.00 2015*

COEX 2H4 (3km W Rural) 46.67679, -1.76899 RCN
Camping La Ferme du Latois, 85220 Coëx [02 51 54 67 30; fax 02 51 60 02 14; ferme@rcn.fr; www.rcn-campings.fr] Exit D948 at Aizenay onto D6 dir St Gilles-Croix-de-Vie; at Coëx take D40 SW sp Brétignolles; site in 1.5km on L. Lge, pt shd, wc (htd); chem disp; shwrs inc; EHU inc (poss rev pol); lndry; shop; rest; snacks; bar; bbq (gas); playgrnd; pool; wifi; 20% statics; dogs €5; phone; Eng spkn; adv bkg acc; quiet; games rm; games area; lake fishing; bike hire. "Spacious pitches; cycle rtes adj; conv Lac du Jaunay & Lac du Gué-Gorand; excel." ♦ 11 Apr-10 Oct. € 45.40 2014*

COGNAC 7B2 (3km NE Rural) 45.70920, -0.31284
Camping de Cognac, Blvd de Châtenay, 16100 Cognac [05 45 32 13 32; fax 05 45 32 15 82; contact@campingdecognac.com; www.campingdecognac.com] Fr N141 foll 'Camping' sp to town cent. Turn R at 'Speedy' g'ge, site immed on R in 2km after x-ing rv; foll sp 'Base de Plein Air'. Take care ent barrier. Med, hdg, mkd, hdstg, pt shd, wc; chem disp; mv service pnt; shwrs inc; EHU (6A) inc (poss long leads req & poss rev pol); lndry; shop; rest; snacks; bar; bbq; playgrnd; pool; red long stay; entmnt; 5% statics; dogs €1.50; phone; bus; Eng spkn; adv bkg acc; ccard acc; games area; rv boating; rv fishing; CKE/CCI. "Excel lge park with many facs; helpful staff; clean modern san facs but dated; gates clsd 2200-0700 (1800 LS); night watchman high ssn; no twin axles; footpath to town; conv Cognac distilleries (vouchers fr site recep); cycle rte to town cent." ♦ 1 May-27 Sep. € 22.40 2018*

COGNAC 7B2 (10km E Rural) 45.67160, -0.22718
Camping De Bourg (formerly Camping du Port), 16200 Bourg-Charente [06 15 16 67 82 or 06 03 06 85 07 (mob)] Exit N141 onto D158 dir Bourg-Charente; turn L in 800m & site on R. Site sp fr D158. Chicane-type ent gates. Sm, pt shd, pt sl, wc; chem disp; shwrs; EHU (6A) €3; shop nr; rest nr; red long stay; dogs; fishing; tennis. "Delightful site on banks of Rv Charante; friendly staff; facs v basic & ltd but clean, poss stretched high ssn; site on 2 levels, lower one sl; gd walks & cycle path to Jarnac & Cognac; gd; find placement, owner will call; vg value; v quiet site."
1 May-15 Sep. € 10.00 2017*

COGNAC 7B2 (16km E Urban) 45.67606, -0.17429
FFCC Camping de l'Ile Madame, 16200 Gondeville [06 26 91 40 92; campingilemadame@orange.fr; camping-jarnac.jimdo.com] Turn E at S end of rv bdge at S end of town. Fr Angoulême on N141, exit junc sp 'Jarnac Est'; foll sp Jarnac thro 1 rndabt into Jarnac; at traff lts (LH lane) turn L sp Tourist Info/Camping; cross rv bdge & immed turn L to site. Lge, pt shd, wc; shwrs inc; EHU (6-10A) €3.20 (rev pol); lndry; shop nr; rest nr; playgrnd; pool; red long stay; entmnt; TV; dogs €2.50; adv bkg acc; golf nr; games area; CKE/CCI. "Pleasant, well-run site; gd sized pitches; easy walk into Jarnac with shops & rests; gd walks along rv; nr Courvoisier bottling plant; excel; boat trips along rv; canoe hire nr; poss noise fr adj sports grnd & disco; site redesigned & new san facs (2015)." 15 Apr-30 Sep. € 14.00 2017*

⊞ COGNAC 7B2 (8km S Rural) 45.60148, -0.36067
Camping Le Chiron (Chainier), 16130 Salles-d'Angles [05 45 83 72 79; fax 05 45 83 64 80; mchainier@voila.fr] Fr Cognac D731 Barbezieux to Salles-d'Angles, R at bottom hill onto D48; then in 3km turn L onto D151; site on L in 500m (foll Chambres d'Hôtes sps). Sm, pt shd, pt sl, wc (htd); chem disp; shwrs inc; EHU (10A) inc (rev pol); shop nr; Eng spkn; quiet. "Vg; meals avail at farm; v basic; own san facs rec."
€ 12.00 2014*

COGNAC LA FORET 7B3 (2km SW Rural) 45.82494, 0.99674
Camping des Alouettes, Les Alouettes, 87310 Cognac-la-Forêt [05 55 03 26 93; info@camping-des-alouettes.com; www.camping-des-alouettes.com] Fr Aixe-sur-Vienne on D10, site W of Cognac-la-Forêt on D10, sp to L. Med, hdg, pt shd, pt sl, wc; chem disp; shwrs inc; EHU (10A) €3; lndry; shop nr; rest; snacks; bar; bbq; playgrnd; pool; paddling pool; sw nr; wifi; 10% statics; dogs €1; Eng spkn; adv bkg acc; quiet; tennis 700m; CKE/CCI. "Beautiful location; friendly Dutch owners; conv war vill Oradour-sur-Glane & Richard Lion Heart sites; excel facs, peaceful, relaxing, vg site; lge pitches; well run site." ♦
1 Apr-30 Sep. € 23.00 2017*

COLMAR 6F3 (2km E Urban) 48.07942, 7.38665
Camping de l'Ill, 1 Allée du Camping, 68180 Horbourg-Wihr [03 89 41 15 94; colmar@camping-indigo.com; www.campingdelill.com] Exit A35 junc 25 onto D415, foll Freibourg sp. At 2nd rndabt turn L to Colmar cent, site on rvside on L bef bdge. Lge, mkd, hdstg, hdg, shd, pt sl, terr, wc (htd); chem disp; mv service pnt; shwrs; EHU (10A) €4.80 (poss rev pol); lndry; shop; rest; snacks; bar; playgrnd; entmnt; wifi; TV; 10% statics; dogs €4; bus/train to city cent; Eng spkn; adv bkg acc; ccard acc; bike hire; CKE/CCI. "Lovely, clean, rvside site; excel san facs; gd rest; some pitches req steel pegs; much noise fr a'route; gd for town; sep area for NH, bus only to town, san facs tired, supmkt 900m." ♦ 21 Mar-31 Dec. € 22.50   2015*

> "I like to fill in the reports as I travel from site to site"
>
> You'll find report forms at the back of this guide, or you can fill them in online at camc.com/europereport.

COLMAR 6F3 (7km S Rural) 48.01613, 7.34983
Camping Clair Vacances, Route de Herrlisheim, 68127 Ste Croix-en-Plaine [03 89 49 27 28; fax 03 89 49 31 37; clairvacances@orange.fr; www.clairvacances.com] Exit D83 at sp Herrlisheim onto D1 bis. Take 2nd rd to vill sp camping, foll site sp thro vill. NB Rd thro vill narr with traff calming bollards. Fr A35 turn off at junc 27 sp Herrlisheim/Ste Croix-en-Plaine onto D1 dir Herrlisheim to site in 1km. Med, hdstg, hdg, mkd, pt shd, wc (htd); chem disp; fam bthrm; shwrs inc; EHU (16A) €4 (long lead poss req); gas; lndry; shop nr; snacks; bbq (gas); playgrnd; pool (htd); paddling pool; entmnt; wifi; phone; Eng spkn; adv bkg acc; quiet; ccard acc; tennis 3km; bike hire; CKE/CCI. "Beautiful site; well-kept & supervised; can be busy, adv bkg rec; service wash; helpful, friendly owners; gd size pitches; excel, clean san facs; gd touring base Alsace wine rte; excel." ♦ 10 Apr-19 Oct. € 37.50   2014*

COLMAR 6F3 (7km SW Rural) 48.04272, 7.29970
Camping des Trois Châteaux, 10 Rue du Bassin, 68420 Eguisheim [03 89 23 19 39; fax 03 89 24 10 19; camping.eguisheim@orange.fr; www.camping-eguisheim.fr] Foll D83 S (Colmar by-pass) R at sp Eguisheim. R into vill to site at top of vill, foll camp sp. Med, mkd, pt shd, pt sl, terr, wc; chem disp; mv service pnt; shwrs inc; EHU (8-10A) €3-5 (poss rev pol); gas; lndry; shop nr; rest nr; bar nr; playgrnd; dogs €3; adv bkg req; ccard acc; CKE/CCI. "Popular, well-run, clean, busy site; no c'vans over 7m (inc draw bar); mv pitches flat but some c'van pitches sl & poss diff; gd touring base; weekly wine-tasting events; stork park adj; rec arr early; excel; cycle rte to cent of Colmar; gd." ♦ 26 Mar-5 Nov & 30 Nov-24 Dec. € 19.00   2018*

COLMAR 6F3 (7km W Urban) 48.08517, 7.27253
Camping Le Medieval (formerly Municipal Les Cigognes), Quai de la Gare, 68230 Turckheim [03 89 27 02 00; fax 03 89 80 86 93; reception@camping-turckheim.fr; en.camping-turckheim.fr] Fr D83 twd Turchkeim turn W onto D11 to Turckheim. On ent vill, turn immed L down 1-way rd after x-ing rlwy lines. Do not cross rv bdge. Site on L bef bdge, adj stadium. Med, hdg, pt shd, wc (htd); chem disp; mv service pnt; fam bthrm; shwrs inc; EHU (16A) €4; lndry; shop nr; bbq; playgrnd; pool; twin axles; entmnt; wifi; TV; dogs €2.50; bus adj, train 250m; Eng spkn; quiet; ccard acc; games rm; CKE/CCI. "Lovely site with med pitches; cycle rtes nr; resident storks; sh walk to interesting, beautiful old vill with rests; gd touring base; gd, excel san facs; poss cr in June, high ssn & w/ends; new management (2016); friendly helpful staff; open 26 Dec-28 Dec for Christmas mkt; vg; close to historic sites and medieval castles; wine tasting & sales; great site; new shwr block (2017); cycle rte to Colmar & vineyards." ♦ 7 Apr-23 Oct & 30 Nov-24 Dec. € 19.00   2018*

COLMARS 9D4 (0km S Rural) 44.17731, 6.62151
Aire Naturelle Les Pommiers, Chemin des Mélèzes, 04370 Colmars-les-Alpes [04 92 83 41 56; fax 04 92 83 40 86; contact@camping-pommier.com; www.camping-pommier.com] Fr N on D908 on ent Colmars take 1st R over rd bdge & foll site sp. Col d'allos on D908 v narr, best to avoid. Sm, pt shd, terr, wc; chem disp; mv service pnt; shwrs inc; EHU (10A) €2; lndry; shop nr; rest nr; bar nr; bbq; dogs €2; phone; adv bkg acc; CKE/CCI. "Beautifully-situated, well-maintained CL-type site nr medieval town; friendly owner; htd pool 800m; gd walking." ♦ 1 May-1 Oct. € 15.50   2014*

> "We must tell the Club about that great site we found"
>
> Get your site reports in by mid-August and we'll do our best to get your updates into the next edition.

COLMARS 9D4 (1km S Rural) 44.17472, 6.61629
Camping Le Bois Joly, Chemin des Buissières, 04370 Colmars-les-Alpes [04 92 83 40 40; fax 04 92 83 50 60; camping-le-bois-joly@sfr.fr; www.colmars-les-alpes.fr] Fr S on D955 & D908 twds Colmars, go thro Beauvezer & Villars-Colmars. Ignore two other sites en rte. Site sp. Sm, hdstg, mkd, shd, wc; chem disp; mv service pnt; shwrs inc; EHU (6A) €2.43; gas; lndry; rest; snacks; bbq; phone; adv bkg acc; quiet; rv fishing adj; CKE/CCI. "Well-kept, wooded site with gd atmosphere; gd facs; ideal base for walking in Haute Provence; bar & shop 1km; friendly owners." 1 May-1 Oct. € 11.00   2014*

COLMARS

COLMARS 9D4 (2km SW Rural) 44.19148, 6.59690
Camping Le Haut Verdon, 04370 Villars-Colmars [04 92 83 40 09; info@lehautverdon.com; www.lehautverdon.com] Only app fr S on D955 & D908 fr St André-les-Alps thro Beauvezer. Clearly sp on ent Villars-Colmars on R. Do not take D908 via Annot/Le Fugeret with a caravan(Do not confuse with Municipal site approx 5km bef this site). Sm, mkd, hdstg, pt shd, wc (htd); chem disp; mv service pnt; shwrs inc; EHU (6-10A) €3-4; gas; lndry; rest; snacks; bar; bbq; playgrnd; pool (htd); paddling pool; sw nr; twin axles; entmnt; wifi; TV; 50% statics; dogs €4; 50m; adv bkg acc; quiet; rv fishing; games area; games rm; bike hire; CKE/CCI. "Superb setting on Rv Verdon; gd, clean san facs; helpful staff; conv Colmars, flower meadows, Allos Lake; site nr Mercantour National Pk; scenic rte to Barcelonnette via Col d'Allos, not suitable for c'vans; ski area at Allos; gd." ♦ 28 Apr-14 Oct. € 28.00   2018*

COMBOURG 2E4 (8km NE Rural) 48.45304, -1.65031 Camping Le Bois Coudrais (Ybert), 35270 Cuguen [02 99 73 27 45; fax 02 99 73 13 08; info@vacancebretagne.com; www.vacancebretagne.com] Fr Combourg take D796 twd Pleine-Fougères, 5km out of Combourg turn L on D83 to Cuguen; 500m past Cuguen, turn L, site sp. Or fr Dol-de-Bretagne, take D795 then turn L onto D9 to Cuguen. Sm, mkd, hdg, pt shd, wc; chem disp; shwrs inc; EHU (10A) €3; shop nr; snacks; bar; bbq; playgrnd; pool; red long stay; wifi; dogs €1; Eng spkn; adv bkg acc; quiet; golf nr; watersports nr; bike hire; fishing nr; CKE/CCI. "CL-type site, friendly British owners, gd clean facs, great for young children, sm animal-petting area, gd touring base; zoo nrby; adventure park nr." ♦ 27 Apr-30 Sep. € 18.50   2013*

COMBOURG 2E4 (6km SW Rural) 48.38090, -1.83490 Camping Domaine du Logis, 35190 La Chapelle-aux-Filtzméens,Ille-et-Vilaine [02 99 45 25 45 or 06 85 78 69 71 (mob); fax 02 99 45 30 40; domainedulogis@wanadoo.fr; www.domainedulogis.com] Fr N176 at junc for Dol-de-Bretagne branch R onto D155 sp Dol & take D795 S to Combourg. Then take D13 twd St Domineuc, go thro La Chapelle-aux-Filtzméens & site on R in 1km. Lge, mkd, hdg, pt shd, wc; chem disp; mv service pnt; shwrs inc; EHU (10A) inc; gas; lndry; shop nr; rest; snacks; bar; bbq; playgrnd; pool (htd); paddling pool; red long stay; entmnt; wifi; TV; 10% statics; dogs €2; phone; Eng spkn; adv bkg acc; quiet; ccard acc; gym; games area; games rm; fishing nr; bike hire; fitness rm; CKE/CCI. "Set in chateau grnds; lge flat grassy pitches; helpful, pleasant staff; gd, clean san facs; gd touring base, conv St Malo, Mont St Michel, Dinan & Channel Islands; mkt Mon; excel; no o'fits over 12m; beautiful; v child oriented; canoe 800m; superb pool." ♦ 1 Apr-2 Oct. € 33.00   2017*

COMPS SUR ARTUBY 10E3 (1km NW Rural) 43.71543, 6.49862 Camp Municipal du Pontet, 83840 Comps-sur-Artuby [04 94 76 91 40; mairie.compsurartuby@wanadoo.fr] Fr Comps-sur-Artuby take D71 sp Grand Canyon du Verdon. Site sp on R in 1km. Med, mkd, pt shd, terr, wc; chem disp; shwrs inc; EHU (6A) €3; shop; rest; bar; dogs; phone; quiet; CKE/CCI. "Vg, well-laid out, wooded site; conv Gorges du Verdon; easy access; ltd san facs at top of site." 1 May-31 Oct. € 8.00   2014*

> **"I need an on-site restaurant"**
>
> We do our best to make sure site information is correct, but it is always best to check any must-have facilities are still available or will be open during your visit.

CONCARNEAU 2F2 (6km S Coastal) 47.85628, -3.89999 Camping Le Cabellou Plage, Ave de Cabellou, Kersaux, 29185 Concarneau [02 98 97 37 41; fax 02 98 60 78 57; info@le-cabellou-plage.com; www.le-cabellou-plage.com] Fr N165 turn onto D70 dir Concarneau. At 5th rndabt (Leclerc supmkt) foll dir Tregunc. After Moros bdge take 2nd exit at next rndabt dir Le Cabellou-Plage. Site sp on L. Lge, mkd, hdg, pt shd, wc cont; chem disp; fam bthrm; shwrs; EHU (10A) inc; lndry; snacks; bar; playgrnd; pool (htd); paddling pool; beach sand adj; wifi; TV; 20% statics; dogs €4; bus at site ent; Eng spkn; adv bkg acc; quiet; ccard acc; games area; bike hire; games rm; watersports. "Pleasant seaside site; vg san facs; gd walking fr site; gd for town via ferry." ♦ 28 Apr-15 Sep. € 36.00   2017*

CONCARNEAU 2F2 (2km NW Urban/Coastal) 47.8807, -3.9311 Camping Les Sables Blancs, Ave du Dorlett, 29900 Concarneau [02 98 97 16 44; contact@camping-lessablesblancs.com; www.camping-lessablesblancs.com] Exit N165 to Concarneau dir 'Centre Ville'. Then foll sp 'La Côte' 300m after traff lts. Site on R, sp. Med, hdstg, mkd, hdg, pt shd, pt sl, terr, wc (htd); chem disp; mv service pnt; fam bthrm; shwrs inc; EHU (10A) €4; lndry; shop nr; rest; snacks; bar; bbq; playgrnd; pool (htd); paddling pool; beach sand 400m; red long stay; entmnt; wifi; TV; 3% statics; dogs €?; phone; bus 300m; Eng spkn; adv bkg acc; quiet; ccard acc; jacuzzi; games rm; games area; CKE/CCI. "Nice, clean, family site in woodland; many sm pitches; friendly staff; excel san facs; superb pool; gd rest; pleasant walk to town, 1.5km; mkt Mon & Thurs; vg; well run; some pitches uneven; steep walk to san facs." ♦ 1 Apr-31 Oct. € 34.00   2017*

CONCARNEAU *2F2* (3km NW Coastal) *47.89054, 3.93847* Camping Les Prés Verts aux 4 Sardines, Kernous-Plage, 29900 Concarneau [02 98 97 09 74 or 07 87 90 90 01 (mob); info@presverts.com; www.presverts-campingconcarneau.com] Exit N165 onto D70 dir Concarneau. At rndabt by Leclerc supmkt foll sp 'Centre Ville' (Town Centre) with Leclerc on L. Strt over at 2nd rndabt then bear R at the next rndabt onto Rue de Kerneach & down slope. Bear L at 1st rndabt & R at next. Keep R to join coast rd & foll sp La Forêt-Fouesnant; pass Hôtel Océans; site 3rd rd on L in 1.5km. Med, hdg, mkd, pt shd, pt sl, serviced pitches; wc; chem disp; mv service pnt; shwrs inc; EHU (6A-10A) inc (poss rev pol & long lead req); lndry; rest nr; bbq (charcoal, gas); playgrnd; pool (htd); paddling pool; wifi; TV; 10% statics; dogs €2; adv bkg acc; quiet; ccard acc; games rm; horseriding 1km; sailing 1km. "Peaceful, scenic, busy site; path to sandy cove below; gd sized pitches, lge pitches extra; family-run, friendly helpful staff; basic san facs, run down, ltd LS; poss unkempt LS; dir access to beach; no o'fits over 8m; gd touring base; walk along coastal path to Concarneau; mkt Mon & Fri; cycle track (old rlwy track) 300m fr site; gd location." 1 May-30 Sep. € 28.00   2017*

CONDE SUR NOIREAU *3D1* (1km W Urban) *48.85146, -0.55703* Camp Municipal du Stade, Rue de Vire, 14110 Condé-sur-Noireau [02 31 69 02 93; fax 02 31 59 15 51; www.conde-sur-noireau.com] On D562 (Flers to Caen rd). In town, turn W on D512 twd Vire. After Zone Industrielle, sports complex on L, no L turn. Go 1 block further & foll lge white sp 'Espace Aquatique' to site. Site 500m on R in grnds of sports cent. Sm, pt shd, wc; chem disp; shwrs inc; EHU (6-10A) inc; lndry; shop nr; rest nr; bar nr; playgrnd; dogs; quiet; tennis; CKE/CCI. "Well-kept clean site in grnds of leisure cent; gd size pitches; gd clean san facs, htd pool adj; staff friendly & helpful; pleasant town; gd NH." 2 May-30 Sep. € 8.00   2013*

CONDOM *8E2* (10km N Rural) *44.03324, 0.36614* Camping Le Mouliat, RD 219, 47600 Moncrabeau [05 53 65 43 28; contact@camping-le-mouliat.fr; www.camping-le-mouliat.fr] N fr Condom on D930 for 9.5km, then R on D219. Site on L in 0.5km, just bef rv bdge. Sm, hdg, mkd, pt shd, wc; chem disp; mv service pnt; shwrs; EHU €4.50; lndry; snacks; bar; bbq; playgrnd; pool; twin axles; wifi; 10% statics; dogs; games area; CKE/CCI. "Quiet LS; conv for Condom/Nerac; takeaway; helpful, cheery owners; vg." ♦ 1 May-1 Oct. € 24.00   2015*

CONDOM *8E2* (4km NE Rural) *43.97491, 0.42038* Camping à la Ferme (Rogalle), Guinland, 32100 Condom [05 62 28 17 85; rogalle.guinland@wanadoo.fr; http://campingdeguinland.monsite-orange.fr] NE fr Condom on D931, turn R onto D41. Pass water tower on R, site ent on L at bottom of hill just bef sm lake on R. Sm, shd, wc; chem disp; shwrs inc; EHU (6-10A) €3; shop nr; rest nr; bbq; playgrnd; 10% statics; dogs; quiet; tennis nr. "Vg CL-type site in pine grove; canoe hire nr; gd views; friendly owner; clean facs." 1 Apr-30 Oct. € 9.00   2017*

⊞ CONDOM *8E2* (7km SE Rural) *43.92929, 0.42698* Camping à la Ferme (Vignaux), Bordeneuve, 32100 Béraut [05 62 28 08 41] E fr Condom on D7 to Caussens; far end of vill turn R on D204, sp St Orens; in 1.2km turn R sp Béraut, bear R at fork, site on L in 400m. Also sp fr D654. Sm, pt shd, pt sl, wc; chem disp; shwrs inc; EHU (12A) €2.50 (long lead poss req); lndry; shop nr; adv bkg acc; quiet. "Peaceful & secluded CL-type site; friendly owners; basic san facs; waymkd trails nr; phone ahead to check open LS - poss not open until Apr." € 12.00   2012*

CONDOM *8E2* (2km SW Rural) *43.94813, 0.36405* Camp Municipal de l'Argenté, Chemin de l'Argenté, Gauge, 32100 Condom [05 62 28 17 32; camping.municipal@condom.org; www.condom.org/index.php/camping-municipal] Fr Condom, take D931 twd Eauze; site ent on L opp municipal sports grnd. Med, mkd, pt shd, wc; chem disp; fam bthrm; shwrs inc; EHU (6A) €3.60; shop nr; rest nr; bar nr; playgrnd; dogs €1.30; phone; fishing; tennis adj. "Pleasant, spacious, well-kept site adj rv; lge pitches; well shd; friendly staff; excel san facs but ltd LS; levelling blocks useful; pool 200m; no twin axles; lots for older children to do; interesting, unspoilt town nr pilgrim rte; rec visit Armagnac distilleries; excel." 1 Apr-30 Sep. € 20.00   2013*

CONDRIEU *9B2* (4km N Rural) *45.50949, 4.77330* Camping Domaine du Grand Bois (Naturist), Tupin et Semons, 69420 Condrieu [04 74 87 89 00 or 04 74 87 04 29; fax 04 74 87 88 48; domainedugrandbois@free.fr; www.domainedugrandbois.fr] Fr Vienne take D502 dir Rive-de-Gier; site well sp after x-ing Rv Rhône. NB Do not app fr Condrieu - v steep with hairpins. Lge, pt shd, sl, wc; chem disp; shwrs inc; EHU (6A) €4.50; snacks; bar; playgrnd; pool; TV; 75% statics; phone; adv bkg acc; quiet; INF card. "Spectacular views; v basic san facs." ♦ 15 Apr-15 Oct. € 17.50   2013*

CONDRIEU *9B2* (6km SE Rural) *45.42413, 4.78251* Camping Le Daxia, Route du Péage, 38370 St Clair-du-Rhône [04 74 56 39 20; fax 04 74 56 45 57; info@campingledaxia.com; www.campingledaxia.com] S fr Vienne on D386; turn L in Condieu sp D28 Les Roches-de-Condrieu & Le Péage-de-Roussillon; foll sp A7 Valance & 'Camping' onto D4. Site on L well sp fr Condrieu. Med, hdg, mkd, pt shd, wc; chem disp; mv service pnt; fam bthrm; shwrs inc; EHU (5-10A) €2.40-2.85; lndry; shop nr; rest; snacks; bar; bbq; playgrnd; pool; paddling pool; wifi; dogs €1.85; adv bkg acc; quiet; games rm; CKE/CCI. "Vg site; on edge of sm rv with beach." ♦ 1 Apr-30 Sep. € 23.00   2017*

CONFOLENS

CONFOLENS 7A3 (1km N Rural) 46.01905, 0.67531 **Camp Municipal des Ribières, Ave de St Germain, 16500 Confolens [05 45 85 35 27 or 05 45 84 01 97 (Mairie); fax 05 45 85 34 10; contact@mairieconfolens.com; http://www.campingdesribieres.fr/]** Fr N foll D951 dir Confolens turn L sp St Germain-de-Confolens, site on R in 7km at edge of town bet rd & rv. NB Diff app fr S thro vill. Med, mkd, pt shd, wc; chem disp; mv service pnt; fam bthrm; shwrs inc; EHU (16A); gas; lndry; shop nr; bbq; playgrnd; sw nr; wifi; 3% statics; dogs; phone; Eng spkn; adv bkg req; bike hire; boating; fishing; games area. "Interesting, pretty town; facs neglected & ltd LS; m'van o'night area outside site; pool 200m; warden calls am & pm; great site; lovely location; excel." ♦ 1 Apr-1 Oct. € 21.00   2018*

CONQUES 7D4 (8km E Rural) 44.55948, 2.46184 **Camping L'Etang du Camp, 12320 Sénergues [05 65 46 01 95; info@etangducamp.fr; www.etangducamp.fr]** Fr S on D901 dir Conques; at St Cyprien turn R onto D46 sp Sénergues; foll sp Sénergues up hill for 6km; 2nd L at the top; foll Camping sp. Med, mkd, hdg, pt shd, wc; chem disp; mv service pnt; fam bthrm; shwrs inc; EHU (6A) €3.70; lndry; shop; bbq (charcoal); playgrnd; wifi; 10% statics; dogs €1.50; Eng spkn; adv bkg acc; quiet; fishing in private lake; ice; bike hire; games area; canoeing nr; games rm; CKE/CCI. "Well-situated, well-kept site; quiet & relaxing; warm welcome, British owners; modern, clean san facs; gd base for touring, walking & cycling; htd pool 6km; conv Conques; highly rec; excel; gd security." ♦ 1 Apr-30 Sep. € 22.00   2018*

CONQUES 7D4 (5km NW Rural) 44.62392, 2.36101 **Camping Du Moulin, Les Passes, 12320 Grand-Vabre [05 65 72 87 28 or 06 82 88 53 33 (mob); campingdumoulin12@orange.fr; www.grand-vabre.fr]** N fr Conques on D901, site sp on banks Rv Dourdou. Sm, mkd, shd, terr, wc; mv service pnt; shwrs; EHU (10A) €2; snacks; bar; playgrnd; pool (htd); TV; 80% statics; quiet; tennis 1km; games area. "Pleasant rvside site; gd, modern san facs; gd." 1 Apr-31 Oct. € 16.00   2012*

CONQUET, LE 2E1 (2km N Coastal) 48.36748, -4.75990 **Camping Les Blancs Sablons, 29217 Le Conquet [02 98 36 07 91; www.les-blancs-sablons.com]** Exit Brest on D789 to Le Conquet. Turn R after 22km (1.8km bef Le Conquet) on D67 twd St Renan, turn L after 700m on D28 twd Ploumoguer. After 2km, turn L at x-rds twd Plage des Blancs Sablons, site on L in 1km. Lge, mkd, unshd, pt sl, wc; chem disp; shwrs inc; EHU (16A) €3 (long lead poss req); lndry; shop; rest nr; bar nr; playgrnd; pool (htd); beach sand 100m; adv bkg acc; ccard acc; CKE/CCI. "Gd views fr some pitches; some soft pitches; ltd facs LS & dated but clean with gd hot water; bar 500m; lovely old fishing town." ♦ 1 Apr-31 Oct. € 21.00   2017*

CORCIEUX 6F3 (8km NE Urban) 48.18436, 6.95784 **Camping Les Acacias, 191 Rue Léonard de Vinci, 88650 Anould [03 29 57 11 06; contact@acaciascamp.com; www.acaciascamp.com]** Site in vill of Anould sp fr all dir; just off main rd. (Annexe Camping Nature Les Acacias 800m fr this site open 15 Jun-15 Sep, terr in woods). Med, pt shd, wc; chem disp; mv service pnt; fam bthrm; shwrs inc; EHU (6-10A) €3.50-6; gas; lndry; shop nr; rest; snacks; bar; playgrnd; pool (htd); wifi; 10% statics; dogs €1; Eng spkn; adv bkg acc; quiet; games rm; rv fishing nrby; CKE/CCI. "Gd standard site; cycle trails; helpful owners; gd, tennis, karting 2km; clean san facs; excel." ♦ 15 Jun-15 Sep. € 21.00   2014*

CORCIEUX 6F3 (1km ESE Rural) 48.16826, 6.89006 **Camping Le Clos de la Chaume, 21 Rue d'Alsace, 88430 Corcieux [03 29 50 76 76 or 06 85 19 62 55 (mob); info@camping-closdelachaume.com; www.camping-closdelachaume.com]** Take D145 fr St Dié, then D8 thro Anould & bear R onto D60. Site in 3km on R at ent to vill. Med, hdstg, hdg, mkd, pt shd, serviced pitches; wc; chem disp; mv service pnt; fam bthrm; shwrs inc; EHU (8-10A) €3.50; gas; lndry; shop nr; rest nr; bar nr; bbq; playgrnd; pool; red long stay; twin axles; wifi; TV; 15% statics; dogs €1.70; phone; Eng spkn; adv bkg acc; quiet; ccard acc; fishing; games area; games rm; CKE/CCI. "Lovely, peaceful site in beautiful area; stream runs thro; friendly & helpful owners; bike hire 800m; san facs poss stetched & busy/noisy high ssn; conv Gérardmer & Alsace wine rte; excel; acess rd vg; highly rec; family owned; v well run; excel covrd pool (new 2016)." ♦ 27 Apr-20 Sep. € 23.00   2016*

See advertisement opposite

CORDES SUR CIEL 8E4 (5km SE Rural) 44.04158, 2.01722 **Camping Redon, Livers-Cazelles, 81170 Cordes-sur-Ciel [09 80 50 42 72 or 06 47 46 13 62 (mob); info@campredon.com; www.campredon.com]** Off D600 Albi to Cordes rd. Exit on D107 to E. Site sp. Sm, hdg, pt shd, pt sl, wc; chem disp; mv service pnt; fam bthrm; shwrs inc; EHU (6-16A) €4.25; gas; lndry; shop nr; rest; snacks; bar; playgrnd; pool; red long stay; wifi; TV; dogs €2.25; phone; bus 1km; Eng spkn; adv bkg acc; quiet; CKE/CCI. "Well-kept, well-run site; views fr some pitches; friendly, helpful Dutch owner; excel facs, poss stretched high ssn; ecological septic tank - environmentally friendly liquid sold on site; conv Bastides in area; highly rec; lovely." ♦ 22 Apr-22 Oct. € 30.00   2017*

CORDES SUR CIEL 8E4 (3km W Rural) 44.06681, 1.92408 **Camping Le Garissou, Les Cabannes, 81170 Cordes-sur-Ciel [05 63 56 27 14; contact@legarissou.fr; www.legarissou.fr]** Take D600 fr Cordes thro Les Cabanes; site sp on L at bottom of hill, 1.5km after Les Cabanes. Med, mkd, pt shd, terr, wc; shwrs inc; EHU (6A) inc; lndry; shop; playgrnd; dogs €1.50; quiet. "Hilltop site; pool complex adj; excel views; clean facs." 15 Mar-10 Nov. € 16.50   2015*

COSNE COURS SUR LOIRE

CORMATIN 9A2 (1km N Rural) 46.54841, 4.68351
Camping Le Hameau des Champs, Route de Chalon, 71460 Cormatin [03 85 50 76 71; fax 03 85 50 76 98; camping.cormatin@wanadoo.fr; www.le-hameau-des-champs.com] Fr Cluny N on D981 dir Cormatin for approx 14km, site N of town sp on L, 300m after chateau. Look for line of European flags. Sm, mkd, hdg, unshd, pt sl, wc (htd); chem disp; mv service pnt; shwrs inc; EHU (13A) €3.70 (long lead poss req); lndry; shop nr; rest; snacks; bar; bbq (elec, gas); cooking facs; playgrnd; sw nr; wifi; TV; 10% statics; dogs €1; phone; Eng spkn; adv bkg acc; quiet; ccard acc; bike hire; CKE/CCI. "Well-kept, secure site in lovely countryside; welcoming, friendly owner; lge pitches; ltd EHU, adv bkg rec; gd facs, poss stretched high ssn; rest open LS; Voie Verte cycling rte adj; excel municipal site; sm town but gd local store; Chateau closeby." ♦
1 Apr-30 Sep. € 18.00   2014*

> "Satellite navigation makes touring much easier"
>
> Remember most sat navs don't know if you're towing or in a larger vehicle – always use yours alongside maps and site directions.

CORMATIN 9A2 (6km NW Rural) 46.57139, 4.66245
Camping du Gué, Messeugne, 71460 Savigny-sur-Grosne [03 85 92 56 86; camping.messeugne@orange.fr; www.camping-messeugne.monsite-orange.fr] Fr Cluny N on D981, 2km N of Cormatin fork L sp Malay. Site 3km on R bef rv bdge. Med, mkd, shd, wc (htd); chem disp; shwrs; EHU €3; snacks; bar; bbq; playgrnd; 90% statics; dogs €1.20; rv; fishing; games area; CKE/CCI. "Pleasant, friendly site; nr St Genoux-le-National (national monument), Cluny & Taizé; on Burgundy wine rte; fairly boggy when wet; c'vans parked on concrete bases." ♦ 29 Mar-27 Oct. € 11.00   2013*

CORNY SUR MOSELLE 5D2 (1km N Rural) 49.03768, 6.05736 Camping Le Pâquis, rue de la Moselle, 57680 Corny-sur-Moselle [03 87 52 03 59 or 03 87 60 68 67; fax 03 87 52 05 78; campinglepaquis@orange.fr; http://campinglepaquis.free.fr]
SW fr Metz on D657; site sp on ent to vill. Or S on A31 take junc 29 Féy & turn R onto D66 into Corny-sur-Moselle; at rndabt in vill turn R & foll sp. Site 300m on L. Lge, pt shd, wc (htd); chem disp; shwrs inc; EHU (6A) inc (long cable poss req); lndry; shop nr; snacks; bar; playgrnd; sw nr; entmnt; TV; dogs €1.30; adv bkg acc; ccard acc; games rm; CKE/CCI. "Gd, well-run site on Rv Moselle; friendly, helpful owners; opening dates vary according to public holidays; rec arr early for quieter pitch at far end site; many pitches long, drive-thro so no need unhitch; pleasant." 1 May-30 Sep.
€ 20.00   2013*

CORPS 9C3 (0km W Urban) 44.81909, 5.94323
Camping Municipal Les Aires, Route du Sautet, 38970 Corps [04 76 30 03 85; fax 04 76 81 12 28; www.isere-tourisme.com] Fr N85, Route de Napoleon, Grenoble to Gap. Vill of Corps turn R on D537, site on L in 400m. Sm, mkd, pt shd, wc; chem disp; shwrs; EHU (6A) inc; lndry; 30% statics; dogs; games rm. "Quiet site; san facs old but clean; in pretty vill on the Route de Napoleon." 6 Apr-30 Sep. € 13.40   2013*

COSNE COURS SUR LOIRE 4G3 (5km SW Rural) 47.40923, 2.91792 Camping de l'Ile, Ile de Cosne, 18300 Bannay [09 72 25 89 83; info@camping-ile-cosne.com; www.camping-ile-cosne.com]
Fr Cosne take Bourges rd, D955, over 1st half of bdge, ent immed on L, 500m strt. On rv island. Lge, shd, wc (htd); chem disp; shwrs inc; EHU (10A) €4; lndry; shop; rest; snacks; bar; bbq; playgrnd; paddling pool; entmnt; TV; 10% statics; dogs €0.90; quiet; ccard acc; bike hire; CKE/CCI. "Helpful staff; views of Rv Loire; gd san facs; gd NH; supmkt Carrefour closeby; gd rest opp; town within walking dist." ♦ 1 Apr-30 Oct.
€ 18.00   2016*

Site report forms at back of guide   *Last year of report

COUHE

⊞ **COUHE** *7A2 (9km SW Rural) 46.25652, 0.08892*
Camping La Grande Vigne, 11 Rue du Paradis, 79120 Messé [05 49 29 39 93 or 0800 073 8385; grande. vigne@orange.fr; www.grande-vigne.com]
Fr N10 exit at Chaunay onto D35/D55 sp Lezay, thro Vanzay & in approx 1.5km turn R onto C11. Site sp. Sm, pt shd, wc (htd); chem disp; shwrs inc; EHU (10A) €3.50; lndry; bbq; pool (htd); twin axles; wifi; dogs €0.75 (by prior agreement); adv bkg acc; quiet; games area; bike hire; CKE/CCI. "Gd walking, cycling; gd birdwatching; 2 gîtes to rent; British owners; friendly welcome; excel." ♦ € 18.50   2013*

COULANGES SUR YONNE *4G4 (9km E Rural) 47.53610, 3.63226* **Camp Municipal Le Petit Port, 89660 Châtel-Censoir [03 86 81 01 98 (Mairie) or 06 80 32 59 50 (mob); campinglepetitport@orange. fr or mairie-de-chatel-censoir@wanadoo.fr; www. chatel-censoir.com]** Fr Auxerre or Clamecy on N151 at Coulanges turn E onto D21, S side of rv & canal to Châtel-Censoir; site sp. Med, pt shd, wc; chem disp; shwrs inc; EHU (6A) €3 (poss rev pol); lndry; shop nr; snacks; bar; bbq; playgrnd; sw nr; twin axles; wifi; 10% statics; dogs €0.50; phone; Eng spkn; fishing adj; CKE/CCI. "Attractive, peaceful site bet rv & canal; friendly, busy resident warden; OK san facs; some pitches muddy when wet; beautiful area with gd cycling; concerts at w/ends; excel." 27 Apr-30 Sep. € 8.50   2018*

COULANGES SUR YONNE *4G4 (1km S Rural) 47.52269, 3.53817* **Camping des Berges de l'Yonne, 89480 Coulanges-sur-Yonne [03 86 81 76 87]** On N151 dir Nevers. Med, pt shd, wc; chem disp; shwrs; EHU (10A) €2.80; shop; snacks; playgrnd; pool; tennis; fishing. "V pleasant site in beautiful area; dated facs but adequate & clean; superb pool." 1 May-30 Sep. € 14.40   2012*

> **"There aren't many sites open at this time of year"**
>
> If you're travelling outside peak season remember to call ahead to check site opening dates – even if the entry says 'open all year'.

COULON *7A2 (1km N Rural) 46.32739, -0.58437*
Camp Municipal La Niquière, Route de Benet, 79510 Coulon [05 49 35 81 19 or 05 49 35 90 26 (Mairie); fax 05 49 35 82 75; tourisme.coulon79@orange.fr; www. ville-coulon.fr] Fr N148 at Benet take D1 to Coulon to site on L at ent to Coulon. Sm, pt shd, wc; chem disp; shwrs inc; EHU (10A) €3.10; gas; shop nr; dogs €0.50; boat hire. "Well-kept site; dated but clean san facs; sports facs adj; ent only with barrier card - collect fr Mairie when site office clsd; 10 min walk to vill; gd NH; gd ctr for Marais Poitevin; Coulon is a v attractive town." 1 Apr-30 Sep. € 16.00   2016*

COULON *7A2 (5km SE Rural) 46.31307, -0.53495*
Camping le Martin-Pêcheur, 155 av. Du Marais Poitevin, 79460 Magné [05 49 35 71 81; info@ camping-le-martin-pecheur.com; www.camping-le-martin-pecheur.com] Fr S take A10, exit 33 dir Marais Poitevin. Then Sansais, La Garette, Magne. Fr Nantes A83, exit 9 twds Marais Poitevin, Coulon & Magne. Med, mkd, hdg, pt shd, wc (htd); mv service pnt; shwrs inc; EHU (10A) inc; lndry; shop; rest nr; bbq; playgrnd; red long stay; bus; Eng spkn; adv bkg acc; quiet; CKE/ CCI. "Excel; beautiful area; interlaced with canals; gd walking & cycling; boats & gondolas for hire, with or without boatman; new facs (2014)." ♦ 1 May-28 Sep. € 27.50   2014*

> **"That's changed – Should I let the Club know?"**
>
> If you find something on site that's different from the site entry, fill in a report and let us know. See camc.com/europereport.

COULON *7A2 (2km W Rural) 46.31444, -0.60888*
Camping La Venise Verte, 178 Route des Bords de Sèvre, 79510 Coulon [05 49 35 90 36; fax 05 49 35 04 69; accueil@camping-laveniseverte.fr; www. camping-laveniseverte.fr] Exit A83 junc 9 onto D148 to Benet. Turn R at rndabt onto D25E sp Benet cent & foll sp for Coulon thro Benet. In Coulon turn R at traff lts onto D123 sp Le Vanneau-Irleau & Arcais. Cont for approx 3km with canal on L to site R bef canal bdge. Site sp. Med, mkd, pt shd, wc; chem disp; mv service pnt; fam bthrm; shwrs inc; EHU (10A) inc (poss rev pol); lndry; rest; snacks; bar; bbq (charcoal, gas); playgrnd; pool; paddling pool; twin axles; entmnt; wifi; 20% statics; dogs €2; phone; Eng spkn; adv bkg acc; ccard acc; canoe hire; fishing; bike hire; games rm; boating; CKE/CCI. "Superb, peaceful site in park-like setting; v friendly helpful owner; excel facs; gd rest; gd sized pitches (some with reinforced plastic grid), but some sm & diff due trees & posts; ACSI; excel touring base for nature lovers; gd walking & cycle paths beside waterways; pretty town; lovely area; much revisited site; well placed pitches; gd facs; beautiful, tranquil location; highly rec; excel family run site; charming vill walkable." ♦ 1 Apr-15 Oct. € 30.40   2017*

COULON *7A2 (6km W Rural) 46.33020, -0.67524*
Camping Le Relais du Pêcheur, 85420 Le Mazeau [02 51 52 93 23; campinglerelaisdupecheur@ orange.fr; www.lerelaisdupecheur.fr] Fr Fontenay-le-Comte take N148 SE. At Benet turn R onto D25 thro vill to Le Mazeau. Turn L in vill then R over canal bdge. Site on L in 500m. Med, hdg, pt shd, wc; chem disp; shwrs inc; EHU (16A) €3.50; lndry; shop nr; playgrnd; paddling pool; wifi; Eng spkn; adv bkg acc; quiet; CKE/CCI. "Pleasant, clean site in delightful location; gd cyling & walks; new owners, resident warden; facs being updated (2016)." ♦ 1 Apr-15 Oct. € 13.00   2017*

COURBIAC 7D3 (2km W Rural) 44.37818, 1.01807
FFCC Le Pouchou, 47370 Courbiac [05 53 40 72 68 or 06 80 25 15 13 (mob); le.pouchou@wanadoo.fr; www.camping-le-pouchou.com] S fr Fumel on D102 thro Tournon-d'Agenais; Courbiac sp to L on S side of town; site on R in 2.5km (1.5km bef Courbiac). Sm, pt shd, pt sl, wc; chem disp; mv service pnt; fam bthrm; shwrs inc; EHU (10A) €4 (poss rev pol); lndry; shop; snacks; bar; playgrnd; pool; paddling pool; wifi; TV (pitch); 10% statics; dogs €1.80; Eng spkn; adv bkg req; quiet; fishing; horseriding; bike hire; site clsd 21 Dec-9 Jan; archery; CKE/CCI. "Vg site in lovely setting; lge pitches each with picnic table; many sl pitches poss diff; gd, clean facs; gd views; friendly, hospitable owners; gd cycling; peaceful location." ♦ 1 Mar-30 Jun, 1 Jul-31 Aug, 1 Sep-30 Nov. € 16.00   2014*

COURPIERE 9B1 (5km NE Rural) 45.79399, 3.60583
Camping Le Grün du Chignore, Les Plaines, 63120 Vollore-Ville [tel/fax 04 73 53 73 37; camping-du-chignore@hotmail.fr; www.campingauvergne.fr] D906 S fr Thiers; at Courpière turn L onto D7 to Vollore-Ville; cont on D7 past vill; site on R in 500m. Sm, mkd, hdg, pt shd, wc; chem disp; mv service pnt; shwrs inc; EHU (10A) €4; lndry; shop nr; rest; snacks; bar; bbq (sep area); playgrnd; pool; wifi; 10% statics; dogs €1.50; Eng spkn; adv bkg acc; quiet; ccard acc; games area. "Situated above fishing lake; rolling hills; helpful & welcoming owners; facs poss stretched high ssn; poss clsd on Weds in April; gd walks; chateau in Vollore-Ville; bar pt of vill life; highly rec; excel; vg, new deep pool; gd size level pitches; gd value pizza rest; hiking guide maps at recep; excel value; some rd noise on upper terrace." ♦ 1 Apr-31 Oct. € 15.40   2018*

> **"I like to fill in the reports as I travel from site to site"**
>
> You'll find report forms at the back of this guide, or you can fill them in online at camc.com/europereport.

⊞ **COURPIERE** 9B1 (10km E Rural) 45.79966, 3.61633 Campsite Le Montbartoux, Montbartoux, 63120 Vollore-Ville, Auvergne [04 73 53 7005; contact@camping-montbartoux.com; www.camping-montbartoux.com] D906 S fr Thiers to Courpiere. Then E on D7 to Vollore-Ville. Cont twd Vollore-Montagne. Sp to camp. Sm, mkd, pt shd, sl, terr, wc; chem disp; fam bthrm; shwrs; EHU (10A); lndry; rest; snacks; bar; bbq; playgrnd; pool; twin axles; entmnt; wifi; TV; dogs €1; Eng spkn; adv bkg acc; quiet; games rm; games area; CCI. "Attractive site, beautiful views of Auvergne Valley and Vocanoes of Puy-de-Dome; helpful owner; gd; lge o'fits should phone for dir to avoid hairpin on app rd; new san fac's being built(2013)." ♦ € 17.00   2014*

COURVILLE SUR EURE

COURSEULLES SUR MER 3D1 (1km NE Coastal) 49.33417, -0.44433 Camp Municipal Le Champ de Course, Ave de la Libération, 14470 Courseulles-sur-Mer [02 31 37 99 26 (Mairie); fax 02 31 37 96 37; camping.courseulles@wanadoo.fr; www.courseulles-sur-mer.com] Fr N814 by-pass thro Caen, take exit 5 onto D7 & D404 dir Courseulles-sur-Mer. On ent to town, foll sp 'Campings' at 1st rndabt Site on D514 on R. Gd sp's for site. Lge, mkd, hdg, unshd, wc; chem disp; mv service pnt; fam bthrm; shwrs inc; EHU (10A) €4.50; lndry; rest nr; bar nr; bbq; playgrnd; beach sand; wifi; TV; 15% statics; dogs €1.90; phone; Eng spkn; adv bkg acc; quiet; ccard acc; games area; horseriding nr; tennis nr; CKE/CCI. "Nice site adj beach; friendly staff; facs clean; boat hire nrby; early dep for ferry catered for; conv D-Day landing beach; gd dog walks; mini golf nr; oyster beds & daily fish mkt; vg; excel modern & clean san facs; pool adj; exit barriers open at 7am; supmkt 0.5 km." ♦ 1 Apr-30 Sep. € 23.50   2015*

> **"We must tell the Club about that great site we found"**
>
> Get your site reports in by mid-August and we'll do our best to get your updates into the next edition.

COURSEULLES SUR MER 3D1 (8km SW Rural) 49.28949, -0.52970 Camp Municipal des Trois Rivières, Route de Tierceville, 14480 Creully [02 31 80 12 00 or 02 31 80 90 17; contact@camping-les-3-rivieres.com; www.camping-les-3-rivieres.com] Fr Caen ring rd, exit junc 8 onto N13 dir Bayeux; in 15km turn R onto D82 to Creully; site on R 500m past cent of Creully. Med, hdg, pt shd, pt sl, wc (htd); chem disp; shwrs inc; EHU (10A) €4.10 (long leads req, poss rev pol); lndry; shop nr; rest nr; bar nr; bbq; playgrnd; beach sand 5km; dogs €1.20; Eng spkn; adv bkg acc; quiet; ccard acc; games area; games rm; CKE/CCI. "clean site; gd pitches; friendly, helpful warden; facs not v clean, stretched high ssn; pool 5km; conv D-Day beaches, Bayeux; barrier clsd 1500-1700; gd cycling; standard of maintenance is poor." ♦ 1 Apr-30 Sep. € 16.00   2014*

COURVILLE SUR EURE 4E2 (1km S Urban) 48.44629, 1.24157 Camp Municipal Les Bords de l'Eure, Ave Thiers, 28190 Courville-sur-Eure [02 37 23 76 38 or 02 37 18 07 90 (Mairie); fax 02 37 18 07 99; secretaria-mairie@courville-sur-eure.fr; www.courville-sur-eure.fr] Turn N off D923 19km W of Chartres. Site on bank of rv. Foll sp. Med, hdg, pt shd, wc (htd); chem disp; shwrs; EHU (16A) €3.30; lndry; shop nr; rest nr; dogs; quiet. "Lovely, peaceful rvside site; spacious pitches; friendly warden; no twin axles; Eng spkn; conv Chartres; mkt Thurs; easy walk into town; gd security, oniste warden; mv service pnt adj; pool 200m; site basic but lge pitches and v well kept; facs gd and spotless." 30 Apr-18 Sep. € 7.80   2016*

COUTANCES

⊞ **COUTANCES** *1D4 (8km NW Rural) 49.09951, -1.48421* **Camping La Renaudière Féret, 50200 Ancteville [02 33 45 57 53; enquiries@renaudiere-feret.com; www.renaudiere-feret.com]**
N fr Coutances on D2; in 6.5km take 1st R after R turn for Servigny; site on R in 200m. App fr N on D2, take 1st L turn after L turn for Ancteville (site on rd bet turnings for Ancteville & Servigny). Sm, unshd, wc; chem disp; mv service pnt; fam bthrm; shwrs inc; EHU (10-16A) inc; shop nr; bbq; red long stay; wifi; dogs; adv bkg acc; quiet; CKE/CCI. "Tranquil, scenic, excel farm site; helpful, friendly British owners; conv NH or longer; vg; only 2 hrs fr Cherbourg; ideal point for Normandy beaches." ♦ € 20.00   2014*

COUTRAS *7C2 (8km NW Rural) 45.07929, -0.20839* **Camping Le Chêne du Lac, 3 Lieu-dit Chateauneuf, 33230 Bayas [05 57 69 13 78 or 06 07 98 92 65 (mob); lechenedulac@orange.fr; www.camping-lechenedulac.com]** Fr Coutras W on D10 to Guitres; N fr Guitres on D247 to Bayas; site 2km N of Bayas, sp. Sm, mkd, pt shd, wc; chem disp; shwrs inc; EHU (10A) €4.30-5; gas; shop; snacks; bar; bbq (sep area); playgrnd; wifi; 25% statics; dogs €2; Eng spkn; adv bkg acc; quiet; CKE/CCI. "Helpful owner; pedalos & canoes adj; vg; red facs in winter; great site; friendly, helpful new owners; v relaxed atmosphere; excel." ♦ 1 Mar-30 Nov. € 24.00   2017*

COUTURES *4G1 (1km NE Rural) 47.37440, -0.34690* **Camping Parc de Montsabert, 49320 Coutures [02 41 57 91 63; fax 02 41 57 90 02; camping@parcdemontsabert.com; www.parcdemontsabert.com]** Easy access on R side of Rv Loire bet Angers & Saumur. Take D751 to Coutures & fr town cent foll sp for site. 1st R after 'Tabac' & foll rd to site (1st on R bef chateau). Med, hdg, hdstg, mkd, pt shd, pt sl, serviced pitches; wc (htd); chem disp; fam bthrm; shwrs inc; EHU (5-10A) inc; lndry; shop nr; rest; snacks; bar; playgrnd; pool (covrd, htd); paddling pool; entmnt; TV; 15% statics; dogs €4; phone; bus 1km; Eng spkn; adv bkg acc; quiet; ccard acc; bike hire; tennis; gym; games area; games rm; CKE/CCI. "Ideal for chateaux & wine cellars; lge pitches." ♦ 12 Apr-8 Sep. € 29.00   2016*

COZES *7B1 (1km NW Urban) 45.58650, -0.83568* **Camping Le Sorlut (formerly Municipal), Rue de Stade, 17120 Cozes [06 45 46 07 90 or 05 46 90 75 99; contact@camping-charente-maritime-cozes.com; www.camping-charente-maritime-cozes.com/]** Fr bypass D730 turn into Cozes at Royan end. Foll sp for camping. Turn L at supmkt, site 400m on L. Med, mkd, pt shd, wc; chem disp; shwrs inc; EHU (6A) €2.50; lndry; shop nr; playgrnd; pool; quiet; tennis; CKE/CCI. "Pleasant site close to Royan; friendly, helpful warden; no twin axles; popular with long stay British; excel new san facs (2016); number plate recognition barrier." 15 Apr-14 Oct. € 16.00   2018*

CRAON *2F4 (2km E Urban) 47.84819, -0.94409* **Camp Municipal du Mûrier, Rue Alain Gerbault, 53400 Craon [02 43 06 96 33 or 02 43 06 13 09 (Mairie); www.campingdecraon53.fr]** Fr Laval take D771 S to Craon. Site sp fr town cent. Sm, hdg, pt shd, wc; shwrs inc; EHU (6-10A) €2.90; lndry; snacks; playgrnd; red long stay; entmnt; wifi; adv bkg acc; quiet; tennis. "Lge pitches; easy walk to town; pool 200m; office clsd Tues & Sun LS, when barrier key req (2010); local chateau gardens; excel; new modern san block (2018)." 1 May-21 Sep. € 12.00   2018*

⊞ **CREMIEU** *9B2 (4km NW Rural) 45.74829, 5.22486* **Camping à la Ferme des Epinettes, 11 Rue de l'Eglise, 38640 St Romain-de-Jalionas [04 74 90 94 90 or 06 19 31 03 50 (mob); info@camping-cremieu.com; www.camping-cremieu.com]** N fr Crémieu on D517; in 3km site sp on R, immed bef rndabt on edge of St Romain-de-Jalionas. 200m after turning R off D517 (into Rue de l'Eglise), turn L into Rue des Epinettes & site ent. Site on R in 100m. Sm, mkd, pt shd, wc (htd); chem disp; shwrs inc; EHU (16A); lndry; shop nr; 20% statics; dogs €1; quiet; jacuzzi. "Gd NH for interesting & historic town of Lyon and Crémieu; helpful owners; ltd facs LS; gd touring base; Pérouges worth visit; trams/metro fr Meyzieu to Lyon; rec; lovely, peaceful site; run down (2014); narr rds; statics mainly for workers; movers needed for lge o'fits; no resident warden." ♦ € 17.00   2014*

CREON *7D2 (3km NW Rural) 44.78372, -0.37108* **FFCC Camping Caravaning Bel Air, 33670 Créon [05 56 23 01 90; fax 05 56 23 08 38; info@camping-bel-air.com; www.camping-bel-air.com]** Fr A10/E70 at junc 24 take D936 E fr Bordeaux sp Bergerac. Approx 15km E turn SE onto D671 sp Créon & cont for 5km. Site on L, 1.5km after Lorient. Med, hdg, mkd, pt shd, wc (htd); chem disp; mv service pnt; shwrs inc; EHU (10A) €3.60; gas; lndry; shop; rest; snacks; bar; playgrnd; pool; red long stay; wifi; 50% statics; dogs €2.50; Eng spkn; adv bkg acc; quiet; ccard acc; CKE/CCI. "Helpful owners; immac, modern san facs; rest sm & ltd; facs v ltd LS; no twin axles; some pitches v restricted and tight; phone ahead to check open LS; gd NH; poss music festival in next field; clsd to vehicles 2200-0800; poss rd noise; nr cycle path to Bordeaux and Sauverne." ♦ 16 Jan-15 Dec. € 22.40   2014*

CROTOY, LE

CRESPIAN *10E1* (0km S Rural) *43.87850, 4.09590*
Kawan Village Le Mas de Reilhe, 30260 Crespian [04 66 77 82 12; fax 04 66 80 26 50; info@camping-mas-de-reilhe.fr; www.camping-mas-de-reilhe.fr]
Exit A9 at Nîmes Ouest N onto N106 dir Alès for 5km. Fork R, then L over bdge onto D999 dir Le Vigan. Foll rd for 24km, R at x-rds onto D6110 to site on R just on ent Crespian. Take care - ent on a bend on busy rd. Med, mkd, pt shd, pt sl, terr, wc (htd); chem disp; mv service pnt; fam bthrm; shwrs inc; EHU (10A) inc; lndry; shop; rest; snacks; bar; bbq (elec, gas); playgrnd; pool (htd); paddling pool; red long stay; entmnt; wifi; TV; dogs €3; Eng spkn; quiet; ccard acc; games area; table tennis; games rm; CKE/CCI. "Quiet, relaxing & lovely site; friendly staff; no o'fits over 7.5m; clean, modern excel san facs; wine-tasting adj; conv Nîmes, Uzès & Cévennes National Park; excel." ♦ 26 Apr-13 Sep. € 42.00   2014*

CREST *9D2* (1km SE Urban) *44.72410, 5.02755*
Camping Les Clorinthes, Quai Soubeyran, 26400 Crest [04 75 25 05 28; fax 04 75 76 75 09; clorinthes@wanadoo.fr; www.lesclorinthes.com]
S fr Crest twd Nyons on D538, cross bdge cont to rndabt,take last exit foll sp to site. Lge, hdg, hdstg, mkd, pt shd, wc; chem disp; fam bthrm; shwrs; EHU (6A) €4.20; gas; lndry; shop; snacks; bar; pool; paddling pool; sw nr; entmnt; wifi; TV; 10% statics; dogs €3-3.50; phone; adv bkg acc; quiet; CKE/CCI. "Well-maintained site in beautiful situation; friendly, family run; dir access rv; gd, modern san facs; easy walk or cycle to vill; sports complex 500m; mkt Tue & Sat, snacks and bar high ssn only." ♦ 28 Apr-14 Sep. € 27.00   2015*

CREST *9D2* (8km W Rural) *44.72717, 4.92664*
Camping Les Quatre Saisons, Route de Roche-sur-Grâne, 26400 Grane [04 75 62 64 17; fax 04 75 62 69 06; contact@camping-4saisons.com; www.camping-4saisons.com]
Exit A7 at junc for Loriol or Crest, take D104 E for 18km. Turn R thro vill twd Roche-sur-Grane, site well sp. If a lge unit, access thro 4th junc to Grane. Site well sp fr Crest. Med, pt shd, pt sl, terr, wc; chem disp; mv service pnt; fam bthrm; shwrs inc; EHU (6A) €4; lndry; shop; rest nr; snacks; bar; bbq; pool (htd); paddling pool; red long stay; wifi; TV; 10% statics; dogs; phone; Eng spkn; adv bkg acc; quiet; ccard acc; games area; bike hire; tennis; CKE/CCI. "Beautiful views; well-run site; pleasant, helpful owner; sm & lge pitches; excel san facs; gd pool; Grane (supmkt, rest etc) in walking dist; some pitches far fr EHU and san facs up steep hill; paths a bit uneven - need attention; pleasant stay." ♦ 1 May-15 Sep. € 27.00   2013*

⊞ **CREVECOEUR LE GRAND** *3C3* (7km SE Rural) *49.59161, 2.16018* **Camping à la Ferme (Fontana), 8 Hameau de la Neuve Rue, 60480 Ourcel-Maison [03 44 46 81 55]** NE fr Beauvais on D1001 to Froissy; turn W at traff lts onto D151. Avoid 1st sp to Francastel but cont to x-rds & turn into vill on D11. Francastel adjoins Ourcel-Maison & site at far end. Or fr A16 exit junc 16 W onto D930 & foll sp. Sm, pt shd, wc; chem disp; shwrs inc; EHU (5A) inc (rev pol); rest; bbq; playgrnd; quiet. "Farm produce avail; no hdstg & poss muddy/diff in wet; gd NH; site yourself, owner calls." € 10.00   2014*

CREVECOEUR LE GRAND *3C3* (13km SW Rural) *49.57569, 1.93899* **Camping du Vieux Moulin, 2 Rue des Larris, 60690 Roy-Boissy [03 44 46 29 46]** Fr Marseille-en-Beauvasis SW onto D930 dir Gournay-en-Bray; in 1.5km site sp to R at Roy-Boissy. Sm, pt shd, wc; chem disp; shwrs inc; EHU inc (poss rev pol); playgrnd; 10% statics; phone; quiet. "Farm site in area with few sites; beautiful countryside; pitch yourself, owner calls eves; excel." ♦ 1 Apr-31 Oct. € 10.00   2017*

⊞ **CRIEL SUR MER** *3B2* (2km N Coastal) *50.02568, 1.30855* **FFCC Camp Municipal Le Mont Joli Bois, 29 Rue de la Plage, 76910 Criel-sur-Mer [02 35 50 81 19 or 06 08 80 67 35 (mob); fax 02 35 50 22 37; camping.criel@wanadoo.fr; www.montjolibois.mobi]** Fr D925 take D222 into Criel cent. Turn R opp church into D126 for 1.6km to beach. Turn L then immed R & foll beach rd to site in 1.5km. Med, hdg, mkd, pt shd, pt sl, terr, wc (htd); chem disp; mv service pnt; shwrs inc; EHU (4-6A) €3-4.60; lndry; shop nr; rest nr; bar nr; playgrnd; beach shgl 500m; TV; 50% statics; dogs €1.60; bus; quiet; CKE/CCI. "Lovely site, facs need refurb." ♦ € 14.50   2015*

CRIEL SUR MER *3B2* (2km NW Coastal) *50.03048, 1.30815* **Camping Les Mouettes, Rue de la Plage, 76910 Criel-sur-Mer [02 35 86 70 73; contact@camping-lesmouettes.fr; www.camping-lesmouettes.fr]** Fr D925 take D222 thro Criel to coast, site sp. Care needed with narr, steep access. Sm, mkd, unshd, terr, wc; chem disp; shwrs; EHU (6A) €3.70; lndry; shop; snacks; bar; bbq; TV; 10% statics; dogs €2; Eng spkn; adv bkg acc; quiet; games area; games rm. "Pleasant, well-kept site; friendly, helpful owner; gd san facs; sea views; 3 min walk to Stoney Beach." 1 Apr-1 Nov. € 16.00   2014*

CROTOY, LE *3B2* (1km N Urban/Coastal) *50.22396, 1.61908* **Camping La Prairie, 2 Rue de Mayocq, 80550 Le Crotoy [03 22 27 02 65; info@camping-laprairie.fr; www.camping-laprairie.fr]** Fr S exit A16 at Abbeville onto D86/D940 to Le Crotoy to rndabt at ent to town. Cont strt for 1.5km then 2nd L, site on L in 500m. Fr N exit A16 for Rue onto D32, then D940, then as above. Lge, hdg, pt shd, wc; chem disp; shwrs; EHU (3A) inc; playgrnd; beach sand 400m; 90% statics; dogs €1; phone; quiet. "Busy site; ltd pitches for tourers; conv beach & town; gd san facs; gd cycle paths; gd tourist train & bird walks; everything in walking dist." ♦ 1 Apr-30 Sep. € 25.00   2014*

CROTOY, LE

CROTOY, LE *3B2* (2km N Rural) *50.22968, 1.64140*
Camping La Ferme de Tarteron, Route de Rue, 80550 Le Crotoy [03 22 27 06 75; fax 03 22 27 02 49; contact@letarteron.fr; www.letarteron.fr]
Fr A16 exit junc 24 onto D32, then D940 around Rue twd Le Crotoy. Pass D4 dir St Firmin site on L. Med, hdg, mkd, pt shd, wc; chem disp; shwrs inc; EHU (4-10A) €3.50-8; gas; shop; snacks; bar; playgrnd; pool (htd); beach sand 1.5km; wifi; 80% statics; quiet. "Conv Marquenterre bird park & steam train fr Le Crotoy; v clean, basic san facs; 2km walk to town, off rd; barrier ent." 1 Apr-31 Oct. € 30.00   2018*

CROTOY, LE *3B2* (3km N Rural/Coastal) *50.23905, 1.63182* Kawan Club Camping Le Ridin, Mayocq, 80550 Le Crotoy [03 22 27 03 22; fax 03 22 27 70 76; leridin@baiedesommepleinair.com; www.campingleridin.com] Fr N exit A16 junc 24 dir Rue & Le Crotoy; at rndabt on D940 on app to Le Crotoy take D4 (due W) to sp St Firmin; take 2nd rd to L, site sp. Or fr S exit A16 junc 23 onto D40/D940 to Le Crotoy; at rndabt cont strt over onto D4; in 800m turn R; site on R in 1km. NB Do not ent Le Crotoy town with c'van. Lge, hdstg, hdg, mkd, unshd, wc (htd); chem disp; mv service pnt; fam bthrm; shwrs inc; EHU (4-10A) €3-5.50; gas; lndry; shop; rest; snacks; bar; playgrnd; pool (htd); paddling pool; beach sand 1km; red long stay; entmnt; wifi; TV; 60% statics; dogs €2; Eng spkn; adv bkg acc; ccard acc; golf 10km; bike hire; games rm; tennis 4km; CKE/CCI. "Some sm, tight pitches bet statics; narr site rds not suitable lge o'fits; helpful staff; fitness rm; clean san facs, unisex LS; bird sanctuary at Marquenterre; quiet except noise fr adj gravel pit/lorries; Le Crotoy interesting town; vg site."
♦ 31 Mar-6 Nov. € 30.00   2012*

CROTOY, LE *3B2* (4km N Coastal) *50.24941, 1.61145*
Camping Les Aubépines, 800 Rue de la Maye, St Firmin, 80550 Le Crotoy [03 22 27 01 34; fax 03 22 27 13 66; lesaubepines@baiedesommepleinair.com; www.baiedesommepleinair.com] Exit A16 junc 23 to Le Crotoy via D40 & D940; then foll sp St Firmin; site sp. Or exit A16 junc 24 onto D32 dir Rue; by-pass Rue but take D4 to St Firmin; sp 1 km after church. Site on rd to beach on W of D4. Med, hdg, mkd, pt shd, wc (htd); chem disp; fam bthrm; shwrs inc; EHU (3-10A) €3-8 (poss long lead req); gas; lndry; shop; bbq; playgrnd; pool (htd); paddling pool; beach sand 1km; entmnt; wifi; 40% statics; dogs €2; phone; Eng spkn; adv bkg acc; ccard acc; horseriding; bike hire; games rm; CKE/CCI. "Peaceful, popular, well-run site; tourers sited with statics; lovely pool; gd cycling & walking; check office opening hrs for early dep; Marquenterre ornithological park 3km; steam train 3km; excel." ♦ 25 Mar-1 Nov. € 29.00   2016*

CROZON *2E2* (7km E Coastal) *48.24204, -4.42932*
Camping L'Aber, Tal-ar-Groas,50 Route de la Plage de l'Aber, 29160 Crozon [02 98 27 02 96 or 06 75 62 39 07 (mob); contact@camping-aber.com; www.camping-aber.com] On D887 turn S in Tal-ar-Groas foll camp sp to site in 1km on R. Med, mkd, pt shd, pt sl, terr, wc; chem disp; shwrs inc; EHU (5A) €3.40; gas; lndry; snacks; bar; pool (htd); beach sand 1km; 50% statics; dogs €1.50; adv bkg acc; quiet; fishing; sailing; windsurfing. "Great views." ♦ 1 Apr-31 Oct. € 20.60   2017*

> **"Satellite navigation makes touring much easier"**
>
> Remember most sat navs don't know if you're towing or in a larger vehicle – always use yours alongside maps and site directions.

CUISEAUX *9A2* (5km W Rural) *46.49570, 5.32662*
Camping Le Domaine de Louvarel, 71480 Champagnat [03 85 76 62 71; info@louvarel.com; www.louvarel.com] Exit A39 junc 9 dir Cuiseaux; foll sp 'Base de Loisirs de Louvarel'. Or fr D1083 exit Champagnat & foll sp to site on lakeside. Med, hdg, mkd, pt shd, terr, wc (htd); chem disp; mv service pnt; fam bthrm; shwrs inc; EHU (10A) incl; lndry; rest; snacks; bar; bbq; playgrnd; pool (htd); paddling pool; beach sand; sw nr; wifi; 7% statics; dogs €2; phone; Eng spkn; adv bkg acc; quiet; bike hire; games area; boating; fishing; CKE/CCI. "Excel, clean site; helpful manager; o'night m'vans area; excel, immac san facs; nice rest & bar; gd walking; free use of canoes; busy."
♦ 12 Apr-27 Sep. € 38.00   2014*

CUVILLY *3C3* (2km N Rural) *49.56750, 2.70790*
Camping de Sorel, 24 Rue St Claude, 60490 Orvillers-Sorel [03 44 85 02 74; fax 03 44 42 11 65; contact@aestiva.fr; www.camping-sorel.com] Exit A1/E15 at junc 12 (Roye) S'bound or 11 (Ressons) N'bound. Site on E of D1017. Med, mkd, pt shd, wc (htd); chem disp; mv service pnt; fam bthrm; shwrs inc; EHU (10A) €3; lndry; shop; rest; snacks; bar; bbq; playgrnd; wifi; TV; 50% statics; quiet; games area. "Pleasant situation; conv NH A1 & Calais; friendly staff; facs need updating (2014); rec early arr in ssn; rv fishing 10km; busy at w/end; 30 mins Parc Astérix; plenty to visit." ♦ 1 Feb-15 Dec. € 32.00   2014*

DAGLAN *7D3* (4km N Rural) *44.76732, 1.17590*
Camping Le Moulin de Paulhiac, 24250 Daglan [05 53 28 20 88; fax 05 53 29 33 45; francis.armagnac@wanadoo.fr; www.moulin-de-paulhiac.com] D57 SW fr Sarlat, across rv into St Cybranet & site in 2km. Fr Souillac W on D703 alongside Rv Dordogne; x-ing rv onto D46 (nr Domme) & D50, to site. Med, mkd, hdg, shd, wc; chem disp; mv service pnt; shwrs; EHU (6-10A) €3.70-4.40; gas; lndry; shop; rest; snacks; bar; playgrnd; pool (htd); beach shgl; entmnt; TV; 20% statics; dogs €1.90; Eng spkn; adv bkg acc; quiet; ccard acc; canoeing; waterslide; rv fishing adj; CKE/CCI. "Pretty site; friendly, helpful staff; vg fruit/veg mkt Sun in vill; highly rec." ♦ 15 May-16 Sep. € 25.00   2017*

DAMAZAN *7D2* (2km S Rural) *44.27966, 0.27739*
Camping Du Lac (formerly Municipal), Lac du Moulineau, 47160 Saint Pierre de Buzet [05 53 89 74 36 or 06 27 11 03 57; contact@campingdulac47.com; www.campingdulac47.com] Fr A62 take junc 6, turn R at rndabt onto D8; almost immed take slip rd sp Damazan/Buzet-dur-Baïse; at top take 2nd R sp Buzet (1st turning goes to lake only). Site 1km on R, sp fr rd. Sm, mkd, hdstg, hdg, pt shd, pt sl, wc; chem disp; shwrs inc; EHU (10A) €3; lndry; shop nr; rest nr; bar nr; bbq; playgrnd; sw nr; wifi; 2% statics; dogs; adv bkg acc; CKE/CCI. "Pretty site by lake; helpful staff; next to cricket club; clean basic san facs; attractive Bastide town; conv NH; needs updating; fair; easy access fr a'route." ♦ 1 Jul-31 Aug. € 24.50   2015*

DANGE ST ROMAIN *4H2* (3km N Rural) *46.96944, 0.60399* **Camp Municipal, 8 Rue des Buxières, 86220 Les Ormes [05 49 21 23 43; les-ormes@cg86.fr; www.tourisme-vienne.com]** Turn W off D910 in cent Les Ormes onto D1a sp Vellèches & Marigny-Marmande, foll site sp to site on rv. Med, mkd, pt shd, pt sl, wc; chem disp; fam bthrm; shwrs inc; EHU (10A) inc; lndry; shop; rest nr; bbq; playgrnd; wifi; 10% statics; dogs €1.20; Eng spkn; adv bkg acc; quiet; tennis 100m; canoe launching area; CKE/CCI. "Lovely, quiet, peaceful setting on rv bank; helpful warden; clean basic modern san facs; poss travellers; quiet vill in walking dist; chateau in walking dist; gd NH; vg." ♦ 1 Apr-30 Sep. € 11.00   2018*

DARBRES *9D2* (10km NE Rural) *44.63370, 4.50740*
Camping Les Charmilles, Le Clapas, 07170 Darbres, Ardèche [04 75 88 56 27; info@campinglescharmilles.fr; www.campinglescharmilles.fr] E fr Aubenas on D259; turn L on D224 at Lussas; fork R after Darbres & site in 2km on L sp. Steep app. Med, pt shd, terr, wc; chem disp; shwrs inc; EHU (5-10A) inc; shop; rest; snacks; pool; 10% statics; dogs €2; Eng spkn; adv bkg acc. "Free tow if in trouble on app." ♦ 27 Apr-30 Sep. € 44.50   2013*

DAX *8E1* (11km W Rural) *43.68706, -1.14687* **FFCC**
Camping à la Ferme Bertranborde (Lafitte), 975 Route des Clarions, 40180 Rivière-Saas-et-Gourby [05 58 97 58 39; bertranborde@orange.fr] Turn S off D824 5km W of Dax onto D113, sp Angoumé; at x-rd in 2km turn R (by water tower); then immed L; site on R in 100m, well sp. Or fr N10/A63, exit junc 9 onto D824 dir Dax; in 5km turn R onto D113, then as bef. Sm, pt shd, pt sl, wc; own san rec; chem disp; mv service pnt; shwrs inc; EHU (4-10A) €2.50-4.50; lndry; shop nr; bbq; playgrnd; dogs €0.50; Eng spkn; adv bkg acc; quiet; ice; CKE/CCI. "Peaceful CL-type site; beautiful garden; friendly, helpful owners; meals on request; min 2 nights high ssn; poss travellers festival time; excel; lovely site." € 16.40   2016*

DAX *8E1* (2km W Rural) *43.71189, -1.07304* **Camping Les Chênes, Allée du Bois de Boulogne, 40100 Dax [05 58 90 05 53; campingleschenes@bala-dax.fr; www.camping-leschenes-dax.com]** Fr D824 to Dax, foll sp Bois de Boulogne, cross rlwy bdge & rv bdge & foll camp sp on rv bank. Well sp. Lge, mkd, shd, serviced pitches; wc (htd); chem disp; mv service pnt; fam bthrm; shwrs inc; EHU (10A) inc; gas; lndry; shop; rest nr; snacks; bar; bbq; playgrnd; pool; wifi; TV; 80% statics; dogs €1.50; Eng spkn; adv bkg acc; ccard acc; games rm; bike hire; CKE/CCI. "Excel position; easy walk along rv into town; poss noise fr school adj; conv thermal baths at Dax; modernised site with uptodate htd, clean san facs; lovely pool and child area; interesting spa town." ♦ 15 Mar-31 Oct. € 19.50   2018*

> **"There aren't many sites open at this time of year"**
>
> If you're travelling outside peak season remember to call ahead to check site opening dates – even if the entry says 'open all year'.

DAX *8E1* (3km NW Rural) *43.72020, -1.09365* **FFCC**
Camping Les Pins du Soleil, Route des Minières, La Pince, 40990 St Paul-les-Dax [05 58 91 37 91; fax 05 58 91 00 24; info@pinsoleil.com; www.pinsoleil.com] Exit N10 junc 11 sp Dax onto D16. Cross D824 & turn R onto D459 S. Cross rndabt & cont on D459, Route des Minières. Site sp in pine forest. Med, mkd, hdg, pt shd, pt sl, serviced pitches; wc (htd); chem disp; mv service pnt; fam bthrm; shwrs inc; EHU (5A) €2; gas; lndry; shop; rest nr; snacks; bar; bbq; playgrnd; pool; paddling pool; red long stay; entmnt; wifi; TV; 25% statics; dogs €2; phone; Eng spkn; ccard acc; tennis 2km; games area; bike hire. "Nice, quiet site (LS); various pitch sizes, some spacious; soft, sandy soil poss problem when wet; helpful, friendly staff; excel pool; spa 2km; conv Pyrenees & Biarritz; vg; not well maintained (2018); NH only." ♦ 1 Apr-31 Oct. € 26.00   2018*

DEAUVILLE

DEAUVILLE *3D4* (3km S Urban) *49.32903, 0.08593*
Camping La Vallée de Deauville, Ave de la Vallée, 14800 St Arnoult [02 31 88 58 17; fax 02 31 88 11 57; www.camping-deauville.com] Fr Deauville take D27 dir Caen, turn R onto D278 to St Arnoult, foll site sp. Lge, mkd, hdg, hdstg, pt shd, wc (htd); fam bthrm; shwrs inc; EHU (10A) €4; gas; lndry; shop; rest; snacks; bar; playgrnd; pool (htd); beach sand 4km; entmnt; wifi; 80% statics; dogs €4; phone; Eng spkn; ccard acc; waterslide; games rm; lake fishing; CKE/CCI. "Easy access to beaches & resorts; conv Le Havre using Pont de Normandie; lake walks & activities on site; excel san facs." ♦ 1 Apr-2 Nov. € 30.00 2017*

See advertisement

DECAZEVILLE *7D4* (9km NE Rural) *44.62920, 2.32030*
Camping La Plaine, Le Bourg, 12300 St Parthem [05 65 64 05 24 or 05 65 43 03 99; infos@camping-laplaine.fr; www.camping-laplaine.fr]
N fr Decazeville on D963; in 6km over narr bdge take 1st turn R onto D42 to St Parthem. Site 1km past vill on R. Med, hdg, mkd, pt shd, wc; chem disp; shwrs inc; EHU (6A) inc; lndry; rest; snacks; bar; bbq; playgrnd; pool; wifi; 5% statics; dogs €1.50; phone; Eng spkn; adv bkg acc; quiet; tennis; CKE/CCI. "Idyllic setting on banks of Rv Lot; friendly Dutch owners; excel walking; vg." ♦ 1 Apr-31 Oct. € 24.50 2017*

⊞ **DECAZEVILLE** *7D4* (3km NW Rural) *44.58819, 2.22145* FFCC Camping Le Roquelongue, 12300 Boisse-Penchot [05 65 63 39 67; info@camping-roquelongue.com; www.camping-roquelongue.com]
Fr D963 N fr Decazeville turn W onto D140 & D42 to Boisse-Penchot. Rte via D21 not rec (steep hill & acute turn). Site mid-way bet Boisse-Penchot & Livinhac-le-Haut on D42. Med, mkd, hdg, pt shd, wc; chem disp; shwrs inc; EHU (6-10A) €4.20-4.80; gas; lndry; shop; snacks; bar; playgrnd; pool (htd); entmnt; wifi; 10% statics; dogs free; phone; adv bkg acc; quiet; canoeing; tennis; fishing; bike hire; CKE/CCI. "Direct access Rv Lot; pitches gd size; san facs clean; no twin axles; excel base for Lot Valley." ♦ € 18.30 2016*

DECIZE *4H4* (1km NE Urban) *46.83487, 3.45552*
Camping des Halles, Allée Marcel Merle, 58300 Decize [03 86 25 14 05 or 03 86 25 03 23 (Mairie); fax 03 86 77 11 48; aquadis1@wanadoo.fr; www.des-vacances-vertes.com or www.aquadis-loisirs.com]
Fr Nevers take D981 to Decize, look for sp for 'Stade Nautique Camping'. Lge, mkd, pt shd, wc; shwrs inc; EHU (6A) €2.30 (poss rev pol); gas; shop; snacks; TV (pitch); dogs €1.60; Eng spkn; quiet; ccard acc; CKE/CCI. "Site on banks of Rv Loire; lge pitches, some by rv; helpful staff; san facs clean but need update; no twin axles; poss diff access pitches due trees; shady, flat walk into town; mkt Fri; town v interesting, 15 min walk." ♦ 1 May-15 Oct. € 18.00 2013*

⊞ **DEYME** *8F3* (0km NE Rural) *43.48672, 1.5322*
Camping Les Violettes, Porte de Toulouse, 31450 Deyme [05 61 81 72 07; fax 05 61 27 17 31; campinglesviolettes@wanadoo.fr; www.campinglesviolettes.com] SE fr Toulouse to Carcassonne on N113, sp on L, 12km fr Toulouse (after passing Deyme sp). Med, mkd, hdstg, pt shd, wc (htd); mv service pnt; shwrs inc; EHU (6A) €4; lndry; shop; rest; snacks; bar; bbq; playgrnd; TV; 60% statics; dogs €0.70; quiet; CKE/CCI. "Helpful, friendly staff; facs run down (Jun 2009); poss muddy when wet; 800m fr Canal du Midi & 10km fr Space City; Park & Ride 2.5km & metro to Toulouse; san facs updated (2018); sw pool nrby." € 25.00 2018*

DIE *9D2* (1km NE Rural) *44.75444, 5.37778* FFCC
Camping La Riou-Merle, Route de Romeyer, 26150 Die [04 75 22 21 31; lerioumerle@gmail.com; www.camping-lerioumerle.com] Fr Gap on D93 heading twd Valence. Cont on D93 twd town cent; R on D742 to Romeyer. Site on L in 200m. On D93 fr Crest foll sp round town cent onto D742. Med, pt shd, pt sl, wc; chem disp; mv service pnt; shwrs inc; EHU (10A) €4.20; lndry; shop nr; rest; playgrnd; pool; wifi; 30% statics; dogs €2; Eng spkn; quiet; fishing. "Clean, well laid out site; friendly, helpful staff; gd san facs; 15 min walk to attractive town; rec." 1 Apr-15 Oct. € 27.00 2016*

DIGNE LES BAINS

DIE *9D2* (2km NW Rural) *44.76250, 5.34674* **Camping de Chamarges, Route de Crest, 26150 Die [04 75 22 14 13 or 04 75 22 06 77; campingchamarges@ orange.fr]** Foll D93 twd Valence, site on L by Rv Drôme. Med, mkd, pt shd, wc; chem disp; shwrs inc; EHU (3-6A) €2.90-3.60; gas; shop nr; rest; snacks; bar; bbq (gas); playgrnd; pool; sw nr; entmnt; wifi; TV; dogs €1.60; phone; Eng spkn; adv bkg rec; quiet; ccard acc; fishing adj; canoeing adj; CKE/CCI. "Beautiful mountainous area; vg; friendly owners." ♦ 1 Apr-13 Sep. € 12.00   2012*

DIEPPE *3C2* (3km S Urban) *49.90040, 1.07472* **Camping Vitamin, 865 Chemin des Vertus, 76550 St Aubin-sur-Scie [02 35 82 11 11; camping-vitamin@ wanadoo.fr; www.camping-vitamin.com]** Fr E or W leave Peripherique (D925) S at D927 (sp Rouen). At rndabt take exit onto Canadiens Ave/N27. About 850m take exit twrds Belvedere. Then R onto Rue de la Briqueterie. Site on the R. Med, hdg, mkd, unshd, wc; mv service pnt; shwrs inc; EHU (10A) inc; lndry; shop nr; snacks; bar; playgrnd; pool (covrd); paddling pool; beach shgl 2km; wifi; 80% statics; dogs €3; adv bkg acc; ccard acc; games area; CKE/CCI. "Lovely, well-kept site; san facs immac; poss boggy in wet; conv ferries; excel; auto barrier for early dep; v useful & gd value; on bus rte to Dieppe; off clsd 1200-1430; lots of statics & ssn workers; lge retail pk nrby; Aldi at ent; fully equipped site; fair." 31 Mar-1 Oct. € 29.50   2018*

DIEPPE *3C2* (5km S Rural) *49.87063, 1.14426* **Camping des 2 Rivières, 76880 Martigny [02 35 85 60 82; fax 02 35 85 95 16; www.camping-2-rivieres.com]** Martigny vill on D154 S fr Dieppe. If appr fr Dieppe, ent is on L bef vill sp. Med, pt shd, wc; EHU (6A) €3.05; lndry; shop; playgrnd; dogs €1.70; adv bkg rec; quiet; horseriding nr; watersports nr. "Attractive, pleasant, spacious site by lge lake; access poss diff long o'fits due parked vehicles; mountain biking nrby; Arques forest nrby; cycle paths; highly rec." 31 Mar-08 Oct. € 20.60   2017*

DIEPPE *3C2* (4km SW Rural) *49.89820, 1.05705* **Camping La Source, 63 Rue des Tisserands, Petit-Appeville, 76550 Hautot-sur-Mer [02 35 84 27 04; fax 02 35 82 25 02; info@camping-la-source.fr; www.camping-la-source.fr]** Fr Dieppe ferry terminal foll sp Paris, take D925 W dir Fécamp. In 2km at Petit Appeville turn L, site in 800m on rvside. NB 4m bdge bef ent & narr rd to site - not suitable v lge o'fits. Med, mkd, pt shd, wc; chem disp; mv service pnt; shwrs inc; EHU (10A) €4.20; lndry; shop nr; bar; playgrnd; pool (htd); beach sand 3km; sw nr; entmnt; wifi; TV; 10% statics; dogs €2.20; adv bkg acc; quiet; ccard acc; golf 4km; bike hire; games area; boating adj; games rm; fishing adj; CKE/CCI. "Lovely, well-kept site in attractive setting; some lge pitches; pleasant, vg, clean san facs; footpath to Le Plessis vill; gd cycling; excel NH for ferry; MH pitches sm, but backs onto delightful stream and fmland." ♦ 15 Mar-15 Oct. € 30.00   2017*

DIEPPE *3C2* (6km SW Rural) *49.90886, 1.04069* **Camping Marqueval, 1210 Rue de la Mer, 76550 Pourville-sur-Mer [02 35 82 66 46; fax 02 35 84 55 03; contact@campinglemarqueval.com; www.campinglemarqueval.com]** Site well sp fr D75. Lge, mkd, hdg, pt shd, wc (htd); chem disp; mv service pnt; fam bthrm; shwrs; EHU (6A) €2.50; lndry; shop; rest; snacks; bar; bbq; playgrnd; pool (htd); paddling pool; beach sand 1.2km; entmnt; wifi; TV; 70% statics; dogs €2; Eng spkn; adv bkg acc; quiet; ccard acc; games rm; lake fishing; CKE/CCI. "Attractive, well-kept site; san facs clean but tired; delightful coastal area close by; Bois Du Moutiers gdns highly rec; spa; dog walk on site." ♦ 20 Mar-15 Oct. € 28.00   2017*

DIEPPE *3C2* (9km SW Urban) *49.87297, 1.04497* **Camp Municipal du Colombier, 453 Rue Loucheur, 76550 Offranville [02 35 85 21 14; fax 02 35 04 52 67]** W fr Dieppe on D925, take L turn on D55 to Offranville, site clearly sp in vill to Parc du Colombier. NB Pt of site cul-de-sac, explore on foot bef towing in. Med, mkd, hdg, pt shd, wc; chem disp; shwrs inc; EHU (10A) €2.20 (poss rev pol); gas; lndry; shop; rest; beach shgl 5km; 80% statics; Eng spkn; CKE/CCI. "Pleasant setting in ornamental gardens; vg clean site & facs; helpful staff; gates clsd 2200-0700; ask warden how to operate in his absence; conv ferries; easy walk to town; rec; gd site; michelin star rest adj." ♦ 1 Apr-15 Oct. € 21.00   2017*

DIEULEFIT *9D2* (1km SW Urban) *44.52129, 5.06126* **Le Domaine des Grands Prés, Chemin de la Bicoque, 26220 Dieulefit [04 75 49 94 36 or 06 30 57 08 43 (mob); info@lesgrandspres-dromeprovencale.com; www.lesgrandspres-dromeprovencale.com]** Fr N of A7 take exit 17 twd Dieulefit/Montelimar. At rndabt, take 2nd exit onto N7. Turn L onto D74. Drive thro the vill of Souzet, La Batie-Rolland & la Begude de Mazenc. Campsite located bef town on S side of the rd on the R. Med, hdstg, mkd, pt shd, wc; chem disp; fam bthrm; shwrs; EHU (10A) €3.90; lndry; bbq; playgrnd; pool; paddling pool; wifi; TV; dogs €2; bus 0.2km; Eng spkn; adv bkg acc; quiet; ccard acc; CCI. "Site on o'skirts of vill (10 min walk) with all facs with unusual accomodations; attractive, well run site." ♦ 20 Mar-1 Nov. € 24.00   2016*

DIGNE LES BAINS *10E3* (2km SE Rural) *44.08646, 6.25028* **Camping Les Eaux Chaudes, 32 Ave des Thermes, 04000 Digne-les-Bains [04 92 32 31 04; fax 04 92 34 59 80; info@campingleseauxchaudes.com; www.campingleseauxchaudes.com]** Fr S foll N85 sp 'Centre Ville' over bdge keeping L to rndabt, turn 1st R sp Les Thermes (D20). Past Intermarché, site on R 1.6km after leaving town. Med, mkd, pt shd, wc (htd); chem disp; shwrs inc; EHU (4-10A) €2-3.50 (poss rev pol); gas; lndry; shop nr; snacks; pool; sw nr; wifi; 50% statics; dogs €1.50; adv bkg acc; quiet; games area; CKE/CCI. "Pleasant site with plenty shd; vg san facs; gd pool; gd touring base; 500m fr thermal baths; National Geological Reserve in town cent; phone ahead LS to check open." ♦ 1 Apr-31 Oct. € 31.50   2013*

DIGOIN

DIGOIN 9A1 (1km W Urban) 46.47985, 3.96780
Camping de la Chevrette, 41 Rue de la Chevrette, 71160 Digoin [03 85 53 11 49; fax 03 85 88 59 70; info@lachevrette.com; www.lachevrette.com]
Fr S exit N79/E62 at junc 24 sp Digoin-la-Grève D994, then on D979 cross bdge over Rv Loire. Take 1st L, sp campng/piscine. Med, hdstg, hdg, pt shd, pt sl, terr, wc (htd); chem disp; mv service pnt; shwrs inc; EHU inc (10A) rev pol; lndry; shop nr; rest; snacks; bar; playgrnd; wifi; 5% statics; dogs €1; Eng spkn; adv bkg acc; quiet; fishing; CKE/CCI. "Pleasant, well-run site by rv; diff sized pitches, some lge; friendly, helpful owner; ltd facs LS; barrier clsd 2200-0700; htd pool adj; pleasant walk & dog walking by rv to town; lovely cycle rides along canals; gd NH; canoe hire avail." ♦ 1 Apr-30 Sep. € 22.00   2018*

DIJON 6G1 (3km W Urban) 47.32127, 5.01108
Camping du Lac Kir, 3 Blvd du Chanoine Kir, 21000 Dijon [03 80 30 54 01; reservation@camping-du-lac-dijon.com; www.camping-du-lac-dijon.com]
Site situated nr N5, Lac Kir. Fr Dijon ring rd take N5 exit (W) sp A38 twd Paris. At traff lts L sp A31, site immed on R under 3m high bdge. Do not tow thro town cent. Med, mkd, hdstg, pt shd, wc; chem disp; shwrs inc; EHU (10-16A) inc (poss rev pol & long lead req); gas; shop nr; sw; dogs €2 vaccinated & on lead; bus adj; Eng spkn; quiet; ccard acc; fishing; boating; CKE/CCI. "Rvside path to town; wonderful surrounding area; easy bus to town; gd security; poss flooding; Aire for MH at ent (€10 per night); one point for chem disp." 1 Apr-31 Oct. € 20.00   2017*

> ### "That's changed – Should I let the Club know?"
> If you find something on site that's different from the site entry, fill in a report and let us know. See camc.com/europereport.

DINAN 2E3 (3km N Rural) 48.48903, -2.00855
Camping Beauséjour, La Hisse, 22100 St Samson-sur-Rance [02 96 39 53 27; fax 02 96 87 94 12; beausejour-stsamson@orange.fr; www.beausejour-camping.com] Fr Dinan take N176/D766 N twd Dinard. In 3km turn R onto D12 dir Taden then foll sp thro Plouer-sur-Rance to La Hisse; site sp. Fr N exit N176/E401 dir Plouer-sur-Rance, then foll sp La Hisse. Med, mkd, hdg, pt shd, pt sl, wc; chem disp; mv service pnt; fam bthrm; shwrs inc; EHU (10A) €3.45 (poss rev pol); lndry; shop; rest; snacks; bar; playgrnd; pool (htd); red long stay; wifi; 40% statics; dogs €2.05; phone; Eng spkn; adv bkg acc; quiet; ccard acc; tennis; games area; sailing; CKE/CCI. "Pleasant, well-kept site; gd pool; quiet & spacious Jun & Sep; no twin axles; excel rv walks; excel well maintained site; footpath down to Rance and rvside walks; gd facs; off open 1000-1230 & 1600-1930." ♦ 1 May-30 Oct. € 20.00   2017*

DINAN 2E3 (4km NE Rural) 48.47138, -2.02277
Camp International de la Hallerais, 4 rue de la Robardais, 22100 Taden [02 96 39 15 93 or 02 96 87 63 50 (Mairie); fax 02 96 39 94 64; contact@camping-lahallerais.com; www.camping-lahallerais.com]
Fr Dinan take N176/D766 N twd Dinard. In 3km turn R onto D12 to Taden. Foll La Hallerais & Taden sp to site. Fr N176 take exit onto D166 dir Taden; turn onto D766 dir Taden, then L onto D12A sp Taden & Camping. At rndabt on ent Taden take 1st exit onto D12 sp Dinan; site rd is 500m on L. Do not ent Dinan. Site adj Rv Rance. Lge, mkd, pt shd, terr, serviced pitches; wc (htd); chem disp; mv service pnt; shwrs inc; EHU (6A) inc (rev pol); gas; lndry; shop nr; rest nr; snacks; bar nr; bbq; playgrnd; pool (htd); paddling pool; beach shgl 10km; wifi; TV; 80% statics; dogs free; Eng spkn; adv bkg acc; quiet; ccard acc; tennis; fishing; horseriding 500m; games rm. "Lovely site, well maintained; clean san facs; vg pool; phone ahead if arr late at night LS; ltd office hrs LS - report to bar; sh walk to Taden; rvside walk to Dinan medieval town; rv trips; no o'fits over 9m (check in adv rec); storage facs; gd walking, cycling; mkt Thur am & Fri eve; rec; excel; san facs refurb (2017); v helpful owner." ♦ 11 Mar-12 Nov. € 22.00   2018*

DINAN 2E3 (1km S Urban) 48.44743, -2.04631
Camp Municipal Châteaubriand, 103 Rue Châteaubriand, 22100 Dinan [02 96 39 11 96 or 02 96 39 22 43 (LS); fax 02 96 87 08 40; campingmunicipaldinan@wanadoo.fr; www.brittanytourism.com]
Fr N176 (E or W) take slip rd for Dinan cent; at lge rndbt in cent take 2nd R; down hill to site on L (500m) after 2nd set of traff lts. Sm, mkd, pt shd, pt sl, wc; chem disp; mv service pnt; shwrs inc; EHU (6A) €2.70; lndry; shop nr; rest nr; bar nr; bbq; dogs €1.50; phone; Eng spkn; adv bkg acc; ccard acc; games area; CKE/CCI. "Pleasant, helpful staff; high kerb onto pitches; poss mkt traders; opening dates vary each year; check time when barrier locked, espec LS; gd cent for Rance valley, St Malo & coast; gd location; bar adj; san facs old but clean; 20 min walk to chateau & town; excel position nr park; more level pitches in lower area of site beyond san block." 1 Jun-30 Sep. € 15.00   2017*

DINARD 2E3 (0km W Coastal) 48.6309, -2.08413
Camping La Touesse, 171 Rue de la Ville Gehan, La Fourberie, 35800 St Lunaire [02 99 46 61 13; fax 02 99 16 02 58; camping.la.touesse@wanadoo.fr; www.campinglatouesse.com] Exit Dinard on St Lunaire coast rd D/86, site sp. Med, mkd, pt shd, wc; mv service pnt; fam bthrm; shwrs inc; EHU (5-10A) €3.30-3.70; lndry; shop; snacks; bar; playgrnd; beach sand 300m; entmnt; TV; dogs €1.50; adv bkg req; golf 2km; tennis 1.5km; CKE/CCI. "Vg well-kept site; gd beach & rocks nr; friendly recep." ♦ 1 Apr-30 Sep. € 30.00   2017*

DOL DE BRETAGNE

France

CAMPING LONGCHAMP**
Aquatic park with water slides
Family campsite, only 100 m from a magnificent sand beach and close to several shops. Covered heated swimming pool. Mobile homes and chalets for rent. Ideally located to discover the Emerald Coast.
CAMPING LONGCHAMP**** • 773, boulevard de saint Cast • 35800 SAINT LUNAIRE - DINARD
tél : 0033 2 99 46 33 98 • www.camping-longchamp.com • contact@camping-longchamp.com

DINARD 2E3 (1km W Coastal) 48.63486, -2.07928
Camping Le Port Blanc, Rue de Sergent Boulanger, 35800 Dinard [02 99 46 10 74; fax 02 99 16 90 91; info@camping-port-blanc.com; www.camping-port-blanc.com] Fr Dinard foll sp to St Lunaire on D786 for 1.5km. Turn R at traff lts by football grnd to site. Lge, mkd, pt shd, pt sl, terr, wc; chem disp; fam bthrm; shwrs inc; EHU (10A) €3.95; lndry; shop; rest nr; snacks; bar; playgrnd; beach sand adj; 40% statics; dogs €1.90; phone; bus; adv bkg acc; ccard acc; CKE/CCI. "O'looks sand beach; gd san facs; excel site; walk along coast to town; well run site; gd pitches; gd access to beach." ♦ 1 Apr-30 Sep. € 33.00   2014*

DINARD 2E3 (5km W Coastal) 48.63406, -2.12039
Camping Longchamp, Blvd de St Cast, 35800 St Lunaire [02 99 46 33 98; fax 02 99 46 02 71; contact@camping-longchamp.com; www.camping-longchamp.com] Fr St Malo on D168 turn R sp St Lunaire, In 1km turn R at g'ge into St Lunaire, site sp to W of vill on D786 dir St Briac. Lge, hdg, mkd, pt shd, wc; chem disp; mv service pnt; fam bthrm; shwrs inc; EHU (4-10A) €3.40-4.20; gas; lndry; shop; rest; snacks; bar; bbq; playgrnd; beach sand 300m; 30% statics; dogs €2; bus 500m; Eng spkn; adv bkg rec; quiet. "Excel, well-run site; clean facs; friendly, helpful staff; clean beach 300m; conv Brittany Ferries at St Malo; site under new ownership, much improved (2013); pool htd; quiet site nr beautiful seaside town." ♦ 1Apr-30 Sep. € 35.00   2013*

See advertisement

DIVONNE LES BAINS 9A3 (3km N Rural) 46.37487, 6.12143 **Camping Indigo Divonne, Quartier Villard, 01220 Divonne-les-Bains [04 50 20 01 95 or 04 42 20 47 25 (LS); fax 04 50 20 00 35; divonne@camping-indigo.com; www.camping-indigo.com]** Exit E62 dir Divonne-les-Bains approx 12km N of Geneva. Fr town on D984, foll sp to site. Lge, hdg, mkd, shd, sl, terr, wc (htd); chem disp; shwrs inc; EHU (4A) €5; gas; lndry; shop; rest; snacks; bar; pool (htd); paddling pool; sw nr; entmnt; TV; 50% statics; dogs €5; Eng spkn; adv bkg acc; quiet; ccard acc; tennis; games area; CKE/CCI. "Helpful owner; levellers req; Lake Geneva 8km; new recep & san facs renovated (2015)." 4 Apr-18 Oct. € 26.00   2014*

DOL DE BRETAGNE 2E4 (7km NE Coastal) 48.60052, -1.71182 **Camping de l'Aumône, 35120 Cherrueix [02 99 48 84 82 or 06 48 64 60 16 (mob); laumone@orange.fr; www.camping-de-laumone.fr]** Exit D797 Pontorson-Cancale rd S onto D82, opp rd leading into vill of Cherrueix. Site in 100m. Med, unshd, wc; chem disp; mv service pnt; fam bthrm; shwrs inc; EHU (10A) €3.50; gas; lndry; shop nr; snacks; bar; bbq; playgrnd; beach 1km; wifi; 20% statics; dogs free; Eng spkn; adv bkg rec; bike hire; CKE/CCI. "Sm chateau; gd sized pitches; modern san facs; noise fr adj rd daytime; sand yachting nrby; beach not suitable for sw; vg; pleasant, friendly owners." 15 Apr-6 Nov. € 22.70   2017*

> "I like to fill in the reports as I travel from site to site"
>
> You'll find report forms at the back of this guide, or you can fill them in online at camc.com/europereport.

DOL DE BRETAGNE 2E4 (6km E Rural) 48.54941, -1.68386 **FFCC Camping du Vieux Chêne, Le Motais, 35120 Baguer-Pican [02 99 48 09 55; vieux.chene@wanadoo.fr; www.camping-vieuxchene.fr]** Leave N176 E of Dol on slip rd sp Baguer-Pican. At traff lts turn L thro vill, site on R of D576 at far end vill adj lake. Lge, mkd, hdg, pt shd, pt sl, wc; chem disp; mv service pnt; fam bthrm; shwrs inc; EHU (10A) inc (poss rev pol & poss long cable req); gas; lndry; shop; rest; snacks; bar; bbq (charcoal, gas); playgrnd; pool (htd); paddling pool; red long stay; entmnt; wifi; TV; dogs €3; phone; Eng spkn; adv bkg acc; quiet; ccard acc; games rm; lake fishing; games area; horseriding; CKE/CCI. "Well-kept site in grnds of former farm; 3 sm unfenced lakes; plenty rm for pitch access; no o'fits over 7.5m high ssn; various pitch sizes, some sm & some with fruit trees; friendly & helpful staff; gd san facs; shop & rest ltd LS; mkt in Dol Sat; gd; boggy when wet." ♦ 1 May-20 Sep. € 30.00   2016*

DOL DE BRETAGNE

DOL DE BRETAGNE *2E4* (7km SE Rural) 48.49150, -1.72990 **Les Ormes, Domaine & Resort, 35120 Epiniac [02 99 73 53 60 or 02 99 73 53 01; fax 02 99 73 53 55; info@lesormes.com; www.lesormes.com]** Exit N176/E401 at W end of Dol-de-Bretagne; then S fr Dol on D795 twd Combourg & Rennes, in 7km site on L of rd, clearly sp. V lge, hdg, mkd, pt shd, pt sl, wc; chem disp; fam bthrm; shwrs inc; EHU (6A) inc (poss long lead req); gas; lndry; shop; rest; snacks; bar; bbq (charcoal, gas); playgrnd; pool (htd); paddling pool; entmnt; wifi; TV; 80% statics; dogs €3; Eng spkn; adv bkg acc; ccard acc; lake fishing; bike hire; tennis; archery; golf; waterslide; canoeing; games rm; horseriding; CKE/CCI. "Busy site set in well-kept chateau grnds; cricket; o'fits 8m & over by request only; helpful staff; clean san facs; covrd aquacentre; conv Mont St Michel, St Malo & Dinan; pedalos; disco at night; mkt Sat; golfing discount for campers; poss noisy (disco); excel all round." ♦ 14 Apr-16 Sep. € 57.00   2017*

DOLE *6H2* (2km E Rural) 47.08937, 5.50339 **FFCC Camping Le Pasquier, 18 Chemin Victor et Georges Thévenot, 39100 Dole [03 84 72 02 61; fax 03 84 79 23 44; camping-pasquier@wanadoo.fr or lola@camping-le-pasquier.com; www.camping-le-pasquier.com]** Fr A39 foll sp dir Dole & Le Pasquier. Fr all dir foll sp 'Centre ville' then foll site name sp & 'Stade Camping' in town; well sp. Site on rvside private rd. Narr app. Lge, mkd, hdg, pt shd, wc (htd); chem disp; mv service pnt; shwrs inc; EHU (10A) inc (rev pol); lndry; shop; snacks; bar; playgrnd; pool; red long stay; twin axles; entmnt; wifi; 10% statics; dogs €1.50; Eng spkn; quiet; ccard acc; fishing; rv; CKE/CCI. "Generous pitches; aqua park 2km; friendly recep; gd clean san facs; pleasant pool; walk along rv (otters!) into Dole; dir access rv 500m; poss mosquito problem; mkt Tues, Thur, Sat; gd NH; poss cr." 15 Mar-25 Oct. € 22.00   2017*

DOLE *6H2* (8km SE Rural) 47.01660, 5.48160 **FFCC Camping Les Bords de Loue, 39100 Parcey [03 84 71 03 82; fax 03 84 71 03 42; contact@jura-camping.fr; www.jura-camping.fr]** Leave A39 at junc 6 onto D905 dir Chalon-sur-Saône. Turn L (SE) at rndabt after going under A39 & in 6km turn R into vill of Parcey at 'Camping' sp. Lge, pt shd, serviced pitches; wc; chem disp; shwrs inc; EHU (6A) inc; lndry; rest; snacks; bar; bbq; playgrnd; pool; paddling pool; beach adj; wifi; 20% statics; dogs €2 must keep on lead; phone; Eng spkn; adv bkg acc; ccard acc; fishing; boating; CKE/CCI. "Pleasant site." ♦ 14 May-15 Sep. € 28.00   2013*

DOMFRONT *4E1* (1km S Urban) 48.58808, -0.65045 **Camp Municipal Champ Passais, 4 Rue du Champ Passais, 61700 Domfront [02 33 37 37 66 or 02 33 38 92 24 (LS); fax 02 33 30 60 67; mairie-de-domfront@wanadoo.fr; http://camping-municipal-domfront.jimdo.com]** Fr N on D962 foll Laval sps into Domfront; then take D976 W dir Mont-St Michel; site turning in 400m on L; well sp bet old quarter & town cent. Fr S on D962 well sp fr edge of town. Sm, hdg, mkd, hdstg, pt shd, terr, wc; chem disp; shwrs inc; EHU (10A) €3; lndry; shop nr; rest nr; bar nr; playgrnd; TV; dogs €0.80; phone; Eng spkn; rv fishing nrby; CKE/CCI. "Pleasant, well-kept terr site; helpful, charming staff; gd security; sh, steep walk to medieval town; no twin axles; vg; site still excel value; shade improving with growing trees." ♦ 1 Apr-30 Sep. € 7.30   2018*

DOMPIERRE SUR BESBRE *9A1* (2km S Urban) 46.51378, 3.68276 **Camp Municipal, La Madeleine, Parc des Sports, 03290 Dompierre-sur-Besbre [04 70 34 55 57 or 04 70 48 11 39 (Mairie); camping@mairie-dsb.fr; www.dompierre-sur-besbre.fr]** At E end of town nr rv behind stadium; sp. Med, hdg, shd, pt sl, wc (htd); chem disp; mv service pnt; fam bthrm; shwrs inc; EHU (10A) inc; lndry; shop nr; bbq; wifi; dogs €1; phone; Eng spkn; adv bkg acc; quiet; CKE/CCI. "Smart, well-run, busy site; v well kept gd san facs, but poss stretched high ssn; excel sports complex; gd for Loire Valley, vineyards & chateaux; highly rec LS; excel; large easy acc pitches; gd adj park for dog walking; rv walks; cycling & running tracks; town v close; full sports facs adj; v friendly recep; rec." ♦ 15 May-15 Sep. € 12.00   2016*

DONJON, LE *9A1* (1km N Urban) 46.35317, 3.79188 **Camp Municipal, 4 Chemin Denys Bournatot, 03130 Le Donjon [04 70 99 56 35 or 04 70 99 50 25 (Mairie); fax 04 74 99 58 02; mairie-le-donjon@wanadoo.fr; www.allier-tourisme.com]** Fr Lapalisse N on D994. Site sp fr town cent on D166 dir Monétay-sur-Loire. Sm, pt shd, pt sl, wc; mv service pnt; shwrs inc; EHU (10A) €2.50; shop nr; rest nr; bar nr; dogs; quiet; fishing 900m; windsurfing 900m; sailing 900m; CKE/CCI♦ 1 May-31 Oct. € 8.00   2016*

DONZENAC *7C3* (2km S Rural) 45.21978, 1.51784 **FFCC Camping La Rivière, Route d'Ussac, 19270 Donzenac [05 55 85 63 95; info@campingdonzenac.com; www.campinglariviere.jimdo.com]** Fr N exit A20 at junc 47 (do not use junc 48); take exit at rndabt dir Donzenac D920. In 3km on ent Donzenac keep on D920 & go down hill to rndabt. Take 2nd exit D170 sp Uzzac, site on R in 500m. NB Avoid app thro Donzenac as narr & diff for lge o'fits. Fr S exit junc 49 to Ussac. Med, mkd, pt shd, wc; chem disp; mv service pnt; shwrs inc; EHU (10A) €3.10; gas; lndry; shop; snacks; bar; playgrnd; pool (htd); wifi; TV; dogs €1.10; adv bkg rec; bike hire; games rm; fishing 5km; tennis; games area. "Excel facs." ♦ 1 May-30 Sep. € 29.00   2014*

DORAT, LE *7A3 (1km S Urban) 46.21161, 1.08237*
Camp Municipal, Route de la Planche des Dames, 87210 Le Dorat [05 55 60 72 20 (Mairie) or 05 55 60 76 81 (TO); fax 05 55 68 27 87] Site sp fr D675 & in town cent. Sm, mkd, hdg, pt shd, wc; shwrs inc; EHU (16A) €3.10; shop nr; rest nr; bar nr; Eng spkn; quiet; CKE/CCI. "Excel, basic site; permanent barrier, code fr TO; clean facs, but ltd & own san rec high ssn; warden calls evenings; public uses footpath as sh-cut; v clean, quiet site, must book in TO in town sq; friendly & helpful." 1 May-30 Sep. € 6.00   2013*

⊞ **DORCEAU** *4E2 (2km N Rural) 48.43717, 0.82742*
Camping Forest View, L'Espérance, 61110 Dorceau [02 33 83 78 55; peter@forestviewfrance.com; www.forestviewleisurebreaks.co.uk] Fr D920 (ring rd) in Rémalard take D38 sp Bretoncelles; site in 4km on corner on L. Sm, pt shd, pt sl, wc; chem disp; shwrs inc; EHU (10A) inc; wifi; 10% statics; dogs €1.40; adv bkg acc; quiet; lake fishing; CKE/CCI. "Simple, well-kept site in beautiful countryside; helpful, friendly British owners; painting workshops; gd touring base or NH; excel; evening meal avail with hosts, reasonable price." € 10.00   2013*

DORMANS *3D4 (9km NE Rural) 49.10638, 3.73380*
Camping Rural (Nowack), 10 Rue de Bailly, 51700 Vandières [03 26 58 02 69 or 03 26 58 08 79; fax 03 26 58 39 62; champagne@nowack.fr; www.champagne-nowack.com] Fr N3, turn N at Port Binson, over Rv Marne, then turn W onto D1 for 3km, then N into Vandières. Site on R about 50m fr start of Rue Bailly, sp 'Champagne Nowack' or 'Camping Nowack.' Sm, pt shd, pt sl, wc; shwrs inc; EHU (6-10A) inc; lndry; bbq; playgrnd; TV; adv bkg acc; ccard acc; tennis 2km; fishing 1km; CKE/CCI. "Charming, peaceful, CL-type site in orchard; friendly owners; lovely, well-kept modern san facs; fresh water tap beside chem disp (2011); boating 6km; site poss muddy when wet; site pt of vineyard, poss grape pickers in Sep, champagne can be bought; pool 8km; excel value." 1 Apr-1 Nov. € 17.00   2017*

DOUAI *3B4 (11km S Rural) 50.29004, 3.04345* **FFCC**
Camp Municipal de la Sablière, Rue du 8 Mai 1945, 62490 Tortequesne [03 21 24 14 94; fax 03 21 07 46 07; camping@tortequesne.fr; www.tortequesne.fr] Fr D643 Douai-Cambrai rd; turn S onto D956 to Tortequesne where site sp. Sm, mkd, hdstg, hdg, pt shd, wc; shwrs inc; EHU (6A) €3; shop nr; playgrnd; wifi; 80% statics; dogs €0.50; tennis; games area; CKE/CCI. "Gd site; park & fishing adj; late night arr area; new & clean san facs (2014); recep open 10:00-12:00 and 16:30-20:00; walking in La Valée de la Sensée; family friendly site; barrier locked when warden leaves (am & pm)." 1 Apr-30 Sep. € 15.00   2017*

DOUAI *3B4 (12km S Rural) 50.27374, 3.10565* **Camp Municipal Les Biselles, Chemin des Bisselles, 59151 Arleux [03 27 89 52 36 or 03 27 93 10 00; fax 03 27 94 37 38; office.tourisme@arleux.com]** Exit A2 junc 14 at Cambrai & take D643 twd Douai, after 5km turn W at Bugnicourt to Arleux. Site sp in vill adj canal La Sensée. Lge, hdg, mkd, shd, wc; shwrs inc; EHU €6.85; playgrnd; pool; 96% statics; dogs; phone; adv bkg acc; quiet; rv fishing; tennis 200m; games area. "Very few touring pitches; basic san facs; gd cycling along canal." ♦ 1 Apr-31 Oct. € 17.50   2015*

DOUARNENEZ *2E2 (14km W Coastal) 48.08416, -4.48194* **Camping Pors Péron, 29790 Beuzec-Cap-Sizun [02 98 70 40 24; fax 02 98 70 54 46; info@campingporsperon.com; www.campingporsperon.com]** W fr Douarnenez take D7 sp Poullan-sur-Mer. Thro Poullan & in approx 4km turn R sp Pors-Piron, foll site & beach sp. Site bef Beuzec-Cap-Sizun vill. Med, mkd, hdg, pt shd, pt sl, wc; chem disp; mv service pnt; fam bthrm; shwrs inc; EHU (10A) inc (long lead req); gas; lndry; shop; snacks; bbq; playgrnd; pool; beach sand 200m; wifi; 5% statics; dogs €1.60; adv bkg acc; quiet; bike hire; games area; CKE/CCI. "Pleasant, quiet site nr beautiful sandy cove; friendly, helpful British owners; immac san facs, poss insufficient high ssn & long way fr some pitches; poss ltd privacy in ladies' facs; gd; excel site leaflet; gd pitches; excel well maintained site; highly rec." ♦ 1 Apr-30 Sep. € 22.00   2017*

DOUARNENEZ *2E2 (2km W Rural) 48.09270, -4.35220* **Camping de Trézulien, Route de Trézulien, 29100 Douarnenez [02 98 74 12 30 or 06 80 01 17 98 (mob); fax 09 70 06 31 74; contact@camping-trezulien.com; www.camping-trezulien.com]** Ent Douarnenez fr E on D7; foll sp 'Centre Ville'; turn L at traff lts sp to Tréboul. Cross rv bdge into Ave de la Gare, at PO turn L, then 1st L. Turn R at island, foll site sp. Lge, pt shd, terr, wc; fam bthrm; shwrs inc; EHU (10A) €3.50; gas; lndry; shop nr; playgrnd; beach sand 1.5km; dogs €2; quiet. "Pleasant site; steep hill fr ent to recep; 1km by foot to Les Sables Blancs; conv Pointe du Raz." 1 Apr-30 Sep. € 14.00   2013*

DOUARNENEZ *2E2 (4km W Urban) 48.09895, -4.36189* **Camping de Kerleyou, 29100 Douarnenez-Tréboul [02 98 74 13 03; fax 02 98 74 09 61; info@camping-kerleyou.com; www.camping-kerleyou.com]** Ent Douarnenez fr E on D7, soll sp 'Cent Ville', L at traff lts past Treboul. Cross over bdge into Ave la Gare, at PO turn L then 1st L, up hill, at rndabt take 3rd exit. Foll sp to site. Med, hdg, mkd, unshd, pt sl, wc; chem disp; mv service pnt; fam bthrm; shwrs; EHU (10A); lndry; shop; snacks; bar; bbq; playgrnd; pool (htd); paddling pool; beach 1km; wifi; TV; 70% statics; dogs €2.50; phone; Eng spkn; adv bkg acc; quiet; games rm; games area. "Excel." 9 Apr-20 Sep. € 23.00   2015*

DOUARNENEZ

DOUARNENEZ *2E2* (6km W Rural) *48.08166, -4.40722*
Camping de la Baie de Douarnenez, Route de Douarnenez, 29100 Poullan-sur-Mer [02 98 74 26 39; fax 02 98 74 55 97; info@pil-koad.com; www.camping-douarnenez.com or www.flowercampings.com]
Fr E take circular rd around Douarnenez on D7/D765 dir Audierne & Poullan-sur-Mer, Tréboul & Pointe-du-Van. Site on L off D7 1km fr Poullan-sur-Mer vill, shortly after church spire becomes visible. Med, hdg, mkd, pt shd, wc (htd); chem disp; mv service pnt; fam bthrm; shwrs inc; EHU (10A) inc; gas; lndry; shop; rest; snacks; bar; bbq (charcoal, gas); playgrnd; paddling pool; beach sand 5km; entmnt; wifi; TV; dogs €4; Eng spkn; adv bkg acc; quiet; ccard acc; bike hire; watersports 4km; games area; tennis; games rm; lake fishing; CKE/CCI. "Tranquil site in woodland; gd sized pitches; staff friendly; ltd facs LS; entmnt well away fr most pitches; gd for families; mkd walks, guided high ssn; no o'fits over 10m high ssn; statics (tour ops); mkt Mon & Fri; pools & water slides great fun." ♦
26 Apr-13 Sep. € 36.00   2013*

> **"I need an on-site restaurant"**
>
> We do our best to make sure site information is correct, but it is always best to check any must-have facilities are still available or will be open during your visit.

DOUCIER *6H2* (6km N Rural) *46.71321, 5.79709*
Camping du Gît, Monnet-le-Bourg, 39300 Montigny-sur-l'Ain [03 84 51 21 17 or 03 84 37 87 58 (LS); christian.olivier22@wanadoo.fr; www.campingdugit.com] W fr Champagnole on D471 foll sp Monnet-la-Ville, foll camp sp thro vill, turn L at x-rds to church; site immed afterwards on R behind church in Monnet-la-Ville (also known as Monnet-le-Bourg). Med, mkd, pt shd, pt sl, wc; chem disp; shwrs inc; EHU (5A) €2.50; lndry; shop nr; rest; snacks; bar; playgrnd; sw nr; dogs €1.50; adv bkg acc; quiet; fishing 1.5km; games area; CKE/CCI. "Peaceful site; beautiful views; kayaking 1.5km; lge pitches; gd san facs." ♦
1 Jun-31 Aug. € 12.00   2012*

DOUE LA FONTAINE *4G1* (1km N Rural) *47.20338, -0.28165* Camp Municipal Le Douet, Rue des Blanchisseries, 49700 Doué-la-Fontaine [02 41 59 14 47 or 06 22 71 25 53 (mob); contact@camping-lesrivesdudouet.fr; www.camping-lesrivesdudouet.fr]
Fr Doué N on D761 twd Angers; site in sports grnd on o'skts of town; sp. Med, mkd, pt shd, wc; chem disp; shwrs inc; EHU (6A) inc; lndry; shop nr; rest nr; wifi; 10% statics; tennis; CKE/CCI. "Clean, well-run site; gd, flat pitches; helpful warden; gd san facs; lovely park & museum; htd pool adj high ssn; conv zoo, rose gardens & Cadre Noir Equestrian Cent; poss ssn workers LS; gd shd; shop will order bread; vg." ♦ 1 Apr-15 Oct.
€ 21.50   2014*

DOUE LA FONTAINE *4G1* (2km SW Rural) *47.17390, -0.34750* Camping La Vallée des Vignes, 49700 Concourson-sur-Layon [02 41 59 86 35; fax 02 44 84 46 95; info@campingvdv.com; www.campingvdv.com]
D960 fr Doué-la-Fontaine (dir Cholet) to Concourson-sur-Layon; site 1st R 250m after bdge on leaving Concourson-sur-Layon. Or fr Angers foll sp dir Cholet & Poitiers; then foll sp Doué-la-Fontaine. Med, mkd, pt shd, serviced pitches; wc (htd); chem disp; fam bthrm; shwrs inc; EHU (10A) €4; gas; lndry; shop; rest; snacks; bar; bbq; playgrnd; pool (htd); paddling pool; red long stay; entmnt; wifi; TV; 5% statics; dogs €3; bus; Eng spkn; adv bkg acc; quiet; ccard acc; bike hire; CKE/CCI. "Peaceful site poss open all yr weather permitting - phone to check; vg, clean, well-maintained facs; pool open & htd early ssn; some pitches diff lge o'fits due o'hanging trees; conv for Loire chateaux & Futuroscope; new French owners (2016), v helpful." ♦
1 Apr-30 Sep. € 28.00   2017*

DOUE LA FONTAINE *4G1* (18km W Rural) *47.18032, -0.43574* Camping KathyDave, Les Beauliers, 49540 La Fosse de Tigné [02 41 67 92 10 or 06 14 60 81 63 (mob); bookings@camping-kathydave.co.uk; www.camping-kathydave.co.uk] Fr Doué-la-Fontaine on D84 to Tigne, turn S thro La Fosse-de-Tigné. Pass chateau, site sp on R. NB Tight turn in, access poss diff lge o'fits. Sm, mkd, pt shd, wc (htd); chem disp; shwrs inc; EHU (16A) (poss rev pol); lndry; rest nr; bbq (gas); wifi; dogs free; adv bkg acc; quiet; CKE/CCI. "Tranquil orchard site in picturesque area; welcoming, helpful British owners; gd san facs; some pitches restricted by trees; gd touring base; adults only preferred; phone ahead rec; excel; sm CL type site in an old orchard."
1 Jun-30 Sep. € 14.50   2015*

DOUE LA FONTAINE *4G1* (8km W Rural) *47.19355, -0.37075* Camping Les Grésillons, Chemin des Grésillons, 49700 St Georges-sur-Layon [02 41 50 02 32; fax 02 41 50 03 16; camping.gresillon@wanadoo.fr; www.camping-gresillons.com]
Fr Doué-la-Fontaine on D84, site sp. In St Georges-sur-Layon turn L opp church. Sm, hdg, hdstg, pt shd, terr, wc (htd); chem disp; fam bthrm; shwrs inc; EHU (6-10A) €2.90-3.50; lndry; shop; rest; bar nr; playgrnd; pool (htd); red long stay; entmnt; 28% statics; dogs free; Eng spkn; adv bkg acc; quiet; ccard acc; rv fishing 200m; games area; CKE/CCI. "Delightful site in area of vineyards; friendly, helpful owner; gem of a site." ♦
1 Apr-30 Sep. € 20.00   2017*

DOUHET, LE *7B2* (2km S Rural) *45.81080, -0.55288*
Camping La Roulerie, 17100 Le Douhet [05 46 96 40 07 or 06 75 24 91 96 (mob); www.camping-laroulerie.fr] Fr Niort to Saintes, site on W side of D150 in vill of La Roulerie. Sm, mkd, hdstg, hdg, pt shd, wc; chem disp; mv service pnt; shwrs inc; EHU (16A) €3.50; lndry; shop; playgrnd; pool; 10% statics; dogs €1; Eng spkn; adv bkg acc; quiet; games area; CKE/CCI. "Sm pitches; full by early eve; friendly, helpful owner; gd san facs; vg value; gd NH."
1 May-15 Oct. € 9.00   2013*

DREUX

DOURDAN *4E3* (1km NE Urban) *48.52572, 2.02878*
Camping Les Petits Prés, 11 Rue Pierre Mendès France, 91410 Dourdan [01 64 59 64 83 or 01 60 81 14 17; fax 01 60 81 14 29; camping@mairie-dourdan.fr; www.mairie-dourdan.fr] Exit A10 junc 10 dir Dourdan; foll by-pass sp Arpajon; after 5th rndabt site 200m on L. Med, mkd, unshd, pt sl, wc (htd); shwrs; EHU (4A) €3.40; rest nr; playgrnd; 75% statics; Eng spkn; adv bkg acc. "Gd NH; friendly welcome; gas & supmkt 500m; clean dated san facs, ltd LS; pool 500m; town worth visit." 1 Apr-30 Sep. € 14.00   2012*

DOUSSARD *9B3* (3km N Rural) *45.80256, 6.20960*
Camping La Ravoire, Route de la Ravoire, Bout-du-Lac, 74210 Doussard [04 50 44 37 80; fax 04 50 32 90 60; info@camping-la-ravoire.fr; www.camping-la-ravoire.fr] Fr Annecy, turn R at traff lts in Bredanaz, then immed L & foll rd across cycle track & uphill for 1km, at vill take L fork, site immed on L. Fr Albertville on B1508, turn L opp Complex Sportif, Bout de Lac sp Lathuile; cont, x-ing cycle track to rndabt; turn R & cont 2km past other sites; at junc turn sharp R, site immed on L. Med, mkd, hdstg, hdg, pt shd, pt sl, serviced pitches; wc (htd); chem disp; mv service pnt; fam bthrm; shwrs inc; EHU (5A) inc (poss rev pol); gas; lndry; shop; rest nr; snacks; bar; playgrnd; pool (htd); paddling pool; sw nr; TV; 10% statics; dogs; phone; Eng spkn; adv bkg rec; quiet; ccard acc; bike hire; sailing adj; horseriding adj; games area; waterslide; fishing adj; windsurfing adj; golf adj; CKE/CCI. "Excel, well-kept, busy site with mountain views; friendly staff & atmosphere; immac facs; lake ferry fr Doussard; cycle paths adj." ♦ 8 May-14 Sep. € 40.40   2014*

DOUSSARD *9B3* (3km N Rural) *45.80302, 6.20608*
Camping Le Taillefer, 1530 Route de Chaparon, 74210 Doussard [04 50 44 30 30; info@campingletaillefer.com; www.campingletaillefer.com]
Fr Annecy take D1508 twd Faverges & Albertville. At traff lts in Bredannaz turn R, then immed L for 1.5km; site immed on L by vill sp 'Chaparon'. Do NOT turn into ent by Bureau but stop on rd & ask for instructions as no access to pitches fr Bureau ent. Or, to avoid Annecy, fr Faverges, along D1508, turn L (sp Lathuile) after Complex Sportif at Bout-du-Lac. Turn R at rndabt (sp Chaparon), site is on R after 2.5km. Sm, mkd, pt shd, pt sl, terr, wc; chem disp; mv service pnt; shwrs inc; EHU (6A) €4.50 (check rev pol); lndry; shop; snacks; bar; bbq (charcoal, gas); playgrnd; beach shgl 3km; sw nr; red long stay; TV; dogs €2.50; Eng spkn; adv bkg acc; quiet; games rm; bike hire; watersports 2km; sailing; tennis 100m; rafting. "Peaceful, simple, family-run site nr Lake Annecy; fantastic mountain views; access some pitches poss diff due steep terraces; friendly, helpful owners; dated, clean san facs; no o'fits over 8m high ssn; canyoning; climbing; vg rest in easy walking dist; mkt Mon; worth another visit." ♦ 1 May-29 Sep. € 21.00   2014*

DOUVILLE *7C3* (2km S Rural) *44.99271, 0.59853*
Camping Lestaubière, Pont-St Mamet, 24140 Douville [05 53 82 98 15 or 06 82 28 23 97; lestaubiere@gmail.com; camping-lestaubiere.fr]
Well sp fr N & S on N21. Approx 21km N of Bergerac. Exit fr N21 sp Pont St. Mamet. Med, mkd, pt shd, wc; mv service pnt; fam bthrm; shwrs inc; EHU (6-10A) €4-5; gas; lndry; rest; snacks; bar; bbq; playgrnd; pool (htd); paddling pool; sw; twin axles; entmnt; wifi; TV; 10% statics; dogs €3.50; phone; Eng spkn; adv bkg acc; quiet; ccard acc; tennis 5km; games area; lake fishing; games rm; CKE/CCI. "Spacious, park-like site with beautiful views; v lge pitches; owned by friendly, helpful Dutch couple; twin axles (high ssn only); vg modern san facs; superb out of ssn; site in 2 sep sections; a few v lge drive thro pitches; excel." ♦ 15 Apr-30 Sep. € 35.00   2018*

DOUZE, LA *7C3* (3km E Rural) *45.06493, 0.88817*
Camping Laulurie en Périgord (Naturist), 24330 La Douze [05 53 06 74 00; fax 05 53 06 77 55; toutain@laulurie.com; www.laulurie.com]
Fr Périgueux S on N221; in 8km turn S on D710 twd Le Bugue. Or exit A89 onto D710 S. On ent La Douze turn L & foll arrow signs. Sm, hdg, mkd, pt shd, pt sl, wc; chem disp; shwrs inc; EHU (3-10A); gas; shop; rest; snacks; bar; playgrnd; pool; dogs €3; adv bkg acc; quiet; ccard acc; sep car park. "Excel site; friendly owners; gd touring base for Dordogne & Périgueux; INF card req." ♦ 15 May-15 Sep. € 34.50   2013*

DRAGUIGNAN *10F3* (4km S Rural) *43.51796, 6.47536* Camping La Foux, Quartier La Foux, 83300 Draguignan [04 94 68 18 27; www.camping-lafoux.com] Fr A8, take Le Muy intersection onto N555 N to Draguignan. Site ent on R at ent to town sp Sport Centre Foux. Fr Draguignan, take N555 S; just after 'End of Draguignan' sp, double back at rndabt & turn R. Lge, unshd, pt sl, wc; shwrs inc; EHU (4-10A) €3.50-5; lndry; shop; rest; bar; playgrnd; entmnt; TV; dogs €3.90; quiet; fishing. "Friendly staff; v poor san facs; care needed long vehicles on ent site; unshd, but many trees planted (2011); poss flooding when wet; easy access to Riviera coast." 20 Jun-30 Sep. € 16.00   2016*

⊞ **DREUX** *4E2* (10km NW Rural) *48.76149, 1.29041*
Camping Etangs de Marsalin, 3 Place du Général de Gaulle, 28500 Vert-en-Drouais [02 37 82 92 23; fax 02 37 82 85 47; contact@campingdemarsalin.fr; www.campingdemarsalin.fr] Fr W on N12 dir Dreux, cross dual c'way bef petrol stn onto D152 to Vert-en-Drouais; on ent turn R to church, site on L. Well sp. Med, hdg, mkd, hdstg, pt shd, pt sl, wc (htd); chem disp; shwrs inc; EHU (6-10A), €4.60 (poss rev pol, long leads poss req, avail at recep); lndry; shop; rest nr; snacks; bar nr; wifi; 80% statics; dogs; Eng spkn; quiet; lake fishing 2km; CKE/CCI. "Peaceful location; working families on site; friendly, helpful staff; basic, clean san facs; touring pitches at far end far fr facs; muddy when wet; lovely vill; conv Versailles; NH only; site tidy and clean; bar 100m; facs refurb (2016)." ♦ € 18.00   2018*

DUNKERQUE

DUNKERQUE *3A3* (12km NE Coastal) *51.07600, 2.55524* **Camping Perroquet Plage, 59123 Bray-Dunes [03 28 58 37 37; fax 03 28 58 37 01; www.camping-perroquet.com]** On Dunkerque-Ostend D601, about 100m fr Belgian frontier, thro vill on D947; cont 1km to traff lts, R on D60 thro vill, past rlwy stn to site on L. NB Take care some speed humps. V lge, hdg, hdstg, pt shd, wc (htd); chem disp; shwrs; EHU (4A) €4.50; lndry; shop; rest; snacks; bar; playgrnd; beach sand adj; entmnt; wifi; 85% statics; dogs €0.50; Eng spkn; adv bkg req; sauna; watersports; gym; tennis; CKE/CCI. "Busy, well-kept site; lge pitches; if parked nr site ent, v long walk to beach; lge bar & rest nr beach (long walk fr ent); gd san facs, poss far; many local attractions; conv NH for ferries; gd." ♦ 1 Apr-1 Oct. € 15.00   2012*

> **"Satellite navigation makes touring much easier"**
>
> Remember most sat navs don't know if you're towing or in a larger vehicle – always use yours alongside maps and site directions.

DUNKERQUE *3A3* (5km NE Coastal) *51.05171, 2.42025* **Camp Municipal La Licorne, 1005 Blvd de l'Europe, 59240 Dunkerque [03 28 69 26 68; fax 03 28 69 56 21; www.campingdelalicorne.com]** Exit A16 junc 62 sp 'Malo'; at end of slip rd traff lts turn L sp Malo-les-Bains; in 2km (at 5th traff lts) turn R at camping sp; at 2nd traff lts past BP g'ge turn L. Site on L (cont strt to rndabt & return on opp side of dual c'way to ent). Lge, mkd, unshd, pt sl, wc (htd); chem disp; mv service pnt; shwrs; EHU (10A) €4.40 (poss long lead); gas; lndry; shop; rest; snacks; bar; playgrnd; pool; beach sand adj; 50% statics; dogs €0.90; bus fr site ent; Eng spkn; adv bkg acc; quiet; clsd 2200-0700; CKE/CCI. "Gd, secure NH for ferries - obtain gate code for early depart; pitches uneven; many site rd humps; promenade along sea front to town cent; site backs onto sand dunes & beach; poss windy; m'van o'night area; gd san facs; bus stop nr site ent; very attractive site; site tired, san facs need refurb." ♦ 1 Apr-11 Nov. € 24.00   2018*

⊞ **DURAS** *7D2* (1km N Rural) *44.68293, 0.18602* **Camping Le Cabri, Malherbe, Route de Savignac, 47120 Duras [05 53 83 81 03; fax 05 53 83 08 91; holidays@lecabri.eu.com; www.lecabri.eu.com]** Fr N on D708, turn R on ent Duras onto D203 at mini-rndabt by tourist info shop; site in 800m. Sm, hdg, hdstg, unshd, terr, wc (htd); chem disp; fam bthrm; shwrs inc; EHU (4-10A) €3-5; lndry; shop nr; rest; snacks; bar; bbq; playgrnd; pool; entmnt; wifi; 30% statics; dogs €2; bus 500m; Eng spkn; adv bkg acc; quiet; ccard acc; games area; tennis 1km; games rm; CKE/CCI. "Spacious site with wide views; lge pitches; British owners (CC members); san facs poss tired high ssn (2011); vg rest; Duras an attractive town; excel." ♦ € 17.00   2012*

DURBAN CORBIERES *8G4* (1km N Rural) *43.00017, 2.81977* **Camping Municipal De Durban-Corbieres, Lespazo, 11360 Durhan-Corbieres [04 68 45 06 81; fax 04 68 45 38 16; mairiededurham@orange.fr]** Fr A61 take exit 25, foll D611 S across to Durban Corbieres. Site sp on R on entering Vill. Sm, hdg, pt shd, pt sl, wc; shwrs inc; EHU (10A); bbq; twin axles; 10% statics; dogs; bus 0.5km; adv bkg acc; quiet; CCI. "Tranquil site surrounded by rugged hills; pool 0.5km; Cathar castle in vill; vg." ♦ 15 Jun-15 Sep. € 11.00   2014*

DURTAL *4G1* (0km W Urban) *47.67115, -0.23798* **Camping Les Portes de l'Anjou, 9 Rue du Camping, 49430 Durtal [02 41 76 31 80; lesportesdelanjou@camp-in-ouest.com; www.lesportesdelanjou.com]** Exit A11 junc 11 dir La Flèche, by-passing Durtal. At D323 turn R for Durtal, site on L at ent to town. Sps not readily visible, look out for 'Motor C'van Parking'. Med, mkd, hdg, pt shd, wc; chem disp; fam bthrm; shwrs inc; EHU (6A) €3.40; gas; lndry; shop nr; snacks; bar; playgrnd; pool (htd); paddling pool; red long stay; entmnt; wifi; TV; 12% statics; dogs €2.50; Eng spkn; adv bkg acc; quiet; ccard acc; games rm; canoeing; fishing; CKE/CCI. "Site in need of TLC, in pleasant position on Rv Loir; office clsd 12.30-3.30; helpful staff; interesting vill." ♦ 12 Apr-27 Oct. € 22.60   2013*

⊞ **EAUX PUISEAUX** *4F4* (1km SW Rural) *48.11696, 3.88317* **Camping à la Ferme des Haut Frênes (Lambert), 6 Voie de Puiseaux, 10130 Eaux-Puiseaux [03 25 42 15 04; fax 03 25 42 02 95; les.hauts.frenes@wanadoo.fr; www.les-hauts-frenes.com]** N fr St Florentin or S fr Troyes on N77. Ignore D374 but take next turning D111 in NW dir. Site in 2km; well sp. Long o'fits take care at ent gate. Med, hdstg, hdg, mkd, pt shd, wc (htd); chem disp; shwrs inc; EHU (6-15A) €2-3 (poss some rev pol); gas; lndry; shop nr; rest nr; snacks; bbq; playgrnd; red long stay; wifi; TV; dogs €2; Eng spkn; adv bkg acc; quiet; games rm; tennis 3km; CKE/CCI. "Well-kept, tidy farm site in beautiful setting; lge, level pitches; helpful, friendly owners; gd san facs; meals on request; own facs adv high ssn; loyalty card; cider museum in vill; conv m'way; excel NH en rte S; super; v quiet site; gd." ♦ € 18.00   2018*

ECHELLES, LES *9B3* (6km NE Rural) *45.45679, 5.81327* **Camping La Bruyère, Hameau Côte Barrier, 73160 St Jean-de-Couz Chartreuse [04 79 65 79 11 or 04 79 65 74 27 (LS) or 06 29 47 27 43 (mob); camping-labruyere@orange.fr; www.campingsavoie.com]** Heading S on D1006 Chambéry-Lyon rd, after x-ing Col de Coux 15km S of Chambéry take D45 to St Jean-de-Couz; site sp. Med, hdg, pt shd, pt sl, wc; chem disp; shwrs inc; EHU (4-10A) €2.90-5.90; gas; lndry; shop; rest; snacks; bar; bbq; playgrnd; TV; 3% statics; dogs €1; adv bkg acc; quiet. "Peaceful site; magnificent scenery; friendly, helpful owner; vg, clean facs; gd walking area; football; volleyball; Chartreuse caves open to public adj; vg base for touring Chartreuse mountains; video games; waymkd walks fr site; site well looked after; lovely." 15 May-30 Sep. € 15.00   2017*

ELNE

ECHELLES, LES 9B3 (0km SE Urban) 45.43462, 5.75615 **Camping L'Arc-en-Ciel, Chemin des Berges, 38380 Entre-Deux-Guiers [04 76 66 06 97; info@camping-arc-en-ciel.com; www.camping-arc-en-ciel.com]** Fr D520 turn W sp Entre-Deux-Guiers. On ent vill turn R into Ave de Montcelet dir Les Echelles & R again in 100m. Site sp fr D520. Med, hdg, mkd, pt shd, pt sl, wc; chem disp; shwrs inc; EHU (2-4A) €2.50-4.30; gas; lndry; shop nr; rest nr; bar nr; 40% statics; dogs €1.10; CKE/CCI. "Conv La Chartreuse area with spectacular limestone gorges; gd." ♦ 1 Mar-15 Oct. € 32.00   2014*

ECHELLES, LES 9B3 (6km S Rural) 45.39107, 5.73656 **Camp Municipal Les Berges du Guiers, Le Revol, 38380 St Laurent-du-Pont [04 76 55 20 63 or 04 76 06 22 55 (LS); fax 04 76 06 21 21; camping.st-laurent-du-pont@wanadoo.fr; www.camping-chartreuse.com]** On D520 Chambéry-Voiron S fr Les Echelles. On ent St Laurent-du-Pont turn R just bef petrol stn on L. Sm, mkd, pt shd, wc; chem disp; mv service pnt; fam bthrm; shwrs inc; EHU (5A) €3.50; lndry; shop nr; rest nr; bar nr; bbq; playgrnd; wifi; dogs €1; Eng spkn; quiet; tennis 100m; CKE/CCI. "Clean & well-kept; pool 300m; pleasant area; gates clsd 1100-1530; vg." 15 Jun-15 Sep. € 17.50   2017*

ECOMMOY 4F1 (0km NE Urban) 47.83367, 0.27985 **Camp Municipal Les Vaugeons, Rue de la Charité, 72220 Ecommoy [02 43 42 14 14 or 02 43 42 10 14 (Mairie); fax 02 43 42 62 80; mairie.ecommoy@wanadoo.fr]** Heading S on D338 foll sp. Turn E at 2nd traff lts in vill; sp Stade & Camping. Also just off A28. Med, pt shd, pt sl, wc; chem disp; shwrs; EHU (6A) €2.35; lndry; shop nr; playgrnd; Eng spkn; adv bkg acc; quiet; tennis; CKE/CCI. "Site full during Le Mans week (nr circuit); gd san facs; new arr no access when recep clsd, hrs 0900-1130 & 1500-2030; coarse sand/grass surface." ♦ 1 May-30 Sep. € 10.00   2014*

ECOMMOY 4F1 (4km SE Rural) 47.81564, 0.33358 **Camp Municipal Le Chesnaie, 72220 Marigné-Laillé [02 43 42 12 12 (Mairie); fax 02 43 42 61 23; mairie.marigne-laille@wanadoo.fr or mairie.marigne-laille.catherine@wanadoo.fr; www.tourisme-en-sarthe.com]** S on D338 Le Mans-Tours, turn E 3km after Ecommoy twds Marigné-Laillé. Site in 1.5km. Sm, mkd, hdstg, pt shd, wc; shwrs; EHU (10A) inc; shop nr; playgrnd; quiet; fishing adj; tennis; CKE/CCI. "Lovely site; clean, adequate san facs; pleasant warden; if hight barrier down, use phone at ent; lake adj; easy access A28; v warm welcome; basic site, but clean; pool 5km; pretty site, great NH." 1 May-30 Sep. € 8.00   2013*

ECRILLE 4H2 (3km WNW Rural) 46.50973, 5.62042 **Camping La Faz, 4 Pont de Vaux 39270 Ecrille [03 08 25 40 27 06 22 48 10 63 (mob); camping.la.faz@sft.fr; www.jura-camping-lafaz.com]** Fr Stye at the rndabt (the only rndabt onmain rd thro Stye) take dir Geneva, then 50m down on R is Ecrille. Site is 1.5km fr Stye. EHU €3.10; dogs €1.40. "Excel." 27 Apr-30 Sep. € 16.50   2013*

⊞ **EGLETONS** 7C4 (2km NE Rural) 45.41852, 2.06431 **Camping du Lac, 10 Le Pont, 19300 Egletons [05 55 93 14 75; campingegletons@orange.fr; www.camping-egletons.com]** Fr Egletons on D1089 for approx 2km, site 300m past Hôtel Ibis on opp site of rd. Med, mkd, pt shd, terr, wc; chem disp; fam bthrm; shwrs inc; EHU (10A) inc; gas; lndry; shop nr; rest; snacks; bar; playgrnd; pool; paddling pool; sw nr; entmnt; TV; 30% statics; dogs €1.30; phone; Eng spkn; quiet; fishing 300m; watersports 300m; CKE/CCI. "Lovely, wooded site in attractive area; lge pitches; friendly owners; vg; san facs dated but clean." € 13.00   2015*

EGUZON CHANTOME 7A3 (2km NE Urban) 46.44556, 1.58314 **Camping Eguzon La Garenne, 1 Rue Yves Choplin, 36270 Éguzon-Chântôme [02 54 47 44 85; info@campinglagarenne.eu; www.campinglagarenne.eu]** Exit A20 junc 20 onto D36 to Eguzon; on ent vill sq cont strt on, foll sp; site on L in 300m. Med, hdg, pt shd, pt sl, wc; chem disp; mv service pnt; fam bthrm; shwrs inc; EHU (6-10A) inc; lndry; shop nr; rest; snacks; bar; bbq; playgrnd; pool (htd); sw nr; entmnt; wifi; TV; 3% statics; dogs €1.50; phone; Eng spkn; adv bkg acc; quiet; watersports 4km; cycling; CKE/CCI. "All you need on site or in vill; excel; well run, attractive site; poss OAY, phone ahead; only 2 hdstg; gas 300m; site is improving; gd; clean, tidy; v friendly Dutch owners; ACSI acc." ♦ 10 Mar-15 Oct. € 26.00   2018*

⊞ **EGUZON CHANTOME** 7A3 (3km SE Rural) 46.43372, 1.60399 **Camp Municipal du Lac Les Nugiras, Route de Messant, 36270 Eguzon-Chântôme [02 54 47 45 22; fax 02 54 47 47 22; nugiras@orange.fr; www.eguzonlaccreuse.com]** Fr A20 exit junc 20, E on D36 to Eguzon; in vill turn R & foll site sp. Lge, mkd, hdg, pt shd, pt sl, terr, wc (htd); shwrs inc; EHU (10A) €3 (rev pol); lndry; shop; rest; snacks; bar; playgrnd; beach sand 300m; entmnt; 10% statics; dogs; games rm; watersports; CKE/CCI. "Scenic site & region; security barrier; ample, clean facs but v ltd LS; site yourself on arr; waterski school; warden avail early eves; gd winter site; muddy after heavy rain." ♦ € 9.40   2014*

⊞ **ELNE** 10G1 (3km E Coastal) 42.60695, 2.99098 **Camping Le Florida, Route Latour-Bas-Elne, 66200 Elne [04 68 37 80 88; fax 04 68 37 80 76; info@campinglefrorida.com; www.campinglefrorida.com]** Exit A9 junc 42 Perpignan-Sud onto D914 dir Argelès-sur-Mer. Exit D914 junc 7 onto D11 dir Elne Centre, then D40 sp St Cyprien to Latour-Bas-Elne, site sp. Lge, mkd, pt shd, wc; chem disp; mv service pnt; fam bthrm; shwrs inc; EHU (6A) €4; lndry; shop nr; rest nr; snacks; bar; bbq; playgrnd; pool; paddling pool; beach sand 4km; entmnt; wifi; TV; 70% statics; dogs; phone; Eng spkn; adv bkg acc; quiet; ccard acc; games area; games rm; tennis; CKE/CCI. "Excel site; bus to beach high ssn." ♦ € 43.00   2016*

ELNE

ELNE *10G1* (4km S Rural) *42.57570, 2.96514* **Kawan Village Le Haras, Domaine St Galdric, 66900 Palau-del-Vidre [04 68 22 14 50; fax 04 68 37 98 93; haras8@wanadoo.fr; www.camping-le-haras.com]** Exit A9 junc 42 sp Perpignan S dir Argelès-sur-Mer on D900 (N9) & then D914; then exit D914 junc 9 onto D11 to Palau-del-Vidre. Site on L at ent to vill immed after low & narr rlwy bdge. Med, shd, wc; chem disp; mv service pnt; fam bthrm; shwrs inc; EHU (10A) €5; lndry; rest; snacks; bar; bbq (elec, gas); playgrnd; pool; paddling pool; entmnt; wifi; TV; 10% statics; dogs €4; Eng spkn; adv bkg acc; ccard acc; tennis 1km; fishing 50m; archery; games rm; CKE/CCI. "Peaceful, well-kept, family-owned site in wooded parkland; helpful, friendly warden; san facs poss red LS; gd rest & pool; 5 mins walk to delightful vill; no o'fits over 7m high ssn; rds around site poss liable to flood in winter; many walks in area; Collioure worth visit; conv Spanish border; excel." ♦ 1 Apr-29 Sep. € 31.50   2013*

EMBRUN *9D3* (6km N Rural) *44.60290, 6.52150* **FFCC Camping Les Cariamas, Fontmolines, 05380 Châteauroux-les-Alpes [04 92 43 22 63 or 06 30 11 30 57 (mob); p.tim@free.fr; http://les.cariamas.free.fr]** Fr Embrun on N94; in 6km slip rd R to Châteauroux & foll sp to site. Site in 1km down narr but easy lane. Med, mkd, pt shd, pt sl, terr, wc; chem disp; mv service pnt; fam bthrm; shwrs inc; EHU (6A) €3.15; lndry; shop nr; rest; snacks; bar; bbq; playgrnd; pool (htd); sw nr; wifi; 20% statics; dogs €2.50; phone; Eng spkn; adv bkg acc; watersports; bike hire; fishing; tennis 500m; CKE/CCI. "Excel for watersports & walking; mountain views; National Park 3km." 1 Apr-30 Oct. € 21.50   2012*

EMBRUN *9D3* (4km S Urban) *44.54725, 6.48852* **Camping le Petit Liou, Ancienne route de Baratier, 05200 Baratier [04 92 43 19 10; info@camping-lepetitliou.fr; www.camping-lepetitliou.com]** On N94 fr Gap to Briancon turn R at rndabt just bef Embrun. First L after 150m then 1st R. Site on L in 250m, sp. Lge, mkd, hdg, pt shd, pt sl, wc; chem disp; mv service pnt; fam bthrm; shwrs; EHU (3-10A) €3.60-4.20; shop; snacks; bar; bbq; playgrnd; pool (htd); paddling pool; wifi; 5% statics; dogs €1.50; Eng spkn; adv bkg acc; games rm; bike hire; CKE/CCI. "Lovely mountain views; vg." ♦ 1 May-21 Sep. € 22.00   2016*

EMBRUN *9D3* (2km SW Urban) *44.55440, 6.48610* **Camping La Vieille Ferme, La Clapière, 05200 Embrun [04 92 43 04 08; fax 04 92 43 05 18; accueil@campingembrun.com; www.campingembrun.com]** On N94 fr Gap, at rndabt 3rd exit sp Embrun cross Rv Durance then take 1st R, sp La Vielle Ferme, keep L down narr lane, site ent on R. Access poss diff for lge o'fits. Med, mkd, pt shd, wc; chem disp; mv service pnt; shwrs inc; EHU (6-10A) €5-6 (pos rev pol); lndry; shop nr; rest; snacks; bar; playgrnd; red long stay; entmnt; dogs €3; Eng spkn; adv bkg acc; rafting; watersports. "Friendly, Dutch family-run site; canyoning; gd facs; pretty town." ♦ 26 Apr-1 Oct. € 33.00   2015*

EMBRY *3B3* (1km NW Rural) *50.49365, 1.96463* **Aire de Service Camping-Cars d'Embryère, 62990 Embry [03 21 86 77 61]** N fr Embry site is just off D108 dir Hucqueliers & Desvres. Sm, hdstg, wc; mv service pnt; shwrs; EHU £2; lndry; bbq. "M'vans only; modern, well-kept site; jetons fr ccard-operated dispenser for services; conv Boulogne & Calais; simple but well equipped; picnic area & gardens; lovely area."
♦ € 6.00   2015*

ENTRAIGUES *9C3* (0km SW Rural) *44.90064, 5.94606* **Camp Municipal Les Vigneaux, 38740 Entraigues [04 76 30 17 05 or 06 43 76 22 66 (mob); camping.murielbillard@orange.fr]** S on D1085 (N85) fr La Mure, turn L on D114, fork R on D26 to Valbonnais. This rd becomes D526. Site on L on ent Entraigues, 4km beyond Lake Valbonnais. Ent on bend in rd, more diff if ent fr Bourg-d'Oisans. Sm, mkd, pt shd, wc; mv service pnt; shwrs inc; EHU (6A) €2 (poss rev pol); lndry; shop nr; red long stay; 15% statics; dogs €1; adv bkg acc; quiet; fishing; CKE/CCI. "Clean facs; National Park adj; warden visits am & pm." ♦ 1 May-30 Sep. € 14.00   2015*

> **"There aren't many sites open at this time of year"**
>
> If you're travelling outside peak season remember to call ahead to check site opening dates – even if the entry says 'open all year'.

ENTRAYGUES SUR TRUYERE *7D4* (4km NE Rural) *44.67777, 2.58279* **Camping Le Lauradiol (Formaly Municipal), Banhars, 12460 Campouriez [05 65 44 53 95; fax 05 65 44 81 37; info@camping-lelauradiol.com; www.camping-lelauradiol.com]** On D34, sp on rvside. Sm, mkd, hdg, pt shd, wc; EHU (6A) inc; lndry; shop nr; pool (htd); paddling pool; 10% statics; dogs €2; quiet; tennis; CKE/CCI. "Beautiful setting & walks; excel; power mover needed for lge o'fits to access pitches; beautiful site; rv adj; v friendly helpful staff; a real gem." ♦ 1 Jul-31 Aug. € 17.50   2013*

ENTRAYGUES SUR TRUYERE *7D4* (2km S Rural) *44.64218, 2.56406* **Camping Le Val de Saures (formerly Municipal), 12140 Entraygues-sur-Truyère [05 65 44 56 92; fax 05 65 44 27 21; info@camping-valdesaures.com; www.camping-valdesaures.com]** Fr town cent take D920 (twds Espalion) & in 200m turn R over narr rv bdge and then R onto D904. In 200m fork R onto new rd and thro sports complex to site. Med, mkd, pt shd, wc; shwrs; EHU (6A) €3.50; lndry; shop nr; playgrnd; entmnt; 10% statics; dogs €1.50; Eng spkn; quiet; ccard acc. "Pleasant, friendly, gd site; in great situation; footbdge to town over rv; vg, well-kept san facs; recep clsd Sun & pm Mon LS; pool adj; gd touring base." ♦ 1 May-30 Sep. € 29.00   2014*

ENTREVAUX *10E4* (2km NW Rural) *43.96163, 6.79830* **Camping Le Brec, 04320 Entrevaux [04 93 05 42 45; info@camping-dubrec.com; www.camping-dubrec.com]** Site sp on R just after bdge 2km W of Entrevaux on N202. Rd (2km) to site narr with poor surface, passing places & occasional lge lorries. Med, mkd, pt shd, pt sl, wc (htd); chem disp; mv service pnt; fam bthrm; shwrs inc; EHU (10A) €3 (poss long lead req); lndry; snacks; bbq; sw nr; wifi; TV; 10% statics; dogs €1; phone; Eng spkn; adv bkg acc; quiet; ccard acc; watersports cent; fishing adj; boating adj; CKE/CCI. "In beautiful area lake on site; friendly family owners; popular with canoeists; easy rv walk to town; beautiful area; gd." ♦ 15 Mar-15 Oct. € 17.00 2013*

EPERNAY *3D4* (1km NW Urban) *49.05734, 3.95042* **Camp Municipal d'Epernay, Allées de Cumières, 51200 Epernay [03 26 55 32 14; fax 03 26 52 36 09; camping.epernay@free.fr; www.epernay.fr]** Fr Reims take D951 twd Epernay, cross rv & turn R at rndabt onto D301 sp Cumières (look for sp 'Stade Paul Chandon'), site sp. Site adj Stadium. Avoid town at early eve rush hr. Med, hdg, mkd, pt shd, wc (htd); chem disp; mv service pnt; shwrs inc; EHU (10A) inc (poss long lead req); lndry; shop; snacks; bar; bbq; playgrnd; red long stay; wifi; dogs €1.80; phone; Eng spkn; adv bkg acc; ccard acc; fishing; tennis; bike hire; games area; canoeing; CKE/CCI. "Attractive, well-run site on Rv Marne in lovely location; generous pitches; friendly, helpful staff; gd spacious san facs; barrier open 0800-2100 & 0700-2200 high ssn; parking outsite; rec arr early; footpaths along rv into town; htd covrd pool 2km; waterslide 2km; Mercier train tour with wine-tasting; site used by grape pickers; no twin axles or c'vans over 6m acc; gd value; boulangerie and cafe nrby." ♦ 28 Apr-1 Oct. € 22.00 2017*

EPESSES, LES *2H4* (1km N Rural) *46.88920, -0.89950* **FFCC Camping La Bretèche, La Haute Bretèche, 85590 Les Epesses [02 51 57 33 34; fax 02 51 57 41 98; contact@campinglabretache.com; www.camping-la-breteche.com]** Fr Les Herbiers foll D11 to Les Epesses. Turn N on D752, site sp on R by lake - sp fr cent Les Epesses. Med, mkd, hdg, pt shd, wc; chem disp; mv service pnt; fam bthrm; shwrs inc; EHU (10A) €3 (poss rev pol); lndry; shop nr; rest; snacks; bar; playgrnd; entmnt; TV; 30% statics; dogs €1.85; Eng spkn; adv bkg acc; ccard acc; fishing; horseriding; tennis; CKE/CCI. "Well-kept, well-run site; htd pool adj inc; busy high ssn; helpful staff; plenty of attractions nr; events staged in park by lake high ssn; conv Puy du Fou; vg; no waste or water on site, long leads req." ♦ 1 Apr-30 Sep. € 22.00 2012*

⊞ **EPINAL** *6F2* (2km E Urban) *48.17930, 6.46780* **Camping Parc du Château, 37 Rue du Petit Chaperon Rouge, 88000 Epinal [03 29 34 43 65 or 03 29 82 49 41 (LS); fax 03 29 31 05 12; parcduchateau@orange.fr]** Sp fr town cent. Or fr N57 by-pass take exit sp Razimont, site sp in 1km. Med, mkd, hdg, hdstg, pt shd, terr, wc (htd); chem disp; mv service pnt; shwrs inc; EHU (6-10A) €5-6; gas; lndry; snacks; bar; bbq; playgrnd; pool; red long stay; TV; 20% statics; dogs €3; Eng spkn; adv bkg acc; ccard acc; tennis; CKE/CCI. "Lge pitches; ltd facs LS; walk thro park to town; helpful new owners who have improved site; sep m'van park adj, fr €12; exceptionally clean." ♦ € 20.00 2016*

⊞ **EPINAL** *6F2* (8km W Rural) *48.16301, 6.35975* **Kawan Village Club Lac de Bouzey, 19 Rue du Lac, 88390 Sanchey [03 29 82 49 41; fax 03 29 64 28 03; lacdebouzey@orange.fr; www.lacdebouzey.com]** Fr Epinal take D460 sp Darney. In vill of Bouzey turn L at camp sp. Site in few metres, by reservoir. Lge, mkd, hdg, hdstg, pt shd, pt sl, terr, wc (htd); chem disp; mv service pnt; fam bthrm; shwrs inc; EHU (10A) €7; gas; lndry; shop; rest; snacks; bar; bbq; playgrnd; pool (htd); paddling pool; red long stay; entmnt; wifi; TV; 15% statics; dogs €4; phone; Eng spkn; adv bkg acc; quiet; ccard acc; bike hire; fishing; horseriding; games area; CKE/CCI. "Excel site; lake adj; sl slightly but pitches fairly level; ACSI discount in LS; gd cycling area; nice cycle ride to Epinal; pleasant position opp lake." ♦ € 22.00 2016*

ERQUY *2E3* (4km NE Coastal) *48.64201, -2.42456* **Camping Les Hautes Grées, Rue St Michel, Les Hôpitaux, 22430 Erquy [02 96 72 34 78; fax 02 96 72 30 15; hautesgrees@wanadoo.fr; www.camping-hautes-grees.com]** Fr Erquy NE D786 dir Cap Fréhel & Les Hôpitaux sp to site. Med, mkd, hdstg, hdg, pt shd, wc (htd); chem disp; mv service pnt; shwrs inc; EHU (10A) €4.70 (rec long lead); gas; lndry; shop; rest; snacks; bar; bbq; playgrnd; pool (htd); beach sand 400m; entmnt; TV; 10% statics; dogs €1.70; adv bkg acc; ccard acc; gym; sauna; fishing; horseriding; tennis; CKE/CCI. "Lovely, well-run site; well-kept pitches, extra charge lge ones; helpful staff; modern facs; excel site." ♦ 6 Apr-3 Oct. € 26.00 2015*

ERQUY *2E3* (5km SSW Coastal) *48.604565, -2.489502* **Camping La Vallée, St Pabu, 22430 Erquy [02 96 72 06 22; contact@campinglavallee.fr; www.campinglavallee.fr]** Foll d786 fr Val Andre twrds Erquy. As dual c'way ends, becoming 2 way, turn L immed. Foll sp for 750m. Sm, mkd, hdg, pt shd, terr, wc; chem disp; mv service pnt; fam bthrm; EHU (10A) €4.50; lndry; shop; bbq; playgrnd; beach 500m; wifi; 20% statics; dogs €2; Eng spkn; adv bkg acc; quiet; sauna; games area; bike hire; CKE/CCI. "Vg site." ♦ 28 Apr-18 Sep. € 26.60 2018*

ERVY LE CHATEL

ERVY LE CHATEL *4F4* (1km E Rural) 48.04018, 3.91900 **Camp Municipal Les Mottes,** 10130 Ervy-le-Châtel [03 25 70 07 96 or 03 25 70 50 36 (Mairie); mairie-ervy-le-chatel@wanadoo.fr; www.ervy-le-chatel.fr] Exit N77 sp Auxon (int'l camping sp Ervy-le-Châtel) onto D374, then D92; site clearly sp. Med, pt shd, wc; shwrs inc; EHU (5A) €2.50; lndry; shop nr; playgrnd; dogs €1.50; adv bkg acc; quiet; tennis; rv fishing 300m; CKE/CCI. "Pleasant, well-kept, grassy site; lge pitches; vg facs; v friendly, helpful staff; no twin axles; rests in vill; rec; excel sm site; v clean." ♦ 15 May-4 Oct. € 16.00   2017*

ESPALION *7D4* (0km E Urban) 44.52176, 2.77098 **Camping Roc de l'Arche,** 12500 Espalion [05 65 44 06 79; info@rocdelarche.com; www.rocdelarche.com] Sp in town off D920 & D921. Site on S banks of Rv Lot 300m fr bdge in town. Med, hdg, mkd, pt shd, wc; mv service pnt; fam bthrm; shwrs inc; EHU (6-10A); lndry; shop nr; snacks; bbq; playgrnd; dogs €0.50; adv bkg acc; quiet; canoeing; fishing; tennis. "Well-kept site; gd sized pitches; water pnts to each; service rds narr; pool adj inc; friendly, helpful warden; clean, modern san facs; excel." 12 May-6 Sept. € 32.00   2014*

ESPALION *7D4* (5km E Rural) 44.51376, 2.81849 **Camping Belle Rive,** 40 rue du Terral Saint Come, 12500 Aveyron [06 98 22 91 59; bellerive12@orange.fr; www.camping-bellerive-aveyron.com] Fr Espalion take D987 to St Côme-d'Olt; cont thro vill to x-rds at far side; turn R by cemetery (small sp to site) down narr rd. Med, pt shd, wc; mv service pnt; shwrs inc; EHU (6-10A) inc (poss rev pol & long lead may be req); lndry; shop nr; rest nr; wifi; 10% statics; dogs €0.70; Eng spkn; quiet. "Pleasant rvside site; friendly, helpful owner; conv acc to delightful medieval vill; excel; gd walking/driving." 1 May-30 Sep. € 14.00   2015*

ESSARTS, LES *2H4* (1km W Urban) 46.77285, -1.23558 **Camp Municipal Le Pâtis,** Rue de la Piscine, 85140 Les Essarts [02 51 62 95 83 or 06 30 02 37 09 (mob); camping.lepatis@wanadoo.fr; www.ville-les-essarts85.fr] Exit A83 junc 5 onto D160. On ent Les Essarts, foll sp to site. Site on L just off rd fr Les Essarts to Chauché. Med, mkd, pt shd, wc (htd); fam bthrm; shwrs inc; EHU (6-10A) €2.80; lndry; shop nr; rest nr; snacks; bbq (charcoal, gas); playgrnd; 40% statics; dogs €1.60; quiet; tennis adj; CKE/CCI. "Excel NH off A83; gd, clean san facs; sports cent adj with 2 pools (1 Olympic size) adj; warden resident." ♦ 15 Apr-15 Sep. € 19.00   2013*

ESSAY *4E1* (1km S Rural) 48.53799, 0.24669 **FFCC Camp Municipal Les Charmilles,** Route de Neuilly, 61500 Essay [02 33 28 40 52; fax 02 33 28 59 43; si-paysdessay@orange.fr] Exit A28 junc 18 (Alençon Nord) onto D31 to Essay (sp L'Aigle); turn R in vill dir Neuilly-le-Bisson; site on R in 400m. Sm, hdg, pt shd, wc; mv service pnt; shwrs; EHU (6A) €1.60; lndry; playgrnd; adv bkg acc; quiet. "Lge pitches, some diff to access; site yourself, warden calls in eve to pay; historical vill; fair NH." 1 Apr-30 Sep. € 9.00   2014*

ESTAGEL *8G4* (3km W Rural) 42.76566, 2.66583 **Camping La Tour de France (formerly La Tourèze),** Route d'Estagel, 66720 Latour-de-France [06 15 14 23 46; camping.latoureze@wanadoo.fr; www.camping-latourdefrance.fr] Fr D117 at Estagel turn S onto D612 then R onto D17 to Latour. Site on R on ent to vill. Med, mkd, shd, wc; chem disp; mv service pnt; fam bthrm; shwrs inc; EHU (10A) €3.50; lndry; shop nr; rest nr; bar nr; playgrnd; sw nr; red long stay; 13% statics; dogs €3; phone; Eng spkn; adv bkg acc; quiet; ccard acc. "Pretty vill & wine 'cave' in walking dist; rec visit Rv Agly barrage nrby; htd pool 3km; helpful staff; excel; peaceful; welcoming, helpful, young owners; many ptiches with trees, diff for lge o'fits." 1 Apr-14 Oct. € 22.50   2018*

ESTANG *8E2* (0km E Rural) 43.86493, -0.10421 **Camping Les Lacs de Courtès,** Courtès, 32240 Estang [05 62 09 61 98; fax 05 62 09 63 13; contact@lacsdecourtes.com; www.lacsdecourtes.com] W fr Eauze site sp fr D30. Fr Mont-de-Marsan D932 take D1 to Villeneuve-de-Marsan, then D1/D30 to Estang. Sm, hdg, mkd, pt shd, terr, wc; chem disp; mv service pnt; fam bthrm; shwrs; EHU (6A) €3; lndry; shop nr; rest nr; snacks; bar; playgrnd; pool (htd); paddling pool; entmnt; wifi; TV; 50% statics; dogs €3; Eng spkn; adv bkg acc; quiet; lake fishing; tennis; games area. "Gd family site; no bar/rest end of Aug; excel walking area; area for m'vans open all yr; gd rest in vill; vg." ♦ 25 Apr-20 Oct. € 28.00   2017*

ETABLES SUR MER *2E3* (1km S Coastal) 48.63555, -2.83526 **Camping L'Abri Côtier,** Rue de la Ville-ès-Rouxel, 22680 Etables-sur-Mer [02 96 70 61 57 or 06 07 36 01 91 (mob LS); fax 02 96 70 65 23; camping.abricotier@wanadoo.fr; www.camping-abricotier.fr] Fr N12 round St Brieuc take D786 N thro Binic & 500m after Super U supmkt turn L to Etables. Go thro vill for approx 3 km & turn L into Rue de la Ville-es-Rouxel just after R turn for Plage-du-Moulin. Site ent just after sm x-rds. NB Long c'vans & big m'vans (to avoid going thro vill): cont on D786, past Chapel, down hill & turn L at boatyard dir Etables; take 2nd turn on R. To avoid manoeuvring, park on rd & go to recep on foot. Med, mkd, pt shd, pt sl, serviced pitches; wc (htd); chem disp; mv service pnt; fam bthrm; shwrs inc; EHU (10A) inc; gas; lndry; shop; snacks; bar; bbq; playgrnd; pool (htd); paddling pool; beach sand 500m; entmnt; wifi; TV; 10% statics; dogs €2; adv bkg acc; quiet; ccard acc; watersports 2km; games rm; jacuzzi; golf 4km; CKE/CCI. "Popular, immac site; tennis in vill; excel beach (poss strong currents); entry narr & steep, narr corners on site rds poss diff lge o'fits; mkt Tues & Sun; vg." ♦ 1 May-14 Sep. € 31.00   2013*

⊞ **ETANG SUR ARROUX** *4H4* (1km SE Rural) *46.86190, 4.19177* **FFCC Camping des 2 Rives, 26-28 Route de Toulon, 71190 Etang-sur-Arroux [03 85 82 39 73; fax 03 85 82 32 97; camping@des2rives.com; www.des2rives.com]** Fr Autun on N81 SW for 11km; turn L onto D994 to Etang-sur-Arroux; site on R after passing thro main pt of town. Med, shd, wc; chem disp; mv service pnt; shwrs inc; EHU (6-10A) €3.60; lndry; shop nr; rest; snacks; bar; playgrnd; sw nr; wifi; 20% statics; dogs €2.40; phone; Eng spkn; adv bkg acc; canoeing; kayaking; CKE/CCI. "Well-kept site bet two rvs; Dutch owners; dated but adequate san facs; gd rv sports; ltd opening Jan & Feb; nice site; pool 500m; helpful owners." ♦ € 27.00 2013*

ETAPLES *3B2* (2km N Rural) *50.53238, 1.6257* **Camp Municipal La Pinède, Rue de Boulogne, 62630 Etaples [03 21 94 34 51; www.etaples-tourisme.com]** Take D940 S fr Boulogne-sur-Mer for 25km, site on R after war cemetary & bef Atac supmkt. Or N fr Etaples for 2km on D940. Med, hdg, pt shd, pt sl, terr, wc; mv service pnt; shwrs; EHU (6A) €6; lndry; shop; rest; snacks; bar; playgrnd; beach 4km; 10% statics; dogs €2.80; phone; adv bkg acc; CKE/CCI. "No twin axles; helpful warden; dated, tired san facs, ltd LS; war cemetery 200m; conv Calais; gd NH." ♦ 15 Feb-15 Nov. € 16.00 2012*

ETRETAT *3C1* (5km E Rural) *49.69840, 0.27580* **Camping de l'Aiguille Creuse, 24 Rue de l'Aiguille, 76790 Les Loges [02 35 29 52 10; fax 02 35 10 86 64; camping@aiguillecreuse.com; www.camping aiguillecreuse.com]** On S side of D940 in Les Loges; sp. Med, mkd, unshd, wc; chem disp; mv service pnt; shwrs; EHU (10A) inc; lndry; shop nr; rest nr; snacks; bar; bbq; playgrnd; pool; beach 3km; wifi; TV; dogs 1st free then €3 each; adv bkg acc; quiet; tennis; games rm. "Facs ltd LS; conv Etretat; gd; gd ctr for cliff top walks and inland villages." ♦ 1 Apr-16 Sep. € 29.50 2018*

ETRETAT *3C1* (1km SE Urban/Coastal) *49.70053, 0.21428* **Camp Municipal, 69 Rue Guy de Maupassant, 76790 Éetretat [02 35 27 07 67]** Fr Fécamp SW on D940 thro town cent of Etretate & site on L. Or fr Le Havre R at 2nd traff lts; site on L in 1km on D39. Med, mkd, hdstg, pt shd, pt sl, wc (htd); chem disp; mv service pnt; shwrs inc; EHU (6A) €6 (poss rev pol); gas; lndry; shop nr; bbq; playgrnd; beach shgl 1km; phone; quiet; ccard acc; CKE/CCI. "Busy, well-kept site; lge pitches; conv Le Havre ferry; friendly & helpful staff; clean san facs but dated; level walk to pleasant seaside resort, attractive beach nr; gd cliff top walks nr; m'van o'night area adj (no EHU) open all yr €8; early arr high ssn rec; excel; lovely site; clsd 1200-1500." ♦ 1 Apr-15 Oct. € 19.00 2018*

EU *3B2* (0km W Rural) *50.05065, 1.40996* **Camp Municipal du Parc du Chateau, Le Parc du Château, 76260 Eu [02 35 86 20 04; camping-du-chateau@ville-eu.fr; www.ville-eu.fr]** App fr Blangy on D1015 turn L at junc with D925 & foll camp sp to site in grnds of Hôtel de Ville (chateau). Fr Abbeville on D925 fork R at 1st rndabt in town S of rlwy then immed strt on over cobbled rd to chateau walls. Turn R at chateau walls into long, narr app rd thro trees. Med, hdstg, hdg, pt shd, terr, wc; chem disp; shwrs inc; EHU (16A) (poss rev pol); gas; lndry; shop nr; beach shgl 3km; 10% statics; Eng spkn. "Louis-Philippe museum in chateau; poor san facs; easy uphill walk to town thro forest behind chateau; Eu worth visit, an alt to seaside towns nrby; vg Fri mkt; gd local dog walks; recep 0900-1200/1400-2100; rec." 1 Apr-31 Oct. € 10.00 2017*

EVIAN LES BAINS *9A3* (6km W Rural) *46.39388, 6.52805* **FFCC Camping Les Huttins, 350 Rue de la Plaine, Amphion-les-Bains, 74500 Publier [04 50 70 03 09; campingleshuttins@gmail.com; www.camping-leshuttins.com]** Fr Thonon on D1005 twds Evian, at start of Amphion turn L onto Rte du Plaine sp; ent 200m on R after rndabt. Fr Evian on D1005 twds Thonon, at end of Amphion turn R & foll sp. Med, mkd, shd, wc; chem disp; mv service pnt; shwrs inc; EHU €3; gas; lndry; shop; rest nr; bar nr; bbq; playgrnd; sw nr; TV; 5% statics; dogs €1; Eng spkn; adv bkg acc; quiet; tennis adj. "Spacious, simple, relaxed site in beautiful area; hypmkt 300m; enthusiastic, helpful owners; pool 200m; sports complex 200m; basic, clean san facs; gd base for Lake Léman; poss unrel opening dates - phone ahead; excel; site run by siblings." 1 May-30 Sep. € 27.00 2014*

> **"That's changed – Should I let the Club know?"**
>
> If you find something on site that's different from the site entry, fill in a report and let us know. See camc.com/europereport.

EVRON *4F1* (9km SE Rural) *48.09423, -0.35642* **Glamping Sainte-Suzanne (formerly Municipal), 10 Rue de la Croix Couverte, 53270 Ste Suzanne [02 43 10 49 60; contact@glamping-saintesuzanne.fr; www.glamping-saintesuzanne.fr]** Take D7 SW fr Evron sp Ste Suzanne. Site 800m S (downhill) after this sm fortified town. Sm, mkd, hdg, pt shd, pt sl, wc; chem disp; shwrs inc; EHU (10A) inc; lndry; shop nr; rest nr; bar nr; bbq; pool; 25% statics; Eng spkn; adv bkg acc; quiet; horseriding adj; CKE/CCI. "Remodelled site with new facs (2017); llovely area; unspoilt town & castle with historic Eng conns; walking adj; 8 EHU pnts; excel; rec." ♦ 1 May-30 Sep. € 10.00 2017*

EVRON

⊞ **EVRON** *4F1* (2km SW Urban) *48.15077, -0.41223*
Camp Municipal de la Zone Verte, Blvd du Maréchal Juin, 53600 Evron [02 43 01 65 36; fax 02 43 37 46 20; camping@evron.fr; www.camping.evron.fr]
Site on ring rd 200 yards fr Super-U supmkt; clearly sp fr all rds into town. Med, hdg, pt shd, wc (htd); chem disp; mv service pnt; shwrs inc; EHU (6-10A) €1.60-2.45; lndry; shop nr; playgrnd; red long stay; 50% statics; dogs €0.80; adv bkg acc; quiet. "Attractive, peaceful, comfortable, well-kept site with many flowers; gd, clean san facs; restricted recep hrs in winter - warden on site lunchtime & early eve only; poss maintenance issues early ssn (2011); no twin axles; some worker's c'vans; sports complex adj; htd pool adj; highly rec for sh or long stay; excel; gd value; san facs dated (2015); gd dog walk." ♦ € 10.00   2015*

EYMET *7D2* (5km SW Rural) *44.63211, 0.39977*
Camping Le Moulin Brûlé, 47800 Agnac [05 53 83 07 56; thebeales@wanadoo.fr; www.campingswfrance.co.uk] Fr S on D933 at Miramont-de-Guyenne (6km S of Eymet) turn E onto D1; in 4km turn L onto C501 dir Eymet; site on L in 2km. Or fr N approx 1km after Eymet turn L onto C1 sp Chateau Pèchalbet. In 1.5km at x-rds turn L sp Bourgougnague, site on R in 2km. NB Narr lanes & bends on app. Sm, mkd, hdstg, pt shd, sl, wc; chem disp; shwrs inc; EHU (10-16A) €4; lndry; bbq (charcoal); playgrnd; pool; 1% statics; adv bkg rec; games area. "Lovely, peaceful, well-kept site in pleasant surroundings; friendly British owners; gd clean san facs; gd cycling & walking; excel; animals not permitted." 1 May-15 Sep. € 19.00   2015*

EYMET *7D2* (0km W Urban) *44.66923, 0.39615*
Camping du Château (formerly Municipal), Rue de la Sole, 24500 Eymet [05 53 23 80 28 or 06 98 16 97 93 (mob); eymetcamping@aol.com; www.eymetcamping.fr] Thro Miramont onto D933 to Eymet. Turn opp Casino supmkt & foll sp to site. Sp on ent to Eymet fr all dirs. Sm, mkd, hdg, pt shd, wc; chem disp; mv service pnt; shwrs inc; EHU (10A) €3 (poss rev pol); lndry; shop nr; rest nr; bar nr; playgrnd; sw nr; red long stay; wifi; dogs; Eng spkn; adv bkg acc; quiet; bike hire; boat hire; CKE/CCI. "Lovely site by rv behind medieval chateau; friendly, helpful owner; clean but tired san facs; pool 1.5km; gas 300m; wine tasting on site; lake nrby; Thur mkt; excel; peaceful site nr lovely Bastide town; no arr bet 1200-1500." ♦ 1 Apr-30 Sep. € 11.20   2016*

EYMOUTIERS *7B4* (8km N Rural) *45.80560, 1.84342*
Camping Les 2 Iles (formerly Municipal Les Peyrades), Auphelle, Lac de Vassivière, 87470 Peyrat-le-Château [05 55 35 60 81; les2iles.camping@orange.fr; www.campingslelacdevassiviere.jimdo.com] Fr Peyrat E on D13, at 5km sharp R onto D222 & foll sp for Lac de Vassivière. At wide junc turn L, site on R. Med, pt shd, pt sl, wc; chem disp; shwrs inc; EHU (5A) €2.50; lndry; shop nr; rest nr; bar nr; bbq; playgrnd; beach sand adj; sw nr; twin axles; wifi; 25% statics; dogs; Eng spkn; adv bkg acc; quiet; games area; games rm. "Helpful warden; some pitches o'look lake; new fac block (2015); v gd." 2 Apr-31 Oct. € 20.70   2016*

EYMOUTIERS *7B4* (1km S Rural) *45.73061, 1.75249*
Camp Municipal, St Pierre-Château, 87120 Eymoutiers [05 55 69 10 21; fax 05 55 69 27 19; mairie-eymoutiers@wanadoo.fr; www.mairie-eymoutiers.fr] On E of D940 S fr Eymoutiers site sp on R. Diff sharp bend bef ent. Sm, pt shd, pt sl, terr, wc; shwrs; EHU (6A) €2 (long lead poss req); shop nr; adv bkg acc; quiet. "Gd views; clean site; site yourself, warden calls; attractive town & area; excel value; vg san facs; rec." 1 Jun-30 Sep. € 9.00   2012*

> **"I like to fill in the reports as I travel from site to site"**
>
> You'll find report forms at the back of this guide, or you can fill them in online at camc.com/europereport.

EYZIES DE TAYAC, LES *7C3* (5km NE Rural) *44.96935, 1.04623* **Camping Le Pigeonnier, Le Bourg, 24620 Tursac [05 53 06 96 90; campinglepigeonnier@orange.fr; www.campinglepigeonnier.fr]**
NE fr Les Eyzies for 5km on D706 to Tursac; site is 200m fr Mairie in vill cent; ent tight. Sm, hdg, mkd, shd, pt sl, terr, wc; shwrs inc; EHU (10A) €3; gas; lndry; shop nr; snacks; bar; playgrnd; pool; beach shgl; sw nr; dogs €1; adv bkg acc; quiet; horseriding; fishing 1km; bike hire; CKE/CCI. "Freshwater pool (v cold); spacious, grass pitches; facs poss stretched high ssn; canoeing 1km; v quiet hideaway site in busy area; chem disp in vill; close to prehistoric sites; friendly Brit owners." 1 Jun-30 Sep. € 20.50   2012*

FALAISE *3D1* (1km W Urban) *48.89545, -0.20476*
FFCC Camp Municipal du Château, 3 Rue du Val d'Ante, 14700 Falaise [02 31 90 16 55 or 02 31 90 30 90 (Mairie); fax 02 31 90 53 38; camping@falaise.fr; www.falaise.fr/tourisme/le-camping] Fr N on N158, at rndabt on o'skirts of town, turn L into vill; at next rndabt by Super U go strt on; at 2nd mini-rndabt turn R; then sp on L after housing estate. Or fr S on D958, at 1st rndabt foll sp town cent & site. Cont down hill thro town then up hill to 1st rndabt, site sp, then sp on L after housing est. Med, hdg, mkd, pt shd, pt sl, terr, wc; chem disp; mv service pnt; shwrs inc; EHU (6-10A) €4.20; lndry; shop nr; rest nr; bar nr; bbq; playgrnd; red long stay; wifi; TV; TV (pitch); dogs €2.20; Eng spkn; adv bkg acc; quiet; ccard acc; tennis; CKE/CCI. "Lovely, peaceful, well-kept site in pleasant surroundings; pitches poss diff lge o'fits; htd pool in town; clean, well kept san facs (lots of hot water) poss ltd LS & stretched high ssn & clsd 2200-0800; pitch self & pay later; uphill walk to town, birthplace of William the Conqueror; vet in Falaise; mkt Sat am; excel; useful for ferry port." ♦ 1 May-30 Sep. € 19.00   2015*

FANJEAUX *8F4* (3km S Rural) *43.16558, 2.02702*
FFCC Camping à la Ferme Les Brugues (Vialaret), 11270 Fanjeaux [04 68 24 77 37; fax 04 68 24 60 21; lesbrugues@free.fr; http://lesbrugues.free.fr] Exit A61 junc 22 onto D4/D119 (dir Mirepoix) to Fanjeaux; cont on D119 dir Mirepoix; at top of hill turn L onto D102 sp La Courtète (past rest La Table Cathare & fuel stn) & in 100m turn R to site in 2.5km. Site well sp fr Fanjeaux. Sm, hdg, mkd, shd, pt sl, terr, wc; chem disp; shwrs inc; EHU (10-16A) inc (rev pol); lndry; shop nr; rest nr; bar nr; playgrnd; wifi; 10% statics; dogs; Eng spkn; adv bkg acc; quiet; games rm; CKE/CCI. "Delightful, peaceful, 'off the beaten track' site adj sm lake; care req sm children; well-kept; v lge pitches, some o'looking lake; friendly, helpful owners; gd clean san facs; many walks; beautful countryside; excel touring base; rec." ♦ 1 Jun-30 Sep. € 19.50   2018*

FAVERGES *9B3* (7km NW Urban) *45.77510, 6.22585*
Camping La Serraz, Rue de la Poste, 74210 Doussard [04 50 44 30 68; info@campinglaserraz. com; www.campinglaserraz.com] Exit Annecy on D1508 twd Albertville. At foot of lake ignore sp on R for Doussard Vill & take next turn R. Site on L in 1km, bef PO, sp. Med, pt shd, wc; chem disp; mv service pnt; fam bthrm; shwrs; EHU (16A) inc; lndry; rest; bbq; playgrnd; pool (htd); paddling pool; sw nr; twin axles; entmnt; wifi; 50% statics; dogs €2.50; Eng spkn; adv bkg acc; quiet; games area; bike hire; games rm; sauna; CCI. "Excel site; diving course for 8-14 year olds in Jul & Aug; spa opening 2014." ♦ 19 Apr-14 Sep. € 49.00   2014*

FAYENCE *10E4* (6km W Rural) *43.3500, 6.39590*
Camping La Tuquette (Naturist), The High Suanes 83440 Fayence [04 94 76 19 40; fax 04 94 76 23 95; robert@tuquette.com; www.tuquette.com] Fr Fayence take N562. At km 64.2 sp turn R, site ent 100m. Sm, mkd, pt shd, terr, wc; chem disp; shwrs inc; EHU (6A) €4.60; lndry; rest; snacks; bar; bbq; playgrnd; pool (htd); wifi; 10% statics; dogs €2; Eng spkn; adv bkg acc; quiet; INF card. "Vg, lovely, clean site; friendly owners, family run." ♦ 10 Apr-26 Sep. € 36.40   2018*

FECAMP *3C1* (6km SE Rural) *49.74041, 0.41660*
Camp Municipal Le Canada, 76400 Toussaint [02 35 29 78 34 or 02 35 27 56 77 (Mairie); fax 02 35 27 48 82; mairie.toussaint@wanadoo.fr; www.commune-de-toussaint.fr] On D926 N of Toussaint. Med, hdg, shd, pt sl, wc (htd); shwrs inc; EHU (4-10A) inc; lndry; bbq; playgrnd; 70% statics; dogs; quiet; games area; CKE/CCI. "Lovely quiet site; helpful warden; clean san facs; gd." ♦ 11 Mar-15 Oct. € 14.80   2017*

FERE, LA *3C4* (2km N Urban) *49.66554, 3.36205* **Camp Municipal du Marais de la Fontaine, Rue Vauban, 02800 La Fère [03 23 56 82 94; fax 03 23 56 40 04]** S on D1044 (St Quentin to Laon); R onto D338; turn E at rndabt; ignore 1st camping sp; turn N at next rndabt; site sp. Or Exit A26 junc 12 onto D1032 SW; in 2km turn R onto D35; in 4km pass under D1044; in 400m turn R; in 800m turn R at traff lts; foll over bdge to sports complex. Sm, hdg, mkd, pt shd, wc; chem disp; shwrs inc; EHU (15A) €3.50; shop; rest nr; bar nr; bbq; red long stay; dogs €1.20; adv bkg rec; CKE/CCI. "Well-kept site adj leisure cent; conv Calais, 2hrs 30mins; clean san facs; pitching awkward due sm pitches & narr site rds; warden lives adj site - on arr open double gates & ring doorbell to register; htd covrd pool adj; gates shut 2200-0700 - no vehicle/ person access; avoid 1st w/end June as Wine & Food Festival held on site; conv A26; gd NH; generous sized pitches." ♦ 1 Apr-30 Sep. € 14.00   2015*

FERRIERES EN GATINAIS *4F3* (0km N Rural) *48.09198, 2.78482* **Camp Municipal Le Perray/ Les Ferrières, Rue du Perray, 45210 Ferrières-en-Gâtinais [06 71 43 25 95 (mob) or 02 38 87 15 44 (Mairie); camping@ferrieresengatinais.fr; www. ferrieresengatinais.fr]** N fr Mantargis on N7; R onto D96/D32 sp Ferrières & foll camp sp. Med, mkd, pt shd, wc; chem disp; mv service pnt; shwrs inc; EHU (10A) inc; lndry; shop nr; rest nr; playgrnd; entmnt; wifi; 50% statics; quiet; tennis; rv fishing adj. "Vg site; direct access to sm rv; sports facs adj; gd facs & security; old pretty town with lovely church; supmkt clsd Sun-Mon; pool adj; call to check if open; free WiFi; off clsd 1200-1500, no access to site at this time." 1 Apr-30 Oct. € 12.00   2018*

FERRIERES SUR SICHON *9B1* (0km SE Rural) *46.02246, 3.65326* **Camp Municipal, 03250 Ferrières-sur-Sichon [04 70 41 10 10; fax 04 70 41 15 22]** Well sp in Ferrières-sur-Sichon. At x-rds of D995 & D122. Sm, pt shd, pt sl, wc (htd); shwrs inc; EHU €2.20; shop nr; playgrnd; dogs; quiet. "CL-type site; friendly warden visits 1930; gd san facs; excel NH; lake adj; pleasant vill." 1 Jun-30 Sep. € 7.00   2014*

FERTE ST AUBIN, LA *4F3* (1km N Urban) *47.72553, 1.93565* **Camp Municipal Le Cosson, Ave Löwendal, 45240 La Ferté-St Aubin [02 38 76 55 90; campingducosson@recrea.fr; www. campingducosson.fr]** S fr Orléans on D2020; ent on R on N o'skts twd Municipal pool. Turning onto Rue Lowendal. Sm, pt shd, wc; chem disp; shwrs inc; EHU (6A) inc (poss rev pol); shop nr; rest nr; pool (htd); wifi; dogs €2; phone; Eng spkn; fishing adj; CKE/CCI. "Agreeable, spacious site; friendly, helpful recep; clean, ltd facs; easy walk to delightful town & gd rests; nr park & chateau; poss travellers LS; conv A71; gd NH." 26 Apr-29 Sep. € 16.00   2014*

FERTE VIDAME, LA *4E2* (1km SW Rural) 48.60760, 0.89005 **Camping Les Abrias du Perche, Route de la Lande, 28340 La Ferte Vidame [02 37 37 64 00; info@campingperchenormandie.fr; www.campingperchenormandie.fr]** Fr N12 take D45 (D24) twds Moussenvilliers and la Ferte Vidame. Site on R (D15.1). Sm, mkd, hdstg, pt shd, wc; chem disp; mv service pnt; fam bthrm; shwrs inc; EHU (6A) €2.50; lndry; snacks; bar; bbq; playgrnd; pool (covrd, htd); twin axles; entmnt; wifi; 50% statics; dogs (€2.50) 2 max; bus 1km; adv bkg acc; quiet; games rm; bike hire; CKE/CCI. "Close to sports ctr, forest walks and fishing; vg; fishing nr; long cable poss req; poss rev pol."
1 Feb-31 Dec. € 17.50   2017*

FEUILLERES *3C3* (0km W Rural) 49.94851, 2.84364 **Camping du Château et de l'Oseraie, 12 Rue du Château, 80200 Feuillères [03 22 83 17 59 or 06 16 97 93 42 (mob-LS); fax 03 22 83 04 14; jsg-bred@wanadoo.fr; www.camping-chateau-oseraie.com]** Fr A1/E15 exit 13.1 Maurepas onto D938 dir Albert & then L onto D146; R at staggered x-rds in Feuillères (by church) & site on R in 500m. Med, hdg, mkd, hdstg, pt shd, wc; chem disp; mv service pnt; shwrs inc; EHU (10A) inc (poss rev pol); gas; lndry; snacks; bar; bbq; playgrnd; pool (htd); red long stay; entmnt; wifi; 10% statics; dogs €1.20; Eng spkn; adv bkg rec; ccard acc; games rm; fishing; tennis; games area; CKE/CCI. "Excel, well-kept, well-run site; gd sized pitches; friendly staff; clean san facs; conv A1 a'route, WW1 battlefields & Disneyland Paris." ♦ 15 Mar-31 Oct. € 24.00   2018*

FEURS *9B2* (1km N Urban) 45.75357, 4.22595 **Camp Municipal Le Palais, Route de Civens, 42110 Feurs [06 63 37 24 57; fax 04 77 26 43 41; www.camping-rhonealpes.com]** Site sp fr D107 on N o'skts of town. Site in corner of sports campus next to Bouldodrome. Lge, pt shd, wc (htd); chem disp; mv service pnt; shwrs inc; EHU (6A) €3.05; gas; shop; snacks; playgrnd; 80% statics; dogs €0.61; phone; quiet; CKE/CCI. "Pleasant, spacious, beautifully-kept site; busy, espec w/ends; pool adj; clean san facs." ♦ 1 Apr-31 Oct. € 17.40   2017*

FIGEAC *7D4* (2km E Rural) 44.60989, 2.05015 **Camping Caravanning Domaine Du Surgie, Domaine du Surgié, 46100 Figeac [05 61 64 88 54; fax 05 61 64 89 17; contact@marc-montmija.com; www.domainedusurgie.com]** Fr Figeac foll sp Rodez (on D840 S) to site by Rv Célé adj leisure complex. Foll sps 'Base Loisirs de Surgie'. Narr ent, light controlled. Or appr fr E on D840, immed after passing under rlwy arch a v sharp R turn into narr rd (keep R thro traff lts); site on L in 700m. NB Recep at beginning of rd to leisure cent & camping. Med, hdg, mkd, pt shd, wc; chem disp; mv service pnt; shwrs; EHU (10A) inc; lndry; shop; rest; snacks; bar; playgrnd; red long stay; entmnt; 30% statics; dogs €2.50; Eng spkn; adv bkg acc; quiet; boating; bike hire; tennis. "Excel pool complex adj (free to campers); peaceful LS; pleasant 2km walk or car park just outside town; ent clsd 1200-1600 LS; adj rv unfenced; htd pool & waterslide adj; mkt Sat; vg." ♦ 1 Apr-30 Sept. € 27.00   2015*

FIGEAC *7D4* (7km SE Urban) 44.57328, 2.07296 **Camp Municipal Les Rives d'Olt, Blvd Paul-Ramadier, 12700 Capdenac-Gare [05 65 80 88 87 or 05 65 80 22 22 (Mairie); camping.capdenac@wanadoo.fr]** Fr Figeac on D840 dir Rodez; at Capdenac turn R onto D994 over rv bdge; immed after x-ing rv bdge turn R onto D86. Site in 200m on R by rv. Med, hdg, mkd, shd, wc; chem disp; mv service pnt; shwrs inc; EHU (9A) €2.90; lndry; shop nr; rest nr; bar nr; playgrnd; TV; 5% statics; dogs; quiet; tennis adj; CKE/CCI. "Site beside Rv Lot; ent clsd 1200-1600 LS; gd fishing, walking & cycling; gas adj; new security barrier." ♦ 10 Apr-30 Sep. € 11.00   2017*

FIGEAC *7D4* (7km SW Rural) 44.57833, 1.93750 **FFCC Camping de Pech-Ibert, Route de Cajarc, 46100 Béduer [05 65 40 05 85; fax 05 65 40 08 33; contact@camping-pech-ibert.com; www.camping-pech-ibert.com]** SW fr Figeac on D662/D19 twds Cajarc. Site well sp on R after Béduer. Sm, pt shd, wc (htd); chem disp; mv service pnt; fam bthrm; shwrs inc; EHU (16A) €3.50 (poss rev pol); snacks; bbq; playgrnd; pool; sw nr; 10% statics; dogs €2; Eng spkn; adv bkg req; quiet; fishing 1km; tennis; bike hire; CKE/CCI. "Peaceful, relaxing site on pilgrimage rte; pleasant, helpful owners; gd clean san facs; gd walking fr site (mkd trails); Sat mkt Figeac; excel; rock pegs req." ♦ 15 Mar-15 Nov. € 16.00   2014*

FISMES *3D4* (1km W Urban) 49.30944, 3.67138 **Camp Municipal de Fismes, Allée des Missions, 51170 Fismes [03 26 48 10 26; fax 03 26 48 82 25; contact@fismes.fr; www.fismes.fr]** Fr Reims NW on N31. At Fismes do not ent town, but stay on N31 dir Soissons. Site on L down little lane at end of sports stadium wall. Or exit A4 junc 22 sp Soissons & Fismes & as bef. Sm, hdstg, unshd, wc; chem disp; fam bthrm; shwrs; EHU (12A) €3.50 (poss rev pol); shop nr; bbq (elec, gas); dogs; train; adv bkg acc; games area; horseriding 5km; CKE/CCI. "Vg site; gd, clean san facs; warden on site ltd hrs; gates locked 2200-0700; train to Reims nr; conv Laon, Epernay, Reims; mkt Sat am; vg NH; site clean and tidy; excel; site nr rd junc."
1 May-15 Sep. € 13.00   2017*

FLECHE, LA *4G1* (10km E Rural) 47.70230, 0.07330 **Camp Municipal La Chabotière, Place des Tilleuls, 72800 Luché-Pringé [tel/fax 02 43 45 10 00; contact@lachabotiere.com; www.lachabotiere.com or www.loir-valley.com]** SW fr Le Mans on D323 twd La Flèche. At Clermont-Créans turn L on D13 to Luché-Pringé. Site sp. Med, mkd, hdg, pt shd, pt sl, wc; chem disp; mv service pnt; fam bthrm; shwrs; EHU (10A) inc (poss rev pol); lndry; shop nr; playgrnd; TV; 10% statics; dogs €1.50; phone; Eng spkn; adv bkg acc; quiet; bike hire; CKE/CCI. "Lovely, well-kept site by Rv Loir; helpful, friendly warden; pool adj high ssn; clean, modern facs; gd site for children; many cycle rtes; conv chateaux; nice vill nrby; avoid Le Mans motor bike week - poss many bikers on site; excel." ♦ 1 Apr-15 Oct. € 16.00   2018*

FLORAC

France

FLECHE, LA *4G1* (1km W Urban) *47.69514, -0.07936*
Camping Municipal de la Route d'Or, Allée du Camping, 72200 La Flèche [02 43 94 55 90; info@camping-laroutedor.com; camping-lafleche.com]
Fr NW dir Laval D306, keep to W of town, leave S on D306 twd Bauge; site on L after x-ing rv; sp. Fr S take dir for A11 & Laval, site clearly sp on R on rvside. Lge, hdg, mkd, hdstg, pt shd, wc (htd); chem disp; mv service pnt; shwrs inc; EHU (10A) €3.80 (poss long lead req); gas; lndry; shop nr; rest nr; bbq; playgrnd; pool (htd); entmnt; wifi; dogs €1; phone; Eng spkn; ccard acc; fishing nr; canoeing nr; games area; tennis; CKE/CCI. "Lovely, busy site in beautiful location by rv; well kept, run & maintained site; lge pitches; v friendly, welcoming, helpful staff; facs ltd LS; ring for ent code if office clsd; no twin axles; attractive, easy, sh walk across rv to attractive town; mkt Wed; rec; mkt Sun & Wed; defibrillator on site; new excel san facs (2016); recep clsd 1200-1400; gd value." ♦ 1 Mar-31 Oct. € 18.00   2018*

FLERS *4E1* (3km E Urban) *48.75451, -0.54341*
Camping du Pays de Flers, 145 La Fouquerie 61100 Flers [02 33 65 35 00; camping.paysdeflers@wanadoo.fr; www.flers-agglomeration.fr]
Fr E on D924 thro town cent, site on L in 2 km. Fr W on D924 dir Centre Ville, site on R. Sm, pt shd, wc; chem disp; fam bthrm; shwrs; EHU (6A); bbq; playgrnd; wifi; 15% statics; dogs; Eng spkn; quiet; bike hire; games area; CCI. "Easy walk to interesting town; excel." ♦ 1 Apr-31 Oct. € 12.00   2014*

⊞ **FLEURAT** *7A4* (1km E Rural) *46.24027, 1.68666*
Camping Les Boueix, Les Boueix, 23320 Fleurat [09 63 61 23 80; info@campinglesboueix.com; www.campinglesboueix.com] Fr N145 N onto D5 take slipway or D6 into Fleurat. Turn E at x-rds to Les Boueix then 2nd L. Site in middle of fork in rd. Sm, mkd, hdg, pt shd, sl, wc; chem disp; shwrs inc; EHU (16A) €3.50 (€5 winter); bbq; dogs €1.50; Eng spkn; adv bkg acc; quiet; fishing; CKE/CCI. "Beautiful, quiet & relaxing CL-type site; lge pitches with views; welcoming, helpful British owners; vg san facs; sl poss diff m'vans; well-stocked fishing lake nrby; lovely walks; ideal for beautiful Creuse Valley; rallies welcome; conv A20; highly rec." € 16.00   2016*

FLEURIE *9A2* (1km S Rural) *46.18758, 4.69895*
Vivacamp La Grappe Fleurie, La Verne, 69820 Fleurie [04 74 69 80 07; fax 04 74 59 85 18; info@beaujolais-camping.com; www.beaujolais-camping.fr] S dir Lyon on D906 turn R (W) at S end of Romanèche onto D32; 4km to vill of Fleurie (beware sharp turn in vill & narr rds) & foll site sp. Med, hdg, mkd, pt shd, terr, serviced pitches; wc; chem disp; mv service pnt; fam bthrm; shwrs inc; EHU (10A) inc; gas; lndry; shop nr; rest nr; bar nr; playgrnd; pool; entmnt; wifi; 10% statics; dogs €3.10; Eng spkn; adv bkg rec; ccard acc; tennis; CKE/CCI. "Clean, well-run, busy site; friendly staff; excel san facs; lovely pool; gates & wash rms clsd 2200-0700; clean, spacious san facs; path to town thro vineyards (uphill); wine tasting; sm mkt Sat; excel." ♦ 8 Apr-8 Oct. € 27.00   2017*

See advertisement

> **"We must tell the Club about that great site we found"**
>
> Get your site reports in by mid-August and we'll do our best to get your updates into the next edition.

FLORAC *9D1* (1km N Rural) *44.33569, 3.59002*
FFCC Camping Le Pont du Tarn, Route de Pont de Montvert, 48400 Florac [04 66 45 18 26 or 04 66 45 17 96 (LS); fax 04 66 45 26 43; contact@camping-florac.com; www.camping-florac.com]
Exit Florac N on N106 & turn R in 500m by by-pass on D998; site on L in 300m. Lge, hdg, mkd, pt shd, wc (htd); chem disp; mv service pnt; shwrs inc; EHU (10A) €4.20; lndry; shop nr; rest nr; bar nr; bbq (charcoal, elec); playgrnd; pool; sw nr; wifi; 60% statics; dogs €2; phone; Eng spkn; adv bkg rec; quiet; rv fishing adj; CKE/CCI. "Nice, well-kept, well-run site in beautiful area; clean san facs, needs updating (2016); no twin axles; 20 min walk to town; gd touring base; lge pitches; lge mkt Thurs; vg value; excel site on rv; well situated." ♦ 1 Apr-1 Nov. € 28.50   2017*

FLORAC

FLORAC *9D1* (3km NE Rural) *44.34528, 3.61008*
FFCC Camping Chantemerle, La Pontèze, 48400 Bédouès [04 66 45 19 66 or 06 73 86 53 16 (mob); chante-merle@wanadoo.fr; www.camping-chantemerle.com] Exit Florac N on N106; in 500m turn R onto D998; in 2.5km site on L, past Bédouès vill cent. Med, mkd, pt shd, pt sl, wc; chem disp; shwrs inc; EHU (6A) €2.80; lndry; shop; snacks; playgrnd; sw nr; wifi; 10% statics; dogs €1.50; Eng spkn; quiet; games rm; CKE/CCI. "Lovely location; helpful owner; gd walking; conv Gorges du Tarn, Cévennes National Park; vg; water and EHU now avail on lower pitches; sm rest, home cooked food; excel site." 14 Apr-16 Oct. € 22.40   2017*

FOIX *8G3* (2km N Rural) *42.98911, 1.61565*
Camping du Lac, Quartier Labarre, 09000 Foix [05 61 65 11 58; fax 05 61 65 32 62; camping-du-lac@wanadoo.fr; www.campingdulac.com] Fr N on N20 foll sp for 'Centre Ville', site on R in 2km. Fr S onto on N20 thro tunnel & take 1st exit N of Foix & foll sp 'Centre Ville', then as above. Site opp Chausson building materials store. Lge, mkd, pt shd, wc; chem disp; mv service pnt; fam bthrm; shwrs inc; EHU (6A) inc; lndry; shop nr; rest; snacks; bar; bbq; playgrnd; pool; paddling pool; entmnt; wifi; TV; 75% statics; dogs €1.50; bus to Foix adj (not Sun); Eng spkn; adv bkg rec; ccard acc; windsurfing; boating; tennis; CKE/CCI. "Busy site w/end; quiet, spacious pitches on L of camp; modern san facs, poss stretched high ssn; site & facs poss uncared for early ssn (2011); gates clsd 2300-0700; pleasant town; NH only LS." ♦ € 27.40   2017*

FOIX *8G3* (4km S Urban) *42.93081, 1.63883* **FFCC Camping Roucateille, 15 Rue du Pradal, 09330 Montgaillard** [05 61 64 05 92; info@roucateille.com; www.camping-roucateille.com] Fr N exit N20 junc 11, fr S exit N20 junc 12; foll sp Montgaillard; site sp fr main rd thro vill. NB Swing wide at ent - sharp turn. Med, mkd, hdg, shd, wc; chem disp; mv service pnt; shwrs inc; EHU (4-10A) €2.50-4.90; lndry; shop nr; rest nr; bbq; playgrnd; red long stay; wifi; 25% statics; dogs free; Eng spkn; adv bkg acc; quiet; ccard acc; CKE/CCI. "Lovely, picturesque, informal site; clean & well cared for; charming, helpful young owners; excel facs; care needed to avoid trees; garden produce in ssn; gd touring base; gd cycling; Forges de Pyène eco-museum worth visit; excel; historical area; pool 3km; nr stream with cherry orchard behind." ♦ 1 May-30 Sep. € 24.00   2014*

FOIX *8G3* (3km NW Rural) *42.97151, 1.57423*
Camp Municipal de Rieutort, 09000 Cos [05 61 65 39 79 or 06 71 18 10 38 (mob); bernard.blazy09@orange.fr; http://camping-municipal-cos09.fr] Fr Foix take D117 dir Tarbes. Turn R onto D17 then at rndabt onto D617, site on L in 3km. NB Narr app rds. Sm, pt shd, pt sl, serviced pitches; wc (htd); chem disp; fam bthrm; shwrs inc; EHU (5A) €1.80; lndry; shop nr; rest nr; playgrnd; pool; dogs; quiet; tennis; CKE/CCI. "Pleasant site amongst trees with gd views; friendly, helpful warden; gd san facs, ltd LS; sm step into disabled facs; no c'vans over 6m." ♦ € 11.00   2015*

FONTAINE SIMON *4E2* (1km N Rural) *48.51314, 1.01941* **Camping du Perche, 3 Rue de la Ferrière, 28240 Fontaine-Simon** [02 37 81 88 11 or 06 23 82 90 28 (mob); info@campingduperche.com; www.campingduperche.com] Fr La Loupe on D929 take D25 N to Fontaine-Simon, site sp. Med, hdg, pt shd, pt sl, wc (htd); chem disp; shwrs inc; EHU €3.60; lndry; shop; bbq; playgrnd; sw nr; wifi; 10% statics; dogs €3; adv bkg acc; quiet; fishing; CKE/CCI. "Undulating, lakeside site; htd covrd pool adj; gd." ♦ € 15.00   2012*

FONTAINEBLEAU *4E3* (5km NE Rural) *48.42215, 2.74872* **Camp Municipal Grange aux Dîmes, Rue de l'Abreuvoir/Rue de l'Eglise, 77210 Samoreau** [01 64 23 72 25; fax 01 64 23 98 31; mairie-de-samoreau@wanadoo.fr; www.samoreau.fr] Fr cent of Fontainebleau take D210 (dir Provins); in approx 4km at rndabt cross bdge over Rv Seine; take R at rndabt; site sp at end of rd thro Samoreau vill; site twd rv. Med, hdg, mkd, pt shd, pt sl, wc (htd); chem disp; mv service pnt; shwrs inc; EHU (10A) inc (poss rev pol); lndry; shop nr; rest nr; snacks; bar nr; phone; bus; adv bkg acc; CKE/CCI. "Peaceful site in attractive location by Rv Seine; gd sized pitches; helpful staff; gd, immac san facs; adj vill hall poss noisy w/end; jazz festival late Jun; conv palace, Paris (by train) & Disneyland; clsd 2200-0700; excel; waterpoints around site could do with upgrade." ♦ 1 Mar-31 Oct. € 22.00   2018*

FONTAINEBLEAU *4E3* (10km S Rural) *48.31740, 2.69650* **Camping Les Prés, Chemin des Prés, 77880 Grez-sur-Loing** [01 64 45 72 75; camping-grez@wanadoo.fr; www.camping-grez-fontainebleau.info] Fr Fontainebleau on D607 twd Nemours (S) for 8km; look for camping sps. At traff island turn L onto D40D, in 1km immed after x-ing bdge turn R; site on L. Do not tow into Grez-sur-Loing. Med, mkd, hdg, pt shd, wc; chem disp; mv service pnt; fam bthrm; shwrs inc; EHU (5A) €3; gas; lndry; shop; rest nr; snacks; bar nr; playgrnd; red long stay; wifi; 80% statics; dogs; phone; Eng spkn; adv bkg acc; ccard acc; fishing; canoe hire; bike hire; CKE/CCI. "In attractive area; helpful British owner; 80% statics; site poss unkempt/scruffy end of ssn; vg." ♦ 20 Mar-11 Nov. € 17.00   2017*

FONTAINEBLEAU *4E3* (14km S Rural) *48.33362, 2.75386* **Camping Le Parc du Gué, Route de Montigny, La Genevraye, 77690 Montigny-sur-Loing** [01 64 45 87 79; fax 01 64 78 31 46; contact@camping-parcdugue.com; www.camping-parcdugue.com] Do not tow thro Montigny-sur-Loing, v narr tight turns. Site is E of Montigny, N of La Genevraye off D104. App fr S Nemours on D40, slow rd but safe, or fr NE, Moret-sur-Loing D606/D104. Lge, hdg, mkd, pt shd, wc (htd); chem disp; fam bthrm; shwrs inc; EHU (10A) €3.60; lndry; shop; snacks; bar; bbq; playgrnd; pool (htd); paddling pool; sw nr; wifi; 70% statics; dogs €3.70; Eng spkn; adv bkg acc; quiet; ccard acc; fishing; games area; watersports; CKE/CCI. "Beautiful, wooded country; kayaks; mkt Sat 2km; excel walking & cycling; new pool (2015); vg." ♦ 15 Mar-30 Nov. € 21.00   2016*

FORCALQUIER

FONTENAY TRESIGNY *4E3* (7km NE Rural) *48.75050, 2.89728* **Camping des Quatre Vents, 77610 Crèvecoeur-en-Brie [01 64 07 41 11; contact@ caravaning-4vents.fr; www.caravaning-4vents.fr]** At Calais take A26/E15 dir Arras; at Arras take A1/E15 dir Paris; next take A104 dir A4 Metz/Nancy/Marne-la-Vallée, then A4 dir Metz/Nancy, exit junc 13 onto D231 dir Provins; after rndabt with lge monument turn R dir Crèvecoeur-en-Brie & foll site sp. Site in 13km. Lge, hdg, mkd, pt shd, serviced pitches; wc (htd); chem disp; mv service pnt; fam bthrm; shwrs inc; EHU (6A) inc; lndry; shop nr; snacks; bbq; playgrnd; pool; wifi; TV; 50% statics; dogs €3; phone; Eng spkn; adv bkg req; quiet; ccard acc; games rm; horseriding; games area; CKE/CCI. "Friendly, well-run, beautiful site; lge, well-kept pitches; welcoming, helpful staff; san facs spacious & v clean; pleasant pool; conv Disneyland & Paris; poss muddy when wet; vg; beautiful countryside ideal for cycling; no o'fits over 10m high ssn; restful even in high ssn." ♦ 20 Mar-1 Nov. € 30.00   2016*

FONTES *10F1* (1km N Rural) *43.54734, 3.37999* **FFCC Camping L'Evasion, Route de Cabrières, 34320 Fontès [04 67 25 32 00; www.campingevasion.com]** Fr A75 exit junc 59 (Pézenas). At rndabt take D124 to Lézignan-la-Cèbe then fork L, cont on D124 to Fontès. In vill foll sp to site. Sm, mkd, hdg, pt shd, pt sl, wc; chem disp; mv service pnt; fam bthrm; shwrs inc; EHU (10A) €3.50; gas; lndry; rest; snacks; bar; bbq; playgrnd; pool; wifi; 75% statics; dogs €2.80; phone; adv bkg acc; quiet; CKE/CCI. "Excel san facs; touring pitches amongst statics (long-term residents); helpful owners." ♦ 14 Mar-2 Nov. € 22.50   2016*

⊞ **FONTES** *10F1* (3km E Rural) *43.54491, 3.41743* **Camping Les Clairettes, Route de Péret, 34320 Fontès [04 67 25 01 31; fax 04 67 25 38 64; www.campinglesclairettes.net]** Sp on D609. Turn onto D128 sp Adissan, Fontès. Fr A75 exit junc 58. Foll sp for Adissan & site. Med, mkd, hdg, pt shd, serviced pitches; wc; chem disp; shwrs inc; EHU (6A); gas; lndry; shop; rest nr; snacks; bar; bbq; playgrnd; pool; entmnt; TV; 50% statics; adv bkg acc. "V quiet; friendly owners; ltd facs LS; nice site; no m'van drive-over drain; convly nr m'way but away fr coastal crowds." ♦ € 23.00   2014*

FORCALQUIER *10E3* (1km E Urban) *43.96206, 5.78718* **Camping Indigo Forcalquier, Route de Sigonce, 04300 Forcalquier [04 92 75 27 94; fax 04 92 75 18 10; forcalquier@camping-indigo.com; www.camping-indigo.com]** Fr A51 exit junc 19 La Brillane onto D4100 to Forcalquier. Site sp. Med, mkd, pt shd, pt sl, serviced pitches; wc; chem disp; mv service pnt; fam bthrm; shwrs inc; EHU (10A) €5.30 (long lead poss req); lndry; shop nr; rest; snacks; bar; playgrnd; pool (htd); paddling pool; wifi; TV; 10% statics; dogs €4; phone; Eng spkn; adv bkg acc; quiet; games area; CKE/CCI. "Pleasant site in lovely location; excel m'van facs; access for lge o'fits & m'vans poss diff due v narr site rds & awkward corners; walking dist fr town cent; v friendly & helpful staff; famous lge mkt on Mon." ♦ 3 Apr-28 Sep. € 29.60   2015*

⊞ **FORCALQUIER** *10E3* (8km SE Rural) *43.89752, 5.80609* **FLOWER Camping La Rivière, Lieu-Dit 'Les Côtes', 04300 St Maime [04 92 79 54 66; fax 04 92 79 51 03; contact@camping-lariviere.com; http://camping-lariviere.com or www.flowercampings.com]** S fr Sisteron on D4085, then D4096. Turn R at Voix onto D13, site on R in about 5km. Med, hdg, mkd, pt shd, wc; chem disp; shwrs; EHU (10A) inc; lndry; shop; rest; snacks; bar; bbq; playgrnd; pool; entmnt; wifi; TV; 50% statics; dogs €2.50; adv bkg acc; ccard acc; games area; games rm; lake fishing adj; CKE/CCI. "Vg, relaxing, friendly site; gd touring base for hilltop towns." ♦ € 35.50   2014*

> **"I need an on-site restaurant"**
>
> We do our best to make sure site information is correct, but it is always best to check any must-have facilities are still available or will be open during your visit.

FORCALQUIER *10E3* (7km S Urban) *43.91096, 5.78210* **FFCC Camping l'Eau Vive, 04300 Dauphin [04 92 79 51 91; info@leauvive.fr; www.leauvive.fr]** S fr Forcalquier on D4100 dir Apt; in 2.5km turn L onto D13 (at Mane); site on R in 3km. Or fr D4096, turn onto D13 at Volx; site on L in 6km (800m past Dauphin). Med, mkd, shd, wc (htd); chem disp; shwrs inc; EHU (3-6A) €3.50-4.50; lndry; shop; snacks; bbq (gas, sep area); playgrnd; pool; paddling pool; entmnt; TV; dogs €3.50; bus 800m; Eng spkn; adv bkg acc; quiet; games area; tennis; games rm; bike hire. "Well-run, super site; helpful owners; vg pools; vg for children; excel." 1 Apr-31 Sep. € 23.50   2016*

FORCALQUIER *10E3* (4km NW Rural) *43.97235, 5.73800* **Camping Le Domaine des Lauzons (Naturist), 04300 Limans [04 92 73 00 60; fax 04 92 73 04 31; leslauzons@wanadoo.fr; www.camping-lauzons.com]** Exit A51 junc 19 onto N100 dir Avignon; in Forcalquier at rndabt turn L onto D950/D313 sp Banon; site on R in approx 6km. Lge site sp. Diff app. Med, mkd, pt shd, pt sl, terr, wc; chem disp; fam bthrm; shwrs inc; EHU (6A) €4.50; gas; lndry; shop; rest; snacks; bar; bbq (charcoal, gas); playgrnd; pool (htd); entmnt; wifi; TV; 25% statics; dogs €4; phone; Eng spkn; adv bkg acc; quiet; ccard acc; waterslide; games area; ice; sauna; games rm; INF card req; archery. "Pleasant site in wooded valley; wonderful scenery; excel family site; helpful, friendly staff; most san facs modern, ltd LS; excel pool area; walks fr site; Forcalquier lovely town; excel touring base; pony rides; many activities; access diff lge o'fits, tractor help avail; INF not compulsory." ♦ 14 Apr-13 Oct. € 37.60   2018*

France

FORET FOUESNANT, LA

FORET FOUESNANT, LA 2F2 (2km SE Coastal) 47.89904, -3.96138 **Camping Les Saules, 54 Route de la Plage, 29940 La Forêt-Fouesnant [02 98 56 98 57; fax 02 98 56 86 60; info@camping-les-saules.com; www.camping-les-saules.com]**
Take N783 Concarneau-Quimper (by-pass) thro Le Poteau Vert, turn L at sp Kerleven. On ent vill, site on R opp Stereden Vor site. Lge, hdg, shd, pt sl, wc (htd); chem disp; mv service pnt; fam bthrm; shwrs inc; EHU (6A) €3; lndry; shop nr; rest nr; bar nr; bbq; playgrnd; pool; beach sand 150m; twin axles; wifi; TV; 60% statics; dogs €2.50; phone; bus adj; Eng spkn; adv bkg acc; quiet; ccard acc; games rm; sailing 150m; windsurfing 150m; fishing 150m; CKE/CCI. "Well run family site; many touring pitches with direct access to beach; yacht marina nrby-boat trips; gd walking on coastal path; excel." ♦ 1 May-28 Sep. € 27.00   2015*

FORGES LES EAUX 3C2 (1km S Urban) 49.60597, 1.54262 **Aire de Service (M'vans only), Blvd Nicolas Thiessé, 76440 Forges-les-Eaux [02 35 90 52 10; officeforgesleseaux@wanadoo.fr; www.forgesleseaux-tourisme.fr]** Fr Forges-les-Eaux cent, take D921 S sp Lyons-la-Forêt. In 500m turn R foll sp, camp on L in 250m opp municipal site. Med, hdstg, mkd, unshd, mv service pnt; EHU (poss rev pol). "No power, water etc Nov to Mar; water points; max 2 nights; warden visits or pay at Municipal site opp; town cent easy walk; views of open countryside; excel."
€ 7.00   2014*

FORGES LES EAUX 3C2 (1km S Urban) 49.60603, 1.54302 **Camp Municipal La Minière, 3 Blvd Nicolas Thiese, 76440 Forges-les-Eaux [02 35 90 53 91; campingforges@gmail.com; www.campingforges.com/en]** Fr Forges-les-Eaux cent, take D921 S sp Lyons-la-Forêt. In 750m turn R foll sp, camp on R in 150m. NB 3,500kg limit in town all dirs. Med, hdg, mkd, pt shd, pt sl, wc; shwrs inc; EHU (6A) inc (rev pol); lndry; shop nr; quiet; CKE/CCI. "Well-presented site; mv service pnt adj; lge pitches; friendly warden, warm welcome; v basic, clean san facs; poss diff access some pitches; m'van o'night area opp; htd pool in town; pleasant town with excel WWII Resistance Museum; gd local vet; useful NH; gd access to town; dog walk on site." ♦ 15 Mar-15 Oct. € 17.00   2017*

FOUGERES 2E4 (3km E Urban) 48.3544, -1.1795 **Camp Municipal de Paron, Route de la Chapelle-Janson, 35300 Fougères [02 99 99 40 81; fax 02 99 99 70 83; campingmunicipal35@orange.fr; www.ot-fougeres.fr]** Fr A84/E3 take junc 30 then ring rd E twd N12. Turn L at N12 & foll sp. Site on D17 sp R after Carrefour. Well sp on ring rd. Med, hdg, hdstg, pt shd, pt sl, serviced pitches; wc; chem disp; shwrs inc; EHU (5-10A) €3.60-4.10 (poss rev pol); lndry; shop nr; rest nr; playgrnd; wifi; dogs; adv bkg acc; quiet; ccard acc; tennis; horseriding adj; CKE/CCI. "Well-kept site in pleasant parkland setting; lge pitches, poss soggy when wet; popular NH; helpful warden; gd clean facs; gates clsd 2200-0900 & 1230-1730 card pass avail, parking avail in adj car park; tours of 12thC castle; old town worth visit; Sat mkt; excel; excel san facs."
27 Apr-16 Sep. € 14.00   2018*

FOURAS 7A1 (1km NE Coastal) 45.99264, -1.08680 **Camp Municipal du Cadoret, Blvd de Chaterny, 17450 Fouras [05 46 82 19 19; fax 05 46 84 51 59; www.campings-fouras.com]**
Fr Rochefort take N137, L onto D937 at Fouras, fork R at sp to site in 1km. At next rndabt take 3rd exit into Ave du Cadoret, then 1st R at next rndabt. Lge, mkd, pt shd, pt sl, wc; chem disp; fam bthrm; shwrs inc; EHU (6-10A) €3.50-5.40 (poss long lead req); gas; lndry; shop nr; rest; bar; pool (htd); paddling pool; beach sand adj; entmnt; wifi; 50% statics; dogs €2.90; bus to La Rochelle, Rochefort, ferry to Ile d'Aix; Eng spkn; adv bkg acc; golf 5km; fishing; games area; tennis 1km; boating; CKE/CCI. "Popular, well-kept site; vg location; well shd; lge pitches; clean san facs, unisex LS; coastal footpath; pleasant town; a favourite; highly rec; gd conv site." ♦ € 24.00   2015*

FOURAS 7A1 (1km E Rural) 45.99023, -1.05184 **Camping Domaine Les Charmilles, Route de l'OcÂcan, 17450 Fouras [05 46 84 00 05; fax 05 46 84 02 84; info@domainedescharmilles.com; www.domainedescharmilles.com]** N fr Rochefort on N137, after 2km L onto D937. Site on L in 2km bef ent Fouras. Lge, hdg, mkd, pt shd, wc (htd); chem disp; mv service pnt; shwrs inc; EHU (6A) €4; gas; lndry; shop; snacks; bar; bbq; playgrnd; pool (covrd, htd); paddling pool; beach sand 3km; red long stay; entmnt; wifi; 20% statics; adv bkg acc; ccard acc; waterslide; bike hire; games rm; CKE/CCI. "Gd site; friendly staff; bus to beach high ssn; unisex facs." ♦ € 37.50   2013*

> "Satellite navigation makes touring much easier"
>
> Remember most sat navs don't know if you're towing or in a larger vehicle – always use yours alongside maps and site directions.

FREJUS 10F4 (10km W Rural) 43.45070, 6.63320 **Village camping Les Pêcheurs, Quartier Verseil, 83520 Roquebrune-sur-Argens [04 94 45 71 25; fax 04 94 81 65 13; info@camping-les-pecheurs.com; www.camping-les-pecheurs.com]** Exit A8 junc 36 dir Le Muy, onto DN7 then D7 sp Roquebrune; camp 800m on L (bef bdge over Rv Argens) at ent to vill. Alt rte, leave A8 at junc 37, turn R at rndabt twrds Le Muy and cont as above. Lge, hdg, mkd, hdstg, pt shd, wc (htd); chem disp; mv service pnt; fam bthrm; shwrs inc; EHU (10A) €5.50; gas; lndry; shop; rest; snacks; bar; bbq (elec, gas); playgrnd; pool (htd); paddling pool; sw nr; entmnt; wifi; TV; 25% statics; dogs €3.20; phone; Eng spkn; adv bkg acc; quiet; ccard acc; horseriding; canoeing adj; tennis 2km; fishing adj; CKE/CCI. "Lovely site; popular with families; helpful staff; sauna; spa; jacuzzi; some pitches v shady; bike hire 1km; some site rds/pitch access tight for lge o'fits, OK with mover; gd walking, cycling." ♦ 5 Apr-29 Sep. € 58.00   2014*

FREJUS *10F4* (12km W Rural) *43.44535, 6.65790*
Camping Le Moulin des Iscles, Chemin du Moulin des Iscles, 83520 Roquebrune-sur-Argens [04 94 45 70 74; fax 04 94 45 46 09; moulin.iscles@wanadoo. fr; www.campingdesiscles.com] Twd Fréjus on DN7, turn R onto D7 to St Aygulf sp Roquebrune. Site on L after passing thro Roquebrune vill. Med, mkd, shd, wc (htd); chem disp; fam bthrm; shwrs inc; EHU (6A) €3.90; lndry; shop; rest; snacks; bar; bbq; playgrnd; entmnt; wifi; TV; 10% statics; dogs €2.50; adv bkg acc; quiet; ccard acc; games rm; rv fishing; canoeing. "Excel well-kept, well-run site by rv; water skiing nrby; helpful owners; gd security." ♦ 1 Apr-30 Sep. € 28.00   2015*

FREJUS *10F4* (3km NW Rural) *43.46335, 6.7247*
Camping Le Fréjus, 3401, rue des Combattants, d'Afrique du Nord, 83600 FREJUS [04 94 19 94 60; fax 04 94 19 94 69; contact@lefrejus.com; www. lefrejus.com] Exit A8 junc 38, at 1st rndabt turn L, then L at 2nd rndabt & L again at 3rd rndabt, Site on R in 200m. Lge, mkd, pt shd, pt sl, terr, wc (htd); chem disp; mv service pnt; fam bthrm; shwrs inc; EHU (10A) inc; lndry; shop; rest; snacks; bar; playgrnd; pool (htd); entmnt; wifi; 80% statics; dogs (leashed) €4; Eng spkn; adv bkg acc; quiet; ccard acc; waterslide; games rm; tennis; CKE/CCI. "Ideal position for coast bet Cannes & St Tropez; lge pitches; pleasant, friendly staff; gd san facs; muddy after rain; quiet; vg site; basin cold water at each pitch." ♦ 15 Jan-15 Dec. € 37.00   2013*

FREJUS *10F4* (4km NW Urban) *43.46616, 6.72203*
Camping La Baume - La Palmeraie, Route de Bagnoles, Rue des Combattants d'Afrique du Nord, 83600 Fréjus [04 94 19 88 88; fax 04 94 19 83 50; reception@labaume-lapalmeraie.com; www. labaume-lapalmeraie.com] Fr A8 exit junc 38 sp Fréjus cent. Fr E'bound dir foll Bagnols sp at 2 rndabts & Fréjus cent/Cais at 3rd. Fr W'bound dir foll Bagnols at 3 rndabts & Fréjus cent/Cais at 4th. Site on L in 300m. V lge, pt shd, pt sl, wc (htd); shwrs; EHU (6A) inc; gas; lndry; shop; rest; snacks; bar; playgrnd; pool (covrd, htd); beach sand 5km; entmnt; 80% statics; dogs €4; adv bkg req; horseriding; tennis; waterslide. ♦ 1 Apr-30 Sep. € 51.00   2012*

FREJUS *10F4* (6km NW Rural) *43.46944, 6.67805*
Camping La Bastiane, 1056 Chemin des Suvières, 83480 Puget-sur-Argens [04 94 55 55 94; fax 04 94 55 55 93; info@labastiane.com; www.labastiane.com] Exit A8 at junc 37 Puget/Fréjus. At DN7 turn R dir Le Muy & in 1km turn R immed after 2nd bdge. Foll sp to site. Fr DN7 turn L at traff lts in Puget, site is 2km N of Puget. Lge, mkd, hdg, shd, pt sl, wc; chem disp; fam bthrm; shwrs inc; EHU (10A) inc; lndry; shop; rest; snacks; bar; bbq (elec); playgrnd; pool (htd); paddling pool; red long stay; entmnt; wifi; TV; 40% statics; dogs €4; phone; Eng spkn; adv bkg acc; quiet; ccard acc; bike hire; tennis; games area; games rm; watersports; CKE/CCI. "Excel, family-run, friendly site; cinema; car wash area; conv m'way (no m'way noise); clean san facs; gd rest." ♦ 21 Apr-9 Oct. € 50.20   2017*

FRESNAY SUR SARTHE *4E1* (0km NW Rural) *48.28297, 0.0158* Camp Municipal Le Sans Souci, Rue du Haut Ary, Ave Victor Hugo, 72130 Fresnay-sur-Sarthe [02 43 97 32 87; fax 02 43 33 75 72; regisseur@camping-fresnaysursarthe.fr; www.camping-fresnaysursarthe.fr] Fr Alençon S on D338; in 14km at La Hutte turn R on D310 to Fresnay; sp in town on traff lts bef bdge; bear R imm after x-ing bdge, then sharp R, sp diff to see, if missed V diff for c'vans to turn fr opp dir. Fr Beaumont-sur-Sarthe NW on D39 to Fresnay. Med, mkd, hdg, pt shd, pt sl, terr, wc; chem disp; shwrs inc; EHU (6A) €3.20 (poss rev pol); lndry; shop; entmnt; wifi; dogs €1.20; Eng spkn; adv bkg acc; quiet; rv fishing adj; bike hire; canoe hire; CKE/CCI. "Pleasant, clean site adj Rv Sarthe; gd rvside pitches; 3 pitches for lge o'fits, mover rec; htd pool adj inc; facs poss stretched high ssn; gd cycling; vg." ♦ 1 Apr-30 Sep. € 16.60   2013*

FRONTIGNAN *10F1* (1km S Coastal) *43.42998, 3.75968* Camping Méditerranée, 11 Ave des Vacances, Quartier L'Entrée, 34110 Frontignan-Plage [04 99 04 92 32 or 06 49 39 03 79 (LS); camping-mediterranee@orange.fr; www.camping-mediterranee34.com] 3km fr Sète on D612 to Montpellier, turn R at rlwy bdge, in approx 1km L at x-rds to site. Or on D129 fr Frontignan to Frontignan-Plage site on R 100m past reclamation area. Med, pt shd, wc; shwrs inc; EHU (6A) €3.50; lndry; shop nr; rest; snacks; bar; playgrnd; beach sand 100m; entmnt; dogs €1.50; bus adj; adv bkg rec; quiet; games area; tennis. " 30 Mar-29 Sep. € 17.00   2013*

FUMEL *7D3* (2km E Rural) *44.48929, 0.99704*
Camping de Condat/Les Catalpas, Route de Cahors, 47500 Fumel [05 53 71 11 99 or 06 30 24 20 04; fax 05 53 71 36 69; les-catalpas@wanadoo.fr; www. les-catalpas.com] Take D811 fr Fumel E twd Cahors. Clearly sp after Condat. Med, hdstg, mkd, pt shd, pt sl, wc (htd); chem disp; mv service pnt; shwrs inc; EHU (10A) €3; lndry; shop nr; rest nr; snacks; bbq; playgrnd; pool; entmnt; wifi; 15% statics; dogs; Eng spkn; adv bkg acc; fishing adj; CKE/CCI. "New owners, friendly helpful, improvements to site, sec barrier, by rv." ♦ 1 Apr-31 Oct. € 21.00   2012*

⊞ **FUMEL** *7D3* (4km E Rural) *44.48925, 1.02048*
Aire Naturelle Le Valenty (Baillargues), Rue de Chantegrue 46700 Soturac, Lot [05 65 36 59 50 or 06 72 57 69 80 (mob); campingdevalenty@gmail.com] Fr Fumel take D911/811 dir Cahors. Thro Soturac, site immed on L outside vill. Sm, pt shd, terr, wc; shwrs inc; EHU (4-10A) €2.50; lndry; shop nr; rest nr; bar nr; playgrnd; pool; 20% statics; dogs €1; bus 200m; Eng spkn; adv bkg acc; quiet; games rm; CKE/CCI. "Delightful CL-type site; helpful owners; tranquil but secure; pony rides; organic produce for sale; mini golf; poss not open LS - phone ahead." € 13.00   2013*

FUMEL

FUMEL 7D3 (8km E Rural) 44.49810, 1.06670 **Camping Le Ch'Timi, La Roque, 46700 Touzac [05 65 36 52 36; fax 05 65 36 53 23; info@campinglechtimi.com; www.campinglechtimi.com]** Exit N20-E9 junc 57 onto D820 dir Cahors; turn R at rndabt onto D811 sp Villeneuve-sur-Lot; in Duravel take 3rd exit at rndabt onto D58, sp Vire-sur-Lot; in 2.5km cross bdge & turn R at rndabt onto D8, sp Touzac; site on R on rvside, on hill, in about 1.5km. Well sp. NB D8 not suitable lge c'vans or m'vans. Med, hdg, mkd, pt shd, pt sl, wc; chem disp; fam bthrm; shwrs inc; EHU (6A) €4.20; gas; lndry; shop; rest; snacks; bar; bbq; playgrnd; pool; paddling pool; twin axles; entmnt; wifi; TV; 13% statics; dogs €1.90; phone; Eng spkn; adv bkg acc; quiet; ccard acc; tennis; games area; games rm; archery; bike hire; fishing 100m; CKE/CCI. "Site in gd position; friendly, helpful Dutch owners; immac facs, ltd LS; rv nr site, down steep steps; access some pitches poss diff lge o'fits; gd local rests; no o'fits over 7m high ssn; canoeing 100m; wine-tasting tours; mkt Puy l'Evêque Tue; wonderful stay, rec; v well kept; rv view fr some pitches; ACSI acc." ♦ 1 Apr-30 Sep. € 28.00 2015*

GACE 4E1 (0km E Urban) 48.79475, 0.29926 **Camp Municipal Le Pressoir, Ave de Tahiti, 61230 Gacé [02 33 35 50 24 or 02 33 35 50 18; fax 02 33 35 92 82; ville.gace@wanadoo.fr]** Exit A28 junc 16 onto D932/D438; in 2km turn R off D438 opp Intermarché onto D724; site immed on L. Foll sp. NB Take care corners on app if o'fit v long. Sm, mkd, hdg, pt shd, sl, wc; chem disp; shwrs inc; EHU (6A) €2.50 (poss long lead req); lndry; shop nr; rest nr; playgrnd; twin axles. "Clean, well-run site; rec early arr; san facs dated but clean; mv service pnt in vill; most pitches gd size, sm pitches poss diff for lge o'fits; pitches rather sl for m'van; warden calls am & pm; conv NH fr A28; nice site, well kept." 1 Jun-8 Sep. € 11.00 2013*

GAILLAC 8E4 (5km E Urban) 43.90929, 1.98311 **Camping Les Pommiers, Aigueleze, 81600 Rivières [05 63 33 02 49; info@camping-lespommiers.com; www.camping-lespommiers.com]** Fr A68, Albi - Toulouse take exit 10, foll sp Espace Loisirs d'Aigueleze. Med, hdstg, mkd, pt shd, pt sl, wc; chem disp; mv service pnt; fam bthrm; shwrs inc; EHU (10-13A) €4.50; lndry; snacks; bar; bbq; playgrnd; pool (htd); paddling pool; sw; twin axles; red long stay; entmnt; wifi; TV; 25% statics; dogs €2; phone; Eng spkn; adv bkg acc; quiet; games area; bike hire; CCI. "Visit Albi by sightseeing boat on Rv Tarn or by train; canoe hire 150m; bike hire 150m; vg; conv Albi, Cordes, P&R Toulose; excel; well kept clean site; friendly, welcoming owners; conv for bastide vill; sm eve mkt Mon in hg ssn nr." ♦ 1 Apr-30 Sep. € 27.00 2018*

GAILLAC 8E4 (2km W Urban) 43.89674, 1.88522 **FFCC Camping des Sources, 9 Ave Guynemer, 81600 Gaillac [05 63 57 18 30; fax 05 49 52 28 58; camping-gaillac@orange.fr; www.camping-gaillac.fr]** Exit A68 junc 9 onto D999 then in 3.5km at rndabt turn onto D968 dir Gaillac. In 100m turn R immed past Leclerc petrol stn, then L by Aldi. Site 200m on R, well sp fr town cent. Sharp turn into ent. Med, hdg, hdstg, mkd, pt shd, terr, wc (htd); chem disp; mv service pnt; fam bthrm; shwrs inc; EHU (10A) €3; lndry; shop nr; snacks; bar; playgrnd; pool; entmnt; TV; 10% statics; dogs €2; quiet; ccard acc; CKE/CCI. "Peaceful, clean & tidy site; friendly, helpful staff; gd, modern san facs; steep walk to recep & bar but san facs at pitch level; purpose-made dog-walk area; gd touring base Tarn & Albi region & circular tour Bastides; cent of wine area; not suitable lge o'fits; gd; call recep fr Aldi carpk to operate barrier." ♦ 1 Apr-31 Oct. € 14.50 2017*

⊞ **GANGES** 10E1 (7km E Rural) 43.92630, 3.78951 **Camp Municipal Le Grillon, Place de l'Eglise, 34190 Montouliou [04 67 73 30 75; camping@montouliou.fr; http://camping.montouliou.fr]** Fr Ganges take D999 E. At La Cadière-et-Cambo turn R onto D195 (site sp). Site on R in 3km. Sm, hdg, hdstg, pt shd, pt sl, wc; mv service pnt; fam bthrm; shwrs inc; EHU (6A) inc; lndry; rest; bar; playgrnd; pool; 40% statics; dogs; quiet. "Gd cent for outdoor activities; gd, modern facs; useful winter NH; fairly isolated." ♦ € 18.50 2014*

GANNAT 9A1 (7km N Rural) 46.16588, 3.18975 **Camp Municipal Champ de la Sioule, Route de Chantelle, 03800 Jenzat [04 70 56 86 35 or 04 70 56 81 77 (Mairie); fax 04 70 56 85 38; mairie-jenzat@pays-allier.com; www.bassin-gannat.com]** D2009 N fr Gannat for 4.5km, turn L onto D42, site in 3km in Jenzat on R, just after rv bdge. Med, pt shd, wc; shwrs inc; EHU (6-10) €1.90-2.95; lndry; shop nr; playgrnd; sw nr; Eng spkn; quiet; CKE/CCI. "Pleasant site on rv bank; helpful warden; clean facs, poss stretched high ssn; clean facs; muddy after heavy rain; pitches nr rv, some mosquitos." ♦ 15 Apr-21 Sep. € 20.00 2014*

GANNAT 9A1 (10km W Rural) 46.11077, 3.08082 **Camp Municipal Les Nières, Rue des Nières, 03450 Ebreuil [04 70 90 70 60 or 04 70 90 71 33 (Mairie); fax 04 70 90 74 90; mairie-ebreuil@wanadoo.fr; www.valdesioule.fr]** Site 1km SW of Ebreuil, sp fr D915. Sm, shd, wc cont; chem disp; shwrs; EHU (4-8A) €1.95-2.80; lndry; shop nr; snacks; playgrnd; quiet; fishing; rv. "Nice setting on Rv Sioule; san facs dated but clean, poss stretched high ssn; warden present 1700-2000 only LS; sh walk into vill." ♦ 1 Jun-30 Sep. € 8.00 2012*

GANNAT *9A1 (10km W Rural) 46.10838, 3.07347*
Camping La Filature de la Sioule, Route de Chouvigny, 03450 Ebreuil [04 70 90 72 01; camping.filature@gmail.com; www.campingfilature.com] Fr A71 exit 12 (not 12.1); foll sp to Ebreuil, after rv bdge in vill turn L onto D998 then cont onto D915. Site on L in abt 1 km. Med, mkd, hdg, pt shd, wc; chem disp; fam bthrm; shwrs inc; EHU (6A) €3.50; gas; lndry; shop; snacks; bar; bbq; playgrnd; red long stay; wifi; TV; 10% statics; dogs free; Eng spkn; adv bkg acc; quiet; ccard acc; canoeing; horseriding; tennis 800m; bike hire; trout fishing; CKE/CCI. "Peaceful, pleasant rvside site in orchard; lge pitches; helpful British owners; clean facs but tired, ltd LS; vg value food high ssn (gd home cooking); vg walking area; mv service pnt 800m; conv A71; no hdstg, v soft grnd; poor water pressure in shwrs; site unkept (2015)." ♦ 15 Apr-1 Oct. € 26.00   2016*

GAP *9D3 (2km N Rural) 44.58030, 6.08270* Camping Alpes-Dauphiné, Route Napoléon, 05000 Gap [04 92 51 29 95; fax 04 92 53 58 42; info@alpesdauphine.com; www.alpesdauphine.com] On N85, sp. Med, hdstg, mkd, pt shd, pt sl, terr, wc (htd); chem disp; mv service pnt; fam bthrm; shwrs inc; EHU (6A) €3; gas; lndry; shop; rest; snacks; bar; playgrnd; pool (htd); paddling pool; wifi; TV; 20% statics; dogs €2.10; phone; Eng spkn; adv bkg rec; quiet; ccard acc; games area; CKE/CCI. "Pleasant site with views; modern, well maintained san facs; m'vans need levellers; gd touring base; lack of maintenance early ssn (2011); conv NH; gd site; excel rest." ♦ 15 Apr-20 Oct. € 27.00   2017*

GAP *9D3 (10km S Rural) 44.45708, 6.04785* Camping Le Chêne, Route de Marseille, 05130 Tallard [04 92 54 13 31; contact@camping-lechene.com; www.camping-lechene.com] Fr S take N85 twds Gap; turn R at traff lts onto D942; site on R after 3km. Fr Gap take N85 S; turn L at traff lts, D942; site on R 3km. Sm, mkd, hdstg, pt shd, sl, terr, wc; shwrs inc; EHU (6A) €3.5; lndry; shop nr; rest; bar; bbq (sep area); playgrnd; pool (htd); entmnt; dogs; phone; adv bkg acc; tennis; CKE/CCI. "Poss unsuitable for lgs o'fits, sm pitches; lovely setting; new san facs (2018), but ltd for site size; site needs tlc;." 6 Apr-13 Oct. € 13.00   2018*

GAVARNIE *8G2 (4km N Rural) 42.75896, 0.00069* Camping Le Pain de Sucre, quartier Couret, 65120 Gavarnie [05 62 92 47 55 or 06 75 30 64 22 (mob); camping-gavarnie@wanadoo.fr or info@camping-gavarnie.com; www.camping-gavarnie.com] N of Gavarnie, across rv by sm bdge; clearly visible & sp fr rd. Med, pt shd, wc; chem disp; mv service pnt; shwrs inc; EHU (2-10A) €2.30-6.50 (long lead poss req); lndry; shop nr; rest nr; bbq; playgrnd; dogs €2.15; quiet; ccard acc. "Gd base for walking; gd facs; access to national park; vg; gd clean san facs; fantastic view of Cirque."
♦ 1 Jan-15 Apr, 1 Jun-30 Sep & 15 Dec-31 Dec. € 20.00   2016*

GERARDMER

GENNES *4G1 (1km NE Rural) 47.34205, -0.22985*
Camping Au Bord de Loire, Ave des Cadets-de-Saumur, 49350 Gennes [02 41 38 04 67 or 06 95 00 24 87; contact@camping-auborddeloire.com; www.camping-auborddeloire.com] At Rv Loire bdge cross S to Gennes on D751B. Site 200m on L. Ent to site thro bus terminus/car park on ent to Gennes. Med, pt shd, pt sl, wc; chem disp; shwrs inc; EHU (10A) €3.40; lndry; shop nr; snacks; bar; bbq; playgrnd; red long stay; entmnt; wifi; 2% statics; dogs €1.60; quiet; CKE/CCI. "Delightful, relaxing, well-kept site by Rv Loire, spacious pitches, main san facs block up 18 steps, vg; htd pool in vill; Loire cycle rte passes gate; new san facs block (2015); v easy walk to vill." 13 Apr-30 Sep. € 16.80   2018*

GERARDMER *6F3 (7km E Rural) 48.06755, 6.94830* FFCC Camping Les Jonquilles, Route du Lac, 88400 Xonrupt-Longemer [03 29 63 34 01; fax 03 29 60 09 28; info@camping-jonquilles.com; www.camping-jonquilles.com] Sp off D417 SE of Xonrupt-Longemer. Fr W thro Gérardmer on D417 (sp Colmar) in approx 1km over bdge & turn R at T-junc (still on D417). After 3km turn R opp hotel Auberge du Lac & almost immed R round W end of lake for 500m to T-junc, turn L, site on S bank 1km. Lge, mkd, unshd, pt sl, wc; chem disp; mv service pnt; fam bthrm; shwrs inc; EHU (6-10A) €3.50-5.20; gas; lndry; shop; rest; snacks; bar; playgrnd; sw nr; wifi; TV; 10% statics; dogs €1.50; phone; bus 1km; Eng spkn; adv bkg acc; quiet; ccard acc; sailing; fishing; CKE/CCI. "Friendly, well-maintained, family-run site; gd views; poss uneven pitches; some noise fr entmnt at night; excel for Haute Vosges region; great lakeside site; busy rd." ♦ 17 Apr-4 Oct. € 18.00   2015*

GERARDMER *6F3 (2km SW Urban) 48.06472, 6.85488* Camping de Ramberchamp, 21 Chemin du Tour du Lac, 88400 Gérardmer [03 29 63 03 82; fax 03 29 63 26 09; info@camping-de-ramberchamp.com; www.camping-de-ramberchamp.com] S bank of Lake Gérardmer. Fr W turn R off D417, 1km bef Gérardmer. Fr E thro cent of town foll sps to La Bresse, fork R onto D69, sp Vagney. Foll lakeside rd & camping sps. Lge, hdg, mkd, pt shd, wc (htd); chem disp; fam bthrm; shwrs inc; EHU (4A) €3.50; lndry; shop nr; rest; snacks; bbq; playgrnd; sw; TV; dogs €1; Eng spkn; quiet; ccard acc; fishing; CKE/CCI. "Comfortable site in excel location; friendly staff; some sm pitches; easy-going walks; walk along lake to town; games for children, giant chessboard, mini golf; excel, stunning area; rec open fr 0830 to 2030, san facs stretched when busy, access rds thro site very narr for lge o'fits, superb location at edge of lake." 4 Apr-30 Sep. € 20.40   2014*

GERARDMER

GERARDMER *6F3 (2km SW Rural) 48.0636, 6.8561* Camping Les Sapins, 18 Chemin de Sapois, 88400 Gérardmer [03 29 63 15 01 or 06 37 35 36 20 (mob); les.sapins@camping-gerardmer.com; www.camping-gerardmer.com] On S side of lake 150m up C17 rd sp Col de Sapois. Med, pt shd, wc; mv service pnt; shwrs inc; EHU (4-6A) €3-4.70; shop; rest; snacks; bar; bbq; playgrnd; sw nr; TV; 10% statics; dogs €1.20; adv bkg rec; quiet; watersports adj; games area; fishing adj. "Well-kept site in lovely area; lge pitches but o'looked by sports stadium; no lake views; walk along lake into pretty town, easy walk to vibrant town, friendly owner." 1 Apr-10 Oct. € 19.60   2014*

GERAUDOT *6E1 (1km E Rural) 48.30268, 4.33752* Camping Les Rives du Lac/L'Epine aux Moines, 10220 Géraudot [03 25 41 24 36; camping.lepineauxmoines@orange.fr; www.campinglesrivesdulac.com] Exit A26 at junc 23 onto D619 to Lusigny-sur-Barse; foll sp Parc de la Forêt d'Orient. Turn N along lake to site. Or fr Troyes D960 E. At Rouilly head S on D43 sp Géraudot. Site 1km E of vill. Lge, mkd, hdg, pt sl, wc (htd); chem disp; mv service pnt; shwrs inc; EHU (6A) inc (poss rev pol & long lead req); lndry; rest nr; bar; playgrnd; sw nr; dogs €2; adv bkg acc; quiet; boat hire; CKE/CCI. "Nice, well-kept site in attractive area; clean san facs; poss mosquitoes; gd walking & cycle paths; nr bird observatory; lovely vill; conv NH." 2 Jan-23 Dec. € 24.00   2013*

GEX *9A3 (1km E Urban) 46.33430, 6.06744* Camping Les Genêts, 400 Ave des Alpes, 01170 Gex [04 50 42 84 57 or 06 79 17 13 69 (mob); fax 04 50 41 68 77; les.2b@hotmail.fr; www.gex.fr/decouvrir-gex/camping] Fr all dir head for 'Centre Ville'; at rndabt take D984 twd Divonne/Lausanne. Site sp to R (tight turn) after rlwy sheds (poor sp in town) & Musée Sapeurs Pompiers. Med, hdg, hdstg, pt shd, pt sl, wc; chem disp; shwrs inc; EHU (16A) €2.90; lndry; shop nr; snacks; bar; playgrnd; TV; dogs €1; phone; Eng spkn; adv bkg acc; quiet; games area; CKE/CCI. "Excel, attractive, well-kept site; excel games facs/playgrnd; friendly, helpful staff; clean san facs; quiet with lots of privacy; conv Geneva; wifi in recep; gates clsd 2200-0800; 20 mins fr Geneva airport." ♦ 1 May-31 Oct. € 17.50   2017*

GIEN *4G3 (3km S Rural) 47.68233, 2.62289* Camping Touristique de Gien, Rue des Iris, 45500 Poilly-lez-Gien [02 38 67 12 50; fax 02 38 67 12 18; info@camping-gien.com; www.camping-gien.com] Off D952 Orléans-Nevers rd; turn R over old rv bdge in Gien & then R again onto D951; site on R on Rv Loire. Alt dir fr D940 (Argent-sur-Sauldre - Gien) at rndbt take rd sp Gien. Take L at traff lts bef old bdge; site on R, 1km S of rv. Lge, hdstg, mkd, hdg, pt shd, pt sl, wc (htd); chem disp; mv service pnt; fam bthrm; shwrs inc; EHU (10A) €5; lndry; shop; rest; snacks; bar nr; bbq; playgrnd; pool (covrd); paddling pool; sw nr; red long stay; entmnt; wifi; TV; 20% statics; dogs €2; phone; Eng spkn; adv bkg acc; quiet; ccard acc; tennis; canoeing; games rm; bike hire; CKE/CCI. "Lovely rvside site; views of old bdge & town some pitches; excel staff; gd san facs; vg facs; no sw allowed in rv; easy walk to town across bdge; porcelain factory 'seconds'; vg value; gd rest; san facs unisex; excel site, highly rec; nice situation; bar adj; gas adj; flock of sheep/goats traverse the site daily." ♦ 3 Mar-4 Nov. € 27.00   2018*

GIEN *4G3 (8km S Rural) 47.64152, 2.61528* **Les Bois du Bardelet, Route de Bourges, Poilly 45500 Gien [02 38 67 47 39; fax 02 38 38 27 16; contact@bardelet.com; www.bardelet.com]** Fr Gien take D940 dir Bourges; turn R onto D53, then R again onto unclassified rd to go back across D940; foll sp to site on L side of this rd. Site well sp fr D940. Lge, mkd, hdstg, hdg, pt shd, pt sl, wc (htd); chem disp; mv service pnt; fam bthrm; shwrs inc; EHU (10-16A) inc (some rev pol); gas; lndry; shop; rest; snacks; bar; bbq; playgrnd; pool (covrd, htd); paddling pool; red long stay; twin axles; entmnt; wifi; TV; 17% statics; dogs €4; phone; adv bkg acc; quiet; ccard acc; archery; bike hire; fitness rm; jacuzzi; canoeing; games area; tennis; lake fishing; horseriding 5km; games rm; CKE/CCI. "Pleasant, well-kept, well-run site; friendly welcome; modern, immac san facs; poss stretched high ssn; some pitches poss diff access; beautiful o'door pool; gd for young children; guided walks; remote site in countryside." ♦ 3 Apr-30 Sep. € 28.00   2015*

See advertisement

GISORS *3D3 (7km SW Rural) 49.25639, 1.70174*
Camp Municipal de l'Aulnaie, Rue du Fond-de-l'Aulnaie, 27720 Dangu [02 32 55 43 42; contact@campingdelaulnaie-dangu.com; www.campingdelaulnaie-dangu.fr] On ent Gisors fr all dirs, take ring rd & exit dir Vernon D10, then L onto D181 dir Dangu. Site on L bef Dangu. Site sp fr D10. NB speed humps. Lge, mkd, pt shd, wc (htd); chem disp; mv service pnt; shwrs inc; EHU (10A) €2.80; gas; lndry; rest nr; bar nr; playgrnd; sw; 90% statics; dogs €2.60; adv bkg acc; fishing; CKE/CCI. "Lakeside site; Gisors attractive town; conv Giverny & Gisors local attractions; beautiful site." ♦ 1 Apr-31 Oct. € 14.00   2014*

⊞ **GIVET** *5B1 (1km N Urban) 50.14345, 4.82614*
Caravaning Municipal La Ballastière, 16 Rue Berthelot, 08600 Givet [03 24 42 30 20; fax 03 24 42 02 44; sa.mairiegivet@wanadoo.fr; http://www.tourisme-champagne-ardenne.com] Site at N end of town on lake. Foll 'Caravaning' sp fr W end of rv bdge or Dinant rd. Med, hdstg, hdg, mkd, pt shd, wc (htd); chem disp; shwrs inc; EHU (10A) inc; lndry; shop nr; rest nr; bar nr; bbq; playgrnd; 60% statics; dogs €0.85; CKE/CCI. "Nr Rv Meuse; adj sports & watersports complex; picturesque town; walking dist to shops & rest; vg; pool adj; conv for Rv Meuse cycleway; fair NH; scruffy & unkept san facs, rundown but clean (2018)." ♦ € 9.00   2018*

GIVET *5B1 (2km SW Rural) 50.12993, 4.80721*
Camping Le Sanglier, 63 Rue des Grands Jardins, 08600 Rancennes [03 24 42 72 61 or 06 47 98 62 41 (mob); fax 09 79 73 72 24; gilbert.gachet0455@orange.fr] Off D949 Givet to Beauraing. Immed after x-ing rv bdge turn R. Turn R again foll sp to site at end narr access rd on rvside. Sm, pt shd, pt sl, terr, wc; chem disp; shwrs; EHU (4A); shop nr; snacks; wifi; 60% statics; phone; Eng spkn; adv bkg acc; quiet; watersports; fishing; CKE/CCI. "Gd touring base; clean, basic facs; gd NH." 1 May-30 Sep. € 9.00   2015*

GIVORS *9B2 (10km NW Urban) 45.61498, 4.67068*
Camping La Trillonnière, Boulevard du General de Gaulle, 69440 Mornant [04 82 29 21 89 or 04 78 44 16 47; contact@la-trillonniere.fr; www.la-trillonniere.fr] Exit A7 at Givors & foll sp for St Etienne via D488, thro Givors onto D2 till sp seen for Mornant via D34, cont on D34 up hill for 7km, cross D342 & cont 1km to o'skts of Mornant, L at junc island & site on L. Med, pt shd, pt sl, wc; chem disp; mv service pnt; fam bthrm; shwrs; EHU (10A) inc; lndry; shop nr; rest nr; playgrnd; twin axles; wifi; 20% statics; dogs €1; Eng spkn; adv bkg acc; CKE/CCI. "Well managed, quiet site on edge of lovely vill in Monts du Lyonnais; walks in hills; Lyon accessible by bus (outside gate) & metro; excell new san facs; 6 chalets;." ♦ 15 May-30 Sep. € 25.00   2018*

⊞ **GIVRE, LE** *7A1 (2km S Rural) 46.44472, -1.39832*
Camping La Grisse, 85540 Le Givre [02 51 30 83 03; info@campinglagrisse.com; www.campinglagrisse.com] Fr Luçon take D949 & turn L at junc with D747 (La Tranche rd). Turn L in 3km & foll sps. Sm, pt shd, wc; chem disp; shwrs inc; EHU (16A) €4; lndry; playgrnd; wifi; 50% statics; dogs €2; Eng spkn; adv bkg acc; ccard acc; games area; CKE/CCI. "Peaceful, friendly, farm site; lge pitches; clean, modern facs; beautiful area/beach; gd for dogs; knowledgeable owner of local area." ♦ € 29.00   2017*

GIVRY EN ARGONNE *5D1 (0km S Rural) 48.94835, 4.88545* **Camp Municipal du Val d'Ante, Rue du Pont, 51330 Givry-en-Argonne** [03 26 60 04 15 or 03 26 60 01 59 (Mairie); fax 03 26 60 18 22; mairie.givryenargonne@wanadoo.fr; www.mairie-givry-en-argonne.fr] Exit A4 junc 29 at Ste Menéhould; S on D382 to Givry-en-Argonne; site sp on R on lakeside. Sm, pt shd, pt sl, wc; chem disp; shwrs inc; EHU (6A) €2.10; shop nr; playgrnd; sw; dogs €1.20; quiet. "Attractive, basic site; boat hire adj; clean san facs; warden calls am & pm; gd birdwatching." 1 May-31 Aug. € 12.40   2013*

GONDRIN *8E2 (3km SE Rural) 43.86936, 0.25844*
Camping La Brouquère, Betbézé, 32330 Gondrin [05 62 29 19 44; camping@brouquere.com; www.brouquere.com] Fr Condom S on D931; pass thro Gondrin & turn S onto D113 dir Courrensan; site sp in 2km. Sm, mkd, shd, pt sl, wc; chem disp; fam bthrm; shwrs inc; EHU (10A) €2.50; lndry; bar; bbq; playgrnd; wifi; TV; dogs €1; Eng spkn; adv bkg acc; quiet; bike hire. "V quiet, CL-type site; friendly Dutch owners; immac san facs; wine-tasting; local produce; inc Armagnac; excel; adults only." 30 Apr-1 Oct. € 17.00   2016*

GORDES *10E2 (2km N Rural) 43.92689, 5.20207*
Camping Les Sources, Route de Murs, 84220 Gordes [04 90 71 12 48; fax 04 90 72 09 43; campingdessources@wanadoo.fr; www.campingdessources.com] Fr A7 junc 24, E on D973; then D22; then D900 twds Apt. After 18km at Coustellet turn N onto D2 then L on D15 twds Murs; site on L in 2km beyond Gordes. Med, mkd, hdstg, pt shd, terr, wc; chem disp; mv service pnt; fam bthrm; shwrs inc; EHU (6A) €4.40 (long lead poss req); lndry; shop; rest; snacks; bar; playgrnd; pool; red long stay; entmnt; 25% statics; dogs €5; Eng spkn; adv bkg acc; quiet; ccard acc; games area; bike hire; games area; CKE/CCI. "Lovely location & views; friendly staff; modern, clean san facs; gd pool; access rds narr; sm pitches v diff lge o'fits; ask for easy pitch & inspect on foot; some steep rds to pitches as site on hillside; 24 hr security barriers; gd walking; mkt Tues." 12 Apr-27 Sep. € 38.40   2014*

GOUAREC

GOUAREC 2E3 (1km SW Rural) 48.22555, -3.18307
Camping Tost Aven, Au Bout du Pont, 22570 Gouarec [02 96 24 87 86; bertrand.cocherel@ orange.fr; www.brittanycamping.com]
Sp fr town cent bet rv & canal. Med, pt shd, wc; chem disp; shwrs inc; EHU (10A) €2.40; lndry; shop nr; rest nr; bar nr; bbq; playgrnd; sw nr; entmnt; dogs; bus 200m; Eng spkn; adv bkg acc; quiet; bike hire; canoe hire. "Clean, relaxed, tidy site bet Nantes-Brest canal & rv on edge of vill; gas adj; towpath for cycling; great!"
♦ 1 May-15 Sep. € 12.00   2018*

> **"There aren't many sites open at this time of year"**
>
> If you're travelling outside peak season remember to call ahead to check site opening dates – even if the entry says 'open all year'.

GOUDARGUES 10E2 (1km NE Rural) 44.22056, 4.47884 **Camping Les Amarines, La Vérune Cornillon, 30630 Goudargues** [04 66 82 24 92; les.amarines@ wanadoo.fr; www.campinglesamarines.com]
Fr D980 foll sp onto D23 & site bet Cornillon & Goudargues. Med, hdg, mkd, shd, wc (htd); fam bthrm; shwrs inc; EHU (6A) €3.50; lndry; snacks; bar; playgrnd; pool (htd); entmnt; dogs €3; adv bkg acc; quiet; rv fishing. "Lge pitches; site liable to flood after heavy rain; excel." ♦ 1 Apr-6 Oct. € 26.00   2014*

GOURDON 7D3 (2km SW Rural) 44.72214, 1.37381
Aire Naturelle Le Paradis (Jardin), La Peyrugue, 46300 Gourdon [05 65 41 65 01 or 06 72 76 32 60 (mob); contact@campingleparadis.com; www. campingleparadis.com] S on D673 Gourdon/Fumel rd, after Intermarché supmkt on L, turn L onto track sp site. If full, overflow area avail – 2 hookups. Sm, pt shd, pt sl, terr, wc; shwrs inc; EHU (6A) €2; lndry; shop nr; rest; 10% statics; dogs €2; adv bkg acc; quiet. "Gd welcome; facs poss stretched if full; farm produce; delightful site; no entmnt; excel san facs."
1 May-31 Aug. € 14.00   2014*

GOURDON 7D3 (10km W Rural) 44.75491, 1.23999
Camping Le Convivial, La Gréze, 24250 St Martial de Nabirat [05 53 28 43 15; contact@campingleconvivial. com; www.campingleconvivial.com] SW fr Gourdon, take D673 twd Salviac. Bef Pont Carral turn R onto D6 which becomes D46. Site 1.5km N St Martial on L. Sm, hdg, pt shd, pt sl, wc (htd); chem disp; fam bthrm; shwrs; EHU (8A); lndry; shop nr; rest; snacks; bar; bbq; playgrnd; pool; twin axles; wifi; 25% statics; dogs €1.60; Eng spkn; quiet; ccard acc; games area; fishing 1km; CCI. "Beautiful, spacious site off tourist track; friendly & welcoming owners; cycle trail in pretty valley of Céon nrby; vg." ♦ 1 Apr-31 Oct.
€ 19.70   2014*

GOURDON 7D3 (2km NW Rural) 44.74637, 1.37700
Camping Domaine La Quercy, Ecoute S'il Pleut, 46300 Gourdon [05 65 41 06 19; fax 05 65 41 31 62; domainequercy@orange.fr; www.domainequercy. com] Fr N site on R of D704 1.5km bef Gourdon. Sp fr Gourdon. Med, mkd, hdstg, pt shd, pt sl, terr, wc; chem disp; mv service pnt; fam bthrm; shwrs inc; EHU (6A) €3.50; lndry; shop; rest; snacks; bar; bbq; cooking facs; playgrnd; pool; paddling pool; entmnt; wifi; TV; 30% statics; dogs €2.50; phone; Eng spkn; adv bkg rec; quiet; ccard acc; waterslide; games area; watersports 200m; tennis; games rm; fishing; sailing 200m. "Gd leisure facs - gd for families; badminton, bowling; volleyball; football; lake adj; ACSI; gd san facs; Gourdon attractive town; vg." ♦ 17 Apr-25 Sep.
€ 24.40   2013*

GOUZON 7A4 (1km S Urban) 46.18785, 2.23913
Camp Municipal de la Voueize, 1 Ave de la Marche, 23230 Gouzon [05 55 81 73 22; camping-gouzon@ orange.fr; www.camping-lavoueize.fr] On E62/N145 Guéret/Montluçon exit at sp for Gouzon. In cent of vill bear R past church & site is sp on edge of Rv Voueize. Sm, pt shd, wc; chem disp; shwrs inc; EHU (10A) inc (poss rev pol); lndry; shop nr; rest nr; bar nr; playgrnd; dogs €0.50; adv bkg acc; quiet; golf 2km; bike hire; fishing. "Lovely aspect; friendly recep; clean site; facs poss tired high ssn; gd walking & cycling rtes; gd NH; birdwatching on lake 8km; snacks/bar Jul & Aug only; gas adj; big trees; adj rv; san facs tired." 1 May-16 Oct.
€ 15.50   2015*

⊞ **GRAMAT** 7D4 (7km SE Rural) 44.74767, 1.79954
Camping Le Teulière, L'Hôpital Beaulieu, 46500 Issendolus [05 65 40 86 71; fax 05 65 33 40 89; laparro.mcv@free.fr; http://laparro.mcv.free.fr]
Site on R on D840 at L'Hôpital, clearly sp. Access fr ent narr & tight corners, not for underpowered. Sm, pt shd, pt sl, wc; shwrs inc; EHU (20A) €2.65 (poss rev pol); lndry; shop; rest; snacks; bar; bbq; playgrnd; pool; TV; 10% statics; adv bkg acc; quiet; tennis; fishing. "Conv Rocamadour; basic san facs; ltd facs LS; site rds unmade, steep & narr - gd traction req; pitches muddy when wet." € 9.35   2016*

GRANDCAMP MAISY 1C4 (1km W Coastal) 49.38814, -1.05204 **Camping Le Joncal, Le Petit Nice, 14450 Grandcamp-Maisy** [02 31 22 61 44; fax 02 31 22 73 99; campingdujoncal@hotmail.fr; www. campingdujoncal.com] Ent on Grandcamp port dock area; visible fr vill. Fr N13 take D199 sp Grandcamp-Maisy & foll Le Port & Camping sps. Lge, hdg, mkd, pt shd, wc; mv service pnt; EHU (6-10A) €5.40-7.50; gas; lndry; shop nr; rest nr; bbq; beach sand adj; 80% statics; dogs €1.10; bus; quiet. "Conv for D Day beaches; some pitches at water's edge; excel morning fish mkt close by; gd NH." ♦ 1 Apr-30 Sep.
€ 23.50   2014*

GRANDE MOTTE, LA 10F1 (2km NW Coastal) 43.56440, 4.07528 **FFCC Camping La Petite Motte à La Grande-Motte, 195 Allée des Peupliers, 34280 La Grande-Motte [04 67 56 54 75; fax 04 67 29 92 58; camping.lagrandemotte@ffcc.fr; www.camping-lapetitemotte.com]** Exit A9 for Lunel or Montpellier Est to La Grande Motte, site sp on D59 & D62 coast rd. Lge, shd, wc; mv service pnt; shwrs; EHU (6A) €4.30; lndry; shop; rest; snacks; bar; playgrnd; beach sand 700m; red long stay; twin axles; entmnt; wifi; 10% statics; dogs €4; adv bkg acc; horseriding nr; watersports nr; games area; tennis nr; golf nr; CKE/CCI. "Walk to beach thro ave of trees & footbdge over rds; helpful staff; clean modern san facs; cycle rtes nrby; m'van o'night area; vg; 2nd san fac modernised (2015)." 29 Mar-30 Sep. € 20.50   2015*

"That's changed – Should I let the Club know?"

If you find something on site that's different from the site entry, fill in a report and let us know. See camc.com/europereport.

GRANVILLE 1D4 (6km NE Coastal) 48.86976, -1.56380 **Kawan Village La Route Blanche, 6 La Route Blanche, 50290 Bréville-sur-Mer [02 33 50 23 31; fax 02 33 50 26 47; larouteblanche@camping-breville.com; www.campinglarouteblanche.com]** Exit A84 junc 37 onto D924 dir Granville. Bef Granville turn L onto D971, then L onto D114 which joins D971e. Site on R bef golf club. Nr Bréville sm airfield. Lge, hdstg, mkd, hdg, pt shd, serviced pitches; wc (htd); chem disp; mv service pnt; fam bthrm; shwrs inc; EHU (6-10A) €4-5; gas; lndry; shop; snacks; bar; bbq; playgrnd; pool (htd); paddling pool; beach sand 500m; red long stay; entmnt; wifi; TV; 40% statics; dogs €3; phone; Eng spkn; adv bkg acc; quiet; ccard acc; tennis nr; waterslide; sailing school; golf nr; games area; CKE/CCI. "Pleasant, busy site with vg clean facs; staff friendly & helpful; disabled seatlift in pool; gd walking, cycling & beach; pleasant old walled town & harbour; vg." ♦ 6 Apr-23 Sep. € 39.50   2018*

GRANVILLE 1D4 (8km SE Rural) 48.79790, -1.5244 **Camping Le Château de Lez-Eaux, 50380 St Pair-sur-Mer [02 33 51 66 09; fax 02 33 51 92 02; bonjour@lez-eaux.com; www.lez-eaux.com or www.les-castels.com]** App site on D973 Granville to Avranches rd (not via St Pair). Cont strt thro 1st rndabt at Geant and next rndabt for 2km, site sp on R. Lge, mkd, pt shd, pt sl, serviced pitches; wc (htd); chem disp; mv service pnt; fam bthrm; shwrs inc; EHU (10-16A) inc; lndry; shop; snacks; bar; bbq; playgrnd; pool (covrd, htd); paddling pool; beach sand 4km; twin axles; wifi; TV; 80% statics; dogs free; quiet; ccard acc; games rm; lake fishing; bike hire; tennis; horseriding 4km; waterslide; games area; CKE/CCI. "Superb, beautiful site in grnds of chateau; children's indoor aqua park; easy access; spacious pitches, various prices; helpful & friendly staff; clean, modern san facs; excel pool complex; gd for children; boat hire 7km; great for dogs; gd cycling & gd cycle rte to beach; gd touring base; conv Mont St Michel, Dol & landing beaches; mkt Thu St Pair; highly rec." ♦ 1 Apr-11 Sep. € 43.80   2016*

See advertisement

GRASSE 10E4 (8km NE Rural) 43.70230, 6.99515 **FFCC Camping des Gorges du Loup, Chemin des Vergers, 06620 Le Bar-sur-Loup [04 93 42 45 06; info@lesgorgesduloup.com; www.lesgorgesduloup.com]** E fr Gasse on D2085 sp Chateauneuf-Grasse; in 4km turn L onto D2210 to Le Bar-sur-Loup. Site well sp. Med, mkd, hdstg, pt shd, terr, wc; chem disp; shwrs inc; EHU (6-10A) €3.50-5.50 (poss rev pol); gas; lndry; shop; playgrnd; pool; beach shgl; TV; 20% statics; dogs €3; phone; bus 1km; Eng spkn; adv bkg acc; quiet; ice; CKE/CCI. "Peaceful, well-kept site with superb views; table tennis; basketball; helpful, pleasant owners; bowls; clean san facs; steep access rds; owner will site c'van; gd hilly cycling; highly rec." 6 Apr-21 Sep. € 27.00   2013*

GRASSE

GRASSE *10E4* (6km SE Urban) *43.63507, 6.94859*
Camping Caravaning La Paoute, 160 Route de Cannes, 06130 Grasse [04 93 09 11 42; fax 04 93 40 06 40; camppaoute@hotmail.com; www.campinglapaoute.com] Sp fr Grasse town cent on Route de Cannes (secondary rd to Cannes, NOT D6185), a 10 min drive. Med, hdg, mkd, pt shd, sl, terr, wc; chem disp; mv service pnt; shwrs inc; EHU (10A) €4; lndry; shop nr; snacks; bar; playgrnd; pool (htd); wifi; 15% statics; dogs; bus 500m; games rm; CKE/CCI. "Gd, quiet site; m'vans acc out of ssn but adv bkg req." 1 Apr-30 Sep. € 23.00 2014*

> ### "I like to fill in the reports as I travel from site to site"
> You'll find report forms at the back of this guide, or you can fill them in online at camc.com/europereport.

GRASSE *10E4* (8km S Rural) *43.60650, 6.90216*
Camping Le Parc des Monges, 635 Chemin du Gabre, 06810 Auribeau-sur-Siagne [04 93 60 91 71; contact@parcdesmonges.fr; www.parcdesmonges.com] Exit A8 junc 40 or 41 onto D6007 dir Grasse; then onto D109 becoming D9; foll sp to Auribeau-sur-Siagne; site on rd to Le Gabre. Med, hdg, shd, wc (htd); chem disp; mv service pnt; fam bthrm; shwrs inc; EHU (4-10A) €3.50-5.50; lndry; shop nr; rest nr; bar nr; playgrnd; pool (htd); sw nr; entmnt; 7% statics; dogs €2.50; phone; bus adj; Eng spkn; adv bkg acc; quiet; ccard acc; ice; fishing nr; CKE/CCI. "Vg site by Rv Siagne; rv not accessible fr site; activities; watch out for branches when manoeurvering." ♦ 4 Apr-26 Sep. € 23.00 2012*

GRAVELINES *3A3* (3km N Coastal) *51.00777, 2.11777*
Camping des Dunes, Rue Victor-Hugo, Plage de Petit-Fort-Philippe, 59820 Gravelines [03 28 23 09 80; fax 03 28 65 35 99; campingdesdunes@campingvpa.fr; www.camping-des-dunes.com] E fr Calais on D940 foll sp to Gravelines. Heading W fr Dunkerque exit D601 E of Gravelines; turn R into Blvd de L'Europe & foll sp for Petit-Fort-Philippe & site. Site on both sides of rd. Lge, hdstg, hdg, mkd, pt shd, wc (htd); chem disp; shwrs inc; EHU (10A) €4.05; lndry; shop; rest nr; bar nr; playgrnd; beach sand adj; entmnt; wifi; TV; 10% statics; dogs €2.10; phone; bus; Eng spkn; adv bkg req; ccard acc; games rm; CKE/CCI. "Site in 2 parts, various prices; gd site rds; helpful, friendly staff; poss uneven pitches & raised manhole covers; conv Dunkerque ferries (15km); vg; excel NH or sh stay; v clean & welcoming." ♦ 1 Apr-31 Oct. € 20.00 2014*

GRAVELINES *3A3* (4km NW Coastal) *51.00250, 2.09694*
Camping de la Plage, 115 Rue du Maréchal-Foch, 59153 Grand-Fort-Philippe [03 28 65 31 95; fax 03 28 65 35 99; campingdelaplage@campingvpa.fr; www.camping-de-la-plage.info] Exit A16 junc 51 dir Grand-Fort-Philippe; at o'skts of town turn R sp Camping ***; cont into town cent; foll rd along quayside; foll rd to L past lge crucifix; turn R at next x-rds; site on R. Med, hdg, hdstg, pt shd, terr, wc (htd); chem disp; mv service pnt; shwrs inc; EHU (10A) €3.70 (poss long lead req); lndry; shop nr; playgrnd; beach sand 500m; entmnt; wifi; 20% statics; dogs €2; adv bkg acc; quiet; ccard acc; CKE/CCI. "Various pitch sizes; ltd EHU; pleasant walk to sea front; night security guard; conv ferries; rec adv bkg; san facs excel; pool 3km; friendly, attractive site." ♦ 1 Apr-31 Oct. € 15.00 2016*

GRAVESON *10E2* (2km SE Rural) *43.84408, 4.78080*
Camping Les Micocouliers, 445 Route de Cassoulen, 13690 Graveson [04 90 95 81 49; micocou@free.fr; www.camping-les-micocouliers-provence.fr] Leave A7 junc 25 onto D99 St Rémy-de-Provence then D5 N past Maillane, site on R. Med, hdg, mkd, unshd, wc; chem disp; mv service pnt; shwrs inc; EHU (4-13A) €4.40-7; lndry; shop nr; rest nr; bar nr; bbq; pool; wifi; 8% statics; dogs €2; phone; Eng spkn; adv bkg rec; bike hire; games area; tennis 1km; CKE/CCI. "Peaceful but busy site; pretty & well-kept; friendly, helpful, welcoming owners; excel, immac san facs; lovely sm pool; vg cycling; attractive, interesting area; excel; additional san facs built (2014)." ♦ 15 Mar-15 Oct. € 31.00 2016*

> ### "We must tell the Club about that great site we found"
> Get your site reports in by mid-August and we'll do our best to get your updates into the next edition.

GRAY *6G2* (1km E Rural) *47.45207, 5.59999*
Camp Municipal Longue Rive, Rue de la Plage, 70100 Gray [03 84 64 90 44; fax 03 84 65 46 26; tourisme-gray@wanadoo.fr; www.ville-gray.fr] S on D67 to Gray. cross rv bdge, L at rndabt, after 300m sp La Plage. Well sp fr all rtes. Med, mkd, hdg, pt shd, wc; mv service pnt; shwrs inc; EHU (10A) €2.45; gas; lndry; shop nr; rest nr; bar nr; playgrnd; dogs €0.85; Eng spkn; tennis; boating; fishing; CKE/CCI. "Lovely setting on Rv Saône; friendly recep; new high quality facs, poss stretched high ssn; twin axles; pool opp; many pitches waterlogged early ssn; several Bastide vills within cycling dist; NH only." 15 Apr-30 Sep. € 14.50 2015*

GRENOBLE *9C3* (19km S Rural) *45.08553, 5.69872* Camping à la Ferme Le Moulin de Tulette (Gaudin), Route du Moulin de Tulette, 38760 Varces-Allières-et-Risset [06 37 74 61 70; campingdetulette@gmail.com; www.camping-moulindetulette.fr] Fr A51, exit junc 12 to join D1075 N, Varces in approx 2km. Turn R at traff lts & foll sp to site, (approx 2km fr D1075). If driving thro Grenoble look for sp Gap - D1075 diff to find; on ent Varce foll site sp. Sm, mkd, pt shd, pt sl, wc; chem disp; fam bthrm; shwrs inc; EHU (5-10A) inc; shop nr; pool; wifi; dogs €1; Eng spkn; adv bkg acc; quiet; CKE/CCI. "Peaceful, picturesque, well-kept site with views; friendly, helpful owners; facs ltd but clean - stretched high ssn; gd base for touring/x-ing Alps; new lge pool." ♦ 1 May-30 Sep. € 19.00   2015*

⊞ **GRENOBLE** *9C3* (5km SW Urban) *45.16687, 5.69897* **Camping Caravaning Les 3 Pucelles, 58 Rue des Allobroges, 38180 Seyssins [04 76 96 45 73; fax 04 38 12 87 51; amico.francoise@gmail.com; www.camping-trois-pucelles.com]** On A480 in dir of rocade (by-pass) S exit 5B, on R after supmkt then foll sp to R then L. Clearly sp. Well sp fr m'way. Sm, hdstg, hdg, pt shd, wc (htd); chem disp; shwrs inc; EHU (16A) meter; lndry; shop; rest; snacks; bar; playgrnd; pool; 70% statics; phone; bus nr; CKE/CCI. "Site pt of hotel campus run by friendly family; sm pitches; san facs need refurb; conv Grenoble by bus/tram; NH only; poorly maintained; tram to city 300m fr site." € 21.00   2015*

GREOUX LES BAINS *10E3* (1km S Rural) *43.75158, 5.88185* **Camping Le Verseau, Route de St Pierre, 04800 Gréoux-les-Bains [04 92 77 67 10 or 06 22 72 93 25 (mob); info@camping-le-verseau.com; www.camping-le-verseau.com]** Fr W on D952 to Gréoux. Go under bdge then bear L just bef petrol stn. Cross rv (narr bdge), site on R in 500m. Med, hdg, pt shd, pt sl, wc; chem disp; mv service pnt; fam bthrm; shwrs inc; EHU (10A) €3.90; lndry; shop nr; rest; snacks; bar; bbq (elec, gas); playgrnd; pool; entmnt; wifi; dogs €2.50; phone; adv bkg acc; quiet; tennis 1km; CKE/CCI. "Friendly owners; interesting spa town; great views." 1 Mar-31 Oct. € 23.00   2016*

⊞ **GREZILLE** *4G1* (1km E Rural) *47.32751, -0.33512* **Ferme du Bois Madame, Frédéric Gauthier, 49320 Grézillé [02 41 54 20 97 or 06 87 23 32 55 (mob); fax 02 41 45 30 37; ferme.boismadame@wanadoo.fr; www.fermeduboismadame.com]** Turn L off D761 (Angers-Poitiers) in Les Alleuds sp Grézillé (D90); in 3.5km turn R sp Grézillé (D276); after 1.4km in Grézillé turn L and immed R sp Gennes (D176). Site on R in 1km. Sm, hdg, pt shd, wc; chem disp; mv service pnt; shwrs; EHU (10-12A); lndry; dogs €0.50; adv bkg acc; bike hire. "Friendly welcome; CL feel to site but lge & more facs; working farm & stables; horse-drawn carrige trip avail in ssn; gd." € 13.00   2015*

GRIGNAN *9D2* (1km S Urban) *44.41731, 4.90950* **Camping de Grignan, 2 Avenue de Grillon, 26230 Grignan [04 75 01 92 23; contact@campingdegrignan.fr; www.campingdegrignan.fr]** N7 S fr Montelimar on N7 N fr Orange, then D133 onto D541, dir Nyons for 17km. Grignan sp Camping Municipal in vill. Sm, lge, mkd, hdg, pt shd, wc; chem disp; shwrs; EHU (6A); lndry; snacks; bar; bbq (htd); paddling pool; twin axles; wifi; dogs; bus; Eng spkn; adv bkg rec; quiet; CKE/CCI. "10 min walk to town & Château and Saint Sauveur Church; excel." ♦ 20 Apr-17 Sep. € 16.00   2017*

GRILLON *9D2* (2km S Rural) *44.38307, 4.93046* **Camping Le Garrigon, Chemin de Visan, 84600 Grillon [04 90 28 72 94; contact@camping-garrigon.com; www.camping-garrigon.com]** A7, exit Montelmar-Sud, twds Gap. Take D541 then Grillon cent & foll sp to site. Med, mkd, pt shd, wc; chem disp; fam bthrm; shwrs; EHU (10A); lndry; shop nr; rest; snacks; bar; bbq (elec, gas); playgrnd; pool (htd); wifi; 10% statics; dogs; Eng spkn; adv bkg acc; ccard acc; games rm; CKE/CCI. "Pleasant site in attractive area; nice pool; updated san facs (2015); level but some rough or uneven grnd; vg." 14 Mar-13 Nov. € 28.50   2016*

> **"I need an on-site restaurant"**
>
> We do our best to make sure site information is correct, but it is always best to check any must-have facilities are still available or will be open during your visit.

GRIMAUD *10F4* (4km E Coastal) *43.28083, 6.58250* **Camping Les Prairies de la Mer, St Pons-les-Mûres, 83360 Grimaud [04 94 79 09 09; fax 04 94 79 09 10; prairies@riviera-villages.com; www.riviera-villages.com]** Leave A8/E80 at Ste Maxime/Draguignan exit. Take DD125/D25 twd Ste Maxime. Site on L of D559 heading SW, 400m bef St Pons-les-Mûres with rndabt at ent. Site opp Marina Village. V lge, hdstg, mkd, pt shd, wc; chem disp; mv service pnt; shwrs inc; EHU (6-10A) inc; gas; lndry; shop; rest; snacks; bar; playgrnd; beach sand adj; entmnt; 85% statics; dogs; phone; bus; adv bkg req; ccard acc; watersports; fishing; CKE/CCI. "Popular, well-run beach site; gd recep; pitches tight for med to lge o'fits & poss dusty high ssn; gd san facs; Port Grimaud sh walk; gd entmnt; gd." ♦ 23 Mar-13 Oct. € 55.00   2013*

GRIMAUD

GRIMAUD *10F4 (5km E Urban) 43.27512, 6.56032*
Camping La Pinède, 1968 route de Ste Maxime, 83310 Grimaud [04 94 56 04 36; fax 04 94 56 04 86; info@lapinede-camping.com; www.lapinede-camping.com] Fr Ste Maxine to St Tropez turn R at St Pons-Les-Mûres on D14 twd Grimaud. Site in 1.6km on L. Lge, hdg, mkd, pt shd, pt sl, wc; chem disp; mv service pnt; shwrs inc; EHU (2A); gas; lndry; shop; rest; snacks; bar; playgrnd; pool; beach sand 2.5km; dogs; quiet. "Vg; excel beaches in easy driving dist; open location with plenty of rm for o'fit." Easter-1 Nov. € 32.50   2013*

GRIMAUD *10F4 (7km E Coastal) 43.28205, 6.58614*
Camping de la Plage, 98 Route National, St Pons-les-Mûres, 83310 Grimaud [04 94 56 31 15; fax 04 94 56 49 61; campingplagegrimaud@wanadoo.fr; www.camping-de-la-plage.fr] Fr St Maxime turn onto D559 sp to St Tropez; site 3km on L on both sides of rd (subway links both parts). Lge, pt shd, wc; chem disp; mv service pnt; shwrs inc; EHU (4-16A) €4.70-14; gas; lndry; shop; rest; snacks; bar; playgrnd; beach sand; entmnt; wifi; dogs €2.50; adv bkg req; ccard acc; tennis; CKE/CCI. "Pitches adj beach or in shd woodland - some sm; site tired but lovely situation & views compensate; clean facs, refurb 2015; cycle tracks; site poss flooded after heavy rain; used every yr for 44 yrs by one CC member (2011); conv for ferry to St Tropez, rec as beautiful, helpful friendly efficient staff." ♦ 11 Apr-13 Oct. € 37.00   2016*

GRUISSAN *10F1 (5km NE Coastal) 43.1358, 3.1424*
Camping Les Ayguades, Ave de la Jonque, 11430 Gruissan [04 68 49 81 59; fax 04 68 49 05 64; loisirs-vacances-languedoc@wanadoo.fr; www.camping-soleil-mer.com] Exit A9 junc 37 onto D168/D32 sp Gruissan. In 10km turn L at island sp Les Ayguades, foll site sp. Lge, hdg, mkd, unshd, wc (htd); chem disp; mv service pnt; fam bthrm; shwrs inc; EHU (6A) inc; lndry; shop; rest; bar; playgrnd; beach sand adj; entmnt; TV; 75% statics; dogs €2.50; Eng spkn; adv bkg acc; quiet; ccard acc; CKE/CCI. "Pleasant site; extensive cycle network, 6 night min stay high ssn." ♦ 1 Apr-4 Nov. € 31.00   2012*

GUDAS 8G3 (2km S Rural) 42.99269, 1.67830
Camping Mille Fleurs (Naturist), Le Tuillier, 09120 Gudas [05 61 60 77 56; info@camping-millefleurs.com; www.camping-millefleurs.com] Do not use SatNav thro Dalou. App Foix on the N20 fr Toulouse foll sp Foix-Tarbes. Pass Camping du lac on R, cont approx 2.2km, at traff lghts turn L sp D1 Laroque d'Olmes, Lieurac, l'Herm). Foll D1 for 6.5km until junc D13 (Care req, sharp bend). Turn L sp Col de Py, Mirepoix, cont past quarry, L fork (sp Gudas, Varhilles). After 2km sp Millefleurs, le Tuilier, turn L over bdge. Site in approx 2km bef Gudas. Sm, hdg, mkd, pt shd, pt sl, terr, wc; chem disp; fam bthrm; shwrs inc; EHU (6-10A) €3.75; lndry; rest; bar; bbq; pool; twin axles; wifi; dogs €2.25; phone; Eng spkn; adv bkg rec; quiet; sauna; INF card req. "Excel, scenic, beautiful, peaceful site; lovely owners; gd pitches; 2 c'vans for hire; clean facs; gd base Andorra, Toulouse & Carcassonne; great touring base." ♦ 1 Apr-1 Nov. € 29.00 2017*

GUEMENE PENFAO 2G4 (1km SE Rural) 47.62575, -1.81857 **Flower Camping L'Hermitage, 46 Ave du Paradis, 44290 Guémené-Penfao [02 40 79 23 48; fax 02 40 51 11 87; camping.hermitage@wanadoo.fr; www.campinglhermitage.com]** On D775 fr cent of Guémené-Penfao, dir Châteaubriant for 500m, turn R, site sp. Med, hdstg, mkd, pt shd, wc; chem disp; mv service pnt; fam bthrm; shwrs inc; EHU (6A) €3.50; gas; lndry; shop nr; rest; snacks; bar; bbq; playgrnd; paddling pool; sw nr; entmnt; TV; 20% statics; dogs €2; phone; Eng spkn; adv bkg acc; quiet; jacuzzi; games rm; waterslide; bike hire; fishing 300m; tennis; canoeing; games area; CKE/CCI. "Gd walking in area; htd covrd pool adj; site not ready early ssn." ♦ 1 Apr-15 Oct. € 22.50 2017*

> **"There aren't many sites open at this time of year"**
>
> If you're travelling outside peak season remember to call ahead to check site opening dates – even if the entry says 'open all year'.

GUERANDE 2G3 (3km N Rural) 47.34954, -2.43170 **Camping La Fontaine, Kersavary, Route de St-Molf, 44350 Guérande [02 40 24 96 19 or 06 08 12 80 96 (mob); lafontaine.guerande@orange.fr; www.camping-lafontaine.com]** Fr Guérande take N774 N sp La Roche-Bernard; in 1 km, opp windmill, fork L onto D233 sp St-Molf; site on L in 500m. Med, hdg, hdstg, mkd, pt shd, wc; chem disp; fam bthrm; shwrs inc; EHU (6A) €4; lndry; shop nr; rest nr; snacks; bbq; playgrnd; pool (htd); paddling pool; twin axles; wifi; 10% statics; dogs €2; Eng spkn; adv bkg rec; quiet; games area; CKE/CCI. "Pleasant, peaceful site; lge pitches; helpful staff; san facs clean & new (2015); gd." ♦ 3 Apr-18 Oct. € 24.00 2016*

GUERANDE 2G3 (2km NE Rural) 47.34340, -2.41935 **Domaine de Bréhadour, Route de Bréhadour, 44350 Guérande [02 43 53 04 33; www.domainedebrehadour.com]** Exit N165 onto D774 to Guérande. After 20km at rndabt take 3rd exit onto D99E. Turn L twd Route de Bréhadour, take first R and site is on L. Lge, hdg, pt shd, wc; mv service pnt; shwrs inc; EHU (4A) €3-4.70; gas; lndry; shop; rest; snacks; bar; bbq; playgrnd; pool (htd); entmnt; 40% statics; dogs €3.70; Eng spkn; adv bkg acc; quiet; ccard acc; golf; tennis; CKE/CCI. "Beautiful, quiet site; redeveloped for 2014." 28 May-18 Sep. € 41.00 2013*

See advertisement opposite

GUERANDE 2G3 (3km S Urban) 47.29797, -2.39988 **Camping Trémondec, 48 Rue du Château Careil, 44350 Guérande [02 40 60 00 07; fax 02 40 60 91 10; camping.tremondec@wanadoo.fr; www.camping-tremondec.com]** Fr Nantes on N165/N171/D213 dir La Baule. Take D192 dir La Baule cent, turn W in 800m dir Brenave, Careil. Site sp. Med, mkd, hdstg, hdg, pt shd, pt sl, wc; chem disp; mv service pnt; fam bthrm; shwrs inc; EHU (16A) inc; lndry; shop; rest; snacks; bar; bbq; playgrnd; pool (htd); beach sand 1.5km; red long stay; entmnt; wifi; TV; 50% statics; dogs €3; Eng spkn; adv bkg acc; quiet; ccard acc; games area; games rm; bike hire; CKE/CCI. "Lovely beaches & coast; interesting walks thro salt marshes; cycle rtes; site poorly maintained (2014); uneven grnd." ♦ 1 Apr-Nov. € 34.00 2014*

GUERANDE 2G3 (7km W Coastal) 47.32856, -2.49907 **Camping Les Chardons Bleus (formerly municipal), Blvd de la Grande Falaise, 44420 La Turballe [02 40 62 80 60; fax 02 40 62 85 40; campingleschardonsbleus@mairielaturballe.fr; www.camping-laturballe.fr]** Foll D99 to La Turballe. Site well sp fr town cent along D92. Lge, hdg, mkd, unshd, wc; chem disp; shwrs inc; EHU (10A) €4.80 (poss rev pol, long lead poss req); gas; lndry; shop; rest; snacks; bar; playgrnd; pool (htd); beach sand adj; entmnt; wifi; dogs €2.55; phone; Eng spkn; ccard acc; CKE/CCI. "Well-run, well-kept site in great location; mv service pnt adj; warm welcome; gd, clean san facs, poss stretched high ssn; ltd EHU when full; variable opening dates, phone ahead to check early ssn; nature reserve adj with bird life; superb beach adj, pt naturist; walk along beach to pretty fishing port of La Turballe with rests; vg modern facs & pool area; pinewoods; gd kids club for younger children; on cycle rte, excel." ♦ 1 Mar-29 Sep. € 22.00 2018*

GUERANDE

CAMPING PARC SAINTE BRIGITTE ★★★★
Deluxe Camping Site
Beside the fishing village of La Turballe and it's sandy beaches. 6 miles from the well-know resort of La Baule. The charm and beauty of a country domain with the fun and sun of the seaside. Four star sanitary facilities. Heated and retractable covered pool and children's one (approx. 2150sq. ft water and 2150sq.ft covered terrace around it).
Website : www.campingsaintebrigitte.com
Contact : saintebrigitte@wanadoo.fr

GUERANDE 2G3 (7km NW Rural) 47.34252, -2.47159 **Camping Le Parc Ste Brigitte, Manoir de Bréhet, 44420 La Turballe [02 40 24 88 91; fax 02 40 15 65 72; saintebrigette@wanadoo.fr; www.campingsaintebrigitte.com]** Take D99 NW fr Guérande twd La Turballe thro vill of Clis. Sp on R in 900m. Lge, mkd, shd, serviced pitches; wc; chem disp; mv service pnt; fam bthrm; shwrs inc; EHU (6-10A) inc; gas; lndry; shop; rest; snacks; bar; playgrnd; pool (covrd, htd); beach sand 2km; entmnt; TV; 10% statics; dogs €1.50; phone; adv bkg acc; ccard acc; fishing; bike hire; CKE/CCI. "V peaceful; excel rest & bar; some sm pitches; poss unkempt LS; gd." ♦ 1 Apr-1 Oct. € 32.00   2014*

See advertisement

GUERET 7A4 (10km S Rural) 46.10257, 1.83528 **Camp Municipal Le Gué Levard, 5 Rue Gué Levard, 23000 La Chapelle-Taillefert [05 55 51 09 20 or 05 55 52 36 17 (Mairie); www.ot-gueret.fr]** Take junc 48 fr N145 sp Tulle/Bourganeuf (D33 thro Guéret); S on D940 fr Guéret, turn off at site sp. Foll sp thro vill, well sp. Sm, hdstg, pt shd, sl, terr, wc; chem disp; mv service pnt; shwrs inc; EHU (16A) €2.50; lndry; bbq (sep area); playgrnd; 20% statics; dogs; adv bkg acc; quiet; fishing in Rv Gartempe; CKE/CCI. "Attractive, peaceful, well-kept site hidden away; vg san facs; site yourself, warden calls 1900; all pitches sl so m'van levelling diff; gd auberge in vill (clsd most of Jul & Aug); gd walking; sports facs nr; phone ahead to check open LS; excel little site." ♦ 1 Apr-1 Nov. € 11.00   2016*

GUERET 7A4 (1km W Rural) 46.16387, 1.85882 **Camp du Plan d'Eau de Courtille (formerly Municipal), Rue Georges Aullon, 23000 Guéret [05 55 81 92 24]** Fr W on N145 take D942 to town cent; then take D914 W; take L turn bef lake sp; site in 1.5km along lakeside rd with speed humps. Site sp. Med, hdg, mkd, pt shd, pt sl, wc; chem disp; mv service pnt; fam bthrm; shwrs inc; EHU (10A) inc; shop nr; rest nr; bar nr; bbq; playgrnd; sw; dogs; phone; quiet; watersports; CKE/CCI. "Pleasant scenery; well-managed site; beach sand; narr ent to pitches; mkd walks nrby; pool 1.5km; ramps needed for m'vans; bread delivered; busy NH." ♦ 1 Apr-30 Sep. € 20.00   2018*

GUIGNICOURT 3C4 (1km SE Urban) 49.43209, 3.97035 **Camping au Bord de l'Aisne (Formaly Municipal), 14b Rue des Godins, 02190 Guignicourt [03 23 79 74 58; campingguignicourt@orange.fr; www.camping-aisne-picardie.fr]** Exit A26 junc 14 onto D925 to Guignicourt; after passing under rlway bdge cont on D925 for 800m; then turn R at Peugeot g'ge down narr rd to site (12% descent at ent & ramp). Site sp in vill on rv bank. Med, mkd, hdg, pt shd, wc (htd); chem disp; mv service pnt; shwrs; EHU (6-10A) inc (poss rev pol, poss long cable req); shop nr; rest nr; snacks; bar; bbq; playgrnd; pool (covrd, htd); red long stay; wifi; 20% statics; dogs €1.70; phone; train 500m; Eng spkn; adv bkg acc; quiet; ccard acc; fishing; CKE/CCI. "Pretty, well-kept/run, excel site in beautiful setting on banks of rv; v pretty & quiet; popular gd NH, conv A26; well-guarded; friendly, v helpful staff; poss muddy when wet; pleasant town; excel touring base Reims, Epernay; easy access despite gradient; excel; v.clean, refurbished & modern facs; facs stretched in high ssn; fair." ♦ 1 Apr-31 Oct. € 31.00   2018*

> **"That's changed – Should I let the Club know?"**
>
> If you find something on site that's different from the site entry, fill in a report and let us know. See camc.com/europereport.

GUILLESTRE 9D4 (2km SW Rural) 44.65854, 6.63836 **Camping La Rochette (formerly Municipal), 05600 Guillestre [04 92 45 02 15 or 06 62 17 02 15 (mob); guillestre@aol.com; www.campingguillestre.com]** Exit N94 onto D902A to Guillestre. In 1km fork R on side rd at camp sps. Site on L in 1km. Lge, mkd, pt shd, wc; shwrs inc; EHU (6-10A) €2.80-3.70; gas; lndry; shop; snacks; bbq; playgrnd; entmnt; wifi; dogs free; phone; adv bkg acc; quiet; tennis adj; fishing; games area. "Spectacular views; lge pitches; Dutch-owned site; helpful staff; superb san facs; dir access to rv; public pool adj; conv Queyras National Park." ♦ 15 May-30 Sep. € 19.50   2015*

GUILVINEC *2F2* (3km W Coastal) *47.80388, -4.31222*
Yelloh! Village la Plage, Chemin des Allemands, Penmarc'h, 29760 Guilvinec [02 98 58 61 90; fax 02 98 58 89 06; info@yellohvillage-la-plage.com; www.villagelaplage.com] Fr Quimper, Pont l'Abbé on D785 SW to Plomeur; turn S onto D57 sp Guilvinec. Bear R on app to town & v soon after turn R sp Chapelle de Tremor. Foll site to site in 1.5km. Lge, pt shd, wc; chem disp; mv service pnt; fam bthrm; shwrs inc; EHU (5A) inc; gas; lndry; shop; rest; snacks; bar; bbq; playgrnd; pool (covrd, htd); paddling pool; beach sand adj; entmnt; wifi; 60% statics; dogs €5; adv bkg acc; quiet; ccard acc; sauna; fitness rm; archery; tennis; games rm; waterslide; bike hire. "Ideal for families; spacious pitches; no o'fits over 8m high ssn; site rds poss diff lge o'fits; excel touring base; mkt Tue & Sun." ♦ 12 Apr-14 Sep. € 51.00 2017*

> **"I like to fill in the reports as I travel from site to site"**
>
> You'll find report forms at the back of this guide, or you can fill them in online at camc.com/europereport.

GUILVINEC *2F2* (4km NW Coastal) *47.81819, -4.30942* **Camping Les Genêts, Rue Gouesnac'h Nevez, 29760 Penmarc'h [02 98 58 66 93 or 06 83 15 85 92 (mob); campinglesgenets29@orange.fr; www.camping-lesgenets.com]** S fr Pont-l'Abbé on D785 to Plomeur; cont on D785 for another 4km, then turn L onto D53 sp Guilvinec; in 300m turn L into Rue Gouesnac'h Nevez to site. Med, mkd, hdg, pt shd, wc (htd); chem disp; fam bthrm; shwrs inc; EHU (10A) €3.40; gas; lndry; rest; snacks; bar; bbq; playgrnd; pool (covrd, htd); beach sand 1.5km; red long stay; entmnt; wifi; TV; 25% statics; dogs €2; phone; bus; Eng spkn; adv bkg acc; games area; horseriding 800m; games rm; waterslide; ice; CKE/CCI. "Peaceful, well-kept site in beautiful, unspoilt area; family-run; friendly atmosphere; welcoming, helpful owners; easy access to spacious pitches; excel, clean, modern san facs; bike hire nrby; gd value; excel." ♦ 1 Apr-30 Sep. € 22.00 2013*

GUINES *3A3* (3km N Urban) *50.88562, 1.87080*
Camping La Belle Pêche, Route de Guînes, 62340 Hames-Boucres [03 21 35 21 07 or 06 18 53 02 69 (mob); fax 03 21 82 51 50; camping-belle-peche@wanadoo.fr] Fr Guînes foll sp Calais on D127; site on L in 1km. Med, hdstg, hdg, pt shd, wc; chem disp; shwrs; EHU (6A) €2.30; shop nr; playgrnd; entmnt; 80% statics; quiet; rv fishing; tennis. "Conv ferries; Eurotunnel 15 mins; some pitches flood in wet weather; NH only; rec use own san facs as poor; scruffy site." 1 May-30 Oct. € 21.00 2016*

GUINES *3A3* (1km SW Rural) *50.86611, 1.85694*
Camping De La Bien Assise, Route D231 62340 Guînes [03 21 35 20 77; fax 03 21 36 79 20; castels@bien-assise.com; www.camping-la-bien-assise.com] Fr Calais or Boulogne, leave A16 at junc 43; foll D305 then D127 to Guines; cont to junc with D231; turn R (across S of vill and cont to rndabt) site ent on L. Fr S (A26 or D943), take D231 to Guines. Lge, mkd, hdg, pt shd, pt sl, wc (htd); chem disp; mv service pnt; fam bthrm; shwrs inc; EHU (10A) inc (poss rev pol); gas; lndry; shop; rest; snacks; bar; bbq (charcoal, gas); playgrnd; pool (covrd, htd); paddling pool; red long stay; twin axles; entmnt; wifi; TV; 20% statics; dogs €3; Eng spkn; adv bkg req; ccard acc; bike hire; games rm; horseriding 3km; waterslide; golf nr; tennis; CKE/CCI. "Pleasant, busy, excel site in grnds of chateau; well-kept & well-run; gd sized pitches with easy access; conv ferries - late arr area; pleasant, cheerful, helpful staff; clean san facs, stretched when site full; excel rest, clsd in Jan; vg pool complex; grass pitches, some soft LS & boggy when wet; vet in Ardres (9km), site will book for you; even if notice says 'Complete' check for sh stay; mkt Fri; ACSI acc; v popular NH stop; one san fac block newly refurb (2016)." ♦ 31 Mar-29 Sep. € 36.20 2018*

GUISE *3C4* (1km SE Urban) *49.89488, 3.63372*
FFCC Camping de la Vallée de l'Oise, 33 Rue du Camping, 02120 Guise [03 23 61 14 86; fax 03 23 61 21 07] Foll Vervin sp in town & camp clearly sp fr all dirs in town. Lge, pt shd, wc; shwrs inc; EHU (6-10A) €5.50 (rev pol); lndry; shop nr; playgrnd; entmnt; TV; 50% statics; dogs; Eng spkn; adv bkg acc; quiet; rv fishing adj; bike hire; games rm; CKE/CCI. "Spacious, beautifully kept, friendly site; busy w/ends; gd san facs; barrier always open, warden not always on site; canoe hire adj; if arr late, pitch & pay next morning; interesting old town; gd value." 15 Apr-15 Oct. € 19.00 2018*

> **"We must tell the Club about that great site we found"**
>
> Get your site reports in by mid-August and we'll do our best to get your updates into the next edition.

GUISE *3C4* (6km NW Rural) *49.92709, 3.57768* **Camp Muncipal de Bovalon, 02120 Vadencourt [03 23 61 07 03 (Mairie); www.vadencourt.com]** Exit Guise NW on D960 dir Bohain-en-Vermandois; in 6km turn R onto D69; site on R in 1km just bef Vadencourt. Or exit D66 S at Vadencourt onto D69; site on L in 150m, just after rv bdg. Site sp in Vadencourt off D66. Sm, hdg, pt shd, wc; chem disp; shwrs inc; EHU (6A) €5; shop nr; bar nr; dogs €0.45; quiet; CKE/CCI. "Site by Rv Oise in pleasant area; height barrier, but call mob number on noticeboard or contact Café du Centre; gd; can't rec due to crowding by travellers (2012)." ♦ 1 May-30 Sep. € 9.50 2012*

HAGUENAU

HAGUENAU 5D3 (3km SW Urban) 48.80233, 7.76439
Camp Municipal Les Pins, 20 Rue de la Piscine, 67500 Haguenau [03 88 73 91 43 or 03 88 93 70 00; fax 03 88 93 69 89; tourisme@ville-haguenau.fr; www.ville-haguenau.fr] Fr S on D263, after passing Haguenau town sp turn L at 2nd set of traff lts (opp Peugeot g'ge). Site sp fr D263. Med, mkd, pt shd, terr, wc (htd); chem disp; shwrs inc; EHU (6A) inc; gas; lndry; shop nr; rest nr; bar nr; bbq; playgrnd; dogs €1; phone; bus 500m; Eng spkn; adv bkg acc; quiet; CKE/CCI. "Lge pitches; helpful staff; clean, modern san facs; meals avail fr warden; grnd firm even after heavy rain; excel; pleasant town." ♦ 1 May-30 Sep. € 13.00 2016*

HAMBYE 1D4 (2km N Rural) 48.9600, -1.2600
Camping aux Champs, 1 Rue de la Ripaudière, 50450 Hambye [02 33 90 06 98; michael.coles@wanadoo.fr; www.campingauxchamps.com] Exit A84 junc 38 onto D999 to Percy; then turn L at town cent rndabt onto D58 to Hambye; at mkt sq proceed to junc, strt sp Le Guislain, past Mairie; site on R in 1.5 km on D51. Sm, hdstg, unshd, wc (htd); chem disp; fam bthrm; shwrs inc; EHU (10A) €3; lndry; shop nr; rest nr; bar nr; red long stay; dogs 1 only; adv bkg req; quiet; CKE/CCI. "Peaceful, CL-type site; friendly, helpful British owners; adults only; excel, clean san facs; Hambye Abbey nrby; bell foundry at Villedieu-les-Poêls worth visit; conv ferry ports; a must if in Normandy." 1 Apr-30 Oct. € 12.00 2018*

HARDELOT PLAGE 3A2 (3km NE Urban) 50.64661, 1.62539 **Caravaning du Château d'Hardelot, 21 Rue Nouvelle, 62360 Condette [03 21 87 59 59; contact@camping-caravaning-du-chateau.com; www.camping-caravaning-du-chateau.com]** Take D901 S fr Boulogne, R turn onto D940 dir Le Touquet; then R at rndabt on D113 to Condette; take 2nd turning to Château Camping, R at next rndabt & site 400m on R. Fr S leave A16 at exit 27 to Neufchâtel-Hardelot, take D940 twd Condette & turn L at 1st rndabt onto D113, then as above. Not well sp last 3km. Tight turn into site ent. Med, hdg, mkd, pt shd, pt sl, wc; chem disp; mv service pnt; fam bthrm; shwrs inc; EHU (10A) €4.70 (poss rev pol); lndry; shop nr; playgrnd; beach sand 3km; entmnt; wifi; 30% statics; dogs free; Eng spkn; adv bkg rec; horseriding; games rm; tennis 500m; golf; CKE/CCI. "Lovely, well-run, wooded site; busy high ssn; vg LS; sm pitches; helpful, friendly owners; sm multi-gym; clean, modern san facs; tight access some pitches; conv Calais (site barrier opens 0800)." ♦ 1 Apr-31 Oct. € 28.60 2016*

HARDINGHEN 3A3 (1km SE Rural) 50.79462, 1.81369
Camping à la Ferme Les Piloteries, Rue de l'Eglise, 62132 Hardinghen [03 21 85 01 85; lespiloteries@free.fr; http://lespiloteries.free.fr] Fr N exit A16 junc 36 at Marquise onto D191 to Hardinghen; turn R onto D127 (where D191 turns sharp L); site in 1km (concealed ent). Sm, pt shd, pt sl, wc; chem disp; shwrs; EHU (6A) €2; bbq; playgrnd; quiet. "Vg CL-type site; friendly owner; lovely site; well looked after; rec; narr ent; gd NH." 16 Apr-2 Oct. € 11.00 2017*

HAUTEFORT 7C3 (3km NE Rural) 45.27248, 1.16861
Camping Belle Vue, La Contie 24390 Boisseuilh [05 53 51 62 71 or 0117 230 2320 (fr UK); cbv@dordogne-camping.org; www.dordogne-camping.org] Fr Limoges take D704 and cont until St Agnan. Take turning for Hautefort and pass supmkt on Land the Chateau on R. At next x-rds turn L onto D72 and cont over 3 bdges until La Contie. Site is last hse on R: Sm, shd, wc; chem disp; mv service pnt; fam bthrm; shwrs inc; EHU (6A); lndry; shop; rest; bar; bbq; pool; twin axles; wifi; 25% statics; dogs €2; Eng spkn; adv bkg acc; quiet; CKE/CCI. "Beautiful views of chateau Hautefort, illuminated at night; excel customer svrs; breakfast delivered to pitch each morning; excel." 1 May-30 Sep. € 23.00 2017*

HAUTEFORT 7C3 (4km NE Rural) 45.28081, 1.15917
Camping La Grenouille, Brégérac, 24390 Hautefort [05 53 50 11 71; info@lagrenouillevacances.com; www.lagrenouillevacances.com] Fr N on D704 at Cherveil-Cubas take D77 dir Boisseuilh/Teillots. In 4km turn R & in 800m turn L to site. Fr S on D704 at St Agnan take D62 sp Hautefort/Badefols d'Ans. Pass 'Vival' (sm shop on L) in Hautefort & turn L dir Boisseuilh. After 1st bdge turn L to La Besse & site in 2km. Sm, pt shd, pt sl, wc; chem disp; shwrs inc; EHU (8A) €3.50; lndry; shop; rest; bbq; playgrnd; pool; wifi; dogs free; Eng spkn; adv bkg acc; quiet; ice; CKE/CCI. "Tranquil, scenic, well-kept CL type site; friendly, helpful, Dutch owners; vg san facs; meals avail; goats, guinea pigs, chickens in pens on site; gd walking; highly rec." 22 Apr-15 Oct. € 21.50 2016*

HAUTEFORT 7C3 (8km W Rural) 45.28032, 1.04845
Camping Les Tourterelles, 24390 Tourtoirac [05 53 51 11 17; les-tourterelles@orange.fr; www.les-tourterelles.com] Fr N or S on D704 turn W at Hautefort on D62/D5 to Tourtoirac. In Tourtoirac turn R over rv then L. Site in 1km. Med, hdg, mkd, pt shd, terr, wc; chem disp; mv service pnt; fam bthrm; shwrs; EHU (6A) €4.50; gas; lndry; shop nr; rest; snacks; bar; playgrnd; pool; TV; 20% statics; dogs €5; phone; bus 1km; Eng spkn; adv bkg acc; quiet; ccard acc; horseriding; tennis; CKE/CCI. "Beautiful Auvézère valley; rallies welcome; owners helpful; equestrian cent; gd walks." ♦ 25 Apr-27 Sep. € 29.00 2014*

HAYE DU PUITS, LA 1D4 (6km N Urban) 49.38725, -1.52755 **FFCC Camp Municipal du Vieux Château, Ave de la Division-Leclerc, 50390 St Sauveur-le-Vicomte [02 33 41 79 06; fax 02 33 95 88 85; basedeloisirs@sslv.fr; www.ville-saint-sauveur-le-vicomte.fr]** Fr Cherbourg on N13/D2 site on R after x-ing bdge at St Sauveur-le-Vicomte, sp. Med, mkd, pt shd, pt sl, wc; shwrs inc; EHU (10A) €2.40 (poss rev pol); lndry; shop nr; rest nr; bbq; playgrnd; TV; dogs €1.50; phone; adv bkg acc; quiet; ccard acc; games area; games rm; tennis 1km; CKE/CCI. "Excel site in chateau grnds; friendly warden; gd clean facs; ideal 1st stop fr Cherbourg; office open until 2200 for late arr; barrier clsd 2200-0800; vg auberge opp; helpful warden; Eng not spkn; sh walk to friendly, nice town." ♦ 15 May-17 Sep. € 14.00 2017*

HAYE DU PUITS, LA *1D4* (3km SW Rural) *49.27292, -1.55896* **Camping La Bucaille, 50250 Montgardon [02 33 07 46 38; fax 09 62 15 99 39; info@labucaille. com; www.labucaille.com]** Fr Cherbourg S on N13 & D2 twd St Sauveur-le-Vicomte, then D900 to La Haye-du-Puits. Fr cent of La Haye turn onto D136 Rte de Bretteville-sur-Ay for approx 2km, site sp at L turn, site on L. Sm, pt shd, pt sl, wc; chem disp; shwrs inc; EHU (10A) €5; shop nr; rest nr; bar nr; bbq; beach sand 4km; wifi; dogs free; adv bkg acc; quiet. "Pleasant quiet, 'hide-way' CL-type site; lge grassy pitches; width restriction 3m; friendly British owners; ideal for walking; excel; peaceful, well kept with super hosts." ♦ 1 Apr-30 Sep. € 17.00   2016*

HEMING *6E3* (5km SW Rural) *48.69130, 6.92769* **Camping Les Mouettes, 4 Rue de Diane Capelle, 57142 Gondrexange [03 87 25 06 01; otsi-gondrexange.pagesperso-orange.fr]** Exit Héming on N4 Strasbourg-Nancy. Foll sp Gondrexange & site sp. App fr W on D955 turn to site sp on L about 1km bef Héming. Lge, mkd, unshd, pt sl, wc (htd); chem disp; mv service pnt; shwrs inc; EHU (10A) inc (rev pol); lndry; shop nr; rest nr; bar nr; playgrnd; sw nr; 60% statics; dogs €1.50; phone; quiet; fishing adj; sailing adj; bike hire; tennis; CKE/CCI. "Pleasant site by lake; basic facs but clean." 1 Apr-30 Sep. € 18.00   2013*

HERBIGNAC *2G3* (0km E Rural) *47.44802, -2.31073* **Camp Le Ranrouet, 7 Allee des Pres Blancs, 44410 Herbignac [02 40 15 57 56; campingleranrouet@ orange.fr; www.camping-parc-de-la-briere.com]** Site at intersection D774 & D33 on E edge of vill. Med, mkd, pt shd, wc; chem disp; mv service pnt; shwrs; EHU (6A); lndry; shop nr; rest nr; bar nr; playgrnd; pool (htd); entmnt; TV; CKE/CCI. "Immac san facs; gd cent for Guérande." Easter-30 Oct. € 18.00   2014*

HERISSON *7A4* (1km WNW Rural) *46.51055, 2.70576* **Camp Municipal de l'Aumance, Rue de Crochepot, 03190 Hérisson [04 70 06 88 22, 04 70 06 80 45 or 06 63 46 21 49 (mob); www.allier-tourisme.com]** Exit A71 junc 9 onto D2144 N; turn R onto D11 dir Hérisson; immed bef T-junc with D3 turn L at blue sp (high on L) into Rue de Crochepot; site on R down hill. NB-Avoid towing thro town. Med, mkd, pt shd, wc; shwrs inc; EHU (6A) €2.80; playgrnd; phone; games area. "Delightful rvside site; idyllic setting; old san facs but gd & clean; warden calls eves; rec; peaceful and picturesque; easy walk to vil; lovely site; sm gd supmkt & fuel at Vallons; rv fishing reserved for campers - permit necessary; remarkable value; site on 2 levels, higher level better in wet weather." 1 Apr-31 Oct. € 8.00   2016*

HONFLEUR

HESDIN *3B3* (4km SE Rural) *50.35950, 2.07650* **Camping Rural St Ladre, 66 Rue Principale, 62770 St Georges [03 21 04 83 34; fax 03 21 30 04 81; bd-martin@wanadoo.fr; http://martinbernard. monsite-orange.fr]** Fr Hesdin SE on D340 for 5.5km. Site on L after St Georges, ent narr lane next cottage on bend. Fr W on D939 or D349 foll sp Frévent, then St Georges. Sp to site poor. Sm, mkd, hdg, pt shd, wc; chem disp; shwrs; EHU (5A) €2.40; adv bkg acc; quiet; CKE/CCI. "Pleasant, peaceful, CL-type site in orchard; basic facs but clean; welcoming, pleasant owner; conv Channel ports, Agincourt & Crécy; usual agricultural noises; gd rests in Hesdin." 1 May-30 Sep. € 9.00   2017*

HIRSON *3C4* (10km N Rural) *50.00585, 4.06195* **FFCC Camping Les Etangs des Moines, 100 rue des Etangs, 59610 Fourmies [03 27 60 04 32; contact@ etangs-des-moines.fr]** Fr D1043 Hirson by-pass head N on D963 to Anor. Turn L onto D156 dir Fourmies, site sp on R on ent town. Site also well sp off D42 & thro Fourmies. Med, hdg, hdstg, pt shd, wc; chem disp; mv service pnt; fam bthrm; shwrs; EHU (10A) €3.30; lndry; shop nr; snacks; bar; bbq; playgrnd; pool (htd); 80% statics; dogs €1; Eng spkn; CKE/CCI. "Textile & eco museum in town; shwrs run down, other facs gd; vg." 1 Apr-7 Nov. € 20.00   2014*

> **"I need an on-site restaurant"**
>
> We do our best to make site information is correct, but it is always best to check any must-have facilities are still available or will be open during your visit.

HONFLEUR *3C1* (6km S Rural) *49.40083, 0.30638* **Camping Domaine Catinière, 910 Route de la Morelle, 27210 Fiquefleur-Equainville [02 32 57 63 51; fax 02 32 42 12 57; info@camping-catiniere. com; www.camping-catiniere.com]** Fr A29/Pont de Normandie (toll) bdge exit junc 3 sp Le Mans, pass under m'way onto D580/D180. In 3km go strt on at rndabt & in 100m bear R onto D22 dir Beuzeville; site sp on R in 500m. Sm, hdg, mkd, pt shd, wc; chem disp; fam bthrm; shwrs inc; EHU (4A) inc or (8-13A) €1-1.50 (long lead poss req, poss rev pol); lndry; shop; snacks; bar; bbq; playgrnd; pool (htd); entmnt; wifi; TV; 15% statics; dogs €2; Eng spkn; adv bkg rec; ccard acc; rv fishing; waterslide; games rm; CKE/CCI. "Attractive, well-kept, busy site; pleasant, helpful, friendly owners; clean but dated unisex san facs, stretched high ssn & ltd LS; some pitches quite sm; unfenced stream on far boundary; gd touring base & NH; gd walks; easy parking for m'vans nr town; 20 mins to Le Havre ferry via Normandy bdge; no o'fits over 8.50m; conv A13; highly rec; lovely pool; ACSI acc." ♦ 1 Apr-15 Oct. € 33.00   2016*

Site report forms at back of guide   *Last year of report   235

HONFLEUR

"Satellite navigation makes touring much easier"

Remember most sat navs don't know if you're towing or in a larger vehicle – always use yours alongside maps and site directions.

HONFLEUR 3C1 (4km SW Rural) 49.39777, 0.20861
Camping La Briquerie, 14600 Equemauville [02 31 89 28 32; fax 02 31 89 08 52; info@campinglabriquerie.com; www.campinglabriquerie.com]
Fr Honfleur head S on D579A. At rndabt cont strt onto D62, site on R. Fr S take D579 dir Honfleur Cent. Pass water tower n turn L at Intermarché rndabt, site on R in 300m. Lge, hdg, pt shd, wc; chem disp; mv service pnt; fam bthrm; shwrs inc; EHU (5-10A) €4-5 (poss rev pol); gas; lndry; shop nr; rest; snacks; bar; bbq; playgrnd; pool (htd); beach sand 2.5km; entmnt; wifi; TV; 50% statics; dogs €3; bus nr; Eng spkn; adv bkg req; games rm; tennis 500m; horseriding 500m; fitness rm; waterslide; CKE/CCI. "Lge pitches; staff helpful; gd clean san facs; late/early ferry arr; local vets geared up for dog inspections, etc; gd; cash only."
♦ 1 Apr-30 Sep. € 34.70   2016*

HONFLEUR 3C1 (1km NW Coastal) 49.42445, 0.22591 Camping du Phare, Blvd Charles V, 14600 Honfleur [02 98 83 45 06; fax 02 31 93 06 05; camping.du.phare@orange.fr; www.camping-du-phare.com] Fr N fr Pont de Normandie on D929 take D144; at ent to Honfleur keep harbour in R; turn R onto D513 sp Trouville-sur-Mer & Deauville (avoid town cent); fork L past old lighthouse to site entry thro parking area. Or fr E on D180; foll sp 'Cent Ville' then Vieux Bassin dir Trouville; at rectangular rndabt with fountain turn R sp Deauville & Trouville, then as above. Med, hdg, pt shd, wc; chem disp; mv service pnt; shwrs; EHU (16A) inc; gas; lndry; shop nr; rest nr; snacks; bar; bbq; playgrnd; beach sand 100m; 10% statics; dogs €3; phone; Eng spkn; fishing; CKE/CCI. "Gd clean site in excel location; conv NH Le Havre ferry; busy high ssn, rec arr early; friendly owners; san facs basic & tired but clean, ltd LS; barrier clsd 2200-0700; m'van pitches narr & adj busy rd; some soft, sandy pitches; easy walk to town/harbour; sep m'van Aire de Service nr harbour; new disabled san facs (2015); conv Honfleur by foot; nice site; own san facs rec." ♦ 1 Apr-30 Sep. € 23.00   2017*

236   ⊞ Site open all year   You can now fill in site reports online

HOULGATE 3D1 (1km E Urban) 49.29223, -0.07428
Camp Municipal des Chevaliers, Chemin des Chevaliers, 14510 Houlgate [02 31 24 37 93; camping-chevaliers.houlgate@orange.fr; www.ville-houlgate.fr] Fr Deauville take D513 SW twds Houlgate; 500m after 'Houlgate' town sp, turn L & foll camping sps to site, 250m after Camping de la Vallée. Lge, mkd, unshd, pt sl, terr, wc; shwrs inc; EHU (6-10A) €3-5; beach sand 800m; 70% statics; dogs €0.85; Eng spkn; adv bkg rec; quiet; fishing 800m. "Well-kept site; pleasant warden; facs simple but adequate & clean; boating 800m; sep area for tourers nr ent; attractive town; excel." ♦ 1 Apr-30 Sep. € 14.00   2014*

HOULGATE 3D1 (1km E Coastal) 49.29390, -0.06820 Camping Yelloh! Village La Vallée, 88 Rue de la Vallée, 14510 Houlgate [02 31 24 40 69; fax 02 31 24 42 42; camping.lavallee@wanadoo.fr; www.campinglavallee.com] Exit junc 29 or 29a fr A13 onto D45 to Houlgate. Or fr Deauville take D513 W. Bef Houlgate sp, turn L & foll sp to site. Lge, mkd, hdg, pt shd, pt sl, terr, serviced pitches; wc (htd); chem disp; mv service pnt; shwrs inc; EHU (6A) inc; gas; lndry; shop; rest; snacks; bar; playgrnd; pool (covrd, htd); paddling pool; beach sand 900m; entmnt; wifi; TV; 85% statics; dogs €5; Eng spkn; adv bkg req; ccard acc; games rm; bike hire; waterslide; lake fishing 2km; tennis; golf 1km; CKE/CCI. "Superb, busy site; friendly recep; clean san facs; some pitches poss sm for lge o'fits; sep area m'vans; 1,5km walk to sandy beach and town; bkg fee; ACSI acc; fam/child orientated site." ♦ 1 Apr-1 Nov. € 47.00   2018*

See advertisement opposite

> "There aren't many sites open at this time of year"
>
> If you're travelling outside peak season remember to call ahead to check site opening dates – even if the entry says 'open all year'.

HOURTIN 7C1 (8km SSW Rural) 45.13915, -1.07096
Aire Naturelle de Camping l'Acacia, Route de Carcans, 33990 (Gironde) [05 56 73 80 80 06 72 94 12 67 (mob); camping.lacacia@orange.fr; www.campinglacacia.com] Fr Carcans on main rd to Hourtin, sp for site about 5km. Turn off rd on L and travel for 1.5km. Sm, pt shd, wc; shwrs; EHU inc; snacks; bar; cooking facs; playgrnd; twin axles; adv bkg acc; games area; games rm. "Site well maintained; immac san facs; owner v helpful, ltd Eng; v lge pitches; volleyball; bicycles; table tennis; v lge field; quiet peaceful site; great for families and couples; excel." Apr-Sep. € 20.00   2013*

HOURTIN 7C1 (10km W Coastal) 45.22296, -1.16472 Camping La Côte d'Argent, Rue de la Côte d'Argent, 33990 Hourtin-Plage [05 56 09 10 25; fax 05 56 09 24 96; info@cca33.com; www.cca33.com] On D1215 at Lesparre-Médoc take D3 Hourtin, D101 to Hourtin-Plage, site sp. V lge, mkd, shd, pt sl, terr, wc; chem disp; mv service pnt; fam bthrm; shwrs inc; EHU (10A) inc; lndry; shop; rest; snacks; bar; bbq; playgrnd; pool (covrd, htd); beach sand 300m; sw nr; red long stay; entmnt; wifi; 30% statics; dogs €5.50; phone; Eng spkn; adv bkg acc; quiet; ccard acc; bike hire; watersports; horseriding; fishing 4km; games area; ice; waterslide; games rm; jacuzzi; CKE/CCI. "Pleasant, peaceful site in pine trees & dunes; poss steel pegs req; conv Médoc region chateaux & vineyards; ideal for surfers & beach lovers." ♦ 14 May-18 Sep. € 53.00   2017*

See advertisement on next page

HOURTIN 7C1 (2km W Rural) 45.17919, -1.07502
Camping Les Ourmes, 90 Ave du Lac, 33990 Hourtin Port [05 56 09 12 76; fax 05 56 09 23 90; info@lesourmes.com; www.lesourmes.com]
Fr vill of Hourtin (35km NW Bordeaux), foll sp Houtin Port. In 1.5km, L at sp to site. Lge, mkd, pt shd, wc; chem disp; mv service pnt; fam bthrm; shwrs inc; EHU (6A) inc; gas; lndry; shop nr; rest nr; bar nr; bbq; playgrnd; pool; sw nr; entmnt; TV; 50% statics; dogs €2; phone; bus; Eng spkn; adv bkg acc; quiet; horseriding; fishing; games rm; watersports; CKE/CCI. "Excel for family holiday; Lake Hourtin shallow & vg for bathing, sailing etc; vg beaches nrby; nr Les Landes & Médoc vineyards." 27 Apr-22 Sep. € 41.00   2013*

HUELGOAT 2E2 (3km E Rural) 48.36275, -3.71532
FFCC Camping La Rivière d'Argent, La Coudraie, 29690 Huelgoat [02 98 99 72 50; fax 02 98 99 90 61; campriviere@orange.fr; www.larivieredargent.com] Sp fr town cent on D769A sp Poullaouen & Carhaix. Med, mkd, hdg, shd, wc; chem disp; mv service pnt; shwrs inc; EHU (6-10A) €3.60-4.30; lndry; shop nr; rest; snacks; playgrnd; pool (htd, indoor); red long stay; entmnt; dogs €1.60; adv bkg acc; quiet; tennis. "Lovely wooded site on rv bank; some rvside pitches; gd walks with maps provided; san facs updated (2017) well maintained, v clean; site self; poss rev pol; excel dog walks fr site; v friendly & helpful new owners (2018); excel." 1 Apr-30 Sep. € 26.00   2018*

HYERES 10F3 (8km E Coastal) 43.1186, 6.24693
Miramar Camping, 1026 Blvd Louis Bernard, 83250 La Londes-les-Maures [04 94 66 80 58 or 04 94 66 83 14; fax 04 94 66 80 98; camping.miramar.lalonde@wanadoo.fr; www.provence-campings.com/azur/miramar] On D98 in cent of La Londes-les-Maures, turn S at traff lts; in 1km turn R over white bdge & foll rd for 1.5km dir Port Miramar; site on R 150m bef port. Lge, mkd, hdg, shd, wc; chem disp; shwrs inc; EHU (4-10A) €4.50-6.50; lndry; shop; rest; snacks; bar; beach sand 200m; 25% statics; phone; Eng spkn; quiet; ccard acc; games rm; CKE/CCI. "Vg shd; beach, port, rests & shops 200m, but food shops 2km; vg marina; excel site out of ssn; vg." ♦ 1 May-30 Sep. € 22.00   2013*

HYERES

HYERES *10F3* (9km S Coastal) *43.02980, 6.15490*
Camping La Tour Fondue, Ave des Arbanais, 83400 Giens [04 94 58 22 86; fax 04 94 58 11 63; info@camping-latourfondue.com; www.camping-latourfondue.com] D97 fr Hyères, site sp. Med, hdg, pt shd, pt sl, terr, wc; chem disp; mv service pnt; shwrs inc; EHU (6A) €4.70; lndry; rest; snacks; bar; beach adj; entmnt; 10% statics; dogs €3 (not allowed on beach); Eng spkn; adv bkg acc; ccard acc; games area. "Pleasant, sister site of Camping Presqu'île de Giens with easier access; sm pitches; only water point at 'Sanitaires' (by recep); superb new san facs (2014)." 5 Apr-2 Nov. € 31.00 2014*

ILE BOUCHARD, L' *4H1* (1km N Urban) *47.12166, 0.42857* Camping Les Bords de Vienne, 4 Allée du Camping, 37220 L'Ile-Bouchard [02 47 95 23 59; fax 02 47 98 45 29; info@campingbordsdevienne.com; www.campingbordsdevienne.com] On N bank of Rv Vienne 100m E of rd bdge nr junc of D757 & D760. Fr E, turn L bet supmkt & pharmacy. Med, mkd, pt shd, pt sl, wc; chem disp; shwrs inc; EHU (6-16A) €3.50; gas; lndry; shop nr; snacks; playgrnd; pool; sw nr; red long stay; wifi; 10% statics; dogs €1.50; Eng spkn; adv bkg acc; quiet; ccard acc; tennis 500m; CKE/CCI. "Lovely, clean rvside site; attractive location; poss travellers; conv Loire chateaux." 15 Mar-25 Oct. € 28.00 2014*

"That's changed – Should I let the Club know?"

If you find something on site that's different from the site entry, fill in a report and let us know. See camc.com/europereport.

ILLIERS COMBRAY *4E2* (2km SW Rural) *48.28667, 1.22697* FLOWER Camping Le Bois Fleuri, Route de Brou, 28120 Illiers-Combray [02 37 24 03 04; infos@camping-chartres.com; www.camping-chartres.com or www.flowercampings.com] S on D921 fr Illiers for 2km twd Brou. Site on L. Med, hdg, hdstg, pt shd, serviced pitches; wc (htd); chem disp; shwrs inc; EHU (6A) €3.50; gas; lndry; shop nr; rest nr; snacks; bar; playgrnd; paddling pool; entmnt; 30% statics; dogs €4; adv bkg acc; quiet; fishing adj; games area; CKE/CCI. "Many pitches wooded & with flowers; popular NH; excel san facs; ltd water/EHU; htd pool 200m; uneven grnd makes access diff; gd security; excel cycle path to vill." ♦ 1 Apr-31 Oct. € 23.00 2018*

INGRANDES *4H2* (1km N Rural) *46.88700, 0.58800*
Camping Le Petit Trianon de St Ustre, 1 Rue du Moulin de St Ustre, 86220 Ingrandes-sur-Vienne [05 49 02 61 47; fax 05 49 02 68 81; petit-trianon@camp-in-ouest.com; www.petit-trianon.com] Leave A10/E5 at Châtellerault Nord exit 26 & foll sp Tours. Cross rv heading N on D910 twd Tours & Dangé-St Romain. At 2nd traff lts in Ingrandes (by church), turn R. Cross rlwy line & turn L at site sp in 300m. After 1.5km turn R at site sp, site at top of hill. NB Site ent narr, poss diff lge o'fits. Med, mkd, pt shd, pt sl, wc; chem disp; mv service pnt; fam bthrm; shwrs inc; EHU (10A) inc; gas; lndry; shop; rest; snacks; bar; bbq; playgrnd; pool (htd); paddling pool; entmnt; wifi; TV; dogs €3; Eng spkn; adv bkg acc; quiet; ccard acc; horseriding 1km; rv fishing 3km; games rm; tennis 1.5km; bike hire; games area; CKE/CCI. "Lovely site in chateau grnds; charming old buildings; gd sized pitches; friendly, helpful staff; excel facs." ♦ 6 Apr-24 Sep. € 30.00   2017*

ISIGNY SUR MER *1D4* (1km NW Rural) *49.31872, -1.10825* Camping Le Fanal, Rue du Fanal, 14230 Isigny-sur-Mer [02 31 21 33 20; fax 02 31 22 12 00; info@camping-lefanal.com] Fr N13 exit into Isigny, site immed N of town. Foll sp to 'Stade' in town, (just after sq & church on narr rd just bef R turn). Med, hdg, mkd, pt shd, wc; chem disp; mv service pnt; shwrs inc; EHU (16A) inc (long cable poss req); lndry; shop; snacks; bar; playgrnd; pool; entmnt; TV; 50% statics; dogs €4; phone; adv bkg acc; quiet; ccard acc; games rm; horseriding; tennis; games area; lake fishing adj; CKE/CCI. "Friendly staff; aqua park; poss boggy in wet weather; vg site." ♦ 1 Apr-30 Sep. € 30.50   2012*

ISLE JOURDAIN, L' *8F3* (1km NW Urban) *43.61569, 1.07839* Camping Municipal du Pont Tourné, 32600 L'Isle Jourdain [05 62 07 25 44; fax 05 62 07 24 81] Exit N124 to town cent. Site well sp. Med, mkd, shd, wc; chem disp; mv service pnt; shwrs; EHU (10A); lndry; bbq; dogs; adv bkg acc; quiet; CCI. "Sports ctr adj to site; shop nr; vg; security barrier; excel Sat mkt; wifi avail at TO;. vg walking & cycling; lakes next to site; v relaxing; hg rec." 6 Jul-1 Sep. € 12.80   2017*

ISLE SUR LA SORGUE, L' *10E2* (2km E Rural) *43.91451, 5.07181* Camping Airotel La Sorguette, 871 Route d'Apt, 84800 L'Isle-sur-la-Sorgue [04 90 38 05 71; fax 04 90 20 84 61; info@camping-sorguette.com; www.camping-sorguette.com] Fr L'Isle-sur-la-Sorgue take D901 twd Apt, on L site in 1.5km, sp. Med, mkd, hdg, pt shd, wc; chem disp; mv service pnt; shwrs inc; EHU (10A) €4.70; gas; lndry; shop; rest nr; bbq; playgrnd; beach adj; wifi; 10% statics; dogs €3.50; Eng spkn; adv bkg acc; quiet; ccard acc; tennis; fishing adj; games area; canoeing; CKE/CCI. "Lovely, well-run site; useful & busy; friendly, helpful staff; beware low trees; dated but clean san facs; rvside walk to attractive town; Sun mkt (shuttle fr site); highly rec." ♦ 15 Mar-15 Oct. € 23.00   2013*

ISLE SUR LA SORGUE, L' *10E2* (7km E Rural) *43.91087, 5.10665* Camping La Coutelière, Route de Fontaine-de-Vaucluse, 84800 Lagnes [04 90 20 33 97; fax 04 90 20 27 22; info@camping-lacouteliere.com; www.camping-lacouteliere.com] Leave L'Isle-sur-la-Sorgue by D900 dir Apt, fork L after 2km sp Fontaine-de-Vaucluse. Site on L on D24 bef ent Fontaine. Med, hdg, shd, wc; shwrs inc; EHU (10A) €4.40; lndry; rest; snacks; bar; playgrnd; pool; entmnt; 40% statics; dogs €4.50; phone; Eng spkn; adv bkg acc; quiet; canoeing nr; tennis; CKE/CCI. "Attractive, busy site by rv; walking/cycling on canal towpath; 2km easy cycle ride to Fontaine; ltd san facs LS; poss unkept LS; lovely area; gd." ♦ 1 Apr-10 Oct. € 32.00   2015*

ISLE SUR LE DOUBS, L' *6G2* (0km N Rural) *47.45288, 6.58338* Camping Les Lûmes, 10 Rue des Lûmes, 25250 L'Isle-sur-le-Doubs [03 81 92 73 05 or 06 85 42 97 81; contact@les-lumes.com; www.les-lumes.com] Well sp fr town edge on D683 bef rv bdge. Med, pt shd, wc; chem disp; shwrs; EHU (10A) €4 (long lead req & poss rev pol); shop; playgrnd; sw; 20% statics; dogs €1.20; Eng spkn; adv bkg acc; CKE/CCI. "Busy site; san facs need upgrade & up steps; gd." 1 May-30 Sep. € 13.50   2018*

ISPAGNAC *9D1* (1km W Rural) *44.37329, 3.53035* FFCC Camp Municipal Le Pré Morjal, 48320 Ispagnac [04 66 45 43 57; lepremorjal@gmail.com; www.campingdupremorjal.com] On D907B 500m W of town, turn L off D907B & then 200m on R, sp. Med, hdg, pt shd, wc (htd); chem disp; mv service pnt; fam bthrm; shwrs inc; EHU (10-16A) €3; lndry; shop nr; rest; snacks; bbq; playgrnd; paddling pool; sw nr; wifi; TV; dogs €1.20; quiet; games area; games rm. "Lovely family site; gd sized pitches on rocky base, poss muddy when wet; pool 50m inc; friendly staff; gd rvside walks; vg base for Tarn & Joute Gorges; early ssn poss unkempt & irreg cleaning of san facs (2010)." ♦ 29 Mar-11 Nov. € 29.00   2014*

ISSOIRE *9B1* (3km E Rural) *45.55113, 3.27423* FFCC Camp Municipal du Mas, Ave du Dr Bienfait, 63500 Issoire [04 73 89 03 59 or 04 73 89 03 54 (LS); fax 04 73 89 41 05; camping-mas@wanadoo.fr; www.camping-issoire.com] Fr Clermont-Ferrand S on A75/E11 take exit 12 sp Issoire; turn L over a'route sp Orbeil; at rndabt, take 1st exit & foll site sp. Med, unshd, wc (htd); chem disp; mv service pnt; fam bthrm; shwrs inc; EHU (10-13A) €3.35 (long lead poss req); gas; lndry; shop nr; snacks; playgrnd; red long stay; wifi; TV; 5% statics; dogs €0.50; phone; Eng spkn; adv bkg rec; quiet; ccard acc; fishing adj; tennis 500m; CKE/CCI. "Lovely, well-kept, basic site in park-like location; lge pitches; helpful warden; new, modern san facs; site poss boggy after rain; conv A75; excel touring base or NH; easy cycle rte to Issoire." ♦ 1 Apr-5 Nov. € 21.00   2016*

ISSOIRE

ISSOIRE *9B1* (6km SE Rural) *45.50908, 3.2848*
FFCC Camping Château La Grange Fort, 63500 Les Pradeaux [04 73 71 05 93 or 04 73 71 02 43; fax 04 73 71 07 69; chateau@lagrangefort.com; www.lagrangefort.com] S fr Clermont Ferrand on A75, exit junc 13 onto D996 sp Parentignat. At 1st rndabt take D999 sp St Rémy-Chargnat (new rd); at next rndabt take 1st exit onto D34 & foll sp to site on hill-top. Narr app rd & narr uphill ent. Med, hdg, mkd, shd, wc (htd); chem disp; mv service pnt; fam bthrm; shwrs inc; EHU (6A) €3.50; gas; lndry; shop nr; rest; snacks; bar; playgrnd; pool (covrd, htd); paddling pool; wifi; TV; 10% statics; dogs €3; phone; Eng spkn; adv bkg req; quiet; ccard acc; bike hire; rv fishing; sauna; canoe hire; tennis; CKE/CCI. "Pleasant, peaceful Dutch-run site in chateau grnds with views; excel san facs but long walk fr some pitches & ltd LS; some sm pitches; most pitches damp & gloomy under lge trees & muddy after rain; bkg fee; mosquito problem on shadiest pitches; ltd parking at recep; conv A75; gd." 1 Apr-31 Oct. € 27.00   2014*

ISSOIRE *9B1* (11km S Rural) *45.47373, 3.27161*
Camping Les Loges, 63340 Nonette [04 73 71 65 82; fax 04 73 71 67 23; les.loges.nonette@wanadoo.fr; www.lesloges.com] Exit 17 fr A75 onto D214 sp Le Breuil, dir Nonette. Turn L in 2km, cross rv & turn L to site. Site perched on conical hill. Steep app. Med, mkd, hdg, pt shd, wc; chem disp; fam bthrm; shwrs inc; EHU (10A) €4.50; gas; lndry; shop; rest; snacks; bar; playgrnd; pool (htd); sw nr; entmnt; TV; 30% statics; dogs €1.80; quiet; fishing adj; CKE/CCI. "Friendly site; conv Massif Cent & A75; gd NH." Easter-10 Sep. € 21.00   2012*

ISSOUDUN *4H3* (3km N Rural) *46.96361, 1.99011*
Camp Municipal Les Taupeaux, 37 Route de Reuilly, 36100 Issoudun [02 54 03 13 46 or 02 54 21 74 02; tourisme@issoudun.fr; www.issoudun.fr] Fr Bourges SW on N151, site sp fr Issoudun on D16 nr Carrefour supmkt. Sm, mkd, hdg, pt shd, wc; shwrs inc; EHU €3.70; playgrnd; dogs; quiet. "Pleasant site off RR; mv service pnt adj; conv A71 & N151." 15 May-15 Sep. € 11.00   2016*

JARD SUR MER *7A1* (2km NE Rural) *46.42624, -1.56564* **Camping La Mouette Cendrée, Les Malécots, 85520 St Vincent-sur-Jard** [02 51 33 59 04; fax 02 51 20 31 39; camping.mc@orange.fr; www.mouettecendree.com] Fr Les Sables-d'Olonne take D949 SE to Talmont-St-Hilaire; then take D21 to Jard-sur-Mer; at rndabt stay on D21 (taking 2nd exit dir La Tranche-sur-Mer & Maison-de- Clemanceau); in 500m turn L onto D19 sp St Hilaire-la-Forêt & foll site sps. Site on L in 700m. Med, hdg, mkd, pt shd, wc; chem disp; shwrs inc; EHU (10A) inc; lndry; shop nr; bbq (elec, gas); playgrnd; pool; paddling pool; beach sand 2km; entmnt; wifi; 30% statics; dogs €3; Eng spkn; adv bkg acc; ccard acc; golf 10km; waterslide; windsurfing 2km; fishing; horseriding 500m; bike hire; games rm; CKE/CCI. "Busy site high ssn; gd pitches; welcoming, helpful owners; san facs poss stretched when site full; no o'fits over 7.5m high ssn; vg pool; gd woodland walks & cycle rtes nr; mkt Mon." ♦ 1 Apr-30 Sept. € 27.50   2016*

JARD SUR MER *7A1* (2km SE Coastal) *46.41980, -1.52580* **Chadotel Camping La Bolée d'Air, Route du Bouil, Route de Longeville, 85520 St Vincent-sur-Jard** [02 51 90 36 05 or 02 51 33 05 05; fax 02 51 33 94 04; info@chadotel.com; www.chadotel.com] Fr A11 junc 14 dir Angers. Take N160 to La Roche-sur-Yon & then D747 dir La Tranche-sur-Mer to Moutier-les-Mauxfaits. At Moutiers take D19 to St Hilaire-la-Forêt & then L to St Vincent-sur-Jard. In St Vincent turn L by church sp Longeville-sur-Mer, site on R in 1km. Lge, hdg, mkd, pt shd, serviced pitches; wc (htd); chem disp; fam bthrm; shwrs inc; EHU (10A) inc; gas; lndry; shop; snacks; bar; bbq (charcoal, gas); playgrnd; pool (covrd, htd); paddling pool; beach sand 900m; red long stay; entmnt; wifi; TV; 25% statics; dogs €3.20; Eng spkn; adv bkg acc; ccard acc; sauna; bike hire; games rm; waterslide; jacuzzi; tennis; CKE/CCI. "Popular, v busy site high ssn; mkt Sun; no o'fits over 8m; whirlpool; access some pitches poss diff lge o'fits; excel." ♦ 1 Apr-24 Sep. € 30.00   2016*

JAULNY *5D2* (1km S Rural) *48.96578, 5.88524*
Camping La Pelouse, 54470 Jaulny [03 83 81 91 67; info@campingdelapelouse.com; www.campingdelapelouse.com] SW fr Metz on D657, cross rv at Corny-sur-Moselle onto D6/D1; in 1.5km turn R onto D952 dir Waville & Thiaucourt-Regniéville; in 6km turn L onto D28 dir Thiaucourt-Regniéville; cont on D28 to Jaulny; site sp to L in Jaulny. Med, pt shd, sl, wc; chem disp; shwrs inc; EHU (6A) €4; lndry; rest; bar; bbq; playgrnd; pool (htd); sw nr; 80% statics; dogs €2; fishing; CKE/CCI. "Vg site; friendly owner and staff; basic san facs; poss stretched high ssn; no fresh or waste water facs for m'vans; conv NH." 1 Apr-30 Sep. € 20.60   2012*

> **"I like to fill in the reports as I travel from site to site"**
>
> You'll find report forms at the back of this guide, or you can fill them in online at camc.com/europereport.

JAUNAY CLAN *4H1* (6km NE Rural) *46.69807, 0.42619*
Camp Municipal du Parc, Rue du Parc 86130 Dissay [05 49 62 84 29 or 05 49 52 34 56 (Mairie); fax 05 49 62 58 72; accueil@dissay.fr; www.dissay.fr] N on D910 Poitiers dir Châtellerault. At rndabt turn R on D15 sp Dissay. Turn R ent Dissay & site on R 50m. Sm, mkd, shd, wc; chem disp; shwrs inc; EHU (10A) €2.65 (poss rev pol); lndry; shop nr; playgrnd; dogs; Eng spkn; quiet; CKE/CCI. "Friendly warden; clean modern facs; conv Futuroscope; 15thC chateau adj; gate locked 2200 but can request key; gd." ♦ 19 Jun-29 Aug. € 10.00   2013*

JOIGNY

JAUNAY CLAN *4H1* (7km NE Rural) *46.72015, 0.45942* Camping Lac de St Cyr, 86130 St Cyr [05 49 62 57 22; fax 05 49 52 28 58; contact@campinglacdesaintcyr.com; www.campinglacdesaintcyr.com] Fr A10 take Châtellerault Sud exit & take D910 dir Poitiers; at Beaumont turn L at traff lts for St Cyr; foll camp sp in leisure complex (Parc Loisirs) by lakeside - R turn for camping. Or fr S take Futuroscope exit to D910. Lge, mkd, hdg, pt shd, pt sl, serviced pitches; wc; chem disp; mv service pnt; shwrs inc; EHU (10A) inc (poss rev pol); gas; lndry; shop; rest; snacks; bar; bbq; playgrnd; sw; red long stay; entmnt; wifi; TV; 15% statics; dogs €3; Eng spkn; adv bkg acc; ccard acc; games area; boat hire; golf adj; watersports; games rm; fishing; sailing; canoeing; tennis; fitness rm; bike hire; CKE/CCI. "Excel, well-kept site in leisure complex; lovely setting by lake; gd sized pitches; helpful recep; no o'fits over 8m; gd, clean san facs, poss stretched high ssn; gd rest; some pitches poss diff lge o'fits; rec long o'fits unhitch at barrier due R-angle turn at barrier - poss diff long o'fits; Futuroscope approx 13km; highly rec; excel site; gd size pitches; friendly helpful staff." ♦ 30 Mar-30 Sep. € 33.00   2017*

⊞ **JAUNAY CLAN** *4H1* (2km SE Urban) *46.66401, 0.39466* Kawan Village Le Futuriste, Rue du Château, 86130 St Georges-les-Baillargeaux [05 49 52 47 52; fax 05 49 37 23 33; camping-le-futuriste@wanadoo.fr; www.camping-le-futuriste.fr] On A10 fr N or S, take Futuroscope exit 28; fr toll booth at 1st rndabt take 2nd exit. Thro tech park twd St Georges. At rndabt under D910 take slip rd N onto D910. After 150m exit D910 onto D20, foll sp. At 1st rndabt bear R, over rlwy, cross sm rv & up hill, site on R. Med, mkd, hdg, pt shd, serviced pitches; wc (htd); chem disp; mv service pnt; shwrs inc; EHU (6A) inc (check earth & poss rev pol); gas; lndry; shop; rest; snacks; bar; bbq; playgrnd; pool (covrd, htd); entmnt; wifi; TV; 10% statics; dogs €2.50; Eng spkn; adv bkg acc; quiet; ccard acc; games area; games rm; lake fishing; waterslide; CKE/CCI. "Lovely, busy, secure site; well-kept; friendly, helpful family owners; vg clean facs, ltd LS - facs block clsd 2200-0700; vg pool; vg for families; hypmkt 2km; ideal touring base for Poitiers & Futuroscope (tickets fr recep); vg value, espec in winter; conv a'route; excel." ♦ € 33.00   2017*

JAUNAY CLAN *4H1* (5km SE Rural) *46.65464, 0.37786* Camp Municipal Parc des Ecluzelles, Rue Leclanché, 86360 Chasseneuil-du-Poitou [05 49 62 58 85 or 05 49 52 77 19 (LS); maire@mairie-chasseneuildupoitou.fr; www.ville-chasseneuil-du-poitou.fr] Fr A10 or D910 N or Poitiers take Futuroscope exit 28/18. Take Chassenueil rd, sp in town to site. Sm, mkd, hdstg, pt shd, wc; chem disp; mv service pnt; shwrs inc; EHU (8A) inc; shop nr; bbq; playgrnd; dogs; quiet. "Vg, clean site; lge pitches; conv Futuroscope; immac; htd pool adj inc; v simple site with the vg san facs, helpful staff; gd bus service into the city." ♦ 11 Apr-27 Sep. € 19.50   2015*

JAVRON LES CHAPELLES *4E1* (1km SW Rural) Camp Municipal, Route de Bagnoles, 53250 Javron-les-Chapelles [02 43 03 40 67; fax 02 43 03 43 43; col360@live.co.uk] Foll sp fr town cent on N12 twds Mayenne. Sm, unshd, terr, wc; chem disp; shwrs inc; EHU (10A) €5; shop nr; rest nr; bbq (charcoal, gas); Eng spkn. "Vg site." Apr-Sep. € 15.00   2013*

> ## "We must tell the Club about that great site we found"
>
> Get your site reports in by mid-August and we'll do our best to get your updates into the next edition.

JOIGNY *4F4* (8km E Urban) *47.95646, 3.50657* Camping Les Confluents, Allée Léo Lagrange, 89400 Migennes [03 86 80 94 55; planethome2003@yahoo.fr; www.les-confluents.com] A6 exit at junc 19 Auxerre Nord onto N6 & foll sp to Migennes & site, well sp. Med, hdg, mkd, hdstg, pt shd, wc (htd); chem disp; mv service pnt; fam bthrm; shwrs inc; EHU (6-10A) €3.50-4.90; gas; lndry; shop; rest; snacks; bar; bbq; playgrnd; pool; red long stay; entmnt; TV; 8% statics; dogs €0.90; phone; bus 10 mins; quiet; ccard acc; bike hire; watersports 300m; games area; canoe hire; CKE/CCI. "Friendly, family-run, clean site nr canal & indust area; no twin axles; medieval castle, wine cellars, potteries nrby; walking dist to Migennes; mkt Thurs; excel." ♦ 1 Apr-1 Nov. € 24.00   2012*

JOIGNY *4F4* (12km SE Rural) *47.92802, 3.51932* Camp Municipal Le Patis, 28 Rue du Porte des Fontaines, 89400 Bonnard [03 86 73 26 25 or 03 86 73 26 91 (Mairie); mairie.bonnard@wanadoo.fr; www.tourisme-yonne.com] Exit A6 junc 19; N on N6 dir Joigny; in 8.5km at Bassou turn R & foll sp Bonnard. Site on L immed after rv bdge. Sm, mkd, shd, wc; chem disp; shwrs inc; EHU (10A) €2.20; lndry; shop nr; rest nr; playgrnd; sw nr; dogs; phone; adv bkg acc; quiet; tennis adj; boating adj; fishing adj. "Super little site on banks of Rv Yonne; well-kept; friendly, helpful warden; immac san facs; gd security; vg fishing." ♦ 15 May-30 Sep. € 8.00   2013*

JOIGNY *4F4* (2km W Rural) *47.98143, 3.37439* FFCC Camp Municipal, 68 Quai d'Epizy, 89300 Joigny [03 86 62 07 55; fax 03 86 62 08 03; camping.joigny@orange.fr; www.ville-joigny.fr/index.php] Fr A6 exit junc 18 or 19 to Joigny cent. Fr cent, over brdg, turn L onto D959; turn L in filter lane at traff lts. Foll sp to site. Sm, hdg, hdstg, pt shd, wc; chem disp; mv service pnt; shwrs; EHU (10A) inc; shop nr; rest nr; sw nr; wifi; quiet; fishing adj; tennis; horseriding; CKE/CCI. "V busy site; liable to flood in wet weather; v helpful warden; pool 4km; interesting town; v modern clean san facs; quiet in May; some sm pitches; v helpful warden; local wine avail to buy." 1 May-30 Sep. € 13.40   2018*

France

JOIGNY

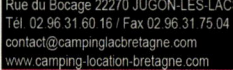

Camping Au Bocage du Lac ★★★★ **Bretagne**

Rue du Bocage 22270 JUGON-LES-LACS
Tél. 02.96.31.60.16 / Fax 02.96.31.75.04
contact@campinglacbretagne.com
www.camping-location-bretagne.com

JOIGNY 4F4 (4km NW Rural) 47.99550, 3.34468
Camp Municipal L'Ile de L'Entonnoir, Route de St Aubin-sur-Yonne, 89210 Cézy [03 86 63 17 87 or 03 86 63 12 58 (LS); fax 03 86 63 02 84; info@camping-cezy.com] Site sp off N6 N & S-bound (Joigny by-pass). Thro St Aubin vill, cross bdge over Rv Yonne. Site on L bank of rv. Or exit N6 Joigny by-pass at N of rndabt onto N2006 twd St Aubin. After St Aubin turn R to Cézy & site in 1km. Rec app via St Aubin - narr bdge 3.5t weight restriction. Alt route for lge o'fits, N6 onto N2006 to St Aubin, sp in vill. Sm, mkd, pt shd, wc; chem disp; mv service pnt; shwrs inc; EHU (6-10A) inc; lndry; shop nr; rest; snacks; bar; bbq; playgrnd; sw nr; dogs €1; Eng spkn; adv bkg acc; quiet; CKE/CCI. "V pleasant, quiet site; helpful staff; conv Chablis area; barrier clsd 2200." 1 May-31 Oct. € 15.40 2012*

JOINVILLE 6E1 (6km E Rural) 48.43018, 5.23077
Camp Municipal La Petite Suisse, Rue de Mélaire, 52230 Poissons [03 23 94 55 75 or 03 25 94 51 78 (Mairie); www.tourisme-hautemarne.com] Fr N67 to Joinville 'Centre Ville'; then onto D60 dir Thonnance; after supmkt turn R onto D427 to Poissons; site on L as exit vill. Site sp in vill. Sm, pt shd, pt sl, wc (htd); own san req; chem disp; shwrs inc; EHU (6A) inc; shop nr; snacks; bar nr; bbq; 20% statics; dogs; quiet; CKE/CCI. "Delightful, peaceful, basic CL-type site in great location; warden calls eves or call at No 7 in same rd to pay; dated but immac san facs; easy to find." 1 May-15 Sep. 2012*

JONZAC 7B2 (4km SW Rural) 45.42916, -0.44833
FFCC Camping Les Castors, 8 Rue Clavelaud, St Simon de Bordes, 17500 Jonzac [05 46 48 25 65; fax 05 46 04 56 76; camping-les-castors@wanadoo.fr; www.campingcastors.com] Fr Jonzac take D19 S twds Montendre, after approx 2km, immed after ring rd rndabt, turn R into minor rd. Site ent adj. Med, hdg, hdstg, pt shd, wc; chem disp; mv service pnt; shwrs inc; EHU (6-10A) €4.20-4.90; lndry; snacks; bar; playgrnd; pool (covrd); sw nr; entmnt; TV; 50% statics; dogs €1.60; quiet; CKE/CCI. "Peaceful, friendly, well-maintained site; gd facs; excel pool; gd; ent & exit gate can be diff for c'vans." ♦ 15 Mar-30 Oct. € 17.60 2015*

JOSSELIN 2F3 (2km W Rural) 47.95340, -2.57338
Domaine de Kerelly, Le bas de la lande, 56120 Guégon [02 97 22 22 20 or 06 27 57 22 79 (mob); domainedekerelly@orange.fr; www.camping-josselin.com] Exit N24 by-pass W of town sp Guégon; foll sp 1km; do not attempt to cross Josselin cent fr E to W. Site on D724 just S of Rv Oust (canal). Med, hdg, pt shd, terr, wc; chem disp; mv service pnt; fam bthrm; shwrs inc; EHU (6-10A) €3.80-4.50; lndry; shop nr; rest; snacks; bar; bbq; playgrnd; pool; wifi; TV; dogs; phone; Eng spkn; adv bkg acc; quiet; ccard acc; bike hire; CKE/CCI. "Vg, clean san facs; site rds steep; pleasant walks; poss diff if wet; walk to Josselin, chateau & old houses; gd cycling; family run; gd food; mini golf." ♦ 1 Apr-31 Oct. € 20.00 2018*

JUGON LES LACS 2E3 (1km S Rural) 48.40166, -2.31678 Camping au Bocage du Lac, Rue Du Bocage, 22270 Jugon-les-Lacs [02 96 31 60 16; fax 02 96 31 75 04; contact@campinglacbretagne.com; www.camping-location-bretagne.com]
Bet Dinan & Lamballe by N176. Foll `Camping Jeux` sp on D52 fr Jugon-les-Lacs. Situated by lakes, sp fr cent of Jugon. Lge, pt shd, pt sl, wc; mv service pnt; fam bthrm; shwrs inc; EHU (10A) €3-4.60; lndry; shop nr; bar; playgrnd; pool (htd); paddling pool; entmnt; TV; 10% statics; dogs €3.20; adv bkg acc; fishing adj; waterslide; games area; watersports adj; games rm. "Well-situated nr pretty vill; many sports & activities; vg, modern san facs; vg, attractive site." 5 Apr-27 Sep. € 25.00 2013*

See advertisement

"I need an on-site restaurant"

We do our best to make sure site information is correct, but it is always best to check any must-have facilities are still available or will be open during your visit.

JUMIEGES *3C2* (1km E Rural) *49.43490, 0.82970*
Camping de la Forêt, Rue Mainberte, 76480 Jumièges [02 35 37 93 43; info@campinglaforet.com; www.campinglaforet.com] Exit A13 junc 25 onto D313/D490 N to Pont de Brotonne. Cross Pont de Brotonne & immed turn R onto D982 sp Le Trait. Cont thro town & in 1km turn R onto D143 sp Yainville & Jumièges. In Jumièges turn L at x-rds after cemetary & church, site on R in 1km. NB M'vans under 3.5t & 3m height can take ferry fr Port Jumièges - if towing do not use sat nav dirs. Med, mkd, hdg, pt shd, wc (htd); chem disp; mv service pnt; fam bthrm; shwrs inc; EHU (10A) €5 (poss rev pol); gas; lndry; shop; rest nr; snacks; bbq; playgrnd; pool (htd); paddling pool; wifi; TV; 30% statics; dogs free; phone; bus to Rouen; adv bkg acc; quiet; ccard acc; watersports; bike hire; games rm; fishing; tennis; games area. "Nice site, well-situated in National Park; busy; some sm pitches; gd, clean san facs but poss stretched high ssn; interesting vill; conv Paris & Giverny; no o'fits over 7m high ssn; gd walking, cycling; ferries across Rv Seine; gd for dogs; children loved it." ♦ 1 Apr-31 Oct. € 29.00   2017*

> **"Satellite navigation makes touring much easier"**
>
> Remember most sat navs don't know if you're towing or in a larger vehicle – always use yours alongside maps and site directions.

KAYSERSBERG *6F3* (1km NW Rural) *48.14899, 7.25405* Camping Municipal de Kayserberg, Rue des Acacias, 68240 Kaysersberg [03 89 47 14 47 or 03 89 78 11 11 (Mairie); camping@villekaysersberg.fr; www.camping-kaysersberg.com] Fr A35/N83 exit junc 23 onto D4 sp Sigolsheim & Kaysersberg; bear L onto N415 bypass dir St Dié; site sp 100m past junc with D28. Or SE fr St Dié on N415 over Col du Bonhomme; turn L into Rue des Acacias just bef junc with D28. Med, mkd, hdg, pt shd, wc; chem disp; fam bthrm; shwrs inc; EHU (8-13A) inc (may need cable); gas; lndry; shop nr; playgrnd; wifi; TV; dogs €2 (no dogs Jul/Aug); quiet; fishing adj; tennis adj. "Excel, well-kept, busy site; rec arr early high ssn; many gd sized pitches; friendly staff; clean san facs; rv walk to lovely town, birth place Albert Schweitzer; bread delivery; many mkd walks/cycle rts; Le Linge WWI battle grnd nr Orbey; excel site; if arr when clsd, choose pitch nbr bef registering." ♦ 1 Apr-30 Sep. € 18.60   2014*

KAYSERSBERG *6F3* (7km NW Rural) *48.18148, 7.18449* Camping Les Verts Bois, 3 Rue de la Fonderie, 68240 Fréland [03 89 47 57 25 or 06 81 71 89 38 (mob); gildas.douault@sfr.fr; www.camping-lesvertsbois.com] Sp off N415 Colmar/St Dié rd bet Lapoutroie & Kaysersberg. Site approx 5km after turn fr main rd on D11 at far end of vill. Turn L into rd to site when D11 doubles back on itself. Sm, pt shd, pt sl, terr, wc (htd); chem disp; shwrs inc; EHU (6-10A) €2.70-3.20; gas; lndry; shop nr; rest; snacks; bar; bbq; dogs €0.70; Eng spkn; adv bkg acc; quiet; ccard acc; CKE/CCI. "Lovely site in beautiful, peaceful setting adj rv; friendly welcome; excel; fishing & bird watching; cheese farms 2 miles away; a must for cheese lovers; v helpful owners, excel rest." 1 Apr-31 Oct. € 19.00   2014*

KRUTH *6F3* (2km N Rural) *47.94355, 6.95418*
Camping du Schlossberg, 19 rue du Bourbach, 68820 Kruth [03 89 82 26 76; camping@schlossberg.fr; www.schlossberg.fr] Fr N66 turn N on D13 for Fellering and Kruth. Leaving Kruth twd Wildenstein, turn L at camping sp. Foll rd round and turn R bef no entry sp. Lge, mkd, pt shd, pt sl, wc; chem disp; mv service pnt; fam bthrm; shwrs; EHU (6A) €3; lndry; shop; bar; playgrnd; wifi; 20% statics; dogs; phone; Eng spkn; adv bkg acc; games area; games rm; CKE/CCI. "Boules & quoytes on site; Go Ape 2km; lake with peddleoes; walking; castle ruins; excel." ♦ 1 Apr-7 Oct. € 17.00   2015*

> **"There aren't many sites open at this time of year"**
>
> If you're travelling outside peak season remember to call ahead to check site opening dates – even if the entry says 'open all year'.

LABENNE *8E1* (4km S Rural) *43.56470, -1.45240*
Camping du Lac, 518 Rue de Janin, 40440 Ondres [05 59 45 28 45 or 06 80 26 91 51 (mob); fax 05 59 45 29 45; contact@camping-du-lac.fr; www.camping-du-lac.fr] Fr N exit A63 junc 8 onto N10 S. Turn R just N of Ondres sp Ondres-Plage, at rndabt turn L & foll site sp. Fr S exit A63 junc 7 onto N10 to Ondres. Cont thro town cent & turn L at town boundary, then as above; tight turns thro housing est. Med, hdg, mkd, pt shd, terr, wc (htd); chem disp; fam bthrm; shwrs inc; EHU (10A) €4; gas; lndry; shop nr; rest; snacks; bar; playgrnd; pool; beach sand 4km; red long stay; entmnt; 60% statics; dogs €5; phone; Eng spkn; adv bkg req; quiet; bike hire; fishing; boating; games area; CKE/CCI. "Peaceful, charming lakeside site by lake; twin axles LS only; gd welcome; helpful staff; ltd facs LS; vg pool; excel." ♦ 21 Mar-2 Oct. € 45.00   2017*

LABENNE

Close to Biarritz, 900m from the beach
Open from 5th April 2019 to 29th September 2019

Yelloh! Village ILBARRITZ ★★★★
Avenue de Biarritz
64210 Bidart - FRANCE
+33 (0)5 59 23 00 29
contact@camping-ilbarritz.com
www.camping-ilbarritz.com

Between the Forest, the dunes and the ocean
Open from 5th April 2019 to 29th September 2019

Yelloh! village SYLVAMAR ★★★★★
Avenue de l'Océan
40530 Labenne Océan
+33 (0)5 59 45 75 16
camping@sylvamar.fr
www.sylvamar.fr

LABENNE 8E1 (3km SW Coastal) 43.59533, -1.45651 Camping Le Sylvamar, Ave de l'Océan, 40530 Labenne [05 59 45 75 16; fax 05 59 45 46 39; camping@sylvamar.fr; www.sylvamar.fr or www.yellohvillage.co.uk] Exit A63 junc 7 onto D85; then take N10 N to Labenne; turn L onto D126; site sp. Lge, hdg, mkd, pt shd, serviced pitches; wc; chem disp; fam bthrm; shwrs inc; EHU (10A) inc; lndry; shop nr; rest; snacks; bar; bbq; playgrnd; pool; paddling pool; beach sand 800m; entmnt; wifi; 50% statics; Eng spkn; adv bkg acc; quiet; ccard acc; waterslide; CKE/CCI. "Site amongst pine trees; sauna; spa; creche; sandy pitches; fitness rm; beauty cent; gd location; vg facs." ♦ 9 Apr-25 Sep. € 43.00   2017*

See advertisement above

LABENNE 8E1 (3km W Coastal) 43.59628, -1.46104 Camp Atlantique Le Boudigau, 45 Avenue de la Plage, 40530 Labenne-Océan [02 51 20 41 94; http://boudigau.camp-atlantique.co.uk] Turn W off N10 in Labenne at traff lts in town cent onto D126 to Labenne-Plage. Site 2km on R. Lge, shd, wc; fam bthrm; shwrs inc; EHU (6A) inc; gas; lndry; shop; rest; snacks; bar; bbq; playgrnd; pool (covrd, htd); beach sand 500m; 90% statics; dogs (1 per pitch); adv bkg rec; games area. "Sm touring area - only 25 pitches; excel san facs; gd site; lively high ssn - gd kids activities." 1 Apr-30 Sep. € 28.00   2014*

LACANAU 7C1 (3km NNW Rural) 45.00178, -1.09241 Camping Les Fougères, Ave de l'Océan, 33680 Talaris [05 56 03 56 76; contact@campinglesfougereslacanau.com; www.campinglesfougereslacanau.com] A630 bypass exit at junc 8 sp Lacanau - Le Verdon. Med, pt shd, wc; chem disp; mv service pnt; shwrs; EHU (4A) inc; bbq; playgrnd; sw nr; twin axles; wifi; 10% statics; dogs €2.10; Eng spkn; adv bkg acc; games area; CKE/CCI. "Excel site; watersports 1.5km; tennis 9km." ♦ 1 Jun-30 Sep. € 33.00   2013*

LACANAU OCEAN 7C1 (1km N Coastal) 45.00823, -1.19531 Airotel Camping de l'Océan, 24 Rue du Repos, 33680 Lacanau-Océan [05 56 03 24 45; fax 05 57 70 01 87; airotel.lacanau@wanadoo.fr; www.airotel-ocean.com] On ent town at end of sq in front of bus stn turn R, fork R & foll sp to site (next to Camping Grand Pins). Lge, pt shd, pt sl, wc; chem disp; shwrs inc; EHU (15A) inc; gas; lndry; shop; rest; snacks; bar; pool; beach sand 600m; entmnt; TV; dogs €4; adv bkg acc; quiet; fishing; watersports; bike hire; tennis. "Attractive site/holiday vill in pine woods behind sand dunes; surfing school nrby; care in choosing pitch due soft sand; gd, modern san facs; some pitches tight access." Easter-27 Sep. € 33.00   2017*

See advertisement opposite

LACAUNE

"That's changed – Should I let the Club know?"

If you find something on site that's different from the site entry, fill in a report and let us know. See camc.com/europereport.

LACANAU OCEAN *7C1* (5km SE Rural) *44.98620, -1.13410* **Camping Le Tedey, Par Le Moutchic, Route de Longarisse, 33680 Lacanau-Océan [05 56 03 00 15; fax 05 56 03 01 90; camping@le-tedey. com; www.le-tedey.com]** Fr Bordeaux take D6 to Lacanau & on twd Lacanau-Océan. On exit Moutchic take L fork twd Longarisse. Ent in 2km well sp on L. V lge, mkd, shd, wc; chem disp; mv service pnt; fam bthrm; shwrs inc; EHU (10A) €4.30; gas; lndry; shop; snacks; bar; playgrnd; sw nr; entmnt; wifi; TV; 10% statics; Eng spkn; adv bkg rec; quiet; ccard acc; bike hire; boating; golf 5km; CKE/CCI. "Peaceful, friendly, family-run site in pine woods - avoid tree sap; golf nr; gd cycle tracks; no EHU for pitches adj beach; access diff some pitches; excel site." ♦ 25 Apr-19 Sep. € 29.40   2013*

See advertisement on next page

LACAPELLE VIESCAMP *7C4* (2km SW Rural) *44.91272, 2.24853* **Camping La Presqu'île du Puech des Ouilhes, 15150 Lacapelle-Viescamp [04 71 46 42 38 or 06 80 37 15 61 (mob); contact@cantal-camping.fr; www.camping-lac-auvergne.com]** W fr Aurillac on D120; at St Paul-des-Landes turn S onto D53 then D18 to Lacapelle-Viescamp. Foll sp Base de Loisirs, Plage-du-Puech des Ouilhes & Camping. Site beside Lake St Etienne-Cantalès. Med, mkd, hdstg, hdg, pt shd, wc; chem disp; fam bthrm; shwrs inc; EHU (16A) €3; lndry; shop nr; rest; snacks; bar; playgrnd; pool; beach sand adj; sw nr; 10% statics; dogs €2; Eng spkn; quiet; fishing; canoeing; tennis; games rm; watersports. "Friendly, helpful young owners; excel." ♦ 15 Jun-15 Sep. € 19.00   2014*

LACAUNE *8E4* (6km E Rural) *43.69280, 2.73790* **Camping Domaine Le Clôt, Les Vidals, 81230 Lacaune [05 63 37 03 59; campingleclot@orange.fr; www.pageloisirs.com/le-clot]** Fr Castres to Lacaune on D622. Cont on D622 past Lacaune then turn R onto unclassified rd to Les Vidals. Site sp 500m on L after Les Vidals. Sm, pt shd, terr, wc (htd); chem disp; shwrs inc; EHU (6-10A) €3.25-4; lndry; shop nr; rest; snacks; playgrnd; dogs €1.50; Eng spkn; quiet; CKE/CCI. "Excel site; modern, immac san facs; gd views; gd walking in Monts de Lacaune; lake sw 12km; fishing 12km; sailing 12km; windsurfing 12km; friendly Dutch owner; site rd steep & narr; vg rest." ♦ 15 Apr-15 Oct. € 22.00   2016*

LAGRASSE

LAGRASSE 8F4 (1km N Rural) 43.09516, 2.61893
Camp Municipal de Boucocers, Route de Ribaute, 11220 Lagrasse [04 68 43 10 05 or 04 68 43 15 18; fax 04 68 43 10 41; mairielagrasse@wanadoo.fr; www.audetourisme.com] 1km on D212 fr Lagrasse to Fabrezan (N). Sm, hdstg, pt shd, pt sl, wc; chem disp; mv service pnt; shwrs inc; EHU (15A) €2.80; shop nr; rest nr; sw nr; wifi; dogs €2.10; phone; adv bkg acc; CKE/CCI. "At cent of 'off-the-beaten-track' beautiful touring area; helpful warden; simple but gd san facs; gd walking; path down to lagrasse cent; o'looks superb medieval town; rec arr early; hillside walk into vill needs care; site run down at then of ssn; no entry barrier, site self, pay when warden calls; excel, well kept site; Lagrasse Abbey & town worth a visit." ♦
15 Mar-15 Oct. € 15.00   2018*

LAGUEPIE 8E4 (1km E Rural) 44.14780, 1.97892
Camp Municipal Les Tilleuls, 82250 Laguépie [05 63 30 22 32 or 05 63 30 20 81 (Mairie); camping.lestilleuls0837@orange.fr; www.camping-les-tilleuls.com] Exit Cordes on D922 N to Laguépie; turn R at bdge, still on D922 sp Villefranche; site sp to R in 500m; tight turn into narr lane. NB App thro Laguépie poss diff lge o'fits. Med, pt shd, terr, wc; shwrs inc; EHU (10A) €2.70; shop nr; bar nr; playgrnd; sw; TV; 44% statics; dogs; phone; adv bkg acc; quiet; canoe hire; fishing; tennis; games area. "Attractive setting on Rv Viaur; friendly welcome; excel playgrnd; gd touring base; conv Aveyron gorges." ♦ May-Oct.
€ 14.00   2018*

LAGUIOLE 7D4 (1km NE Rural) 44.68158, 2.85440
Camp Municipal Les Monts D'Aubrac, 12210 Laguiole [05 65 44 39 72 or 05 65 51 26 30 (LS); fax 05 65 51 26 31; http://campinglesmontsdaubraclaguiole.jimdo.com] E of Laguiole on D15 at top of hill. Fr S on D921 turn R at rndabt bef ent to town. Site sp. Med, hdg, mkd, pt shd, pt sl, wc; chem disp; mv service pnt; shwrs inc; EHU (16A) inc; lndry; shop nr; rest nr; bar nr; dogs; phone; quiet; CKE/CCI. "Clean & well cared for site; pleasant vill." 15 May-15 Sep. € 10.00   2014*

LAISSAC 7D4 (3km SE Rural) 44.36525, 2.85090
FLOWER Camping La Grange de Monteillac, Chemin de Monteillac, 12310 Sévérac-l'Eglise [05 65 70 21 00 or 06 87 46 90 83 (mob); fax 05 65 70 21 01; info@le-grange-de-monteillac.com; www.la-grange-de-monteillac.com or www.flowercampings.com] Fr A75, at junc 42, go W on N88 twds Rodez; after approx 22km; bef Laissac; turn L twds Sévérac-l'Eglise; site sp. Med, mkd, hdg, unshd, pt sl, terr, wc; chem disp; mv service pnt; shwrs inc; EHU (6A) inc (long lead poss req); lndry; rest; playgrnd; pool; paddling pool; entmnt; wifi; TV; 10% statics; dogs €1.50; phone; Eng spkn; adv bkg rec; quiet; bike hire; tennis; horseriding; CKE/CCI. "Beautiful, excel site; bar & shops high ssn." ♦
7 May-15 Sep. € 42.00   2014*

LALINDE 7C3 (2km E Urban) 44.83956, 0.76298
Camping Moulin de la Guillou, Route de Sauveboeuf, 24150 Lalinde [09 61 46 06 96 or 05 53 73 44 60 (Mairie); fax 05 53 57 81 60; la-guillou@wanadoo.fr; www.pays-de-bergerac.com] Take D703 E fr Lalinde (Rv Dordogne on R) & keep strt where rd turns L over canal bdge. Site in 300m; sp. Med, shd, wc; shwrs inc; EHU (5A) €2.60; shop nr; playgrnd; pool; sw nr; entmnt; dogs €2; adv bkg rec; tennis adj; fishing adj. "Charming, peaceful site on bank of Rv Dordogne; lovely views; clean san facs, in need of upgrade; poss travellers; vg."
1 May-30 Sep. € 15.00   2012*

LALLEY 9D3 (0km S Rural) 44.75490, 5.67940 **Camping Belle Roche**, Chemin de Combe Morée, 38930 Lalley [04 76 34 75 33 or 06 86 36 71 48 (mob); camping.belleroche@gmail.com or contact@camping-belleroche.com; www.campingbelleroche.com] Off D1075 at D66 for Mens; down long hill into Lalley. Site on R thro vill. Med, hdstg, hdg, pt shd, pt sl, wc; chem disp; mv service pnt; fam bthrm; shwrs inc; EHU (10A) €4 (poss rev pol, poss long lead req); gas; lndry; shop nr; rest; snacks; bar; bbq; playgrnd; pool (htd); entmnt; wifi; TV; 10% statics; dogs €1.50; adv bkg acc; quiet; ccard acc; games area; tennis 500m; CKE/CCI. "Well-kept, scenic site; spacious pitches but little shd; friendly, welcoming owners; clean, vg modern san facs, poss stretched high ssn; pleasant pool area; nr Vercors National Park; vg walking/cycling; don't miss The Little Train of La Mure; conv NH; v nice site; highly rec superb in every way." ♦ 26 Mar-15 Oct. € 30.00   2014*

LAMALOU LES BAINS *10F1* (2km SE Rural) *43.57631, 3.06842* **Camping Domaine de Gatinié, Route de Gatinié, 34600 Les Aires [04 67 95 71 95 or 04 67 28 41 69 (LS); fax 04 67 95 65 73; gatinie@wanadoo.fr; www.domainegatinie.com]** Fr D908 fr Lamalou-les-Bains or Hérépian dir Poujol-sur-Orb, site sp. Fr D160 cross rv to D908 then as above. Med, mkd, hdg, pt shd, pt sl, wc; chem disp; fam bthrm; shwrs inc; EHU (6A) inc; lndry; rest; snacks; bar; bbq; playgrnd; pool; paddling pool; sw nr; red long stay; entmnt; 10% statics; dogs €2; Eng spkn; adv bkg acc; quiet; fishing; horseriding 2km; tennis 2km; canoeing; games area; golf 2km; CKE/CCI. "Beautiful, peaceful situation; many leisure activities; vg; helpful staff, leafy pleasant site in a lovely area." ♦ 1 Apr-31 Oct. € 19.00   2014*

LAMASTRE *9C2* (5km NE Rural) *45.01353, 4.62366* **Camping Les Roches, 07270 Le Crestet [04 75 06 20 20; fax 04 75 06 26 23; camproches@nordnet.fr; www.campinglesroches.com]** Take D534 fr Tournon-sur-Rhône dir Lamastre. Turn R at Le Crestet & foll sp for site, 3km fr vill. Sm, hdstg, mkd, pt shd, terr, wc; chem disp; mv service pnt; fam bthrm; shwrs inc; EHU (6A) €5; lndry; shop; rest; snacks; bar; bbq; playgrnd; pool (htd); sw nr; TV; 30% statics; dogs €4.50; bus 1km; Eng spkn; adv bkg acc; quiet; ccard acc; games area; tennis 3km; fishing; CKE/CCI. "Friendly family-run site; clean facs; lovely views; gd base for touring medieval vills; gd walking; site rd steep." ♦ 1 May-30 Sep. € 32.00   2013*

LANDEDA *2E1* (2km NW Coastal) *48.59333, -4.60333* **Camping des Abers, 51 Toull Tréaz, Plage de Ste Marguerite, 29870 Landéda [02 98 04 93 35; fax 02 98 04 84 35; info@camping-des-abers.com; www.camping-des-abers.com]** Exit N12/E50 at junc with D788 & take D13 to Lannilis. Then take D128A to Landéda & foll green site sp. Lge, mkd, hdg, pt shd, terr, wc; chem disp; mv service pnt; fam bthrm; shwrs; EHU (10A) €3 (long lead poss req); gas; lndry; shop; rest nr; snacks; bar nr; bbq; playgrnd; beach sand adj; red long stay; entmnt; wifi; TV; 10% statics; dogs €2.20; Eng spkn; adv bkg rec; quiet; ccard acc; bike hire; fishing; games rm; CKE/CCI. "Attractive, landscaped site on wild coast; views fr high pitches; friendly, helpful manager; san facs clean, some new, others old; some pitches muddy when wet; no o'fits over 8m high ssn; access to many pitches by grass tracks, some sl; gd walks, cycling; excel; some problems with voltage." ♦ 1 May-30 Sep. € 20.50   2014*

LANDEDA *2E1* (3km NW Coastal) *48.60310, -4.59882* **Camp Municipal de Penn-Enez, 29870 Landéda [02 98 04 99 82; info@camping-penn-enez.com; www.camping-penn-enez.com]** Proceed NW thro Landéda, turn R in 1km sp Penn-Enez then L in 600m. Site sp. Med, hdg, unshd, pt sl, wc; chem disp; shwrs; EHU (16A) €2.80; playgrnd; beach sand 500m; 2% statics; dogs €1.65; Eng spkn; quiet. "Site on grassy headland; beach views fr some pitches; site self if warden absent; friendly, helpful staff; vg clean san facs; gd walks; excel." ♦ 25 Apr-30 Sep. € 16.00   2014*

LANDIVISIAU *2E2* (9km NE Urban) *48.57724, -4.03006* **Camp Municipal Lanorgant, 29420 Plouvorn [02 98 61 32 40 (Mairie); www.plouvorn.com/aire-de-camping-cars]** Fr Landivisiau, take D69 N twd Roscoff. In 8km turn R onto D19 twd Morlaix. Site sp, in 700m turn R. NB Care req entry/exit, poss diff lge o'fits. Sm, hdg, mkd, pt shd, terr, wc; mv service pnt; shwrs; EHU (10A) inc; lndry; shop nr; rest nr; bar nr; bbq; playgrnd; beach sand; sw; adv bkg acc; quiet; tennis; fishing; canoe hire. "Ideal NH for ferries; lge pitches; sailboards hire; nr lake." 26 Jun-15 Sep. € 5.20   2016*

LANGEAC *9C1* (1km NE Rural) *45.10251, 3.49980* **Camp Municipal du Pradeau/Des Gorges de l'Allier, 43300 Langeac [04 71 77 05 01; fax 04 71 77 27 34; infos@campinglangeac.com; www.campinglangeac.com]** Exit N102 onto D56 sp Langeac; in 7km join D585 into Langeac; pass under rlwy; at 2nd rndabt in 1km turn L to site, just bef junc with D590. Fr S on D950 to Langeac, take 1st R after rv bdge; then 1st exit at rndabt in 100m. Lge, pt shd, wc; chem disp; mv service pnt; shwrs inc; EHU (10A) €2.60 (poss long lead req); lndry; shop nr; rest nr; snacks; playgrnd; pool; sw nr; entmnt; TV; 10% statics; dogs €1.05; phone; bus 1km; Eng spkn; quiet; bike hire; fishing adj; canoeing adj; CKE/CCI. "Beautiful location on Rv Allier; tourist train thro Gorges d'Allier fr Langeac; walking rtes adj; barrier to site poss clsd after sept 11am-5pm; gd san facs; gd local mkt; excel NH." ♦ 1 Apr-31 Oct. € 13.00   2015*

LANGEAIS *4G1* (1km E Urban) *47.32968, 0.41848* **Camp Municipal du Lac, rue Carnot, 37130 Langeais [02 47 96 85 80; fax 02 47 96 69 23; patrimoine@langeais.fr; www.langeais.fr]** Exit A85 junc 7 onto D952 dir Langeais & foll 'Camping Municipal' sp. Med, mkd, pt shd, wc; chem disp; shwrs inc; EHU (6A) €3.50; shop nr; rest nr; snacks; playgrnd; pool (htd); 5% statics; dogs; ccard acc; fishing nr; CKE/CCI. "Busy site high ssn; easy walk to town; dated san facs, inadequate when busy; nr Rv Loire cycle path; lovely chateau; gd; poss rd/rlwy noise." 1 Jun-15 Sep. € 19.00   2013*

LANGOGNE *9D1* (2km W Rural) *44.73180, 3.83995* **Camping Les Terrasses du Lac, 48300 Naussac [04 66 69 29 62; fax 04 66 69 24 78; info@naussac.com; www.naussac.com]** S fr Le Puy-en-Velay on N88. At Langogne take D26 to lakeside, site sp. Lge, pt shd, terr, wc; chem disp; mv service pnt; fam bthrm; shwrs; EHU (6A) €2.50; lndry; shop nr; rest; snacks; bar; bbq; playgrnd; pool; paddling pool; sw nr; entmnt; wifi; TV; 10% statics; dogs €3.30; phone; Eng spkn; adv bkg acc; quiet; horseriding 3km; games area; sailing school; bike hire; golf 1km; watersports adj; CKE/CCI. "Vg views; steep hill bet recep & pitches; vg cycling & walking." ♦ 15 Apr-1 Oct. € 23.30   2018*

LANGRES

LANGRES *6F1* (6km NE Rural) *47.89505, 5.39510*
Camping Hautoreille, 6 Rue du Boutonnier, 52360 Bannes [03 25 84 83 40; campinghautoreille@orange.fr; www.campinghautoreille.com] N fr Dijon on D974/D674 to Langres; foll rd around Langres to E; onto D74 NE to Bannes; site on R on ent vill. Or exit A31 junc 7 Langres Nord onto D619, then D74 NE to Bannes. Med, mkd, hdstg, pt shd, pt sl, wc (htd); chem disp; mv service pnt; shwrs inc; EHU (10A) €4; lndry; shop; rest; snacks; bar; playgrnd; sw nr; wifi; 10% statics; dogs €1; phone; Eng spkn; adv bkg acc; quiet; horseriding 5km; tennis 5km; bike hire; CKE/CCI. "Peaceful, clean, tidy site; basic facs, ltd LS & poss inadequate high ssn; pleasant owner; gd rest; site muddy when wet - parking on hdstg or owner will use tractor; on Sundays site yourself - recep opens 1700; gd NH." ♦ 2 Jan-30 Nov. € 24.30 2013*

LANGRES *6F1* (6km E Rural) *47.87190, 5.38120* **Kawan Village Le Lac de la Liez, Rue des Voiliers, 52200 Peigney** [03 25 90 27 79; fax 03 25 90 66 79; contact@camping-liez.fr; www.campingliez.com] Exit A31 at junc 7 (Langres Nord) onto DN19; at Langres turn L at traff lts onto D74 sp Vesoul, Mulhouse, Le Lac de la Liez; at rndabt go strt on sp Epinal, Nancy; after Champigny-lès-Langres cross over rlwy bdge & canal turning R onto D52 sp Peigney, Lac de la Liez; in 3km bear R onto D284 sp Langres Sud & Lac de la Liez; site on R in 800m. Well sp fr N & S. Lge, mkd, hdg, hdstg, pt shd, terr, wc (htd); chem disp; mv service pnt; fam bthrm; shwrs inc; EHU (10A) €5.50; lndry; shop; rest; snacks; bar; bbq; playgrnd; pool (covrd, htd); paddling pool; sw nr; entmnt; wifi; TV; 15% statics; dogs €3; phone; Eng spkn; ccard acc; bike hire; sauna; golf 10km; boat hire; watersports; fishing; horseriding 10km; tennis; games rm; CKE/CCI. "Popular, well-run, secure site; lake views fr some pitches; various sized pitches; helpful, friendly staff; san facs ltd LS; blocks poss req some pitches; some sm pitches & narr access rds diff manoeuvre lge o'fits; no o'fits over 10m; spa; vg rest; rec arr bef 1600 high ssn; gd walks & cycle rte by picturesque lake; interesting & historic town; poor." ♦ 1 Apr-25 Sep. € 37.00 2016*

LANGRES *6F1* (15km S Rural) *47.74036, 5.30727*
Camping du Lac, 14 rue Cototte, 52190 Villegusien le Lac [(07) 70 05 87 19; richard-emmanuel@hotmail.fr; www.tourisme-langres.com] Take N19, foll N19 to Ave de Capitaine Baudoin, then foll Ave du Général de Gaulle, foll D974 to D26 in Villegusien-le-Lac, cont on D26, turn L onto D26, turn L, turn R,site on L. Med, mkd, shd, pt sl, wc (htd); chem disp; mv service pnt; fam bthrm; shwrs; EHU; lndry; shop nr; rest; snacks; bar; bbq (gas); playgrnd; pool; beach; sw; twin axles; wifi; dogs; adv bkg acc; windsurfing; trekking; games rm; tennis; fishing; sailing. "V pleasant site in lovely setting, some slight rd noise; beach lifeguard." 15 Mar-15 Oct. € 20.00 2014*

LANGRES *6F1* (8km S Rural) *47.81210, 5.32080*
Camping de la Croix d'Arles, 52200 Bourg [03 25 88 24 02; croix.arles@yahoo.fr; www.campingdelacroixdarles.com] Site is 4km S of Langres on W side of D974 (1km S of junc of D974 with D428). Site opp junc of D51 with D974. Fr Dijon poss no L turn off D974 - can pull into indust est N of site & return to site, but memb reported that L turn now poss (2011). Med, hdg, mkd, pt shd, pt sl, wc (htd); chem disp; mv service pnt; shwrs inc; EHU (10A) €4 (poss rev pol) (long cable req); lndry; shop; rest; snacks; bar; playgrnd; pool; wifi; dogs free; phone; Eng spkn; ccard acc; CKE/CCI. "Popular site, fills up quickly after 1600; friendly staff; some lovely secluded pitches in woodland; gd san facs; access poss diff lge o'fits; muddy after rain; unkempt LS; poss haphazard pitching when full; conv NH Langres historic town; nice, sm rest on site; easy to reach." ♦ 15 Mar-31 Oct. € 22.00 2018*

LANGRES *6F1* (1km SW Urban) *47.86038, 5.32894*
Camp Municipal Navarre, 9 Blvd Maréchal de Lattre de Tassigny, 52200 Langres [03 25 87 37 92 or 06 10 74 10 16; contact@campingnavarre.fr; www.camping-navarre-langres.fr] App fr N or S on D619/D674, cont on main rd until lge rndabt at top of hill & go thro town arched gateway; site well sp fr there. NB Diff access for lge o'fits thro walled town but easy access fr D619. Med, pt shd, pt sl, wc (htd); chem disp; shwrs inc; EHU (10A) €3.10 (long lead req & poss rev pol); lndry; shop nr; bbq; wifi; dogs free; phone; Eng spkn; CKE/CCI. "Well-situated, busy NH, gd views fr some pitches; on arr site self & see warden; rec arr bef 1630; helpful staff, excel, modern unisex san facs; lovely walk round citadel ramparts; delightful town; vg site, views and location; warden mulit-lingual and helpful; conv for shops, rest, Friday mkt, cathedral." ♦ 10 Mar-5 Nov. € 18.30 2017*

⊞ **LANGRES** *6F1* (13km SW Rural) *47.79528, 5.23278*
Camping de la Croisée, 3 Route De Auberive, 52250 Flagey [03 25 88 01 26; yannick.durenne52@orange.fr; www.campingdelacroisee.com] Exit A31 at J6 direction Langres D428. Campsite 1km on L (opp junc to Flagey). Med, mkd, hdg, hdstg, pt shd, wc (htd); chem disp; mv service pnt; shwrs inc; rest; snacks; bar; bbq (charcoal, gas); playgrnd; dogs; quiet; ccard acc; red low ssn.. "Conv NH stop as 2km fr A31 m'way; farm animals; gd." € 17.00 2018*

LANILDUT *2E1* (1km N Coastal) *48.48012, -4.75184*
Camping du Tromeur, 11 Route du Camping, 29840 Lanildut [02 98 04 31 13; tromeur@vive-les-vacances.com; www.vive-les-vacances.com/tromeur] Site well sp on app rds to vill. Med, wc; chem disp; shwrs inc; EHU €3 (poss long lead req & poss rev pol); lndry; shop nr; rest nr; bar nr; bbq; dogs €1; phone; quiet. "Clean, sheltered site; san facs gd; harbour & sm beach; LS warden am & pm only - site yourself; wooded walk into vil." 1 May-30 Sep. € 16.00 2014*

LANLOUP 2E3 (0km W Rural) 48.71369, -2.96711
FFCC Camping Le Neptune, 22580 Lanloup [02 96 22 33 35; fax 02 96 22 68 45; contact@leneptune.com; www.leneptune.com] Take D786 fr St Brieuc or Paimpol to Lanloup, site sp. NB Take care sat nav dirs (2011). Med, mkd, hdg, pt shd, wc; chem disp; mv service pnt; fam bthrm; shwrs inc; EHU inc; gas; lndry; shop; rest nr; snacks; bar; bbq; playgrnd; pool (covrd, htd); beach sand 2km; wifi; TV; 15% statics; dogs €3; phone; Eng spkn; adv bkg acc; horseriding 4km; bike hire; tennis 300m; CKE/CCI. "Excel, well-maintained site nr beautiful coast; various pitch sizes; clean san facs; friendly, helpful owner; highly rec." ♦ 31 Mar-9 Oct. € 30.00   2017*

LANNE 8F2 (1km NW Rural) 43.17067, 0.00186
Camping La Bergerie, 79 Rue des Chênes, 65380 Lanne [05 62 45 40 05; camping-la-bergerie@orange.fr; www.camping-la-bergerie.com] Fr Lourdes take N21 N dir Tarbes; turn R onto D16 (Rue des Chênes) dir Lanne; site on R in 200m. Med, mkd, shd, wc (htd); shwrs; EHU (10A) €3.8 (poss rev pol); gas; shop; snacks; bar; playgrnd; pool; dogs €2; bus 200m; Eng spkn; adv bkg acc; quiet; tennis; CKE/CCI. "Well-run site; friendly owners; some rd noise & aircraft noise at night; gd san facs; poss unkempt LS; poss flooding wet weather." ♦ 15 Mar-15 Oct. € 19.00   2017*

⊞ **LANNION** 1D2 (3km SE Urban) 48.72300, -3.44600
Camp Municipal Les Deux Rives, Rue du Moulin du Duc, 22300 Lannion [02 96 46 31 40 or 02 96 46 64 22; fax 02 96 46 53 35; infos@ville.lannion.fr; www.ville-lannion.fr] SW fr Perros-Guirec on D788 to Lannion; fr Lannion town cent foll dir Guincamp on D767; site well sp, approx 1.5km, turn R at Leclerc supmkt (do not confuse with hypmkt). Fr S on D767 sp at rndabts; turn L at Leclerc supmkt. Med, mkd, unshd, wc; chem disp; shwrs inc; EHU (6A) €2.50; lndry; shop; bar; playgrnd; dogs €1.10; adv bkg acc; CKE/CCI. "Rvside walk to old town; vg, clean san facs; phone ahead LS to check open; security barrier; warden lives on site but poss no arr acc Sun." ♦ € 20.00   2014*

LANNION 1D2 (9km NNW Coastal) 48.73833, -3.54500
FFCC Camping Les Plages de Beg-Léguer, Route de la Côte, 22300 Lannion [02 96 47 25 00; fax 02 96 47 27 77; info@campingdesplages.com; www.campingdesplages.com] Fr Lannion take D786 out of town twd Trébeurden then twd Servel on D65, then head SW off that rd twd Beg Léguer (sp). Lge, hdg, mkd, pt shd, wc; chem disp; mv service pnt; fam bthrm; shwrs inc; EHU (6A) €3.50 (poss long lead req); gas; lndry; shop; rest; snacks; bar; playgrnd; pool (covrd, htd); paddling pool; beach sand 500m; red long stay; wifi; TV; 20% statics; dogs €1; phone; bus 400m; Eng spkn; adv bkg acc; quiet; ccard acc; windsurfing; fishing; sailing; tennis; CKE/CCI. "Pleasant, peaceful, wel-run family site; charming French owner who speaks excel Eng; superb pool complex & vg children's play area; lge grass pitches; immac, modern san facs; one of the best sites in France; many superb rest in nrby seaside resorts; stunning beaches, cliftop location; adj to GR34 coastal path; phone LS." ♦ 1 May-30 Sep. € 29.00   2015*

LANSLEBOURG MONT CENIS 9C4 (0km SW Rural) 45.28417, 6.87380 **Camp Municipal Les Balmasses, Chemin du Pavon, 73480 Lanslebourg-Mont-Cenis [04 79 20 52 77 or 06 19 46 28 18 (mob); info@camping-les-balmasses.com; www.camping-les-balmasses.com]** Fr Modane, site on R on rv on ent to town. Med, mkd, pt shd, wc; shwrs inc; EHU (6-10A) €4.50-5.40; lndry; shop nr; bbq; playgrnd; dogs; phone; Eng spkn; CKE/CCI. "Pleasant, quiet site by rv; mountain views; clean facs; conv NH bef/after Col du Mont-Cenis." ♦ 1 Jun-20 Sep. € 14.00   2014*

LAON 3C4 (3km W Rural) 49.56190, 3.59583 **Camp La Chênaie (formerly Municipal), Allée de la Chênaie, 02000 Laon [03 23 23 38 63 or 03 23 20 25 56; contact.camping.laon@gmail.com; www.camping-laon.com]** Exit A26 junc 13 onto N2 sp Laon; in 10km at junc with D1044 (4th rndabt) turn sp Semilly/Laon, then L at next rndabt into site rd. Site well sp. Sm, hdstg, hdg, mkd, pt shd, sl, terr, wc (htd); chem disp; mv service pnt; fam bthrm; shwrs inc; EHU (10A) €3.40 (poss rev pol); lndry; shop; bbq; playgrnd; red long stay; twin axles; wifi; 10% statics; dogs €2; phone; Eng spkn; adv bkg acc; quiet; fishing 50m; CKE/CCI. "Peaceful, pleasant site in gd location; popular NH; well-mkd pitches - lgest at end of site rd; pool (2.5km); extremely helpful staff; no twin axles; if travelling Sept phone to check site open; m'van parking nr cathedral; vg; woodland glades; gd NH; site now privately owned, pool under construction (2016)." ♦ 1 Apr-30 Sep. € 21.00   2016*

> "I like to fill in the reports as I travel from site to site"
>
> You'll find report forms at the back of this guide, or you can fill them in online at camc.com/europereport.

LAPALISSE 9A1 (0km S Urban) 46.24322, 3.63950
Camping de la Route Bleue, Rue des Vignes, 03120 Lapalisse [04 70 99 26 31, 04 70 99 76 29 or 04 70 99 08 39 (LS); office.tourisme@cc-paysdelapalisse.fr; www.cc-paysdelapalisse.fr] S fr Moulins on N7; at rndabt junc with D907 just bef Lapalisse, take 3rd exit onto Ave due Huit Mai 1945 (to town cent), foll rd for 1.5km, over rv bdg, round RH bend onto Rue des Vignes, site on R in 500m. Med, mkd, pt shd, wc (htd); mv service pnt; shwrs inc; EHU (6-9A) €2.40; lndry; shop nr; playgrnd; dogs €1; Eng spkn; quiet; CKE/CCI. "Popular, excel NH off N7 in pleasant parkland setting; gd clean san facs; pleasant 10 min walk thro adj park to town; no twin axles; poss flooding after heavy rain; adequate sans but need upgrade." ♦ 1 Apr-30 Sep. € 15.00   2014*

LARGENTIERE

LARGENTIERE 9D2 (5km SE Rural) 44.50347, 4.29430
Camping Les Châtaigniers, Le Mas-de-Peyrot, 07110 Laurac-en-Vivarais [04 75 36 86 26; chataigniers@ hotmail.com; www.chataigniers-laurac.com]
Fr Aubenas S on D104 dir Alès; site sp fr D104. Site on one of minor rds leading to Laurac-en-Vivarais. Med, mkd, pt shd, pt sl, wc; chem disp; fam bthrm; shwrs; EHU (10A) €3; lndry; bbq (gas); playgrnd; pool; 15% statics; dogs €2; adv bkg acc; quiet. "Attractive, great, clean site; some pitches deep shd; sun area; gd pool; sh uphill walk to vill shops & auberge; vg." ♦
1 Apr-30 Sep. € 25.00   2016*

LARGENTIERE 9D2 (2km NW Rural) 44.56120, 4.28615 **Domaine Les Ranchisses, Route de Rocher, Chassiers, 07110 Largentière [04 75 88 31 97; fax 04 75 88 32 73; reception@lesranchisses.fr; www.lesranchisses.fr]** Exit A7/E15 junct 17/18 (Montelimar N or S) on to N7 dir Montelimar to take N102.
Fr Aubenas S on D104 sp Alès. 1km after vill of Uzer turn R onto D5 to Largentière. Go thro Largentière on D5 in dir Rocher/Valgorge; site on L in 1.5km. DO NOT use D103 bet Lachapelle-Aubenas & Largentière - too steep & narr for lge vehicles & c'vans. NB Not rec to use sat nav dirs to this site. Lge, mkd, pt shd, wc; chem disp; mv service pnt; fam bthrm; shwrs inc; EHU (10A) inc; gas; lndry; shop; rest; snacks; bar; bbq (elec, gas); playgrnd; pool (covrd, htd); paddling pool; sw; entmnt; wifi; TV; 30% statics; dogs €3.60; adv bkg req; ccard acc; games rm; fishing; tennis; bike hire; games area; canoeing. "Lovely, well-run, busy site adj vineyard; gd sized pitches; friendly, helpful staff; gd, immac san facs; o'fits over 7m by request; excel rest & takeaway; lovely pools; gd choice of sporting activities; wellness cent; poss muddy when wet; noisy rd adj to S end of site; mkt Tues am; first class; 5 star site in lovely location." ♦ 12 Apr-21 Sep. € 48.00   2014*

⊞ **LARUNS** 8G2 (6km N Rural) 43.02085, -0.42043
FFCC Camp Municipal de Monplaisir, Quartier Monplaisir, 64260 Gère-Bélesten [05 59 82 61 18]
Site sp on E side of D934 S of Gère-Bélesten. Med, mkd, pt shd, wc (htd); shwrs inc; EHU (6A) €3.90; shop nr; bar nr; TV; 75% statics; Eng spkn; adv bkg acc; quiet; fishing. "Helpful warden calls am & pm; htd pool 4km." € 10.00   2014*

LARUNS 8G2 (6km SE Rural) 42.96972, -0.38220
Camping d'Iscoo, 64440 Eaux-Bonnes [05 59 05 36 81 or 06 98 23 54 93 (mob); camping.iscoo@live.fr; http://iscoo.free.fr] Site is on R 1.4km fr Eaux-Bonnes on climb to Col d'Aubisque. Site ent in middle of S-bend so advise cont 500m & turn on open grnd on L. Sm, mkd, pt shd, pt sl, wc; shwrs; EHU (2-5A) €2.50; shop nr; playgrnd; dogs; quiet; CKE/CCI. "V pleasant location; friendly owner; beautiful sunny site in hills; pool 3km; excel shwrs." 1 Jun-30 Sep. € 12.00   2014*

⊞ **LARUNS** 8G2 (1km S Rural) 42.98241, -0.41591
Camping Les Gaves, Quartier Pon, 64440 Laruns [05 59 05 32 37; fax 05 59 05 47 14; campingdesgaves@wanadoo.fr; www.campingdesgaves.com]
Site on S edge of town, N of Hôtel Le Lorry & bdge. Fr town sq cont on Rte d'Espagne (narr exit fr sq) to end of 1-way system. After Elf & Total stns turn L at site sp immed bef bdge (high fir tree each side of bdge ent). Ignore 1st site on L. At v constricted T-junc at ent to quartier 'Pon', turn R & foll rd into site. App no suitable lge o'fits. Med, mkd, pt shd, serviced pitches; wc (htd); chem disp; shwrs inc; EHU (3-10A) €2.60-4.50; lndry; shop nr; bar; playgrnd; TV; 75% statics; dogs €3; quiet; fishing; games area; games rm; rv fishing adj; CKE/CCI. "Beautiful, lovely site; nr vill; htd covrd pool 800m; facs tired (2015); level walk to vill."
€ 24.00   2015*

⊞ **LAURENS** 10F1 (1km S Rural) 43.53620, 3.18583
Camping L'Oliveraie, Chemin de Bédarieux, 34480 Laurens [04 67 90 24 36; fax 04 67 90 11 20; oliveraie@free.fr; www.oliveraie.com]
Clearly sp on D909 Béziers to Bédarieux rd. Sp reads Loisirs de L'Oliveraie. Med, hdstg, mkd, pt shd, terr, wc (htd); chem disp; fam bthrm; shwrs inc; EHU (10A) €3.20-4.60 (poss rev pol); lndry; shop; rest; snacks; bar; playgrnd; pool; wifi; TV; 30% statics; dogs free €2 (high ssn); phone; adv bkg acc; quiet; ccard acc; site clsd 15 Dec-15 Jan; games rm; CKE/CCI. "Helpful staff; gd, clean san facs; sauna high ssn; site becoming tatty (2011); in wine-producing area; gd winter NH." ♦
€ 28.00   2014*

> "We must tell the Club about that great site we found"
>
> Get your site reports in by mid-August and we'll do our best to get your updates into the next edition.

LAVAL 2F4 (17km N Rural) 48.17367, -0.78785 **Camp Municipal Le Pont, 53240 Andouillé [02 43 69 72 72 (Mairie); fax 02 43 68 77 77]** Fr Laval N on D31 dir Ernée. In 8km turn R onto D115 to Andouillé. Site on L bef hill to vill cent. Sm, hdg, pt shd, wc; chem disp; shwrs inc; EHU (3A) inc; lndry; shop nr; playgrnd; quiet. "Pretty, busy, basic site; vg, clean san facs; warden on site am & pm; site liable to flood." 1 Apr-31 Oct.
€ 6.00   2015*

LAVANDOU, LE

France

LAVANDOU, LE *10F3 (2km E Coastal) 43.14471, 6.38084* Caravaning St Clair, Ave André Gide, 83980 Le Lavandou [04 94 01 30 20; fax 04 94 71 43 64; patrick.martini@wanadoo.fr or lesmandariniers@orange.fr; www.caravaningsaintclair.com] N559 thro Le Lavandou twd St Raphaël; after 2km at sp St Clair turn R immed after bend 50m after blue 'caravaning' sp (easy to overshoot). Med, mkd, shd, wc (htd); mv service pnt; shwrs inc; EHU (16A) €4.10 (rev pol); lndry; shop nr; rest nr; bar nr; playgrnd; beach sand adj; wifi; TV; dogs €2; adv bkg req; boat hire; fishing. "Popular with British; pitch & ent screened by trees; conv beach & rests; no tents; quiet site." ♦ Apr-Oct. € 30.00   2013*

LAVANDOU, LE *10F3 (9km E Coastal) 43.15645, 6.44821* Parc-Camping de Prasmousquier, Ave du Capitaine Ducourneau, Pramousquier, 83980 Le Lavandou [04 94 05 83 95; fax 04 94 05 75 04; camping-lavandou@wanadoo.fr; www.campingpramousquier.com] Take D559 E fr Le Lavandou. At Pramousquier site sp on main rd; awkward bend. Lge, pt shd, terr, wc; shwrs inc; EHU (3-6A) €3.304; gas; lndry; shop; snacks; bar; playgrnd; beach sand 400m; dogs €2.10; Eng spkn. "Pleasant, relaxing, clean site; site lighting poor; gd cycle track to Le Lavandou; excel." 14 Apr-30 Sep. € 28.00   2014*

LAVANDOU, LE *10F3 (2km S Coastal) 43.11800, 6.35210* Camping du Domaine, La Favière, 2581 Route de Bénat, 83230 Bormes-les-Mimosas [04 94 71 03 12; fax 04 94 15 18 67; mail@campdudomaine.com; www.campdudomaine.com] App Le Lavandou fr Hyères on D98 & turn R on o'skts of town clearly sp La Favière. Site on L in 2.3km about 200m after ent to Domaine La Favière (wine sales) - ignore 1st lge winery. If app fr E do not go thro Le Levandou, but stay on D559 until sp to La Favière. V lge, mkd, pt shd, terr, wc; chem disp; mv service pnt; fam bthrm; shwrs inc; EHU (10A) inc (long lead poss req); gas; lndry; shop; rest; snacks; bar; bbq (gas); playgrnd; beach sand adj; entmnt; wifi; TV; 10% statics; dogs (not acc Jul/Aug); phone; Eng spkn; adv bkg req; quiet; ccard acc; tennis; games rm; CKE/CCI. "Lge pitches, some with many trees & some adj beach (direct access); well-organised site with excel facs; gd walking & attractions in area." ♦ 30 Mar-31 Oct. € 48.00   2013*

See advertisement

LAVANDOU, LE *10F3 (2km SW Coastal) 43.13386, 6.35224* Camping Beau Séjour, Quartier St Pons, 83980 Le Lavandou [04 94 71 25 30; beause jourvar@orange.fr] Take Cap Bénat rd on W o'skts of Le Lavandou. Site on L in approx 500m. Med, mkd, pt shd, wc; shwrs inc; EHU (3A) €4; shop nr; rest nr; bar nr; beach 900m. "Well-kept, clean site; rd noise on W side; gd sized pitches." ♦ Mid Apr-30 Sep. € 17.60   2014*

LAVANDOU, LE

LAVANDOU, LE *10F3 (3km W Urban) 43.13630, 6.35439* Camping St Pons, Ave Maréchal Juin, 83960 Le Lavandou [04 94 71 03 93; campingstpons@netcourrier.com; www.campingstpons.com] App fr W on D98 via La Londe. At Bormes keep R onto D559. At 1st rndabt turn R sp La Favière, at 2nd rndabt turn R, then 1st L. Site on L in 200m. Med, mkd, shd, wc; chem disp; shwrs inc; EHU (6A) inc; lndry; shop nr; rest; snacks; bar; playgrnd; beach sand 800m; entmnt; 10% statics; dogs €3.90; phone; Eng spkn; CKE/CCI. "Much improved site; helpful owner."
29 Apr-1 Oct. € 26.00   2017*

⊞ **LAVANDOU, LE** *10F3 (8km NW Rural) 43.16262, 6.32152* Camping Manjastre, 150 Chemin des Girolles, 83230 Bormes-les-Mimosas [04 94 71 03 28; fax 04 94 71 63 62; manjastre@infonie.fr; www.campingmanjastre.com] App fr W on D98 about 3km NE of where N559 branches off SE to Le Lavandou. Fr E site is 2km beyond Bormes/Collobrières x-rds; sp. Lge, mkd, hdg, pt shd, sl, terr, wc (htd); chem disp; mv service pnt; fam bthrm; shwrs inc; EHU (10A) €4.70; lndry; shop; rest; snacks; bar; bbq; playgrnd; pool; paddling pool; wifi; TV; 10% statics; dogs €1.50 (not acc Jul/Aug); Eng spkn; adv bkg acc; quiet; CKE/CCI. "Lovely site in vineyard on steep hillside with 3 san facs blocks; c'vans taken in & out by tractor; facs poss stretched in ssn; winter storage avail." ♦
€ 30.00   2015*

LAVELANET *8G4 (1km SW Urban) 42.92340, 1.84477* Camping Le Pré Cathare, Rue Jacquard, 09300 Lavelanet [05 61 01 55 54; leprecathare@orange.fr; www.leprecathare.fr] Fr Lavelanet, take D117 twd Foix & foll sp (foll sp for sports complex). Adj 'piscine'. Med, mkd, pt shd, wc (htd); chem disp; shwrs; EHU (15A) €3; lndry; shop nr; snacks; bbq; playgrnd; entmnt; wifi; TV; 80% statics; dogs €1; adv bkg acc; quiet; games area; tennis 800m; CKE/CCI. "Gd sized pitches, some with mountain views; excel san facs; poss open in winter with adv bkg; pool adj; gates locked 2200; quiet town; vg." ♦ 15 Mar-31 Oct.
€ 20.00   2017*

LEGE *2H4 (7km S Rural) 46.82899, -1.59368* Camp Municipal de la Petite Boulogne, 12 Rue du Stade, 85670 St Etienne-du-Bois [02 51 34 52 11 or 02 51 34 54 51; fax 02 51 34 54 10; la.petite.boulogne@wanadoo.fr; www.stetiennedubois-vendee.fr] S fr Legé on D978 dir Aizenay. Turn E onto D94 twd St Etienne-du-Bois. Foll sp to site. Sm, mkd, pt shd, pt sl, terr, wc; chem disp; shwrs inc; EHU (10A) €2.70; lndry; shop nr; pool; TV; dogs €2.10; Eng spkn; adv bkg acc; quiet; CKE/CCI. "Pleasant, clean site; helpful warden; san facs would be stretched if site full." ♦
1 May-1 Oct. € 15.00   2014*

⊞ **LEGE** *2H4 (10km SW Rural) 46.82121, -1.64844* Camp Municipal Les Blés d'Or, 10 rue de la Piscine, 85670 Grand'Landes [02 51 98 51 86; fax 02 51 98 53 24; mairiegrandlandes@wanadoo.fr; www.vendee-tourisme.com] Take D753 fr Legé twd St Jean-de-Monts. In 4km turn S on D81 & foll sp. Fr S on D978, turn W sp Grand-Landes. 3km N of Palluau. Sm, pt shd, pt sl, wc; chem disp; shwrs inc; EHU (16A) €2.30; gas; rest nr; bar nr; playgrnd; 30% statics; Eng spkn; adv bkg acc; quiet. "V pleasant site; height barrier only, cars 24hr access; immac but dated facs; pay at Mairie adj; v useful." € 10.50   2017*

"I need an on-site restaurant"

We do our best to make sure site information is correct, but it is always best to check any must-have facilities are still available or will be open during your visit.

LEMPDES SUR ALLAGNON *9C1 (1km N Rural) 45.38699, 3.26598* Camping Le Pont d'Allagnon (formerly CM au Delà de l'Eau), Rue René Filiol, off Route de Chambezon, 43410 Lempdes-sur-Allagnon [04 71 76 53 69; centre.auvergne.camping@orange.fr; www.campingenauvergne.com] Going S on A75 exit junc 19 (ltd access) onto D909; turn R on D654 bef vill, site sp at junc. Or fr junc 20 going N; foll sp. Site just outside vill. Med, hdg, pt shd, wc; chem disp; mv service pnt; fam bthrm; shwrs inc; EHU (16A) €3.40; lndry; shop nr; bar; playgrnd; phone; adv bkg acc; quiet; ccard acc; games rm; tennis; rv fishing; games area. "Pleasant site in beautiful area; pool 100m; conv NH A75; gd." ♦ 28 Mar-19 Oct.
€ 25.00   2014*

LEON *8E1 (4km N Rural) 43.90260, -1.31030* Camping Sunêlia Le Col Vert, Lac de Léon, 40560 Vielle-St Girons [08 90 71 00 01; fax 05 58 42 91 88; contact@colvert.com; www.colvert.com] Exit N10 junc 12; at Castets-des-Landes turn R onto D42 to Vielle-St Girons. In vill turn L onto D652 twd Léon sp Soustons. In 4km, bef Vielle, take 2nd of 2 RH turns twd Lac de Léon. Site on R at end of rd in 1.5km. V lge, shd, serviced pitches; wc; chem disp; mv service pnt; fam bthrm; shwrs inc; EHU (3A) inc; gas; lndry; shop; rest; snacks; bar; bbq (elec, gas); playgrnd; pool (covrd, htd); paddling pool; sw nr; red long stay; entmnt; wifi; TV; 60% statics; dogs €4.70; adv bkg acc; ccard acc; canoeing nr; games rm; windsurfing nr; archery; tennis; sailing nr; bike hire; fishing nr; horseriding; CKE/CCI. "Lakeside site in pine forest; fitness rm; some pitches 800m fr facs; ideal for children & teenagers; wellness cent; no c'van/m'van over 6.5m; daily mkt in Léon in ssn; excel location." ♦
12 Apr-20 Sep. € 57.40   2013*

LEON *8E1* (9km NW Coastal) *43.90830, -1.36380* **Domaine Naturiste Arna (Naturist), Arnaoutchot, 5006 Route de Pichelèbe, 40560 Vielle-St Girons [05 58 49 11 11; fax 05 58 48 57 12; contact@arna.com; www.arna.com]** Fr St Girons turn R onto D328 at Vielle sp Pichelèbe. Site in 5km on R. Lge, hdstg, shd, pt sl, wc; chem disp; mv service pnt; fam bthrm; shwrs inc; EHU (3-10A) €4.50-6.10 inc; gas; lndry; shop; rest; snacks; bar; bbq (elec, gas); playgrnd; pool (covrd, htd); paddling pool; beach sand adj; red long stay; entmnt; wifi; TV; 80% statics; dogs €3.50; Eng spkn; adv bkg acc; quiet; ccard acc; games area; golf nr; bike hire; waterslide; games rm; tennis; watersports 5km; archery. "Excel site in pine forest; Arna Forme Spa; some pitches soft sand; clean san facs, ltd LS; no o'fits over 6.5m; lake adj; spa cent; excel LS site; access lge o'fits poss diff due trees; superb beach; daily mkt in Léon in ssn; new hdstg pitches with elec/water for MH's; great facs." ♦ 9 Apr-25 Sep. € 40.00   2018*

LERAN *8G4* (2km E Rural) *42.98368, 1.93516* **Camping La Régate, Route du Lac, 09600 Léran [05 61 03 09 17; campinglaregate@gmail.com; www.campinglaregate.com]** Fr Lavelanet go N on D625, turn R onto D28 & cont to Léran. Site sp fr vill. Ent easily missed - rd past it is dead end. Med, hdg, mkd, shd, terr, wc; chem disp; fam bthrm; shwrs; EHU (8A) €3.70; lndry; shop nr; rest nr; bar; bbq; playgrnd; entmnt; 10% statics; dogs €1; phone; adv bkg acc; quiet; ccard acc; watersports. "Conv Montségur chateau; leisure cent nr; pony trekking; clean san facs; lake adj; gd location; pool adj; mkd walking & cycle rtes around adj lake." 30 Mar-26 Oct. € 33.60   2014*

LESCHERAINES *9B3* (3km SE Rural) *45.70279, 6.11158* **Camp Municipal de l'Ile, Base de Loisirs, Les Iles du Chéran, 73340 Lescheraines [04 79 63 80 00; contact@iles-du-cheran.com; www.iles-du-cheran.com]** Fr Lescheraines foll sp for Base de Loisirs. Lge, mkd, pt shd, wc; chem disp; mv service pnt; fam bthrm; shwrs inc; EHU (6-10A) €2.40-3.50; lndry; shop; rest nr; snacks; bar; bbq; playgrnd; sw; entmnt; wifi; 5% statics; dogs €1.50; phone; Eng spkn; quiet; boat hire; fishing; canoe hire; CKE/CCI. "Beautiful, scenic, lakeside setting; v helpful staff; gd walks." ♦ 19 Apr-28 Sep. € 16.50   2014*

LEUCATE PLAGE *10G1* (0km S Coastal) *42.90316, 3.05178* **Camp Municipal du Cap Leucate, Chemin de Mouret, 11370 Leucate-Plage [04 68 40 01 37; fax 04 68 40 18 34; cap.leucate@wanadoo.fr; www.mairie-leucate.fr/capleucate]** Exit A9 junc 40 onto D627 thro Leucate vill to Leucate-Plage approx 9km. Site sp. Lge, hdg, shd, wc; chem disp; mv service pnt; fam bthrm; shwrs inc; EHU (6A) €2.10 long lead req; lndry; shop nr; rest nr; bar nr; bbq; playgrnd; beach sand 100m; entmnt; TV; 60% statics; dogs €2; phone; adv bkg acc; quiet; games area; CKE/CCI. "Nice, spacious, sandy site in gd position; popular with surfers; htd pool 100m; m'van area outside; gd NH; immac new san facs (2012)." 1 Feb-30 Nov. € 18.50   2013*

LEZIGNAN CORBIERES *8F4* (10km S Rural) *43.11727, 2.73609* **Camping Le Pinada, Rue des Rousillous, 11200 Villerouge-la-Crémade [04 68 43 32 29; contact@camping-le-pinada.com; www.camping-le-pinada.com]** Fr Lézignan-Corbières on D611 S, pass airfield & fork L thro Ferrals-les-Corbières (steep, narr) on D106. Site sp & on L after 4km. Alt rte to avoid narr rd thro Ferrals: exit A61 junc 25 & foll D611 thro Fabrezan. At T-junc turn L onto D613 & after 2km turn L onto D106. Site on R after Villerouge-la-Crémade. Med, hdg, mkd, shd, pt sl, terr, wc; chem disp; fam bthrm; shwrs inc; EHU (6A) €5; lndry; shop; snacks; bar; playgrnd; pool; sw nr; entmnt; TV; 25% statics; dogs €2; Eng spkn; adv bkg req; quiet; fishing 3km; games area; tennis; CKE/CCI. "Friendly owners; gd base for Carcassonne & Med coast; bkg fee; well-run site; dated san facs; excel." ♦ 1 Mar-30 Oct. € 18.50   2012*

LEZIGNAN CORBIERES *8F4* (1km NW Urban) *43.20475, 2.75255* **Camp Municipal de la Pinède, Ave Gaston Bonheur, 11200 Lézignan-Corbières [04 68 27 05 08; reception@campinglapinede.fr; www.campinglapinede.fr]** On D6113 fr Carcassonne to Narbonne on N of rd; foll 'Piscine' & 'Restaurant Le Patio' sp. Med, hdstg, hdg, pt shd, pt sl, terr, wc; chem disp; mv service pnt; shwrs inc; EHU (6A) inc; gas; lndry; shop nr; rest; snacks; bar; bbq (gas); wifi; 5% statics; dogs €2.10; adv bkg acc; quiet; tennis; CKE/CCI. "Well-run, clean, popular site; helpful, friendly staff; gd san facs; gd m'van facs; htd pool adj; some pitches diff due high kerb; no o'fits over 5m; superb pool; mkt Wed; gd touring base or NH." ♦ 1 Apr-30 Oct. € 19.00   2015*

LEZINNES *4F4* (0km S Urban) *47.79955, 4.08957* **La Graviere du Moulin, 7 route de Frangey, 89160 Lezinnes [03 86 75 68 67 or 02 29 59 27 (mob); lagravieredumoulin@lezinnes.fr; www.gravieredumoulin.lezinnes.fr]** Fr N on Route Nationale D905 turn L onto D200, foll rd round to the R onto Route de Frangey to site. Sm, wc; shwrs inc; EHU €2.70; lndry; playgrnd; tennis; canoeing. "Gated site; football; basketball; handball; strictly run; great café in vill." 29 Mar-7 Oct. € 7.00   2013*

LICQUES *3A3* (3km E Rural) *50.77905, 1.95567* **Camping-Caravaning Le Canchy, Rue de Canchy, 62850 Licques [03 21 82 63 41; camping.lecanchy@wanadoo.fr; www.camping-lecanchy.com]** Fr Calais D127 to Guînes, then D215 sp Licques; site sp in vill on D191; site on L in 1km with narr app rd. Or fr Ardres take D224 to Liques then as above. Or A26 fr Calais exit junc 2 onto D217 dir Zouafques/Tournehem/Licques. Foll site sp in vill. Med, hdg, mkd, pt shd, wc; chem disp; shwrs; EHU (6A) €3.70; lndry; shop nr; snacks; bar; bbq; playgrnd; entmnt; 50% statics; Eng spkn; adv bkg acc; quiet; ccard acc; fishing nr; CKE/CCI. "Busy site; friendly, helpful owners; dated san facs, ltd LS; gd walking/cycling; conv Calais & ferries; vg." 15 Mar-31 Oct. € 18.00   2012*

Site report forms at back of guide

LICQUES

LICQUES *3A3* (2km SE Rural) *50.77974, 1.94766*
Camping Les Pommiers des Trois Pays, 273 Rue du Breuil, 62850 Licques [03 21 35 02 02; contact@ pommiers-3pays.com; www.pommiers-3pays.com] Fr Calais to Guînes on D127 then on D215 to Licques; take D191 fr vill & foll sp; site on L in 1km. Or exit A26 junc 2 onto D217 to Licques; turn L onto D215; cont strt on & site on L on far side of vill. NB sloping ent, long o'fits beware grounding. Med, mkd, hdg, pt shd, sl, wc; chem disp; mv service pnt; fam bthrm; shwrs inc; EHU (16A) €4.80; lndry; shop nr; rest; snacks; bar; bbq; playgrnd; pool (covrd, htd); red long stay; entmnt; wifi; TV; 65% statics; dogs €1; Eng spkn; adv bkg acc; quiet; ccard acc; games rm; golf 25km; fishing 2km; sailing 25km; games area. "Site v full early Jun, adv bkg rec; lge pitches; friendly, helpful owners; gd quality facs, ltd LS, rest clsd; gd beaches nr; gd walking; conv Calais/Dunkerque ferries; gd; excel san facs; busy, well-run site; sm pool for children; clean facs; only 0.75h fr Calais ferry." ♦ 1 Apr-31 Oct. € 19.00   2016*

LIGNY EN BARROIS *6E1* (1km W Rural) *48.68615, 5.31666* **Camp Municipal Chartel, Rue des Etats-Unis, 55500 Ligny-en-Barrois [03 29 77 09 36 or 03 29 78 02 22 (Mairie)]** If app fr E, leave N4 at Ligny-en-Barrois N exit, turn S twd town; in approx 500m turn R at junc (bef rd narr); foll sm sp, site 500m on L. If app fr W, leave N4 at exit W of town onto N135 (Rue des Etats-Unis); site sp on R. Sm, hdstg, pt shd, terr, wc (cont); own san rec; chem disp; shwrs; EHU inc; shop nr; playgrnd; sw nr; dogs; Eng spkn; fishing 500m; CKE/CCI. "Poss diff lge o'fits; modern san facs; further modernisation planned (2010); gd NH; great site and location." 1 Jun-30 Sep. € 11.00   2012*

> **"Satellite navigation makes touring much easier"**
>
> Remember most sat navs don't know if you're towing or in a larger vehicle – always use yours alongside maps and site directions.

LIGNY LE CHATEL *4F4* (1km SW Rural) *47.89542, 3.75288* **Camp Municipal La Noue Marrou, 89144 Ligny-le-Châtel [03 86 47 56 99 or 03 86 47 41 20 (Mairie); fax 03 86 47 44 02; camping.lignylechatel@ orange.fr; www.mairie-ligny-le-chatel-89.fr]** Exit A6 at junc 20 Auxerre S onto D965 to Chablis. In Chablis cross rv & turn L onto D91 dir Ligny. On ent Ligny turn L onto D8 at junc after Maximart. Cross sm rv, foll sp to site on L in 200m. Sm, mkd, pt shd, wc; chem disp; mv service pnt; shwrs inc; EHU (10A) inc (poss rev pol, poss long lead req); lndry; shop; rest; snacks; bar; playgrnd; sw nr; wifi; dogs; phone; bus 200m; quiet; tennis; CKE/CCI. "Well-run site; lge pitches; no twin axles; friendly warden lives on site; san facs dated but clean; pleasant vill with gd rests; popular NH; excel." ♦ 1 May-30 Sep. € 12.00   2014*

LIGUEIL *4H2* (2km N Rural) *47.05469, 0.84615* **Camping de la Touche, Ferme de la Touche, 37240 Ligueil [02 47 59 54 94; booklatouche@hotmail. co.uk; www.theloirevalley.com]** Fr Loches SW on D31; turn L at x-rds with white cross on R 2km after Ciran; in 500m turn R, site on R bef hotel. Fr A10 exit junc 25 Ste Maure-de-Touraine & foll sp to Ligueil; then take D31 dir Loches; turn L at white cross. Sm, mkd, hdstg, pt shd, wc; chem disp; shwrs; EHU (10A) €5; lndry; shop; snacks; playgrnd; pool; wifi; dogs free; adv bkg acc; quiet; ccard acc; bike hire; fishing; CKE/CCI. "Well-maintained, relaxed CL-type site; lge pitches; welcoming, helpful British owners; c'van storage; excel san facs; gd walking & touring base; much wild life; conv m'way; gd; cycling dist fr pleasant vill." € 15.50   2015*

⊞ **LILLEBONNE** *3C2* (4km W Rural) *49.53024, 0.49576* **Camping Hameau des Forges, 76170 St Antoine-la-Forêt [02 35 39 80 28 or 02 35 91 48 30]** Fr Le Havre take rd twds Tancarville bdge, D982 into Lillebonne, D81 W to site on R in 4km, sp (pt winding rd). Fr S over Tancarville bdge onto D910 sp Bolbec. At 2nd rndabt turn R onto D81, site 5km on L. NB Concealed ent by phone box. Med, pt shd, wc; chem disp; shwrs; EHU (5A) inc; 90% statics; dogs; adv bkg acc; quiet; CKE/CCI. "Basic, clean, open site; staff welcoming & helpful; poss statics only LS & facs ltd; site muddy when wet; conv NH for Le Havre ferries late arr & early dep; Roman amphitheatre in town worth visit." € 10.00   2015*

LIMOGES *7B3* (5km N Rural) *45.86949, 1.27625* **Camping d'Uzurat, 40 Ave d'Uzurat, 87280 Limoges [05 55 38 49 43; contact@campinglimoges.fr; www.campinglimoges.fr]** Fr N twd Limoges on A20 take exit 30 sp Limoges Nord Zone Industrielle, Lac d'Uzurat; foll sp to Lac d'Uzurat & site. Fr S twd Limoges on A20 exit junc 31 & foll sp as above. Well sp fr A20. Lge, hdstg, pt shd, serviced pitches; wc (htd); chem disp; mv service pnt; fam bthrm; shwrs inc; EHU (10A) €3.60; lndry; shop nr; playgrnd; red long stay; wifi; 10% statics; dogs €1.50; phone; bus; Eng spkn; quiet; ccard acc; lake fishing; CKE/CCI. "Lovely site by lake; gd sized pitches; friendly & helpful staff; clean modern san facs; pitch on chippings - awnings diff; hypmkt 500m; poss red opening dates - phone ahead LS; poss mkt traders;m'van o'night area; conv martyr vill Oradour-sur-Glane; gd touring base; conv m'way; popular NH; frequent bus into city." ♦ 15 Mar-31 Oct. € 19.00   2017*

LIMOGNE EN QUERCY *7D4* (1km W Rural) *44.39571, 1.76396* **Camp Municipal Bel-Air, 46260 Limogne-en-Quercy [05 65 24 32 75; fax 05 65 24 73 59; camping. bel-air@orange.fr]** E fr Cahors on D911 just bef Limogne vill. W fr Villefranche on D911 just past vill; 3 ents about 50m apart. Sm, mkd, shd, sl, wc; shwrs inc; EHU (6A) inc; lndry; shop nr; bar nr; pool; adv bkg rec; quiet. "Friendly welcome; if warden absent, site yourself; pleasant vill." 1 Apr-1 Oct. € 18.00   2014*

LIMOUX *8G4* (0km SE Urban) *43.04734, 2.22280*
Camp Municipal du Breilh, Ave Salvador Allende, 11300 Limoux [04 68 31 13 63; fax 04 68 31 18 43; limoux@limoux.fr] Fr D118 cross bdge to E side of Rv Aude, then S on D129 Ave de Corbières & foll site sp. Not well sp on ent town fr N. Sm, pt sl, wc; shwrs; EHU (6A) €2.90; shop nr; quiet; boating; tennis adj; fishing. "Basic rvside site; pleasant town; suitable sh stay; pool adj; staff exceptionally kind & helpful; san facs poor." 1 Jun-30 Sep. € 15.00   2014*

LION D'ANGERS, LE *2G4* (1km N Rural) *47.63068, -0.71190* Camp Municipal Les Frênes, Route de Château-Gontier, 49220 Le Lion-d'Angers [02 41 95 31 56; fax 02 41 95 34 87; mairie.lelionangers@wanadoo.fr; www.leliondangers.fr] On N162 Laval-Angers rd, site on R bef bdge over Rv Oudon app Le Lion-d'Angers, easily missed. Med, mkd, pt shd, wc; chem disp; shwrs inc; EHU (10A) €2.75; lndry; shop nr; rest; bbq; playgrnd; phone; Eng spkn; adv bkg acc; quiet; rv fishing adj; CKE/CCI. "Excel site; friendly staff; gd location; wc block up 2 flights steps; no m'vans; unrel opening dates - phone ahead." ♦ 18 May-1 Sep. € 6.40   2013*

LISIEUX *3D1* (2km N Rural) *49.16515, 0.22054* Camp Municipal de La Vallée, 9 Rue de la Vallée, 14100 Lisieux [02 31 62 00 40 or 02 31 48 18 10 (LS); fax 02 31 48 18 11; tourisme@cclisieuxpaysdauge.fr; www.lisieux-tourisme.com] N on D579 fr Lisieux twd Pont l'Evêque. Approx 500m N of Lisieux take L to Coquainvilliers onto D48 & foll sp for Camping (turn L back in Lisieux dir). Site on D48 parallel to main rd. On app to site look for Volvo dealer & Super U supmkt. Med, hdstg, pt shd, wc; chem disp; shwrs inc; EHU (6A) €2.50-4.50; gas; shop nr; rest nr; bar nr; 20% statics; bus fr ent; CKE/CCI. "Interesting town, childhood home of St Thérèse; helpful warden; v clean san facs; gd." 1 Apr-30 Sep. € 14.30   2017*

LISLE *7C3* (6km SW Rural) *45.25731, 0.49573* Camp Municipal Le Pré Sec, 24350 Tocane-St Apre [05 53 90 40 60 or 05 53 90 70 29; fax 05 53 90 25 03; commune-de-tocane-st-apre@orange.fr; www.campingdupresec.com] Fr Ribérac E on D710 sp Brantôme. Fr E or W at Tocane St Apre, take bypass rd at rndabt. Site sp at both rndabts - dist 500m. Site is on N side of D710 (fr Riberac dir, there is a gab bet cent reservation to turn L.) Ent thro lge car park for Tocan Sports, barrier to site 100m back. Med, hdg, shd, wc; chem disp; mv service pnt; fam bthrm; shwrs; EHU (6-10A) €1.80; shop nr; bbq; playgrnd; twin axles; wifi; 10% statics; dogs; phone; bus 200m; Eng spkn; adv bkg acc; quiet; CKE/CCI. "Gd; canoeing nrby on Rv Dronne." ♦ 2 May-30 Sep. € 9.00   2014*

LOCHES *4H2* (1km S Urban) *47.12255, 1.00175*
Kawan Village La Citadelle, Ave Aristide Briand, 37600 Loches [02 47 59 05 91 or 06 21 37 93 06 (mob); fax 02 47 59 00 35; camping@lacitadelle.com; www.lacitadelle.com] Fr any dir take by-pass to S end of town & leave at Leclerc rndabt for city cent; site well sp on R in 800m. Lge, hdg, mkd, pt shd, wc (htd); chem disp; mv service pnt; shwrs inc; EHU (10A) €4.70 (poss rev pol) (poss long lead req); gas; lndry; shop; rest; snacks; bar; bbq; playgrnd; pool (htd); red long stay; entmnt; wifi; TV; 30% statics; dogs €3; Eng spkn; adv bkg rec; ccard acc; golf 9km; tennis nr; boating; games area; bike hire; fishing; CKE/CCI. "Attractive, well-kept, busy site nr beautiful old town; views of citadel; gd sized pitches, poss uneven; helpful staff; facs poss stretched; barrier clsd 2200-0800; poss no night security (2010); rvside walk into town; poss mosquitoes; site muddy after heavy rain; mkt Wed & Sat am; excel site; lge serviced pitches; sh walk to a beautiful medieval town." ♦ 26 Mar-7 Oct. € 31.70   2016*

LOCMARIAQUER *2G3* (2km S Coastal) *47.55598, 2.93939* Camp Municipal de la Falaise, Route de Kerpenhir, 56740 Locmariaquer [02 97 57 31 59 or 02 97 57 32 32 (LS); campinglafalaise@wanadoo.fr; www.campingmunicipallafalaise.com]
Site sp fr Locmariaquer. On ent vill, site sp R avoiding narr cent (also sp fr vill cent). Lge, mkd, pt sl, wc; chem disp; mv service pnt; shwrs; EHU (6A) inc; gas; lndry; shop nr; rest; playgrnd; beach sand adj; entmnt; wifi; dogs €2.10; ccard acc. "Gd, quiet, well run site in pleasant countryside; clean san facs, some modern & some dated; archaeological remains; gd fishing, boating, cycling & coastal walking; rest simple but superb food." ♦ 15 Mar-15 Oct. € 16.50   2014*

LOCMARIAQUER *2G3* (2km NW Coastal) *47.57982, - 2.97394* Camping Lann Brick, Lieu Dit Lann-Brick, 56740 Locmariaquer [02 97 57 32 79 or 06 42 22 29 69 (mob); camping.lanbrick@wanadoo.fr; www.camping-lannbrick.com] N165/E60, exit Crach via D28 dir Locmariaquer. L Onto D781. Sp on R 2km bef Locmariaquer. Med, mkd, hdg, shd, wc cont; chem disp; mv service pnt; fam bthrm; shwrs inc; EHU (6/10A); lndry; shop nr; snacks; bar; bbq; playgrnd; pool (htd); paddling pool; beach 0.5km; twin axles; entmnt; wifi; TV; 40% statics; dogs €2.60; phone; bus adj; Eng spkn; adv bkg acc; quiet; ccard acc; bike hire; CKE/CCI. "Gd; quiet well managed site; helpful & friendly owners; facs well maintained & spotless; easy walk to beach; delightful site; gd location for Gulf of Morbihan; easy cycle rte; hg hdg." ♦ 17 Mar-31 Oct. € 26.00   2014*

LOCQUIREC

⊞ **LOCQUIREC** *2E2* (2km SW Coastal) **48.67940, -3.65320** Camping Municipal Du fond de la Baie, Route de Plestin, 29241 Locquirec [02 98 67 40 85; campingdufonddelabaie@gmail.com; www.campinglocquirec.com] Fr D786 Morlaix-Lannion, turn L (traff lts) at Plestin-Les-Graves onto D42. At T junc on reaching Bay turn L onto D64. Site on R on app Locquirec. Lge, mkd, pt shd, wc; chem disp; mv service pnt; shwrs; gas; lndry; shop; rest; snacks; bar; bbq; beach sand adj; twin axles; entmnt; wifi; 6% statics; dogs €1; phone; bus adj; Eng spkn; adv bkg acc; quiet; ccard acc. "Beautifully situated beachside site; vill 1.5km; flat site; fishing, boating & shellfishing; gd." ♦ € 19.00   2016*

LOCRONAN *2E2* (1km ESE Urban) **48.09657, -4.19774** Camping de Locronan, Rue de la Troménie, 29180 Locronan [02 98 91 87 76 or 06 28 80 44 74; contact@camping-locronan.fr; www.camping-locronan.fr] Fr Quimper/Douarnenez foll sp D7 Châteaulin; ignore town sp, take 1st R after 3rd rndabt. Fr Châteaulin, turn L at 1st town sp & foll site sp at sharp L turn. NB Foll sp around town, do not ent Locronan. Med, hdg, pt shd, terr, wc; chem disp; fam bthrm; shwrs; EHU (10A) €4.30; lndry; shop nr; rest nr; bar nr; playgrnd; pool (covrd, htd); paddling pool; wifi; dogs €2.20; phone; Eng spkn; adv bkg rec; quiet; ccard acc; games area; CKE/CCI. "Gd touring cent with gd views; gd walks; historic town; excel; ltd san facs LS." ♦ 13 Apr-10 Nov. € 32.00   2013*

⊞ **LODEVE** *10E1* (6km SE Rural) **43.69198, 3.35030** Camping Les Peupliers, Les Casseaux, 34700 Le Bosc [04 67 44 38 08; contact@camping-les-peupliers-salagou.com; www.camping-les-peupliers-salagou.com] Take exit 54 on A75; sp Le Bosc. Med, mkd, pt shd, pt sl, terr, wc; shwrs inc; EHU (5A) €2; gas; shop nr; snacks; bar; playgrnd; pool; wifi; 90% statics; dogs €1; Eng spkn; adv bkg acc; CKE/CCI. "Friendly staff; ltd facs LS; recep clsd LS, phone ahead; windsurfing Lac du Salagou; easy access fr m'way; conv winter NH." ♦ € 20.00   2014*

LODEVE *10E1* (3km S Urban) **43.71247, 3.32179** Camping Les Vals, 2000 route de Puech, 34700 Lodève [04 30 40 17 80 or 06 04 01 18 78; camping lesvals@yahoo.fr; www.camping-les-vals.org] Fr N: A75 exit 52 dir Lodéve. Foll av. Fumel, not the cent. R over Vinas bdge dir Puech. Fr S: A75 exit 53 dir Lodéve cent dir Puech on Vinas bdge. 2km on the D148. Med, hdg, mkd, pt shd, pt sl, terr, wc; chem disp; mv service pnt; shwrs; EHU (6A); lndry; shop; rest; snacks; bar; playgrnd; pool; paddling pool; sw nr; entmnt; wifi; TV; 30% statics; dogs; phone; Eng spkn; adv bkg acc; quiet; games area; watersports adj; games rm; bike hire; tennis; rv fishing adj; CKE/CCI. "Gd site; v ltd facs LS." ♦ 15 Apr-30 Oct. € 26.00   2015*

LODEVE *10E1* (9km S Rural) **43.67182, 3.35429** Camp Municipal Les Vailhés, Baie des Vailhes, Lac du Salagou, 34700 Lodève [04 11 95 01 82; camping@lodevoisetlarzac.fr; www.campinglesvailhes.com] Fr N exit A75 junc 54 onto D148 dir Octon & Lac du Salagou. Foll site sp. Fr S exit A75 junc 55. Lge, hdg, mkd, pt shd, terr, wc; chem disp; shwrs inc; EHU (16A) inc; lndry; bbq; playgrnd; sw; 20% statics; dogs; Eng spkn; quiet; fishing; watersports; CKE/CCI. "Peaceful, remote site by lake; pleasant staff; no facs nrby; excel walks; gd." ♦ 1 Apr-30 Sep. € 8.00   2018*

LODEVE *10E1* (6km W Rural) **43.73631, 3.26443** Camping Domaine de Lambeyran (Naturist), Lambeyran, 34700 Lodève [04 67 44 13 99; fax 04 67 44 09 91; lambeyran@wanadoo.fr; www.lambeyran.com] Fr N or S on N9 take sliprd to Lodève. Leave town on D35 W twd Bédarieux. In 2km take 2nd R, sp L'Ambeyran & St Martin. Foll sp 3.7km up winding hill to site. Lge, hdg, mkd, pt shd, pt sl, terr, wc; chem disp; shwrs inc; EHU (6A) €4.20; gas; lndry; shop nr; rest; snacks; bar; bbq; playgrnd; pool; red long stay; 5% statics; dogs; phone; Eng spkn; adv bkg acc; quiet; ccard acc; windsurfing 10km; CKE/CCI. "Superb location with views; lge pitches; sailing 10km; gd walking, inc on site; gates clsd 2000; Lac du Salagou with sports facs 12km." 20 May-20 Sep. € 33.00   2014*

LONGEVILLE SUR MER *7A1* (2km S Coastal) **46.40402, -1.50673** Camp Le Petit Rocher, 1250 Ave du Dr Mathevet, 85560 Longeville-sur-Mer [02 51 20 41 94; fax 02 51 22 11 09; info@campinglepetitrocher.com; www.campinglepetitrocher.com] Fr La Tranche-sur-Mer take D105 N. In 8km note clearly sp 'Le Rocher' at 3rd exit fr rndabt (Ave du Dr Mathevet). Site on R in 1km at beginning of beach rd. Lge, mkd, hdg, shd, pt sl, wc; chem disp; shwrs inc; EHU (6A) inc; gas; shop nr; rest nr; playgrnd; beach sand 150m; entmnt; 10% statics; dogs €3; adv bkg acc; quiet; bike hire; games area; games rm; CKE/CCI. "Gd beach holiday; gd facs." 1 May-20 Sep. € 33.00   2014*

LONGEVILLE SUR MER *7A1* (2km S Coastal) **46.39499, -1.48736** Camping Le Sous-Bois, La Haute Saligotière, 85560 Longeville-sur-Mer [02 51 33 32 73 or 02 51 33 36 90 or 06 71 63 39 62 (mob)] Sp fr D105 fr La Tranche-sur-Mer. Med, hdg, shd, wc; chem disp; shwrs inc; EHU (10A) €4 (poss rev pol); lndry; shop; playgrnd; beach sand 1km; TV; 15% statics; dogs €1.60; phone; quiet; tennis; CKE/CCI. "Nice, well-managed, family site; pleasant 1km woodland walk to beach; gd walks; cycle tracks; excel; great for cycling; lovely sandy beach." ♦ 1 Jun-30 Sep. € 19.00   2013*

LONGEVILLE SUR MER *7A1* (3km SW Coastal) *46.41310, -1.52280* **Camping Les Brunelles, Rue de la Parée, Le Bouil, 85560 Longeville-sur-Mer [02 51 33 50 75; fax 02 51 33 98 21; camping@les-brunelles.com; www.les-brunelles.com]** Site bet Longeville-sur-Mer & Jard-sur-Mer; foll D21. Lge, mkd, pt shd, pt sl, wc; mv service pnt; fam bthrm; shwrs inc; EHU (10A) inc; lndry; shop; rest nr; snacks; bar; playgrnd; pool (covrd, htd); paddling pool; beach sand 800m; entmnt; wifi; TV; 75% statics; dogs €5; adv bkg acc; ccard acc; gym; sauna; bike hire; horseriding 2km; games area; waterslide; watersports; tennis; golf 15km. "Gd san facs." ♦ 7 Apr-22 Sep. € 25.00   2017*

LONS LE SAUNIER *6H2* (3km NE Rural) *46.68437, 5.56843* **Camping La Marjorie, 640 Blvd de l'Europe, 39000 Lons-le-Saunier [03 84 24 26 94; fax 03 84 24 08 40; info@camping-marjorie.com; www.camping-marjorie.com]** Site clearly sp in town on D1083 twd Besançon. Fr N bear R dir 'Piscine', cross under D1083 to site. Lge, hdstg, hdg, pt shd, terr, wc; chem disp; fam bthrm; shwrs inc; EHU (10A) inc (poss rev pol); gas; lndry; shop; snacks; bar; playgrnd; pool (covrd, htd); twin axles; entmnt; wifi; dogs €2.60; phone; Eng spkn; ccard acc; golf 8km; games area; CKE/CCI. "Lovely site in beautiful area; conv location; lge pitches; welcoming, friendly, helpful owners; excel, spotless san facs; 20 mins walk to interesting old town & Laughing Cow Museum; ideal touring base; rec; excel; by busy main rd; well run; aquatic cent adj; red facs in LS." ♦ 1 Apr-15 Oct. € 24.00   2015*

⊞ **LORIENT** *2F2* (6km N Rural) *47.82041, -3.40689* **Camping Ty Nénez, Route de Lorient, 56620 Pont-Scorff [02 97 32 51 16; fax 02 97 32 43 77; contact@camping-tynenez.com; www.lorient-camping.com]** N fr N165 on D6, look for sp Quéven in approx 5km on R. If missed, cont for 1km & turn around at rndabt. Site sp fr Pont-Scorff. Med, hdg, pt shd, wc (htd); chem disp; mv service pnt; fam bthrm; shwrs inc; EHU (16A) €3; lndry; shop nr; rest; bar; bbq; pool (htd); wifi; 10% statics; dogs €1; Eng spkn; adv bkg acc; quiet; games area. "Site barrier locked 2200-0800; excel LS; peaceful NH; tidy, organised site; excel htd facs; gd base for S Brittany." ♦ € 29.00   2017*

LORIENT *2F2* (10km NE Rural) *47.80582, -3.28347* **Camp Municipal St Caradec, Quai St Caradec, 56700 Hennebont [02 97 36 21 73; camping.municipal.stcaradec@wanadoo.fr; www.morbihan.com]** Fr S on D781 to Hennebont. In town cent turn L & cross bdge, then sharp R along Rv Blavet for 1km. On R on rv bank. Med, mkd, pt shd, wc; chem disp; shwrs inc; EHU inc; lndry; shop nr; playgrnd; 10% statics; adv bkg acc; quiet; CKE/CCI. "Pretty site; excel fishing; peaceful; pleasant sh walk into sm town." ♦ 15 Jun-15 Sep. € 13.00   2015*

LOUDEAC *2E3* (2km E Urban) *48.17764, -2.72834* **Campsite Seasonova Aquarev, Les Ponts es Bigots, 22600 Loudéac [02 96 26 21 92; contact@camping-aquarev.com; www.vacances-seasonova.com]** Fr Loudeac take N164 twrds Rennes. Site on L by lake. Med, mkd, pt shd, wc; chem disp; mv service pnt; fam bthrm; shwrs; EHU (10A) inc; lndry; snacks; playgrnd; wifi; 10% statics; dogs; adv bkg acc; games area; CKE/CCI. "Walks; tennis; fishing; archery; vg." ♦ 31 Mar-15 Oct. € 19.00   2017*

LOUDUN *4H1* (1km W Rural) *47.00379, 0.06337* **Camp Municipal de Beausoleil, Chemin de l'Etang, 86200 Loudun [05 49 98 14 22 or 05 49 98 15 38; fax 05 49 98 12 88; mairie@ville-loudun.fr; www.ville-loudun.fr]** On main rte fr Poitiers to Saumur/Le Mans; N on D347 around Loudun, foll sp; turn L just N of level x-ing, then on R approx 250m. Sm, hdg, mkd, pt shd, terr, wc; shwrs inc; EHU (10A) €3.15; shop nr; playgrnd; bus adj; Eng spkn; quiet; lake fishing adj; CKE/CCI. "Beautiful, well-kept site; lge pitches; site yourself, warden calls am & pm; friendly & helpful; excel; long way fr the town." ♦ 15 May-31 Aug. € 12.00   2014*

> **"There aren't many sites open at this time of year"**
>
> If you're travelling outside peak season remember to call ahead to check site opening dates – even if the entry says 'open all year'.

LOUHANS *6H1* (2km W Urban) *46.62286, 5.21733* **Camp Municipal de Louhans, 10, Chemin de la Chapellerie, 71500 Louhans [03 85 75 19 02 or 03 85 76 75 10 (Mairie); fax 03 85 76 75 11; mairiedelouhanschateaurenaud@yahoo.fr]** In Louhans foll sp for Romenay on D971. Go under rlwy & over rv. Site on L just after stadium. Med, hdg, mkd, hdstg, shd, wc; chem disp; shwrs inc; EHU €3.60; lndry; snacks; playgrnd; sw nr; adv bkg acc; CKE/CCI. "Rv location; clean & well-appointed; sports complex adj; lovely cycling area; tennis courts adj; mv service pnt nr; lge town mkt Mon am; poss travellers; vg." ♦ 1 Apr-30 Sep. € 7.40   2012*

LOURDES *8F2* (1km N Urban) *43.09697, -0.04336* **Camping de la Poste, 26 Rue de Langelle, 65100 Lourdes [05 62 94 40 35]** Fr NW take D940/D914 sp Centre Ville. At traff lts turn R. Go under rlwy bdge, at rndabt take 2nd exit sp Centre Ville. In 400m at La Poste turn L into Rue de Langelle. Site on R in 400m sp "Camping". Entry thro archway. Fr NE take N21/D914 sp Cent Ville. Sm, pt shd, wc; mv service pnt; shwrs; EHU (3-10A); train 500m; bus 1km; adv bkg acc; quiet; CKE/CCI. "Well supervised by friendly, helpful owners; excel food mkt; basic facs; gd NH." ♦ 1 Apr-30 Sep. € 12.50   2016*

LOURDES

LOURDES 8F2 (1km NE Urban) 43.10247, -0.02789
Camping de Sarsan, 4 Ave Jean Moulin, 65100 Lourdes [05 62 94 43 09; camping.sarsan@wanadoo.fr; www.lourdes-camping.com] Fr N on N21 past airport, on app to Lourdes turn L sp 'Zone Indust du Monge'. Pass Cmp Le Moulin du Monge & foll site sp for approx 2km. Site on L immed after x-rds. Med, pt shd, pt sl, wc; chem disp; mv service pnt; shwrs inc; EHU (4-10A) pos rev pol €2.50-4.60; lndry; shop; pool; wifi; TV; 10% statics; dogs free; adv bkg acc; quiet; games rm; games area. "Easy 25min walk to town cent." 15 Apr-15 Oct. € 13.00   2012*

LOURDES 8F2 (3km W Rural) 43.09561, -0.07463 **Camping La Forêt, Route de la Forêt, 65100 Lourdes [05 62 94 04 38; fax 05 62 42 14 86; campingdelaforet65@orange.fr; www.campingdelaforet.fr]** Fr N on N21 exit onto D914 to Lourdes; on ent Lourdes turn L off D914 under rlwy bdge dir Cent Ville & hospital; in 100m turn R onto Rue de Pau sp St Pé & Bétharram; in 1km turn L over rv bdge; site in 1km. Med, mkd, pt shd, wc; mv service pnt; shwrs; EHU (3-10A) €2.60-7.60; gas; lndry; shop; rest; snacks; bar; playgrnd; 10% statics; dogs €1.30; Eng spkn; adv bkg acc; quiet; ccard acc; CKE/CCI. "Lovely site; helpful owners; conv town cent & grotto (1km); poss open outside stated dates - adv bkg req; ideal site to visit Lourdes." 29 Mar-31 Oct. € 27.00   2014*

LOUROUX, LE 4G2 (0km N Rural) 47.16270, 0.78697 **Camping à la Ferme La Chaumine (Baudoin), 37240 Le Louroux [02 47 92 82 09 or 06 85 45 68 10 (mob); bruno.baudoin@free.fr]** Fr Tours, take D50 S for 30km. Site immed on R bef Le Louroux. Sm, hdg, shd, wc; chem disp; shwrs inc; EHU (10A) inc; bbq; playgrnd; dogs; bus 200m; Eng spkn; adv bkg acc; quiet. "Superb CL-type site nr quaint vill; helpful owners; gd, clean san facs; gd walks fr site." 1 May-15 Oct. € 11.50   2013*

LOUVIE JUZON 8F2 (1km E Rural) 43.08940, -0.41019 **FFCC Camping Le Rey, Quartier Listo, Route de Lourdes, 64260 Louvie-Juzon [05 59 05 78 52; fax 05 59 05 78 97; nadia@camping-pyrenees-ossau.com; www.camping-pyrenees-ossau.com]** Site on L at top of hill E fr Louvie; v steep app. Sm, mkd, pt shd, pt sl, wc (htd); chem disp; shwrs inc; EHU (6A) €3.30; lndry; shop nr; rest nr; snacks; bar; playgrnd; pool; entmnt; wifi; 50% statics; dogs €2; phone; adv bkg acc; quiet; site clsd last 2 weeks Nov & last 2 weeks Jan; watersports nr; fishing nr; games area; CKE/CCI. "Fascinating area; chateau nr; lovely, friendly site; not all facs open in LS; nice town." ♦ 1 Jan-15 Jan, 1 Feb-15 Nov & 1 Dec-31 Dec. € 22.00   2015*

LOUVIE JUZON 8F2 (1km S Rural) 43.08277, -0.42050 **Camp Municipal de la Vallée d'Ossau, Route d'Ossau, 64260 Izeste [05 59 05 68 67; fax 05 59 05 73 82; mairie.izeste@9business.fr]** Site 300m fr rv bdge in Louvie-Juzon, on L heading S on D934. Sm, mkd, shd, wc; shwrs inc; EHU (6A) inc; shop nr; rest nr; adv bkg acc; quiet; CKE/CCI. "Vg, attractive site adj fast-flowing rv & weir; ideal for access to Vallée d'Ossau; some rd & water noise; incredibly helpful & friendly site manager." 1 Jun-15 Sep. € 14.60   2014*

LOUVIERS 3D2 (4km W Rural) 49.21490, 1.13279 **Camping Le Bel Air, Route de la Haye-Malherbe, Hameau de St-Lubin, 27400 Louviers [02 32 40 10 77; contact@camping-lebelair.fr; www.camping-lebelair.fr]** Site well sp in Louviers. Fr cent foll D81 W for 2.5km dir La Haye-Malherbe; twisting rd uphill; site on R. Or if travelling S leave A13 at junc 19 to Louviers & as bef. NB In town cent look for sm green sp after Ecole Communale (on L) & bef Jardin Public - a narr rd (1-way) & easy to miss. Med, mkd, hdg, hdstg, shd, wc; chem disp; mv service pnt; shwrs inc; EHU (6A) €4.90; gas; lndry; shop nr; playgrnd; pool (htd); wifi; 30% statics; dogs €2.50; Eng spkn; adv bkg acc; quiet; ccard acc; CKE/CCI. "Access to pitches diff long o'fits, poss mover req; check barrier opening times; bowling; poss NH only (2013); gd site and dog walks on site; handy for Newhaven Dieppe rte." 15 Mar-15 Oct. € 24.00   2016*

LUCHON 8G3 (2km N Rural) 42.80806, 0.59667 **Camping Pradelongue, 31110 Moustajon [05 61 79 86 44; fax 05 61 79 18 64; contact@camping-pradelongue.com; www.camping-pradelongue.com]** Site is on D125c on W of D125 main rd fr Luchon. Ent at Moustajon/Antignac going S. Site adj Intermarché; sp. Lge, mkd, hdg, pt shd, wc; chem disp; mv service pnt; fam bthrm; shwrs inc; EHU (2-10A) €2-4; lndry; shop nr; bbq; playgrnd; pool (htd); wifi; 10% statics; dogs €2; Eng spkn; adv bkg acc; quiet; ccard acc; games area; CKE/CCI. "Excel, well-run, tidy, big site; mountain views; gd sized pitches; friendly, helpful owners; rec; excel clean san facs; big supmkt adj; 20mins walk to lovely town; excel for walking, mountain & rd cycling." ♦ 1 Apr-30 Sep. € 26.00   2015*

LUCON 7A1 (11km E Rural) 46.46745, -1.02792 **Camp Municipal Le Vieux Chêne, Rue du Port, 85370 Nalliers [02 51 30 91 98 or 02 51 30 90 71; fax 02 51 30 94 06; nalliers.mairie@wanadoo.fr]** Fr Luçon E on D949 dir Fontenay-le-Comte; 500m after ent Nalliers turn R onto D10 (Rue de Brantome); after level x-ing cont strt on for 50m (leaving D10); then Rue du Port on L. Site sp on D949 but easy to miss. Sm, hdg, mkd, pt shd, wc; chem disp; shwrs inc; EHU (4-13A) €3.90; shop nr; playgrnd; adv bkg acc; quiet; CKE/CCI. "Excel, clean site; site yourself on lge pitch; in LS contact Mairie for ent to site; vg NH; conv for rd to Bordeaux." 15 May-15 Sep. € 14.50   2015*

LUCON *7A1 (17km SE Rural) 46.39174, -01.01952*
Camping l'île Cariot, Rue Du 8 Mai, 85450 Chaillé-les-Marais [02 5156 7527; camping.ilecariot@gmail.com; camping-chaille-les-marais.com]
In Chaille take D25, sp in town. Sm, mkd, pt shd, wc (htd); chem disp; mv service pnt; fam bthrm; shwrs; EHU (10A) €3.90; lndry; shop nr; snacks; bar; bbq; playgrnd; pool (htd); entmnt; wifi; TV; dogs €1.65; bus adj; Eng spkn; adv bkg acc; quiet; games area; games rm; CKE/CCI. "Cycle & walking rtes fr site; nr 'Green Venice'; free canoeing on canal; excel." ♦ 1 Apr-30 Sep. € 19.00   2016*

LUDE, LE *4G1 (1km NE Rural) 47.65304, 0.16221*
Camp Municipal au Bord du Loir, Route du Mans, 72800 Le Lude [02 43 94 67 70; camping@ville-lelude.fr; www.camping-lelude.com]
Fr town cent take D305 (E); in 1km take D307 (N) sp 'Le Mans'; site immed on L. Well sp. Fr E on D305, avoid cent of Vaas, use HGV route. Med, mkd, hdg, pt shd, wc; chem disp; mv service pnt; shwrs inc; EHU (10A) inc; lndry; shop nr; rest nr; bbq (gas); playgrnd; pool; entmnt; wifi; TV; 10% statics; dogs; phone; Eng spkn; adv bkg acc; ccard acc; fishing; cycling; tennis; canoeing; CKE/CCI. "Well-kept, well-run site; warm welcome, helpful staff; modern san facs; vg walk to town; Château du Lude & excel rest nrby; highly rec; gd." ♦ 1 Apr-4 Oct. € 13.00   2016*

LUNEL *10E2 (3km S Rural) 43.65666, 4.14111*
Camping Le Bon Port, 383 Chemin de Mas St Angé, 34400 Lunel [04 67 71 15 65; fax 04 67 83 60 27; contact@campingbonport.com; www.campingbonport.com] Exit A9 junc 27 S dir La Grande Motte, D61. Site sp on L. Lge, mkd, hdg, pt shd, wc; fam bthrm; shwrs inc; EHU (5A) €4; lndry; shop; rest; snacks; bar; bbq (gas); playgrnd; pool; paddling pool; entmnt; wifi; TV; 50% statics; dogs €3.50; adv bkg acc; quiet; games area; waterslide. "Site scruffy; ltd facs out of ssn; narr site rds; new leisure pools being completed (2015)." ♦ 4 Apr-30 Sep. € 37.00   2015*

LUNEVILLE *6E2 (1km NE Urban) 48.59650, 6.49871*
Camping Les Bosquets, 63 Quai des petit, 54300 Lunéville [03 83 74 05 00; fax 03 83 74 16 27; camping@cc-lunevillois.fr; www.cc-lunevillois.fr]
Exit N333 Lunéville by-pass sp `Lunéville-Château' & foll sp to Lunéville. Fr traff lts in sq in front of chateau, take rd to L of chateau (Quai des Bosquets). At sm rndabt do not ent site on R but cont round rndabt to L to yard opp warden's house. Warden will open barrier. Sm, mkd, pt shd, terr, wc; chem disp; shwrs inc; EHU (10-15A) €2.55; lndry; shop nr; wifi; dogs; CKE/CCI. "Friendly staff; rec visit adj chateau gardens; rd noise on bottom pitches; pool 200m; vg." ♦ 20 Apr-30 Sep. € 14.00   2014*

LUSIGNAN *7A2 (1km N Rural) 46.43712, 0.12369*
Camp Municipal de Vauchiron, Chemin de la Plage, 86600 Lusignan [05 49 43 30 08 or 05 49 43 31 48 (Mairie); fax 05 49 43 61 19; lusignan@cg86.fr; www.lusignan.fr] Site sp fr D611, 22km SW of Poitiers; foll camp sp in Lusignan to rvside. Med, pt shd, wc; chem disp; fam bthrm; shwrs inc; EHU (15A) €2.40 (poss rev pol); lndry; shop nr; snacks; bar nr; bbq; playgrnd; sw nr; entmnt; wifi; dogs free; phone; adv bkg acc; quiet; ccard acc; fishing; boat hire; CKE/CCI. "Beautiful, peaceful site in spacious park; lge pitches; forest & rv walks adj; friendly, helpful resident warden; excel clean san facs; steep walk to historic town; highly rec; rv fishing." ♦ 15 Apr-30 Sep. € 13.50   2017*

LUSSAC LES CHATEAUX *7A3 (13km SW Rural) 46.32231, 0.67384* Camp Municipal du Renard, 8 route de la Mairie, 86150 Queaux [05 49 48 48 32 or 05 49 48 48 08 (Mairie); fax 05 49 48 30 70; contact@queaux.fr; www.queaux.fr] Fr Lussac cross rv bdge sp Poitiers & immed turn L. Foll sp to Gouex & Queaux. Site on D25 S of vill. Med, mkd, pt shd, pt sl, wc; mv service pnt; shwrs inc; EHU (6A) €2.50; shop nr; bar; playgrnd; paddling pool; 10% statics; Eng spkn; quiet. "Lovely rvside site nr pleasant vill; manned high ssn or apply to Mairie." 15 Jun-15 Sep. € 9.00   2017*

LUSSAC LES CHATEAUX *7A3 (6km SW Rural) 46.36912, 0.69330* Camp Municipal du Moulin Beau, 86320 Gouex [05 49 48 46 14; fax 05 48 48 50 01; www.tourisme-vienne.com] Fr Lussac on N147/E62 dir Poitiers, cross rv bdge sp Poitiers & immed turn L on D25; foll sp to Gouex; site on L in 4km at sw pool/camping sp. Sm, pt shd, wc; chem disp; shwrs inc; EHU (15A) €1.60 (check pol); quiet; CKE/CCI. "Excel site on bank Rv Vienne; bakery in vill; facs clean but ltd; bollards at site ent, care needed if van over 7m or twin axles; pool 300m; highly rec." 15 Jun-15 Sep. € 4.00   2012*

LUXEUIL LES BAINS *6F2 (1km N Rural) 47.82315, 6.38200* FFCC Camping du Domaine de Chatigny, 14 Rue Grammont, 70300 Luxeuil-les-Bains [03 84 93 97 97; fax 03 84 40 56 44; camping.lechatigny@chainethermale.fr; www.camping.luxeuil.fr]
N fr Vesoul on N57; turn L at rndabt into Luxeuil-les-Bains; foll Camping sp. Vehicular access fr Rue Ste Anne. Med, mkd, hdstg, hdg, pt shd, terr, wc (htd); chem disp; mv service pnt; fam bthrm; shwrs inc; EHU (15A) €3.50-4.50; gas; lndry; shop; rest; snacks; bar; bbq; playgrnd; pool; wifi; TV; 20% statics; dogs €1.70; bus 300m; Eng spkn; adv bkg acc; quiet; ccard acc; CKE/CCI. "New (2009), high standard site; indoor tennis court; gd." 1 Mar-31 Oct. € 18.00   2014*

LUZ ST SAUVEUR

LUZ ST SAUVEUR *8G2* (1km N Rural) *42.88140, -0.01258* **Airotel Camping Pyrénées, 46 Ave du Barège, La Ferme Theil, 65120 Esquièze-Sère [05 62 92 89 18; fax 09 70 06 59 56; contact@airotel-pyrenees.com; www.airotel-pyrenees.com]** On main rd fr Lourdes to Luz on L past Int'l Campsite. L U-turn into ent archway needs care - use full width of rd & forecourt. Med, mkd, shd, pt sl, wc (htd); chem disp; mv service pnt; fam bthrm; shwrs inc; EHU (3-10A) €3.50-6.50 (rev pol); gas; lndry; shop; rest; snacks; bar; playgrnd; pool (covrd); entmnt; wifi; TV; 30% statics; dogs €1.50; Eng spkn; adv bkg acc; quiet; ccard acc; horseriding; sauna; site clsd Oct & Nov; fishing; CKE/CCI. "Beautiful area; facs poss stretched highs ssn; ski in winter; walking; excel walking & wildlife; lovely vill; well organised; ACSI discount." ♦ 1 May-24 Sep. € 37.00   2017*

LUZ ST SAUVEUR *8G2* (2km N Rural) *42.88285, -0.01354* **Camping International, 50 Ave de Barège, 65120 Esquièze-Sère [05 62 92 82 02; fax 05 62 92 96 87; camping.international.luz@wanadoo.fr; www.international-camping.fr]** On E side of D921, clearly sp. Ave de Barège is pt of D921. Lge, hdg, mkd, pt shd, pt sl, wc (htd); chem disp; mv service pnt; fam bthrm; shwrs inc; EHU (2-6A) €2-5; lndry; shop; rest nr; snacks; bar; playgrnd; pool (htd); paddling pool; entmnt; wifi; TV; 10% statics; dogs free; phone; Eng spkn; adv bkg acc; quiet; tennis; horseriding; games area; games rm; waterslide; CKE/CCI. "Beautiful views fr site; friendly, helpful owners; vg clean san facs, ltd LS; gd walking; gd base for cycling inc Col du Tourmalet; skiing; mkt Mon; vg; Excel modern san facs." ♦ 20 May-30 Sep. € 41.00   2013*

LUZ ST SAUVEUR *8G2* (0km E Urban) *42.87342, -0.00057* **Camping Toy, 17 Place du 8 mai 1945, 65120 Luz Saint Sauveur [05 62 92 86 85; campingtoy@gmail.com; www.camping-toy.com]** Fr Lourdes D921, at Luz St Sauveur turn L onto sq after x-ing rv. Site in 100m. Med, mkd, pt shd, pt sl, wc; chem disp; shwrs inc; EHU (1-10A); lndry; shop nr; rest nr; bar nr; bbq; playgrnd; wifi; dogs; bus adj; Eng spkn; quiet. "In cent of town; helpful, friendly owners; pool 0.5km; magnificent views; gd walking/cycling area; st foot of Col du Tourmalet; excel." ♦ € 15.00   2015*

LUZ ST SAUVEUR *8G2* (1km E Rural) *42.87362, 0.00293* **Camping Le Bergons, Route de Barèges, 65120 Esterre [05 62 92 90 77; info@camping-bergons.com; www.camping-bergons.com]** On D918 to Col du Tourmalet, site on R. Med, mkd, pt shd, pt sl, terr, wc (htd); chem disp; shwrs inc; EHU (2-6A) €2.10-5; gas; lndry; shop nr; bbq; playgrnd; red long stay; 10% statics; dogs €0.80; phone; CKE/CCI. "Well-kept site; friendly, helpful owner; gd san facs; levelling blocks poss req; v tight ent for lge o'fits; excel walking; Donjon des Aigles at Beaucens worth visit; pool 500m; mkt Mon; vg." ♦ 2 May-26 Oct. € 20.00   2014*

LUZ ST SAUVEUR *8G2* (8km E Rural) *42.89451, 0.05741* **Camping La Ribère, Route de Labatsus, 65120 Barèges [05 62 92 69 01 or 06 80 01 29 51 (mob); contact@laribere.com; www.laribere.com]** On N side of rd D918 on edge of Barèges, site sp as `Camping Caraveneige'. Phone kiosk at ent. Sm, pt shd, pt sl, wc (htd); chem disp; shwrs inc; EHU (2-6A) €2-6; lndry; shop; rest nr; wifi; 10% statics; dogs €0.95; quiet; site clsd end Oct-mid Dec. "Conv, attractive site; gd facs; magnificent views; site refurb (2015)." ♦ € 23.00   2013*

LUZ ST SAUVEUR *8G2* (2km NW Rural) *42.88218, -0.02270* **Camping Le Pyrénévasion, Route de Luz-Andiden 65120 Sazos [05 62 92 91 54; fax 05 62 92 98 34; camping-pyrenevasion@wanadoo.fr; www.campingpyrenevasion.com]** Fr Lourdes S on D921 twd Gavarnie. Shortly bef Luz-St Sauveur after petrol stn & campsites sp, take R fork onto D12 sp Sazos. Cont thro vill & turn R sp Luz-Andiden, then immed R again sp Sazos (D12) & Luz-Andiden. Cont uphill, site on R just after Sazon sp. Med, mkd, hdg, pt shd, wc (htd); chem disp; fam bthrm; shwrs inc; EHU (3A/6A/10A) €3.5/€7/€8; gas; lndry; shop nr; rest; snacks; bar; bbq (charcoal, elec, gas); playgrnd; pool; paddling pool; wifi; 60% statics; dogs €2.50; Eng spkn; quiet; fishing; games rm; site clsd 20 Oct-19 Nov. "Fair site in mountains; no o'fits over 7.5m high ssn; long, steep trek to/fr shops." ♦ € 28.00   2017*

LUZY *4H4* (1km NE Rural) *46.79622, 3.97685* **Camping La Bédure, Route d'Autun, 58170 Luzy [03 86 30 68 27; info@campinglabedure.com; www.campinglabedure.com]** Foll sps on D981 to site. Med, mkd, pt shd, pt sl, wc; fam bthrm; shwrs inc; EHU (6A) €3 (poss rev pol); shop nr; playgrnd; dogs 1.50; Eng spkn; quiet. "Pleasant site; pool adj; gd walking & touring base; adjoins Lidl." 14 Apr-30 Sep. € 18.60   2018*

LUZY *4H4* (7km NE Rural) *46.81680, 4.05650* **Camping Domaine de la Gagère (Naturist), 58170 Luzy [03 86 30 48 11; fax 03 86 30 45 57; info@la-gagere.com; www.la-gagere.com]** Fr Luzy take D981 dir Autun; in 6.5km over rlwy, turn R onto unclassified rd sp 'La Gagère'. Site at end of rd in 3.5km on L; this rd narr in places. Med, hdstg, mkd, pt shd, pt sl, terr, wc; chem disp; mv service pnt; fam bthrm; shwrs inc; EHU (6A) €4.50; lndry; shop; rest; snacks; bar; bbq; playgrnd; pool (htd); entmnt; wifi; TV; 20% statics; dogs €4; phone; bus 10km; Eng spkn; adv bkg acc; quiet; ccard acc; INF card req; sauna; ACSI acc. "Excel, wooded, scenic site in beautiful area; gd views; friendly, helpful owners; superb san facs; gd touring base." ♦ 1 Apr-30 Sep. € 42.60   2014*

LYON *9B2* (12km E Rural) *45.79282, 4.99223* **Camping Le Grand Large, 81 Rue Victor Hugo, 69330 Meyzieu [04 78 31 42 16; fax 04 72 45 91 78; rhtgrandlarge@gmail.com; www.legrandlargerht.fr]** Exit N346 junc 6, E onto D6 dir Jonage. In approx 2 km turn L twd Le Grand Large (lake), site in 1km. Lge, pt shd, wc (htd); chem disp; mv service pnt; shwrs inc; EHU (5A) inc; gas; lndry; shop nr; snacks; sw nr; entmnt; TV; 90% statics; dogs €1; bus 1km; adv bkg acc; quiet; ccard acc; fishing; boating; games area; CKE/CCI. "Pleasant location; san facs scruffy & unclean (2011); stn 2km for trains to Lyon; mainly statics and chalets; NH only high ssn." 1 Apr-31 Oct. € 28.00   2014*

"That's changed – Should I let the Club know?"
If you find something on site that's different from the site entry, fill in a report and let us know. See camc.com/europereport.

⊞ **LYON** *9B2* (8km NW Urban) *45.81948, 4.76168* **Camping Indigo Lyon, Ave de la Porte de Lyon, 69570 Dardilly [04 78 35 64 55; fax 04 72 17 04 26; lyon@camping-indigo.com; www.camping-indigo.com]** Fr D306 Paris rd, take Limonest-Dardilly-Porte de Lyon exit at Auchan supmkt. Fr A6 exit junc 33 Porte de Lyon. Site on W side of A6 adj m'way & close to junc, foll sp (poss obscured by trees) for 'Complexe Touristique'. Fr E take N ring rd dir Roanne, Paris, then as above. Lge, mkd, hdg, hdstg, pt shd, serviced pitches; wc (htd); chem disp; mv service pnt; fam bthrm; shwrs inc; EHU (6-10A) €4.70-7.50; lndry; shop nr; rest nr; bar nr; playgrnd; pool; twin axles; wifi; TV; 10% statics; dogs €4; phone; bus/train to city nr; Eng spkn; adv bkg acc; ccard acc; games rm; CKE/CCI. "Well-run, secure site; Lyon easy by bus & metro, tickets can be bought fr recep; bar 100m; gd touring base for interesting area; helpful recep; gd, clean san facs; gas 100m; cafes nrby." ♦ € 30.00   2017*

MACHECOUL *2H4* (1km SE Urban) *46.98987, -1.81562* **Camp Municipal La Rabine, Allée de la Rabine, 44270 Machecoul [02 40 02 30 48 or 06 08 49 22 88; camprabine@wanadoo.fr; camping-la-rabine.com]** Sp fr most dirs. Look out for prominent twin-spired church in cent; take sm one-way rd that leads away fr spire end; site on R in 400m. Med, pt shd, wc; chem disp; shwrs; EHU (4-13A) €2-3.20; lndry; shop nr; bbq (gas); playgrnd; entmnt; wifi; dogs €0.90; adv bkg acc; quiet. "Pleasant site with lge generous size pitches & gd facs; excel base for birdwatching & cycling over marshes; pleasant town; mkt Wed & Sat; pool adj; lovely friendly well managed site; excel facs; lovely site rv fishing." 1 Apr-30 Sep. € 15.00   2017*

MACON *9A2* (4km N Urban) *46.33023, 4.84491* **Camp Municipal Les Varennes, 1 Route des Grandes Varennes, Sancé, 71000 Mâcon [03 85 38 16 22 or 03 85 38 54 08; fax 03 85 39 39 18; camping@ville-macon.fr; www.macon.fr]** Fr both N & S exit A6 junc 28 & cont S on N6 twd Mâcon; site on L in approx 3km, sp. (Fr S, leaving A6 at junc 28 avoids long trip thro town). Lge, mkd, pt shd, pt sl, wc (htd); chem disp; mv service pnt; fam bthrm; shwrs inc; EHU (5-10A) inc (poss rev pol); gas; lndry; shop; rest; snacks; bar; playgrnd; pool; red long stay; twin axles; wifi; TV; dogs €1.40; phone; bus; Eng spkn; adv bkg acc; ccard acc; golf 6km; tennis 1km; CKE/CCI. "Well-kept, busy NH nr A6; rec arr early as poss full after 1800; friendly staff; vg, immac san facs; hypmkt 1km; excel rest; gates clsd 2200-0630; poss flooding bottom end of site; long level walk to town; excel; perfect new facs (2014)." ♦ 15 Mar-31 Oct. € 25.00   2015*

MACON *9A2* (8km S Rural) *46.25167, 4.82610* **Base de loisirs du lac de Cormoranche, Les Luizant, 01290 Cormoranche-sur-Saône [03 85 23 97 10; fax 03 85 23 97 11; contact@lac-cormoranche.com; www.lac-cormoranche.com]** Exit A26 junc 29 sp Mâcon Sud onto N6 S to Crêches-sur-Saône. Turn L in town at traff lts onto D31 sp Cormoranche, then D51A. Cross rv, site sp on L. Alt rte: exit N6 in Mâcon & turn E onto D1079 dir St Laurent-sur-Saône then take D933 S to Pont-de-Veyle. Cont on D933 & foll sp to Cormoranche. Med, mkd, hdg, pt shd, wc (htd); chem disp; mv service pnt; shwrs inc; EHU (10A) inc; lndry; shop; rest; snacks; bar; playgrnd; sw nr; entmnt; wifi; TV; 25% statics; dogs €2.20; Eng spkn; adv bkg acc; quiet; ccard acc; fishing; bike hire; CKE/CCI. "Spacious pitches, some with narr access; vg; tight access to some pitches; gd for families." ♦ 1 May-30 Sep. € 21.00   2018*

MACON *9A2* (8km S Rural) *46.24106, 4.80643* **Camp Municipal du Port d'Arciat, Route du Port d'Arciat, 71680 Crêches-sur-Saône [03 85 37 11 83 or 03 85 37 48 32 (LS); fax 03 85 36 51 57; campingduportdarciat@wanadoo.fr; http://campingduportdarciat.pagesperso-orange.fr]** S fr Mâcon on N6 to Crêches-sur-Saône. Site sp (1 sm sp) at 3rd set of traff lts in cent vill on N6, turn E, cross m'way bdge; site on R by rv, sp on rndabt. Lge, mkd, pt shd, pt sl, wc; chem disp; mv service pnt; shwrs inc; EHU (6A) €4; gas; lndry; shop; rest; snacks; bar; playgrnd; entmnt; dogs €1.40; Eng spkn; adv bkg acc; ccard acc; fishing; boating; CKE/CCI. "Gd touring base; gd facs; gates clsd 2200-0700; gate to lake/beach clsd bef 1900; twin axles; poss flooding in heavy rain; conv a'route; ideal NH, espec LS; vg." ♦ 15 May-15 Sep. € 23.00   2014*

MAICHE

⊞ **MAICHE** 6G3 (1km S Rural) 47.24705, 6.79952
Camp Municipal St Michel, 23 Rue St Michel, 25120
Maîche [03 81 64 12 56 or 03 81 64 03 01 (Mairie);
contact@mairie-maiche.fr; www.mairie-maiche.fr]
Fr S turn R off D437 onto D442. App on D464 L on
o'skts of town. Sp fr both dir. Med, pt shd, sl, terr, wc
(htd); chem disp; shwrs inc; EHU (6A) inc; lndry; shop
nr; playgrnd; 10% statics; dogs; phone; adv bkg acc;
games area; site clsd 3rd week Nov & Dec; games rm.
"Beautiful, neat, well-run site with lovely views; many
trees & wild flowers; lower pitches are quieter; pool
adj; clean facs; phone ahead LS to check open; gd
walks in woods." ♦ € 18.00   2017*

MAILLEZAIS 7A2 (0km S Rural) 46.36921, -0.74054
Camp Municipal de l'Autize, Rue du Champ de Foire,
85420 Maillezais [02 51 00 70 79 or 06 43 19 14 90
(mob); camping.lautize@orange.fr; www.maillezais.fr]
Fr Fontenay take D148 twd Niort; after 9km, turn R
onto D15 to Maillezais; pass church in vill on L, site
on R after 200m. Or fr A83, exit junc 9 onto D148,
then D15 (do not use v minor rds, as poss directed by
sat nav). Sm, hdg, mkd, pt shd, wc; chem disp; shwrs
inc; EHU (4-13A) €3-5; lndry; shop nr; playgrnd; twin
axles; wifi; TV; adv bkg acc; quiet; ccard acc; games
rm; games area; CKE/CCI. "Lovely, clean site; spacious
pitches, gd views fr some; friendly, helpful warden;
excel, immac san facs; warden calls am & pm; some
low branches (2010); excel mkd cycle paths; conv
Marais Poitevin area & Venise Verte; nrby abbey worth
a visit; vg NH fr A83; excel; boat rides fr Vieux Port." ♦
1 Jun-30 Sep. € 17.00   2018*

MAILLEZAIS 7A2 (6km S Rural) 46.31308,
-0.73342 FFCC Camping Les Conches, Route
du Grand Port, 85420 Damvix [02 51 87 17
06; campingdesconches@orange.fr; http://
campingdesconches.free.fr] Fr Fontenay-le-Comte
exit D148 at Benet then W on D25 thro Le Mazeau
to sp on L for Damvix. Or exit A83 junc 8 then S on
D938 & E on D25 dir Benet. Site 1km thro vill on R
over bdge (sp). Med, mkd, shd, wc; chem disp; mv
service pnt; shwrs; EHU (6-10A) €3; lndry; shop nr; rest
nr; playgrnd; pool; dogs €1; adv bkg rec; quiet; golf;
rv fishing adj; boating adj; tennis; horseriding; CKE/
CCI. "Gd rest; friendly staff; gd cycling." 1 May-15 Oct.
€ 17.50   2014*

⊞ **MAILLY LE CHATEAU** 4G4 (5km S Rural)
47.56327, 3.64671 Camping Merry Sur Yonne
(formerly Municipal Escale), 5 Impasse de
Sables, 89660 Merry-sur-Yonne [03 86 34 59
55; gite.merrysuryonne@wanadoo.fr; www.
campingmerrysuryonne.com] Fr N on D100, turn R
over bdge, sp Merry Sur Yonne. At t-junc in vill turn L.
At end of vill bear L at war memorial into site. Med,
hdstg, mkd, pt shd, wc; chem disp; mv service pnt;
fam bthrm; shwrs; EHU; lndry; shop; rest; snacks; bar;
bbq; cooking facs; playgrnd; sw nr; twin axles; wifi;
dogs; Eng spkn; adv bkg acc; quiet; games rm; games
area; CCI. "New British owners; takeaway; beautiful
location nr rv and canal; canal walks adj; excel." ♦
€ 15.00   2016*

MAINTENON 4E2 (6km NW Rural) 48.60890, 1.54760
Camping Les Ilots de St Val, Le Haut Bourray,
28130 Villiers-le-Morhier [02 37 82 71 30; fax 02
37 82 77 67; lesilots@campinglesilotsdestval.com;
www.campinglesilotsdestval.com] Take D983 N
fr Maintenon twd Nogent-le-Roi, in 5km 2nd L onto
D101 sp Néron/Vacheresses-les-Basses/Camping
to site in 1km on L at top of hill. NB New by-pass
around Nogent le Roi fr N. Lge, mkd, hdstg, hdg, pt
shd, wc (htd); chem disp; mv service pnt; shwrs inc;
EHU (6-10A) €4-7; gas; lndry; shop nr; bbq; playgrnd;
red long stay; wifi; 50% statics; dogs €2; Eng spkn;
adv bkg acc; quiet; games rm; rv fishing 1km; tennis;
CKE/CCI. "Pleasant, peaceful site in open countryside;
lge private pitches; some vg, modern san facs;
helpful staff; gd value site; conv Chartres, Versailles,
Maintenon Château, train to Paris; dog walking fr the
site is gd; improved access for lge o'fits; pool 4km;
phone ahead late Dec to mid Feb as site may be clsd
to tourers." ♦ 1 Feb-22 Dec. € 32.00   2016*

> **"I like to fill in the reports as I travel from site to site"**
>
> You'll find report forms at the back of this guide, or you can fill them in online at camc.com/europereport.

MALAUCENE 10E2 (4km N Rural) 44.20101, 5.12535
FFCC Camping Aire Naturelle La Saousse (Letilleul),
La Madelaine, 84340 Malaucène [04 90 65 14 02]
Fr Malaucène take D938 N dir Vaison-la-Romaine &
after 3km turn R onto D13 dir Entrechaux where site
sp. After 1km turn R, site 1st on R. Sm, hdg, shd, terr,
wc; chem disp; shwrs inc; EHU (5A) €2.50; lndry; shop
nr; rest nr; dogs; adv bkg rec; quiet; CKE/CCI. "CL-type
site o'looking vineyards with views to Mt Ventoux;
some pitches in woods with steep incline - rec pitch
on lower level for easy access; friendly, helpful
owners; pool 4km; basic, clean facs; v peaceful, excel."
1 Apr-30 Sep. € 14.00   2012*

MALAUCENE 10E2 (0km NW Rural) 44.17789,
5.12533 Camping Le Bosquet, Route de Suzette,
84340 Malaucène [04 90 65 24 89 or 04 90 65 29 09;
fax 04 90 65 12 52; camping.lebosquet@wanadoo.
fr; www.provence.guideweb.com/camping/
bosquet] Fr S on D938 dir Vaison-la-Romaine turn
L onto D90 at Malaucène dir Suzette. Site on R in
300m. Do not tow thro Malaucène. Sm, hdg, hdstg,
pt shd, terr, wc (htd); chem disp; fam bthrm; shwrs
inc; EHU (10A) €3.20 (poss rev pol); gas; lndry; shop
nr; snacks; bar; playgrnd; pool; wifi; 2% statics; dogs
€1; phone; adv bkg acc; quiet; CKE/CCI. "Clean san
facs; friendly owner; gd touring base Mt Ventoux; mkt
Wed; easy 15 min walk to the town." ♦ 4 Apr-12 Oct.
€ 16.00   2014*

MALBUISSON *6H2* (2km S Rural) *46.77449, 6.27370* **Camping du Lac, 10 Rue du Lac, 25160 Labergement-Ste Marie [03 81 69 31 24; camping. lac.remoray@wanadoo.fr; www.camping-lac-remoray.com]** Exit N57/E23 junc 2 onto D437 thro Malbuisson to Labergement. Site sp to R of D437 after x-ing Rv Doubs. Med, mkd, pt shd, wc; chem disp; mv service pnt; fam bthrm; shwrs inc; EHU (6A) €3.50; gas; lndry; rest; snacks; bar; playgrnd; beach adj; wifi; TV; 5% statics; dogs €1.50; phone; Eng spkn; adv bkg acc; quiet; ccard acc; fishing; tennis nr; cycling; games area; CKE/CCI. "Roomy site by Lake Remoray with forest views; kind & helpful owner; clean san facs; walking; statics sep area; vill 500m with gd shops; excel." ♦ 1 May-30 Sep. € 21.00   2014*

MALBUISSON *6H2* (1km SW Urban) *46.79176, 6.29257* **Camping Les Fuvettes, 24 Route de la Plage et des Perrières, 25160 Malbuisson [03 81 69 31 50; fax 03 81 69 70 46; les-fuvettes@wanadoo.fr; www. camping-fuvettes.com]** Site 19km S of Pontarlier on N57 & D437 to Malbuisson, thro town, R down rd to Plage. Lge, pt shd, pt sl, wc (htd); shwrs inc; EHU (4-6A) €3.60-4; gas; lndry; shop; rest; snacks; bar; playgrnd; sw; 30% statics; dogs €1,50; quiet; fishing; games rm; boating; CKE/CCI. "Popular, lakeside, family site; mkd walks/cycle paths in adj woods; petting zoo (llamas etc) nrby." 1 Apr-30 Sep. € 34.00   2014*

MALENE, LA *9D1* (0km W Rural) *44.30120, 3.31923* **FFCC Camp Municipal Le Pradet, 48210 La Malène [04 66 48 58 55 or 04 66 48 51 16 (LS); fax 04 66 48 58 51; camping.lamalene@gmail.com; www. gorgesdutarn-camping.com]** W fr La Malène on D907B dir Les Vignes. Site on L in 200m. Well sp. Sm, hdstg, mkd, pt shd, pt sl, wc; chem disp; mv service pnt; shwrs inc; EHU (10A) €2.50; lndry; shop nr; rest nr; bar nr; bbq; playgrnd; sw; dogs €0.30; phone; adv bkg acc; quiet; ccard acc; fishing; CKE/CCI. "Kayak hire; boat trips fr vill; helpful warden; excel; v narr pitches; rvside site; steep slope down to recep; spectacular scenery." 1 Apr-30 Sep. € 27.00   2017*

⊞ **MALESHERBES** *4E3* (5km S Rural) *48.25659, 2.43574* **FFCC Camping Ile de Boulancourt, 6 Allée des Marronniers, 77760 Boulancourt [01 64 24 13 38; fax 01 64 24 10 43; info@ camping-iledeboulancourt.com; www.camping-iledeboulancourt.com]** Exit A6 at junc 14 Ury & Fontainebleau. SW on D152 to Malesherbes, S on D410 for 5km into Boulancourt. Site sp fr D410 & in vill. Med, pt shd, wc (htd); chem disp; mv service pnt; shwrs inc; EHU (3-6A) €2.70; lndry; shop nr; rest; bbq; playgrnd; 90% statics; dogs €1; Eng spkn; quiet; waterslide 5km; fishing 3km; tennis; CKE/CCI. "Attractive rv thro site; well-maintained facs, ltd LS; sep field for tourers; friendly, helpful staff; golf course in vill; chateau nr; excel." € 15.70   2016*

MANDRES AUX QUATRE TOURS

MALESTROIT *2F3* (1km E Urban) *47.80865, -2.37922* **Camp Municipal de la Daufresne, Chemin des Tanneurs, 56140 Malestroit [02 97 75 13 33 or 02 97 75 11 75 (Mairie); fax 02 97 75 06 68; etat.civil@ malestroit.fr; www.villedemalestroit.bzh]** S fr Ploërmel on N166 dir Vannes for 9km. Turn L onto D764 to Malestroit; site sp just off Blvd du Pont Neuf on E bank of Rv Oust, not well sp. Sm, hdg, pt shd, wc; chem disp; mv service pnt; shwrs inc; EHU (10A) €2.70 (poss long lead req); lndry; shop nr; rest nr; bar nr; playgrnd; wifi; dogs free; adv bkg acc; ccard acc; rv fishing adj; tennis; canoeing nr; CKE/CCI. "Pleasant site in excel location; narr site rds, some pitches poss diff to manoeuvre; no twin axles; clean san facs, basic but ok, poss stretched high ssn; canal towpath adj; gd cycle rtes; Museum of Breton Resistance in St Marcel; v nice, pretty site, highly rec." ♦ 1 May-15 Sep. € 10.00   2017*

MAMERS *4E1* (1km N Rural) *48.35778, 0.37181* **Camp Municipal du Saosnois, Route de Contilly, 72600 Mamers [02 43 97 68 30; fax 02 43 97 38 65; camping.mamers@free.fr; www.mairie-mamers.fr]** Fr W on D311, at rndabt at top of hill on circular rd, turn R (sp); then easy L (sp). Fr E on D311, strt thro rndabt (at Super U), ignore 1st camping sp, turn R at traff its & 2nd camping sp; at mini-rndabt turn L, sp Contilly; see lake & site. Sm, hdg, hdstg, pt shd, pt sl, terr, wc (htd); mv service pnt; shwrs inc; EHU (10A) inc (long lead poss req); lndry; shop; snacks; wifi; TV; 30% statics; dogs €0.50; adv bkg acc; quiet; games area; CKE/CCI. "Well-kept, secure site; admittance LS 1700-1900 only; Mamers pretty; pool 200m; lakeside; easy walk to town." ♦ 15 Apr-30 Sep. € 15.00   2016*

> "We must tell the Club about that great site we found"
>
> Get your site reports in by mid-August and we'll do our best to get your updates into the next edition.

MANDRES AUX QUATRE TOURS *5D2* (2km S Rural) *48.82739, 5.78936* **Camp Municipal Orée de la Forêt de la Reine, Route Forêt de la Reine, 54470 Mandres-aux-Quatre-Tours [03 83 23 17 31; mandres.54470@wandoo.fr]** On D958 Commercy to Pont-à-Mousson, sp as Camping Mandres. Turn R at sp in Beaumont & foll sp to vill Mandres-aux-Quatre-Tours. Sm, mkd, hdg, pt shd, wc; chem disp; shwrs inc; EHU (10A) inc (poss long lead req); playgrnd; red long stay; wifi; 10% statics; dogs; quiet; tennis; sailing 500m; watersports 500m; horseriding adj. "Gd, peaceful site; basic san facs; site poss muddy when wet; gd birdwatching, walking, cycling; popular NH." 1 Apr-31 Oct. € 17.00   2018*

MANOSQUE

MANOSQUE *10E3* (4km E Rural) *43.82352, 5.85424*
Camping Oxygene, 04210 Valensole [04 92 72 41 77; info@camping-oxygene.com; www.camping-oxygene.com] Exit A51 junc 18 onto D907 E dir Vinon-sur-Verdon; in 1km turn L at rndabt onto D4 N dir Oraison; site in 2.5km on L, at Les Chabrands, just bef Villedieu. Med, hdg, mkd, pt shd, wc; chem disp; mv service pnt; fam bthrm; shwrs inc; EHU (6-10A) €3.50-4.50; lndry; snacks; bar; bbq (elec, gas); pool; dogs €2.50; quiet; gym; horseriding nr; games area. "Peaceful, well-kept site with hill views; excel well-run site; vg pool; many places of interest nrby, inc Gorges du Verdon; canyoning, angling & rafting nr; paragliding nr; vg farm shop nr." ♦
20 Apr-17 Sep. € 33.50   2014*

MANOSQUE *10E3* (2km W Rural) *43.82986, 5.76384*
FFCC Camping Les Ubacs, 1138 Ave de la Repasse, 04100 Manosque [04 92 72 28 08; fax 04 92 87 75 29; lesubacs.manosque@ffcc.fr] Exit A51 junc 18 onto D907 dir Manosque; then D907 dir Apt; site sp at last rndabt on W side of Manosque. NB easy to overshoot. Med, mkd, hdg, pt shd, pt sl, wc cont; mv service pnt; shwrs inc; EHU (3-9A) €3.34-4.20; lndry; shop; rest; snacks; bar; playgrnd; pool; sw nr; red long stay; entmnt; dogs €1; ccard acc; tennis; CKE/CCI. "Conv Gorges du Verdon; helpful." 1 Apr-30 Sep.
€ 15.40   2013*

"I need an on-site restaurant"

We do our best to make sure site information is correct, but it is always best to check any must-have facilities are still available or will be open during your visit.

MANS, LE *4F1* (8km NE Rural) *48.01904, 0.27996*
Camping Le Pont Romain, Allée des Ormeaux, Lieu-dit La Châtaigneraie, 72530 Yvré-l'Evêque [02 43 82 25 39; contact@campinglepontromain.fr] Fr Le Mans take D314 to Yvré-l'Evêque - but do not ent town; just after rv bdge take 1st L into Allée des Ormeaux; site on L in 800m. Or exit A28 junc 23 onto D314 dir 'Le Mans Cent'; site on R just bef Yvré-l'Evêque. Avoid direct rte into vill over bridge. Med, hdstg, mkd, hdg, pt shd, wc (htd); chem disp; mv service pnt; fam bthrm; shwrs inc; EHU (16A) inc; gas; lndry; shop; rest; snacks; bbq; playgrnd; pool (htd); paddling pool; wifi; 15% statics; dogs €1; phone; bus; Eng spkn; adv bkg acc; quiet; games rm; CKE/CCI. "Excel modern san facs but ltd number of toilets; sep car park; conv Le Mans & m'way; vg; uneven pitches, need TLC; pleasant rural site; easy access to city; recep open 0830-1200 & 1430-2000; gd; bus to Le Mans 1.5km; beautiful site; easy access to bus; excel pitches." ♦ 16 Mar-11 Nov. € 28.60   2018*

⊞ **MANS, LE** *4F1* (20km SW Urban) *47.88985, 0.03038* **Aire De Camping Car, Rue de La Port, Suze Sur Sarthe** Fr A11 Lemans-Angers take exit 9 twds Tours/Allonnes on A11.1, 1st exit on rndabt onto D309. Then take D233 to La Suze-sur-Sarthe. Turn L immed bef Rv brdg onto site. Sm, hdstg, pt shd, wc cont; own san rec; chem disp; mv service pnt; EHU (6A) inc; shop nr; rest nr; bar nr; dogs; bus/train. "Excel site; no c'vans allowed; on edge of rv bank with views; conv for Le Mans." € 5.00   2014*

⊞ **MANS, LE** *4F1* (20km SW Urban) **Camp Municipal Le Port, Ave de la Piscine, 72210 La Suze-sur-Sarthe [02 43 77 32 74 or 02 43 77 39 48; contact@lasuzero.fr; www.lasuze.fr]** Fr A11 take exit 9 twrds Tours/Allonnes on A11.1, 1st exit on rndabt onto D309. Foll sp to La Suze Sur Sarthe on D233. Cross rlwy and turn L as you come into town, foll sp for MH. Turn R into Ave de la Piscine, then right into parking area. Pay at barrier to be let thro to site. Med, mkd, pt shd, wc; chem disp; mv service pnt; shwrs inc; EHU (10A) €2.30; shop; snacks; bbq; playgrnd; pool (htd); red long stay; TV; dogs €0.45; boating; rv adj; own san; tennis; adv bkg; fishing. "Narr gate to site; ample hdstg for m'vans in adj car park." ♦ € 4.50   2018*

MANSLE *7B2* (0km NE Urban) *45.87841, 0.18175*
Camp Municipal Le Champion, Rue de Watlington, 16230 Mansle [05 45 20 31 41 or 05 45 22 20 43; fax 05 45 22 86 30; mairie.mansle@wanadoo.fr; www.mansle.fr] N on N10 fr Angoulême, foll sp Mansle Ville. Leave N10 at exit to N of town, site rd on L, well sp. Rec ent/leave fr N as rte thro town diff due to parked cars. Site beside Rv Charente. Med, hdg, pt shd, wc; chem disp; mv service pnt; shwrs inc; EHU (16A) €2.80 (poss long lead req); lndry; shop nr; rest; bar nr; bbq; playgrnd; sw nr; entmnt; 5% statics; phone; Eng spkn; adv bkg acc; quiet; fishing; boating adj; CKE/CCI. "Popular, peaceful, well-kept NH nr N10; lge pitches, choose own; helpful warden; immac san facs; grnd poss boggy after heavy rain; mkt Tues, Fri am; great site in excel location, well run; vg; gd rest; easy walk to town." ♦ 15 May-15 Sep. € 16.40   2017*

⊞ **MANSLE** *7B2* (10km SE Rural) *45.84137, 0.27319*
Camping Devezeau, 16230 St Angeau [05 45 94 63 09; ask@campingdevezeau.com; www.campingdevezeau.com] N or S on N10 exit Mansle; in cent vill at traff lts foll sp twd La Rochefoucauld (D6); past Super U supmkt; over bdge; 1st R onto D6. In approx 9km at T-junc turn R, site sp. App down narr rd. Sm, hdstg, hdg, pt shd, sl, wc (htd); chem disp; shwrs inc; EHU (6A-10A) €2; gas; lndry; shop nr; rest; snacks; bar; bbq; pool; twin axles; wifi; 25% statics; dogs; Eng spkn; adv bkg acc; quiet; cycling; canoeing; horseriding; fishing; CKE/CCI. "Nice CL-type site; v friendly British owners; excel san facs modernised (2015); traction diff in wet (4x4 avail); blocks & steel pegs needed; gd cycling country; phone ahead in winter; lovely tranquil site; walking; vg; friendly atmosphere; bar snacks & English breakfast." ♦ € 20.00   2017*

MARENNES

MARANS *7A1* (1km N Rural) *46.31682, -0.99158*
Camp Municipal Le Bois Dinot, Route de Nantes, 17230 Marans [05 46 01 10 51; fax 05 46 66 02 65; campingmarans@orange.fr; www.ville-marans.fr] Heading S, site on L of D137 bef ent Marans. Heading N, site is well sp on R 300m after supmkt on L. Lge, shd, wc, shwrs inc; EHU (10A) €3; shop nr; rest nr; bar nr; red long stay; wifi; dogs €1.10; Eng spkn; adv bkg rec; fishing; boat hire; CKE/CCI. "Well-kept, wooded site; v helpful, efficient staff; quieter pitches at back of site; vg pool adj; poss mosquitoes; gd cycling; mkt Tues & Sat; excel; v clean san facs; grass pitch avail subj to rainfall; woodland pitches quietest; poss diff lger o'fits." 1 Apr-30 Sep. € 17.50   2018*

> **"Satellite navigation makes touring much easier"**
> Remember most sat navs don't know if you're towing or in a larger vehicle – always use yours alongside maps and site directions.

⊞ **MARANS** *7A1* (10km NE Rural) *46.38196, -0.97186* **Camping à la Ferme Le Pont Grenouilles (Berjonneau), 24 Rue du Port d'Aisne, 85450 Vouillé-les-Marais [02 51 52 53 96]** Fr N/S use D137 to Le Sableau N of Marans; at rndabt take D25A twds Vouille les Marais; site on L in 3.8km. Sm, pt shd, wc; shwrs inc; EHU (3-6A); lndry; playgrnd; quiet. "Friendly, helpful owners; peaceful site; toilet block old but clean; charming area; nightingales in Spring; gd NH or sh stay." € 12.50   2014*

MARCENAY *6F1* (1km N Rural) *47.87070, 4.40560*
Camping Les Grèbes du Lac de Marcenay, 5 Route du Lac, 21330 Marcenay [03 80 81 61 72; fax 03 25 81 02 64; info@campingmarcenaylac.com; www.campingmarcenaylac.com] On D965 bet Laignes & Châtillon-sur-Seine. Fr Châtillon sp on R 8km after vill of Cérilly. Foll sp to lake & camp. Med, hdstg, hdg, mkd, shd, wc (htd); chem disp; mv service pnt; fam bthrm; shwrs inc; EHU (10A) €3; gas; lndry; shop; rest nr; snacks; bar nr; bbq; playgrnd; pool; sw nr; wifi; TV; 5% statics; dogs €1; phone; Eng spkn; adv bkg rec; quiet; ccard acc; horseriding; games rm; boat hire; watersports; fishing; canoe hire; games area; golf; bike hire; CKE/CCI. "Lovely, peaceful, well-run site by lake; beautiful area; friendly, helpful Dutch owners; excel san facs; pitches poss soft after rain; bar adj; gd touring base; gd walking & cycling; Châtillon museum & Abbey de Fontenay worth visit." ♦ 1 May-30 Sep. € 30.00   2013*

MARCIAC *8F2* (2km NW Rural) *43.53228, 0.16633*
FFCC Camping du Lac, Bezines, 32230 Marciac [05 62 08 21 19; camping.marciac@wanadoo.fr; www.camping-marciac.com] E fr Maubourguet take D943 to Marciac. Take D3 to lake dir Plaisance. At lake turn R & R again at sp. Site on L in 200m. Fr N exit A62 at junc 3 & foll D932 sp Pau to Aire-sur-Adour then E on D935 & D3 & foll sp. Med, hdstg, mkd, pt shd, pt sl, wc; chem disp; mv service pnt; fam bthrm; shwrs inc; EHU (6A) inc; gas; lndry; shop; rest nr; snacks; bar; bbq; playgrnd; pool; red long stay; wifi; 8% statics; dogs €1.50; phone; adv bkg acc; ccard acc; CKE/CCI. "Friendly British owners; peaceful site; lge pitches with easy access; interesting old town; lake adj; jazz festival 1st 2 weeks Aug (extra charge); Wed mkt." ♦ 20 Mar-17 Oct. € 25.00   2013*

MARCIGNY *9A1* (7km W Rural) *46.26489, 3.95706*
Camping La Motte aux Merles, 71110 Artaix [03 85 25 37 67] Leave D982 (Digoin-Roanne) at Marcigny by-pass. Take D989 twd Lapalisse. In 2km at Chambilly cont on D990, site sp in 5km on L, 200m down side rd. Sm, pt shd, pt sl, wc; shwrs inc; EHU (8A) €2.40; lndry; snacks; playgrnd; pool; dogs €1; quiet; fishing nr; tennis nr; golf nr. "Friendly owners; gd sightseeing in peaceful area; site diff in wet; excel." ♦ 1 Apr-15 Oct. € 10.00   2012*

MARCILLAC LA CROISSILLE *7C4* (2km SW Rural) *45.26896, 2.00838* **Camp Municipal Le Lac, 28 Route du Viaduc, 19320 Marcillac-la-Croisille [05 55 27 81 38 or 05 55 27 82 05 (Mairie); campingdulac19@wanadoo.fr; www.campingdulac19.com]** S fr Egletons on D16 & D18. Site sp at S end of vill at intersection with D978. Lge, shd, pt sl, wc; shwrs; EHU (6A) €2.80; lndry; shop nr; snacks; playgrnd; entmnt; TV; 10% statics; dogs €0.90; adv bkg acc; quiet; tennis adj. "Spacious park like setting; lake adj." 1 Jun-1 Oct. € 11.50   2012*

MARENNES *7B1* (11km SE Rural) *45.77324, -0.96301*
Camping Le Valerick, La Petite Mauvinière, 17600 St Sornin [05 46 85 15 95; camplevalerick@aol.com; www.camping-le-valerick.fr] Fr Marennes take D728 sp Saintes for 10km; L to St Sornin; site sp in vill. Fr Saintes D728 W for 26km; take 2nd R turn R in vill D118, site on L sp La Gripperie. Sm, mkd, pt shd, pt sl, wc; chem disp; shwrs inc; EHU (4-6A) €3-€3.80 (poss rev pol); lndry; shop; rest; snacks; bar; bbq; playgrnd; entmnt; dogs €1.40; adv bkg acc; quiet; CKE/CCI. "Nice, friendly site; gd san facs; plenty of bird life - herons, storks etc; poss mosquito problem; excel; spotless san facs; lge pitches; v warm welcome; highly rec." 1 Apr-30 Sep. € 14.00   2017*

MARENNES

MARENNES 7B1 (5km SE Rural) 45.81083, -1.06027
Camping Séquoia Parc, La Josephtrie, 17320 St Just-Luzac [05 46 85 55 55; fax 05 46 85 55 56; info@sequoiaparc.com; www.sequoiaparc.com] Fr A10/E05 m'way exit at Saintes, foll sp Royan (N150) turning off onto D728 twd Marennes & Ile d'Oléron; site sp to R off D728, just after leaving St Just-Luzac. Or fr Rochefort take D733 & D123 S; just bef Marennes turn L on D241 sp St Just-Luzac. Best ent to site fr D728, well sp fr each dir. Lge, mkd, hdg, unshd, sl, wc; chem disp; mv service pnt; fam bthrm; shwrs inc; EHU (6A) inc (poss rev pol); gas; lndry; shop; rest; snacks; bar; bbq; playgrnd; pool; paddling pool; red long stay; entmnt; wifi; TV; 50% statics; dogs €7 - max 1; adv bkg acc; ccard acc; fishing 1.5km; bike hire; watersports 3km; games area; horseriding; tennis; games rm; CKE/CCI. "High standard site; aqua park: o'fits over 8m on request; waterslides, waterjets & whirlpool; barrier clsd 2230-0700; 3 pools (2 htd); lge pitches; cash machine; clean san facs; superb pools; excel free club for children." ♦ 5 May-5 Sep. € 54.00   2017*

See advertisement

> **"There aren't many sites open at this time of year"**
>
> If you're travelling outside peak season remember to call ahead to check site opening dates – even if the entry says 'open all year'.

MARENNES 7B1 (2km NW Coastal) 45.83139, -1.15092 Camp Municipal La Giroflée, 17560 Bourcefranc-le-Chapus [05 46 85 06 43 or 05 46 85 02 02 (Mairie); fax 05 46 85 48 58; campinglagiroflee@orange.fr; www.bourcfranc-le-chapus.fr] Fr Saintes on D728/D26 to Boucefranc, turn L at traff lts. Site on L after 1km (after sailing school) opp beach. Med, pt shd, wc; shwrs; EHU (6A) €3; lndry; shop nr; snacks; playgrnd; beach adj; quiet; 1 May-30 Sep. € 7.60   2017*

MAREUIL 7B2 (5km N Rural) 45.49504, 0.44860
FFCC Camping Les Graulges, Le Bourg, 24340 Les Graulges [05 53 60 74 73; info@lesgraulges.com; www.lesgraulges.com] Fr D939 at Mareuil turn L onto D708 & foll sp to Les Graulges in 5km. Sm, mkd, pt shd, pt sl, terr, wc; chem disp; fam bthrm; shwrs inc; EHU (6A) €3.50; lndry; rest; snacks; bar; bbq; playgrnd; pool; red long stay; 10% statics; dogs €2; Eng spkn; adv bkg acc; quiet; lake fishing. "Tranquil site in forested area; ideal touring base; friendly Dutch owners; excel rest; not suitable for elderly; pool dirty; lge dog lives on site (2012)." ♦ 1 Apr-15 Sep. € 20.50   2012*

MAREUIL 7B2 (4km SE Rural) 45.44481, 0.50474
Camping L'Etang Bleu, 24340 Vieux-Mareuil [05 53 60 92 70; letangbleu@ornage.fr; www.letangbleu.com] On D939 Angoulême-Périgueux rd, after 5km turn L cent of Vieux-Mareuil onto D93, foll camping sp to site in 2km. Narr app thro vill, care needed. Lge, hdg, mkd, pt shd, wc; chem disp; mv service pnt; fam bthrm; shwrs inc; EHU 6-10A (poss rev pol); gas; lndry; shop; rest; snacks; bar; bbq; playgrnd; pool; paddling pool; entmnt; TV; 10% statics; dogs €3; adv bkg acc; quiet; ccard acc; lake fishing 500m; CKE/CCI. "Pleasant site in unspoilt countryside; lge pitches, but narr site rds; access diff lge o'fits without mover; friendly British owners; gd san facs, ltd LS; gd walking/cycling area; excel." ♦ 1 Apr-20 Oct. € 23.50   2018*

MAREUIL 7B2 (8km SE Rural) 45.42429, 0.53070
Camping La Charrue, Les Chambarrières, 24340 Vieux-Mareuil [05 53 56 65 59; bookings@lacharrue.biz; or clive.davie@sfr.fr; www.lacharrue.biz] SE fr Angoulême on D939 sp Périgueux to Mareuil. Fr Mareuil stay on D939 twds Brantôme, thro Vieux-Mareuil then in 2km site immed on L after passing a lge lay-by on R with white stone chippings. Awkward turn. Sm, mkd, pt shd, wc; chem disp; shwrs inc; EHU (4A) €3; lndry; shop nr; rest nr; snacks; bar nr; bbq; playgrnd; pool; beach sand nrby; red long stay; dogs (LS only); adv bkg req; watersports nr; fishing 3km; bike hire; golf nr; CKE/CCI. "CL-type site in Regional Park; friendly, helpful British owners; bar 500m; immac facs; gd touring base for beautiful area; lakes nrby; B&B & gîtes avail; excel." 1 May-31 Oct. € 14.50   2015*

MAREUIL *7B2* (1km SW Rural) *45.44680, 0.45153*
Camp Municipal Vieux Moulin, Rue des Martyrs/ Rue Arnaud de Mareuil; 24340 Mareuil [05 53 60 91 20 (Mairie) or 05 53 60 99 80; fax 05 53 60 51 72; mariemareuil@wanadoo.fr] Fr town cent take D708 (sp Ribérac); after 300m turn L on D99 (sp 'La Tour Blanche'); after 100m turn L opp lge school, site 100m ahead. Well sp all dirs. Sm, mkd, shd, wc; shwrs; EHU (6A) €1.70; shop nr; rest nr; bar nr; playgrnd; dogs €0.50; adv bkg acc; quiet. "Clean, tidy site; friendly warden; ltd, well-kept facs; lovely walk by stream to vill; interesting chateau; vg, immac site." ♦ 1 Jun-30 Sep. € 8.00   2012*

MARNAY (HAUTE SAONE) *6G2* (1km SE Urban) *47.28975, 5.77628* **Camping Vert Lagon, Route de Besançon, 70150 Marnay [03 84 31 73 16 or 06 40 78 58 13; accueil@camping-vertlagon.com; www.camping-vertlagon.com]** Fr N stay on D67 Marnay by-pass; ignore old camping sp into town. Proceed to S of town on by-pass then turn L at junc. Bef bdge in 1km take gravel rd on S side, round under bdge to site (app thro town fr N v narr). Med, hdg, mkd, pt shd, wc; chem disp; mv service pnt; fam bthrm; shwrs inc; EHU (10A) €4; lndry; shop nr; rest nr; snacks; bar; bbq; playgrnd; pool (htd); wifi; 40% statics; dogs €1; adv bkg acc; quiet; ccard acc; games area; canoeing; fishing; CKE/CCI. "Pleasant, popular, family site by Rv Ognon; gd san facs; lake adj; tree-top walks; vg." ♦ 2 May-30 Sep. € 21.00   2017*

MARQUION *3B4* (3km NE Rural) *50.22280, 3.10863* **FFCC Camping de l'Epinette, 7 Rue du Calvaire, 62860 Sauchy-Lestrée [03 21 59 50 13; lepinette62@wanadoo.fr; www.lepinette62.com]** Fr A26 exit junc 8 onto D939 to Marquion. On ent Marquion turn R at x-rds to Sauchy-Lestrée; on ent vill turn R at 1st T-junc & site on L in 100m. Fr Cambrai take D939 twd Arras, then as above. Sm, pt shd, pt sl, wc; own san rec; chem disp; shwrs; EHU (10A) €3 (poss rev pol); gas; lndry; shop nr; playgrnd; 80% statics; dogs free; adv bkg acc; games area; CKE/CCI. "Charming, well-kept site in tranquil spot; sm CL-type area for tourers; clean, simple, dated but adequate facs, ltd LS; levelling blocks ess for m'vans; conv Calais/Dunkerque; quiet but some military aircraft noise; WW1 cemetary nr; gd value; popular excel NH." 1 Apr-31 Oct. € 9.00   2015*

MARQUISE *3A3* (5km SW Rural) *50.78389, 1.66917* **FFCC Camping L'Escale, 15 Route Nationale, 62250 Wacquinghen [03 21 32 00 69; camp-escale@wanadoo.fr; www.escale-camping.fr]** Fr A16 S fr Calais exit junc 34. Fr A16 N fr Boulogne exit junc 33. Foll sp. Lge, pt shd, wc cont; chem disp; mv service pnt; shwrs inc; EHU (4A) €3.50 (poss rev pol); gas; lndry; shop; rest; snacks; bar; playgrnd; entmnt; wifi; 90% statics; dogs; quiet; ccard acc. "Pleasant, busy site; open 24 hrs; conv NH nr ferries, A16, Channel tunnel & WW2 coastal defences; o'fits staying 1 night pitch on meadow at front of site for ease of exit (but some noise fr m'way); m'van 'aire' open all yr; vg; site relandscaped (2017), vg; comfort pitches." ♦ 1 Apr-15 Oct. € 25.00   2017*

MARSANNE *9D2* (3km NE Rural) *44.65769, 4.89098* **Camping Les Bastets, Quartier Les Bastets, 26740 Marsanne [04 75 90 35 03; fax 04 75 90 35 05; contact@campinglesbastets.com; www.campinglesbastets.com]** Exit A7 junc 17 onto N7; pass thro Les Tourettes & La Coucourde to Marsanne. In La Coucourde turn L onto D74 & in 6km L onto D105 thro Marsanne. Site sp fr D105. App fr N on D57 not rec. Med, mkd, hdg, pt shd, sl, terr, wc (htd); chem disp; mv service pnt; fam bthrm; shwrs inc; EHU (10A); lndry; shop; rest; snacks; bar; bbq; playgrnd; pool; entmnt; wifi; TV; 10% statics; dogs €4; Eng spkn; adv bkg acc; games rm; archery; bike hire; games area. "Pleasant site; gd views; beautiful area; vg; infinity pool with views over Valdaine Plaine; 30 new easy access level hdg pitches, some in woods; welcoming site; mini golf, golf 10km; highly rec." ♦ 1 Apr-1 Oct. € 24.50   2016*

⊞ **MARSEILLAN PLAGE** *10F1* (1km NE Coastal) *43.32158, 3.55932* **Camping Le Paradou, 2 Impasse Ronsard, 34340 Marseillan-Plage [06 15 49 09 90 or 04 67 21 90 10 ls; info@paradou.com; www.paradou.com]** Exit A9 junc 34 or 35 onto N113/N312 dir Agde & Sète. Fr Agde foll sp Sète to Marseillan-Plage. Site well sp on N112. Med, hdg, pt shd, wc (htd); chem disp; mv service pnt; fam bthrm; shwrs inc; EHU (10A) €3.50; gas; lndry; shop nr; rest nr; snacks; bar nr; playgrnd; beach sand adj; wifi; 15% statics; dogs €1.50; phone; bus 1km; CKE/CCI. "Gd area for cycling; ltd pitches avail for long o'fits; gd clean facs, maybe stretched in ssn; superb san facs; cycle rte to Sete; highly rec." ♦ € 29.00   2014*

MARSEILLAN PLAGE *10F1* (7km SE Coastal) *43.31904, 3.55655* **Flower Camping Robinson, Quai de Plaisance, 34340 Marseillan Plage [04 67 21 90 07; reception@camping-robinson.com; www.camping-robinson.com]** Fr Agde take D612 twds Sete. In Marseillan Plage cont on D612 & cross canal bdge. In abt 300m turn R and foll sp to site. Med, mkd, pt shd, wc; chem disp; mv service pnt; fam bthrm; shwrs; EHU (10A); lndry; shop; snacks; bar; playgrnd; beach opp; twin axles; wifi; 33% statics; Eng spkn; adv bkg acc; games area; CKE/CCI. "Gd." ♦ 23 Apr-23 Sep. € 38.00   2016*

MARSEILLAN PLAGE *10F1* (1km SW Urban/Coastal) *43.31365, 3.54779* **Camping Beauregard Plage, 250 Chemin de l'Airette, 34340 Marseillan-Plage [04 67 77 15 45; fax 04 67 01 21 78; campingbeauregardplage@orange.fr; www.camping-beauregard-plage.com]** On N112 Agde-Sète rd, turn S at rndabt to Marseillan-Plage onto D51 & foll camping sp thro town. Site immed on leaving town cent. Lge, hdg, pt shd, wc; chem disp; mv service pnt; fam bthrm; shwrs inc; EHU (6A) inc; lndry; shop nr; rest nr; bar nr; bbq; playgrnd; beach sand adj; entmnt; wifi; TV; 5% statics; dogs €2 (allowed LS only); Eng spkn; adv bkg acc; quiet; fishing. "Superb sand beach sheltered by dunes; some pitches soft & sandy; excel for beach holiday; delightful staff; onsite bistro gd value; town is tourist resort & v new; plenty of bars, rest, supermrkt & shops nr." ♦ 26 Mar-15 Oct. € 40.00   2013*

MARSEILLAN PLAGE

MARSEILLAN PLAGE 10F1 (1km SW Coastal) 43.31275, 3.54638 **Camping La Créole, 74 Ave des Campings, 34340 Marseillan-Plage [04 67 21 92 69; fax 04 67 26 58 16; campinglacreole@wanadoo.fr; www.campinglacreole.com]** Fr Agde-Sète rd N112, turn S at rndabt onto D51 & foll sp thro town. Narr ent easily missed among lger sites. Med, hdg, hdstg, mkd, pt shd, wc; chem disp; mv service pnt; fam bthrm; shwrs inc; EHU (6A) €3.50; lndry; shop; rest nr; bar nr; playgrnd; beach sand adj; entmnt; 10% statics; dogs €3; phone; adv bkg acc; quiet; tennis 1km; games area; CKE/CCI. "Vg, well-kept site; min stay 7 nights Jul-Aug; dir access to excel beach; naturist beach 600m." ♦
1 Apr-15 Oct. € 34.50   2012*

MARSEILLAN PLAGE 10F1 (1km SW Coastal) 43.31036, 3.54601 **Camping La Plage, 69 Chemin du Pairollet, 34340 Marseillan-Plage [04 67 21 92 54; fax 04 67 01 63 57; info@laplage-camping.net; www.laplage-camping.net]** On D612 fr Agde to Sète, turn R at rndabt dir Marseillan-Plage. Foll sp for site at 2nd rndabt. Site on L in 150m. Med, hdg, pt shd, wc; chem disp; mv service pnt; fam bthrm; shwrs inc; EHU (10A) inc; gas; lndry; rest; snacks; bar; bbq; playgrnd; beach sand adj; entmnt; TV; 1% statics; dogs €4; phone; Eng spkn; adv bkg acc; quiet; ccard acc; games area; watersports; CKE/CCI. "Excel, popular, family-run site; superb beach; extra for beach front pitches; sm pitches, some diff for lge o'fits; gd, friendly atmosphere." ♦ 14 Mar-31 Oct. € 42.00   2015*

MARTEL 7C3 (5km SE Rural) 44.88538, 1.59929 **Camping du Port, 46600 Creysse [05 65 32 20 82 or 05 65 32 27 59; fax 05 65 38 78 21; contact@campingduport.com; www.campingduport.com]** Exit A20 at Junc 55 foll D803 to Le Pigeon, then take D15 to Saint Sozy, then D114 to Creysse then foll signs to site. Med, pt shd, pt sl, wc; shwrs inc; EHU (6A) inc; lndry; shop nr; rest nr; playgrnd; pool; dogs €1.50; adv bkg acc; quiet; bike hire; canoe hire. "Lovely grnds; gd access to rv; friendly; v peaceful LS; ltd facs LS; Creysse beautiful vill." 1 May-20 Sep. € 26.40   2013*

MARTRES TOLOSANE 8F3 (2km S Rural) 43.19060, 1.01840 **Camping Le Moulin, 31220 Martres-Tolosane [05 61 98 86 40; fax 05 61 98 66 90; info@domainelemoulin.com; www.domainelemoulin.com]** Exit A64 junc 22 (fr N or S) & foll camping sps. Site sp adj Rv Garonne. Med, pt shd, pt sl, wc; chem disp; mv service pnt; fam bthrm; shwrs inc; EHU (6-10A) €4-6; gas; lndry; shop nr; snacks; bar; bbq; playgrnd; pool (htd); paddling pool; red long stay; entmnt; wifi; TV; 20% statics; dogs €2.50; Eng spkn; adv bkg rec; quiet; ccard acc; games area; tennis; games rm; bike hire; rv fishing inc; CKE/CCI. "Excel, well-maintained site; friendly welcome; gd, modern san facs; water on all pitches; gd touring base for Spain, Lourdes, etc." ♦
31 Mar-5 Oct. € 23.00   2012*

MARVEJOLS 9D1 (1km NE Rural) 44.55077, 3.30440 **Camping Village Le Coulagnet, Quartier de l'Empery, 48100 Marvejols [04 66 32 03 69]** Exit A75 junc 38 onto D900 & N9. Foll E ring rd onto D999, cont over rv & foll sp to site; no R turn into site, cont 500m to Aire de Retournement, & turn L into site. Foll sp 'VVF', camping pt of same complex. NB U-turn bef ent impossible long o'fits; nasty speed humps on app rd. Sm, hdg, pt shd, wc; shwrs inc; EHU (5A) inc (poss rev pol); lndry; shop; bbq (sep area); playgrnd; pool; TV; 50% statics; phone; Eng spkn; adv bkg acc; quiet; ccard acc; games rm; tennis; games area. "Well equiped site; san facs immac; sep area for tourers; interesting walled town; rv adj; excel; ent too tight to make u-turn." ♦ 15 May-15 Sep. € 26.00   2014*

> **"I like to fill in the reports as I travel from site to site"**
>
> You'll find report forms at the back of this guide, or you can fill them in online at camc.com/europereport.

MARVILLE 5C1 (1km N Rural) 49.46294, 5.45859 **Camp Syndicat Mixte de la Vallée de l'Othain, 55500 Marville [03 29 88 19 06 or 03 29 88 15 15; fax 03 29 88 14 60; marville.accueil@wanadoo.fr]** Sp on D643 on app Marville fr both dirs. Med, hdg, pt shd, wc; shwrs; EHU (3A); lndry; shop; rest; snacks; playgrnd; entmnt; 20% statics; quiet; CKE/CCI. "Easy access adj lake; htd covrd pool adj; gd NH."
1 Feb-30 Nov.   2012*

MASEVAUX 6F3 (1km N Urban) 47.77820, 6.99090 **Camping de Masevaux, 3 Rue du Stade, 68290 Masevaux [03 89 82 42 29; contact-masevaux@tv-com.net; www.camping-masevaux.com]** Fr N83 Colmar-Belfort rd take N466 W to Masevaux; site sp. NB D14 fr Thann to Masevaux narr & steep - not suitable c'vans. Med, mkd, pt shd, wc (htd); chem disp; mv service pnt; fam bthrm; shwrs inc; EHU (3-6A) €3.20-3.80; lndry; shop nr; snacks; bar; playgrnd; red long stay; entmnt; wifi; TV; 40% statics; dogs €0.50; Eng spkn; adv bkg acc; quiet; ccard acc; CKE/CCI. "Pleasant walks; htd pool adj; interesting town - annual staging of Passion Play; helpful, friendly owners; excel facs; sports complex adj; gd cycle rtes; excel; gd site in nice little town; supmkt nrby; close to Ballon d'Alsace."
♦ 15 Mar-31 Oct. € 19.00   2014*

MATHES, LES

MASSERET *7B3* (11km N Rural) *45.61142, 1.50110*
Camping de Montréal, Rue du Petit Moulin, 87380 St Germain-les-Belles [05 55 71 86 20; fax 05 55 71 00 83; contact@campingdemontreal.com; www.campingdemontreal.com] S fr Limoges on A20; exit junc 42 onto D7B to St Germain-les-Belles; turn R onto D216; site on L in 500m. Site sp in vill. NB Care needed due narr rds. Med, mkd, hdg, pt shd, terr, wc (htd); chem disp; mv service pnt; shwrs inc; EHU (10A) €3; lndry; shop nr; rest; snacks; bar; bbq; playgrnd; pool (htd); sw nr; entmnt; wifi; 12% statics; dogs €2.60; phone; Eng spkn; adv bkg acc; quiet; ccard acc; tennis; fishing; watersports; CKE/CCI. "Peaceful, lovely, well-run site in attractive setting o'looking lake; excel, modern, spotless san facs; bike hire 1km; conv A20; a gem of a site; gd rest; vg NH; shops 10 min walk." ♦ € 19.00   2018*

MASSERET *7B3* (5km E Rural) *45.53880, 1.57790*
Camping Domaine des Forges (formerly Camping Plan l'Eau), Complexe Touristique Bourg, 19510 Lamongerie [05 55 73 44 57; fax 05 55 73 49 69; www.domaine-des-forges.fr] Exit A20 at junc 43 sp Masseret & foll sp Lamongerie. At rndabt turn R, site sp. Site ent bet 2 lge stone pillars. Med, shd, sl, wc; chem disp; shwrs; EHU (5A) €2.30 (poss long lead req some pitches); lndry; shop; rest; snacks; playgrnd; sw; TV; quiet; ccard acc; fishing; golf nr; tennis. "Pleasant situation; fitness course thro woods & round lake; clean facs; gd NH & longer." ♦ 1 Apr-30 Sep. € 19.00   2014*

MASSEUBE *8F3* (0km E Rural) *43.42914, 0.58516*
Camping Berges du Gers, Route de Simorre, 32140 Masseube [05 62 66 01 75; camping.masseube@orange.fr; www.camping-masseube-lesbergesdugers.fr] S fr Auch on D929 to Masseube; turn L onto D27 dir Simorre; site on L in 500m. Med, shd, wc; chem disp; shwrs inc; EHU (6A) €3; lndry; shop nr; rest nr; bar nr; bbq; playgrnd; entmnt; wifi; TV; 10% statics; dogs free; Eng spkn; adv bkg acc; quiet; ccard acc; games area; tennis; bike hire; games rm; CKE/CCI. "Well-run site in pleasant setting; security barrier; htd pool adj; access to rv; vg." ♦ 1 May-31 Oct. € 13.00   2017*

MASSEUBE *8F3* (2km E Rural) *43.42748, 0.61142*
Camping Aux Mêmes, 32140 Bellegarde [05 62 66 91 45 or 06 83 62 02 22; info@gascogne-camping.fr; www.gascogne-camping.fr] Fr Masseube take D27 E dir Simorre & Bellegarde; in 2.5km turn L (having past sports stadium & driven up hill thro trees); site is 1st farm on R in 300m. Site sp. Sm, unshd, pt sl, wc; chem disp; shwrs inc; EHU (6A) €3; lndry; shop; snacks; bar; bbq; playgrnd; pool; wifi; TV; dogs; Eng spkn; adv bkg acc; quiet; tennis nr; canoeing; games rm; sailing nr; golf nr; watersports; bike hire; windsurfing nr; fishing. "Excel; v friendly & helpful Eng owners." ♦ 1 Apr-15 Sep. € 25.00   2017*

MATHES, LES *7B1* (1km WSW Urban) *45.71517, -1.15520* Camping Monplaisir, 26 avenue de la Palmyre, 17250 Les Mathes [05 46 22 50 31; camping-monplaisir@orange.fr; www.camping monplaisirlesmathes.fr] Fr Saujon take D14 to the o'skirts of Tremblade, avoid vill of Arvert & Etaule if towing c'van, rd surface poor & narr. At rndabt take D25 for a sh dist & take L onto D268 twrds La Palmyre. Cont along D141 to o'skirts of Les Mathes, then L at rndabt. Site on L within approx 450m opp cycle hire. Med, pt shd, pt sl, wc; chem disp; mv service pnt; fam bthrm; shwrs; EHU €4.50; lndry; shop nr; rest nr; snacks; bar nr; bbq; playgrnd; pool; beach beach 3.5km; wifi; TV; dogs; Eng spkn; quiet; ccard acc; games area; games rm. "Bike hire nrby; crazy golf & childrens car track on site; friendly family owned site, clean & tidy; gd cycle tracks in area; bar 300m; zoo 4km; vg; v clean san facs; open mkt in vill most days." Apr-Sep. € 20.00   2016*

MATHES, LES *7B1* (3km N Rural) *45.72333, -1.17451*
Camping La Palombière, 1551 Route de la Fouasse, 17570 Les Mathes [05 46 22 69 25; fax 05 46 22 44 58; contact@camping-lapalombiere.com; www.camping-lapalombiere.com] Fr La Tremblade bypass foll sp Dirée on D268; site on R in 5km just past Luna Park. Med, pt shd, wc (htd); chem disp; mv service pnt; fam bthrm; shwrs inc; EHU (6-10A) €4.50-5; gas; lndry; shop; rest; snacks; bar; bbq; playgrnd; pool (htd); beach sand 5km; wifi; 10% statics; dogs €3; phone; bus; Eng spkn; quiet; ice; games area; CKE/CCI. "Spacious, tranquil site under oaks & pines; lge pitches; palatial san facs; superb beaches 5km (some naturist); excel, spacious site, helpful staff; immac maintained." ♦ 1 Apr-15 Oct. € 35.00   2013*

> ### "That's changed – Should I let the Club know?"
> If you find something on site that's different from the site entry, fill in a report and let us know. See camc.com/europereport.

MATHES, LES *7B1* (1km SW Rural) *45.70256, -1.15638* Camping Palmyre Loisirs, 28 Ave des Mathes, 17570 La Palmyre [05 46 23 67 66; www.palmyreloisirs.com] S fr La Tremblade on D14; at Arvert take D141 SW thro Les Mathes; site on L of rd 1km fr Les Mathes. Lge, pt shd, wc; shwrs inc; EHU (6A) inc; shop; rest; snacks; bar; pool; beach sand 3km; dogs €4.5 (1 per pitch); adv bkg acc; quiet. "Excel new san facs; new pool complex for 2015; pitches away fr bar/rest are quiet; barrier clsd 12-6am." Apr-Sep. € 51.50   2015*

MATHES, LES

MATHES, LES 7B1 (3km SW Urban) 45.70133, -1.16613 **Camping Atlantique Parc, 26 Ave des Mathes, 17570 La Palmyre [05 46 02 17 17; fax 05 46 02 52 30; info@camping-atlantique-parc.com; www.camping-atlantique-parc.com]** Fr N150, in Saujon turn R onto D14 sp Les Mathes for 22km. At 3rd rndabt take 3rd exit sp D14 Ètaules. In Arvert turn L on D141 sp Les Mathes, La Palmyre Zoo. Foll D141 thro Les Mathes, at rndabt take 3rd exit onto Ave des Mathes sp La Palmyre, site ent on L after 1.5km, sp fr rd. Lge, pt shd, wc; shwrs inc; EHU (10A) €7 (poss rev pol); gas; lndry; shop; snacks; bar; playgrnd; pool (htd); beach sand 2km; wifi; TV; 80% statics; dogs (€5, 1 per pitch); waterslide; fishing 3km; watersports 3km; games rm. "€30 refundable deposit for card for barriers and san fac access; gd site, espec for families; gd san fac." Apr-Sep. € 49.00   2013*

MATHES, LES 7B1 (6km SW Coastal) 45.6974, -1.2286 **Camping Parc de la Côte Sauvage, Phare de la Coubre, 17570 La Palmyre [05 46 22 40 18 or 05 49 35 83 60; contact@parc-cote-sauvage.com; www.parc-cote-sauvage.com]** D25 fr Royan, thro La Palmyre, at rndabt foll sp 'Phare de la Coubre'. Turn L at junc sp as bef, turn L on R-hand bend. Ent nr lighthouse. Lge, hdg, pt shd, terr, wc; chem disp; mv service pnt; fam bthrm; shwrs inc; EHU (6-10A) €5; gas; lndry; shop; rest nr; snacks; bar nr; playgrnd; pool; beach sand 500m; entmnt; wifi; TV; 25% statics; dogs €3 (not acc Jul/Aug); Eng spkn; ccard acc; tennis; boating; CKE/CCI. "Lge pitches; surfing school; poss v cr (NH area); bike hire adj; beach can be v windy." ♦ 1 May-15 Sep. € 63.00   2014*

MATHES, LES 7B1 (3km NW Rural) 45.72098, -1.17165 **Camping La Clé des Champs, 1188 Route de la Fouasse, 17570 Les Mathes [05 46 22 40 53; fax 05 46 22 56 96; contact@la-cledeschamps.com; www.la-cledeschamps.com]** S of La Tremblade, take D141 twd La Palmyre, site sp. Lge, mkd, pt shd, wc (htd); chem disp; fam bthrm; shwrs; EHU (6-10A) inc; gas; lndry; shop; rest; snacks; bar; bbq; playgrnd; pool (covrd, htd); paddling pool; beach sand 3.5km; entmnt; wifi; TV; 30% statics; dogs €3.80; Eng spkn; adv bkg acc; quiet; ccard acc; fishing 3km; jacuzzi; games area; gym; watersports 3km; games rm; bike hire; sauna; CKE/CCI. "Well-equipped, busy site; many excel beaches in area; modern san facs; local oysters avail; Cognac region; Luna Park nrby." ♦ 30 Mar-15 Nov. € 40.00   2013*

MATOUR 9A2 (1km W Rural) 46.30475, 4.47858 **Camp Municipal Le Paluet, Rue de la Piscine, 71520 Matour [03 85 59 70 92; lepaluet@matour.fr; www.matour.com]** On W o'skts of Matour off Rte de la Clayette D987. Med, hdg, mkd, pt shd, wc; chem disp; shwrs inc; EHU (10A) inc; lndry; shop nr; snacks; bar; bbq; playgrnd; pool; entmnt; wifi; TV; adv bkg acc; quiet; ccard acc; lake fishing adj; tennis; games area; waterslide; CKE/CCI. "Conv touring vineyards; highly rec; facs poss inadequate high ssn." ♦ 1 May-30 Sep. € 18.50   2012*

MAUBEUGE 3B4 (10km NE Rural) 50.34525, 4.02842 **Camping Les Avallées, 19 Rue du Faubourg, 59600 Villers-Sire-Nicole [03 27 67 92 56; fax 03 27 67 45 18; loisirs-les-avallees@wanadoo.fr; www.loisirs-les-avallees.fr]** N fr Maubeuge on N2; in 5km R onto D259 to Villers-Sire-Nicole. Site well sp. Last 4km narr country rd. Lge, pt shd, pt sl, terr, wc; chem disp; shwrs; EHU (4A) €2; lndry; shop; rest; snacks; bar; bbq; playgrnd; 80% statics; dogs; quiet. "Friendly owners; lake fishing; no twin axles; vg; lovely site." 1 Apr-14 Oct. € 11.00   2015*

MAULEON LICHARRE 8F1 (2km S Rural) 43.20795, -0.89631 **Camping Uhaitza Le Saison, Route de Libarrenx, 64130 Mauléon-Licharre [05 59 28 18 79; fax 05 59 28 06 23; camping.uhaitza@wanadoo.fr; www.camping-uhaitza.com]** Fr Sauveterre take D936 twd Oloron. In 500m turn R onto D23 to Mauléon, then take D918 dir Tardets, site on R. Sm, hdg, mkd, pt shd, wc; chem disp; mv service pnt; fam bthrm; shwrs inc; EHU (6A) €2.65-4.90; lndry; shop nr; snacks; bar; bbq; playgrnd; 10% statics; dogs €2; adv bkg acc; quiet; tennis 2km; rv fishing adj; games rm; CKE/CCI. "Lovely, quiet site beside rv; lge pitches; friendly owners." ♦ 1 Apr-15 Oct. € 25.00   2015*

> "I like to fill in the reports as I travel from site to site"
>
> You'll find report forms at the back of this guide, or you can fill them in online at camc.com/europereport.

MAURS 7D4 (1km S Rural) 44.70522, 2.20586 **Camp Municipal Le Vert, Route de Decazeville, 15600 Maurs [04 71 49 04 15; fax 04 71 49 00 81; camping@ville-maurs.fr; www.ville-maurs.fr/tourisme/camping]** Fr Maurs take D663 dir Decazeville. Site on L 400m after level x-ing thro sports complex. Narr ent. Med, mkd, shd, wc; chem disp; fam bthrm; shwrs inc; EHU (15A) inc; lndry; shop nr; playgrnd; pool; adv bkg acc; quiet; rv fishing; tennis. "V pleasant on side of rv; sports complex adj; friendly helpful warden." ♦ 1 May-30 Sep. € 11.00   2014*

MAYENNE 4E1 (2km N Rural) 48.31350, -0.61296 **Camp Municipal du Gué St Léonard, 818 Rue de St Léonard, 53100 Mayenne [02 43 04 57 14 or 02 43 04 19 37; www.campingduguesaintleonard.fr]** Fr N, sp to E of D23 & well sp fr cent of Mayenne on rvside. Med, hdg, mkd, pt shd, serviced pitches; wc (htd); chem disp; shwrs inc; EHU (10A) €2.20; lndry; shop; rest nr; snacks; bbq; playgrnd; pool (htd); twin axles; 8% statics; phone; adv bkg acc; rv fishing adj; CKE/CCI. "Peaceful, well-kept site by rv; pleasant location adj parkland walks; modern san facs with piping hot water; some pitches sm & access poss diff; vg value." ♦ 15 Mar-30 Sep. € 13.70   2015*

MEGEVE

France

MAZAMET *8F4* (2km E Urban) *43.49634, 2.39075*
FFCC Camp Municipal de la Lauze, Chemin de la Lauze, 81200 Mazamet [05 63 61 24 69; camping.mazamet@imsnet.fr; www.camping-mazamet.com]
Exit Mazamet dir St Pons on D612, site on R past rugby grnd. Med, hdstg, pt shd, pt sl, wc; chem disp; mv service pnt; fam bthrm; shwrs inc; EHU (15A) €3.50; lndry; bbq; red long stay; dogs; adv bkg acc; tennis; CKE/CCI. "Well-kept site in 2 adj parts, 1 flat & other sl; office thro gateway - warden needed for access; htd pool adj; san facs excel; gd touring base 'Black Mountain' region." ♦ 1 Jun-30 Sep. € 16.00   2014*

"We must tell the Club about that great site we found"

Get your site reports in by mid-August and we'll do our best to get your updates into the next edition.

MEAUX *3D3* (4km NE Rural) *49.00301, 2.94139*
Camping Village Parisien, Route des Otages, 77910 Varreddes [02 51 20 41 94; fax 01 60 22 89 84; direction@villageparisien.com; http://villageparisien.camp-atlantique.nl] Fr Meaux foll sp on D405 dir Soissons then Varreddes, site sp on D121 dir Congis. Med, mkd, hdg, pt shd, wc; chem disp; mv service pnt; fam bthrm; shwrs inc; EHU (6-10A) €2; gas; lndry; shop; rest; snacks; bar; bbq; playgrnd; pool; paddling pool; red long stay; entmnt; wifi; TV; 85% statics; dogs free; Eng spkn; adv bkg acc; waterslide; games area; golf 5km; tennis; games rm; fishing; bike hire; CKE/CCI. "Conv Paris cent (drive to metro), Parc Astérix & Disneyland - tickets avail fr site; friendly, helpful staff; cash only; sm pitches; narr site rds; v busy, well-used site." 1 Apr-5 Nov. € 41.00   2017*

MEAUX *3D3* (10km SW Rural) *48.91333, 2.73416*
Camping L'International de Jablines, 77450 Jablines [01 60 26 09 37; fax 01 60 26 43 33; welcome@camping-jablines.com; www.camping-jablines.com] Fr N on A1 then A104 exit Claye-Souilly. Fr E on A4 then A104 exit Meaux. Fr S on A6, A86, A4, A104 exit Meaux. Site well sp 'Base de Loisirs de Jablines'. Lge, mkd, pt shd, pt sl, wc (htd); chem disp; mv service pnt; fam bthrm; shwrs inc; EHU (10A) inc; lndry; shop; rest nr; snacks; bar; bbq; playgrnd; sw nr; wifi; dogs €3; bus to Eurodisney; Eng spkn; adv bkg req; quiet; ccard acc; horseriding; windsurfing; bike hire; tennis 500m; fishing; sailing; CKE/CCI. "Clean, well-run, well-guarded site; vg pitches; pelasant staff; san facs poss tired high ssn; ideal for Disneyland (tickets for sale), Paris & Versaille." ♦ 31 Mar-29 Sep. € 28.00   2017*

See advertisement

MEES, LES *10E3* (11km S Rural) *43.95377, 5.93304*
Camping Les Olivettes, Hameau-Les-Pourcelles, 04190 Les Mées [04 92 34 18 97; campingolivette@club-internet.fr; www.campinglesolivettes.com]
Exit A51 junc 20 (fr N) or 19 (fr S) & cross Rv Durance onto D4. Site bet Oraison & Les Mées. Turn onto D754 to Les Pourcelles & foll site sp. Sm, hdg, mkd, pt shd, pt sl, terr, wc; mv service pnt; fam bthrm; shwrs inc; EHU (6-10A) €4.90; playgrnd; pool; 5% statics; dogs €1.50; Eng spkn; adv bkg acc; quiet. "Views over beautiful area; friendly owners; occasional out of ssn pitches avail; unrel opening; vg." ♦ 29 Apr-30 Sep. € 33.50   2016*

MEGEVE *9B3* (2km SW Rural) *45.84120, 6.58887*
FFCC Camping Gai Séjour, 332 Route de Cassioz, 74120 Megève [04 50 21 22 58] On D1212 Flumet-Megève rd, site on R 1km after Praz-sur-Arly, well sp. Med, mkd, pt shd, sl, wc; chem disp; shwrs inc; EHU (4A); lndry; shop nr; rest nr; bar nr; dogs; Eng spkn; adv bkg acc; quiet; CKE/CCI. "Pleasant site with gd views, lge pitches; gd walks; 40km fr Mont Blanc; helpful owners; no free parking in Megeve." 6 Jan-15 Sep. € 15.00   2014*

MEHUN SUR YEVRE

MEHUN SUR YEVRE *4H3* (1km N Urban) 47.14797, 2.21725 **Camp Municipal, Ave Jean Châtelet, 18500 Mehun-sur-Yèvre [02 48 57 44 51 or 02 48 57 30 25 (Mairie); fax 02 48 57 34 16; http://www.ville-mehun-sur-yevre.fr/Le-camping]** Leave A71 junc 6 onto D2076 (N76) dir Bourges. App Mehun & turn L into site at 2nd traff lts. Ave Jean Châtelet is pt of D2076. Sm, mkd, pt shd, wc; chem disp; mv service pnt; shwrs inc; EHU (6A) €2.80 (poss rev pol & long lead req some pitches); lndry; shop nr; rest nr; bar nr; playgrnd; twin axles; quiet; tennis adj. "Excel NH conv for m'way; clean, modern san facs; water pnts poss long walk; gates locked 2200-0700 (high ssn); facs open to elements; pool adj; town rather run down, nice park."
♦ 8 May-30 Sep. € 13.00   2017*

MELE SUR SARTHE, LE *4E1* (1km SE Rural) 48.50831, 0.36298 **Camp Intercommunal La Prairie, La Bretèche, St Julien-Sarthe, 61170 Le Mêle-sur-Sarthe [02 33 27 18 74]** Turn off N12 onto D4; site sp in vill. Med, mkd, pt shd, wc; chem disp; mv service pnt; shwrs; EHU (6A) inc; lndry; shop nr; playgrnd; adv bkg acc; sailing; tennis; CKE/CCI. "Pt of excel sports complex; vg." 1 May-30 Sep. € 11.00   2014*

MELISEY *6F2* (3km N Rural) 47.77560, 6.58020 **Camping La Pierre, Route de Melay, 70270 Melisey [03 84 63 23 08 or 03 84 22 11 10; office-tourisme-melisey.fr]** Fr Lure on D486 to Melisey, L in vill onto D293 sp Melay. Site on L in 2.5km. Med, hdstg, hdg, mkd, pt shd, wc; chem disp; mv service pnt; fam bthrm; shwrs inc; EHU (6A)€2.60; lndry; shop nr; rest nr; bbq; playgrnd; TV; 40% statics; dogs; phone; adv bkg acc; quiet; games area; games rm; CKE/CCI. "V quiet, well-kept site; site yourself, warden calls; local c'van club organises reg social events and visitors are invited; pool (3km); gd site; conv Rochamp Courbusier Chapel; not suitable for lge units; all facs vg; peaceful."
♦ 1 May-30 Sep. € 16.00   2014*

MELISEY *6F2* (1km E Rural) 47.75484, 6.58683 **Camping La Bergereine, 17bis Route des Vosges, 70270 Mélisey [06 23 36 87 16 (mob); isabelle.schweizer0704@orange.fr]** Fr Lure (or by-pass) take D486 dir Le Thillot; site sp. Sm, pt shd, wc; chem disp; shwrs; EHU inc; gas; 25% statics; adv bkg acc; quiet; rv fishing adj; CKE/CCI. "Ok NH; simple farm site; leisure cent 500m; attractive scenery; improvd san block; pool 500m; v scruffy." 1 Apr-30 Sep. € 8.00   2015*

MELISEY *6F2* (8km E Rural) 47.75525, 6.65273 **Camping La Broche, Le Voluet, 70270 Fresse [03 84 63 31 40; www.camping-broche.com]** Fr Lure head NE on D486 twd Melisey. Fr Mélisey stay on D486 twd Le Thillot, in 2.5km turn R onto D97 dir Plancher-les-Mines. In approx 5.5km site sp on R in Fresse. Sm, mkd, pt shd, pt sl, terr, wc; chem disp; shwrs inc; EHU (10A) €2.50; lndry; shop nr; bbq; playgrnd; sw nr; 10% statics; dogs €1; phone; adv bkg acc; quiet; games rm; fishing adj; ice; games area; CKE/CCI. "Secluded, relaxing site next to lake, in attractive setting in regional park; friendly owner; conv Rte of 1000 lakes; great site; vg." ♦ 15 Apr-15 Oct. € 12.00   2015*

MELLE *7A2* (8km S Rural) 46.15127, -0.12022 **Camping La Maison de Puits, 14 Rue de Beauchamp, 79110 Tillou [05 49 07 20 28 or 06 74 21 11 78 (mob); janethall@mail.com; www.hallmarkholidays.eu]** Fr Niort on D948. At Melle foll sp Angoulême, R turn (to ring rd & avoids Melle cent). At Total stn rndabt turn R onto D948 dir Chef-Boutonne. In 3.5km turn R onto D737 sp Chef-Boutonne. After approx 5km at x-rds of D111 & D737, strt over & take 2nd turn R in 1km (sm sp to Tillou) along narr rd sp Tillou. In 1.6km site on L. Sm, unshd, sl, wc; chem disp; shwrs; EHU (6A) €3; bbq; pool; adv bkg acc; quiet. "CL-type site in meadow/orchard (6 vans only); quiet & peaceful; friendly, helpful British owners - help with househunting avail; ring ahead to book; interesting area." 1 Apr-30 Sep. € 12.00   2013*

MELLE *7A2* (11km SW Rural) 46.14421, -0.21983 **Camp Municipal, Rue des Merlonges, 79170 Brioux-sur-Boutonne [05 49 07 50 46; fax 05 49 07 27 27]** On ent Brioux fr Melle on D150 turn R immed over bdge; site on R in 100m. Sm, pt shd, wc; shwrs inc; EHU (6A) €1.80; lndry; shop nr; playgrnd; quiet. "Pleasant rural setting; tidy, well-cared for site; ltd facs but clean; choose own pitch & pay at Mairie on dep if no warden; conv for town; great value; vg sh stay/NH." 1 Apr-31 Oct. € 8.00   2018*

MENAT *7A4* (2km E Rural) 46.09579, 2.92899 **Camp Municipal des Tarteaux, 63560 Menat [04 73 85 52 47 or 04 73 85 50 29 (Mairie); fax 04 73 85 50 22; mairiemenat@wanadoo.fr; www.ville-menat.com]** Heading SE fr St Eloy-les-Mines on D2144 foll sp Camping Pont de Menat. Exit D2144 at Menat opp Hôtel Pinal. Site alongside Rv Sioule. Med, shd, pt sl, terr, wc cont; mv service pnt; shwrs inc; EHU (16A) €2.70; lndry; shop nr; playgrnd; wifi; adv bkg acc; quiet; rv fishing 2km; CKE/CCI. "Beautiful site beside rv; Chateau Rocher ruins nrby; boating 2km; OK NH; delightful site; modern san facs in new block (2014)" 1 Apr-30 Sep. € 8.00   2013*

> ### "I need an on-site restaurant"
>
> We do our best to make sure site information is correct, but it is always best to check any must-have facilities are still available or will be open during your visit.

MENDE *9D1* (3km W Rural) 44.51409, 3.47363 **Camping Tivoli, Route des Gorges du Tarn, 48000 Mende [04 66 65 31 10; camping.tivoli0601@orange.fr; www.camping-tivoli.com]** Sp fr N88, turn R 300m downhill (narr but easy rd). Site adj Rv Lot. Med, pt shd, wc; chem disp; mv service pnt; shwrs inc; EHU (6A) inc; lndry; shop; bar; playgrnd; pool; TV; 10% statics; dogs €1; adv bkg rec; quiet; rv fishing. "Gd site nr town at back of cent commerciale; hypmkt 1km; v narr ent with little rm to park." € 20.00   2015*

MERDRIGNAC 2E3 (2km N Rural) 48.19786, -2.41622
**Camping Le Val de Landrouët, 14 rue du Gouède,
22230 Merdrignac** [02 96 28 47 98; fax 02 96
26 55 44; contact@valdelandrouet.com; www.
valdelandrouet.com] Sp fr town cent, 500m fr town
on D793 twd Broons, site on L. Med, mkd, hdg, pt shd,
pt sl, wc; chem disp; fam bthrm; shwrs inc; EHU (4A)
€3; lndry; shop nr; bar; bbq; playgrnd; pool (htd); sw
nr; twin axles; entmnt; 5% statics; dogs; bus adj; adv
bkg acc; quiet; ccard acc; fishing; tennis; CKE/CCI.
"Superb, spacious site; mv service pnt (emptying only);
gd touring ctr; activities adj; excel." 1 May-30 Sep.
€ 15.00   2014*

> "Satellite navigation makes touring much easier"
>
> Remember most sat navs don't know if you're towing or in a larger vehicle – always use yours alongside maps and site directions.

⊞ **MERENS LES VALS** 8G4 (1km W Rural) 42.64633,
1.83083 **Camp Municipal Ville de Bau, Ville de Bau,
09110 Mérens-les-Vals** [05 61 02 85 40 or 05 61
64 33 77; fax 05 61 64 03 83; camping.merens@
wanadoo.fr; merenslesvals.fr] Fr Ax-les-Thermes on
N20 sp Andorra past Mérens-les-Vals turn R nr start of
dual c'way sp Camp Municipal. Site on R in 800m. Med,
hdg, wc (htd); shwrs inc; EHU (6-10A) inc (poss rev
pol); lndry; shop; bar; bbq; playgrnd; wifi; 20% statics;
dogs €0.70; quiet; ccard acc; CKE/CCI. "Excel site; gd
clean san facs; gd walks fr site; conv Andorra, Tunnel
de Puymorens; all pitches have water taps; pool 8km;
lovely walk fr site past Eglise Romane in vill to hot
spring with natural bathing pools." € 17.00   2017*

MERS LES BAINS 3B2 (2km NE Rural) 50.07730,
1.41540 **Camping Le Rompval, Lieudit Blengues,
154 Rue André Dumont, 80350 Mers-les-
Bains** [02 35 84 43 21 or 06 50 02 79 57 (mob);
lerompval@baiedesommepleinair.com; www.
campinglerompval.com] Fr Calais on A16, exit junc
23 at Abbeville onto A28. In 5km exit junc 2 onto D925
dir Friville-Escarbotin, Le Tréport. In approx 20km at
rndabt junc with D19 foll sp Ault & at next rndabt take
D940 twd Mers-les-Bains. In St Quentin-la-Motte turn
R, site on R, sp. Fr S on A28 exit junc 5 onto D1015
to Mers-les-Bains & foll sp Blengues & site. Med, hdg,
hdstg, mkd, unshd, wc (htd); chem disp; mv service
pnt; fam bthrm; shwrs inc; EHU (6-13A) €4-6.50; gas;
lndry; shop; snacks; bar; bbq; playgrnd; pool (covrd,
htd); paddling pool; beach sand 2.5km; red long stay;
entmnt; wifi; TV; 25% statics; dogs €3; Eng spkn; adv
bkg acc; quiet; ccard acc; tennis 3km; games rm; bike
hire; games area; CKE/CCI. "Vg site; library; gd facs." ♦
29 Mar-11 Nov. € 22.50   2014*

METZ

MESNIL ST PERE 6F1 (2km NE Rural) 48.26329,
4.34633 **Kawan Village Camping Lac d'Orient, Rue
du Lac, 10140 Mesnil-St Père** [03 25 40 61 85 or
03 85 72 27 21 (LS); fax 03 25 70 96 87 or 03 85 72
66 07 (LS); info@camping-lacdorient.com; www.
camping-lacdorient.com] On D619 foll sps Lac de la
Forêt d'Orient. Approx 10km fr Vendeuvre or 20km
fr Troyes turn N on D43A, to Mesnil-St Père; site sp.
Sp at ent to site: 'Camping Lac d'Orient' (with 'Kawan
Village' in v sm lettering). Lge, hdstg, hdg, mkd, pt
shd, pt sl, wc (htd); chem disp; mv service pnt; fam
bthrm; shwrs inc; EHU (10A) inc; lndry; shop; rest nr;
snacks; bar; bbq; playgrnd; pool (covrd, htd); paddling
pool; sw nr; entmnt; wifi; 10% statics; dogs €3; phone;
Eng spkn; adv bkg acc; quiet; ccard acc; watersports
500m; games rm; fishing; games area; tennis; jacuzzi;
CKE/CCI. "Peaceful site with mature trees next to
lake & forest; lge pitches; 1st class san facs; no o'fits
over 10m high ssn; poss muddy when wet; conv
Nigloland theme park & Champagne area; conv A26;
excel spacious site; excel cycle rte; private san facs
some pitches; fantastic rest over looking lake; vg." ♦
9 Apr-23 Sep. € 36.00   2016*

MESSANGES 8E1 (2km SW Coastal) 43.79790,
-1.40135 **Airotel Camping Le Vieux Port, Plage Sud,
40660 Messanges** [01 76 76 70 00; fax 05 58 48 01 69;
contact@levieuxport.com; www.levieuxport.com]
Fr S take D652 past Vieux-Boucau; site sp. Turn W
at Super U rndabt. V lge, hdstg, mkd, shd, wc; chem
disp; mv service pnt; fam bthrm; shwrs inc; EHU (6A)
inc; gas; lndry; shop; rest; snacks; bar; bbq; playgrnd;
pool (htd); paddling pool; beach sand 400m; red
long stay; entmnt; wifi; TV; 10% statics; dogs €5.50;
Eng spkn; adv bkg acc; quiet; ccard acc; horseriding;
waterslide; tennis; bike hire; games area; CKE/CCI. "V
pleasant, clean site; dir access to sand beach; quad
bikes; superb, v lge pool complex; excel touring base."
♦ 24 Mar-4 Nov. € 85.00   2017*

METZ 5D2 (2km NW Urban) 49.12402, 6.16917
**Camp Municipal Metz-Plage, Allée de Metz-Plage,
57000 Metz** [03 87 68 26 48; fax 03 87 38 03 89;
campingmetz@mairie-metz.fr; www.mairie-metz.fr]
Fr W exit A31 junc 33 Metz-Nord/Pontiffroy exit; cross
rv bdges Pont Canal & Pont des Morts; then immed
turn L into Allée de Metz-Plage; site in 200m (or after
leaving A31 at junc 33, at rndabt turn R & foll sps).
Fr E foll 'Autres Directions' over A31 & Rv Moselle,
then as above. Lge, hdstg, mkd, pt shd, pt sl, wc; chem
disp; mv service pnt; fam bthrm; shwrs inc; EHU (10A)
inc (poss rev pol); lndry; shop; snacks; playgrnd; twin
axles; wifi; dogs €0.50; Eng spkn; adv bkg acc; ccard
acc; rv fishing adj; CKE/CCI. "Spacious, well-situated
on rv with views; some gd sized pitches; helpful staff;
poss long walk to san facs; rv unfenced; facs stretched
if site full; early arr ess high ssn; vg; fac's need
updating; wifi in designated areas; pool adj; excel." ♦
15 Apr-1 Oct. € 21.00   2015*

France

MEYRIEU LES ETANGS

MEYRIEU LES ETANGS *9B2* (1km SE Rural) *45.50790, 5.20850* **Camping Base de Loisirs du Moulin, Commune du Pays St Jeannais, 38440 Meyrieu-les-Etangs [04 74 59 30 34; fax 04 74 58 36 12; contact@camping-meyrieu.com; www.camping-meyrieu.com]** Exit A43 at junc 8. Enter Bourgoin & foll sp for La Gare to pick up D522 SW twd St Jean-de-Bournay. Site next to lake 1km fr D522, sp. Med, hdstg, mkd, pt shd, terr, wc; shwrs; EHU (6-10A) €2.90-4.50; lndry; shop; rest; sw; entmnt; TV; dogs €1.80; phone; adv bkg acc; quiet; fishing; archery; games rm; canoeing. "Views across lake; pedalos; sm pitches; hdstg on all pitches for car; clean san facs & site; vg, nice site." ♦ 6 Apr-30 Sep. € 15.00   2013*

MEYRUEIS *10E1* (1km E Rural) *44.18075, 3.43540* **Camping Le Champ d'Ayres, Route de la Brèze, 48150 Meyrueis [04 66 45 60 51; campinglechampdayres@wanadoo.fr; www.campinglechampdayres.com]** Fr W on D907 dir Gorges de la Jonte into Meyrueis. Foll sp Château d'Ayres & site. Med, mkd, hdg, pt shd, pt sl, wc; chem disp; mv service pnt; fam bthrm; shwrs inc; EHU (6A) €3; lndry; shop; snacks; bar; bbq; playgrnd; pool (htd); wifi; 15% statics; dogs €1; phone; Eng spkn; adv bkg acc; ccard acc; games rm; games area; bike hire; CKE/CCI. "Helpful owners; rec." ♦ 11 Apr-19 Sep. € 26.50   2012*

MEYSSAC *7C3* (2km NE Rural) *45.06150, 1.66402* **Intercommunal Moulin de Valane, Route de Collonges-la-Rouge, 19500 Meyssac [05 55 25 41 59; fax 05 55 84 07 28; mairie@meyssac.fr; www.meyssac.fr]** Well sp on D38 bet Meyssac & Collonges-la-Rouge. Med, mkd, pt shd, pt sl, wc; chem disp; shwrs; EHU (10A) €2.80; lndry; shop; rest; snacks; bar; playgrnd; pool; 80% statics; adv bkg acc; tennis; CKE/CCI. "Within walking dist of attractive vill; vg san facs; rec." ♦ 1 May-30 Sep. € 13.00   2012*

MEZE *10F1* (1km N Coastal) *43.43019, 3.61070* **Kawan Village Beau Rivage, 113 Route Nationale, 34140 Mèze [04 67 43 81 48; fax 04 67 43 66 70; reception@camping-beaurivage.fr; www.camping-beaurivage.fr]** Fr Mèze cent foll D613 dir Montpellier, site on R 100m past rndabt on leaving town; well sp. Lge, mkd, pt shd, wc; chem disp; mv service pnt; fam bthrm; shwrs inc; EHU (3-6A) inc; lndry; shop; rest; snacks; bar; bbq; playgrnd; pool (htd); paddling pool; beach sand 700m; entmnt; wifi; TV; 50% statics; dogs €6; phone; Eng spkn; adv bkg acc; quiet; ccard acc; sailing; tennis 900m; fishing; CKE/CCI. "Well equipped site; trees & narr access rds poss diff lge o'fits; vg modern san facs; lovely pool; pitches poss worn end of ssn; fitness rm; poor security - rear of site open to public car park; diff exit onto busy coast rd; conv Sète & Noilly Prat distillery; vg; excel site; close to town with gd mkt, marina and rest." ♦ 10 Apr-17 Sep. € 40.00   2013*

MEZE *10F1* (3km N Rural) *43.44541, 3.61595* **Camp Municipal Loupian, Route de Mèze, 34140 Loupian [04 67 43 57 67 or 04 67 43 82 07 (LS); camping@loupian.fr; www.loupian.fr]** Fr Mèze tak D613 & turn L at 1st Loupian sp, then foll sp for site. Med, hdg, mkd, pt shd, wc; chem disp; fam bthrm; shwrs; EHU (6A); lndry; snacks; bar; bbq; playgrnd; beach sand 3km; entmnt; dogs €1; phone; Eng spkn; adv bkg acc; quiet; tennis; CKE/CCI. "Pleasant site in popular area; plenty shd; friendly, helpful staff; vg san facs; takeaway; gd beaches; excel fisherman's rest; gd rests at Mèze & Bouziques; superb cycling on old rlwy rte fr site to Mèze (Voie Verte); rec; cent to main attractions; vg." ♦ 6 Apr-14 Oct. € 19.00   2018*

MEZIERES EN BRENNE *4H2* (6km E Rural) *46.79817, 1.30595* **Camping Bellebouche, 36290 Mézières-en-Brenne [02 54 38 32 36; fax 02 54 38 32 96; v.v.n@orange.fr; www.village-vacances-bellebouche.com]** Sp on D925. Med, mkd, pt shd, pt sl, wc cont; chem disp; fam bthrm; shwrs inc; EHU €3.50; lndry; rest; bar; bbq (elec); playgrnd; sw nr; 10% statics; phone; quiet; ccard acc; fishing; watersports; CKE/CCI. "In country park; gd walking, cycling, birdwatching; vg; san facs dated." 30 Apr-30 Sep. € 11.00   2013*

MEZOS *8E1* (1km SE Rural) *44.07980, -1.16090* **Le Village Tropical Sen Yan, 40170 Mézos [05 58 42 60 05; fax 05 58 42 64 56; reception@sen-yan.com; www.sen-yan.com]** Fr Bordeaux on N10 in 100km at Laharie turn W onto D38 dir Mimizan; in 12km turn L onto D63 to Mézos; turn L at mini-rndabt; site on L in approx 2km. Site 1.5km fr D63/D38 junc NE of Mézos. Lge, hdg, mkd, shd, wc; chem disp; fam bthrm; shwrs inc; EHU (6A) inc; gas; lndry; shop; rest; snacks; bar; bbq (gas); playgrnd (covrd, htd); paddling pool; entmnt; wifi; TV; 80% statics; dogs €5; phone; Eng spkn; adv bkg acc; quiet; ccard acc; waterslide; tennis; watersports 15km; jacuzzi; bike hire; rv fishing adj; games rm; sauna; CKE/CCI. "Attractive, restful site; many plants, inc banana trees; fitness cent; no o'fits over 8m; canoe hire 1km; modern, many sports & games; clean san facs; excel facs for families; mkt Mimizan Fri & Morcenx Wed." ♦ 1 Jun-9 Sep. € 47.00   2012*

MILLAS *8G4* (7km SW Urban) *42.67165, 2.62907* **Camp Municipal Le Colomer, Rue Colonel Fabien, 66130 Ile-sur-Tet [04 68 84 72 40; camping@ille-sur-tet.com; www.ille-sur-tet.com]** Exit N116 on NE of town, R twds Ille sur Tet on D916, L at next rndabt foll sp to site. Med, hdg, pt shd, wc; shwrs inc; EHU (10A) €4; lndry; playgrnd; wifi; 30% statics; dogs €1.50; bus adj, train 0.5km; Eng spkn; adv bkg req; games area; CKE/CCI. "Conv for Les Orgues cliffs & Prieure de Serrabone; gd rests in attractive town; pool 200m; adj rlwy not busy but conv for Perpignan; vg." 1 Nov-30 Sep. € 11.30   2016*

MILLAU *10E1 (7km N Rural) 44.15188, 3.09899*
Camping La Belle Etoile (formerly Camping d'Aguessac), Chemin des Prades, 12520 Aguessac [05 65 72 91 07 ou 06 72 23 10 56 (mob); fax 05 65 59 08 72; contact@camping-labelleetoile.fr; www.camping-labelleetoile.fr] Site on N907 in vill; ent on R v soon after level x-ing when app fr Millau. Alt app fr J44.1 on A75 via D29, unmade rd fr A75 to Aguessa. Med, mkd, pt shd, wc; chem disp; shwrs inc; EHU (6A) inc; gas; lndry; shop nr; bar; entmnt; wifi; dogs €2; quiet; canoeing; games area; rv fishing adj; CKE/CCI. "Nice, spacious, clean rvside site; gd position with mountain views; gd sized pitches; helpful & friendly staff; public footpath thro site along rv to picturesque vill; poss youth groups high ssn; sports grnd adj; excel touring base; vg location; vg quiet site."
♦ 1 May-30 Sep. € 23.00   2015*

> **"There aren't many sites open at this time of year"**
>
> If you're travelling outside peak season remember to call ahead to check site opening dates – even if the entry says 'open all year'.

MILLAU *10E1 (1km NE Urban) 44.10500, 3.08833*
Camping du Viaduc, Millau-Cureplat, 121 Ave du Millau-Plage, 12100 Millau [05 65 60 15 75; fax 05 65 61 36 51; info@camping-du-viaduc.com; www.camping-du-viaduc.com] Exit Millau on N991 (sp Nant) over Rv Tarn via Cureplat bdge. At rndabt take D187 dir Paulhe, 1st campsite on L. Lge, mkd, hdg, shd, serviced pitches; wc (htd); chem disp; fam bthrm; shwrs inc; EHU (6A) €4 (poss long lead req); gas; lndry; shop; rest; snacks; bar; bbq; playgrnd; pool (htd); paddling pool; sw; red long stay; entmnt; wifi; 20% statics; dogs €3; Eng spkn; ccard acc; CKE/CCI. "Peaceful, well-run site; helpful, welcoming staff; excel, clean san facs; barrier clsd 2200-0700; many sports & activities in area; conv for gorges & viaduct tours; quiet; super site." ♦ 8 Apr-26 Sep.
€ 36.00   2014*

MILLAU *10E1 (2km NE Urban) 44.10240, 3.09100*
Camping Indigo Millau, Ave de l'Aigoual, 12100 Millau [05 65 61 18 83; millau@camping-indigo.com; www.camping-indigo.com] Fr N exit A75 junc 45 to Millau. Turn L at 2nd traff island sp 'Camping'. Site on R over bdge in 200m. Fr S exit A75 junc 47 onto D809 & cross rv on by-pass, turn R at 1st traff island sp Nant on D991, cross bdge, site on R in 200m, sp. Site a S confluence of Rv Dourbie & Rv Tarn. Med, mkd, shd, pt sl, wc; chem disp; shwrs inc; EHU (5A) €3.50; gas; lndry; shop; snacks; playgrnd; pool; paddling pool; sw nr; 10% statics; dogs €1.50; Eng spkn; adv bkg acc; fishing nr; CKE/CCI. "Excel site; gd san facs, renovated 2015; hang-gliding nrby; pleasant, helpful owner; canoe hire nr; conv Tarn Gorges; lge mkt Fri."
1 Apr-30 Sep. € 20.50   2012*

MILLAU *10E1 (2km NE Rural) 44.10640, 3.08800*
Camping Les Erables, Route de Millau-Plage, 12100 Millau [05 65 59 15 13; fax 05 65 59 06 59; camping-les-erables@orange.fr; www.campingleserables.fr] Exit Millau on D991 (sp Nant) over Rv Tarn bdge; take L at island sp to Millau-Plage & site on L immed after Camping du Viaduc & bef Camping Larribal. On ent Millau fr N or S foll sps 'Campings'. Med, mkd, hdg, shd, wc (htd); chem disp; fam bthrm; shwrs inc; EHU (10A) €3 (rev pol); lndry; shop; snacks; bar; bbq; playgrnd; sw nr; entmnt; wifi; TV; dogs €1.20; phone; Eng spkn; adv bkg acc; ccard acc; canoeing adj; CKE/CCI. "Peaceful, well-kept, clean site on banks of Rv Tarn; lge shd pitches; friendly, helpful owners; excel modern san facs; some pitches poss diff lge o'fits; excel walking; beavers nrby; Millau Viaduct Vistor Cent a must; excel." ♦ 1 Apr-30 Sep. € 21.00   2017*

MILLAU *10E1 (1km E Urban) 44.10287, 3.08732*
Camping des Deux Rivières, 61 Ave de l'Aigoual, 12100 Millau [05 65 60 00 27 or 06 07 08 41 41 (mob); fax 05 65 60 76 78; camping.deux-rivieres@orange.fr or camp2rivieres@yahoo.fr; www.camping-des-deux-rivieres.fr] Fr N on D911 foll sp for Montpellier down to rv. At rndabt by bdge turn L over bdge, site immed on L well sp. Fr S on D992 3rd bdge, sp camping. Sm, mkd, shd, wc (htd); chem disp; mv service pnt; shwrs inc; EHU (8-10A) €3 (poss long lead req); gas; lndry; shop; snacks; playgrnd; wifi; dogs €1.50; phone; quiet; fishing; CKE/CCI. "Basic site in gd situation by rv; friendly, helpful owners; gd san facs; gd base for touring gorges." 1 Apr-29 Oct.
€ 29.00   2014*

MILLAU *10E1 (1km E Rural) 44.10166, 3.09611*
Camping Les Rivages, Ave de l'Aigoual, 12100 Millau [05 65 61 01 07 or 06 10 75 65 94 (mob); fax 05 65 59 03 56; info@campinglesrivages.com; www.campinglesrivages.com] Fr Millau take D991 dir Nant (sp Gorges de la Dourbie & Campings). Cross Rv Tarn & cont on this rd, site is 500m after bdge on R. Lge, pt shd, serviced pitches; wc (htd); chem disp; mv service pnt; fam bthrm; shwrs inc; EHU (10A) inc (poss rev pol); lndry; shop; rest; snacks; bar; bbq; playgrnd; pool; sw nr; red long stay; twin axles; entmnt; wifi; TV; 10% statics; dogs €4; phone; Eng spkn; adv bkg acc; quiet; ccard acc; canoeing nr; squash; fishing; games area; tennis; games rm; CKE/CCI. "Pleasant, busy, scenic site - esp rv/side pitches; helpful & friendly staff; immac, clean san facs; vg rest/snack bar - home cooked & inexpensive; gd security; views of Millau viaduct; hang-gliding; spa; easy access to town; mkt Wed & Fri; pleasant cycle ride along rvbank; v nice site." ♦ 15 Apr-30 Sep. € 37.00   2015*

MILLAU

MILLAU 10E1 (3km E Rural) 44.10029, 3.11099 **FFCC**
Camping St Lambert, Ave de l'Aigoual, 12100 Millau [05 65 60 00 48; contact@campingsaintlambert.fr; www.campingsaintlambert.fr] Fr N on either D809 or D11 foll dir D992 St Affrique/Albi. Turn L at rndabt over bdge onto D991 dir Nant. Site on R, sp. Fr S on D992 turn R at rndabt & dir as above. Med, mkd, shd, wc; chem disp; mv service pnt; shwrs inc; EHU (6A); gas; lndry; shop; bar; playgrnd; pool; sw nr; wifi; 10% statics; dogs €1; adv bkg acc; quiet; ccard acc; CKE/CCI. "Spacious, gd site; sm pitches, all under trees; stretched high ssn; site needed gd tidy up, but nice atmosphere; 30min walk into Millau; gd LS; owners pleasant & helpful; lovely area." 30 Apr-26 Sep. € 20.50   2014*

> **"That's changed – Should I let the Club know?"**
>
> If you find something on site that's different from the site entry, fill in a report and let us know. See camc.com/europereport.

MIMIZAN 7D1 (2km N Rural) 44.21997, -1.22968
Camping du Lac, Ave de Woolsack, 40200 Mimizan [05 58 09 01 21; fax 05 58 09 43 06; lac@mimizan-camping.com; www.mimizan-camping.com] Fr Mimizan N on D87, site on R. Lge, mkd, pt shd, wc; chem disp; mv service pnt; fam bthrm; shwrs inc; EHU (3A) inc; gas; lndry; shop; rest; snacks; bar; bbq; playgrnd; entmnt; 10% statics; dogs €1.70; adv bkg acc; quiet; boating; fishing. "Nice site in lovely location; lake adj - no sw; o'night m'vans area; rec." ♦ 27 Apr-20 Sep. € 20.00   2012*

MIMIZAN 7D1 (3km E Rural) 44.22296, -1.19445
Camping Aurilandes, 1001 Promenade de l'Etang, 40200 Aureilhan [05 58 09 10 88 or 05 46 55 10 01; fax 05 46 55 10 00; www.village-center.com] Fr N10 S of Bordeaux take D626 W fr Labouheyre twds Mimizan. Site 1km fr D626 by Lake Aureilhan. V lge, mkd, pt shd, wc; mv service pnt; shwrs inc; EHU (6-10A) inc; lndry; shop; rest; playgrnd; pool (htd); paddling pool; entmnt; dogs €3; Eng spkn; adv bkg acc; quiet; ccard acc; watersports; sauna; tennis; games rm. "Dir access to lake; spa." ♦ 27 Apr-9 Sep. € 44.00   2013*

MIMIZAN PLAGE 7D1 (1km E Coastal) 44.21629, -1.28584 Camping de la Plage, Blvd d'Atlantique, 40200 Mimizan-Plage [05 58 09 00 32; fax 05 58 09 44 94; contact@mimizan-camping.com; www.mimizan-camping.com] Turn off N10 at Labouheyre on D626 to Mimizan (28km). Approx 5km after Mimizan turn R. Site in approx 500m. V lge, mkd, pt shd, wc; mv service pnt; fam bthrm; shwrs; EHU (10A) inc; lndry; shop; bbq; playgrnd; beach sand 850m; entmnt; wifi; 20% statics; dogs €1.80; games area. "Gd facs; town nrby; big busy coastal site; many cycle paths; excel." 7 Apr-30 Sep. € 24.00   2018*

MIMIZAN PLAGE 7D1 (3km E Coastal) 44.20420, -1.2908 Club Marina-Landes, Rue Marina, 40202 Mimizan-Plage-Sud [05 58 09 12 66; fax 05 58 09 16 40; contact@clubmarina.com; www.marinalandes.com] Turn R off N10 at Labouheyre onto D626 to Mimizan (28km). Approx 5km fr Mimizan-Plage turn L at Camping Marina sp on dual c'way. Site sp on S bank of rv. V lge, hdg, hdstg, pt shd, wc; chem disp; mv service pnt; fam bthrm; shwrs inc; EHU (10A) €7; gas; lndry; shop; rest; snacks; bar; bbq; playgrnd; pool (covrd, htd); paddling pool; beach sand 500m; entmnt; wifi; TV; 10% statics; dogs €5; Eng spkn; adv bkg acc; quiet; ccard acc; ice; golf 7km; games area; horseriding; games rm; bike hire; waterslide; fitness rm; tennis; CKE/CCI. "Excursions to Dax, Biarritz & Bordeaux areas; excel leisure facs; excel; great location." ♦ 15 May-16 Sep. € 61.00   2017*

MIRAMBEAU 7C2 (1km N Urban) 45.37822, -0.56874 Camp Municipal Le Carrelet, 92 Ave de la République, 17150 Mirambeau [06 71 77 30 38; campingcarrelet@hotmail.fr; www.mirambeau-tourisme.fr] Exit 37 fr A10 onto D730/D137 dir Mirambeau. Site opp Super U supmkt, behind TO. Sm, pt shd, pt sl, wc cont; chem disp; mv service pnt; shwrs inc; EHU (10A) €4.50 (poss rev pol); gas; lndry; shop nr; rest nr; snacks; bar; 80% statics; dogs €1.50; phone; quiet. "Basic site; clean but tired facs; obliging warden; site yourself & warden calls evening; v muddy when wet; poss neglected LS; conv NH for A10."
1 Apr-31 Oct. € 19.00   2014*

MIRAMBEAU 7C2 (8km S Rural) 45.31830, -0.60290
Camping Chez Gendron, 33820 St Palais [05 57 32 96 47; info@chezgendron.com; www.chezgendron.com] N fr Blaye on N137; turn to St Palais, past church 1km; turn L twd St Ciers. Site sp R down narr lane. Or N fr Bordeaux on A10 exit juncs 37 or 38 onto N137 to St Palais & as above. Sm, mkd, pt shd, pt sl, terr, wc (htd); chem disp; fam bthrm; shwrs; EHU (6A) inc; lndry; shop nr; rest; snacks; bar; bbq; playgrnd; pool; paddling pool; wifi; TV; dogs free; phone; Eng spkn; adv bkg rec; quiet; games rm; tennis 3km; games area; CKE/CCI. "Peaceful & relaxed site in vineyards; lovely ambience; friendly, helpful Dutch owners; sep car park high ssn; superb san facs; ltd facs LS; pitches nr bar/recep poss noisy till late peak ssn; poss waterlogged after heavy rain; chem disp poor; excel Sun mkt." ♦
1 Mar-31 Oct. € 25.70   2014*

⊞ **MIRAMBEAU** 7C2 (15km W Coastal) 45.38333, -0.72250 Camping L'Estuaire, La Grange Godinet, 17150 St Thomas-de-Cônac [05 46 86 08 20; info@lestuaire.com; www.lestuaire.com] Exit A10 junc 37 Mirambeau onto D730 dir Royan. At St Ciers-du-Taillon foll sp St Thomas-de-Cônac, site sp. Lge, hdg, mkd, unshd, wc (htd); chem disp; mv service pnt; fam bthrm; shwrs inc; EHU (16A) inc; lndry; shop; rest; snacks; bar; bbq; playgrnd; pool; paddling pool; entmnt; TV; 60% statics; dogs €4; adv bkg acc; quiet; games area; gym; bike hire; watersports nr; fishing; tennis. "Interesting area nr Gironde estuary; gd walking & cycling." ♦ € 20.00   2016*

MIRAMONT DE GUYENNE *7D2 (7km NW Rural) 44.62877, 0.29135* **Camp Municipal Le Dropt, Rue du Pont, 47800 Allemans-du-Dropt [05 53 20 25 59 or 05 53 20 23 37 (Mairie); fax 05 53 20 68 91]** Fr D668 site well sp in vill. Sm, shd, wc; chem disp; shwrs inc; EHU (20A) €2; shop nr; rest nr; bar nr; playgrnd; quiet; canoeing; kayaking; CKE/CCI. "Attractive site on opp side of Rv Dropt to vill; friendly warden; ltd pitches for c'vans & lge o'fits due trees & o'hanging branches; basic but clean facs; excel." 1 Apr-15 Oct. € 7.00 2014*

MIRANDE *8F2 (1km NE Rural) 43.55235, 0.31371* **Camping Pouylebon (Devroome), Pouylebon, 32320 Montesquiou [05 62 66 72 10; campingpouylebon2@wanadoo.fr; http://campingpouylebon.pagesperso-orange.fr]** Exit N21 NW at Mirande onto D159; in 10km, at Pouylebon, turn R onto D216; in 900m site on R, 600m down track. Sm, pt shd, pt sl, wc; chem disp; shwrs inc; EHU (6A) €2.85; lndry; shop; snacks; bar; bbq; playgrnd; pool; wifi; TV; dogs free; Eng spkn; adv bkg acc; games area; games rm; tennis nr; horseriding nr; fishing nr. "Rural retreat; charming, Dutch owners; meals on request; excel." 15 Apr-15 Oct. € 26.00 2013*

MIRANDE *8F2 (1km E Rural) 43.51322, 0.40990* **Camp Municipal L'Ile du Pont, Au Batardeau, 32300 Mirande [05 62 66 64 11; fax 05 62 66 69 86; info@camping-gers.com; www.groupevla.fr]** On N21 Auch-Tarbes, foll sp to site on island in Rv Grande Baise. Med, pt shd, wc (htd); chem disp; mv service pnt; fam bthrm; shwrs inc; EHU (6A) inc; lndry; rest; snacks; bar; bbq; playgrnd; pool; entmnt; wifi; 20% statics; dogs €1; adv bkg rec; quiet; bike hire; games rm; sailing; canoeing; windsurfing; tennis; waterslide; fishing; CKE/CCI. "Excel site; helpful staff; quiet location; 5min walk to town; gd stopover if heading to pyrenees." 15 Apr-30 Sep. € 20.00 2016*

MIREPOIX (ARIEGE) *8F4 (1km E Rural) 43.08871, 1.88585* **Camping Les Nysades, Route de Limoux, 09500 Mirepoix [05 61 60 28 63; fax 05 61 68 89 48; campinglesnysades@orange.fr; www.camping-mirepoix-ariege.com]** E fr Pamiers on D119 to Mirepoix. Site well sp on D626. Med, hdg, mkd, shd, wc; chem disp; shwrs; EHU (6A) €3.50; shop nr; pool; 10% statics; dogs €2; quiet; fishing 1km; tennis. "Lge pitches; san facs ok; site a bit tired; interesting medieval town; mkt Mon rec; gd little site, walks along rv; barrier open 0700-2300, if warden not on site he will collect fees later." ♦ 16 Apri-31 Oct. € 15.00 2017*

MIRMANDE *9D2 (3km SE Rural) 44.68705, 4.85444* **Camping La Poche, 26270 Mirmande [04 75 63 02 88; fax 04 75 63 14 94; camping@la-poche.com; wwwcamping-lapoche.com]** Fr N on N7, 3km after Loriol turn L onto D57 sp Mirmande. Site sp in 7km on L. Fr S on N7 turn R onto D204 in Saulce & foll sp. Med, hdg, hdstg, mkd, shd, terr, wc; chem disp; fam bthrm; shwrs; EHU (6A) €3; lndry; shop; rest; snacks; bar; playgrnd; pool; paddling pool; entmnt; TV; 90% statics; adv bkg acc; quiet; games area; CKE/CCI. "Pleasant, scenic, gd site in wooded valley; gd walking/cycling; v friendly, helpful Dutch owners." 1 Apr-1 Oct. € 26.00 2015*

MODANE *9C4 (12km ENE Rural) 45.22870, 6.78116* **Camp Municipal Val d'Ambin, Plan de l'Eglise, 73500 Bramans-le-Verney [04 79 05 03 05 or 06 16 51 90 91 (mob); fax 04 79 05 03 03; campingbramans@gmail.com; www.camping-bramansvanoise.com]** 10km after Modane on D1006 twd Lanslebourg, take 2nd turning R twd vill of Bramans, & foll camping sp, site by church. App fr Lanslebourg, after 12km turn L at camping sp on D306 at end of vill. Med, unshd, wc (htd); mv service pnt; fam bthrm; shwrs; EHU (12-16A) €3.70-5.20; lndry;`shop; rest nr; bar nr; bbq; playgrnd; entmnt; wifi; TV; dogs €1.60; quiet; games area. "Away-fr-it-all site worth the climb; beautiful area, mountain views; gd dog walk adj; excel, brilliant site; great for walkers & outdoor enthusiasts; v well rec; friendly staff." 20 Apr-30 Oct. € 17.00 2015*

⊞ **MODANE** *9C4 (1km W Rural) 45.19437, 6.66413* **Camping Les Combes, Refuge de La Sapinière, Route de Bardonnèche, 73500 Modane [04 79 05 00 23 or 06 10 16 54 61 (mob); fax 04 79 05 00 23; camping-modane@wanadoo.fr; http://camping-modane.chez-alice.fr]** Exit A43 junc 30 onto D1006 thro Fourmeaux to o'skirts Modane; at Casino supmkt turn R onto D215; site in 500m on bend on hill (at junc with D216). Fr Fréjus tunnel site on L 1km bef Modane. Med, pt shd, pt sl, wc (htd); chem disp; shwrs inc; EHU (6A) €3; lndry; shop nr; snacks; bar; playgrnd; wifi; 10% statics; dogs €1.50; quiet; tennis. "Excel & conv NH for Fréjus tunnel; warm welcome; winter sports; superb scenery; ltd san facs; LS recep opens 1700 - site yourself." € 13.00 2014*

MOISSAC

MOISSAC *8E3* (2km S Rural) *44.09664, 1.08878*
Camping Le Moulin du Bidounet, St Benoît, 82200 Moissac [05 63 32 52 52; info@camping-moissac. com; www.camping-moissac.com] Exit A62/E72 at junc 9 at Castelsarrasin onto D813 dir Moissac. Or fr N on D813 cross Rv Tarn, turn L at 1st rndabt & foll camp sp, site on L by rv. NB Height restriction 3.05m for tunnel at ent & tight turn lge o'fits. Med, hdg, mkd, hdstg, shd, wc; chem disp; mv service pnt; fam bthrm; shwrs inc; EHU (6A) €3.10; lndry; shop nr; rest nr; bar; bbq; playgrnd; pool; red long stay; entmnt; wifi; 10% statics; dogs €1.50; phone; Eng spkn; adv bkg acc; quiet; ccard acc; canoe hire; fishing; bike hire; watersports; boat hire; CKE/CCI. "Excel, pleasant, rvside site in lovely area; extra for twin axles; helpful staff; basic, clean san facs; conv lovely town & abbey; gd fishing; walking/cycling; vg cycle track by canal; gd NH; entry tight for lge o'fits; passport identity needed." ♦ 1 Apr-30 Sep. € 24.20   2018*

"We must tell the Club about that great site we found"

Get your site reports in by mid-August and we'll do our best to get your updates into the next edition.

MOLIETS ET MAA *8E1* (2km W Coastal) *43.85166, -1.38375* **Camping Les Cigales, Ave de l'Océan, 40660 Moliets-Plage [05 58 48 51 18; fax 05 58 48 53 27; reception@camping-les-cigales.fr; www. camping-les-cigales.fr]** In Moliets-et-Maa, turn W for Moliets-Plage, site on R in vill. Lge, shd, pt sl, wc; chem disp; mv service pnt; shwrs inc; EHU (5A) €3.50; lndry; shop; rest; snacks; bar; bbq; playgrnd; beach sand 300m; TV; 80% statics; dogs €2; adv bkg acc; quiet; ccard acc; games area; CKE/CCI. "Site in pine wood - sandy soil; narr access tracks; excel beach & surfing; many shops, rests 100m; gd forest walk to N." 1 Apr-30 Sep. € 36.00   2014*

MOLIETS ET MAA *8E1* (2km W Coastal) *43.85210, -1.38730* **Camping St Martin, Ave de l'Océan 40660 Moliets-Plage [05 58 48 52 30; fax 05 58 48 50 73; contact@camping-saint-martin.fr; www.camping-saint-martin.fr]** On N10 exit for Léon, Moliets-et-Maa. At Moliets foll sp to Moliets-Plage. Camp site after Les Cigales, by beach. V lge, mkd, hdg, pt shd, pt sl, terr, serviced pitches; wc (htd); chem disp; fam bthrm; shwrs inc; EHU (10A) €5.30; gas; lndry; shop; rest; snacks; bar; playgrnd; pool (covrd, htd); paddling pool; beach sand 300m; entmnt; TV; dogs €5 (free LS); Eng spkn; adv bkg rec; quiet; ccard acc; games area; jacuzzi; tennis nr; watersports; golf nr; sauna; CKE/CCI. "Excel family site; cycle paths; vg san facs; gd for teenagers; gd cycling, walking." 8 Apr-1 Nov. € 43.00   2017*

See advertisement

MOLSHEIM *6E3* (1km SE Urban) *48.54124, 7.50003* **Camp Municipal de Molsheim, 6 Rue des Sports, 67120 Molsheim [03 88 49 82 45 or 03 88 49 58 58 (LS); fax 03 88 49 58 59; camping-molsheim@ orange.fr; www.mairie-molsheim.fr]** On ent town fr Obernai on D1422 site sp on R immed after x-ing sm rv bdge. Med, mkd, pt shd, wc; chem disp; mv service pnt; shwrs inc; EHU (10A) €3.40; lndry; bbq; wifi; dogs €1.30; train to Strasbourg 700m; Eng spkn; adv bkg acc; bike hire; CKE/CCI. "Pleasant site; excel san facs; pool adj; easy walk to town cent & shops; Bugatti museum in town; vg." ♦ 7 Apr-29 Oct. € 18.00   2017*

MONASTIER SUR GAZEILLE, LE *9C1* (1km SW Rural) *44.93662, 3.98453* **Camping Estela, Route du Moulin de Savin, 43150 Le Monastier-sur-Gazeille [06 87 48 60 28 04 71 03 82 24 (mob); contact@ campingestela.com]** Fr Le Puy-en-Velay E on D535; in 4km fork R continuing on D535 to Le Monastier-sur-Gazeille; site sp fr ent to vill. App only fr N end of vill. Site in bottom of valley; gd power-weight ratio needed on dep. Sm, pt shd, wc; shwrs; EHU (3-10A) €3.20; lndry; snacks; bbq; playgrnd; sw; wifi; dogs €2.50; quiet. "Lovely rvside site in beautiful area; friendly staff; Le Monastier was start of RL Stevenson's 'Travels with a Donkey'." 1 Jun-30 Sep. € 18.00 2013*

MONESTIER DE CLERMONT 9C3 (1km SW Urban) 44.91515, 5.62809 **Camping Les Portes du Trièves, Chemin de Chambons, 38650 Monestier-de-Clermont [04 76 34 01 24 or 04 76 34 06 20 (LS); fax 04 76 34 19 75; camping.lesportesdutrieves@wanadoo.fr; www.campingisere.com]** Turn W off D1075. Sp in vill. 700m up hill adj sw pool & school. Fr Grenoble take A51 to S end of vill & foll sps to site. Sm, hdg, hdstg, mkd, pt shd, terr, wc (htd); chem disp; mv service pnt; shwrs inc; EHU (10A); lndry; shop nr; rest nr; bar nr; playgrnd; red long stay; wifi; dogs free; bus 500m; Eng spkn; adv bkg acc; quiet; tennis adj; games rm; CKE/CCI. "Attractive, immac, well-run site; friendly, helpful staff; clean san facs but sm; watersports at lake; htd pool 200m; spectacular countryside; train to Grenoble; gd NH; off clsd 1200-1530, site self." 1 May-30 Sep. € 15.00 2015*

MONETIER LES BAINS, LE 9C3 (1km NW Rural) 44.98059, 6.49537 **Camp Municipal Les Deux Glaciers, 05220 Le Monêtier-les-Bains [07 89 56 58 77; camping.monetier@orange.fr; www.monetier.com]** On D1091 12km NW of Briançon; pass thro Le Monêtier-les-Bains, in 1km site sp on L. Med, hdstg, mkd, shd, terr, wc (htd); chem disp; mv service pnt; fam bthrm; shwrs inc; EHU (16A) €3.50; lndry; shop nr; rest nr; bar nr; playgrnd; dogs €1; bus 1km; adv bkg acc; CKE/CCI. "Excel, scenic site bef x-ing Montgenèvre pass; gd base for Ecrins National Park; easy access fr D1091; footpath to vill; v friendly helpful staff; immac gd facs; excel for hiking, cycling, wildlife & flowers; fantastic loc; clean." ♦ 1 Jun-30 Sep. € 15.50 2017*

MONFORT 8E3 (0km N Urban) 43.79628, 0.82315 **Camp Municipal de Monfort, 32120 Monfort [05 62 06 83 26 (Mairie); mairiemonfort@orange.fr]** SE fr Fleurance on D654 to Monfort, then foll sp to 'Cent Ville' & camping sp. Town has narr rds so foll sp & v narr app rd. Sm, hdg, pt shd, pt sl, wc; chem disp; shwrs inc; EHU (5A) €1.50; shop nr; rest nr; bar nr; bbq; playgrnd; dogs €0.50; quiet; CKE/CCI. "Well-kept, scenic, CL-type site on ramparts of attractive Bastide vill; pitch yourself, warden calls am & pm; ltd pitches big enough for c'van; long walk to waste disposal; excel; pitches well prepared and solid." 1 May-15 Oct. € 9.50 2013*

MONISTROL D'ALLIER 9C1 (4km N Rural) 44.99148, 3.67781 **Camp Municipal Le Marchat, 43580 St Privat-d'Allier [04 71 57 22 13; fax 04 71 57 25 50; info@mairie-saintprivatdallier.fr; www.mairie-saintprivatdallier.fr]** Fr Le Puy-en-Velay W on D589. Turn R in cent of vill at petrol stn, site on R in 200m. Sm, hdg, shd, terr, wc; chem disp; shwrs inc; EHU (10A) €1.10; shop nr; bar nr; playgrnd; quiet. "Beautifully-kept, superb sm site; friendly warden; not suitable lge o'fits; bars & shop within 200mtrs." ♦ 1 May-1 Nov. € 6.00 2018*

MONISTROL D'ALLIER 9C1 (0km E Rural) 44.96912, 3.64793 **Camp Municipal Le Vivier, 43580 Monistrol-d'Allier [04 71 57 24 14 or 04 71 57 21 21 (Mairie); fax 04 71 57 25 03; mairie-monistroldallier@wanadoo.fr; www.monistroldallier.fr/camping.php]** Fr Le Puy-en-Velay W on D589 to Monistrol-d'Allier. Turn L in vill immed after rlwy stn & cont down steep entry rd bef x-ing bdge. Site sp in town cent. Sm, mkd, pt shd, wc; chem disp; shwrs inc; EHU (5-10A) €2.60; shop; rest; snacks; bar nr; bbq; dogs; phone; train 500m; quiet; CKE/CCI. "Vg site steep valley; bar 200m." ♦ 15 Apr-15 Sep. € 12.00 2014*

MONISTROL SUR LOIRE 9C1 (7km SE Rural) 45.21630, 4.21240 **Kawan Village Camping de Vaubarlet, 43600 Ste Sigolène [04 71 66 64 95; fax 04 71 66 11 98; camping@vaubarlet.com; www.vaubarlet.com]** Fr Monistrol take D44 SE twd Ste Sigolène & turn R into vill. In vill take D43 dir Grazac for 6km. Site by Rv Dunière, ent L bef bdge. Site well sp fr vill. Med, mkd, pt shd, wc; chem disp; mv service pnt; shwrs inc; EHU (6A) €3 (poss rev pol); lndry; shop; rest; snacks; bar; bbq; playgrnd; pool (htd); paddling pool; sw nr; entmnt; wifi; TV; 15% statics; dogs €1; phone; Eng spkn; adv bkg acc; quiet; ccard acc; trout fishing; games area; bike hire; CKE/CCI. "Friendly, helpful staff; well-run site; excel, spotless san facs; interesting museums nrby; ideal for families." ♦ 1 May-30 Sep. € 28.00 2014*

MONISTROL SUR LOIRE 9C1 (8km NW Urban) 45.31087, 4.12004 **Camping Municipal La Garenne, Route du Camping, 43210 Bas-en-Basset [04 71 66 72 37 or 04 71 66 70 01; contact@basenbasset.fr; www.basenbasset.fr]** Fr N88 take the S exit (D47) sp Monistrol-sur-Loire. L at 1st rndabt; downhill on D12 dir Gourdon & Bas-en-Basset. Immed after Rv Loire turn R on D46. At rndabt turn R & foll sp to site. Med, hdg, mkd, pt shd, wc; chem disp; mv service pnt; shwrs; EHU (10A); lndry; shop nr; bar; bbq; playgrnd; pool (htd); twin axles; wifi; 95% statics; dogs; phone; quiet; games rm; games area; CKE/CCI. "Fishing adj; bustling static site, sm quiet area next to rv for tourers; takeaway; clean modern san facs; vg value; gd NH." ♦ 15 Apr-30 Sep. € 7.00 2015*

MONNERVILLE 4E3 (2km S Rural) 48.33256, 2.04702 **Camping Le Bois de la Justice, Méréville, 91930 Monnerville [01 64 95 05 34; fax 01 64 95 17 31; leboisdelajustice@gmail.com; www.campingleboisdelajustice.com]** Fr N20 S of Etampes, turn onto D18 at Monnerville, site well sp. Long narr app rd. Med, hdg, mkd, pt shd, pt sl, wc (htd); chem disp; shwrs inc; EHU (5A) inc; lndry; snacks; bar; bbq; cooking facs; playgrnd; pool (htd); TV; 50% statics; dogs €1; phone; Eng spkn; adv bkg acc; quiet; ccard acc; tennis; games area. "Delightful woodland oasis in open countryside; beware caterpillars in spring (poisonous to dogs); friendly welcome; clean san facs; ideal for Chartres, Fontainebleau, Orléans, Paris or excel NH just off N20; excel." ♦ 7 Feb-24 Nov. € 25.00 2015*

MONPAZIER

MONPAZIER *7D3* (3km SW Rural) *44.65875, 0.87925* Camping Moulin de David, Route de Villeréal, 24540 Gaugeac-Monpazier [05 53 22 65 25 or 04 99 57 20 25; fax 05 53 23 99 76; contact@moulindedavid. com; www.moulindedavid.com] Fr Monpazier, take D2 SW twd Villeréal, site sp on L after 3km. Narr app rds. Lge, hdg, mkd, pt shd, serviced pitches; wc (htd); chem disp; mv service pnt; fam bthrm; shwrs inc; EHU (10A) inc gas; lndry; shop; rest; snacks; bar; bbq; playgrnd; pool; paddling pool; sw; entmnt; wifi; TV; 80% statics; dogs €3; Eng spkn; adv bkg acc; quiet; ccard acc; games rm; waterslide; archery; bike hire; tennis; fishing adj; games area; CKE/CCI. "Charming site nr lovely town; welcoming, helpful owners; excel facs, ltd LS; poss mosquitoes nr rv thro site; mkt Thur Monpazier; highly rec; v rural; superb rest." ♦ 30 Mar-30 Sep. € 35.00   2014*

⊞ **MONS LA TRIVALLE** *10F1* (3km SE Rural) *43.56247, 2.97306* Camp Municipal de Tarassac, 34390 Mons-la-Trivalle [04 67 97 72 64; commune demonslatrivalle@orange.fr] Fr D908 turn S onto D14, sp Béziers; site off D14 on Rv Orb. Lge, mkd, hdstg, shd, pt sl, wc; shwrs inc; EHU; lndry; shop; rest; snacks; bar; playgrnd; sw nr; 10% statics; dogs; phone; quiet; fishing adj. "Fair sh stay; watersports cent adj; pitches bounded by boulders; beautiful area; site a bit unkept; v natural enviroment; vg." € 14.50   2012*

MONT DORE, LE *7B4* (4km SE Rural) *45.571474, 2.817692* Domaine de la Grande Cascade, Route de Besse, 63240 Le Mont-Dore [04 73 65 06 23; contact@camping-grandecascade.com; www.camping-grandecascade.com] Fr Le Mont-Dore take D36 (12% incline) via col rte twd Besse-en-Chandesse. Site on R visible fr rd after 4km. App fairly steep & winding with poor surface. Med, mkd, hdg, pt shd, pt sl, wc; chem disp; mv service pnt; fam bthrm; EHU (6A); lndry; snacks; cooking facs; playgrnd; wifi; 5% statics; dogs €1; Eng spkn; adv bkg acc; quiet; games area; CKE/CCI. "Excel; simple with magnificent, stunning mountain views; walk to waterfall; modern clean san facs; helpful staff." ♦ 1 Jun-30 Sep. € 15.00   2018*

MONT LOUIS *8G4* (5km W Rural) *42.50636, 2.04671* Camping Huttopia Font-Romeu, Route de Mont-Louis, 66120 Font-Romeu [04 68 30 09 32; fax 04 68 04 56 39; font-romeu@huttopia.com; www.huttopia.com] W fr Mont-Louis on D618. Site on L bef Font-Romeu, opp stadium. Fr Aix-les-Thermes or Puigcerdà turn E at Ur up longish hill, thro town to site on R at o'skts. Lge, pt shd, sl, wc (htd); shwrs; EHU (6-10A) €4.20-6.20; lndry; shop; rest; bar; pool (htd); paddling pool; entmnt; wifi; 10% statics; dogs €3.50; phone; adv bkg acc; quiet; tennis 500m; horseriding 1km. "Gd cent for mountain walks; site at 1800m altitude." 19 Jun-13 Sep. € 22.00   2013*

MONT ST MICHEL, LE *2E4* (10km E Rural) *48.62822, -1.41508* Camping St Michel, Route du Mont-St Michel, 50220 Courtils [02 33 70 96 90; fax 02 33 70 99 09; infos@campingsaintmichel.com; www.campingsaintmichel.com] Fr A84 exit J33. Foll sp for Courtils on Mont St Michel rd. Site on L at far end of vill. Med, mkd, hdg, pt shd, pt sl, wc (htd); chem disp; mv service pnt; fam bthrm; shwrs inc; EHU (6A) €3.50; gas; lndry; shop; snacks; bar; bbq; playgrnd; pool (htd); entmnt; wifi; TV; 40% statics; dogs €2-3; phone; bus adj; Eng spkn; adv bkg acc; quiet; ccard acc; bike hire; games area; games rm; CKE/CCI. "Excel, flat site; helpful, friendly owner; excel modern san facs (unisex); cycle paths adj; gd NH for St Malo; attractive; vg." ♦ 31 Mar-1 Nov. € 29.00   2017*

MONT ST MICHEL, LE *2E4* (4km S Rural) *48.59622, -1.51244* Camping aux Pommiers, 28 Route du Mont-St Michel, 50170 Beauvoir [02 33 60 11 36; pommiers@aol.com; www.camping-auxpommiers.com] N fr Pontorson foll D976 sp Le Mont St Michel. Site 5km on R on ent vill of Beauvoir. Med, mkd, hdstg, hdg, pt shd, wc (htd); chem disp; mv service pnt; shwrs inc; EHU (6A) €4; gas; lndry; shop; snacks; bar; bbq; playgrnd; pool (htd); beach shgl 2km; entmnt; wifi; TV; 30% statics; dogs €1.20; Eng spkn; adv bkg acc; quiet; ccard acc; games area; waterslide; bike hire; games rm; tennis 900m; CKE/CCI. "Busy site, rec arr early; friendly, helpful staff & owner; tired clean facs; gd touring base; easy cycle ride to Mont St Michel or pleasant walk; excel site; modern; v highly rec." 27 Mar-11 Nov. € 27.00   2014*

MONTAGNAC *10F1* (4km SE Rural) *43.45175, 3.51600* Camping Domaine St Martin-du-Pin, 34530 Montagnac [04 67 24 00 37; fax 04 67 24 47 50; www.saint-martin-du-pin.com] Exit A75 junc 59 onto D113 to Montagnac; 2km past Montagnac turn R immed past picnic site at end of dual c'way, site sp. Sm, hdg, pt shd, pt sl, wc; chem disp; mv service pnt; fam bthrm; shwrs inc; EHU €3.50; lndry; shop nr; bbq; playgrnd; pool; 10% statics; Eng spkn; adv bkg rec; quiet; games area; CKE/CCI. "Delightful, relaxing site; lge pitches, blocks req on most; clean facs; gd touring base; beautiful views." ♦ 1 Mar-12 Oct. € 23.00   2014*

⊞ **MONTAIGU** *2H4* (10km SE Rural) *46.93769, -1.21575* Camping L'Eden, La Raillière, 85600 La Boissière-de-Montaigu [02 51 41 62 32; fax 02 51 41 56 07; contact@camping-domaine-eden.fr; www.domaine-eden.fr] Fr Montaigu S on D137, in 8km turn E on D62, thro Le Pont-Legé. Site sp on L off D62. Med, mkd, shd, wc; shwrs inc; EHU (10A) inc; gas; lndry; shop; rest; snacks; bar; playgrnd; pool (htd); entmnt; TV; 40% statics; dogs €2; adv bkg acc; tennis; CKE/CCI. "Pleasant, quiet site in woodlands; site poss open all year; clean facs; motor mover useful; site looking a bit tired." ♦ € 23.00   2017*

MONTBARD 6G1 (1km N Urban) 47.6314, 4.33303
Camp Municipal Les Treilles, Rue Michel Servet, 21500 Montbard [03 80 92 69 50; fax 03 80 92 21 60; camping.montbard@wanadoo.fr; www.montbard.com] Lies off N side D980. Camping sp clearly indicated on all app including by-pass. Turn onto by-pass at traff lts at rndabt at junc of D905 & D980. Site nr pool. Med, hdg, pt shd, wc; chem disp; shwrs inc; EHU (16A) €4; lndry; shop nr; snacks; bbq; playgrnd; sw nr; dogs €2; phone; bike hire; CKE/CCI. "Pleasant & well-kept site; gd pitches; lge, smart san facs; poss contract worker campers; pool complex adj inc; quiet but rd/rlwy noise at far end; interesting area; excel NH." ♦ 26 Mar-30 Oct. € 20.00   2016*

MONTBARREY 6H2 (1km SW Rural) 47.01230, 5.63761 FLOWER Camping Les Trois Ours, 28 Rue du Pont, 39380 Montbarrey [03 84 81 50 45; h.rabbe@orange.fr; www.camping-les3ours-jura.com or www.flowercampings.com] Exit A39 junc onto D905 E; 1km after Mont-sur-Vaudrey on D472 turn L dir Montbarrey. Cross rv, site on L at rvside on edge of vill. Med, hdg, mkd, shd, wc (htd); chem disp; mv service pnt; fam bthrm; shwrs inc; EHU (10A) inc; lndry; shop nr; rest; snacks; bar; bbq; playgrnd; pool; wifi; TV; 10% statics; dogs; phone; bus; Eng spkn; adv bkg acc; quiet; ccard acc; games rm. "Improvements planned; vg walking/cycling fr site; excel menu in rest."
♦ 15 Apr-30 Sep. € 34.00   2014*

MONTBAZON 4G2 (1km N Rural) 47.29044, 0.71595
Camping de la Grange Rouge, 37250 Montbazon [02 47 26 06 43; fax 02 47 26 03 13; infos@camping-montbazon.com; www.camping-montbazon.com] On D910 thro Montbazon fr S to N, after x-ing bdge (pt of D910) immed turn L to site. Clearly visible & clearly sp on W side of rd at N end of town. Med, mkd, pt shd, wc; chem disp; shwrs inc; EHU (10A) €4; lndry, shop nr; rest nr; bar nr; playgrnd; pool (htd); TV; 10% statics; dogs €2; Eng spkn; adv bkg acc; quiet; ccard acc; fishing; tennis; CKE/CCI. "Lovely, spacious rvside site in pretty town (walkable); helpful, friendly owner; bar adj; basic facs dated but clean; conv Tours & a'routes; poorly maintained." ♦ 1 Apr-15 Oct. € 20.50   2016*

MONTBERT 2H4 (1km SE Rural) 47.05133, -1.47930
Camping Le Relais des Garennes (Gendron), La Bauche Coiffée, 44140 Montbert [02 40 04 78 73; lerelaisdesgarennes@gmail.com; www.camping-lerelaisdesgarennes.com] Fr Nantes on N937 dir La Roche, at Geneston turn L dir Montbert & foll site sp. Or fr Nantes on N137 dir La Rochelle turn R at Aigrefeuille-sur-Maine for Montbert. Sm, mkd, pt shd, pt sl, wc (htd); chem disp; fam bthrm; shwrs inc; EHU (10A) inc; lndry; wifi; dogs; Eng spkn; adv bkg acc; quiet; lake fishing adj; tennis nr; CKE/CCI. "Peaceful, picturesque site; lge pitches; friendly owners; immac facs, but no individual wash rms; rabbits & hens on site; toys for children; many attractions nrby; pleasant walk to town; gd value; sports facs nrby; excel; highly rec; bus avail to Nantes fr vill; excel." ♦ 1 Jun-30 Sep. € 13.00   2018*

MONTBRISON 9B1 (2km S Urban) 45.59133, 4.07806
Camp Municipal Le Surizet, 31 Rue du Surizet, Moingt, 42600 Montbrison [04 77 58 08 30]
Fr St Etienne on D8, at rndabt junc with D204 turn L sp St Anthème & Ambert. Cross rlwy & turn R in 400m, site sp. Med, pt shd, wc; chem disp; mv service pnt; shwrs; EHU (5-10A) inc; lndry; shop nr; bbq; playgrnd; pool; 10% statics; dogs €0.85; bus (every hr); adv bkg acc; quiet; fishing; tennis 2km; CKE/CCI. "Pleasant, well-kept site; no twin axles; vg value; highly rec NH or sh stay; bird reserve (20km)." 15 Apr-15 Oct. € 13.00   2017*

MONTBRON 7B3 (11km NE Rural) 45.74042, 0.58678 Camping de l'Etang, Les Geloux, 16310 Le Lindois [05 45 65 02 67; fax 05 45 65 08 96; www.campingdeletang.com] Fr S take D16 N fr Montbron, in 9km turn R onto D13, in 3km turn R onto D27. Site sp in vill opp lake. Sm, hdg, mkd, pt shd, pt sl, wc (htd); chem disp; fam bthrm; shwrs inc; EHU (16A) €4.50; gas; lndry; shop; rest; snacks; bar; playgrnd; beach adj; sw; dogs €1.50; phone; Eng spkn; adv bkg rec; quiet; ccard acc; fishing; CKE/CCI. "Loads of wildlife in attractive surroundings; sm library; v pleasant & restful; gd quality rest; gd value; rec." 1 Apr-1 Nov. € 17.50   2013*

> **"I need an on-site restaurant"**
> We do our best to make sure site information is correct, but it is always best to check any must-have facilities are still available or will be open during your visit.

MONTBRON 7B3 (6km SE Rural) 45.65972, 0.55805
Camping Les Gorges du Chambon, Le Chambon, 16220 Eymouthiers [05 45 70 71 70; fax 05 45 70 80 02; info@gorgesduchambon.fr; www.gorgesduchambon.fr or www.les-castels.com] Fr N141 turn SE onto D6 at La Rochefoucauld; cont on D6 out of Montbron; after 5km turn L at La Tricherie onto D163; foll camp sp to site in approx 1.9km. NB Fr La Tricherie narr in places & some sharp bends. Med, mkd, hdstg, pt shd, pt sl, wc (htd); chem disp; mv service pnt; fam bthrm; shwrs inc; EHU (10A) inc; gas; lndry; shop; rest; snacks; bar; bbq (charcoal, gas); playgrnd; pool; paddling pool; twin axles; red long stay; entmnt; wifi; TV; 25% statics; Eng spkn; adv bkg acc; quiet; ccard acc; horseriding nr; games rm; tennis; bike hire; games area; golf nr; canoe hire; rv fishing; CKE/CCI. "Beautiful, 'away fr it all', scenic site in grnds of old farm; welcoming, helpful & friendly staff; lge pitches but some sl; excel san facs; superb rest; gd mkd walks; birdwatching & wildlife; poss motorbike rally on site end June; excel." ♦ 19 Apr-13 Sep. € 45.00   2012*

MONTECH

MONTECH *8E3* (1km E Rural) *43.96608, 1.24003* Camping de Montech (formerly Camping Paradis), Chemin de la Pierre, 82700 Montech [05 63 31 14 29; fax 05 62 65 68 69; contact@camping-montech.fr; www.camping-montech.fr] Exit A20 junc 65 Montauban Sud onto D928 dir Auch. In Montech turn R just bef canal, site well sp. Lge, mkd, hdg, unshd, wc; chem disp; mv service pnt; shwrs inc; EHU (16A) €4; lndry; shop; rest; snacks; bar; bbq; playgrnd; pool; twin axles; entmnt; 60% statics; dogs €2.80; Eng spkn; adv bkg acc; games area; lake fishing nrby; CKE/CCI. "Gd cycle paths." 1 Mar-31 Oct. € 24.00   2014*

⊞ MONTENDRE *7C2* (4km NW Rural) *45.30037, -0.43495* Camping Twin Lakes, La Faïencérie, 17130 Souméras [05 46 49 77 12 or 0114 2463800 (UK); twinlakesinfo@hotmail.co.uk; www.twinlakesfrance.com] Exit N10/E606 at Montlieu-la-Garde onto D730 thro Montendre dir Mirambeau, go past Souméras vill on R, site sp on L. Or exit A10 junc 37; turn R onto D730; at rndabt turn R onto N137; in Mirambeau turn L onto D730; site on R in approx 14 km. Sm, hdg, pt shd, pt sl, wc; chem disp; fam bthrm; shwrs inc; EHU (10-16A) €3; gas; shop nr; snacks; bar; bbq; playgrnd; pool (htd); paddling pool; red long stay; TV; 15% statics; dogs €1.50; Eng spkn; adv bkg acc; quiet; clsd 15 Dec-1 Jan; lake fishing; games rm. "Vg British-owned site; meals arranged; gd touring base; vg; best to pitch on field beside lake." ♦ € 25.00   2017*

MONTESQUIOU *8F2* (4km W Rural) *43.57705, 0.29111* Camping l'Anjou, L'Anjou 32380 Montesquiou [05 62 70 95 24; clemens.van-voorst@wanadoo.fr; www.camping-anjou.com] Campsite is bet Montesquiou & Bassoues on the D943. Site is well mkd. A sm lane leads to site ent. Sm, hdg, hdstg, mkd, pt shd, pt sl, wc; chem disp; mv service pnt; fam bthrm; shwrs; EHU (6A) € 2.50; lndry; snacks; bar; bbq; pool; paddling pool; wifi; 50% statics; dogs €2.50; Eng spkn; adv bkg acc; games area; playgd; CCI. "Excel; no twin axles; friendly welcoming owners; mini farm; ideally situated for those attending Marciac Jazz Festival." ♦ 1 May-30 Sep. € 19.50   2015*

MONTFAUCON *7D3* (3km W Rural) *44.69197, 1.53480* Kawan Village Domaine de la Faurie, 46240 Sénierguès [05 65 21 14 26; fax 05 65 31 11 17; contact@camping-lafaurie.com; www.camping-lafaurie.com] Fr N20 turn E onto D2 sp Montfaucon, or fr A20 exit junc 56. In 5km site sp. Rd to site (off D2) is 500m long, single-track with passing places & steep but passable. Well sp fr A20. Med, mkd, pt shd, pt sl, terr, wc (htd); chem disp; mv service pnt; fam bthrm; shwrs inc; EHU (6-10A) €4.50-6.70; lndry; shop; rest; playgrnd; pool (htd); paddling pool; twin axles; wifi; TV; 30% statics; dogs €3; Eng spkn; adv bkg acc; quiet; ccard acc; games area; bike hire. "Superb, pretty site with great views; quiet & peaceful; lge pitches; excel facs & rest; gd touring base; poss intermittent elec supply some pitches (2010); many walks; conv A20; award winning site; one of the best sites." ♦ 5 Apr-31 Oct. € 30.00   2015*

MONTFERRAND *8F4* (5km N Rural) *43.39007, 1.82788* FFCC Domaine St Laurent, Les Touzets, 11320 Montferrand [04 68 60 15 80 or 06 76 60 58 42 (mob); info@camping-carcassonne-toulouse.com; www.camping-carcassonne-toulouse.com] S fr Toulouse on N113/D1113 past Villefranche-de-Lauragais. Turn L onto D43 for 4.2km; then R to St Laurent. Or turn L onto D218 bypassing Montferrand & cont directly to St Laurent; turn L at church. Site well sp. Sm, hdg, pt shd, wc; chem disp; shwrs inc; EHU (6A) inc; lndry; shop; rest; snacks; bar; playgrnd; pool; entmnt; wifi; TV; 10% statics; dogs €2; Eng spkn; adv bkg acc; quiet; tennis; bike hire; games rm; sauna; archery. "Attractive, peaceful, well-kept site; clean san facs; friendly owners; gd views; woodland walks; vg site but narr access rds." 1 Apr-15 Oct. € 26.00   2017*

> **"Satellite navigation makes touring much easier"**
>
> Remember most sat navs don't know if you're towing or in a larger vehicle – always use yours alongside maps and site directions.

MONTFERRAND *8F4* (6km SE Rural) *43.31451, 1.80246* Camping Le Cathare, Château de la Barthe, 11410 Belflou [04 68 60 32 49; fax 04 68 60 37 90; info@auberge-lecathare.com; www.auberge-lecathare.com] Fr Villefranche-de-Lauragais on N113/D6113, foll D622 sp Toulouse/Carcassonne over rlwy, canal, then immed L on D625 for 7km. Thro St Michel-de-Lanes then take D33 to Belflou; foll sp to Le Cathare. Sm, hdg, pt shd, wc; chem disp; shwrs inc; EHU (3-10A) €3-7.50; rest nr; beach shgl; sw nr; 10% statics; dogs €1.20; quiet; CKE/CCI. "Poss long walk to basic san facs - sh timer for lts & might prefer to use your own facs; Cent Nautique on lake; dramatic position o'looking lake." 15 Apr-1 Nov. € 18.00   2012*

MONTIGNAC *7C3* (7km E Rural) *45.05375, 1.23980* Yelloh! Village Lascaux Vacances, Route des Malénies, 24290 St Amand-de-Coly [05 53 50 81 57; fax 05 53 50 76 26; mail@campinglascauxvacances.com; www.campinglascauxvacances.com or www.yellohvillage.co.uk] Exit A89 junc 17 (Peyrignac) SE onto D6089 to Le Lardin-St Lazare. Join D62 S to Coly & then foll sp to Saint Amand-de-Coly. Site well sp. Med, mkd, hdg, pt shd, wc; chem disp; mv service pnt; fam bthrm; shwrs; EHU (10A) inc; lndry; shop; rest; snacks; bar; bbq; playgrnd; pool; paddling pool; red long stay; entmnt; wifi; TV; 60% statics; dogs €4; phone; adv bkg acc; quiet; ccard acc; fishing nr; waterslide; games area; sauna; games rm. "Excel, peaceful, renovated site in superb location; warm welcome; lge pitches; excel touring base." ♦ 15 Apr-11 Sep. € 33.00   2017*

MONTIGNAC

MONTIGNAC *7C3* **(8km SE Rural)** *45.07211, 1.23431*
Camping La Tournerie Ferme, La Tournerie, 24290 Aubas [05 53 51 04 16; la-tournerie@orange.fr; www.la-tournerie.com] Fr Montignac on D704 dir Sarlat-la-Canéda; in 5.5km turn L onto C1 sp St Amand-de-Coly; in 1.6km at x-rds turn L sp Malardel & Drouille; in 400m at Y-junc foll rd to R sp Manardel & La Genèbre; cont on this rd ignoring minor rds; in 1.6km at elongated junc take rd to R of post box; immed after passing Le Treuil farm on R turn R at x-rds La Tournerie. Site opp farm. Sm, hdstg, unshd, sl, terr, wc (htd); chem disp; shwrs inc; EHU (6A) inc; lndry; rest nr; bar nr; bbq; twin axles; dogs; Eng spkn; adv bkg req. "Lovely, tranquil site; adults only; lge pitches with beautiful views; friendly, helpful British owners (CC members); excel san facs; request detailed dirs or see website - sat nav not rec; excel touring base; excel site; fenced dog pitches." ♦
1 Mar-30 Nov. € 23.00   2016*

MONTIGNAC *7C3* **(1km S Urban)** *45.05980, 1.15860*
Camping Le Moulin du Bleufond, Ave Aristide Briand, 24290 Montignac [05 53 51 83 95; fax 05 53 51 19 92; info@bleufond.com; www.bleufond.com] S on D704, cross bdge in town & turn R immed of rv on D65; site sp in 500m nr stadium, adj Rv Vezere. Med, hdg, pt shd, wc; shwrs inc; EHU (10A) €3.50; shop nr; rest; snacks; bar; bbq; pool (htd); paddling pool; entmnt; wifi; dogs €2; quiet; ccard acc; fishing; tennis adj. "Pleasant site; pleasant, helpful owners; facs excel; poss diff lge o'fits due trees; conv Lascaux caves & town; gd walking area; lovely site." 1 Apr-15 Oct. € 31.40   2012*

MONTIGNAC *7C3* **(9km S Rural)** *45.01765, 1.18811*
FFCC Camping La Fage, 24290 La Chapelle-Aubareil [05 53 50 76 50 or 06 87 37 5 891 (Mob); contact@camping-lafage.com; www.camping-lafage.com] Fr Montignac take D704 twd Sarlat. In about 8km turn R onto La Chapelle-Aubareil & foll camp sp. Med, hdstg, pt shd, pt sl, wc; mv service pnt; fam bthrm; shwrs inc; EHU (10A); lndry; shop; rest; snacks; bar; bbq; playgrnd; pool (htd); paddling pool; entmnt; wifi; TV; 30% statics; dogs €1.80; adv bkg acc; games area; CKE/CCI. "Excel site; helpful owners; vg, clean san facs; red facs LS; gd rest at auberge in vill; conv Lascaux 2 & other pre-historic sites; gd walking."
11 Apr-10 Oct. € 30.00   2015*

MONTIGNAC *7C3* **(14km SW Rural)** *45.00178, 1.07555*
Camping Le Paradis, La Reybeyrolle, 24290 St Léon-sur-Vézère [05 53 50 72 64; fax 05 53 50 75 90; le-paradis@perigord.com; www.le-paradis.fr] On W bank of Rv Vézère on D706 Montignac-Les Eyzies rd, 1km fr Le Moustier. D706 poss rough rd. Med, hdg, pt shd, wc (htd); chem disp; mv service pnt; fam bthrm; shwrs inc; EHU (10A); lndry; shop; rest; snacks; bar; bbq; playgrnd; pool (htd, indoor); paddling pool; beach adj; sw; red long stay; entmnt; wifi; TV; 25% statics; dogs €2.50; phone; Eng spkn; adv bkg acc; ccard acc; boat hire; tennis; fishing; sauna; games area; bike hire; CKE/CCI. "Excel, high standard site in gd location; friendly, conscientious Dutch owners; immac san facs; gd pool, rest & takeaway; vg for families; tropical vegetation around pitches, grnds like a garden; excel, espec LS; ACSI acc." ♦ 1 Apr-20 Oct. € 38.00   2017*

See advertisement

> **"There aren't many sites open at this time of year"**
>
> If you're travelling outside peak season remember to call ahead to check site opening dates – even if the entry says 'open all year'.

MONTIGNAC *7C3* **(8km SW Rural)** *45.04107, 1.11915*
Camping La Castillonderie, 24290 Thonac [05 53 50 76 79; fax 05 53 51 59 13; castillonderie@wanadoo.fr; www.castillonderie.nl] Take D706 dir Les Eyzies. At rndabt in Thonac turn R onto D65 sp Fanlac in 1km after x-rd take R, site is sp 1.5km. Narr app rd. Med, mkd, hdstg, hdg, pt shd, pt sl, wc (htd); chem disp; mv service pnt; fam bthrm; shwrs inc; EHU (10A) €4; lndry; shop; rest; snacks; bar; bbq; playgrnd; pool; paddling pool; entmnt; wifi; TV; 10% statics; dogs €0.50; phone; Eng spkn; adv bkg acc; quiet; ccard acc; CKE/CCI. "Peaceful, well-kept site; friendly, helpful Dutch owners; on site lake fishing; canoeing 3km; gd cent for historic visits & walks." ♦ 15 May-15 Sep. € 23.00   2013*

MONTIGNY LE ROI

MONTIGNY LE ROI *6F2* (1km N Rural) *48.00084, 5.49637* Camping du Château, Rue Hubert Collot, 52140 Montigny-le-Roi [03 25 87 38 93; campingmontigny52@wanadoo.fr; www.campingduchateau.com] Fr A31 junc 8 for Montigny-le-Roi. Site well sp in cent vill on D74. Med, pt shd, terr, wc (htd); chem disp; mv service pnt; fam bthrm; shwrs inc; EHU (5A) €3; lndry; shop; snacks; bar; bbq; playgrnd; entmnt; tennis; bike hire. "Modern facs; steep ent; rests & shops in vill." ♦ 15 Apr-30 Sep. € 22.00 2014*

MONTLUCON *7A4* (12km NW Rural) *46.37795, 2.46695* Camp Municipal Le Moulin de Lyon, 03380 Huriel [06 11 75 05 63 or 04 70 28 60 08 (Mairie); fax 04 70 28 94 90; mairie.huriel@wanadoo.fr] Exit A71 junc 10 & foll sp Domérat, then D916 to Huriel. Site well sp. Or fr N D943 turn SW at La Chapelaude to Huriel on D40, foll sp to site. Last km single track (but can pass on level grass) with steep incline to site ent. Site adj Rv Magieure. Med, hdg, pt shd, pt sl, wc; chem disp; shwrs; EHU (10A) inc (poss rev pol); gas; lndry; shop; bar nr; bbq; playgrnd; TV; 10% statics; Eng spkn; quiet; lake fishing; tennis. "Peaceful, wooded site in lovely setting by lake; well-kept; friendly; site yourself, warden calls am & pm; no apparent security; uphill walk to vill (1km); lovely quiet site, clean facs." 15 Apr-15 Oct. € 9.00 2016*

MONTMARAULT *9A1* (11km NE Rural) *46.38107, 3.03926* Camp Municipal, 03240 Deux-Chaises [04 70 47 12 33 or 04 70 47 12 74 (Mairie); fax 04 70 47 31 33; mairie-deux-chaises@pays-allier.com; www.auvergne-tourisme.info] Exit A71 junc 11 onto N79 dir Moulins; in 8km turn off N79 to Deux-Chaises. Site in vill, well sp. Sm, hdg, unshd, pt sl, terr, wc; shwrs; EHU (16A) €2; shop; rest nr; bar nr; playgrnd; lake fishing adj; tennis. "Well-kept site in beautiful setting; gd, basic facs; warden calls for fees pm; phone to check open bef arr, esp LS; vg rest nrby; gd NH." 1 Apr-30 Sep. € 10.50 2013*

⊞ **MONTMAUR** *9D3* (7km SE Rural) *44.55003, 5.95114* Camping au Blanc Manteau, Route de Céüse, 05400 Manteyer [92 57 82 56 or 92 57 85 89; pierre.wampach@wanadoo.fr; www.camping aublancmanteau.fr] Take D994 fr Veynes twd Gap, past Montmaur; site sp fr vill of La Roche-des-Arnauds on D18 in 1km. Sm, hdg, pt shd, wc (htd); chem disp; fam bthrm; shwrs inc; EHU (10A) €5.35; lndry; shop nr; snacks; bar; playgrnd; pool (htd); adv bkg rec; tennis. "Gd sized pitches; pleasant owner; pretty, in wooded area with beautiful views of mountains." ♦ € 24.00 2014*

MONTMEDY *5C1* (1km NW Urban) *49.52126, 5.36090* Camp Municipal La Citadelle, Rue Vauban, 55600 Montmédy [03 29 80 10 40 (Mairie); fax 03 29 80 12 98; mairie.montmedy@wanadoo.fr; www.montmedy.fr] Fr D643 foll sp to Montmedy cent & foll site sp. Steep app. Sm, hdg, pt shd, pt sl, wc; chem disp; shwrs inc; EHU (4-10A) €2.80-3.97; lndry; shop nr; playgrnd; red long stay; dogs €2.24; quiet; CKE/CCI. "Warden calls am & pm; facs clean, ltd LS; nr Montmedy Haut fortified town; 10A hook-up not avail high ssn; vg; lovely little site; gd views." 1 May-30 Sep. € 9.00 2015*

MONTMIRAIL *3D2* (1km E Rural) *48.87299, 3.55147* Camp Municipal Les Châtaigniers, Rue du Petit St Lazare, 51210 Montmirail [03 26 81 25 61; fax 03 26 81 14 27; mairie.montmirail@wanadoo.fr; www.montmirail.fr] Site sp at junc of D933 & D373 at E o'skts of town. By sports stadium 150m twds town by Gendarmerie. Med, mkd, pt shd, wc cont; own san rec; shwrs inc; EHU (20A) €4; shop nr; playgrnd; golf; tennis; CKE/CCI. "Peaceful, clean site approx 1 hr fr Paris; warm welcome, helpful warden; dated, clean san facs; call at warden's house L of ent for removal of barrier; barrier v nr main rd; pool 500m; fees collected pm (cash only); vg NH." 1 Apr-31 Oct. € 9.50 2013*

MONTMORILLON *7A3* (1km S Urban) *46.42035, 0.87554* Camp Municipal de l'Allochon, 31 Ave Fernand Tribot, 86500 Montmorillon [05 49 91 02 33 or 05 49 91 13 99 (Mairie); fax 05 49 91 58 26; www.montmorillon.fr] On D54 to Le Dorat, approx 400m SE fr main rd bdge over rv at S of town. Site on L. Fr S v sharp RH turn into site. Med, mkd, pt shd, terr, wc (htd); mv service pnt; shwrs inc; EHU (10A); lndry; shop nr; rest nr; bar nr; bbq; playgrnd; wifi; TV; dogs; Eng spkn; adv bkg acc; ccard acc; games area; fishing; CKE/CCI. "Delightful, peaceful, well-kept site; lge pitches; friendly, hard-working warden; gd touring base; vg value; v clean facs, old but working shwrs; htd covrd pool adj; relaxing; rec; security barrier; gd walking area, maps fr TO; ltd facs LS." ♦ 1 Mar-31 Oct. € 12.00 2018*

MONTOIRE SUR LE LOIR *4F2* (1km S Rural) *47.74750, 0.86351* Camp Municipal Les Reclusages, Ave des Reclusages, 41800 Montoire-sur-le Loir [02 54 85 02 53; camping.reclusages@orange.fr; www.mairie-montoire.fr] Foll site sp, out of town sq, over rv bdge & 1st L on blind corner at foot of old castle. Med, mkd, pt shd, pt sl; mv service pnt; shwrs inc; EHU (6-10A) €3.10-3.93; lndry; shop nr; snacks; bar; playgrnd; wifi; 5% statics; dogs €0.97; Eng spkn; adv bkg acc; quiet; ccard acc; canoeing; fishing; CKE/CCI. "Lovely location nr Rv Loir; peaceful, well-kept, secure site; some rvside pitches; friendly, helpful warden; excel clean san facs, ltd LS; gd cycling; conv troglodyte vills; excel; pleasant sh walk into town across rv; htd pool adj; attractive town; Int'l Folk Festival mid Aug." ♦ 1 Apr-30 Sep. € 14.00 2017*

⊞ **MONTPELLIER** *10F1* (10km SE Rural) *43.57611, 3.92583* FFCC Camping Le Parc, Route de Mauguio, 34970 Lattes [04 67 65 85 67; fax 04 67 20 20 58; camping-le-parc@wanadoo.fr; www.leparccamping.com] Exit A9 junc 29 for airport onto D66. In about 4km turn R onto D172 sp Lattes & campings, cross over D21. Site ent in 200m on R. Med, hdg, shd, wc; chem disp; shwrs inc; EHU (10A) inc; gas; lndry; shop; snacks; playgrnd; pool; beach sand 4km; wifi; 15% statics; dogs €3; Eng spkn; adv bkg req; quiet; CKE/CCI. "Friendly, helpful owners; lge pitches but dusty; gd facs, excel pool & snack bar; conv Cévennes mountains & Mediterranean beaches; hiking & mountain biking; barrier locked 2200." ♦ € 28.00 2014*

MONTPON MENESTEROL 7C2 (1km N Rural) 45.01280, 0.15828 **Camping La Cigaline, 1 Rue de la Paix, Route de Ribérac, 24700 Montpon-Ménestérol [05 53 80 22 16; contact@lacigaline.fr; www.lacigaline.fr]** Fr Montpon town cent traff lts take D730 N to Ménestérol. Site on L bef bdge beside Rv Isle. Med, hdg, mkd, shd, wc; chem disp; shwrs inc; EHU (10A) inc; lndry; shop nr; rest; snacks; bar; bbq; playgrnd; sw nr; wifi; 1% statics; dogs €1.50; train 1km; Eng spkn; adv bkg acc; quiet; ccard acc; fishing; tennis 200m; boat hire; CKE/CCI. "Gd touring base for St Emilion region; gd walking, cycling; vg; new young owners (2014); leisure park nrby; bike hire 500m; gd food in bar/rest; terr o'looks rv; site improving." ♦ 12 Apr-30 Sep. € 16.00 2014*

"That's changed – Should I let the Club know?"

If you find something on site that's different from the site entry, fill in a report and let us know. See camc.com/europereport.

MONTREJEAU 8F3 (7km S Rural) 43.02864, 0.57852 **Camping Es Pibous, Chemin de St Just, 31510 St Bertrand-de-Comminges [05 61 88 31 42; fax 05 61 95 63 83; contact@es-pibous.fr; www.espibous.fr]** Turn S fr D817 onto D825 sp Bagnères-de-Luchon & Espagne. Foll past 'Super U' to lge rndabt & turn R sp St Bertrand-de-Comminges/Valcabrère then at 1st traff lts turn R & foll sp for St Bertrand. Turn R off N125 onto D825 to roman excavation site. Site on L. Or exit A64 junc 17 onto A645 sp Bagnères-de-Luchon to lge rndabt, then as above. Med, mkd, hdg, pt shd, wc (htd); chem disp; mv service pnt; fam bthrm; shwrs inc; EHU (10A) inc; gas; lndry; shop; rest nr; bar nr; playgrnd; pool; TV; 20% statics; dogs; adv bkg acc; quiet; ccard acc; fishing 3km; tennis 3km. "Peaceful, friendly site; pitches among trees; clean dated san facs, ltd LS; lndry is owner's washing machine, not always avail (2010); gd touring area nr mountains; picturesque town in walking dist." ♦ 1 Apr-31 Oct. € 20.40 2017*

MONTREJEAU 8F3 (1km W Rural) 43.08624, 0.55414 **Camping Couleurs Garonne (formerly Camping Les Hortensias), Route de Tarbes, 31210 Montréjeau [05 61 88 52 30; campingcouleursgaronne@orange.fr; www.campingcouleursgaronne.com]** Fr St Gaudens on D817, R at foot of steep hill, sp 'Tarbes Poids Lourds' to avoid Montréjeau cent. Site on L in 1km. On W o'skirts of town, well sp on rd to Tarbes. Sm, pt shd, wc; chem disp; shwrs; EHU (15A) inc; shop nr; bbq; playgrnd; CKE/CCI. "Gd NH; no twin axles; spacious grassy site; friendly." 15 Apr-31 Oct. € 15.00 2015*

MONTRESOR 4H2 (3km W Rural) 47.15782, 1.16026 **Camping Les Coteaux du Lac, 37460 Chemillé-sur-Indrois [02 47 92 77 83; fax 02 47 92 72 95; lescoteauxdulac@wanadoo.fr; www.lescoteauxdulac.com]** Fr Loches on D764; then D10 dir Montrésor; cont to Chemillé-sur-Indrois. Med, pt sl, wc; chem disp; mv service pnt; fam bthrm; shwrs inc; EHU (6A) €3.90; lndry; shop; rest; snacks; bar; bbq; playgrnd; pool (htd); paddling pool; entmnt; wifi; TV; dogs €1.70; phone; Eng spkn; quiet; fishing; games rm; boating. "Excel setting by lake; immac, modern san facs; beautiful vill 600m; trekking in Val d'Indrois; 3km along cycle track (old rlwy)." ♦ 3 Mar-15 Oct. € 34.00 2013*

See advertisement

"I like to fill in the reports as I travel from site to site"

You'll find report forms at the back of this guide, or you can fill them in online at camc.com/europereport.

MONTREUIL

⊞ **MONTREUIL** 3B3 (1km W Rural) 50.46853, 1.76280 FFCC Camping La Fontaine des Clercs, 1 Rue de l'Eglise, 62170 Montreuil [03 21 06 07 28; desmarest.mi@wanadoo.fr; www.campinglafontainedesclercs.fr] Fr N or S turn SW off D901 at rndabt onto D349 to Montreuil; turn R immed after rlwy x-ing (onto Rue des Préaux); in 120m turn R; site in 100m on R; sp on Rv Canche. Or take 2nd R ALMOST immed after (20m) rlwy-xing (onto Grande Ville Basse); in 50m fork R (Rue de l'Eglise); site in 200m on R. NB Poss difff access lge o'fits. Med, mkd, hdstg, pt sl, terr, wc (htd); chem disp; mv service pnt; shwrs inc; EHU (6-10A) €3.70-€4.80; shop nr; bbq; wifi; 60% statics; dogs €2; adv bkg rec; quiet; rv fishing adj; site clsd over New Year; games rm; CKE/CCI. "Busy, basic site in beautiful spot; helpful, friendly owner; gd san facs; steep & narr site rd with tight turns to terr pitches, some sm; pool 1.5km; not suitable lge o'fits; some generous pitches beside rv; vet in Montreuil; attractive, historic town with amazing restaurants- uphill walk; conv NH Le Touquet, beaches & ferry; wine society outlet; excel site; some Eng spkn." € 19.50   2017*

⊞ **MONTREUIL BELLAY** 4H1 (4km E Rural) 47.15263, -0.13599 FFCC Camping Le Thouet, Les Côteaux-du-Chalet, route Bron 49260 Montreuil-Bellay [02 41 38 74 17 or 06 19 56 32 75 (mob); campinglethouet@alicepro.fr; www.campinglethouet.com] Fr D347 N of Montreuil-Bellay take dir 'Cent Ville'; turn L immed bef rv bdge & foll sp to Les Côteaux-du-Chalet. Access via narr, rough rd for 1km. Med, pt shd, wc; chem disp; shwrs inc; EHU (10A) €3; gas; shop nr; bar; bbq; playgrnd; pool; 5% statics; dogs €2; phone; adv bkg acc; quiet; ccard acc; boating; fishing; CKE/CCI. "Peaceful, spacious, British-owned site; lge area grass & woods surrounded by vineyards; pitches in open grass field; poss unkempt LS; gd walks; vill not easily accessed by foot; unguarded rv bank poss not suitable children; v lge pitches." ♦ € 26.00   2013*

MONTREUIL BELLAY 4H1 (1km W Urban) 47.13191, -0.15897 Camping Les Nobis D'Anjou, Rue Georges Girouy, 49260 Montreuil-Bellay [02 41 52 33 66; fax 02 41 38 72 88; camping-les-nobis@orange.fr; www.campinglesnobis.com] Fr S on D938 turn L immed on ent town boundary & foll rd for 1km to site; sp fr all dir. Fr N on D347 ignore 1st camping sp & cont on D347 to 2nd rndabt & foll sp. Fr NW on D761 turn R onto D347 sp Thouars to next rndabt, foll site sp. Lge, hdg, mkd, pt shd, wc; chem disp; mv service pnt; shwrs inc; EHU (10A) €3 (poss long cable req, rev pol); gas; lndry; shop; rest; snacks; bar; playgrnd; pool (htd); red long stay; wifi; TV; 50% statics; dogs; phone; Eng spkn; adv bkg acc; quiet; ccard acc; bike hire; CKE/CCI. "Spacious site bet castle & rv; gd, modern san facs; local chateaux & town worth exploring; 'aire de service' for m'vans adj; gd patisserie in town; some pitches o'look rv Thouet; extremely well managed, friendly site; nr Saumur vineyards; excel." ♦ 31 Mar-30 Sep. € 29.00   2018*

See advertisement

MONTREVEL EN BRESSE 9A2 (1km E Rural) 46.33911, 5.13615 Camping La Plaine Tonique, Base de Plein Air, 01340 Montrevel-en-Bresse [04 74 30 80 52; fax 04 74 30 80 77; plaine.tonique@wanadoo.fr; www.laplainetonique.com] Exit A40 junc 5 Bourg-en-Bresse N onto D975; at Montrevel-en-Bresse turn E onto D28 dir Etrez & Marboz; site sp on L in 400m. Or exit A6 junc 27 Tournus S onto D975. V lge, hdg, mkd, shd, wc; chem disp; mv service pnt; fam bthrm; shwrs inc; EHU (10A) inc; lndry; shop; rest; snacks; bar; bbq; playgrnd; pool (covrd, htd); paddling pool; sw nr; entmnt; TV; dogs €2.10; Eng spkn; adv bkg acc; quiet; ccard acc; waterslide; fishing; watersports; bike hire; games area; tennis. "Excel, busy, family site; superb leisure facs; mountain biking; archery; vg clean san facs; some pitches boggy after rain." ♦ 11 Apr-25 Sep. € 30.00   2012*

MONTRICHARD *4G2* (1km S Rural) *47.33384, 1.18766* **Camping Couleurs du Monde, 1 Rond Point de Montparnasse, 41400 Faverolles-sur-Cher [02 54 32 06 08 or 06 74 79 56 29 (mob); fax 02 54 32 61 35; touraine-vacances@wanadoo.fr; www.camping-couleurs-du-monde.com]** E fr Tours on D796 thro Bléré; at Montrichard turn S on D764 twd Faverolles-sur-Cher, site 200m fr junc, adj to Carrefour supmkt - on L by 2nd rndabt. Med, mkd, hdstg, pt shd, wc; chem disp; mv service pnt; fam bthrm; shwrs inc; EHU (10A) €4; lndry; shop nr; rest; snacks; bar; bbq; playgrnd; pool (htd); paddling pool; sw nr; entmnt; wifi; TV; dogs €2; Eng spkn; adv bkg acc; quiet; ccard acc; tennis 500m; games rm; sauna; bike hire; games area; waterslide 500m; CKE/CCI. "Level site in gd location nr vineyards; beauty cent; gd sports activities; vg; excel facs; gd sw pool with canopy; ideal for exploring Cher & Loire Valley." ♦ 31 Mar-29 Sep. € 30.00   2017*

MONTRICOUX *8E3* (1km W Rural) *44.07660, 1.61103* **FFCC Camping Le Clos Lalande, Route de Bioule, 82800 Montricoux [05 63 24 18 89; contact@camping-lecloslalande.com; www.camping-lecloslalande.com]** Fr A20 exit junc 59 to Caussade; fr Caussade take D964 to Montricoux, where site well sp. Med, hdg, mkd, pt shd, wc; chem disp; mv service pnt; fam bthrm; shwrs inc; EHU (6A) €3.60; lndry; shop nr; snacks; bar; bbq; playgrnd; pool; wifi; TV; 10% statics; dogs €2.50; phone; bus 400m; Eng spkn; adv bkg rec; games area; rv fishing 400m; canoe hire; watersports; tennis; bike hire; CKE/CCI. "Peaceful, quiet, well-kept site by rv at mouth of Aveyron gorges; beautiful area, inc Bastide vills; great family site; friendly, helpful owners; mkt Weds; easy walk to town; highly rec." ♦ 29 Mar-28 Sep. € 33.00   2014*

MONTROLLET *7B3* (0km N Rural) *45.98316, 0.89702* **Camping Auberge La Marchadaine, Beaulieu, 16420 Montrollet [05 45 71 09 88 or 06 63 07 82 48 (mob); aubergedelamarchadaine@gmail.com]** N fr St Junien on D675, turn W onto D82 to Montrollet. Auberge sp in vill. Sm, pt shd, wc; chem disp; mv service pnt; fam bthrm; shwrs; EHU (6A) inc; gas; shop nr; rest; bar; bbq; playgrnd; twin axles; wifi; dogs free; phone; adv bkg acc; quiet; games area; fishing; CKE/CCI. "Delightful CL-type site nr beautiful lake; vg rest; many mkd walks; Oradour sur Glane nrby (wartime museum); Vienne rv; gd; rund down (2017)." ♦ € 12.00   2017*

MONTSAUCHE LES SETTONS *4G4* (5km SE Rural) *47.19276, 4.06047* **FFCC Camping de la Plage des Settons, Rive Gauche, Lac des Settons, 58230 Montsauche-les-Settons [03 86 84 51 99; fax 03 86 84 54 81; camping@settons-tourisme.com; www.settons-tourisme.com]** Fr Montsauche foll sp Château-Chinon. In 500m fork L to Les Settons. After 2km foll sp for Rive Gauche, after 1km L at bend for site. Med, hdg, mkd, pt shd, terr, wc; chem disp; mv service pnt; shwrs inc; EHU (4A) inc (long lead req); lndry; shop nr; bbq; playgrnd; sw; dogs free; Eng spkn; ccard acc; bike hire; fishing; CKE/CCI. "In cent of Parc du Morvan; lake adj; direct access to Lac des Settons; pedalos; access rd busy pm." ♦ 15 Apr-15 Oct. € 20.00   2015*

MONTSAUCHE LES SETTONS *4G4* (7km SE Rural) *47.18175, 4.05293* **FFCC Camping Les Mésanges, Rive Gauche, 58230 Montsauche-les-Settons [03 86 84 55 77; info@campinglesmesanges.fr; www.campinglesmesanges.fr]** Fr Montsauche take D193 twds Les Settons, just bef Les Settons fork R onto D520 dir Chevigny. After 1km turn L and foll sp to site on R on W side of lake. Med, mkd, shd, pt sl, terr, wc; chem disp; mv service pnt; fam bthrm; shwrs inc; EHU (16A) inc; gas; lndry; shop; rest nr; snacks; playgrnd; sw; wifi; dogs €0.80; Eng spkn; adv bkg acc; quiet; games rm; fishing; games area; CKE/CCI. "Beautiful site; well-maintained; gd for families - lge play areas; excel." ♦ 14 May-15 Sep. € 22.00   2015*

> **"We must tell the Club about that great site we found"**
>
> Get your site reports in by mid-August and we'll do our best to get your updates into the next edition.

MONTSAUCHE LES SETTONS *4G4* (8km SE Rural) *47.18578, 4.07056* **Camping Plage du Midi, Lac des Settons Les Branlasses, 58230 Montsauche-les-Settons [03 86 84 51 97; fax 03 86 84 57 31; campplagedumidi@aol.com; www.settons-camping.com]** Fr Salieu take D977 bis to Montsauche, then D193 'Rive Droite' to Les Settons for 5km. Cont a further 3km & take R fork sp 'Les Branlasses' Cent du Sport. Site on L after 500m at lakeside. Med, mkd, pt shd, terr, wc (htd); chem disp; mv service pnt; fam bthrm; shwrs inc; EHU (10A) €3.60; gas; lndry; shop; rest nr; snacks; bar; bbq; playgrnd; pool (covrd, htd); beach sand adj; sw; entmnt; wifi; dogs €1; phone; Eng spkn; adv bkg acc; ccard acc; horseriding 2km; watersports; bike hire; CKE/CCI. "Site in gd situation; muddy when wet." ♦ 19 Apr-15 Sep. € 20.00   2015*

MONTSOREAU *4G1* (1km NW Rural) *47.21805, 0.05270* **Kawan Village L'Isle Verte, Ave de la Loire, 49730 Montsoreau [02 41 51 76 60 or 02 41 67 37 81; fax 02 41 51 08 83; isleverte@cvtloisirs.fr; www.campingisleverte.com]** At Saumur on S side of rv turn R immed bef bdge over Rv Loire; foll sp to Chinon & site. Fr N foll sp for Fontevraud & Chinon fr Rv Loire bdge; site on D947 in vill on banks of Loire opp 'Charcuterie' shop. Med, mkd, pt shd, wc; chem disp; mv service pnt; fam bthrm; shwrs inc; EHU (16A) €3.50 (poss long lead req); gas; lndry; shop nr; rest; snacks; bar; playgrnd; pool; paddling pool; entmnt; wifi; TV; 10% statics; dogs €2; bus to Saumur; Eng spkn; adv bkg rec; ccard acc; games area; rv fishing; bike hire; watersports; golf 13km; tennis; CKE/CCI. "Pleasant rvside site in beautiful situation; v busy high ssn; various sized/shaped pitches; car hire; adequate san facs, poss irreg cleaning LS; vg rest; barrier clsd 2200-0700; gd security; pleasant vill; gd; excel; helpful staff." ♦ 3 Apr-14 Oct. € 29.00   2017*

MOREE

MOREE *4F2* (3km SW Urban) *47.88932, 1.20109*
Camping La Maladrerie, Rue du Plessis, 41160 Fréteval [06 50 23 11 88 or 06 67 31 55 52]
E fr Le Mans on D357 to Fréteval; turn L in vill. Sp. Med, mkd, pt shd, wc; chem disp; mv service pnt; shwrs inc; EHU (4-6A) €1.55-2.30; gas; lndry; shop nr; bar; bbq; playgrnd; pool; sw nr; 60% statics; Eng spkn; ccard acc; lake fishing; CKE/CCI. "Delightful, well-kept, quiet site; friendly owner; unisex wc; poss ltd facs LS; site was a medieval leper colony; new owners but site still run down (2017)." ♦ 1 Apr-30 Oct. € 12.00   2017*

MORESTEL *9B3* (8km S Urban) *45.63521, 5.57231*
Camping Les Avenières (formerly Les Epinettes), 6 Rue du Stade, 38630 Les Avenières [04 74 33 92 92; infos@camping-les-avenieres.com] S fr Morestel on D1075, turn onto D40 to Les Avenières, site well sp. Med, mkd, hdstg, hdg, pt shd, wc (htd); chem disp; mv service pnt; fam bthrm; shwrs inc; EHU (10A); lndry; shop; rest; snacks; bar; bbq; playgrnd; sw nr; entmnt; TV; 35% statics; dogs; phone; adv bkg acc; ccard acc; CKE/CCI. "Phone ahead LS to check open; pool adj; noise fr adj stadium." ♦ 1 May-30 Sep. € 27.00   2014*

MOREZ *9A3* (9km S Rural) *46.48368, 5.94885* **Camping Le Baptaillard, 39400 Longchaumois [03 84 60 62 34; camping-lebaptaillard@orange.fr; www.haut-jura.com]** Foll D69 S, site sp on R. Med, mkd, pt shd, pt sl, wc (htd); chem disp; shwrs inc; EHU (6A) €2.50; lndry; shop; rest nr; playgrnd; paddling pool; wifi; 10% statics; adv bkg req; quiet; tennis; fishing 3km; games rm. "Beautiful CL-type site; skiing; views; lge pitches; friendly staff." 1 Jan-30 Sep & 1 Dec-31 Dec. € 30.50   2014*

MORLAIX *2E2* (13km N Coastal) *48.65950, -3.84847*
Camping De La Baie de Terenez, 29252 Plouezoch [02 98 67 26 80; campingbaiedeterenez@wanadoo.fr; www.campingbaiedeterenez.com] Take D46 on exit Morlaix, turn L on D76 to site. Lge, pt shd, pt sl, wc; mv service pnt; fam bthrm; shwrs inc; EHU (6A) €3.20; gas; lndry; shop; snacks; bar; playgrnd; pool (htd); beach sand 2km; wifi; TV; dogs; adv bkg acc; quiet; fishing; windsurfing; games rm. ♦ 5 Apr-28 Sep. € 26.50   2014*

MORLAIX *2E2* (11km E Rural) *48.60283, -3.73833*
Camping Aire Naturelle la Ferme de Croas Men (Cotty), Garlan, 29610 Plouigneau [02 98 79 11 50; info@ferme-de-croasmen.com; www.ferme-de-croasmen.com] Fr D712 rndabt W of Plouigneau twd Morlaix (exit fr N12) 2km R sp Garlan; thro Garlan site 1km on L, well sp. Sm, hdg, pt shd, serviced pitches; wc; chem disp; mv service pnt; fam bthrm; shwrs; EHU (6A) €3.50; lndry; shop; playgrnd; 10% statics; dogs €1; Eng spkn; quiet; horseriding 200m; CKE/CCI. "Lovely, well-kept CL-type farm site; excel facs; farm museum; donkey/tractor rides; ideal for children; produce avail inc cider & crêpes; vg." ♦ 1 Apr-31 Oct. € 19.00   2017*

MORMOIRON *10E2* (4km E Rural) *44.05713, 5.22798*
Camping Les Verguettes, Route de Carpentras, 84570 Villes-sur-Auzon [04 90 61 88 18; fax 04 90 61 97 87; info@provence-camping.com; www.provence-camping.com] E on D942 fr Carpentras dir Sault. Site at ent to Villes-sur-Auzon beyond wine cave. Or at Veulle-les-Roses turn E onto D68. Cont thro Sottenville-sur-Mer. Site on L in 2km. Lge, hdg, mkd, pt shd, pt sl, wc (htd); chem disp; shwrs inc; EHU (6A) inc; lndry; shop nr; rest; pool; paddling pool; wifi; TV; dogs €2.60- 3.60; adv bkg rec; quiet; tennis; fishing 300m; games rm. "Scenic location; gd walking & cycling; friendly, helpful owner; families with children sited nr pool, others at end of camp away fr noise; poss muddy when it rains; sm pitches not suitable lge o'fits; red facs LS; new san facs block." ♦ 23 Mar-30 Sep. € 24.50   2013*

MORTAGNE SUR GIRONDE *7B2* (1km SW Coastal) *45.47600, -0.79400* **Aire Communale Le Port, 17120 Mortagne-sur-Gironde [05 46 90 63 15; fax 05 46 90 61 25; mairie-mortagne@smic17.fr]**
Fr Royan take D730 dir Mirambeau for approx 28km. Turn R in Boutenac-Touvent onto D6 to Mortagne, then foll sp Le Port & Aire de Camping-Car. M'vans only. Sm, unshd, chem disp; mv service pnt; shwrs; EHU (10A) inc; shop nr; rest nr; bar nr; dogs; quiet. "Car/c'vans poss acc; shwrs & mv service pnt 800m fr site; fees collected 0900; all pitches have views; excel." € 6.00   2013*

MORTAIN *2E4* (12km S Rural) *48.57039, -0.94883*
Camping Les Taupinières, La Raisnais, 50140 Notre-Dame-du-Touchet [02 33 69 49 36 or 06 33 26 78 82 (mob); belinfrance@fsmail.net; www.lestaupinieres.com] Fr Mortain S on D977 sp St Hilaire-du-Harcouët; shortly after rndabt take 2nd L at auberge to Notre-Dame-deTouchet. In vill turn L at PO, sp Le Teilleul D184, then 2nd R sp La Raisnais. Site at end of lane on R (haycart on front lawn). Sm, hdstg, pt shd, pt sl, wc; chem disp; shwrs inc; EHU (10A) inc (poss long lead req); shop nr; rest nr; wifi; dogs; adv bkg acc; quiet. "Pleasant, tranquil, spacious CL-type site adj farm; lovely outlook; washing machine on request; adults only; NB no wc or shwrs Dec-Feb but water & EHU all year; DVD library; friendly, helpful British owners; htd pool 8km; well-kept, clean san facs; adv bkg rec; highly rec." 1 Mar-31 Oct. € 15.00   2017*

MOSNAC *7B2* (0km E Rural) *45.50557, -0.52304*
Camp Municipal Les Bords de la Seugne, 34 Rue de la Seugne, 17240 Mosnac [05 46 70 48 45; fax 05 46 70 49 13; mosnac@mairie17.fr] Fr Pons S on N137 for 4.5km; L on D134 to Mosnac; foll sp to site behind church. Sm, mkd, pt shd, wc (htd); shwrs inc; EHU (10A) inc; gas; red long stay; dogs free; Eng spkn; adv bkg acc; quiet; CKE/CCI. "Charming, clean, neat site in sm hamlet; site yourself, warden calls; helpful staff; excel, spotless san facs; conv Saintes, Cognac & Royan." 1 May-30 Sep. € 13.50   2017*

MOUSTIERS STE MARIE

MOTHE ACHARD, LA *2H4 (5km NW Rural) 46.65285, -1.74759* **Camping La Guyonnière, 85150 St Julien-des-Landes [02 51 46 62 59; fax 02 51 46 62 89; info@laguyonniere.com; www.laguyonniere.com]** Leave A83 junc 5 onto D160 W twd La Roche-sur-Yon. Foll ring rd N & cont on D160 twd Les Sables-d'Olonne. Leave dual c'way foll sp La Mothe-Achard, then take D12 thro St Julien-des-Landes twd La Chaize-Giraud. Site sp on R. Lge, hdg, pt shd, pt sl, wc; chem disp; shwrs inc; EHU (6A) €3.50 (long lead rec); gas; lndry; shop; rest; snacks; bar; bbq; playgrnd; pool (covrd, htd); wifi; TV; 10% statics; dogs €3; phone; Eng spkn; adv bkg acc; ccard acc; waterpark; lake fishing 400m; waterslide; windsurfing 400m; bike hire. "V lge pitches; canoe hire 400m; gd views; friendly owners; gd walking area." ♦ 26 Apr-28 Sep. € 23.50   2013*

MOTHE ACHARD, LA *2H4 (6km NW Rural) 46.64469, -1.73346* **FLOWER Camping La Bretonnière, 85150 St Julien-des-Landes [02 51 46 62 44 or 06 14 18 26 42 (mob); fax 02 51 46 61 36; camp.la-bretonniere@wanadoo.fr; www.la-bretonniere.com or www.flowercampings.com]** Fr La Roche-sur-Yon take D160 to La Mothe-Achard, then D12 dir St Gilles-Croix-de-Vie. Site on R 2km after St Julien. Med, mkd, pt shd, pt sl, wc; chem disp; mv service pnt; fam bthrm; shwrs inc; EHU (6-12A) €2-4.50; lndry; bar nr; bbq; playgrnd; pool (covrd, htd); sw nr; entmnt; wifi; TV; 20% statics; dogs €2-5; Eng spkn; adv bkg acc; ccard acc; bike hire; fishing; ice; games area; sailing 2km; tennis; games rm; CKE/CCI. "Excel, friendly site adj dairy farm; v lge pitches; san facs stretched in high ssn; 10 mins fr Bretignolles-sur-Mer sand dunes." ♦ 9 Apr-30 Sep. € 33.00   2017*

MOTHE ACHARD, LA *2H4 (7km NW Rural) 46.66280, -1.71380* **Camping La Garangeoire, 85150 St Julien-des-Landes [02 51 46 65 39; fax 02 51 46 69 85; info@garangeoire.com; www.camping-la-garangeoire.com or www.les-castels.com]** Site sp fr La Mothe-Achard. At La Mothe-Achard take D12 for 5km to St Julien, D21 for 2km to site. Or fr Aizenay W on D6 turn L dir La Chapelle-Hermier. Site on L, well sp. Lge, mkd, hdg, shd, pt sl, serviced pitches; wc; chem disp; mv service pnt; fam bthrm; shwrs inc; EHU (16A) inc (poss rev pol); gas; lndry; shop; rest; snacks; bar; bbq (elec, gas); playgrnd; pool (htd); paddling pool; twin axles; entmnt; wifi; 50% statics; dogs €4; phone; Eng spkn; adv bkg rec; ccard acc; lake fishing 400m; waterslide; bike hire; games area; tennis; horseriding; CKE/CCI. "Busy, well-run site set in chateau parkland; some v lge pitches; pleasant helpful owners; excel, clean facs; gd for families & all ages; pitches quiet - entmnt well away fr pitches; super site; gd site in every way." ♦ 19 Apr-19 Sep. € 37.00   2012*

⊞ **MOURIES** *10E2 (2km E Rural) 43.68207, 4.91769* **Camping à la Ferme Les Amandaies (Crouau), Mas de Bou Malek, 13890 Mouriès [04 90 47 50 59; fax 04 90 47 61 79; www.les-amandaies.fr]** Fr Mouriès take D17 E sp Salon-de-Provence. Site sp on R 200m past D5 junc. Foll site sp to farm in 2km. Sm, pt shd, wc; shwrs inc; EHU €2 (rec long lead) (poss rev pol); bbq; dogs; quiet. "Simple CL-type site; a few lge pitches; friendly owners; dated, dimly-lit san facs, conv coast & Avignon; book in using intercom on LH wall at ent to shwr block." € 15.40   2018*

MOURIES *10E2 (7km NW Urban) 43.72138, 4.80950* **Camp Municipal Les Romarins, Route de St Rémy-de-Provence, 13520 Maussane-les-Alpilles [04 90 54 33 60; fax 04 90 54 41 22; camping-municipal-maussane@wanadoo.fr; www.maussane.com]** Fr Mouriès N on D17, turn onto D5 on o'skts of vill dir St Rémy-de-Provence, turn immed L site on R adj municipal pool. Med, hdg, mkd, pt shd, wc; chem disp; mv service pnt; fam bthrm; shwrs inc; EHU (10A) €3.80; lndry; shop nr; red long stay; twin axles; wifi; TV; dogs €3; phone; bus in ssn; Eng spkn; adv bkg rec; quiet; ccard acc; bike hire; games area; games rm; tennis; CKE/CCI. "Well-kept, well-run site in lovely area; on edge of vill; excel san facs; pool adj inc; some pitches diff m'vans due low trees; gd security; in Natural Park; hiking; mountain biking; excel." ♦ 15 Mar-3 Nov. € 26.00   2017*

MOUSTIERS STE MARIE *10E3 (1km W Rural) 43.84497, 6.21555* **Camping Manaysse, 04360 Moustiers-Ste Marie [04 92 74 66 71; fax 04 92 74 62 28; www.camping-manaysse.com]** Fr Riez take D952 E, pass g'ge on L & turn L at 1st rndabt for Moustiers; site on L off RH bend; strongly advised not to app Moustiers fr E (fr Castellane, D952 or fr Comps, D71) as these rds are diff for lge vehicles/c'vans - not for the faint-hearted. Med, mkd, pt shd, pt sl, wc; chem disp; mv service pnt; shwrs inc; EHU (6-10A) €2.50-3.50; shop nr; playgrnd; dogs €0.50; adv bkg acc; quiet; CKE/CCI. "Welcoming, family-run site; super views; gd unisex san facs; cherry trees on site - avoid parking under during early Jun; steep walk into vill; lge o'fits do not attempt 1-way system thro vill, park & walk; gd." ♦ 1 Apr-24 Oct. € 14.00   2012*

MOUSTIERS STE MARIE *10E3 (1km W Rural) 43.84371, 6.21475* **FFCC Camping St Jean, Route de Riez, 04360 Moustiers-Ste Marie [04 92 74 66 85; camping-saint-jean@wanadoo.fr; www.camping-st-jean.com]** On D952 opp Renault g'ge & petrol stn. Med, hdg, pt shd, pt sl, wc (htd); chem disp; mv service pnt; fam bthrm; shwrs inc; EHU (6-10A) €3.60-4.70; gas; lndry; shop; snacks; bbq (elec, gas); playgrnd; sw nr; wifi; TV; 10% statics; dogs €2.10; Eng spkn; adv bkg acc; quiet; ccard acc; games rm; fishing; games area; CKE/CCI. "Excel site in lovely location by rv; climbing nr; dated san facs (2010); boating 4km; some pitches diff lge o'fits; easy uphill walk to beautiful vill; conv Gorges du Verdon; cycle rtes; gd value." ♦ 28 Mar-11 Oct. € 23.00   2015*

Site report forms at back of guide   *Last year of report

MOYAUX

MOYAUX *3D1* (3km NE Rural) *49.20860, 0.39230*
Camping Château Le Colombier, Le Val Séry, 14590 Moyaux [02 31 63 63 08; fax 02 31 61 50 17; mail@camping-lecolombier.com; www.camping-lecolombier.com] Fr Pont de Normandie on A29, at junc with A13 branch R sp Caen. At junc with A132 branch R & foll sp Lisieux, D579. Turn L onto D51 sp Blangy-le-Château. Immed on leaving Moyaux turn L onto D143 & foll sp to site on R in 3km. Lge, mkd, pt shd, wc; chem disp; mv service pnt; fam bthrm; shwrs inc; EHU (10A) inc (poss lead req); gas; lndry; shop; rest; snacks; bar; bbq; playgrnd; pool (htd); red long stay; entmnt; wifi; TV; dogs free; phone; Eng spkn; adv bkg acc; quiet; ccard acc; excursions; games rm; bike hire; tennis; horseriding nr; games area; CKE/CCI. "Beautiful, peaceful, spacious site in chateau grnds; ltd san facs LS; lge pool, but no shd, seats or sunshades around; vg for children; gd shop & crêperie; some static tents/tour ops; shgl paths poss diff some wheelchairs/pushchairs; if dep bef 0800 must move to car park o'night; mkt Sun; gd site; some pitches boggy when wet; no o'fits over 7m high ssn; gd facs; excel site to explore Normandy landing beaches; easy walk to vill with shops and rest and sh drive to larger town, lovely site, v helpful owners." ♦ 1 May-14 Sep. € 39.00 2015*

MUIDES SUR LOIRE *4G2* (1km N Rural) *47.67191, 1.52596* Camp Municipal Belle Vue, Ave de la Loire, 41500 Muides-sur-Loire [02 54 87 01 56 or 02 54 87 50 08 (Mairie); fax 02 54 87 01 25; contact.muides@orange.fr; www.muides.fr] Fr A10/E5/E60 exit junc 16 S onto D205. Turn R onto D2152 then D112 over rv. Site on S bank of rv on D112 W of bdge. Tight U-turn into site fr N. Med, mkd, pt shd, wc; chem disp; mv service pnt; shwrs inc; EHU (6A) €4.80 (poss long lead req),(poss rev pol); lndry; shop nr; rest nr; playgrnd; sw nr; dogs €2.55; quiet; rv fishing adj; cycling; CKE/CCI. "Neat, clean, basic, spacious site; ladies shwrs need upgade (2011); vehicle barrier; gd views over rv; some pitches by fast-flowing (unfenced) rv; little shd; excel cycling; site self when off clsd (open 0800-1000 & 1700-1900)." ♦ 1 May-15 Sep. € 14.00 2018*

MUIDES SUR LOIRE *4G2* (6km E Rural) *47.64803, 1.61125* Camp Municipal du Cosson, Route de la Cordellerie, 41220 Crouy-sur-Cosson [02 54 87 08 81; fax 02 54 87 59 44; mairie-de-crouy-sur-cosson@wanadoo.fr] Fr Muides-sur-Loire, take D103 E dir Crouy-sur-Cosson. In vill, turn R onto D33 dir Chambord. Site 200m fr vill, well sp. Med, mkd, pt shd, wc; shwrs inc; EHU (6A) inc (poss rev pol); lndry; shop nr; rest nr; snacks; bar nr; bbq; playgrnd; 10% statics; dogs; phone; adv bkg acc; quiet; rv fishing nrby; CKE/CCI. "V pleasant site; woodland setting; nr Rv Loire; poss long-stay workers; attractive site in nice vill; bar 300m; excel." 1 Apr-15 Oct. € 13.00 2014*

MUIDES SUR LOIRE *4G2* (1km S Rural) *47.66611, 1.52916* Camping Le Château des Marais, 27 Rue de Chambord, 41500 Muides-sur-Loire [02 54 87 05 42; fax 02 54 87 05 43; chateau.des.marais@wanadoo.fr; www.chateau-des-marais.com] Exit A10 at junc 16 sp Chambord & take D2152 sp Mer, Chambord, Blois. At Mer take D112 & cross Rv Loire; at Muides-sur-Loire x-rds cont strt on for 800m; then turn R at Camping sp; site on R in 800m. Lge, mkd, shd, pt sl, serviced pitches; wc (htd); chem disp; mv service pnt; fam bthrm; shwrs inc; EHU (6A) inc (poss rev pol); gas; lndry; shop; rest; snacks; bar; bbq; playgrnd; pool (covrd, htd); paddling pool; twin axles; wifi; TV; 50% statics; dogs €6; Eng spkn; adv bkg acc; ccard acc; watersports nr; lake fishing; games area; bike hire; waterslide; tennis; jacuzzi; games rm; sauna; CKE/CCI. "Busy lively site in wooded area in chateau grnds; gd sized pitches; excel, clean san facs; friendly staff; plenty of gd quality children's play equipment; sh walk to rv; conv Loire chateaux; plenty to do in area; mkt Sat Blois; pitches grass, can be a problem when wet." ♦ 8 May-13 Sep. € 49.00 2014*

"I need an on-site restaurant"

We do our best to make sure site information is correct, but it is always best to check any must-have facilities are still available or will be open during your visit.

MULHOUSE *6F3* (10km SW Rural) *47.72225, 7.22590* FFCC Camping Parc La Chaumière, 62 Rue de Galfingue, 68990 Heimsbrunn [03 89 81 93 43 or 03 89 81 93 21; reception@camping-lachaumiere.com; www.camping-lachaumiere.com] Exit A36 junc 15; turn L over m'way; at rndabt exit on D166 sp Heimsbrunn; in vill turn R at rndabt; site end of houses on R. Med, hdg, hdstg, mkd, pt shd, pt sl, wc (htd); chem disp; mv service pnt; fam bthrm; shwrs inc; EHU (10A) €3.50 (poss rev pol); lndry; shop nr; snacks; bbq; playgrnd; pool; twin axles; wifi; 50% statics; dogs €1; phone; bus 1km; Eng spkn; adv bkg acc; quiet; ccard acc; CKE/CCI. "Sm pitches not suitable long o'fits; beautiful wine vills on La Route des Vins; museum of trains & cars in Mulhouse; conv; vg san facs." ♦ € 11.00 2015*

MULHOUSE *6F3* (2km SW Rural) *47.73405, 7.3235* Camping de l'Ill, 1 Rue de Pierre Coubertin, 68100 Mulhouse [03 89 06 20 66; fax 03 89 61 18 34; campingdelill@wanadoo.fr; www.camping-de-lill.com] Fr A36 take Mulhouse/Dornach exit & foll sp Brunstatt at 1st traff lts. At 2nd traff lts turn R, foll University/Brunstatt/Camping sps, site approx 2.5km on rvside. Lge, mkd, pt shd, pt sl, wc; chem disp; mv service pnt; fam bthrm; shwrs inc; EHU (10A); gas; shop nr; rest nr; snacks; pool; wifi; dogs €1.50; tram 500m; CKE/CCI. "Welcoming recep; cycle/walk along rv to town cent; OK NH." 1 Apr-30 Sep. € 22.30 2017*

MULHOUSE 6F3 (30km W Rural) 47.73554, 7.01497
Flower Camping du Lac de la Seigneurie, 3 Rue de la Seigneurie, 90110 Leval [03 84 23 00 13; contact@camping-lac-seigneurie.com; www.camping-lac-seigneurie.com] Off N83 dir Belfort-Mulhouse. D11 NW Petitefontaine twds Roughmont sp to Leval. Med, hdg, mkd, pt shd, pt sl, wc; chem disp; mv service pnt; shwrs; EHU (6-10A); lndry; shop; rest; bar; bbq; playgrnd; pool (htd); paddling pool; wifi; 6% statics; dogs; adv bkg acc; ccard acc; games area. 1 Apr-31 Oct. € 21.00   2016*

MUNSTER 6F3 (4km E Rural) 48.05160, 7.20527
Camping La Route Verte, 13 Rue de la Gare, 68230 Wihr-au-Val [03 89 71 10 10; info@camping-routeverte.com; www.camping-routeverte.com] Take D417 out of Colmar twd Munster & turn R int Wihr-au-Val. Site on L 800m. Well sp. Med, mkd, shd, pt sl, wc; chem disp; mv service pnt; shwrs inc; EHU (6A) €2.80-3.95; lndry; shop nr; rest nr; bar nr; red long stay; dogs €1.50; phone; adv bkg acc; quiet; games rm; CKE/CCI. "Delightful, popular, clean site amid vineyards; owner helpful & friendly; not suitable lge c'vans (6m max); pool 4km; excel san facs; highly rec; excel." ♦ 26 Apr-30 Sep. € 17.50   2014*

MUNSTER 6F3 (13km SW Rural) 47.98250, 7.01865
Camp Municipal de Mittlach Langenwasen, 68380 Mittlach [03 89 77 63 77; fax 03 89 77 74 36; mairiemittlach@wanadoo.fr; www.mittlach.fr] Fr Munster on D10 to Metzeral then R onto D10. Site at end rd in 6km. Med, mkd, hdg, pt shd, pt sl, wc; chem disp; shwrs inc; EHU (6-10A) €2.45-6; gas; lndry; shop; playgrnd; 10% statics; dogs €0.80; Eng spkn; adv bkg acc; quiet; CKE/CCI. "Peaceful, wooded site at bottom of valley; helpful staff; san facs gd & clean; gd walking base; plenty of interest locally; excel." ♦ 20 Apr-10 Oct. € 14.00   2015*

> **"Satellite navigation makes touring much easier"**
>
> Remember most sat navs don't know if you're towing or in a larger vehicle – always use yours alongside maps and site directions.

MUNSTER 6F3 (2km SW Rural) 48.03105, 7.11350
FFCC Camping Les Amis de la Nature, 4 Rue du Château, 68140 Luttenbach-près-Munster [03 89 77 38 60; fax 03 89 77 25 72; an-munster@wanadoo.fr; www.camping-an.fr] Fr Munster take D10 sp Luttenbach; site sp. Lge, mkd, pt shd, wc (htd); chem disp; mv service pnt; fam bthrm; shwrs inc; EHU (4-6A) €3.25-4.40/6.20; lndry; shop; rest; snacks; bar; bbq; playgrnd; pool (htd); entmnt; wifi; TV; 50% statics; dogs €1.50; Eng spkn; quiet; ccard acc; games rm; sauna; fishing; tennis 1km; games area. "Lovely setting by stream; dir access to rv; gd value; new san facs (2017); pleasant walk to town; excel rest; gd touring area." ♦ 21 Mar-11 Nov. € 16.50   2018*

⊞ **MUR DE BRETAGNE** 2E3 (6km N Rural) 48.25568, -2.98801 Camping Le Boterff d'en Haut, 22320 St Mayeux [02 96 24 00 65; info@leboterff.com; www.brittanyforholidays.com] N fr Mur-de-Bretagne on D767 to St Mayeux. Turn R into vill & R after vill hall (Salle Municipal); to T-junc, turn R & site on L. App via 750m single-track lane. Car parking in rd outside. Sm, unshd, wc; chem disp; shwrs inc; EHU (6A) inc; shop nr; rest nr; bar nr; bbq; red long stay; dogs €1 (2 max); adv bkg acc; quiet; watersports 8km. "Peaceful, remote CL-type site; gd san facs; gd touring cent; gd walks & cycling; when wet, cars parked off site; excel; (2013) new owner, still British, very welcoming; superb CL type site; beautiful area." € 20.00   2013*

MUR DE BRETAGNE 2E3 (2km SW Rural) 48.19872, -3.01282 Camping Le Point de Vue, 104 Rue du Lac, 22530 Mur-de-Bretagne [02 96 26 01 90; fax 02 96 28 59 44; camping-lepointdevue@orange.fr; www.camping-lepointdevue.fr] Fr Mur-de-Bretagne take D18 & foll site sp; ent opp view point of Lake Guerlédan. Med, pt shd, pt sl, terr, wc; chem disp; shwrs inc; EHU (10A) inc; lndry; shop nr; rest nr; bar nr; playgrnd; wifi; dogs €1; quiet; CKE/CCI. "Gd watersports; hot water may be ltd to a few hrs a day in LS; gd walking & cycling around lake." ♦ 15 Feb-15 Nov. € 15.00   2013*

MUR DE BRETAGNE 2E3 (4km NW Rural) 48.20950, -3.05150 Camping Nautic International, Route de Beau Rivage, 22530 Caurel [02 96 28 57 94; fax 02 96 26 02 00; contact@campingnautic.fr; www.campingnautic.fr] Fr Loudéac on N164 into Caurel. Fork L 100m past church, site is 1st on L, beside Lac de Guerlédan. NB App fr Pontivy on D767 via Mur-de-Bretagne v steep in places & not rec when towing. Med, mkd, pt shd, terr, wc; chem disp; mv service pnt; fam bthrm; shwrs inc; EHU (10A)€4.90; lndry; shop; bbq; playgrnd; pool (htd); paddling pool; TV; dogs €2.50; adv bkg acc; quiet; ccard acc; lake fishing; games rm; horseriding nr; bike hire; watersports nr; jacuzzi; sauna; tennis; CKE/CCI. "Peaceful site in attractive countryside by lake; gd pitches, some poss diff lge o'fits; dated facs, poss stretched when site full; fitness rm; no o'fits over 8m; wonderful pool & lake." ♦ 15 May-25 Sep. € 24.00   2013*

MURAT 7C4 (1km SW Urban) 45.10303, 2.86599
Camp Municipal de Stalapos, 8 Rue de Stade, 15300 Murat [04 71 20 01 83 or 04 71 20 03 80; fax 04 71 20 20 63; agyl@camping-murat.com; www.murat.fr] Fr N122 site sp fr cent of Murat dir Aurillac (thro indus est), adj Rv Alagnon. Lge, hdstg, pt shd, pt sl, wc cont; chem disp; shwrs inc; EHU (6-16A) €2.50-6.30; lndry; shop nr; playgrnd; dogs free; quiet; rv fishing adj; CKE/CCI. "Peaceful location; winter ssn, phone ahead; basic but clean san facs; warden lives on site; excel touring base; gd views medieval town." ♦ 1 May-30 Sep. € 14.00   2014*

MURAT

MURAT *7C4* (5km SW Rural) *45.07781, 2.83047* **Aire Naturelle Municipal, 15300 Albepierre-Bredons [04 71 20 20 49]** SW fr Murat on D39 dir Prat-de-Bouc; site sp fr cent of Albepierre. Sm, pt shd, wc; chem disp; shwrs inc; EHU (10A) €2; shop nr; rest nr; bar nr; dogs free; quiet; CKE/CCI. "Excel, peaceful location; basic, clean facs; warden visits am & pm; bar 300m; vg walking amidst extinct volcanoes; gd; beautiful sm friendly site." 15 Jun-15 Sep. € 9.00   2016*

MURAT *7C4* (5km W Rural) *45.11697, 2.81275* **Camp Municipal Le Vallognon, 15300 Laveissière [04 71 20 11 34; fax 04 71 20 20 48; campinglaveissiere@orange.fr]** Site sp fr N122 W fr Murat Sp Aurilla, after 4km turn R onto D439 site on L after 300m. Med, pt shd, wc; shwrs inc; EHU inc; lndry; shop nr; playgrnd; quiet; CKE/CCI. "Conv for Cantal Mountains; htd pool adj; gd hill walking; gd site." ♦ 1 Jan-3 Apr, 1Jun-4 Sep, 20 Dec-31 Dec. € 14.60   2013*

MUROL *7B4* (1km S Rural) *45.57400, 2.95735* **FFCC Camp Le Repos du Baladin, Groire, 63790 Murol [04 73 88 61 93; reposbaladin@free.fr; www.camping-auvergne-france.com]** Fr D996 at Murol foll sp 'Groire' to E, site on R in 1.5km just after vill. Med, hdg, mkd, shd, pt sl, terr, wc (htd); chem disp; fam bthrm; shwrs inc; EHU (6A); lndry; shop nr; snacks; bar; playgrnd; pool (htd); sw nr; wifi; dogs €3; Eng spkn; sauna; CKE/CCI. "Lovely site with immac san facs; friendly, helpful owners; easy walk into town thro fields." 29 Apr-16 Sep. € 28.00   2018*

MUROL *7B4* (2km W Rural) *45.57516, 2.91428* **Camping Le Pré Bas, 63790 Chambon-sur-Lac [04 73 88 63 04; fax 04 73 88 65 93; prebas@campingauvergne.com; www.campingauvergne.com]** Take D996 W fr Murol twd Mont-Dore. Site 1.5km on L, twd lake. Lge, hdg, mkd, pt shd, pt sl, serviced pitches; wc; chem disp; mv service pnt; fam bthrm; shwrs inc; EHU (6A) €4.70; lndry; shop; snacks; bar; bbq; playgrnd; pool (covrd, htd); sw; entmnt; TV; 40% statics; dogs €2.10; phone; Eng spkn; adv bkg acc; quiet; games area; waterslide; ice; CKE/CCI. "Excel family-run site by Lac Chambon; library; superb views; friendly, helpful staff; immac san facs; excel pool complex; rock pegs ess; access to sm pitches poss diff lge o'fits; excel walking area." ♦ 24 Apr-30 Sep. € 24.00   2012*

MUROL *7B4* (5km W Rural) *45.56979, 2.90185* **Camping Les Bombes (formerly Municipal), Chemin de Pétary, 63790 Chambon-sur-Lac [04 73 88 64 03 or 06 88 33 25 94 (mob); les-bombes-camping@orange.fr; www.camping-les-bombes.com]** Site is on D996. Nr exit fr vill Chambon. Well sp. Med, mkd, pt shd, wc; chem disp; mv service pnt; shwrs; EHU (6A) €4.50; lndry; shop; rest nr; snacks; bar; bbq; playgrnd; pool; sw nr; TV; 5% statics; dogs €2.20; phone; Eng spkn; adv bkg acc; quiet; CKE/CCI. "Beautiful area; gd, clean, well-maintained facs stretched in high ssn; lge pitches; friendly, helpful owners; excel." ♦ 15 May-30 Sep. € 24.00   2012*

MUZILLAC *2G3* (8km SW Coastal) *47.51780, -2.55539* **Camping Ty Breiz, 15 Grande Rue, Kervoyal, 56750 Damgan [02 97 41 13 47; info@campingtybreiz.com; www.campingtybreiz.com]** Fr Muzillac on D153 dir Damgan, turn S for Kervoyal; site on L opp sm church. Med, hdg, mkd, pt shd, wc; shwrs inc; EHU (6-10A) €3-3.50; lndry; playgrnd; beach sand 300m; wifi; dogs €1.50; Eng spkn; adv bkg rec; quiet; ccard acc; CKE/CCI. "Pleasant, welcoming, family-run site; excel san facs; quiet; cycle path to Damgan; mkt Wed; vg."
♦ 26 Apr-15 Oct. € 21.00   2012*

NAJAC *8E4* (2km W Rural) *44.22011, 1.96985* **Camping Le Païsserou, 12270 Najac [05 65 29 73 96; fax 05 65 29 72 29; info@camping-le-paisserou.com; www.camping-le-paisserou.com]** Take D922 fr Villefranche-de-Rouergue. Turn R on D39 at La Fouillade to Najac. Site by rv, sp in vill. Or fr A20 exit junc 59 onto D926. At Caylus take D84 to Najac. All appr v steep. Med, hdg, shd, wc; chem disp; shwrs inc; EHU €3; lndry; shop nr; rest nr; snacks; bar; 10% statics; dogs €1.50; phone; Eng spkn; adv bkg acc; quiet; tennis adj; CKE/CCI. "Conv for Aveyron gorges; friendly owners; ltd facs LS; lovely vill; unrel opening LS, phone ahead; htd covrd pool adj (free); site yourself if recep clsd, avail pitches listed." 30 Apr-1 Oct. € 23.00   2012*

NAMPONT ST MARTIN *3B3* (3km W Rural) *50.33595, 1.71230* **La Ferme des Aulnes, 1 Rue du Marais, Fresne-sur-Authie, 80120 Nampont-St Martin [03 22 29 22 69 or 06 22 41 86 54 (mob LS); fax 03 22 29 39 43; contact@fermedesaulnes.com; www.fermedesaulnes.com]** D901 S fr Montreuil 13km thro Nampont-St Firmin to Nampont-St Martin; turn R in vill onto D485; site in 3km; sp fr D901. Med, hdg, pt shd, pt sl, wc (htd); chem disp; mv service pnt; fam bthrm; shwrs inc; EHU (6-10A) €6-12; lndry; shop nr; rest; snacks; bar; bbq (charcoal, gas); playgrnd; pool (covrd, htd); entmnt; wifi; 80% statics; dogs €4; Eng spkn; adv bkg acc; quiet; games area; golf 1km; archery; CKE/CCI. "Attractive site nr Calais; some pitches sm, some very sl; friendly welcoming staff; clsd 2200-0800; cinema rm; old fm bldgs retain character of an old fmstead; clean san facs." ♦ 1 Apr-31 Oct. € 32.50   2017*

NANCAY *4G3* (1km NW Rural) *47.35215, 2.18522* **Camp Municipal des Pins, Route de Salbris, La Chaux, 18330 Nançay [02 48 51 81 80 or 02 48 51 81 35 (Mairie); campingdenancay@orange.fr; www.nancay.a3w.fr]** Site on D944 fr Salbris twd Bourges on L immed bef ent Nançay. Med, mkd, hdstg, shd, wc (htd); chem disp; shwrs inc; EHU (6A) inc; gas; lndry; shop nr; playgrnd; adv bkg acc; quiet; golf 2km; fishing; tennis; CKE/CCI. "Lovely spot in pine woods; friendly recep; clean san facs; poor site lighting; beautiful vill; gd walking; rec open am and pm." 1 May-30 Sep. € 8.50   2017*

NANTES

NANCY *6E2* (7km SW Rural) *48.65730, 6.14028*
Campéole Le Brabois, 2301 Ave Paul Muller, 54600 Villers-lès-Nancy [03 83 27 18 28; fax 03 83 40 06 43; brabois@campeole.com; www.campeole.nl/le-brabois] Fr A33 exit junc 2b sp Brabois onto D974 dir Nancy; after 400m turn L at 2nd traff lts; at slip rd after 2nd further traff lts turn R on slip rd & site on R; site well sp. Lge, mkd, pt shd, wc (htd); chem disp; mv service pnt; shwrs inc; EHU (4-15A) €4.50-5.25 (poss rev pol)(ask for pitch with 15A if req); gas; lndry; shop; rest; snacks; bar; bbq; playgrnd; wifi; TV; 10% statics; dogs €2.60; bus adj; Eng spkn; adv bkg acc; quiet; ccard acc; games area; CKE/CCI. "Popular, well-run site; mostly lge pitches, but some sm, all grass; supmkt & petrol 2km; friendly, helpful staff; gd, clean, all new san facs; no twin axles over 5.5m (m'vans OK); interesting town; rec arr early; vg NH; excel." ♦
30 Mar-14 Oct. € 21.30   2018*

NANCY *6E2* (10km NW Rural) *48.74333, 6.05700*
Camping Les Boucles de la Moselle, Ave Eugène Lerebourg, 54460 Liverdun [03 83 24 43 78 or 06 03 27 69 71 (mob); fax 03 83 24 89 47; francis.iung@orange.fr] Fr A31 exit junc 22 to Frouard. In Frouard bear L onto D90 to Liverdun; cross rv bdge (sp Liverdun); under rlwy bdge L at traff lts, thro town, fork L & foll sp to site by on rvside by sports area. Do not turn L at site exit when towing. Lge, pt shd, wc (htd); fam bthrm; shwrs inc; EHU (6A) €3.20; lndry; shop; rest; snacks; bar; playgrnd; pool; entmnt; 10% statics; dogs €1.20; CKE/CCI. "Lovely site & area; helpful staff, Nancy worth visit; pleasant rvside site."
1 May-30 Sep. € 23.00   2017*

NANT *10E1* (2km N Rural) *44.03578, 3.29008*
Camping Le Roc Qui Parle, Les Cuns, 12230 Nant [05 65 62 22 05; contact@camping-roc-qui-parle-aveyron.fr; www.camping-roc-qui-parle-aveyron.fr] Fr Millau take D991E to site passing Val de Cantobre. Fr La Cavalerie take D999E to Nant & at T-junc on o'skts of Nant turn N; Millau & Les Cuns approx 2km; site on R. NB Steep decent into site. Med, hdg, mkd, pt shd, pt sl, serviced pitches; wc; chem disp; mv service pnt; shwrs inc; EHU (10A) €3.50; lndry; shop; bbq; playgrnd; sw; wifi; dogs free; adv bkg acc; quiet; fishing; CKE/CCI. "Excel, well-run site in magnificent surroundings; lge pitches with views; warm welcome, friendly & helpful; excel facs; rv walk; rec; same price year round." ♦ 13 Mar-21 Oct. € 15.00   2016*

NANT *10E1* (11km E Rural) *44.01117, 3.20457*
Camping La Dourbie, Route de Nant, 12230 Saint-Jean-du-Bruel, Aveyron [05 65 46 06 40; fax 05 65 46 06 50; campingladourbie@orange.fr; www.camping-dourbie-aveyron.com] Fr A75 take exit 47, twrds la cavalerie, Nat, St-Eulalie-de-Cernon. At rndabt take 3rd exit onto D999, go thro next rndabt, turn R cont D999 to site. Med, hdg, pt shd, wc; chem disp; mv service pnt; shwrs; EHU (10A); lndry; rest; bar; bbq; playgrnd; pool (htd); wifi; 20% statics; dogs (1 per pitch, leashed); canoeing. "Excel site, such a lot to do & see; very friendly; bungee jumping; paragliding; clean san facs; spa; rest open Fri & Sat nights in LS." ♦
14 Apr-30 Sep. € 25.00   2018*

NANT *10E1* (1km S Rural) *44.01698, 3.30125*
Camping Les Deux Vallées, 12230 Nant [05 65 62 26 89 or 05 65 62 10 40; fax 05 65 62 17 23; contact@lesdeuxcallees.com; www.lesdeuxvallees.com] Exit A75 junc 47 onto D999 for 14km to Nant; site sp. Med, mkd, pt shd, serviced pitches; wc; own san req; chem disp; mv service pnt; shwrs inc; EHU (6A) €2 (poss rev pol); lndry; shop nr; rest; snacks; bar; playgrnd; entmnt; TV; dogs €1; phone; adv bkg acc; quiet; rv fishing; CKE/CCI. "Peaceful, well-kept, scenic site; friendly; clean, modern san facs; pool 500m; 15 mins walk fr vill cent; gd walking; rec." ♦
15 Apr-17 Oct. € 21.50   2016*

NANT *10E1* (1km SW Rural) *44.02105, 3.29390*
Camping Les Vernèdes, Route St Martin-Le Bourg, 12230 Nant [05 65 62 15 19; http://patocheperso.pagesperso-orange.fr/camping/accueil.htm] Site sp fr vill cent. Sm, shd, wc; chem disp; shwrs inc; EHU (10A) inc (long lead req); lndry; bbq; playgrnd; dogs; Eng spkn; adv bkg acc; quiet; CKE/CCI. "Orchard site set in beautiful location; pleasant stroll to Nant cent; gd trout rest adj; gd touring base; very helpful owners; excel and great site to stay on; CL style, not modern but idyilic; gd rest next door." 1 Mar-31 Oct.
€ 13.50   2015*

⊞ **NANTES** *2G4* (3km N Urban) *47.24261, -1.55703*
Nantes Camping, 21 Blvd de Petit Port, 44300 Nantes [02 40 74 47 94; fax 02 40 74 23 06; nantes-camping@nge-nantes.fr; www.nantes-camping.fr] Fr ring rd exit junc 39 sp Porte de la Chapelle & foll sp Cent Ville, Camping Petit Port or University when ent o'skts of Nantes. Site ent opp Hippodrome & nr racecourse & university; well sp. Take care tram lines. Lge, mkd, hdg, hdstg, pt shd, serviced pitches; wc (htd); chem disp; mv service pnt; fam bthrm; shwrs inc; EHU (16A) €5; gas; lndry; shop; rest; snacks; bar; bbq (charcoal); playgrnd; twin axles; red long stay; entmnt; wifi; TV; 30% statics; dogs €3.10; bus & tram to city cent adj; Eng spkn; adv bkg req; quiet; ccard acc; bike hire; CKE/CCI. "Well kept and maintained; htd covrd pool adj; waterslide adj inc; excel san facs; tram stop next to site, easy access to Nantes cent; excel site, great location; o'night m'van area; ACSI red LS; popular; recep clsd 1230-1500." ♦ € 41.00   2018*

NANTES *2G4* (20km E Urban) *47.24930, -1.37118*
Camping Le Chêne, 44450 St Julien-de-Concelles [02 40 54 12 00; contact@campingduchene.fr; www.campingduchene.fr] Fr Nantes, cross Rv Loire dir Poitiers; immed turn E sp St Sébastien; thro town onto D751 to Le Bout-des-Pont; turn S onto D57 sp Camping. Site on L immed after lake. Med, shd, wc; mv service pnt; shwrs; EHU (10A) €2.60; shop nr; rest; bar; bbq; playgrnd; pool (covrd); wifi; dogs €1; adv bkg rec; fishing; sailing; golf; windsurfing; tennis; bike hire. "Under new ownership (2013); lake adj; very helpful staff." 1 Apr-31 Oct. € 16.00   2014*

NANTES *2G4* (6km E Rural) *47.25416, -1.45361*
Camping Belle Rivière, Route des Perrières, 44980 Ste Luce-sur-Loire [02 40 25 85 81; belleriviere@ wanadoo.fr; www.camping-belleriviere.com]
Fr 'Nantes Périphérique Est' take exit 43 (at Porte d'Anjou) onto A811; exit A811 junc 24 dir Thouaré-sur-Loire on D68; at double rndabt by car showroom turn S & foll sp over rlwy bdge; site sp. Fr E via D68, thro Thouaré dir Ste Luce; at double rndabt by car showroom, S over rlwy bdge twd rv; site sp. Med, mkd, hdstg, hdg, pt shd, wc (htd); chem disp; shwrs inc; EHU (3-10A) €2.70-3.90 (extra charge in winter); gas; lndry; shop nr; rest nr; snacks; bar; bbq; playgrnd; wifi; 50% statics; dogs €1.45; Eng spkn; adv bkg acc; quiet; CKE/CCI. "Beautifully-kept site; helpful owners; gd clean san facs; rvside walks; conv Nantes Périphérique & city cent; gd touring base; excel."
♦ € 17.00   2017*

NANTUA *9A3* (1km W Urban) *46.14999, 5.60017*
Camping du Signal, 17 Ave du Camping, 01130 Nantua [04 74 75 02 09 or 06 71 76 36 17 (mob); contact@ camping-nantua.fr; www.camping-nantua.fr]
E on D1084 fr Pont d'Ain, rd passes alongside Nantua lake on R. At end of lake bef ent town turn R & foll sps. Sm, mkd, hdg, unshd, wc; mv service pnt; shwrs inc; EHU (16A) €3 (rev pol); shop nr; rest; snacks; playgrnd; sw nr; wifi; 10% statics; dogs free; quiet. "Attractive, spacious, well-kept site in lovely setting; nice lrg pitches; friendly staff; town & shops mins away; conv for m'way; sports cent nr; Lidl store 3 mins away; gd shwrs." 1 Apr-31 Oct. € 17.60   2017*

NAPOULE, LA *10F4* (3km N Urban/Coastal) *43.5234, 6.9308*
Camping Coté Mer (formaly Camping de la Ferme), Blvd du Bon Puits, 06210 Mandelieu-la-Napoule [04 93 49 94 19; fax 04 93 49 18 52; info@ campingcotemer.fr; www.campingdelaferme.com]
Fr A8 exit junc 40 & turn L in Mandelieu cent sp Fréjus; 200m after rndabt with palm tree cent, fork R into Ave Maréchal Juin & strt into Blvd du Bon Puits. Avoid La Napoule vill when towing. Med, shd, wc; shwrs; EHU (10A) inc; gas; lndry; shop; rest; snacks; bar; beach sand 700m; 10% statics; dogs €4; adv bkg acc; quiet. "Nice atmosphere; some pitches very sm; friendly, helpful staff; dated but clean facs; pleasant sm bar & rest." ♦ 25 Mar-1 Oct. € 36.00   2013*

NAPOULE, LA *10F4* (5km N Urban/Coastal) *43.52547, 6.93354*
Camping L'Argentière, 264 Blvd du Bon-Puits, 06210 Mandelieu-la-Napoule [04 93 49 95 04; www.campingdelargentiere.com]
Fr A8 turn L in Mandelieu cent (sp Fréjus). At rndabt with fountains take 2nd exit, at next rndabt take 2nd exit to L of BP stn, at next rndabt take 2nd exit, site on R in 150m. Avoid La Napoule vill when towing. Med, mkd, hdstg, hdg, pt shd, wc; chem disp; mv service pnt; shwrs inc; EHU (10A) €2.90; lndry; shop; rest; snacks; bar; beach sand 800m; entmnt; TV; 80% statics; dogs €3; bus; Eng spkn; adv bkg req; quiet; fishing; CKE/CCI. "Clean san facs; hypmkt 1km; lovely local beaches, conv to town." ♦ € 31.00   2012*

NARBONNE *10F1* (10km N Rural) *43.26009, 2.95552*
Camp Municipal, Rue de la Cave Coopérative, 11590 Sallèles-d'Aude [04 68 46 68 46 (Mairie); fax 04 68 46 91 00; ot.sallelesdaude@wanadoo.fr; www. salleles-daude.com]
Fr A9/E15 exit junc 36 onto D64 N & in approx 4km turn L to join D11 W. Cont on this rd for approx 18km, then turn L onto D13 S to Ouveillan. In vill, turn R onto D418 SW to Sallèles-d'Aude. Site in vill. NB Nr Canal du Midi some narr app rds. Sm, hdg, mkd, pt shd, wc; chem disp; EHU €2.50; shop nr; bbq; dogs; adv bkg acc; quiet. "Clean site nr canal; 16 pitches; warden calls am; phone warden bef pitching; site not maintained but nice." 1 May-30 Sep. € 16.00   2014*

NARBONNE *10F1* (6km S Rural) *43.13662, 3.02595*
Village-Camping Les Mimosas, Chaussée de Mandirac, 11100 Narbonne [04 68 49 03 72; fax 04 68 49 39 45; info@lesmimosas.com; www. lesmimosas.com] Leave A9 junc 38 at Narbonne Sud & at rndabt foll sp La Nautique. Turn L opp ent to Camping La Nautique & foll sp Mandirac & site. Lge, mkd, hdg, hdstg, pt shd, serviced pitches; wc (htd); chem disp; mv service pnt; fam bthrm; shwrs inc; EHU (6A) inc; gas; lndry; shop; rest; snacks; bar; bbq (elec, gas); playgrnd; pool (htd); paddling pool; red long stay; entmnt; wifi; TV; 6% statics; dogs €4; Eng spkn; adv bkg acc; quiet; ccard acc; sauna; games rm; horseriding adj; lake fishing 300m; waterslide; bike hire; rv fishing adj; jacuzzi; watersports; games area; gym; tennis; CKE/CCI. "Attractive site, lge pitches; gd choice of pitches; friendly, helpful staff; vg san facs, poss ltd LS; excel pool complex; vg for children; lge o'fits rec phone in adv high ssn; excel touring base in historic area; gd birdwatching; cycle path to Narbonne." ♦
17 Mar-31 Oct. € 46.00   2017*

See advertisement opposite

NARBONNE *10F1* (12km SW Rural) *43.16296, 2.89186*
Camping La Figurotta, Route de Narbonne, 11200 Bizanet [04 68 45 16 26 or 06 88 16 12 30 (mob); fax 04 68 48 98 22; camping.figurotta@ gmail.com; www.camping-figurotta.com]
Exit A9 at Narbonne Sud onto slip rd N9/D6113 twd Lézignan-Corbières; in 3km at new rndabt head L twd D613 & then D224 sp Bizanet & site. App fr W not rec due narr D rds. Sm, mkd, hdstg, shd, pt sl, terr, wc (htd); chem disp; shwrs; EHU (4-10A) €2.50-3.50 (poss long lead req); gas; lndry; shop; rest; snacks; bar; playgrnd; pool; red long stay; wifi; 5% statics; dogs €3 (sm dogs only); phone; Eng spkn; adv bkg acc; games area; CKE/CCI. "Pleasant, simple, well-run, scenic site; friendly & helpful owners; gd pool with new snack bar o'looking; gusty & stony site - steel pegs req; excel drainage; gd NH en rte Spain; vg; new san facs (2018)."
♦ € 25.00   2018*

NARBONNE *10F1* **(4km SW Urban)** *43.14702, 3.00424* **Camping La Nautique, Chemin de la Nautique,11100 Narbonne [04 68 90 48 19; fax 04 68 90 73 39; info@campinglanautique.com; www.campinglanautique.com]** Exit junc 38 fr A9 at Narbonne Sud. After toll take last rndabt exit & foll sp La Nautique. Site on R 2.5km fr A9 exit. Lge, hdstg, mkd, hdg, pt shd, wc; chem disp; mv service pnt; shwrs inc; EHU (10A) inc; gas; lndry; shop; rest; snacks; bar; bbq (elec); playgrnd; pool (htd); paddling pool; red long stay; entmnt; wifi; 30% statics; dogs €6; Eng spkn; adv bkg acc; quiet; ccard acc; waterslide; windsurfing; canoeing; tennis; CKE/CCI. "Helpful, friendly Dutch owners; caution - hot water very hot; individual san facs on each pitch inc; some pitches lge but narr; steel pegs req; pitches sheltered but some muddy after heavy rain; excel rest; many sports activities avail; cycle trips; gd walks nrby." ♦ 1 Mar-31 Oct. € 47.70   2018*

NARBONNE PLAGE *10F1* **(8km NE Coastal)** *43.20592, 3.21056* **Camping La Grande Cosse, St Pierre-sur-Mer, 11560 Fleury-d'Aude [04 68 33 61 87; fax 04 68 33 32 23; grande-cosse@franceloc.fr; www.camping-grandecosse.fr]** Exit A9 junc 37 & foll sp Narbonne-Plage. Cont thro Narbonne-Plage to St Pierre-sur-Mer, pass municipal site & turn R twd L'Oustalet, site sp. Lge, hdg, mkd, pt shd, serviced pitches; wc; chem disp; mv service pnt; shwrs inc; EHU (10A); gas; lndry; shop; rest; snacks; bar; playgrnd; pool (htd); beach sand 300m; red long stay; entmnt; wifi; TV; 20% statics; dogs €6-9 (high ssn); phone; Eng spkn; adv bkg acc; ccard acc; boat hire; INF card req; games rm; fishing; games area; tennis; gym. "Excel; gd pitches; helpful, friendly staff; excel san facs; lovely walk to beach thro lagoons & dunes (poss flooded early ssn); mosquitoes poss problem Jun-Sep; ACSI; flood risk after heavy rain; gd mkt St Pierre-sur-Mer; access rds can be diff, very narr; new owners, no longer a naturist site (2017)." ♦ 15 Apr-30 Oct. € 50.00   2017*

NASBINALS *9D1* **(1km N Rural)** *44.67016, 3.04036* **Camp Municipal, Route de St Urcize, 48260 Nasbinals [02 46 32 51 87 or 04 66 32 50 17; mairie.nasbinals@laposte.net; www.mairie-nasbinals.info]** Fr A75 exit 36 to Aumont-Aubrac, then W on D987 to Nasbinals. Turn R onto D12, site sp. Med, pt sl, wc (htd); chem disp; mv service pnt; shwrs inc; EHU (16A) €3; shop nr; rest nr; bbq; dogs; quiet; CKE/CCI. "Lovely location; gd views; no shd; facs inadequate peak ssn; excel communal rm." ♦ 15 May-30 Sep. € 12.00   2016*

NAVARRENX *8F1* **(0km S Urban)** *43.31988, -0.76143* **Camping Beau Rivage, Allée des Marronniers, 64190 Navarrenx [05 59 66 10 00; beaucamping@free.fr; www.beaucamping.com]** Fr E exit A64 junc 9 at Artix onto D281 dir Mourenx, then Navarrenx. Fr N on D947 thro Orthez to Navarrenx (D947 fr Orthez much improved). Site well sp bet walled (Bastide) town & rv. Med, hdstg, hdg, mkd, pt shd, pt sl, terr, serviced pitches; wc (htd); chem disp; mv service pnt; fam bthrm; shwrs inc; EHU (6-10A) inc; lndry; shop nr; rest nr; snacks; bar nr; bbq; playgrnd; pool; wifi; 15% statics; dogs €1.50; phone; Eng spkn; adv bkg acc; quiet; ccard acc; rv fishing; games rm; rafting; tennis; CKE/CCI. "Lovely, peaceful, well-run site; no d'fits over 9m high ssn; nr interesting walled town; helpful, friendly, British owners; bike hire in town; clean san facs; gd pool; bar 300m; gd area for walking, cycling; conv local shops & rests; mkt Wed; rec; outstanding." ♦ 25 Mar-8 Oct. € 28.70   2017*

NAY *8F2* **(2km N Rural)** *43.20027, -0.25722* **Camping Les Ô Kiri, Ave du Lac, 64800 Baudreix [05 59 92 97 73; fax 05 59 13 93 77; les-okiri@wanadoo.fr; www.lesokiri.net]** Exit A64 junc 10 onto Pau ring rd D317 S, then D938 dir Nay & Lourdes. Exit sp Baudreix & in 2km turn R at rndabt & foll sp to lake & site. Med, hdg, mkd, pt shd, wc (htd); chem disp; mv service pnt; shwrs inc; EHU (6-10A) €4-5.50; lndry; shop; rest; snacks; bar; bbq; playgrnd; sw; wifi; 50% statics; dogs €2; adv bkg acc; quiet; ccard acc; tennis; waterslide; bike hire. "Conv Biarritz, N Spain & Pyrennees; lake sw complex booking ess; on arr use carpark for recep; excel rest; superb lake facs; picturesque; basic but OK san facs, poss stretched if site full." ♦ 1 Apr-30 Sep. € 19.50   2014*

NEBOUZAT

NEBOUZAT 9B1 (2km NW Rural) 45.72569, 2.89008
Camping Les Domes, Les Quatre Routes de Nébouzat, 63210 Nébouzat [04 73 87 14 06 or 04 73 93 21 02 (LS); fax 04 73 87 18 81; camping-les-domes@wanadoo.fr; www.les-domes.com] Exit 5 fr A75 onto D213 twd Col de la Ventouse; turn L on D2089 sp Tulle. Do not ent vill of Nébouzat but cont for 1km. Take L onto D216 sp Orcival then immed L. Site on L in 100m. Med, mkd, hdstg, pt shd, wc; chem disp; fam bthrm; shwrs inc; EHU (10-15A) €6 (poss long lead req); gas; lndry; shop; snacks; playgrnd; pool (covrd, htd); entmnt; TV; dogs free; phone; Eng spkn; adv bkg acc; quiet; sailing; windsurfing; CKE/CCI. "Immac site; walking; boules area; warm welcome; friendly, helpful staff; sm pitches; gd san facs; conv Vulcania; excel rest nrby; gd base for Auvergne." 23 Apr-3 Oct. € 26.50   2016*

NEMOURS 4F3 (5km S Urban) 48.24073, 2.70389
FFCC Camping de Pierre Le Sault, Chemin des Grèves, 77167 Bagneaux-sur-Loing [01 64 29 24 44; camping.bagneaux-sur-loing@orange.fr] Well sp bef town fr both dir off D607. Med, hdg, mkd, pt shd, wc; shwrs inc; EHU (3-6A) €2-3.10; lndry; shop nr; playgrnd; 30% statics; Eng spkn; tennis; CKE/CCI. "Lovely site by canal & rv; excel clean facs; site a bit run down, but pleasant; ent barrier clsd 2200-0700." ♦ 1 Apr-31 Oct. € 16.20   2014*

NERAC 8E2 (6km SW Rural) 44.09948, 0.31028 Aire Naturelle Les Contes d'Albret, 47600 Nérac [05 53 65 18 73; fax 05 53 97 18 62; lescontesdalbret@orange.fr; www.albret.com] Exit A62 junc 7 onto D931 to Laplume. Then turn W onto D15 & D656 to Nérac. Cont on D656 dir Mézin & foll site sp 'Les Contes d'Albert' to end of rd in 3km. Sm, pt shd, pt sl, wc (htd); fam bthrm; shwrs inc; EHU (6A) €2; shop; rest; playgrnd; pool; Eng spkn; adv bkg acc; quiet; kayaking. "Vg, peaceful, CL-type site; farm shop; excel views; glorious garden." 1 May-30 Sep. € 13.00   2014*

> ### "There aren't many sites open at this time of year"
> If you're travelling outside peak season remember to call ahead to check site opening dates – even if the entry says 'open all year'.

NERET 4H3 (3km N Rural) 46.58885, 2.13425
Campsite Le Bonhomme, Mulles 36400 Neret [02 54 31 46 11; info@camping-lebonhomme.com; www.camping-lebonhomme.com] Fr Vierzon on the A20 take exit 12 to Chateauroux, then the D943 twds Montlucon. Turn L at Neret exit and foll Aire Naturelle signs. Site is 2km beyond Neret on L. Sm, mkd, hdstg, pt shd, sl, wc; chem disp; mv service pnt; shwrs; EHU (16A); lndry; rest; bbq; wifi; Eng spkn; adv bkg acc; quiet; games area. "Excel; lovely rural, quiet site; food avail fr owners." 1 Apr-1 Oct. € 20.50   2016*

NERIS LES BAINS 7A4 (1km NW Urban) 46.28695, 2.65215 Le Camping du Lac (formerly Municipal), Ave Marx Dormoy, 03310 Néris-les-Bains [04 70 03 17 59 or 04 70 03 24 70 (recep); fax 04 70 03 79 99; campingdulac-neris@orange.fr; www.ville-neris-les-bains.fr] Site on N side of Néris off D2144. Turn W at rndabt by blue TO, opp park, & foll sp round 1 way system to site in 500m. Med, mkd, hdg, hdstg, pt shd, pt sl, terr, wc; chem disp; shwrs inc; EHU (10A); gas; shop nr; snacks; bar; playgrnd; red long stay; 10% statics; dogs €1; quiet. "6 pitches for m'vans at ent to site; covrd pool 500m; space to wait on car park if barrier clsd; pleasant town; vg; gd facs, quiet lower pitches, gd NH." 1 Apr-22 Oct. € 15.00   2013*

> ### "That's changed – Should I let the Club know?"
> If you find something on site that's different from the site entry, fill in a report and let us know. See camc.com/europereport.

NEUF BRISACH 6F3 (1km E Urban) 48.01638, 7.53565 Camp Municipal Vauban, Entrée Porte de Bâle, 68600 Neuf-Brisach [03 89 72 54 25 or 03 89 72 51 68 (Mairie); contact@camping-vauban.fr; www.camping-vauban.fr] Fr D415 (Colmar-Freiburg) at E of Neuf-Brisach turn NE on D1 bis (sp Neuf-Brisach & Camping Vauban). At next junc turn L & immed R into site rd. Med, pt shd, wc; mv service pnt; shwrs; EHU (10A) €4; shop nr; playgrnd; 5% statics; dogs €1; adv bkg acc; quiet; CKE/CCI. "Gd, well-run site; fascinating ramparts around town; lge pitches; friendly, helpful staff; excel cycle rtes fr site along Rhine & thro historic vill; pool 3km; site won many awards; long elec leads req; ideal long stay; supmkt 2km." 1 Apr-31 Oct. € 17.00   2018*

NEUF BRISACH 6F3 (6km SE Rural) 47.97988, 7.59639 FFCC Camping L'Orée du Bois, 5 Rue du Bouleau, 68600 Geiswasser [03 89 72 80 13; valerie.schappler@orange.fr; valerieschappler1.wixsite.com/campingaloreedubois] Site in vill cent; rd name on bungalow; ent bet bungalow & vegetable garden - tight turn, watch out bungalow gutters. Sm, hdg, pt shd, wc (htd); chem disp; shwrs inc; EHU (10A) €3.60; lndry; bbq; playgrnd; wifi; 60% statics; dogs free; bus adj; Eng spkn; adv bkg acc; quiet; CKE/CCI. "Gd touring base; friendly owner; gd." ♦ 1 Apr-30 Sep. € 6.60   2017*

NEUVIC (CORREZE)

NEUFCHATEL EN BRAY *3C2* (1km NW Urban) *49.73781, 1.42803* **Camping Sainte Claire, 19 rue Grande Flandre, 76220 Neufchâtel-en-Bray [02 35 93 03 93 or 06 20 12 20 98 (mob); fancelot@ wanadoo.fr; www.camping-sainte-claire.com]** Fr N & S exit A28 junc 9 onto D928 sp Neufchâtel; in 1km at mini rndabt at bottom hill, turn L into Rue de la Grande Flandre, foll Leclerc supmkt sp; cont past supmkt for 400m to Rue Ste Claire. (NB Motorvan aire immed bef site ent, do not turn in by mistake as there are charges). Med, hdstg, mkd, hdg, pt shd, pt sl, terr, serviced pitches; wc; chem disp; mv service pnt; fam bthrm; shwrs inc; EHU (6-10A) inc; lndry; shop; rest; bar; bbq; playgrnd; red long stay; twin axles; wifi; 20% statics; dogs free LS; phone; bus 400m; Eng spkn; adv bkg acc; quiet; ccard acc; bike hire; fishing; CKE/CCI. "Beautiful, spacious, well-run, well-kept, busy site by rv; lge, med & sm pitches; not all pitches have 10A, poss 6A pitches better; friendly, helpful owner; excel clean san facs - poss long walk LS; wet rm for disabled; wheelchair access/easy walking; pleasant walk along cycle rte (old rlwy line) to town & vet; Sat mkt; conv Le Havre/ Dieppe ferries & A28; sep o'night area; some drive-thro pitches; gd value sh or long stay; popular NH; excel; nice site as always; Aire for m'vans now open adj (OAY, €12, all hdstg, full facs, 10A elec & acc ccards only); busy, efficient site; gd easy access fr a'route; ent tight for lge o'fits; best book for twin axles; excel rest; adj 40km greenway cycle ride; ACSI acc." ♦ 1 Apr-15 Oct. € 17.00 2018*

NEUNG SUR BEUVRON *4G3* (1km NE Rural) *47.53893, 1.81488* **FFCC Camp Municipal de la Varenne, 34 Rue de Veilleas, 41210 Neung-sur-Beuvron [02 54 83 68 52 or 06 27 92 39 14 (mob); camping.lavarenne@wanadoo.fr; www.neung-sur-beuvron.fr/camping]** On A10 heading S take Orléans Sud exit & join N20 S. At end of La Ferté-St Aubin take D922 SW twd Romorantin-Lanthenay. In 20km R onto D925 to Neung. Turn R at church pedestrian x-ing in cent of vill ('stade' sp), R at fork (white, iron cross) & site on R in 1km. Site by rvside. Fr A71 exit junc 3 onto D923; turn R onto D925 & as above. Sm, mkd, hdg, pt shd, pt sl, wc; chem disp; mv service pnt; shwrs inc; EHU (6A) €3.10; gas; lndry; shop nr; rest nr; bar nr; playgrnd; 10% statics; dogs; Eng spkn; adv bkg acc; quiet; ccard acc; tennis. "Friendly, helpful warden; gd, immac facs; lge pitches; barrier clsd 2200-0800; vg cent for hiking, cycling, birdwatching; mkt Sat; excel well maintained site." Easter-20 Oct. € 12.00 2017*

NEUVE LYRE, LA *3D2* (0km W Urban) *48.90750, 0.74486* **Camp Municipal La Salle, Rue de l'Union, 27330 La Neuve-Lyre [02 32 60 14 98 or 02 32 30 50 01 (Mairie); fax 02 32 30 22 37; mairie.la-neuve-lyre@wanadoo.fr]** Fr NE on D830 into vill turn R at church (sp not visible), fr S (Rugles) foll sp. Well sp fr vill. Med, pt shd, wc; chem disp; mv service pnt; shwrs; EHU (5A) inc (poss long lead req); shop nr; 2% statics; dogs; quiet; fishing; CKE/CCI. "Delightful, peaceful, clean site; site yourself, warden calls; excel sh stay/NH." ♦ 15 Mar-15 Oct. € 10.00 2017*

NEUVEGLISE *9C1* (5km S Rural) *44.89500, 3.00157* **Flower Camping Le Belvédère, Le Pont-de-Lanau, 15260 Neuvéglise [04 71 23 50 50; fax 04 71 23 58 93; contact@campingbelvedere.com; www.campingbelvedere.com]** S on A75/E11 exit junc 28 at St Flour; take D921 S twd Chaudes-Aigues. Turn R sp 'Villages de Vacances de Lanau' & site - do not app site thro Neuvéglise. Steep access poss diff lge o'fits. Med, pt shd, terr, wc; chem disp; mv service pnt; fam bthrm; shwrs inc; EHU (6A) inc; gas; lndry; shop; rest; snacks; bar; bbq (charcoal, gas); playgrnd; pool (htd); paddling pool; red long stay; twin axles; entmnt; wifi; TV; 25% statics; dogs free; adv bkg acc; quiet; ccard acc; sauna; fishing; windsurfing nr; horseriding 20km; canoeing nr; games rm; tennis nr; sailing 15km; CKE/CCI. "Views over Rv Truyère; fitness rm; friendly, peaceful, family-run site; steep terrs & tight pitches poss diff; gd, clean san facs; mkt Neuvéglise Fri; excel site, beautiful views." ♦ 30 Mar-29 Sep. € 39.00 2013*

NEUVIC (CORREZE) *7C4* (4km N Rural) *45.38245, 2.22901* **Camping Domaine de Mialaret, Route d'Egletons, 19160 Neuvic [05 55 46 02 50; fax 05 55 46 02 65; info@lemialaret.com; www.lemialaret.com]** Fr N on A89 exit 23 twds St Angel then D171 to Neuvic or foll sp fr Neuvic on D991. Med, hdg, pt shd, pt sl, wc (htd); chem disp; mv service pnt; fam bthrm; shwrs inc; EHU (10A) €3-4; lndry; shop; rest; snacks; bar; playgrnd; pool; red long stay; entmnt; wifi; TV; 30% statics; dogs free; phone; bus 4km; Eng spkn; adv bkg acc; quiet; games rm; watersports nr; CKE/CCI. "Excel site in grnds of chateau; 2 carp fishing pools; charming owner, friendly staff; facs ltd LS; blocks req most pitches; mini farm; walking tours; mountain bike trails; children's mini zoo & rare sheep breeds nrby." 26 Apr-5 Oct. € 42.60 2014*

> "I like to fill in the reports as I travel from site to site"
>
> You'll find report forms at the back of this guide, or you can fill them in online at camc.com/europereport.

NEUVIC (CORREZE) *7C4* (8km NE Rural) *45.40586, 2.32078* **Camping à la Ferme Chez Père Jules (Van Boshuysen), Prentegarde, 19160 Liginiac [05 55 95 84 49; rob_ykie@hotmail.com]** Exit A89 junc 23 onto D979 dir Bort-les-Orgues; in 5km (just after La Serre) turn R onto D982; in 10km turn L to Liginiac; cont thro vill & then turn R uphill onto D20. Site sp to R in 1.5km. Sm, pt shd, pt sl, wc; chem disp; shwrs inc; EHU (4A) inc; lndry; shop nr; rest; bar; bbq; playgrnd; pool; sw nr; 5% statics; dogs; Eng spkn; adv bkg acc; quiet; CKE/CCI. "Beautiful CL-type site; helpful Dutch owners; rallies welcome; mv service pnt in Liginiac; vg; highly rec." 1 Apr-30 Sep. € 15.00 2012*

NEVERS

NEVERS *4H4* (1km S Rural) *46.98210, 3.16110* **FFCC Camping de Nevers, Rue de la Jonction, 58000 Nevers [03 86 36 40 75; campingdenevers@orange.fr; www.aquadis-loisirs.com/camping-de-nevers]** Fr E exit A77 junc 37 & foll dir 'Cent Ville'. Site on R immed bef bdge over Rv Loire. Fr W (Bourges) on D976 foll sp 'Nevers Centre' onto D907. In approx 3km bef bdge turn R, site on L. Sm, mkd, hdg, hdstg, shd, pt sl, terr, wc cont; chem disp; mv service pnt; fam bthrm; shwrs inc; EHU (10A); lndry; shop nr; rest nr; snacks; bar; bbq; playgrnd; beach sand 200m; wifi; TV; 3% statics; dogs €1.50; phone; bus 20m; Eng spkn; adv bkg acc; ccard acc; rv fishing; bike hire; CKE/CCI. "Pleasant, scenic site on bank of Rv Loire; on 3 levels - ltd EHU on lower; gd clean san facs, poss stretched high ssn; cycle paths along Loire; no twin axles; poss noisy when events at Nevers Magny-Cours racing circuit; gd site; easy walk over bdge to interesting town; nr town; excel recep staff; ltd no of elec pitches, arr early." ♦ 6 Mar-5 Nov. € 23.00 2017*

NEVERS *4H4* (7km NW Urban) *47.01222, 3.07822* **FFCC Camping La Loire, 2 Rue de la Folie, 58600 Fourchambault [03 86 60 81 59 or 06 11 05 18 69 (mob); fax 03 86 60 96 24; campingdelaloire@dbmail.com; www.camping-de-loire.fr.st]** Fr Nevers on D40 thro town, site on L bef rv bdge. Med, pt shd, wc; chem disp; mv service pnt; shwrs inc; EHU (6-10A) €3-4.50; lndry; shop nr; rest nr; snacks; bar; bbq; red long stay; dogs €0.50; bus; CKE/CCI. "Friendly, helpful staff; rv adj; san facs need update & poss unclean; NH only." ♦ 9 Apr-31 Oct. € 17.50 2017*

NEXON *7B3* (6km SSW Rural) *45.63471, 1.16176* **Flower Camping L'Air Du Lac, Impasse du Lac Plaisance, 87800 St Hilaire-les-Places [05 55 58 79 18; campinglairdulac@flowercampings.com; www.campinglairdulac.com]** S fr Nexon on D11. Soon after ent St Hilaire-les-Places take a L sp Lac Plaisance & Camping. Site adj to lake. Med, hdg, shd, pt sl, wc; chem disp; mv service pnt; fam bthrm; shwrs inc; EHU (10A) inc; lndry; shop; snacks; bar; bbq; playgrnd; beach adj; sw; entmnt; wifi; TV; 20% statics; dogs €2; Eng spkn; adv bkg acc; quiet; ccard acc; games rm; games area; CKE/CCI. "Pleasant site adj to lake sw beach; dep req; very helpful staff; gd sized pitches; clean facs; vg for families; interesting touring area; excel." ♦ 15 Apr-30 Sep. € 14.50 2017*

NEXON *7B3* (1km SW Rural) *45.67104, 1.18059* **Camp Municipal de l'Etang de la Lande, 87800 Nexon [05 55 58 35 44 or 05 55 58 10 19 (Mairie); fax 05 55 58 33 50; campingdelalande.nexon@orange.fr; www.nexon.fr]** S fr Limoges on D704, take D15 W twd Nexon. Exit Nexon by D11 sp Ladignac-le-Long & Camping, site 3km S at junc with D17. Med, mkd, pt shd, sl, wc (htd); shwrs; EHU (5-10A); lndry; shop; rest nr; bar; playgrnd; sw nr; entmnt; TV; Eng spkn; quiet; bike hire. "Excel base for Limoges; site open to adj leisure park." 1 Jun-30 Sep. € 10.00 2013*

NIEDERBRONN LES BAINS *5D3* (2km SW Rural) *48.92958, 7.60428* **Camping Oasis Oberbronn, 3 Rue de Frohret, 67110 Oberbronn [03 88 09 71 96; fax 03 88 09 97 87; contact@opale-dmcc.com; www.opale-dmcc.fr]** Fr D1062 turn S on D28 away fr Niederbronn; thro Oberbronn, site sp. Lge, mkd, pt shd, pt sl, wc; chem disp; mv service pnt; shwrs inc; EHU (6A) €4.30; lndry; shop; rest; snacks; bar; bbq; playgrnd; pool (covrd, htd); paddling pool; red long stay; 20% statics; dogs €2.65; adv bkg rec; quiet; ccard acc; golf; cycling; fishing 2km; sauna; games rm; clsd 1200-1300; tennis; CKE/CCI. "Vg site with views; pt of leisure complex; sl area for tourers; horseriding rtes; some san facs tired; walking; wellness cent; fitness rm; site gravel paths not suitable wheelchair users." ♦ 1 Apr-30 Sep. € 15.00 2016*

NIMES *10E2* (8km S Rural) *43.78776, 4.35196* **Camp La Bastide (formerly Municipal), route de Générac, 30900 Nîmes [04 66 62 05 82; bastide@capfun.com; www.camping-nimes.com]** Fr A9 exit junc 25 onto A54 dir Arles; in 2km exit A54 junc 1 onto D42 sp St Gilles; in 1.5km (at 2nd rndabt) turn R onto D135; in 2.5km at rndabt turn R onto D13; site on L. Or N fr Montpellier on N113/D6113 to Nimes; at Périphique Sud turn S onto D13 sp Générac; site on R 500m after rndabt junc with D613. Site well sp fr town cent. Lge, hdstg, hdg, mkd, shd, wc (htd); chem disp; mv service pnt; fam bthrm; shwrs inc; EHU (10A) inc; gas; lndry; shop nr; rest; snacks; bar; playgrnd; wifi; TV; 10% statics; dogs €2.70; phone; bus; Eng spkn; adv bkg acc; quiet; games area; CKE/CCI. "Excel, well-run site; lge pitches; friendly, helpful recep; Nîmes 20 mins by bus fr site; gd site; exciting water complex; vg bistro on site; child's entmnt; old san facs; busy, used by workers." ♦ € 30.00 2017*

> **"We must tell the Club about that great site we found"**
>
> Get your site reports in by mid-August and we'll do our best to get your updates into the next edition.

NOIRETABLE *9B1* (1km S Rural) *45.80817, 3.76844* **Camp Municipal de la Roche, Route de la Roche, 42440 Noirétable [04 77 24 72 68; fax 04 77 24 92 20; www.noiretable.fr/plan_eau_camping_Roche.aspx]** Leave A72/E70 junc 4 sp Noirétable; thro toll & turn SW onto D53. Ignore narr tourist rte sp to W; cont downhill to T-junc & turn R onto D1089. Take next L & site on R in 750m. Sm, hdstg, mkd, pt shd, pt sl, terr, wc (htd); own san rec; shwrs; EHU (10A) €2.80; shop nr; bar nr; playgrnd; 40% statics; Eng spkn. "Warden lives on site, but barrier poss locked LS; recep open 0900-1230, 1800-1930; camperstop 100m; lake adj; €3 for water & chem disp, token fr site." 1 Apr-1 Nov. € 10.00 2017*

NOIRMOUTIER EN L'ILE *2H3* (2km E Coastal) *46.99697, -2.22057* **Huttopia Noirmoutier, Bois de la Chaize, 23 Rue des Sableaux, 85330 Noirmoutier-en-l'Ile [02 51 39 06 24; fax 02 51 35 97 63; www.europe.huttopia.com]** Ent Noirmoutier on D948, strt on over bdge & foll sp for Bois-de-la-Chaize, then 'campings'. Lge, pt shd, wc; chem disp; mv service pnt; fam bthrm; shwrs inc; EHU (10A) €4.80; lndry; snacks; bar; playgrnd; beach sand adj; wifi; 10% statics; dogs €4; phone; adv bkg acc; quiet; bike hire; fishing; boat launch; CKE/CCI. "Peaceful site in pine forest nr salt water marshes; gd for children." 1 Apr-1 Oct. € 21.00 2017*

NOIRMOUTIER EN L'ILE *2H3* (6km SE Coastal) *46.96659, -2.22027* **Domaine Les Moulins, 54 Rue des Moulins, 85680 La Guérinière [0251 39 51 38; fax 0251 39 57 97; moulins@originalcamping.com; www.domaine-les-moulins.com]** Cross to island on D38, sp to La Guérinière, imm turn L, site dir ahead. Lge, mkd, hdg, pt shd, pt sl, wc (htd); chem disp; mv service pnt; fam bthrm; shwrs; EHU (10A); lndry; shop nr; rest; bar; playgrnd; pool; beach; wifi; 40% statics; dogs; adv bkg acc; quiet; ccard acc; games area; games rm; CKE/CCI. "Excel site; bike hire 100m." 1 Apr-30 Sep. € 67.00 2014*

NOIRMOUTIER EN L'ILE *2H3* (8km W Coastal) *47.02409, -2.30374* **Camp Municipal La Pointe, L'Herbaudière, 85330 Noirmoutier-en-l'Ile [02 51 39 16 70; fax 02 51 39 74 15]** Fr bdge to island foll sp to Noirmoutier town, then to L'Herbaudière & port. At port turn L, 500m to site. Lge, mkd, unshd, wc; chem disp; mv service pnt; shwrs inc; EHU (10A) €3.65 (long leads poss req); gas; lndry; playgrnd; beach adj; wifi; dogs €1.60; adv bkg acc; quiet; ccard acc; CKE/CCI. "Excel site in beautiful location; peaceful; sea views some pitches; poss windy (exposed to sea on 3 sides); helpful staff; clean, adequate facs; grnd poss soft in some areas; shop; rest, snacks & bar in town; gd cycle rtes on island; sh walk to fishing/pleasure harbour; rec; very busy." 18 Mar-15 Oct. € 19.00 2014*

⊞ **NOLAY** *6H1* (1km NW Rural) *46.95084, 4.62266* **Camping La Bruyère, Rue du Moulin Larché, 21340 Nolay [03 80 21 87 59 or 06 88 16 06 18 (mob); www.nolay.com/fr/?/Logement/Les-campings]** Fr Beaune take D973 W dir Autun. In approx 20km, arr in vill of Nolay & cont on D973 thro vill. Site on L in 1km after vill, opp supmkt. Sm, mkd, hdg, pt shd, terr, wc (htd); chem disp; mv service pnt; shwrs inc; EHU (10-12A) €3.60-4; lndry; shop nr; rest nr; bar nr; bbq; 10% statics; bus adj; Eng spkn; quiet; ccard acc; CKE/CCI. "Lovely, peaceful, well-kept site; friendly staff; gd, clean san facs, poss stretched if site busy; poss grape pickers in Sep; poss school & youth groups; attractive walk to bustling old town; gd touring base in wine area or NH; excel." ♦ € 19.00 2016*

NONANCOURT *4E2* (4km E Urban) *48.76410, 1.23686* **Camp Municipal du Pré de l'Eglise, Rue Pré de l'Eglise, 28380 St Rémy-sur-Avre [02 37 48 93 87 or 02 37 62 52 00 (LS); fax 02 37 48 80 15; mairiesaintremy2@wanadoo.fr; www.ville-st-remy-sur-avre.fr]** Fr Dreux take N12 W to St Rémy; strt over 1st rndabt & at traff lts complex in 500m turn R & then immed R & foll site sp. Fr Evreux (W) on N12 to St Rémy; after x-ing rv bdge at traff lts complex strt ahead to rndabt (no L turn at traff lts), then immed R at end rv bdge to cross N12 as above. Site clearly sp in vill cent, sp 'Oscar' is for sports cent adj. NB Speed ramps on site app rd. Sm, mkd, hdg, pt shd, wc; chem disp; fam bthrm; shwrs inc; EHU (6-10A) €2.83 (poss rev pol); lndry; rest nr; playgrnd; TV; dogs; phone; Eng spkn; adv bkg acc; tennis adj; fishing adj; CKE/CCI. "Pleasant, popular, well-kept NH nr rv; welcoming warden; clean, fair facs, some modern, ltd LS; no twin axles (but negotiable); some pitches poss diff access; factory adj poss noisy; vill in walking dist; a gd find; Carrefour with fuel 1km; excel site in middle of vill; site van, warden will call." ♦ 1 Apr-30 Sep. € 14.60 2017*

NONTRON *7B3* (11km NE Rural) *45.55138, 0.79472* **Kawan Village Le Château Le Verdoyer, 24470 Champs-Romain [05 53 56 94 64; fax 05 53 56 38 70; chateau@verdoyer.fr; www.verdoyer.fr]** Fr Limoges on N21 twd Périgueux. At Châlus turn R sp Nontron (D6 bis-D85). After approx 18km turn L twd Champs Romain on D96 to site on L in 2km. Lge, pt shd, terr, wc; chem disp; mv service pnt; fam bthrm; shwrs inc; EHU (5-10A) inc (poss rev pol); gas; lndry; shop; rest; snacks; bar; bbq (charcoal, gas); playgrnd; pool (htd); paddling pool; entmnt; wifi; TV; 20% statics; dogs €3; phone; Eng spkn; adv bkg acc; quiet; ccard acc; lake fishing; games rm; waterslide; bike hire; tennis; golf 25km; boating; CKE/CCI. "Peaceful, Dutch-run site in grnds of chateau; B&B in chateau; lovely location; no o'fits over 10m; gd sized pitches, but terr; friendly staff; superb facs; poss steep access some pitches; grnd hard, but awnings poss; excel; highly rec." ♦ 19 Apr-29 Sep. € 42.00 2013*

NONTRON *7B3* (8km NE Rural) *45.56185, 0.71979* **Camping Manzac Ferme, Manzac, 24300 Augignac [05 53 56 31 34; info@manzac-ferme.com; www.manzac-ferme.com]** Fr Nontron take D675 N dir Rochechouart & after 7km on ent Augignac turn R sp Abjat-sur-Bandiat then immed R sp Manzac. Site on R 3.5km. Sm, mkd, hdstg, pt shd, pt sl, wc (htd); chem disp; shwrs inc; EHU (6A) inc; shop nr; rest nr; bbq; sw nr; wifi; dogs by arrangement; Eng spkn; adv bkg acc; quiet; rv fishing; CKE/CCI. "Superb, peaceful, well-kept CL-type, adults only site; helpful British owners; excel san facs; phone ahead in winter; ideal for birdwatching & wildlife; highly rec; most pitches in dense shd; excel." ♦ 15 May-15 Sep. € 24.00 2016*

NONTRON

⊞ **NONTRON** 7B3 (1km S Urban) 45.51992, 0.65876
Camping de Nontron, St Martiel-de-Valette, 24300 Nontron [05 53 56 02 04 or 06 30 66 25 74 (mob); camping-de-nontron@orange.fr; www.campingdenontron.com] Thro Nontron S twd Brantôme on D675. Site on o'skts of town on L nr stadium. Sp. Med, hdg, mkd, pt shd, wc (htd); mv service pnt; shwrs; EHU (10A) €3.50; gas; lndry; shop nr; rest nr; bar nr; playgrnd; paddling pool; entmnt; TV; dogs €1; Eng spkn; quiet; games area; games rm; CKE/CCI. "Pleasant owners; site clsd mid-Dec to early Jan; excel, modern san facs; gd touring base; town 1km walk along footpath." € 22.50   2018*

NORT SUR ERDRE 2G4 (1km S Rural) 47.42770, -1.49877 Camping Seasonova du Port Mulon (formaly Municipal), Rue des Mares Noires, 44390 Nort-sur-Erdre [02 36 81 00 01 or 02 40 72 23 57; fax 02 40 72 16 09; contact@camping-portmulon.com; www.camping-portmulon.com] Sp fr all ents to town; foll 'Camping' & 'Hippodrome' sp. NB: C'vans banned fr town cent, look for diversion sp. Med, shd, wc; chem disp; shwrs inc; EHU (6A) €2.40; lndry; shop nr; playgrnd; dogs €0.90; adv bkg acc; quiet; fishing; boating; tennis; CKE/CCI. "Delightful, spacious, under-used site; gd walking & cycling area, espec along Nantes canal & Rv Erdre; Barrier perm locked, access when warden on site only; new site rd & toilet block (2014); friendly staff." 5 Apr-15 Oct. € 24.00   2014*

> **"I need an on-site restaurant"**
> We do our best to make sure site information is correct, but it is always best to check any must-have facilities are still available or will be open during your visit.

NOUAN LE FUZELIER 4G3 (1km S Urban) 47.53328, 2.03508 Camping La Grande Sologne, Rue des Peupliers, 41600 Nouan-le-Fuzelier [02 54 88 70 22; fax 02 54 88 41 74; info@campingrandesologne.com; www.campingrandesologne.com] On E side of D2020, at S end of Nouan opp rlwy stn. Sp fr town cent & opp rlwy stn. NB sat nav not rec. Med, mkd, pt shd, wc; chem disp; mv service pnt; fam bthrm; shwrs inc; EHU (10A) €3; lndry; shop nr; playgrnd; red long stay; wifi; 2% statics; dogs €1; Eng spkn; adv bkg; quiet; golf 15km; tennis; fishing; games area; CKE/CCI. "Pretty site adj lake (no sw); some pitches boggy when wet; facs poss stretched high ssn; ltd facs end of ssn & poss unclean; htd pool adj; public park at ent to site, but quiet; rec arr early; excel NH; phone for entry LS; excel site; office open 0700-1500; voucher for nrby sw pool; san facs dated; friendly owners." 1 Apr-15 Oct. € 24.50   2014*

NOUVION EN THIERACHE, LE 3B4 (2km S Rural) 50.00538, 3.78292 Camp Municipal du Lac de Condé, Promenade Henri d'Orléans, Rue de Guise (Le Lac), 02170 Le Nouvion-en-Thiérache [03 23 98 98 58; fax 03 23 98 94 90; campinglacdeconde@gmail.com; www.camping-thierache.com] Sp fr cent of Le Nouvion fr D1043 on D26, dir Guise opp chateau. Sm, hdstg, hdg, mkd, pt shd, pt sl, wc; chem disp; mv service pnt; shwrs inc; EHU (4-8A) €2.50; lndry; shop nr; rest nr; bar nr; bbq; playgrnd; red long stay; 70% statics; dogs €0.80; phone; Eng spkn; adv bkg acc; ccard acc; tennis nr; horseriding nr; CKE/CCI. "Beautiful, spacious, lakeside site; busy even LS - rec phone ahead; gd sized pitches; warm welcome, staff helpful; htd pool adj; gd san facs; gd for families; canoe hire nr; some pitches not suitable m'vans due slope; muddy when wet; walk around lake; conv NH; excel; coarse fishing in adj lake."
♦ 1 Apr-30 Sep. € 12.50   2017*

NOYERS 4G4 (0km S Rural) 47.69423, 3.99421 Camp Municipal, Promenade du Pré de l'Echelle, 89310 Noyers-sur-Surein [03 86 82 83 72 (Mairie); fax 03 86 82 63 41; mairie-de-noyers@wanadoo.fr] Exit A6 at Nitry & turn R onto D944. In 2km at N edge of Nitry, turn R onto D49 sp Noyers. In 10km in Noyers, turn L onto D86 sp Cent Ville/Camping. Immed after x-ing rv & bef gate, turn L bet 2 obelisks. Site at end of track. Sm, mkd, shd, terr, wc; own san req; chem disp; shwrs nr; EHU €1.05; shop nr; rest nr; bar nr; bbq; playgrnd; dogs; quiet. "Attractive, secluded site nr Rv Serein (6 pitches); ent key fr Mairie on R after going thro town gate; pretty old vill; ltd san facs." € 4.00   2014*

⊞ **NOYON** 3C3 (5km E Rural) 49.58882, 3.04370 FFCC Camping L'Etang du Moulin, 54 Rue du Moulin, 60400 Salency [03 44 09 99 81; fax 03 44 43 06 78] Take D1032 fr Noyon dir Chauny. On ent Salency turn L & foll site sp. Site in 1km. Sm, shd, pt sl, wc (htd); chem disp; mv service pnt; shwrs; EHU (10A) €1.60; gas; shop nr; rest nr; bar; bbq; playgrnd; 75% statics; dogs €1; quiet; fishing; tennis; CKE/CCI. "Site adj to fishing lake; gd facs; very clean & tidy; elec french 2 pin; security barrier card; pool 3km; v quiet location."
♦ € 13.00   2016*

NOYON 3C3 (10km S Rural) 49.50667, 3.01765 FFCC Camping Les Araucarias, 870 Rue du Général Leclerc, 60170 Carlepont [03 44 75 27 39; fax 03 44 38 12 51; camping-les-araucarias@wanadoo.fr; www.camping-les-araucarias.com] Fr S, fr A1 exit junc 9 or 10 for Compiègne. There take D130 sp Tracy-le-Val & Carlepont. Site on L 100m fr Carlepont vill sp. Or fr N on D934 Noyon-Soissons rd take D130 dir Carlepont & Tracy-le-Val. Site on R after vill on SW twd Compiegne - not well sp. Sm, mkd, pt shd, pt sl, wc (htd); chem disp; mv service pnt; fam bthrm; shwrs inc; EHU (6-10A) €3 (poss rev pol); gas; lndry; shop nr; rest nr; bar nr; bbq; playgrnd; 80% statics; dogs €1; Eng spkn; adv bkg acc; quiet; CKE/CCI. "Secluded site, previously an arboretum; close Parc Astérix & La Mer-de-Sable (theme park); 85km Disneyland; san facs poss scruffy LS; vg." ♦ 1 Apr-31 Oct. € 12.50   2016*

NUITS ST GEORGES 6G1 (5km S Urban) 47.10323, 4.94148 Camping Le Moulin de Prissey, 14 rue du Moulin de Prissey, 21700 Premeaux-Prissey [03 80 62 31 15; fax 03 80 61 37 29; cpg.moulin.prissey@free.fr; www.cpg-moulin-prissey.fr] Exit Beaune on D974 twd Nuits-St Georges & Dijon; app Premeaux-Prissey turn R soon after vill sp, under rlwy bdge & foll site sp. Fr A31 exit at Nuits-St Georges & foll camp sp for Saule-Guillaume, thro Premeaux-Prissey & foll site sp. Sm, mkd, pt shd, pt sl, wc; chem disp; mv service pnt; shwrs inc; EHU (6A) inc; gas; lndry; shop nr; rest nr; snacks; bar nr; bbq; playgrnd; dogs €0.90; adv bkg acc; ccard acc; CKE/CCI. "Popular NH - arr early; sm pitches; access poss diff lge o'fits; basic facs; gd cycling; noisy rlwy adj; site well laid out & tidy (2015)." ♦ 4 Apr-15 Oct. € 18.00 2016*

NYONS 9D2 (12km NE Rural) 44.42569, 5.21904 Camping de Trente Pas, 26110 St Ferréol-Trente-Pas [04 75 27 70 69; contact@campingtrentepas.com; www.campingtrentepas.com] Exit A7 junc 19 Bollène onto D994 & D94. L on D70 to St Ferréol-Trente-Pas. Site 100m fr vill on banks of stream. Med, shd, wc; shwrs; EHU (6A) €3.10; lndry; shop nr; rest nr; snacks; bar; playgrnd; pool; entmnt; TV; 5% statics; dogs €2; quiet; bike hire; tennis; games rm; horseriding 4km. "Peaceful site nr rv; scenic area, views fr site; gd, clean san facs; gd pool; on flood plain; excel value; rec." 1 May-31 Aug. € 22.80 2017*

NYONS 9D2 (12km NE Rural) 44.43507, 5.21248 FFCC Camping Le Pilat, 26110 St Ferréol-Trente-Pas [04 75 27 72 09; fax 04 75 27 72 34; info@campinglepilat.com; www.campinglepilat.com] Fr D94 N or Nyons turn N at La Bonté onto D70 to St Ferréol, site sp 1km N of vill. Med, hdg, shd, wc; chem disp; shwrs inc; EHU (6A) €4; lndry; shop; snacks; playgrnd; pool; paddling pool; entmnt; TV; 25% statics; dogs €1.50 high ssn; phone; Eng spkn; quiet; games area; CKE/CCI. "Site among lavender fields; pleasant, helpful owners; gd clean san facs; outdoor gym; gd walking & off-rd cycling; Thurs mkt Nyons; excel." ♦ 1 Apr-30 Sep. € 23.60 2012*

NYONS 9D2 (18km E Rural) 44.34319, 5.28357 Camp Municipal Les Cigales, Allée des Platanes, 26110 Ste Jalle [04 75 27 34 88 or 04 75 27 32 78 (mairie); mairie.saintejalle@orange.fr] Fr Nyons take D94 dir Serres; in 10 km at Curnier turn R onto D64 to Ste-Jalle. In vill turn R onto D108 dir Buis-les-Baronnies. Site on R in 300m. NB Dist by rd fr Nyons is 20km. Sm, hdg, pt shd, wc; chem disp; shwrs inc; EHU (10A) €2.20; lndry; shop nr; rest nr; bar nr; playgrnd; 15% statics; dogs; adv bkg acc; quiet. "Vg site in attractive old vill; friendly warden; facs dated but clean." 1 May-30 Sep. € 13.00 2016*

OBERNAI 6E3 (17km ESE Urban) 48.41413, 7.66983 Camping Municipal Le Wagerlott, 1 rue de la Sucrerie, 67150 Erstein [33 88 98 09 88 or 33 88 98 14 33 (Municipal); campingerstein@gmail.com] Fr Strasbourg on A35 then D1083. R onto D426. At rndabt turn L then 1st R to site. Med, mkd, hdg, unshd, wc (htd); shwrs inc; EHU (16A) €3.50; lndry; shop nr; rest nr; beach; wifi; 50% statics; dogs €2.30; phone; Eng spkn; adv bkg acc; ccard acc. "Gd municipal site; cls to Strasbourg; gd cycle rts; clean facs." 1 Apr-30 Sep. € 16.00 2018*

> **"Satellite navigation makes touring much easier"**
>
> Remember most sat navs don't know if you're towing or in a larger vehicle – always use yours alongside maps and site directions.

OBERNAI 6E3 (2km W Urban) 48.46460, 7.46750 Camp Municipal Le Vallon de l'Ehn, 1 Rue de Berlin, 67210 Obernai [03 88 95 38 48; fax 03 88 48 31 47; camping@obernai.fr; www.obernai.fr] Fr N exit A35 junc 11 onto D426 sp Obernai. Foll D426 W around Obernai & foll sp Mont St Odile & Camping VVF; at final rndabt turn R & immed L to site. Fr S on A35 exit junc 12 sp Obernai. At 3rd rndabt turn L onto D426 Ottrott-Mont Ste Odile (look for sp Camping VVF). Do not tow into Obernai. Lge, hdstg, mkd, pt shd, pt sl, serviced pitches; wc (htd); chem disp; mv service pnt; fam bthrm; shwrs inc; EHU (10-16A) €4.50; lndry; shop; bbq; playgrnd; twin axles; red long stay; wifi; dogs €1.10; phone; bus to Strasbourg & Obernai adj, train; Eng spkn; adv bkg acc; quiet; ccard acc; horseriding adj; tennis adj; CKE/CCI. "Attractive, well-kept, busy site on edge of picturesque town; sm pitches; welcoming, helpful staff; superb, excel, modern clean san facs; no entry after 1930; rec arr early high ssn; lge pool 200m;10% red CC members LS; c'vans, m'vans & tents all sep areas; excel bus/train links; ideal NH; highly rec; very well run, gd site; office clsd 1230-1400; popular." ♦ 1 Jan-8 Jan & 17 Mar-31 Dec. € 21.00 2017*

OCTON 10F1 (2km NE Rural) 43.65948, 3.32052 Camping Le Village du Bosc (Naturist), Chemin de Ricazouls, 34800 Octon [04 67 96 07 37; fax 04 67 96 35 75; r.villagedubosc@free.net; www.villagedubosc.net] Exit 54 or 55 fr N9/A75 dir Octon onto D148, foll sp to Ricazouls/site. Med, mkd, hdg, pt shd, pt sl, terr, wc; chem disp; mv service pnt; fam bthrm; shwrs; EHU (10A)inc; lndry; shop; rest; snacks; bar; playgrnd; pool (htd); sw; red long stay; entmnt; wifi; TV; 5% statics; dogs €3 (restricted area only); Eng spkn; adv bkg acc; quiet; watersports; INF card; games area; games rm. "Lovely, quiet site with wooded walks; friendly owners; clean facs; tight turns on terr access for lge o'fits; Octon vill pretty; wheelchair facs in san facs." ♦ 21 Apr-30 Sep. € 30.00 2017*

OCTON

OCTON *10F1* (1km SE Rural) 43.65100, 3.30877
Camping Le Mas des Carles, 34800 Octon [04 67 96 32 33] Leave A75 at junc 54, foll sp for Octon, 100m after vill sp turn L & foll white site sp keeping L. Ent on L opp tel kiosk (sharp turn). Sm, mkd, hdg, pt shd, pt sl, terr, wc; chem disp; shwrs inc; EHU (6-10A) inc; lndry; shop nr; rest nr; playgrnd; pool; 30% statics; dogs; phone; adv bkg acc; quiet; watersports 800m; CKE/CCI. "Pleasant site with views; helpful owner; facs a little tired (2006); boating 800m; take care low branches on pitches; Lac de Salagou with abandoned vill of Celles 1km." 1 Apr-10 Oct. € 21.30   2012*

> **"There aren't many sites open at this time of year"**
>
> If you're travelling outside peak season remember to call ahead to check site opening dates – even if the entry says 'open all year'.

OLARGUES *8F4* (0km N Rural) 43.55798, 2.91440
Camp Municipal Le Baoüs, 34390 Olargues [04 67 97 71 50; otsi.olargues@wanadoo.fr; www.olargues.org] Take D908 W fr Bédarieux, site immed bef ent Olargues. Site sp over sm bdge on L. At end of bdge turn R to site. Last 50m rough track & narr turn into site. Sm, pt shd, wc cont; chem disp; shwrs inc; EHU (6A); shop nr; playgrnd; wifi; adv bkg req; quiet; canoeing; bike hire. "Helpful warden; hill climb to services block; site poss flooded by Rv Jaur in spring; sh walk to amazing hilltop vill." 1 Jul-15 Sep.   2014*

OLLIERGUES *9B1* (4km N Rural) 45.69008, 3.63289
Camping Les Chelles, 63880 Olliergues [04 73 95 54 34; info@camping-les-chelles.com; www.camping-les-chelles.com] Fr Olliergues take D37 N up hill dir Le Brugeron; then sharp L onto D87 dir La Chabasse; site sp. Med, hdg, mkd, shd, terr, wc; chem disp; shwrs inc; EHU (15A) €2.80; lndry; shop nr; rest; snacks; bar; playgrnd; pool (htd); wifi; TV; dogs €1; phone; Eng spkn; adv bkg acc; ccard acc; games area; games rm. "Facs excel for families with young children; enthusiastic, helpful & kind Dutch owners; gd walking; gd touring base; excel." ♦ 1 Apr-31 Oct. € 19.00   2015*

OLONZAC *8F4* (9km E Rural) 43.28372, 2.82688
FFCC Camping Les Auberges, 11120 Pouzols-Minervois [04 68 46 26 50; vero.pradal@neuf.fr; www.camping-lesauberges.fr] Fr D5 site 500m S of vill of Pouzols-Minervois. Sm, mkd, pt shd, wc; chem disp; shwrs inc; EHU (5A) €3.50; lndry; shop nr; playgrnd; pool; 30% statics; dogs; Eng spkn; adv bkg rec; quiet; CKE/CCI. "V popular site; friendly owners; gas adj; sm Sat mkt at 'cave' opp." 15 Mar-15 Nov. € 16.00   2012*

OLORON STE MARIE *8F2* (3km SW Urban) 43.17886, -0.62328 **Camping-Gîtes du Stade, Chemin de Lagravette, 64400 Oloron-Ste Marie [05 59 39 11 26 or 06 08 35 09 06 (mob); fax 05 59 36 12 01; camping-du-stade@wanadoo.fr; www.camping-du-stade.com]** Fr N on ring rd foll sp to Saragosse (Spain); at rndabt take 2nd exit onto D6 still sp Saragosse, site sp on R just after sports field. Fr S on D55 join ring rd & turn W at rndabt by McDonalds; sp. Med, hdg, mkd, pt shd, wc; chem disp; shwrs inc; EHU (6-10A) €4-6 (some rev pol); lndry; shop nr; rest; snacks; bbq; playgrnd; sw nr; twin axles; entmnt; wifi; TV; dogs €1.20; adv bkg acc; quiet; tennis; rv fishing 1km; bike hire; CKE/CCI. "Well-kept site; lge pitches; helpful staff; clean facs but ltd LS & stretched high ssn; take care low tree; grnd poss soft & damp after rain; barrier clsd 1200-1500; excel base for Pyrenees; pool adj; gd walking." ♦ 1 May-30 Sep. € 19.00   2014*

ONESSE ET LAHARIE *8E1* (1km N Rural) 44.06344, -1.07257 **FFCC Camping Le Bienvenu, 259 Route de Mimizan, 40110 Onesse-et-Laharie [05 58 07 30 49 or 06 81 32 12 56 (mob); www.camping-onesse.fr]** On N10 Bordeaux-Bayonne rd, turn W onto D38 at Laharie. Site in 5km. Med, mkd, pt shd, wc; chem disp; mv service pnt; shwrs inc; EHU (10A) €4; lndry; shop nr; rest nr; bar nr; playgrnd; red long stay; TV; 10% statics; dogs €1; adv bkg acc; quiet; CKE/CCI. "Well-run, nice, family site; gd facs; very helpful staff." 1 Mar-30 Sep. € 18.00   2014*

> **"That's changed – Should I let the Club know?"**
>
> If you find something on site that's different from the site entry, fill in a report and let us know. See camc.com/europereport.

ONZAIN *4G2* (6km W Rural) 47.51030, 1.10400
Yelloh! Village Le Parc du Val de Loire, 155 Route de Fleuray, 41150 Mesland [02 54 70 27 18; fax 02 54 70 21 71; parcduvaldeloire@orange.fr; www.parcduvaldeloire.com or www.yellohvillage.co.uk] Fr Blois take D952 SW twd Amboise. Approx 16km outside Blois turn R to Onzain & foll sp to Mesland; go thro Mesland vill & turn L dir Fleuray; site on R after 1.5km. Lge, hdg, mkd, pt shd, pt sl, serviced pitches; wc; chem disp; mv service pnt; fam bthrm; shwrs inc; EHU (10A) inc; gas; lndry; shop; rest; snacks; bar; bbq (charcoal, gas); playgrnd; pool (covrd, htd); paddling pool; entmnt; wifi; TV; 30% statics; dogs €4; Eng spkn; adv bkg acc; ccard acc; waterslide; bike hire; tennis; games area; games rm; CKE/CCI. "Secluded site; wine-tasting; excursions to vineyards; mkt Thur Onzain; excel." ♦ 11 Apr-20 Sep. € 35.00   2016*

ORANGE 10E2 (12km NE Rural) 44.16222, 4.93531
Camping des Favards (formerly Aire Naturelle Domaine), 1335 Route d'Orange, 84150 Violès [04 90 70 90 93; campingfavards@gmail.com; www.favards.com] Fr N exit A7 junc 19 Bollène. Foll D8 dir Carpentras & Violès. In Violès foll dir Orange & look for camp sp. Fr S exit A7 junc 22 sp Carpentras, take dir Avignon, then dir Vaison-la-Romaine to Violès. Avoid cent of Orange when towing. Sm, hdg, mkd, unshd, wc (htd); fam bthrm; shwrs inc; EHU (6-10A) €3.65 (poss rev pol); lndry; snacks; bar; playgrnd; pool; wifi; dogs €1.70-€1.90; Eng spkn; adv bkg acc; quiet; ccard acc; CKE/CCI. "Well-kept site; excel pitches - some very lge (extra charge); superb san facs, poss stretched; wine-tasting on site high ssn; gd touring base; poss dust clouds fr Mistral wind; pitches muddy when wet; gd."
♦ 13 Apr-30 Sep. € 23.50   2018*

ORANGE 10E2 (9km SE Urban) 44.11472, 4.90314
Camp Municipal Les Peupliers, Ave Pierre-de-Coubertin, 84150 Jonquières [04 90 70 67 09; fax 04 90 70 59 01; mairie@jonquieres.fr; www.jonquieres.fr] Exit junc 22 fr A7 onto N7 S. In 2km turn L (E) onto D950. In 5km at rndabt turn L onto D977. In 200m turn L sp Jonquières, site on L in 2km, sp in vill. Site behind sports complex. Sp not obvious. Med, mkd, pt shd, wc; chem disp; shwrs inc; EHU (4A) inc; lndry; shop nr; rest nr; bar nr; playgrnd; dogs €2.50; phone; adv bkg acc; ccard acc; tennis adj; CKE/CCI. "Excel, well-run, busy site; friendly, helpful & welcoming owners; vg, clean san facs; noise fr airfield (week days); need care with high o'fits due trees; gates close 2200; Roman ruins nrby; pool adj; popular long stay; vg o'night stop." 1 May-31 Aug. € 16.50   2014*

ORBEC 3D1 (2km N Urban) 49.02829, 0.40857 **Camp Municipal Les Capucins, Rue des Frères Bigot, 14290 Orbec [02 31 32 76 22; camping.sivom@orange.fr]** Exit A28 junc 15 to Orbec; on ent town foll site sp. If app fr D519 or D819 steep drag up to site & care req down to town. Sm, pt shd, wc; chem disp; shwrs inc; EHU (10A) €2; shop nr; playgrnd; dogs free; quiet. "Well-kept site; site yourself if office clsd; san facs old but clean; no twin axles; access easy for lge o'fits; delightful countryside; excel." 25 May-8 Sep. € 12.00   2015*

ORBEY 6F3 (7km SE Rural) 48.09198, 7.19341
Camping des Deux Hohnack, Giragoutte 68910 Labaroche [03 89 49 83 72; camping-labaroche@orange.fr; www.camping-labaroche.fr] Fr Colmar take D11 thro Turckheim (do not turn off on D10). Cont thro Trois Epis. At fork turn L sp Linge. In half km turn R. Med, mkd, hdg, hdstg, pt shd, pt sl, wc; chem disp; shwrs; EHU (6A) €4; lndry; rest; bar; bbq; playgrnd; TV; dogs €1; games area; CKE/CCI. "Gd walks; rural museum at Labaroche 1.5km; vg." ♦ 1 Apr-30 Sep. € 17.50   2015*

ORLEANS 4F3 (11km E Rural) 47.88830, 2.02744
Camp Municipal Les Pâtures, 55 Chemin du Port, 45430 Chécy [02 38 91 13 27; camping@checy.fr; www.checy.fr] Take D960 E twd Châteauneuf. In Chécy, foll site sp. Access thro town via narr rds. Sm, hdg, pt shd, wc; chem disp; mv service pnt; shwrs; EHU (16A) €3.80; lndry; shop nr; bbq; twin axles; red long stay; wifi; dogs €1; Eng spkn; adv bkg acc; fishing; golf 5km; tennis; CKE/CCI. "Excel, well-run site on Rv Loire; vg location; friendly, helpful warden; gd san facs; conv Orléans, park & ride tram; poss open bef & after dates given; popular NH." ♦ 12 May-25 Sep. € 19.00   2018*

ORLEANS 4F3 (5km S Rural) 47.85603, 1.92555 **Camp Municipal d'Olivet, Rue du Pont-Bouchet, 45160 Olivet [02 38 63 53 94; fax 02 38 63 58 96; infos@camping-olivet.org; www.camping-olivet.org]** To avoid height restriction, best app fr A71 exit junc 2 onto N271 dir Orléans-La Source. Cont on N271 until rd crosses N20 into Rue de Bourges. Pass commercial estate & hotel on L & turn L at traff lts into Rue de Châteauroux. Pass university (Parc Technologique), cross tramway & turn L at traff lts onto D14, Rue de la Source, then in 500m turn R (watch for pharmacy on L & green site sp) into Rue du Pont-Bouchet (narr rd). Site well sp on D14. NB Beware height restrictions on junc underpasses in Orléans cent. Sm, hdg, pt shd, pt sl, wc (htd); chem disp; mv service pnt; fam bthrm; shwrs inc; EHU (16A) €3.10 (rev pol); lndry; shop; snacks; playgrnd; wifi; dogs €2; bus 400m; Eng spkn; adv bkg rec; quiet; CKE/CCI. "Well-run, busy site by Rv Loiret; friendly; excel clean san facs; guided tours of Orléans by site staff; gd walking; vineyards nr; vg." ♦ 1 Apr-30 Sep. € 21.70   2018*

> "I like to fill in the reports as I travel from site to site"
>
> You'll find report forms at the back of this guide, or you can fill them in online at camc.com/europereport.

ORLEANS 4F3 (15km SW Urban) 47.85539, 1.75352
Camp Municipal Fontaine de Rabelais, Chemin de la Plage, 45130 St Ay [02 38 88 44 44 (Mairie); fax 02 38 88 82 14; maire@ville-saint-ay.fr; www.ville-saint-ay.fr] Exit A10/E60 at junc 15 Meung-sur-Loire onto N152 dir Orléans, sp La Chapelle-St Mesmin; site sp on app to St Ay on N bank Rv Loire. Fr A71 exit junc 1 dir Blois & Beaugency onto N152. Lge, pt shd, pt sl, wc; chem disp; mv service pnt; shwrs inc; EHU (6A) inc (poss rev pol); gas; shop nr; rest nr; bbq; playgrnd; red long stay; dogs; phone; bus 500m; Eng spkn; adv bkg acc; rv fishing adj; boating adj; CKE/CCI. "Pleasant, clean, tidy, flat site on Rv Loire; excel modern facs for sm site but poss stretched high ssn; rvside cycling/walking; conv Orléans & chateaux; poss early closure or late opening - rec call in adv to check; perfect NH; lge spaces." ♦ 15 Apr-31 Oct. € 14.00   2016*

ORNANS

ORNANS *6G2* (1km E Rural) *47.10064, 6.16036*
Camping La Roche d'Ully, Allée de la Tour de Peiltz, 25290 Ornans [03 81 57 17 79; contact@ larochedully.com; www.camping-larochedully.com] Fr Ornans foll blue sps to site nr rvside. Med, mkd, unshd, wc (htd); chem disp; mv service pnt; fam bthrm; shwrs; EHU (10A) €4; lndry; shop; rest; snacks; bar; bbq; playgrnd; pool (covrd, htd); paddling pool; wifi; 20% statics; dogs €3; adv bkg acc; quiet; ccard acc; rv fishing; bike hire; sauna; canoeing; games area. "Pleasant, family-run site in gd location in rv valley; popular with students; some noise in ssn." ♦ 2 Apr-9 Oct. € 36.00   2016*

ORNANS *6G2* (11km SE Rural) *47.04132, 6.26024*
Camp Municipal Le Champaloux, 25930 Lods [03 81 60 90 11 (Mairie) or 06 72 54 51 41 (mob); fax 03 81 60 93 86; mairie.lods@wanadoo.fr; www.camping-champaloux.fr] Fr Ornans SE on D67. In Lods turn R across Rv Loue. Site in 150m beside rv. Or N fr Pontarlier on N57/E23 to St Gorgon then W on D67 to Lods. Med, hdstg, pt shd, wc; chem disp; mv service pnt; shwrs inc; EHU (6A) €2.80; shop nr; playgrnd; quiet; fishing. "Lovely, peaceful site by rv; on disused rlwy stn in attractive area; site yourself, office opens 1830-2000; friendly, helpful warden; clean, adequate san facs; dog shwrs; vg rest 200m; woodland walks; excel." 15 Jun-30 Sep. € 12.80   2012*

ORPIERRE *9D3* (1km E Rural) *44.31110, 5.69650*
Camping Les Princes d'Orange, Flonsaine, 05700 Orpierre [04 92 66 22 53; fax 04 92 66 31 08; campingorpierre@wanadoo.fr; www.camping-orpierre.com] N75 S fr Serres for 11km to Eyguians. Turn R in Eyguians onto D30, 8km to Orpierre, turn L in vill to site (sp). Med, hdstg, mkd, pt shd, pt sl, terr, wc; chem disp; mv service pnt; fam bthrm; shwrs inc; EHU (10A) €4.50; gas; lndry; shop; snacks; bar; playgrnd; pool (htd); entmnt; TV; 10% statics; dogs €1.60; adv bkg acc; fishing; games area; waterslide; tennis. "Rock-climbing area; gd walking, beautiful, interesting vill." ♦ 1 Apr-31 Oct. € 44.70   2014*

ORTHEZ *8F1* (2km SE Rural) *43.48793, -0.75882*
Camping La Source, Blvd Charles de Gaulle, 64300 Orthez [05 59 67 04 81; fax 05 59 67 02 38; campingdelasource@orange.fr; www.camping-orthez.com] Leave Orthez on D817 twd Pau, turn L at sp Mont-de-Marsan & site on R in 300m at crossrds bet pedestrian x-ings. Sm, hdstg, shd, pt sl, wc; chem disp; mv service pnt; shwrs inc; EHU (10A) €3.50; snacks; playgrnd; wifi; 10% statics; dogs €1.80; phone; quiet; fishing; CKE/CCI. "Peaceful, basic but well-maintained site; friendly & helpful staff; gd, clean facs but need updating; some pitches soft in wet weather; interesting historical town; gd security; rec; gd NH."
1 Apr-31 Oct. € 18.40   2014*

OUISTREHAM *3D1* (1km S Urban) *49.26909, -0.25498*
Camping Le Riva Bella, Rue de la Haie Breton, 14150 Ouistreham [02 31 97 12 66; camping-rivabella@ vacances-seasonova.com; www.vacances-seasonova.com/camping-riva-bella] Fr ferry terminal foll sp Caen on D84 (Rue de l'Yser/ Ave du Grand Large); in approx 1.5km site sp at rndabt; take 3rd exit. Lge, hdg, pt shd, wc (htd); chem disp; mv service pnt; fam bthrm; shwrs inc; EHU (10A) inc; gas; lndry; shop; snacks; bar; playgrnd; pool (htd); beach sand 1.8km; twin axles; entmnt; wifi; 40% statics; dogs €1.50; bus; Eng spkn; adv bkg acc; quiet; ccard acc; games area; tennis; bike hire; CKE/CCI. "V conv for late or early ferry (5 mins to terminal), site stays open for late Brittany ferry; busy high ssn; gd sized pitches; sandy soil; gates open 0630-2300 (dep out of hrs, by request); opens for late arr; no twin axles; nice walk/cycle along canal to town; wonderful beaches; interesting area; mkt Thur; conv & sep area for NH without unhitching; British twin axle c'vans acc; gd for long stay; takeaway food and bread shop on site; new management has improved site (2017); new san facs & pool." 30 Mar-4 Nov. € 30.00   2018*

> ### "We must tell the Club about that great site we found"
>
> Get your site reports in by mid-August and we'll do our best to get your updates into the next edition.

⊞ **OUISTREHAM** *3D1* (7km S Rural) *49.23838, -0.25763* **FFCC Camping des Capucines, rue de la Côte Fleurie,14860 Ranville [02 31 78 69 82; fax 02 31 78 16 94; campingdescapucines.14@orange.fr; www.campingdescapucines.com]** App Caen fr E or W, take Blvd Péripherique Nord, then exit 3a sp Ouistreham car ferry (D515). In approx 8.5km turn R onto D514 sp Cabourg, cross Pegasus Bdge & foll sp Ranville across 2 rndabts; at x-rds in 500m turn L (at sm campsite sp); site in 300m on L. Fr Ouistreham foll D514 dir Caborg to Pegasus Bdge, then as above. Med, hdg, mkd, pt shd, terr, wc (htd); chem disp; mv service pnt; fam bthrm; shwrs inc; EHU (10A) inc (poss rev pol); gas; lndry; shop; rest nr; bar nr; playgrnd; beach sand 3km; wifi; 60% statics; dogs €1.80; phone; bus 500m; Eng spkn; adv bkg rec; quiet; ccard acc. "Excel, well established site in pleasant position; some pitches sm; helpful, friendly owner; gd clean san facs but dated; barrier open 0600-2400 but if clsd LS use intercom at recep; conv ferries (if arr late fr ferry, phone in adv for pitch number & barrier code); take care o'hanging trees; conv vill, Pegasus Bdge, museum & war cemetery; vg, quiet well run site; hypmkt 4.8km; site run down in LS; reliable freq visited stop nr port." € 21.40   2018*

OUISTREHAM *3D1 (5km SW Urban) 49.24970, -0.27190* **Camping Les Hautes Coutures, avenue de la Côte de Nacre, 14970 Bénouville [02 31 44 73 08 or 06 07 25 26 90 (mob LS); fax 02 31 95 30 80; info@campinghautescoutures.com; www.campinghautescoutures.com]**
Leave Ouistreham ferry & foll sp Caen & A13 over 2 rndabts. After 2nd rndabt join dual c'way. Leave at 1st exit (D35) sp St Aubin d'Arquenay & ZA de Bénouville. Turn R at end of slip rd, then L at T-junc; site in 200m uphill on R. Or fr Caen twd port on dual c'way, site has own exit shortly after Pegasus Memorial Bdge exit; site clearly visible on R of dual c'way. Lge, hdg, pt shd, pt sl, wc (htd); chem disp; mv service pnt; fam bthrm; shwrs inc; EHU (10A) €5.50 (rev pol)(adaptors avail €18); lndry; rest; snacks; bar; bbq; playgrnd; pool (covrd, htd); paddling pool; beach 2km; entmnt; wifi; TV; 30% statics; dogs €3; Eng spkn; adv bkg acc; ccard acc; jacuzzi; golf 4km; bike hire; fishing; horseriding 1km; games rm; windsurfing 1km; waterslide; CKE/CCI. "Busy, poss noisy holiday complex o'looking Caen Canal; friendly staff; sm pitches; access tight some pitches when busy; recep 0800-2000 high ssn, but staff will open for late ferry arr if req in adv; no o'fits over 12m high ssn; ltd EHU (2009); cycle path to Caen; daily mkt in Ouistreham; conv NH; access to pitches diff as high kerbs, some pitches on steep slopes; excel pool." ♦ 25 Mar-25 Sep. € 35.00 2016*

OUISTREHAM *3D1 (12km NW Coastal) 49.31799, -0.35824* **Camp Municipal La Capricieuse, 2 Rue Brummel, 14530 Luc-sur-Mer [02 31 97 34 43; fax 02 31 97 43 64; info@campinglacapricieuse.com; www.campinglacapricieuse.com]** Fr ferry terminal turn R at 3rd traff lts (D514) into Ave du G. Leclerc. Cont to Luc-sur-Mer; 1st turn L after casino; site on R in 300m. Ave Lecuyer is sp & Rue Brummel is off that rd. Lge, hdg, mkd, pt shd, terr, wc; chem disp; mv service pnt; shwrs inc; EHU (6-10A) €4.65-6.25; gas; lndry; shop nr; playgrnd; beach sand adj; entmnt; wifi; TV; dogs €2.50; Eng spkn; adv bkg rec; quiet; ccard acc; games rm; tennis; excursions; CKE/CCI. "Excel location; some lge pitches with easy access; clean, ltd facs LS; conv beach & Luc-sur-Mer; conv WW2 beaches; excel site; conv for ferries." ♦ 1 Apr-30 Sep. € 26.40 2013*

OUNANS *6H2 (1km N Rural) 47.00290, 5.66550* **Kawan Village La Plage Blanche, 3 Rue de la Plage, 39380 Ounans [03 84 37 69 63; fax 03 84 37 60 21; plageblanche@camping-indigo.com; www.la-plage-blanche.com]** Exit A39 junc 6 sp Dole Cent. Foll N5 SE for 18km dir Pontarlier. After passing Souvans, turn L on D472 sp Mont-sous-Vaudrey. Foll sp to Ounans. Site well sp in vill. Lge, mkd, hdstg, pt shd, wc; chem disp; mv service pnt; shwrs inc; EHU (6A) €4 (poss rev pol); lndry; shop nr; rest; snacks; bar; playgrnd; pool; paddling pool; sw nr; entmnt; wifi; TV; 1% statics; dogs €2; Eng spkn; adv bkg rec; quiet; ccard acc; lake fishing; bike hire; horseriding; canoeing; CKE/CCI. "Superb rvside pitches; trout & carp fishing; friendly recep; excel san facs, recently updated (2013); gd rest; excel." ♦ 1 May-29 Sep. € 24.00 2013*

OUST *8G3 (12km SE Rural) 42.81105, 1.25558* **Camping Le Montagnou, Route de Guzet, 09140 Le Trein-d'Ustou [05 61 66 94 97 or 06 07 85 37 65; campinglemontagnou@wanadoo.fr; www.lemontagnou.com]** Fr St Girons S on D618 & D3 to Oust. Fr Oust SE on D3 & D8 thro Seix & at Pont de la Taule turn L onto D8 twd Le Trein-d'Ustou. Site on L just bef vill, sp. Med, hdg, pt shd, wc (htd); chem disp; shwrs inc; EHU (6-10A) €3.50-5.50; lndry; shop; rest nr; snacks; bbq; playgrnd; pool; sw nr; wifi; 30% statics; dogs €1.50; phone; adv bkg acc; quiet; ccard acc; tennis; fishing; CKE/CCI. "Well-situated, well-run, delightful rvside site; mountain views; skiing 9km; gd sized pitches; friendly, helpful French owners; gd walking; highly rec." ♦ 1 Jan-31 Oct & 1 Dec-31 Dec. € 22.00 2015*

⊞ **OUST** *8G3 (1km S Rural) 42.87042, 1.21947* **Camping Les Quatre Saisons, Route d'Aulus-les-Bains, 09140 Oust [05 61 96 55 55; camping.ariege@gmail.com; www.camping4saisons.com]** Take D618 S fr St Girons; then D3 to Oust; on N o'skts of town turn L (sp Aulus) onto D32; in 1km site on R nr Rv Garbet. Med, hdg, pt shd, wc (htd); chem disp; shwrs inc; EHU (10A) inc; lndry; shop nr; bar; playgrnd; pool; wifi; TV; 25% statics; dogs €1.50; phone; Eng spkn; adv bkg rec; quiet; ccard acc; games area; CKE/CCI. "In beautiful, unspoilt area; friendly site; excel boulangerie 5mins walk on footpath to vill; excel." € 20.00 2016*

OYONNAX *9A3 (13km E Rural) 46.25530, 5.55705* **Camping Les Gorges de l'Oignin, Rue du Lac, 01580 Matafelon-Granges [04 74 76 80 97; camping.lesgorgesdeloignin@wanadoo.fr; www.gorges-de-loignin.com]** Exit A404 junc 9 onto D979 dir Bourg-en-Bresse; in 700m turn R onto D18 to Matafelon-Granges; foll sp. NB Fr Oyonnax 22km by rd. Med, hdg, mkd, hdstg, pt shd, terr, wc (htd); chem disp; fam bthrm; shwrs inc; EHU (10A) €3.40; lndry; shop; rest; snacks; bar; bbq; playgrnd; pool; paddling pool; sw nr; wifi; TV; 10% statics; dogs €2.40; phone; Eng spkn; adv bkg acc; quiet; games area; CKE/CCI. "Beautiful site on lake - boat launching; friendly, helpful staff; Jura National Park; Rv Ain gorges; excel." 15 Apr-20 Sep. € 29.00 2015*

PACAUDIERE, LA *9A1 (0km E Rural) 46.17512, 3.87539* **Camp Municipal Beausoleil, Route de Vivans, 42310 La Pacaudière [04 77 64 11 50 or 04 77 64 30 18 (Mairie); fax 04 77 64 14 40; lapacaudiere@wanadoo.fr; www.camping-rhonealpes.com]** NW on N7 Roanne to Lapalisse; turn R in La Pacaudière, D35; site well sp; fork R in 50m; site ent in 400m. Sm, hdg, hdstg, unshd, sl, wc; chem disp; shwrs inc; EHU (10A); gas; lndry; shop; playgrnd; TV; quiet. "Pleasant NH in beautiful countryside; public pool high ssn; ltd facs LS; interesting area; Sat mkt." 1 May-30 Sep. € 15.50 2017*

PAIMPOL

PAIMPOL 1D3 (3km SE Coastal) 48.76966, -3.02209
Camp Municipal Crukin, Rue de Crukin, Kérity, 22500 Paimpol [02 96 20 78 47 or 02 96 55 31 70 (Mairie); fax 02 96 20 75 00; contact@camping-paimpol.com; www.camping-paimpol.com]
On D786 fr St Brieuc/Paimpol, site sp in vill of Kérity 80m off main rd shortly bef abbey. Med, hdg, pt shd, wc (htd); chem disp; mv service pnt; fam bthrm; shwrs inc; EHU (6A) €3.90 (poss rev pol); lndry; shop nr; playgrnd; beach shgl 250m; wifi; TV; 10% statics; dogs €2.10; bus 100m; quiet; watersports; fishing; CKE/CCI. "Sep m'van area; Beaufort Abbey nrby; excel sh stay/NH; plenty of space; facs ltd LS; walk to town along coast rd gd views; site unkept; boggy when wet; gd; tourist train runs past site ent to/fr Paimpol, hourly svrs." ♦ 1 Apr-30 Sep. € 23.00   2018*

⊞ **PALAVAS LES FLOTS** 10F1 (1km N Coastal) 43.53000, 3.92400 Aire Communale/Camping-Car Halte, Base Fluviale Paul Riquer, 34250 Palavas-les-Flots [04 67 07 73 45 or 04 67 07 73 48; fax 04 67 50 61 04] Fr Montpellier on D986 to Palavas. On ent town at 1st rndabt 'Europe' foll sp Base Fluviale & site sp. Med, hdstg, mkd, pt shd, wc; chem disp; mv service pnt; shwrs inc; EHU (16A) €2; lndry; shop nr; rest nr; bar nr; beach sand 500m; phone; bus 200m; ccard acc; CKE/CCI. "M'vans only; special elec cable req - obtain fr recep (dep); some pitches on marina quay; conv Montpellier, Camargue; 3 night max stay." € 10.00   2012*

PALAVAS LES FLOTS 10F1 (1km NE Coastal) 43.53346, 3.94820 Camping Montpellier Plage, 95 Ave St Maurice, 34250 Palavas-les-Flots [04 67 68 00 91; fax 04 67 68 10 69; camping.montpellier.plage@wanadoo.fr; www.camping-montpellier-plage.com]
Site on D21ES on o'skts of vill twd Carnon. V lge, mkd, pt shd, wc; chem disp; mv service pnt; shwrs inc; EHU (4A) inc; gas; lndry; shop; rest; snacks; bar; bbq; playgrnd; pool; paddling pool; beach sand adj; 50% statics; dogs; bus high ssn; Eng spkn; adv bkg rec; games area; CKE/CCI. "Gd location;spa facs; basic san facs, but lge pitches & friendliness of site outweigh this; gd security; poss somewhat unkempt; easy walk into Palavas - interesting sm port; flamingoes on adjoining lake; gd." ♦ 16 Apr-18 Sep. € 36.00   2017*

PALAVAS LES FLOTS 10F1 (2km E Urban/Coastal) 43.53867, 3.96076 Camping Les Roquilles, 267b Ave St Maurice, 34250 Palavas-les-Flots [04 67 68 03 47; fax 04 67 68 54 98; roquilles@wanadoo.fr; www.camping-les-roquilles.fr] Exit A9 junc 30 onto D986 dir Palavas. In Palavas foll sp Carnon-Plage on D62, site sp. V lge, hdstg, mkd, pt shd, serviced pitches; wc; chem disp; mv service pnt; shwrs inc; EHU (6A) €3.90; lndry; rest; snacks; bar; playgrnd; pool (htd); beach sand 100m; red long stay; entmnt; TV; 30% statics; phone; bus; Eng spkn; adv bkg acc; ccard acc; waterslide; CKE/CCI. "Excel pizza bar on site; gas 100m; vg sw pools."
15 Apr-15 Sep. € 40.00   2014*

PARAY LE MONIAL 9A1 (1km NW Urban) 46.45750, 4.10472 Camping de Mambré, Route du Gué-Léger, 71600 Paray-le-Monial [03 85 88 89 20; fax 03 85 88 87 81; camping.plm@gmail.com; www.campingdemambre.com] Fr N79 Moulin to Mâcon; site at W end of town; just after level x-ing turn NE into Rte du Gué-Léger. Turn R into site after x-ing rv; well sp. Lge, mkd, pt shd, wc; chem disp; shwrs inc; EHU (10A) €3.40; lndry; shop; snacks; bar; playgrnd; pool; dogs €2; quiet; CKE/CCI. "Paray-le-Monial is pilgrimage cent; ltd facs & poorly maintained LS (2011); no designated fresh water pnts (2011); 15min walk to town along rv; excel cycling cent."
3 May-4 Oct. € 25.60   2014*

PARENTIS EN BORN 7D1 (6km SW Rural) 44.34562, -1.09241 Camping L'Arbre d'Or, 75 Route du Lac, 40160 Landes [05 58 78 41 56; fax 05 58 78 49 62; contact@arbre-dor.com; www.arbre-dor.com]
Leave the Bordeaux m'way A63/N10 in Liposthey and drive twds Parentis (D43). The campsite is sp in Parentis. Med, mkd, pt shd, wc; chem disp; mv service pnt; fam bthrm; shwrs inc; EHU inc (10A); lndry; shop nr; rest; snacks; bar; bbq; playgrnd; pool; sw nr; twin axles; entmnt; wifi; 25% statics; dogs free; phone; Eng spkn; adv bkg acc; quiet; ccard acc; games area; CKE/CCI. "Vg; lake 500m fr site, watersports in lake; v friendly mgmt; bike hire." ♦ 1 Apr-30 Oct. € 30.00   2017*

> ## "I need an on-site restaurant"
>
> We do our best to make sure site information is correct, but it is always best to check any must-have facilities are still available or will be open during your visit.

PARIS 3D3 (12km E Urban) 48.85385, 2.53794 Camp Municipal La Haute Ile, Chemin de l'Ecluse, 93330 Neuilly-sur-Marne [01 43 08 21 21; fax 01 43 08 22 03; campingmunicipal.nsm@wanadoo.fr; www.tourisme93.com] Fr Périphérique (Porte de Vincennes) foll N34 sp Vincennes. Shortly after passing Château de Vincennes on R, L at fork, sp Lagny. At next major x-rds sharp L (still N34) sp Chelles. Thro Neuilly-Plaisance to Neuilly-sur-Marne. In cent lge x-rds turn R sp N370 Marne-la-Vallée & A4 Paris. In 200m, bef rv bdge, foll Camp Municipal sp (no tent or c'van symbols on sp) turn L. Site at junc of rv & canal. Lge, mkd, pt shd, wc; shwrs inc; EHU (10A) inc (check rev pol); gas; shop; rest nr; bbq; playgrnd; 25% statics; dogs €2.85; bus/train 900m; Eng spkn; adv bkg rec; quiet; rv fishing. "Lovely location bet rv & canal (almost on an island); additional; wooden posts on pitches poss diff manoeuvring lge o'fits; some sm pitches; lndry adj; poss unkempt (2011); soft after rain; gd base & transport for Paris & Disney; gd dog walks adj; gd NH; san facs are run down."
1 Apr-30 Sep. € 25.00   2014*

PAU

⊞ **PARIS** *3D3* (11km W Urban) *48.86843, 2.23471*
Camping Indigo Paris Bois de Boulogne, 2 Allée du Bord de l'Eau, 75016 Paris [01 45 24 30 00; fax 01 42 24 42 95; paris@camping-indigo.com; www.camping-indigo.com] Site bet bdge of Puteaux & bdge of Suresnes. App fr A1: take Blvd Périphérique W to Bois de Boulogne exit at Porte Maillot; foll camp sp. App fr A6: Blvd Périphérique W to Porte Dauphine exit at Porte Maillot; foll camp sp. App fr Pont de Sèvres (A10, A11): on bdge take R lane & take 2nd rd R mkd Neuilly-sur-Seine; rd runs parallel to Seine; cont to site ent. App fr A13: after St Cloud Tunnel foll sp twd Paris; immed after x-ing Rv Seine, 1st R sp Bois de Boulogne; foll camp sps; traff lts at site ent. NB Sharp turn to site, poorly sp fr N - watch for lge 'Parking Borne de l'Eau 200m'. V lge, mkd, hdg, hdstg, pt shd, pt sl, wc (htd); chem disp; mv service pnt; fam bthrm; shwrs inc; EHU (10A) inc; gas; lndry; shop nr; rest nr; playgrnd; twin axles; TV; 10% statics; dogs €2; phone; bus to metro; Eng spkn; adv bkg rec; ccard acc; CKE/CCI. "Busy site in excel location; easy access A13; conv cent Paris - Metro Porte Maillot 4km; some v sm pitches; walk over Suresne bdge for shops, food mkt, supmkt etc; some tour ops on site; gd security; refurbished san facs (2014); vg; food truck; new rest (2015)." € 45.00   2016*

> **"Satellite navigation makes touring much easier"**
>
> Remember most sat navs don't know if you're towing or in a larger vehicle – always use yours alongside maps and site directions.

PARIS *3D3* (22km NW Urban) *48.94001, 2.14563*
Camping International Maisons Laffitte, Ile de la Commune, 1 Rue Johnson, 78600 Maisons-Laffitte [01 39 12 21 91; fax 01 39 12 70 50; maisonslaffitte@sandaya.fr; www.sandaya.fr] Easy access fr A13 sp Poissy; take D308 to Maisons-Laffitte; foll site sp bef town cent. Fr A15 take N184 S fr Poissy, foll sp St Germain; approx 6km after x-ing Rv Seine & approx 300m after x-ing lge steel bdge, take L lane ready for L turn onto D308 to Maison-Laffitte; foll camp sp. Or D301 to St Denis, then A86 exit Bezons, then dir Poissy, Noailles, Sartrouville & Maisons-Laffitte. NB Narr app rd diff due parked cars & high kerbs. Lge, hdg, mkd, pt shd, wc (htd); chem disp; mv service pnt; shwrs inc; EHU (6A) €3.20 (poss rev pol); gas; lndry; shop; rest; snacks; bar; playgrnd; TV; 50% statics; dogs €2.60; Eng spkn; adv bkg acc; ccard acc; games area; CKE/CCI. "V busy, popular site on island in Rv Seine; ideal for visiting Paris (20 min by RER), Disneyland & Versailles; RER stn 1km; mobilis ticket covers rlwy, metro & bus for day in Paris; friendly, helpful staff; poss ltd facs LS." ♦ 3 Apr-1 Nov. € 38.00   2015*

PARTHENAY *4H1* (1km SW Urban) *46.64160, -0.26740*
Camping Flower du Bois Vert, 14 Rue Boisseau, Le Tallud, 79200 Parthenay [05 49 64 78 43; fax 05 49 95 96 68; campingboisvert@orange.fr; www.camping-boisvert.com] Site on D743 to Niort. Sp fr N & S. Fr S 1km bef town turn L at sp La Roche-sur-Yon immed after rv bdge turn R; site on R in 500m. Med, hdg, hdstg, mkd, pt shd, pt sl, wc (htd); chem disp; mv service pnt; fam bthrm; shwrs inc; EHU (6 or 10A) inc; lndry; shop nr; rest; snacks; bar; bbq; playgrnd; pool (htd); paddling pool; entmnt; wifi; TV; 10% statics; phone; adv bkg acc; fishing; games rm; bike hire; tennis; boating; CKE/CCI. "1 hr rvside walk to town; m'van o'night area adj; noisy nr main rd & bar; Wed mkt; gd NH to Spain; conv Futuroscope; new facs, plenty hot water; well spaced hdg grass pitches; excel facs." ♦ 4 Apr-31 Oct. € 28.50   2017*

PARTHENAY *4H1* (9km W Urban) *46.62214, -0.35139*
Camp Municipal Les Peupliers, 79130 Azay-sur-Thouet [05 49 95 37 13 (Mairie); fax 05 49 95 36 14; mairie-azaysurthouet@cc-parthenay.fr; www.tourisme-gatine.com] Fr Parthenay take D949 dir Secondigny to Azay-sur-Thouet; turn L onto D139 dir St Pardoux; site on L in 200m. Site adj stadium on rvside. Sm, mkd, pt shd, wc; shwrs inc; EHU (10A) €3.50; shop nr; bbq; playgrnd; quiet. "Pleasant, peaceful site; barrier open ltd hrs; clean dated san facs, poss inadequate number high ssn; MH area outside of campsite; gd." 15 Jun-30 Sep. € 9.00   2017*

⊞ **PARTHENAY** *4H1* (9km W Rural) *46.65738, -0.34816* **FFCC Camping La Chagnée (Baudoin), 79450 St Aubin le Cloud [05 49 95 31 44 or 06 71 10 09 66 (mob); gerard.baudoin3@wanadoo.fr; www.lachagneevacances.fr]** Fr Parthenay on D949BIS dir Secondigny. Turn R in Azay-sur-Thouet onto D139 dir St Aubin, site on R in 2km, look for 'Gîte' sp. Sm, hdg, pt shd, terr, wc; chem disp; mv service pnt; fam bthrm; shwrs; EHU (10A) €3.50; lndry; shop nr; dogs; Eng spkn; quiet; fishing. "Charming, CL-type organic fm site o'looking lake; friendly, extremely helpful & welcoming owners; v clean, modern facs; OAY providing use own san in winter; maps loaned for walks; excel; m'van only during period Nov-Mar; fmhse meal avail weekly; vg lake fishing; rec." ♦ € 15.00   2017*

⊞ **PAU** *8F2* (5km E Rural) *43.28909, -0.26985* **FFCC Camping Les Sapins, Route de Tarbes, 64320 Ousse [05 59 81 79 03 or 05 59 81 74 21 (LS); lessapins64@orange.fr]** Site adj Hôtel des Sapins on S side of D817 (Pau-Tarbes rd). Sm, pt shd, wc; mv service pnt; shwrs inc; EHU (4-6A) €2-3; shop nr; rest nr; fishing. "Popular, pleasant NH; red facs LS; helpful owners; NH only." € 10.00   2014*

France

Site report forms at back of guide   *Last year of report

PAUILLAC

PAUILLAC *7C2* (1km S Rural) *45.18515, -0.74218*
FFCC Camp Municipal Les Gabarreys, Route de la Rivière, 33250 Pauillac [05 56 59 10 03 or 05 56 73 30 50; fax 05 56 73 30 68; camping.les.gabarreys@ wanadoo.fr; www.pauillac-medoc.com]
On ent Pauillac on D206, turn R at rndabt, sp site. On app Quays, turn R bef 'Maison du Vin'. Site on L in 1km. Med, hdg, hdstg, mkd, pt shd, wc; chem disp; mv service pnt; shwrs inc; EHU (5-10A) €5-6; lndry; shop nr; bbq; playgrnd; TV; 6% statics; dogs €3; Eng spkn; adv bkg acc; quiet; ccard acc; games rm; CKE/CCI. "Peaceful, well-kept, well-equipped site on estuary; nice clean san facs; conv wine chateaux; cycle rtes; mkt Sat; excel." ♦ 3 Apr-8 Oct. € 23.00   2017*

⊞ **PAYRAC** *7D3* (1km N Rural) *44.80574, 1.47479*
Camping Panoramic, Route de Loupiac, 46350 Payrac-en-Quercy [05 65 37 98 45; fax 05 65 37 91 65; info@campingpanoramic.com; www.campingpanoramic.com] N fr Payrac on D820, turn L onto D147 sp Loupiac (200m after 'end of vill' sp), site 300m on R. Sm, hdstg, pt shd, pt sl, wc (htd); chem disp; fam bthrm; shwrs inc; EHU (5A) €3 (poss rev pol); gas; lndry; shop nr; rest; snacks; bar; bbq; playgrnd; sw nr; entmnt; wifi; TV; 10% statics; phone; Eng spkn; adv bkg acc; quiet; bike hire; canoe hire; CKE/CCI. "Well-run, clean site; OK san facs - poss inadequate if site full; poss muddy in bad weather but hdstg avail; pool 400m; friendly, helpful Dutch owner; gd walking; excel winter NH." ♦ € 15.00   2015*

PAYRAC *7D3* (6km N Rural) *44.83527, 1.46008*
Camping Les Hirondelles, Al Pech, 46350 Loupiac [05 65 37 66 25; fax 05 65 37 66 65; camp.les-hirondelles@orange.fr; www.les-hirondelles.com]
Fr Souillac foll D820 for about 12km. Site on R bef dual c'way. Sm, hdg, mkd, shd, pt sl, wc (htd); chem disp; fam bthrm; shwrs inc; EHU (6A) inc (poss rev pol); gas; lndry; shop; rest; snacks; bar; playgrnd; pool (htd); paddling pool; entmnt; wifi; TV; 40% statics; dogs €2.50; phone; Eng spkn; adv bkg acc; quiet; bike hire; games area; CKE/CCI. "Vg friendly, helpful owners; clean site; gd views fr some pitches; excel." ♦ 1 Apr-15 Sep. € 23.00   2012*

PEILLAC *2F3* (2km N Rural) *47.72635, -2.21430* **Camp Municipal du Pont d'Oust, 56220 Peillac [02 99 91 39 33 or 02 99 91 26 76 (Mairie); fax 02 99 91 31 83; www.peillac.fr]** SW fr La Gacilly on D777; in 6km turn L onto D14 sp Les Fougerêts; cont thro Les Fougerêts, site on R in 1km opp canal. Or N fr Peillac on D14, folls sp Pont d'Oust; site on L. Med, pt shd, wc (htd); shwrs inc; EHU (10A) €3.20 (poss rev pol); lndry; shop nr; rest nr; bar nr; bbq; quiet. "Nice, peaceful site by Rv Oust & canal; spacious pitches, soft when wet; helpful warden calls, site yourself; v flat, ideal for cycling; pretty vill; vg; mkd cycling and walking rtes fr site; pool adj; pay at Mairie during May." 1 May-30 Sep. € 12.70   2017*

PELUSSIN *9B2* (1km SE Rural) *45.41375, 4.69143*
Camping Bel'Epoque du Pilat, La Vialle, Route de Malleval, 42410 Pélussin [04 74 87 66 60; contact@ camping-belepoque.fr; www.camping-belepoque.fr]
Exit A7 junc 10 just S of Lyon foll N86 dir Serrières; in Chavanay turn R onto D7 to Pélussin, then at rndabt turn L and foll D79 S & foll site sp. Rec do not use sat nav! Sm, hdg, pt shd, pt sl, wc (htd); chem disp; mv service pnt; fam bthrm; shwrs inc; EHU (6A) €3.50; gas; lndry; shop nr; rest; snacks; bar; bbq; playgrnd; pool (htd); paddling pool; entmnt; wifi; dogs €2.50; phone; train 10km; Eng spkn; adv bkg acc; quiet; ccard acc; games area; tennis; CKE/CCI. "In nature reserve; excel touring base; vg walking; vg, peaceful site; supmkt in Pelussin; friendly, helpful owners." 1 Apr-30 Sep. € 28.00   2017*

PENESTIN *2G3* (3km E Rural) *47.47687, -2.45204*
Camping Les Pins, Chemin du Val au Bois de la Lande, 56760 Pénestin [02 99 90 33 13; camping. lespins@wanadoo.fr; www.camping-despins.com]
Fr Roche-Bernard take D34 dir Pénestin, 2km bef town turn L sp Camping Les Pins. Site on R in 250m. Med, mkd, hdg, pt shd, pt sl, wc (htd); chem disp; mv service pnt; fam bthrm; shwrs inc; EHU (10A) €3; lndry; shop; snacks; bar; bbq; playgrnd; pool (covrd, htd); paddling pool; beach sand 3km; red long stay; twin axles; entmnt; wifi; TV; 33% statics; dogs €1.50; Eng spkn; adv bkg acc; quiet; waterslide; games area; bike hire; games rm; CKE/CCI. "Sun mkt; excel; fab countryside; sandy beaches nrby; gd facs, exceptionally clean; gd welcome." ♦ 1 Apr-18 Oct. € 26.00   2015*

PENESTIN *2G3* (3km S Coastal) *47.44527, -2.48416* **Camping Les Iles, La Pointe du Bile, 56760 Pénestin [02 99 90 30 24; fax 02 99 90 44 55; lesiles@seagreen.fr; www.seagreen-campinglesiles.com]** Fr La Roche Bernard take D34 to Pénestin; cont on D201 for 2.5km & foll site sp. Lge, mkd, hdg, pt shd, serviced pitches; wc; chem disp; mv service pnt; fam bthrm; shwrs inc; EHU (10A) inc (poss rev pol); gas; lndry; shop; rest; snacks; bar; bbq (charcoal, elec); playgrnd; pool (htd); paddling pool; beach sand nrby; entmnt; wifi; TV; 10% statics; dogs €4; Eng spkn; adv bkg acc; ccard acc; bike hire; waterslide; fishing adj; horseriding; tennis; games rm; CKE/CCI. "Lovely site o'looking sea; no o'fits over 7m high ssn; direct access to shoreline; some pitches sm; helpful staff; clean modern unisex san facs; mkt Sun (also Wed in Jul/Aug); gd cycling, walking; vg." ♦ 12 Apr-30 Sep. € 43.00   2018*

See advertisement opposite

⊞ **PERIERS** *1D4* (6km NE Rural) *49.21581, -1.35093*
Camping Le Clos Castel, 50500 Raids [02 33 17 23 61 or 07789 227484 (mob); lecloscastel@live.com; www.camping-france-normandy.com]
S fr Carentan on D791 to Raids; cont past vill on D791 for 300m; turn R to site, ent on R in 100m. Or N fr Periers on D791; turn L 300m bef Raids & then as bef. Site well sp. Sm, hdstg, unshd, wc; chem disp; shwrs inc; EHU (6A) inc; shop nr; bar; bbq; dogs free; Eng spkn; adv bkg acc. "Site has B&B; helpful British owners; conv D-day beaches; excel." € 17.50 2016*

PERIERS *1D4* (5km SE Rural) *49.16338, -1.34916*
FFCC Aire Naturelle Municipale Le Clos Vert, 50190 St Martin-d'Aubigny [02 33 46 57 03 or 02 33 07 73 92 (Mairie); fax 02 33 07 02 53; mairie-st-martin-daubigny@wanadoo.fr; www.gites-de-france-manche.com] E fr Périers on D900 dir St Lô; in 4km turn R sp St Martin-d'Aubigny; site on L in 500m adj church. Sm, pt shd, wc; chem disp; shwrs inc; EHU (6A) €2.50; lndry; shop nr; rest nr; bar nr; bbq; playgrnd; quiet; golf 2km; fishing 2km; tennis 2km; CKE/CCI. "Charming, sm, well-kept, useful site; facs basic but OK; easy 70km run to Cherbourg; no twin axles; basic quiet site in vill, bar & rest within walking dist; conv for ports; pay at Marie if no one calls for payment." ♦ 15 Apr-15 Oct. € 10.50 2018*

⊞ **PERIGUEUX** *7C3* (13km NE Rural) *45.21975, 0.86383* **Camping Le Bois du Coderc, Route des Gaunies, 24420 Antonne-et-Trigonant [05 53 05 99 83; coderc-camping@wanadoo.fr; www.campinglecoderc.com]** NE fr Périgueux on N21 twd Limoges, thro Antonne approx 1km turn R at x-rds bet car park & rest. Site in 500m. Med, hdg, pt shd, wc; chem disp; mv service pnt; fam bthrm; shwrs inc; EHU (10A) inc; lndry; shop nr; rest nr; snacks; bar; bbq; playgrnd; pool (htd); beach shgl adj; sw nr; wifi; TV; 10% statics; dogs €1; phone; Eng spkn; adv bkg acc; quiet; ccard acc; games rm; ice; games area; CKE/CCI. "Secluded, pleasant, peaceful site; most pitches spacious, rallies welcome; gd value, inc rest; highly rec; quiet; well maintained; excel site; view of website a must; gd birdwatching; v helpful owners, v eager to please; excel htd pool; excel wifi fr some pitches; new san block (2018); excel." ♦ € 22.00 2018*

PERIGUEUX *7C3* (20km SE Rural) *45.13165, 0.92867* **Camping de la Pélonie, La Bourgie, 24330 St Antoine-d'Auberoche [05 53 07 55 78; fax 05 53 03 74 27; info@campinglapelonie.com; www.lapelonie.com]** Fr Périgueux on A89 twd Brive; 5km past St Pierre-de-Chignac, site sp on L; turn L at picnic area - go under rlwy bdge; site ent on L. Med, mkd, pt shd, wc; chem disp; shwrs inc; EHU (10A) €3.80 (poss req long cable); gas; lndry; shop; rest; snacks; bar; playgrnd; pool (htd); paddling pool; wifi; TV; 20% statics; dogs €2; phone; Eng spkn; adv bkg acc; ccard acc; CKE/CCI. "Delightful site; pleasant, welcoming owners; gd, clean, well kept facs; excel facs for children; some pitches diff lge o'fits; gd touring base." ♦ 18 Apr-10 Oct. € 22.00 2015*

PERIGUEUX *7C3* (8km SE Rural) *45.14900, 0.77880* **Camping Le Grand Dague, Route du Grand Dague, 24750 Atur [05 53 04 21 01; fax 05 53 04 22 01; info@legranddague.fr; www.legranddague.fr]** Fr cent Périgueux, take N21 & A89 twd Brive. Fork L onto D2 to Atur (main rd bears R). In Atur turn L after bar/tabac; foll site sp for 2.5km. Lge, shd, pt sl, wc (htd); chem disp; fam bthrm; shwrs inc; EHU (6A) inc; lndry; shop; rest; snacks; bar; bbq; playgrnd; pool (htd); paddling pool; entmnt; wifi; TV; 70% statics; dogs €2; phone; Eng spkn; adv bkg acc; quiet; ccard acc; games rm; bike hire; games area; CKE/CCI. "Gd family site; friendly owners; site immac, even end of ssn; poss unkempt early ssn; lots to do; ltd touring pitches; excel." ♦ 22 Apr-25 Sep. € 39.00 2016*

PERONNE *3C3* (1km NE Urban) *49.93424, 2.94140* **Camp Municipal du Brochet, Rue Georges Clémenceau, 80200 Péronne [03 22 84 02 35; fax 03 22 73 31 01; peter.v.gent@orange.fr]** Fr N on D1017 turn R into town. L at lights & L immed after footbdge. 1st R & site on L. Well sp fr all dirs. Go to town cent then foll 'Intn'l Camping Site' sps. Sm, hdstg, pt shd, pt sl, terr, wc; chem disp; mv service pnt; EHU (16A) inc; lndry; shop nr; rest nr; playgrnd; dogs free; phone; bus 500m; Eng spkn; adv bkg acc; quiet; CKE/CCI. "Pleasant, basic site nr park & attractive town; grass pitches soft when wet; rec arr early high ssn; conv WW1 museum; NH, vg." 8 Apr-30 Oct. € 16.00 2015*

PERONNE

PERONNE 3C3 (3km S Rural) 49.91805, 2.93227
Camping du Port de Plaisance, Route de Paris, 80200 Péronne [03 22 84 19 31; fax 03 22 73 36 37; contact@camping-plaisance.com; www.camping-plaisance.com] Exit A1/E15 junc 13 dir Peronne on D1029 to D1017. Site on L o'looking canal. Well sp fr all dirs. Med, mkd, pt shd, wc (htd); chem disp; mv service pnt; shwrs inc; EHU (6-10A) €4.30-7.95 (some rev pol & long lead poss req); lndry; shop; rest nr; snacks; bar; playgrnd; pool (htd); red long stay; wifi; dogs €1.30; Eng spkn; ccard acc; jacuzzi; fishing. "Popular NH; helpful, pleasant staff & owners; gd play park & pool; gates locked 2200-0800 - when clsd, park outside; vg rest adj; rec visit to war museum in Péronne castle; popular with ralliers; facs need upgrading; vg site, pleasant situation nr a canal; gd size pitches; gd dog walk along canal; hypmkt 3km; san facs clean but tired; site self if recep clsd." ♦ 1 Mar-31 Oct. € 27.00   2017*

PERONNE 3C3 (2km NW Rural) 49.94409, 2.90826
Camping La Tortille, L'Orgibet, 80200 Cléry-sur-Somme [03 22 83 17 59 or 03 22 84 10 45 (LS); fax 03 22 83 04 14; jsg-bred@wanadoo.fr]
Exit A1/E15 junc 13.1 onto D938 to Cléry, dir Péronne. Site sp on rvside in 5km. Med, hdstg, hdg, pt shd, wc; shwrs inc; EHU (10A) €3.60; shop nr; bbq; playgrnd; red long stay; 10% statics; dogs €1.30; adv bkg acc; quiet; rv fishing; games area; CKE/CCI. "Peaceful site; sm, uneven pitches; clean modern san facs; conv for A1 m'way." ♦ 1 Apr-31 Oct. € 21.50   2017*

PERPIGNAN 8G4 (6km S Rural) 42.63754, 2.89819
Camping Les Rives du Lac, Chemin de la Serre, 66180 Villeneuve-de-la-Raho [04 68 55 83 51; fax 04 68 55 86 37; camping.villeneuveraho@wanadoo.fr]
Fr A9 exit Perpignan Sud, dir Porte d'Espagne. In 3km turn R onto N9 dir Le Boulou. In 1km after Auchan supmkt take slip rd to N91 dir Villeneuve-de-la-Raho. In 2km rd becomes D39, turn R to site, site on L in 1km. Beware ford on D39 in v wet weather (usually dry). Med, mkd, hdstg, pt shd, pt sl, wc (htd); chem disp; mv service pnt; shwrs inc; EHU (6A) inc; lndry; shop; rest; snacks; bar; bbq (elec, gas); playgrnd; pool (htd); beach 1.5km; sw nr; 10% statics; dogs €1.60; phone; Eng spkn; adv bkg acc; ccard acc; tennis 2km; watersports 1.5km; fishing 1.5km; CKE/CCI. "Lakeside site with views; poor san facs & insufficient for site size; busy cycling/jogging path adj; conv trips to Spain; busy public beach nr." ♦ 15 Mar-15 Nov. € 17.50   2014*

PERROS GUIREC 1D2 (1km SE Coastal) 48.79657, -3.42689 Camp Municipal Ernest Renan, 22700 Louannec [02 96 23 11 78; fax 02 96 49 04 47; www.camping-louannec.fr] 1km W of Louannec on D6. Lge, unshd, wc; chem disp; mv service pnt; shwrs inc; EHU (6A) inc; gas; shop; rest; bar; playgrnd; pool (htd); beach sand adj; TV; dogs €1.35; Eng spkn; adv bkg acc; watersports adj; fishing adj; games rm. "Well-kept site; pitches on seashore; clean san facs; clsd 1200-1530, little parking space outside; highly rec." ♦ 1 Jun-30 Sep. € 17.00   2017*

PERS 7C4 (5km NE Rural) 44.90619, 2.25568
Camping Du Viaduc, Le Ribeyres Village, 15290 Pers [04 71 64 70 08; infos@camping-cantal.com; www.camping-cantal.com] Fr Aurillac take N122 S twrds Figeac. After Sansac turn R onto D61 sp Pers. Site well sp fr here. Final 2km narr rd with passing places. Med, hdg, mkd, pt shd, terr, wc; chem disp; mv service pnt; shwrs inc; EHU (10A) €3.60; lndry; shop; snacks; bar; bbq; playgrnd; pool; twin axles; wifi; 20% statics; dogs €2-3.10; adv bkg acc; CKE/CCI. "Adj to lge lake with watersports avail; takeaway; nearest town for shops is Aurillac 25km; local shops in Le Rouget 7km; beautiful location; many pitches with lake view; excel." ♦ 26 Apr-11 Nov. € 26.50   2014*

⊞ **PERTUIS** 10E3 (8km N Rural) 43.75860, 5.50407
Camping de La Bonde, 84290 Cabrières-d'Aigues [04 90 77 63 64; campingdelabonde@wanadoo.fr; www.campingdelabonde.com] NE fr Pertuis on D956, fork L onto D9 (sp Cabrières & Etang de la Bonde). At x-rds in 8km turn R onto D27. Site on L in 200m. Med, pt shd, wc; shwrs; EHU (6A) (poss rev pol) €3.20; gas; shop; rest; snacks; playgrnd; sw; 80% statics; dogs €1.80; adv bkg acc; quiet; ccard acc; tennis; fishing; watersports; games area; CKE/CCI. "Lovely lakeside & beach; ltd facs LS; phone ahead to check site open; pool 8km; gd cycling area." € 18.00   2017*

> ## "There aren't many sites open at this time of year"
>
> If you're travelling outside peak season remember to call ahead to check site opening dates – even if the entry says 'open all year'.

PESMES 6G2 (1km S Rural) 47.27612, 5.56451
Camp Municipal La Colombière, Route de Dole, 70140 Pesmes [03 84 31 20 15; fax 03 84 31 20 54; campcolombiere@aol.com] On D475 halfway bet Gray & Dole. S fr Pesmes immed on L after x-ing rv bdge. N fr Dole, site sp on R immed bef rest at rv bdge. Med, hdg, pt shd, wc; chem disp; shwrs; EHU (6-10A) €2.30-3.60; lndry; shop nr; rest nr; snacks; bar; dogs €1.20; phone; Eng spkn; adv bkg rec; ccard acc; bike hire. "Picturesque vill; helpful, friendly staff; gd san facs; vg; no twin axles." 1 May-31 Oct. € 12.60   2018*

PEYRELEAU 10E1 (1km N Rural) 44.19126, 3.20470
Camp Municipal de Brouillet, 48150 Le Rozier [05 65 62 63 98; fax 05 65 62 63 98; contact@campinglerozier.com; www.camping-lerozier.com] Fr Millau take D809 N to Aguessac, onto D907; in Le Rozier, cross bdge over Rv Tarn onto D996 & in 200m (opp church); take rd on R to site; sp. Lge, mkd, pt shd, wc; chem disp; fam bthrm; shwrs inc; EHU (6A) €3.50; lndry; shop nr; playgrnd; pool (htd); wifi; adv bkg rec; quiet; CKE/CCI. "V pleasant, busy, spacious site adj rv; friendly recep; vg for m'vans; poss facs stretched & unclean; gd base for Tarn Gorges; gd area walking & birdwatching." ♦ 1 Apr-30 Sep. € 22.00   2012*

PICQUIGNY

PEYRELEAU *10E1* (1km W Rural) *44.19470, 3.20210*
Camping Saint Pal, Route des Gorges du Tarn, 12720 Mostuéjouls [05 65 62 64 46 or 05 65 58 79 82 (LS); saintpal@orange.fr; www.campingsaintpal.com] Exit A75 exit junc 44.1 onto D29 to Aguessac then L onto D907 to Mostuéjouls. Or fr Millau take D809 N to Aguessac, turn R onto D907 to Mostuéjouls. Site in 10km 500m fr Rozier bdge. Med, mkd, hdg, shd, wc; chem disp; mv service pnt; fam bthrm; shwrs; EHU (6A) €3.20; gas; lndry; shop; snacks; bar; bbq; playgrnd; pool; sw nr; red long stay; TV; 20% statics; dogs €2; phone; Eng spkn; adv bkg acc; quiet; ccard acc; games rm; CKE/CCI. "Excel site & facs; organised walks; gd walks, canoeing, fishing & birdwatching, beavers on rv bank opp; poss diff for lge o'fits." ♦
1 May-30 Sep. € 27.50   2012*

PEYRELEAU *10E1* (1km NW Rural) *44.19810, 3.19442* FFCC Camping Les Bords du Tarn, 12720 Mostuéjouls [05 65 62 62 94; lesbordsdutarn@orange.fr; www.campinglesbordsdutarn.com] Exit A75 junc 44.1 onto D29 to Aguessac; turn L onto D907 dir Le Rozier & Peyreleau; site on R 1km bef Le Rozier. NB Do not use exit 44 fr A75 (as sat nav might instruct). Med, mkd, pt shd, pt sl, wc; chem disp; fam bthrm; shwrs inc; EHU (10A) €3.50; lndry; shop; rest; snacks; bar; bbq (charcoal, gas); playgrnd; pool (htd); sw nr; entmnt; wifi; 10% statics; dogs €2; phone; Eng spkn; adv bkg acc; quiet; ccard acc; cycling; fishing; games rm; canoe hire; tennis; CKE/CCI. "Site in beautiful area by rv; some v lge pitches; climbing; gd for rv sports; paragliding; modern san facs; gd walking; conv Gorges du Tarn & Gorges de la Jonte; excel." ♦
7 May-12 Sep. € 40.00   2014*

> ### "That's changed – Should I let the Club know?"
> If you find something on site that's different from the site entry, fill in a report and let us know. See camc.com/europereport.

PEZENAS *10F1* (1km SW Urban) *43.45419, 3.41573*
Campotel Municipal de Castelsec, Chemin de Castelsec, 34120 Pézenas [04 67 98 04 02; fax 04 67 98 35 40; contact@camping-pezenas.com; www.camping-gites-herault.com] Fr Béziers take N9 to Pézenas; foll Cent Ville sps fr rndabt at edge of town onto Route de Béziers; in 600m at next rndabt (at junc with D13) go strt over into Ave de Verdun; in 400m take 1st L after McDonalds & pharmacy at ent to Carrefour supmkt; foll Campotel sps; site on L in 300m. Sm, mkd, pt shd, pt sl, terr, wc; chem disp; shwrs inc; EHU (10A) €2.90; lndry; shop nr; playgrnd; TV; 30% statics; dogs €1.40; adv bkg acc; quiet; tennis adj; CKE/CCI. "Great little site; friendly staff; clean, dated san facs; some pitches unsuitable lge o'fits; easy walk/cycle to interesting town; toy museum worth visit; vg." ♦ 1 Apr-30 Oct. € 16.00   2014*

PHALSBOURG *5D3* (3km N Rural) *48.78300, 7.25020*
FFCC Camping de Bouleaux (CC de F), 5 Rue des Trois Journeaux, 57370 Vilsberg [03 87 24 18 72; fax 03 87 24 46 52; info@campinglesbouleaux.fr; www.campinglesbouleaux.fr or www.campingclub.asso.fr] Fr A4 exit junc 44 dir Phalsbourg. At x-rds turn L sp D661 Sarreguemines. Site on R in 2km. NB Site ent off steep descent on D661. Lge o'fits take care leaving site & turning L - watch rear overhangs. Lge, pt shd, wc; chem disp; mv service pnt; fam bthrm; shwrs inc; EHU (6A) inc; lndry; shop; bbq; playgrnd; 15% statics; dogs €2; phone; Eng spkn; adv bkg acc; quiet; CKE/CCI. "Peaceful, well-kept site; welcoming, helpful Dutch owners; barrier clsd 1930; gd facs; access to some pitches poss diff, some uneven; conv m'way & NH to/fr Germany/Austria; gd NH." ♦ 1 Apr-18 Oct.
€ 18.50   2015*

> ### "I like to fill in the reports as I travel from site to site"
> You'll find report forms at the back of this guide, or you can fill them in online at camc.com/europereport.

PHALSBOURG *5D3* (6km SW Rural) *48.71922, 7.22643* Camping du Plan Incliné, Hoffmuhl, 57820 Henridorff [03 87 25 30 13 or 06 71 21 86 91 (mob); campingplanincline@wanadoo.fr; www.campingplanincline.fr] Exit A4 at junc 44. In Phalsbourg take D38 twds Lutzelbourg; turn R onto D98 dir Arzviller & foll sp to Henridorff & site on R adj rv (narr ent). Med, hdg, hdstg, pt shd, wc; chem disp; shwrs inc; EHU (6A) €3; gas; lndry; shop nr; rest; snacks; bar; playgrnd; pool; sw nr; red long stay; entmnt; wifi; 60% statics; dogs €1; phone; Eng spkn; adv bkg acc; fishing adj; boating adj; CKE/CCI. "In wooded valley; friendly, helpful owner; vg rest; grnd soft when wet; cycle path to Strasbourg; adj to unique canal; poss dif ent for lge units; v poor, run-down site; gd for NH or short stay." ♦ 1 Apr-15 Oct.
€ 18.40   2018*

PICQUIGNY *3C3* (0km E Urban) *49.9345, 2.1458*
Camping De L'Abime (formerly Municipal), 66 Rue du Marais, 80310 Picquigny [03 22 51 25 83 or 06 51 64 40 25; fax 03 22 51 30 98; contact@campingdelabime-picquigny.fr; www.campingdelabime-picquigny.fr] Site sp fr town cent. Med, pt shd, wc; chem disp; shwrs inc; EHU (10A) inc; lndry; shop nr; playgrnd; wifi; 80% statics; dogs; adv bkg rec; quiet; rv; fishing. "Pleasant, well laid out site; gd, clean, modern san facs; some shd pitches bet statics; occasional noise fr rlwy line; WW1 war cemetery nr town; nice, small, simple site; easy walking dist fr town; many places to visit."
1 Apr-31 Oct. € 26.00   2018*

France

Check any essential information with the site before you travel

les alicourts
resort by nature ★★★★★

LES ALICOURTS RESORT, Glamping Loire-Valle
Spa, Golf, Pool Complex, Fishing
www.lesalicourts.com
Member of the Leading Campings of Europe

PIEUX, LES

PIERRE BUFFIERE *7B3 (2km SE Rural) 45.68937, 1.37101* **Camp Intercommunal Chabanas, 87260 Pierre-Buffière [05 55 00 96 43; www.pierre-buffiere.com]** Approx 20km S of Limoges on A20, take exit 40 onto D420 S bound; site on L in 500m. Foll sps for 'Stade-Chabanas'. Med, hdg, mkd, pt shd, pt sl, wc; chem disp; shwrs inc; EHU (10A) inc (poss rev pol); lndry; shop nr; playgrnd; dogs €1.14; phone; adv bkg acc; fishing; CKE/CCI. "Clean, quiet site; helpful staff; excel clean san facs; some pitches diff for lge o'fits; no twin axles; warden on site 1600-2200, but gate poss locked all day LS (code issued, phone ahead); conv Limoges; excel NH fr A20; conv for Oradour Sur Glane; gd size plots." ♦ 15 May-30 Sep. € 13.00   2018*

PIERREFITTE SUR SAULDRE *4G3 (6km NE Rural) 47.54483, 2.19133* **Les Alicourts Resort, Domaine des Alicourts, 41300 Pierrefitte-sur-Sauldre [02 54 88 63 34; fax 02 54 88 58 40; info@lesalicourts.com; www.lesalicourts.com]** Fr S of Lamotte-Beuvron, turn L on D923. After 14km turn R on D24E sp Pierrefitte. After 750m turn L, foll sp to site approx 750m on R. Med, pt shd, wc; chem disp; mv service pnt; fam bthrm; shwrs inc; EHU (6A) inc; lndry; shop; rest; snacks; bar; bbq; playgrnd; pool; sw; entmnt; 10% statics; dogs €7; Eng spkn; adv bkg acc; quiet; ccard acc; waterslide; bike hire; games rm; tennis; CKE/CCI. "Excel, peaceful site; skating rink; kayak/pedalo hire; extra for lakeside pitches; fitness cent; gd, clean facs; v lge pitches." ♦ 29 Apr-6 Sep. € 52.00   2016*

See advertisement opposite

PIERREFONDS *3D3 (1km N Urban) 49.35427, 2.97564* **Camp Municipal de Batigny, 34 Rue de l'Armistice, 60350 Pierrefonds [03 44 42 80 83 or 09 71 20 42 08 (mob); fax 03 44 42 87 73; camping-de-pierrefonds@orange.fr]** Take D973 fr Compiegne; after 14km site on L adj sp for Pierrefonds at ent to vill. Med, hdg, pt shd, serviced pitches; wc (htd); chem disp; mv service pnt; shwrs inc; EHU (10A) €2.80 (poss rev pol); lndry; shop nr; rest nr; red long stay; dogs €1; adv bkg acc; CKE/CCI. "Attractive, well-run, busy site; tight pitches for lge o'fits; clean san facs; poss unkempt LS; site yourself if recep clsd; cycle paths; nr Armistice train & museum; gd site; walking dist to vill." 6 Apr-30 Sep. € 19.00   2014*

PIEUX, LES *1C4 (3km SW Coastal) 49.49444, -1.84194* **Le Grand Large, 11 Route de Grand Large, 50340 Les Pieux [02 33 52 40 75; fax 02 33 52 58 20; info@legrandlarge.com; www.legrandlarge.com]** Fr ferry at 1st rndabt take 1st exit sp Cent Ville. Closer to town cent foll old N13 sp Caen. In about 1.5km branch R onto D900 then L onto D650 sp Carteret. Foll this rd past Les Pieux, cont on D650 to sp Super U. Turn R & foll site sp onto D517, then D117 for 3km until reaching beach rd to site, site on L in 2km. Lge, mkd, hdg, pt shd, wc (htd); chem disp; mv service pnt; fam bthrm; shwrs inc; EHU (10A) €4; gas; lndry; shop; snacks; bar; bbq; playgrnd; pool (htd); paddling pool; beach sand adj; red long stay; entmnt; wifi; TV; 40% statics; dogs free (1 per pitch); phone; Eng spkn; adv bkg acc; quiet; ccard acc; tennis; horseriding 4km; games rm. "Well-run site; rec for families; dir access to superb lge beach; friendly staff; clean modern san facs; o'fits over 8m by request; barrier clsd 2100-0900; conv Cherbourg ferries but arr not rec after dark due sm country lanes; outside pitches avail for early dep for ferries; mkt Fri." ♦ 12 Apr-20 Sep. € 33.00   2013*

See advertisement above

PIEUX, LES *1C4 (4km SW Coastal) 49.48022, -1.84216* **Camping Le Ranch, 50340 Le Rozel [02 33 10 07 10; fax 02 33 10 07 11; contact@camping-leranch.com; www.camping-leranch.com]** S fr Cherbourg on D650 & turn R to Les Pieux, then take D117 to Le Rozel. Turn L thro Rozel, foll sps to site. Site is on R at end rd. Med, unshd, pt sl, wc; chem disp; fam bthrm; shwrs inc; EHU (10A) €4.50; lndry; shop; rest; snacks; bar; playgrnd; pool (htd); beach sand adj; red long stay; entmnt; wifi; 80% statics; dogs €3.20; quiet; fishing; waterslide; games area; watersports; CKE/CCI 1 Apr-30 Sep. € 46.60   2013*

PIRIAC SUR MER

PIRIAC SUR MER *2G3* (4km E Rural/Coastal) *47.38705, -2.51021* Camping Parc du Guibel, Route de Kerdrien, 44420 Piriac-sur-Mer [02 40 23 52 67; fax 02 40 15 50 24; camping@parcduguibel.com; www.parcduguibel.com] Fr Guérande take D99 to La Turballe, D333 to St Sébastien. In St Sébastien turn R to Kerdrien over x-rds & site on R in approx 500m. Lge, mkd, hdstg, pt shd, pt sl, serviced pitches; wc; chem disp; mv service pnt; shwrs inc; EHU (3-10A) €2.90-4.30 (poss rev pol); gas; lndry; shop; rest; snacks; bar; bbq; playgrnd; pool (htd); paddling pool; beach sand 1km; entmnt; TV; 30% statics; dogs €2; phone; adv bkg acc; ccard acc; bike hire; tennis; games area; CKE/CCI. "Helpful owner; mini waterslide; lovely, quiet location in woods; gd touring base; site split by rd; san facs need upgrade." ♦ 22 Mar-21 Sep. € 19.50   2012*

PISSOS *7D1* (1km E Rural) *44.30831, -0.76987* Camp Municipal l'Arriu, 40410 Pissos [05 58 08 90 38 or 05 58 04 41 40 (LS); fax 05 58 08 92 93; mairie.pissos@wanadoo.fr; www.pissos.fr] Fr N exit N10 junc 18 onto D834 to Pissos; at x-rds turn L onto D43 sp Sore; site on R in 500m, sp. Med, shd, wc; chem disp; shwrs inc; EHU €2.10; playgrnd; red long stay; quiet; ice; rv fishing 300m. "Lge pitches; pool 500m; excel." 1 Jul-15 Sep. € 11.50   2012*

PITHIVIERS *4F3* (8km S Rural) *48.10365, 2.24142* Camping Le Clos des Tourterelles, Rue des Rendillons, 45300 Bouzonville-aux-Bois [02 38 33 01 00] S fr Pithiviers on D921 twds Jargeau; enter Bouzonville; turn R immed bef cafe; site 500m on R; sp in vill. Med, pt shd, wc (htd); chem disp; shwrs inc; EHU (16A) inc; lndry; playgrnd; 90% statics; adv bkg acc; quiet; CKE/CCI. "Ltd space for tourers - phone ahead rec; friendly, helpful owners; gd NH; cash only." ♦ € 15.00   2014*

PLAISANCE *8F2* (1km S Urban) *43.92511, 2.54616* Camping Municipal Le Moulin De L'Horte, 12550 Plaisance [05 65 99 72 07 or 05 65 99 75 07; mairie.plaisance12@laposte.net; www.plaisance12.com/camping htm] Fr D999 Albi-Millau, exit at D127 to Plaisance. R onto D77. Site on R after bdge. Sm, mkd, pt shd, wc; shwrs inc; EHU (6A); gas; lndry; bbq; pool; sw nr; twin axles; wifi; TV; 10% statics; dogs; phone; Eng spkn; adv bkg acc; quiet; games rm. " Vg, great quiet site with rv adj to swim in; excel rest & café nrby 0.2km; sm town but v pleasant." 15 Jun-15 Sep. € 12.00   2014*

⊞ **PLELAN LE GRAND** *2F3* (7km SW Rural) *47.95950, -2.15160* Camping du Château d'Aleth, Rue de l'Ecole, 56380 St Malo-de-Beignon [06 78 96 10 62 (mob); contact@camping-aleth.com; www.camping-aleth.com] Fr N24 twds Rennes exit N onto D773 to St Malo-de-Beignon in 5km, site L by church. Sm, pt shd, pt sl, wc; chem disp; mv service pnt; shwrs inc; EHU (10A) inc; lndry; shop; snacks; bbq; playgrnd; wifi; dogs free; quiet. "Pleasant, tranquil, well-kept site by lake; clean san facs; themed cowboy & indian site." ♦ € 19.50   2013*

PLESTIN LES GREVES *2E2* (4km NE Coastal) *48.66805, -3.60060* Camp Municipal St Efflam, Rue Lan-Carré, 22310 Plestin-les-Grèves [02 96 35 62 15; fax 02 96 35 09 75; campingmunicipalplestin@wanadoo.fr; www.camping-municipal-bretagne.com] Fr Morlaix on D786 thro Plestin-les-Grèves; foll D786 sp St Efflam down hill to bay; site on R 850m along bay; sp. Lge, mkd, pt shd, pt sl, terr, wc; chem disp; mv service pnt; shwrs inc; EHU (10A) €2.50; gas; lndry; shop nr; rest; bar; bbq; playgrnd; beach sand 150m; sw nr; pool €1.30; Eng spkn; adv bkg req; ccard acc; boating adj; fishing adj; CKE/CCI. "Excel; helpful recep; v well kept; modern san facs; municipal pool on site; superb beach nrby; grass pitches liable to waterlogging in wet weather." ♦ 26 Mar-3 Oct. € 14.00   2016*

> **"We must tell the Club about that great site we found"**
>
> Get your site reports in by mid-August and we'll do our best to get your updates into the next edition.

PLOERMEL *2F3* (2km N Rural) *47.94866, -2.42077* Camping du Lac, Les Belles Rives, 56800 Taupont [02 97 74 01 22; contact@camping-du-lac-ploermel.com; www.camping-du-lac-ploermel.com] Fr N24 foll D766e around Ploërmel or foll sp for Taupont (D8). Cent, take D8 twds Taupont & Lac-au-Duc 3km. Site clearly sp on R on edge of lake. Med, hdg, mkd, pt shd, wc (htd); chem disp; mv service pnt; shwrs inc; EHU (5A) €3.50; gas; lndry; shop; snacks; bar; bbq; playgrnd; sw nr; 10% statics; dogs €2.40; Eng spkn; adv bkg acc; quiet; ccard acc; tennis; waterslide nr; watersports adj; CKE/CCI. "Pleasant site in lovely location; golf 1km; horseriding 1km; friendly staff; vg; excel shopping in Ploermel; excel cent to explore Brittany." ♦ 1 Apr-30 Sep. € 15.00   2014*

⊞ **PLOERMEL** *2F3* (8km N Rural) *47.98425, -2.38191* FFCC Camping Parc Merlin l'Enchanteur, 8 Rue du Pont, Vallée de l'Yvel, 56800 Loyat [02 97 93 05 52 or 02 97 73 89 45; fax 02 97 73 89 37; camelotpark@wanadoo.fr; www.campingmerlin.com] Fr Ploermel take D766 N sp St Malo. In 5km turn L to Loyat. Site on L on ent vill opp g'ge, adj sm lake. Med, hdg, mkd, pt shd, wc (htd); chem disp; mv service pnt; shwrs inc; EHU (10-16A) €3.50-6 (poss rev pol); gas; lndry; shop; rest nr; bar nr; bbq; pool (covrd, htd); sw nr; red long stay; wifi; 10% statics; dogs €2; adv bkg acc; quiet; ccard acc; games area; tennis; bike hire; fishing; watersports 4km; CKE/CCI. "Peaceful site; spacious pitches; welcoming British owners; vg clean facs; gd indoor pool; poss soggy in winter; new 60km tarmac cycle trail adj; conv Château Josselin, Lizio & Brocéliande forest with legend of King Arthur; pleasant site; excel walking and cycling; site rather unkept." ♦ € 20.00   2018*

PLOERMEL 2F3 (10km S Rural) 47.86354, -2.44612
Camping Domaine du Roc, Rue Beaurivage, 56460 Le Roc-St André [02 97 74 91 07 or 06 48 07 68 05 (mob); contact@domaine-du-roc.com; www.domaine-du-roc.com] Fr N on N166 turn R onto D764/D4 to Le Roc-St André. Site in approx 3km at end of bdge over Nantes & Brest Canal. Med, mkd, hdg, pt shd, wc; fam bthrm; shwrs inc; EHU (6A) €3.50; lndry; shop nr; rest nr; bar nr; bbq; playgrnd; pool (covrd, htd); 50% statics; dogs €3; adv bkg acc; quiet; ccard acc; CKE/CCI. "Peaceful, well-situated site; gd touring base; excel cycle rtes adj canal; v helpful staff." 1 Apr-1 Nov. € 18.00   2015*

PLOERMEL 2F3 (10km NW Rural) 47.96932, -2.47010
Camping La Vallée du Ninian, Route du Lac, Le Rocher, 56800 Taupont [02 97 93 53 01; fax 02 97 93 57 27; infos@camping-ninian.com; www.camping-ninian.com] Fr Ploërmel cent foll sp to Taupont or Lac au Duc; N on D8. Thro vill Taupont take L hand turn sp La Vallée du Ninian; site on L 1km fr Helléan. Sm, hdg, pt shd, wc; chem disp; fam bthrm; shwrs inc; EHU (3-10A) €2-3.50; lndry; shop; bar; playgrnd; pool (htd); paddling pool; beach sand 4km; sw nr; entmnt; dogs €1; adv bkg rec; quiet; watersports 4km. "Farm produce; helpful, friendly owners; peaceful; gd facs for children; vg." ♦ 1 Apr-30 Sep. € 21.50   2015*

PLOMBIERES LES BAINS 6F2 (10km S Rural) 47.92460, 6.47545 **Camp Municipal Le Val d'Ajol, Rue des Oeuvres, 88340 Le Val-d'Ajol [03 29 66 55 17; camping@valdajol.fr; www.valdajol.fr]** Fr N on N57 after Plombières-les-Bains turn onto D20 sp Le Val-d'Ajol. Site sps in vill. Sm, hdg, pt shd, wc; chem disp; shwrs inc; EHU (6A) €2.50; lndry; shop nr; wifi; TV; dogs; phone; adv bkg acc; quiet; CKE/CCI. "Excel site; excel, clean san facs; vg touring base; lovely; htd covrd pool adj; attractive area." ♦ 15 Apr-30 Sep. € 13.00   2017*

> ## "I need an on-site restaurant"
> We do our best to make sure site information is correct, but it is always best to check any must-have facilities are still available or will be open during your visit.

PLONEVEZ PORZAY 2E2 (4km W Coastal) 48.14458, -4.26915 **Camping La Plage de Tréguer, Plage de Ste Anne-la-Palud, 29550 Plonévez-Porzay [02 98 92 53 52; fax 02 98 92 54 89; camping-treguer-plage@wanadoo.fr; www.camping-treguer-plage.com]** On D107 S fr Châteaulin. After 8km turn R to Ste Anne-la-Palud & foll sp. Lge, hdstg, mkd, hdg, pt shd, wc; chem disp; mv service pnt; shwrs inc; EHU (6A) €3.90; gas; lndry; shop; snacks; bar; bbq; playgrnd; beach sand adj; entmnt; TV; 10% statics; dogs €2.20; Eng spkn; adv bkg acc; ccard acc; games area; games rm; CKE/CCI. "Well-situated touring base; vg, friendly site; excel beach." ♦ 4 Apr-24 Sep. € 34.50   2013*

PLOUGUENAST

PLOUGASNOU 1D2 (2km SE Coastal) 48.68548, -3.78530 **Camping Le Trégor, 130 route du Cosquerou, 29630 Plougasnou [02 98 67 37 64; bookings@campingdutregor.com; www.campingdutregor.com]** At junc of D46 to Plougasnou. Site is on L just bef town sp. Sm, mkd, hdg, pt shd, wc; chem disp; shwrs inc; EHU (6-10A) inc; gas; lndry; shop nr; bbq; playgrnd; beach sand 1.2km; sw nr; 40% statics; dogs €1; adv bkg acc; quiet; watersports 3km; CKE/CCI. "Well-run site in beautiful area; dated but clean facs; ideal for walking, cycling & fishing; conv Roscoff ferries & Morlaix; phone if req NH after end Oct." Easter-11 Nov. € 15.00   2014*

> ## "Satellite navigation makes touring much easier"
> Remember most sat navs don't know if you're towing or in a larger vehicle – always use yours alongside maps and site directions.

PLOUGASNOU 1D2 (3km NW Coastal) 48.71421, -3.81563 **Camp Municipal de la Mer, 29630 Primel-Trégastel [02 98 72 37 06 or 02 98 67 30 06; fax 02 98 67 82 79; primel-tregastel.camping-de-la-mer@wanadoo.fr]** Fr Morlaix take D46 to Plougastel on to Primel-Trégastel. Bear R in vill & 1st L opp cafe to site on R in 100 m. Med, unshd, wc; chem disp; mv service pnt; shwrs; EHU (10A) inc; lndry; shop nr; rest nr; bar nr; playgrnd; beach sand 500m; dogs €1; phone; quiet; CKE/CCI. "Fine coastal views; gd walking & cycling; ltd facs LS." ♦ 1 Jun-30 Sep. € 17.00   2014*

PLOUGASTEL DAOULAS 2E2 (5km NE Coastal) 48.40134, -4.35419 **Camping Saint Jean, 29470 Plougastel-Daoulas [02 98 40 32 90; fax 02 98 04 23 11; info@campingsaintjean.com; www.campingsaintjean.com]** Fr Brest, take N165 E for approx 12km then leave m'way after Plougastel exit & foll sp. Site in 2km at end of rd by rv. Med, hdstg, hdg, pt shd, pt sl, terr, wc (htd); chem disp; mv service pnt; fam bthrm; shwrs; EHU (6A) €3 (poss rev pol); lndry; shop; snacks; bar; bbq; playgrnd; pool (covrd, htd); paddling pool; entmnt; wifi; TV; 10% statics; dogs €2; quiet; waterslide; games area. "Nice site by rv; steep in places; gd facs." ♦ 11 Apr-26 Sep. € 25.00   2015*

PLOUGUENAST 2E3 (2km NW Rural) 48.28653, -2.72145 **Pinâbre Camping & Caravaning, Lingouet 22150 [02 96 26 80 04; campgite-brittany.com]** Site is 50 miles fr St. Malo ferry port, bet Loudeac and Moncontour off the D768. Sm, pt shd, pt sl, wc; chem disp; fam bthrm; shwrs; EHU (16A) €3; lndry; bbq; wifi; Eng spkn; adv bkg acc; CKE/CCI. "Gd for walks & cycling; sm friendly site; excel facs; close to N & S coast; open plan, grassy site; quiet; excel." Apr-Sep. € 12.00   2018*

France

PLOUGUERNEAU

PLOUGUERNEAU *2E2* (3km N Coastal) *48.63048, -4.52402* **Camping La Grève Blanche, St Michel, 29880 Plouguerneau [02 98 04 70 35 or 02 98 04 63 97 (LS); fax 02 98 04 63 97; lroudaut@free.fr; www.campinggreveblanche.com]** Fr Lannilis D13 to Plouguerneau, D32 sp La Grève, St Michel (look out for lorry rte sp). Avoid Plouguerneau vill when towing - tight RH bend. Med, mkd, hdg, unshd, pt sl, terr, wc (htd); chem disp; mv service pnt; shwrs; EHU (9A) €2.80 (long cable poss req, rev pol); lndry; shop nr; bar; bbq (charcoal, elec, gas); playgrnd; beach sand; twin axles; entmnt; wifi; 20% statics; dogs; bus adj; Eng spkn; adv bkg acc; quiet; games area; games rm; CCI. "Excel location; sea views; helpful staff; facs clean & well-kept; LS recep open eves only; in fog lighthse sounds all night otherwise quiet; walking coastal rte; san facs clean but dated." ♦ 23 Mar-8 Oct. € 16.50 2018*

PLOUGUERNEAU *2E2* (7km NE Coastal) *48.63112, -4.44972* **Camping du Vougot, Route de Prat-Leden, 29880 Plouguerneau [02 98 25 61 51; campingduvougot@hotmail.fr; www.campingplageduvougot.com]** Fr N12 at Landerneau exit N onto D770 to Lesneven, then D28/D32 to Plouguerneau. Fr Plouguerneau take D10 dir Guisseny then turn W onto D52 dir Grève-du-Vougot, site sp. Med, hdg, mkd, pt shd, wc; chem disp; mv service pnt; shwrs; EHU (10A) €3.30; lndry; snacks; playgrnd; beach sand 250m; red long stay; entmnt; wifi; 30% statics; dogs €2.60; adv bkg acc; quiet; ccard acc; watersports nr; CKE/CCI. "Gd walking (GR34); interesting area; excel touring base; excel site; v lge pitches; friendly staff." ♦ 4 Apr-24 Oct. € 20.60 2015*

PLOUHARNEL *2F3* (7km S Coastal) *47.55458, -3.13118* **Camping Municipal De Penthievre, Avenue Duquesne, Penthievre 56510 St Pierre, Quiberon [02 07 52 33 86; fax 02 97 52 49 14; www.saintpierrequiberon.fr]** Take D768 fr N165 at Auray dir Quiberon. Foll sp at Penthievre. V lge, pt shd, pt sl, wc; chem disp; mv service pnt; fam bthrm; shwrs inc; EHU (10A) €1.83; gas; lndry; shop; rest; snacks; bar; bbq; playgrnd; beach adj; twin axles; entmnt; wifi; dogs €1.04; phone; bus, train; Eng spkn; quiet; ccard acc; games area. "Traditional French municipal; v friendly; ideal watersports & cycling; coastal scenery; Quiberon magnificent; rests, mkt; park & ride; ideal base for visiting southern Brittany; pool 6km; excel." ♦ 1 Apr-30 Sep. € 15.00 2016*

POET LAVAL, LE *9D2* (2km SE Rural) *44.52889, 5.02300* **Camp Municipal Lorette, 26160 Le Poët-Laval [04 75 91 00 62 or 04 75 46 44 12 (Mairie); fax 04 75 46 46 45; camping.lorette@wanadoo.fr; www.campinglorette.fr]** Site 4km W of Dieulefit on D540. Sm, mkd, pt shd, pt sl, wc (htd); chem disp; mv service pnt; shwrs inc; EHU (1A) €3; lndry; shop nr; rest nr; bar nr; playgrnd; pool; wifi; dogs €1.80; bus; Eng spkn; adv bkg acc; quiet; ccard acc; tennis; CKE/CCI. "Well-kept site with views; lge pitches; clean, modern facs; nr lavender fields (Jun/Jul); mkt in Dieulefit Fri; excel; gd welcome." ♦ 1 May-30 Sep. € 12.50 2016*

POITIERS *7A2* (12km N Rural) *46.65611, 0.30194* **Camping du Futur, 9 Rue des Bois, 86170 Avanton [05 49 54 09 67; contact@camping-du-futur.com; www.camping-du-futur.com]** Exit A10 junc 28. After toll take 1st exit at rndabt sp Avanton. Site well sp fr Avanton, but care needed thro Martigny & hotel complex. Med, hdg, mkd, pt shd, wc; chem disp; mv service pnt; shwrs inc; EHU (6-10A) €3.50-3.8; lndry; shop nr; rest nr; bar; playgrnd; pool; wifi; TV; dogs €1.50; adv bkg acc; quiet; games area; games rm; CKE/CCI. "Attractive, spacious site in rural setting; well-kept & well-run; helpful French owners; vg clean san facs, ltd early ssn; c'van storage; 5 mins Futuroscope & A10; ideal NH or longer; bread, pastries and breakfast can be ordered; mv service pnt; nr Futurscope attraction; ltd shd; lovely & peaceful; quiet parkland setting; conv for Poitiers; excel." ♦ 1 Apr-31 Oct. € 19.00 2016*

POITIERS *7A2* (5km S Rural) *46.54367, 0.33230* **Saint-Benoît Camping, 2 Rue de Passe Lourdain, 86280 St Benoît [05 49 88 48 55; camping.stbenoit@orange.fr; www.ville-saint-benoit.fr]** Fr N or S turn W off D741 to St Benoît, site well sp. Med, mkd, pt shd, wc; shwrs; EHU (4A) €3; shop nr; rest nr; bar nr; playgrnd; dogs €0.50; adv bkg acc; rv fishing adj; watersports adj; CKE/CCI. "Pleasant 10 min walk into vill; gd cheap bus service fr vill to Poitiers." 1 Jun-6 Sep. € 16.00 2015*

POIX DE PICARDIE *3C3* (0km SW Rural) *49.77621, 1.97561* **Camp Municipal Le Bois des Pêcheurs, Route de Forges-les-Eaux, 80290 Poix-de-Picardie [03 22 90 11 71 or 03 22 90 32 90 (Mairie); fax 03 22 90 32 91; camping@ville-poix-de-picardie.fr; www.ville-poix-de-picardie.fr]** Fr town cent on D901 dir Beauvais, in 100m turn R onto D919 opp Citroën agent sp Camping; site on R in 500m. Fr Beauvais, turn L at bottom of steep hill opp Citroën agent; site in 500m on R. Med, hdg, mkd, hdstg, pt shd, wc; chem disp; mv service pnt; shwrs inc; EHU (6A) €4 (poss long lead req); lndry; shop nr; rest nr; bar nr; bbq; playgrnd; red long stay; wifi; TV; dogs €1.50; Eng spkn; adv bkg acc; quiet; rv fishing adj; tennis 800m; bike hire; games rm; CKE/CCI. "Pleasant, peaceful, tidy site in delightful area; v clean modern san facs; htd covrd pool 800m; gd touring base; vg walking & cycling; bar 500m; train to Amiens; lovely mkt Sun; rec; every 3rd night free; gas 300m; sh walk to town and supmkt; vg." ♦ 1 Apr-30 Sep. € 18.00 2018*

POLIGNY *6H2* (1km SW Rural) *46.83455, 5.69840* **Camp Communautaire de la Croix du Dan, 39800 Poligny [03 84 37 01 35; fax 03 84 73 77 59; cccgrimont@wanadoo.fr; www.ville-poligny.fr]** Fr SW on N83 turn R at rndabt sp 'Centre'; site on R immed bef town sp Poligny. Fr N & NW take D905 into & thro town cent (no L turn on N83 S of Poligny), then foll sp Lons-Le Saunier. Site on L bef sportsgrnd - look for m'van sp. Do not overshoot ent, as diff to see. N5 fr E not rec as steep & hairpins. Med, mkd, pt shd, wc; chem disp; shwrs inc; EHU (10A) €6.40; lndry; shop nr; playgrnd; twin axles; dogs; phone; Eng spkn; quiet; CKE/CCI. "Excel, clean, tidy site; helpful warden; pretty town; if recep clsd ring number on board to open barrier." ♦ 15 Jun-20 Sep. € 15.00 2017*

PONS (CHARENTE MARITIME) 7B2 (1km W Urban) 45.57791, -0.55552 **Camp Municipal Le Paradis, 1 Ave de Poitou, 17800 Pons [05 46 91 36 72; fax 05 46 96 14 15; campingmunicipalpons@voila.fr; www.pons-ville.org]** Well sp fr town o'skts. Med, mkd, pt shd, wc; mv service pnt; shwrs inc; EHU (6-10A) inc (poss rev pol); shop nr; wifi; TV; dogs €1.76; rv fishing 200m. "Excel site in attractive grnds; helpful super wardens, Eng spkn; interesting town; conv for Saintes, Cognac, Royan; free wifi in snack bar; gd sized pitches; pool 100m; waterslide 100m; v friendly staff; easy walk to old city; excel." ♦ 1 May-30 Sep. € 15.00 2017*

"There aren't many sites open at this time of year"

If you're travelling outside peak season remember to call ahead to check site opening dates – even if the entry says 'open all year'.

PONT AUDEMER 3D2 (8km W Rural) 49.31433, 0.40344 **Camping La Lorie (Lehaye), 5 La Lorie, 27210 Fort-Moville [02 32 57 15 49]** Fr Pont-Audemer take D675 twrds Beauzeville. Then L onto D27. Take 3rd exit at rndabt to stay on D27. Then 3rd exit at next rndabt onto Haut Rue de Fort Moville; slight L then strt on; site on L. Sm, pt shd, wc; chem disp; shwrs inc; EHU (10A) inc; rest nr; bar nr; bbq; playgrnd; 10% statics; dogs; quiet; CKE/CCI. "CL-type site in attractive area; basic facs but clean; conv Le Havre, Honfleur; gd base." Easter-1 Nov. € 13.50 2012*

PONT AUDEMER 3D2 (2km NW Rural) 49.36660, 0.48739 **Camp Municipal Risle-Seine Les Etangs, 19 Route des Etangs, 27500 Toutainville [02 32 42 46 65; fax 02 32 42 24 17; camping@ville-pont-audemer.fr; www.ville-pont-audemer.fr]** Fr Le Havre on A131/E05 cross rv at Pont de Normandie (toll). Take D580 & at junc 3 branch R & take 2nd exit onto D22 sp Beuzeville. At edge of Fiquefleur take D180, then D675 dir Pont-Audemer. In Toutainville foll site sp, turn L just bef A13 underpass, then immed R. Site approx 2km on R. Med, mkd, hdg, pt shd, serviced pitches; wc; chem disp; mv service pnt; shwrs inc; EHU (5-10A) €3.95; lndry; shop nr; snacks; bar; bbq; playgrnd; red long stay; wifi; TV; dogs free; bus; Eng spkn; adv bkg acc; quiet; ccard acc; fishing; bike hire; watersports; games area; tennis 1.5km; games rm; canoeing. "Lovely, well-run site; helpful warden; barrier clsd 2200-0830 but flexible for ferry; many leisure activities; htd pool 1.5km; poss school groups at w/end; vg for dogs; 1hr Le Havre ferry; Fri mkt Pont-Audemer; conv NH; excel; facs stretched LS; boggy when wet; pitches are narr which means car has to go at the front of your pitch." ♦ 25 Mar-31 Oct. € 21.00 2016*

PONT AVEN

PONT AVEN 2F2 (13km N Rural) 47.92512, -3.68888 **Camping Les Genêts d'Or, KermerourPont Kereon 29380 Bannalec [02 98 39 54 35; info@holidaybrittany.com; www.holidaybrittany.com]** Fr Pont Aven/Bannalec exit on N165 N to Bannalec on D4; after rlwy x-ing turn R sp Quimperlé. In 1km turn R, sp Le Trévoux; site on L 500m. Sm, hdg, mkd, pt shd, pt sl, wc; chem disp; shwrs inc; EHU (6A) €3.50; lndry; shop nr; rest; snacks; bar; bbq (gas); playgrnd; red long stay; 10% statics; dogs €1.50; Eng spkn; adv bkg acc; games rm; bike hire; CKE/CCI. "Lovely, peaceful, well-kept site in orchard; ACSI acc; lge pitches; welcoming, helpful, friendly, lovely British owners; immac san facs; Bannalec in walking dist; lovely area - excel touring base; highly rec." 31 May-30 Sep. € 19.00 2015*

PONT AVEN 2F2 (8km SE Coastal) 47.78799, -3.70064 **Camping de l'Ile Percée, Plage de Trénez, 29350 Moëlan-sur-Mer [02 98 71 16 25; camping-ilepercee-am@orange.fr; www.camping-ile-percee.fr]** App thro Moëlan-sur-Mer, 6km SE of Pont-Aven or 6km SW of Quimperlé - watch for R turn after Moëlan. Take D116 sp to Kerfany. Keep strt at Kergroës, turn L after 500m sp L'Ile Percée. Med, unshd, pt sl, wc; fam bthrm; shwrs; EHU (4-6A) €2.60-3.70; lndry; snacks; bar; bbq; playgrnd; beach shgl adj; sw nr; entmnt; TV; 10% statics; dogs €1; phone; adv bkg acc; quiet; watersports adj; fishing adj; games area. "Well-run site; sea views; ent narr & winding; sm pitches; manhandling ess; not suitable lge o'fits; san facs poss stretched high ssn." 1 Apr-19 Sep. € 17.50 2013*

PONT AVEN 2F2 (10km S Coastal) 47.80492, -3.74510 **Camping Le St Nicolas, Port Manec'h, 29920 Névez [02 98 06 89 75; fax 02 98 06 74 61; info@campinglesaintnicolas.com; www.campinglesaintnicolas.com]** Take D783 W fr Pont-Aven for 2km, turn L onto D77 S thro Névez to Port Manech. Site well sp. Narr app to site. Lge, hdg, mkd, pt shd, pt sl, wc; chem disp; shwrs inc; EHU (6-10A) €3.70-4.70; gas; lndry; rest nr; bar nr; playgrnd; pool (htd); paddling pool; beach sand 200m; entmnt; TV; dogs €1.70; Eng spkn; adv bkg acc; quiet; ccard acc; tennis nr; games rm; watersports; games area; horseriding nr; CKE/CCI. "Pleasant, wooded site; friendly owners; sh walk to beach & cliff walks; gd touring base." ♦ 1 May-19 Sep. € 29.00 2014*

PONT AVEN 2F2 (11km SSW Coastal) 47.79640, -3.77489 **Camping Les Chaumières, 24 Hameau de Kerascoët, 29920 Névez [02 98 06 73 06; fax 02 98 06 78 34; info@camping-des-chaumieres.com; www.camping-des-chaumieres.com]** S fr Pont-Aven thro Névez to Kerascoët. Med, hdg, mkd, pt shd, serviced pitches; wc; chem disp; mv service pnt; shwrs inc; EHU (4-10A) €3.40-4.70; lndry; shop nr; rest nr; bar nr; bbq; playgrnd; beach sand 800m; dogs €1.50; Eng spkn; adv bkg req; quiet; CKE/CCI. "Excel, well-organised, peaceful, beautiful site; immac facs poss stretched high ssn; gd play & games areas; sandy bay/beaches, cliff walks; san facs refurbished and upgraded; highly rec; friendly owner; recep clsd LS, but owner avail via mob." ♦ 15 May-19 Sep. € 18.00 2018*

Check any essential information with the site before you travel   *Last year of report

PONT AVEN

PONT AVEN 2F2 (5km SW Rural) 47.81749, -3.79959
Camping Les Genêts, Route St Philibert, 29920 Névez [02 98 06 86 13 or 02 98 06 72 31; campinglesgenets@aol.com; www.campinglesgenets-nevez.com]
Turn S off D783 onto D77 to Névez. At church in town, bear R & turn immed R to exit Névez with PO on R. Site on L, clearly sp. Med, hdg, mkd, pt shd, wc; fam bthrm; shwrs inc; EHU (3-6A) €2.40-5; lndry; shop nr; playgrnd; beach sand; 10% statics; dogs €1; Eng spkn; adv bkg acc; quiet; CKE/CCI. "Excel beaches adj; vg."
15 Jun-15 Sep. € 15.00   2012*

PONT AVEN 2F2 (6km SW Coastal) 47.79906, -3.79033 **Camping Les Deux Fontaines, Raguenès, 29920 Névez** [02 98 06 81 91; fax 02 98 06 71 80; info@les2fontaines.fr; www.les2fontaines.fr]
Leave N165/E60 at Kérampaou foll sp D24 twds Pont Aven. In approx 4.5km turn R (S) foll sp Névez then Raguenès. Site 3km fr Névez. Lge, mkd, pt shd, wc; fam bthrm; shwrs inc; EHU (10A) €4.90; lndry; shop; rest; bar; pool (htd); beach sand 800m; 80% statics; dogs €3.40; adv bkg acc; tennis. "Busy high ssn; popular with British families; o'night facs for m'vans; 25 meter conn lead req'd; price inc waterpark acc & kids club." ♦ 27 Apr-7 Sep. € 33.00   2013*

PONT AVEN 2F2 (8km SW Coastal) 47.79597, -3.79877 **Camping du Vieux Verger, Raguenès-Plage, 29920 Névez** [02 98 06 86 08; contact @campingduvieuxverger.com; www.campingduvieuxverger.com] Fr Pont-Aven take D783 dir Concarneau; in 2.5km L onto D77 to Névez; foll sp Raguenès-Plage; 1st site on R. Foll 'Vieux Verger' sps. Med, hdg, mkd, pt shd, wc; chem disp; shwrs inc; EHU (4-10A) €3.20-4.20 (poss rev pol); shop; rest; playgrnd; beach sand 500m; dogs free; phone; quiet; CKE/CCI. "Well-run, well-kept site with pool & waterslides; statics (sep area); highly rec LS; excel; gd for young children; excel site; gd value; many attractive beaches nrby." 14 Apr-15 Sep. € 23.70   2018*

PONT AVEN 2F2 (8km SW Coastal) 47.79330, -3.80110 **Camping Raguénès-Plage, 19 Rue des Îles à Raguénès, 29920 Névez** [02 98 06 80 69; fax 02 98 06 89 05; leraguenesplage@orange.fr; www.camping-le-raguenes-plage.com] Fr Pont-Aven take D783 dir Trégunc; in 2.5km turn L for Névez, foll sps to Raguénès fr Névez. Or fr N165 take D24 at Kérampaou exit; in 3km turn R to Nizon; at church in vill turn R onto D77 to Névez; site on L 3km after Névez. Lge, mkd, hdstg, pt shd, wc (htd); chem disp; mv service pnt; fam bthrm; shwrs inc; EHU (6-15A) €4-6.90; gas; lndry; shop; rest; bar; bbq; playgrnd; pool (covrd, htd); paddling pool; beach sand adj; entmnt; wifi; 20% statics; dogs €3.20; Eng spkn; adv bkg rec; quiet; ccard acc; games rm; watersports school adj; sauna; tennis nr; bike hire; games area; waterslide; horseriding; CKE/CCI. "Pretty, wooded, family-run site; trampoline; statics sep area; private path to beach; clean facs; 1st class site." ♦
20 Apr-30 Sep. € 33.00   2017*

See advertisement

PONT D'AIN 9A2 (1km SE Urban) 46.04680, 5.34446 **Camping de l'Oiselon, Rue E'mile Lebreüs, 01160 Pont-d'Ain** [04 74 39 05 23; campingoiselon@free.fr; www.campingpontdain.e-monsite.com] Fr A42 exit Pont-d'Ain foll D90 to vill. In vill cent turn R on D1075. Turn L immed after x-ing Rv L'Ain. Foll rd passing tennis club on L. Site on L, clearly sp. Lge, pt shd, wc; chem disp; fam bthrm; shwrs inc; EHU (6-10A) €2.40-3.10 (poss rev pol); shop; rest; snacks; bbq; playgrnd; pool; sw; entmnt; 30% statics; dogs free; Eng spkn; adv bkg acc; quiet; fishing; canoeing; tennis adj; games area; horseriding 5km; bike hire; CKE/CCI. "Gd, well-run site with easy access, v lge; helpful, friendly staff; gd clean san facs; cash only; site needs TLC (early ssn 2010); gd NH; excel site." ♦ 17 Mar-14 Oct. € 17.50   2018*

PONT DU CHATEAU

PONT DE L'ARCHE *3D2* (1km N Urban) *49.3060, 1.1546* **Camp Municipal Eure et Seine, Quai Maréchal Foch, 27340 Pont-de-l'Arche [02 35 23 06 71 or 02 32 98 90 70 (Mairie); fax 02 32 98 90 89; campeure@ orange.fr or campeure@pontdelarche.fr; www. pontdelarche.fr]** Fr Rouen S on D6015 turn 1st L after x-ing rv bdge, drive downhill then L under bdge & strt on for 300m (foll Camping Car sp at traff lts, do not go into town), site on R. Restricted width on app. Or exit A13 junc 20 onto D321 to Pont-de-l'Arche; turn L at War Memorial onto Place du Souvenir; in 300m to R at rv; site on L in 200m. Med, mkd, pt shd, wc; chem disp; shwrs inc; EHU (6-10A) €6-6.60; lndry, shop nr; rest; bar; playgrnd; red long stay; wifi; 4% statics; dogs €1.20; phone; adv bkg rec; ccard acc; rv fishing adj; CKE/CCI. "Pleasant, peaceful, clean rvside site in attractive medieval town; sm pitches; helpful warden; gd, modern san facs; recep 1000-1200 & 1600-2000; access only after 1600, Aire outside site accessible 24/7; many shops clsd Wed pm; bus fr town to Rouen; popular NH & longer; beautiful site nr Gothic church; excel; superb setting; v busy so arrive early or ring ahead; sh walk to town." ♦ 1 Apr-30 Oct. € 12.00   2017*

⊞ **PONT DE L'ARCHE** *3D2* (10km S Rural) *49.22513, 1.22406* **FFCC Camping Le St Pierre, 1 Rue du Château, 27430 St Pierre-du-Vauvray [02 32 61 01 55; eliane.darcissac@wanadoo.fr; www. lecampingdesaintpierre.com]** Fr S exit A154 junc 3 or A13 junc 18 (Louviers) onto D6155 E until junc with D6015. Turn L & in 4km turn R to St Pierre. Fr N on D6015 after x-ing Rv Seine at Pont-de-l'Arche cont for approx 6km & turn L to St Pierre. Do not ent St Pierre fr E on D313 due low bdge under rlwy line. Med, hdg, mkd, pt shd, wc; chem disp; shwrs inc; EHU (6-10A) €2.80 (poss rev pol); lndry; shop nr; bbq; playgrnd; pool (htd); 25% statics; dogs €1.20; Eng spkn; adv bkg rec; site clsd 2 weeks at Xmas/New Year; CKE/CCI. "In grnds sm chateau; TGV rlwy line adj site; conv Giverny; friendly staff; noise fr rlwy adj; ltd facs; site tired, expensive but OK for NH; not enough facs, scruffy and dirty." € 13.00   2013*

PONT DE SALARS *7D4* (2km N Rural) *44.29150, 2.72571* **Parc Camping du Lac, 12290 Pont-de-Salars [05 65 46 84 86; fax 05 65 46 60 39; contact@parc-du-lac.com; www.campingpontdesalars.fr]** Fr Rodez on D911 La Primaube-Millau rd, turn L bef ent Pont-de-Salars. Site sp. Lge, mkd, pt shd, pt sl, terr, wc; chem disp; fam bthrm; shwrs inc; EHU (3-6A) €2.50-3.50; gas; lndry; shop; rest; snacks; bar; bbq; playgrnd; pool; paddling pool; sw; entmnt; TV; 90% statics; phone; adv bkg acc; ccard acc; fishing; sailing. "Beautiful situation; poor for c'vans, OK m'vans; diff lge o'fits; blocks req; site poss unclean end of ssn; ltd facs." ♦ 1 Jun-30 Sep. € 17.00   2017*

PONT DE SALARS *7D4* (8km S Rural) *44.21500, 2.77777* **Camping Soleil Levant, Lac de Pareloup, 12290 Canet-de-Salars [05 65 46 03 65; contact@ camping-soleil-levant.com; www.camping-soleil-levant.com]** Exit A75 junc 44.1 onto D911 to Pont-de-Salars, then S on D993 dir Salles-Curan. Site in 8km bef bdge on L. Lge, mkd, pt shd, pt sl, terr, wc (htd); chem disp; fam bthrm; shwrs inc; EHU (6A) inc; gas; lndry; shop nr; snacks; bar; bbq; playgrnd; sw nr; entmnt; wifi; TV; 50% statics; dogs €2; Eng spkn; adv bkg acc; quiet; ccard acc; watersports; games area; tennis; games rm; fishing; CKE/CCI. "Lovely lakeside site; excel san facs; vg; well run by friendly couple." ♦ 1 May-30 Sep. € 30.00   2017*

PONT DE VAUX *9A2* (4km NE Rural) *46.44394, 4.98313* **Camping Les Ripettes, St Bénigne, 01190 Chavannes-sur-Reyssouze [03 85 30 66 58; info@ camping-les-ripettes.com; camping-les-ripettes. pagesperso-orange.fr]** Take D2 fr Pont-de-Vaux sp St Trivier-des-Courtes for 3km. Immed after water tower on R turn L onto D58 sp Romenay, then immed L. Site well sp on L in 100m. Med, hdg, mkd, pt shd, pt sl, wc (htd); chem disp; mv service pnt; shwrs inc; EHU (10A) €4; lndry; shop; snacks; playgrnd; pool; wifi; 1% statics; dogs €1.50; phone; Eng spkn; adv bkg rec; quiet; ccard acc; games area; CKE/CCI. "Lovely, popular site in beautiful location; spacious pitches; friendly, helpful owner; immac facs; gd pool area; gd touring base; hard to beat; ACSI card acc; one of the best; cycle rte maps at TO in Pont de Vaux; memb of La Via Natura; promoting many eco ideas; excel." ♦ 1 Apr-30 Sep. € 23.70   2018*

PONT DE VAUX *9A2* (1km W Urban) *46.42979, 004.93296* **Camping Champ d'Été, Lieu-dit Champ D'Eté, 01190 Reyssouze [0033 385 23 96 10; info@ camping-champ-dete.com; www.camping-champ-dete.com]** Fr A6 N J27, take D906 dir Pont-de-Vaux. In town, foll Base-de-Loisirs & camping sp. Med, hdstg, mkd, pt shd, wc (htd); chem disp; mv service pnt; fam bthrm; shwrs; EHU (10A) inc; lndry; shop nr; rest nr; bar nr; bbq; playgrnd; entmnt; wifi; TV; 20% statics; dogs €3; bus adj; Eng spkn; adv bkg acc; quiet; ccard acc; games rm; CKE/CCI. "Walking dist to town; adj to pk & free sw pool; v clean san facs; friendly owners; htd pool adj; gd for touring Burgundy area; gd for long or sh stays; some pitches tight for lge o'fits; vg." ♦ 25 Mar-15 Oct. € 23.90   2016*

PONT DU CHATEAU *9B1* (5km SSW Urban) *45.77546, 3.24197* **Camping Les Ombrages, Rue Pont du Château, 63111 Dallet [04 73 83 10 97; lesombrages@hotmail.com; www.lesombrages.nl]** E fr Clermont Ferrand on D769; 200m bef x-ing Rv Allier turn R onto D783/D769A; 50m after x-ring rv turn L into Rue Pont du Château; site on L in 400m. Sm, shd, wc; shwrs inc; EHU (6A) (rev pol) €3.50; lndry; shop; rest; snacks; bar; playgrnd; pool; paddling pool; sw nr; entmnt; wifi; TV; quiet; canoeing; fishing; games rm. "Peaceful, pretty, gd site; excel pitches by rv; gd for fishing & canoeing; mosquitoes; gd san facs." 14 May-15 Sep. € 25.00   2015*

PONT FARCY

PONT FARCY *1D4* (1km N Rural) *47.46810, 4.35709*
Camp Municipal Pont-Farcy, Quai de la Vire, 14380 Pont-Farcy [02 31 68 32 06 or 02 31 68 86 48; pontfarcy@free.fr; www.pont-farcy.fr]
Leave A84 junc 39 onto D21 to Pont-Farcy; site on L at ent to vill. Med, hdg, mkd, pt shd, terr, wc; chem disp; mv service pnt; fam bthrm; shwrs inc; EHU (10A) €2.50; shop nr; rest nr; bar nr; playgrnd; 30% statics; dogs €1; phone; adv bkg acc; quiet; boating adj; rv fishing adj; tennis; bike hire; CKE/CCI. "Barrier poss locked periods during day but parking avail; bar 500m; helpful, friendly warden; clean facs; mosquitoes at dusk." ♦ 3 April-30 Sep. € 10.00   2018*

PONT L'ABBE *2F2* (7km S Rural) *47.81241, -4.22147*
Camping L'Océan Breton, Route Kerlut, 29740 Lesconil [02 98 82 23 89; fax 02 98 82 26 49; info@yellohvillage-loceanbreton.com; www.camping-bretagne-oceanbreton.fr or www.yellohvillage.co.uk]
Fr Pont l'Abbé S on D102 to Plobannalec & head for Lesconil; site on L after supmkt. Lge, mkd, hdstg, hdg, pt shd, serviced pitches; wc (htd); chem disp; mv service pnt; shwrs inc; EHU (5A) inc; gas; lndry; shop; rest; snacks; bar; playgrnd; pool (covrd, htd); beach sand 2km; het real long stay; 80% statics; dogs €4; phone; Eng spkn; adv bkg acc; quiet; ccard acc; tennis; games area; sauna; waterslide; bike hire; CKE/CCI. "Excel site for families; fitness rm; spacious pitches." ♦ 28 May-18 Sep. € 39.00   2014*

PONT L'ABBE *2F2* (9km S Rural/Coastal) *47.79715, -4.22868* Camping des Dunes, 67 Rue Paul Langevin, 29740 Plobannalec-Lesconil [02 98 87 81 78; fax 02 98 82 27 05; contact@camping-lesdunes.com; www.camping-lesdunes-29.com] Fr Pont l'Abbé, S on D102 for 5km to Plobannelec; over x-rds; in 1km turn R, 100m after sports field; green sp to site in 1km. Med, mkd, hdg, pt shd, wc; chem disp; mv service pnt; fam bthrm; shwrs inc; EHU (8A) €3.70; lndry; shop; rest nr; snacks; bar; bbq; playgrnd; beach sand 100m; dogs €2.10; adv bkg acc; ccard acc; games area; games rm; CKE/CCI. "Helpful owner; nr fishing port; gd walking, cycling & birdwatching; site gd for children; access to beach with amazing granite rock formations; red early ssn; well cared for." ♦ 4 Apr-30 Sep. € 25.00   2014*

PONT L'ABBE *2F2* (3km W Rural) *47.86113, -4.26766*
Aire Naturelle Keraluic, 29120 Plomeur [02 98 82 10 22; camping@keraluic.fr; www.keraluic.fr]
Leave Quimper S on D785 to o'skts Pont L'Abbe; turn R at 1st rndabt (junc with D44); strt on at 2nd rndabt (junc with D2); in 1km turn R at 3rd rndabt up narr rd sp St Jean-Trolimon; site on R in 1.5km. Site 2km NE of Plomeur & well sp. Sm, pt shd, wc; chem disp; fam bthrm; shwrs inc; EHU (6A) €2.90; gas; lndry; shop; bbq; playgrnd; wifi; dogs (except high ssn) £1.50 LS; Eng spkn; adv bkg rec; quiet; ccard acc; games area; games rm; CKE/CCI. "Excel, well-kept, family-run site; friendly, helpful Dutch owners; spacious pitches; gd leisure facs; ideal for children; gd walking; gd surfing nrby; surfing 5km; facs poss stretched high ssn, highly rec LS; no motorhomes." ♦ 1 May-31 Oct. € 19.00   2014*

PONT L'ABBE *2F2* (10km NW Rural) *47.89462, -4.32863* Camping Kerlaz, Route de la Mer, 29670 Tréguennec [02 98 87 76 79; contact@kerlaz.com; www.kerlaz.com] Fr Plonéour-Lanvern take D156 SW to Tréguennec. Med, hdg, pt shd, wc; chem disp; mv service pnt; shwrs inc; EHU (10A); lndry; shop nr; snacks; bbq; playgrnd; pool (covrd, htd); beach sand 2km; 30% statics; dogs €1.30; Eng spkn; adv bkg acc; quiet; ccard acc; bike hire. "Nice, friendly site; pleasant owners; attractive site; gd for cycling." 1 Apr-30 Sep. € 24.00   2017*

PONT ST ESPRIT *9D2* (5km W Rural) *44.27306, 4.57944* Camping Les Oliviers, Chemin de Tête Grosse, 30130 St Paulet-de-Caisson [04 66 82 14 13; info@camping-lesoliviers.net; www.camping-lesoliviers.net] Exit A7 junc 19 & foll D994 to Pont-St Esprit, then sp to St Paulet-de-Caisson. Turn R into vill & foll sp to St Julien-de-Peyrolas on D343, site sp 1.5km off narr rd - unsuitable lge o'fits. Sm, mkd, hdg, pt shd, terr, wc; chem disp; shwrs inc; EHU (4A) €3; lndry; shop nr; rest; snacks; bar; playgrnd; pool; sw nr; dogs free; Eng spkn; adv bkg acc; quiet; CKE/CCI. "Ardèche, Roman sites nr; helpful Dutch owners; painting tuition; ltd water points & long way fr lower levels; v attractive vill; gd cent for walking, cycling & driving." 1 Apr-30 Sep. € 35.00   2014*

⊞ **PONT ST ESPRIT** *9D2* (10km NW Rural) *44.29808, 4.56535* Camping Les Cigales, 30760 Aiguèze [04 66 82 18 52; fax 04 66 82 25 20; www.camping-cigales.fr] N fr Pont-St Esprit on D6086 take D901 NW twd Barjac & D141 to St Martin-d'Ardèche. Site on L bef rv bdge. Avoid app fr St Martin-d'Ardèche over narr suspension bdge. Care at ent. Diff for lge units. Sm, mkd, shd, wc; mv service pnt; shwrs inc; EHU (4-10A) €3.13-5.88; gas; lndry; shop nr; rest nr; bbq; pool (htd); sw nr; wifi; 25% statics; dogs €2; adv bkg acc; ccard acc; CKE/CCI. "Helpful, friendly owner; easy walk to St Martin-d'Ardèche." € 21.00   2015*

PONT ST ESPRIT *9D2* (6km NW Rural) *44.30388, 4.58443* Camping Le Pontet, 07700 St Martin-d'Ardèche [04 75 04 63 07 or 04 75 98 76 24; fax 04 75 98 76 59; contact@campinglepontet.com; www.campinglepontet.com] N86 N of Pont-St Esprit; turn L onto D290 at sp Gorges de l'Ardèche & St Martin-d'Ardèche, site on R after 3km, sp. Med, mkd, pt shd, wc; chem disp; mv service pnt; shwrs inc; EHU (6A) €3.60 (rev pol); gas; lndry; shop; rest; snacks; bar; playgrnd; pool; sw nr; wifi; 5% statics; dogs €3; phone; Eng spkn; adv bkg acc; quiet; CKE/CCI. "Vg; helpful owners; peaceful out of ssn; facs stretched when busy; online bkg fee €10." ♦ 8 Apr-25 Sep. € 22.00   2017*

PONT ST ESPRIT *9D2* (8km NW Rural) *44.28950, 4.58923* **Camping Le Peyrolais, Route de Barjac, 30760 St Julien-de-Peyrolas [04 66 82 14 94; fax 04 66 82 31 70; contact@camping-lepeyrolais.com; www.camping-lepeyrolais.com]** N fr Pont-St. Esprit on D6086 turn L onto D901 sp Barjac. In 2.5km turn R at site sp, site in 500m up narr track on bank of Rv Ardèche. Med, mkd, pt shd, wc; chem disp; mv service pnt; shwrs inc; EHU (3-10A) €2.30-3.80; lndry; shop; rest; bar; playgrnd; sw nr; entmnt; wifi; TV; dogs €2; phone; adv bkg acc; quiet; ccard acc; horseriding; kayaking; fishing; bike hire; games area; canoe hire; CKE/CCI. "Attractive, well-maintained site in beautiful location; clean facs; hiking; friendly owners; vg; great site." ♦ 1 Apr-30 Sep. € 32.00 2014*

⊞ **PONT ST ESPRIT** *9D2* (8km NW Rural) *44.34423, 4.60534* **FFCC Camping Les Truffières, 201 Route de St Ramèze, 07700 St Marcel-d'Ardèche [04 75 04 68 35 or 06 82 01 28 30 (mob); soulier.valerie@wanadoo.fr; www.camping-les-truffieres.com]** S fr Bourg-St Andéol, turn W on D201; in vill foll sp to site located approx 3km W of vill. Med, mkd, pt shd, terr, wc (htd); mv service pnt; shwrs inc; EHU (6A) €6.60 (poss rev pol); gas; lndry; shop nr; rest; snacks; bar; playgrnd; pool; entmnt; 70% statics; dogs €1.60; adv bkg acc; quiet; CKE/CCI. "Friendly owners; glorious views; gd san facs; conv NH nr A7; v pleasant; tricky without motor mover (trees)." ♦ € 17.00 2017*

PONTAILLER SUR SAONE *6G1* (1km E Rural) *47.30817, 5.42518* **Camping La Chanoie, 46 Rue de la Chanoie, 21270 Pontailler-sur-Saône [03 80 36 10 58; fax 03 80 47 84 42; otpontailler@wanadoo.fr; www.pontailler-tourisme.fr]** E fr Pontailler-sur-Saône on D959; pass town hall & TO on R; after bdg take 1st L sp Camping; site in 500m. Fr W on D959 turn R bef bdg & bef ent town. Med, mkd, hdg, pt shd, wc (htd), chem disp; mv service pnt; fam bthrm; shwrs inc; EHU (6-10A) €2.85-4.10; lndry; shop nr; rest; snacks; bar; bbq; playgrnd; sw nr; red long stay; 80% statics; dogs €1.55; bus; adv bkg acc; quiet; games area; tennis; watersports adj; games rm; fishing adj; CKE/CCI. "Attractive sm town; polite & helpful owner; clean san facs; poss stretched high ssn; vg; OK NH." ♦ 15 Apr-15 Oct. € 21.00 2014*

PONTARLIER *6H2* (1km SE Rural) *46.90024, 6.37425* **FFCC Camping Le Larmont, Rue du Toulombief, 25300 Pontarlier [03 81 46 23 33; lelarmont.pontarlier@wanadoo.fr; www.camping-pontarlier.fr]** Leave N57 at Pontarlier Gare & foll site sp. Site uphill, turning nr Nestlé factory. Med, hdstg, unshd, terr, wc (htd); chem disp; mv service pnt; shwrs inc; EHU (10A) €4; gas; lndry; shop; snacks; bar; playgrnd; wifi; 20% statics; dogs €1; Eng spkn; adv bkg acc; horseriding adj; CKE/CCI. "Friendly; easy access; clean san facs; ltd pitches for awnings; site self out of office hrs; skiing winter; well-behaved zebra on site; excel; horseriding next to site; rec." ♦ 1 Jan-15 Nov & 15 Dec-31 Dec. € 25.00 2014*

PONTARLIER *6H2* (12km S Rural) *46.81176, 6.30326* **Camp Municipal, 8 Rue du Port, 25160 St Point-Lac [03 81 69 61 64 or 03 81 69 62 08 (Mairie); fax 03 81 69 65 74; camping-saintpointlac@orange.fr; www.camping-saintpointlac.fr]** Exit Pontarlier S on N57 dir Lausanne, turn R on D437 dir Malbuisson; in 6km turn R onto D129 thro Les Grangettes to St Point-Lac. Site sp on L. Med, mkd, hdstg, pt shd, wc (htd); chem disp; mv service pnt; shwrs inc; EHU (16A) €4.50; lndry; shop; rest nr; snacks; bar; bbq; playgrnd; beach adj; entmnt; wifi; 5% statics; dogs €1.50; Eng spkn; adv bkg rec; quiet; ccard acc; games area; CKE/CCI. "Delightful, well-kept lakeside site in beautiful position; sm pitches, some may be diff for large units to get in to; friendly staff; vg, clean san facs; m'van o'night area with facs opp; gd fishing, walking, birdwatching; sw; gd touring rec adv bkg wkends/high ssn; excel." ♦ 1 May-30 Sep. € 20.00 2017*

PONTAUBAULT *2E4* (4km E Rural) *48.61690, -1.29475* **Camp Municipal La Sélune, Rue de Boishue, 50220 Ducey [02 33 48 46 49 or 02 33 48 50 52; fax 02 33 48 87 59; ducey.tourisme@wanadoo.fr; www.ducey-tourisme.com]** Exit A84 junc 33 onto N176 E fr Pontaubault. In Ducey turn R onto D178 twd St Aubin-de-Terregatte. Ent at sports grnd in 200m. Sm, hdg, shd, pt sl, wc; chem disp; shwrs inc; EHU (5A) €1.85 (poss rev pol, poss long lead req); gas; lndry; shop; rest nr; bar nr; playgrnd; 10% statics; dogs €1.30; phone; bus; Eng spkn; adv bkg acc; quiet; tennis adj; CKE/CCI. "Well-maintained site; warden calls am & pm; poss travellers; excel; v clean facs; friendly, helpful owners." ♦ 1 Apr-30 Sep. € 17.50 2014*

PONTAUBAULT *2E4* (6km SW Coastal) *48.56583, -1.47111* **Campéole Camping St Grégoire, Le Haut Bourg, 50170 Servon [02 33 60 26 03; fax 02 33 60 68 65; saint-gregoire@campeole.com; www.camping-mont-saint-michel.com or www.campeole.com]** Foll N175 fr Pontaubault twd Pontorson. After 6km site sp on R twd Servon vill. Med, mkd, hdg, hdstg, pt shd, wc; chem disp; fam bthrm; shwrs; EHU (6A) inc; lndry; shop; bbq; playgrnd; pool; wifi; TV; 30% statics; dogs €2.60; adv bkg acc; ccard acc; games rm; CKE/CCI. "Conv ferries; quiet but some rd noise on S side of site; useful stop en rte to Cherbourg." 5 Apr-21 Sep. € 35.00 2014*

PONTAUBAULT *2E4* (0km W Urban) *48.62983, -1.35205* **Camping La Vallée de la Sélune, 7 Rue Maréchal Leclerc, 50220 Pontaubault [02 33 60 39 00; campselune@wanadoo.fr; www.camping-manche.com]** Foll sp to Pontaubault (well sp fr all dirs). In vill head twd Avranches. Turn L immed bef bdge over Rv Sélune. In 100m turn L, site strt in 100m, well sp. Med, mkd, pt shd, pt sl, wc; chem disp; shwrs inc; EHU (10A) inc; lndry; shop; snacks; bar; playgrnd; red long stay; wifi; 10% statics; dogs €1.30; adv bkg rec; ccard acc; horseriding nr; fishing adj; golf nr; tennis adj; CKE/CCI. "Relaxing, clean, tidy, pleasant site in sm vill; vg, clean san facs; conv Mont St Michel & Cherbourg ferries; gd NH; cycling nr; friendly Yorkshire owner; on cycle rte." ♦ 1 Apr-20 Oct. € 15.00 2018*

PONTCHATEAU

PONTCHATEAU 2G3 (7km W Rural) 47.44106, -2.15981
Le Château du Deffay, Ste Reine-de-Bretagne, 44160 Pontchâteau [02 40 88 00 57; fax 02 40 01 66 55; info@camping-le-deffay.com; www.camping-le-deffay.com] Leave N165 at junc 13 onto D33 twd Herbignac. Site on R approx 1.5km after Le Calvaire de la Madeleine x-rds, 270m past Chateau ent. Site sp fr by-pass. Lge, hdg, mkd, pt shd, pt sl, terr, wc; chem disp; mv service pnt; fam bthrm; shwrs inc; EHU (6-10A) inc poss rev pol; lndry; shop; rest; snacks; bar; bbq (charcoal, gas); playgrnd; pool (covrd, htd); paddling pool; entmnt; wifi; TV; 18% statics; dogs €1; Eng spkn; adv bkg acc; quiet; ccard acc; lake fishing; bike hire; tennis; games rm; golf 10km; CKE/CCI. "Excel, beautiful site with trees in grnds of chateau by lake; free pedalos; friendly, helpful, welcoming staff; excel clean san facs; some pitches lakeside & not fenced; mkt Mon; gd value rest." ♦ 1 May-30 Sep. € 30.00 2015*

> **"That's changed – Should I let the Club know?"**
>
> If you find something on site that's different from the site entry, fill in a report and let us know. See camc.com/europereport.

PONTGIBAUD 7B4 (3km NE Rural) 45.84436, 2.87672
Camping Bel-Air, 63230 St Ours [04 73 88 72 14; contact@campingbelair.fr; www.campingbelair.fr] Exit A89 junc 26 onto D941 dir Pontgibaud; cont past Pontigibaud; in 1.5km turn L onto D943; site in 1.3km on L. Site sp. Med, mkd, shd, pt sl, wc; chem disp; mv service pnt; fam bthrm; shwrs inc; EHU (6A) €3.30; gas; lndry; shop nr; rest; snacks; bar; bbq; playgrnd; 5% statics; dogs €1; Eng spkn; adv bkg acc; quiet; golf; games area; CKE/CCI. "Peaceful, basic site in beautiful area; helpful owner; clean facs, ltd LS; conv Vulcania; excel." ♦ 1 May-27 Sep. € 18.00 2013*

PONTGIBAUD 7B4 (0km S Rural) 45.82978, 2.84517
FFCC Camp Municipal La Palle, 3 Avenue du General de Gaulle, 63230 Pontgibaud [04 73 88 96 99 or 04 73 88 70 42 (LS); fax 04 73 88 77 77; mairie. pontgibaud@wanadoo.fr; www.ville-pontgibaud.fr/camping-municipal] At W end of Pontgibaud turn S over bdge on D986 & site in 500m on L, past site for La Palle Chalets. Med, hdg, mkd, hdstg, pt shd, wc (htd); chem disp; mv service pnt; shwrs inc; EHU (10-16A) inc; lndry; shop nr; rest; bbq; playgrnd; sw nr; red long stay; entmnt; wifi; dogs; Eng spkn; adv bkg acc; games area; tennis 400m; CKE/CCI. "Pleasant, clean, tidy site nr sm rv; helpful staff; gd touring base; pop concerts once a week high ssn; conv Vulcania exhibition cent; bike hire 400m; v lge hdg plots; minimal rd & rlwy noise; well maintained; friendly; easy flat walk to town; gd base for Puy de Dome." ♦ 15 Apr-30 Sep. € 17.00 2018*

PONTORSON 2E4 (1km NW Rural) 48.55805, -1.51444 **Camping Haliotis**, Chemin des Soupirs, 50170 Pontorson [02 33 68 11 59; fax 02 33 58 95 36; camping.haliotis@wanadoo.fr; www.camping-haliotis-mont-saint-michel.com] Exit A84 junc 33 onto N175 dir Pontorson; foll sp Cent Ville/Mont-St-Michel. Site well sp. Lge, mkd, hdg, pt shd, pt sl, wc (htd); chem disp; mv service pnt; fam bthrm; shwrs inc; EHU (10-16A) inc (poss rev pol); gas; lndry; shop; rest nr; snacks; bar; bbq; playgrnd; pool (htd); paddling pool; wifi; 25% statics; dogs €2; phone; bus 400m; Eng spkn; adv bkg rec; ccard acc; boating; games area; tennis; rv fishing; games rm; bike hire; sauna; CKE/CCI. "Popular, well-kept, busy, superb site; lge pitches; friendly, helpful owners; immac, unisex san facs; lovely pool & bar; rvside walk to town; cycle rte/bus to Mont St Michel; highly rec; serviced pitches; pitches with private bthrms avail; spa; library; avoid pitches 77-89 due to noise fr bins; excel." ♦ 30 Mar-4 Nov. € 30.00 2018*

PONTORSON 2E4 (8km NW Rural) 48.59415, -1.59855 **Camping Les Couesnons**, Route de St Malo, 35610 Roz-sur-Couesnon [02 99 80 26 86; contact@les-couesnons.com; www.lescouesnons.com] Exit N175/N176 NW onto D797 dir St Malo on coastal rd; site sp 700m past Roz-sur-Couesnon on R. Turn R at Les Couesnons Rest. Site behind. Sm, hdg, mkd, pt shd, wc (htd); chem disp; fam bthrm; shwrs inc; EHU (6A) €3; lndry; rest; snacks; bar; bbq (charcoal, gas); playgrnd; red long stay; wifi; TV; 10% statics; dogs €2; Eng spkn; adv bkg acc; quiet; ccard acc; games rm; games area; CKE/CCI. "Excel site; Mont St Michel 8km; ACSI acc; vg, spotless, htd facs; gd rest & bar; highly rec." ♦ 1 Apr-31 Oct. € 23.00 2017*

⊞ **PONTRIEUX** 2E3 (1km W Rural) 48.69493, -3.16365 **Camping de Traou Mélédern (Moisan)**, Traou Mélédern, 22260 Pontrieux [02 96 95 69 27; campingpontrieux@free.fr; www.camping-pontrieux.com] N on D787 fr Guingamp; on ent town sq turn sharp L sp Traou Mélédern, cross rv bdge & turn R alongside church. Site in 400m. Access poss diff for lge o'fits; steep exit on 1-way system. Med, mkd, hdg, pt shd, pt sl, wc; chem disp; shwrs inc; EHU (8A) €3.50; lndry; shop nr; bbq; playgrnd; dogs €1; phone; Eng spkn; adv bkg acc; CKE/CCI. "In orchard; excel touring base; friendly owner; quiet but some daytime factory noise; steep junc nr site poss problem for lge o'fits; gd." ♦ € 17.50 2016*

PORGE, LE 7C1 (9km W Coastal) 44.89430, -1.20181 **Camping La Grigne**, Ave de l'Océan, 33680 Le Porge [05 56 26 54 88; fax 05 56 26 52 07; info@lagrigne.com; www.camping-leporge.fr] Fr Bordeaux ring rd take N215 twd Lacanau. In 22km at Ste Hélène D5 to Saumos & onto Le Porge. Site on L of rd to Porge-Océan in approx 9km. V lge, mkd, shd, pt sl, terr, wc; chem disp; shwrs inc; EHU (10A) €5; gas; lndry; shop; snacks; bar; playgrnd; beach 600m; red long stay; TV; dogs €1.90; adv bkg acc; quiet; tennis; games area. "Vg facs; great beach; excel cycle path network." ♦ 1 Apr-30 Sep. € 22.00 2016*

PORNIC 2G3 (10km N Urban) 47.20315, -2.03716
**Camping du Grand Fay, Rue du Grand Fay, 44320
St Père-en-Retz** [02 40 21 72 89; fax 02 40 82 40 27;
legrandfay@aol.com; www.camping-grandfay.com]
Fr Mairie in cent St Père-en-Retz take D78 E twds
Frossay. After 500m turn R into Rue des Sports, after
200m turn L into Rue du Grand Fay. Site on L in 200m
adj sports cent. Med, mkd, pt shd, pt sl, wc; shwrs inc;
EHU (6A) €3.80; lndry; shop nr; playgrnd; pool (htd);
10% statics; dogs €2; quiet; lake fishing adj; games
area; CKE/CCI. "Pleasant site nr sandy beaches." ♦
1 Apr-15 Oct. € 20.00   2014*

> "I like to fill in the reports as I travel from site to site"
>
> You'll find report forms at the back of this guide, or you can fill them in online at camc.com/europereport.

PORNIC 2G3 (4km E Rural) 47.11885, -2.07296
**Camping Le Patisseau, 29 Rue du Patisseau, 44210
Pornic** [02 40 82 10 39; fax 02 40 82 22 81; contact@
lepatisseau.com; www.lepatisseau.com]
Fr N or S on D213, take slip rd D751 Nantes. At
rndabt take exit sp to Le Patisseau, foll sp. Med,
mkd, hdstg, hdg, pt shd, pt sl, wc (htd); chem disp;
mv service pnt; fam bthrm; shwrs inc; EHU (6A)
inc; lndry; shop; rest; snacks; bar; bbq; playgrnd;
pool (covrd, htd); paddling pool; beach sand 2.5km;
entmnt; wifi; TV; 35% statics; dogs €6; Eng spkn;
adv bkg rec; quiet; ccard acc; sauna; fitness rm;
waterslide; golf 2km; tennis 1km; bike hire; games
area; games rm; jacuzzi. "Excel, modern, family
site; modern san facs block - lovely shwrs; 1hr walk
on path fr back of site to Pornic." ♦ 7 Apr-12 Sep.
€ 42.00   2017*

See advertisement above

PORNIC 2G3 (5km E Coastal) 47.09748, -2.0525
**Airotel Camping Village La Boutinardière, 23 Rue
de la Plage de la Boutinard, 44210 Pornic** [02 40 82
05 68; fax 02 40 82 49 01; info@laboutinardiere.
com; www.camping-boutinardiere.com]
SW fr Nantes on D723; after abt 6km turn L on D751
sp Pornic; after abt 30km L at 2nd rndabt onto D13
sp la Bernerie en Retz; site rd on R after abt 3km in
la Rogere abt 50m bef rndabt; recep on R; park on
gravel next to low walls on R. Lge, hdg, pt shd, pt sl,
serviced pitches; wc; chem disp; mv service pnt; fam
bthrm; shwrs inc; EHU (6-10A) €5-6 (poss rev pol);
gas; lndry; shop; rest; snacks; bar; bbq; playgrnd;
pool (covrd, htd); paddling pool; beach sand 200m;
sw nr; red long stay; entmnt; wifi; TV; 15% statics;
dogs €5; bus nrby; Eng spkn; adv bkg acc; quiet; ccard
acc; waterslide; bike hire; tennis; sauna; golf 5km;
games rm; jacuzzi; CKE/CCI. "Excel family site; vg pool
complex; activities; v busy high ssn; Pornic interesting
town." ♦ 1 Apr-30 Sep. € 62.00   2014*

See advertisement on next page

PORNIC 2G3 (6km SE Rural/Coastal) 47.08450,
-2.03650 **Camping Les Ecureuils, 24 Ave Gilbert
Burlot, 44760 La Bernerie-en-Retz** [02 40 82 76
95; fax 02 40 64 79 52; camping.les-ecureuils@
wanadoo.fr; www.camping-les-ecureuils.com]
Fr Pornic take D13 S for 5km, then D66 for 1km; site sp.
Lge, hdg, pt shd, pt sl, wc; chem disp; fam bthrm; shwrs
inc; EHU (6-10A) €4; lndry; shop nr; snacks; bar; bbq;
playgrnd; pool (htd); paddling pool; beach sand 350m;
entmnt; 30% statics; dogs (up to 10kg only) €4; Eng
spkn; adv bkg acc; quiet; ccard acc; waterslide; golf 5km;
tennis; CKE/CCI. "Excel; children's club; v clean modern
san facs; hg rec." ♦ 1 Apr-30 Sep. € 48.00   2017*

PORNIC 2G3 (10km S Coastal) 47.07500, -2.00741
**Campsite Les Brillas, Le Bois des Treans, 44870
Les Moutiers-en-Retz** [02 40 82 79 78; fax 02 40
64 79 60; info@campinglesbrillas.com; www.
campinglesbrillas.com] Fr Nantes ring rd, take D723
SW. Take exit D751 twd Pornic. Turn L on D66. Foll sp.
Med, mkd, hdg, wc; chem disp; fam bthrm; EHU (6A);
lndry; Eng spkn; quiet; CCI. "Sm coastal vill; easy walk
to beach; excel; lovely location & beach; basic facs."
14 Apr-1 Oct. € 31.00   2017*

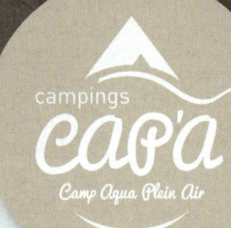

campings cap'a
Camp Aqua Plein Air

5 Camping villages on the Atlantic coast

LE PALACE
★★★★
F-33780 Soulac-sur-Mer
(400 m from the beach)
☎ 0033 5 56 09 80 22
www.camping-palace.com

LA BOUTINARDIÈRE
★★★★
F-44210 Pornic
(200 m from the beach)
☎ 0033 2 40 82 05 68
www.camping-boutinardiere.com

LE DOMAINE D'INLY
★★★★★
F-56760 Pénestin
(1,8 km from the beach)
☎ 0033 2 99 90 35 09
www.camping-inly.com

L'OCÉAN
★★★★★
F-44490 Le Croisic
(150 m from the beach)
☎ 0033 2 40 23 07 69
www.camping-ocean.com

LE DOMAINE DE LÉVENO
★★★★
F-44350 Guérande
(7 km from La Baule beach)
☎ 0033 2 40 24 79 30
www.camping-leveno.com

www.campaquapleinair.com

fannygraphisme@gmail.com

PORNIC 2G3 (5km W Rural) 47.14079, -2.15306
Camping La Tabardière, 44770 La Plaine-sur-Mer [02 40 21 58 83; fax 02 40 21 02 68; info@camping-la-tabardiere.com; www.camping-la-tabardiere.com] Take D13 NW out of Pornic sp Préfailles & La Plaine-sur-Mer. In about 5.5km turn R (nr water tower). Foll sps to site, about 1km fr main rd. NB C'vans not allowed in Pornic town cent, use by-pass. Lge, mkd, hdg, hdstg, pt shd, terr, wc (htd); chem disp; mv service pnt; fam bthrm; shwrs inc; EHU (8A) €5; gas; lndry; shop; snacks; bar; bbq (charcoal, gas); playgrnd; pool (covrd, htd); paddling pool; beach sand 3km; entmnt; wifi; TV; 40% statics; dogs €3.50; Eng spkn; adv bkg acc; quiet; ccard acc; tennis; games rm; fishing 3km; waterslide; horseriding 5km; CKE/CCI. "Excel, peaceful site; multi-sport area; no o'fits over 7.5m high ssn; vg facs for families; v clean unisex san facs; gates clsd 2230-0800; recep clsd lunchtime." ♦ 12 Apr-20 Sep. € 47.00   2014*

> **"We must tell the Club about that great site we found"**
>
> Get your site reports in by mid-August and we'll do our best to get your updates into the next edition.

PORNIC 2G3 (9km NW Coastal) 47.15995, -2.16813
Camping Thar-Cor, 43 Ave du Cormier, 44730 St Michel-Chef-Chef [02 40 27 82 81; fax 02 40 27 81 51; camping@letharcor.com; www.camping-le-thar-cor.com] Fr Pornic take D213 twds Saint Michel Chef Chef. Turn L onto Rue de la Dalonnerie. L at rndabt onto D96. Foll sp to site. Lge, hdg, mkd, pt shd, wc (htd); chem disp; mv service pnt; fam bthrm; shwrs inc; EHU (10A) €5; lndry; shop nr; rest; snacks; bar; bbq; playgrnd; pool; beach sand 200m; twin axles; entmnt; wifi; TV; 50% statics; dogs €3; phone; Eng spkn; adv bkg rec; quiet; ccard acc; games area. "Vg town site, mkt at Tharon-Plage high ssn; 200m to promenade & sandy beach; friendly staff; mainly French; beach excel." ♦ 10 Apr-25 Sep. € 26.50   2016*

PORT EN BESSIN HUPPAIN 3D1 (1km N Coastal) 49.34693, -0.77095 **Camping Port'land, Chemin du Sémaphore, 14520 Port-en-Bessin [02 31 51 07 06; fax 02 31 51 76 49; campingportland@wanadoo.fr; www.camping-portland.com]** Site sp fr D514 W of Port-en-Bessin. Lge, mkd, hdg, hdstg, pt shd, wc (htd); chem disp; mv service pnt; shwrs inc; EHU (16A) €5; lndry; shop; rest; snacks; bar; bbq; playgrnd; pool (covrd, htd); paddling pool; beach sand 4km; red long stay; entmnt; wifi; TV; 30% statics; dogs €3; Eng spkn; adv bkg acc; ccard acc; waterslide; tennis 800m; games area; games rm; CKE/CCI. "Pleasant site; friendly, helpful staff; vg san facs; extra charge lger pitches; excel touring base for landing beaches etc; well kept clean, well spaced lge hdged pitches; well positioned for Bayeaux, Arromanche and D Day museums and cemetaries." ♦ 1 Apr-30 Oct. € 37.50   2016*

PORTIRAGNES PLAGE

PORT LESNEY 6H2 (0km N Rural) 47.00358, 5.82366
Camping Les Radeliers, 1 Rue Edgar Faure, 39600 Port-Lesney [03 84 73 81 44; camp.portlesney@aliceadsl.fr; www.camping-les-radeliers.com] N fr Arbois on N83, cross junc with D472 & turn L in 1.5km sp Port-Lesney. Site sp. Med, mkd, pt shd, wc; chem disp; shwrs inc; EHU (13A) €4; lndry; shop nr; rest nr; snacks; bar nr; playgrnd; sw nr; twin axles; 2% statics; dogs €2; bus adj; Eng spkn; adv bkg acc; quiet; canoeing, kayak hire; CKE/CCI. "Tranquil site in delightful rvside setting; helpful staff; poss youth groups high ssn; gd walking & cycling; Salt Mine Museum in Salins-les-Bains worth visit; canyoning; bar 200m; plenty rvside pitches." ♦ 1 May-30 Sep. € 23.00   2016*

PORT SUR SAONE 6F2 (1km S Rural) 47.68056, 6.03937 **Camp Municipal Parc de la Maladière, 70170 Port-sur-Saône [03 84 78 18 00 (Mairie); fax 03 84 78 18 09; serviceculturel@gmail.com; www.ville-port-sur-saone.fr]** Take N19 SE fr Langres or NW fr Vesoul. Site sp in vill bet rv & canal off D6 at municipal bathing area. Med, hdg, pt shd, wc (cont); own san rec; chem disp; shwrs inc; EHU (6A) €3 (poss rev pol); lndry; shop nr; rest nr; bar nr; playgrnd; adv bkg acc; quiet; ccard acc; fishing; tennis; CKE/CCI. "Peaceful site on island; rvside cycle path; gd walks; gd sh stay/NH; san facs basic & tired; pool adj; 25m cable needed; vg value." ♦ 15 May-15 Sep. € 15.40   2017*

⊞ **PORT VENDRES** 10G1 (2km E Urban) 42.51775, 3.11314 **Aire Communale des Tamarins, Route de la Jetée, 66660 Port-Vendres [04 68 82 07 54]** Fr D914 at Port-Vendres at Banyuls side of town turn N on D86B sp Port de Commerce & Aire de Camping-Cars. Foll sp to site on R in 700m. Sm, hdstg, pt shd, wc; own san req; chem disp; mv service pnt; shop nr; rest nr; bar nr; playgrnd; beach shgl 100m. "NH, m'vans only; walking dist rlwy stn; a bit run down (Jun 2009); gd; payment collected am; popular." € 10.00   2016*

PORTIRAGNES PLAGE 10F1 (1km N Coastal) 43.28003, 3.36593 **Camping Les Sablons, Plage-Est, 34420 Portiragnes-Plage [04 67 90 90 55; fax 04 67 90 82 91; les.sablons@wanadoo.fr; www.les-sablons.com]** Fr A9 exit Béziers Est junc 35 onto N112. Then take D37 S to Portiragnes-Plage & foll sp. V lge, mkd, shd, wc; chem disp; mv service pnt; fam bthrm; shwrs inc; EHU (6A) inc; gas; lndry; shop; rest; snacks; bar; bbq; playgrnd; pool (htd); beach sand adj; entmnt; 50% statics; dogs €4; phone; Eng spkn; adv bkg acc; quiet; ccard acc; waterslide; boating; games area; tennis; bike hire; fishing. "Gd site on beach; modern san facs; diving; nightly disco but quiet after midnight." ♦ 1 Apr-30 Sep. € 46.00   2012*

Les Embruns — LE POULDU PLAGES | CAMPING CARAVANING | CLOHARS-CARNOËT — BRETAGNE

- 250 m from sandy beaches, Gwénaelle welcomes you in her particulary well maintained campsite - in the heart of Le Pouldu Village
- First class facilities and amenities in a green and floral environment
- Covered swimming pool heated - Waterslides
- Sauna - hammam - fitness - beauty salon
- Restaurant & take-away service • Mini market and fresh bread

www.camping-les-embruns.com
(0033) 2 98 39 91 07
BRETAGNE SUD

POSES 3D2 (2km SE Urban) 49.29552, 1.24914 **Base de Loisirs, Rue du Souvenir French, 27740 Poses [02 32 59 13 13; lery.poses@wanadoo.fr; www.lery-poses.fr]** Fr Poses head NE on Rue du Bac twrd Rue das Masures, take 1st R onto Rue des Masures, turn R onto Rue du Roussillon, after 350m turn L onto Rue du Souvenir Francais, site after 220m on L. Lge, pt shd, wc; chem disp; shwrs; EHU (16A); beach; table tennis; canoeing. "Gd san facs; gravel rdway throughout site; water ski; hiking; pedalo hire; mini golf; site adj to & overlooking the Rv Seine with direct access to the rvside; plenty of pitches for tourers; beach volleyball; supmkt 5km; older san block needs updating (2018)." 1 Apr-31 Oct. € 15.00   2018*

POUANCE 2F4 (2km N Rural) 47.74850, -1.17841 **Camp Muncipal La Roche Martin, 23 Rue des Etangs, 49420 Pouancé [02 41 92 43 97 or 02 41 92 41 08 (Mairie); fax 02 41 92 62 30]** Take D6 (sp St Aignan) N fr town. After level x-ing turn L onto D72 (sp La Guerche-de-Bretagne). In 300m, site on L. Sm, mkd, pt sl, terr, wc; mv service pnt; shwrs; EHU (10A); gas; shop nr; rest nr; bar nr; playgrnd; adv bkg rec; watersports; tennis; games area. "Well-kept, friendly site o'looking lge lake; dir access to lake; noise fr rd & sailing school." 1 Apr-30 Sep.   2012*

POUILLY EN AUXOIS 6G1 (1km NW Urban) 47.26534, 4.54804 **Camping Vert Auxois, 15 Voûte du Canal du Bourgogne, 21320 Pouilly-en-Auxois [03 80 90 71 89; contact@camping-vert-auxois.com; www.camping-vert-auxois.fr]** Exit A6 at Dijon/Pouilly-en-Auxois onto A38. Exit A38 at junc 24. Thro vill & turn L after church on R, site sp adj Burgandy canal. Sm, hdg, pt shd, wc; chem disp; mv service pnt; shwrs inc; EHU (6-10A) long cable req; lndry; shop; rest; snacks; bar; playgrnd; wifi; 10% statics; dogs; bus 300m; Eng spkn; adv bkg acc; quiet; ccard acc; rv fishing adj; CKE/CCI. "Beautiful position, relaxed & peaceful; lge pitches, unusual layout; run by delightful, friendly couple; gd cycling; interesting area; sh walk to sm town; vg; san facs poss stretched." ♦ 1 Apr-7 Oct. € 23.00   2018*

POUILLY SUR LOIRE 4G3 (1km N Rural) 47.28742, 2.94627 **Camp Municipal Le Malaga, Rue des Champs-sur-Loire, Les Loges, 58150 Pouilly-sur-Loire [03 86 39 14 54 or 03 86 58 74 38 (LS); www.ot-pouillysurloire.fr]** Fr S exit A77 junc 26 onto D28a, turn L onto D59/D4289 W, bef rv bdge turn R, site in 1km on rv. Fr N on ent vill turn R at site sp into narr rd. Turn R along rv as above. Med, pt shd, wc; chem disp; shwrs inc; EHU (10A) inc (poss long lead req & poss rev pol); lndry; shop; snacks; bar; bbq; playgrnd; dogs €1; phone; Eng spkn. "Beautifully kept site on banks of Loire; busy NH; spacious but uneven pitches; mixed reports san facs; poss youth groups; beautiful area; wine tasting nrby; no twin axles or o'fits over 5m; poss mosquitoes; excel; delightful site adj to the Loire, spacious and leafy areas, wonderful wines in Pouilly and Sancerre, excel museum closeby." ♦ 1 Jun-10 Sep. € 14.00   2014*

POULDU, LE 2F2 (0km N Coastal) 47.76850, -3.54540 **Camping Les Embruns, 2 Rue du Philosophe Alain, Clohars-Carnoët, 29360 Le Pouldu [02 98 39 91 07; fax 02 98 39 97 87; camping-les-embruns@wanadoo.fr; www.camping-les-embruns.com]** Exit N165 dir Quimperlé Cent, onto D16 to Clohars-Carnoët. Cont on D16/D24/D1214 to Le Pouldu. Site on R on ent 1-way traff system. Site sp. Lge, hdstg, mkd, hdg, pt shd, terr, serviced pitches; wc (htd); chem disp; mv service pnt; fam bthrm; shwrs inc; EHU (10A) inc; gas; lndry; shop; rest; snacks; bar; bbq; playgrnd; pool (covrd, htd); paddling pool; beach sand 250m; TV; 40% statics; dogs €2.70; bus nrby; Eng spkn; adv bkg acc; quiet; ccard acc; watersports; games area; tennis; horseriding nr; tennis 200m; games rm; bike hire; fishing; CKE/CCI. "Excel family-run site in great location; children's farm; luxury pitches extra charge; friendly, helpful owners; vg clean san facs; superb facs; gd walking along coastal paths; cycle rtes; great for dogs; town was home of Paul Gauguin; highly rec." ♦ 6 Apr-22 Sep. € 31.50   2017*

See advertisement

POULDU, LE *2F2* (2km N Coastal) *47.78401, -3.54463*
FFCC Camping de Croas An Ter, Quelvez, Le Pouldu, 29360 Clohars-Carnoët [02 98 39 94 19 or 06 24 88 68 20 (mob); campingcroasanter@orange.fr; www.campingcroasanter.com] On D49 fr Quimperlé to Le Pouldu. Site on L 3km after junc with D224. Med, pt shd, pt sl, wc; chem disp; mv service pnt; shwrs inc; EHU (6A) €3.20; lndry; shop nr; rest nr; bar nr; playgrnd; beach 1.5km; wifi; dogs; Eng spkn; quiet; CKE/CCI. "Lge pitches; friendly owners; cash only; gd bathing & sailing; walks in wood & rv fr site; Tues mkt; vg." ♦ 1 May-15 Sep. € 13.60   2016*

POULDU, LE *2F2* (1km NE Rural) *47.77274, -3.54433*
Camping Keranquernat, 29360 Keranquernat [02 98 39 92 32; fax 02 98 39 99 84; camping.keranquernat@wanadoo.fr; www.camping-keranquernat.com] Fr Quimperlé D16 to Clohars-Carnoët, then D24 to Le Pouldu - twd port; turn R at x-rds nr Ar Men Résidence; site ent immed on R. Fr S on N165 exit junc 45 sp Guidel; in 1km turn W onto D162/D224, then foll sp Le Pouldu; site sp at town ent. Med, mkd, hdg, pt shd, wc; chem disp; fam bthrm; shwrs; EHU (3-5A) €3-4; lndry; shop nr; rest nr; bbq; playgrnd; pool (htd); paddling pool; beach sand 700m; TV; dogs €0.50; adv bkg acc; quiet; bike hire; fishing; sailing; tennis; games rm; CKE/CCI. "Beautifully-kept, pretty site; welcoming owners; highly rec." 1 May-6 Sep. € 27.30   2014*

POULDU, LE *2F2* (2km E Rural/Coastal) *47.77466, -3.50616* Camping Les Jardins de Kergal, Route des Plages, 56520 Guidel [02 97 05 98 18; fax 02 97 32 88 27; jardins.kergal@wanadoo.fr; www.camping-lorient.com] Fr N165 Brest-Nantes take Guidel exit; thro Guidel & onto Guidel-Plages; camp sp in 1km. Lge, hdg, hdstg, mkd, pt shd, pt sl, wc; chem disp; fam bthrm; shwrs inc; EHU (10A) inc; gas; lndry; shop nr; rest; snacks; bar; bbq; playgrnd; pool (covrd); beach sand 1.5km; entmnt; wifi; TV; 75% statics; dogs €3; adv bkg acc; quiet; waterslide; games area; tennis; games rm; bike hire; CKE/CCI. "Friendly, helpful, welcoming staff; well-run, peaceful site; conv beaches & touring." ♦ 29 Mar-30 Sep. € 41.00   2013*

POULE LES ECHARMEAUX *9A2* (2km W Rural) *46.15028, 4.45419* Camp Municipal Les Echarmeaux, 69870 Poule-les-Echarmeaux [06 89 90 33 64 (mob) or 06 79 30 46 62; fax 04 74 03 68 71; www.poulelesecharmeaux.eu] Turn E off D385 to Poule-les-Echarmeaux, site sp. Sm, hdg, pt shd, terr, wc; shwrs inc; EHU inc; shop nr; playgrnd; adv bkg rec. "Beautifully situated site adj lake; nr Beaujolais wine area; excel sh stay; mkd walks." 1 May-30 Sep. € 11.00   2013*

PRATS DE MOLLO LA PRESTE

PRADES *8G4* (10km NE Urban) *42.64269, 2.53367*
Camping Lac De Vinca (formerly Municipal Les Escoumes), Rue des Escoumes, 66320 Vinça [04 68 05 84 78 or 06 72 32 27 07 (mob); campinglesescoumes@orange.fr; www.camping-lac-de-vinca.com/EN] Fr Perpignan take N116 W twd Andorra. 10km E of Prades in vill of Vinça take 1st L foll camp sps to site (400m). Vinca 32km W of Perpignan. Med, mkd, pt shd, pt sl, wc; chem disp; mv service pnt; shwrs inc; EHU (6-10A) €3; gas; lndry; shop nr; rest nr; bar nr; sw; wifi; 20% statics; dogs €3.50; Eng spkn; quiet; fishing; bike hire. "Beautiful, quiet, excel site; helpful staff; gd sized pitches; gd touring base; lake not suitable for toddlers (no sand, entry via steps); rec." ♦ 1 Apr-31 Oct. € 17.00   2017*

PRALOGNAN LA VANOISE *9B4* (1km S Rural) *45.37667, 6.72236* Camping Le Parc Isertan, Route de l'Isertan, 73710 Pralognan-la-Vanoise [04 79 08 75 24; fax 04 79 08 76 13; camping@camping-isertan.com; www.camping-isertan.com] Fr Moûtiers, take D915 E to Pralognan. Pass under concrete bdge & foll camping sp. Site behind pool adj municipal site. Lge, hdstg, pt shd, terr, wc (htd); chem disp; mv service pnt; fam bthrm; shwrs inc; EHU (2-10A) €4-6.50; shop nr; rest; snacks; bar; bbq; playgrnd; red long stay; 10% statics; dogs €1.50; phone; Eng spkn; adv bkg acc; quiet; ccard acc; horseriding 500m; CKE/CCI. "Peaceful site with superb scenery; recep in hotel on site; vg walking; sports cent adj; htd covrd pool adj; cable car in vill; drying rm & ski boot rm; cross country skiing at side of site; free naveltte to ski lift; new spa facs (2012); excel site." ♦ 18 Dec-18 Apr & 21 May-24 Sep. € 24.00   2012*

PRALOGNAN LA VANOISE *9B4* (14km NW Rural) *45.44274, 6.64874* Camp Municipal Le Chevelu, Route de Chevelu, 73350 Bozel [06 49 23 10 34 or 04 79 55 03 06 (LS); camping.lechevelu.bozel@gmail.com; www.camping-bozel.com] Foll D915 thro Bozel dir Pralognan. Site on R immed beyond vill. Med, mkd, hdstg, shd, pt sl, terr, wc; chem disp; mv service pnt; shwrs inc; EHU (6-10A) €3.50-4.50; lndry; shop nr; rest; snacks; playgrnd; sw nr; dogs €1.50; phone; Eng spkn; adv bkg acc; quiet; lake fishing 1km; CKE/CCI. "In wood by rv; excel walking & climbing; vg; pleasant vill; lunchtime rest v popular with locals." ♦ 1 Jun-30 Sep. € 16.40   2014*

PRATS DE MOLLO LA PRESTE *8H4* (12km E Rural) *42.41200, 2.61800* Camping Domaine Le Clols (Naturist), 66260 St Laurent-de-Cerdans [04 68 39 51 68; info@leclols.com; www.leclols.com] Fr A9 at Le Boulou take D115 dir Prats-de-Mollo; 6km past Arles-sur-Tech take D3 on L sp St Laurent-de-Cerdans; at La Forge-del-Mitg turn sharp L sp Le Clols; site on R in 3km (narr, winding rd). Sm, pt shd, pt sl, wc; chem disp; shwrs inc; EHU (5-10A) €3-3.95; gas; lndry; shop; snacks; playgrnd; pool; red long stay; TV; 10% statics; dogs €2; adv bkg acc; quiet; CKE/CCI. "Gd views; friendly British owners; gd walks fr site." ♦ 1 May-30 Sep. € 24.00   2013*

PRAZ SUR ARLY

⊞ **PRAZ SUR ARLY** *9B3* (1km W Urban) *45.83628, 6.56747* **Chantalouette, 384 Route du Val d'arly, 74120 Praz sur Arly [04 50 21 90 25 or 06 70 06 19 71 (mob); chantalouette@prazarly.fr; www. prazarly.fr]** On D1212, Ugine to Megeve. Site on L at southern end of vill. Sm, hdstg, pt shd, wc (htd); chem disp; shwrs inc; EHU (6-10A) €4.60-€8.50; gas; lndry; shop nr; rest nr; bar nr; twin axles; wifi; dogs €0.40; bus adj; Eng spkn; adv bkg acc; quiet; ccard acc; games rm; CKE/CCI. "Walking dist to ski bus; vg." € 19.00   2015*

> **"I need an on-site restaurant"**
>
> We do our best to make sure site information is correct, but it is always best to check any must-have facilities are still available or will be open during your visit.

PRECY SOUS THIL *6G1* (0km NW Rural) *47.38721, 4.30645* **Camp Municipal du Parc de l'Hôtel de Ville, 17 Rue de l'Hôtel de Ville, 21390 Précy-sous-Thil [03 80 64 57 18 (Mairie); fax 03 80 64 43 37; precysousthil@ orange.fr; www.cotedor-tourisme.com]** Exit A6 at junc 23 Bierre-lès-Semur exit onto D980 to Précy. Site sp in vill. Sm, pt shd, pt sl, wc; shwrs inc; EHU (6A) inc; lndry; shop nr; rest nr; bar nr; playgrnd; entmnt; TV; 10% statics; dogs €1.30; quiet; tennis nr; horseriding. "In grnds of Town Hall; warden calls 1900-2100; bar 300m; rv adj; mostly sl pitches; conv NH on way S." Easter-1 Nov. € 12.00   2013*

PREMERY *4G1* (1km NW Urban) *47.17804, 3.33692* **Camp Municipal Le Plan D'eau (Les Prés de la Ville), 58700 Prémery [03 86 37 99 42 or 03 86 68 12 40 (Mairie); fax 03 86 37 98 72; mairie-premery@ wanadoo.fr; www.mairie-premery.fr]** N fr Nevers on D977 to Prémery; turn R after 2nd rndabt. Site sp on D977. Med, pt shd, wc; chem disp; shwrs inc; EHU (8-10A) €1-1.80; shop nr; sw nr; red long stay; adv bkg acc; quiet; tennis adj; boating; fishing. "Lovely, well-run lakeside site in town park; lake adj; clean, excel, htd, unisex san facs; popular NH; nice walk to interesting town; poss mkt traders; excel value." ♦ 1 May-30 Sep. € 9.30   2016*

⊞ **PRESSAC** *7A3* (8km SW Rural) *46.09696, 0.48081* **Camping Rural des Marronniers, La Bussière, 16490 Pleuville [05 45 71 42 19; sgbann@btinternet.com; www.campingruraldesmarronniers.com]** S fr Poitiers on D741 to Pressac; turn R onto D34 to Pleuville then turn onto D30 dir Charroux, site on L in 1.5km - look for sp La Bùssière. Sm, unshd, pt sl, wc (htd); chem disp; fam bthrm; shwrs inc; EHU (10A) €2.50; lndry; shop nr; snacks; bar nr; bbq; playgrnd; pool; twin axles; dogs; adv bkg acc; quiet; games rm; CKE/CCI. "Friendly, British-owned, peaceful, lovely sm CL-type farm site; open field - chickens & ducks roaming; gd touring base; ideal for exploring SW France; fam/couples welcome; excel." ♦ € 12.00   2017*

PRIVAS *9D2* (2km S Urban) *44.72668, 4.59730* **Kawan Village Ardèche Camping, Blvd de Paste, Quartier Ouvèze, 07000 Privas [04 75 64 05 80; fax 04 75 64 59 68; jcray@wanadoo.fr; www.ardechecamping.fr]** Exit A7 junc 16 dir Privas. App Privas cross rv bdge & at rndabt take 2nd exit. Site ent opp supmkt, sp. Lge, mkd, pt shd, pt sl, wc; chem disp; mv service pnt; fam bthrm; shwrs inc; EHU (10A) inc; lndry; shop nr; rest; snacks; bar; bbq; playgrnd; pool (htd); paddling pool; red long stay; entmnt; wifi; TV; 80% statics; dogs €3.30; Eng spkn; adv bkg acc; ccard acc; rv fishing; tennis adj; CKE/CCI. "Very gd, friendly owners; gd rest and shady pitches; interesting area to visit; pleasant site; walk to town up extremely steep rd."; ♦ ;-- 11 Apr-27 Sep. € 33.00   2015*

PUGET THENIERS *10E4* (2km NW Rural) *43.95801, 6.85980* **Camping L'Origan (Naturist), 2160 Route de Savé, 06260 Puget-Théniers [04 93 05 06 00; fax 04 93 05 09 34; origan@orange.fr; www.origan-village.com]** On N202 fr Entrevaux (dir Nice) at Puget-Théniers, immed turn L at rlwy x-ing (sp), site approx 1km up track. Med, hdg, mkd, hdstg, pt shd, pt sl, terr, wc (htd); shwrs inc; EHU (6A) €4; lndry; shop; rest; snacks; bar; bbq; playgrnd; pool (htd); paddling pool; wifi; TV; 50% statics; dogs €2.50; phone; train to Nice; Eng spkn; adv bkg acc; ccard acc; INF card; tennis; fishing; waterslide; sauna; archery. "Sm pitches not suitable o'fits over 6m; hilly site but pitches level; san facs dated (2018); interesting area; great views; ent noise poss high ssn; attractive bar/rest; tourist steam train bet Puget-Theniers & Annot on certain days." ♦ Easter-3 Oct. € 36.00   2018*

PUIMOISSON *10E3* (7km NE Rural) *43.89836, 6.18011* **Camping à la Ferme Vauvenières (Sauvaire), 04410 St Jurs [04 92 74 44 18; contact@ferme-de-vauvenieres.fr; www.ferme-de-vauvenieres.fr]** Fr Riez take D953 N to 1km beyond Puimoisson then fork R onto D108 sp St Jurs & site sp. Sm, pt shd, wc; chem disp; shwrs inc; EHU (6A) €2.90; lndry; shop nr; rest; bbq; sw nr; dogs €0.75; Eng spkn; adv bkg acc; quiet; games area; CKE/CCI. "Peaceful, basic site off beaten track; wonderful views; lavendar fields; friendly Dutch owner; clean san facs, poss stretched if site full; gd for mountain walking; D17 to Majastres v narr; vg mkt on Wed & Sat in Riez; sm supmkt at filling stn at ent Puimoisson; v lge mkd pitches." 1 Apr-15 Oct. € 18.00   2014*

PUIVERT *8G4* (1km S Rural) *42.91596, 2.0441* **Camping de Puivert, Fontclaire, 11230 Puivert [04 68 20 00 58 or 06 22 45 15 74 (mob); fax 04 68 20 82 29; camping-de-puivert@orange.fr]** Take D117 W fr Quillan dir Lavelanet for 16km; at Puivert turn L onto D16; site in 500m by lake; well sp. Or E fr Foix on D117 for 45km; at Puivert turn R onto D16 & as bef. Med, hdg, hdstg, pt shd, terr, wc; chem disp; mv service pnt; shwrs inc; EHU (16A) €3; lndry; shop; rest nr; snacks; bar; bbq (sep area); sw nr; entmnt; wifi; dogs; quiet; fishing adj. "Attractive area; lge pitches, some lakeside, some hill views; dated san facs but adequate & clean; museum in vill; chateau nrby; vg." 24 Apr-27 Sep. € 12.00   2014*

QUETTEHOU

PUY EN VELAY, LE *9C1* (1km N Urban) *45.05014, 3.88044* **Camping de Bouthezard, Chemin de Bouthezard, Ave d'Aiguilhe, 43000 Le Puy-en-Velay [04 71 09 55 09 or 06 15 08 23 59 (mob); camping. puyenvelay@orange.fr; www.aquadis-loisirs.com/ camping-de-bouthezard]** Fr Le Puy heading NW on N102 to city cent; look for sp Clermont & Vichy; turn R at traff lts in Place Carnot at sp for Valence; site on L on bank of rv. Site ent immed opp Chapel St Michel & 200m fr volcanic core. Med, hdg, pt shd, wc; chem disp; mv service pnt; shwrs inc; EHU (6A) inc (rev pol); lndry; shop; snacks; playgrnd; wifi; dogs €0.85; Eng spkn; adv bkg acc; tennis adj; games rm; CKE/ CCI. "Popular, well-kept site in gd location; busy - rec arr early; efficient staff; gates clsd 2100-0700 LS; no twin axles; may flood & grnd soft in v heavy rain; unrel opening dates - phone ahead LS; vg touring base on pilgrim rte to Spain; immac; very helpful owners; spectacular town; highly rec; pool adj; excel." ♦
3 Apr-25 Oct. € 16.00   2014*

PUY EN VELAY, LE *9C1* (9km N Rural) *45.12473, 3.92177* **Camp Municipal Les Longes, Route des Rosières, 43800 Lavoûte-sur-Loire [04 71 08 18 79; campinglavoutesurloire@orange.fr; www. lavoutesurloire.fr]** Fr Le Puy take N on D103 sp Lavoûte & Retournac. In Lavoûte turn R onto D7 bef rv bdge, site on L in 1km on rvside. Med, mkd, shd, wc; mv service pnt; shwrs; EHU (6A) €2.50; lndry; playgrnd; sw nr; dogs €1.50; quiet; tennis; fishing 50m. "Gd, friendly site; gd walking; lovely quiet site by Haute Loire; san facs clean; rec; mostly statics." ♦
1 May-14 Sep. € 17.00   2017*

PUY EN VELAY, LE *9C1* (3km E Urban) *45.04431, 3.93050* **Camp Municipal d'Audinet, Ave des Sports, 43700 Brives-Charensac [04 71 09 10 18; camping. audinet@wanadoo.fr; www.camping-audinet.fr]** Fr Le Puy foll green sp E twd Valence. Fr S on N88 foll sp twd Valence & on E side of town foll white sp. Lge, pt shd, wc; chem disp; mv service pnt; fam bthrm; shwrs inc; EHU (6A) €3.30; lndry; shop; rest; snacks; bar; bbq; playgrnd; pool; sw; red long stay; wifi; bus to town; quiet; fishing. "Spacious site on rvside; friendly, helpful staff; gd san facs; poss stretched high ssn; poss travellers - but not a prob; no twin axles; vg; 12 min bus to town every 1/2 hr." ♦ 30 Apr-17 Sep.
€ 19.00   2017*

PUY L'EVEQUE *7D3* (3km S Rural) *44.47780, 1.14214* **FFCC Village-Camping Les Vignes, Le Méoure, Le Cayrou, 46700 Puy-l'Evêque [05 65 30 81 72; contact@camping-lesvignes.fr; www.camping-lesvignes.fr]** App fr E on D911 dir Villeneuve-sur-Lot, just bef ent Puy-l'Evêque turn L, foll sp for 3km. Site adj Rv Lot. Avoid town cent while towing. Med, shd, wc; fam bthrm; shwrs; EHU (10A) €2.90; gas; lndry; shop nr; snacks; bar; playgrnd; pool; entmnt; TV; dogs €1.50; quiet; games area; tennis; fishing; bike hire. "Lovely, peaceful site in beautiful countryside; well-kept; warm welcome, friendly owners; gd san facs."
1 Apr-30 Sep. € 18.00   2012*

PUYSSEGUR *8E3* (0km N Rural) *43.75064, 1.06065* **FFCC Camping Namasté, 31480 Puysségur [05 61 85 77 84; camping.namaste@free.fr; http:// camping.namaste.free.fr]** Fr Toulouse NW on N224/ D1 sp Cadours; at Puysségur in 30km foll Camping Namasté sp. (Puysségur is 1km NE of Cadours). Sm, pt shd, wc; fam bthrm; shwrs; EHU (4-10A) €3-5; lndry; shop; rest; snacks; bar; bbq; playgrnd; pool; paddling pool; entmnt; wifi; 10% statics; dogs €1.50; quiet; sauna; bike hire; games area; games rm; fishing. ♦
1 May-15 Oct. € 40.50   2014*

PYLA SUR MER *7D1* (7km S Coastal) *44.58517, -1.20868* **Camping Village Centre La Forêt, Route de Biscarrosse, 33115 Pyla-sur-Mer [05 56 22 73 28; fax 05 56 22 70 50; contact@village-center.com; www. village-center.com]** Fr Bordeaux app Arcachon on A660 by-pass rd; at La Teste-de-Buch at rndabt foll sp for Dune du Pilat & 'campings'. At T-junc in 4km turn L; foll 'plage' & camping sp on D218. Site on R. Lge, hdg, mkd, shd, sl, wc; chem disp; mv service pnt; shwrs inc; EHU (6A) inc; lndry; shop; rest; snacks; bar; bbq; playgrnd; pool; beach sand 600m; 80% statics; dogs €2; adv bkg acc; ccard acc; solarium; tennis; bike hire; CKE/CCI. "Forest setting at foot of sand dune (own steps); well-organised; many facs; hang-gliding, surfing, sailing, cycle rtes nrby." ♦ 4 Apr-20 Sep.
€ 20.00   2018*

PYLA SUR MER *7D1* (8km S Rural/Coastal) *44.57474, -1.22217* **Yelloh! Village Panorama du Pyla, Route de Biscarrosse, 33115 Pyla-sur-Mer [05 56 22 10 44; fax 05 56 22 10 12; mail@camping-panorama.com; www. camping-panorama.com or www.yellohvillage.co.uk]** App Arcachon fr Bordeaux on A63/A660, at rndabt foll sp for Dune-du-Pilat & 'campings'. Foll sp for 'plage' & 'campings' on D218. Site on R next to Camping Le Petit Nice. Lge, mkd, hdstg, shd, sl, terr, wc; chem disp; mv service pnt; shwrs inc; EHU (3-10A) inc; gas; lndry; shop; rest; snacks; bar; bbq; playgrnd; pool (htd); paddling pool; beach sand adj; entmnt; wifi; TV; 20% statics; dogs €5; Eng spkn; games area; tennis; games rm; sauna; waterslide; CKE/CCI. "Pleasant site on wooded dune; pitches clsd together; adv bkg not acc; some pitches poor; direct steep access to excel beach; site rds v narr; ltd pitches for v lge o'fits; some pitches sandy; gd facs; paragliding adj." ♦ 9 Apr-3 Oct.
€ 46.00   2016*

QUETTEHOU *1C4* (3km E Urban/Coastal) *49.58520, -1.26858* **Camping La Gallouette, Rue de la Gallouette, 50550 St Vaast-la-Hougue [02 33 54 20 57; contact@camping-lagallouette.fr; www. camping-lagallouette.fr]** E fr Quettehou on D1, site sp in St Vaast-la-Houge to S of town. Lge, hdg, mkd, pt shd, wc; chem disp; mv service pnt; fam bthrm; shwrs; EHU (6-10A) €3.80-4.60; gas; lndry; shop; rest; snacks; bar; bbq; playgrnd; pool (htd); beach sand 300m; 10% statics; dogs €1.80; phone; adv bkg acc; quiet; games area; games rm; CKE/CCI. "Lovely friendly site; some lge pitches; gd range of facs; sh walk to interesting town; excel site." ♦ 1 Apr-30 Sep.
€ 31.00   2017*

QUIBERON

QUIBERON *2G3* (4km N Coastal) *47.49978, -3.12021*
Camping Do Mi Si La Mi, 31 Rue de la Vierge, 56170 Quiberon [02 97 50 22 52; fax 02 97 50 26 69; camping@domisilami.com; www.domisilami.com] Take D768 down Quiberon Peninsular, 3km after St Pierre-Quiberon & shortly after sp for rlwy level x-ing turn L into Rue de la Vierge, site on R in 400m. Lge, hdg, mkd, pt shd, pt sl, serviced pitches; wc; chem disp; mv service pnt; fam bthrm; shwrs inc; EHU (3-10A) €2.80-4.30; gas; lndry; shop nr; bar nr; bbq; playgrnd; beach shgl 100m; wifi; 40% statics; dogs €2.40; Eng spkn; quiet; ccard acc; bike hire; tennis nr; horseriding nr; sailing nr; games area; CKE/CCI. "Gd touring base; vg; excel site; great location; excel rest." ♦ 31 Mar-30 Sep. € 32.00   2018*

QUIBERON *2G3* (2km SE Coastal) *47.47424, -3.10563*
Camp Municipal Le Goviro, Blvd du Goviro, 56170 Quiberon [02 97 50 13 54 or 02 97 30 24 00 (LS); www.ville-quiberon.fr] Fr D768 at Quiberon foll sp Port Maria & 'Cent Thalassothérapie'. Site 1km on L nr Sofitel hotel. Lge, hdg, mkd, pt shd, terr, wc; chem disp; mv service pnt; shwrs; EHU (13A) €3; gas; lndry; rest nr; playgrnd; beach sand adj; dogs €1.65; quiet; fishing adj; watersports adj. "Popular, well-run site in excel location; lovely bay, gd sea views & coastal path into town; smallish pitches; clean, adequate san facs, ltd LS." ♦ 1 Apr-12 Oct. € 16.00   2015*

QUIBERON *2G3* (2km SE Rural/Coastal) *47.47641, -3.10441* **Camping Le Bois d'Amour, Rue St Clément, 56170 Quiberon [02 97 50 13 52; camping. boisdamour@flowercampings.com; www.quiberon-camping.com]** Exit N165 at Auray onto D768. In Quiberon foll sp 'Thalassothérapie', site sp. Lge, mkd, hdg, pt shd, wc; chem disp; mv service pnt; fam bthrm; shwrs inc; EHU (16A) €5; gas; lndry; shop; rest; snacks; bar; bbq; playgrnd; pool (htd); beach 200m; entmnt; dogs €5; Eng spkn; adv bkg acc; quiet; ccard acc; tennis; horseriding; bike hire; games area; CKE/CCI. "Shwrs clean but hot water can be temperamental; lovely friendly clubhse with reasonable food prices." ♦ 2 Apr-24 Sep. € 20.00   2016*

QUILLAN *8G4* (1km W Urban) *42.87358, 2.17565*
FFCC Camp Municipal La Sapinette, 21 Ave René Delpech, 11500 Quillan [04 68 20 13 52; fax 04 68 20 27 80; campingsapinette@wanadoo.fr; www.camping-la-sapinette.com] Foll D118 fr Carcassonne to Quillan; turn R at 2nd traff lts in town cent; site sp in town. Med, mkd, hdstg, hdg, pt shd, sl, terr, wc (htd); chem disp; mv service pnt; shwrs inc; EHU (6A) €3.10; lndry; shop nr; playgrnd; pool; wifi; TV; 25% statics; dogs €1.60; adv bkg acc; quiet; ccard acc; CKE/CCI. "Gd touring base; sm pitches, some level, mostly sl; early arr rec; helpful staff; san facs a little tired; excel pool; site poss tired end ssn; mkt Wed & Sat; leisure cent 500m; vet adj; highly rec; 15min walk to nice town." 1 Apr-30 Oct. € 25.00   2016*

QUIMPER *2F2* (10km SE Rural) *47.94133, -4.02453*
Camping de Keromen, 38 Rue de Cornouaille, 29170 Saint-Evarzec [02 98 64 09 59; contact@campingdekeromen.fr; www.campingdekeromen.fr] Heading S fr Quimper on D783 at end of dual c'way fork R sp Evarzec. Cont over mini rndabt, site on R in 1.5km, well sp. Med, hdg, mkd, pt shd; wc; chem disp; shwrs; EHU (10A); lndry; playgrnd; twin axles; wifi; TV; 40% statics; dogs; bus; adv bkg acc; quiet; games area; games rm. "Adj lake area; donkeys & goats in enclosure; free fishing on sm lake; gd." ♦ 1 Apr-30 Oct. € 18.50   2017*

QUIMPER *2F2* (9km SE Rural) *47.93811, -3.99959*
Camping Vert de Creac'h-Lann (Hemidy), 202 Route de Concarneau, 29170 St Evarzec [02 98 56 29 88 or 06 68 46 97 25 (mob); contact@campingvertcreachlann.com; www.campingvertcreachlann.com] S fr Quimper on D783, 1.5km fr St Evarzec rndabt at brow of hill (easily missed). Sm, hdg, pt shd, pt sl, wc; chem disp; mv service pnt; shwrs; EHU (4-13A) €3-3.50; lndry; shop nr; rest nr; bbq; playgrnd; pool (htd); wifi; 60% statics; dogs; Eng spkn; adv bkg acc; quiet; games rm. "Lovely spacious site; lge pitches; friendly, helpful owner; gd playgrnd; poss to stay after end Sep by arrangement; lovely old town; gd touring base; daily mkt; excel." 1 Jun-30 Sep. € 13.00   2017*

QUIMPER *2F2* (4km S Rural) *47.97685, -4.11060*
Camping L'Orangerie de Lanniron, Château de Lanniron, 29000 Quimper [02 98 90 62 02; fax 02 98 52 15 56; camping@lanniron.com; www.lanniron.com] Fr Rennes/Lorient: on N165 Rennes-Quimper, Quimper-Centre, Quimper-Sud exit, foll dir Pont l'Abbé on S bypass until exit sp Camping de Lanninon on R. At top of slip rd turn L & foll site sp, under bypass then 2nd R to site. Recep at Old Farm 500m bef site. Lge, mkd, pt shd, serviced pitches; wc; chem disp; mv service pnt; fam bthrm; shwrs inc; EHU (10A) inc; gas; lndry; shop; rest; snacks; bar; bbq; playgrnd; pool (htd); paddling pool; beach; entmnt; wifi; TV; 40% statics; dogs €5.70; phone; bus; Eng spkn; adv bkg acc; ccard acc; bike hire; tennis; golf; canoeing; rv fishing; games rm; CKE/CCI. "Excel, busy, family-run site in grnds of chateau by Rv Odet; 9-hole golf on site; aqua park; well-spaced pitches; vg san facs; vg leisure facs; easy walk to town." ♦ 31 Mar-5 Nov. € 37.00   2018*

QUIMPER *2F2* (3km W Urban) *47.99198, -4.12536*
Camp Municipal Bois du Séminaire, Ave des Oiseaux, 29000 Quimper [02 98 55 61 09; camping-municipal@quimper.bzh; www.mairie-quimper.fr] Fr E on D765 to Quimper, bear L on 1-way system along rv. In 1km bear R over rv into Blvd de Boulguinan - D785. In 500m turn R onto Blvd de France (lge junc). In 1km bear R into Ave des Oiseaux, site on R in front of Auberge de Jeunesse. Med, hdg, pt shd, terr, wc; chem disp; shwrs inc; EHU (5A) €3.30; lndry; shop nr; rest nr; bar nr; bbq; 10% statics; phone; bus adj; quiet; ccard acc; CKE/CCI. "Conv NH/sh stay." ♦ 1 Jun-30 Sep. € 12.00   2015*

QUIMPERLE *2F2* (7km NE Rural) *47.90468, -3.47477*
Camping Le Ty-Nadan, Route d'Arzano, 29310 Locunolé [17 46 78 51 00 or 02 98 71 75 47; info@tynadan-vacances.fr; www.irisparc.com] To avoid Quimperlé cont exit N165 dir Quimperlé. As ent town turn R onto D22 dir Arzano. In 9km turn L at W end of Arzano (un-numbered rd) sp Locunolé & Camping Ty Nadan; site on L just after x-ing Rv Elle. Or fr Roscoff on D69 S join N165/E60 but take care at uneven level x-ing at Pen-ar-Hoat 11km after Sizun. Lge, hdg, mkd, pt shd, serviced pitches; wc (htd); chem disp; mv service pnt; fam bthrm; shwrs inc; EHU (10A) inc (long lead poss req); gas; lndry; shop; rest; snacks; bar; bbq (charcoal, gas); playgrnd; pool (covrd, htd); paddling pool; entmnt; wifi; TV; 40% statics; dogs €5.50; Eng spkn; adv bkg acc; ccard acc; waterslide; games area; horseriding; rv fishing adj; tennis; archery; games rm; sauna; bike hire; canoeing adj; CKE/CCI. "Excel, peaceful site by rv; pitches poss narr for lge o'fits; friendly staff; spa; no o'fits over 8.5m high ssn; barrier clsd 2300-0800; many activities; gd touring base." ♦ 18 Apr-31 Aug. € 46.00   2016*

QUINTIN *2E3* (1km SE Urban) *48.40128, -2.90672* Camp Municipal du Lac, Chemin des Côtes, 22800 Quintin [02 96 74 92 54 or 02 96 74 84 01 (Mairie); fax 02 96 74 06 53; mairie@quintin.fr; www.quintin.fr] Fr N exit D790 at rndabt & foll sp 'Cent Ville'; at 2nd rndabt site sp; site on L 200m after 5th ped x-ing (narr rd, easy to miss). Fr S on D790 do not slip rd (D7) but cont to rndabt - narr rds in town; then as above. Site N (100m) of town gardens & boating lake. Sm, pt shd, pt sl, wc; mv service pnt; shwrs; EHU (6A) €2.50; shop nr; rest nr; bar nr; bbq; playgrnd; quiet; fishing. "Fair site; helpful warden; poss insufficient of security (2011); interesting town." ♦ 15 Apr-30 Sep. € 8.50   2016*

> **"Satellite navigation makes touring much easier"**
>
> Remember most sat navs don't know if you're towing or in a larger vehicle – always use yours alongside maps and site directions.

RABASTENS *8E3* (2km NW Rural) *43.83090, 1.69805* Camp Municipal des Auzerals, Route de Grazac, 81800 Rabastens [05 63 33 70 36 or 06 23 81 85 69 (mob); fax 05 63 33 64 05; mairie.rabastens@libertysurf.fr] Exit A68 junc 7 onto D12. In Rabastens town cent foll sp dir Grazac, site sp. Sm, hdg, mkd, pt shd, pt sl, terr, wc; chem disp; shwrs inc; EHU (10A) inc; lndry; shop nr; rest nr; playgrnd; adv bkg req; quiet; CKE/CCI. "Attractive lakeside site; facs old but clean; office 0900-1200 & 1500-1900, otherwise height barrier in place; conv m'way NH; pool adj high ssn; highly rec; gd hedges around plots; call to check if site open." 1 Apr-30 Sep. € 11.00   2017*

RAMBOUILLET *4E3* (3km SE Rural) *48.6252, 1.84495* Camping Huttopia Rambouillet, Route du Château d'Eau, 78120 Rambouillet [01 30 41 07 34; fax 01 30 41 00 17; rambouillet@huttopia.com; www.huttopia.com] Fr N exit D910 at 'Rambouillet Eveuses' & foll sp to site in 2.5km. Fr S exit at 'Rambouillet Cent' & foll sp to site back onto D910 (in opp dir), exit 'Rambouillet Eveuses' as above. Avoid Rambouillet town cent. Lge, hdg, pt shd, wc (htd); chem disp; mv service pnt; fam bthrm; shwrs inc; EHU (10A) inc; lndry; shop; rest; snacks; bar; bbq (elec, gas); playgrnd; 10% statics; dogs €4.20; phone; Eng spkn; adv bkg rec; quiet; ccard acc; fishing adj; sep car park; CKE/CCI. "Excel, busy, wooded site; conv Paris by train - parking at stn 3km; gd cycling rtes; interesting town." ♦ 30 Mar-3 Nov. € 41.00   2017*

> **"There aren't many sites open at this time of year"**
>
> If you're travelling outside peak season remember to call ahead to check site opening dates – even if the entry says 'open all year'.

RAON L'ETAPE *6E3* (2km SE Rural) *48.39474, 6.86232* Camping Vosgina, 1 Rue la Cheville, 88420 Moyenmoutier [03 29 41 47 63; info@camping-vosgina.com; www.camping-vosgina.com] On N59 St Dié-Lunéville rd, take exit mkd Senones, Moyenmoutier. At rndabt take rd twd St Blaise & foll camping sp. Site is on minor rd parallel with N59 bet Moyenmoutier & Raon. Med, pt shd, pt sh, terr, wc; chem disp; shwrs inc; EHU (4-10A) €3-6; gas; lndry; shop; snacks; bar; wifi; TV; 20% statics; dogs €1.50; Eng spkn; adv bkg acc; quiet; ccard acc; CKE/CCI. "Gd site for quiet holiday in a non-touristy area of Alsace; friendly recep; lovely countryside; many cycle/walking rtes in area; barrier clsd 2200-0700; park like setting; beautifully maintained; friendly Swiss owners; excel for sh stay or NH." 25 Mar-31 Oct. € 20.00   2016*

⊞ **RAON L'ETAPE** *6E3* (9km S Rural) *48.36355, 6.83861* Camping Beaulieu-sur-l'Eau, 41 Rue de Trieuche, 88480 Etival-Clairefontaine [03 29 41 53 51; camping-beaulieu-vosges@orange.fr; www.camping-beaulieu-vosges.com] SE fr Baccarat on N59 turn R in vill of Etival-Clairefontaine on D424 sp Rambervillers & Epinal & foll sp for 3km. Ent on L. Med, mkd, pt shd, terr, wc (htd); mv service pnt; shwrs inc; EHU (4-10A) €3.05-7.90; gas; shop; rest nr; bar; playgrnd; sw nr; 10% statics; dogs; adv bkg rec; quiet; CKE/CCI. "Lovely, peaceful, clean site; 80% statics; dedicated touring area; gd rural views." € 10.50   2015*

France

RAON L'ETAPE

RAUZAN

RAUZAN 7D2 (0km N Rural) 44.78377, -0.12712
Camping du Vieux Château, 6 Blabot-Bas, 33420 Rauzan [05 57 84 15 38; fax 05 57 84 18 34; contact@ vieuxchateau.fr; www.camping-levieuxchateau.com]
Fr Libourne S on D670, site is on D123 about 1.5km fr D670, sp. Sm, mkd, shd, wc; chem disp; fam bthrm; shwrs inc; EHU (6A) €5 (poss rev pol); gas; lndry; shop; rest nr; snacks; bar; playgrnd; pool; entmnt; wifi; TV; 10% statics; dogs €2; Eng spkn; adv bkg acc; quiet; ccard acc; tennis; bike hire; horseriding; CKE/CCI. "Lovely site but take care tree roots on pitches; quiet wooded area; pleasant family run site; helpful owners; basic san facs - ltd LS & poss not well-maintained, & poss stretched high ssn; access to some pitches diff when wet; conv vineyards; walking dist to vill; nice sw pool; wine-tasting; TV rm & bar open to 9pm; events avail." ♦ 30 Mar-18 Oct. € 27.00   2018*

REALMONT 8E4 (3km SW Rural) 43.77092, 2.16336
Camp Municipal La Batisse, Route Graulhet, 81120 Réalmont [05 63 55 50 41; camping-realmont@ wanadoo.fr; www.realmont.fr/decouvrir/camping-municipal-realmont] On D612 fr Albi heading S thro Réalmont. On exit Réalmont turn R on D631 where site sp. Site 1.5km on L on Rv Dadou. Sm, pt shd, wc; shwrs; EHU (3A) inc; gas; shop nr; rest nr; bar nr; playgrnd; 10% statics; quiet; rv fishing adj. "Pleasant, peaceful, well-kept site in rv valley; friendly, pleasant warden; dated but clean san facs; nr Albi-Castres cycle rte; excel value; mkt Wed; gd; hg rec." 1 Apr-30 Sep. € 12.00   2017*

REGUINY 2F3 (1km S Urban) 47.96928, -2.74083
Camp Municipal de l'Etang, Rue de la Piscine, 56500 Réguiny [02 97 38 66 11; fax 02 97 38 63 44; mairie. requiny@wanadoo.fr; www.reguiny.com]
On D764 fr Pontivy to Ploërmel, turn R into D11 to Réguiny then foll sp. Med, pt shd, wc; chem disp; mv service pnt; fam bthrm; shwrs inc; EHU (10A) €2.50; lndry; shop nr; rest nr; bar nr; playgrnd; dogs €2; phone; Eng spkn; quiet; ccard acc. "Gd facs; htd pool 500m; gd touring base; deposit for gate remote control (€100); v pleasant site; rec rest in vill; gd acc to S Brittany." 15 Jun-15 Sep. € 10.40   2018*

REIMS 3D4 (19km SE Rural) 49.16687, 4.21416
Camping Intercommunalité Val de Vesle (formerly Municipal), 8 Rue de Routoir, Courmelois, 51360 Val-de-Vesle [03 26 03 91 79; valdevesle.camping@ orange.fr; www.reims-tourism.com]
Fr Reims twd Châlons-en-Champagne on D944, turn L by camp sp on D326 to Val-de-Vesle, foll camp sp; look for tall grain silos by canal. NB do not turn L bef D326 due narr lane. Med, mkd, shd, wc; chem disp; shwrs inc; EHU (6-10A) inc €3 (long lead poss req); lndry; shop nr; bbq; playgrnd; pool; dogs €1; adv bkg acc; ccard acc; rv fishing; CKE/CCI. "Charming, well-kept, busy site amongst trees; popular NH, rec arrive early; informal pitching; friendly, helpful staff; new security gate, booking in req for code (2011); in sm vill (no shops); poss mosquito prob; cycle rte to Reims along canal; gd touring base; lge pitches; lovely, clean facs; well sp fr D944." ♦ 1 Apr-15 Oct. € 15.00   2018*

REMOULINS 10E2 (2km NW Rural) 43.94805, 4.54583 **Camping La Sousta, Ave du Pont de Gard, 30210 Remoulins [04 66 37 12 80; fax 04 66 37 23 69; info@lasousta.fr; www.lasousta.fr]**
Fr A9 exit Remoulins, foll sp for Nîmes, then sp 'Pont du Gard par Rive Droite' thro town. Immed over rv bdge turn R sp 'Pont du Gard etc'; site on R 800m fr Pont du Gard. Lge, hdstg, mkd, shd, pt sl, wc; chem disp; mv service pnt; fam bthrm; shwrs inc; EHU (6A); gas; lndry; shop; rest nr; snacks; bar; bbq (sep area); playgrnd; pool; sw nr; entmnt; wifi; TV; 20% statics; dogs €2; Eng spkn; adv bkg acc; quiet; ccard acc; bike hire; fishing; watersports; tennis; CKE/CCI. "Friendly, helpful staff; poss diff lge o'fits due trees; excel touring base; in walking dist Pont-du-Gard; set in lovely woodland with plenty of shd; vg; can be dry & dusty in Jul & Aug; bar & rest open in LS; sw pool clsd until 5th May." ♦
12 Mar-1 Nov. € 34.00   2018*

REMOULINS 10E2 (4km NW Rural) 43.95594, 4.51588 **Camping International Les Gorges du Gardon, Chemin de la Barque Vieille, Route d'Uzès, 30210 Vers-Pont-du-Gard [04 66 22 81 81; fax 04 66 22 90 12; camping.international@wanadoo.fr; www. le-camping-international.com]**
Exit A9 junc 23 Remoulins & head NW twd Uzès on D981. Pass turn for Pont-du-Gard & site on L in 1.5km. Or fr E on N100 turn N onto D6086 then D19A to Pont-du-Gard (avoiding Remoulins cent). Lge, hdg, mkd, pt shd, wc; chem disp; fam bthrm; shwrs inc; EHU (6A) inc; gas; lndry; shop; rest; snacks; bar; playgrnd; pool (htd); sw nr; red long stay; entmnt; wifi; TV; 10% statics; dogs €2; Eng spkn; adv bkg acc; quiet; ccard acc; tennis; games rm; boating; fishing; games area; CKE/CCI. "Beautiful location; many sm pitches - some lge pitches to back of site; friendly, cheerful owners; excel san facs, ltd LS; no twin axles or o'fits over 5m; beavers in rv; site poss subject to flooding & evacuation; superb, conv for the Pont du Gard; thoroughly rec staying several nights, unique site." ♦
15 Mar-30 Sep. € 29.00   2018*

⊞ **RENNES** 2F4 (4km NE Urban) 48.13529, -1.64597
Camp Municipal des Gayeulles, Rue du Maurice Audin, 35700 Rennes [02 99 36 91 22; fax 02 23 20 06 34; info@camping-rennes.com; www.camping-rennes.com] Exit Rennes ring rd N136 junc 14 dir Maurepas & Maison Blanche, foll sp 'Les Gayeules' & site. Narr app to site. Med, mkd, hdstg, pt shd, pt sl, serviced pitches; wc; chem disp; mv service pnt; fam bthrm; shwrs; EHU (10A) inc; lndry; shop nr; snacks; bbq; playgrnd; red long stay; wifi; dogs €1; phone; bus; Eng spkn; adv bkg acc; quiet; ccard acc; tennis nr; CKE/CCI. "Lovely, well-kept, well-run site adj activity park; friendly, helpful staff; lge pitches; slight sl for m'vans; 1st class facs; office clsd 1200-1400; reg bus to Rennes, a lovely city; sm m'van Aire de Service adj; excel; mini golf nr; archery nrby; no dogs allowed in park adj; m'van o'night area; pool adj; noise fr disco & football; great location; new san facs close to ent." ♦
€ 19.00   2018*

REOLE, LA 7D2 (2km SE Urban) 44.57778, -0.03360 **Camp Municipal La Rouergue, Bords de Garonne, 33190 La Réole [05 56 61 13 55; fax 05 56 61 89 13; lareole@entredeuxmers.com; www.entredeuxmers.com]** On N113 bet Bordeaux & Agen or exit A62 at junc 4. In La Réole foll sps S on D9 to site on L immed after x-ing suspension bdge. Med, pt shd, wc; shwrs inc; EHU (3A) inc; gas; shop; snacks; dogs €2; boating; fishing. "Resident warden; 2m barrier clsd 1200-1500; pool 500m; Sat mkt on rv bank." 1 May-30 Sep. € 16.00   2015*

> **"That's changed – Should I let the Club know?"**
>
> If you find something on site that's different from the site entry, fill in a report and let us know. See camc.com/europereport.

RETHEL 5C1 (19km E Urban) 49.48234, 4.57589 **Camping Le Vallage (formerly Municipal), 38 Chemin de l'Assaut, 08130 Attigny [03 24 71 23 06; camping.levallage@orange.f; www.camping-levallage.fr]** E on D983 fr Rethel to Attigny; fr town cent take D987 twd Charleville; over rv bdge; 2nd turn on L; sp. Med, mkd, hdg, hdstg, pt shd, wc; chem disp; shwrs inc; EHU (10A) inc; lndry; shop nr; playgrnd; 50% statics; dogs; phone; fishing; tennis; CKE/CCI. "Lovely quiet site; lge pitches; sports facs adj; helpful staff; pool adj; gd facs." 1 Apr-15 Oct. € 16.00   2015*

REVEL 8F4 (1km E Urban) 43.45454, 2.01515 **Camp Municipal Le Moulin du Roy, Tuilerie de Chazottes, off Ave de Sorèze, 31250 Revel [05 61 83 32 47 or 05 62 18 71 40 (Mairie); mairie@mairie-revel.fr; www.tourisme-revel.fr]** Fr Revel ring rd take D1/D85 dir Sorèze, site sp. Med, hdg, pt shd, mv service pnt; shwrs inc; EHU €320; shop nr; playgrnd; sw nr; dogs €0.90; phone; bus; Eng spkn; tennis adj; CKE/CCI. "Pleasant, immac site; htd pool adj; helpful staff; Sat mkt; vg." 2 Jun-7 Sep. € 16.00   2017*

REVEL 8F4 (6km E Urban) 43.45446, 2.06953 **Camping St Martin, Les Vigariés, 81540 Sorèze [05 63 50 20 19; fax 05 63 73 28 99; campingsaintmartin@gmail.com; www.campingsaintmartin.com]** Fr Revel take D85 sp Sorèze; site sp on N side of vill; turn L at traff lts; site on R in 100m. Sm, mkd, hdstg, hdg, pt shd, wc; chem disp; mv service pnt; shwrs inc; EHU (10A) €3.60; lndry; shop; snacks; bar; bbq; playgrnd; pool; sw nr; entmnt; wifi; TV; 20% statics; dogs €1.50; quiet; tennis; games rm; CKE/CCI. "Vg, well-kept site; friendly staff; excel san facs; fascinating medieval town; nr Bassin de St Ferréol; excel mkt in Revel; rec; noise fr adj sports facs & pitches nr san fac beware of being hit by footballs." ♦ 30 Mar-14 Oct. € 24.60   2017*

RIBEAUVILLE

REVIGNY SUR ORNAIN 5D1 (0km S Urban) 48.82663, 4.98412 **Camping Municipal du Moulin des Gravières, Rue du Stade, 55800 Revigny-sur-Ornain [03 29 78 73 34; contact@ot-revigny-ornain.fr; www.ot-revigny-ornain.fr]** N fr Bar-le-Duc on D994 to Revigny-sur-Ornain; fr town cent take D995 twd Vitry-le-François. Site on R, sp. Sm, hdg, mkd, pt shd, wc; chem disp; mv service pnt; fam bthrm; shwrs inc; EHU (6A) €2.70; lndry; shop nr; snacks; playgrnd; TV; 3% statics; dogs; Eng spkn; adv bkg acc; quiet; CKE/CCI. "Pleasant, well-kept site; lge pitches; vg, modern facs; trout stream runs thro site; bike hire in town; tennis in town; gd cycling along canal; mkt Wed adj; highly rec; excel site, beautifully kept; park like setting; far better than any other municipal site we have stayed on." ♦ 1 May-30 Sep. € 13.00   2016*

RHINAU 6E3 (1km NW Rural) 48.32123, 7.69788 **Camping Ferme des Tuileries, 1 Rue des Tuileries, 67860 Rhinau [03 88 74 60 45 or 06 85 74 98 97; camping.fermetuileries@neuf.fr; www.fermedestuileries.com]** Take D1083 (between Strasbourg and Selestat). Exit at Benfield or Sand and take D5 through Boofzheim to Rhinau. Site sp. Med, hdstg, mkd, pt shd, wc; chem disp; mv service pnt; fam bthrm; shwrs inc; EHU (6A) €3.20; gas; lndry; shop nr; rest; snacks; bar; bbq; playgrnd; pool (htd); sw; entmnt; wifi; 20% statics; Eng spkn; quiet; games area; games rm; bike hire; tennis. "Spacious site with excel facs; regimented; free ferry across Rv Rhine adj; vg; excel for cycling; hdstg for MH's." ♦ 1 Apr-30 Sep. € 16.50   2018*

RIBEAUVILLE 6E3 (2km E Urban) 48.19490, 7.33648 **Camp Municipal Pierre-de-Coubertin, Rue de Landau, 68150 Ribeauville [03 89 73 66 71; camping.ribeauville@wanadoo.fr; www.camping-alsace.com]** Exit N83 junc 20 at Ribeauville onto D106 & foll rd to o'skts; at traff lts turn R & then immed R again. Site on R in 500m. Camp at sports grnd nr Lycée. Lge, mkd, pt shd, pt sl, wc (htd); chem disp; fam bthrm; shwrs inc; EHU (16A) €3.50; gas; lndry; shop; wifi; dogs €1; quiet; CKE/CCI. "Well-run site; friendly, helpful staff; park outside site bef checking in; clean, excel san facs; resident storks; gd size pitches; gd touring base; mkt Sat; pool adj; highly rec; excel." ♦ 15 Mar-15 Nov. € 17.00   2017*

RIBEAUVILLE 6E3 (5km S Rural) 48.16200, 7.31691 **Camping de Riquewihr, 1 Route du Vin, 68340 Riquewihr [03 89 47 90 08; fax 03 89 49 05 63; camping.riquewihr@wanadoo.fr; www.ribeauville-riquewihr.com]** Fr Strasbourg on N83/E25, take junc 21 (fr opp dir take junc 22) to Blebenheim/Riquewihr. D416 & D3 thro Blebenheim. At T-junc turn R onto D1B, site on R at rndabt. Lge, mkd, hdg, hdstg, pt shd, pt sl, wc (htd); chem disp; mv service pnt; fam bthrm; shwrs inc; EHU (6A) €3.50 (poss rev pol); gas; lndry; shop nr; playgrnd; wifi; dogs €1.20; ccard acc; tennis; CKE/CCI. "Rec arr early; friendly staff; san facs clean; gd for sm children; lovely town; games area adj; m'van o'night area; office clsd 1200-1400." 28 Mar-31 Dec. € 21.00   2015*

RIBERAC

RIBERAC 7C2 (1km N Rural) 45.25755, 0.34128 **Camp Municipal La Dronne, Route d'Angoulême, 24600 Ribérac [05 53 92 41 61; ot.riberac@perigord.tm.fr]** Site on W of main rd D708 immed N of bdge over Rv Dronne on o'skts of Ribérac. Med, hdg, pt shd, wc; shwrs inc; EHU (10A) €2.50; lndry; shop nr; snacks; playgrnd; dogs €0.50; quiet. "Vg, well-run site; pitches in cent hdgd & shady; facs gd & clean but inadequate high ssn; Fri mkt." ♦ 1 Jun-15 Sep. € 14.00   2017*

RIBES 9D2 (1km S Rural) 44.29545, 4.12436 **Camping Les Cruses, Ribes 07260 Joyeuse [33 04 75 39 54 69; les-cruses@wanadoo.fr; www.campinglescruses.com]** Head NW on rue du Mas de Laffont twd Le Chateâu after 120m turn L onto Le Chateâu. Turn R onto D550, sharp R twds Laffont, L onto Laffont, sharp R twd D450 after 40m turn L onto D450. Sm, mkd, shd, wc (htd); chem disp; mv service pnt; fam bthrm; shwrs; EHU (10A) €4.30; lndry; rest; snacks; bar; bbq; playgrnd; pool; beach 1km; entmnt; wifi; TV; dogs; Eng spkn; adv bkg acc; quiet; ccard acc; games area; CCI. "Excel on site pool and jacuzz; v helpful and friendly owners; nr lively town and places to see." 1 Apr-30 Sep. € 29.00   2014*

RICHELIEU 4H1 (1km S Rural) 47.00774, 0.32078 **Camp Municipal, 6 Ave de Schaafheim, 37120 Richelieu [02 47 58 15 02 or 02 47 58 10 13 (mob); commune-de-richelieu@wanadoo.fr; www.tourisme-richelieu.fr]** Fr Loudun, take D61 to Richelieu, D749 twd Châtellerault; site sp. Sm, hdg, mkd, pt shd, wc; chem disp; shwrs inc; EHU (5-15A) lndry; shop nr; playgrnd; quiet; fishing; tennis; CKE/CCI. "Phone ahead to check site open LS; clean site and facs; pool 500m; gd value." ♦ 15 May-15 Sep. € 10.00   2014*

RIEL LES EAUX 6F1 (2km W Rural) 47.97050, 4.64990 **Camp Municipal du Plan d'Eau, 21570 Riel-les-Eaux [03 80 93 72 76; bar-camping-du-marais@wanadoo.fr]** NE fr Châtillon-sur-Seine on D965 twd Chaumont: after 6km turn N onto D13 at Brion-sur-Ource; cont thro Belan-sur-Ource. Site almost opp junc with D22 turning to Riel-les-Eaux; site well sp. Sm, hdg, pt shd, wc; chem disp; shwrs inc; EHU (5A) €3; snacks; bar; playgrnd; Eng spkn; quiet; fishing; CKE/CCI. "Conv Champagne area; lake adj; excel; vg, simple site; lge hdg pitches." ♦ 1 Apr-31 Oct. € 12.00   2015*

RIEUX 2G3 (1km E Urban) 47.59801, -02.10131 **Le Parc du Château, 56350 Rieux, France [02999 19785; contact@mariederriex.fr; rieux-morbihan.fr]** Turn R off D114 at R angled bend E of town. Sm, mkd, hdg, pt shd, terr, wc; chem disp; mv service pnt; shwrs; EHU (10A) €2.60; lndry; rest; bar; bbq; playgrnd; wifi; TV; 5% statics; dogs; phone; bus 200m; Eng spkn; adv bkg acc; canoeing; fishing; sailing; tennis; CKE/CCI. "Beside Vilaine canal; pretty, well kept site; vg." ♦ 1 Apr-31 Oct. € 13.40   2016*

RIEZ 10E3 (1km SE Urban) 43.81306, 6.09931 **Camping Rose de Provence, Rue Edouard Dauphin, 04500 Riez [04 92 77 75 45; info@rose-de-provence.com; www.rose-de-provence.com]** Exit A51 junc 18 onto D82 to Gréoux-les-Bains then D952 to Riez. On reaching Riez strt across rndabt, at T-junc turn L & immed R, site sp. Med, mkd, pt shd, wc; chem disp; shwrs inc; EHU (6A) inc (rev pol); lndry; rest nr; bar nr; playgrnd; 5% statics; dogs €1.60-2.10; phone; adv bkg acc; tennis adj; CKE/CCI. "Beautiful, well-kept site; helpful, friendly owners; gd san facs; nice vill; conv Verdon Gorge; mkd walks around vill; trampoline & gym equipmnt; gate clse 1230-1500 & 2100-0830." ♦ 12 Apr-1 Oct. € 21.00   2015*

RILLE 4G1 (4km W Rural) 47.45750, 0.21840 **Camping Huttopia Rillé, Base de Loisirs de Pincemaille, Lac de Rillé, 37340 Rillé [02 47 24 62 97; fax 02 47 24 63 61; rille@huttopia.com; www.huttopia.com]** Fr N or S D749 to Rillé, foll sp to Lac de Pincemaille, site sp on S side of lake. Med, shd, wc (htd); chem disp; mv service pnt; fam bthrm; shwrs inc; EHU (6-10A) €4.20-6.20; shop; rest; snacks; bar; playgrnd; pool (htd); sw nr; 10% statics; dogs €3.50; adv bkg rec; sep car park; watersports; fishing; games rm; tennis. "Peaceful site; vg walking, excel." 24 Apr-5 Nov. € 24.00   2014*

RIOM 9B1 (5km NW Rural) 45.91597, 3.07682 **Camping Le Ranch des Volcans (formerly Clos de Balanède), Route de la Piscine, 63140 Châtel-Guyon [04 73 86 02 47; fax 04 73 86 05 64; contact@ranchdesvolcans.com; www.ranchdesvolcans.com]** Fr Riom take D227 to Châtelguyon, site on R on o'skts of town. Tight turn into ent. Lge, pt shd, pt sl, wc; shwrs inc; EHU (6-10A) €3-3.50; gas; lndry; shop; rest; snacks; bar; playgrnd; pool; red long stay; dogs €1.50; Eng spkn; adv bkg acc; quiet; tennis; poss open until 31 Dec. "Pleasant, well-run site; san facs dated; some pitches steep & poss uneven; sh walk to town; m'vans/campers not allowed up to Puy-de-Dôme - must use bus provided; conv for A71, gd NH; gd quiet site; conv for Clermont-Ferrand and Puy de Dôme." ♦ 21 Mar-1 Nov. € 17.00   2015*

RIOM 9B1 (6km NW Rural) 45.90614, 3.06041 **Camping de la Croze, St Hippolyte, 63140 Châtel-Guyon [04 73 86 08 27 or 06 87 14 43 62 (mob); fax 04 73 86 08 51; info@campingcroze.com; www.campingcroze.com]** Fr A71 exit junc 13; ring rd around Riom sp Châtel-Guyon to Mozac, then D455. Site L bef ent St Hippolyte. Fr Volvic on D986 turn L at rndabt after Leclerc supmkt & L again to D455. NB Not rec to tow thro Riom. Lge, mkd, pt shd, pt sl, wc (htd); chem disp; shwrs inc; EHU (6-10A) €3.80; lndry; shop nr; playgrnd; pool (htd); wifi; 10% statics; dogs €1.80; quiet; CKE/CCI. "Gd sightseeing area; mini-bus to Châtel-Guyon (2km) high ssn; vg; supmkt nrby; gd rest." 26 Mar-30 Oct. € 18.50   2017*

RIOM ES MONTAGNES 7C4 (1km E Rural) 45.28214, 2.66707 **Camp Municipal Le Sédour, 15400 Riom-ès-Montagnes [04 71 78 05 71]** Site on W of D678 Riom N to Condat rd, 500m out of town over bdge, sp fr all dirs, opp Clinique du Haut Cantal. Med, mkd, pt shd, pt sl, wc; chem disp; mv service pnt; fam bthrm; shwrs inc; EHU (6A); lndry; shop nr; bbq; playgrnd; twin axles; TV; Eng spkn; adv bkg acc; games area. "Vg; takeaway." ♦ 1 May-30 Sep. € 16.00   2015*

RIOZ 6G2 (1km E Rural) 47.42525, 6.07524 **Camp Municipal du Lac, Rue de la Faïencerie, 70190 Rioz [03 84 91 91 59, 03 84 91 84 84 (Mairie) or 06 33 78 63 75 (mob); fax 03 84 91 90 45; camping@rioz.fr; camping.rioz.fr]** Site sp off D15. Med, hdstg, hdg, pt shd, wc (htd); fam bthrm; shwrs inc; EHU (16A) €2.50; gas; shop nr; rest nr; playgrnd; dogs €1.50; quiet. "Site yourself, warden calls; some lge pitches; gd facs; pool adj; footpath to vill shops." 1 Apr-30 Sep. € 10.40   2016*

RIVIERE SUR TARN 10E1 (3km E Rural) 44.20319, 3.15806 **FFCC Camping Le Pont, Boyne, 12640 Rivière-sur-Tarn [05 65 62 61 12; nicolas.garlenq@orange.fr; www.campinglepont.com]** Fr Millau head N on N9, R after 7km onto D907 sp Gorges du Tarn, site in 9km on R on ent to vill. Sm, pt shd, wc; chem disp; mv service pnt; shwrs inc; EHU (8A) €2.50; lndry; shop nr; rest nr; playgrnd; sw nr; dogs €1; quiet; fishing adj; CKE/CCI. "Gd base for Tarn gorges; canoeing & climbing nrby; facs dated but clean; helpful owner; excel." 1 Apr-30 Sep. € 14.00   2012*

> "I like to fill in the reports as I travel from site to site"
>
> You'll find report forms at the back of this guide, or you can fill them in online at camc.com/europereport.

RIVIERE SUR TARN 10E1 (0km SW Rural) 44.18530, 3.13060 **Camping Les Peupliers, Rue de la Combe, 12640 Rivière-sur-Tarn [05 65 59 85 17; fax 05 65 61 09 03; lespeupliers12640@orange.fr; www.campinglespeupliers.fr]** Heading N on N9 turn R dir Aguessac onto D907 twd Rivière-sur-Tarn. Site on R bef vill. Or fr A75 exit junc 44.1 sp Aguessac/Gorges du Tarn. In Aguessac, foll sp Rivière-sur-Tarn for 5km, site clearly sp. Med, mkd, hdg, hdstg, pt shd, wc; chem disp; mv service pnt; fam bthrm; shwrs inc; EHU (6A) inc; gas; lndry; shop nr; rest; snacks; bar; bbq; playgrnd; pool (htd); paddling pool; sw nr; entmnt; wifi; TV; 10% statics; dogs €3; Eng spkn; adv bkg acc; quiet; ccard acc; canoeing; fishing; horseriding; waterslide; games area; tennis; watersports; CKE/CCI. "Lovely rural site alongside rv Tarn; friendly staff and owners; beautiful scenery; kayaking avail; adv bkg rec; excel site for gorges."; ♦ ;-- 1 Apr-30 Sep. € 34.00   2015*

ROCHE BERNARD, LA

ROANNE 9A1 (5km SW Rural) 45.98830, 4.04531 **Camping L'Orée du Lac, 68 Route du Barrage, 42300 Villerest [04 77 69 60 88; loreedulac@wanadoo.fr; www.loreedulac.net]** Take D53 SW fr Roanne to Villerest; site sp in vill. Sm, mkd, pt shd, pt sl, wc; chem disp; shwrs inc; EHU (6A) €3.50; shop nr; rest; snacks; bar; playgrnd; pool; entmnt; wifi; TV; dogs (€1); phone; Eng spkn; adv bkg rec; quiet; watersports; fishing; CKE/CCI. "Attractive site nr medieval vill; much of site diff lge/med o'fits; lower pt of site diff when wet; sandy sw beach 800m on lake." 14 Apr-28 Oct. € 26.00   2018*

ROCAMADOUR 7D3 (3km N Rural) 44.81040, 1.61615 **FFCC Camping Ferme Branche, Route de Souillac, Les Campagnes, 46500 Rocamadour [05 65 33 63 37 or 06 75 19 69 90 (mob); campingfermebranche@yahoo.fr; www.campingfermebranche.com]** Site on D247, 1km N of Rocamadour. Sm, pt shd, wc; mv service pnt; shwrs inc; EHU (6A) €2; lndry; shop nr; bbq; playgrnd; dogs free; phone; quiet. "Lovely, open, spacious site; gd, clean facs; gd for dogs; nr chateau; facs stretched in ssn; friendly owner; great site for price." 10 Apr-15 Nov. € 8.50   2015*

ROCAMADOUR 7D3 (7km E Rural) 44.81805, 1.68638 **Campsite Padimadour, La Châtaigneraie-Varagne, 46500 Rocamadour [05 65 33 72 11; camping@padimadour.fr; www.uk.padimadour.fr]** Fr N of A20, take exit 54 dir Gramat D840. Turn L onto Pounou. Sharp L onto La Chataigneraie after Pounou. Sm, mkd, pt shd, pt sl, wc (htd); chem disp; mv service pnt; fam bthrm; shwrs inc; EHU (10A) inc; lndry; shop; snacks; bar; bbq; pool; entmnt; wifi; 30% statics; dogs; phone; Eng spkn; adv bkg acc; quiet; ccard acc; games rm; games area; CCI. "Excel & clean san facs & pool; helpful, friendly owners; homemade pizza's in high ssn; highly rec; new level pitches (2016)." ♦ 29 Apr-2 Oct. € 35.00   2014*

ROCHE BERNARD, LA 2G3 (0km NW Urban) 47.51946, -2.30517 **Camp Municipal Le Patis, Chemin du Patis, 56130 La Roche-Bernard [02 99 90 60 13 or 02 99 90 60 51 (Mairie); fax 02 99 90 88 28; camping.lrb56@gmail.com; www.camping-larochebernard.com]** Leave N165 junc 17 (fr N) junc 15 (fr S) & foll marina sp. NB Arr/exit OK on mkt day (Thurs) if avoid town cent. Med, hdstg, hdg, mkd, pt shd, wc cont; chem disp; mv service pnt; shwrs inc; EHU (6A) €4; lndry; shop nr; playgrnd; red long stay; dogs €2.30; Eng spkn; adv bkg acc; quiet; ccard acc; boating adj; games area; sailing adj. "Excel clean site in lovely spot on rv bank; helpful staff; facs poss stretched high ssn; grass pitches poss soft - heavy o'fits phone ahead in wet weather; Thurs mkt; m'van o'night area; organic mkt Sat; ancient, pretty town up steep hill; gd walks; highly rec." ♦ 1 Apr-30 Sep. € 19.00   2015*

France

ROCHE CHALAIS, LA

ROCHE CHALAIS, LA *7C2* (1km S Rural) *45.14892, -0.00245* **Camp Municipal Les Gerbes, Rue de la Dronne, 24490 La Roche-Chalais [05 53 91 40 65 or 06 38 82 40 08 (mob); fax 05 53 90 32 01; campinggerbes@orange.fr; www.larochechalais.com]** Fr S on D674 turn sharp L in vill at site sp. Site on R in 500m. Fr N take Coutras-Libourne rd thro vill; site sp on L beyond sm indus est. Med, mkd, pt shd, terr, wc; shwrs inc; EHU (5-10A) €2.60-3.60 (poss rev pol); lndry; shop nr; playgrnd; pool; sw nr; red long stay; wifi; adv bkg acc; canoeing adj; fishing adj; boating adj; CKE/CCI. "Pleasant, well-kept, well-run site nr rv; gd sized pitches, some rvside; leisure pk 5km; gd clean san facs; rec pitch N side of site to avoid factory noise; mkt Sat am; rec." ♦ 15 Apr-30 Sep. € 14.00 2014*

ROCHE POSAY, LA *4H2* (2km N Rural) *46.7989, 0.80961* **Camping La Roche-Posay, Route de Lésigny. 86270 La Roche-Posay [05 49 86 21 23; info@larocheposay-vacances.com; www.larocheposay-vacances.com]** On A10 take exit 26 Châtellerault-Nord, La Roche-Posay; foll sp La Roche-Posay; foll the D725 to La Roche-Possay; at rndabt foll sp for 'Camping-Hippodrome'. Lge, hdg, mkd, shd, wc (htd); mv service pnt; shwrs inc; EHU (10A) inc; gas; lndry; shop nr; rest; snacks; bar; bbq (elec, gas); playgrnd; pool (covrd, htd); sw nr; red long stay; entmnt; 10% statics; dogs €1.50; Eng spkn; adv bkg acc; quiet; bike hire; fishing 1.5km; tennis; waterslide; CKE/CCI. "Excel, popular, well-maintained site; aquatic park; 1st class facs; barrier locks automatically 2300; parking avail outside; walk to town on busy rd with no pavement; spa town." ♦ 7 Apr-23 Sep. € 40.00 2017*

ROCHE POSAY, LA *4H2* (3km E Rural) *46.78274, 0.86942* **Camp Municipal Les Bords de Creuse, Rue de Pont, 37190 Yzeures-sur-Creuse [02 47 94 48 32 or 02 47 94 55 01 (Mairie); www.yzeuressurcreuse.com]** Fr Châtellerault take D725 E twds La Roche-Posay; after x-ing Rv Creuse, turn L onto D750 twds Yzeures-sur-Creuse; at traff lts in vill turn S onto D104; site on R in 200m at T-junc. Med, mkd, pt shd, pt sl, wc; chem disp; shwrs inc; EHU (6A) inc; lndry; shop nr; bbq; sw nr; dogs; quiet; games rm; tennis adj. "Pool adj." ♦ 15 Jun-31 Aug. € 15.40 2013*

ROCHE SUR YON, LA *2H4* (8km SW Rural) *46.62281, 1.44983* **Campilo, L'Auroire, 85430 Aubigny [02 51 31 68 45; accueil@campilo.com; www.campilo.com]** Take Rue du Maréchal Joffre, D248 Rue du Maréchal Lyautey and D747 to Les Gâts in Aubign, take Rue des Mésanges and Le Champt des Landes to La Guyonnière, turn R onto Les Gâts, turn L onto Route de l'Auroire, cont onto Rue des Mésanges, turn L onto Le Champt des Landes, take the 2nd R onto La Guyonnière. Med, mkd, pt shd, sl, chem disp; shwrs; EHU (10A); lndry; bar; bbq; playgrnd; pool; dogs (€3); Eng spkn. "Tow cars not allowed besides c'vans sep car park; fishing lake on site; walks and cycling rtes; lge sports area; bicycles; sm gym; friendly staff; new san facs and pool." ♦ € 19.00 2014*

⊞ **ROCHECHOUART** *7B3* (13km SW Rural) *45.73390, 0.68070* **Camping Chez Rambaud, 87440 Les Salles-Lavauguyon [05 55 00 08 90; camping@chez-rambaud.com; www.chez-rambaud.com]** Fr Rochechouart on D675 then immed R onto D10 dir Videix & Verneuil; in 11km at Verneuil turn L to Les Salles-Lavauguyon. At Salles turn R at bottom of hill (leaving church on L) onto D34 sp Sauvagnac; in 300m turn L sp Chez Rambaud, site on L in 1km along narr rd. Sm, hdg, hdstg, mkd, pt shd, sl, wc (htd); chem disp; shwrs inc; EHU (10A) €3.50 (long lead poss req); lndry; shop nr; rest nr; bar nr; bbq; dogs €1.50; Eng spkn; adv bkg acc; quiet; ice; CKE/CCI. "Tranquil, CL-type site in National Park; views over wooded valley; enthusiastic, friendly & helpful British owners; excel, immac facs; levelling blocks poss req; some pitches inadequate for awnings; farm animals in pens on site; horseriding nr; kayaking nrby; gd touring base; gd walking & cycling; easy walk to vill (1.5km); Richard The Lion Heart rte in vill; mkt in Rochechouart Sat; superb." ♦ € 18.00 2012*

ROCHEFORT *7B1* (2km N Coastal) *45.94386, -0.99499* **Camping Le Bateau, Rue des Pêcheurs d'Islande, 17300 Rochefort [05 46 99 41 00; fax 05 46 99 91 65; lebateau@wanadoo.fr; www.campinglebateau.com]** Exit A837/E602 at junc 31 & take D733 dir Rochefort. At 1st rndabt by McDonalds, take D733 dir Royan. At next rndabt 1st R onto Rue des Pêcheurs d'Islande. Site at end of rd on L. Med, hdg, pt shd, wc; chem disp; shwrs inc; EHU (8A) €4; lndry; shop; rest; snacks; bar; playgrnd; pool; entmnt; 25% statics; dogs €1.70; quiet; watersports; tennis; fishing; waterslide; games rm; CKE/CCI. "Sm pitches, a few o'look estuary; helpful staff; basic, clean san facs; poss scruffy LS - ducks & geese on site; no twin axles; gd cycling, walking; mkt Tues & Sat; lake fishing; Lidl 10 mins walk; intersting town; friendly non-english speaking owners; site adj to rv." 1 Apr-1 Nov. € 22.50 2014*

ROCHEFORT *7B1* (1km S Urban) *45.93013, -0.95826* **Camping Municipal Le Rayonnement, 3, Avenue de la Fosse Aux Mâts, 17300 Rochefort [05 46 82 67 70; camping.municipal@ville-rochefort.fr; www.ville-rochefort.fr/decouvrir/camping]** Exit E602 at junc 31 & take D733 dir Rochefort. At rndabt by McDonalds, take D733 dir Royan. Cont on D733. At rndabt with plane take 3rd exit onto Bd Edouard Pouzet. At rndabt take 3rd exit onto Bd de la Résistance, at next rndabt take 1st exit & then turn L onto ave de la Fosse aux Mâts. Site on L. Med, hdstg, hdg, shd, wc; chem disp; mv service pnt; fam bthrm; shwrs inc; EHU (15A) inc; lndry; shop nr; bbq; playgrnd; entmnt; wifi; TV; 15% statics; dogs €1.05; phone; bus 100m; Eng spkn; adv bkg rec; games rm; bike hire. "Bikes hire free; rv Charente & cycle path to cent 800m away; v helpful staff; no c'vans over 6m & twin axles; san facs v clean; Ecolabel campsite; vg; excel transporter bdge & access to town; excel." ♦ 27 Feb-3 Dec. € 18.00 2016*

ROCROI

ROCHEFORT 7B1 (8km W Coastal) 45.94828, -1.09592
Camp Municipal de la Garenne, Ave de l'Ile-Madame, 17730 Port-des-Barques [05 46 84 80 66 or 06 08 57 08 75 (mob); fax 05 46 84 98 33; camping@ville-portdesbarques.fr; www.camping-municipal-portdesbarques.com] Fr Rochefort S on D773, cross Rv Charente bdge & take 1st exit sp Soubise & Ile Madame. Cont strt thro Port-des-Barques, site on L opp causeway to Ile-Madame. Lge, mkd, unshd, wc; chem disp; mv service pnt; fam bthrm; shwrs inc; EHU (10A) inc; lndry; shop nr; rest nr; snacks; bar nr; playgrnd; pool (htd); beach shgl adj; red long stay; wifi; 25% statics; dogs €1.26; phone; bus adj; adv bkg acc; quiet; ccard acc; CKE/CCI. "Pleasant site; lge pitches; pitches a little scruffy, but level; facs dated but clean; refurb (2016) nice location to sea." ♦ 1 Apr-31 Oct. € 22.00　　　　　　　　　　　　　　　2017*

ROCHEFORT EN TERRE 2F3 (10km NE Urban) 47.74455, -2.25997 Camp Municipal de La Digue, Route 77 Le Guélin, 56200 St Martin sur Oust [02 99 91 55 76 or 02 99 91 49 45; fax 02 99 91 42 94; st-martin-oust@wanadoo.fr; www.tourismebretagne.com] On D873 14km N of Redon at Gacilly, turn W onto D777 twd Rochefort-en-Terre; site sp in 10km in St Martin. Med, pt shd, wc; shwrs; EHU (3-5A) €3.20; lndry; shop nr; bbq; playgrnd; dogs €0.50; adv bkg acc; quiet; rv fishing 50m. "Towpath walks to vill & shops; clean facs but ltd LS; well-maintained site; site yourself, warden calls am & eve; excel, refurbished facs (2013)." 1 May-30 Sep. € 10.00　　　2018*

ROCHEFORT EN TERRE 2F3 (1km S Rural) 47.695193, -2.349117 Camping Au Gré des Vents (formerly du Moulin Neuf), Chemin de Bogeais, Route de Limerzel, 56200 Rochefort-en-Terre [02 97 43 37 52; fax 02 97 43 35 45; gredesvents@orange.fr; www.campingaugredesvents.com] Fr Redon W on D775 twd Vannes, approx 23km turn R onto D774 sp Rochefort-en-Terre; immed after vill limit sp, turn sharp L up slope to ent. NB Do not drive thro vill. Med, hdg, mkd, pt shd, pt sl, terr, wc; chem disp; mv service pnt; shwrs inc; EHU ltd (10A) €4.50; lndry; shop nr; rest nr; bbq; pool (htd); sw nr; 10% statics; dogs €3; adv bkg acc; quiet; ccard acc; games area; CKE/CCI. "Peaceful base for touring area; helpful, lovely owners; no vehicle movement or shwrs 2200-0700 (0800 LS), but wcs open; no twin axles; excel; bit scruffy; v nr vill." ♦ 31 Mar-30 Sep. € 26.00　　　　　　2018*

ROCHEFORT SUR LOIRE 4G1 (1km N Urban) 47.36021, -0.65611 Camping Seasonova Les Plages de Loire, route de Savennières, 49190 Rochefort-sur-Loire [02 41 68 55 91; www.camping-lesplagesdeloire.com] Fr Angers: S on A87. Exit 24 onto D160 dir Beaulieu for 1km. At rndabt 1st R onto D54 to Rochfort. Thro town cent over rv. Site on L. Med, wc (htd); chem disp; mv service pnt; fam bthrm; shwrs inc; EHU (10A); lndry; rest; snacks; bar; playgrnd; twin axles; 10% statics; dogs €2; Eng spkn; adv bkg acc; CKE/CCI. "New site, nice facs up steps; interesting area." ♦ 3 Apr-1 Nov. € 19.00　　　　　　　　　　2015*

ROCHELLE, LA 7A1 (12km N Rural/Coastal) 46.25239, -1.11972 Camp Municipal Les Misottes, 46 Rue de l'Océan, 17137 Esnandes [07 68 16 70 20; www.campinglesmisottes.fr] Fr N on D938 or N1327 turn W at Marans onto D105. In 7.5km turn S onto D9 then D202 to Esnandes. Enter vill, at x-rds strt, site on R in 200m. Fr La Rochelle D105 N to cent Esnandes, site sp. Med, mkd, pt shd, wc cont; shwrs inc; EHU (6-10A) €2.85; lndry; shop nr; rest nr; snacks; bar nr; playgrnd; beach shgl 2km; 5% statics; dogs €1.60; Eng spkn; adv bkg acc; quiet; fishing; CKE/CCI. "Site on the edge of marshlands; v nice & quiet; excel bus svrs; canal fishing; liable to flood; vg; new manager (2018) enthusiastic and determined to update site; v clean basic san facs; vg for La Rochelle and area; rec for sh stay." 1 Apr-15 Oct. € 15.50　　　　　　　　2018*

ROCHELLE, LA 7A1 (5km S Rural/Coastal) 46.11659, -1.11939 Camping Les Sables, Chemin du Pontreau, 17440 Aytré [05 46 45 40 30; fax 05 46 27 89 02; camping_les_sables@yahoo.fr; www.camping-les-sables.com] Fr S (Rochefort) on D137, exit sp Aytré. At 2nd traff lts turn L & foll site sp. Lge, hdg, pt shd, wc; chem disp; mv service pnt; fam bthrm; shwrs inc; EHU (6A) €3; lndry; shop; rest; snacks; bar; bbq; playgrnd; pool (covrd, htd); paddling pool; entmnt; wifi; 50% statics; dogs €1.50; phone; Eng spkn; adv bkg acc; ccard acc; bike hire; games area; games rm; waterslide; CKE/CCI. "Vg." ♦ 1 May-15 Oct. € 35.00　　　　　　　　　　　　　　　2017*

ROCHELLE, LA 7A1 (5km NW Rural/Coastal) 46.19583, -1.1875 Camping au Petit Port de l'Houmeau, Rue des Sartières, 17137 L'Houmeau [05 46 50 90 82; fax 05 46 50 01 33; info@aupetitport.com; www.aupetitport.com] Exit N237 onto D104/D105 sp Lagord; at rndabt in 1km turn L onto D104; in 2.5km fork L onto D106 to L'Houmeau; at ent to town turn R into Rue des Sarthières sp Camping; site on R in 100m. Med, mkd, hdstg, hdg, shd, terr, wc; chem disp; mv service pnt; fam bthrm; shwrs inc; EHU (10A) €4.60 (poss rev pol); lndry; shop nr; rest nr; snacks; bar; bbq (gas); playgrnd; beach shgl 1.5km; wifi; dogs €2; bus 400m; Eng spkn; adv bkg rec; quiet; ccard acc; bike hire; games rm; CKE/CCI. "Pleasant, friendly site; helpful owners; clean facs; no vehicle access 2230-0730; gd walking & cycling; under new management (2013); conv Ile de Ré bdge; excel." ♦ 1 Apr-30 Sep. € 30.00　　　　　　　　　　　　　　　2014*

ROCROI 5C1 (12km SE Rural) 49.87200, 4.60446 Camp Départemental du Lac des Vieilles Forges, 08500 Les Mazures [03 24 40 17 31; fax 03 24 41 72 38; cmpingvieillesforges@cg08.fr] Fr Rocroi take D1 & D988 fr Les Mazures/Renwez. Turn R D40 at sp Les Vieilles Forges. Site on R nr lakeside. Lge, mkd, hdstg, shd, pt sl, wc (htd); mv service pnt; shwrs inc; EHU (6-10A) €2.50-4.30 (long leads req); lndry; shop; snacks; playgrnd; sw; entmnt; TV; 20% statics; dogs €1; adv bkg acc; quiet; bike hire; boating; tennis; fishing. "Attractive walks; lake views fr some pitches; vg site; recep clsd 1200-1500." ♦ 11 Apr-15 Sep. € 20.00　　　　　　　　　2016*

France

Site report forms at back of guide　　　　　　　　　　*Last year of report

ROCROI

ROCROI *5C1* (3km SE Rural) *49.89446, 4.53770* **Camping La Murée, 35 Rue Catherine-de-Clèves, 08230 Bourg-Fidèle [03 24 54 24 45; campingdelamuree@wanadoo. fr; www.campingdelamuree.com]** Site sp fr Rocroi on R. Sm, hdstg, mkd, pt shd, pt sl, wc (htd); chem disp; fam bthrm; shwrs inc; EHU (10A) €4; lndry; shop nr; rest; bar; bbq; playgrnd; sw pool; twin axles; 60% statics; dogs €1.50; Eng spkn; adv bkg acc; quiet; ccard acc; CKE/CCI. "Two fishing lakes on site; pleasant site; gd sh stay/NH; gd san facs, new management helpful & friendly; gd rest; scenic location." ♦ 01 Mar-30 Nov. € 19.00 2013*

RODEZ *7D4* (1km NE Urban) *44.35323, 2.58708* **Camp Municipal Layoule, 12000 Rodez [05 65 67 09 52; fax 05 65 67 11 43; contact@mairie-rodez.fr]** Clearly sp in Rodez town cent & all app rds. Access at bottom steep hill thro residential area. Med, hdg, hdstg, mkd, pt shd, wc; chem disp; mv service pnt; shwrs inc; EHU (6A) inc; lndry; shop nr; playgrnd; dogs; phone; bus adj; quiet; golf nr; tennis nr; CKE/CCI. "Site by lake & rv; gd sized pitches; helpful warden; clean facs; steep walk to historic town; gates clsd 2000-0700; ent is down steep twisty rds & exit is up the same hill; interesting wild life; gd walks & cycling; excel NH; excel for town."
♦ 1 May-30 Sep. € 14.00 2018*

ROHAN *2F3* (0km NW Rural) *48.07078, -2.75525* **Camp Municipal du Val d'Oust, Rue de St Gouvry, 56580 Rohan [02 97 51 57 58 or 02 97 51 50 33 (Mairie); fax 02 97 51 52 11; mairie.rohan@wanadoo.fr; www.morbihan.com]** Rue de St Gouvry runs NW fr Rohan parallel to D11, but other side of canal. Sm, mkd, pt shd, wc; chem disp; shwrs inc; EHU €3.10; lndry; shop nr; rest nr; bar nr; bbq; playgrnd; dogs €0.90; phone; adv bkg acc; CKE/CCI. "Pleasant site beside Nantes/Brest canal; gd cycling; market in vill; some rd noise." ♦ 1 Jun-15 Sep. € 12.00 2018*

ROMIEU, LA *8E2* (0km NE Rural) *43.98299, 0.50183* **Kawan Village Le Camp de Florence, 32480 La Romieu [05 62 28 15 58; fax 05 62 28 20 04; info@lecampdeflorence.com; www.lecampdeflorence.com]** Take D931 N fr Condom & turn R onto D41, where La Romieu sp next to radio mast. Go thro La Romieu & turn L at sp just bef leaving vill. Lge, hdstg, hdg, pt shd, wc; chem disp; mv service pnt; fam bthrm; shwrs inc; EHU (10A) inc (poss rev pol); lndry; shop nr; rest nr; snacks; bar; bbq; playgrnd; pool; paddling pool; twin axles; entmnt; wifi; TV; 80% statics; dogs €2.30; Eng spkn; adv bkg req; quiet; ccard acc; bike hire; games area; games rm; tennis; CKE/CCI. "Peaceful, Dutch-run site in pleasant location; gd sized pitches, most with views; welcoming, helpful staff; waterslide; jacuzzi; leisure complex 500m; gd clean san facs; gd rest; poss muddy when wet; archery; some noise fr disco, ask for pitch away fr bar; rest in 16thC farmhouse; gd pool but take care sl ent; gd cycling; historic 11thC vill; mkt Wed Condom." ♦ 28 Apr-24 Sep. € 36.60 2015*

⊞ **ROMILLY SUR SEINE** *4E4* (4km W Rural) *48.5259, 3.6646* **Camping du Domaine de la Noue des Rois, Chemin des Brayes, 10100 St Hilaire-sous-Romilly [03 25 24 41 60; fax 03 25 24 34 18; contact@lanouedesrois.com; www.lanouedesrois.com]** Site sp fr D619, on rvside. Lge, mkd, pt shd, wc (htd); mv service pnt; fam bthrm; shwrs; EHU (16A) €3.50-5; gas; lndry; shop; rest; bar; playgrnd; pool (covrd, htd); paddling pool; red long stay; entmnt; 90% statics; dogs (on lead) €3.50; Eng spkn; adv bkg acc; quiet; ccard acc; waterslide; fishing; games area; watersports; sailing; tennis; CKE/CCI. "Gd situation in wooded area; conv Paris & Disneyland; ltd pitches/facs for tourers." ♦ € 32.00 2012*

ROMORANTIN LANTHENAY *4G2* (1km E Urban) *47.35586, 1.75568* **Camping de Tournefeuille, Rue de Long Eaton, 41200 Romorantin-Lanthenay [02 54 76 16 60; fax 02 54 76 00 34; camping.romo@wanadoo.fr]** Fr town cent on D724 to Salbis, foll sp thro several traff lts over bdge turn R into Rue de Long-Eaton, site sp. Med, pt shd, wc (htd); shwrs inc; EHU (10A) €3; gas; shop nr; snacks; playgrnd; wifi; dogs free; quiet; fishing; bike hire. "Rv walk to town rec; pool adj; excel modern san facs; helpful staff." 1 Apr-30 Sep. € 16.00 2016*

ROQUEBRUN *10F1* (0km SE Rural) *43.49775, 3.02834* **Camping Campotel Le Nice de Roquebrun, Rue du Temps Libre, 34460 Roquebrun [04 67 89 61 99 or 04 67 89 79 97; fax 04 67 89 78 15; camping-campotel@wanadoo.fr; www.Camping-lenice.com]** N112 to St Chinian & take D20 dir Cessenon-sur-Orb, turn L onto D14 twd Roquebrun; site on L bef bdge over rv. Narr app rd. Sm, mkd, hdstg, pt shd, pt sl, terr, wc; chem disp; mv service pnt; shwrs inc; EHU (6A) €2.50; lndry; shop nr; rest nr; bar nr; playgrnd; sw nr; entmnt; 15% statics; dogs €1.30; phone; adv bkg acc; quiet; ccard acc; fishing adj; tennis; sailing adj; CKE/CCI. "Excel cent for walking & cycling; beautiful scenery; ltd touring pitches; some gd, modern san facs; canoe hire adj; not suitable for lge o'fits; need key for WC block; off clsd Sundays LS." 15 Mar-15 Nov. € 14.00 2012*

ROSANS *9D3* (3km SW Rural) *44.38273, 5.46172* **Camping des Rosieres, Quartier des Coings, 05150 Rosans [04 92 66 62 06 or 06 70 10 69 99 (mob); fax 04 92 66 68 90; contact@camping-rosieres.com; www.camping-rosieres.com/fr]** On D94 Nyons to Gap on RH side just prior to ent Rosans. Sm, hdg, shd, wc; chem disp; shwrs; EHU (6A); lndry; rest; snacks; bar; playgrnd; pool (htd); twin axles; entmnt; wifi; dogs; Eng spkn; adv bkg acc; games area; CKE/CCI. "Horseriding; canyoning; tennis; boules; steep narr rd fr recep & sw pool to pitches; gd." 1 May-30 Sep. € 24.00 2017*

ROSCOFF *1D2* (7km SW Rural/Coastal) *48.67246, -4.05326* Camp Municipal du Bois de la Palud, 29250 Plougoulm [02 98 29 81 82 or 02 98 29 90 76 (Mairie); contact@plougoulm.bzh; www.plougoulm.bzh]
Fr D58 turn W on D10 sp Cléder/Plouescat; after 3km on ent Plougoulm foll sp to site. Sm, mkd, hdg, pt shd, terr, wc; chem disp; shwrs inc; EHU (8A) €3.50; lndry; shop nr; playgrnd; beach sand 500m; phone; Eng spkn; adv bkg acc; quiet; ccard acc; CKE/CCI. "Clean, tidy site in delightful area; lovely views to sandy inlet; conv ferry; if arr late, site yourself; warden calls am & pm; access all hrs with c'van; walk in first, turning diff inside; also lower field with EHU; sh walk to vill; excel; late arr & late dep; beautiful beaches to the west." ♦
15 Jun-4 Sep. € 14.00   2016*

ROSIERS SUR LOIRE, LES *4G1* (1km N Rural) *47.35908, -0.22500* FLOWER Camping Val de Loire, 6 Rue Ste Baudruche, 49350 Les Rosiers-sur-Loire [02 41 51 94 33; fax 02 41 51 89 13; contact@ camping-valdeloire.com; www.camping-valdeloire.com or www.flowercampings.com]
Take D952 fr Saumur in dir Angers. Site on D59 1km N of vill cent on L dir Beaufort-en-Vallée. Med, mkd, hdg, hdstg, pt shd, serviced pitches; wc; chem disp; mv service pnt; fam bthrm; shwrs inc; EHU (10A) €4.50; gas; lndry; rest; snacks; bar; bbq; playgrnd; pool (htd); paddling pool; red long stay; entmnt; wifi; TV; 15% statics; dogs €3; Eng spkn; adv bkg acc; quiet; waterslide; tennis; games rm; CKE/CCI. "Close to Rv Loire; lge pitches; friendly, helpful staff; excel san facs; gd touring base for chateaux region; excel." ♦
1 Apr-30 Sep. € 38.00   2014*

ROSIERS SUR LOIRE, LES *4G1* (6km NW Rural) *47.39231, -0.27381* Camping Port St Maur, 49250 La Ménitré [02 41 45 60 80; fax 02 41 45 65 65; 0611417561@sfr.fr] Exit Les Rosiers on D952 sp Angers. At rndabt 3km past St Mathhurin sur Loire take 1st exit sp Port St Maur. Site on R in 200m. Med, mkd, pt shd, wc; chem disp; shwrs inc; EHU (5A) inc; lndry; shop nr; rest; snacks; bar; bbq; playgrnd; entmnt; 10% statics; dogs €1; Eng spkn. "Access to san facs by steps; helpful warden; boat trips on Loire; lovely rvside setting with view of St Maur Abbey; gd walking & cycling; gd." ♦ 1 May-15 Sep.
€ 12.50   2016*

ROSNAY *4H2* (1km N Rural) *46.70647, 1.21161* Camp Municipal Les Millots, Route de St Michel-en-Brenne, 36300 Rosnay [02 54 37 80 17 (Mairie); rosnay-mairie@wanadoo.fr] NE on D27 fr Le Blanc to Rosnay; site sp 500m N of Rosnay on D44. Sm, mkd, pt shd, wc (htd); chem disp; fam bthrm; shwrs inc; EHU (6-10A) inc (poss rev pol); lndry; shop nr; rest nr; bbq; playgrnd; dogs; phone; adv bkg acc; quiet; lake fishing; tennis; cycling; CKE/CCI. "Lovely, tranquil, popular site; well-kept; excel modern san facs; warden collects fees twice daily; lakeside walks; excel walking, cycling, birdwatching & fishing; gd base for exploring Brenne National Park; vg value; excel; friendly." ♦
16 Feb-15 Nov. € 11.40   2018*

⊞ **ROUEN** *3C2* (5km E Urban) *49.43154, 1.15387* Camping L'Aubette, 23 Rue du Vert-Buisson, 76160 St Léger-du-Bourg-Denis [02 32 08 32 40; accueil@ rouentourisme.com; www.rouentourisme.com]
Fr Rouen E on N31 dir Darnétal & Beauvais; in 1km cont strt on onto D42/D138 dir St Léger-du-Bourg-Denis; in 400m turn L onto Rue du Vert Buisson; site on r in 800m just past stop sp. Site well sp as 'Camping' fr Rouen cent. Med, pt shd, pt sl, terr, wc; chem disp; mv service pnt; shwrs; EHU (3-10A) €1.50-3; lndry; shop nr; 40% statics; dogs; bus 150m; CKE/CCI. "In attractive rv valley; conv city cent; conv bus to town; v ltd touring pitches; cash only; v basic site; gd NH only; v poor." ♦ € 15.00   2018*

ROUEN *3C2* (14km NW Rural) *49.50553, 0.98409* Camping Les Nenuphars, 765 Rue des Deux Tilleuls, Le Bout du Haut, 76480 Roumare [02 35 33 80 75; www.camping-les-nenuphars.com] S on D6015/A150 dir Rouen, foll sp Roumare & site. Fr Rouen take A150/D6015 N to St Jean-du-Cardonnay; turn L to Roumare; site sp. 500m bef Roumare. Med, mkd, hdg, pt shd, pt sl, wc; chem disp; shwrs inc; EHU (5-10A); lndry; playgrnd; twin axles; dogs €1.70; phone; bus 1km; Eng spkn; adv bkg acc; games area; CKE/CCI. "Pleasant grassy site, handy for Rouen; v ltd sports facs; lge pitches; vg." 28 Mar-15 Dec. € 18.00   2015*

> **"We must tell the Club about that great site we found"**
>
> Get your site reports in by mid-August and we'll do our best to get your updates into the next edition.

ROUSSILLON *10E2* (3km SW Rural) *43.88973, 5.27596* Camping L'Arc-en-Ciel, Route de Goult, 84220 Roussillon [04 90 05 73 96; contact@camping-arc-en-ciel.fr; www.camping-arc-en-ciel.fr] Take D900 W out of Apt, then R on D201 sp Roussillon, then R on D4 for 1.5km, then L on D104 twd Roussillon. Take L fork twd Goult, site well sp 2.5km on L. No access for c'vans & m'vans in Roussillon vill. Med, hdstg, mkd, pt shd, pt sl, terr, wc; chem disp; shwrs inc; EHU (4A) €3.80; gas; lndry; shop; snacks; bar; playgrnd; pool; paddling pool; dogs €3.50; phone; adv bkg acc; quiet; games area; CKE/CCI. "Tranquil woodland site; tight access some pitches; poss diff lge o'fits due trees; helpful staff; old san facs; beware rd humps & drainage channels on site access rds; some pitches poss diff lge o'fits; worth a detour; vg." ♦ 15 Mar-31 Oct. € 16.00   2014*

ROYAN 7B1 (9km NE Rural) 45.64796, -0.95847 **FFCC Camping Le Bois Roland,** 82 Route de Royan, 17600 Médis [05 46 05 47 58; contact@le-bois-roland.com; www.le-bois-roland.com] On N150 Saintes-Royan rd, site sp on R 100m beyond Médis vill sp. Med, pt shd, wc; chem disp; shwrs inc; EHU (5-10A) €4.20-5.20; gas; lndry; shop; snacks; bar; playgrnd; pool; paddling pool; beach sand 4km; entmnt; TV; dogs €2.80; phone; Eng spkn; adv bkg acc; quiet; ccard acc; CKE/CCI. "Attractive, wooded site; friendly, family-run; facs poss stretched high ssn; waiting area avail; vg; shop/rest/bar open in July when tradsmn will call." ♦
1 May-30 Sep. € 19.00   2015*

ROYAN 7B1 (16km SE Coastal) 45.55713, -0.94655 **Camping Soleil Levant,** Allée de la Langée, 17132 Meschers-sur-Gironde [05 46 02 76 62; fax 05 46 02 50 56; info@camping-soleillevant.com; www.camping-soleillevant.com] Take D145 coast rd fr Royan to Talmont. At Meschers turn R foll camp sp twd port; sp. Med, pt shd, wc; chem disp; shwrs inc; EHU (10A) €5.10; lndry; shop; snacks; bar; playgrnd; pool; paddling pool; beach sand 1.5km; entmnt; 20% statics; dogs €3.50; adv bkg acc; quiet; ccard acc; horseriding adj; watersports adj; CKE/CCI. "Gd, busy site; v clean san facs; port & rest 300m; vill shop & daily mkt 500m; visits to Cognac & Bordeaux distilleries; v friendly, helpful family run site."
1 Apr-30 Sep. € 31.00   2015*

⊞ **ROYAN** 7B1 (2km SE Coastal) 45.61817, -1.00425 **Camping La Triloterie,** 44 ter, Ave Aliénor d'Aquitaine, 17200 Royan [05 46 05 26 91; fax 05 46 06 20 74; info@campingroyan.com; www.campingroyan.com] Fr Royan PO, foll sp Bordeaux N730, on E of rd. Med, shd, wc (htd); chem disp; mv service pnt; fam bthrm; shwrs inc; EHU (4-12A) €4-6 (poss rev pol); shop nr; bbq; playgrnd; beach sand 900m; entmnt; wifi; 10% statics; dogs €1.50; phone; waterslide. "Excel site; conv for Royan town cent & St George de Didonne; site a bit tired, ok for NH."
€ 23.00   2017*

ROYAN 7B1 (5km SE Coastal) 45.58345, -0.98720 **Camping Bois-Soleil,** 2 Ave de Suzac, 17110 St Georges-de-Didonne [05 46 05 05 94; fax 05 46 06 27 43; camping.bois.soleil@wanadoo.fr; www.bois-soleil.com] Fr A10 exit junc 35 dir Saintes & Royan; on app Royan foll St Georges-de-Didonne sp onto bypass D25/D730/D25/D25E; go over 2 rndabts (with underpass bet); at 3rd rndabt turn L sp Meschers-sur-Gironde; site on R in 500m. Site well sp. Lge, mkd, hdstg, hdg, pt shd, terr, wc (htd); chem disp; mv service pnt; fam bthrm; shwrs inc; EHU (6A) inc (poss rev pol); gas; lndry; shop; rest; snacks; bar; bbq (gas); playgrnd; pool (htd); paddling pool; beach sand adj; entmnt; wifi; TV; 30% statics; dogs €3 (not acc end Jun-Aug inc); phone; Eng spkn; adv bkg rec; ccard acc; bike hire; tennis; games area; CKE/CCI. "Superb wooded site in vg location nr beach; popular & busy; generous pitches, some sandy; excel, clean san facs; vg shop & rest; many sandy beaches nrby." ♦
2 Apr-9 Oct. € 42.00   2012*

See advertisement

> **"I need an on-site restaurant"**
>
> We do our best to make sure site information is correct, but it is always best to check any must-have facilities are still available or will be open during your visit.

ROYAN 7B1 (6km SE Coastal) 45.59253, -0.98713 **Camping Idéal,** Ave de Suzac, 17110 St Georges-de-Didonne [05 46 05 29 04; fax 05 46 06 32 36; info@ideal-camping.com; www.ideal-camping.com] Fr Royan foll coast rd sp St Georges-de-Didonne. Site sp on D25 2km S of St Georges, opp Cmp Bois-Soleil. Lge, mkd, shd, wc; chem disp; shwrs inc; EHU (6-10A) €4.50-5.50; gas; lndry; shop; rest; snacks; bar; playgrnd; pool (htd); paddling pool; beach sand 200m; entmnt; 10% statics; phone; ccard acc; bike hire; games area; horseriding 300m; tennis 500m; games rm; jacuzzi; waterslide; CKE/CCI. "Helpful staff; site popular with families." ♦ 7 May-5 Sep. € 37.00   2014*

ROYAN 7B1 (4km NW Urban/Coastal) 45.6309, -1.0498 **Campéole Camping Clairefontaine, 6 Rue du Colonel Lachaud, Pontaillac, 17200 Royan [05 46 39 08 11; fax 05 46 38 13 79; clairefontaine@ campeole.com; www.camping-clairefontaine.com or www.campeole.com]** Foll Pontaillac sp fr Royan. Site sp in Clairefontaine (& Pontaillac). Lge, mkd, pt shd, serviced pitches; wc; chem disp; mv service pnt; fam bthrm; shwrs inc; EHU (10A); gas; lndry; shop; rest; snacks; bar; bbq; playgrnd; pool; beach sand 300m; wifi; TV; 80% statics; dogs €3; phone; Eng spkn; adv bkg req; quiet; ccard acc; tennis; CKE/CCI. "Lovely coastline; gd for family holiday; helpful owner; clean, unisex san facs; ltd touring pitches, some sm; gd security; site poss dusty; vg walking & cycling; casino 300m; coastal path Pontaillac to Royan; gd site; easy walk/bike/bus into town; nice sw; bar & shop onsite; conv for city; vg." ♦ 31 Mar-1 Oct. € 41.00   2017*

ROYBON 9C2 (2km S Rural) 45.24639, 5.24806 **Camping de Roybon, Route de St Antoine, 38940 Roybon [04 76 36 23 67 or 06 86 64 55 47; campingroybon38@gmail.com; www.campingroybon.com]** Fr Roybon go S on D71 & foll sp. Med, mkd, pt shd, pt sl, wc; chem disp; shwrs inc; EHU (10A) €3.50; shop nr; playgrnd; sw nr; dogs €2.65; adv bkg acc; quiet; watersports adj. "V peaceful; gd, modern facs new; vg; can be boggy when wet." ♦ 1 May-30 Sep. € 18.40   2016*

ROYERE DE VASSIVIERE 7B4 (6km SW Rural) 45.78869, 1.89855 **Camping Les Terrasses du Lac, Vauveix, 23460 Royère-de-Vassivière [05 55 64 76 77; lesterrasses.camping@free.fr; www.campings-vassiviere.com]** Fr Eymoutiers take D43 for approx 10km then take D36 to Vauveix & foll sp. Med, mkd, hdg, pt shd, terr, wc (htd); chem disp; shwrs inc; EHU (10A) €3.10 (poss rev pol); lndry; rest nr; bar nr; beach adj; TV; 50% statics; dogs €1; quiet; cycling; horseriding; watersports adj; CKE/CCI. "Helpful staff; walking; lovely setting." ♦ 2 Apr-31 Oct. € 22.00   2017*

RUE 3B2 (6km N Rural) 50.31367, 1.69472 **Kawan Village Le Val d'Authie, 20 Route de Vercourt, 80120 Villers-sur-Authie [03 22 29 92 47; fax 03 22 29 92 20; camping@valdauthie.fr; www.valdauthie.fr]** Exit 24 on A16 twrds Vron, foll sp Camping Vercourt thro town. Lge, mkd, hdg, pt shd, pt sl, wc (htd); chem disp; mv service pnt; fam bthrm; shwrs inc; EHU (6-10A) (rev pol); gas; lndry; shop; rest; snacks; bar; playgrnd; pool (covrd, htd); paddling pool; entmnt; wifi; TV; 60% statics; dogs €1.50; phone; Eng spkn; adv bkg acc; quiet; ccard acc; games area; games rm; fitness rm; tennis; CKE/CCI. "Set in pleasant countryside; sauna; steam rm; helpful, friendly owners; clean, unisex facs & spacious shwrs; sm sep area for tourers, but many touring pitches bet statics (2009); poss diff for lge o'fits; gd pool; v cr & noisy high ssn; excel." ♦ 1 Apr-30 Sep. € 31.00   2017*

RUE 3B2 (4km SE Rural) 50.25278, 1.71224 **Camping de la Mottelette, Ferme de la Mottelette, 80120 Forest-Montiers [03 22 28 32 33 or 06 72 85 73 77 (mob); contact@la-mottelette.com; www.la-mottelette.com]** Exit A16 junc 24 onto D32 dir Rue & L Crotoy; at rndabt junc with D235 cont on D32; site on L in 1.5km. Site sp on leaving A16. Sm, mkd, hdg, unshd, wc; chem disp; fam bthrm; EHU (6A) €4; lndry; shop nr; bbq; playgrnd; 50% statics; dogs €1; Eng spkn; adv bkg acc; quiet; games area; games rm; CKE/CCI. "Basic, CL type, clean site on wkg fm; welcoming, friendly owners; mkt Sat; conv A16; gd touring base or NH; vg; pleasant atmosphere; new facs (2015)." ♦ 1 Apr-31 Oct. € 20.00   2017*

⊞ **RUFFEC** 7A2 (3km SE Rural) 46.01500, 0.21304 **Camping Le Réjallant, Les Grands Champs, 16700 Condac [05 45 31 29 06; fax 09 70 60 01 33; cdc-ruffec-charente@wanadoo.fr]** Site sp fr N10 & fr town. App 1km fr turn-off. Med, mkd, hdg, shd, pt sl, wc; chem disp; shwrs inc; EHU (10A) inc; lndry; rest nr; snacks; playgrnd; sw nr; wifi; dogs; Eng spkn; quiet; fishing 100m; CKE/CCI. "Friendly, sm nbr of touring sites; lovely vill 2km, gd Leclerc and Lidl supmkt; gd pool; clean facs; bar 100m; great for families." € 21.00   2017*

RUMILLY 9B3 (4km S Rural) 45.84083, 5.96277 **Camping Le Madrid, Route de St Félix, 74150 Rumilly [04 50 01 12 57; contact@camping-le-madrid.com; www.camping-le-madrid.com]** S fr Rumilly on D910, take D3 L dir St Marcel for approx 600m & at 2nd rndabt turn R, site sp. Med, hdstg, mkd, hdg, pt shd, wc (htd); chem disp; mv service pnt; fam bthrm; shwrs; EHU (6-10A) €2.80-4.30; lndry; shop nr; rest; snacks; bar; bbq; playgrnd; pool; paddling pool; entmnt; wifi; 50% statics; dogs €2; adv bkg acc; quiet; games rm; fishing; bike hire; games area. "Pleasant owners; chosen for proximity to m'way; ideal for NH." ♦ 1 Apr-24 Oct. € 28.00   2014*

RUOMS 9D2 (4km SW Urban) 44.43101, 4.32945 **Camping La Chapoulière, 07120 Ruoms [04 75 39 64 98 or 04 75 93 90 72; camping@lachapouliere.com; www.lachapouliere.com]** Exit Ruoms S on D579. At junc 2km S, foll D111 sp St Ambroix. Site 1.5km fr junc. Med, mkd, shd, pt sl, wc; mv service pnt; fam bthrm; shwrs inc; EHU (6A) €4; gas; lndry; shop; rest; snacks; bar; pool; paddling pool; sw nr; entmnt; wifi; TV; dogs €2.50; Eng spkn; adv bkg rec; quiet; games area; tennis 2km; canoeing; fishing adj. "Beautiful pitches on rv bank; friendly; ltd facs LS; vg; excel modern san facs; lge pitches demarcated by trees." ♦ Easter-30 Sep. € 37.00   2014*

SABLE SUR SARTHE *4F1* (1km S Rural) *47.83101, -0.33101* **Camp Municipal de l'Hippodrome, Allée du Québec, 72300 Sable-sur-Sarthe [02 43 95 42 61; fax 02 43 92 74 82; camping@sablesursarthe.fr; camping.sablesursarthe.fr]** Sp in town (foll sm, white sp with c'van symbols or Hippodrome). Fr N on D306; at traff lts at junc with D309, go strt over & under rlwy brdg sp Centre Ville; foll camping sps. Med, hdg, pt shd, wc; shwrs inc; EHU (15A) €2.40; gas; lndry; shop; snacks; bbq; playgrnd; pool; red long stay; entmnt; TV; Eng spkn; quiet; ccard acc; boat hire; canoeing; rv fishing; bike hire. "Excel site next to racecourse; gd, clean facs; helpful staff; conv for town; some pitches diff for lge fits." ♦ 3 Apr-15 Oct. € 16.40   2018*

SABLES D'OLONNE, LES *7A1* (2km E Rural) *46.48098, -1.73146* **Camping Le Puits Rochais, 25 Rue de Bourdigal, 85180 Château-d'Onne [02 51 21 09 69; fax 02 51 23 62 20; info@puitsrochais.com; www.puitsrochais.com]** Fr Les Sables-d'Olonne take D949 twd La Rochelle. Pass rndabt with lge hypermrkt 'Magasin Géant' & turn R at 1st traff lts at Mercedes g'ge, then 1st L to site. Med, hdg, mkd, pt shd, wc; chem disp; fam bthrm; shwrs inc; EHU (6-10A) inc; lndry; shop; rest; snacks; bar; bbq (gas); playgrnd; pool (htd); paddling pool; beach sand 2km; entmnt; wifi; TV; 60% statics; dogs €3.30; phone; adv bkg acc; quiet; ccard acc; games area; waterslide; bike hire; games rm; tennis; CKE/CCI. "Friendly, welcoming site; gd for families; san facs gd but ltd." ♦ 19 Apr-30 Sep. € 46.00   2014*

SABLES D'OR LES PINS *2E3* (1km NW Rural/Coastal) *48.63230, -2.41229* **Camping Les Salines (formerly Mun Sables), Rue du Lac, 22240 Plurien [02 96 72 17 40 or 06 28 22 43 36; campinglessalinesplurien@gmail.com; www.campinglessalines.fr]** Fr D786 turn N at Plurien onto D34 to Sables-d'Or. In 1km turn L & site on L after 200m. Med, pt shd, pt sl, terr, wc; chem disp; shwrs inc; EHU (6A) €2.35; lndry; shop nr; playgrnd; beach sand 400m; dogs €0.50; phone; Eng spkn; adv bkg acc; quiet; CKE/CCI. "Lovely, quiet, tranquile hillside site; some sea views; vg san facs; gates clsd 2200-0700; no pitching when office clsd, but lge car park opp; excel access to nature reserve & beautiful beaches; enthusiastic, helpful new owners (2017); lge pitches; lovely estuary walks; conv St Malo; wonderful coast; highly rec." ♦ 1 Apr-12 Nov. € 16.00   2017*

SACQUENAY *6G1* (1km S Rural) *47.58924, 5.32178* **Aire Naturelle La Chênaie (Méot), 16 Rue du 19 Mars, 21260 Sacquenay [03 80 75 89 43 or 03 80 75 97 07; eric.meot@wanadoo.fr; www.cotedor-tourisme.com]** S on D974 turn L onto D171A sp Occey & Sacquenay, site sp. Sm, pt shd, pt sl, wc; shwrs inc; EHU (6A); lndry; shop nr; playgrnd; red long stay; Eng spkn; adv bkg acc; quiet; CKE/CCI. "Peaceful site in orchard." 1 Apr-1 Oct. € 12.00   2013*

SAILLANS 9D2 (2km W Rural) 44.69511, 5.18124
Camping Les Chapelains, 26340 Saillans [04 75 21 55 47; camping@chapelains.fr; www.chapelains.fr] Fr W on D93 turn onto D493. Site well sp just bef Saillans vill boundary adj Rv Drôme. Sm, hdg, mkd, pt shd, wc; shwrs inc; EHU (4-10A); gas; lndry; shop; rest; snacks; playgrnd; beach shgl; dogs; Eng spkn; adv bkg acc; quiet; games area; CKE/CCI. "Attractive, well-run rvside site; some v sm pitches; friendly, helpful warden; rv walk to vill; rest open LS; san facs clean & updated (2015); gd." 18 Apr-15 Sep. € 22.60   2015*

ST AFFRIQUE 8E4 (1km E Urban) 43.95025, 2.89248
Camp Municipal, Parc des Sports, La Capelle Basse, 12800 St Affrique [05 65 98 20 00; fax 05 65 49 02 29] Site on D99 Albi-Millau rd to St Affrique sp fr all dir in E end of town. Nr stn & sports complex. Med, pt shd, wc; shwrs; EHU €2.75; shop nr; rest nr; bar nr; pool; sw; adv bkg acc; quiet; rv fishing; tennis. "Gd clean facs; NH." 14 Jun-13 Sep. € 12.00   2012*

> "Satellite navigation makes touring much easier"
>
> Remember most sat navs don't know if you're towing or in a larger vehicle – always use yours alongside maps and site directions.

⊞ **ST AIGNAN SUR CHER** 4G2 (9km N Rural) 47.32361, 1.36983 FFCC Camping Domaine du Bien Vivre, 13-15 Route du Petit Village, 41140 St Romain-sur-Cher [02 54 71 73 74; fax 02 54 71 72 81; domainedubienvivre@free.fr; www.domainedubienvivre.fr] Fr St Aignan-sur-Cher N on D675; in 6km in St Romain-sur-Cher site sp to L; foll sps for 3km. Sm, mkd, pt shd, pt sl, wc; chem disp; shwrs inc; EHU (6A) inc; shop nr; rest nr; bbq; playgrnd; dogs; Eng spkn; quiet; ccard acc; CKE/CCI. "A vineyard site; helpful owner; ltd facs in winter; sale of wines; conv Blois; gd." € 16.50   2016*

ST AIGNAN SUR CHER 4G2 (2km SE Rural) 47.26530, 1.38875 Camping Les Cochards, 1 Rue du Camping, Seigy, 41110 St Aignan-sur-Cher [02 54 75 15 59 or 06 72 09 45 24 (mob); fax 02 54 75 44 72; camping@lesclochards.com; www.lescochards.com] On D17 heading SE fr St Aignan twd Seigy on S bank of Rv Cher. Lge, mkd, pt shd, wc (htd); chem disp; mv service pnt; fam bthrm; shwrs inc; EHU (5-10A) €4.50; lndry; shop; snacks; bar; bbq; playgrnd; pool; sw nr; entmnt; wifi; TV; 20% statics; dogs €1.60; phone; Eng spkn; quiet; ccard acc; games area; horseriding 3km; rv fishing; canoeing; CKE/CCI. "Attractive, open site; helpful owners; gd san facs; recep clsd 2000; some pitches waterlogged after rain; easy walk to attractive town; excel; discount vouchers avail for local attractions; san facs being upgraded (2015)." ♦ 1 Apr-15 Oct. € 28.00   2015*

ST AIGNAN SUR CHER 4G2 (4km NW Rural) 47.29411, 1.33041 Camp Municipal Le Port, 3 rue du Passeur, 41110 Mareuil-sur-Cher [02 54 75 10 01; camping-leport@orange.fr; www.camping-leport.fr] Fr St Aignan take D17 twd Tours (on S bank of Cher); site in 4km in vill of Mareuil-sur-Cher behind church, thro new archway, on Rv Cher. By Mareuil chateau. Or fr A85 sp. Sm, mkd, pt shd, wc (htd); chem disp; shwrs inc; EHU (16A) €5.50; shop; rest nr; playgrnd; sw; dogs €2; Eng spkn; recce hire; fishing; CKE/CCI. "Beautiful, simple, rvside site; friendly staff; clean san facs but ltd; opening/closing dates variable, phone ahead to check; if office clsd enquire at supmkt adj (same owners); gas 50m; no access 1300-1500; diff lge o'fits; no twin axles; m'vans extra; gd touring area." ♦ 15 Apr-30 Sep. € 28.60   2013*

ST AMAND EN PUISAYE 4G4 (1km NE Urban) 47.53294, 3.07333 Camp Municipal La Vrille, Route de St Sauveur, 58310 St Amand-en-Puisaye [03 86 39 72 21 or 03 86 39 63 72 (Mairie); fax 03 86 39 64 97; saintam.mairie@wanadoo.fr; www.ot-puisaye-nivernaise.fr] Fr N7 take D957 Neuvy-sur-Loire to St Amand, at rd junc in vill take D955 sp St Sauveur-en-Puisaye, site on R in 500m; clearly sp on all app to vill. Sm, mkd, pt shd, wc; shwrs inc; EHU €2.30; shop nr; rest nr; bar nr; sailing adj; fishing in adj reservoir. "Vg simple site; gates clsd 2200-0700." 1 Jun-30 Sep. € 12.50   2015*

ST AMAND LES EAUX 3B4 (4km SE Rural) 50.43535, 3.46290 FFCC Camping du Mont des Bruyères, 806 Rue Basly, 59230 St Amand-les-Eaux [03 27 48 56 87; info@campingmontdesbruyeres.com; www.campingmontdesbruyeres.com] Exit A23 m'way at junc 5 or 6 onto ring rd D169, site sp. Fr N exit E42 junc 31 onto N52/N507 then D169. Avoid St Amand cent. Med, mkd, hdg, shd, pt sl, terr, wc (htd); mv service pnt; shwrs inc; EHU (6A-10A) inc; lndry; shop; bar; bbq; playgrnd; wifi; 60% statics; dogs €1.50; adv bkg acc; quiet; CKE/CCI. "Attractive site on forest edge; most touring pitches under trees; access to some pitches diff due slopes; gd cycling; excel birdlife on site; fac gd & clean." 15 Mar-30 Oct. € 24.00   2015*

ST AMAND MONTROND 4H3 (3km SW Rural) 46.71258, 2.49000 Camp Municipal La Roche, Rue de la Roche, 18200 St Amand-Montrond [02 48 96 09 36; camping-la-roche@wanadoo.fr; www.st-amand-tourisme.com] Exit A71/E11 junc 8 dir St Amand-Montrond on D300. Then foll sp to Montluçon on D2144 until rndabt on canal, turn R onto Quai Pluviôse/Rue de la Roche, site on R. Site sp on far side of town. Med, shd, pt sl, wc (htd); chem disp; shwrs inc; EHU (6A) €2.90 (poss rev pol); lndry; shop nr; playgrnd; entmnt; wifi; dogs; phone; quiet; rv fishing; tennis; CKE/CCI. "Popular NH, rec arr by 1700 high ssn; helpful warden; clean facs; tight for lge o'fits; rvside walk to pleasant town; gd." ♦ 1 Apr-30 Sep. € 17.00   2015*

ST ANDRE DE CUBZAC

CÔTE DE JADE | SOUTH BRITTANY | FRANCE

ST ANDRE DE CUBZAC 7C2 (4km NW Rural) 45.00703, -0.47724 **FFCC Camping Le Port Neuf, 1125 Route du Port Neuf, 33240 St André-de-Cubzac [05 57 43 16 44; contact@camping-port-neuf.com; www.camping-port-neuf.com]** Fr A10 or N10 take exit sp St André. Well sp fr St André (narr rds) on D669. Sm, mkd, hdg, hdstg, pt shd, wc (htd); chem disp; mv service pnt; shwrs inc; EHU (6A) €3.50 (poss long lead req); lndry; rest; snacks; bar; wifi; dogs €1; train to Bordeaux fr vill; Eng spkn; adv bkg acc; quiet; bike hire; lake fishing 100m; boating 100m; horseriding nr; CKE/CCI. "Lovely spot; friendly, helpful staff; san facs clean; pedalo hire; scruffy site (2015)." ♦ 1 May-30 Sep. €15.00 2016*

STE ANNE D'AURAY 2F3 (2km SW Rural) 47.69842, -2.96226 **Camp Municipal du Motten, Allée des Pins, 56400 Ste Anne-d'Auray [02 97 57 60 27 or 02 97 57 63 91; fax 02 97 57 72 33; contact@sainte-anne-auray.com or campingmotten@orange.fr; www.sainte-anne-auray.com]** Fr W on N165 take D17bis N to St Anne-d'Auray; then L onto D19 to town. This rte avoids Pluneret. Foll site sp. Med, mkd, pt shd, wc; chem disp; shwrs inc; EHU (10A) inc; lndry; shop nr; snacks; playgrnd; wifi; TV; dogs; Eng spkn; adv bkg acc; quiet; tennis; games area. "Peaceful, well-kept site, best pitches immed R after ent; welcoming, helpful warden; gd clean san facs; excel touring base; conv Basilica Ste Anne d'Auray; excel." ♦ 13 Jun-14 Sep. €16.00 2015*

ST ANTONIN NOBLE VAL 8E4 (2km N Rural) 44.1595, 1.7564 **FFCC Camp Municipal Le Ponget, Route de Caylus, 82140 St Antonin-Noble-Val [05 63 68 21 13 or 05 63 30 60 23 (Mairie); camping-leponget@wanadoo.fr]** Fr Caylus take D19 S to St Antonin; site on R, well sp. Sm, hdg, pt shd, wc (htd); mv service pnt; shwrs inc; EHU (3-6A) €2.50-3.70; gas; lndry; shop nr; rest nr; bar nr; playgrnd; sw nr; dogs €1.20; phone; quiet; CKE/CCI. "Well-kept site adj sports field; modern san facs; poss diff lge o'fits; gd walking; vg friendly site; excel mkt Sun; discount for 7 days; lovely medival town; gd for Aveyron Gorges & Bastide towns." ♦ 2 May-30 Sep. €11.70 2017*

ST ASTIER 7C3 (1km E Rural) 45.14735, 0.53308 **Flower Camping Le Pontet, Route de Montanceix, 24110 St Astier [05 53 54 14 22; fax 05 53 04 39 36; camping.lepontet@flowercampings.com; www.camping-dordogne-lepontet.com]** Take D6089 SW fr Périgueux; in 14km turn R sp St Astier; site on R on D41 on banks of Rv Isle. Med, mkd, shd, wc; chem disp; shwrs inc; EHU (6A) €2.55; gas; lndry; shop nr; snacks; bbq; playgrnd; pool; paddling pool; beach sand adj; entmnt; dogs; adv bkg acc; quiet; canoeing; fishing; CKE/CCI. "Some areas soft in wet weather." 1 Apr-30 Sep. €25.00 2012*

ST AUBIN DU CORMIER 2E4 (0km E Urban) 48.25990, -1.39609 **Camp Municipal, Rue de l'Etang, 35140 St Aubin-du-Cormier [06 15 49 51 83 (mob) or 02 99 39 10 42 (Mairie); mairie@ville-staubinducormier.fr; www.ville-staubinducormier.fr]** NE fr Rennes on A84; in 20km exit junc 28 dir St Aubin-du-Cormier. Foll sp 'Centre Ville' then site sp. Poss diff for lge o'fits - narr app. Sm, pt shd, pt sl, wc; shwrs inc; EHU (6-10A) inc; shop nr; 10% statics; dogs €0.65; adv bkg acc; quiet; lake fishing; CKE/CCI. "Pleasant, beautifully kept site adj lake; friendly; forest walks & around lake; pretty vill, with excel shops; mkt Thur; vet 1km; lovely site; san facs renovated 2014; vg disabled facs; recycling; dog health certs check on arr; excel for sh or long stay." ♦ 5 May-30 Sep. €12.00 2015*

ST AVOLD 5D2 (2km N Urban) 49.11017, 6.71059 **FFCC Camping Le Felsberg, Centre International de Séjour, Rue en Verrerie, 57500 St Avold [03 87 92 75 05; fax 03 87 92 20 69; cis.stavold@wanadoo.fr; www.mairie-saint-avold.fr]** Fr N on A4 exit junc 39 onto D633 to St Avold, stay in L hand lane at 2nd traff lts & turn L; pass under D603 for 2km & turn R. Site well sp in & around town; app up steep incline. Sm, hdstg, hdg, mkd, pt shd, pt sl, wc; chem disp; mv service pnt; shwrs inc; EHU (6-10A) €3-5; lndry; shop nr; rest; bar; playgrnd; red long stay; 50% statics; dogs €1; adv bkg acc; ccard acc; CKE/CCI. "German border 10km; sm pitches; gd facs; coal mine & archaeological park nrby worth visit; hypmkt 1.5km; awkward, heavy duty security gate at site ent; conv NH nr m'way; gd; walking dist of town facs." ♦ €14.00 2015*

344 ⊞ Site open all year

ST BREVIN LES PINS

ST AYGULF *10F4* (1km N Coastal) *43.39151, 6.72648* Camping de St Aygulf Plage, 270 Ave Salvarelli, 83370 St Aygulf Plage [04 94 17 62 49 or 06 12 44 36 52 (mob); fax 04 09 81 03 16; info@campingdesaintaygulf.fr; www.campingdesaintaygulf.fr] Fr Roquebrunne on D7 at rndabt 100m after vill sp St Aygulf take 3rd exit leading to Rue Roger Martin du Gard. Keep turning L. Fr Fréjus on D559, rd bends R after bdge over beach access, turn R bef rd climbs to L. V lge, hdg, mkd, shd, wc; chem disp; shwrs inc; EHU (5A) €3.50; gas; lndry; shop; rest; snacks; bar; playgrnd; beach sand adj; red long stay; twin axles; entmnt; dogs €3; adv bkg acc; ccard acc; fishing; watersports nr; games area; CKE/CCI. "Gd; shop clsd LS; sports facs nrby; pool (2017)." 1 Apr-28 Oct. € 34.00   2017*

ST AYGULF *10F4* (4km S Coastal) *43.40963, 6.72491* Camping Le Plage d'Argens, 541 route Départementale 559 (RN 98), 83370 St Aygulf [04 94 51 14 97; fax 04 94 51 29 44; camping.lepontdargens@yahoo.fr; www.camping-caravaning-lepontdargens.com] Well sp fr D559 bet Fréjus & St Aygulf, by Rv Argens. If app fr W pass site on R & return via next rndbt. Lge, mkd, pt shd, wc (htd); chem disp; mv service pnt; fam bthrm; shwrs; EHU (6A) €2; gas; lndry; shop; rest; snacks; bar; playgrnd; pool (htd); paddling pool; beach sand adj; wifi; TV; 5% statics; dogs €2.50; Eng spkn; adv bkg acc; ccard acc; bike hire; CKE/CCI. "Excel, well-run site by rv; sh walk to uncrowded beach (pt naturist); excel facs & pool; hypmkt 1km; cycle track to St Aygulf & pt way to Fréjus." 1 Apr-20 Oct. € 30.00   2013*

ST AYGULF *10F4* (3km W Coastal) *43.36566, 6.71264* Camping Au Paradis des Campeurs, La Gaillarde-Plage, 83380 Les Issambres [04 94 96 93 55; fax 04 94 49 62 99; www.paradis-des-campeurs.com] Exit A8/E80 junc 37 at Puget-sur-Argens onto DN7 to by-pass Fréjus, then onto D559 twd Ste Maxime. Site on R 2km after passing thro St Aygulf, on LH bend bef hill. Or exit junc 36 onto D125 to Ste Maxime, then D559 dir Fréjus. Site on L after ent Les Issambres. Med, hdstg, mkd, pt shd, pt sl, terr, serviced pitches; wc (htd); chem disp; mv service pnt; fam bthrm; shwrs inc; EHU (6A) €4 (poss rev pol); lndry; shop; rest; snacks; bar; bbq; playgrnd; beach sand adj; wifi; TV; dogs €3; Eng spkn; quiet; ccard acc; golf 4km; games rm; bike hire; CKE/CCI. "V popular LS; direct access via underpass to beach; excel san facs; superb views fr top level pitches - worth extra; gates shut at night & guarded; helpful owners; old rd to St Aygulf suitable for cycling; excel; adj beach small." ♦ 1 Apr-5 Oct. € 43.00   2014*

ST AYGULF *10F4* (5km NW Rural) *43.41626, 6.70598* Camping L'Etoile d'Argens, Chemin des Etangs, 83370 St Aygulf [04 94 81 01 41; fax 04 94 81 21 45; info@etoiledargens.com; www.etoiledargens.com] Exit A8 at junc 37 Puget-sur-Argens onto DN7 to Fréjus & D559 to St Aygulf, or fr DN7 take D7 to St Aygulf by-passing Fréjus & turn onto D8 to site. Lge, mkd, shd, serviced pitches; wc; chem disp; fam bthrm; shwrs inc; EHU (10A) inc; gas; lndry; shop; rest; snacks; bar; playgrnd; pool (htd); beach sand 3km; entmnt; wifi; 40% statics; dogs €5; Eng spkn; adv bkg acc; quiet; ccard acc; tennis; rv fishing; archery; golf 1.5km; CKE/CCI. "Friendly, helpful owners; gd facs, poss unclean LS; excel pool complex; ferry down rv to beach in ssn; vg."
♦ 1 Apr-30 Sep. € 59.00   2015*

⊞ **ST BREVIN LES PINS** *2G3* (2km N Coastal) *47.26553, -2.16918* FFCC Camping de Mindin, 32-40 Ave du Bois, 44250 St Brévin-les-Pins [02 40 27 46 41; fax 02 40 39 20 53; info@camping-de-mindin.com; www.camping-de-mindin.com] On beach rd at N end of St Brevin. Med, shd, wc (htd); chem disp; mv service pnt; fam bthrm; shwrs inc; EHU (16A) €5.05; lndry; shop; rest; snacks; bar; playgrnd; pool (htd); paddling pool; beach sand adj; 80% statics; dogs €2.35; adv bkg acc; ccard acc; CKE/CCI. "Sm, sandy pitches; 6 touring pitches, area unkept; san facs being updated." € 16.80   2017*

⊞ **ST BREVIN LES PINS** *2G3* (2km S Coastal) *47.21375, -2.15409* Camping Les Rochelets, Chemin des Grandes Rivières, 44250 St Brévin-les-Pins [02 40 27 40 25; info@rochelets.com; www.rochelets.com] Fr N or S on D213 exit sp Les Rochelets, site sp. Lge, hdg, mkd, pt shd, wc; shwrs; EHU (6-10A) €5-6.50; lndry; rest; snacks; bar; playgrnd; pool (htd); beach 100m; entmnt; wifi; 30% statics; dogs €4; adv bkg acc; quiet; ccard acc; games rm; games area; bike hire. "Gd site for families; lots of entmnt & activities in high ssn; great location." € 29.60   2014*

ST BREVIN LES PINS *2G3* (2km S Coastal) *47.23514, -2.16739* Camping Sunêlia Le Fief, 57 Chemin du Fief, 44250 St Brévin-les-Pins [02 40 27 23 86; fax 02 40 64 46 19; camping@lefief.com; www.lefief.com] Fr Nantes dir St Nazaire. After St Nazaire bdge S on D213. Pass Leclerc & exit sp St Brévin-l'Océan/La Courance. At rndabt foll sp Le Fief. Lge, mkd, hdstg, pt shd, wc; chem disp; mv service pnt; fam bthrm; shwrs inc; EHU (6A) €6; gas; lndry; shop; rest; snacks; bar; bbq (charcoal, gas); playgrnd; pool (covrd, htd); paddling pool; beach sand 800m; red long stay; entmnt; wifi; TV; 30% statics; dogs €11; Eng spkn; adv bkg acc; quiet; ccard acc; sauna; gym; games area; waterslide; tennis; games rm; jacuzzi; CKE/CCI. "Excel for families; wellness cent; fitness rm; waterpark & waterslide etc adj; vg leisure facs." ♦ 7 Apr-30 Sep. € 41.00   2017*

See advertisement opposite

ST BRIAC SUR MER 2E3 (1km N Urban) 48.62765, -2.13056 FFCC Camping Emeraude, 7 Chemin de la Souris, 35800 St Briac-sur-Mer [02 99 88 34 55; emeraude@seagreen.fr; www.seagreen-campingemeraude.com] SW fr Dinard to St Lunaire on N786, after passing Dinard golf course, site is sp to L. Lge, hdg, pt shd, wc; chem disp; mv service pnt; fam bthrm; shwrs inc; EHU (6A) €3.80; gas; lndry; shop; snacks; bar; playgrnd; pool (htd); paddling pool; beach 700m; entmnt; wifi; 40% statics; dogs €2.50; adv bkg acc; bike hire; games area; waterpark; games rm. "Excel, well-run site, quiet LS." ♦ 3 Apr-19 Sep. € 26.00   2016*

ST BRIAC SUR MER 2E3 (1km S Coastal) 48.61493, -2.12779 Camping Le Pont Laurin, Route de la Vallée Gatorge, 35800 St Briac-sur-Chem [02 99 88 34 64; fax 02 99 16 38 19; lepontlaurin@ouest-camping.com; www.ouest-camping.com] Fr St Briac, 500m S on D3. Lge, hdstg, hdg, mkd, pt shd, wc; chem disp; mv service pnt; fam bthrm; shwrs inc; EHU (10A) €3 (poss rev pol); lndry; shop; snacks; playgrnd; beach sand 1km; wifi; 40% statics; dogs €1.50; Eng spkn; adv bkg acc; ccard acc; games area; sailing; tennis nr; CKE/CCI. "Peaceful site; welcoming, helpful staff; clean, modern san facs; excel beaches; canoe hire nr; sports cent adj; gd walking; walking dist to shops, rest etc; interesting town; highly rec." ♦ 1 Apr-30 Sep. € 26.00   2017*

ST BRIEUC 2E3 (2km S Rural) 48.50066, -2.75938 Camping des Vallées, Blvd Paul-Doumer, 22000 St Brieuc [02 96 94 05 05; campingdesvallees@wanadoo.fr; www.camping-desvallees.com] Fr N12 take exit sp D700 Trégueux, Pleufragan & foll sp 'Des Vallées'. Site nr Parc de Brézillet. Sm, hdstg, mkd, hdg, pt shd, wc; chem disp; mv service pnt; fam bthrm; shwrs inc; EHU (10A) €4; lndry; shop; snacks; bar; playgrnd; beach sand 3km; 25% statics; dogs €2.40; Eng spkn; adv bkg acc; quiet; waterslide adj; CKE/CCI. "High kerbs to pitches; htd pool adj; excel." ♦ 2 Mar-18 Dec. € 25.00   2015*

ST CALAIS 4F2 (1km N Urban) 47.92691, 0.74413 Camp Municipal du Lac, Rue du Lac, 72120 St Calais [02 43 35 04 81; fax 02 43 35 15 13; campingstcalais@orange.fr] E fr Le Mans on D357 to St Calais; after sharp (90 degree) L/H bend away fr town cent take L/H lane for next junc in 100m; do not foll D357 bend to R but go strt ahead on D429; in 200m turn R onto sm rd sp 'Conflans/Plan d'Eau'. Site on R after football grnd. Fr N exit A11 junc 5 onto D1 to St Calais; turn R onto D357 dir Le Mans; in 200m turn R onto D429 N; in 400 turn R onto sm rd sp 'Confland/Plan d'Eau to site; leave D357 at R angle bend by Champion supmkt; site in 100m. Site by lake on N edge of town, well sp fr cent. Ent easy to miss. Med, hdg, mkd, pt shd, wc; chem disp; mv service pnt; shwrs inc; EHU (6A) inc; lndry; shop nr; bar nr; bbq; playgrnd; sw nr; 10% statics; dogs; adv bkg acc; quiet; CKE/CCI. "Delightful, well-kept site; friendly, helpful warden; spacious pitches, espec nr lake; easy rvside walk to town; pool adj; gd touring base." ♦ 26 Mar-15 Oct. € 14.00   2017*

ST CAST LE GUILDO 2E3 (1km N Coastal) 48.63690, -2.26900 Camping Le Châtelet, Rue des Nouettes, 22380 St Cast-le-Guildo [02 96 41 96 33; fax 02 96 41 97 99; info@lechatelet.com; www.lechatelet.com] Site sp fr all dir & in St Cast-le-Guildo but best rte: fr D786 at Matignon take D13 into St Cast-le-Guildo, turn L after Intermarché supmkt on R; foll sm site sp. Or app on D19 fr St Jaguel. Care needed down ramp to main site. (NB Avoid Matignon cent Wed due to mkt). Lge, mkd, hdg, pt shd, pt sl, terr, wc; chem disp; mv service pnt; fam bthrm; shwrs inc; EHU (10A) inc; gas; lndry; shop; snacks; bar; bbq (charcoal, elec); playgrnd; pool (covrd, htd); paddling pool; beach sand 300m; entmnt; wifi; TV; 50% statics; dogs €4.20; adv bkg acc; ccard acc; games rm; golf 2km; fishing. "Site o'looks coast; o'fits over 7m by req; extra for sea view pitches; gd for families; helpful staff; modern unisex san facs; bike hire 500m; gates clsd 2230-0700; access to some pitches diff lge o'fits; mkt Mon; excel site." ♦ 16 Apr-15 Sep. € 50.00   2017*

ST CAST LE GUILDO 2E3 (4km S Rural) 48.58441, -2.25691 Camping Le Château de Galinée, Rue de Galinée, 22380 St Cast-le-Guildo [02 96 41 10 56; fax 02 96 41 03 72; contact@chateaudegalinee.com; www.chateaudegalinee.com] W fr St Malo on D168 thro Ploubalay. At La Ville-es-Comte branch onto D786 & go thro Notre Dame-du-Guildo. Approx 2km after Notre Dame-du-Guildo turn 3rd L into Rue de Galinée & foll sp to site. Do not go into St Cast. Lge, hdg, mkd, pt shd, wc (htd); chem disp; mv service pnt; fam bthrm; shwrs inc; EHU (10A) inc; lndry; shop; rest; snacks; bar; bbq; playgrnd; pool (covrd, htd); paddling pool; beach sand 4km; red long stay; entmnt; wifi; TV; 30% statics; dogs €4; Eng spkn; adv bkg acc; quiet; ccard acc; sauna; games area; waterslide; horseriding 6km; games rm; tennis; golf 3km; CKE/CCI. "Peaceful, family site in lovely area; spacious, well laid-out pitches; helpful staff; modern, clean, excel san facs; pitches poss muddy after rain; fishing pond; excel rest; mkt Fri & Mon; identity bracelet to be worn at all times." ♦ 10 May-5 Sep. € 54.50   2014*

ST CAST LE GUILDO 2E3 (6km SW Rural) 48.59111, -2.29578 Camping Le Vallon aux Merlettes, Route de Lamballe, 22550 Matignon [02 96 80 37 99; contact@campingdematignon.com; www.campingdematignon.com] Fr E & W take D786 to Matignon; 500m fr town cent turn SW on D13 twds Lamballe. Med, pt shd, pt sl, wc cont; chem disp; mv service pnt; shwrs inc; EHU (8A); gas; lndry; shop; snacks; playgrnd; pool; wifi; 10% statics; dogs €0.75; adv bkg rec; quiet; tennis; CKE/CCI. "Lovely site on playing fields outside attractive town; vg clean facs; new hard working private owners (2015); excel & popular." ♦ 4 Apr-30 Sep. € 19.00   2015*

ST CLAUDE

ST CHELY D'APCHER *9D1* (3km N Rural) *44.81644, 3.27074* Cosy Camping (formerly Municipal Croix des Anglais, 48200 St Chély-d'Apcher [06 42 10 49 04; cosycamping48@gmail.com; cosy-camping.com] Fr N on A75 J33 onto D809, 2nd exit of rndabt, site 100m on L. Fr S J34 onto D809 thro vill dir Clermont Ferand. Site 1km on R after vill. Med, hdg, pt shd, wc; chem disp; mv service pnt; shwrs; EHU (10A) inc; shop nr; rest nr; bar nr; playgrnd; twin axles; wifi; TV; 5% statics; dogs €1; Eng spkn; adv bkg acc; quiet; games area; games rm; CKE/CCI. "Friendly, helpful staff; gd walks; gd NH/long stay; horse riding adj; gd." ♦ 1 Apr-6 Oct. € 14.00   2018*

ST CHELY D'APCHER *9D1* (10km E Rural) *44.77506, 3.37203* Camping Le Galier, Route de St Chély, 48120 St Alban-sur-Limagnole [04 66 31 58 80; accueil@campinglegalier.fr; campinglozere.net/en] Exit A75 junc 34 onto D806, then E on D987 for 3km. Site 1.5km SW of St Alban on rvside. Sm, mkd, pt sl, wc (htd); chem disp; shwrs inc; EHU (6A) inc; lndry; shop nr; snacks; bar; bbq; playgrnd; pool; paddling pool; wifi; 10% statics; dogs €1.60; Eng spkn; adv bkg acc; quiet; tennis 800m; games rm; CKE/CCI. "Lovely, quiet setting by rv; friendly owners; clean san facs - stretched high ssn, ltd LS; gd walking, fishing; vg NH; rec; pretty site with rv running thro; grass pitches." ♦ 1 Mar-30 Sep. € 19.00   2015*

ST CHERON *4E3* (4km SE Rural) *48.54341, 2.13791* Camping Le Parc des Roches, La Petite Beauce, 91530 St Chéron [01 64 56 65 50; fax 01 64 56 54 50; info@camping-parcdesroches.com; www.camping-parcdesroches.com] N20 S to Arpajon; then D116 to St Chéron. Site bet Arpajon & Dourdan. Sp in town. Lge, mkd, hdg, hdstg, pt shd, wc (htd); chem disp; mv service pnt; fam bthrm; shwrs inc; EHU (10A) €3; lndry; shop nr; rest; snacks; bar; bbq; playgrnd; pool (htd); paddling pool; wifi; 70% statics; dogs €2; Eng spkn; adv bkg acc; quiet; ccard acc; solarium; games area; tennis; games rm; CKE/CCI. "Pleasant, wooded site; helpful, friendly owner; gd san facs; o'night pitches lge & nr ent; gd walking; great site; v conv for train to Paris." ♦ 1 Mar-15 Dec. € 27.00   2014*

ST CHINIAN *10F1* (2km W Rural) *43.42082, 2.93395* Camp Municipal Les Terrasses, Route de St Pons, 34360 St Chinian [04 67 38 28 28 (Mairie); fax 04 67 38 28 29; mairie@saintchinian.fr; www.campinglesterrasses.net] On main Béziers-St Pons rd, D612, heading W on o'skts of St Chinian. Site on L. Med, unshd, terr, wc; shwrs inc; EHU (10A) €4; shop nr; pool; quiet. "Attractive site with gd views; sm pitches; diff access some pitches; terraced site; quiet until school hols; pool; friendly hosts." 1 Apr-6 Nov. € 12.00   2016*

ST CHRISTOPHE *7A3* (3km NE Rural) *46.01467, 0.87679* Camping En Campagne, Essubras, 16420 St Christophe [05 45 31 67 57; info@encampagne.com; www.encampagne.com] Fr Bellac take D675 direction Saint-Junien. In Chene Pignier turn R on D9/D82 to Confolens. In Saint-Christophe turn R on D330 to Nouic. Site on L in 2.6km. Sm, mkd, hdg, pt shd, wc (htd); chem disp; mv service pnt; fam bthrm; shwrs inc; EHU (6-10A) inc; lndry; rest; snacks; bar; bbq; playgrnd; pool (covrd, htd); paddling pool; wifi; dogs €2; Eng spkn; adv bkg acc; quiet; games area; games rm; bike hire; pingpong table; petanque court; CCI. "Vg; tourist attractions info avail; hiking/biking rtes; excel." ♦ 1 Apr-1 Oct. € 23.80   2018*

ST CIRQ LAPOPIE *7D3* (2km N Rural) *44.46926, 1.68935* Camping La Plage, Porte Roques, 46330 St Cirq-Lapopie [05 65 30 29 51; fax 05 65 30 23 33; camping-laplage@wanadoo.fr; www.campingplage.com] Exit Cahors on D653, in Vers take D662 sp Cajarc. In 20km turn R at Tour-de-Faure over narr bdge, sp St Cirq-Lapopie, site 100m on R beside Rv Lot. Med, mkd, shd, wc; fam bthrm; shwrs inc; EHU (6-16A) €4-5; lndry; shop; rest; snacks; bar; bbq; playgrnd; pool; entmnt; wifi; 5% statics; dogs €2; Eng spkn; adv bkg acc; quiet; watersports; canoeing; CKE/CCI. "Pleasant, clean & tidy rvside site; v shady; LS site yourself, pay later; friendly, helpful owner; gd walking; excel." ♦ 1 Apr-15 Oct. € 19.00   2012*

ST CIRQ LAPOPIE *7D3* (3km S Rural) *44.44871, 1.67468* FFCC Camping La Truffière, Route de Concots, 46330 St Cirq-Lapopie [05 65 30 20 22; fax 05 65 30 20 27; contact@camping-truffiere.com; www.camping-truffiere.com] Take D911, Cahors to Villefranche rd; in 20km turn N onto D42 at Concots dir St Cirq for 8km - site clearly sp. NB Do not app fr St Cirq-Lapopie. Med, shd, pt sl, terr, wc (htd); chem disp; mv service pnt; fam bthrm; shwrs inc; EHU (10A) €4; lndry; shop; rest; snacks; bar; playgrnd; pool (htd); paddling pool; entmnt; TV; dogs €1.50; phone; Eng spkn; adv bkg acc; quiet; ccard acc; fishing 3km; bike hire; CKE/CCI. "Well-kept site in gd location; friendly owners; excel but dated san facs (2014), ltd LS; most pitches in forest clearings; muddy when wet; lovely pool; gd; 2m fr fairytale vill of St Cirq Lapopie, a must see; site 11m fr nearest supmkt." ♦ 12 Apr-28 Sep. € 33.00   2014*

ST CLAUDE *9A3* (2km S Rural) *46.37153, 5.87171* Campsite Flower Camping Le Martinet, 12 le Martinet, 39200 St Claude [03 84 45 00 40 or 03 84 41 42 62 (LS); contact@camping-saint-claude.fr; www.camping-saint-claude.fr] On ent town foll 1-way, under bdge mkd 4.1m high, then take R turn 'Centre Ville' lane to next traff lts. Turn R then immed L sp Genève, turn R 300m after Fiat g'ge onto D290, site on R. Med, pt shd, wc; chem disp; shwrs inc; EHU (5A) €2.30; gas; lndry; shop nr; rest; Eng spkn; adv bkg acc; quiet; ccard acc; tennis; fishing; CKE/CCI. "Site now pt of Flower camping group (2014), completely renovated; htd pool adj; has 3 modern san blocks; excel walking; v attractive town; gd." 1 Apr-30 Sep. € 19.00   2014*

ST CYPRIEN PLAGE

Camping Yelloh! Village Saint-Emilion

France

NEW indoor pool

A range of free activities and services on site, in the heart of nature, surrounded by the world famous Bordeaux wine region
Come and enjoy the French Art de Vivre!
www.camping-saint-emilion.com

ST CYPRIEN PLAGE 10G1 (3km S Coastal) *42.59939, 3.03761* **Camping Cala Gogo, Ave Armand Lanoux, Les Capellans, 66750 St Cyprien-Plage [04 68 21 07 12; fax 04 68 21 02 19; contact@camping-le-calagogo.fr; www.camping-le-calagogo.fr]** Exit A9 at Perpignan Nord onto D617 to Canet-Plage, then D81; site sp bet St Cyprien-Plage & Argelès-Plage dir Les Capellans. V lge, hdg, mkd, pt shd, wc (htd); chem disp; mv service pnt; fam bthrm; shwrs inc; EHU (6A) €2-4; lndry; shop; rest; snacks; bar; playgrnd; pool; paddling pool; beach sand adj; entmnt; TV; 30% statics; dogs €3-4; Eng spkn; adv bkg acc; ccard acc; tennis; games area; CKE/CCI. "Excel site; gd pitches; lovely beach; v helpful staff." ♦ 8 Apr-30 Sep. € 48.00   2017*

ST DENIS D'OLERON 7A1 (4km S Coastal) *46.00480, -1.38480* **Camping Les Seulières, 1371 Rue des Seulières, 17650 Saint-Denis-d'Oléron [33 546 479 051; campinglesseulieres@wanadoo.fr; www.campinglesseulieres.fr]** Fr D734 Cheray-Saint-Denis-d'Oleron. L twd La Jausiere, cont onto Grande Rue a Chaucre and foll sp to campsite. Med, mkd, pt shd, wc; fam bthrm; shwrs inc; EHU (10A); gas; lndry; shop nr; bar; pool; beach sand 0.3km; entmnt; wifi; 45% statics; dogs €2; Eng spkn; adv bkg acc; quiet; ccard acc; CCI. "Very nice beach; sep cycling rtes (plan provided)." ♦ 1 Apr-31 Oct. € 30.50   2014*

"That's changed – Should I let the Club know?"

If you find something on site that's different from the site entry, fill in a report and let us know. See camc.com/europereport.

ST DONAT SUR L'HERBASSE 9C2 (1km S Rural) *45.11916, 4.99690* **Camping Domaine Les Ulèzes, Route de Romans, 26260 St Donat-sur-l'Herbasse [04 75 47 83 20; contact@domaine-des-ulezes.com; www.domaine-des-ulezes.com]** Exit A7 junc 13 onto D532 dir Romans-sur-Isère. In 5km turn N onto D67 thro St Donat. Site on edge of vill off D53 dir Peyrins, well sp. Med, mkd, hdg, pt shd, wc; chem disp; mv service pnt; shwrs inc; EHU (6-10A) €3.50-4.50; lndry; shop; rest; snacks; bar; bbq (elec, gas); playgrnd; pool (htd); entmnt; wifi; TV; 10% statics; dogs €2; Eng spkn; adv bkg acc; quiet; ccard acc; games rm; ice; games area; CKE/CCI. "Lovely rvside site; gd size pitches; immac; excel facs; welcoming, friendly owners; canal-side walk to town; gd touring base; vg; rec; serviced pitches." ♦ 1 Apr-31 Oct. € 33.00   2014*

ST EMILION 7C2 (3km N Rural) 44.91695, -0.14160
Camping Yelloh Saint Emilion, 2 lieu dit Les Combes, 33330 St Emilion [05 57 24 75 80; fax 05 57 24 69 68; info@camping-saint-emilion.com; www.camping-saint-emilion.com] NB Trailer c'vans not permitted in cent of St Emilion. Fr A10 exit junc 39a sp Libourne onto D670. In Libourne turn E on D243 twd St Emilion. On o'skts of St Emilion turn L onto D122 dir Lussac & Montagne; site on R by lake in 3km. Or fr S, foll site sp off D670 to Libourne, nr Les Bigaroux. NB D122 S of St Emilion unsuitable for c'vans. Lge, hdg, hdstg, mkd, shd, wc; chem disp; mv service pnt; fam bthrm; shwrs inc; EHU (10A) inc; gas; lndry; shop; rest; snacks; bar; bbq (gas); playgrnd; pool (htd); paddling pool; entmnt; wifi; TV; 40% statics; dogs €4; phone; Eng spkn; adv bkg acc; quiet; ccard acc; horseriding 8km; games rm; waterslide; bike hire; watersports nr; tennis; canoeing; fishing; CKE/CCI. "Lovely, peaceful, well-run lakeside site; owners friendly & helpful; gd sized & shd pitches; pedalos avail; suitable lge o'fits; no o'fits over 10m; mountain bike circuit; clean, modern san facs but inadequate; free shuttle bus service to St Emilion; gd cycle rtes; poss boggy when wet; excel." ♦ 28 Apr-25 Sep. € 40.00   2017*

See advertisement opposite

⊞ **ST EMILION** 7C2 (9km SE Rural) 44.85138, -0.10683 **Aire St Emilion Domaine du Château Gerbaud, 33000 St Pey-d'Armens [06 03 27 00 32 (mob); fax 05 57 47 10 53; contact@chateau-gerbaud.com; www.chateau-gerbaud.com]** Fr Libourne SE on D670/D936 dir Castillon-la-Bataille. In St Pey-d'Armens at bar/tabac foll sp Château Gerbaud vineyard. Mv service pnt; Eng spkn. "Parking for max 48 hrs; friendly, lovely site among the vines." € 5.00   2016*

> **"I like to fill in the reports as I travel from site to site"**
>
> You'll find report forms at the back of this guide, or you can fill them in online at camc.com/europereport.

STE ENGRACE 8F1 (5km NW Rural) 43.01600, -0.85786 **FFCC Camping Ibarra, Quartier Les Casernes, 64560 Ste Engrâce [05 59 28 73 59; maryse@ibarra-chantina.com; www.ibarra-chantina.com]** D918 S fr Tardets-Sorholus; in 2km turn R onto D26; in 6km to L onto D113 sp Ste Engrâce; site on R in 5km. Site clearly sp just bef La Caserne. NB not suitable car+c'van. Sm, mkd, pt shd, wc; chem disp; shwrs inc; EHU (5A) €1.80; lndry; bar; bbq (sep area); playgrnd; 8% statics; dogs; quiet; CKE/CCI. "Pleasant site on rv bank; scenic views; spectacular Kakuetta gorges nrby; vg; narr rd thro gorge for several kms bef site." ♦ 1 Apr-30 Sep. € 11.50   2013*

ST ETIENNE DE BAIGORRY 8F1 (1km N Rural) 43.18370, -1.33569 **Camp Municipal L'Irouleguy, Borciriette, 64430 St Etienne-de-Baïgorry [05 59 37 43 96 or 05 59 37 40 80 (Mairie); fax 05 59 37 48 20; comstetiennebaigorry@wanadoo.fr]** W on D15 fr St Jean-Pied-de-Port to St Etienne-de-Baigorry; site on R 300m bef junc with D948; ent next to wine co-operative. Fr N on D948, on ent St Etienne-de-Baïgorry turn L onto D15; site in 300m on L. NB Don't be put off by entry down track L of winery - can't see site fr rd. Med, shd, wc; chem disp; shwrs inc; EHU (6A) €2.70; lndry; shop nr; adv bkg acc; quiet; trout fishing; tennis adj. "Scenic site by rv; lge pitches; plenty hot water; gas 100m; gd hill walking cent; birdwatching; htd pool adj; out of ssn call at Mairie to open site for NH; gd modern san facs." ♦ 1 May-30 Nov. € 9.00   2013*

⊞ **ST ETIENNE DE MONTLUC** 2G4 (0km N Rural) 47.28002, -1.77967 **Camp Municipal de la Colettrie, Rue de Tivoli, 44360 St Etienne-de-Montluc [02 40 86 97 44 or 02 40 86 80 26 (Mairie); campinglacoletterie@st-etienne-montluc.net; www.st-etienne-montluc.net]** Well sp fr N165 (E60) in both dirs. Sm, mkd, hdg, pt shd, pt sl, wc (htd); chem disp; fam bthrm; shwrs inc; EHU (15A) €3.80; lndry; shop nr; rest nr; bar nr; playgrnd; dogs €1.20; phone; adv bkg acc; quiet; fishing; games area; CKE/CCI. "Vg; check open bef travelling." ♦ € 10.00   2013*

ST FARGEAU 4G4 (6km SE Rural) 47.60941, 3.11961 **Camp Municipal La Calangue, 89170 St Fargeau [03 86 74 04 55; campingmunicipallacalanque@nordnet.fr; www.camping-lacalanque.fr]** Take D85 fr St-Fargeau, after 1km turn R on D185, after 2km turn R onto D485. Site on L (by circus) after 2 km. Lge, mkd, shd, wc (htd); chem disp; shwrs inc; EHU (6-10A) €3.80; lndry; bar nr; bbq; playgrnd; sw nr; twin axles; 2% statics; dogs; adv bkg rec; quiet; canoeing; games area; horseriding nr; fishing; CKE/CCI. "Pleasant site in woods; tight manoeuvring round trees; sm pitches; gd; shops & rest 6km; conv for Guedelon; san facs not clean." ♦ 1 Apr-30 Sep. € 10.50   2015*

ST FLORENTIN 4F4 (1km S Rural) 47.99252, 3.73450 **Camping L'Armançon, 89600 St Florentin [03 86 35 08 03 13 or 03 86 35 11 86 (mob); ot.saint-florentin @wanadoo.fr; www.camping-saint-florentin.fr]** N fr Auxerre on N77 site on R app rv bdge S of town. Fr N pass traff islands, exit town up slope, x-ing canal & rv. Site immed on S side of rv bdge - turn R immed at end of bdg then under bdg to site. Site well sp fr all dirs. Med, hdg, pt shd, pt sl, wc cont; chem disp; shwrs inc; EHU (10A) inc (poss long lead req); gas; lndry; shop; snacks; playgrnd; dogs €0.20; fishing. "Well-kept site; excel. lge pitches; friendly manager; dated but clean san facs; diff, steep exit to main rd; gd NH." ♦ 2 Apr-11 Oct. € 14.50   2015*

ST FLOUR

ST FLOUR *9C1* (4km N Rural) *45.05120, 3.10778*
Camping International La Roche Murat, N9 15100 St Flour [04 71 60 43 63; fax 04 71 60 02 10; courrier@camping-saint-flour.com; www.camping-saint-flour.com] Fr N or S on A75 exit junc 28; sp off rndabt on St Flour side of m'way. Site ent visible 150m fr rndabt. Med, hdg, mkd, pt shd, terr, wc (htd); chem disp; mv service pnt; shwrs inc; EHU (16A) inc (poss rev pol); gas; lndry; shop nr; playgrnd; dogs; Eng spkn; adv bkg acc; quiet; CKE/CCI. "Busy site with gd views; sunny & secluded pitches; gd, clean facs; some pitches sm; when pitches waterlogged use site rds; old town high on hill worth visit; excel touring cent & conv NH fr A75; v clean facs." ♦ 1 Apr-1 Nov. € 16.50   2016*

ST FORT SUR GIRONDE *7B2* (4km SW Rural) *45.43278, -0.75185* Camping Port Maubert, 8 Rue de Chassillac, 17240 St Fort-sur-Gironde [05 46 04 78 86; fax 05 46 04 16 79; bourdieu.jean-luc@wanadoo.fr; www.campingportmaubert.com] Exit A10 junc 37 onto D730 dir Royan. Foll sp Port Maubert & site. Sm, hdg, mkd, shd, wc; chem disp; mv service pnt; shwrs inc; EHU (10A) €3.50; gas; lndry; shop nr; bar; bbq; playgrnd; pool; red long stay; TV; 10% statics; dogs €2; Eng spkn; adv bkg acc; quiet; ccard acc; bike hire; games rm; CKE/CCI. "Pleasant, well-run site; LS ltd facs, OK NH." 1 Apr-30 Oct. € 12.40   2014*

STE FOY LA GRANDE *7C2* (1km NE Rural) *44.84426, 0.22468* Camping de la Bastide, Allée du Camping, 2 Les Tuileries, Pineuilh, 33220 Ste Foy-la-Grande [05 57 46 13 84; contact@camping-bastide.com; www.camping-bastide.com] Fr W go thro town & turn off at D130 to site, well sp on Rv Dordogne. Med, mkd, pt shd, wc; chem disp; mv service pnt; fam bthrm; shwrs inc; EHU (10A) €3 (poss rev pol); lndry; shop nr; bar nr; playgrnd; pool; wifi; 10% statics; dogs €2; phone; Eng spkn; adv bkg acc; quiet; ccard acc; canoeing; games rm; jacuzzi; fishing; CKE/CCI. "Pretty, well-cared for site; sm pitches; helpful, lovely British owners; immac, modern san facs; high kerb stones onto pitches - poss diff lge o'fits; mkt Sat; excel; ACSI acc; walking dist to supmkt & town; v clean site." ♦ 1 Apr-31 Oct. € 25.00   2017*

STE FOY LA GRANDE *7C2* (6km W Rural) *44.82954, 0.12290* FLOWER Camping La Rivière Fleurie, 180 Rue Théophile, 24230 St Antoine-de-Breuilh [05 53 24 82 80; info@la-riviere-fleurie.com; www.la-riviere-fleurie.com or www.flowercampings.com] Turn S off D936 at W end of St Antoine-de-Breuilh; site 2.7km fr main rd in vill of St Aulaye adj Rv Dordogne. Well sp. Med, mkd, pt shd, wc; chem disp; fam bthrm; shwrs inc; EHU (10A) inc; gas; lndry; shop nr; rest; bar; bbq; playgrnd; pool (htd); paddling pool; sw nr; red long stay; entmnt; wifi; TV; 10% statics; dogs €2; phone; Eng spkn; adv bkg acc; quiet; tennis; fishing nr; golf; canoeing nr; horseriding; games rm; CKE/CCI. "Peaceful, well-maintained site; some spacious pitches; welcoming, helpful owners; excel san facs; church bells during day; vg cycling; mkt Sat in Ste Foy; highly rec." ♦ 10 Apr-20 Sep. € 27.00   2014*

ST GALMIER *9B2* (2km E Rural) *45.59266, 4.33528* Campéole Camping Val de Coise, Route de la Thiéry, 42330 St Galmier [04 77 54 14 82; fax 04 77 54 02 45; val-de-coise@campeole.com; www.camping-valdecoise.com or www.campeole.com] Fr St Etienne take D1082 N. In 7km turn R onto D12 sp St Galmier; after x-ing rv bdge on o'skirts of vill turn R & foll Camping sp for 2km. Or fr N on D1082 look for sp to St Galmier about 1.5km S of Montrond-les-Bains & turn L onto D6 to St Galmier. On D12 in St Galmier at floral rndabt with fountain if app fr N go L & fr S go R, uphill & foll site sp. Site approx 1.5km fr rndabt. Med, hdstg, mkd, pt shd, pt sl, wc; chem disp; fam bthrm; shwrs inc; EHU (16A) €4.10; gas; lndry; shop; rest nr; bbq; playgrnd; pool (htd); paddling pool; entmnt; wifi; TV; 20% statics; dogs €2.60; phone; Eng spkn; adv bkg acc; quiet; ccard acc; bike hire; tennis 2km; fishing; games area; games rm; CKE/CCI. "Pleasant rvside site; helpful staff; facs poss stretched high ssn; highly rec; mainly statics." ♦ 11 Apr-11 Oct. € 21.50   2015*

ST GAUDENS *8F3* (1km W Rural) *43.11000, 0.70839* Camp Municipal Belvédère des Pyrénées, Rue des Chanteurs du Comminges, 31800 St Gaudens [05 62 00 16 03; www.st-gaudens.com] Foll camping sp fr St Gaudens town cent on D817 dir Tarbes. Site ent at top of hill on N side. Last rd sp is 'Belvédère'. Med, pt shd, wc (htd); mv service pnt; shwrs inc; EHU (4-13A) €3.50-6; gas; rest nr; playgrnd; dogs €1.50. "Pleasant site; facs clean; gates clsd 1200-1500 & 2300-0700." 1 Jun-30 Sep. € 15.00   2013*

ST GAULTIER *4H2* (0km W Rural) *46.63470, 1.42172* Camp Municipal L'Illon, Rue de Limage, 36800 St Gaultier [02 54 47 11 22 or 02 54 01 66 00 (Mairie); fax 02 54 01 66 09; st-gaultier.mairie@wanadoo.fr; www.mairie-saintgaultier.fr] Site well sp in town. V narr thro town - best app fr W. NB App down sh, steep hill with sharp R turn into site ent. Med, mkd, pt shd, pt sl, wc; shwrs inc; EHU inc; gas; shop nr; playgrnd; quiet; rv; fishing 50m. "Lovely, peaceful setting nr rv; site ent poss too narr for twin axles/lge o'fits; gd cycle path on old rlwy track nrby; site now has barriers, if off clse call warden; gd." Easter-30 Sep. € 13.00   2016*

ST GAULTIER *4H2* (1km W Rural) *46.63406, 1.40863* Camping L'Oasis du Berry, Rue de la Pierre Plate, 36800 St Gaultier [02 54 47 17 04; www.campoasisduberry.com] Appr fr W (fr Le Blanc) on D951; turn R at sp St Gaultier, then foll sp L'Oasis du Berry. Look out for sp in vill. Med, mkd, hdg, pt shd, terr, wc; chem disp; shwrs inc; EHU (4-10A) €2.50-3.50; lndry; shop; rest; snacks; bar; bbq; playgrnd; pool (htd); wifi; 60% statics; dogs €1.40; Eng spkn; adv bkg acc; quiet; games area; CKE/CCI. "Pleasant site in wooded surroundings; nice clean san facs; takeaway; gd pool; gd walks nrby; nr Voie Verte track; nr Brenne Regional Park; most pitches sl; gd." 1 Apr-6 Nov. € 19.00   2014*

ST GEOURS DE MAREMNE

Open all year, panoramic view of the Futuroscope, heated swimming pool, fishing lake, snack bar, restaurant.

www.camping-le-futuriste.fr

+33(0)5 49 52 47 52

86130 St Georges les Baillargeaux - Fax. +33(0)5 49 37 23 33 - camping-le-futuriste@wanadoo.fr

France

ST GENIX SUR GUIERS *9B3* (0km SE Urban) *45.58878, 5.64152* **Les Bords du Guiers, Route de Pont Beauvoisin, 73240 Saint Genix sur Guiers [04 76 31 71 40; info@lesbordsduguiers.com; www.lesbordsduguiers.com]** On reaching vill on D1516 foll sp Le-Pont-de-Beauvoisin, site 300m on R. Med, hdg, mkd, pt shd, wc; chem disp; mv service pnt; shwrs; EHU (8-10A); bbq; pool; twin axles; wifi; dogs; Eng spkn; quiet; games area; games rm. "Excel, quiet site; bike hire; v helpful owners; gd base for site seeing or star watching; town cent 5 mins walk; mkt day Wed." 30 Apr-25 Sep. € 21.00 2014*

"We must tell the Club about that great site we found"

Get your site reports in by mid-August and we'll do our best to get your updates into the next edition.

ST GEORGES DU VIEVRE *3D2* (0km W Rural) *49.24248, 0.58040* **Camp Municipal du Vièvre, Route de Noards, 27450 St Georges-du-Vièvre [02 32 42 76 79 or 02 32 56 34 29 (LS); fax 02 32 57 52 90; camping.stgeorgesduvievre@wanadoo.fr; www.saintgeorgesduvievre.org]** Fr traff lts on D130 in Pont Authou turn W onto D137 to St Georges-du-Vièvre; turn L after town square uphill sp camping; site 200m on L. If app fr S on N138 at Bernay take D834 sp Le Havre to Lieurey. Turn R onto D137 to St Georges, then turn R at camping sp by sw pool. Sm, hdg, pt shd, serviced pitches; wc (htd); chem disp; shwrs inc; EHU (5A) inc; lndry; shop nr; bbq; playgrnd; sw nr; dogs; Eng spkn; adv bkg rec; quiet; bike hire; tennis 50m; CKE/CCI. "Peaceful; gd facs & pitches; pool 150m; well-run site; interesting area; gd cycling; vg; basic but attractive site on edge of v picturesque vill; gd sized pitches." ♦ 1 Apr-30 Sep. € 11.00 2018*

⊞ **ST GEORGES LES BAILLARGEAUX** *4H1* (1km S Rural) *46.66452, 0.39477* **Camping Le Futuriste, Rue du Château, 86130 St Georges-les-Baillargeaux [05 49 52 47 52; fax 05 49 37 23 33; camping-le-futuriste.@wanadoo.fr; www.camping-le-futuriste.fr]** On A10 fr N or S, take Futuroscope exit 28; fr toll booth at 1st rndabt take 2nd exit. Thro tech park twd St Georges. At rndabt under D910 take slip rd N onto D910. After 150m exit D910 onto D20, foll sp. At 1st rndabt bear R, over rlwy, cross sm rv & up hill, site on R. Med, hdg, mkd, pt shd, serviced pitches; wc (htd); chem disp; mv service pnt; shwrs inc; EHU (6A) inc (check earth & poss rev pol); gas; lndry; shop; rest; snacks; bar; bbq; playgrnd; pool (covrd, htd); twin axles; entmnt; wifi; TV; 10% statics; dogs €2.50; Eng spkn; adv bkg acc; quiet; ccard acc; games area; waterslide; games rm; lake fishing; CKE/CCI. "Lovely, busy, secure site; well-kept; friendly, helpful family owners; vg clean facs, ltd LS - facs block clsd 2200-0700; vg poolwith waterslide for kids & adults; hypmkt 2km; vg for families; ideal touring base for Poitiers & Futuroscope (tickets fr recep); vg value, espec in winter; conv a'route; excel." ♦ € 33.00 2017*

See advertisement

ST GEOURS DE MAREMNE *8E1* (1km W Rural) *43.68981, -1.23376* **Camping Les Platanes, 3 Route de Lecoume, 40230 St Geours-de-Maremne [05 58 57 45 35; fax 05 58 57 37 85; info@platanes.com; www.platanes.com]** Fr N10 take junc sp St Geours-de-Maremne. Site sp fr town cent. Med, pt shd, pt sl, wc (htd); chem disp; shwrs inc; EHU (6A) €4.70; gas; lndry; shop nr; rest; snacks; bar; bbq; playgrnd; pool; red long stay; wifi; TV; 50% statics; dogs €1.50; phone; adv bkg acc; quiet; ccard acc; tennis; games rm; games area; CKE/CCI. "Friendly British owners; useful NH on N10." 1 Mar-15 Nov. € 27.50 2012*

ST GERVAIS D'AUVERGNE

ST GERVAIS D'AUVERGNE *7A4* (8km E Rural) *46.02741, 2.89894* **Camp Municipal Les Prés Dimanches, 63390 Châteauneuf-les-Bains [04 73 86 41 50 or 04 73 86 67 65 (LS); fax 04 73 86 41 71; mairie-chat-les-bains@wanadoo.fr]** Fr Montaigut take N144 S twd Riom & Clermont-Ferrand. In 9km at La Boule S onto D987 to St Gervais. Take D227 E to Chateuneuf-les-Bains. In 7km L onto D109. Site thro vill on R. Sm, hdg, mkd, pt shd, wc (htd); shwrs inc; EHU (6A) inc; lndry; shop nr; rest nr; playgrnd; adv bkg acc; quiet; fishing nr; canoeing nr; tennis nr; CKE/CCI. "Lovely, well-kept site; helpful warden; spa baths 500m; excel; gd walks." ♦ 30 Apr-15 Oct. € 13.00   2012*

ST GERVAIS LES BAINS *9B4* (10km SE Rural) *45.80275, 6.72207* **Camping Le Pontet, 2485 Route de Notre-Dame-de-la-Gorge, 74170 Les Contamines-Montjoie [04 50 47 04 04; fax 04 50 47 18 10; welcome@campinglepontet.fr; www.campinglepontet.fr]** Fr St Gervais take D902 to Les Contamines-Montjoie (sp); go thro vill & foll sp to Notre Dame-de-la-Gorge; site in 2km on L, clearly sp. Lge, hdstg, mkd, pt shd, wc (htd); chem disp; fam bthrm; shwrs inc; EHU (2-10A) €3-9.90; lndry; shop nr; rest; snacks; playgrnd; dogs free; phone; Eng spkn; adv bkg acc; quiet; ccard acc; tennis; horseriding; fishing. "Mkd alpine walks; ski lift 200m; leisure/sports park adj; lake adj; excel new owners; owner is a ski instructor & mountain guide." ♦ 1 May-26 Sep & 1 Dec-30 Apr. € 25.00   2014*

ST GERVAIS LES BAINS *9B3* (3km S Rural) *45.87333, 6.72000* **Camping Les Dômes de Miage, 197 Route des Contamines, 74170 St Gervais-les-Bains [04 50 93 45 96; fax 04 50 78 10 75; info@camping-mont-blanc.com; www.natureandlodge.fr]** Exit A40 junc 21; fr N thro St Gervais, at sm rndabt in cent foll sp Les Contamines onto D902, site 2km on L. Med, mkd, pt shd, wc (htd); chem disp; mv service pnt; fam bthrm; shwrs inc; EHU (6A) €3.50 (poss rev pol); gas; lndry; shop; rest nr; snacks; bar nr; bbq; playgrnd; wifi; TV; dogs €2 (free LS); bus adj; Eng spkn; adv bkg req; quiet; ccard acc; tennis 800m; fishing 1km; games area; CKE/CCI. "Superb, well-kept, perfect, family-owned site in beautiful location at base of Mt Blanc; welcoming, helpful & friendly; lux chalet to rent; bike hire 800m; immac san facs; conv Tramway du Mont Blanc excursions; mkt Thurs; bkg fee; htd pool 800m; excel; free bus service to delightful sm town." ♦ 15 May-16 Sep. € 31.00   2017*

ST GILLES *10E2* (0km SW Urban) *43.67569, 4.42946* **Camping de la Chicanette, Rue de la Chicanette, 30800 St Gilles [04 66 87 28 32; camping@campinglachicanette.fr; www.campinglachicanette.fr]** Site on D6572 W fr Arles, sp in cent of town, behind Auberge de la Chicanette. Narr app rd, tight turn to ent. Med, hdg, pt shd, wc; chem disp; shwrs inc; EHU (6A) €3 (rev pol); lndry; shop nr; snacks; bar; playgrnd; pool; entmnt; 20% statics; dogs €2; quiet; CKE/CCI. "Useful site; sm pitches; facs poss stretched high ssn; site poss unkempt LS; interesting old town; bus to Nîmes; mkt Sun." 1 Apr-30 Oct. € 22.00   2015*

ST GILLES CROIX DE VIE *2H3* (4km SE Coastal) *46.67095, -1.90874* **Camping Les Cyprès, 41 Rue du Pont du Jaunay, 85800 St Gilles-Croix-de-Vie [02 51 55 38 98; fax 02 51 54 98 94; contact@camping-lescypres85.com; www.campinglescypres.com]** Site on S end of St Gilles-Croix-de-Vie off D38, after rndabt sp Le Jaunay turn sharp L - hard to spot. Lge, hdg, shd, wc; chem disp; mv service pnt; shwrs inc; EHU (10A) €3; gas; lndry; shop; rest; snacks; bar; playgrnd; pool (covrd, htd); beach sand 600m; red long stay; 12% statics; dogs €3.30; Eng spkn; adv bkg req; quiet; ccard acc; jacuzzi; CKE/CCI. "Excel for family hols; family-run site; red facs LS; footpath along rv to town cent; busy & noisy in high ssn." ♦ 9 Apr-28 Sep. € 43.00   2014*

ST GILLES CROIX DE VIE *2H3* (4km SE Urban/Coastal) *46.67113, -1.90356* **Chadotel Le Domaine de Beaulieu, Rue du Parc, Route des Sables-d'Olonne, 85800 Givrand [02 51 55 59 46 or 02 51 33 05 05 (LS); info@chadotel.com; www.chadotel.com]** S on D38 fr St Gilles Croix-de-Vie, site sp on L. Lge, hdg, mkd, pt shd, serviced pitches; wc; fam bthrm; shwrs inc; EHU (6A) inc (poss long lead req); gas; lndry; shop; snacks; bar; bbq (gas); playgrnd; pool; beach sand 1km; red long stay; entmnt; wifi; TV; dogs €3.20; adv bkg acc; quiet; ccard acc; waterslide; tennis; golf 5km; CKE/CCI. "Gd site for families; red facs LS; low trees poss diff; gd; excel value for money; lovely site; friendly, helpful Eng spkn staff." ♦ 5 Apr-20 Sep. € 39.00   2014*

ST GIRONS PLAGE *8E1* (1km NE Coastal) *43.95436, -1.35689* **Campéole Camping Les Tourterelles, 40560 St Girons-Plage [05 58 47 93 12; tourterelles@campeole.com; www.camping-tourterelles.com or www.campeole.com]** Exit N10 at Castets & take D42 W to St Girons, then to St Girons-Plage. Lge, shd, pt sl, wc; shwrs inc; EHU (6A) €3.90; lndry; shop nr; bbq; playgrnd; beach sand 200m; entmnt; dogs €1; quiet; games rm; games area. "Site in pine trees; footpath to dunes & beach." 15 Mar-15 Oct. € 20.00   2012*

ST GIRONS PLAGE *8E1* (1km E Coastal) *43.95105, -1.35276* **Camping Eurosol, Route de la Plage, 40560 St Girons-Plage [05 58 47 90 14 or 05 58 56 54 90; fax 05 58 47 76 74; contact@camping-eurosol.com; www.camping-eurosol.com]** Turn W off D652 at St Girons on D42. Site on L in 4km. Lge, pt shd, pt sl, serviced pitches; wc; chem disp; fam bthrm; shwrs inc; EHU (10A) inc; gas; lndry; shop; rest; snacks; playgrnd; pool; paddling pool; beach sand 700m; entmnt; TV; 10% statics; dogs €4; quiet; tennis; games rm; bike hire; games area; horseriding adj. "Pitches poss tight for long vans; excel for beach." ♦ 10 May-13 Sep. € 43.00   2017*

See advertisement opposite

ST HILAIRE DE RIEZ

"I need an on-site restaurant"

We do our best to make sure site information is correct, but it is always best to check any must-have facilities are still available or will be open during your visit.

STE HERMINE *2H4* (11km NE Rural) *46.59764, -0.96947* **FFCC Camping Le Colombier (Naturist), 85210 St Martin-Lars [02 51 27 83 84; fax 02 51 27 87 29; info@lecolombier-naturisme.com; www.lecolombier-naturisme.com]** Fr junc 7 of A83 take D137 N; 3km past Ste Hermine turn R onto D52 to Le Poteau; turn L onto D10 to St Martin-Lars; 150m past St Martin-Lars turn R sp Le Colombier. Site ent on L in 200m. Lge, hdg, mkd, hdstg, pt shd, pt sl, wc; chem disp; shwrs inc; EHU (16A) €4.50; gas; lndry; shop nr; rest; snacks; bar; playgrnd; pool; wifi; 50% statics; dogs €4.50; Eng spkn; adv bkg acc; quiet; ccard acc; jacuzzi; sauna. "Well-run site; diff areas diff character; lge pitches; friendly Dutch owners; san facs clean but tired; gd walking in site grnds & local area; conv Mervent National Park; excel; superb facs; gd loc." ♦
1 Apr-1 Oct. € 29.00   2018*

ST HILAIRE DE RIEZ *2H3* (6km N Rural) *46.76332, -1.95839* **Camping La Puerta del Sol, 7 Chemin des Hommeaux, 85270 St Hilaire-de-Riez [02 51 49 10 10; fax 02 51 49 84 84; info@campinglapuertadelsol.com; www.campinglapuertadelsol.com]** N on D38 fr Les Sables-d'Olonne; exit onto D69 sp Soullans, Challans, Le Pissot. At next rndabt take 3rd exit & foll lge sp to site. Site on R in 1.5km. Lge, hdg, mkd, pt shd, pt sl, serviced pitches; wc; chem disp; fam bthrm; shwrs inc; EHU (10A) inc (poss rev pol); lndry; shop; rest; snacks; bar; bbq (elec, gas); playgrnd; pool (htd); paddling pool; beach sand 4.5km; entmnt; wifi; TV; 50% statics; dogs €4; Eng spkn; adv bkg acc; quiet; ccard acc; tennis; games area; watersports 5km; horseriding; sauna; games rm; jacuzzi; bike hire; waterslide; fishing 2km; golf; CKE/CCI. "Vg site; med sized pitches, some diff lge o'fits due odd shape; clean san facs; gd for families; no o'fits over 10m high ssn; gd touring base; lovely pools and playgrnd." ♦
1 Apr-30 Sep. € 33.00   2016*

"Satellite navigation makes touring much easier"

Remember most sat navs don't know if you're towing or in a larger vehicle – always use yours alongside maps and site directions.

Check any essential information with the site before you travel

ST HILAIRE DE RIEZ

Campsite for nature lovers with direct access to the beach and with the distinction "clef vert" for its eco friendliness. Pitches for tents or caravans and rental of tent bungalows or mobile homes. Organised leisure for everybody. Heated swimming pool.
Avenue des Mimosas. F-85270 St Hilaire de Riez.
Tel.: 00 33 (0)2 51 54 36 59.
Fax: 00 33 (0)2 51 54 99 0 • riez85@free.fr
www.campingsainthilairederiez.com

ST HILAIRE DE RIEZ 2H3 (4km W Coastal) 46.72289, -1.97131 **Camp Municipal de La Plage de Riez, Allée de la Plage de Riez, Ave des Mimosas, 85270 St Hilaire-de-Riez [02 51 54 36 59; fax 02 51 60 07 84; www.souslespins.com]** Fr St Hilaire take D6A sp Sion-sur-l'Océan. Turn R at traff lts into Ave des Mimosas, site 1st L. V lge, mkd, shd, pt sl, serviced pitches; wc; shwrs inc; EHU (10A) €3.40; gas; lndry; shop; rest; snacks; bar; playgrnd; beach sand adj; entmnt; wifi; TV; 30% statics; dogs €3.90; Eng spkn; bike hire. "Vg for dogs; pool 5km; exceptionally helpful manager." 30 Mar-31 Oct. € 22.00   2016*

See advertisement

ST HILAIRE DU HARCOUET 2E4 (1km W Urban) 48.58105, -1.09771 **FFCC Camp Municipal de la Sélune, 50600 St Hilaire-du-Harcouët [02 33 49 43 74 or 02 33 49 70 26; fax 02 33 49 59 40; info@st-hilaire.fr; www.st-hilaire.fr]** Sp on N side of N176 twd Mont St Michel/St Malo/Dinan, on W side of town; well sp. Med, hdg, pt shd, pt sl, wc; chem disp; shwrs inc; EHU (16A) €1.95; lndry; shop nr; playgrnd; red long stay; wifi; dogs €0.70; CKE/CCI. "Peaceful, beautifully maintained site; pool 300m; easy access; helpful, pleasant warden; superb san facs; gate locked 2200-0730; excel.". 23 Apr-16 Sep. € 22.50   2014*

ST HILAIRE LA FORET 7A1 (4km SW Rural) 46.44836, -1.52860 **Camping Les Batardières, Rue des Bartardières, 85440 St Hilaire-la-Forêt [02 51 33 33 85]** Fr Sables d'Olonne take D949 twd Avrillé. 7km after Talmont-St-Hilaire fork R on D70 to St Hilaire-la-Forêt. In 3km turn R on ent vill. Site 70m on L. Med, hdg, pt shd, serviced pitches; wc; chem disp; shwrs inc; EHU (6A) €3.50; lndry; shop nr; playgrnd; beach sand 5km; dogs €1.50; adv bkg acc; quiet; tennis; cycling; CKE/CCI. "Excel; spacious pitches; clean facs; excel for families; rec.". 9 Apr-22 Sep. € 20.00   2012*

ST HILAIRE LA PALUD 7A2 (4km NW Rural) 46.28386, -0.74344 **Flower Camping Le Lidon, Le Lidon, 79210 St Hilaire-la-Palud [05 49 35 33 64; fax 05 49 35 32 63; info@le-lidon.com; www.le-lidon.com]** Exit A10 junc 33 onto E601 then N248 & N11 S. At Epannes foll D1 N to Sansais, then D3 to St Hilaire-la-Palud. Foll sp Canal du Mignon & site. NB Access to site over narr angled bdge, extreme care needed - v diff lge o'fits. Med, mkd, hdg, pt shd, wc; chem disp; mv service pnt; fam bthrm; shwrs inc; EHU (10A) inc; lndry; shop; rest; snacks; bar; bbq; playgrnd; pool (htd); paddling pool; entmnt; wifi; 5% statics; dogs €2.50; Eng spkn; adv bkg acc; quiet; ccard acc; canoe hire; ice; rv fishing; bike hire; CKE/CCI. "Secluded site in Marais Poitevin Regional Park (marsh land); gd sized pitches; excel clean san facs; gd walking, cycling, birdwatching; vg; might not be suitable for lge o'fits due to many trees." ♦ 11 Apr-19 Sep. € 20.00   2015*

> "There aren't many sites open at this time of year"
>
> If you're travelling outside peak season remember to call ahead to check site opening dates – even if the entry says 'open all year'.

ST HONORE LES BAINS 4H4 (0km W Urban) 46.90413, 3.83919 **Camp Municipal Plateau du Guet, 13 Rue Eugène Collin, 58360 St Honoré-les-Bains [03 86 30 76 00 or 03 86 30 74 87 (Mairie); fax 03 86 30 73 33; mairie-de-st-honore-les-bains@wanadoo.fr; www.st-honore-les-bains.com]** On D985 fr Luzy to St Honoré-les-Bains. In cent vill turn L on D106 twd Vandenesse. Site on L in 150m. Or N fr Château-Chinon 27km. Then D985 to St Honoré. Med, hdstg, mkd, pt shd, terr, wc (htd); mv service pnt; shwrs inc; EHU (10A) €2.90; lndry; shop nr; rest nr; bar nr; playgrnd; adv bkg acc; quiet; CKE/CCI. "Gd, modern san facs; htd pool 300m; pleasant, conv site town, gd walking." ♦ 1 Apr-26 Oct. € 8.60   2012*

ST JEAN DE LUZ

France

ST HONORE LES BAINS *4H4* (2km W Rural)
46.90580, 3.82843 Camping & Gîtes Les Bains, 15 Ave Jean Mermoz, 58360 St Honoré-les-Bains [03 86 30 73 44; fax 03 86 30 61 88; campinglesbains@ gmail.com; www.campinglesbains.com]
Fr St Honoré-les-Bains foll site sp as 'Village des Bains' fr town cent on D106 twd Vandenesse. Med, mkd, hdg, hdstg, pt shd, pt sl, wc; chem disp; fam bthrm; shwrs; EHU (10A) €4; gas; lndry; shop nr; rest; snacks; bar; bbq; playgrnd; pool; paddling pool; twin axles; entmnt; wifi; TV; 20% statics; dogs; phone; Eng spkn; adv bkg acc; quiet; ccard acc; bike hire; fishing; horseriding 300m; tennis; games rm; waterslide; CKE/CCI. "Helpful staff; poor maintenance & san facs need refurb; gd walking; sm pitches & poss waterlogged after rain; mkt Thu; new British owners." ♦ 1 Apr-31 Oct.
€ 20.80   2015*

> **"That's changed – Should I let the Club know?"**
> If you find something on site that's different from the site entry, fill in a report and let us know. See camc.com/europereport.

ST JEAN D'ANGELY *7B2* (3km WNW Rural) *45.94868, -0.53645* Camping Val de Boutonne, 56 Quai de Bernouet, 17400 St Jean-d'Angély [05 46 32 26 16; fax 05 46 32 29 54; info@camping-charente-maritime-17. com; www.campingcharentemaritime17.org]
Exit A10 at junc 34; head SE on D939; turn R at 1st rndabt into town. Site sp. Med, mkd, shd, wc; chem disp; mv service pnt; shwrs inc; EHU (10A) €4; lndry; shop; rest nr; bar nr; playgrnd; red long stay; wifi; TV; 10% statics; dogs €2; Eng spkn; adv bkg acc; quiet; ccard acc; CKE/CCI. "Pleasant, friendly, well-kept site by Rv Boutonne; helpful owners; aquatic cent 500m; lovely pool, strict rules, men must wear speedos; gd, clean san facs, outdated; poss open in Oct - phone ahead; vg; lake with sm boating facs; rec; gd NH just off the A10; 10min walk to historic town; lge Sat mkt; no admittance until 14:30; gd rests." ♦ 1 Apr-30 Sep.
€ 19.50   2018*

ST JEAN DE LUZ *8F1* (2km NE Coastal) *43.40563, -1.64216* Camping de la Ferme Erromardie, 40 Chemin d'Erromardie, 64500 St Jean-de-Luz [05 59 26 34 26; fax 05 59 51 26 02; contact@camping-erromardie.com; www.camping-erromardie.com]
Exit A63 junc 3 onto D810 sp St Jean-de-Luz. After 1km cross rlwy and turn immed sharp R sp Erromardie. Site ent on R in 3km just bef rest/bar. Lge, mkd, hdg, shd, wc; chem disp; mv service pnt; fam bthrm; shwrs inc; EHU (6-16A) €3.80-4.30; gas; lndry; rest; snacks; bar; playgrnd; beach sand adj; 80% statics; dogs €1.50; Eng spkn; adv bkg acc; CKE/CCI. "Well-run, popular site; cheerful, helpful staff; ltd water pnts in 2nd field; lovely, sandy beaches; coastal walk into St Jean-de-Luz; Basque museum nrby; site in 3 sections, lge o'fits should ask for pitch on touring field; excel modern san facs." ♦
15 Mar-30 Sep. € 36.00   2014*

See advertisement

ST JEAN DE LUZ *8F1* (3km NE Coastal) *43.40549, -1.64222* Camping Bord de Mer, 71 chemin d'Erromardie, 64500 St Jean-de-Luz [05 59 26 24 61; bord-de-mer64@orange.fr; www.camping-le-bord-de-mer.fr] Exit A63 junc 3 onto D810 dir St Jean-de-Luz. In 1km cross rlwy & immed turn sharp R sp Erromardie. Site on sharp turn L bef beach. Ent by plastic chain fence bef ent to prom, but easy to miss. App poss diff lge o'fits due hairpin turn - drive on to car park where may be poss to turn. Med, hdg, pt sl, wc; chem disp; mv service pnt; shwrs inc; EHU (10A) €3,50; lndry; snacks; bar; bbq; beach sand adj; dogs; quiet. "Nice site in excel position; owner connects EHU; cliff walk to town; NH en rte Spain; san facs refurbished; wonderful location; site on 2 levels, sea views on top level." ♦ 10 Apr-1 Nov. € 34.00   2015*

> **"I like to fill in the reports as I travel from site to site"**
> You'll find report forms at the back of this guide, or you can fill them in online at camc.com/europereport.

Site report forms at back of guide   *Last year of report   355

ST JEAN DE LUZ

ST JEAN DE LUZ *8F1* (3km NE Coastal) *43.41339, -1.61710* **Camping Itsas-Mendi, Acotz, 64500 St Jean-de-Luz [05 59 26 56 50; fax 05 59 26 54 44; itsas@wanadoo.fr; www.itsas-mendi.com]**
Exit A63 junc 3 sp St Jean-de-Luz; take D810 dir Biarritz; in 3km turn L sp Acotz Plage & Camping; site well sp. Lge, hdg, shd, pt sl, terr, wc (htd); chem disp; mv service pnt; fam bthrm; shwrs inc; EHU (10A) inc; lndry; shop; rest; snacks; bar; bbq; playgrnd; pool (htd); paddling pool; beach 500m; wifi; TV; dogs €2.20; phone; Eng spkn; games area; tennis; sauna; CKE/CCI. "Friendly staff; excel; waterslides & aquatic area." ♦ 3 Apr-13 Oct. € 40.00   2012*

ST JEAN DE LUZ *8F1* (10km SE Rural) *43.35748, -1.57465* **Camping d'Ibarron, 64310 St Pée-sur-Nivelle [05 59 54 10 43; fax 05 59 54 51 95; camping.dibarron@wanadoo.fr; www.camping-ibarron.com]**
Fr St Jean take D918 twd St Pée, site 2km bef St Pée on R of rd. Lge, shd, wc; chem disp; mv service pnt; shwrs inc; EHU (6A) €3.95; lndry; shop; snacks; playgrnd; pool; wifi; TV; 5% statics; dogs €1.60; phone; Eng spkn; adv bkg acc; quiet; games rm; CKE/CCI. "Well-kept site in scenic location; spacious pitches; welcoming, helpful owner; gd san facs; on main rd & no footpath to vill; walk along rv into vill; mkt Sat; excel." ♦ 23 Apr-30 Sep. € 29.00   2017*

ST JEAN DE LUZ *8F1* (8km SE Rural) *43.34591, -1.61724* **Camping Chourio, Luberriaga, 64310 Ascain [05 59 54 06 31 or 05 59 54 04 32; www.tourisme-aquitaine.fr]**
Fr St Jean-de-Luz take D918 sp Ascain. In 6km turn R at traff lts, in 250m over rv bdge & turn L at mini-rndabt. Site sp in town. Med, pt shd, wc; chem disp; mv service pnt; shwrs inc; EHU (6A) €2.80; rest nr; bar nr; phone; quiet; CKE/CCI. "Friendly, family-owned, relaxed site in lovely countryside; conv Spanish border, Tues & Sat mkt St Jean-de-Luz; vg; v helpful owners; bar only 300mtrs." 20 Mar-15 Nov. € 12.00   2018*

⊞ **ST JEAN DE LUZ** *8F1* (3km SW Rural) *43.37064, -1.68629* **Camping Larrouleta, 210 Route de Socoa, 64122 Urrugne [05 59 47 37 84; fax 05 59 47 42 54; info@larrouleta.com; www.larrouleta.com]**
Exit A63 junc 2 St Jean-de-Luz Sud. Pass under D810 & take 1st L sp Urrugne. Loop back up to N10 & turn R, site sp in 500m. Or fr S on D810, 2km beyond Urrugne vill (by-pass vill), turn L into minor rd, site 50m on R. Lge, hdg, hdstg, mkd, pt shd, wc (htd); chem disp; fam bthrm; shwrs inc; EHU (10A) inc (poss rev pol); gas; lndry; shop; rest; snacks; bar; playgrnd; pool (covrd, htd); beach sand 3km; sw; entmnt; wifi; dogs €2; phone; bus 200m; Eng spkn; adv bkg req; ccard acc; games area; boating; tennis; fishing; CKE/CCI. "Pleasant, well-run family site nr lake; satisfactory san facs (unisex LS) & pool; friendly & helpful (ask for dir on dep to avoid dangerous bend); some pitches unrel in wet but can park on site rds/hdstg; poss ltd facs LS; conv A63, Biarritz & en rte Spain; gd; conv m'way & hypmkt/fuel 1.5km; nice walk to Urrugne & St Jean to Luz." ♦ € 30.00   2017*

See advertisement

ST JEAN DE LUZ *8F1* (9km SW Rural) *43.33277, -1.68527* **Le Camping du Col d'Ibardin, Route d'Ascain, 64122 Urrugne [05 59 54 31 21; fax 05 59 54 62 28; info@col-ibardin.com; www.col-ibardin.com]**
Exit A63 junc 2, ignore slip rd to R 50m, turn L & in 100m turn R onto D810 S. In 2km at rndabt foll sp Col d'Ibardin, Ascain; after 4km site on R immed past minor rd to Col d'Ibardin. Med, mkd, hdstg, hdg, pt shd, pt sl, terr, serviced pitches; wc; chem disp; fam bthrm; shwrs inc; EHU (10A) inc; gas; lndry; shop; rest; snacks; bar; bbq; playgrnd; pool (htd); paddling pool; red long stay; entmnt; wifi; TV; 50% statics; dogs €3; phone; Eng spkn; adv bkg acc; quiet; ccard acc; games rm; tennis; games area; CKE/CCI. "Lovely, well-run site in woodland; fair sized pitches; helpful, friendly owner; gd san facs; pleasant bar/rest; mountain rlwy nr; gd touring base for Pyrenees & N Spain; excel." ♦ 1 Apr-1 Oct. € 50.00   2017*

ST JEAN DE MAURIENNE 9C3 (1km SE Urban) 45.27034, 6.35023 **Camp Municipal des Grands Cols**, 422 Ave du Mont-Cenis, 73300 St Jean-de-Maurienne [04 79 64 28 02 or 06 64 09 77 48 (mob); info@campingdesgrandscols.com; www.campingdesgrandscols.com] Site sp fr D1006 in St Jean-de-Maurienne; site behind shops 100m fr town cent behind trees/parking. Med, hdg, hdstg, mkd, pt shd, pt sl, serviced pitches; wc; chem disp; mv service pnt; shwrs inc; EHU (16A) €3; lndry; shop nr; snacks; bar; playgrnd; TV; dogs €1; Eng spkn; quiet; games rm; CKE/CCI. "Warm welcome; helpful staff; clean san facs; pool 1.5km; interesting town; excel for serious cycling; gd NH for Fréjus tunnel; excel." 17 May-30 Sep. € 31.00   2014*

ST JEAN DE MONTS 2H3 (8km SE Coastal) 46.75638, -2.00749 **Camping La Yole**, Chemin des Bosses, Orouët, 85160 St Jean-de-Monts [02 51 58 67 17; fax 02 51 59 05 35; contact@la-yole.com; www.vendee-camping.eu] Take D38 S fr St Jean-de-Monts dir Les Sable d'Olonne & Orouet. At Orouet turn R at L'Oasis rest dir Mouette; in 1.5km turn L at campsite sp; site on L. Situated bet D38 & coast, 1km fr Plage des Mouettes. On arr, park in carpark on R bef registering. Lge, hdg, mkd, pt shd, serviced pitches; wc; chem disp; fam bthrm; shwrs inc; EHU (10A) inc; lndry; shop; rest; snacks; bar; bbq (gas); playgrnd; pool (covrd, htd); paddling pool; beach sand 2km; entmnt; wifi; TV; 80% statics; dogs €7 (only small dogs); Eng spkn; adv bkg req; ccard acc; tennis; watersports 6km; fishing; jacuzzi; games rm; waterslide; horseriding 3km; CKE/CCI. "Busy, gd, well-run site; no o'fits over 8m; san facs clean, not spacious; excel cycle paths; mkt Wed & Sat; vg; friendly & helpful staff." ♦ 11 Apr-24 Sep. € 36.50   2015*

> **"We must tell the Club about that great site we found"**
>
> Get your site reports in by mid-August and we'll do our best to get your updates into the next edition.

ST JEAN DE MONTS 2H3 (1km W Coastal) 46.79931, -2.07378 **Camping Le Bois Joly**, 46 Route de Notre Dame-de-Monts, 85165 St Jean-de-Monts [02 51 59 11 63; fax 02 51 69 11 06; contact@camping-leboisjoly.com; www.camping-leboisjoly.com] N on D38 circular around St Jean-de-Monts; at rndabt past junc with D51 turn R dir Notre Dame-de-Monts, site on R in 300m. Lge, hdg, mkd, pt shd, wc; chem disp; fam bthrm; shwrs inc; EHU (6A) inc rev pol; lndry; shop nr; rest; snacks; bar; playgrnd; pool (covrd, htd); beach sand 1km; entmnt; wifi; TV; 25% statics; dogs €3; phone; Eng spkn; adv bkg acc; ccard acc; games area; waterslide; sauna; CKE/CCI. "Ideal for families; ACSI; gd san facs; lge pitches; coastal & inland cycleways nrby; excel." ♦ 13 Apr-29 Sep. € 34.00   2012*

ST JEAN DE MONTS

ST JEAN DE MONTS 2H3 (1km NW Rural) 46.80083, -2.08013 **Camping La Buzelière**, 79 Rue de Notre Dame, 85169 St Jean-de-Monts [02 51 58 64 80; fax 02 28 11 03 61; buzeliere@aol.com; www.buzeliere.com] Take D38 fr St Jean-de-Monts to Notre Dame-de-Monts. Site on L. Med, mkd, hdg, pt shd, pt sl, serviced pitches; wc; chem disp; fam bthrm; shwrs inc; EHU (10A) inc; gas; lndry; shop nr; snacks; bar; bbq; playgrnd; pool (htd); beach sand 1km; TV; 20% statics; dogs €2.50; Eng spkn; adv bkg acc; quiet; ccard acc; games area; games rm; CKE/CCI. "Many sports inc golf nrby; clean san facs; red facs LS; excel." ♦ 1 May-30 Sep. € 30.00   2012*

ST JEAN DE MONTS 2H3 (3km NW Coastal) 46.80311, -2.09300 **La Prairie**, 146 Rue du Moulin Casse, 85160 Saint-Jean-de-Monts [02 51 58 16 04; contact@campingprairie.com; campingprairie.com] Fr St Jean de Monts take D38 twds Notre Dame de Monts. Site abt 1.5km N of St Jean de Monts. Foll sp. Sm, mkd, pt shd, wc; chem disp; mv service pnt; fam bthrm; shwrs; EHU (6A); lndry; rest; snacks; bar; bbq; playgrnd; pool; paddling pool; beach sand; twin axles; entmnt; wifi; 40% statics; dogs; bus adj; Eng spkn; adv bkg acc; bike hire; games rm; sauna; games area. "Gd site." ♦ 1 Apr-9 Oct. € 34.00   2016*

ST JEAN DE MONTS 2H3 (4km NW Coastal) 46.80978, -2.10971 **Camping Les Places Dorées**, Route de Notre Dame de Monts, 85160 St Jean-de-Monts [02 51 59 02 93 or 02 40 73 03 70 (LS); fax 02 51 59 30 47; abridespins@aol.com; www.placesdorees.com] Fr Nantes dir Challons & St Jean-de-Monts. Then dir Notre Dame-de-Monts. Med, shd, pt sl, wc; chem disp; shwrs inc; EHU (10A) inc; gas; lndry; shop nr; rest; snacks; pool (htd); beach sand 800m; entmnt; dogs €2.80; Eng spkn; adv bkg acc; quiet; games area; games rm; waterslide; CKE/CCI. "Vg; free entmnt children/adults; organised excursions; friendly family-run site; mountain views." ♦ 1 Jun-10 Sep. € 32.00   2016*

ST JEAN DE MONTS 2H3 (6km NW Coastal) 46.81831, -2.13006 **Camping La Forêt**, 190 Chemin de la Rive, 85160 St Jean-de-Monts [02 51 58 84 63; camping-la-foret@wanadoo.fr; www.hpa-laforet.com] Fr St Jean-de-Monts, take D38 twd Notre-Dame-de-Monts for 6km, over rndabt then turn L (last turning bef Notre-Dame-de-Monts) sp Pont d'Yeu, then immed L, site on L in 200m, on parallel rd to main rd. Med, mkd, hdg, pt shd, wc; chem disp; shwrs inc; EHU (10A) €3.80; gas; lndry; shop; snacks; bbq; playgrnd; pool (htd); beach sand 500m; TV; 30% statics; dogs €2.50; phone; Eng spkn; adv bkg acc; quiet; horseriding nr; CKE/CCI. "Friendly, helpful owners; clean san facs; not suitable twin axles; some pitches diff c'vans; excel; great cycling area fr site." ♦ 1 May-20 Sep. € 36.00   2015*

ST JEAN DU GARD

ST JEAN DU GARD *10E1* (4km W Rural) *44.11250, 3.85320* Camping Mas de La Cam, Route de St André-de-Valborgne, 30270 St Jean-du-Gard [04 66 85 12 02; fax 04 66 75 32 07; camping@masdelacam.fr] On S side of D 907, 1.1km W of W end of town by-pass, W of sp Camping les Baigneurs on non-Corniche rd to Florac. NB: Due to acute angle of slip rd off D907, if app fr W on D907 must go 500m past slip rd & make U-turn at layby opp D907-D9 junc. Slip rd sh but v narr; turn L after x-ing rv, L twd tennis court. Med, hdg, mkd, shd, pt sl, wc; shwrs; EHU (6A) €4.5; lndry; shop nr; rest; snacks; playgrnd; pool; entmnt; TV; quiet; bike hire; tennis. "Excel site; friendly owners." Easter-30 Sep. € 16.00 2013*

ST JEAN PIED DE PORT *8F1* (1km S Urban) *43.16126, -1.23662* Camp Municipal de Plaza Berri, Ave de Fronton, 64220 St Jean-Pied-de-Port [05 59 37 11 19 or 05 59 37 00 92; fax 05 59 37 99 78; mairie.stjeanpieddeport@wanadoo.fr; www.saintjeanpieddeport-paysbasque-tourisme.com] Fr N on D933 thro town & cross rv. In 50m bear L at sm rndabt, site in 200m, sp. Enquire at Hôtel de Ville (Town Hall) off ssn. Narr app rds. Med, mkd, pt shd, pt sl, wc; chem disp; mv service pnt; shwrs inc; EHU (5A) €2.50 (poss rev pol); shop nr; quiet; CKE/CCI. "Nice site; busy, rec arr early high ssn; dogs; friendly warden; if recep unmanned, site yourself & report later; san facs still need refurb (2015); gd walks & scenery; used by walkers on pilgrim rte; pelota court adj; mkt Mon; gd NH; pool 500m; lovely site." ♦ 23 Apr-1 Nov. € 13.00 2016*

ST JEAN PIED DE PORT *8F1* (3km W Rural) *43.17745, -1.25970* Camping Narbaïtz Vacances Pyrénées Basques, Route de Bayonne, 64220 Ascarat [05 59 37 10 13 or 06 09 39 30 42 (mob); camping-narbaitz@wanadoo.fr; www.camping-narbaitz.com] Site on L of D918 St Jean to Bayonne 3km fr St Jean, sp. Med, hdg, mkd, pt shd, pt sl, wc (htd); chem disp; mv service pnt; fam bthrm; shwrs inc; EHU (6-10A) €4.50-5.50 (poss rev pol); lndry; shop; snacks; bar; playgrnd; pool (htd); entmnt; wifi; 5% statics; dogs free; phone; Eng spkn; adv bkg acc; quiet; ccard acc; trout fishing; kayaking, canoeing; cycling; CKE/CCI. "Attractive, clean, pleasant, family-run site; lovely views; helpful owners; vg facs; rec m'vans use top of site when wet; nr Spanish border (cheaper petrol); excel; gd san facs." ♦ 29 Apr-24 Sep. € 41.00 2017*

ST JEAN PIED DE PORT *8F1* (2km NW Rural) *43.17304, -1.25416* Europ Camping, 64220 Ascarat [05 59 37 12 78; fax 05 59 37 29 82; europ camping64@orange.fr; www.europ-camping.com] Site on D918 bet Uhart-Cize & Ascarat. Well sp. Med, hdg, mkd, pt shd, wc; chem disp; mv service pnt; shwrs inc; EHU (6A) €4 (poss rev pol); lndry; shop nr; rest; snacks; bar; playgrnd; pool; paddling pool; 30% statics; dogs €2.50; adv bkg acc; quiet; ccard acc; sauna; games area; games rm; CKE/CCI. "Beautiful location; helpful staff; ltd facs LS; only basic food in bar/rest; grnd v soft when wet; vg." ♦ 4 Apr-30 Sep. € 33.00 2016*

ST JULIEN EN GENEVOIS *9A3* (5km SE Rural) *46.12015, 6.10565* Kawan Village La Colombière, 166 Chemin Neuf-Chef-Lieu, 74160 Neydens [04 50 35 13 14; fax 04 50 35 13 40; la.colombiere@wanadoo.fr; www.camping-la-colombiere.com] Exit A40 junc 13 onto D1201 dir Cruseilles; in 1.75km turn L to Neydens; turn R at church; site on R in 200m. Site sp. NB: Do not go into St Julien-en-Genevois when towing. Med, hdstg, hdg, mkd, pt shd, pt sl, wc (htd); chem disp; mv service pnt; fam bthrm; shwrs inc; EHU (6-10A) inc, extra for 15A; gas; lndry; shop; rest; snacks; bar; bbq; playgrnd; pool (covrd, htd); paddling pool; entmnt; wifi; TV; 10% statics; dogs €2.50; Eng spkn; adv bkg acc; ccard acc; bike hire; lake fishing 1km; games rm; CKE/CCI. "Family-owned site; friendly, helpful staff; boggy after heavy rain; farm produce; conv Geneva - guided tours high ssn; no o'fits over 10m high ssn; park & ride bus; open for m'vans all year; gd NH; excel; highly rec." ♦ 1 Apr-31 Oct. € 39.70 2017*

ST JUNIEN *7B3* (4km E Rural) *45.88078, 0.96539* FFCC Camp Municipal de Chambery, 87200 St Brice-sur-Vienne [05 55 02 18 13; fax 05 55 02 93 36; mairiest-brice@wanadoo.fr; www.tourismelimousin.fr] Fr St Junien take D32 E sp St Brice & St Victurnien; on leaving St Brice on D32 turn L & foll sp; site on L in 500m, on E edge of vill. Or app on D32 fr E, turn R onto C2 bef St Brice-sur-Vienne town sp, sp 'Campings & Gîte Rural'. Sm, mkd, hdstg, hdg, pt shd, pt sl, serviced pitches; wc (htd); shwrs inc; EHU (10A) €3.40; lndry; shop nr; playgrnd; dogs; adv bkg acc; CKE/CCI. "Peaceful, clean site in park; spacious pitches o'look lake & countryside; site yourself, office open 1hr am & pm; barrier clsd 2200-0700; conv Oradour-sur-Glane; excel; beautiful location; excel san facs; each pitch has own tap & drain; call to check if open." ♦ 1 May-1 Sep. € 10.00 2014*

> **"I need an on-site restaurant"**
>
> We do our best to make sure site information is correct, but it is always best to check any must-have facilities are still available or will be open during your visit.

ST JUST (CANTAL) *9C1* (0km W Urban) *44.89035, 3.21079* FFCC Camp Municipal, 15320 St Just [04 71 73 72 57, 04 71 73 70 48 or 06 31 47 05 15 (mob); fax 04 71 73 71 44; info@saintjust.com; www.saintjust.com] Exit junc 31 fr A75, foll sp St Chély-d'Apcher D909; turn W onto D448 twds St Just (approx 6km); sp with gd access. Med, mkd, pt shd, pt sl, terr, wc (htd); chem disp; mv service pnt; shwrs inc; EHU (10A) €2.30; lndry; shop; snacks; bar; pool; red long stay; dogs; phone; Eng spkn; quiet; ccard acc; tennis; bike hire; fishing. "Vg site; friendly, helpful warden; ltd facs LS; excel tennis & pool; gd touring base; area for m'vans." Easter-30 Sep. € 10.20 2017*

ST LEONARD DE NOBLAT

ST JUST EN CHEVALET 9B1 (1km NW Rural)
45.91459, 3.84026 **Camp Municipal Le Verdillé, 42430 St Just-en-Chevalet [04 77 65 17 82 or 04 77 65 00 62 (Mairie); campingleverdille@sfr.fr]** Exit A72 at junc 4, join D53 NE twd St Just-en-Chevalet. Foll sp in town to camping/piscine. Due to steep gradients avoid D1 when towing. Med, hdg, pt shd, pt sl, wc; chem disp; mv service pnt; shwrs inc; EHU (16A) €3; lndry; shop nr; rest nr; bar nr; 10% statics; dogs €1.70; phone; Eng spkn; adv bkg acc; quiet; tennis adj; CKE/CCI. "Friendly owners; htd pool adj." 1 May-30 Sep. € 19.00   2013*

ST JUSTIN 8E2 (3km NW Rural) 44.00166, -0.23502
Camping Le Pin, Route de Roquefort, 40240 St Justin [05 58 44 88 91; camping.lepin@orange.fr; www.campinglepin.com] Fr D933 in St Justin take D626 sp Requefort, site on L in 2km (sp says 3). Sm, hdg, mkd, pt shd, wc; chem disp; mv service pnt; fam bthrm; shwrs inc; EHU (6-10A) £3 (rev pol poss); lndry; shop; rest; snacks; bar; bbq; playgrnd; pool; entmnt; wifi; TV; 10% statics; dogs €2.50; Eng spkn; adv bkg acc; quiet; rv fishing 2km; games area; bike hire; horseriding; CKE/CCI. "Pleasant, spacious site; new facs (2016); beautiful vill; rustic wooded setting; gd welcome; helpful owner; bread avail daily; sm pond, free fishing for campers; highly rec; excel modern clean san facs; Bastide town nrby; conv to & fr Spain; excel." ♦ 3 Mar-1 Dec. € 23.00   2018*

⊞ **ST LARY SOULAN** 8G2 (4km NE Rural) 42.84482, 0.33836 **Camping Le Lustou, 89 Chemin d'Agos, 65170 Vielle-Aure [05 62 39 40 64; fax 05 62 39 40 72; contact@lustou.com; www.lustou.com]** Exit A64 junc 16 & head S on D929. Thro Arreau & Guchen turn R onto D19 dir Vielle-Aure. Site on R just bef Agos. Med, hdg, pt shd, pt sl, wc (htd); chem disp; fam bthrm; shwrs inc; EHU (6-10A) €6.80; gas; lndry; shop nr; snacks; bar; bbq; playgrnd; wifi; TV; 5% statics; dogs €1.80; phone; adv bkg acc; quiet; canoeing nr; fishing nr; tennis nr; games area; CKE/CCI. "Organised walks in mountains by owner; excel skiing; immac facs; communal meals organised weekly (high ssn); excel site." ♦ € 19.00   2016*

⊞ **ST LAURENT DE CERIS** 7B3 (5km NE Rural) 45.95902, 0.52880 **Camp Laurent, Le Fournet, 16450 St Laurent de Ceris Charente [06 02 22 37 15; lecamplaurent@gmail.com]** Fr St Claud on D174. Fr St Laurent de Ceris turn R at rest onto D15. Take 2nd L on D345, Le Fournet sp at junc. Site on R in about 1km. Sm, pt shd, pt sl, wc; chem disp; mv service pnt; shwrs; EHU (10A) €3; shop nr; rest nr; bar nr; bbq; pool; twin axles; wifi; dogs; Eng spkn; adv bkg acc; quiet. "Adults only site; suitable for all units; Eng owners; beside sm rv; v clean facs; helpful, friendly welcome; lakes with beach nrby; new owners; ideal walking & cycling country." ♦ € 25.00   2015*

ST LAURENT EN GRANDVAUX 6H2 (1km SE Rural)
46.57645, 5.96214 **Camp Municipal Le Champs de Mars, 8 Rue du Camping, 39150 St Laurent-en-Grandvaux [03 84 60 19 30 or 06 03 61 06 61; fax 03 84 60 19 72; champmars.camping@wanadoo.fr or champmars.camping@orange.fr; www.st-laurent39.fr]** E thro St Laurent on N5 twd Morez, site on R, sp `Caravaneige' at ent. Med, hdstg, mkd, pt shd, pt sl, serviced pitches; wc (htd); chem disp; mv service pnt; shwrs inc; EHU (4-10A) €5-6.4; lndry; shop nr; playgrnd; TV; 20% statics; dogs; phone; adv bkg acc; quiet; CKE/CCI. "Gd site; peaceful LS; gd NH; friendly staff." ♦ 15 Dec-1 Oct. € 26.00   2014*

ST LAURENT SUR SEVRE 2H4 (1km W Rural)
46.95790, -0.90290 **Camping Le Rouge Gorge, Route de la Verrie, 85290 St Laurent-sur-Sèvre [02 51 67 86 39; campinglerougegorge@wanadoo.fr; www.camping-lerougegorge-vendee.com]** Fr Cholet on N160 dir La Roche-sur-Yon; at Mortagne-sur-Sèvre take N149 to St Laurent-sur-Sèvre. In St Laurent foll sp La Verrie on D111. Site on R at top of hill. Or take 762 S fr Cholet to St Laurent. Site sp in town. Med, hdg, mkd, pt shd, pt sl, wc (htd); chem disp; mv service pnt; fam bthrm; shwrs inc; EHU (4-13A) €2.95-4.10; lndry; shop; snacks; bar; playgrnd; pool; paddling pool; wifi; 30% statics; dogs €2.10; adv bkg acc; quiet; lake fishing 800m; golf 15km; games area; CKE/CCI. "Peaceful family site; woodland walks & mountain biking; attractive sm town; close to Puy du Fou Theme Park." ♦ 1 Apr-30 Sep. € 24.00   2017*

ST LEGER SOUS BEUVRAY 4H4 (1km N Rural)
46.93157, 4.10088 **Camping De La Boutière, 71990 St Léger-sous-Beuvray [06 80 40 81 28 or 03 85 82 48 86 (LS); camping@la-boutiere.com; www.la-boutiere.com]** Take N81 SW fr Autun dir Bourbon-Lancy & in approx 10km, turn R onto D61 to St Léger. Site sp in vill. Sm, mkd, pt shd, pt sl, wc; chem disp; shwrs inc; EHU (6-10A) €3.70; shop nr; twin axles; wifi; 5% statics; dogs €2.70; phone; quiet; CKE/CCI. "Pleasant, well-kept, Dutch-owned site; gd, modern san facs; vg." 1 Apr-31 Aug. € 16.00   2013*

ST LEONARD DE NOBLAT 7B3 (15km N Rural)
45.94311, 1.51459 **Camping Pont du Dognon (formerly Municipal), 87240 St Laurent-les-Eglises [06 75 73 25 30 or 05 55 56 57 25; www.aupontdudognon.fr]** Take D941 fr St Léonard-de-Noblat; after 1.5km turn L (N) on D19 thro Le Châtenet-en-Dognon. Site in approx 4km, bef St Laurent-les-Eglises. Med, mkd, hdg, pt shd, terr, wc (htd); chem disp; shwrs inc; EHU (6-16A) €3.50; gas; lndry; shop; rest; snacks; bar; bbq; playgrnd; pool; beach shgl; twin axles; entmnt; dogs €2; adv bkg acc; quiet; tennis; bike hire; canoeing. "Vg site." 2 Apr-1 Oct. € 13.00   2016*

ST LEONARD DE NOBLAT

ST LEONARD DE NOBLAT 7B3 (2km S Rural) 45.82300, 1.49200 Camping de Beaufort, 87400 St Léonard-de-Noblat [05 55 56 02 79; info@campingdebeaufort.com; www.campingdebeaufort.com] Leave A20 S-bound at junc 34 dir St Léonard, onto D941. In 18km on ent St Léonard, 300m after x-ing Rv Vienne, fork R (sp). Site on R in 2km. Med, hdg, pt shd, pt sl, wc (htd); chem disp; shwrs inc; EHU (15A) €3-4; lndry; shop; bar; playgrnd; dogs €1.50; phone; adv bkg acc; ccard acc; fishing; CKE/CCI♦ Easter-30 Sep. € 13.00   2012*

ST LOUIS 6G3 (2km N Rural) 47.59428, 7.58930 Camping au Petit Port, 10 Allée des Marronniers, 68330 Huningue [03 89 69 05 25 or 03 89 70 01 71; contact@campinghuningue.fr; www.campinghuningue.fr] S fr Mulhouse on A35, exit onto D105 & foll sps to Huningue; after level x-ing site sp on rvside. Med, pt shd, wc; chem disp; mv service pnt; fam bthrm; shwrs inc; EHU (6A) €3; lndry; shop nr; rest; snacks; bar nr; bbq; cooking facs; playgrnd; TV; 50% statics; dogs; bus to Basle; Eng spkn; adv bkg acc; quiet; games rm; bike hire; CKE/CCI. "Excel NH on banks of Rv Rhine; helpful staff; htd pool 2km; clean facs; poss diff access lge o'fits; bar 500m; canoeing." ♦ 15 Apr-15 Oct. € 20.00   2018*

ST MAIXENT L'ECOLE 7A2 (2km SW Urban) 46.40836, -0.21856 Camp Municipal du Panier Fleuri, Rue Paul Drévin, 79400 St Maixent-l'Ecole [05 49 05 53 21; fax 05 49 76 50 90] Take D611 twd Niort, at 2nd set of traff lts nr top of hill out of town turn L. Foll camping sps into ent. Med, mkd, pt shd, pt sl, wc; mv service pnt; shwrs inc; EHU (10A); rest nr; bar nr; playgrnd; wifi; dogs; quiet; tennis. "Warden on site am & eve, if office locked go to hse nr wc block; ltd/basic facs LS; htd pool adj; interesting town; NH en rte Spain; immac new htd san facs (2014)." 1 Apr-15 Oct. € 10.50   2014*

⊞ **ST MALO** 2E4 (10km NE Rural) 48.67368, -1.92732 Camping a la ferme La Vignette, 35350 St Coulomb [02 99 89 08 42; francoise.morin600@orange.fr; www.facebook.com/campinglavignette] Fr St Malo foll D355 E twds St Coulomb. Just bef vill turn L, sp 'Camping a la ferme'. Site in 400m on R. Sm, pt shd, pt sl, wc; chem disp; shwrs; EHU (10A); beach 1km; dogs; quiet. "Vg site." € 14.00   2015*

ST MALO 2E4 (11km NE Coastal) 48.69000, -1.94200 Camping des Chevrets, La Guimorais, 35350 St Coulomb [02 99 89 01 90; fax 02 99 89 01 16; contact@campingdeschevrets.fr; www.campingdeschevrets.fr] St Malo to Cancale coast rd D201; La Guimorais on L 3km E of Rothéneuf, strt thro vill; fairly narr app. V lge, hdg, mkd, pt shd, pt sl, wc; chem disp; mv service pnt; fam bthrm; shwrs inc; EHU (6A) €3.35 (poss rev pol); gas; lndry; shop; rest; snacks; bar; bbq; playgrnd; beach sand adj; red long stay; entmnt; wifi; 50% statics; dogs; Eng spkn; adv bkg acc; quiet; ccard acc; games area; bike hire; CKE/CCI. "Vg, beautiful location with 2 bays; vg, busy, well run site; bus fr St Malo to Cancale in the summer; statics in sep area; vg value LS; vg facs; conv for ferry." ♦ 30 Mar-16 Oct. € 28.00   2017*

⊞ **ST MALO** 2E4 (5km E Urban) 48.65762, -1.95932 Camping De La Fontaine, 40 Rue de la Fontaine aux Pèlerins, 35400 St Malo [02 99 81 62 62; fax 02 99 81 68 95; contact@campinglafontaine.com; www.campinglafontaine.com] N fr Rennes on D137 turn R onto D301 sp Cancale. Turn R onto D155 sp Mont-St Michel, site in L in 100m. Med, mkd, hdg, pt shd, wc (htd); chem disp; mv service pnt; fam bthrm; shwrs inc; EHU (10A) €3.80 (poss rev pol); gas; lndry; shop; rest; snacks; bar; bbq; pool (htd); beach sand 5km; entmnt; wifi; 80% statics; dogs €3; phone; Eng spkn; quiet; ccard acc; bike hire; games area; table tennis; CKE/CCI. "Gd touring base; conv ferry; excel site; looks like garden cent fr rd; v clean & tidy site; gd covrd pool; clean san facs; supmkt nrby; san facs poss stretched in high ssn; bouncy castle; pleasant site very friendly; gd wifii coverage." € 28.00   2014*

ST MALO 2E4 (5km SE Rural) 48.60916, -1.98663 Camping Le P'tit Bois, La Chalandouze, 35430 St Jouan-des-Guérets [02 99 21 14 30; fax 02 99 81 74 14; camping.ptitbois@wanadoo.fr; www.ptitbois.com] Fr St Malo take D137 dir Rennes; after o'skts of St Malo turn R twd St Jouan-des-Guérets, site sp. Lge, mkd, hdg, pt shd, wc; chem disp; mv service pnt; fam bthrm; shwrs inc; EHU (10A) inc; gas; lndry; shop; rest; snacks; bar; bbq (elec, gas); playgrnd; pool (covrd, htd); paddling pool; beach sand 2km; entmnt; wifi; TV; 50% statics; dogs €4-6; adv bkg acc; ccard acc; waterslide; games rm; tennis; bike hire; watersports 2km; CKE/CCI. "Well-kept, well-run site; lge o'fits by request; busy even LS; min 3 persons high ssn; tidal rv fishing 2km; jacuzzi; turkish bath; friendly, helpful staff; gd clean san facs, can book unisex; some narr site rds poss diff lge o'fits; conv Le Mont-St Michel & ferries; excel." ♦ 11 Apr-20 Sep. € 59.00   2013*

ST MALO 2E4 (3km S Coastal) 48.63558, -2.02731 Camp Municipal Cité d'Alet, Allée Gaston Buy, Saint-Servan 35400 St Malo [02 99 81 60 91 or 02 99 40 71 11 (LS); fax 02 99 40 71 37; camping@ville-saint-malo.fr; www.ville-saint-malo.fr/campings] Fr ferry terminal go twd St Malo, site sp at rndabt immed past docks. Fr all other dir foll sp for port/ferry, then site sp. Site off Place St Pierre, St Servan-sur-Mer. App thro old pt of city poss diff for lge o'fits. Lge, hdstg, pt shd, pt sl, wc; chem disp; mv service pnt; shwrs inc; EHU (10A) inc (poss rev pol & long elec cable poss req); shop nr; rest nr; bar nr; bbq (charcoal, elec, gas); playgrnd; beach sand 500m; twin axles; dogs €2.95; phone; bus 1km; Eng spkn; adv bkg acc; quiet; ccard acc; CKE/CCI. "Well-run, scenic site; staff helpful & friendly; sm pitches, access to some diff lge o'fits; san facs basic but OK (poss v slippery); WW2 museum adj; noise fr harbour when foggy; mkt Fri; parts of site steep, lovely walks, cliff top views of Dinard & St Malo, walk to St Malo worth while; site feels cosy." ♦ 26 Apr-21 May & 1 Jul-25 Sep. € 22.50   2018*

STES MARIES DE LA MER

ST MALO 2E4 (6km S Rural) 48.61469, -1.98663
Camping Domaine de la Ville Huchet, Rue de la Passagère, Quelmer, 35400 St Malo [02 99 81 11 83; fax 02 99 81 51 89; info@lavillehuchet.com; www.lavillehuchet.com] Fr ferry port, foll sps for D137 dir Rennes; site sp fr 'Madeleine' rndabt on leaving St Malo. Or fr S on D137 take D301 sp St Malo cent. Take 1st exit at next 2 rndabts (thro indus est) & cont on this rd (sharp R-hand bend), then under bdge, site on R. Fr S head N on D137, merge onto D301, at rndabt take 1st exit onto Rue de la Grassinais, thro next rndabt. At next rndabt take 1st exit. Site on the L. Lge, mkd, hdg, pt shd, pt sl, wc; chem disp; mv service pnt; fam bthrm; shwrs inc; EHU (6A) inc; lndry; shop; rest; snacks; bar; bbq (charcoal, gas, sep area); playgrnd; pool (covrd, htd); paddling pool; beach sand 4km; entmnt; wifi; TV; 40% statics; dogs €3.50; Eng spkn; adv bkg acc; quiet; waterpark; games area; games rm; bike hire. "Spacious site in grnds of sm chateau; helpful owner; modern san facs; no o'fits over 7.5m except by request; lge pitches avail; some pitches v shady; conv ferries & Mont St Michel; excel; bus to St Malo adj." ♦ 2 Apr-18 Sep. € 37.00   2016*

See advertisement

ST MARCELLIN 9C2 (7km E Rural) 45.12122, 5.33775
Camping Château de Beauvoir, 38160 Beauvoir-en-Royans [04 76 64 01 79; fax 04 76 38 49 60; chateaudebeauvoir@wanadoo.fr] On D1092 Romans to Grenoble, turn into narr uphill rd D518 to vill; L into site, sp. Care needed on app rd & ent gate narr. Sm, shd, wc (htd); shwrs inc; EHU (10A) €2; lndry; rest nr; bar; 10% statics; dogs; adv bkg rec; quiet. "Vg site on château lawn; gd walking." 1 Apr-31 Oct. € 11.60   2013*

⊞ **STE MARIE AUX MINES** 6E3 (2km SW Urban) 48.23520, 7.16695 FFCC Camping Les Reflets du Val d'Argent, 20 Rue d'Untergrombach, 68160 Ste Marie-aux-Mines [03 89 58 64 31; reflets@calixo.net; www.les-reflets.com] Fr Sélestat N59 into Ste Marie. Go thro vill to traff lts & turn L. 1km to site; sp. Med, hdg, mkd, pt shd, pt sl, wc (htd); chem disp; mv service pnt; shwrs inc; EHU (5-15A) €3.30-9.90; lndry; shop; rest; snacks; bar; bbq; playgrnd; pool; wifi; TV; 5% statics; dogs €3.50; phone; adv bkg acc; quiet; games rm; CKE/CCI. "Pleasant site; winter skiing 5km; new san facs; grnds could be improved." ♦ € 21.00   2015*

> **"Satellite navigation makes touring much easier"**
>
> Remember most sat navs don't know if you're towing or in a larger vehicle – always use yours alongside maps and site directions.

STES MARIES DE LA MER 10F2 (1km E Coastal) 43.45633, 4.43576 Camping La Brise, Rue Marcel Carrière, 13460 Les Stes Maries-de-la-Mer [04 90 97 84 67; fax 04 90 97 72 01; info@camping-labrise.fr; www.camping-labrise.fr] Sp on o'skts on all rds. Take N570 fr Arles or D58 fr Aigues-Mortes. V lge, unshd, wc (htd); mv service pnt; shwrs inc; EHU (16A) €4.90; lndry; shop; rest nr; snacks; bbq; pool (htd); paddling pool; beach adj; entmnt; wifi; TV; 10% statics; dogs €5.20; fishing; site clsd mid-Nov to mid-Dec. "Gd facs; v cr Aug; poss mosquitoes; gd security; beach improved with breakwaters; m'vans can use free municipal car park with facs; fitness area; recep open fr 0900-1700 but clsd 1200-1400; vg winter NH; pitches poorly mrkd, dirty & dusty." ♦ 1 Jan-12 Nov & 15 Dec-31 Dec. € 17.00   2016*

STES MARIES DE LA MER 10F2 (3km W Coastal) 43.45014, 4.40163 **Camping Le Clos du Rhône, Route d'Aigues-Mortes, 13460 Stes Maries-de-la-Mer [04 90 97 85 99; fax 04 90 97 78 85; info@camping-leclos.fr; www.camping-leclos.fr]** Fr Arles take D570 to Stes Maries; fr Aigues Mortes, D58/D570. Lge, mkd, pt shd, serviced pitches; wc; chem disp; mv service pnt; fam bthrm; shwrs inc; EHU (16A) €5.10; gas; lndry; shop; rest; snacks; bar; bbq; cooking facs; playgrnd; pool (htd); paddling pool; beach sand; twin axles; entmnt; wifi; TV; 30% statics; dogs €5.50; phone; Eng spkn; adv bkg acc; quiet; ccard acc; horseriding adj; games area; games rm; bike hire; waterslide; CKE/CCI. "Excel pool & facs; san facs clean, poss ltd & stretched LS; popular with families; private gate to beach; mosquitoes; rv boat trips adj; off rd bike & foot paths to town; vg." ♦ 4 Apr-6 Nov. € 33.00 2015*

See advertisement

ST MARTIN DES BESACES 1D4 (1km W Rural) 49.00889, -0.85955 **Camping Le Puits, La Groudière, 14350 St Martin-des-Besaces Calvados [02 31 67 80 02; enquiries@lepuits.com; www.lepuits.com]** Fr Caen SW on A84 dir Rennes, Villers-Bocage & exit junc 41 to St Martin-des-Besaces. At traff lts in vill turn R & foll site sp, site on L at end of vill in 500m. Fr Cherbourg foll sp St Lô onto m'way. After Torini-sur-Vire at junc with A84 foll sp Caen & exit junc 41, then as above. Sm, mkd, hdg, pt shd, pt sl, wc; chem disp; mv service pnt; shwrs inc; EHU (6A) €5 (poss rev pol); gas; lndry; shop nr; rest nr; snacks; bar; bbq; playgrnd; entmnt; dogs €1.50; adv bkg acc; quiet; ccard acc; fishing; cycling; CKE/CCI. "Pleasant CL-type orchard site; welcoming, helpful Irish owners; no arr bef 1400; lge pitches with garden; 'super' pitches extra cost; san facs v basic & inadequate if site full - little privacy; B&B in farmhouse; equestrian trails; lake adj; suitable for rallies up to 30 vans; c'van storage; war museum in vill; conv Caen ferries; excel." ♦ 1 Mar-31 Oct. € 29.00 2013*

ST MARTIN EN CAMPAGNE 3B2 (2km N Coastal) 49.96631, 1.20469 **Camping Domaine Les Goélands, Rue des Grèbes, 76370 St Martin-en-Campagne [02 35 83 82 90; fax 02 35 83 21 79; domainelesgoelands@orange.fr; www.camping-les-goelands.fr]** Fr Dieppe foll D925 twd Le Tréport & Abbeville. Turn L at rndabt on D113 twd St Martin-en-Campagne. Cont thro vill to St Martin-Plage (approx 3km) & foll 'Camping' sp to site on L. Lge, hdg, hdstg, mkd, pt shd, pt sl, terr, serviced pitches; wc (htd); chem disp; fam bthrm; shwrs inc; EHU (16A) inc (poss rev pol); gas; lndry; shop nr; bar nr; bbq; playgrnd; beach shgl 500m; TV; 40% statics; dogs €2; Eng spkn; adv bkg acc; quiet; ccard acc; bike hire; waterslide 1km; tennis; fishing; CKE/CCI. "Gd touring area; ltd recep hrs LS; no late arr area; poss resident workers LS; mkt Dieppe Sat; golf 20km; horseriding 15km; vg site; immac modern san facs(2017); v helpful recep." ♦ 1 Apr-31 Oct. € 23.00 2017*

> **"There aren't many sites open at this time of year"**
>
> If you're travelling outside peak season remember to call ahead to check site opening dates – even if the entry says 'open all year'.

⊞ ST MARTIN SUR LA CHAMBRE 9B3 (0km N Rural) 45.36883, 6.31458 **Camping Le Petit Nice, Notre Dame-de-Cruet, 73130 St Martin-sur-la-Chambre [04 79 56 37 72 or 06 76 29 19 39 (mob); campinglepetitnice@yahoo.fr; www.campinglepetitnice.com]** Fr N on A43 exit junc 26 & foll sp to cent of La Chambre, thro town to rndabt & turn R into Rue Notre Dame-du-Cruet. Foll site sp & in 2km turn R thro housing, site on L in 200m. Sm, pt shd, terr, wc (htd); chem disp; shwrs inc; EHU (3-10A); lndry; shop; rest; snacks; bar; playgrnd; pool; wifi; 80% statics; dogs €1; Eng spkn; adv bkg acc; quiet; CKE/CCI. "By stream with mountain views; clean, dated facs; gd location for hilly cycling; fair." ♦ € 16.00 2016*

ST MAURICE L'EXIL

ST MARTIN SUR LA CHAMBRE *9B3* (1km SW Rural) *45.36146, 6.31300* Camping Le Bois Joli, 73130 St Martin-sur-la-Chambre [04 79 56 21 28; fax 04 79 56 29 95; camping.le.bois.joli@wanadoo.fr; www.campingleboisjoli.com] Leave A43 at junc 26 onto D213 sp La Chambre & Col de la Madeleine; foll camping sp (rd narr & winding in places); site on L. Med, mkd, pt shd, pt sl, terr, wc; chem disp; fam bthrm; shwrs inc; EHU (6A) inc; gas; lndry; shop; rest; snacks; bbq; playgrnd; pool; red long stay; entmnt; 20% statics; dogs €4; phone; Eng spkn; adv bkg acc; quiet; fishing; CKE/CCI. "Helpful staff; mountain scenery; gd walking, skiing; guided walks; ltd facs LS; conv Fréjus Tunnel." ♦ 5 Apr-6 Oct. € 13.00   2017*

ST MATHIEU *7B3* (3km E Rural) *45.71413, 0.78835* Camp Municipal du Lac, Les Champs, 87440 St Mathieu [05 55 00 34 30 (Mairie); fax 05 55 48 80 62] On D699 heading E in dir of Limoges 1.8km fr vill turn on L (N). Sp fr vill cent. Med, mkd, hdg, pt shd, terr, wc; fam bthrm; shwrs; EHU €3; lndry; shop nr; rest nr; playgrnd; sw; dogs €3.50; quiet; windsurfing. "Attractive, well-kept site; pleasant situation on lakeside; lge pitches; pedalos; site yourself, warden calls; beautiful lake with lots of activities." 1 May-30 Sep. € 14.00   2014*

STE MAURE DE TOURAINE *4H2* (6km NE Rural) *47.14831, 0.65453* Camping Le Parc de Fierbois, 37800 Ste Catherine-de-Fierbois [02 47 65 43 35; fax 02 47 65 53 75; contact@fierbois.com; www.fierbois.com or www.les-castels.com] S on D910 fr Tours, thro Montbazon & cont twd Ste Maure & Châtellerault. About 16km outside Montbazon nr vill of Ste Catherine look for site sp. Turn L off main rd & foll sp to site. Or exit A10 junc 25 onto D760E, then D910 N sp Tours; in 6.5 km turn R to Ste Catherine-de-Fierbois; site on L 1.5km past vill. Lge, hdg, mkd, pt shd, wc; chem disp; mv service pnt; fam bthrm; shwrs inc; EHU (10A) €5; lndry; shop; rest; snacks; bar; bbq; playgrnd; pool (covrd, htd); paddling pool; twin axles; entmnt; wifi; TV; dogs free; Eng spkn; adv bkg acc; ccard acc; games area; waterslide; tennis; bike hire; games rm; boating; fishing; CKE/CCI. "Excel, well-kept family site; helpful staff; gd touring base; peaceful LS; rec." ♦ 19 May-6 Sep. € 44.00   2017*

STE MAURE DE TOURAINE *4H2* (2km SE Rural) *47.10483, 0.62574* Camp Municipal Marans, Rue de Toizelet, 37800 Ste Maure-de-Touraine [02 47 65 44 93 or 06 72 18 05 41; fax 02 47 65 65 76; www.tourisme-saintemauredetouraine.fr] Fr A10 take Ste Maure exit junc 25 & foll D760 twd Loches. At 4th rndabt turn L & then immed R. Site on R in 500m. Site sp fr m'way. Med, mkd, pt shd, wc; chem disp; mv service pnt; shwrs inc; EHU (10A) €3.20 (poss long cables req); shop nr; rest nr; bar nr; bbq; playgrnd; wifi; dogs €1.42; phone; Eng spkn; adv bkg acc; quiet; fishing; tennis. "Well-kept, basic site; cheerful staff; gd, clean facs - poss stretched when busy; pool 1.5km; if office clsd site yourself; barrier down 2200-0700; roller blade court; late arr area outside barrier; no twin axles; poss travellers in sep area; vg; wifi around office area; lovely peaceful site." ♦ 10 Apr-30 Sep. € 9.00   2017*

⊞ **STE MAURE DE TOURAINE** *4H2* (2km S Rural) *47.10861, 0.61440* Aire de Service Camping-Cars Bois de Chaudron, 37800 Ste Maure-de-Touraine [02 47 34 06 04] Fr S on D910 dir Tours, as ent town, site on R adj junc at traff lts; sm sp on dual-c'way. Sm, wc; mv service pnt; shwrs; EHU €2 (on only some pitches); lndry; wifi; Eng spkn. "M'vans only; New Aire de Service (2009); warden calls; conv N/S journeys; easy to park; level, grass; friendly." € 5.00   2017*

STE MAURE DE TOURAINE *4H2* (10km W Rural) *47.10705, 0.51016* Camping du Château de la Rolandière, 37220 Trogues [02 47 58 53 71; contact@larolandiere.com; www.larolandiere.com] Exit A10 junc 25 onto D760 dir Chinon & L'Ile-Bouchard. Site on S side of rd in 5.5km. Sm, mkd, hdg, pt shd, pt sl, wc; chem disp; fam bthrm; shwrs inc; EHU (10A) €4.40 (poss long lead req); lndry; shop nr; snacks; bar; bbq; playgrnd; pool (htd); paddling pool; wifi; TV; dogs €3; Eng spkn; adv bkg acc; quiet; games area; games rm; CKE/CCI. "Beautiful, well-maintained, family-run site in chateau grnds; friendly, helpful owners; gd clean san facs; excel for young families, sh or long stay; gd dog walking; conv Loire chateaux; excel pool & sports field; highly rec; Villandry gdns to N; Richlieu worth a visit; secluded and peaceful; gd size pool; football pitch & games for children; great location for Loire chateaux; gd for o'night stay." ♦ 30 Apr-18 Sep. € 24.00   2016*

⊞ **ST MAURICE LES CHARENCEY** *4E2* (0km N Rural) *48.64747, 0.75575* Camp Municipal de la Poste, Rue de Brest, 61190 St Maurice-lès-Charencey [02 33 25 72 98; mairie.stmaurice-charencey@wanadoo.fr] Vill on N12 halfway bet Verneuil-sur-Avre & Mortagne-au-Perche. Site in vill cent, opp Mairie & church. Sm, hdg, mkd, pt shd, wc; shwrs inc; EHU; shop nr; rest nr; bar nr; bbq; 50% statics; phone; fishing. "Phone ahead LS to check open; helpful warden; facs basic but adequate; gd NH; lake adj; site self; gd site." € 7.60   2016*

ST MAURICE L'EXIL *9B2* (2km E Urban) *45.39760, 4.78836* Camping La Colombière, 20 Rue Mata, La Colombier, 38550 Saint-Maurice l'Exile [(033) 474 862 567; contact@camping-lacolombiere.com; www.camping-lacolombiere.com] Fr N7 turn off at exit St Maurice-l'Exile, foll sp to vill. Take exit rd sp Vienne (toll Free) via RN7 exit to vill and foll sp to site. Sm, hdg, pt shd, wc cont; mv service pnt; fam bthrm; shwrs; EHU 9A; lndry; playgrnd; pool (htd, indoor); entmnt; wifi; dogs; Eng spkn; quiet; ccard acc; tennis; games area; waterslide. "Lovely warm welcome." ♦ 1 Apr-31 Oct. € 18.50   2012*

France

SAINT MAURICE SOUS LES COTES

SAINT MAURICE SOUS LES COTES *5D2* (0km N Rural) *49.01796, 5.67539* Camping Du Bois Joli, 12 rue haute Gaston Parant, 55210 St Maurice-sous-les-Côtes [03 29 89 33 32; campingduboisjoli@voila.fr; www.forest-campingbj.com] Well sp in vill. If app on D23, turn R at t-junc & foll sp. Sm, pt shd, sl, wc; shwrs inc; EHU (7A) €2.20; rest nr; bar nr; bbq; playgrnd; dogs; Eng spkn; quiet. "Conv Verdun & WW1 sites; gd view during World Air Balloon Festival." ♦ 1 Apr-15 Oct. € 13.00 2015*

ST MAURICE SUR MOSELLE *6F3* (5km NE Urban) *47.88888, 6.85758* Sunêlia Domaine de Champé, 14 Rue des Champs Navés, 88540 Bussang [03 29 61 51; fax 03 29 61 56 90; info@domaine-de-champe.com; domaine-de-champe.fr] Fr N66/E512 in Bussang, site sp fr town sq. Opp Avia filling stn. Med, mkd, pt shd, pt sl, terr, wc (htd); chem disp; mv service pnt; fam bthrm; shwrs inc; EHU (6-10A) €5-6; lndry; shop nr; rest; snacks; bbq; playgrnd; pool (covrd, htd); paddling pool; entmnt; wifi; TV; 50% statics; dogs €3; phone; bus 1km; Eng spkn; adv bkg acc; quiet; ccard acc; sauna; waterslide; games rm; bike hire; tennis; games area; CKE/CCI. "Excel site behind hospital grnds; lovely views; welcoming, helpful owners; fitness rm; facs vg; vg rest; excel walks, cycle path." ♦ 1 Apr-15 Nov. € 34.00 2018*

ST MAURICE SUR MOSELLE *6F3* (14km E Rural) *47.88170, 6.94435* Camp Municipal Bénélux-Bâle, Rue de la Scierie, 68121 Urbès [03 89 82 78 76 or 03 89 82 60 91 (Mairie); fax 03 89 82 16 61; mairie.urbes@wanadoo.fr; camping-urbes.fr] Site off N66 on N side of rd at foot of hill rising W out of Urbès. At foot of Col de Bessang. Fr Bussang on N66, immed on ent Urbes turn L doubling back & foll rd, site on L. Lge, mkd, pt shd, wc (htd); chem disp; mv service pnt; fam bthrm; shwrs inc; EHU (6-10A) €6.80; lndry; rest; snacks; bar; bbq; playgrnd; sw nr; entmnt; wifi; 10% statics; dogs; phone; adv bkg rec; quiet; fishing adj; games area; CKE/CCI. "Gd sh stay/NH; beautiful area; friendly, welcoming staff; meals avil on site; facs bit cramped & ltd with poor shwrs; horse riding; hang gliding; cycle paths fr site; walks." 1 May-30 Sep. € 9.00 2017*

ST MAURICE SUR MOSELLE *6F3* (2km W Rural) *47.8555, 6.8117* Camping Les Deux Ballons, 17 Rue du Stade, 88560 St Maurice-sur-Moselle [03 29 25 17 14; stan0268@orange.fr; www.camping-deux-ballons.fr] On N66 on E side of rd in vill, site on L bef petrol stn. Clearly sp. Lge, mkd, pt shd, pt sl, wc; chem disp; mv service pnt; fam bthrm; shwrs inc; EHU (4-15A) €4.15-5.20; gas; lndry; shop nr; snacks; bar; pool; wifi; TV; dogs €3.20; phone; Eng spkn; adv bkg acc; quiet; waterslide; tennis; games rm; CKE/CCI. "Some pitches sm; excel site & facs; cycle path fr site." ♦ 19 Apr-27 Sep. € 32.00 2015*

ST MAXIMIN LA STE BAUME *10F3* (3km S Rural) *43.42848, 5.86498* Camping Caravaning Le Provençal, Route de Mazaugues, 83470 St Maximin-la-Ste Baume [04 94 78 16 97; fax 04 94 78 00 22; camping.provencal@wanadoo.fr; www.camping-le-provencal.com] Exit St Maximin on N560 S twd Marseilles. After 1km turn L onto D64. Site on R after 2km. Lge, mkd, shd, pt sl, wc; mv service pnt; shwrs inc; EHU (6-10A) €3.40-4.40; gas; lndry; shop; rest; snacks; bar; playgrnd; pool; TV; 10% statics; adv bkg acc; CKE/CCI. "Gd NH." 1 Apr-30 Sep. € 16.00 2012*

> ### "That's changed – Should I let the Club know?"
> If you find something on site that's different from the site entry, fill in a report and let us know. See camc.com/europereport.

STE MENEHOULD *5D1* (1km E Rural) *49.08937, 4.90969* Camp Municipal de la Grelette, Chemin de l'Alleval, 51800 Ste Ménéhould [03 26 60 24 76; mairie@ste-menehould.fr; www.ste-menehould.fr] Exit A4 junc 29 to Ste Menéhould; foll sp 'Centre Ville' thro town to Mairie & cent sq on D3; then foll sp 'Piscine' & 'Camping' on D3; cont uphill with rlwy on R; turn R over narr rlwy bdge, then L to site in 200m. Sm, pt shd, pt sl, wc; chem disp; shwrs inc; EHU (4A) €3.40; shop nr; rest nr; bar nr; dogs €1.05; Eng spkn; adv bkg acc; CKE/CCI. "Delightful site; helpful warden; recep 0800-1000 & 1800-2000, access to o'fits over 2m poss restricted at other times, confirm dep with warden; vg, clean but dated san facs(2017); interesting old town; under new ownership (2013); well maintained site; new indoor pool opened nrby; conv for Reims & Verdun; ok for NH." 1 May-30 Sep. € 16.00 2017*

STE MERE EGLISE *1C4* (10km NE Coastal) *49.46650, -1.23540* Camping Le Cormoran, 2 Rue du Cormoran, 50480 Ravenoville-Plage [02 33 41 33 94; fax 02 33 95 16 08; lecormoran@wanadoo.fr; www.lecormoran.com] NE on D15 fr Ste Mère-Eglise to Ravenoville, turn L onto D14 then R back onto D15 to Ravenoville Plage. Turn R on D421, Rte d'Utah Beach, site on R in 1km. Or fr N13 sp C2 Fresville & ent Ste Mère-Eglise, then take D15. Lge, mkd, hdstg, hdg, unshd, wc; chem disp; mv service pnt; fam bthrm; shwrs inc; EHU (6A) inc; gas; lndry; shop; snacks; bar; bbq (charcoal, gas); playgrnd; pool (covrd, htd); paddling pool; beach sand adj; twin axles; entmnt; wifi; TV; 60% statics; dogs €3; Eng spkn; adv bkg acc; quiet; ccard acc; jacuzzi; games rm; archery; tennis; bike hire; games area; horseriding; sauna; CKE/CCI. "Popular, family-run site; lge pitches; warm welcome, helpful recep; well-kept san facs, poss tired end of ssn; poss v windy; vg children's facs; special pitches for early dep for ferry; m'van o'night area; excel." ♦ 31 Mar-30 Sep. € 33.00 2017*

ST MIHIEL

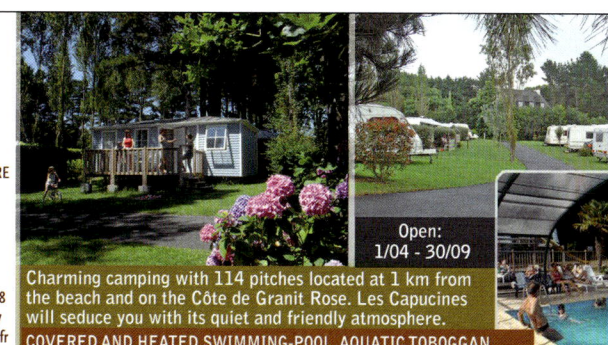

STE MERE EGLISE *1C4* (1km E Urban) *49.41006, -1.31078* **Camping De Sainte-Mere Eglise (formerly Municipal), 6 Rue due 505eme Airborne, 50480 Ste Mère-Eglise [02 33 41 35 22; fax 02 33 41 79 15; www.camping-sainte-mere.fr]** Fr Cherbourg S on N13 to cent of Ste Mère-Eglise (avoiding by-pass); at vill sq turn L on D17 to site, next adj sports grnd. Med, hdstg, pt shd, pt sl, wc; chem disp; shwrs inc; EHU (12A) €4 (poss rev pol); lndry; shop nr; rest; snacks; bar nr; bbq; playgrnd; 5% statics; dogs €1.50; phone; Eng spkn; adv bkg acc; games rm; bike hire; tennis; CKE/CCI. "Nice, basic site; clean facs; friendly warden; if warden absent site yourself & pay later; conv ferries & D-Day beaches etc; gates open 6am for early dep; rec; san facs improving (2014)." ♦ 15 Mar-1 Oct. € 22.00   2015*

> **"I like to fill in the reports as I travel from site to site"**
>
> You'll find report forms at the back of this guide, or you can fill them in online at camc.com/europereport.

⊞ **ST MICHEL DE MAURIENNE** *9C3* (1km SE Rural) *45.21276, 6.47858* **FFCC Camping Le Marintan, 1 Rue de la Provalière, 73140 St Michel-de-Maurienne [04 79 59 17 36; contact@gite-lemarintan.com; http://gite-lemarintan.com/camping]** Fr D1006 foll sp in town to 'Centre Touristique' & 'Maison Retraite'. Rue de la Provalière is a L turn fr D1006 immed bef rlwy bdge. Sm, hdg, unshd, wc (htd); chem disp; shwrs inc; EHU inc; lndry; shop nr; rest; bar; pool; 10% statics; dogs €1; quiet. "Gd touring base, but no character; conv for skiing at Val Thorens via gondola lift at Orelle." € 12.00   2013*

ST MICHEL EN GREVE *2E2* (1km NE Coastal) *48.69277, -3.55694* **Camping Les Capucines, Voie Romaine, Kervourdon, 22300 Trédez-Locquémeau [02 96 35 72 28; fax 02 96 35 78 98; les.capucines@wanadoo.fr; www.lescapucines.fr]** Fr Lannion on D786 SW twd St Michel-en-Grève, sp Morlaix; in approx 700m, after steep descent & 'Landebouch' sp, turn R & R again in 100m at x-rds. Fr Roscoff take D58 to join N12 at junc 17; NE of Morlaix at next junc turn onto D786 twd Lannion; site down narr app rd on L on leaving St Michel-en-Grève (slow down at town exit sp), then R at x-rds. Med, hdg, mkd, pt shd, pt sl, serviced pitches; wc; chem disp; mv service pnt; fam bthrm; shwrs inc; EHU (10A) inc; gas; lndry; shop; snacks; bar; bbq (charcoal, gas); playgrnd; pool (covrd, htd); paddling pool; beach sand 1km; red long stay; wifi; TV; 15% statics; dogs €2.10; phone; Eng spkn; adv bkg acc; quiet; ccard acc; games area; watersports 1km; bike hire; games rm; CKE/CCI. "Excel, peaceful, well-kept site; no o'fits over 9.5m high ssn; gd sized pitches; helpful owners; clean san facs; gd pool; gd touring base; mkt Lannion Thu." ♦ 1 Apr-30 Sep. € 30.00   2017*

See advertisement

ST MIHIEL *5D2* (1km NW Rural) *48.90209, 5.53978* **Camping Base de Plein Air, 1Chemin du Gué Rappeau, 55300 St Mihiel [03 29 89 11 70 or 06 75 10 18 94 (mob); fax 03 29 89 07 18; base.de.plein.air@wanadoo.fr; www.tourisme-lorraine.fr]** Site on W bank of rv. Sp app St Mihiel. Fr town cent take rd sp Bar-le-Duc (D901) 1st R after rv bdge. Med, mkd, pt shd, wc (htd); chem disp; mv service pnt; shwrs inc; EHU (10A) €2.60; lndry; shop nr; rest nr; bar nr; playgrnd; TV; 10% statics; bus 1km; adv bkg acc; quiet; sailing; games area; canoeing; CKE/CCI. "Site developed as youth cent; facs clean but tired; pleasant scenery; htd pool 1km; lge pitches; v friendly." 1 Apr-1 Nov. € 9.00   2013*

ST NAZAIRE LE DESERT 9D2 (0km E Rural) 44.56952, 5.27750 Camp Municipal, 26340 St Nazaire-le-Désert [04 75 26 42 99 or 04 75 27 52 31 (LS); info@camping-stnazaire.com; www.campingstnazaire.fr] Well sp in St Nazaire-le-Désert. Med, mkd, shd, terr, wc; own san rec; chem disp; shwrs inc; EHU €3.50; shop nr; rest; snacks; bar; bbq; playgrnd; pool (htd); entmnt; wifi; dogs €2; phone; Eng spkn; adv bkg rec; games rm. "Busy, friendly site in beautiful location; v lge o'fits poss diff to pitch; gd." 1 May-30 Sep. € 15.00 2016*

ST NECTAIRE 9B1 (1km SE Rural) 45.57971, 3.00173 Camping Le Viginet, chemin du Manoir, 63710 St Nectaire [04 73 88 53 80 or 08 25 80 14 40; fax 04 73 88 41 93; info@camping-viginet.com; www.camping-viginet.com] Exit A75/E11 junc 14 onto D996 dir Mont-Doré. In E side of St Nectaire (opp Ford g'ge) turn sharp L up v steep hill; rd widens after 100m; site on R after bends. Car park at site ent. Med, mkd, hdg, pt shd, pt sl, wc; chem disp; mv service pnt; fam bthrm; shwrs inc; EHU (10A) €4; gas; lndry; shop nr; rest nr; snacks; bar nr; playgrnd; pool; dogs €2; Eng spkn; adv bkg acc; quiet; CKE/CCI. "Nice pitches; gd views; gd sm pool; gd walking in hills around site." ♦ 1 Apr-30 Sep. € 30.00 2013*

ST NECTAIRE 9B1 (1km S Rural) 45.57556, 3.00169 Camping La Clé des Champs, Les Sauces, Route des Granges, 63710 St Nectaire [04 73 88 52 33; campingcledechamps@free.fr; www.campingcledeschamps.com] S bound exit A75 at junc 6 to join D978 sp Champeix; N bound exit junc 14 to join D996 sp Champeix/St Nectaire. In St Nectaire turn L at g'ge on L (site sp); site 300m on L. Med, mkd, hdg, pt shd, pt sl, wc; chem disp; mv service pnt; shwrs inc; EHU (2-6A) €2.10-3.50 (poss rev pol); gas; lndry; shop nr; playgrnd; pool; wifi; 10% statics; dogs €2; adv bkg acc; CKE/CCI. "Well-kept, clean site; spectacular scenery; helpful owner; vg san facs." ♦ 1 Apr-30 Sep. € 37.00 2014*

ST NECTAIRE 9B1 (1km S Rural) 45.57541, 2.99942 Camping La Vallée Verte, Route des Granges, 63710 St Nectaire [04 73 88 52 68; lavalleeverte@neuf.fr; www.valleeverte.com] Fr A75 exit junc 6 onto D978 & D996 to St Nectaire. On ent o'skts St Nectaire turn L immed at site sp, site in 300m. Med, pt shd, wc (htd); chem disp; mv service pnt; fam bthrm; shwrs inc; EHU (5-8A) €3-3.50; lndry; shop; snacks; bar; playgrnd; sw nr; 20% statics; dogs €3; phone; Eng spkn; adv bkg acc; quiet; CKE/CCI. "Vg, friendly, well-maintained, family-run site." ♦ 15 Apr-18 Sep. € 21.00 2017*

ST NICOLAS DU PELEM 2E3 (2km SW Rural) 48.30983, -3.17923 Camp Municipal de la Piscine, Croas-Cussuliou, Rue de Rostrenen, 22480 St Nicolas-du-Pélem [02 96 29 51 27; fax 02 96 29 59 73] Fr Rostrenen, take D790 NE twd Corlay. In 11km, turn L sp St Nicolas-du-Pélem. Site in 500m on R, opp pool. Med, pt shd, wc; chem disp; shwrs inc; EHU (10A) inc; shop nr; dogs; quiet; CKE/CCI. "Clean, well-kept site; choose own pitch, warden will call; htd pool opp; excel touring base." ♦ 15 Jun-15 Sep. € 10.00 2012*

ST OMER 3A3 (15km NE Rural) 50.80152, 2.33924 Camping La Chaumière, 529 Langhemast Straete, 59285 Buysscheure [03 28 43 03 57; camping.lachaumiere@wanadoo.fr; www.campinglachaumiere.com] Take D928 fr St Omer (see NOTE) twd Bergues & Watten & foll sp St Momelin. Stay on rd until Lederzeele & turn R onto D26 twds Cassel. After approx 2km turn R just bef rlwy bdge sp Buysscheure & site. Turn L after church, R, then site on L 500m. Single-track rd after church. NOTE on D928 fr St Omer height limit 3m; use adj level x-ing sp rte for vehicles over 3m. NB app fr Cassel diff, espec for wide or long o'fits; also rd thro Cassel cobbled & poss more diff to find. Sm, hdstg, hdg, mkd, unshd, pt sl, wc; chem disp; mv service pnt; fam bthrm; shwrs inc; EHU (6A) inc; lndry; shop nr; rest; snacks; bar; bbq; playgrnd; pool (htd); paddling pool; entmnt; wifi; TV; dogs €1; Eng spkn; adv bkg acc; archery; bike hire; lake fishing; CKE/CCI. "Lovely, well-kept site; friendly, welcoming, family-run; conv ferries - but poss no exit bef 0800; gd sized pitches - some may req o'fit manhandling due hedges; gd san facs, ltd in number, stretched when site full; no arr bef 12 noon; close to WW1/WW2 sites; local vet; excel; gd bar & food; rest open only w/end in LS." ♦ 1 Apr-30 Sep. € 23.00 2015*

ST OMER 3A3 (11km E Rural) 50.73490, 2.37463 FFCC Camping Le Bloem Straete, 1 Rue Bloemstraete, 59173 Renescure [03 28 49 85 65 or 06 50 01 08 16 (mob); lebloemstraete@gmail.com; www.lebloemstraete.fr] E fr St Omer on D642 thro Renescure dir Hazebrouck; turn L (site sp) onto D406 Rue André Coo on bend on leaving Renescure; over level x-ing; site on L thro gates. Sm, hdstg, hdg, mkd, pt shd, wc (htd); chem disp; mv service pnt; shwrs inc; EHU (2-6A) €2.50 (poss rev pol); lndry; shop nr; rest nr; bar nr; bbq (charcoal, gas); playgrnd; wifi; 20% statics; dogs; Eng spkn; adv bkg acc; quiet; tennis; games area; CKE/CCI. "Conv Calais ferry & tourist sites; manoeuvring poss diff due high kerbs; m'van area; site clean and tidy; worth finding!; excel facs; easy access to ports; new owners, v helpful & planning on improving site (2015)." ♦ 15 Apr-15 Oct. € 27.00 2016*

ST OMER 3A3 (7km E Urban) 50.74612, 2.30566 Camp Municipal Beauséjour, Rue Michelet, 62510 Arques [03 21 88 53 66; camping@ville-arques.fr; www.camping-arques.fr] Fr junc 4 of a A26 foll sp Arques to town cent. Foll sp Hazebrouck. After x-ing canal site sp 'Camping ***' on L. NB Drive 25m bef correct turning to site. Site signs sm and easily missed. Med, hdg, pt shd, wc; chem disp; mv service pnt; fam bthrm; shwrs; EHU (6-10A) €3 (poss rev pol); lndry; shop nr; rest nr; bar nr; bbq; playgrnd; wifi; 80% statics; dogs; phone; Eng spkn; adv bkg acc; ccard acc; lake fishing; CKE/CCI. "Neat, tidy site; well-run; lge pitches but tight access; friendly, helpful warden; excel, clean facs; m'van o'night area adj (no EHU); gd cycling along canal; lakes & nature park nrby; conv Cristal d'Arques; canal lift & preserved rlwy in town; Calais & Dunkerque 50 mins drive; useful NH; vg." ♦ 1 Apr-31 Oct. € 17.50 2018*

ST OMER 3A3 (13km SW Rural) 50.66938, 2.16490
Camping du Moulin, 14 bis rue Bernard Chochoy, 62380 Remilly- Wirquin [03 21 93 05 99; www.campingdumoulin.ex-flash.com] Fr A26 N or S take exit 3 sp St Omer; at rndabt take D342 sp Lumbres; in 2m at Setques turn L onto D211 sp Esquerdes; in 2m at Esquerdes turn R onto D192E to Crehem; at Crehem turn R on D192; site on L in 1m; sharp turn into site. Med, hdg, pt shd, wc; chem disp; shwrs; EHU (3A) €2.50; lndry; bbq; playgrnd; twin axles; 75% statics; dogs €1; phone; bus 45m; adv bkg acc; quiet; games rm; CKE/CCI. "Rando rail 6km; horseriding 5km; gd walking country; rv fishing on site; golf 10mins away." ♦ 1 Jan-31 Nov. € 13.00   2014*

> "We must tell the Club about that great site we found"
>
> Get your site reports in by mid-August and we'll do our best to get your updates into the next edition.

ST OMER 3A3 (10km NW Rural) 50.81890, 2.17870
Kawan Village Château du Gandspette, 133 Rue du Gandspette, 62910 Eperlecques [03 21 93 43 93; fax 03 21 95 74 98; contact@chateau-gandspette.com; www.chateau-gandspette.com] Fr Calais SE on A26/E15 exit junc 2 onto D943 foll sp Nordausques-St Omer. 1.5km after Nordausques turn L onto D221 twd Eperlecques; site 5km on L. Do not ent Eperlecques. (Larger o'fts should cont on D943 fr Nordausques to Tilques; at rndabt foll sp for Dunkerque (D300) then D221 dir Eperlecques, site on R. Med, hdstg, mkd, hdg, pt shd, pt sl, wc; chem disp; mv service pnt; fam bthrm; shwrs inc; EHU (6A) €5.20 (some rev pol); gas; lndry; shop nr; rest; snacks; bar; bbq (charcoal, gas); playgrnd; pool (htd); entmnt; wifi; TV; 15% statics; dogs €2; phone; Eng spkn; adv bkg acc; quiet; ccard acc; tennis; bike hire; fishing 3km; golf 5km; games rm; horseriding 5km; CKE/CCI. "Beautiful, well-kept, busy site; spacious, mainly sl pitches; charming, helpful friendly owners; superb, clean san facs; excel rest; site poss muddy in wet; gd for dogs; no o'fits over 8m; rec visit WW2 'Le Blockhaus' nr site; conv A26; highly rec; conv for Calais & for ferry to Dover; spectacular location; excel ctr for visits & activities; vg; security guard with dog; excel site." ♦ 1 Apr-30 Sep. € 34.00   2018*

ST PABU 2E1 (2km NW Coastal) 48.57643, -4.62854
Camping FFCC de L'Aber Benoît, 89 Rue de Corn ar Gazel, 29830 St Pabu [02 98 89 76 25; info@camping-aber-benoit.com; www.camping-aber-benoit.com] E fr Ploudalmézeau on D28; in 5km L to St Pabu. Site sp in vill. Med, hdg, pt shd, wc; chem disp; mv service pnt; fam bthrm; shwrs inc; EHU (6A) €3; lndry; shop; rest; snacks; bbq; playgrnd; beach 100m; entmnt; wifi; TV; 10% statics; dogs €1; CKE/CCI. "Facs stretched high ssn; vg." ♦ Easter-30 Sep. € 12.00   2013*

ST PALAIS SUR MER 7B1 (7km N Rural) 45.67550, -1.09560 Camping Le Logis du Breuil, 17570 St Augustin [05 46 23 23 45; fax 05 46 23 43 33; info@logis-du-breuil.com; www.logis-du-breuil.com] N150 to Royan, then D25 dir St Palais-sur-Mer. Strt on at 1st rndabt & 2nd rndabt; at next rndabt take 2nd exit dir St Palais-sur-Mer. At next traff lts turn R dir St Augustin onto D145; site on L. NB sat nav can direct thro diff & narr alt rte. Lge, mkd, pt shd, pt sl, wc; chem disp; mv service pnt; fam bthrm; shwrs inc; EHU (6-10A) €6-8 (50m cable poss req); gas; lndry; shop, rest; snacks; bar; bbq (elec, gas); playgrnd; pool; paddling pool; beach sand 5km; entmnt; wifi; TV; 10% statics; dogs €4.25; phone; Eng spkn; adv bkg acc; ccard acc; tennis; fishing 1km; golf 3km; excursions; games area; bike hire; games rm; horseriding 400m; CKE/CCI. "Nice peaceful site; lge pitches in wooded area; gd alt to cr beach sites; friendly owner; san facs clean; no c'vans over 12m; gd for young families; excel." ♦ 5 May-30 Sep. € 28.00   2017*

ST PALAIS SUR MER 7B1 (1km NE Coastal) 45.64245, -1.07577 Camping de Bernezac, 2 Ave de Bernezac, 17420 St Palais-sur-Mer [05 46 39 00 71; fax 05 46 38 14 46; acccf-bernezac@acccf.com; bernezac.acccf.com] Leave A10 at junc 35 fr N. N150 then D25, at 2nd rndabt take 3rd exit (Rue de la Roche), cross 2 rndabt then L onto Ave de Bernezac. Site on R in under 1km. Med, hdg, mkd, pt shd, pt sl, serviced pitches; wc; chem disp; mv service pnt; fam bthrm; shwrs inc; EHU (6A) €4.60 (poss rev pol); lndry; shop nr; rest; snacks; bbq; playgrnd; beach adj; twin axles; entmnt; wifi; TV; 60% statics; dogs €1; Eng spkn; adv bkg acc; quiet; lake fishing 1km; games area. "Helpful, friendly staff; clean, spacious pitches; new shwrs (2016); free wifi; cycle rtes nr; sm quiet site; direct access to beach; pleasant coastal walks; off rd bike rides fr beach gate; lots of activities in area; vg." 15 Mar-15 Oct. € 33.00   2017*

ST PALAIS SUR MER 7B1 (2km E Coastal) 45.64396, -1.06325 Camping Le Val Vert, 108 Ave Frédéric Garnier, 17640 Vaux-sur-Mer [05 46 38 25 51; fax 05 46 38 06 15; camping-val-vert@wanadoo.fr; www.val-vert.com] Fr Saintes on N150 dir Royan; join D25 dir St Palais-sur-Mer; turn L at rndabt sp Vaux-sur-Mer & Centre Hospitaliers; at traff lts ahead; at 2nd rndabt take 3rd exit & then turn immed R. Site on R in 500m. Med, hdg, wc; chem disp; mv service pnt; fam bthrm; shwrs inc; EHU (10A) €6; gas; lndry; shop; rest; snacks; bbq (elec, gas); playgrnd; pool (htd); paddling pool; beach sand 900m; entmnt; wifi; dogs €3.40; adv bkg acc; ccard acc; tennis 400m; bike hire; horseriding 5km; games rm; fishing; watersports; games area; golf 5km. "Well-kept, family-run site; no o'fits over 6.5m high ssn; gd sized pitches; unisex san facs; a stream runs alongside site; sh walk to pleasant vill; daily mkt in Royan." ♦ 27 Apr-30 Sep. € 36.00   2017*

ST PALAIS SUR MER

ST PALAIS SUR MER 7B1 (2km E Rural/Coastal) 45.64656, -1.07300 **Camping Les Ormeaux**, 44 Ave de Bernezac, 17420 St Palais-sur-Mer [05 46 39 02 07; fax 05 46 38 56 66; campingormeaux@aliceadsl.fr; www.camping-ormeaux.com] Foll sp fr D25 Royan-St Palais rd. Rec app rent fr R. Ent & camp rds narr. Lge, pt shd, wc; fam bthrm; shwrs inc; EHU (6-10A) €7.50; gas; lndry; shop; bar; playgrnd; pool (htd); beach sand 800m; wifi; TV; 98% statics; dogs €4; quiet. "Ltd touring area & access diff for lge o'fits or m'vans - tents or sm m'vans only; one of the best campsites we have stayed in; clean spacious pitches, amazing staff, new san facs; dir access to 41km cycle rtes, mostly off-rd; no TV on pitches." ♦ 1 Apr-31 Oct. € 25.00 2016*

ST PALAIS SUR MER 7B1 (2km SE Urban/Coastal) 45.64272, -1.07183 **Camping Nauzan-Plage**, 39 Ave de Nauzan-Plage, 17640 Vaux-sur-Mer [05 46 38 29 13; fax 05 46 38 18 43; info@campinglenauzanplage.com; www.camping lenauzanplage.com] Take either coast rd or inland rd fr Royan to Vaux-sur-Mer; site not well sp. Lge, mkd, pt shd, wc; chem disp; fam bthrm; shwrs inc; EHU (10A) €5.50; gas; lndry; shop; rest; snacks; bar; playgrnd; pool; beach sand 450m; red long stay; TV; 10% statics; dogs €5; adv bkg rec; quiet; tennis 200m; games rm; CKE/CCI. "Gd site, busy high ssn; helpful staff; gd cycling rte; pt of Flower Camping group." ♦ 1 Apr-15 Oct. € 45.00 2017*

ST PALAIS SUR MER 7B1 (3km NW Coastal) 45.6500, -1.1193 **Camping La Côte de Beauté**, 157 Ave de la Grande Côte, 17420 St Palais-sur-Mer [05 46 23 20 59; fax 05 46 23 37 32; campingcotedebeaute@wanadoo.fr; www.camping-cote-de-beaute.com] Fr St Palais-sur-Mer foll sp to La Tremblade & Ronce-les-Bains. Site on D25, 50m fr beach, look for twin flagpoles of Camping Le Puits de l'Auture & lge neon sp on R; site in 50m. Med, mkd, pt shd, wc (htd); fam bthrm; shwrs inc; EHU (6A) €4.20; lndry; rest; playgrnd; beach sand 200m; 10% statics; dogs €3; adv bkg acc; quiet; tennis adj; golf 2km. "Clean, tidy site; friendly staff; steep descent to beach opp - better beach 600m twd La Tremblade; bike hire adj; cycle track to St Palais & Pontaillac; town 3km; clean san facs; gd pitches." 1 May-30 Sep. € 26.00 2017*

ST PALAIS SUR MER 7B1 (7km NW Coastal) 45.64930, -1.11785 **Camping Le Puits de l'Auture, La Grande Côte**, 17420 St Palais-sur-Mer [05 46 23 20 31; fax 05 46 23 26 38; contact@camping-puitsdelauture.com; www.camping-puitsdelauture.com] Fr Royan take D25 onto new rd past St Palais foll sp for La Palmyre. At 1-way section turn back L sp La Grande Côte & site is 800m; rd runs close to sea, flags at ent. Lge, pt shd, serviced pitches; wc (htd); fam bthrm; shwrs inc; EHU (10A) inc; gas; lndry; shop; snacks; bar; playgrnd; pool (htd); beach sand adj; wifi; 25% statics; Eng spkn; adv bkg rec; quiet; ccard acc; fishing; games area; CKE/CCI. "Well-maintained, well laid-out, excel site; san facs stretched high ssn & 'tired'; poss cr but carefully controlled; friendly, helpful staff; gd cycle paths." ♦ 28 Apr-3 Oct. € 38.00 2016*

ST PANTALEON 7D3 (4km NE Rural) 44.36760, 1.30634 **Camping des Arcades, Moulin de St Martiel**, 46800 St Pantaléon [05 65 22 92 27 or 06 80 43 19 82 (mob); fax 05 65 31 98 89; info@des-arcades.com; www.des-arcades.com] Fr N20 3km S of Cahors take D653 sp Montcuq, after 17km site in hamlet of St Martial on L. Med, mkd, pt shd, pt sl, wc; chem disp; shwrs inc; EHU (6A) €4; lndry; shop; rest; snacks; bar; bbq; playgrnd; pool (htd); paddling pool; sw nr; wifi; 5% statics; dogs €1.50; Eng spkn; adv bkg acc; quiet; ccard acc; fishing adj; CKE/CCI. "Vg Dutch-owned site with restored 13thC windmill; sm lake; clean facs." ♦ 23 Apr-30 Sep. € 20.00 2012*

ST PANTALEON LES VIGNES 9D2 (2km E Rural) 44.39752, 5.06099 **Camping Les Cyprès, Hameau Font de Barral**, 26770 Saint Pantaleon les Vignes [06 81 53 78 03 or 06 82 27 19 14; contact@lescypres-camping.com; www.lescypres-camping.com] D541 fir Nyons. Fr highway A7 exit Montélimar-Sud Bollène or Orange Cent. Sm, pt shd, pt sl, wc; chem disp; shwrs inc; EHU (4,6,10A) €2.50-3.60; shop nr; rest nr; bbq; playgrnd; twin axles; wifi; dogs €1.80; quiet; games rm. "Beautiful surroundings; friendly owners." ♦ 1 Apr-31 Oct. € 11.00 2014*

ST PARDOUX 7A3 (2km S Rural) 46.04955, 1.27893 **Campsite Fréaudour, Site de Freaudour** 87250 St Pardoux [05 55 76 57 22; camping.freaudour@orange.fr; www.aquadis-loisirs.com] Fr A20 dir Limonges, take exit 25, onto D219. Cont onto D44 thro Razes & foll sp to Lac De Saint-Pardoux. Turn R onto D103A to Freaudour. Med, mkd, pt shd, wc; chem disp; shwrs; EHU (6A); lndry; shop; snacks; bar; bbq; playgrnd; pool; wifi; TV; 20% statics; dogs; Eng spkn; adv bkg rec; games area. "Fair site." 9 Mar-8 Nov. € 18.00 2014*

ST PARDOUX 9A1 (8km SW Rural) 46.03202, 2.95704 **Camping La Coccinelle (formerly Camping Elan), Route de Villemorie**, 63440 Blot-l'Eglise [04 73 64 93 15; info@campingcoccinelle.com; www.campingcoccinelle.com] Fr N on N144 take D16 to Blot, fr S take D50, foll site sp. Sm, mkd, hdg, pt shd, wc; chem disp; shwrs inc; EHU (5-10A) €2.50-4.50; lndry; shop nr; rest; snacks; bar; playgrnd; red long stay; wifi; TV; dogs €1; Eng spkn; adv bkg acc; quiet; tennis; games area; CKE/CCI. "In beautiful area; lge pitches; friendly Dutch owners; clean but basic san facs; site open LS by arrangement; gd touring base, conv Vulcania; gd." 1 Mar-31 Oct. € 18.00 2014*

ST PAUL DE FENOUILLET 8G4 (7km E Rural) 42.80811, 2.6058 **Camping Le Maurynate, La Caunette Basse**, 66460 Maury [04 68 67 11 01; lemaurynate@orange.fr; www.lemaurynate.fr] W fr St-Paul-de-Fenouillet on D117 to Maury in 6km; cont past Maury on D117; site on L in 1km, just bef level x-ing. Sm, hdg, mkd, pt shd, wc (htd); chem disp; mv service pnt; fam bthrm; shwrs inc; EHU (10A) €3.50; lndry; shop; bbq; playgrnd; dogs €2; Eng spkn; adv bkg acc; quiet; CKE/CCI. "Vg site; prehistoric history region." 1 Apr-31 Aug. € 25.00 2013*

ST PIERRE LE MOUTIER

ST PAUL DE FENOUILLET *8G4* (7km E Rural) *42.80782, 2.60579* **Camping Le Maurynate (formerly Municipal Les Oliviers), 66460 Maury [04 68 67 11 01; fax 04 68 59 08 74; lemaurynate@orange.fr; www.lemaurynate.fr]** Heading W on D117. Site immed after level x-ing on R 500m bef Maury. Sm, mkd, shd, wc cont; shwrs inc; EHU; shop nr; rest nr; bar nr; playgrnd; CKE/CCI. "Some rd noise fr level x-ing; immac san facs." 1 Apr-30 Aug. € 16.50   2012*

⊞ **ST PAUL DE FENOUILLET** *8G4* (0km S Rural) *42.80762, 2.50235* **Camping de l'Agly, Ave 16 Août 1944, 66220 St Paul-de-Fenouillet [04 68 59 09 09; fax 04 68 59 11 04; contact@camping-agly.com; www.camping-agly.com]** Heading W on D117; turn L at traff lts in St Paul; site on R in 200m, well sp. Sm, mkd, hdg, pt shd, pt sl, wc; chem disp; shwrs inc; EHU (16A) €4.50; shop nr; sw nr; dogs; quiet; site clsd Jan; CKE/CCI. "Vg site; friendly warden; mountain scenery; gd climbing & cycling; conv for Château's Payrepertuse & Quéribus; sm pitches, diff access for lge o'fits; conv NH." ♦ € 16.00   2017*

ST PAUL EN FORET *10E4* (4km N Rural) *43.58449, 6.69016* **Camping Le Parc, Quartier Trestaure, 83440 St Paul-en-Forêt [04 94 76 15 35; contact@campingleparc.com; www.campingleparc.com]** Exit A8 at junc 39, foll D37 (dir Fayence) for 8.4km to lge rndabt on D562. Take 3rd exit at rndabt (sp draguignan/Fayence). Foll D562 for 4.8km thro 4 more rndabts. At 5th rndabt (Intermarche Supmkt on L) take 3rd exit D562 sp Draguignan. After 4.2km take 3rd exit at rndabt onto D4, after 2km turn L at bus stop. Foll rd to site. Sm, mkd, shd, sl, wc (htd); chem disp; mv service pnt; fam bthrm; shwrs inc; EHU (10A) €5 high ssn only; lndry; shop; rest; snacks; bar; playgrnd; pool (htd); paddling pool; twin axles; entmnt; wifi; TV; 65% statics; dogs €4.50 high ssn only; phone; Eng spkn; adv bkg acc; quiet; games rm; fishing; games area; tennis; CKE/CCI. "Conv hill vills of Provence; gd rests in St Paul; many medieval vill; excel." ♦ 2 Apr-30 Sep. € 29.00   2016*

ST PAULIEN *9C1* (3km SW Rural) *45.12041, 3.79357* **Camping de la Rochelambert, 43350 St Paulien [04 71 00 54 02; infos@camping-rochelambert.com; www.camping-rochelambert.com]** Fr St Paulien take D13; turn L onto D25 sp La Rochelambert; site on L in 1.5km. Med, mkd, pt shd, terr, wc; chem disp; mv service pnt; shwrs inc; EHU (10A) €3.10; lndry; shop nr; snacks; bar; bbq; playgrnd; pool; paddling pool; wifi; 15% statics; dogs €1.50; phone; Eng spkn; adv bkg acc; quiet; tennis; CKE/CCI. "Gd touring base; gd walking & fishing; app poss diff lge/long o'fits; gd." ♦ 1 Apr-30 Sep. € 30.00   2014*

ST PHILBERT DE GRAND LIEU *2H4* (1km N Rural) *47.04202, -1.64021* **Camping La Boulogne, 1 Ave de Nantes, 44310 St Philbert-de-Grand-Lieu [32 40 78 88 79; fax 32 40 78 76 50; accueil@camping-la-boulogne.com]** Fr Nantes on A83 exit junc 1 or 2 onto D178 - D117 dir St Philbert; turn L onto D65 (Ave de Nantes) to St Philbert; site on R in 500m adj rv & sp. Or fr Machecoul take bypass to St Philbert & then D65 as narr rds thro town. Med, hdg, mkd, pt shd, wc; chem disp; fam bthrm; shwrs inc; EHU (6A) inc; lndry; shop nr; bar; bbq; playgrnd; entmnt; wifi; 10% statics; dogs €1; phone; bus adj; Eng spkn; adv bkg acc; quiet; ccard acc; fishing; games area; CKE/CCI. "Well-kept, secure site; htd covrd pool 200m; lake adj; new enthusiastic, helpful owners (2010); gd; ACSI acc." ♦ 1 Apr-31 Oct. € 13.50   2016*

ST PIERRE DE CHARTREUSE *9C3* (2km S Rural) *45.32570, 5.79700* **Camping de Martinière, Route du Col de Porte, 38380 St Pierre-de-Chartreuse [04 76 88 60 36; fax 04 76 88 69 10; camping-de-martiniere@orange.fr; www.campingdemartiniere.com]** Site is situated on D520B thro Gorge-du-Guiers-Mort after St Pierre-de-Chartreuse. Med, mkd, pt shd, wc (htd); chem disp; mv service pnt; fam bthrm; shwrs inc; EHU (2-10A) €2-7.20; gas; lndry; shop; rest; snacks; bar; bbq; playgrnd; pool; paddling pool; 15% statics; dogs €1.50; phone; Eng spkn; adv bkg req; quiet; ccard acc; rv fishing 500m; CKE/CCI. "Excel site; lge pitches; friendly owner; excel mountain/hill walking, cycling; Grand Chartreuse Monastery 4km; vg; rte to site and area demanding, gd car/c'van ratio advised; beautiful site in lovely setting." 1 May-11 Sep. € 9.00   2013*

ST PIERRE EN PORT *3C2* (1km N Coastal) *49.80943, 0.49354* **Les Falaises, 130 rue du Camping, 76540 St Pierre-en-Port [02 35 29 51 58; lesfalaises@cegetel.net; www.campinglesfalaises.com]** Fr D925 turn onto D79 bet St Valery & Fecamp. Site sp in St Pierre. Med, hdg, unshd, wc; chem disp; mv service pnt; fam bthrm; shwrs inc; EHU (10A); lndry; shop nr; snacks; bar; bbq; playgrnd; beach 2km; wifi; 60% statics; dogs; bus 0.5km; Eng spkn; quiet; games area; games rm; CKE/CCI. "Cliff top site; path to beach steep with steps; narr app rd; facs dated but clean; well kept site; takeaway snacks avail high ssn only; v quiet, pleasant site; gd." ♦ 1 Apr-5 Oct. € 19.00   2017*

ST PIERRE LE MOUTIER *4H4* (8km SW Rural) *46.75722, 3.03328* **Camp Municipal de St Mayeul, Rue de Saint-Mayeul, 03320 Le Veurdre [04 70 66 40 67 (Mairie); fax 04 70 66 42 88; mairie.le.veurdre@wanadoo.fr; www.allier-tourisme.com]** Fr N7 at St Pierre-le-Moûtier SW onto D978A to Le Veurdre. Site sp on far side of Le Veurdre. Sm, hdg, mkd, pt shd, pt sl, wc; shwrs inc; EHU €4; shop nr; bbq; adv bkg acc; quiet. "Pleasant spot; site yourself, warden calls; friendly staff; clean, basic facs; shops in pleasant vill; rec NH; vg." ♦ 1 May-15 Sep. € 11.40   2018*

ST POL DE LEON

ST POL DE LEON *1D2* (2km E Coastal) *48.69103, -3.96730* Camping Ar Kleguer, Plage de Ste Anne, 29250 St Pol-de-Léon [02 98 69 18 81; fax 02 98 29 12 84; info@camping-ar-kleguer.com; www.camping-ar-kleguer.com] In St Pol-de-Léon foll Centre Ville sp. At cathedral sq (2 towers) with cathedral on L descend hill & in 150m, bef church with tall belfry, turn L foll Plage & camping sp. On reaching sea turn L (N); site at end, well sp. NB Narr, busy rds in town. Med, mkd, pt shd, pt sl, terr, wc; chem disp; mv service pnt; fam bthrm; shwrs inc; EHU (10A) (long lead poss req); lndry; shop nr; snacks; bar; pool (htd); paddling pool; beach adj; wifi; 40% statics; dogs €2.80; adv bkg acc; waterslide; games rm; tennis; CKE/CCI. "Well-kept, attractive site; modern facs; gd views; conv Roscoff ferry." 2 Apr-25 Sep. € 31.00   2015*

> **"I need an on-site restaurant"**
>
> We do our best to make sure site information is correct, but it is always best to check any must-have facilities are still available or will be open during your visit.

ST POL DE LEON *1D2* (2km E Coastal) *48.69355, -3.96930* Camping de Trologot, Grève du Man, 29250 St Pol-de-Léon [02 98 69 06 26 or 06 62 16 39 30 (mob); fax 02 98 29 18 30; camping-trologot@wanadoo.fr; www.camping-trologot.com] Fr the port of Roscoff take D58 go briefly on the D769 then back on to the D58 foll the sp to Morlaix over six rndabts (approx 4miles/6.5km). Just after passing under a rlwy bdge, take the exit for the D769 (sp St Pol de Léon, Kerlaudy, Penzé) then turn L. Stay on the D769 for 1.8 km, just past the graveyard turn R at the rndabt and go strt over the next rndabt (sp Campings/Plage) at the end of the rd turn L and the turning for the site will be on L after 1km and is sp. Do not use sat nav. Fr the E on the N12 take the exit for the D19 (sp Morlaix St pol de Leon) at the rndabt take the 2nd exit cont twds St-Pol-de Leon on the D58. Take the exit to the D769 (SP St-Pol-de Leon) then foll above dirs fr the graveyard. Med, hdg, mkd, unshd, wc; chem disp; mv service pnt; fam bthrm; shwrs inc; EHU (10A) €3.65; lndry; shop; snacks; bar; bbq (charcoal, gas); playgrnd; pool (htd) paddling pool; beach sand adj; red long stay; entmnt; wifi; TV; 20% statics; dogs €2.05; adv bkg acc; quiet; ccard acc; games rm; CKE/CCI. "Lovely, well-kept site; ideal NH for Roscoff ferry; gd sized pitches; helpful owners; clean, modern facs; no o'fits over 7m high ssn; gd for family beach holiday; peaceful area, many walks nrby; beautiful town; highly rec." ♦ 1 May-29 Sep. € 18.50   2013*

ST POL DE LEON *1D2* (5km SE Coastal) *48.65805, -3.92805* Yelloh! Village Les Mouettes, La Grande Grève, 29660 Carantec [02 98 67 02 46; fax 02 98 78 31 46; camping@les-mouettes.com; www.les-mouettes.com] Fr Morlaix take D58 N sp Roscoff; at lge rndabt turn R sp Carantec on D173; turn L at 1st rndabt; strt on at 2nd & 3rd rndabt past Casino supmkt; turn L next rndabt; site on L. Or fr Roscoff take D58 sp Mortaix, then D173 to Carantec; foll sp town cent, then site. Lge, mkd, pt shd, wc; chem disp; mv service pnt; fam bthrm; shwrs inc; EHU (10A) inc (poss rev pol); gas; lndry; shop; snacks; bar; bbq (charcoal); playgrnd; pool (covrd, htd); paddling pool; beach shgl 1km; entmnt; wifi; TV; 50% statics; dogs €6; Eng spkn; adv bkg acc; ccard acc; tennis; bike hire; fishing; games area; golf 1.5km; waterslide; games rm; CKE/CCI. "Attractive site with sea views; no o'fits over 8m; clean, modern san facs; sauna; jaccuzi; impressive pool complex; plenty to do on site; mkt Thu; noise fr boatyard; conv Carnac." ♦ 20 Apr-10 Sep. € 46.00   2017*

ST POL DE LEON *1D2* (9km SE Rural) *48.64912, -3.92126* Camping Les Hortensias (Jacq), Kermen, 29660 Carantec [02 98 67 08 63 or 02 98 67 96 34; contact@leshortensias.fr; www.leshortensias.fr] Fr Roscoff on D58 dir Morlaix. Turn L after approx 10km onto D173, then turn R at 1st rndabt, site in 200m, site sp. Sm, mkd, unshd, wc; chem disp; mv service pnt; shwrs inc; EHU (6A) €3; lndry; shop nr; playgrnd; beach 2.5km; dogs €0.80; adv bkg acc; quiet; CKE/CCI. "Conv Roscoff ferry; views of bay; friendly staff; poss unkempt LS; organic produce in shop; gd touring base; no gates allows early departure; excel NH; no o'fits over 6m." ♦ 1 May-30 Sep. € 12.50   2015*

ST PONS DE THOMIERES *8F4* (2km E Rural) *43.49055, 2.78527* Camping Village Les Cerisiers du Jaur, Les Marbrières-du-Jaur, Route de Bédarieux, 34220 St Pons-de-Thomières [04 67 95 30 33; fax 04 67 28 09 96; info@cerisierdujaur.com; www.cerisierdujaur.com] Fr Castres on D612 to St Pons; go thro town cent under rlwy bdge; turn L onto D908 sp Olargues. Site on R in 500m. Med, mkd, hdg, pt shd, terr, wc; chem disp; mv service pnt; fam bthrm; shwrs inc; EHU (10A) €4; lndry; shop; rest nr; snacks; bbq; playgrnd; pool; wifi; dogs €1.50; phone; Eng spkn; quiet; ccard acc; games area; bike hire; CKE/CCI. "Excel site nr Rv Jaur; welcoming, friendly, helpful owner; cycle rte fr site; an oasis!; hot water not v hot; expensive in LS; san facs unkept." ♦ 29 Mar-26 Oct. € 33.00   2017*

ST PONS DE THOMIERES *8F4* (11km W Rural) *43.47776, 2.65768* Camp Municipal de Cabanes, Route de St Pons, 81270 Labastide-Rouairoux [05 63 98 49 74 or 05 63 98 07 58; tourisme@labastide-rouairoux.com; www.labastide-rouairoux.com] E fr Labastide-Rouairoux twd St Pons on D612. Site adj D612 immed after leaving Labastide vill. Sm, hdg, mkd, pt shd, terr, wc; chem disp; shwrs; EHU inc; shop nr; adv bkg acc; CKE/CCI. "Lovely site; poss diff lge o'fits due to terr; sans block small." 15 Jun-15 Sep. € 11.00   2014*

ST QUENTIN EN TOURMONT

ST POURCAIN SUR SIOULE *9A1* (1km SE Urban) *46.30643, 3.29207* Camp Municipal de l'île de la Ronde, Quai de la Ronde, 03500 St Pourçain-sur-Sioule [04 70 35 13 69 or 07 61 52 33 72 (mob); camping.ronde@ville-saint-pourcain-sur-sioule.com; www.ville-saint-pourcain-sur-sioule.com] On D2009, 31km S of Moulins; in St Pourçain-sur-Sioule town cent turn R immed bef rv bdge; site ent on L in 100m. NB Sp in town easily missed. Med, hdg, pt shd, wc; chem disp; mv service pnt; shwrs; EHU (10A) inc; lndry; shop nr; playgrnd; dogs; adv bkg acc; quiet; CKE/CCI. "Well-run, magnificent, busy, pleasant site in pretty town; extra charge for lger pitches; barrier clsd 2000-0800; gd rest nr; mkt Sat; great value; excel; recep and barrier clsd 1200-1400; 2 supmkt in town; 2 pin adapter ess; set amongst trees; walks/rvside path adj; san facs stretched at times; gd value." ♦ 31 Mar-1 Oct. € 14.00   2017*

> **"Satellite navigation makes touring much easier"**
>
> Remember most sat navs don't know if you're towing or in a larger vehicle – always use yours alongside maps and site directions.

ST QUAY PORTRIEUX *2E3* (3km NW Coastal) *48.66269, -2.84550* Camping Bellevue, 68 Blvd du Littoral, 22410 St Quay-Portrieux [02 96 70 41 84; fax 02 96 70 55 46; info@campingbellevue.net; www.campingbellevue.net] Foll D786 thro St Quay-Portrieux twd Paimpol; turn R at traff lts sp St Quay-Portrieux; foll site sp; site in 2.5km. Lge, hdg, hdstg, mkd, pt shd, pt sl, terr, wc; chem disp; mv service pnt; fam bthrm; shwrs inc; EHU (6A) €3; gas; lndry; shop; snacks; bbq; playgrnd; pool (htd); paddling pool; beach sand adj; wifi; TV; 8% statics; dogs free; Eng spkn; adv bkg acc; quiet; ccard acc; games area; golf 3km; CKE/CCI. "Beautiful position with sea views; direct access to sm cove; friendly staff; gd, clean facs; vg; excel pool; gd exercise area for dogs." ♦ 8 May-15 Sep. € 23.00   2015*

ST QUENTIN *3C4* (12km SW Urban) *49.78222, 3.21333* Camping du Vivier aux Carpes, 10 Rue Charles Voyeux, 02790 Seraucourt-le-Grand [03 23 60 50 10; contact@camping-picardie.com; www.camping-picardie.com] Fr A26 take exit 11 St Quentin/Soissons; S 4km on D1 dir Tergnier/Soissons. Fork R onto D8 to Essigny-le-Grand & in vill foll camping sp W to Seraucourt. Fr St Quentin, S 10km on D930 to Roupy, E on D32 5km to Seraucourt-le-Grand. Site N of Seraucourt on D321. Narr ent fr rd unsuitable lge o'fits. Med, hdstg, hdg, mkd, pt shd, wc; chem disp; mv service pnt; fam bthrm; shwrs inc; EHU (10A) inc (poss rev pol); gas; lndry; shop; snacks; bbq; playgrnd; wifi; 30% statics; dogs €1.50; Eng spkn; adv bkg acc; quiet; tennis adj; golf adj; horseriding adj; games rm; CKE/CCI. "Delightful, lovely, well-run site; busy, even LS - rec arr early; ltd hdstg; peaceful LS; gd, lge pitches; narr site rds; friendly, helpful staff; pitches by lake poss boggy when wet; poss flooding; mkd footpaths round lakes; vg angling; mosquito probs; Disneyland 90 mins; conv Channel ports; c'van storage; warn staff night bef if v early dep; excel; facs stretched but clean & gd; lovely cycle rte along canal to St Quentin; nice bistro in vill; new coded security barrier (2015)." ♦ 20 Mar-20 Oct. € 23.50   2018*

ST QUENTIN EN TOURMONT *3B2* (1km S Rural) *50.26895, 1.60263* Camping Le Champ Neuf, 8 Rue du Champ Neuf, 80120 St Quentin-en-Tourmont [03 22 25 07 94; fax 03 22 25 09 87; campinglechampneuf@orange.fr; www.camping-lechampneuf.com] Exit D1001 or A16 onto D32 to Rue, take D940 around Rue & foll sp St Quentin-en-Tourmont, Parc Ornithologique & Domaine du Marquenterre to site. Site sp fr D204. Lge, mkd, hdg, pt shd, wc (htd); chem disp; mv service pnt; fam bthrm; shwrs inc; EHU (5-10A) inc; lndry; shop; snacks; bar; bbq; playgrnd; pool (covrd, htd); paddling pool; beach 2km; entmnt; wifi; 80% statics; dogs €1.50; phone; adv bkg acc; quiet; ccard acc; horseriding 500m; bike hire; games area. "Excel Ornithological Park nrby; well-kept, pleasant site; friendly, helpful owner; gd cycle paths." ♦ 1 Apr-1 Nov. € 30.00   2017*

See advertisement

ST REMY DE PROVENCE

ST REMY DE PROVENCE *10E2* (1km NE Rural) *43.79622, 4.83878* **FFCC Camping Le Mas de Nicolas, Ave Plaisance-du-Touch, 13210 St Rémy-de-Provence [04 90 92 27 05; fax 04 90 92 36 83; contact@camping-masdenicolas.com; www.camping-masdenicolas.com]** Fr town ctr take D99 eastwards for abt 0.5km. Turn L at 2nd rndabt & foll sp to campsite. Lge, hdg, mkd, hdstg, pt shd, wc (htd); chem disp; mv service pnt; fam bthrm; shwrs inc; EHU (6A) €3.80; lndry; shop; snacks; bar; bbq; playgrnd; pool (htd); entmnt; wifi; TV; TV (pitch); 20% statics; dogs €2.15-€2.80; bus 1km; Eng spkn; adv bkg req; quiet; ccard acc; games area; games rm; CKE/CCI. "Family-owned site; gd clean modern san facs; some pitches diff access long o'fits; excel; v helpful staff; interesting town." ♦ 1 Apr-14 Oct. € 33.00 2017*

ST REMY DE PROVENCE *10E2* (1km E Urban) *43.78836, 4.84093* **Camping Pégomas, Ave Jean Moulin, 13210 St Rémy-de-Provence [04 90 92 01 21; contact@campingpegomas.com; www.campingpegomas.com]** On D99 fr W dir Cavaillon, ignore R fork to St Rémy 'Centre Ville' (& sat nav!). Pass twin stone sculptures on rndabt, at 2nd rndabt turn into Ave Jean Moulin, site on R in 400m - v sharp turn into site. Fr E Exit A7 junc 25 on D99 W dir St Rémy. Ignore sp 'Centre Ville', pass under aquaduct & across rndabt. At next rndabt turn L into Ave Jean Moulin, then as above. Do not attempt to tow thro town. Med, hdg, mkd, shd, wc (htd); chem disp; mv service pnt; fam bthrm; shwrs inc; EHU (6A) €3.50 (poss rev pol & long lead req); gas; lndry; shop nr; snacks; bar; playgrnd; pool; paddling pool; entmnt; wifi; TV; dogs €1.70; phone; Eng spkn; adv bkg acc; quiet; ccard acc; games area; CKE/CCI. "Well-run, busy site; clean san facs; lge o'fits poss diff some sm pitches; gd pool; gd touring base; recep clsd 2000 hrs, lge lay-by outside; mkt Wed am; excel for walking; lovely site." 15 Mar-24 Oct. € 31.00 2015*

ST REMY DE PROVENCE *10E2* (2km NW Rural) *43.7967, 4.82378* **Camping Monplaisir, Chemin Monplaisir, 13210 St Rémy-de-Provence [04 90 92 22 70; fax 04 90 92 18 57; reception@camping-monplaisir.fr; www.camping-monplaisir.fr]** Exit D99 at St Rémy onto D5 going NW dir Maillane, in 110m turn L & foll sp in 500m. Avoid going thro town. Med, hdstg, hdg, shd, wc (htd); chem disp; mv service pnt; fam bthrm; shwrs inc; EHU (10A) €4.20; gas; lndry; shop; snacks; bar; bbq (elec, gas); playgrnd; pool; paddling pool; red long stay; entmnt; wifi; dogs €2; phone; bus 1km; Eng spkn; adv bkg acc; quiet; ccard acc; bike hire; CKE/CCI. "Immac, well-run site; mostly gd sized pitches; clean, modern san facs; gd touring base; highly rec; site clsd last Sat in Oct; excel site; lovely pool; walk to nice town; fills up quickly." ♦ 11 Mar-21 Oct. € 37.00 2017*

See advertisement

⊞ **ST ROME DE TARN** *8E4* (0km N Rural) *44.05302, 2.89578* **Camping de la Cascade des Naisses, Route du Pont, 12490 St Rome-de-Tarn [05 65 62 56 59; fax 05 65 62 58 62; contact@camping-cascade-aveyron.com; www.camping-cascade-aveyron.com]** Fr Millau take D992 to St Georges-de-Luzençon, turn R onto D73 & foll sp to St Rome. In St Rome turn R along Ave du Pont-du-Tarn, site sp. Diff, steep app for sm/underpowered car+c'van o'fits. Med, hdg, hdstg, mkd, pt shd, terr, wc (htd); own san req; chem disp; mv service pnt; fam bthrm; shwrs inc; EHU (6A) inc; lndry; shop; rest; bar; playgrnd; pool; paddling pool; entmnt; wifi; 40% statics; dogs €6; Eng spkn; adv bkg acc; quiet; boating; rv fishing; tennis; bike hire; CKE/CCI. "Lovely rvside pitches; pleasant vill; friendly, helpful staff; each level has a wc but steep walk to shwr block; owners will site vans; conv Millau viaduct; excel tranquil, scenic site." ♦ € 35.00 2016*

ST SAVIN *7A3* (1km N Rural) *46.56892, 0.86772* Camp Municipal Moulin de la Gassotte, 10 Rue de la Gassotte, 86310 St Savin-sur-Gartempe [05 49 48 18 02; fax 05 49 48 28 56; campingdumoulin@aol.com; saintsavin.com/camping-moulin-de-la-gassotte] E fr Chauvigny on D951 to St Savin; fr St Savin N on D11; well sp. Fr S on D5 cross rv; meet D951, turn R & site on R. Fr S on D11 use 'poids lourds' (heavy vehicles) rec rte to meet D951. Sm, pt shd, wc; chem disp; mv service pnt; shwrs inc; EHU (12A) inc; lndry; shop nr; rest nr; bar nr; playgrnd; TV; quiet; rv fishing adj; CKE/CCI. "Beautiful, peaceful, park like site by rv; views of Abbey; helpful warden; san facs old but clean; sh walk to vill; murals in Abbey restored by UNESCO; no defined pitches." ♦ 8 May-30 Sep. € 11.00   2016*

ST SEINE L'ABBAYE *6G1* (2km SE Rural) *47.44073, 4.79256* Camp Municipal, Rue de la Foire aux Vaches, 21440 St Seine-l'Abbaye [03 80 35 00 09 or 03 80 35 01 64 (Mairie)] On D971 in vill of St Seine-l'Abbaye, turn N onto D16. Turn R uphill, sp camping & turn R thro gateway in stone wall. Narr rds in vill. Or fr N on D974, avoiding Dijon, turn R onto D959 at Til-Châtel, then D901 Moloy/Lamargelle. Turn L in Lamargelle onto D16 St Seine-l'Abbaye. Turn L uphill at edge of vill & as above (avoids narr rds). Sm, hdstg, pt sl, wc cont; chem disp; shwrs inc; EHU (10A) €2.50 (rev pol); shop nr; dogs; quiet; CKE/CCI. "Pleasantly situated & peaceful site; basic but immac san facs; fees collected fr 1900 hrs; lovely vill; conv Dijon or as NH; pool 4km; excel; not suitable for o'fits over 7m." 1 May-30 Sep. € 12.00   2015*

ST SYMPHORIEN *7D2* (1km S Rural) *44.41831, -0.49232* Camping Vert Bord'Eau (formerly Camping La Hure), Route de Sore, 33113 St Symphorien [05 56 25 79 54 or 06 07 08 37 28 (mob); camping@vertbordeau.com; www.vertbordeau.com] S thro Langon on app. Foll sp Villandraut, St Symphorien. Sp fr vill 1km S on D220, opp Intermarché. Sm, shd, wc (htd); chem disp; mv service pnt; shwrs inc; EHU (10A) €2.50; lndry; shop; rest; snacks; bar; playgrnd; pool; wifi; 80% statics; dogs €1.30; Eng spkn; adv bkg acc; games area; tennis; rv fishing. "Helpful staff; basic facs; site in pinewoods; gd cycling, walks, beaches, vg cycle path run thro St Symphorien, gd level surface thro woods and vineyard; excel." 2 Apr-29 Oct. € 23.50   2016*

ST TROPEZ *10F4* (11km SW Rural) *43.21804, 6.57830* Camping Moulin de Verdagne, Route du Brost, 83580 Gassin [04 91 09 10 27; www.domaine-verdagne.com] Foll N559 N fr Cavalaire for 6km. Take 1st R after town traff lts in La Croix-Valmer, site sp. Site in 2km, surrounded by vineyards. Rough app rd/track. Med, mkd, pt shd, terr, wc; chem disp; shwrs inc; EHU (6A) €4; lndry; shop nr; rest; snacks; bar; playgrnd; pool; beach sand 5km; red long stay; 60% statics; dogs €3; phone; Eng spkn; quiet; ccard acc. "Vg, lovely site; tight bends & narr pitches poss diff long o'fits; pool 2m deep; c'van best app fr La Croix vill; new owners (2016); helpful; new pool (2017)." 1 Apr-31 Oct. € 37.50   2017*

ST VALERY SUR SOMME

ST VALERY EN CAUX *3C2* (2km N Coastal) *49.86839, 0.71154* Aire Communale, Quai d'Aval, Plage Ouest, 76460 St Valery-en-Caux [02 35 97 00 22 or 02 35 97 00 63 (TO); servicetourisme@ville-saint-valeryen-caux.fr] Sp fr cent of St Valery-en-Caux along rv/seafront to harbour. Sm, chem disp; mv service pnt; shop nr; rest nr; phone. "M'vans only; rec arr early; LS free except Fri, Sat & Sun; water fill €4; free parking for 48 hrs." € 4.00   2012*

ST VALERY SUR SOMME *3B2* (5km S Rural) *50.15333, 1.63583* Le Domaine du Château de Drancourt, 80230 Estréboeuf [03 22 26 93 45; fax 03 22 26 85 87; chateau.drancourt@wanadoo.fr; www.chateau-drancourt.com] Exit A28/E402 junc 1 at Abbeville onto D40 twd Noyelles-sur-Mer. At rndbt with D940 turn L sp St Valery-sur-Somme. At next rndabt go strt over dir Le Tréport, then at next rndabt at junc with D48 take last exit (sp Estréboeuf), turn immed L & foll sps to site. NB.1-way system at recep area. Lge, mkd, hdg, pt shd, pt sl, wc; chem disp; mv service pnt; fam bthrm; shwrs inc; EHU (10A) inc (poss rev pol); gas; lndry; shop; rest; snacks; bar; bbq; playgrnd; pool (covrd, htd); paddling pool; entmnt; 80% statics; dogs €3.80; Eng spkn; adv bkg acc; ccard acc; bike hire; fishing adj; golf driving range; tennis; horseriding 12km; games rm; watersports 2km; CKE/CCI. "Conv, busy, popular NH in grnds of chateau; friendly staff; facs poss stretched when site full; red facs LS; bird sanctuary in estuary nrby; gd." ♦ 13 Apr-24 Sep. € 40.00   2017*

ST VALERY SUR SOMME *3B2* (1km SW Urban/Coastal) *50.18331, 1.61786* Camping Le Walric, Route d'Eu, 80230 St Valery-sur-Somme [03 22 26 81 97; fax 03 22 60 77 26; info@campinglewalric.com; www.campinglewalric.com] Ringrd round St Valery D940 dir Le Tréport. Cont to 3rd rndabt (1st rndabt Carrefour supmkt on L) 3km & take 1st exit (R) sp St Valery & Cap Hornu D3. Site on R in 2km at ent to town sp. Lge, hdstg, hdg, mkd, pt shd, wc; chem disp; mv service pnt; fam bthrm; shwrs inc; EHU (6A) inc; gas; lndry; shop; bar; bbq; playgrnd; pool (htd); paddling pool; red long stay; entmnt; wifi; 70% statics; dogs €3; phone; Eng spkn; adv bkg acc; quiet; ccard acc; tennis; games area; bike hire; games rm; boat hire; fishing; CKE/CCI. "Well-kept, well-run, busy site in excel location; clean dated san facs; cycle rtes, canal track; steam train; beach nrby; delightful medieval town; mkt Sun; excel; easy to find." ♦ 1 Apr-30 Oct. € 37.00   2017*

ST VALERY SUR SOMME *3B2* (3km SW Rural) *50.17632, 1.58969* Camping de la Baie, Routhiaville, 80230 Pendé [03 22 60 72 72; contact@campingdelabaie.eu; www.campingdelabaie.net] Just off D940 twd Tréport, well sp. Sm, hdg, wc; chem disp; shwrs inc; EHU (6A) €4; lndry; shop nr; playgrnd; 95% statics; adv bkg acc; quiet; CKE/CCI. "Well-run, clean, tidy site & san facs; friendly, helpful owners; low trees in places need care; cycle rte to St Valery; adequate NH." 27 Mar-16 Oct. € 15.50   2013*

ST VALERY SUR SOMME

ST VALERY SUR SOMME *3B2* (1km W Urban) *50.18447, 1.62263* **Camping de la Croix l'Abbé**, Place de la Croix l'Abbé, 80230 St Valery-sur-Somme [03 22 60 81 46; w.a.georges@wanadoo.fr] Ringrd round St Valery D940 dir Le Tréport. Cont to 2nd rndabt (1st rndabt Champion supmkt on L) 3km & take exit sp St Valery & Cap Hornu D3. Site 250m beyond Camping Le Walric. Lge, hdg, mkd, unshd, pt sl, wc; chem disp; shwrs inc; EHU (10A) inc; shop nr; rest; snacks; bar; playgrnd; pool (covrd, htd); beach shgl 1km; TV; 90% statics; bus adj; Eng spkn; quiet. "San facs needs updating (2017); gd location for walk to town; sh stay/NH only; super town; rec steam rlwy to Le Crotoy." 1 Apr-30 Nov. € 20.00   2017*

> "There aren't many sites open at this time of year"
>
> If you're travelling outside peak season remember to call ahead to check site opening dates – even if the entry says 'open all year'.

ST VALLIER *9C2* (2km N Rural) *45.18767, 4.81225* **Camp Municipal Les Iles de Silon**, 26240 St Vallier [04 75 23 22 17 or 04 73 23 07 66; camping.saintvallier@orange.fr; www.saintvallier.fr/decouvrir/camping] On N7 just N of town, clearly sp in both dirs on rvside. Med, hdg, pt shd, wc; chem disp; shwrs inc; EHU (10A) €2.30 (poss long cable req); lndry; shop; snacks; bbq; playgrnd; wifi; 10% statics; dogs €2.30; Eng spkn; adv bkg acc; ccard acc; watersports; tennis adj; CKE/CCI. "Attractive, gd quality site; views over rv; lge pitches; friendly warden; gd immac san facs; rec arr bef 1600 high ssn; gd value; cycle/walking track adj, along Rhône; excel well managed site; vg facs and staff; free WiFi." ♦ 15 Mar-15 Nov. € 13.00   2018*

ST VINCENT DE BARRES *9D2* (1km SW Rural) *44.65659, 4.69330* **Camping Le Rieutord**, 07210 St Vincent-de-Barrès [04 75 20 86 17; campinglerieutord@orange.fr; www.camping-le-rieutord.com] Fr N exit A7 junc 16 Loriol onto D104 & foll sp Le Pouzin then Chomérac (do not foll 1st sp St Vincent-de-Barrès - narr rd). At rndabt foll D2 dir Le Teil-Montélimar for 6km. When arr at St Vincent (vill on L), turn R & foll site sp for 1.5km. Fr S exit junc 18 Montélimar Sud, foll sps Montélimar then Privas. Cross Rv Rhône, go thro Rochemaure sp Privas. At Meysse turn L after bdge dir Privas. Foll D2 for 4.5km then turn L dir St Bauzile to site in 3km. Med, hdg, pt shd, pt sl, wc (htd); shwrs inc; EHU (16A) €3; lndry; shop; snacks; bar; cooking facs; playgrnd; pool; paddling pool; 10% statics; dogs €2; Eng spkn; adv bkg acc; quiet; tennis; games area; waterslide; CKE/CCI. "Tranquil site in beautiful setting nr old walled town; pleasant owners; no c'vans over 6m or twin axles; gd touring base." 4 Apr-31 Oct. € 20.00   2016*

ST VINCENT LES FORTS *9D3* (1km N Rural) *44.45682, 6.36529* **Campéole Camping Le Lac**, Le Fein, 04340 St Vincent-les-Forts [04 92 85 51 57; fax 04 92 85 57 63; lac@campeole.com; www.camping-montagne.com or www.campeole.com] W fr Barcelonnette on D900/D900b, past St Vincent-les-Forts dir Le Lautaret. Turn R onto D7 & foll narr steep winding rd to end, site sp o'looking lake. Lge, mkd, pt shd, sl, terr, wc; chem disp; mv service pnt; fam bthrm; shwrs inc; EHU (6A) €4.10; lndry; shop; rest; snacks; bar; bbq; playgrnd; pool; paddling pool; sw nr; entmnt; wifi; 30% statics; dogs €3.50; phone; Eng spkn; adv bkg acc; quiet; ccard acc; horseriding; fishing; watersports; games area; games rm; tennis; CKE/CCI. "Simple site in superb scenic location; many leisure activities; vg walking in area; vg." ♦ 20 May-25 Sep. € 25.00   2012*

SAINTES *7B2* (1km N Urban) *45.75511, -0.62871* **Camp Municipal au Fil de l'Eau**, 6 Rue de Courbiac, 17100 Saintes [05 46 93 08 00 or 06 75 24 91 96 (mob); fax 05 46 93 61 88; campingaufildeleau@sfr.fr; www.camping-saintes-17.com] Well sp as 'Camping Municipal' fr rndbts on by-pass N & S on D150 & D137 (thro indus area), adj rv. If app fr W on D128 (N side of Saintes), turn R at rndabt onto Rue de l'Abbatoir; in 800m turn L into Rue de Courbiac; site on R in 200m. NB 1st Mon in month st mkt & many rds clsd. Lge, pt shd, wc; chem disp; shwrs inc; EHU (10A) €3.60; lndry; shop; rest; snacks; bar; bbq; playgrnd; pool; sw nr; red long stay; wifi; dogs €1.60; Eng spkn; adv bkg acc; ccard acc; boating adj; fishing adj; CKE/CCI. "Excel site; vg, clean san facs; excel rest; grnd poss boggy when wet; gd touring base; easy walk to attractive Roman town; huge open site, efficent recep; site being upgraded (2014); friendly staff; gd NH just off A10; rest clsd on Sundays." ♦ 20 Apr-15 Oct. € 22.80   2014*

SALBRIS *4G3* (1km N Urban) *47.43006, 2.05427* **Camping de Sologne**, 8 Allée de la Sauldre, Route de Pierrefitte, 41300 Salbris [02 54 97 06 38; fax 02 54 97 33 13; campingdesologne@wanadoo.fr; www.campingdesologne.fr] Exit A71 junc 4; take D724 bypass, then take D2020 N (do not take D724 into town); turn E onto D55 (Route de Pierrefitte); Impasse de la Sauldre leading to Allée de la Sauldre is 2nd turning on R in 200m (narr & easy to miss). Med, hdg, mkd, pt shd, wc; chem disp; fam bthrm; shwrs inc; EHU (10A) inc (some rev pol); gas; lndry; shop nr; rest; snacks; bar; playgrnd; wifi; TV; 25% statics; dogs €1; phone; Eng spkn; adv bkg acc; ccard acc; fishing; boat hire; CKE/CCI. "Excel, well-kept site in pleasant lakeside location; friendly, helpful owners; karting 6km; lake adj; gd san facs poss stretched if site busy & ltd LS; gd rest; gd dog walks adj; conv NH for m'way; hypmkt 1km; beautiful site; easy access to town; new shwr block (2015)." ♦ 1 Apr-30 Sep. € 23.00   2016*

SALERS 7C4 (1km NE Rural) *45.14756, 2.49857* **Camp Municipal Le Mouriol, Route de Puy-Mary, 15410 Salers [04 71 40 73 09 or 04 71 40 72 33 (Mairie); fax 04 71 40 76 28; www.salers.fr]** Take D922 SE fr Mauriac for Aurillac; turn onto D680 E dir Salers; site 1km NE of Salers on D680 dir Puy Mary, opp Hôtel Le Gerfaut; sp fr all dir. Med, hdg, mkd, pt shd, sl, wc; chem disp; shwrs inc; EHU (16A) €4.60 (long lead poss req); lndry; shop nr; rest nr; bar nr; bbq; playgrnd; red long stay; wifi; dogs; phone; bus 1km; quiet; tennis; CKE/CCI. "Generous pitches; san facs gd but stretched if site full; peaceful LS; hill walking; excel cycling & walking; beautiful medieval vill; vg; well kept; footpath fr site to Salers." ♦ 1 Apr-30 Oct. € 19.80   2017*

SALERS 7C4 (1km W Rural) *45.13304, 2.48762* **Camping à la Ferme (Fruquière), Apcher, 15140 Salers [04 71 40 72 26]** D922 S fr Mauriac for 17km; L on D680 sp Salers; in lane on R sp Apcher - immed after passing Salers town sp. Sm, pt shd, wc; shwrs inc; EHU (10A) €2.30; shop nr; dogs; quiet; CKE/CCI. "Sm farm, CL type site; welcoming, friendly owner; excel clean san facs, plenty hot water; beautiful countryside; gd; run down end of ssn." 1 May-30 Sep. € 10.00   2017*

SALIES DE BEARN 8F1 (3km S Rural) *43.45277, -0.92055* **Domaine d'Esperbasque, Chemin de Lagisquet, 64270 Salies de Béarn [05 59 38 21 04; info@esperbasque.com; www.esperbasque.com]** Site well sp on D933. E of rd bet Salies de Bearn and Sauveterre. Fr N pass the site, turn at next exit & app fr southern side. Med, hdstg, mkd, pt shd, sl, terr, wc; chem disp; mv service pnt; fam bthrm; shwrs inc; EHU (6A) €3.50; lndry; shop nr; rest; snacks; bar; bbq; playgrnd; pool; paddling pool; twin axles; wifi; TV; dogs €1.50-€3.50; Eng spkn; adv bkg acc; quiet; ccard acc; games area; games rm; CKE/CCI. "Gd touring; horse riding at site highly rec; excel; go-karts; petanque; scenic, rural, visits to wine growers & Salies de Bearn; gd." 1 Mar-31 Oct. € 23.40   2017*

SALIES DU SALAT 8F3 (2km S Rural) *43.07621, 0.94683* **Complex Touristique de la Justale, Chemin de St Jean, 31260 Mane [05 61 90 68 18; fax 05 61 97 40 18; contact@village-vacances-mane.fr; www.village-vacances-mane.fr]** Fr A64 exit 20 onto D117, turn R in vill at sp 'Village de Vacances'. Site on R in approx 500m. Sm, pt shd, wc; chem disp; mv service pnt; shwrs inc; EHU (6A) €3.60 (poss rev pol); lndry; shop nr; playgrnd; pool; wifi; TV; dogs €1.20; phone; adv bkg rec; horseriding; tennis; fishing. "Lovely, peaceful site; lge pitches; helpful staff; excel facs; sinage poss diff to foll." 1 Apr-31 Oct. € 12.00   2013*

SALINS LES BAINS 6H2 (1km N Rural) *46.94650, 5.87896* **Camp Municipal, 39110 Salins-les-Bains [03 84 37 92 70; campingsalins.kanak.fr; www.salinscamping.com]** SE fr Besançon on N83. At Mouchard take D472 E to Salins. Turn L at rndabt at N of Salins, well sp nr old stn. If app fr E take 2nd exit fr rndabt (blind app). Sm, pt shd, wc; shwrs inc; EHU (10A) €3.10; lndry; shop nr; playgrnd; 10% statics; adv bkg acc. "Well-run site; clean, modern san facs; excel touring base N Jura; not often visited by British; far end of site quieter; htd pool adj; gd NH; barrier locked 1000-0700; chalets being built (2016)." ♦ 31 Mar-1 Oct. € 13.50   2017*

SALLANCHES 9A3 (4km SE Rural) *45.92388, 6.65042* **Camping Village Center Les Iles, Lac de Passy 245 Chemin de la Cavettaz, 74190 Passy [04 30 05 15 04; www.campinglesiles.fr]** E fr Geneva on A40, exit junc 21 onto D339 dir Passy; in 400m turn L onto D39 dir Sallanches; at rndabt in 1.5km turn L onto D199 dir Domancy; immed after rlwy x-ing in 500m turn R into Chemin de Mont Blanc Plage; site at end of rd in 1km. Or E fr Sallanches on D1205 dir Chamonix; in 3km turn L (1st into filter to turn L) onto D199; in 1km turn L immed bef level x-ing; site at end of rd. Lge, hdg, hdstg, pt shd, wc; fam bthrm; shwrs inc; EHU (8A) inc; lndry; shop; snacks; playgrnd; pool (htd); sw nr; entmnt; dogs €3; phone; Eng spkn; adv bkg acc; quiet; ccard acc; fishing; CKE/CCI. "Mountain views; conv Chamonix; vg site; v overgrown; nr rlwy and m'way; pitches bare of grass, some v muddy after rain, v shady; not rec." ♦ 1 Apr-1 Oct. € 16.00   2016*

> **"That's changed – Should I let the Club know?"**
>
> If you find something on site that's different from the site entry, fill in a report and let us know. See camc.com/europereport.

SALLE EN BEAUMONT, LA 9C3 (4km SE Rural) *44.87593, 5.83710* **Camping Belvédère de l'Obiou, Les Egats, 38350 St Laurent-en-Beaumont [04 76 30 40 80; info@camping-obiou.com; www.camping-obiou.com]** Clearly sp on D1085. Sm, pt shd, pt sl, terr, wc (htd); chem disp; mv service pnt; fam bthrm; shwrs; EHU (4-10A) €3-6 (poss rev pol); lndry; rest; snacks; playgrnd; pool (covrd, htd); red long stay; wifi; TV; 5% statics; dogs €2; Eng spkn; games rm; CKE/CCI. "Superb, immac, family-run site; excel facs; helpful owners; excel rest & pool; picturesque & interesting area; gd local walks." ♦ 15 Apr-15 Oct. € 30.00   2013*

SALLES (GIRONDE)

SALLES (GIRONDE) *7D1* (1km SW Rural) *44.54475, -0.87506* **FFCC Camping Parc du Val de l'Eyre, 8 Route du Minoy, 33770 Salles [05 56 88 47 03; fax 05 56 88 47 27; levaldeleyre2@wanadoo.fr; www.camping-parcduvaldeleyre.com]** Exit junc 21 fr A63, foll dir to Salles on D3. On edge of Salles turn L on D108 at x-rds. Ent to site on L after ´rv opp Super U supmkt building. Lge, pt shd, wc; chem disp; mv service pnt; fam bthrm; shwrs inc; EHU (6A) €4 (poss rev pol); gas; lndry; shop nr; rest; snacks; bar; bbq; playgrnd; pool (htd); sw; entmnt; 80% statics; dogs €4; quiet; ccard acc; tennis 500km; games area; canoeing; fishing; horseriding 8km. "Attractive site; gd san facs but poss stretched when site busy; ltd facs LS; gd NH only; peaceful site by rv; gd size mkd pitches with access to water & drainage; refurbished unizex san facs (2013) v clean; conv for m'way; Carrefour opp; gd for long/sh stay." ♦ 1 Apr-15 Oct. € 50.00 2014*

SALLES (GIRONDE) *7D1* (4km SW Rural) *44.52039, -0.89631* **Camping Le Bilos, 37 Route de Bilos, 33770 Salles [05 56 88 36 53; fax 05 56 88 45 14; lebilos@aol.com; www.lebilos.com]** Exit A63 junc 21; foll sp Salles on D3; turn L onto D108/D108E3 sp Lugos; pass Carrefour supmkt on R; in 2km bear R & site on R in 2km. Med, pt shd, wc (htd); chem disp; shwrs inc; EHU (3-6A) €2.20-3.50; gas; lndry; shop; bbq (sep area); playgrnd; 80% statics; dogs; adv bkg acc; quiet. "Pleasant, peaceful site in pine forest; sm, well-drained pitches, ltd space for tourers, friendly owners, old but clean san facs, ltd LS; cycle lane thro forest, vg NH en rte Spain; friendly welcome; site cr." € 13.00 2016*

SALLES CURAN *8E4* (3km N Rural) *44.20167, 2.77705* **Camping Beau Rivage, Route des Vernhes, 12410 Salles-Curan [05 65 46 33 32; fax 05 65 46 33 96; camping-beau-rivage@orange.fr; www.beau-rivage.fr]** Fr Rodez D911 turn S onto the D993 sp Salles Curan. Foll rd for approx 7km; turn R after lake bdge to site on R in approx 1.5km. Med, pt shd, wc; chem disp; shwrs inc; EHU (6A) inc; lndry; shop; rest; playgrnd; pool; TV; dogs €3.90; adv bkg rec; quiet; fishing; watersports nr; games rm; horseriding nr. "Excel site on lake location; lovely area, gd walks & lots of activities nrby." Jun-Sep. € 35.00 2013*

SALLES CURAN *8E4* (2km NW Rural) *44.18933, 2.76693* **Camping Les Genêts, Lac de Pareloup, 12410 Salles-Curan [05 65 46 35 34; fax 05 65 78 00 72; contact@camping-les-genets.fr; www.camping-les-genets.fr]** Fr D911 Rodez-Millau rd take D993 S for approx 9km, then R onto D577, site sp on R by lake. Lge, shd, pt sl, wc; mv service pnt; fam bthrm; shwrs; EHU (10A) inc; lndry; shop; rest; snacks; bar; pool (htd); paddling pool; sw; red long stay; entmnt; wifi; 40% statics; dogs €4; adv bkg acc; fishing; sailing; bike hire; games area. "Beautiful area; ltd facs LS; excel site." ♦ 10 May-11 Sep. € 36.00 2013*

SALLES SUR VERDON, LES *10E3* (2km N Rural) *43.78129, 6.21298* **Camp Municipal Les Ruisses, 83630 Les Salles-sur-Verdon [04 98 10 28 15; fax 04 98 10 28 16; lesruissescamping@orange.fr; www.sallessurverdon.com]** Fr Moustiers foll D957, site on L just bef Les Salles. Lge, mkd, pt shd, wc; fam bthrm; shwrs inc; EHU (6A) €3.20; lndry; shop; snacks; bar; playgrnd; dogs €1.70; quiet; ccard acc; fishing; CKE/CCI. "Pleasant site; lake nrby; ltd facs LS but gd hot shwrs & clean facs." ♦ 15 Feb-15 Nov. € 19.00 2013*

> "I like to fill in the reports as I travel from site to site"
>
> You'll find report forms at the back of this guide, or you can fill them in online at camc.com/europereport.

SALLES SUR VERDON, LES *10E3* (1km W Rural) *43.77552, 6.20719* **Camping La Source, Lac de Sainte Croix, Quartier Margaridon, 83630 Les Salles-sur-Verdon [04 94 70 20 40; fax 04 94 70 20 74; contact@camping-la-source.eu; www.camping-la-source.eu]** Fr Moustiers on D957, foll sp Camping Les Pins (adj) via rd round vill. Med, hdg, hdstg, mkd, pt shd, terr, serviced pitches; wc; chem disp; fam bthrm; shwrs inc; EHU (10A) €3.80 (poss rev pol); gas; lndry; shop nr; rest nr; bar nr; bbq; playgrnd; sw nr; TV; dogs €2.20; phone; Eng spkn; adv bkg acc; quiet; ccard acc; watersports; canoe hire; CKE/CCI. "Excel facs; superb situation; well-run site conv Gorges du Verdon; dir access to lake; friendly, helpful owners; gates clsd 2200-0700; some sm pitches - manhandling poss req; highly rec." ♦ 20 Apr-10 Oct. € 25.00 2014*

SALON DE PROVENCE *10E2* (12km NE Rural) *43.72125, 5.20495* **FFCC Camping Durance Luberon, Domaine du Vergon, 13370 Mallemort [04 90 59 13 36; fax 04 90 57 46 62; duranceluberon@orange.fr; www.campingduranceluberon.com]** Exit A7 junc 26 onto D7n dir Aix-en-Provence. In 11km turn L at rndabt onto D561 dir Charleval (passing Pont-Royal golf course). In 1km turn L dir Mallemort, site on R in 1km, sp. Med, mkd, hdg, pt shd, wc (htd); chem disp; mv service pnt; shwrs inc; EHU inc (6-10A) €3.80-4.50; gas; lndry; shop; rest nr; snacks; bar; bbq; playgrnd; pool (htd); paddling pool; wifi; 5% statics; dogs €2; phone; Eng spkn; adv bkg acc; quiet; rv fishing 1km; horseriding adj; tennis; bike hire; CKE/CCI. "Gd site with lge pitches; friendly owners; clean, modern san facs; gd touring base; excel." ♦ 1 Apr-30 Sept. € 22.00 2013*

SALON DE PROVENCE *10E2* (5km NW Rural) *43.67820, 5.06480* **Camping Nostradamus, Route d'Eyguières, 13300 Salon-de-Provence [04 90 56 08 36; fax 04 90 56 65 05; gilles.nostra@gmail.fr; www.camping-nostradamus.com]** Exit A54/E80 junc 13 onto D569 N sp Eyguières. After approx 1.5km turn R opp airfield onto D72d, site on R in approx 4km just bef T-junc. Or fr N exit A7 junc 26 dir Salon-Provence. Turn R onto D17 for 5km dir Eyguières, then L onto D72, site on L. Med, hdg, mkd, pt shd, wc; chem disp; mv service pnt; fam bthrm; shwrs inc; EHU (4-6A) €2.95-5.15; gas; lndry; shop nr; rest; snacks; bar; bbq; playgrnd; pool; paddling pool; entmnt; wifi; TV; 15% statics; dogs €3; phone; Eng spkn; adv bkg req; quiet; ccard acc; games area; CKE/CCI. "Pleasant site; busy high ssn; welcoming owner with vg sense of humour!; bkg fee; poss diff access lge o'fits; dusty when dry; gd walking." ♦ 1 Mar-30 Nov. € 23.60   2014*

⊞ **SAMOENS** *9A3* (1km S Rural) *46.07731, 6.71851* **Camping Caravaneige Le Giffre, La Glière, 74340 Samoëns [04 50 34 41 92; fax 04 50 34 98 84; camping.samoens@wanadoo.fr; www.camping-samoens.com]** Leave A40 at junc 15 sp Fillinges/St Jeoire. Foll D907 thro Taninges E for 11km, sp Samoëns. At W town boundary turn R immed after wooden arch over rd, foll sp to Parc des Loisirs. Site on R after sw pool & park. Lge, mkd, pt shd, wc (htd); chem disp; mv service pnt; fam bthrm; shwrs inc; EHU (6-10A) €3.20-4.75; lndry; shop nr; rest nr; bbq; playgrnd; wifi; TV; 5% statics; dogs €2; phone; adv bkg req; quiet; ccard acc; bike hire; tennis; lake fishing adj; CKE/CCI. "Friendly staff; some facs ltd LS; on arr, park on rdside bef checking in; htd pool adj; htd ski storage/drying rm; private san facs avail; Samoëns ski gondola 150m; excel winter site." ♦ € 31.00   2014*

> **"We must tell the Club about that great site we found"**
>
> Get your site reports in by mid-August and we'll do our best to get your updates into the next edition.

⊞ **SAMOENS** *9A3* (6km W Rural) *46.08944, 6.67874* **Camp Municipal Lac et Montagne, 74440 Verchaix [06 79 57 69 59; fax 04 50 90 10 12; www.verchaix.com]** Fr Taninges take D907 sp Samoëns for 6km, site to R of main rd in Verchaix. Med, shd, shwrs; EHU (10A) €4.10; lndry; shop nr; rest nr; bar nr; playgrnd; 10% statics; dogs €1.40; phone; adv bkg acc; quiet; tennis. "Gd touring base; clean facs; rv & lake adj; barrier locked 2200-0700." ♦ € 21.00   2016*

SANARY SUR MER *10F3* (4km NE Urban) *43.13147, 5.81483* **Campasun Mas de Pierredon, 652 Chemin Raoul Coletta, 83110 Sanary-sur-Mer [04 94 74 25 02; fax 04 94 74 61 42; pierredon@campasun.com; www.campasun-pierredon.fr]** Take D11 fr Sanary, cross m'way & 1st L. Site on R in approx 1km. Med, shd, wc (htd); chem disp; mv service pnt; shwrs inc; EHU (10A) inc; lndry; shop; rest; snacks; bar; playgrnd; pool (htd); paddling pool; beach 3km; entmnt; wifi; TV; dogs €4; adv bkg rec; tennis; waterslide; CKE/CCI. "Gd family site." ♦ 19 Apr-30 Sep. € 47.00   2013*

SANCERRE *4G3* (4km N Rural) *47.34215, 2.86571* **Flower Camping Les Portes de Sancerre, Quai de Loire, 18300 St Satur [02 48 72 10 88; camping.sancerre@flowercampings.com; www.camping-cher-sancerre.com]** Fr Sancerre on D955 thro cent St Satur & St Thibault. Turn L immed bef Loire bdge. Site on R in 100m. Med, hdg, shd, wc; chem disp; mv service pnt; shwrs inc; EHU (16A) inc (long lead poss req); lndry; shop nr; rest nr; playgrnd; sw; entmnt; wifi; TV; 50% statics; dogs €2; Eng spkn; adv bkg acc; bike hire; games area; tennis; CKE/CCI. "Nice site; some pitches sm, some with rv view; friendly & helpful staff; pool adj; canoe hire adj; gd clean excel san facs, rec own in peak ssn; rvside walks; gd touring cent; vg; highly rec; gd rest nrby." ♦ 1 Apr-1 Oct. € 23.00   2017*

SANCERRE *4G3* (9km SW Rural) *47.30353, 2.74555* **Camping Crezancy en Sancerre, 9 Route de Veagues, 18300 Crezancy en Sancerre [06 12 55 69 98; campingcrezancy@orange.fr]** Fr Sancerre take D955 dir Bourges. In 5km turn R onto D22 sp Crezancy, Henrichemont. After 5km at vill turn L onto D86 sp Veagues. Site 100m on L. Sm, hdg, mkd, shd, wc; chem disp; fam bthrm; shwrs; EHU (6A); lndry; bbq; cooking facs; playgrnd; twin axles; dogs; phone; bus 100m; Eng spkn; adv bkg acc; CKE/CCI. "Site in Sancerre vineyards with wine tasting & to buy; gd walks & cycling, but a bit hilly; easy acc to Sancerre and The Loire; hospitable site manager; excel; lovely sm friendly site; indiv hdg bays; rural, quiet & clean; new shwrs (2016)." ♦ 1 Apr-31 Oct. € 10.00   2017*

SANGUINET *7D1* (3km N Rural) *44.49915, -1.07911* **Camping Lou Broustaricq, 2315 Route de Langeot, 40460 Sanguinet [05 58 82 74 82; fax 05 58 82 10 74; loubrousta@wanadoo.fr; www.lou-broustaricq.com]** Take Arcachon exit off Bordeax-Bayonne m'way. After 5km twd S on D3 & D216 to Sanguinet. Site sp in town off Bordeaux rd. V lge, mkd, pt shd, wc (htd); chem disp; shwrs inc; EHU (10A) inc; lndry; shop; rest; snacks; bar; bbq; playgrnd; pool; sw nr; entmnt; wifi; TV; 60% statics; Eng spkn; adv bkg acc; quiet; ccard acc; watersports; games area; golf nr; bike hire; waterslide; tennis; sailing school; CKE/CCI. "In lovely wooded area; gd cycle tracks; gd for children; vg; touring pitches sep fr statics; nice pool; nr army base, some aircraft noise." ♦ 1 Apr-30 Sep. € 51.00   2013*

SANGUINET

SANGUINET 7D1 (2km SW Rural) 44.48402, -1.09098 **Camping Les Grands Pins**, Ave de Losa, Route du Lac, 40460 Sanguinet [05 58 78 61 74; fax 05 58 78 69 15; info@campinglesgrandspins.com; www.campinglesgrandspins.com] Foll Le Lac sp at rndabt in Sanguinet. Turn L at lakeside. Site on L in 450m opp yacht club. Lge, hdg, shd, wc; chem disp; fam bthrm; shwrs inc; EHU (3-10A) inc; lndry; rest; snacks; bar; playgrnd; pool; sw nr; TV; 50% statics; dogs €2; Eng spkn; adv bkg acc; canoeing; bike hire; fishing; tennis; boating; windsurfing; CKE/CCI. "Clean site; rest & bar poss clsd LS; parking for m'vans adj." ♦ 1 Apr-31 Oct. € 37.00   2016*

See advertisement above

SARLAT LA CANEDA 7C3 (12km N Rural) 44.97450, 1.18732 **Camping Les Tailladis**, 24200 Marcillac-St Quentin [05 53 59 10 95; fax 05 53 29 47 56; info@tailladis.com; www.tailladis.com] N fr Sarlat on D704 dir Montignac. After 7km turn L & foll sp to site. NB Access along fairly narr lane. Med, hdg, pt shd, pt sl, terr, wc; chem disp; mv service pnt; shwrs inc; EHU (10A) €4.20; gas; lndry; shop; rest; snacks; bar; pool; sw; 6% statics; dogs €2.20; phone; Eng spkn; adv bkg acc; ccard acc; canoeing; fishing. "Excel site; friendly & helpful Dutch owners; immac san facs, ltd early ssn; vg food in rest; c'van storage." ♦ 1 Mar-30 Nov. € 22.00   2014*

SARLAT LA CANEDA 7C3 (10km NE Rural) 44.91905, 1.27789 **Camping Domaine des Mathévies, Les Mathévies**, 24200 Ste Nathalène [05 53 59 20 86 or 06 14 10 95 86 (mob); info@mathevies.com; www.mathevies.com] Exit A20 junc 55 Souillac & foll sp Roufillac. At Roufillac, foll sp to Carlux & cont to Ste Nathalène, site sp N of Ste Nathèlene. Sm, hdg, mkd, pt shd, wc; chem disp; mv service pnt; shwrs; EHU (10A) €4; snacks; bar; playgrnd; pool; paddling pool; wifi; TV (pitch); 10% statics; dogs €1.50; adv bkg acc; quiet; tennis; games area. "Gd, British-owned site; lge pitches, most with views; excel site; gd for kids." ♦ 18 Apr-19 Sep. € 46.00   2014*

SARLAT LA CANEDA 7C3 (10km NE Rural) 44.95778, 1.27580 **Camping Les Péneyrals, Le Poujol**, 24590 St Crépin-et-Carlucet [05 53 28 85 71; fax 05 53 28 80 99; camping.peneyrals@wanadoo.fr; www.peneyrals.com] Fr Sarlat N on D704; D60 E dir Salignac-Eyvignes to Le Poujol; S to St Crépin. Site sp. Lge, hdg, pt shd, pt sl, terr, serviced pitches; wc (htd); chem disp; mv service pnt; fam bthrm; shwrs inc; EHU (5-10A) €3.40-3.90; lndry; shop; rest; snacks; bar; playgrnd; pool (covrd, htd); paddling pool; entmnt; 50% statics; dogs €2.40; Eng spkn; adv bkg acc; quiet; ccard acc; games area; waterslide; fishing; tennis. "Friendly owners; superb family & touring site; excel aquatic ctr; some pitches require mover." ♦ 12 May-13 Sep. € 41.00   2017*

> ## "I need an on-site restaurant"
>
> We do our best to make sure site information is correct, but it is always best to check any must-have facilities are still available or will be open during your visit.

SARLAT LA CANEDA 7C3 (8km NE Rural) 44.90404, 1.28610 **Camping Les Grottes de Roffy**, 24200 Ste Nathalène [05 53 59 15 61; fax 05 53 31 09 11; contact@roffy.fr; www.roffy.fr] Fr N end of Sarlat take D47 NE for Ste Nathalène. Site on R 1km bef vill. Or fr A20 exit junc 55 onto ND804/D703 dir Carlux. Turn R onto D61B then D47 to Ste Nathalène, site thro vill on L. Lge, mkd, hdg, pt shd, terr, wc (htd); chem disp; fam bthrm; shwrs inc; EHU (6A) €3; gas; lndry; shop; rest; snacks; bar; bbq; playgrnd; pool; paddling pool; entmnt; 40% statics; dogs €2.10; Eng spkn; adv bkg rec; canoeing; games rm; tennis; bike hire; games area; CKE/CCI. "Excel rest, bar & shop; extra for 'comfort' pitches; helpful staff, lovely site." ♦ 25 Apr-13 Sep. € 33.50   2015*

See advertisement

SARLAT LA CANEDA

SARLAT LA CANEDA *7C3* (12km E Rural) *44.86345, 1.37350* Camping Le Mondou, Le Colombier, 24370 St Julien-de-Lampon [05 53 29 70 37; lemondou@ camping-dordogne.info; www.camping-dordogne.info] Fr Sarlat-la-Canéda take D704/D703 E; cross rv at Rouffillac, ent St Julien-de-Lampon & turn L at x-rds; site sp on R in 2km. Med, hdg, mkd, pt shd, wc; chem disp; mv service pnt; fam bthrm; shwrs inc; EHU (6A) €3.50; lndry; shop nr; rest; snacks; bar; bbq; playgrnd; pool; paddling pool; sw nr; wifi; 10% statics; dogs €1; phone; Eng spkn; adv bkg acc; quiet; games rm; bike hire; fishing 300m; games area; watersports 300m. "Beautiful views; friendly, helpful owners; gas 700m; sm, uneven pitches; gd cycle paths." ♦ 1 May-15 Oct. € 21.00 2012*

"Satellite navigation makes touring much easier"

Remember most sat navs don't know if you're towing or in a larger vehicle – always use yours alongside maps and site directions.

SARLAT LA CANEDA *7C3* (2km E Rural) *44.89328, 1.22756* Camping Indigo Sarlat Les Périères, Rue Jean Gabin, 24200 Sarlat-la-Canéda [05 53 59 05 84; fax 05 53 28 57 51; sarlat@camping-indigo. com; www.camping-indigo.com] Site on R of D47 to Proissans & Ste Nathalène. NB steep access rds. Med, mkd, shd, terr, wc; mv service pnt; fam bthrm; shwrs inc; EHU (6A); gas; lndry; shop; bar; bbq (charcoal, gas); playgrnd; pool (covrd, htd); wifi; 10% statics; dogs; Eng spkn; adv bkg acc; quiet; ccard acc; games rm; sauna; tennis. "Lovely site; friendly, helpful staff; san facs clean; excel pool complex; steep site rds; access poss diff med & lge o'fits; excel; great facs & location; v easy walk to Old City; site extended (2015); new san facs (2016); excel site." ♦ 24 Mar-2 Nov. € 37.00 2015*

SARLAT LA CANEDA *7C3* (20km E Rural) *44.86732, 1.35796* Camping Les Ombrages, Rouffillac, 24370 Carlux [09 53 53 25 55; ombragesperigord@free.fr; www.ombrages.fr] 12km W thro Souillac on D703. Turn L at x-rds in Rouffillac & immed turn L bef rv bdge into site. Med, mkd, pt shd, wc; chem disp; shwrs inc; EHU (6A) €2.70; lndry; shop nr; rest nr; snacks; bar; bbq; playgrnd; sw nr; wifi; TV; 2% statics; dogs €2; phone; Eng spkn; adv bkg acc; quiet; ccard acc; fishing; tennis; bike hire; games area; canoe hire; CKE/ CCI. "Pleasant, well-kept, rvside site; enthusiastic new owners live on site; pitching poss diff due trees; san facs (open air) poss stretched high ssn; cycle track; vg; lovely peaceful site; pool adj; lots of entmnt." 19 Apr-15 Oct. € 20.00 2015*

SARLAT LA CANEDA *7C3* (10km SE Rural) *44.81536, 1.29245* Camping Les Granges, 24250 Groléjac [05 53 28 11 15; fax 05 53 28 57 13; contact@ lesgranges-fr.com; www.lesgranges-fr.com] Fr Sarlat take D704 SE, sp Gourdon. Site sp nr cent of Groléjac on R. Care on acute corner after rlwy bdge. Med, hdg, pt shd, terr, serviced pitches; wc; chem disp; fam bthrm; shwrs inc; EHU (6A) €3.80; gas; lndry; shop; rest; snacks; bar; playgrnd; pool (htd); paddling pool; entmnt; wifi; TV; 40% statics; dogs €3; Eng spkn; adv bkg acc; ccard acc; lake fishing 1km; bike hire; waterslide; games rm; CKE/CCI. "Historical & beautiful area; vg site & facs." ♦ 23 Apr-11 Sep. € 26.50 2014*

SARLAT LA CANEDA *7C3* (11km SE Rural) *44.83274, 1.26626* Camping Le Plein Air des Bories, 24200 Carsac-Aillac [05 53 28 15 67; camping.lesbories@ wanadoo.fr; www.camping-desbories.com] Take D704 SE fr Sarlat sp Gourdon; diff RH turn to site after Carsac vill. Easier access on D703 fr Vitrac. Med, shd, pt sl, wc; fam bthrm; shwrs; EHU (16A) €4.50; gas; lndry; shop; snacks; bar; pool (htd); sw; dogs €3; Eng spkn; quiet; canoe hire; fishing; boating; tennis 700m; CKE/CCI. "Clean, shady rvside site; friendly owners." ♦ 1 Jun-15 Sep. € 24.00 2018*

SARLAT LA CANEDA

SARLAT LA CANEDA 7C3 (10km S Rural) 44.81521, 1.22362 **Camping La Rivière de Domme, 24250 Domme** [05 53 28 33 46; fax 05 53 29 56 04; contact@camping-riviere-domme.com; www.camping-riviere-domme.com] Fr Sarlat take D46 to Vitrac. Cross rv bdge on D46E. In 1km at T-junc turn R on D50 & in 1km turn R at sp into site. Sm, pt shd, wc; chem disp; shwrs inc; EHU (10A) €2.50 (poss rev pol); lndry; shop nr; playgrnd; pool; 10% statics; Eng spkn; adv bkg acc; quiet; games area. "Generous pitches; pleasant owner; modern san facs; many walks fr site." ♦ 4 Apr-3 Oct. € 32.00   2014*

SARLAT LA CANEDA 7C3 (10km S Rural) 44.82181, 1.22587 **Camping Le Bosquet, La Rivière, 24250 Domme** [05 53 28 37 39; fax 05 53 29 41 95; info@lebousquet.com; www.lebosquet.com] Fr Sarlat take D46 S to Vitrac cross rv on D46E. Sp at junc, site 500m on R. Sm, hdg, mkd, pt shd, wc; chem disp; shwrs inc; EHU (6A) €2.50 (long lead poss req); gas; lndry; shop; snacks; pool; sw nr; wifi; 50% statics; dogs €2; Eng spkn; adv bkg acc; quiet; fishing 500m; CKE/CCI. "Lovely peaceful site with friendly, helpful owners; excel updated san facs but poss stretched high ssn; gd shd but sm pitches; gd views of Domme." ♦ 11 Apr-27 Sep. € 27.70   2014*

SARLAT LA CANEDA 7C3 (10km S Rural) 44.81725, 1.21944 **Camping Le Perpetuum, 24250 Domme** [05 53 28 35 18; fax 05 53 29 63 64; leperpetuum.domme@orange.fr; www.campingleperpetuum.com] Fr Sarlat take D46 to Vitrac; cross rv bdge to D46E; in 1km turn R onto D50, R again in 1km at site sp. Med, mkd, hdstg, hdg, pt shd, wc; chem disp; mv service pnt; fam bthrm; shwrs inc; EHU (10A) €3.50; lndry; shop; snacks; bar; bbq; playgrnd; pool; sw nr; entmnt; wifi; TV; dogs €2; Eng spkn; adv bkg acc; quiet; ccard acc; games area; canoeing; CKE/CCI. "Site fronts rv; busy high ssn; relaxed, friendly atmosphere; gd sized pitches; cheerful, helpful owners; gd san facs; gd pool; Rv Dordogne adj; gd local dog walks; late arr area at ent." ♦ 1 May-10 Oct. € 36.20   2014*

See advertisement

SARLAT LA CANEDA 7C3 (10km S Rural) 44.82525, 1.25360 **Domaine de Soleil-Plage, Caudon-par-Montfort, 24200 Vitrac** [05 53 28 33 33; fax 05 53 28 30 24; info@soleilplage.fr; www.soleilplage.fr] On D46, 6km S of Sarlat twd Vitrac, turn L onto D703 to Château Montfort, R to site dir Caudon, sp. Site beyond Camping La Bouysse on rvside, 2km E of Vitrac. If coming fr Souillac on D703, when app Montfort rd v narr with overhanging rock faces. Narr access rds on site. Lge, hdg, pt shd, serviced pitches; wc (htd); chem disp; mv service pnt; fam bthrm; shwrs inc; EHU (16A) inc (poss rev pol); gas; lndry; shop; rest; snacks; bar; bbq; playgrnd; pool (htd); paddling pool; entmnt; wifi; TV; 45% statics; dogs €3.50; phone; Eng spkn; adv bkg req; quiet; ccard acc; waterslide; bike hire; tennis; golf 1km; canoeing; rv fishing adj; horseriding 5km; games rm; CKE/CCI. "Lovely site in beautiful location; friendly, welcoming owner; variety of pitches - extra for serviced/rvside (shady); no o'fits over 7m Jun-Aug; san facs clean; superb aquatic complex; poss muddy when wet; red groups; highly rec; first class comprehensive site." ♦ 8 Apr-29 Sep. € 42.00   2017*

SARLAT LA CANEDA 7C3 (12km S Rural) 44.79175, 1.16599 **Camping Bel Ombrage, 24250 St Cybranet** [05 53 28 34 14; fax 05 53 59 64 64; belombrage@wanadoo.fr; www.belombrage.com] Fr Sarlat take D46 sp Bergerac, rd then conts as D57; after 8km turn L at Vézac sp Castelnaund. After 1.6km at T-junc turn L onto D703 & in 180m turn R onto D57. Cont thro Castelnaund on D57; site on L in 3km. Lge, hdg, shd, wc; chem disp; fam bthrm; shwrs inc; EHU (10A) inc; lndry; shop nr; bar nr; bbq; playgrnd; pool; paddling pool; beach; sw; red long stay; wifi; TV; dogs free; adv bkg acc; quiet; ccard acc; tennis 800m; horseriding 2km; fishing; games area; bike hire; games rm; CKE/CCI. "Attractive, well-run site by rv; popular with British; lge pitches; no o'fits over 8m high ssn; modern san facs; peaceful early ssn; library; ideal base for Dordogne; mkt Thur; excel." ♦ 1 Jun-5 Sep. € 25.00   2017*

SARLAT LA CANEDA

Caudon 24200 VITRAC - France
info@labouysse.com - www.labouysse.com

Site owned by French family. English spoken.

Along the river Dordogne near the well known Caudon rock, direct access to beach area where you can swim or go canoeing. Beautiful site near Montfort château, Sarlat (6km.) and many other Dordogne sights.
Green pitches, with trees and hedges giving some shade.
Lovely swimming pool. A wide range of accommodations available (country cottages, mobile homes, gîtes and pitches).
On the site: grocery´s, bar and snack bar (open from 15th June until 31st August) – washing machine, dryer and iron - WiFi

France

SARLAT LA CANEDA 7C3 (6km S Rural) 44.82375, 1.25080 **Camping La Bouysse de Caudon, 24200 Vitrac [05 53 28 33 05; fax 05 53 30 38 52; info@ labouysse.com; www.labouysse.com]** S fr Sarlat on D46 dir Vitrac. At Vitrac 'port' bef bdge turn L onto D703 sp Carsac. In 2km turn R & foll site sp, site on L. Well sp. Med, mkd, hdg, pt shd, wc; chem disp; fam bthrm; shwrs inc; EHU (10A) €4.80; gas; lndry; shop; rest; snacks; bar; bbq; playgrnd; pool; sw; entmnt; wifi; 8% statics; dogs €2; phone; Eng spkn; adv bkg req; quiet; ccard acc; canoe hire; tennis; fishing; games area; CKE/CCI. "Beautiful family-run site on Rv Dordogne; helpful owner; plenty gd clean san facs; gd access rv beach; muddy when wet; many Bastides in area; excel." ♦ 2 Apr-25 Sep. € 21.70   2014*

See advertisement

SARLAT LA CANEDA 7C3 (9km S Rural) 44.81628, 1.21508 **Camping Beau Rivage, Gaillardou, 24250 La Roque-Gageac [05 53 28 32 05; fax 05 53 29 63 56; camping.beau.rivage@wanadoo.fr; www. beaurivagedordogne.com]** On S side of D703, 1km W of Vitrac adj Rv Dordogne. Lge, mkd, pt shd, wc (htd); chem disp; fam bthrm; shwrs inc; EHU (6A) €3.50; gas; lndry; shop; rest nr; snacks; bar; playgrnd; pool (htd); entmnt; wifi; TV; 10% statics; dogs €3; phone; Eng spkn; adv bkg rec; quiet; games area; horseriding; bike hire; rv; archery; canoeing; tennis; golf 2km. "Gd touring base." ♦ 4 Apr-20 Sep. € 23.60   2013*

SARLAT LA CANEDA 7C3 (9km S Rural) 44.82442, 1.16759 **Camping La Plage, 83 Près La Roque-Gageac, 24220 Vézac [05 53 29 50 83 or 06 85 23 22 16 (mob); campinglaplage24@orange.fr; www. camping-laplage.fr]** On banks of Rv Dordogne, 500m W of La Roque-Gageac on D703. Med, mkd, shd, wc; chem disp; shwrs inc; EHU (3A) €2.40; gas; shop nr; bbq; playgrnd; pool; sw; 10% statics; adv bkg acc; quiet; canoeing; fishing; CKE/CCI. "Attractive site; excel pitches; kind, helpful owers; ltd facs LS; highly rec; upgraded (2014) immac, well kept san facs."
1 Apr-30 Sep. € 20.00   2014*

SARLAT LA CANEDA 7C3 (9km S Rural) 44.78648, 1.20930 **Camping Le Pech de Caumont, 24250 Cénac-et-St-Julien [05 53 28 21 63 or 05 53 28 30 67; fax 05 53 29 99 73; jmilhac@pech-de-caumont.com; www.pech-de-caumont.com]** D46 fr Sarlat to Cénac, cross rv & cont on D46 thro Cénac; site ent on L 500m past End of Vill sp. Do not go thro Domme. Med, hdg, mkd, pt shd, pt sl, terr, wc; chem disp; shwrs inc; EHU (6A) €3.10; lndry; shop nr; bar; bbq; playgrnd; pool; sw nr; TV; 20% statics; dogs; phone; Eng spkn; adv bkg acc; quiet; ccard acc; CKE/CCI. "Views fr most pitches; modern, clean san facs; helpful owners; popular, tidy, family-run site; excel." 15 Jun-15 Sep. € 15.40   2012*

"There aren't many sites open at this time of year"

If you're travelling outside peak season remember to call ahead to check site opening dates – even if the entry says 'open all year'.

SARLAT LA CANEDA 7C3 (10km SW Rural) 44.83819, 1.14846 **Camping Le Capeyrou, 24220 Beynac-et-Cazenac [05 53 29 54 95; fax 05 53 28 36 27; lecapeyrou@wanadoo.fr; www.campinglecapeyrou. com]** Fr W on D703 on R (opp sm supmkt & baker) immed past vill of Beynac. Or fr N on D57 fr Sarlat; in vill immed on L on rv. Med, hdg, hdstg, pt shd, wc; chem disp; mv service pnt; fam bthrm; shwrs inc; EHU (6-10A) €3.50-4.20; lndry; shop nr; rest nr; snacks; bar; playgrnd; pool; wifi; dogs €2; Eng spkn; adv bkg acc; ccard acc. "View of chateau most pitches; helpful, friendly owners; clean san facs; excel lge pool; rvside walk to attractive vill; excel NH; canoeing; hot air ballooning; v muddy when wet." ♦ Apr-30 Sep. € 28.00   2015*

SARLAT LA CANEDA

SARLAT LA CANEDA 7C3 (10km SW Rural) 44.80519, 1.15852 **Camping Maisonneuve, Vallée de Céou, 24250 Castelnaud-la-Chapelle [05 53 29 51 29; fax 05 53 30 27 06; contact@campingmaisonneuve. com; www.campingmaisonneuve.com]** Take D57 SW fr Sarlat sp Beynac. Cross Rv Dordogne at Castelnaud; site sp 500m on L out of Castelnaud on D57 twd Daglan. Foll narr rd across bdge (or alt ent - cont on D57 for 2km, sp on L for c'vans. Med, mkd, hdstg, hdg, pt shd, wc (htd); chem disp; mv service pnt; fam bthrm; shwrs inc; EHU (6-10A) €4-4.90; gas; lndry; shop; rest; snacks; bar; bbq; playgrnd; pool; paddling pool; entmnt; wifi; TV; 10% statics; dogs €2; Eng spkn; adv bkg req; quiet; ccard acc; rv; games rm; tennis 2km; bike hire; fishing; CKE/CCI. "Vg, spacious site; helpful owners; modern, clean facs; gd walking, cycling." ♦ 27 Mar-2 Nov. € 20.40   2017*

See advertisement

"That's changed – Should I let the Club know?"

If you find something on site that's different from the site entry, fill in a report and let us know. See camc.com/europereport.

SARLAT LA CANEDA 7C3 (12km SW Rural) 44.82585, 1.15322 **Camping La Cabane, 24220 Vézac [05 53 29 52 28; contact@lacabanedordogne.com; www. lacabanedordogne.com]** Fr Sarlat-La-Canéda take D57 thro Vézac. On leaving Vézac turn L immed bef rlwy bdge, site sp on R on bank of Rv Dordogne. Lge, hdg, mkd, pt shd, wc; shwrs inc; EHU (6-10A) €2.60-3.15; gas; lndry; shop; rest nr; bbq; playgrnd; pool (covrd, htd); sw nr; wifi; TV; 10% statics; dogs €1; phone; Eng spkn; adv bkg acc; quiet; ccard acc; CKE/ CCI. "Well-shd, rvside site; lge pitches; clean facs; friendly, helpful family owners; rvside walk to Beynac Château; gd; 2nd san facs block modernised (2015)." ♦ 1 Apr-30 Sep. € 18.00   2015*

SARLAT LA CANEDA 7C3 (8km SW Rural) 44.83560, 1.15873 **Camping Les Deux Vallées, La Gare, 24220 Vézac [05 53 29 53 55; fax 05 53 31 09 81; contact@ campingles2vallees.com; www.campingles2vallees. com]** Exit A20 junc 55 onto D804 dir Sarlat-La-Caneda; cont onto D703/D704A/D704 to Sarlat; then take D57 SW to Vézac; immed after sp for vill take 1st R to site. Or fr E leave D703 onto D57; 250m after junc with D49 turn L & foll sp to site. Med, mkd, hdstg, hdg, pt shd, wc (htd); chem disp; fam bthrm; shwrs inc; EHU (6-10A) €4.10; gas; lndry; shop; rest; snacks; bar; bbq; playgrnd; pool; red long stay; TV; 6% statics; dogs €2; Eng spkn; adv bkg req; ccard acc; games area; bike hire; games rm; ice; CKE/CCI. "Excel site; helpful, friendly Dutch owners; ltd san facs LS; poss muddy when wet; entmnt July/Aug (in Dutch); gd local walks; poss long leads req; some reverse polarity; ltd water points; pitch 71,72 &73 too restricted for c'van access." ♦ 17 Feb-12 Nov. € 41.00   2013*

SARLAT LA CANEDA 7C3 (9km W Rural) 44.90805, 1.11527 **Camping Le Moulin du Roch, Le Roch, Route des Eyzies, 24200 Sarlat-la-Canéda [05 53 59 20 27; fax 05 53 59 20 95; moulin.du.roch@ wanadoo.fr; www.moulin-du-roch.com or www. les-castels.com]** Fr A20 take exit 55 at Souillac dir Sarlat. Head for D704 twds Sarlat La Caneda. At rndabt in Sarlat (just under rlwy viaduct) take 2nd exit onto bypass. Take 2nd exit at next rndabt staying on D704. At next rndabt take 2nd exit onto D6 dir Les Eyzies (becomes D47). Site on L in approx 9 km on D47. Fr N on D704 to Sarlat, turn R at hypmkt, then as above. Lge, mkd, hdg, pt shd, terr, serviced pitches; wc (htd); chem disp; mv service pnt; fam bthrm; shwrs inc; EHU (6A) inc; gas; lndry; shop; rest; snacks; bar; bbq (charcoal, gas); playgrnd; pool (htd); paddling pool; red long stay; twin axles; entmnt; wifi; TV; 45% statics; Eng spkn; adv bkg rec; quiet; ccard acc; horseriding nr; games rm; canoeing nr; lake fishing; tennis; CKE/ CCI. "Well-run, family owned site; lge pitches; clean facs but poss long, steep walk; some noise fr adj rd; gd rest & pool; m'vans poss not acc after prolonged heavy rain due soft grnd; mkt Sat." ♦ 17 May-20 Sep. € 52.00   2014*

SARZEAU 2G3 (8km SE Coastal) 47.50551, -2.68308
Camping Manoir de Ker An Poul, 1 Route de la Grée, Penvins, 56370 Sarzeau [02 57 62 04 65; manoirdekeranpoul@wanadoo.fr; www.manoirdekeranpoul.com] Fr E exit N165 1km E of Muzillac, sp Sarzeau D20 & cont approx 20km to junc of D20 & D199, S on D199 sp Penvins. Fr W, 6km E of Vannes, exit N165 onto N780 sp Sarzeau, in 9.5km S onto D199 sp Penvins. Lge, hdg, pt shd, pt sl, wc; chem disp; fam bthrm; shwrs inc; EHU (6-10A) €4; lndry; shop; rest nr; snacks; bar; bbq; playgrnd; pool (htd, indoor); beach sand 1km; entmnt; wifi; TV; 30% statics; dogs €4; Eng spkn; adv bkg acc; quiet; tennis; games area; bike hire; CKE/CCI. "Spacious pitches; warm welcome; excel staff; no dog walk on site; san facs recently renovated (2015); noisy weekend nr pool, quieter mid week." ♦ 7 Apr-23 Sep. € 41.00   2018*

SARZEAU 2G3 (3km S Coastal) 47.50720, -2.76083
Camping La Ferme de Lann Hoëdic, Rue Jean de la Fontaine, Route de Roaliguen, 56370 Sarzeau [02 97 48 01 73; contact@camping-lannhoedic.fr; www.camping-lannhoedic.fr] Fr Vannes on N165 turn onto D780 dir Sarzeau. Do not ent Sarzeau, but at Super U rndabt foll sp Le Roaliguen. After 1.5km turn L to Lann Hoëdic. Med, mkd, pt shd, wc (htd); chem disp; mv service pnt; fam bthrm; shwrs inc; EHU (16A); gas; lndry; shop nr; rest nr; snacks; bar nr; playgrnd; beach sand 800m; wifi; 10% statics; dogs €2; phone; Eng spkn; adv bkg acc; quiet; ccard acc; bike hire; CKE/CCI. "Peaceful, well-managed, popular, family-run site; warm welcome; excel, clean facs; beautiful coastline - beaches & dunes; highly rec." ♦ 1 Apr-31 Oct. € 24.50   2017*

SARZEAU 2G3 (2km SW Rural) 47.52355, -2.79713
Lodge Club Presqu'île de Rhuys (formerly Le Bohat), Route d'Arzon Lower Bohat, 56370 Sarzeau [02 97 41 78 68; fax 02 97 41 71 97; info@lodgeclub.fr; www.lodgeclub.fr] Fr Vannes on N165, exit onto D780 to Sarzeau. Do not turn off this main rd to Sarzeau (town not suitable for m'vans or c'vans) but cont twd Arzon; 1km after 2nd rndabt turn L for Le Bohat & Spernec, then take 1st R. Fr S on N165 take D20 at Muzillac, thro Surzur & cont to join D780 to Sarzeau. Then as above. Lge, hdg, mkd, pt shd, wc; chem disp; mv service pnt; fam bthrm; shwrs inc; EHU (10A) inc; gas; lndry; shop; rest; snacks; bar; bbq (charcoal, gas); playgrnd; pool (covrd, htd); paddling pool; beach sand 4km; entmnt; wifi; TV; 4% statics; dogs €3.70; phone; Eng spkn; adv bkg acc; quiet; ccard acc; bike hire; fishing; golf 6km; waterslide; horseriding 2km; games rm; watersports 4km; CKE/CCI. "Busy, well-kept, Dutch-owned site; pony rides; lge pitches; excel, helpful staff; clean san facs; excel pools; gd for families; cycle tracks; gd touring base; mkt Thu; vg." ♦ 5 Apr-29 Sep. € 34.00   2012*

SAULIEU 6G1 (1km N Rural) 47.28936, 4.22401
Camping Le Perron/Camping de Saulieu, Route de Paris, 21210 Saulieu [03 80 64 16 19; camping.salieu@wanadoo.fr; www.aquadis-loisirs.com] On D906 on L of rd on ent fr N. Sp. Lge, mkd, hdg, pt shd, pt sl, wc (htd); chem disp; mv service pnt; shwrs inc; EHU (10A) €3.90; gas; lndry; shop; rest; bar; playgrnd; pool; paddling pool; wifi; dogs €1.50; adv bkg acc; tennis; lake fishing; CKE/CCI. "Nr town but rural feel; quiet at far end of site, away fr pool & playgrnd; no twin axles; many rests in town; gd walking area; gd." ♦ 15 Mar-30 Oct. € 25.00   2014*

> **"I like to fill in the reports as I travel from site to site"**
>
> You'll find report forms at the back of this guide, or you can fill them in online at camc.com/europereport.

SAUMUR 4G1 (2km N Urban) 47.25990, -0.06440
Flower Camping de L'Ile d'Offard, Rue de Verden, 49400 Saumur [02 41 40 30 00; fax 02 41 67 37 81; iledoffard@flowercampings.com; www.saumur-camping.com or www.flowercampings.com] Exit A85 junc 3 onto D347 and then D347E; ent town past rlwy stn & cross Rv Loire bdge; turn L immed over bdge & alongside rv. At rndabt turn L & take 1st L to site; foll sp. Site on island facing Saumur castle. Lge, mkd, hdg, hdstg, pt shd, pt sl, wc (htd); chem disp; mv service pnt; fam bthrm; shwrs inc; EHU (10A) (poss rev pol); gas; lndry; shop; rest; snacks; bar; playgrnd; pool (htd); paddling pool; sw nr; entmnt; wifi; TV; 20% statics; dogs €1.50; Eng spkn; adv bkg req; ccard acc; tennis; boating adj; fishing adj; games area; jacuzzi; bike hire; CKE/CCI. "Pleasant, busy, well-run site; ideal for children; hdstg pitches in winter; helpful staff; clean, most pitches lge but some v sm pitches bet statics - lge o'fits check in advance; gd bar & rest; can be muddy when wet; gd cycle rtes; nice rvside and bdge walk to town; excel, but busy; great facs; easy acc to city; san facs refurb, modern & clean (2015); recep clsd 1200-1400; lovely loc; gd base for visiting Loire Valley; 35 placement municiple area adj, acc by card." ♦ 17 Mar-28 Oct. € 36.00   2018*

SAUMUR 4G1 (7km NE Rural) 47.29937, -0.01218
Camping Le Pô Doré, 49650 Allonnes [02 41 38 78 80 or 06 09 26 31 28 (mob); camping.du.po.dore@wanadoo.fr; www.camping-lepodore.com] NE fr Saumur on N347 & turn R onto D10. Site 3km W of Allonnes on R. Med, mkd, hdg, hdstg, pt shd, wc; chem disp; mv service pnt; shwrs inc; EHU (6-10A) €3-4 (poss rev pol); lndry; rest; snacks; bar; playgrnd; pool (htd); entmnt; wifi; 25% statics; dogs €1.50; phone; Eng spkn; ccard acc; bike hire; CKE/CCI. "Gd, clean & tidy site; helpful staff; dirty, sandy soil; conv wine rtes, caves, museums & a'route; conv NH/sh stay; excel san facs; spectacular laggon." ♦ 15 Mar-15 Nov. € 29.00   2017*

SAUMUR

SAUMUR 4G1 (6km E Rural) 47.24755, -0.00033
Camping Domaine de la Brèche, 5 Impasse de la Brèche, 49730 Varennes-sur-Loire [02 41 51 22 92; fax 02 41 51 27 24; mail@etang-breche.com; www.domainedelabreche.com or www.les-castels.com]
Exit 3 of A85, then D767 & D347 twrds Saumur, then D952 twd Tours & site sp fr either dir. Site on N side of rd (6km W of Varennes) app fr lge lay-by giving easy ent. Lge, hdg, pt shd, serviced pitches; wc; chem disp; mv service pnt; fam bthrm; shwrs inc; EHU (16A); gas; lndry; shop; rest; snacks; bar; playgrnd; pool (htd); entmnt; wifi; TV; 30% statics; dogs; phone; Eng spkn; adv bkg rec; ccard acc; waterslide; tennis; bike hire; games rm; CKE/CCI. "Spacious site & pitches; well-organised; excel facs; auto barrier clsd 2300-0700; helpful staff; excel." ♦
14 Apr-09 Sep. € 45.00   2017*

SAUMUR 4G1 (8km NW Rural) 47.29440, -0.14120
Camping de Chantepie, Route de Chantepie, 49400 St Hilaire-St Florent [02 41 67 95 34; fax 02 41 67 95 85; info@campingchantepie.com; www.campingchantepie.com] Fr Saumer take D751 on S bank of Rv Loire sp Gennes. Turn L 3km N of St Hilaire-St-Florent just bef lge sp for a supmkt & bef mushroom museum. Site sp. Or fr N after x-ing rv on N347, take turn sp St Hilaire-St-Florent & join D751 for Gennes; site is 3km N of St Hilaire-St Florent, well sp fr D751. NB Easy to miss turning. Lge, mkd, hdg, pt shd, wc (htd); chem disp; mv service pnt; fam bthrm; shwrs inc; EHU (10A) inc (poss rev pol); gas; lndry; shop; snacks; bar; bbq; playgrnd; pool (covrd, htd); paddling pool; entmnt; wifi; TV; 10% statics; dogs €4; Eng spkn; adv bkg acc; quiet; ccard acc; golf 2km; games rm; horseriding 5km; tennis 2km; bike hire; fishing; CKE/CCI. "Excel well-run site nr rv; well-spaced, lge pitches, some with excel rv views, ltd access to some pitches diff lge o'fits; friendly, helpful staff; no o'fits over 10m; boating 5km; excel san facs, conv Loire cycle rte; mkt Sat Saumur; excel views, bar & rest; excel cycle track; TV recep may be diff due to many trees." ♦ 4 May-26 Sep. € 39.00   2016*

SAUMUR 4G1 (9km NW Rural) 47.30982, -0.14492
Camping Terre d'Entente (formerly La Croix Rouge), Lieu dit de la Croix Rouge, 49160 St Martin-de-la-Place [09 72 30 31 72 or 07 70 07 69 37; fax 09 72 30 31 70; contact@terre-dentente.fr; terre-dentente.fr]
Exit A85 junc 3 sp Saumur. Take slip rd immed bef bdge then L sp 'Angers Touristique'. Site on L at vill sp. Fr Saumur take D347 N across rv then turn L onto D952 dir Angers. At St Martin-de-la-Place foll sp for site. Med, mkd, pt shd, wc; chem disp; mv service pnt; shwrs; EHU (6-10A) €3-4; lndry; shop nr; rest nr; bar nr; playgrnd; sw nr; wifi; dogs €1.50; bus 150m; Eng spkn; adv bkg acc; quiet; sailing adj; CKE/CCI. "Beautiful, tranquil site on Rv Loire; friendly, helpful owners; 26 steps to spacious san facs; disabled facs at grnd level; 2m high security fence by rv; barrier clsd 2200-0700; no twin axles; conv Saumur; bar 200m; v pleasant site; poor." ♦ 8 Apr-30 Sep. € 18.00   2017*

SAVENAY 2G3 (3km E Rural) 47.35651, -1.92136
Camp Municipal du Lac de Savenay, Route du Lac, 44260 Savenay [02 40 58 31 76; www.camping-lac-savenay.fr] Site well sp in Savenay. Can avoid Savenay Town by turning off N165 SW of town on new rd, dir LAC. Med, mkd, pt shd, terr, wc (htd); shwrs inc; EHU (10A) €2.07; lndry; snacks; playgrnd; dogs €1.20; Eng spkn; quiet; fishing. "Vg, clean site in attractive lakeside park; lge pitches; gas adj; pool adj; excel modern san block; terr pitches req long elec leads." ♦
1 Mar-31 Oct. € 26.00   2016*

SAVERNE 6E3 (2km SW Urban) 48.73329, 7.35371
Camping Les Portes d'Alsace (formerly Camping de Saverne), Rue du Père Libermann, 67700 Saverne [03 88 91 35 65; contact@camping-lesportesdalsace.com; www.vacances-seasonova.com]
Take Saverne exit fr A4, junc 45. Site well sp nr town cent. Med, hdg, mkd, hdstg, pt shd, pt sl, terr, wc (htd); chem disp; mv service pnt; shwrs inc; EHU (6-10A) €3.10-5.70 (poss rev pol); lndry; shop nr; playgrnd; wifi; 20% statics; dogs €1.60; adv bkg acc; quiet; ccard acc; CKE/CCI. "Pleasant, busy, well-run site; pitches mostly terr; warm welcome, friendly staff; long steep walk back fr town; m'van aire de service nr ent; trains to Strasbourg fr town; poss travellers; gd." ♦
31 Mar-4 Nov. € 27.00   2018*

SAVIGNY EN VERON 4G1 (1km W Rural) 47.20059, 0.13932 FFCC Camping La Fritillaire, Rue Basse, 37420 Savigny-en-Véron [02 47 58 03 79; fax 02 47 58 03 81; www.aquadis-loisirs.com]
Fr Montsoreau on D751 or D7 on S bank of Rv Loire, foll sp to Savigny-en-Véron & site. Med, mkd, pt shd, wc (htd); chem disp; mv service pnt; fam bthrm; shwrs inc; EHU (10A) inc (poss rev pol); lndry; rest nr; bar nr; bbq; playgrnd; 10% statics; dogs €1; adv bkg acc; quiet; bike hire; horseriding; tennis; CKE/CCI. "Excel, peaceful site; htd covrd pool 4km; friendly owners; gd clean facs, ltd LS; gd touring base Loire chateaux; vg cycle rtes; games area (under-7s); poss workers staying on site (2009)." ♦ 29 Mar-20 Oct.
€ 13.00   2013*

SEDAN 5C1 (1km S Urban) 49.69868, 4.93848 Camp Municipal La Prairie, Prairie de Torcy, Blvd Fabert, 08200 Sedan [03 24 27 13 05 or 03 24 27 73 42; fax 03 24 22 14 78; christophe.lagnier@mairie-sedan.fr]
Fr A34(A203) exit junc 4 dir Sedan cent. Cont strt thro town & over rlwy bdge; in 500m cont over viaduct, site visible on R, turn R at next traff lts at end of viaduct, site 100m on R. Easy to find. Med, pt shd, wc; chem disp; mv service pnt; shwrs inc; EHU (10A) €3.15; lndry; shop nr; rest nr; bar nr; bbq; playgrnd; red long stay; dogs €1; phone; adv bkg acc; CKE/CCI. "Pleasant, peaceful site in lovely spot by rv; haphazard parking; rough/uneven grnd; friendly, helpful staff; san facs dated but clean; poss muddy when wet; pleasant walk to interesting town; mkt traders for fair mid-Sep; gd value; highly rec; pool 500m; local Patisserie comes to site." ♦ 1 Apr-30 Sep. € 8.50   2016*

SEES *4E1* (1km S Urban) *48.59875, 0.17103* **Camp Municipal Le Clos Normand, Ave du 8 mai 1945, 61500 Sées [02 33 28 87 37 or 02 33 28 74 79 (LS); fax 02 33 28 18 13; contact@camping-sees.fr; www.ville-sees.fr]** C'vans & lge m'vans best app fr S - twd rndabt at S end of by-pass (rec use this rndabt as other rtes diff & narr). Well sp. Narr ent. Sm, hdg, pt shd, wc; chem disp; mv service pnt; shwrs inc; EHU (10A) €2.50; gas; lndry; shop nr; rest nr; bar nr; playgrnd; wifi; 10% statics; dogs €1.25; Eng spkn; adv bkg acc; fishing; CKE/CCI. "Spacious, well-cared for pitches; helpful, friendly warden; gd san facs, poss stretched if site full; excel mv service pnt; gates clsd 2100 (2000 LS); easy walk to town; shop nr; vg." ♦ 16 Apr-30 Sep. € 13.00   2018*

SEGRE *2F4* (7km NW Rural) *47.71003, -0.95165* **Camping Parc de St Blaise, 49520 Noyant-la-Gravoyère [02 41 61 93 09; fax 02 41 61 44 68; campingstblaise@orange.fr; www.camping saintblaise.fr]** Fr Segré take D775 dir Pouancé to Noyant, site/park sp in vill on R. Sm, hdg, pt shd, terr, wc; chem disp; shwrs inc; EHU (6A) inc; shop; rest; bar; playgrnd; sw nr; entmnt; dogs; phone; horseriding; fishing; CKE/CCI. "Clean, well-maintained site in leisure park; gd views; aquatic park; slate mine worth visit." ♦ 15 Jun-30 Sep. € 17.00   2014*

SEILHAC *7C4* (4km SW Rural) *45.35018, 1.64642* **Camp Municipal du Pilard, La Barthe, 19700 Lagraulière [05 55 73 71 04; fax 05 55 73 25 28; mairie.lagrauliere@wanadoo.fr; www.lagrauliere.correze.net]** Exit A20 junc 46 onto D34 to Lagraulière, site sp. NB Lge o'fits rec take D44 & D167E fr Seilhac. Sm, mkd, pt shd, wc; chem disp; shwrs inc; EHU (3-6A) €3 (poss rev pol); shop nr; rest nr; bar nr; bbq; playgrnd; dogs €1; Eng spkn; quiet; tennis; CKE/CCI. "Quiet, clean site nr pleasant interesting vill; htd pool adj; warden calls; mkts on Thurs." ♦ 15 Jun-15 Sep. € 10.00   2014*

SEISSAN *8F3* (2km WNW Rural) *43.49554, 0.57815* **Domaine Lacs de Gascogne, Route Du Lac, 32260 Seissan [05 62 66 27 94; info@domainelacsdegascogne.eu; www.domaine lacsdegascogne.eu]** V lge, mkd, pt shd, pt sl, wc; chem disp; mv service pnt; fam bthrm; EHU (16A); lndry; rest; snacks; bar; bbq; playgrnd; pool; twin axles; entmnt; wifi; TV; 25% statics; dogs (max 1 per reservation, €3 per night); bus 2km; Eng spkn; adv bkg acc; HCAP ltd; bike hire; games area; showrs; games rm; pool paddling; CKE/CCI. "Tennis, separate carpk; walks; watersports; tourist attractions; table tennis; pool; sauna; carp fishing; vg." 31 Mar-30 Sep. € 32.00   2018*

SELESTAT *6E3* (7km N Rural) *48.30647, 7.50057* **Camping Rural (Weiss), 17 Rue du Buhl, 67600 Ebersheim [06 85 10 95 54; theo.sonntag@wanadoo.fr]** Fr S or N on N83 in vill of Ebersheim foll green Camping Rural sps. Sm, pt shd, wc; shwrs inc; EHU (16A) inc; shop nr; bbq; dogs free; bus 0.5km; Eng spkn; adv bkg acc; quiet; CKE/CCI. "Gd touring base; friendly, helpful staff; excel Boulangerie in vill; site self, staff visit pm." ♦ 15 Jun-15 Sep. € 13.00   2017*

SELESTAT *6E3* (1km SW Urban) *48.25470, 7.44781* **Camp Municipal Les Cigognes, Rue de la 1ère D.F.L, 67600 Sélestat [03 88 92 03 98; fax 03 88 92 88 63; camping@ville-selestat.fr; http://camping.selestat.fr]** Site sp D1083 & D424. Fr S town cent turn E off D1083 & foll sps to site adj schools & playing fields. Med, mkd, pt shd, wc; chem disp; mv service pnt; shwrs inc; EHU (6-16A) inc; gas; lndry; shop; rest nr; bar; playgrnd; entmnt; wifi; dogs €1; train to Strasbourg nrby; Eng spkn; adv bkg rec; quiet; CKE/CCI. "Great, well-run site; helpful staff; pool 300m; some noise fr local football area; excel new san blocks; easy walk to old town; mkt Sat; rec." ♦ 1 Apr-15 Oct & 15 Nov-24 Dec. € 15.50   2016*

SELESTAT *6E3* (12km W Rural) *48.27287, 7.29052* **Camping du Haut-Koenigsbourg, Rue de la Vancelle, 68660 Lièpvre [03 89 58 43 20; fax 03 89 58 98 29; camping.haut-koenigsbourg@wanadoo.fr; www.liepvre.fr/camping]** Fr Sélestat W on N59 twd Lièpvre vill then R at factory car park & foll site sps. Fr Ste Marie-aux-Mines on N59 turn L at rndabt after tunnel. Med, mkd, pt sl, wc (htd); mv service pnt; shwrs inc; EHU (4-8A) €3-4.20; lndry; shop nr; bar; bbq; playgrnd; TV; 10% statics; dogs €2; quiet; CKE/CCI. "V well maintained site; gd location; rec; gd walks & cycling; lovely site." ♦ 15 Mar-15 Oct. € 12.50   2012*

⊞ **SEMUR EN AUXOIS** *6G1* (4km S Rural) *47.46812, 4.35589* **FFCC Camping Lac de Pont, 16 Rue du Lac, 21140 Pont-et-Massène [03 80 97 01 26 or 03 80 97 01 26 (LS); contact@camping-lacdepont.fr or camping-lacdepont@orange.fr; www.campinglacdepont.fr]** Exit A6 junc 23 twd Semur-en-Auxois on D980; after sh dist turn R sp 'Lac de Pont' D103. Med, hdg, pt shd, pt sl, wc; chem disp; mv service pnt; fam bthrm; shwrs inc; EHU (6A) €3.50; gas; lndry; shop; rest nr; snacks; bar; bbq; playgrnd; sw nr; dogs €2; phone; Eng spkn; quiet; ccard acc; tennis; watersports; games rm; bike hire; CKE/CCI. "Warm welcome, helpful owners; generous pitches, some shady; san facs dated; vg for teenagers - games/meeting rm; 'Petit Train' goes round site & into Semur; cycle rte/walks adj; gd touring base; nr A6 m'way; diving platform; walled, medieval town; muddy pitches; site neglected (2017), NH only." € 15.00   2017*

SENNECEY LE GRAND

PICTURE YOURSELF..ON A SANDY SHORELINE

Le Sérignan Plage

34410 Sérignan France - Tel : +33 4 67 32 35 33
info@leserignanplage.com - www.leserignanplage.com

SENNECEY LE GRAND 6H1 (7km E Rural) 46.65480, 4.94061 **Château de L'Epervière, Rue du Château, 71240 Gigny-sur-Saône [03 85 94 16 90; fax 03 85 94 16 97; info@domaine-eperviere.com; www.domaine-eperviere.com]** Fr N exit A6 junc 26 (Chalon Sud) onto N6 dir Mâcon & Tournus; at Sennecey-le-Grand turn E onto D18 sp Gigny-sur-Saône; site sp 1km S of Gigny-sur-Saône. Or fr S exit A6 junc 27 (Tournus) onto N6 N to Sennecey-le-Grand, then as above. NB Diff to find signs fr main rd. Lge, hdstg, hdg, mkd, pt shd, wc (htd); chem disp; mv service pnt; fam bthrm; shwrs inc; EHU (6A) inc; gas; lndry; shop; rest; snacks; bar; bbq; playgrnd; pool (covrd, htd); paddling pool; entmnt; wifi; TV; dogs €3; Eng spkn; adv bkg acc; quiet; ccard acc; sauna; bike hire; tennis 400m; fishing; games rm; jacuzzi; CKE/CCI. "Superb, spacious, well-run site in grnds of chateau nr sm lake; lovely, lge pitches; warm welcome, pleasant staff; excel san facs; gd pools & rest; vg for families; wine tasting; tour op statics; lake nrby; interesting wild life; no o'fits over 18m high ssn; boggy when wet; conv NH fr a'route; fantastic site; level pitches; great facs." ♦ 1 Apr-30 Sep. € 40.00 2016*

SENNECEY LE GRAND 6H1 (5km NW Rural) 46.67160, 4.83301 **Camping La Héronnière, Les Lacs de Laives, 71240 Laives [03 85 44 98 85; camping.laives@wanadoo.fr; www.camping-laheronniere.com]** Exit A6 junc 26 (fr N) or junc 27 (fr S) onto N6. Turn W at Sennecey-le-Grand to Laives. Foll sp 'Lacs de Laives'. Sp on D18. Med, hdg, mkd, hdstg, pt shd, wc; chem disp; shwrs inc; EHU (6A) €4.80; lndry; shop; rest nr; snacks; playgrnd; pool (htd); sw nr; dogs €1.60; Eng spkn; adv bkg acc; quiet; fishing; windsurfing; bike hire; watersports; CKE/CCI. "Lovely, level, lakeside site; busy NH; may fill up after 1500; popular with bikers; vg; pretty site; laid back helpful staff; gd NH; romantic rest by lakeside 3 mins walk (high ssn); excel facs; san facs ok but dirty." ♦ 3 Mar-4 Nov. € 27.00 2018*

SENS 4F4 (1km S Urban) 48.18312, 3.28803 **Camp Municipal Entre Deux Vannes, Ave de Senigallia, 89100 Sens [03 86 65 64 71 or 03 86 65 37 42 (LS); fax 03 86 95 39 41; http://ville-sens.fr]** D606/D1060 S of town. Take D606a sp sens. Site on R in 600m. Med, mkd, pt shd, wc; chem disp; mv service pnt; fam bthrm; shwrs inc; EHU (16A) inc; lndry; shop nr; rest nr; playgrnd; adv bkg rec; ccard acc; CKE/CCI. "Excel site; opp rv & superb park area; friendly, helpful warden; san facs old but clean; gate locked 2200; easy walk to town; ensure height barrier moved bef ent." 15 May-15 Sep. € 13.50 2014*

SERIGNAC 7D3 (5km W Rural) 44.43103, 1.06902 **Camping Le Clos Barrat (Naturist)**, 46700 Sérignac [06 47 50 09 78 or 04 74 24 60 82; info@ leclosbarrat.fr; www.leclosbarrat.fr] Fr Fumel by-pass turn S on D139 to Montayral, rd cont but becomes D4. Site sp bet Mauroux & St Matré. Med, mkd, pt shd, pt sl, wc (htd); own san rec; chem disp; fam bthrm; shwrs inc; EHU (6A) inc; gas; lndry; rest; snacks; bar; bbq (gas); playgrnd; pool; paddling pool; twin axles; entmnt; wifi; TV; 2% statics; dogs €2.50; phone; Eng spkn; adv bkg acc; quiet; ccard acc; games rm; CKE/CCI. "Nr Rv Lot; INF card req - can be bought on site; new owners (2015); helpful staff; excel & friendly site; beautiful area." 1 May-25 Sep. € 29.00   2017*

SERIGNAN PLAGE 10F1 (1km W Coastal) 43.26398, 3.3210 **Yelloh! Village Le Sérignan Plage, Les Orpelières, 34410 Sérignan-Plage** [04 67 32 35 33; fax 04 67 32 26 36; info@leserignanplage.com; www. leserignanplage.com or www.yellohvillage.co.uk] Exit A9 junc 35. After toll turn L at traff lts onto N112 & at 1st rndabt strt on to D64. In 5km turn L onto D37E Sérignan-Plage, turn R on narr 1-way rd to site. Adj to Camping Sérignan-Plage Nature (Naturist site). V lge, mkd, hdg, pt shd, wc; chem disp; mv service pnt; fam bthrm; shwrs inc; EHU (5A) inc; gas; lndry; shop; rest; snacks; bar; bbq; playgrnd; pool (covrd, htd); paddling pool; sw; entmnt; wifi; TV; 80% statics; dogs €4; Eng spkn; adv bkg acc; tennis; horseriding; CKE/CCI. "Busy, even LS; excel pool; Club Nautique - sw, sailing & water-ski tuition on private beach; use of naturist private beach & facs adj; some tourers amongst statics & sm sep touring area." 21 Apr-2 Oct. € 48.00   2016*

See advertisement opposite

SERIGNAN PLAGE 10F1 (2km W Coastal) 43.26308, 3.31976 **Camping Le Sérignan-Plage Nature (Naturist), Les Orpelière, 34410 Sérignan-Plage** [04 67 32 09 61; fax 04 67 32 26 36; info@leserignan nature.com; www.leserignannature.com] Exit A9 junc 36 Beziers Est onto D64. At Sérignan town turn L on D37E to Sérignan-Plage. After 4km turn R on single-lane dual c'way. At T-junc turn L & immed L again in 50m to site. Lge, mkd, pt shd, wc; chem disp; mv service pnt; fam bthrm; shwrs inc; EHU (5A) inc (poss rev pol); gas; lndry; shop; rest; snacks; bar; bbq; playgrnd; pool; beach sand; red long stay; wifi; TV; 75% statics; dogs €6; Eng spkn; adv bkg rec; golf 15km; bike hire; CKE/CCI. "Lovely, clean site & facs; helpful staff; Cmp Le Sérignan Plage (non-naturist) adj with use of same private beach & facs; pool also shared - for naturists' use 1000-1200 only; beauty cent; cycle rtes adj; excel." 21 Apr-2 Oct. € 47.00   2017*

SERIGNAN PLAGE 10F1 (5km W Rural) 43.26965, 3.28631 **FFCC Camping Le Paradis, Route de Valras-Plage, 34410 Sérignan** [04 67 32 24 03; www. camping-leparadis.com] Exit A9 junc 35 Béziers Est onto D64 dir Valras-Plage. Site on L on rndabt at S end of Sérignan by-pass, 1.5km S of Sérignan. Med, mkd, pt shd, wc; chem disp; shwrs; EHU (6A) inc; gas; lndry; shop; rest; snacks; bar; playgrnd; pool; beach sand 2km; red long stay; Eng spkn; adv bkg rec; CKE/ CCI. "Excel, well-kept, family-run site; immac san facs; nr gd beaches; vg value LS; EHU poss no earth." ♦ 1 Apr-30 Sep. € 33.50   2012*

SERRES 9D3 (1km S Rural) 44.41941, 5.71840 **Camping des Barillons, Route de Nice, 05700 Serres** [04 92 67 17 35 or 06 30 50 31 58; campingdesbarillons@free. fr; campingdesbarillons.free.fr] D4075 dir Sistoron fr town ctr. Sm, pt shd, chem disp; shwrs; EHU (6A); lndry; snacks; bar; bbq; playgrnd; pool (covrd, htd); entmnt; wifi; dogs €1.60; adv bkg acc;.; CKE/CCI. "Gd" 1 Apr-30 Sep. € 20.00   2017*

SERRIERES

SERRIERES *9C2* (3km W Rural) 45.30872, 4.74622 **Camping Le Bas Larin, 88 Route de Larin Le Bas, 07340 Félines [04 75 34 87 93 or 06 80 05 13 89 (mob); camping.baslarin@wanadoo.fr; www.camping-bas-larin.com]** Exit A7 junc 12 Chanas or fr N7, exit at Serrieres onto D1082; cross canal & rv; cont over rndabt up winding hill, camp on L nr hill top. Sp fr N7 & D1082, but easily missed - foll sp Safari de Peaugres. Med, shd, terr, wc; chem disp; fam bthrm; shwrs inc; EHU (4-10A) €2.50-3.80; lndry; shop nr; rest nr; playgrnd; pool; paddling pool; entmnt; wifi; 10% statics; dogs free; Eng spkn; games area; games rm; CKE/CCI. "Friendly, family-run site; beautiful views; helpful staff; easy access pitches; popular with Dutch; excl; v nice site but ent to pitches may be diff." ♦ 1 Apr-30 Sep. € 18.50 2018*

SETE *10F1* (11km SW Coastal) 43.34194, 3.58440 **Camping Le Castellas, Cours Gambetta, 34200 Sète [04 67 51 63 00; fax 04 67 51 63 01; www.le-castellas.com www.village-center.com]** On D612/N112 bet Agde and Sète. Foll sp for 'Plages-Agde'. Lge, hdg, pt shd, wc; chem disp; shwrs inc; EHU (6A) inc; gas; lndry; shop; rest; snacks; bar; playgrnd; pool (htd); beach sand 150m; red long stay; entmnt; dogs €3; Eng spkn; adv bkg acc; bike hire; tennis; games area; CKE/CCI. "Bull-fighting in ssn; superb beach; twin axles welcome." ♦ 6 Apr-29 Sep. € 59.00 2013*

SEVERAC LE CHATEAU *9D1* (15km SE Rural) 44.27302, 3.21538 **Camp Municipal, 48500 St Rome-de-Dolan [04 66 44 03 81 or 04 66 48 83 59; camping-stromededolan@orange.fr; www.saint-rome-de-dolan.com]** Exit A75 junc 42 to Sévérac, then take D995 fr Séverac-le-Château then E thro le Massegros to St Rome-de-Dolan. Site on R at ent to vill, sp. NB Rec not to use GPS. Sm, pt shd, pt sl, terr, wc; chem disp; shwrs inc; EHU (6A); lndry; shop nr; rest nr; bbq; playgrnd; sw nr; wifi; dogs €0.80; Eng spkn; adv bkg acc; quiet; CKE/CCI. "Simple, well-kept, well-run site in beautiful location nr Gorges du Tarn; fantastic views some pitches; friendly, helpful warden; clean san facs; some pitches sm & need mover; bird watching, inc vultures, walking; highly rec." ♦ 1 May-30 Sep. € 13.50 2015*

SEVERAC LE CHATEAU *9D1* (1km SW Urban) 44.31841, 3.06412 **FFCC Camping Les Calquières, Ave Jean Moulin, 12150 Sévérac-le-Château [05 65 47 64 82; contact@camping-calquieres.com; www.camping-calquieres.com]** Exit A75 junc 42 sp Sévérac & Rodez; foll 'Camping' sps to avoid narr town rds. Med, hdg, pt shd, serviced pitches; wc (htd); mv service pnt; fam bthrm; shwrs inc; EHU (6-16A) €4.20 (poss long lead & rev pol); lndry; shop nr; rest; snacks; bar; bbq; playgrnd; pool (covrd, htd); red long stay; wifi; 10% statics; dogs €1.50; adv bkg acc; tennis; fishing; games area; CKE/CCI. "Lovely, spacious site with gd views; lge pitches; friendly, v helpful owners; v gd touring base & NH; conv A75; busy NH, espec w/end; gd for main holiday stay; new excel san facs (2015); vg rest; chge for wifi." ♦ 1 Apr-30 Sep. € 28.50 2018*

SEYNE *9D3* (1km S Rural) 44.34270, 6.35896 **Camping Les Prairies, Haute Gréyère, 04140 Seyne-les-Alpes [04 92 35 10 21; fax 04 92 35 26 96; info@campinglesprairies.com; www.campinglesprairies.com]** Fr Digne-les-Bains, take D900 N to Seyne. Turn L on ent Seyne onto D7, site sp beside Rv La Blanche. Med, mkd, pt shd, wc (htd); chem disp; mv service pnt; fam bthrm; shwrs inc; EHU (10A) €3.50; gas; lndry; shop nr; rest nr; snacks; bar; bbq; playgrnd; pool (htd); dogs €2; phone; Eng spkn; adv bkg acc; quiet; ccard acc; tennis 300m; horseriding 500m; CKE/CCI. "Immac, tidy, peaceful site; excel; beautifully sited and maintained; rest fr mid June; highly rec." 18 Apr-12 Sep. € 34.00 2014*

SEZANNE *4E4* (2km NW Rural) 48.72115, 3.70247 **Camp Municipal, Route de Launat, 51120 Sézanne [03 26 80 57 00 or 03 26 80 57 00 (mob); campingdesezanne@wanadoo.fr]** W'bound on N4 Sézanne by-pass onto D373 & foll site sp. Fr E turn R at 1st junc on Sézanne bypass & foll sps 'Camping & Piscine'. Avoid town cent. Med, pt shd, sl, serviced pitches; wc; shwrs inc; EHU (10A) inc; shop nr; rest nr; playgrnd; dogs €1.05; waterslide; CKE/CCI. "Nice, well-kept site, v busy high ssn; generous pitches, some v sl; helpful manager; excel, immac san facs; levelling blocks req some pitches; request gate opening/closing at back bungalow of 2 opp site; nice vill; vg; well run site; pool adj; excel value; barrier clsd until 1500 unless adj pool open." ♦ 1 Apr-30 Sep. € 11.00 2018*

SIERCK LES BAINS *5C2* (2km W Rural) 49.44544, 6.34599 **Camp Municipal les Tilleuls, Allée des Tilleuls, 57480 Sierck-les-Bains [03 82 83 72 39; camping@siercklesbains.fr; www.siercklesbains.fr]** Fr S on D654 turn L onto D64 sp Contz. Fr Schengen (Lux) turn L immed bef Moselle Bdge sp Contz. Well sp on banks of Moselle. Sm, mkd, hdg, pt shd, wc; chem disp; mv service pnt; shwrs; EHU (16A); bbq; playgrnd; Eng spkn; adv bkg acc; bike hire; CKE/CCI. "Excel site." ♦ 1 May-15 Oct. € 14.00 2014*

⊞ **SIGEAN** *10G1* (5km N Rural) 43.06633, 2.94100 **Camping La Grange Neuve, 17 La Grange Neuve Nord, 11130 Sigean [04 68 48 58 70; info@camping-sigean.com; www.campingsigean.com]** Exit junc 39 fr A9; pass over A9 (fr N) then 1st R sp La Réserve Africaine, then turn R just bef entering Sigean sp La Grange Neuve. Med, hdstg, hdg, mkd, pt shd, pt sl, terr, wc; chem disp; mv service pnt; shwrs inc; EHU (6A) inc; lndry; shop; rest; snacks; bar; playgrnd; pool; beach sand 5km; wifi; TV; 5% statics; dogs €3; adv bkg acc; quiet; waterslide; CKE/CCI. "Easy access; gd san facs; excel pool; ltd facs LS; phone ahead to check open LS; gd NH." ♦ € 30.00 2017*

SIGEAN *10G1* (10km S Rural) *42.95800, 2.99586*
Camping Le Clapotis (Naturist), 11480 La Palme [04 68 48 15 40 or 05 56 73 73 73; info@leclapotis.com; www.leclapotis.com] On D6009 S fr Narbonne turn L 8km S of Sigean. After 350m turn R at camping sp. Site in 150m. Final app rd narr but negotiable for lge vans. Lge, mkd, pt shd, wc cont; shwrs inc; EHU (4A) €4; gas; rest; bar; pool; wifi; 80% statics; dogs €2; Eng spkn; adv bkg acc; quiet; ccard acc; games area; tennis. "Pleasant, basic, friendly site; sm pitches; Naturists INF card req; helpful owners; san facs dated but clean; gd pool; poss strong winds - gd windsurfing; La Palme vill 15 mins walk; great location." 11 Apr-10 Oct. € 31.00   2017*

SIGNY L'ABBAYE *5C1* (1km N Urban) *49.70123, 4.41971* **Camp Municipal de l'Abbaye, 08460 Signy-l'Abbaye [03 24 52 87 73; mairie-signy-Labbaye@wanadoo.fr; www.sud-ardennes-tourisme.com]** Take D985 N twd Belgium fr Rethel to Signy-l'Abbaye. Foll sp fr town cent to Stade & Camping. Site by sports stadium. Sm, hdstg, hdg, pt shd, pt sl, wc (htd); chem disp; shwrs inc; EHU (10A) €3.20 (poss rev pol); lndry; shop nr; rest nr; playgrnd; dogs €0.60; Eng spkn; adv bkg acc; quiet; rv fishing adj; CKE/CCI. "Lovely site in gd location; friendly warden; sports cent adj; san facs excel (shared with public); strong awning pegs req on gravel hdg pitches, or can park on open grassed area." ♦ 1 May-30 Sep. € 6.40   2016*

SILLE LE GUILLAUME *4F1* (3km N Rural) *48.20352, -0.12774* **Camping Indigo Les Mollières, Sillé-Plage, 72140 Sillé-le-Guillaume [02 43 20 16 12; molieres@camping-indigo.com; www.camping-indigo.com]** Fr Sillé-le-Guillaume take D5 N, D203 to site. Med, shd, wc (htd); chem disp; mv service pnt; shwrs inc; EHU (13A) inc; lndry; shop; snacks; playgrnd; pool (htd); paddling pool; sw; wifi; 10% statics; dogs; quiet; ccard acc; watersports; fishing; bike hire; games area. "Site in pine forest; gd dog walk around lake." ♦ 30 Apr-28 Sep. € 25.00   2015*

SILLE LE GUILLAUME *4F1* (3km N Rural) *48.20928, -0.13444* **FFCC Camping La Forêt, Sillé-Plage, 72140 Sillé-le-Guillaume [02 43 20 11 04; fax 02 43 20 84 82; campingsilleplage@wanadoo.fr or info@campingsilleplage.com; www.campingsilleplage.com]** Exit Sillé on D304 sp Mayenne. After 2km at x-rds turn R; across next x-rds & turn L at next x-rds; sp Sillé-Plage; site on R in 500m, visible. Sp fr other dir. Med, pt shd, wc; mv service pnt; shwrs inc; EHU (10A) €4.10; gas; shop; playgrnd; sw; 40% statics; dogs €1.15; boating; tennis; fishing; CKE/CCI. "Pleasant lakeside & forest scenery (some pitches amongst trees); highly rec." 31 Mar-31 Oct. € 18.00   2013*

SILLE LE GUILLAUME *4F1* (2km NW Rural) *48.18943, -0.14130* **Camping Les Tournesols, Route de Mayenne, Le Grez, 72140 Sillé-le-Guillaume [02 43 20 12 69; campinglestournesols@orange.fr; www.campinglestournesols.com]** Exit Sillé on D304/D35 sp Mayenne; in 2km at x-rds turn R; site in 150m on L, easily visible & sp. Med, mkd, hdg, pt shd, pt sl, wc; chem disp; mv service pnt; shwrs inc; EHU (6A) inc (poss long lead req); lndry; shop; snacks; bar; bbq (gas); playgrnd; sw nr; red long stay; entmnt; wifi; TV; 20% statics; dogs €2 rabies cert req'd; Eng spkn; adv bkg acc; quiet; ccard acc; bike hire; fishing 1km; CKE/CCI. "Beautiful site; friendly, new owners (2013); facs dated but spotless; badminton; bouncy castle; pleasant town; canoeing 2km; mini golf; football; volleyball; jeux de boules; conv Le Mans; gd; welcoming, helpful owner; excel value; pretty, 'natural' site; onsite family owners." ♦ 1 May-30 Sep. € 18.00   2016*

SILLE LE PHILIPPE *4F1* (1km W Rural) *48.10880, 0.33730* **Camping Le Château de Chanteloup, Parc de l'Epau Sarl, 72460 Sillé-le-Philippe [02 43 27 51 07 or 02 43 89 66 47; fax 02 43 89 05 05; chanteloup.souffront@wanadoo.fr; www.chateau-de-chanteloup.com]** Leave A11/E50 at junc 7 Sp Le Mans Z1 Nord. After toll turn L onto N338. Foll this & turn L onto D313 sp Coulaines, Mamers & Ballon. Take D301 (at lge supmkt) & in approx 13km site is sp just after ent to Sillé-le-Philippe. Avoid cent Sillé-le-Philippe. Med, mkd, pt shd, pt sl, wc (htd); chem disp; fam bthrm; shwrs inc; EHU (10A) €4 (poss rev pol); gas; lndry; shop; rest; snacks; bar; bbq; playgrnd; pool; paddling pool; twin axles; entmnt; wifi; TV; dogs €2; Eng spkn; adv bkg acc; quiet; ccard acc; golf 10km; games area; lake fishing; games rm; horseriding 10km; CKE/CCI. "Lovely, tranquil, spacious site in chateau grnds; pleasant, helpful staff; some pitches in wooded areas poss tight lge o'fits; gd rest; twin axles & lge o'fits by request; gd for Le Mans; sep o'night area with elec & water; rec; no facs to drain waste water fr m'van; higher charge during Le Mans events; excel new san facs (2014); clean & well maintained park." ♦ 29 May-31 Aug. € 41.50   2015*

SISTERON *10E3* (3km N Rural) *44.21467, 5.93643* **Camp Municipal Les Prés Hauts, 44 Chemin des Prés Hauts, 04200 Sisteron [04 92 61 00 37 or 04 92 61 19 69; contact@camping-sisteron.com; www.camping-sisteron.com]** On W of D951. Lge, hdg, pt shd, pt sl, serviced pitches; wc; chem disp; shwrs inc; EHU (10A) €4 (poss rev pol); lndry; shop; playgrnd; pool; entmnt; dogs €2; Eng spkn; quiet; ccard acc; fishing; tennis; CKE/CCI. "Lovely, well-kept, busy, excel site; excel location, gd views; lge pitches & gd for m'vans; site yourself LS; vg facs, ltd LS; interesting old town, gd mkt; conv a'route; vg; ent Barrier clsd at 2000; stunning pool; huge pitches; gd facs; friendly helpful staff; handy for m'way; 30min walk to Sisteron." ♦ 1 Apr-30 Sep. € 21.50   2018*

SIZUN

SIZUN *2E2* (1km S Rural) *48.40038, -4.07635* **Camp Municipal du Gollen, 29450 Sizun [02 98 24 11 43 or 02 98 68 80 13 (Mairie); fax 02 98 68 86 56; mairie. sizun@wanadoo.fr; www.mairie-sizun.fr]**
Fr Roscoff take D788 SW onto D69 to Landivisiau, D30 & D764 to Sizun. In Sizun take D18 at rndabt. At end of by-pass, at next rndabt, take 3rd exit. Site adj pool. Sm, pt shd, wc; shwrs inc; EHU (10A) €3 (poss rev pol); lndry; shop nr; playgrnd; phone; quiet; CKE/CCI. "Lovely little site; simple & restful by rv in nature park; friendly recep; htd pool adj high ssn; site yourself if warden not avail; vg." 16 Apr-30 Sep. € 13.50   2017*

SOISSONS *3D4* (2km N Urban) *49.39295, 3.32701* **Camp Municipal du Mail, 14 Ave du Mail, 02200 Soissons [03 23 74 52 69; fax 03 23 75 05 21; campingdumail@gmail.com; www.tourisme-soissons.fr]** Fr N on D1; foll town cent sp to 1st rndabt; turn R, cross rv & immed R into Ave du Mail. Foll sp 'Camping Piscine'. Site well sp beside sw pool. Rd humps & tight ent on last 500m of access rd. (Poss to avoid tight ent by going 150m to rndabt & returning). Or fr S on D1, turn R sp Centre Ville along Ave de Château-Thiery; at 3rd rndabt turn R into Rue du Général Leclerc to Place de la Republique; cont strt over into Blvd Gambette for 500m, then turn L into Ave de l'Aisne, leading into Ave du Petit Mail; then as above. Med, hdstg, hdg, mkd, pt shd, wc (htd); chem disp; mv service pnt; shwrs inc; EHU (6A) inc (poss rev pol); lndry; shop; snacks; bar nr; bbq; playgrnd; wifi; 5% statics; dogs €1; phone; quiet; ccard acc; bike hire; clsd 1 Jan & 25 Dec; CKE/CCI. "Pleasant, excel, clean & well-run site in interesting area; gd sized pitches, some nr rv; poss muddy, park on site rds in winter; m'van pitches all hdstg; helpful, friendly staff; gd clean, modern san facs, updated (2015); rvside walks/cycling; gate clsd 2200-0700; pool adj; lge mkt Wed & Sat; vg winter NH; conv for town (15mins)." ♦ 2 Jan-24 Dec & 26 Dec-31 Dec. € 16.00   2016*

SOMMIERES *10E1* (2km SE Rural) *43.77550, 4.09280* **Camping Domaine de Massereau, 1990 Route d'Aubais, 30250 Sommières [04 66 53 11 20 or 06 03 31 27 21 (mob); fax 04 11 71 50 20; camping@massereau.com; www.massereau.com]** Exit A9 junc 26 at Gallargues, foll sp Sommières; site sp on D12. NB Danger of grounding at ent fr D12. Use this rte 24/7 - 03/08 (due to festival in Sommières). Otherwise exit A9 junc 27 onto D34 to Sommières, foll sps to "Centre Historique" dir Aubias; cross bdge (sharp turn) & turn R onto D110; site on L in 3km. Med, hdg, mkd, pt shd, pt sl, serviced pitches; wc; chem disp; mv service pnt; fam bthrm; shwrs inc; EHU (16A) inc; gas; lndry; shop; rest; snacks; bar; bbq (gas); playgrnd; pool; paddling pool; sw nr; entmnt; wifi; TV; 50% statics; dogs €3.90; phone; Eng spkn; adv bkg acc; quiet; ccard acc; games rm; jacuzzi; bike hire; waterslide; canoeing nr; sauna; games area; tennis; horseriding nr; CKE/CCI. "Lovely, tranquil, well-run site adj vineyard; lge pitches, some uneven; pleasant, cheerful staff; running track; no o'fits over 7m high ssn; trampoline; modern san facs; narr site rds, sl/uneven pitches & trees diff lge o'fits; tight ents, diff without mover; excel; pool not htd." ♦ 12 Apr-1 Nov. € 47.00   2014*

SOMMIERES *10E1* (3km SE Rural) *43.76120, 4.11961* **Camping Les Chênes, Les Teullières Basses, 30250 Junas [04 66 80 99 07 or 06 03 29 36 32 (mob); fax 04 66 51 33 23; chenes@wanadoo.fr; www.camping-les-chenes.com]** Fr Sommières take D12 S (sp Gallargues) 3km to junc with D140 L (N) for 1km. Site on R 300m up side rd. Sp. Med, mkd, pt shd, pt sl, wc; chem disp; fam bthrm; shwrs inc; EHU (10A) €5.40 (long lead poss req); gas; lndry; shop; snacks; bbq (charcoal, gas); playgrnd; pool; sw nr; wifi; 10% statics; dogs €4; adv bkg acc; quiet; games area; sep car park; CKE/CCI. "Gd shd; gd san facs; friendly, helpful staff; vg; 2km fr disused rlwy cycle track; vg site." 7 Apr-14 Oct. € 23.40   2018*

SOMMIERES *10E1* (6km SE Urban) *43.77052, 4.12592* **Camping L'Olivier, 112 Route de Congénies Junas, 30250 Sommieres [04 66 80 39 52; camping. lolivier@wanadoo.fr; www.campinglolivier.fr]** Fr Nîmes, take D40 twd Sommières. At Congenies take D140 L to Junas, site sp in vill. Sm, mkd, pt shd, pt sl, wc; chem disp; mv service pnt; fam bthrm; shwrs inc; EHU (6-10A) €5, poss inc on certain pitches; shop nr; snacks; bar; cooking facs; playgrnd; pool; paddling pool; wifi; 40% statics; dogs (€3); phone; Eng spkn; adv bkg acc; quiet; fishing; tennis; games area; CKE/CCI. "Excel home made pizzas; jazz festival in summer; elec BBQ for hire; excel; lovely site; ping pong; entmnt (Thur eves); trampoline; homemade jams & olive oil for sale; less than 1km fr Nimes-Sommiere Voie Verte; mini golf; new owners (2017)." ♦ 30 Mar-20 Oct. € 24.30   2017*

SOMMIERES *10E1* (1km NW Urban) *43.78672, 4.08702* **Camp Municipal Le Garanel, 110 Rue Eugène Rouché, 30250 Sommières [04 66 80 33 49; campingmunicipal.sommieres@wanadoo.fr; www.sommieres.fr]** Fr S on A9 exit junc 27 N & foll D34 then take D610 twd Sommières. By-pass town on D610, over rv bdge; turn R for D40, Rue Condamine. After L turn for Nîmes pull out to make sharp R turn sp 'Camping Arena' (easy to miss this R turn). At T-junc turn R, site thro car park. Fr N on D610 turn L at 4th junc sp 'Ville Vieille' & site adj rv. Site sp fr D610 fr N. NB Narr rds nr site. Sm, hdg, mkd, pt shd, wc (htd); chem disp; mv service pnt; shwrs inc; EHU (10A) inc; lndry; shop nr; rest nr; bar nr; bbq; pool; dogs €2; bus 500m; Eng spkn; adv bkg acc; tennis adj; CKE/CCI. "Well-kept site in great location nr medieval town cent & rv; some open views; friendly, helpful warden; nice sm pool; poss some workers' statics LS; rv walks; bar 200m; Voie Verte cycle rte; interesting town & area; site subject to flooding at any time; mkt Sat; twin axle restrictions; diff in/out for lge o'fits; email for avail in Jul/Aug; san facs updated (2018)." 1 Apr-30 Sep. € 18.50   2018*

SOUILLAC

SONZAY *4G1* (1km W Rural) *47.52620, 0.45390*
Kawan Village L'Arada Parc, 88 Rue de la Baratière, 37360 Sonzay [02 47 24 72 69; fax 02 47 24 72 70; info@laradaparc.com; www.laradaparc.com] Exit A28 junc 27 to Neuillé-Pont-Pierre; then D766 & D6 to Sonzay; turn R in town cent. Site on R on o'skirts immed past new houses; sp. Med, mkd, hdg, pt shd, pt sl, serviced pitches; wc; chem disp; mv service pnt; fam bthrm; shwrs inc; EHU (10A) €4.10 (poss rev pol); gas; lndry; shop; rest; snacks; bar; bbq; playgrnd; pool (covrd, htd); paddling pool; red long stay; entmnt; wifi; TV; 15% statics; dogs €2; phone; bus to Tours; Eng spkn; adv bkg acc; quiet; ccard acc; bike hire; rv fishing 500m; gym; games area; CKE/CCI. "Peaceful, well-kept site; spa; friendly, helpful owners & staff; clean, modern facs; gd views; vg rest; poss diff for lge o'fits when site full/cr; barrier clsd 2300-0800; many walks, inc in attractive orchards; 60km fr Le Mans circuit; rec." ♦ 26 Mar-1 Nov. € 31.00   2012*

SORGUES *10E2* (7km NW Rural) *44.04163, 4.82493*
Camping L'Art de Vivre, Islon St Luc, 84230 Châteauneuf-du-Pape [04 90 02 65 43; contact@camping-artdevivre.com; www.camping-artdevivre.com] Exit A7 junc 22 onto D907 S dir Sorgues; in 11km (just bef Sorgues) turn R onto D17 dir Châteauneuf-du-Pape; in 4km, bef vill, turn L at site sp; site in 1km. Site well fr D17. Med, mkd, shd, wc; chem disp; mv service pnt; shwrs inc; EHU (10A) €4; lndry; rest; snacks; bar; bbq; pool; wifi; dogs €2.50; Eng spkn; ccard acc; games area; games rm. "Site situated in woodland nr rv; new enthusiastic owners (2011); gd walks & cycling; wine-growing area; m'van o'night area; gd; pleasant site; gd rest." 4 Apr-27 Sep. € 26.00   2015*

SOSPEL *10E4* (4km NW Rural) *43.89702, 7.41685*
Camping Domaine Ste Madeleine, Route de Moulinet, 06380 Sospel [04 93 04 10 48; fax 04 93 04 18 37; camp@camping-sainte-madeleine.com; www.camping-sainte-madeleine.com] Take D2566 fr Sospel NW to Turini & site 4km on L; sp fr town. Rd to site fr Menton steep with many hairpins. Med, mkd, shd, pt sl, terr, wc; chem disp; mv service pnt; shwrs; EHU (10A) €2.90; gas; lndry; pool; dogs €1.50; Eng spkn; adv bkg rec; quiet; CKE/CCI. "Friendly, busy site; gd pool but has no shallow end; stunning scenery; beautifully kept site; gd, immac facs; v well run;." 28 Mar-3 Oct. € 25.40   2018*

SOUILLAC *7C3* (9km N Rural) *44.95178, 1.46547*
Camping Le Lac Rouge, 46200, Lachapelle Auzac [06 82 92 55 67 or 06 82 92 55 67 (mob); jo.campinglelacrouge@gmail.com] Fr Souillac foll D15, sp Salignac, at La Forge turn R on D15 sp Gignac. Site on R by junc for Lhom, 500m past golf club. Sm, pt shd, pt sl, wc; chem disp; fam bthrm; shwrs inc; EHU inc; lndry; bar; bbq; playgrnd; twin axles; 50% statics; dogs; adv bkg acc; games area; CKE/CCI. "Gd site." ♦ 1 Apr-31 Oct. € 14.00   2015*

SOUILLAC *7C3* (7km SE Rural) *44.87716, 1.57361*
Camping Les Borgnes, 46200 St Sozy [05 65 32 21 48; info@campinglesborgnes.fr; www.campinglesborgnes.fr] Exit A20 junc 55; foll sp Martel on D803; in 5km turn R onto D15 to St Sozy; site just bef rv bdge. Med, pt shd, wc; chem disp; mv service pnt; shwrs inc; EHU €3; gas; lndry; shop nr; rest nr; snacks; bar; bbq; playgrnd; pool; paddling pool; sw nr; 60% statics; dogs €1; phone; Eng spkn; adv bkg acc; quiet; ccard acc; canoe hire; CKE/CCI. "Helpful British owners; gd." ♦ 1 May-30 Sep. € 12.00   2013*

> **"We must tell the Club about that great site we found"**
>
> Get your site reports in by mid-August and we'll do our best to get your updates into the next edition.

SOUILLAC *7C3* (1km S Rural) *44.88197, 1.48253*
Camp Municipal du Pont de Lanzac, 46200 Lanzac [05 65 37 02 58; fax 05 65 37 02 31; mairie.lanzac@wanadoo.fr; www.lanzac.fr] S on D820 thro Souillac; immed after x-ing Rv Dordogne site visible on R of D820. Sm, shd, wc; chem disp; shwrs inc; EHU (6A) €3; gas; shop nr; rest; snacks; playgrnd; sw; TV; 10% statics; dogs; adv bkg acc; canoe hire; fishing; CKE/CCI. "Gd site in lovely location; free-style pitching; helpful warden; clean, basic san facs; easy stroll into Souillac along rv; unrel opening dates - phone ahead; gd NH." ♦ July-Aug. € 11.00   2014*

SOUILLAC *7C3* (5km S Rural) *44.86602, 1.49715*
Camping Verte Rive, 46200 Pinsac [05 65 37 85 96; www.camping-laverterive.com] Fr Souillac S on D820. Turn L immed bef Dordogne rv bdge on D43 to Pinsac. Site on R in 2km on rvside. Med, mkd, hdg, shd, wc; chem disp; fam bthrm; shwrs inc; EHU (10A) €4; gas; lndry; shop; rest; snacks; bar; playgrnd; pool; 20% statics; dogs €2; Eng spkn; adv bkg req; quiet; ccard acc; games rm; canoeing; CKE/CCI. "Pleasant, peaceful, wooded site on Rv Dordogne; gd san facs; poss mosquitoes by rv; gd pool; excel." ♦ 1 Apr-15 Sep. € 31.00   2013*

SOUILLAC *7C3* (5km SW Rural) *44.87340, 1.43389*
Camp Municipal La Borgne, 24370 Cazoulès [05 53 29 81 64 or 05 53 31 45 25 (Mairie); fax 05 53 31 45 26; campingcazoules@orange.fr; http://cazoules.pagesperso-orange.fr] Fr Souillac, take D804/D703 twd Sarlat. In 4km in vill of Cazoulès turn L & foll site sps. Site on R just bef rv bdge & adj Rv Dordogne. Lge, pt shd, wc; fam bthrm; shwrs inc; EHU (10A) €3; lndry; shop; bbq; playgrnd; pool; paddling pool; 15% statics; dogs €1; quiet; fishing; tennis adj; boat hire. "Poss mosquito problem; canoe trips; helpful staff." ♦ 15 Jun-15 Sep. € 15.00   2013*

SOUILLAC

Campsite Les Lacs ★★★★★
Soulac sur mer

France

www.camping-les-lacs.com

SOUILLAC *7C3* (1km W Urban) 44.88895, 1.47418
FLOWER Camping Les Ondines, Ave de Sarlat, 46200 Souillac [05 65 37 86 44 or 06 33 54 32 00; fax 05 65 32 61 15; camping.les.ondines@flowercampings. com; www.camping-lesondines.com or www. flowercampings.com] Turn W off D820 in cent Souillac onto D804/D703 sp Sarlat. In 200m turn L at sp into narr rd. Ent 400m on R adj rv. Lge, mkd, pt shd, pt sl, wc; chem disp; shwrs inc; EHU (5A) inc; lndry; shop; rest nr; bbq; playgrnd; entmnt; wifi; 10% statics; dogs €2; phone; Eng spkn; quiet; horseriding; tennis; canoeing; fishing; CKE/CCI. "Gd touring base nr rv; helpful staff; clean facs; conv NH Rocamadour & caves; easy access fr D820; aquatic park nrby; vg." ♦
1 May-28 Sep. € 34.20   2014*

SOUILLAC *7C3* (7km NW Rural) 44.93599, 1.43743
Camping La Draille, La Draille, 46200 Souillac [05 65 32 65 01; fax 05 65 37 06 20; la.draille@wanadoo. fr; www.ladraille.com] Leave Souillac on D15 sp Salignac-Evvigues; at Bourzoles in 6km take D165; site sp in 500m on L. Med, hdg, pt shd, pt sl, wc; chem disp; fam bthrm; shwrs inc; EHU (4A) €4; lndry; shop; rest; snacks; bar; bbq; pool; 25% statics; dogs €3; phone; Eng spkn; adv bkg acc; quiet; ccard acc; CKE/CCI. "Lovely location; friendly; gd walks; highly rec." ♦
27 Apr-5 Oct. € 26.00   2013*

SOUILLAC *7C3* (8km NW Rural) 44.94510, 1.44140
Domaine de la Paille Basse, 46200 Souillac [05 65 37 85 48; fax 05 65 37 09 58; info@lapaillebasse. com; www.lapaillebasse.com] Exit Souillac by D15 sp Salignac, turn onto D165 to D15 at Bourzolles foll sp to site in 3km. NB Narr app, few passing places. Lge, hdg, pt shd, terr, wc; chem disp; mv service pnt; shwrs inc; EHU (3-10A) €4-6; gas; lndry; shop; rest; snacks; bar; bbq; playgrnd; pool; paddling pool; entmnt; wifi; TV; dogs €4; adv bkg acc; quiet; ccard acc; golf 5km; tennis; bike hire; games area; waterslide. "Excel site in remote location; friendly, helpful staff; clean facs; organised outdoor activities; cinema rm; some shwrs unisex; restored medieval vill." ♦ 15 May-14 Sep.
€ 25.00   2016*

SOULAC SUR MER *7B1* (1km S Coastal) 45.50136, -1.13585 Camping Le Palace, 65 Blvd Marsan-de-Montbrun, Forêt Sud, 33780 Soulac-sur-Mer [05 56 09 80 22; fax 05 56 09 84 23; info@camping-palace. com; www.camping-palace.com]
Fr ferry at Le Verdon-sur-Mer S on D1215, site sp. Or fr S on D101. V lge, mkd, hdg, shd, wc; mv service pnt; fam bthrm; shwrs inc; EHU; lndry; shop; rest; snacks; bar; bbq; playgrnd; pool (covrd, htd); paddling pool; beach sand 400m; entmnt; wifi; 65% statics; dogs €3-6; adv bkg acc; quiet; waterslide; bike hire. "Ideal for family beach holiday." 1 May-27 Sep. € 36.00   2014*

SOULAC SUR MER *7B1* (13km S Coastal) *45.41600, -0.12930* **Centre Naturiste Euronat (Naturist), 33590 Grayan-l'Hôpital [05 56 09 33 33; fax 05 56 09 30 27; info@euronat.fr; www.euronat.fr]** Fr Soulac, take D101 twd Montalivet, turn W at camp sp onto rd leading direct to site. Fr Bordeaux, take D1215 sp Le Verdon-sur-Mer. Approx 8km after Lesparre-Médoc turn L onto D102. In Venday-Montalivet bear R onto D101. In 7.5km turn L sp Euronat. V lge, hdstg, mkd, shd, serviced pitches; wc (htd); chem disp; mv service pnt; fam bthrm; shwrs inc; EHU (10A) inc; gas; lndry; shop; rest; snacks; bar; bbq; playgrnd; pool (covrd, htd); paddling pool; beach sand adj; entmnt; wifi; TV; 30% statics; dogs €3; phone; Eng spkn; adv bkg acc; quiet; bike hire; horseriding; tennis; archery; INF card req; golf driving range. "Expensive, but well worth it; cinema; thalassotherapy & beauty treatment cent; gd lge pitches, many with elec/water; shwrs basic/dated; excel." ♦ 1 Apr-29 Oct. € 55.50   2017*

SOULAC SUR MER *7B1* (2km SW Coastal) *45.49958, -1.13899* **Camping Les Sables d'Argent, Blvd de l'Amélie, 33780 Soulac-sur-Mer [05 56 09 82 87; fax 05 56 09 94 82; sables@lelilhan.com; www.sables-d-argent.com]** Drive S fr Soulac twd L'Amélie-sur-Mer. Clearly sp on R. Med, mkd, pt shd, pt sl, wc; shwrs inc; EHU (10A) inc (poss long lead req); lndry; shop; rest; snacks; bar; beach sand adj; entmnt; wifi; TV; 60% statics; dogs €2.95; tennis; fishing. "Nice area, but major erosion of coast so no access to beach; poss diff lge o'fits; Soulac sm, lively mkt town." 1 Apr-30 Sep. € 25.00   2018*

SOULAINES DHUYS *6E1* (1km N Rural) *48.37661, 4.73829* **Camping La Croix Badeau, 6 Rue Croix Badeau, 10200 Soulaines-Dhuys [03 25 27 05 43 or 03 26 82 35 31 (LS); responsable@croix-badeau.com; www.croix-badeau.com]** 500m N of junc D960 & D384, behind lge church of Soulaines-Dhuys, well sp. Sm, mkd, hdg, hdstg, pt shd, wc; chem disp; shwrs inc; EHU (10A) €2.50; lndry; shop nr; playgrnd; dogs €1; phone; Eng spkn; quiet; tennis; CKE/CCI. "Excel, clean site in interesting vill." 1 Apr-15 Oct. € 14.00   2012*

SOUSTONS *8E1* (7km NE Rural) *43.78340, -1.30473* **Camping Azu'Rivage, 720 Route des Campings, 40140 Azur [05 58 48 30 72; info@campingazurivage.com; www.campingazurivage.com]** Exit m'way A10 at exit Magescq & take D150 W for 8km to Azur, site sp fr church adj La Paillotte. Med, pt shd, wc; fam bthrm; shwrs inc; EHU (10A) €7.40; lndry; shop; rest; snacks; playgrnd; pool; paddling pool; sw; red long stay; entmnt; TV; dogs €2; adv bkg acc; ccard acc; boating; tennis; watersports. "Delightful forest setting adj lake; v busy high ssn; san facs poss stretched high ssn; rec; lovely pool; no easy access to lake." ♦ 15 May-30 Sep. € 15.00   2017*

STENAY

⊞ **SOUTERRAINE, LA** *7A3* (2km NE Rural) *46.24368, 1.50606* **Camping Suisse Océan, Etang-du-Cheix, 23300 La Souterraine [05 55 63 33 32 or 05 55 63 59 71; fax 05 55 63 21 82]** Fr N145/E62 take D72 sp La Souterraine. Strt over 1st rndabt, at 2nd rndabt turn R, then L to L'Etang de Cheix. Fr N exit A20 junc 22 onto D912 sp La Souterraine; at T-junc turn L & foll outer rd D912b; at rndabt turn L to Etang-du-Cheix; in 50m turn L to site. Sp fr D912b. Sm, hdg, hdstg, mkd, pt shd, pt sl, terr, wc (htd); chem disp; mv service pnt; shwrs inc; EHU (10A) €3.50; lndry; shop; rest; snacks; bar; playgrnd; 10% statics; dogs €1.20; Eng spkn; adv bkg acc; tennis; fishing adj; sailing adj; CKE/CCI. "Superb location by lake; lge pitches; sl rds on site could grnd lge o'fits - walk site bef pitching; san facs in portacabin; diving (summer); ltd facs LS inc EHU & inadequate when site full; quiet but night noise fr factory nrby; lake adj; pleasant sm town; mkt Thur & Sat; site fair." ♦ € 15.00   2012*

SOUTERRAINE, LA *7A3* (6km E Rural) *46.24534, 1.59083* **Camp Municipal Etang de la Cazine, 23300 Noth [05 55 63 31 17; mairiedenoth@wanadoo.fr]** Exit A20 junc 23 onto N145 dir Guéret; turn L on D49 sp Noth. Site opp lake. Sm, mkd, pt shd, pt sl, wc; chem disp; mv service pnt; shwrs inc; EHU (16A) €3; bar; playgrnd; sw nr; dogs €1.50; quiet; lake fishing adj; CKE/CCI. "Gd touring base; gd; san facs portacabins; excel NH and sh stay; rural location." 31 Mar-7 Nov. € 16.00   2013*

SOUTERRAINE, LA *7A3* (10km S Rural) *46.15129, 1.51059* **Camp Municipal, 23290 St Pierre-de-Fursac [05 55 63 65 69 or 05 55 63 61 28 (Mairie); fax 05 55 63 68 20; www.communes-fursac.fr]** Exit A20 at junc 23.1 onto D1 S twd St Pierre-de-Fursac. Site on L at ent to vill dir 'Stade'. Sm, mkd, pt shd, pt sl, wc; shwrs inc; EHU (6A) €2 (poss rev pol); shop nr; playgrnd; phone; quiet. "Pleasant, well-kept site o'looking vill; san facs basic but clean; fine NH; gd." ♦ 15 Jun-15 Sep. € 8.00   2013*

> **"I need an on-site restaurant"**
>
> We do our best to make sure site information is correct, but it is always best to check any must-have facilities are still available or will be open during your visit.

⊞ **STENAY** *5C1* (0km W Urban) *49.49083, 5.18333* **Port de Plaisance - Motor Caravan Parking Area, Rue du Port, 55700 Stenay [03 29 80 64 22 or 03 29 74 87 54; fax 03 29 80 62 59; otsistenayaccueil@orange.fr]** Off D947 fr town cent. Foll sp to rv port. NB M'vans only. Sm, hdstg, mv service pnt; shwrs inc; EHU (6A) inc; shop nr; rest nr; quiet. "Adj to rv; excel san facs; NH only; sh walk to Beer Museum, rest, shop." ♦ € 8.00   2015*

STRASBOURG

⊞ **STRASBOURG** *6E3* (3km W Urban) 48.57537, 7.71724 **Camping Indigo Strasbourg**, 9 rue de l'Auberge de Jeunesse, 67200 Strasbourg [03 88 30 19 96; strasbourg@camping-indigo.com; www.citykamp.com] Fr A35 exit junc 4, then foll (white) sp to Montagne Verte. Then foll D392 to site. Lge, hdg, pt shd, pt sl, wc; chem disp; mv service pnt; fam bthrm; shwrs; EHU (10A); lndry; snacks; bar; bbq; playgrnd; pool (htd); paddling pool; red long stay; twin axles; entmnt; wifi; TV; 50% statics; dogs; bus; Eng spkn; adv bkg req; quiet; bike hire; games area; games rm; CKE/CCI. "Excel site; site renovated (2015); bus/tram/cycle path to city." ♦ € 32.90   2018*

⊞ **SULLY SUR LOIRE** *4F3* (2km NW Rural) 47.77180, 2.36100 **Camping Le Jardin de Sully**, 1Route Orleans, 45600 Saint-Pere-Sur-Loire [02 38 67 10 84 or 07 81 11 47 65 (mob); lejardindesully@gmail.com; www.camping-bord-de-loire.com] Fr N on D948 to Sully then turn R at rndabt immed bef x-ing bdge over Rv Loire onto D60 in St Père-sur-Loire, dir Châteauneuf-sur-Loire. Sp to site in 200m. Fr S thro Sully on D948, cross Rv Loire & turn L at rndabt onto D60. Well sp fr town. Med, hdstg, mkd, hdg, pt shd, serviced pitches; wc (htd); chem disp; mv service pnt; fam bthrm; shwrs inc; EHU (10-16A) inc (poss rev pol); gas; lndry; shop; rest; snacks; bar; bbq; playgrnd; beach sand adj; red long stay; entmnt; wifi; TV (pitch); 18% statics; dogs €2; phone; bus; Eng spkn; adv bkg rec; quiet; ccard inc; tennis; bike hire; games rm; CKE/CCI. "Pleasant, well-kept, well laid-out site on rvside adj nature reserve; pleasant walk along rv to town; long dist footpath (grande randonnée) along Loire passes site; gd dog walks; htd covrd pool 500m; gd cycling; gd winter site & NH en rte S; recep might be clsd LS, need to phone for barrier code ent; fairy-tale chateau in Sully; gd loc; helpful, friendly new owner keen to bring the standards up; excel new san fac (2018); excel." ♦ € 25.00   2018*

SURGERES *7A2* (1km S Urban) 46.10180, -0.75376 **Camping de La Gères**, 10 Rue de la Gères, 17700 Surgères [05 46 07 79 97 or 06 64 03 89 32 (mob); fax 05 46 27 16 78; contact@campingdelageres.com; www.campingdelageres.com] Site sp in Surgères, on banks of Rv Gères, & fr Surgères by-pass. Sm, mkd, hdg, shd, wc cont; chem disp; mv service pnt; shwrs; EHU (6A) €3.50; lndry; shop nr; rest nr; bar nr; bbq; pool (htd); wifi; dogs €1.50; phone; ccard acc; tennis 800m; CKE/CCI. "Adj to park; m'vans extra charge; poss travellers; excel; park with rv walks, shops and rests via traff free walk in town cent." 12 Jan-11 Dec. € 20.00   2015*

SURGERES *7A2* (13km SW Rural) 46.07123, -0.86742 **Aire Naturelle de Loisirs**, Le Pré Marechat, 17290 Landrais [46 27 87 29 or 46 27 73 69] Fr D911 dir Rochefort, turn R au Muron onto D112 sp Landrais. Foll camping sp (not Loisirs). Site on L at NW end of vill. Sm, hdg, mkd, shd, wc; shwrs inc; shop nr; bar nr; bbq; playgrnd; twin axles; dogs; adv bkg acc; quiet; games area. "Delightful peaceful site conv for La Rochells & Rochefort; site yourself & pay at Marie or staff; vg." 15 Jun-15 Sep. € 9.50   2015*

SURIS *7B3* (1km N Rural) 45.85925, 0.63739 **Camping La Blanchie**, 16270 Suris [05 45 89 33 19 or 06 35 43 21 39 (mob); contact@lablanchie.co.uk; www.lablanchie.co.uk] Fr N141 halfway bet Angoulême & Limoges take D52 S at La Péruse to Suris; in 3km turn E up a narr lane to site. Sm, hdstg, pt shd, pt sl, wc; chem disp; shwrs inc; EHU (10A) €4; bbq; sw nr; twin axles; red long stay; wifi; 10% statics; dogs; Eng spkn; adv bkg acc; quiet; golf nr; tennis nr; CKE/CCI. "Welcoming, friendly British owners; clean site in lovely area; Futuroscope nrby; ltd facs; c'van storage; gd touring base; poor." ♦ 1 Apr-30 Sep. € 20.40   2014*

SURZUR *2G3* (2km NE Urban) 47.58775, -2.61913 **Camping Ty-Coët**, 38 rue du Bois, 56450 Surzur [02 97 42 09 05; contact@camping-tycoet.com; www.camping-tycoet.com] N165/E60 Vannes-Nantes. Take Exit 22. D183 twd Surzur. At rndabt bef Surzur cont onto D183, then 1st L onto Rue des Lutins. Foll sp to site. Med, hdg, mkd, pt shd, wc; chem disp; mv service pnt; fam bthrm; shwrs; EHU (16A) €3.20; lndry; snacks; bar; bbq; playgrnd; sw nr; twin axles; wifi; 30% statics; dogs €1; bus 0.5km; Eng spkn; adv bkg acc; quiet; games area; CCI. "BBQ except Jul & Aug; conv for Golfe de Morbihan; gd mkt in Vannes (Sat & Tue); lovely, quiet, well-kept site with super clean san facs; excel; gd touring area; v pleasant warden." ♦ 1 Mar-15 Nov. € 18.60   2015*

TAGNIERE, LA *6H1* (2km SW Rural) 46.77728, 3.56283 **Camping Le Paroy**, 71190 La Tagnière [03 85 54 59 27 or 603 56 64 82 (mob); info@campingleparoy.com; www.campingleparoy.com] Fr Autun SW on D681, after 11km S on D994. 3km after Etang L onto D224 to La Tagniere and foll sp. Sm, hdg, pt shd, terr, wc; chem disp; mv service pnt; shwrs; EHU (10A) €4; lndry; shop; bbq; playgrnd; twin axles; wifi; TV; dogs; Eng spkn; adv bkg acc; quiet; bike hire; CKE/CCI. "Fishing at Sm adj lake; takeaway; vg." 1 Apr-30 Sep. € 23.00   2015*

⊞ **TAIN L'HERMITAGE** *9C2* (5km NE Rural) 45.10715, 4.89105 **Camping Chante-Merle**, 26600 Chantemerle-les-Blés [04 75 07 49 73; fax 04 75 07 45 15; campingchantemerle@wanadoo.fr; www.campingchante-merle.fr] Exit A7 at Tain-l'Hermitage. After exit toll turn L twd town, next turn R (D109) to Chantemerle; site sp. Cont for 5km, site on L. Sm, hdg, mkd, pt shd, serviced pitches; wc (htd); chem disp; fam bthrm; shwrs inc; EHU (10A) €4.50; lndry; shop nr; rest; snacks; bar; playgrnd; pool; wifi; 10% statics; dogs €2; adv bkg req; quiet; tennis 500m; site clsd Jan; CKE/CCI. "Helpful manager; popular site; excel facs." ♦ € 23.00   2017*

TARASCON SUR ARIEGE

TAIN L'HERMITAGE 9C2 (1km S Urban) 45.06727, 4.84880 Camp Municipal Les Lucs, 24 Ave du Président Roosevelt, 26600 Tain-l'Hermitage [04 75 08 32 82 or 04 75 08 30 32; camping.tainlhermitage@ wanadoo.fr; www.campingleslucs.fr] Fr N or S exit A7 junc 13 dir Tain-l'Hermitage onto N7. Cont N twd town cent; at fuel stn on R & Netto supmkt sp prepare to turn L in 80m; ent to site in 35m. Fr N on N7 prepare to turn R after fuel stn on R. Site alongside Rv Rhône via gates (locked o/night). Well sp adj sw pool/ petrol stn. Med, hdstg, hdg, mkd, pt shd, wc; chem disp; mv service pnt; shwrs inc; EHU (6A) inc (poss rev pol); lndry; shop nr; rest nr; playgrnd; dogs €1.40; phone; Eng spkn; CKE/CCI. "Pretty, well-kept, well-run site by Rhône; lovely views; secure site; friendly staff; excel, clean san facs; no twin axles, no c'vans over 5.5m & no m'vans over 6m (poss high ssn only); rvside walk to town; Valrhona chocolate factory shop nrby; mkt Sat; gd touring base; popular NH; highly rec; access gate with PIN; v sm pitches;." ♦ 1 Mar-31 Oct. € 20.00 2018*

⊞ **TANINGES** 9A3 (1km S Rural) 46.09899, 6.58806 Camp Municipal des Thézières, Les Vernays-sous-la-Ville, 74440 Taninges [04 50 34 25 59; fax 04 50 34 39 78; camping.taninges@wanadoo.fr] Take D902 N fr Cluses; site 1km S of Taninges on L - just after 'Taninges' sp on ent town boundary; sp Camping-Caravaneige. Lge, pt shd, wc (htd); chem disp; mv service pnt; shwrs inc; EHU (6-10A) €2.50-4; lndry; shop; rest nr; bar nr; bbq; playgrnd; wifi; TV; dogs €1.30; phone; Eng spkn; quiet; ccard acc; tennis; CKE/CCI. "Splendid site with magnificent views; pool at Samoens 11km; peaceful & well-kept; lge pitches; friendly, helpful staff; excel facs; conv for N Haute Savoie & Switzerland to Lake Geneva; excel; wooded site; bit of rd noise." ♦ € 13.40 2017*

⊞ **TARASCON** 10E2 (5km SE Urban) 43.78638, 4.71789 Camp Municipal du Grès, 33 Ave du Docteur Barbarin, 13150 St Etienne-du-Grès [04 90 49 00 03 or 06 11 42 45 68; campingmunicipaldugres@ wanadoo.fr; www.campingalpilles.com] Fr Arles take N570 dir Avignon D99 E dir St Rémy. Site sp on o'skts of St Etienne. Sm, hdg, pt shd, wc; chem disp; mv service pnt; EHU (16A) €4; shop nr; wifi; dogs €1; quiet; CKE/CCI. "Gd, peaceful site; lge pitches; friendly staff; gd san facs, recently updated." € 14.00 2014*

TARASCON 10E2 (5km SE Rural) 43.76744, 4.69331 Camping St Gabriel, Route de Fontvieille, 13150 Tarascon [04 90 91 19 83; contact@camping saintgabriel.com; www.campingsaintgabriel.com] Take D970 fr Tarascon, at rndabt take D33 sp Fontvieille, site sp 100m on R. Med, hdg, shd, wc (htd); chem disp; mv service pnt; shwrs inc; EHU (6A) €3.3; gas; lndry; shop; rest nr; snacks; bar; playgrnd; pool (htd); wifi; TV; 30% statics; dogs €2; adv bkg acc; quiet; games rm; site clsd mid-Feb & Xmas/New Year; rv fishing; CKE/CCI. "Well-kept, charming site; excel base for Camargue & Arles; modern san facs; sm pitches poss not suitable lge o'fits; gd; 10 min walk into cent." ♦ 14 Mar-14 Nov. € 27.00 2016*

TARASCON SUR ARIEGE 8G3 (4km N Rural) 42.87910, 1.62829 Camping du Lac, 1 Promenade du Camping, 09400 Mercus-Garrabet [05 61 05 90 61 or 06 86 07 24 18 (mob); info@campinglac.com; www. campinglac.com] N20 S fr Foix, after 10km exit Mercus over N20 sp, cross rlwy line. At T-junc turn R thro Mercus, site of R over level x-ing. Tight bend into site off long, narr ent drive. Med, mkd, hdg, shd, terr, wc; chem disp; fam bthrm; shwrs inc; EHU (6-10A) €3.40-4.90; lndry; shop; rest nr; bar nr; bbq; pool (htd); sw nr; red long stay; 20% statics; dogs €2; phone; Eng spkn; adv bkg req; fishing adj; games rm; watersports adj; CKE/CCI. "Clean facs; friendly owners; sm pitches; bkg fee; steep entry rd with tight turn to get thro barrier; 60km Andorra; a real find!" ♦ 11 Apr-19 Sep. € 26.00 2014*

TARASCON SUR ARIEGE 8G3 (2km SE Rural) 42.83981, 1.61215 Kawan Village Le Pré-Lombard, Route d'Ussat, 09400 Tarascon-sur-Ariège [05 61 05 61 94; fax 05 61 05 78 93; leprelombard@wanadoo. fr; www.prelombard.com] Travelling S twd Andorra join N20 to Tarascon. Approx 17km S of Foix after 3 rndabts & x-ing a bdge, at 4th rndabt turn L, after rlwy on D618 foll site sp. This rte avoids cent of Tarascon. Lge, hdg, mkd, pt shd, wc (htd); chem disp; mv service pnt; shwrs inc; EHU (10A) inc; gas; lndry; shop; rest; snacks; bar; bbq; playgrnd; pool (htd); paddling pool; sw nr; entmnt; wifi; TV; 50% statics; dogs €4; Eng spkn; adv bkg rec; ccard acc; rv fishing adj; games rm; bike hire; archery; tennis; CKE/CCI. "Busy, well-run, family site in lovely location by rv; spacious pitches; helpful owner; san facs tired (2015), poss stretched high ssn; no o'fits over 6m; plenty for teenagers to do; canyoning & climbing nrby; gd base for exploring area; excel winter NH en rte to Spain; kayaking adj; poss rallies LS; excel; nice walk to town." ♦ 2 Mar-4 Oct. € 38.60 2015*

> **"Satellite navigation makes touring much easier"**
>
> Remember most sat navs don't know if you're towing or in a larger vehicle – always use yours alongside maps and site directions.

TARASCON SUR ARIEGE 8G3 (3km SW Rural) 42.81311, 1.58908 Camping Les Grottes, Dumaines de la Hille, 09400 Alliat [05 61 05 88 21; fax 05 61 03 89 91; info@campingdesgrottes.com; www. campingdesgrottes.com] S fr Foix on N20 dir Andorra, turn R onto D8 just past Tarascon-sur-Ariège sp Niaux/Vicdessos. Site on R in 2km. Med, hdg, hdstg, mkd, pt shd, wc; chem disp; mv service pnt; shwrs inc; EHU (6-10A) €2; lndry; shop; rest nr; snacks; bar; playgrnd; pool (htd); paddling pool; entmnt; TV; 20% statics; dogs €2; phone; adv bkg acc; quiet; waterslide; games area. "Lovely, peaceful site in valley; ideal NH for Andorra or long stay; Miglos Castle & Niaux cave nr; excel modern san facs; excel." 1 Mar-15 Oct. € 28.00 2017*

Camping Sites & Paysages LE PANORAMIC ★★★★ BRITTANY

On the Crozon peninsula and the bay of Douarnenez, this is a family campsite bordering the sea, where English is spoken and everything is well maintained. There are many holiday activities available, including a swimming pool, children's play area, tennis, bathing, sailing, mountain biking, etc., and a further choice of cultural activities in the Armorique Regional Park – the coast, the local ports, museums, and of course the richness of the Breton culture itself.

Family JACQ.
F-29560 Telgruc-sur-Mer – France
Tel. 0033 298 27 78 41 – Fax: 0033 298 27 36 10
Email: info@camping-panoramic.com
Internet: www.camping-panoramic.com

⊞ **TARDETS SORHOLUS** *8F1* (1km S Rural) *43.11143, -0.86362* **Camping du Pont d'Abense, 64470 Tardets-Sorholus** [05 59 28 58 76 or 06 78 73 53 59 (mob); camping.abense@wanadoo.fr; www.camping-pontabense.com] Take D918 S to Tardets, turn R to cross bdge onto D57. Site sp on R. Tardets cent narr. Med, shd, wc; chem disp; shwrs inc; EHU (3A) €3.20; lndry; shop nr; rest nr; bar nr; 10% statics; dogs €2; adv bkg acc; quiet; rv fishing nr; CKE/CCI. "Informal pitching; facs old; gd birdwatching; lovely, quaint site, a gem; nr gorges; heavenly!" € 26.00 2017*

TEICH, LE *7D1* (2km W Rural) *44.63980, -1.04272* **Camping Ker Helen, Ave de la Côte d'Argent, 33470 Le Teich** [05 56 66 03 79; fax 05 56 66 51 59; camping.kerhelen@wanadoo.fr; www.kerhelen.com] Fr A63 take A660 dir Arcachon & exit junc 2 onto D3 then D650 thru Le Teich. Site sp on L. Med, hdg, pt shd, wc (htd); chem disp; mv service pnt; fam bthrm; shwrs inc; EHU (10A) €3.70; lndry; rest; snacks; bar; playgrnd; pool; entmnt; wifi; TV; 75% statics; adv bkg acc; canoeing; horseriding; CKE/CCI. "Less cr than coastal sites in Arcachon region; bird reserve nrby; vg; rest and snacks bar only open in July and August." ♦ 16 Apr-16 Oct. € 25.30 2015*

TELGRUC SUR MER *2E2* (1km S Coastal) *48.22386, -4.37123* **Camping Le Panoramic, 130 Route de la Plage, 29560 Telgruc-sur-Mer** [02 98 27 78 41; fax 02 98 27 36 10; info@camping-panoramic.com; www.camping-panoramic.com] Fr D887 Crozon-Châteaulin rd, turn W on D208 twd Trez-Bellec Plage, site sp on R in approx 1.5km. Med, hdg, mkd, pt shd, terr, wc; chem disp; mv service pnt; fam bthrm; shwrs inc; EHU (6-10A) €3.50-4.50; lndry; shop; rest; snacks; bar; bbq; playgrnd; pool (covrd, htd); paddling pool; beach sand 700m; wifi; TV; 10% statics; dogs €2; adv bkg acc; quiet; ccard acc; jacuzzi; bike hire; tennis; games rm; CKE/CCI. "Vg, well-run, welcoming site; access to pitches poss diff due trees & narr site rds; rec; some facs tired need updating; sea views; excel rest, pool & all facs; helpful owner." ♦ 1 May-15 Sep. € 34.50 2014*

See advertisement

THANN *6F3* (9km NW Rural) *47.85071, 7.03058* **FFCC Camping La Mine d'Argent, Rue des Mines, 68690 Moosch** [03 89 82 30 66 or 03 89 60 34 74; fax 03 89 42 15 12; moosch@camping-la-mine-argent.com; www.camping-la-mine-argent.com] Turn L off N66 Thann-Thillot rd in cent of Moosch opp church; foll sps for 1.5km, ent on R, narr app. Med, mkd, pt shd, pt sl, terr, wc; chem disp; mv service pnt; shwrs inc; EHU (6-10A) €3-5.60; gas; lndry; shop nr; playgrnd; 10% statics; dogs €0.60; phone; adv bkg acc; quiet; ccard acc; CKE/CCI. "Well-kept site in wooded valley; busy w/end; helpful staff; excel walking; highly rec." 5 Apr-15 Oct. € 12.50 2015*

THENON *7C3* (3km SE Rural) *45.11883, 1.09119* **Camping Le Verdoyant, Route de Montignac, 24210 Thenon** [05 53 05 20 78; fax 05 53 44 05 00; contact@campingleverdoyant.fr; www.campingleverdoyant.fr] Sp fr A89, take D67 fr Thenon to Montignac. Site on R in 4km. Med, mkd, pt shd, sl, terr, wc; chem disp; shwrs inc; EHU (10A) €3.15 (rev pol) may req long lead; gas; lndry; shop nr; snacks; bar; playgrnd; pool; wifi; 20% statics; dogs €1.75; Eng spkn; adv bkg acc; quiet; lake fishing; CKE/CCI. "Beautiful setting away fr tourist bustle; friendly owners; excel base for area." ♦ 1 Apr-30 Sep. € 16.50 2017*

THIERS *9B1* (7km NE Rural) *45.89874, 3.59888* **Camping Les Chanterelles, Chapon 63500 St Rémy-sur-Durolle** [04 73 93 60 00; fax 04 73 94 31 71; contact@revea-vacances.com; www.revea-vacances.fr] On A72/E70 W dir Clermont-Ferrand, exit at junc 3 sp Thiers. Foll sp twd Thiers on N89 into L Monnerie. Fr vill, take D20 & foll sp St Rémy. In St Rémy, foll 'Camping' sp. Do not app thro Thiers as narr rds v diff for lge o'fits. Med, pt shd, terr, wc (htd); chem disp; mv service pnt; shwrs inc; EHU (10A) €3.50; gas; lndry; shop; bbq; playgrnd; pool (htd); paddling pool; sw nr; TV; 10% statics; dogs €1.50; adv bkg acc; quiet; ccard acc; waterslide; tennis 600m; windsurfing; CKE/CCI. "Vg site in beautiful situation with views; modern, clean facs; some noise at w/end fr statics; excel." ♦ 30 Apr-15 Sep. € 26.00 2013*

⊞ **THIEZAC** 7C4 (1km E Rural) 45.01360, 2.67027
Camping La Bédisse, 3 Rue de la Bédisse, 15800 Thiézac [0471 47 00 41; camping.thiezac@orange.fr; camping-thiezac.pagesperso-orange.fr]
Fr Murat, take N122 twds Vic sur Cere & Aurillac. In approx 24km foll sp to Thiezac. Site posted fr vill cent. EHU €4; lndry; bbq; playgrnd; sw; twin axles; wifi; 10% statics; dogs; Eng spkn; adv bkg acc; quiet; games area; CKE/CCI. "Tennis court; lovely rvside site; sh uphill walk to vill & shops; view of mountains; gd walks; rec; excel." ♦ € 13.00   2016*

> **"There aren't many sites open at this time of year"**
> If you're travelling outside peak season remember to call ahead to check site opening dates – even if the entry says 'open all year'.

⊞ **THILLOT, LE** 6F3 (4km NNE Rural) 47.90694, 6.78138 **Camping l'Oree du Bois, 51 Bis Grande Rue, 88160 Le Ménil** [03 29 25 04 88; contact@loree-du-bois.fr; www.loree-du-bois.fr]
Fr N66 bet Ramonchamp & St Maurice, in Le Thillot turn L (N) on D486. After 3km ent Le Menil. In middle of vill, immed opp church turn L to enter site behind hse selling honey. Gd sp after Le Thillot. Sm, unshd, terr, wc; chem disp; shwrs; EHU (10A) €5; lndry; rest; bar; playgrnd; 75% statics; dogs €1; phone; bus; Eng spkn; adv bkg acc; games rm; games area; CKE/CCI. "Gd walking & cycling, mkd trails fr site; htd pool adj; access to winter sports nrby; vg." ♦ € 18.00   2015*

⊞ **THILLOT, LE** 6F3 (1km NW Rural) 47.88893, 6.75683 **Camp Municipal du Clos de Chaume, 36 Rue de la Chaume, 88160 Le Thillot** [03 29 25 10 30; fax 03 29 25 25 87; campingmunicipal@ville-lethillot88.fr; www.ville-lethillot88.fr] Site sp on N o'skts of town N on N66, on R behind sports cent. Med, pt shd, pt sl, wc (htd); shwrs inc; EHU (6A) €1.80; gas; lndry; shop nr; playgrnd; 10% statics; adv bkg acc; quiet; tennis adj. "Attractive, well-maintained site; friendly staff; vg san facs; excel touring base." € 6.00   2012*

THIONVILLE 5C2 (1km NE Urban) 49.36127, 6.17534 **Camp Municipal Touristique, 6 Rue du Parc, 57100 Thionville** [03 82 53 83 75; fax 03 82 53 91 27; camping.municipal@mairie-thionville.fr; www.thionville.fr/fr/content/camping-municipal-touristique-1] Exit A31 at sp Thionville Cent; foll sp 'Centre Ville'; foll site sp dir Manom. Sm, hdstg, mkd, pt shd, wc; chem disp; mv service pnt; shwrs inc; EHU (3-10A) €2.40-4.65; shop nr; rest nr; bar nr; playgrnd; red long stay; wifi; dogs €1.20; Eng spkn; adv bkg acc; fishing; boating; CKE/CCI. "Well-kept site; some rvside pitches which can be noisy in eve; friendly warden; gd san facs; rec arr early high ssn; 5 min walk thro lovely adj park to town; vg; walk alongside rv as adj." ♦ 1 May-30 Sep. € 16.50   2017*

THIVIERS

⊞ **THIVIERS** 7C3 (10km N Rural) 45.50255, 0.91447
Camping Moulin du Touroulet, Moulin du Tourelet, 24800 Chaleix [05 53 55 23 59; touroulet@hotmail.com; www.camping-touroulet.com]
Fr Limoges on N21 S twd Périgueux, thro vill of La Coquille, in about 4.5km turn R onto D98 twd St Jory-de-Chalais & Chaleix. In 4km turn L to vill & site 1km further on. Take care narr bdge & site ent. Sm, hdstg, pt shd, pt sl, wc (htd); chem disp; shwrs inc; EHU (8A) €3; lndry; shop nr; rest; bar; bbq; pool; entmnt; wifi; dogs €0.50; adv bkg acc; quiet; fishing; games rm; CKE/CCI. "Beautiful site in tranquil rvside setting; spacious & well-kept; welcoming, helpful British owners; fishing avail on site; basic, ltd san facs, stretched high ssn; excel bar/rest; hdstg pitches sl & uneven; Xmas package; excel."
1 Mar-31 Dec. € 18.00   2012*

⊞ **THIVIERS** 7C3 (7km N Rural) 45.47390, 0.93808
Camping La Petite Lande, Lieu-dite La Petitie Lande, 24800 St Jory-de-Chalais [09 64 44 82 79; fax 05 53 62 42 89; info@la-petite-lande.com; www.la-petite-lande.com] N fr Thiviers on D21; in 6km turn L after La Poste onto unclassified rd sp 'La Petite Lande' campsite; foll sps to site in 500m. Sm, unshd, wc (htd); chem disp; mv service pnt; shwrs inc; EHU (6-10A) €3.75; lndry; shop nr; rest nr; bbq; playgrnd; pool; dogs €1; Eng spkn; quiet; ccard acc. "Relaxing, CL-type site; new site (2011); helpful Dutch owners; vg, clean facs plans to expand." ♦ € 11.00   2016*

> **"That's changed – Should I let the Club know?"**
> If you find something on site that's different from the site entry, fill in a report and let us know. See camc.com/europereport.

THIVIERS 7C3 (2km E Rural) 45.41299, 0.93209
Camping Le Repaire, Ave de Verdun, 24800 Thiviers [05 53 52 69 75; contact@camping-le-repaire.fr; www.camping-le-repaire.fr] N21 to Thiviers; at rndabt take D707 E dir Lanouaille; site in 1.5km on R. Med, mkd, hdg, pt shd, pt sl, terr, wc (htd); chem disp; mv service pnt; shwrs inc; EHU (12A) €3; lndry; shop nr; snacks; bbq; playgrnd; pool (covrd); entmnt; TV; 5% statics; dogs €2; phone; Eng spkn; adv bkg acc; quiet; games rm; lake fishing; CKE/CCI. "Lovely site, one of best in area; friendly owners; clean san facs; some pitches unrel in wet weather; excel; v nice tree shd plots." ♦ 1 Apr-4 Nov. € 20.00   2017*

THONNANCE LES MOULINS

St Disdille Camping Locations

Enjoy the Geneva Lake area, between the beach and the montains !

+33 (0)4.50.71.14.11
www.disdille.com

THONNANCE LES MOULINS *6E1* (2km W Rural) *48.40630, 5.27110* **Camping La Forge de Ste Marie, 52230 Thonnance-les-Moulins [03 25 94 42 00; fax 03 25 94 41 43; info@laforgedesaintemarie.com; www.laforgedesaintemarie.com or www.les-castels.com]** Fr N67 exit sp Joinville-Est, foll D60 NE sp Vaucouleurs. In 500m turn R onto D427 sp Poissons & Neufchâteau. Site on R in 11km. NB Swing wide at turn into site fr main c'way, not fr what appears to be a run in. Site ent narr. Lge, hdg, mkd, pt shd, pt sl, terr, serviced pitches; wc; chem disp; mv service pnt; fam bthrm; shwrs inc; EHU (6A) inc; gas; lndry; shop; rest; snacks; bar; bbq; pool (covrd, htd); paddling pool; entmnt; wifi; TV; 25% statics; dogs €2; phone; Eng spkn; adv bkg acc; ccard acc; games rm; bike hire; boating; lake fishing; games area; CKE/CCI. "Vg, well-kept, busy site; friendly, helpful owners; freshwater fishing; access poss diff to some terr pitches/sharp bends on site rds; muddy after rain; vg rest; no o'fits over 8m; mkt Fri; lovely spacious, well run site, beautiful area; swing wide at ent; poss no mob phone recep; san facs fair." ♦ 18 Apr-4 Sep. € 40.00 2015*

THONON LES BAINS *9A3* (3km NE Rural) *46.39944, 6.50416* **Camping Le Saint Disdille, 117 Ave de St Disdille, 74200 Thonon-Les-Bains [04 50 71 14 11; fax 04 50 71 93 67; camping@disdille.com; www.disdille.com]** Exit A41/A40 junc 14 Annemasse onto D1005 & foll sp Thonon twd Evian. At Vongy rndabt foll sp St Disdille & site. Site 200m fr Lake Geneva. V lge, mkd, shd, wc; fam bthrm; shwrs; EHU (6-10A) €4; gas; lndry; shop; rest; snacks; bar; bbq; playgrnd; sw nr; entmnt; wifi; 30% statics; dogs €3; adv bkg req; quiet; ccard acc; fishing; watersports; tennis; games area; bike hire; games rm; CKE/CCI. "Well-situated; well-equipped site; gd touring base for v nice area." ♦ 1 Apr-30 Sep. € 35.00 2013*

See advertisement

THONON LES BAINS *9A3* (13km W Rural) *46.35638, 6.35250* **Campéole Camping La Pinède, 74140 Excenevex [04 50 72 85 05 or 04 50 72 81 27 (Mairie); fax 04 50 72 93 00; pinede@campeole.com; www.camping-lac-leman.info or www.campeole.com]** On D1005 to Geneva, 10km fr Thonon, turn R at Camping sp. V lge, mkd, shd, wc (htd); chem disp; mv service pnt; fam bthrm; shwrs inc; EHU (10A) €4.10; gas; lndry; shop; rest; snacks; bar; bbq; playgrnd; beach sand adj; sw nr; entmnt; wifi; TV; 75% statics; dogs €3.50; adv bkg acc; quiet; horseriding 1km; games area; tennis; watersports adj; fishing adj. "Excel lakeside site; friendly & efficient staff; ltd touring emplacements." 28 Apr-30 Sep. € 30.00 2016*

THURY HARCOURT *3D1* (1km NE Rural) *48.98930, -0.46966* **FFCC Camping Vallée du Traspy, Rue du Pont Benoît, 14220 Thury-Harcourt [02 31 29 90 86; contact@campingdutraspy.com; www.campingdutraspy.com]** App fr N on D562 fr Caen, take L fork into town after pool complex. In 100m turn L at Hôtel de la Poste, 1st L to site, clearly sp adj Rv Orne. Med, mkd, pt shd, terr, wc; chem disp; mv service pnt; shwrs inc; EHU (4A) inc; gas; lndry; shop nr; snacks; bar; bbq; playgrnd; entmnt; 20% statics; dogs €2.90; phone; Eng spkn; adv bkg rec; quiet; fishing; canoeing; CKE/CCI. "Friendly owners; well-maintained pitches; o'night m'vans area; gd walking; site under new management with some refurbishment (2014); rec." ♦ 1 Apr-30 Sep. € 16.00 2014*

TIL CHATEL *6G1* (2km E Rural) *47.53042, 5.18700* **Camping Les Sapins, 21120 Til-Châtel [03 80 95 16 68; www.restaurantlessapins.eresto.net]** Leave A31 junc 5 onto D974 dir Til-Châtel. Site on R in 500m adj Rest Les Sapins. Sm, pt shd, pt sl, serviced pitches; wc; shwrs inc; EHU (10A) inc; shop nr; Eng spkn; adv bkg acc; CKE/CCI. "Clean, CL type site; basic san facs; no twin axles; conv NH fr a'route." 1 Apr-30 Sep. € 16.50 2016*

TINTENIAC 2E4 (1km N Rural) 48.33111, -1.83315
Camp Municipal du Pont L'Abbesse, Rue du 8 Mai 1945, 35190 Tinténiac [02 99 68 09 91 or 02 99 68 02 15 (Mairie); fax 02 99 68 05 44] Fr D137 turn E onto D20 to Tinténiac; go strt thro vill to canal; sp just bef canal bdge; turn L. Site behind Brit Hôtel La Guinguette, on Canal d'Ille et Rance. Sm, hdg, mkd, pt shd, pt sl, wc (htd); shwrs; EHU inc; shop nr; rest nr; bar nr; playgrnd; 10% statics; quiet; fishing; CKE/CCI. "Delightful, busy site; gd san facs; lovely walks/cycling along canal; vg; unreliable end of ssn closing; clsd at night by barrier; NH." ♦ 1 Mar-30 Sep. € 10.00   2017*

TINTENIAC 2E4 (2km S Rural) 48.31058, -1.82027
Camping Les Peupliers, Manoir de la Besnelais, 35190 Tinténiac [02 99 45 49 75; contact@domainelespeupliers.fr; www.domainelespeupliers.fr]
On D137 Rennes to St Malo rd; after Hédé foll rd to Tinténiac about 2km; site on main rd on R, sp. Med, hdg, mkd, pt shd, pt sl, wc; chem disp; mv service pnt; shwrs inc; EHU (6A) €2.90 (poss rev pol); lndry; shop nr; rest; snacks; bar; playgrnd; pool (htd); wifi; TV; 30% statics; dogs €1.60; phone; adv bkg acc; games area; tennis; lake fishing; CKE/CCI. "Pleasant, quiet, well-kept site; gd pool & park; on pilgrim rte to Spain; conv for acc to canal." ♦ 1 Apr-1 Oct. € 25.50   2018*

TONNERRE 4F4 (2km NE Urban) 47.86003, 3.98429
Camp Municipal de la Cascade, Ave Aristide Briand, 89700 Tonnerre [03 86 55 15 44 or 03 86 55 22 55 (Mairie); fax 03 86 55 30 64; ot.tonnerre@wanadoo.fr; www.revea-camping.fr or www.tonnerre.fr]
Best app via D905 (E by-pass); turn at rndabt twd town cent L after x-ing 1st rv bdge. Foll site sp to avoid low bdge (height 2.9m, width 2.4m). On banks of Rv Armançon & nr Canal de l'Yonne, 100m fr junc D905 & D944. Med, pt shd, wc (htd); chem disp; mv service pnt; fam bthrm; shwrs inc; EHU (6A) inc; lndry; shop; bar; playgrnd; sw nr; entmnt; wifi; TV; 10% statics; Eng spkn; adv bkg acc; ccard acc; fishing; CKE/CCI. "Pleasant, spacious, shady site in arboretum; friendly warden; lge pitches; excel clean san facs; often damp underfoot; no twin axles; interesting town; gd cycling/walking along canal; conv site; excel." ♦ 15 Apr-30 Oct. € 15.00   2015*

TORIGNI SUR VIRE 1D4 (1km S Rural) 49.02833, -0.97194 Camping Le Lac des Charmilles, Route de Vire, 50160 Torigny-sur-Vire [02 33 75 85 05 or 06 08 85 15 99; contact@camping-lacdescharmilles.com; www.camping-lacdescharmilles.com]
Exit A84 junc 40 onto D974 dir Torigni-sur-Vire/St Lô; site on R in 4km. Opp municipal stadium. Med, hdg, hdstg, mkd, pt shd, pt sl, wc (htd); chem disp; mv service pnt; fam bthrm; shwrs inc; EHU (10A) inc (long lead poss req); gas; lndry; shop; rest; snacks; bar; bbq; playgrnd; pool (htd); sw nr; twin axles; wifi; TV; 30% statics; dogs €2; phone; Eng spkn; adv bkg acc; quiet; ccard acc; games area; bike hire; games rm; CKE/CCI. "Lovely, well-kept, well-laid out site; clean, modern san facs, new shwr (2016); attractive, interesting town; excel; excel shopping in the town within walking dist; v helpful,friendly new owner (2016); picturesque lakes; tree-lined walks." ♦ 1 Apr-30 Sep. € 31.00   2017*

TORREILLES PLAGE 10G1 (1km N Coastal) 42.76750, 3.02972 Camping Sunêlia Les Tropiques, Blvd de la Méditerranée, 66440 Torreilles-Plage [04 68 28 05 09; fax 04 68 28 48 90; contact@campinglestropiques.com; www.campinglestropiques.com] Exit A9 junc 41 onto D83 E dir Le Barcarès, then D81 dir Canet-Plage. At 1st rndabt turn L onto D11 sp Torreilles-Plage, site sp. Lge, mkd, hdg, shd, wc; chem disp; mv service pnt; fam bthrm; shwrs inc; EHU (6A) inc; gas; lndry; shop; rest; snacks; bar; playgrnd; pool; paddling pool; beach sand 400m; red long stay; entmnt; wifi; TV; 80% statics; dogs €4; Eng spkn; ccard acc; waterslide; gym; bike hire; tennis; games area; CKE/CCI. "Vg family site; excel leisure & san facs." ♦ 9 Apr-1 Oct. € 48.50   2017*

TOUCY 4F4 (1km S Urban) 47.73159, 3.29677
Camping des Quatre Merlettes, Rue du Pâtis, 89130 Toucy [03 86 44 13 84; fax 03 86 44 28 42; 4merlettestoucy@orange.fr; www.ville-toucy.fr/public/?code=camping-municipal] On D3, 25km SW of Auxerre to Toucy. After rv x-ing take 1st L sp 'Base de Loisirs'. Site on S bank of Rv Quanne. Med, pt shd, wc; mv service pnt; shwrs inc; EHU (8A) €3.50; shop nr; pool (htd); 10% statics; adv bkg acc; quiet; fishing. "Pleasant vill; pleasant, helpful warden; no twin axles; mkt Sat; rests in walking dist; gd." 1 Apr-14 Oct. € 12.00   2016*

TOUL 6E2 (10km E Rural) 48.65281, 5.99260
Camping de Villey-le-Sec, 34 Rue de la Gare, 54840 Villey-le-Sec [03 83 63 64 28; info@campingvilleylesec.com; www.campingvilleylesec.com]
Exit Toul E on D909 or exit A31 junc 15 ondo D400 (W, in dir Hôpital Jeanne d'Arc); at rndabt turn L onto D909 to Villey-le-Sec; in vill site S by Rv Moselle, sp. V steep app rd. Med, hdg, mkd, hdstg, pt shd, wc; chem disp; mv service pnt; fam bthrm; shwrs inc; EHU (6-10A) €3.70-4.50; gas; lndry; shop; rest; snacks; bar; bbq; playgrnd; red long stay; dogs €1.80; phone; Eng spkn; quiet; ccard acc; games area. "Peaceful, well-kept site on rvside; lovely location; lge pitches; friendly; vg san facs, poss stretched; gd cycle paths; popular NH, ess arr bef 1800 high ssn." ♦ 1 Apr-15 Oct. € 22.00   2015*

TOULON SUR ARROUX 4H4 (1km W Urban) 46.69419, 4.13233 Camp Municipal Le Val d'Arroux, Route d'Uxeau, 71320 Toulon-sur-Arroux [03 85 79 51 22 or 03 85 79 42 55 (Mairie); fax 03 85 79 62 17] Fr Toulon-sur-Arroux NW on D985 over rv bdge; rturn L in 100m, site sp. Med, pt shd, wc; chem disp; mv service pnt; shwrs inc; EHU (6A) €3.25; lndry; shop nr; playgrnd; sw nr; 30% statics; dogs; quiet. "Rvside site; boules park adj; beautiful Buddhist temple 6km; gd." ♦ 16 Apr-15 Oct. € 9.50   2013*

TOULOUSE

⊞ **TOULOUSE** 8F3 (5km N Urban) 43.65569, 1.41585
Camping Toulouse Le Rupé, 21 Chemin du Pont de Rupé, 31200 Toulouse [05 61 70 07 35; fax 05 61 70 93 17; campinglerupe31@wanadoo.fr; www.camping-toulouse.com] N fr Toulouse on D820, sp. Poss tricky app fr N for long vans, suggest cont past Pont de Rupé traff lts to next rndabt & double back to turn. Fr S on ring rd exit junc 33A (after junc 12), turn immed R & foll sp. Lge, hdg, hdstg, mkd, pt shd, wc (htd); chem disp; mv service pnt; fam bthrm; shwrs inc; EHU (10A) €4; lndry; shop; rest; snacks; bar; playgrnd; wifi; TV; 50% statics; dogs €1.50; phone; bus; Eng spkn; ccard acc; games rm; lake fishing; CKE/CCI. "If site clsd 1200-1500, park in layby just bef site & use speakerphone; gd clean san facs; rock pegs poss req; ssn workers camp opp but no probs, site security excel; conv Airbus factory tours; space theme park 10km; well maintained; v helpful staff; ideal for dogs, children or walkers." € 28.00 2017*

⊞ **TOUQUET PARIS PLAGE, LE** 3B2 (5km N Rural) 50.55270, 1.61887 Camping La Dune Blanche, Route d'Etaples, 62176 Camiers [03 21 09 78 48 or 06 86 15 69 32 (mob); fax 03 21 09 79 59; duneblanche@wanadoo.fr; www.lesdomaines.org] Leave A16 junc 26 dir Etaples or junc 27 dir Neufchâtel onto D940 dir Etables, Le Touquet. Site well sp. Lge, mkd, shd, pt sl, wc (htd); chem disp; fam bthrm; shwrs inc; EHU (6A) €6; gas; lndry; shop nr; bar; bbq; playgrnd; beach sand 3km; red long stay; entmnt; TV; 90% statics; dogs €2.50; phone; adv bkg acc; quiet; ccard acc; CKE/CCI. "Amongst trees; remote, quiet by rlwy line; bus to beach at Ste Cécile; staff friendly & helpful." ♦ € 17.50 2014*

TOUQUET PARIS PLAGE, LE 3B2 (2km S Coastal) 50.51091, 1.58867 Camping Caravaning Municipal Stoneham, Ave François Godin, 62520 Le Touquet-Paris-Plage [03 21 05 16 55; fax 03 21 05 06 48; caravaning.stoneham@letouquet.com; www.letouquet.com] Fr Etaples on D939; stay in L-hand lane at traff lts dir airport & cont strt on (Ave du Général de Gaulle); L at traff lts sp Golf (Ave du Golf); foll rd to rndabt; turn R onto Ave François Godin (site sp); at next rndabt site on R. Or cont another 500m along Ave du Général de Gaulle to x-rds; turn L into Ave Louis Quetelart; in 500m at T-junc turn L into Ave François Godin; site on L in 200m. Lge, hdg, mkd, pt shd, wc; shwrs inc; EHU (16A) €5.80 (poss rev pol); lndry; shop nr; playgrnd; beach sand 1km; 82% statics; dogs €2; adv bkg rec; ccard acc; CKE/CCI. "Pleasant & well kept site; conv for town; helpful staff; excel facs; recep closes 1800 (LS 2010); htd pool 2km; m'van 'aires' nr harbour & equestrian cent; mkt Thu/Sat; walking & cycle paths to South Beach; town has many rest; gd sh stay." 2 Feb-15 Nov. € 26.40 2017*

TOUQUET PARIS PLAGE, LE 3B2 (6km S Coastal) 50.47343, 1.59178 Camping La Forêt, 149 Blvd de Berck, 62780 Stella-Plage [03 21 94 75 01; info@laforetstella.fr; www.laforetstella.fr] Exit A16 junc 26 onto D393 to Etaples; turn L onto D940 dir Berck; foll sp Stella-Plage. Blvd de Berck is turning S off D144 W to Stella-Plage. Med, hdg, mkd, unshd, wc; fam bthrm; shwrs; EHU €5; gas; lndry; shop; playgrnd; beach sand 2km; entmnt; wifi; 90% statics; dogs €2.50; phone; bus adj; Eng spkn; adv bkg acc; quiet; games rm; fishing nr; sailing; tennis 900m; windsurfing; games area. "Gd site; tourist attractions nrby; narr aves to pitches with tight corners; not suitable for lge o'fits; unisex facs; not a touring site." 1 Apr-30 Sep. € 27.00 2014*

TOUQUIN 4E4 (3km W Rural) 48.73305, 3.04697 Camping Les Etangs Fleuris, Route de la Couture, 77131 Touquin [01 64 04 16 36; fax 01 64 04 12 28; contact@etangs-fleuris.com; www.etangsfleuris.com] On D231 fr Provins, turn R to Touquin. Turn sharp R in vill & foll sp to site on R in approx 2km. Or fr Coulommiers, take D402 SW twd Mauperthuis, after Mauperthuis L twd Touquin. Foll sp in vill. NB Beware two unmkd speed bumps on entering vill. Med, hdstg, hdg, mkd, pt shd, wc (htd); chem disp; mv service pnt; shwrs inc; EHU (10A) inc; gas; lndry; shop; snacks; bar; bbq; playgrnd; pool (htd); paddling pool; entmnt; wifi; TV; 20% statics; dogs €1.50; phone; adv bkg acc; quiet; ccard acc; games rm; fishing; games area; CKE/CCI. "Peaceful site; no twin axles high ssn; conv Paris & Disneyland; helpful, supportive staff; no noise after 11pm." 5 Apr-15 Sep. € 31.00 2014*

> "I like to fill in the reports as I travel from site to site"
>
> You'll find report forms at the back of this guide, or you can fill them in online at camc.com/europereport.

⊞ **TOURNIERES** 1D4 (1km S Rural) 49.23017, -0.93256 Camping Le Picard, 14330 Tournières [02 31 22 82 44; fax 02 31 51 70 28; paulpalmer@orange.fr; www.normandycampsite.com] Fr Bayeux foll D5/D15 W to Tournières, 5km past Le Molay-Littry. Fr N13 Cherbourg-Bayeux, E of Carentan turn S onto N174 then E on D15 to Tournières. Site sp opp Tournières church. Sm, hdg, pt shd, serviced pitches; wc (htd); chem disp; shwrs inc; EHU (10A) €4.30; shop nr; rest; snacks; bar; playgrnd; pool (htd); wifi; 10% statics; phone; adv bkg acc; quiet; ccard acc; fishing; boating; CKE/CCI. "Delightful, British-owned site; conv Normandy beaches, Bayeux, Cherbourg ferry; friendly, helpful owners bake croissants & will do laundry; san facs need refurb/update; c'van storage; clean well maintained site; nice fishing pool with carp; home cooked food avail; themed evenings inc food." ♦ € 21.00 2013*

TOURS

⊞ **TOURNON SUR RHONE** *9C2* (0km N Rural) *45.07000, 4.83000* **FFCC Camping de Tournon HPA, 1 Promenade Roche-de-France, 07300 Tournon-sur-Rhône [04 75 08 05 28; camping@camping-tournon.com; www.camping-tournon.fr]** Fr Tain l'Hermitage cross Rhône, turn R onto D86; In approx 1km R at end of car park; turn L after 50m, site on R on Rv Rhône. Or fr N on D86, sp on L by car park. Med, shd, wc (htd); chem disp; mv service pnt; shwrs inc; EHU (6-10A) €4-6.50; gas; lndry; shop nr; rest nr; bar nr; playgrnd; red long stay; wifi; 10% statics; dogs €2; phone; Eng spkn; adv bkg rec; canoeing; CKE/CCI. "Pleasant, well-kept site in wooded location; rvside pitches; friendly owners; clean, dated san facs (unisex LS); m'van o'night area; c'van storage avail; some sm pitches & narr site rds poss diff lge o'fits; gd security; footbdge to Tain-l'Hermitage; fr mid-Jun rock concerts poss held nrby at w/end; gd; conv NH; interesting old town." ♦ € 24.00   2016*

TOURNON SUR RHONE *9C2* (4km W Rural) *45.06786, 4.78516* **Camping Le Castelet, 113 Route du Grand Pont, 07300 St Jean-de-Muzols [04 75 08 09 48; fax 04 75 08 49 60; courrier@camping-lecastelet.com; www.camping-lecastelet.com]** Exit Tournon on D86 N; in 500m turn L on D532 twd Lamastre; in 4km turn R on D532 over bdge & turn immed R into site. Med, hdstg, mkd, pt shd, terr, wc; chem disp; fam bthrm; shwrs inc; EHU (10A) €4.50; gas; lndry; shop; bar; bbq; playgrnd; pool; paddling pool; entmnt; wifi; TV; dogs €2; adv bkg acc; quiet; fishing; games rm. "Lovely, family-run site in beautiful setting; excel facs." 5 Apr-13 Sep. € 37.00   2014*

TOURNUS *9A2* (1km N Urban) *46.57244, 4.90854* **Camping de Tournus, 14 Rue des Canes, 71700 Tournus [03 85 51 16 58; camping-tournus@orange.fr; www.camping-tournus.com]** Fr N6 at N of town turn E opp rlwy stn & rest 'Le Terminus;' foll site sp. Med, hdstg, mkd, pt shd, pt sl, wc; chem disp; mv service pnt; shwrs inc; EHU (10A) €4.70 (long lead poss req)(poss rev pol); gas; lndry; snacks; bar; bbq; playgrnd; wifi; TV; dogs €2.60; Eng spkn; rv fishing 100m; CKE/CCI. "Peaceful, rvside site in nice position; popular NH, conv A6 - rec arr early; helpful staff; clean facs poss stretched high ssn & ltd LS; htd pools adj; poss extra charge twin axles; rv walk into town; gd cycling nrby; quiet but rd & rlwy noise some pitches; abbey worth visit; vg; well kept site; helpful staff." ♦ 1 Apr-30 Sep. € 27.00   2017*

TOURNUS *9A2* (9km S Rural) *46.48768, 4.91286* **Camping International d'Uchizy - Le National 6, 71700 Uchizy [03 85 40 53 90; camping.uchizylen6@wanadoo.fr; www.camping-lenational6.com]** Exit A6 junc 27 & foll N6 S; sp on L, turn L over rwly bdge on lane to site on L. Adj Rv Saône. Med, shd, wc; shwrs inc; EHU (6A) €3.90; gas; shop; snacks; playgrnd; pool; dogs €1; adv bkg acc; fishing; boat hire. "Attractive, well-maintained site; gd, modern san facs; pitches soft & muddy in rain; cash only; arr early for rvside pitch; lovely position." 1 Apr-30 Sep. € 26.40   2017*

⊞ **TOURS** *4G2* (8km E Rural) *47.40226, 0.77845* **Camping Les Acacias, Rue Berthe Morisot, 37700 La Ville-aux-Dames [02 47 44 08 16; fax 02 47 46 26 65; contact@camplvad.com; www.camplvad.com]** Fr Tours take D751 E sp Amboise; after 6km at rndabt where La Ville-aux-Dames sp to R, go strt on for 200m, then turn R, site sp. Med, shd, serviced pitches; wc (htd); chem disp; mv service pnt; fam bthrm; shwrs; EHU (10A) inc; gas; lndry; shop; rest; snacks; bar; bbq; playgrnd; wifi; 30% statics; dogs €2; bus nr; Eng spkn; adv bkg acc; ccard acc; tennis 600m; fishing 100m; games rm; CKE/CCI. "Well-kept, well-run, level site; excel san facs, ltd LS; conv town cent; fitness trail; many long-term residents; gd site; conv NH; lovely friendly helpful English speaking owners; mountain bike circuit; lge supmkt nr; bus to city nr; childrens playgrnd; pool 500m; gd for long or sh stays." ♦ € 22.00   2017*

> ## "We must tell the Club about that great site we found"
> Get your site reports in by mid-August and we'll do our best to get your updates into the next edition.

TOURS *4G2* (8km E Rural) *47.39273, 0.81085* **Camping Les Peupliers, 37270 Montlouis-sur-Loire [02 47 50 81 90 or 03 86 37 95 83; aquadis1@wanadoo.fr; www.aquadis-loisirs.com]** On D751, 2km W of vill of Montlouis. Fr N foll sp to Vouvray (keep on N side of Rv Loire to avoid Tours) & cross rv by bdge to Montlouis. Sp at last min. NB App fr E a 'Q-turn' to get into site. Lge, hdg, pt shd, wc (htd); chem disp; mv service pnt; fam bthrm; shwrs inc; EHU (6A) €2; lndry; shop nr; playgrnd; 12% statics; dogs €1.90; Eng spkn; adv bkg acc; ccard acc; tennis; CKE/CCI. "Clean, tidy site; poss clsd mid-Oct; lge pitches; mkt Sun in Amboise; vg." ♦ 1 Apr-31 Oct. € 15.50   2012*

TOURS *4G2* (5km SE Urban) *47.37070, 0.72305* **Camping Les Rives du Cher, 61 Rue de Rochepinard, 37550 St Avertin [02 47 27 87 47; fax 02 47 25 82 89; contact@camping-lesrivesducher.com; www.camping-lesrivesducher.com]** Fr Tours, take D976 S of rv sp Bléré/Vierzon into St Avertin vill. Take next L at traff lts over 1st of 2 bdges. Site on R in 450m, not well sp. Med, hdg, hdstg, mkd, pt shd, wc; chem disp; mv service pnt; shwrs inc; EHU (10A) €4.20 (poss rev pol); lndry; shop nr; rest nr; bar nr; playgrnd; red long stay; wifi; dogs €1.20; phone; bus nrby; Eng spkn; adv bkg acc; quiet; ccard acc; tennis; fishing; CKE/CCI. "Clean & tidy site but needs updating; some lge pitches; friendly owner; htd pool adj; some resident workers; frequent bus to Tours." ♦ 1 Apr-15 Oct. € 19.00   2013*

TOURS

TOURS *4G2* (8km SW Urban) *47.35530, 0.63401*
Camping La Mignardière, 22 Ave des Aubépines, 37510 Ballan-Miré [02 47 73 31 00; fax 09 56 64 93 87; info@mignardiere.com; www.mignardiere.com] Fr A10 exit junc 24 onto N585 & D37 by-pass. At exit for Joué-lès-Tours foll sp Ballan-Miré onto D751. Turn R at 1st set traff lts & foll site sp to W of lake. Lge, hdstg, mkd, hdg, pt shd, serviced pitches; wc (htd); chem disp; mv service pnt; fam bthrm; shwrs inc; EHU (6-10A) €3.50; lndry; shop; snacks; bar nr; bbq; playgrnd; pool (covrd, htd); entmnt; wifi; TV; dogs; phone; Eng spkn; adv bkg acc; squash; bike hire; tennis; windsurfing 1km; fishing 1km; CKE/CCI. "Conv Loire valley & chateaux; friendly, helpful staff; unisex facs LS; gd cycle paths; vg site; rec; bar 200m; gd san facs; v conv for bus/tram to Tours." ♦ 1 Apr-25 Sep. € 27.00   2018*

See advertisement

> **"I need an on-site restaurant"**
>
> We do our best to make sure site information is correct, but it is always best to check any must-have facilities are still available or will be open during your visit.

TOURS *4G2* (10km W Rural) *47.35054, 0.54964*
Camping de la Confluence, Route de Bray, 37510 Savonnières [02 47 50 00 25; contact@campinglaconfluence.fr; www.onlycamp.fr] Fr Tours take D7 on S of Rv Cher. Site on R on ent Savonnières on rvside. Med, hdg, mkd, hdstg, pt shd, wc; chem disp; mv service pnt; fam bthrm; shwrs; EHU (10A) €4.20; lndry; shop nr; rest nr; bar nr; bbq; playgrnd; dogs €1.20; phone; bus 200m; Eng spkn; adv bkg acc; quiet; tennis adj; canoe hire; CKE/CCI. "Well-kept, clean, pleasant site; friendly, efficient staff; modern unisex san facs (a bit dated, 2018); some pitches narr & awnings diff; lovely vill with basic facs; gd touring base; gd birdwatching, cycling; bar adj; highly rec; gd touring base; on cycle rte." ♦ 30 Apr-30 Sep. € 23.00   2018*

TOURS *4G2* (8km W Rural) *47.38950, 0.59616*
Camping L'Islette, 23 Rue de Vallières, 37230 Fondettes [02 47 42 26 42; www.camping-de-lislette.ruedesloisirs.com] Foll D952 W fr Tours twd Saumur. In approx 6km turn R at traff lts onto D276 at Port-de-Vallières. Site on L in approx 2km. Sm, hdg, pt shd, wc; mv service pnt; shwrs inc; EHU (10A) €2.50; shop nr; playgrnd; dogs; bus; adv bkg acc; quiet; CKE/CCI. "Pleasant site; helpful owners; facs poss stretched if site full; poss boggy when wet; pool 4km; conv for Langeais & Luynes chateaux." ♦ 1 Apr-31 Oct. € 9.40   2013*

TOURY *4F3* (1km S Urban) *48.19361, 1.93260* **Camp Municipal, Rue de Boissay, 28310 Toury** [02 37 90 50 60 (Mairie); fax 02 37 90 58 61; mairie-toury@wanadoo.fr; www.ville-toury.fr] Fr Orléans take N20 N. Site well sp. Sm, pt shd, wc; chem disp; shwrs inc; EHU (6A) €3; shop nr; rest nr; bar nr; bbq; playgrnd; dogs. "NH only; warden calls; poss travellers LS & unclean san facs; bar 100m; high ssn rec arrive bef 1600 to ensure pitch." 15 Apr-15 Oct. € 10.00   2014*

> **"Satellite navigation makes touring much easier"**
>
> Remember most sat navs don't know if you're towing or in a larger vehicle – always use yours alongside maps and site directions.

TRANCHE SUR MER, LA *7A1* (1km E Coastal) *46.34945, -1.43280* **Camping Bel, Rue de Bottereau, 85360 La Tranche-sur-Mer** [02 51 30 47 39; fax 02 51 27 72 81; campbel@wanadoo.fr; www.campingbel.com] Ent La Tranche on D747, take 2nd R at rndabt, R at traff lts, ent on L. Med, hdg, mkd, pt shd, wc; chem disp; fam bthrm; shwrs inc; EHU (10A) inc; lndry; shop nr; rest nr; snacks; bar; playgrnd; pool; paddling pool; TV; 70% statics; phone; Eng spkn; adv bkg acc; quiet; table tennis; CKE/CCI. "Ideal for families with young children; bike hire nrby." ♦ 26 May-3 Sep. € 20.00   2017*

TRANCHE SUR MER, LA *7A1 (1km E Coastal) 46.34611, -1.43225* **Camping La Baie d'Aunis, 10 Rue de Pertuis-Breton, 85360 La Tranche-sur-Mer [02 51 27 47 36; fax 02 51 27 44 54; info@camping-baiedaunis.com; www.camping-baiedaunis.com]**
Fr La Roche-sur-Yon on D747 to La Tranche-sur-Mer; at 1st rndabt turn R, at 2nd rndabt (by Super U) turn L, at 3rd rndabt turn R - (all sp Centre Ville); ahead at min-rndabt & site on L in 100m. Med, mkd, hdg, hdstg, pt shd, wc (htd); chem disp; mv service pnt; fam bthrm; shwrs inc; EHU (10A) inc; gas; lndry; shop nr; rest; snacks; bar; bbq; playgrnd; pool (htd); beach sand adj; entmnt; TV; 10% statics; dogs (not Jul/Aug) €2.30; Eng spkn; adv bkg rec; quiet; ccard acc; sea fishing; watersports; games rm; tennis 500m; sailing; CKE/CCI. "Vg, friendly site; bike hire adj; helpful staff; excel san facs; excel rest; poss diff ent for lge o'fits; gd beaches, lovely area." ♦ 26 Apr-15 Sep. € 35.00   2013*

> **"There aren't many sites open at this time of year"**
>
> If you're travelling outside peak season remember to call ahead to check site opening dates – even if the entry says 'open all year'.

TRANCHE SUR MER, LA *7A1 (4km E Coastal) 46.34781, -1.38303* **Camping La Grande Vallée, 145 blvd de Lattre de Tassigny, 85360 La Tranche-sur-Mer [02 51 30 12 82; c.lagrandevallee@orange.fr; www.campinglagrandevallee.com]** Fr La Roche Sur Yon on D747 to Latranche. At rndabt turn L onto D46, in 5km at rndabt turn R sp Le Gote L'Aiguillon. R at next rndabt. Site sp on R past Spar. Med, mkd, pt shd, wc; chem disp; mv service pnt; fam bthrm; shwrs inc; EHU (4-10A); lndry; snacks; bar; bbq; playgrnd; beach 700m; red long stay; 10% statics; dogs; bus; Eng spkn; adv bkg acc; quiet; ccard acc. "Vg; rec long stay; bike hire; coastal bus Jul-Aug; friendly young owners; bkg fee for mid/high ssn." 1 Apr-30 Sep. € 30.00   2014*

TREBEURDEN *1D2 (4km NW Coastal) 48.79905, -3.58386* **Camp Municipal Le Dourlin, L'Île Grande, 22560 Pleumeur-Bodou [02 96 91 92 41 or 02 96 23 91 17 (Mairie); infos.tourisme@pleumeur-bodou.com; www.pleumeur-bodou.com]**
Off D788 N fr Trébeurden. Foll minor rd thro vill to site on coast. Well sp. Med, mkd, unshd, wc; chem disp; mv service pnt; shwrs inc; EHU (6A) €2.35; lndry; shop nr; rest; snacks; bar; bbq; playgrnd; beach shgl adj; wifi; dogs €0.60; phone; bus; Eng spkn; quiet; sailing; games area; fishing; CKE/CCI. "Popular site in excel location - fine sea views; excel facs; gd walking, cycling; ornithological cent nr; 8km circular coast rd round peninsula; gd; lovely coastal walk; well stocked shop in vill." ♦ 30 Apr-27 Sep. € 9.00   2017*

TREGUNC

TREGASTEL *1D2 (3km NE Coastal) 48.82549, -3.49135* **Tourony Camping, 105 Rue de Poul-Palud, 22730 Trégastel [02 96 23 86 61; fax 02 96 15 97 84; contact@camping-tourony.com; www.camping-tourony.com]** On D788 fr Trébeurden dir Perros Guirec, site on R imm after exit Trégastel town sp & imm bef bdge over Traouieros inlet, opp Port de Ploumanac'h. Med, hdg, mkd, pt shd, wc; chem disp; mv service pnt; fam bthrm; shwrs inc; EHU (6A) €3; gas; lndry; shop nr; snacks; bar; bbq; playgrnd; beach sand adj; red long stay; entmnt; TV; 15% statics; dogs €1.50; Eng spkn; adv bkg acc; quiet; ccard acc; tennis; bike hire; games area; horseriding nr; lake fishing; golf nr; CKE/CCI. "Pleasant, lovely sm site in gd location; friendly, helpful staff; gd touring base Granit Rose coast; sm pitches dif for lge o'fits; clean but dated san facs (2015)." ♦ 31 Mar-22 Sep. € 25.00   2018*

TREGASTEL *1D2 (4km SW Rural/Coastal) 48.80995, -3.54140* **Camping du Port, 3 Chemin des Douaniers, 22560 Landrellec [02 96 23 87 79 or 06 73 78 32 64 (mob); renseignements@camping-du-port-22.com; www.camping-du-port-22.com]** Turn off D788 to Landrellec & foll rd thro vill past shop for 100m, take care tight turn L. Site in 500m. Med, mkd, hdg, pt shd, pt sl, serviced pitches; wc (htd); chem disp; mv service pnt; fam bthrm; shwrs inc; EHU (10-15A) €3.20-3.50; gas; lndry; shop; rest; snacks; bar; bbq; playgrnd; beach sand; entmnt; wifi; TV; 25% statics; dogs €2.50; Eng spkn; adv bkg acc; quiet; ccard acc; waterskiing; games rm; bike hire; boating; fishing; CKE/CCI. "Immac, family-owned site; beautiful location; direct access beach; beach front pitches extra charge but narr; coastal path runs thro site; lots of lovely beaches nrby; telecoms museum worth visit; excel." ♦ 21 Mar-8 Nov. € 22.00   2015*

TREGUIER *1D3 (10km N Coastal) 48.85810, -3.22013* **FFCC Camping Le Varlen, 4 Pors-Hir, 22820 Plougrescant [02 96 92 52 15; fax 02 96 92 50 34; info@levarlen.com; www.levarlen.com]**
Take D8 N out of Tréguier to Plougrescant. Go past old chapel then imm bef church turn R sp Pors-Hir to site in 1km on R. Sm, mkd, pt shd, pt sl, wc; mv service pnt; fam bthrm; shwrs inc; EHU (6-10A) €3.50-3.90 (poss rev pol); lndry; shop; bar; playgrnd; beach shgl 300m; 90% statics; dogs €1.50; adv bkg acc; quiet; ccard acc; games area. "Friendly, helpful owners; some pitches sm & poss diff lge o'fits/m'vans; coastal walks." 1 Mar-15 Nov. € 15.00   2013*

TREGUNC *2F2 (4km SW Coastal) 47.83384, -3.89173* **Camping La Plage Loc'h Ven, Plage de Pendruc, 29910 Trégunc [02 98 50 26 20; fax 02 98 50 27 63; contact@lochven.com; www.lochven.com]**
Fr N165 exit at Kérampaou sp Trégunc. At rndbt W of Trégunc foll Loc'h Ven sp thro Lambell, site on coast. Med, hdg, mkd, pt shd, pt sl, wc (htd); chem disp; fam bthrm; shwrs inc; EHU (4-10A) €3.50-4.70; gas; lndry; shop nr; rest nr; playgrnd; beach shgl adj; TV; 40% statics; dogs free (€1.60 high ssn); Eng spkn; adv bkg acc; quiet; games area. "Easy walk to beach, rock pools & coastal footpath; helpful owners." 28 Apr-20 Sep. € 18.50   2014*

TREIGNAC

TREIGNAC *7B4* (5km N Rural) *45.56023, 1.81369*
Camping La Plage, Lac des Barriousses, 19260 Treignac [05 55 98 08 54; fax 05 55 98 16 47; camping.laplage@flowercampings.com; www.laplagecamping.com] On D940 opp Lac des Barriousses. Med, mkd, shd, pt sl, terr, wc (htd); chem disp; mv service pnt; shwrs inc; EHU (6A) €2.80; lndry; shop; rest nr; snacks; sw nr; 5% statics; dogs €1.20; adv bkg acc; quiet; fishing adj; boating adj; CKE/CCI. "Beautiful area & outlook; friendly; facs unclean LS." ♦ 30 Mar-29 Sep. € 22.70   2013*

TREIGNAC *7B4* (10km SE Rural) *45.50262, 1.86911*
Camping Le Fayard (Naturist), Cors, 19260 Veix [05 55 94 00 20 or 0031 113301245 (N'lands); veen514@zonnet.nl; www.le-fayard.com] Fr Treignac take D16 dir Lestards. 1km after Lestards take D32 S & in 2km turn R dir Cors, site sp. Sm, mkd, pt shd, pt sl, wc; chem disp; fam bthrm; shwrs inc; EHU (6A) €3.50; lndry; bar; playgrnd; pool (htd); dogs €2; adv bkg acc; quiet; games area; CKE/CCI. "Friendly Dutch owners; relaxing site in National Park of Limousin." ♦ 1 May-19 Sep. € 16.00   2012*

TREPORT, LE *3B2* (1km N Urban) *50.05805, 1.38860*
Camp Municipal Les Boucaniers, Rue Pierre Mendès-France, 76470 Le Tréport [02 35 86 35 47; fax 02 27 28 04 10; camping@ville-le-treport.fr; www.ville-le-treport.fr] Fr Eu take minor rd sp to Le Tréport under low bdge. On ent o'skts of Le Tréport, turn R at traff lts, camp ent 100m on R. Site nr stadium. Lge, hdstg, pt shd, wc (htd); shwrs inc; EHU (6A) €4.60; lndry; shop; rest; snacks; bar; playgrnd; beach sand 2km; entmnt; wifi; TV; 10% statics; dogs €1.60; quiet; games rm. "Busy, well-kept, well-run site; some lge pitches; gd, clean san facs; gd sep m'van area; lots to see in Le Tréport; m'van Aire de Service adj; gd value; excel; check elec lead is long enough bef unhitching." ♦ 28 Mar-30 Sep. € 18.00   2017*

TREPT *9B2* (3km E Rural) *45.68701, 5.35190*
Camping les 3 Lacs du Soleil, La Plaine de Serrières, 38460 Trept [04 74 92 92 06; fax 04 74 83 43 81; info@les3lacsdusoleil.com; www.camping-les3lacsdusoleil.com] Exit A432 at junc 3 or 3 & head twd Crémieu then Morestel. Trept bet these 2 towns on D517, site sp by lakes. Lge, pt shd, wc; chem disp; fam bthrm; shwrs inc; EHU (6A) inc; lndry; shop; rest; snacks; bar; bbq (gas); playgrnd; pool; paddling pool; sw nr; entmnt; wifi; TV; 5% statics; dogs €2.50; phone; Eng spkn; adv bkg acc; quiet; ccard acc; waterslide; fishing; tennis; games area; archery; horseriding 2km. "Gd family site; gd, modern san facs; fitness rm; lge & busy site with lots of activities." ♦ 26 Apr-7 Sep. € 35.50   2014*

TRETS *10F3* (4km SW Rural) *43.44178, 5.62847*
Camping Le Devançon, Chemin de Pourachon, 13790 Peynier [04 42 53 10 06; fax 04 42 53 04 79; reservation@ledevancon.fr; www.ledevancon.fr] Leave A8 at Canet or Pas-de-Trets or leave D6 at Trets & take D908 to Peynier. In vill cont on D908 sp Marseille. Site on R at end vill after g'ge. Med, mkd, hdstg, shd, pt sl, wc (htd); chem disp; mv service pnt; shwrs inc; EHU (3-10A) €3-5; gas; lndry; shop; rest; snacks; bar; bbq; playgrnd; pool; paddling pool; red long stay; entmnt; TV; 50% statics; dogs €1; Eng spkn; adv bkg acc; quiet; ccard acc; tennis; CKE/CCI. "Excel facs & site; helpful owner; poss diff manoeuvring onto pitches for lge o'fits; few water points; gd touring area." ♦ 1 Mar-5 Nov. € 27.00   2017*

TREVIERES *1D4* (1km NE Rural) *49.31308, -0.90578*
Camp Municipal Sous Les Pommiers, Rue du Pont de la Barre, 14710 Trévières [02 31 22 57 52 or 02 31 92 89 24; fax 02 31 22 19 49; mairie@ville-trevieres.fr] Turn S off N13 onto D30 sp Trévières. Site on R on ent to vill. Med, mkd, hdg, pt shd, wc cont; chem disp; mv service pnt; shwrs inc; EHU (10A) €3; lndry; shop nr; rest; playgrnd; wifi; adv bkg rec; quiet; rv fishing adj; CKE/CCI. "Delightful site in apple orchard; lge pitches; vg san facs; conv D-Day beaches; excel site; sm town in walking dist." ♦ 1 Apr-30 Sep. € 14.00   2014*

TRIE SUR BAISE *8F2* (3km NE Rural) *43.34400, 0.36970* **Camping Fontrailles, Le Quartier Lanorbe, 65220 Fontrailles** [05 62 35 62 52; detm.paddon@orange.fr; www.fontraillescamping.com] Fr N on N21 leave Mirande & turn L (S) at end of town sp Trie-sur-Baïse onto D939; after St Michel look out for silos on R after 7km, site sp. Fr S at Miélan turn onto D3/D17 sp Trie-sur-Baïse to Fontrailles. Sm, pt shd, pt sl, wc; chem disp; shwrs inc; EHU (9A) €2.50; shop nr; rest nr; bbq; playgrnd; pool; red long stay; wifi; dogs; Eng spkn; adv bkg acc; quiet; fishing; tennis; CKE/CCI. "Delightful, well-kept CL-type site in orchard; friendly, helpful British owners; excel pool & tennis nrby; gd walking; conv Lourdes, Pyrenees & Spain; mkt Trie-sur-Baïse Tues; excel site; beautiful views." 1 Jul-30 Sep. € 17.00   2012*

TRIE-SUR-BAISE *8F2* (22km WNW Urban) *43.388595, 0.155504* **Camping Municipal La Galotte, 44 Rue de Mirande, 65140 Rabastens de Bigorre** [05 62 36 57 64 or 06 10 35 34 95; camping.lagalotte@gmail.com; www.camping-lagalotte.com] Turn R (fr Tarbes, S) in ctr of Rabastens-de-Bigorre and foll N21. Site on R on outskirts of town abt 1km. Sm, shd, wc; chem disp; mv service pnt; shwrs inc; EHU (10A); gas; lndry; shop nr; bbq (charcoal, elec, gas, sep area); twin axles; Eng spkn; adv bkg acc; quiet; CKE/CCI. "Gd, basic site on edge of vill; suitable for short stays." 1 Apr-30 Sep. NP 19.8   2018*

TULLE

TROYES *4E4* (3km NE Urban) *48.31150, 4.09630*
Camp Municipal de Troyes, 7 Rue Roger Salengro, 10150 Pont-Ste Marie [03 25 81 02 64; info@troyescamping.net; www.troyescamping.net]
Fr N exit A26 junc 22 onto D677. site on R opp stadium & adj Esso g'ge, just pass junc with D960. Fr S exit A26 junc 23 for Pont-Ste-Mairie. Pont-Ste-Marie & site 'municipal' well sp fr all dirs & in town. NB Queues form onto rd outside site, use Esso g'ge to turn if queue too long. Med, hdstg, hdg, mkd, pt shd, wc (htd); chem disp; mv service pnt; shwrs inc; EHU (10A) (long lead poss req); gas; lndry, shop; rest nr; snacks; bbq; playgrnd; pool (htd); red long stay; wifi; TV; dogs €1.15; bus opp; Eng spkn; adv bkg acc; ccard acc; games area; bike hire; games rm; CKE/CCI. "Busy, popular, transit site in parkland - rec arr early; can be noisy at w/ends; vg pool; some lge pitches; some pitches soft when wet; diff access some pitches; twin axles acc at recep's discretion; red facs LS; takeaway; Troyes Cathedral, museums & old quarter worth visit; Lac d'Orient & Lac du Temple nrby; conv NH; gd rest by rv bdge 3 min fr site; conv for m'way; pleasant friendly site; clean facs; excel snacks/rest; stay 7 nights pay for 6." ♦
1 Apr-16 Oct. € 27.00   2017*

TROYES *4E4* (16km E Rural) *48.28998, 4.28279*
Camping La Fromentelle, Ferme Fromentelle, 10220 Dosches [03 25 41 52 67; fax 03 25 40 78 38; www.tourisme-champagne-ardenne.com] Exit A26 junc 23 onto D619 dir Bar-sur-Aube. In 8.5km turn L onto D1 sp Géraudot (take care bends). Site on L in 5km. Sm, mkd, pt shd, pt sl, wc; chem disp; mv service pnt; shwrs inc; EHU (6-10A) €3 (long lead poss req)(poss rev pol); shop nr; bbq; playgrnd; beach sand 5km; sw nr; dogs €1.50; adv bkg acc; quiet; games area; CKE/CCI. "Beautiful, lovely farm/CL-type site in old orchard; well-kept & well-run; warm welcome, charming owner; v clean san facs; gd for birdwatching, sailing, watersports on lakes; excel cycle tracks; nr nature reserve, lakes & forest; conv A26; excel spacious pitches; gd facs; some rd noise; hg rec old town in Troyes." ♦ 30 Apr-15 Oct. € 15.00   2018*

TROYES *4E4* (14km SE Rural) *48.20106, 4.16620* Le Base de Loisirs au Plan d'Eau 'Les Terres Rouges', 10390 Clérey [06 70 00 76 75; terres-rouges@wanadoo.fr; www.les-terres-rouges.com]
Exit A5 junc 21 onto D671 S dir Bar-sur-Seine & Dijon; site on R in 3.5km. Or SE fr Troyes on D671 dir Bar-sur-Seine, foll sp Clérey; then as bef. Site well sp. App over gravel track thro gravel quarry area. Sm, hdstg, pt shd, wc (htd); chem disp; shwrs; EHU (5-10A) €3.20 (poss rev pol); shop nr; rest; snacks; bar; playgrnd; sw; wifi; 10% statics; dogs; phone; adv bkg acc; tennis; waterskiing; fishing; boating; CKE/CCI. "Gd, basic NH; clean, v basic san facs; friendly, helpful new owners(2017); gate opens 0600, recep clsd 1900; conv fr a'route to Calais; commuter traff noise." ♦
2 April-30 Sep. € 19.00   2017*

TUCHAN *8G4* (1km S Rural) *42.88302, 2.71861*
Camping La Peiriere, route de Paziols, 11350 Tuchan [04 68 45 46 50; fax 04 68 45 03 39; lapeiriere@lapeiriere.com; www.lapeiriere.com]
Fr Tuchan dir Paziols on L, 200m fr edge of town. Med, hdg, mkd, shd, wc; chem disp; mv service pnt; shwrs; EHU (9A); rest; snacks; bar; bbq; playgrnd; pool; paddling pool; wifi; 10% statics; dogs €3; bus adj; Eng spkn; adv bkg acc; CKE/CCI. "Mini farm & free lake fishing on site; excel base; access rds are v tight; vg." ♦
1 Apr-30 Sep. € 26.00   2016*

> **"That's changed – Should I let the Club know?"**
>
> If you find something on site that's different from the site entry, fill in a report and let us know. See camc.com/europereport.

TUFFE *4F1* (1km N Urban) *48.11866, 0.51148* FFCC
Camping du Lac, Route de Prévelles, 72160 Tuffé [02 43 93 88 34; fax 02 43 93 43 54; campingdulac.tuffe@orange.fr; www.camping.tuffe.fr]
Site on D33, sp. Med, mkd, hdg, pt shd, wc (htd); chem disp; mv service pnt; fam bthrm; shwrs inc; EHU (6A) €2.50; lndry; snacks; bar; bbq; playgrnd; sw nr; wifi; TV; 10% statics; dogs €2; Eng spkn; adv bkg acc; fishing; CKE/CCI. "Well-kept, pretty lakeside site; adj tourist train; clean san facs; friendly staff." ♦ 30 Mar-30 Sep. € 24.70   2013*

TULETTE *9D2* (2km S Rural) *44.26485, 4.93180*
Camping Les Rives de L'Aygues, 142 chemin des rives de l'Eygues, 26790 Tulette [04 75 98 37 50; camping.aygues@wanadoo.fr; www.lesrivesdelaygues.com] Exit D94 at Tulette onto D193 S; site in 2.2km on L. Site sp. Med, hdg, mkd, hdstg, shd, wc; chem disp; shwrs inc; EHU (6A) €4.20; gas; snacks; bar; playgrnd; pool (htd); wifi; 5% statics; dogs €2.50; phone; Eng spkn; adv bkg acc; quiet; ccard acc; games area; CKE/CCI. "Lovely, peaceful, family-run site in woodland by Rv Aygue; gd san facs; gd pool; vineyards & lavender fields nr; dir access to rv; excel."
♦ 1 May-25 Sep. € 35.00   2013*

TULLE *7C4* (12km NE Rural) *45.39658, 1.86223*
Camping L'Etang de Ruffaud, 19800 St Priest-de-Gimel [06 81 85 83 27 or 05 55 21 32 81; dominique.dorme@gmail.com; www.campingdeletang.sitew.com]
Sp on D1089 Tulle-Clermont-Ferrand rd & 3km S of this rd. Med, pt shd, pt sl, wc; chem disp; shwrs; EHU (10A); gas; lndry; rest; snacks; bbq; playgrnd; beach shgl adj; entmnt; TV; dogs; phone; Eng spkn; adv bkg acc; quiet; bike hire; rv fishing; tennis; boating; windsurfing; CKE/CCI. "Vg site; canoe/pedalo hire; set in woodland next to lake; owner runs rest with reasonably priced menu; beautiful location; Gimel Cascades 4km." ♦ 15 May-30 Sep. € 19.00   2014*

France

UGINE

UGINE *9B3* (7km NW Rural) 45.76141, 6.33702
Camping Champ Tillet, 28 Rue Chenevier, 74210 Marlens [04 50 44 33 74; fax 04 50 66 23 44; duchamptillet@wanadoo.fr; www.champtillet.com] D1508 S fr Annecy after leaving Lake. Take by-pass past Faverges dir Ugine. After rndabt, site on R at junc bef Marlens, sp. Med, hdg, pt shd, wc (htd); chem disp; fam bthrm; shwrs inc; EHU (10A) €4 (poss rev pol); lndry; shop nr; rest; snacks; playgrnd; pool; paddling pool; wifi; 10% statics; dogs €1; ccard acc; bike hire; rv fishing 500m; CKE/CCI. "Gd walks; lovely views; barrier clsd 2300-0700; some rd noise - adj extensive cycle track; helpful staff; shops 4km." ♦ 1 Apr-30 Sep. € 39.00   2013*

URCAY *4H3* (6km NE Rural) 46.6430, 2.6620
Camping Champ de la Chapelle, St Bonnet-Tronçais, 03360 Braize [00 33 470 07 82 46; simon.swinn@sfr.fr; www.champdelachapelle.com] Fr D2144 take D978A for Tronçais. 1.5km on L fr rndabt(Montaloyer) x-ing D28. Site sp. Med, mkd, pt shd, pt sl, wc; chem disp; shwrs; EHU (10A) inc; lndry; shop; rest nr; snacks; bar; playgrnd; pool; sw nr; wifi; 10% statics; dogs €1; Eng spkn; adv bkg acc; ccard acc; games area; CKE/CCI. "Excel walking & flora/fauna in ancient oak forest; some lge pitches; peaceful site; new British owner (2016)." 16 Apr-17 Oct. € 20.00   2014*

URDOS *8G2* (1km N Rural) 42.87705, -0.55670 **Camp Municipal Le Gave d'Aspe, 64490 Urdos** [05 59 34 88 26; fax 05 59 34 88 86; guittonb@hotmail.com] Turn W off N134 onto site access rd by disused Urdos stn approx 1km bef vill, clear sp. Other access rds in vill v diff lge o'fits. Sm, mkd, pt shd, pt sl, wc; chem disp; mv service pnt; shwrs inc; EHU (10A) €2.40; lndry; shop nr; rest nr; bar nr; bbq; playgrnd; paddling pool; phone; Eng spkn; adv bkg acc; quiet; ccard acc; rv; CKE/CCI. "Adj Rv Aspe; 14km fr Col du Somport/Tunnel; surrounded by mountains; conv x-ing into Spain; vg; lovely sm site; beautiful mountain scenery; gd facs; gd walking." 1 May-15 Sep. € 16.00   2017*

> **"I like to fill in the reports as I travel from site to site"**
>
> You'll find report forms at the back of this guide, or you can fill them in online at camc.com/europereport.

URT *8F1* (1km E Rural) 43.49353, -1.27960
Camping Ferme Mimizan, 64240 Urt [05 59 56 21 51; contact@lafermedemimizan.fr; www.lafermedemimizan.fr] E fr Bayonne on A64/E80, exit junc 4 sp Urt; in vill turn sharp R at PO & foll sps; site on R in 1km. Fr N on D12 cross Rv Adour by metal bdge & turn L immed past church, site on R in 1.5km. Med, pt shd, wc; shwrs inc; EHU (10A) €3.50; playgrnd; pool; paddling pool; wifi; 10% statics; adv bkg acc; CKE/CCI. "V peaceful out of ssn; friendly owners; gd walking & cycling; conv coast & Pyrenees; gd NH." € 19.50   2017*

UZERCHE *7B3* (8km NE Rural) 45.45200, 1.65056
Camping Aimée Porcher (Naturist), 19140 Pingrieux Eyburie [05 55 73 20 97 or 06 01 11 51 90; aimeeporcher@hotmail.com; www.aimee-porcher.com] Fr Uzerche take D3 NE to Eyburie & in Eyburie turn R at site sp (Cheyron/Pingrieux). In 1km turn L at site sp; site at end of narr lane. Sm, mkd, pt shd, terr, wc; chem disp; fam bthrm; shwrs inc; EHU (6A) (poss long lead req); lndry; snacks; bar; bbq; playgrnd; sw nr; red long stay; wifi; dogs; adv bkg acc; quiet; games area; INF card. "Beautiful views; wonderful location; INF not req; excel san facs; spacious pitches; basic; site rd steep in places; superb; v friendly Dutch owners." ♦ 20 May-11 Sep. € 26.50   2017*

UZERCHE *7B3* (0km SE Rural) 45.42148, 1.56592
Camp Municipal La Minoterie, Route de la Minoterie, 19140 Uzerche [05 55 73 12 75; nicolas@uzerche.fr; http://camping.uzerche.fr/] Fr N exit A20 at junc 44 for Uzerche on D920; proceed thro tunnel & cross town bdge. Site clearly sp on ent to town on rvside. Steep app rd & sharp bend. NB Narr app rd used by lorries fr nrby quarry. Site well sp. NB Steep exit. Sm, mkd, shd, pt sl, wc; chem disp; shwrs inc; EHU (10A) €2.90; lndry; shop nr; bbq; playgrnd; TV; Eng spkn; quiet; watersports; fishing; tennis; games rm; kayak hire; CKE/CCI. "Lovely pitches on rv's edge; helpful warden; rock climbing; clean san facs; not suitable lge o'fits or lge m'vans; sh walk along rv to beautiful old vill; gd local walks; poss risk of flooding; v quiet end of ssn with ltd pitches; conv NH; excel." 1 May-2 Oct. € 13.00   2014*

UZERCHE *7B3* (9km SW Rural) 45.36861, 1.53849
Camp Municipal du Lac du Pontcharal, 19410 Vigeois [05 55 98 90 86 or 05 55 98 91 93 (Mairie); fax 05 55 98 99 79; mairievigeois@wanadoo.fr; www.vigeois.com] Fr A20 exit 45 onto D3 to Vegeois then D7. Site is 2.5km SE of Vigeois. Med, shd, pt sl, wc; chem disp; shwrs inc; EHU (15A) €3.50 (poss rev pol); gas; lndry; shop; rest; snacks; bar; playgrnd; sw; entmnt; TV; dogs €0.90; adv bkg acc; quiet; watersports; fishing; tennis 2km; games area. "Delightful, well-kept site in picturesque setting; excel san facs." ♦ 1 Jun-15 Sep. € 10.70   2012*

UZES *10E2* (2km E Rural) 44.03202, 4.45557 **Camping Le Moulin Neuf, 30700 St Quentin-la-Poterie** [04 66 22 17 21; fax 04 66 22 91 82; lemoulinneuf@yahoo.fr; www.le-moulin-neuf.fr] N fr Uzès on D982; after 3km turn L onto D5; in 1.5km fork R, keeping on D5; in 200m turn R onto D405 (Chemin du Moulin Neuf); site on L in 500m. Med, mkd, pt shd, wc; chem disp; mv service pnt; shwrs inc; EHU (5A) €3.50; lndry; shop; snacks; bar; playgrnd; pool (htd); wifi; 10% statics; dogs €1.50; quiet; fishing; horseriding; bike hire; tennis. "Site off beaten track; busy high ssn, rec phone in adv; conv touring base; o'night m'van area; barrier clsd 2230-0700; poss mosquito problem; Uzès a lovely town; wonderful helpful staff; excel facs." ♦ 1 Apr-22 Sep. € 24.50   2017*

UZES *10E2* (3km SW Rural) *43.99843, 4.38424*
Camping Le Mas de Rey, Route d'Anduze, 30700 Arpaillargues [04 66 22 18 27; info@campingmasderey.com; www.campingmasderey.com]
Sp fr Uzès. Exit by D982 sp Anduze. After 2.5km cross narr bdge, turn L in 100m on site app rd. Med, mkd, hdg, hdstg, pt shd, pt sl, wc; chem disp; fam bthrm; shwrs inc; EHU (10A) €4 (rev pol); lndry; shop; rest; snacks; bar; bbq; playgrnd; pool; TV; dogs €2; phone; Eng spkn; adv bkg acc; quiet; CKE/CCI. "Clean, comfortable, busy site; helpful Dutch owners; some v lge pitches; gd for sm children; excel cycling; Uzès interesting; LS red for snr citizens." ♦ 23 Mar-15 Oct. € 41.00   2014*

> **"We must tell the Club about that great site we found"**
>
> Get your site reports in by mid-August and we'll do our best to get your updates into the next edition.

VAISON LA ROMAINE *9D2* (2km NE Urban) *44.24472, 5.07861* **Camping du Théâtre Romain, Chemin du Brusquet, 84110 Vaison-la-Romaine [04 90 28 78 66; fax 04 90 28 78 76; info@camping-theatre.com; www.camping-theatre.com]**
Fr D975, cont onto Ave de Martigny to Chemin du Brusquet. Foll sp for Théâtre Romain & site. Ent to Chemin du Busquet on rndabt at Théâtre Romain. Or site sp off Orange-Nyons rd thro town (do not ent town cent). Med, hdg, mkd, pt shd, serviced pitches; wc (htd); chem disp; mv service pnt; fam bthrm; shwrs inc; EHU (5-10A); lndry; shop nr; bar; bbq; playgrnd; pool; wifi; 10% statics; dogs €2; Eng spkn; adv bkg req; quiet; ccard acc; games rm; CKE/CCI. "Excel, well-kept, friendly site; busy LS due long stay residents, rec book in adv; mainly gd sized pitches but some sm; most pitches suitable m'vans; clean, unisex san facs; attractive sw; mkt Tues; highly rec; excel as usual; old Roman town cent, 10 mins walk fr campsite; conv for town; refurbed sw & new paddling pool (2016); long stay red." ♦ 15 Mar-5 Nov. € 31.00   2016*

VAISON LA ROMAINE *9D2* (4km NE Rural) *44.26240, 5.12950* **Camping L'Ayguette, 84110 Faucon [04 90 46 40 35 or 06 18 47 33 42 (mob); fax 04 90 46 46 17; info@ayguette.com; www.ayguette.com]**
Exit Vaison NE on D938, R on D71, thro St Romain-en-Viennois. Then R onto D86 sp Faucon. Site on R, well sp. Med, mkd, shd, terr, wc (htd); chem disp; fam bthrm; shwrs inc; EHU (10A) €2.50 (poss long lead req); lndry; shop nr; snacks; bar; bbq; playgrnd; pool (htd); red long stay; wifi; dogs €1.80; adv bkg acc; quiet; ccard acc; CKE/CCI. "Excel, well-run site; lge pitches in forest setting; friendly, helpful owners; excel mod facs inc hairdryers & children's shwrs; tractor tow avail." 19 Apr-27 Sep. € 38.00   2014*

VAISON LA ROMAINE *9D2* (5km NE Rural) *44.26806, 5.10651* **Camping Le Soleil de Provence, Route de Nyons, Quartier Trameiller, 84110 St Romain-en-Viennois [04 90 46 46 00; fax 04 90 46 40 37; info@camping-soleil-de-provence.fr; www.camping-soleil-de-provence.fr]** Leave A7 at junc 19 Bollène onto D94 dir Nyons. After Tullette turn R onto D20 & then D975 to Vaison-la-Romaine; fr Vaison take D938 sp Nyons; in 4km R & in 150m L to site; well sp. Lge, mkd, hdg, pt shd, terr, serviced pitches; wc (htd); chem disp; shwrs inc; EHU (10A) €4.50; gas; lndry; shop; rest; snacks; bar; playgrnd; pool; paddling pool; entmnt; wifi; dogs; adv bkg acc; CKE/CCI. "Popular, scenic, attractive, well-kept, family-run site; gd pools; lovely town; poss strong Mistral winds Sep; mkt Tues; excel; newly extended section & new san block (2014)." ♦ 15 Mar-31 Oct. € 30.00   2014*

⊞ **VAISON LA ROMAINE** *9D2* (1km SE Rural) *44.23440, 5.08955* **FFCC Camping Club International Carpe Diem, Route de St Marcellin, 84110 Vaison-la-Romaine [04 90 36 02 02; fax 04 90 36 36 90; contact@camping-carpe-diem.com; www.camping-carpe-diem.com or www.campings-franceloc.fr]**
S on A7 exit Orange; foll sp to Vaison; at Vaison on Nyons rd (D938) turn S at rndabt by supmkt dir Carpentras. In 1km turn L at junc to St Marcellin, site immed on L. Lge, mkd, hdg, pt shd, terr, wc; chem disp; mv service pnt; shwrs inc; EHU (6-10A) €4.70-5.70; gas; lndry; shop; snacks; bar; playgrnd; pool; paddling pool; entmnt; wifi; TV; 10% statics; dogs €5; Eng spkn; adv bkg acc; ccard acc; waterslide; site clsd 21 Dec-16 Jan; CKE/CCI. "Lively site; helpful staff; poss dust fr nrby quarry; poss muddy pitches; gd san facs; gd cent for Provence." ♦ € 31.00   2013*

VAISON LA ROMAINE *9D2* (4km SE Rural) *44.22357, 5.10428* **Camping Le Voconce, route de St Marcellin, 84110 St Marcellin [04 90 36 28 10; fax 04 90 36 20 35; contact@camping-voconce.com; www.camping-voconce.com]** Fr Vaison S on D977. Turn L onto D938 after 1km. Turn R onto D151 after 0.5km to St Marcellin-les-Vaison. Turn R at rndabt by a chapel & foll sp to site. Med, mkd, hdg, pt shd, wc; chem disp; fam bthrm; shwrs inc; EHU (10A) €5; gas; lndry; shop nr; snacks; bar; playgrnd; pool; entmnt; wifi; 15% statics; dogs €3-4; Eng spkn; adv bkg acc; quiet; ccard acc; games area; CKE/CCI. "Tranquil site bet 2 vineyards; friendly, fam run site; vg base for cycling, walking & exploring; boules; great views; acc to rv; vg." ♦ 1 Apr-15 Oct. € 24.00   2016*

VAISON LA ROMAINE *9D2* (5km NW Rural) *44.26446, 5.05242* **Camping Domaine de La Cambuse, Route de Villedieu, 84110 Vaison-la-Romaine [04 90 36 14 53 or 06 32 18 15 54 (mob); dom.lacambuse@wanadoo.fr; www.domainelacambuse.com]**
Fr Vaison-la-Romaine N on D51 sp Villedieu. After 4km fork R onto D94 sp Villedieu. Site on R after 300m. Sm, pt shd, terr, wc; chem disp; shwrs inc; EHU (6A) €3; snacks; bar; pool; paddling pool; 5% statics; dogs €1.52; phone; quiet; CKE/CCI. "Site in vineyard on hillside; friendly, helpful owners." 1 May-15 Oct. € 12.00   2014*

VAL D'ISERE

VAL D'ISERE *9B4* (1km E Rural) *45.44622, 6.99218*
Camping Les Richardes, Le Laisinant, 73150 Val-d'Isère [04 79 06 26 60; campinglesrichardes@free.fr; www.campinglesrichardes.free.fr]
Leave Val d'Isère going E twds Col de l'Iseran on D902, site on R 1.5km bef Le Fornet vill. Med, unshd, pt sl, wc; shwrs; EHU (3-6A) €1.90-3.80; dogs €0.50; quiet; CKE/CCI. "Peaceful site; pool 1.5km; delightful owner."
15 Jun-15 Sep. € 13.00   2016*

VALENCAY *4H2* (2km W Urban) *47.15656, 1.55202*
Camp Municipal Les Chênes, Route de Loches, 36600 Valençay [02 54 00 03 92 or 02 54 00 32 32; www.valencay.fr] App town fr E on D960 or N/S on D956, foll sp for D960 Luçay-le-Mâle. D960 is next L in town. Foll sp for pool & camping. Site adj pool mkd by flags. Sm, hdg, mkd, pt shd, wc; chem disp; shwrs inc; EHU (6A) €3.20 (poss rev pol); lndry; shop nr; bbq; playgrnd; red long stay; TV; dogs; adv bkg acc; quiet; fishing; tennis adj; CKE/CCI. "Excel, well-kept site in parkland with lake; lge pitches; gd, clean facs; poss muddy after heavy rain; htd pool adj (high ssn); gate clsd 2100-0700; sh walk to impressive chateau; day's drive to Calais or Le Havre ferries; motor museum & vill 1km." ♦ 1 May-30 Sep. € 15.00   2015*

VALENCE *9C2* (9km N Rural) *44.99323, 4.89383*
Camping Le Soleil Fruité, Les Pêches, 26300 Chateauneuf-sur-Isère [04 75 84 19 70; fax 04 75 78 05 85; contact@lesoleilfruite.com; www.lesoleilfruite.com] Exit A7 junc 14 Valence Nord onto D67 sp Chateauneuf-sur-Isère, site sp to W of vill. Alt rte foll N7 turn onto D877 twrds Chateauneuf and foll sp to campsite. Med, mkd, hdg, pt shd, wc; chem disp; mv service pnt; fam bthrm; shwrs inc; EHU (10A) €4; lndry; rest; snacks; bar; bbq; playgrnd; pool; paddling pool; entmnt; wifi; TV; 15% statics; dogs €2 (not acc high ssn); phone; Eng spkn; adv bkg acc; quiet; ccard acc; CKE/CCI. "Vg, family-run site; lge pitches; friendly owner; excel, clean, modern san facs; rest/takeaway open early Jun (2011); ltd water pnts; cycle friendly; gd bar/rest; smart site; v busy HS; gd for families with young children." ♦ 26 Apr-15 Sep. € 33.00   2016*

VALENCE *9C2* (9km NW Rural) *45.00726, 4.84862*
Camping Municipal Les Vernes, 26600 La Roche-de-Glun [04 75 84 54 11 or 04 75 84 60 52 (Mairie); mairie.rdg@wanadoo.fr; www.ladrometourisme.com]
Turn W off N7 at Pont-d'Isère. On ent La Roche-de-Glun foll camping sp. Sm, mkd, hdg, shd, serviced pitches; wc; chem disp; shwrs inc; EHU (10A) €1.40; lndry; shop nr; bbq; 50% statics; phone; adv bkg acc; quiet; CKE/CCI. "Pleasant site; friendly resident warden; htd pool adj in ssn inc; sports cent adj; gd, clean san facs; vg municipal pool adj; barrier clsd 2200-0700; vg value; vg NH." ♦ 1 May-30 Apr.
€ 17.00   2015*

VALENSOLE *10E3* (5km E Rural) *43.83862, 6.02029*
Domaine du Petit Arlane (Naturist), Route de Riez, 04210 Valensole [04 92 74 82 70; fax 04 92 74 99 35; contact@domainepetitarlane.fr; www.domainepetitarlane.fr] Leave A51 junc 18 to Valensole 15km, fr Valensole take D6 signed Riez, site on L 5km (v bendy rds). Med, hdstg, mkd, pt sl, chem disp; mv service pnt; shwrs; EHU (6- 15A) €3.90-8; lndry; rest; snacks; bar; bbq; playgrnd; pool; twin axles; wifi; TV; 10% statics; dogs leashed €3.30; Eng spkn; adv bkg acc; ccard acc; games area. "Beautiful site, many pitches face lakes; INF card advised;gd local walks fr local villages; bkg ess." ♦ 26 Apr-30 Sep.
€ 25.00   2013*

VALLOIRE *9C3* (1km N Rural) *45.17000, 6.42960*
Camp Caravaneige Municipal Ste Thècle, Route des Villards, 73450 Valloire [04 79 83 30 11; fax 04 79 83 35 13; camping-caravaneige@valloire.net; www.valloire.net] Exit A43 junc 29 onto D306 to St Michel-de-Maurienne, then onto D902 to Valloire. At vill mkt turn R over rv to site. Climb fr valley 15% gradient max. Med, hdstg, mkd, pt shd, wc (htd); chem disp; mv service pnt; fam bthrm; shwrs inc; EHU (13A) €3.60; lndry; shop nr; rest nr; bar nr; playgrnd; pool; paddling pool; red long stay; wifi; TV; dogs free; bus; Eng spkn; adv bkg acc; quiet; ccard acc; waterslide; tennis; fishing. "Superb mountain scenery for walking & cycling; fitness rm; bar 200m; excel, well kept site."
♦ 12 Dec-23 Apr & 1 Jun-30 Sep. € 20.00   2015*

> **"I need an on-site restaurant"**
>
> We do our best to make sure site information is correct, but it is always best to check any must-have facilities are still available or will be open during your visit.

VALLON EN SULLY *7A4* (1km SE Rural) *46.53019, 2.61547* Camp Municipal Les Soupirs, Allée des Soupirs, 03190 Vallon-en-Sully [04 70 06 50 96 or 04 70 06 50 10 (LS); fax 04 70 06 51 18; mairie.vallonensully@wanadoo.fr] N fr Montluçon on D2144; in 23km at traff lts where D11 crosses D2144 turn L & foll camping sp for Vallon-en-Sully. After bdge over Rv Cher turn L in 50m. Site in 500m. If N or S on A71 exit at junc 9 Vallon-en-Sully; turn N on D2144; in 3km at traff lts turn L. Med, pt shd, wc cont; chem disp; shwrs; EHU (6-20A) €2-4; shop nr; rest nr; bar nr; TV; dogs; bus 500m; adv bkg acc; quiet. "Peaceful, spacious site on banks of rv & canal; immac san facs; lge pitches; risk of flooding in wet; gd cycling along canal; gd NH; vg." 1 Jul-12 Sep. € 10.40   2017*

VALLON PONT D'ARC *9D2* (6km N Rural) *44.46611, 4.4125* **Domaine de Chadeyron, 07150 Lagorce Vallon-Pont-d'Arc** [04 75 88 04 81 or 06 70 67 88 78 (mob); infos@campingchadeyron.com; www.campingdechadeyron.com] Fr S Vallon Pont d'Arc take D390 sp St Remeze/Lagorce. R onto D1, foll sp to site. (NB Rd thro vill narr). Fr N (rec large o'fits) Vogue foll D579 sp Ruoms/Vallon Pont d'Arc, after 1.5km turn L D1 Rochecolmbe/Lagorce, 8km to site. Sm, mkd, pt shd, wc; chem disp; mv service pnt; fam bthrm; shwrs; EHU (10A); lndry; snacks; bar; playgrnd; pool (htd); paddling pool; twin axles; entmnt; wifi; TV; 50% statics; dogs; Eng spkn; adv bkg acc; CCI. "Gd walks; canoeing; vg site." ♦ 3 Apr-16 Oct. € 32.50   2014*

VALLON PONT D'ARC *9D2* (1km SE Rural) *44.39783, 4.40005* **Camping Le Provençal, Route des Gorges, 07150 Vallon-Pont-d'Arc** [04 75 88 00 48; fax 04 75 88 02 00; camping.le.provencal@wanadoo.fr; www.camping-le-provencal.fr] Fr Aubenas take D579 thro Vallon-Pont-d'Arc to S. Turn L on D290 N of rv; site on R in 500m (middle of 3 sites). Fr Alès, N on D904/D104. At St Ambroix turn R onto D51 then D579 to Vallon-Pont-d'Arc. Lge, pt shd, wc (htd); shwrs inc; EHU (8A) €3.90; gas; lndry; shop; rest; snacks; bar; playgrnd; pool (htd); wifi; 10% statics; dogs €4; Eng spkn; adv bkg acc; quiet; ccard acc; tennis; fishing; sailing; canoeing. "Friendly, helpful staff; site at NW end of spectacular Gorges de l'Ardèche." ♦ 13 Apr-20 Sep. € 59.00   2014*

VALLON PONT D'ARC *9D2* (1km SE Rural) *44.39777, 4.39861* **Camping Nature Park L'Ardéchois, Route des Gorges de l'Ardèche, 07150 Vallon-Pont-d'Arc** [04 75 88 06 63; fax 04 75 37 14 97; ardecamp@bigfoot.com; www.ardechois-camping.com or www.les-castels.com] Fr Vallon take D290 Rte des Gorges & site on R bet rd & rv. Lge, mkd, hdg, hdstg, shd, pt sl, serviced pitches; wc (htd); chem disp; mv service pnt; fam bthrm; shwrs inc; EHU (6-10A) inc; gas; lndry; shop; rest; snacks; bar; bbq; playgrnd; pool (htd); paddling pool; entmnt; wifi; TV; dogs €7.70; Eng spkn; adv bkg acc; quiet; ccard acc; tennis; bike hire; canoeing; games area; CKE/CCI. "Spectacular scenery; private bthrm avail (by reservation); excel rvside site; helpful staff; price depends on size of pitch; gd san facs; 5 star site." ♦ 15 Apr-30 Sep. € 49.00   2017*

See advertisement

"Satellite navigation makes touring much easier"

Remember most sat navs don't know if you're towing or in a larger vehicle – always use yours alongside maps and site directions.

VALLON PONT D'ARC

VALLON PONT D'ARC 9D2 (2km SE Rural) 44.39467, 4.39909 Mondial Camping, Route des Gorges, 07150 Vallon-Pont-d'Arc [04 75 88 00 44; fax 04 75 37 13 73; reserv-info@mondial-camping.com; www.mondial-camping.com] Fr N exit A7 Montélimar Nord junc 17 onto N7 then N102 dir Le Teil, Villeneuve-de-Berg. Turn S onto D103/D579 dir Vogüé, Ruoms then Vallon-Pont-d'Arc. Take D290, Rte des Gorges de l'Ardèche to site in 1.5km. Fr S exit A7 junc 19 at Bollène, dir Bourg-St Andéol, then D4 to St Remèze & Vallon-Pont-d'Arc. App to Vallon fr E thro Gorges de l'Ardeche not rec. Lge, mkd, hdg, shd, serviced pitches; wc (htd); chem disp; mv service pnt; fam bthrm; shwrs inc; EHU (6-10A) inc; gas; lndry; shop; rest; snacks; bar; playgrnd; pool (htd); paddling pool; entmnt; wifi; TV; 10% statics; dogs €4.50; phone; Eng spkn; adv bkg acc; quiet; ccard acc; tennis adj; canoeing; games rm; CKE/CCI. "Dir access to rv, Ardèche gorges & canoe facs; gd touring base; waterslides & aqua park; excel site." ♦ 1 Apr-30 Sep. € 42.00 2017*

See advertisement

VALLON PONT D'ARC 9D2 (5km S Rural) 44.39333, 4.39465 Camping Le Clapas, La Vernède, 07150 Salavas [04 75 37 14 76; contact@camping-le-clapas.com; www.camping-le-clapas.com] D579 S fr Vallon-Pont-d'Arc to Salavas; 250m after Salavas turn L. Well sp. Med, mkd, shd, pt sl, wc; chem disp; mv service pnt; shwrs inc; EHU (10A) €3; lndry; shop; rest nr; snacks; bar; bbq (elec, gas); playgrnd; sw; entmnt; wifi; TV; dogs €2; Eng spkn; adv bkg acc; quiet; ccard acc; games rm; rafting; fishing; canoeing; games area; CKE/CCI. "Beautiful, well-kept site by Rv Ardèche with beach; friendly, helpful staff; poss diff lge o'fits; canyoning; conv Ardèche Gorges; excel; French adaptor needed, site sells or loans." ♦ 17 Apr-27 Sep. € 27.50 2015*

VALLON PONT D'ARC 9D2 (2km W Rural) 44.41517, 4.37796 Domaine de L'Esquiras, chemin du Fez, 07150 Vallon-Pont-d'Arc [04 75 88 00 16; esquiras@orange.fr; www.camping-esquiras.com] Fr Ruoms L at rndabt bef the Lidl nr the vill. Foll sp. Fr Vallon foll dir Ruoms. R after Lidl. Med, mkd, pt shd, pt sl, wc; chem disp; mv service pnt; fam bthrm; shwrs inc; gas; lndry; shop; rest; snacks; bar; pool; twin axles; entmnt; wifi; TV; dogs €3.50; phone; Eng spkn; adv bkg acc; quiet; ccard acc; games area; games rm; CKE/CCI. "Lovely vill (10 min walk) with lots of bars & rest; caving, climbing or kayaking; excel; ACSI acc." ♦ 25 Mar-30 Sep. € 40.00 2016*

VALLON PONT D'ARC 9D2 (4km W Rural) 44.41251, 4.35018 Camping L'Arc en Ciel, Route de Ruoms, Les Mazes, 07150 Vallon-Pont-d'Arc [04 75 88 04 65; fax 04 75 37 16 99; camping.arcenciel@wanadoo.fr; www.arcenciel-camping.fr] Fr Ruoms take D579 dir Vallon. After 4km bear R for Les Mazes. Pass thro vill & in about 1.7km bear L at camp sp. Lge, pt shd, pt sl; wc; chem disp; fam bthrm; shwrs inc; EHU (10A) €4; lndry; shop; rest; snacks; bar; bbq (elec, gas); playgrnd; pool; paddling pool; entmnt; wifi; 10% statics; dogs €3.50; bus; adv bkg acc; quiet; ccard acc; games rm; rv; canoeing; horseriding nr; tennis nr; fishing. "Pleasant site on rv bank; excel; some pitches diff to access." ♦ 29 Apr-18 Sep. € 41.00 2016*

VALLORCINE 9A4 (1km SE Rural) 46.0242, 6.92430 Camping des Montets, Le Buet, 74660 Vallorcine [06 79 02 18 81; b.stam@orange.fr; http://camping-montets.com] N fr Chamonix on D1506 via Col de Montets; Le Buet 2km S of Vallorcine; site sp nr Le Buet stn. Fr Martigny (Switzerland) cross border via Col de la Forclaz; then D1506 to Vallorcine; cont to Le Buet in 1km. Med, hdg, mkd, pt shd, wc; chem disp; shwrs inc; EHU (3-6A) €2-3; lndry; shop nr; rest; snacks; red long stay; dogs; train 500m; Eng spkn; quiet; tennis adj; CKE/CCI. "Site with spectacular views; friendly owners; ltd flat pitches for o'fits (others for tents in field), rec phone ahead; clean san facs; excel walking direct fr site; free train pass to Chamonix; vg." ♦ 1 Jun-15 Sep. € 16.00 2016*

VALOGNES 1C4 (1km N Urban) 49.51154, -1.47534
Camp Municipal Le Bocage, Rue Neuve, 50700 Valognes [02 33 95 82 03 or 06 10 84 59 33 (mob); environement@mairie-valognes.fr; www.mairie-valognes.fr] Off N13 Cherbourg to Carentan take 1st exit to Valognes, turn L just past Champion at Lidl sp; site sp bef & in town. Fr Carentan dir, take 3rd R after 4th set traff lts. Sm, hdg, hdstg, mkd, pt shd, wc; chem disp; shwrs inc; EHU (10A) €3.55 (poss rev pol); gas; shop nr; rest nr; bar nr; dogs €0.66; quiet; CKE/CCI. "Super little site; clean san facs; friendly staff; conv Cherbourg ferries (17km) & town; poss travellers; warden calls 1900-2000, site self if office clsd; gates clsd 2200-0600; ideal NH; excel as always."
♦ 1 Apr-15 Oct. € 14.60   2012*

VALRAS PLAGE 10F1 (3km SW Coastal) 43.23750, 3.26166 Camping Domaine de la Yole, 34350 Valras-Plage [04 67 37 33 87; fax 04 67 37 44 89; infocamping@layolewineresort.com; www.campinglayole.com] Leave A9/E15 at Béziers-Ouest junc 36; foll D64 twd coast dir Valras-Plage, then Valras-Plage-Ouest & site sp. V lge, hdg, hdstg, mkd, shd, wc; chem disp; mv service pnt; fam bthrm; shwrs inc; EHU (4A) inc; gas; lndry; shop; rest; snacks; bar; bbq (charcoal, gas); playgrnd; pool; paddling pool; beach sand 400m; entmnt; wifi; TV; dogs €4.50 (not on beach); Eng spkn; adv bkg acc; quiet; ccard acc; games rm; bike hire; tennis; horseriding 3km; waterslide; games area; CKE/CCI. "Lovely, excel site; v busy high ssn; some gd sized pitches with plenty of shd - book ahead high ssn; gd for all age groups; mkt Mon & Fri; lge clean sw pool complex; site extremely lge; tour ops statics; gd beach in 15 mins walk." ♦ 26 Apr-20 Sep. € 63.00   2014*

VALRAS PLAGE 10F1 (3km W Coastal) 43.23502, 3.26845 Camping La Plage et du Bord de Mer, Route de Vendres, 34350 Valras Plage [04 67 37 34 38; fax 04 67 37 33 74; contact@camping-plage-mediterranee.net; www.camping-plage-mediterranee.com] Leave A9 at Junc 9 onto D64. Foll signs for Valras Plage Ouest. Site on R, past La Yole. Lge, mkd, pt shd, wc; chem disp; mv service pnt; fam bthrm; shwrs; EHU (6A) inc; lndry; shop; rest; snacks; bar; bbq; cooking facs; playgrnd; pool (htd); paddling pool; beach adj; twin axles; entmnt; wifi; 20% statics; dogs €4.50; phone; Eng spkn; adv bkg acc; bike hire; games area; waterslide; games rm; tennis; CCI. "Excel site; watersports mkt Mon & Fri (am)." ♦ 28 Apr-21 Sep. € 54.00   2014*

VALRAS PLAGE 10F1 (6km NW Rural) 43.29273, 3.26710 Camping La Gabinelle, 7 Rue de la Grille, 34410 Sauvian [04 67 39 50 87; info@lagabinelle.com; www.lagabinelle.com] Exit A9 at Béziers Ouest, turn R twd beaches sp S to Sauvian on D19. Site 500m on L thro town. Med, pt shd, wc; chem disp; shwrs inc; EHU (6A) €3; lndry; shop nr; rest nr; bar; playgrnd; pool; beach sand 5km; red long stay; entmnt; TV; dogs €3.50; adv bkg acc; quiet; fishing 1km; tennis; games area; games rm. "Friendly, helpful staff; suitable lge m'vans; canoeing 2km; LS ltd san facs & poss unkempt; sh walk to delightful old vill; popular; bar/pool shut LS." ♦ 12 Apr-12 Sep. € 13.80   2016*

VALREAS 9D2 (1km N Rural) 44.39264, 4.99245
Camping La Coronne, Route de Pègue, 84600 Valréas [04 88 70 00 13; contact@lacoronne.com; www.vaucluse-camping.fr] Fr Nyons take D538 W to Valréas. Exit town on D10 rd to Taulignan, immed after x-ing bdge over Rv Coronne turn R into D196 sp Le Pègue. Site on R in 100m on rvside. Sp app fr E but easy to miss; app fr W; well sp in Valréas. Med, hdg, mkd, pt shd, wc; chem disp; mv service pnt; shwrs inc; EHU (6A) inc; gas; lndry; shop; rest; snacks; bar; bbq; playgrnd; pool; paddling pool; entmnt; wifi; TV; dogs €4; phone; Eng spkn; adv bkg acc; quiet; ccard acc; fishing; CKE/CCI. "Sm pitches; excel pool; facs need refurb & poss unclean; site clsd 2200-0700." ♦ 31 Mar-15 Oct. € 25.70   2017*

VALREAS 9D2 (8km W Rural) 44.41131, 4.89112
Camping Les Truffières, 1100 Chemin de Bellevue-d'Air, Nachony, 26230 Grignan [04 75 46 93 62; info@lestruffieres.com; www.lestruffieres.com] Fr A7 take D133 E twds Grignan. On W o'skts of vill turn S on D71. In 1km turn L at sp. Site is 200m on R. Fr Nyons take D538 W to Grignan. Sm, mkd, shd, wc; chem disp; mv service pnt; shwrs inc; EHU (10A) €4.20; gas; lndry; shop nr; rest; snacks; bar; bbq; playgrnd; pool; 5% statics; Eng spkn; adv bkg acc; quiet; fishing; CKE/CCI. "Excel, well-wooded site by lavendar fields; pleasant owners; immac san facs; gd pool; some pitches diff access; site poss dusty; 20 min stroll to town." ♦ 20 Apr-30 Sep. € 31.50   2013*

> **"There aren't many sites open at this time of year"**
>
> If you're travelling outside peak season remember to call ahead to check site opening dates – even if the entry says 'open all year'.

VANDENESSE EN AUXOIS 6G1 (3km NE Rural) 47.23661, 4.62880 Camping Le Lac de Panthier, 21320 Vandenesse-en-Auxois [03 80 49 21 94; fax 03 80 49 25 80; info@lac-de-panthier.com; www.lac-de-panthier.com] Exit A6 junc 24 (A38) at Pouilly-en-Auxois; foll D16/D18 to Vandenesse; turn L on D977bis, cross canal bdge & cont strt for 3km to site on L. Fr SW (Autun) on D981 approx 12km after Arnay-le-Duc turn R onto D994 sp Châteauneuf. At x-rds cont onto D977bis then as above. Lge, hdg, mkd, pt shd, pt sl, terr, wc; chem disp; fam bthrm; shwrs inc; EHU (6A) inc (some rev pol); lndry; shop; rest; snacks; bar; bbq; playgrnd; pool (covrd, htd); paddling pool; entmnt; wifi; TV (pitch); dogs €3; adv bkg req; fishing; waterslide; bike hire; sauna; CKE/CCI. "Lovely area; Oct open Fri, Sat & Sun; views fr higher pitches; well-run site operating with Les Voiliers adj; lge pitches, most sl & blocks req; facs poss stretched high ssn, adequate; gd cycling & walks round lake; popular NH; vg." ♦ 9 Apr-8 Oct. € 29.00   2014*

VANNES

⊞ **VANNES** 2F3 (5km N Rural) 47.73035, -2.72795
Camping du Haras, 5 Kersimon-Vannes/Meucon, 56250 Monterblanc [02 97 44 66 06 or 06 71 00 05 59 (mob); fax 02 97 44 49 41; contact@ campingvannes.com; www.campingvannes.com]
App fr N165 turn L onto D767 sp Airport. Go N for 7km & turn R onto D778 for 1km & turn R again. After 1km approx, turn L onto Airport Perimeter Rd, site sp on W side. App fr N on D767, join D778 & as above. Med, hdg, mkd, hdstg, pt shd, wc (htd); chem disp; mv service pnt; fam bthrm; shwrs inc; EHU (4-16A) €3-8; gas; lndry; shop; snacks; bar; bbq; playgrnd; pool (covrd, htd); paddling pool; sw nr; red long stay; wifi; 30% statics; dogs €4; Eng spkn; adv bkg acc; quiet; ccard acc; horseriding 300m; fishing; tennis; waterslide; bike hire; games rm; CKE/CCI. "Lovely site; outdoor fitness; ltd facs LS; NH; sauna; wellness cent; trampoline; ltd space for tourers; rec."
♦ € 36.00 2013*

VANNES 2F3 (3km S Rural) 47.62754, -2.74117 FFCC
Camping Moulin de Cantizac, 2 Rue des Orchidées, 56860 Séné [02 98 92 53 52; info@camping-vannes. com; www.camping-vannes.com] S fr Vannes on D199 twds Séné. Site on L at rndabt beside rv. Med, hdg, pt shd, pt sl, wc; chem disp; fam bthrm; shwrs inc; EHU (10A) €3.90; gas; lndry; shop; snacks; playgrnd; pool (htd); beach sand 4km; wifi; 10% statics; dogs €2.30; quiet; ccard acc; games rm; boating; games area. "Superb cent for birdwatching; excel new facs; buses to Vannes." 1 May-15 Oct. € 22.00 2014*

> **"That's changed – Should I let the Club know?"**
> If you find something on site that's different from the site entry, fill in a report and let us know. See camc.com/europereport.

VANNES 2F3 (4km SW Coastal) 47.63365, -2.78008
Flower Camping Le Conleau (formerly Municipal), 188 Ave Maréchal Juin, 56000 Vannes [02 97 63 13 88; fax 02 97 40 38 82; camping.conleau@ flowercampings.com; en.vannes-camping.com]
Exit N165 at Vannes Ouest junc; Conleau sp on R. Site twd end of rd on R. If on N165 fr Auray take 1st exit sp Vannes & at 2nd rndabt R (sp) to avoid town cent. C'vans not allowed thro town cent. Lge, mkd, hdg, pt shd, pt sl, wc; chem disp; mv service pnt; shwrs; EHU (6A) €3.50 (some rev pol); lndry; snacks; bar; bbq; playgrnd; pool (covrd, htd); paddling pool; beach sand 300m; twin axles; entmnt; wifi; TV; 20% statics; dogs €3; phone; bus adj; Eng spkn; adv bkg acc; quiet; ccard acc; games area; bike hire; CKE/CCI. "Most pitches sl; sep area for m'vans by rd - little shd & poss long walk to san facs; v busy/noisy in high ssn; sea water pool nr; lovely easy walk to Port Conleau; site full of atmosphere - rec; excel; great location & facs." ♦
1 Apr-1 Oct. € 32.00 2017*

VANNES 2F3 (5km SW Coastal) 47.62190, -2.80056
Camping de Penboch, 9 Chemin de Penboch, 56610 Arradon [02 97 44 71 29; fax 02 97 44 79 10; camping. penboch@wanadoo.fr; www.camping-penboch.fr]
Exit Brest-Nantes N165 Vannes by-pass at junc with D127 sp Ploeren & Arradon. Foll sp Arradon. Site well sp. Lge, mkd, hdg, pt shd, wc; chem disp; mv service pnt; fam bthrm; shwrs inc; EHU (10A) inc (poss rev pol); gas; lndry; shop; snacks; bar; bbq; playgrnd; pool (covrd, htd); paddling pool; beach sand 200m; wifi; TV; 10% statics; dogs €3.50; Eng spkn; adv bkg rec; quiet; ccard acc; games rm; waterslide; games area; CKE/ CCI. "Excel site; gd clean san facs; bike hire 2km; some pitches sm; steel pegs req; o'flow area with facs; no o'fits over 7m high ssn; plenty for youngsters; 20 mins walk to Arradon; gd coast walks." ♦ 12 Apr-26 Sep. € 58.50 2012*

VANNES 2F3 (6km SW Coastal) 47.62108, -2.84025
Camping de l'Allée, 56610 Arradon [02 97 44 01 98; fax 02 97 44 73 74; contact@camping-allee.com; www.camping-allee.com] Fr Vannes take D101 & D101A to Arradon. Take by-pass & take 1st exit at rndabt & foll sp. Site to SW of Arradon. Fr Auray on D101 turn R on C203 immed after Moustoir. App rd to site is narr. Med, mkd, hdg, pt shd, pt sl, wc; chem disp; fam bthrm; shwrs inc; EHU (10A) €4.60 (poss long leads req); gas; lndry; shop; snacks; playgrnd; pool (htd); beach shgl 600m; TV; 5% statics; dogs €2; Eng spkn; adv bkg acc; quiet; games rm; CKE/CCI. "Delightful, helpful, family-run site partly in orchard; site yourself if office clsd; immac modern san facs; gd walks; gd touring base; highly rec; roomy site with gd atmosphere; rec." ♦ 1 Apr-30 Sep. € 34.50 2014*

VANS, LES 9D1 (3km E Rural) 44.40953, 4.16768
Camping Domaine des Chênes, 07140 Chassagnes-Haut [04 75 37 34 35; fax 04 75 37 20 10; reception @domaine-des-chenes.fr; www.domaine-des-chenes.fr] Fr town cent take D104A dir Aubenas. After Peugeot g'ge turn R onto D295 at garden cent twd Chassagnes. Site on L after 2km; sp adj Rv Chassezac. Med, pt shd, pt sl, terr, wc; mv service pnt; fam bthrm; shwrs inc; EHU (10A) inc; lndry; shop; rest; snacks; bar; bbq; playgrnd; pool; 80% statics; dogs €2.50; adv bkg acc; quiet; ccard acc; rv fishing 500m; CKE/CCI. "Lovely shady site; ideal for birdwatchers; gd rest; rec." 4 Apr-27 Sep. € 18.00 2016*

VARENNES EN ARGONNE 5D1 (0km N Rural) 49.22935, 5.03424 **Camp Municipal Le Pâquis, Rue St Jean, 55270 Varennes-en-Argonne [03 29 80 71 01 (Mairie); fax 03 29 80 71 43; mairievarennesnargonne@wanadoo.fr; www. varennesenargonne.fr/pages/annexe/reglement-du-camping]** On D946 Vouziers/Clermont-en-Argonne rd; sp by bdge in vill, on banks of Rv Aire, 200m N of bdge. NB Ignore sp by bdge to Camping Lac Vert (not nr). Med, pt shd, wc; shwrs inc; EHU (6-16A) €3.65; lndry; shop nr; bbq; playgrnd; wifi; pool €0.40; Eng spkn; quiet; rv fishing. "Pleasant site with gd facs; gd (hilly) cycle ride taking in US WWI cemetary." 9 Apr-9 Oct. € 10.00 2014*

⊞ **VARILHES** *8G3* (0km NE Urban) *43.04714, 1.63096*
FFCC Camp Municipal du Parc du Château, Ave de 8 Mai 1945, 09120 Varilhes [05 61 67 42 84 or 05 61 60 55 54 (TO); campingdevarilhes@orange.fr; www.campingdevarilhes.com] Exit N20/E9 at sp Varilhes. Turn N in town on D624. Site 250m on L (sp) just bef leisure cent adj Rv Ariège. Med, mkd, pt shd, terr, wc (htd); mv service pnt; fam bthrm; shwrs inc; EHU (5-10A) €5.90-6.40; lndry; shop nr; rest nr; snacks; bar nr; playgrnd; wifi; 20% statics; dogs; adv bkg acc; quiet; rv fishing adj; games area. "Shwr & sinks locked 2100-0700; hot water unreliable." ♦ € 13.00   2018*

⊞ **VARILHES** *8G3* (3km NW Rural) *43.06258, 1.62101*
FFCC Camping Les Mijeannes, Route de Ferriès, 09120 Rieux-de-Pelleport [05 61 60 82 23; fax 05 61 67 74 80; www.vap-camping.fr] Exit N20 sp Varilhes; on app Varilhes cent join 1-way system; 1st R at Hôtel de Ville; over rv bdge; foll camp sps; site 2km on R. Med, hdg, pt shd, wc (htd); chem disp; mv service pnt; shwrs inc; EHU (10A) €4.60; bar; bbq; playgrnd; pool; entmnt; wifi; TV; dogs €1.10; Eng spkn; adv bkg acc; quiet; fishing; games area; CKE/CCI. "Peaceful site by rv, on island formed by rv; ACSI; helpful owner; kids club; badminton; gd size pitches; excel san facs; weekly theme nights high ssn; volley; excel; ltd facs LS." € 27.00   2017*

VATAN *4H3* (9km N Rural) *47.13479, 1.85121* Camp Municipal St Phalier, 2 Chemin Trompe-Souris, 18310 Graçay [02 48 51 24 14 or 02 48 51 42 07 (Mairie); fax 02 48 51 25 92; camping-gracay@wanadoo.fr; www.camping.gracay.info] Leave A20 at junc 9 & take D83 to Graçay. On o'skts of vill turn L & immed turn L foll sp to Cent Omnisport & site. Sm, pt shd, wc; chem disp; shwrs; EHU (10A) €2.69; playgrnd; dogs €1.02; phone; Eng spkn; quiet; fishing; CKE/CCI. "Lovely, peaceful, well-kept, pleasant site by sm unfenced lake & park; plenty of space lge o'fits - site yourself; excel clean san facs; poss travellers, but no problem; rest nr; bar nr; pool adj; shop nr; vill in walking dist; gd NH fr A20." 1 Apr-15 Sep. € 8.70   2016*

VATAN *4H3* (1km W Urban) *47.07131, 1.80573*
Camp Municipal de la Ruelle au Loup, Rue du Collège, 36150 Vatan [02 54 49 91 37 or 02 54 49 76 31 (Mairie); fax 02 54 49 93 72; vatan-mairie1@wanadoo.fr; www.vatan-en-berry.com] Exit A20 junc 10 onto D922 to town cent. Take D2 dir Guilly & foll site sp - 2nd on L (easily missed). Med, mkd, hdg, pt shd, wc; mv service pnt; shwrs inc; EHU (10A) €3 (rev pol); lndry; shop nr; rest nr; playgrnd; adv bkg acc; quiet; CKE/CCI. "Pleasant, well-kept site in park; spacious pitches; basic but clean san facs; twin axles; site yourself, warden calls pm; easy access fr a'route; pool adj; conv Loire chateaux." ♦ 15 Apr-15 Sep. € 15.00   2014*

VAUVERT *10E2* (6km SE Rural) *43.65440, 4.29610* FLOWER Camping Le Mas de Mourgues, Gallician, 30600 Vauvert [04 66 73 30 88; info@masdemourgues.com; www.masdemourgues.com or www.flowercampings.com] Exit A9 junc 26 onto D6313/D6572. Site on L at x-rds with D779 sp to Gallician & Stes Marie-de-la-Mer. Med, mkd, pt shd, wc; chem disp; mv service pnt; shwrs inc; EHU (6A) inc; lndry; shop; snacks; bbq; pool; wifi; 15% statics; dogs €3; phone; Eng spkn; adv bkg acc; ccard acc; games area; CKE/CCI. "Enthusiastic, helpful British owners; some diff, long narr pitches; grnd stony; rd & farming noise; clean facs but poss stretched high ssn; excel pool; excel cycling; vg site." ♦ 15 Mar-15 Oct. € 27.00   2015*

VAYRAC *7C4* (4km S Rural) *44.93462, 1.67981*
FFCC Camping Les Granges, Les Granges-de-Mezel, 46110 Vayrac [05 65 32 46 58; fax 05 65 32 57 94; info@les-granges.com; www.les-granges.com] App Vayrac on D803; turn S at sq in town sp "Campings"; site in 3.5km on banks of Rv Dordogne. Sp in Vayrac. Alt rte fr D803 in St Denis-les-Martel on D80 S - shorter on narr rds; site sp. Lge, pt shd, wc; shwrs; EHU (10A) €4; gas; lndry; shop; rest; snacks; bar; playgrnd; pool; paddling pool; entmnt; TV; dogs €1.60; adv bkg acc; quiet; cycling; fishing; canoeing; games area. "Vg children's amenities; facs fair; poss mosquitoes." 8 May-20 Sep. € 20.00   2012*

VENACO *10G2* (3km E Rural) *42.22388, 9.19364*
Camping La Ferme de Peridundellu, 20231 Venaco [04 95 47 09 89 or 06 12 95 51 65 (mob); campingvenaco@wanadoo.fr; http://campingvenaco.monsite-orange.fr] S on N200 fr Corte for 15km; R on D143; at bdge keep R twds Venaco; site on L in 1.5km on bend. Sm, pt shd, pt sl, wc (htd); chem disp; shwrs inc; EHU (6-10A) €5; lndry; shop nr; rest nr; bar nr; quiet; CKE/CCI. "CL-type site; beautifully situated; gd walking country; friendly owner; highly rec." Apr-Sep. € 17.00   2013*

VENAREY LES LAUMES *6G1* (1km W Urban) *47.54448, 4.45043* Camp Municipal Alésia, Rue du Docteur Roux, 21150 Venarey-les-Laumes [03 80 96 07 76 or 03 80 96 01 59 (Mairie); camping@ville-venareyleslaumes.fr; www.venareyleslaumes.fr] SE fr Montbard on D905, site well sp fr Venarey on D954. Med, mkd, hdg, hdstg, pt shd, wc (htd); shwrs inc; EHU (16A) €3; lndry; shop nr; bbq; playgrnd; sw; red long stay; TV; 10% statics; dogs €1; phone; Eng spkn; adv bkg acc; ccard acc; bike hire; CKE/CCI. "Well-kept site in scenic area; lge pitches; pleasant wardens gd, sm htd refurbished san facs; barrier clsd 2200-0700; cycle tracks to Canal de Bourgogne, ltd facs in LS." ♦ 1 Apr-15 Oct. € 14.70   2015*

VENCE

Tél : +33 (0)4 98 11 45 45
Roquebrune sur Argens
Var - Côte d'Azur - FRANCE

France

⊞ **VENCE** *10E4* (3km W Rural) *43.7117, 7.0905*
Camping Domaine La Bergerie, 1330 Chemin de la Sine, 06140 Vence [04 93 58 09 36; fax 04 93 59 80 44; info@camping-domainedelabergerie.com; www.camping-domainedelabergerie.com] Fr A8 exit junc 47 & foll sp Vence thro Cagnes-sur-Mer. Take detour to W around Vence foll sp Grasse/Tourrettes-sur-Loup. At rndabt beyond viaduct take last exit, foll site sp S thro La Sine town; long, narr rd to site, up driveway on R. Lge, hdstg, mkd, shd, pt sl, wc; chem disp; mv service pnt; fam bthrm; shwrs inc; EHU (5A); gas; lndry; shop; rest; snacks; bar; bbq (gas); playgrnd; pool; paddling pool; red long stay; dogs; Eng spkn; adv bkg acc; quiet; ccard acc; lake fishing; games area; tennis; CKE/CCI. "Shady site; helpful staff; clean san facs; no twin axles or c'vans over 5m; gd dog walks; Vence lovely & excel touring base." ♦ 25 Mar-15 Oct. € 27.00   2014*

See advertisement

"I like to fill in the reports as I travel from site to site"

You'll find report forms at the back of this guide, or you can fill them in online at camc.com/europereport.

VENCE *10E4* (6km W Rural) *43.69348, 7.00785*
Camping Les Rives du Loup, Route de la Colle, 06140 Tourrettes-sur-Loup [04 93 24 15 65; fax 04 93 24 53 70; info@rivesduloup.com; www.rivesduloup.com] Exit A8 junc 47 at Cagnes-sur-Mer. Foll sp La Colle-sur-Loup, then Bar-sur-Loup (D6). Site in Gorges-du-Loup valley, 3km bef Pont-du-Loup. Sm, pt shd, wc; fam bthrm; shwrs inc; EHU (5A) €3.50 (poss rev pol); lndry; shop; rest; snacks; bar; playgrnd; pool; wifi; 60% statics; dogs €3.50; adv bkg acc; quiet; horseriding 5km; tennis; fishing. "Many activities avail; guided walks; beautiful location; cramped pitches."
1 Apr-30 Sep. € 29.50   2013*

⊞ **VENDAYS MONTALIVET** *7C1* (9km W Coastal) *45.36325, -1.14696* Camping CHM Montalivet (Naturist), 46 Ave de l'Europe, 33930 Vendays-Montalivet [05 33 09 20 92; fax 05 56 09 32 15; infos@socnat.fr; www.chm-montalivet.com] D101 fr Soulac to Vendays-Montalivet; D102 to Montalivet-les-Bains; site bef ent to vill; turn L at petrol stn; site 1km on R. V lge, hdstg, mkd, pt shd, pt sl, wc; chem disp; mv service pnt; shwrs inc; EHU (6A) inc; gas; lndry; shop; rest; snacks; bar; playgrnd; pool (htd); beach sand adj; red long stay; entmnt; wifi; TV; 50% statics; dogs €6.90; phone; Eng spkn; adv bkg acc; quiet; ccard acc; games rm; bike hire; INF card; games area. "Vast, peaceful site in pine forest; superb lge naturist beach adj; excel facs for children of all ages; vg; excel; hdstg with elec for MH's." ♦ € 48.00   2018*

⊞ **VENDOIRE** *7B2* (3km W Rural) *45.40860, 0.28079*
Camping du Petit Lion, 24320 Vendoire [05 53 91 00 74; contact@camping-petit-lion.com; www.camping-petit-lion.com] S fr Angoulême on D939 or D674, take D5 to Villebois-Lavalette, then D17 to Gurat. Then take D102 to Vendoire, site sp. Sm, hdg, hdstg, pt shd, wc (htd); shwrs inc; EHU (10A) €4; lndry; shop; rest; snacks; bar; playgrnd; pool; paddling pool; wifi; 10% statics; dogs €3; adv bkg acc; quiet; lake fishing; tennis; CKE/CCI. "British owners; rally fields." ♦ € 17.00   2016*

VENDOME *4F2* (1km E Urban) *47.79122, 1.07586*
Camping au Coeur de Vendôme, Rue Geoffroy-Martel, 41100 Vendôme [02 54 77 00 27 or 09 70 35 83 31; fax 02 54 89 41 01; aucoeurdevendome@camp-in-ouest.com; www.aucoeurdevendome.com] Fr N10 by-pass foll sp for town cent; in town foll sp Camping; site adj to pool 500m. Lge, mkd, pt shd, wc; chem disp; fam bthrm; shwrs inc; EHU (10A) inc; lndry; shop nr; rest nr; bar nr; bbq; playgrnd; red long stay; wifi; 5% statics; dogs €2.50; phone; Eng spkn; quiet; rv fishing adj; tennis; CKE/CCI. "Pleasant rvside setting; clean san facs - a trek fr outer pitches; sports cent, pool & theatre adj; statics sep area; recep 0900-2100; htd pool adj; games area adj; barrier clsd 2200-0630; vg; friendly; bar 500m; level site; narr ent/exit over bdge, poss diff for lge o'fits." ♦ 15 Apr-30 Oct. € 20.00   2017*

VERDUN 5D1 (2km SW Urban) 49.15428, 5.36598
Camping Les Breuils, 8 Allée des Breuils, 55100
Verdun [03 29 86 15 31; fax 03 29 86 75 76;
contact@camping-lesbreuils.com; www.camping-lesbreuils.com] Fr W (Paris) on A4/E50, exit junc 30 onto D1916/D603/D330; cont over rndabt junc with D34 onto D330; at next rndabt in 100m turn R into Allée des Breuils. Or fr E (Metz) exit junc 31 onto D964/D330; cont on D330 past junc with D34A; at rndabt in 150m turn L into Allée des Breuils. Site sp nr Citadel. Avoid Verdun town cent due to 1-way rds. Allée des Breuils runs parallel to D34 on E side of rwly. Site well sp fr D603 & all other dirs. Steepish ent. Lge, hdg, mkd, hdstg, pt shd, pt sl, wc; chem disp; mv service pnt; fam bthrm; shwrs inc; EHU (16A) €4.55 (poss some rev pol); gas; lndry; shop; rest; snacks; bar; playgrnd; pool; red long stay; wifi; dogs €2.10; phone; Eng spkn; adv bkg rec; ccard acc; fishing; bike hire; waterslide; CKE/CCI. "Pleasant, clean, well-kept, lovely, busy site; grass pitches beside lge pond, some lge; poss long walk to water taps; some site rds tight for lge o'fits; gd pool; poss lge youth groups Sept; interesting historial town; cycle rtes around WWI battlefields; easy walk to Citadel with WWI museum; excel; gd rest; friendly staff; sports cent; bus tours fr site; san facs block refurbished (2018); facs expanding." ♦ 15 Mar-15 Oct. € 25.00   2018*

VERDUN SUR LE DOUBS 6H1 (1km W Rural) 46.90259, 5.01777 Camp Municipal La Plage, Quai du Doubs Prolongé, 71350 Verdun-sur-le-Doubs [03 85 91 55 50 or 03 85 91 52 52; fax 03 85 91 90 91; mairie.verdunsurledoubs@wanadoo.fr; www.tourisme-verdun-en-bourgogne.com]
SE on D970 fr Beaune to Verdun-sur-le-Doubs & foll sp in town. Or on D973 or N73 twd Chalon fr Seurre, turn R onto D115 to Verdun; site on bank of Rv Saône. Lge, mkd, shd, pt sl, wc; chem disp; shwrs inc; EHU (10A) €2.10; shop nr; rest nr; bar nr; bbq; playgrnd; wifi; dogs €1; phone; quiet; waterslide; tennis; fishing. "Lovely rvside location; lge pitches; helpful warden; interesting sm town; confluence of 3 rvs: La Saône, Le Doubs & La Dheune; htd pool adj; fishermen's paradise; excel."
1 May-15 Sep. € 16.50   2017*

VERMENTON 4G4 (1km S Rural) 47.65897, 3.73087
Camp Municipal Les Coullemières, route de Coullemières, 89270 Vermenton [03 86 81 53 02; fax 03 86 81 63 95; contact@camping-vermenton.com; www.camping-vermenton.com]
Lies W of D606 - turn off D606 into Rue Pasteur (tight turn & narr rd), strt on at x-rds into Ave de la Gare. Turn R at stn, L over level x-ing. Well sp in vill adj to rv but sps low down & easy to miss. Med, mkd, hdg, pt shd, wc (htd); chem disp; shwrs inc; EHU (6A) inc; lndry; shop nr; rest nr; playgrnd; wifi; TV; 5% statics; dogs €1; bus; adv bkg rec; quiet; ccard acc; fishing; boating; tennis; bike hire. "Peaceful, well-run rvside site; excel san facs; absolutely immac; weight limit on access rds & pitches; no twin axles; gd walks & cycling; conv Chablis vineyards; beautiful town with 12thC church; excel site; staff helpful; delightful site in interesting area." ♦
1 Apr-30 Sep. € 17.00   2017*

VERNANTES 4G1 (7km NW Rural) 47.43717, 0.00641 Camping La Fortinerie, La Fortinerie, 49390 Mouliherne [02 41 67 59 76; north.john.a@gmail.com; www.lafortinerie.com] Fr Vernantes take D58 dir Mouliherne; opp Château Loroux (Plaissance) turn L; at x-rds turn R, site over 1.5km on L. Sm, pt shd, wc, chem disp; shwrs inc; EHU (16A) €5 (poss rev pol); shop nr; rest nr; bbq; dogs free (by arrangement); adv bkg acc; quiet. "Peaceful CL-type site; only sound is crickets!; lge pitches; helpful, friendly British owners; B&B avail; beautiful chateau town; conv Loire valley & vineyards; excel." ♦ 1 May-30 Sep. € 12.00   2016*

VERNET LES BAINS 8G4 (4km S Rural) 42.53330, 2.39847 Domaine-St-Martin, 6 Boulevard de la Cascade 66820 Casteil [04 68 05 52 09; info@domainestmartin.com] Fr Prade to Villefranche on N116. Twd Vernet-les-Bains/Casteil at rndabt. Sp to campsite. Med, hdstg, mkd, shd, terr, wc; chem disp; fam bthrm; shwrs inc; EHU (10A); lndry; shop nr; rest; bar; bbq; cooking facs; playgrnd; pool; wifi; TV; 20% statics; dogs; phone; bus adj; Eng spkn; adv bkg acc; quiet; games rm; CCI. "Mountain hiking/biking; Grottoes 6km; Abbey in vill; friendly, helpful staff; excel rest; vg." ♦ 1 Apr-11 Oct. € 29.00   2014*

VERNET LES BAINS 8G4 (8km NW Rural) 42.56255, 2.36050 Camping Le Rotja, Ave de la Rotja, 66820 Fuilla [04 68 96 52 75; info@camping-lerotja.com; www.camping-lerotja.com] Take N116 fr Prades dir Mont-Louis, 500m after Villefranche-de-Conflens turn L onto D6 sp Fuilla; in 3km just bef church, turn R at sp to site. D6 narr but passing places. Sm, mkd, pt shd, pt sl, terr, wc (htd); chem disp; fam bthrm; shwrs inc; EHU (10A) €3.25; gas; lndry; shop nr; rest nr; snacks; bbq (gas); playgrnd; pool; red long stay; 10% statics; dogs €2; phone; Eng spkn; adv bkg acc; quiet; ccard acc; CKE/CCI. "Peaceful site; views of Mount Canigou; friendly, helpful Dutch owners; gd hiking/walks." ♦
1 Apr-17 Oct. € 27.50   2015*

VERNET, LE 9D3 (1km N Rural) 44.28170, 6.39080
Camping Lou Passavous, Route de Roussimat, 04140 Le Vernet [04 92 35 14 67; fax 04 92 35 09 35; loupassavous@orange.fr; www.loupassavous.com]
Fr N on A51 exit junc 21 Volonne onto N85 sp Digne. Fr Digne N on D900 to Le Vernet; site on R. Fr S exit A51 junc 20 Les Mées onto D4, then N85 E to Digne, then as above. Sm, pt shd, pt sl, wc (htd); chem disp; fam bthrm; shwrs inc; EHU (6A) €4; lndry; shop; rest; snacks; bar; playgrnd; pool; entmnt; wifi; TV; 10% statics; dogs €1.50; Eng spkn; adv bkg acc; quiet; fishing; games area; CKE/CCI. "Scenic location; gd, clean facs; Dutch owners; gd walking, mkd walks fr site, escorted walks by owner; excel; highly rec." ♦
1 May-15 Sep. € 24.00   2016*

VERNEUIL SUR SEINE

VERNEUIL SUR SEINE *3D3* (2km N Rural) *48.99567, 1.95681* Camping-Caravaning 3* du Val de Seine, Chemin du Rouillard, 78480 Verneuil-sur-Seine [01 39 71 88 34 or 01 39 28 16 20; fax 01 39 71 18 60; vds78@orange.fr; www.vds78.com] Exit A13 junc 8 & foll sp to Verneuil; site sp twd rvside. Med, mkd, hdstg, pt shd, wc (htd); chem disp; mv service pnt; shwrs inc; EHU (6A) €4.25; lndry; shop; rest; snacks; bbq; playgrnd; sw nr; 10% statics; dogs €2; Eng spkn; quiet; ccard acc; horseriding; watersports; fishing; games area. "V pleasant site adj Rv Seine; friendly, helpful staff; gd facs & activities; Paris 20 mins by train; site and area run down." ♦ 15 Apr-30 Sep. € 17.30 2012*

VERNON *3D2* (2km W Rural) *49.09625, 1.43851* Camping Les Fosses Rouges, Chemin de Réanville, 27950 St Marcel [02 32 51 59 86 or 06 22 42 19 11 (LS); camping@cape27.fr; www.cape27.fr] Exit A13/E5 junc 16 dir Vernon onto D181; in 2km at rndabt turn L onto D64e dir St Marcel; in 2km at 5-exit rndabt take 1st R onto Chemin de Réanville (D64) & foll camping sp. At 1st major bend to R, cont strt ahead, site on L in 50m. Med, mkd, pt shd, pt sl, wc (htd); chem disp; shwrs inc; EHU (6-10A) €3.20-4.20; gas; shop nr; bbq; playgrnd; 10% statics; dogs €0.50; adv bkg acc; quiet; CKE/CCI. "Well-kept, well-run scenic site; gd clean san facs but tired; parking for m'vans at St Marcel - cont past site over rndabt for 900m, turn sharp L past hotel on R & parking on R; lovely little vill; conv Giverny, but access diff lge o'fits; pool 4km; gd size pitches; peaceful site." ♦ 1 Mar-31 Oct. € 11.00 2017*

VERSAILLES *4E3* (3km E Urban) *48.79455, 2.16038* Camping Huttopia Versailles, 31 Rue Berthelot, Porchefontaine, 78000 Versailles [01 39 51 23 61; fax 01 39 53 68 29; versailles@huttopia.com; www.huttopia.com] Foll sp to Château de Versailles; fr main ent take Ave de Paris dir Porchefontaine & turn R immed when fr when gate lodges; sp. Narr access rd due parked cars & sharp bends. No sp rec use sat nav. Lge, mkd, pt shd, pt sl, terr, wc (htd); chem disp; mv service pnt; fam bthrm; shwrs inc; EHU inc (6-10A) €4.60-6.80; gas; lndry; shop nr; rest; snacks; bar; bbq; playgrnd; pool (htd); red long stay; TV; 20% statics; dogs €4; bus 500m; Eng spkn; adv bkg acc; quiet; ccard acc; bike hire; games area; CKE/CCI. "Wooded site; sm, sl, uneven pitches poss diff lge o'fits; friendly, helpful staff; excel, clean san facs, stretched high ssn; conv Paris trains & Versailles Château; bus 171 to town." ♦ 24 Mar-2 Nov. € 45.30 2016*

VERVINS *3C4* (9km N Rural) *49.90676, 3.91477* FFCC Camping du Val d'Oise, 3 Rue du Mont d'Origny, 02580 Etréaupont [03 23 97 48 04; www.campingduvaldoisern2.com] Site to E of Etréaupont off N2, Mons-Reims rd. Site adj football pitch on banks of Rv Oise. Well sp fr main rd. Sm, mkd, hdg, pt shd, wc; chem disp; mv service pnt; shwrs inc; EHU (10A) €4 (poss rev pol); lndry; shop nr; playgrnd; wifi; dogs €0.30; Eng spkn; adv bkg acc; quiet; rv fishing adj; tennis; CKE/CCI. "Pretty, tidy site; sports field adj; warm welcome; v clean san facs; site self if recep clsd; conv rte to Zeebrugge ferry (approx 200km); gd walking & cycling; gd; delightful site; canoe hire adj; vg." 1 Apr-31 Oct. € 16.00 2017*

VESOUL *6G2* (3km W Rural) *47.63026, 6.12858* Camping International du Lac, Ave des Rives du Lac, 70000 Vesoul [03 84 76 22 86; camping_dulac@yahoo.fr; www.camping-vesoul.com] 2km fr D619, sp fr W end of by-pass, pass indus est to lge lake on W o'skts. Ent opp Peugeot/Citroën factory on lakeside. Lge, mkd, pt shd, wc (htd); mv service pnt; fam bthrm; shwrs inc; EHU (6A) €3; gas; lndry; shop nr; rest; bar; playgrnd; 10% statics; dogs €2; adv bkg acc; ccard acc; tennis; fishing; waterslide 300m; games area; CKE/CCI. "Super site screened fr indus est by trees; pool & paddling pool 300m; site clsd mid-Dec to early Jan; gd size pitches but poss soft after rain; excel aqua park nr; gd cycle rtes; vg." ♦ € 19.00 2016*

VEULES LES ROSES *3C2* (4km E Rural) *49.88351, 0.85188* Camp Municipal Le Mesnil, Route de Sotteville, 76740 St Aubin-sur-Mer [02 35 83 02 83; lemesnil76@orange.fr; www.campinglemesnil.com] On D68 2km W of St Aubin-sur-Mer. Med, hdg, unshd, terr, wc (htd); mv service pnt; shwrs inc; EHU (10A) €3.70 (pos rev pol); lndry; shop; playgrnd; beach sand 1.5km; wifi; 30% statics; ccard acc; CKE/CCI ♦ 1 Apr-31 Oct. € 23.00 2012*

> "We must tell the Club about that great site we found"
>
> Get your site reports in by mid-August and we'll do our best to get your updates into the next edition.

VEULES LES ROSES *3C2* (6km E Rural) *49.86083, 0.89079* Camping Les Garennes de la Mer, 12 Route de Luneray, 76740 Le Bourg-Dun [02 35 83 10 44; camping_lesgarennesdelamer@hotmail.fr; www.lesgarennes.fr] Fr Veules-les-Roses, take D925 twd Dieppe. Site sp in Le Bourg-Dun - 1km SE. Sm, mkd, pt shd, pt sl, wc; shwrs inc; EHU (16A) €4; gas; lndry; shop nr; beach shgl 3km; 60% statics; dogs €1; Eng spkn; adv bkg acc; quiet; ccard acc; CKE/CCI. "Well-kept site; vg san facs." ♦ 1 Apr-15 Oct. € 26.00 2013*

VEULES LES ROSES *3C2* (0km S Rural/Coastal) *49.87586, 0.80314* Camping Les Mouettes, 7 Ave Jean Moulin, 76980 Veules-les-Roses [02 35 97 61 98; fax 02 35 97 33 44; camping.les.mouettes0509@orange.fr; www.camping-lesmouettes-normandie.com] On ent vill fr Dieppe on D925, turn R onto D68, site in 500m up hill (14%). Lge, hdg, mkd, pt shd, wc (htd); chem disp; mv service pnt; fam bthrm; shwrs inc; EHU (6A) €4.70; gas; lndry; shop; snacks; bar; bbq; playgrnd; pool (covrd, htd); paddling pool; beach shgl 800m; red long stay; entmnt; wifi; TV; 10% statics; dogs €2; Eng spkn; adv bkg acc; quiet; ccard acc; games area; games rm; fitness rm; CKE/CCI. "Pleasant area; peaceful, well-kept site; vg; site a bit scruffy start of ssn (2017)." ♦ 1 Apr-15 Oct. € 29.30 2017*

VIAS

www.camping-farret.com
"The best holidays ever!"
LE CLUB FARRET ★★★★★ | 34450 VIAS-PLAGE
info@farret.com | +33 4 67 21 64 45
Yelloh! VILLAGE

France

VEYNES 9D3 (2km SW Rural) 44.51889, 5.79880
FFCC Camping Les Rives du Lac, Les Iscles, 05400 Veynes [04 92 57 20 90; contact@camping-lac.com; www.camping-lac.com] Off D994. Sp on lakeside. Med, mkd, hdstg, pt shd, pt sl, wc; chem disp; mv service pnt; fam bthrm; shwrs; EHU (10A) €3.50; lndry; snacks; bar; bbq; playgrnd; pool (covrd); paddling pool; sw nr; wifi; dogs €2.50; phone; bus 500m; adv bkg acc; quiet; ccard acc; watersports; CKE/CCI. "Attractive, well-run site on shore of sm lake; welcoming staff; beach games in high ssn; climbing; mountain biking; open air cinema twice weekly; san facs excel; something for all ages."
1 May-30 Sep. € 23.00   2013*

VEZELAY 4G4 (2km SE Rural) 47.45879, 3.77150
Camp Municipal, 89450 St Père [03 86 33 36 58 or 03 86 33 26 62 (Mairie); fax 03 86 33 34 56; mairie-saint-pere@wanadoo.fr; www.saint-pere.fr] Fr Vézelay take D957, turn onto D36 to St Père. Site sp. Med, pt shd, wc cont; shwrs inc; EHU (10A) €2.20 (poss rev pol); shop nr; playgrnd; 10% statics; quiet; tennis; rv fishing adj; canoeing. "Pleasant site; conv Morvan National Park; warden comes am & pm; basic san facs need update; gd walking area." 1 Apr-30 Sep. € 11.00   2014*

VEZELAY 4G4 (5km S Rural) 47.45675, 3.78768 FFCC Camping de Vézelay L'Ermitage, 1 Route de l'Étang, 89450 Vézelay [03 86 33 24 18; auberge.jeunesse. vezelay@orange.fr; www.camping-auberge-vezelay. com] Foll sp fr cent of Vézelay to 'Camping Vézelay' & Youth Hostel. Sm, pt shd, pt sl, serviced pitches; wc; chem disp; mv service pnt; shwrs inc; EHU (4-6A) €3; shop nr; Eng spkn; quiet; CKE/CCI. "Pleasant, peaceful, scenic site; welcoming; gd, clean facs; some pitches diff lge o'fits & blocks req; recep eve only - site self & sign in when open; some pitches muddy after heavy rain; Vézelay the starting point of one of the pilgrim rtes - superb abbey; excel." 1 Apr-31 Oct.
€ 8.50   2015*

VIAS 10F1 (3km S Coastal) 43.29055, 3.39863
Camping Californie Plage, 34450 Vias-Plage [04 67 21 64 69; fax 04 67 21 54 62; info@californie-plage. fr; www.californie-plage.fr] W fr Agde on D612 to Vias; turn S in town & foll sps 'Mer' over canal bdge & sp to site. Lge, mkd, shd, wc; chem disp; shwrs inc; EHU (5-10A) €1.50-3.50; gas; lndry; shop; rest; snacks; bar; playgrnd; pool (covrd, htd); paddling pool; beach sand adj; entmnt; wifi; TV; 10% statics; dogs €4.60; Eng spkn; adv bkg acc; ccard acc; bike hire; waterslide; CKE/CCI♦ 1 Apr-30 Oct. € 33.00   2016*

VIAS 10F1 (3km S Coastal) 43.29800, 3.41750
Camping Les Salisses, Route de la Mer, 34450 Vias-Plage [04 67 21 64 07; fax 04 67 21 76 51; info@ salisses.com; www.salisses.com]
Turn S off D612 (Agde-Béziers rd) in Vias & foll sp to Vias-Plage. Cross Canal du Midi bdge & site on R. Lge, mkd, pt shd, wc; chem disp; fam bthrm; shwrs inc; EHU (6A) inc; gas; lndry; shop; rest; snacks; bar; bbq; playgrnd; pool (covrd, htd); beach sand 1km; entmnt; wifi; TV; 80% statics; dogs €3.50; quiet; ccard acc; bike hire; waterslide; tennis; games area. "Vg family hols; sauna; steam rm; interesting town & mkt in Agde; sm pitches." ♦ 16 Apr-17 Sep. € 42.00   2012*

VIAS 10F1 (3km S Coastal) 43.29083, 3.41783
Yelloh! Village Le Club Farret, Farinette-Plage, 34450 Vias-Plage [04 67 21 64 45; fax 04 67 21 70 49; info@farret.com; www.camping-farret.com]
Fr A9, exit Agde junc 34. Foll sp Vias-Plage on D137. Sp fr cent of Vias-Plage on L, immed after Gendarmerie. V lge, mkd, pt shd, wc; chem disp; mv service pnt; fam bthrm; shwrs inc; EHU (6A) inc; gas; lndry; shop; rest; snacks; bar; playgrnd; pool (htd); beach sand adj; entmnt; TV; 10% statics; dogs €6; Eng spkn; adv bkg acc; quiet; ccard acc; games rm; bike hire; fitness rm; games area; tennis; watersports; CKE/CCI. "Excel facs, entmnt; excursions; gd security." ♦ 12 Apr-29 Sep.
€ 65.00   2017*

See advertisement

VIAS

Cherished moments make great memories

Camping village club *****

Open from April to November

High standing accommodations for unique holidays

Fully equipped camping pitches with private heated bathroom

3 heated **aquatic complexes** including 1 indoor

Natural Lagoon of thin sand

Entertainment 7/7

SPA, services & **shops** in all seasons

Use the promo code **CAMC-19** for free booking fees

www.dragonniere.com
+33 (0)4 67 01 03 10

France / Méditerranée / Vias

VIAS *10F1 (3km W Rural) 43.31222, 3.36367* **Camping Sunêlia Le Domaine de la Dragonnière, 34450 Vias** [04 67 01 03 10; fax 04 67 21 73 39; contact@dragonniere.com; www.dragonniere.com] Exit A9 junc 35 onto D64 twd Valras-Plage, then D612 dir Agde & Vias. Site on R bef Vias. Or exit junc 34 onto D612A. At Vias turn R onto D612 sp Béziers, site on L. NB Take care high speed humps at sh intervals. V lge, mkd, hdg, pt shd, wc; chem disp; mv service pnt; shwrs inc; EHU (16A) inc; gas; lndry; shop; rest; snacks; bar; bbq; playgrnd; pool (htd); paddling pool; beach sand 3km; entmnt; wifi; TV; 80% statics; dogs €5; phone; Eng spkn; adv bkg acc; ccard acc; games area; sauna; bike hire; tennis; CKE/CCI. "Vg site in botanical reserve; excel for children & teenagers high ssn; Canal du Midi nrby; opp Béziers airport; free bus to beach high ssn; site poss flooded after heavy rain; touring pitches have individual shwr block on pitch (new 2014); v busy at w/ends." ♦ 4 Apr-2 Nov. € 72.00   2016*

See advertisement

"I need an on-site restaurant"

We do our best to make sure site information is correct, but it is always best to check any must-have facilities are still available or will be open during your visit.

VICHY *9A1 (4km S Rural) 46.11555, 3.43006* **Camping Beau Rivage, Rue Claude Decloître, 03700 Bellerive-sur-Allier** [04 70 32 26 85; fax 04 70 32 03 94; camping-beaurivage@wanadoo.fr; www.camping-beaurivage.com] Fr Vichy cross rv bdge over Rv Allier onto D1093, turn L at rndabt foll sp Campings, sp to Beau Rivage. Site on L on rv bank, past Cmp Les Acacias. Med, shd, wc; chem disp; mv service pnt; fam bthrm; shwrs inc; EHU (10A) €3.10; gas; lndry; shop; snacks; bbq; playgrnd; pool (covrd, htd); entmnt; wifi; TV; 50% statics; dogs €1; quiet; tennis 2km; games area; bike hire; archery; waterslide; canoeing; fishing. "Lovely rvside site, but no rv sw allowed; lge o'fits have diff pitching; easy cycle ride to lovely city." ♦ 1 Apr-8 Oct. € 23.60   2016*

VICHY 9A1 (4km S Urban) 46.10756, 3.43670 **FFCC Camping La Croix St Martin, Allée du Camping, 99 Ave des Graviers, 03200 Abrest [04 70 32 67 74 or 06 10 94 70 90 (mob); camping-vichy@orange.fr; www.camping-vichy.com]** Exit D906 at Abrest onto D426 N (Ave des Graviers); in 900m turn L into Allée du Camping. Site sp fr D906, both N & S of Abrest. Med, mkd, hdg, pt shd, wc; chem disp; mv service pnt; fam bthrm; shwrs inc; EHU (10A) €3.80; lndry; snacks; playgrnd; pool (htd); paddling pool; wifi; 15% statics; dogs; phone; Eng spkn; adv bkg acc; quiet; ccard acc; games area; CKE/CCI. "Gd cycling along rv allier thro Vichy; san facs clean; well maintained, well run, attractive site; friendly staff; flat walking dist fr a v attractive town; free wifi over all site; pool now covrd."
♦ 2 Apr-2 Oct. € 20.00   2015*

VICHY 9A1 (1km SW Rural) 46.11648, 3.42560 **Camping Les Acacias, Rue Claude Decloître, 03700 Bellerive-sur-Allier [04 70 32 36 22; fax 04 70 32 88 52; camping-acacias03@orange.fr; www.camping-acacias.com]** Cross bdge to Bellerive fr Vichy & foll Hauterive sp onto D1093. Strt over at 1st rndabt & turn L at 2nd rndabt onto D131 dir Hauterive. At 3rd rndabt turn L sp Vichy 'piscine'. Foll sm camping sps along rv side. Or fr S leave D906 at St Yorre & cross Rv Allier, then foll sp to Bellerive. Site sp at rndabt on app to Bellerive adj Rv Allier. On final app, at sp showing site in either dir, keep L & foll site sp along rv bank to recep. NB Many other sites in area, foll sp carefully. Med, mkd, hdg, shd, wc; chem disp; fam bthrm; shwrs inc; EHU (10A) €3.40; gas; shop nr; snacks; bbq; playgrnd; pool; wifi; TV; 20% statics; dogs €1; adv bkg acc; ccard acc; boating; fishing; CKE/CCI. "Well-run site; helpful owner; gd san facs; free Vichy Célestins water at spring in lovely town." 7 Apr-7 Oct. € 19.00   2015*

VIERZON 4G3 (3km SW Urban) 47.20937, 2.08079 **Camp Municipal de Bellon, Route de Bellon, 18100 Vierzon [02 48 75 49 10 or 02 48 53 06 14 (LS); fax 02 48 71 40 94; campingmunicipal-vierzon@wanadoo.fr or ot-vierzon@wanadoo.fr; www.officedetourismedevierzon.com]** Fr N on A71 take A20 dir Châteauroux, leave at junc 7 onto D2020 & then D27 dir Bourges; pass Intermarché supmkt on L, after next traff lts turn L into Route de Bellon; site in 1km on R, sp. NB Do not go into town cent. Med, mkd, hdg, pt shd, pt sl, wc; chem disp; mv service pnt; shwrs inc; EHU (6A) €3 (some rev pol); gas; lndry; shop nr; rest; snacks; bar; bbq (elec, gas); playgrnd; wifi; dogs; phone; Eng spkn; adv bkg acc; boat hire; fishing; CKE/CCI. "Attractive, well-kept site by rv; gd sized pitches but some poss diff to negotiate; nice little rest o'looking rv; gates clsd 2300-0700; warden on site 1700-2200; poss travellers; ideal NH; gd site; friendly recep; new facs, v clean (2017)." ♦ 1 May-30 Sep. € 13.00   2017*

VIEURE 7A4 (2km NE Rural) 46.50305, 2.90754 **Plan d'eau de Vieure, La Borde, 03430 Vieure [04 70 02 04 46; plandeau03@orange.fr; www.loctionschaletscampingdelaborde.fr]** Exit A71-E11 at junc 10. Take D94 NE to Cosne d'Allier, then R onto D11. L onto D459, 1st R onto La Bordé. Foll sp to campsite. Med, hdg, pt shd, pt sl, wc; fam bthrm; shwrs inc; EHU (10A) €3.10; lndry; rest; snacks; bar; playgrnd; sw; twin axles; 35% statics; dogs; phone; quiet; ccard acc; CCI. "Large, open & shd pitches; dated san facs; v pleasant remote site by lake; fishing & canoeing; family friendly; gd." ♦ 11 Apr-30 Sep. € 11.50   2014*

⊞ **VIHIERS** 4G1 (15km SE Rural) 47.07419, -0.41104 **Camping Le Serpolin, St Pierre-à-Champ, 49560 Cléré-sur-Layon [02 41 52 43 08; fax 02 41 52 39 18; info@loirecamping.com; www.loirecamping.com]** Take D748 S fr Vihiers by-pass sp Argenton Château. In 2km turn L at sp Cléré-sur-Layon onto D54. Cont thro vill to 1st mkd x-rd, turn R, site last house along this lane. Sm, hdstg, pt shd, wc (htd); chem disp; shwrs inc; EHU (10A) €4; lndry; bbq; playgrnd; pool; wifi; dogs free; Eng spkn; adv bkg rec; quiet; bike hire; fishing; CKE/CCI. "Peaceful, CL-type site; clean san facs; helpful British owners; rallies by arrangement; conv chateaux, Futuroscope; vg." € 15.00   2015*

VILLARD DE LANS 9C3 (12km N Rural) 45.12951, 5.53215 **Camping Caravaneige Les Buissonnets, 38112 Méaudre [04 76 95 21 04; fax 04 76 95 26 14; camping-les-buissonnets@wanadoo.fr; www.camping-les-buissonnets.com]** Fr Grenoble take D1532 to Sassenage then D531 to Lans-en-Vercors. Turn R at rndabt onto D106 twrds Meaudre. Turn L just bef rndabt in vill off D106. Approx 30km SW of Grenoble by rd & 18km as crow flies. Med, unshd, sl, wc (htd); chem disp; mv service pnt; shwrs inc; EHU (6-10A) €4-6; lndry; shop nr; rest nr; snacks; playgrnd; bus to ski slopes; quiet; games area; clsd 1 Dec-10 Nov. "Gd skiing cent; conv touring Vercours; levellers ess; highly rec; friendly, v well managed site; higher price in winter; pool 300m; lovely area; slightly sl, levelling necessary; v pleasant." ♦ 1 Jan-31 Oct & 12 Dec-31 Dec. € 21.00   2017*

⊞ **VILLARD DE LANS** 9C3 (2km N Rural) 45.07750, 5.55620 **Camping Caravaneige L'Oursière, 38250 Villard-de-Lans [04 76 95 14 77; fax 04 76 95 58 11; oursiere@franceloc.fr; www.camping-oursiere.fr]** Site clearly visible on app to town fr D531 Gorges d'Engins rd (13km SW Grenoble). App fr W on D531 not rec for c'vans & m'vans due o'hangs. Lge, unshd, terr, wc (htd); chem disp; mv service pnt; fam bthrm; shwrs inc; EHU (10A) €4-6; lndry; shop; rest; snacks; bbq; playgrnd; wifi; 20% statics; dogs €5; Eng spkn; adv bkg acc; quiet; ccard acc; CKE/CCI. "Excel all winter sports; friendly owners; drying rm; san facs need upgrade (2010); pool 800m; waterpark 800m; new htd indoor sw pool (2015)." ♦ € 26.00   2016*

VILLARS LES DOMBES

VILLARS LES DOMBES *9A2* (0km S Urban) *45.99763, 5.03163* Camping Indigo Parc des Oiseaux, 164 Ave des Nations, 01330 Villars-les-Dombes [04 74 98 00 21 or 04 92 75 27 94; fax 04 74 98 05 82; camping@ parcdesoiseaux.com; www.camping-indigo.com] N fr Lyon on N83, site in town cent on R by sw pool. Lge, hdstg, pt shd, wc; mv service pnt; shwrs inc; EHU (10A) €4.50; lndry; shop nr; rest; snacks; bar; bbq (gas); playgrnd; paddling pool; entmnt; 60% statics; dogs €3; games area; rv fishing adj; bike hire; tennis. "Excel site; lge pitches; modern, gd san facs; htd pool adj inc; gd security; bird park 10 mins walk; popular NH." ♦ 29 Mar-3 Nov. € 33.00   2014*

VILLEDIEU LES POELES *1D4* (1km S Urban) *48.83638, -1.21694* Camping Les Chevaliers de Malte, 2 Impasse Pré de la Rose, 50800 Villedieu-les-Poêles [02 33 59 49 04; contact@camping-deschevaliers.com; www.camping-deschevaliers.com] Exit A84 junc 38 onto D999 twd Villedieu, then R onto D975 & R onto D924 to avoid town cent. Foll sp fr car park on R after x-ing rv. Site behind PO & cinema. Med, hdstg, hdg, mkd, pt shd, wc (htd); chem disp; mv service pnt; fam bthrm; shwrs inc; EHU (6A) inc (poss rev pol); lndry; shop nr; snacks; bar; bbq; playgrnd; pool (htd); entmnt; wifi; TV; 40% statics; dogs €1.50; phone; Eng spkn; adv bkg acc; quiet; games area; boating; games rm; rv fishing; tennis; CKE/CCI. "Peaceful, lovely site; lge pitches but kerbs poss diff lger o'fits; interesting historic town; avoid arr Tue am due mkt; conv A84 & Cherbourg ferry; vg; gd modern facs, all new; well worth a visit to town; excel site; rest extended 2011; staff v helpful; bell foundry worth a visit; new owners (2016); vg." ♦ 1 Apr-15 Oct. € 28.00   2017*

VILLEFORT (LOZERE) *9D1* (1km S Rural) *44.43536, 3.93123* Les Sédariès (formerly Municipal), Ave des Cévennes, 48800 Villefort [04 66 46 25 20; vacances48@gmail.com; www.sedaries.com] On D906 heading S fr Villefort twd Alès. Sm, pt shd, terr, wc; chem disp; shwrs inc; EHU (6A) €2; lndry; shop nr; rest nr; bar nr; bbq; sw nr; phone; quiet; fishing 2km; CKE/CCI. "Attractive, scenic site; bureau clsd 1000-1830; privately owned now (2014); not many touring places." 1 Jun-30 Sep. € 15.00   2014*

⊞ **VILLEFRANCHE DE LAURAGAIS** *8F3* (8km SW Rural) *43.35498, 1.64762* Camping Le Lac de la Thésauque, Naillowx, 31560 Montgeard [05 61 81 34 67; fax 05 61 81 00 12; camping@thesauque.com; www.camping-thesauque.com] Fr S exit A61 at Villefrance-de-Lauragais junc 20 onto D622, foll sp Auterive then Lac after Gardouch vill, site sp. Fr N turn off A61 at 1st junc after tolls S of Toulouse onto A66 (sp Foix). Leave A66 at junc 1 & foll sp Nailloux. Turn L on ent vill onto D662 & in 2km turn R onto D25 & immed R to site, sp. Med, hdstg, mkd, pt shd, terr, wc (htd); chem disp; shwrs inc; EHU (10A) inc; lndry; shop; rest; snacks; bar; bbq; playgrnd; pool; wifi; 70% statics; dogs; ccard acc; boating; fishing; tennis; CKE/CCI. "Scenic, peaceful location, conv NH for A61; helpful owners; ltd facs LS; gd security; steep app to sm terr pitches poss diff lge o'fits; facs basic but adequate." ♦ € 28.50   2014*

VILLEFRANCHE DE ROUERGUE *7D4* (9km SE Rural) *44.26695, 2.11575* Camping Le Muret, 12200 St Salvadou [05 65 81 80 69 or 05 65 29 84 87; info@lemuret.com; www.lemuret.com] Fr Villefranche on D911 twd Millau, R on D905A sp camping & foll camping sp 7km. Sm, mkd, hdg, shd, wc; shwrs inc; EHU (16A) €4.50; lndry; rest; snacks; bar; red long stay; wifi; dogs €2; phone; adv bkg acc; quiet; fishing; CKE/CCI. "Lovely setting; gas & ice at farm; lake adj; gd sized pitches." ♦ 5 Apr-22 Oct. € 23.00   2017*

> ### "Satellite navigation makes touring much easier"
>
> Remember most sat navs don't know if you're towing or in a larger vehicle – always use yours alongside maps and site directions.

VILLEFRANCHE DE ROUERGUE *7D4* (1km SW Urban) *44.34207, 2.02731* FFCC Camping du Rouergue, 35 Ave de Fondies, Le Teulel, 12200 Villefranche-de-Rouergue [05 65 45 16 24; campingrouergue@wanadoo.fr; www.campingdurouergue.com] Best app fr N on D922, then D47 dir Monteils & Najac; avoid 1-way system in town; ent thro sports stadium. Site well sp. Med, hdstg, hdg, mkd, shd, serviced pitches; wc; chem disp; mv service pnt; fam bthrm; shwrs inc; EHU (16A) €3.50; lndry; shop; rest; snacks; bar; playgrnd; pool; red long stay; twin axles; entmnt; wifi; TV; 15% statics; dogs €1; bus high ssn; Eng spkn; adv bkg req; quiet; ccard acc; tennis 1km; CKE/CCI. "Well-kept, peaceful site; easy access; lge pitches; pleasant, friendly owner; excel clean san facs; pool v sm; gd security; sports stadium adj; easy walk/cycle to town; m'van services outside site; rec; v hot water, gd supply; excel." ♦ 12 Apr-30 Sep. € 23.70   2014*

VILLEFRANCHE DU PERIGORD *7D3* (1km E Urban) *44.62757, 1.08159* FFCC Camping La Bastide, Route de Cahors, 24550 Villefranche-du-Périgord [05 53 28 94 57; fax 05 53 29 47 95; campinglabastide@wanadoo.fr; www.camping-la-bastide.com] On N660 fr Villefranche-du-Périgord dir Cahors; site past PO on R nr top of hill on town o'skts. Med, hdg, mkd, pt shd, terr, wc; chem disp; mv service pnt; fam bthrm; shwrs inc; EHU (6-10A) €3-4; lndry; shop nr; rest; snacks; bar; playgrnd; pool; entmnt; wifi; 25% statics; dogs €1; adv bkg acc; quiet; tennis 300m; fishing; CKE/CCI. "Steep, terr site but easy access, can be soft in wet weather; charming owners; ACSI; excel touring base; vg; v nice town within walking dist." ♦ 3 Apr-16 Oct. € 22.00   2012*

VILLEFRANCHE SUR SAONE

VILLEFRANCHE DU PERIGORD *7D3* (8km SW Rural) *44.59025, 1.04799* **Moulin du Périé Camping - Caravaning, 47500 Sauveterre-la-Lémance [05 53 40 67 26; fax 05 53 40 62 46; moulinduperie@ wanadoo.fr; www.camping-moulin-perie.com or www.flowercampings.com]** Fr N fr Villefranche-du-Périgord take D710 S dir Fumel. At Sauveterre-la-Lémance turn L at traff lts, cross level x-ing & in 400m turn L sp Loubejac & site; site on R in 4km. Tight ent bet tall hedges 2.6m apart for 30m. Fr E fr Cahors on D660 & turn L onto D46 sp Loubejac. Cont thro Loubejac & turn L at T-junc, foll sp Sauveterre. Site on R in 4km. Med, pt shd, pt sl, wc; chem disp; mv service pnt; fam bthrm; shwrs inc; EHU (6-10A) €3 (poss rev pol); gas; lndry; shop; rest; snacks; bar; playgrnd; pool; paddling pool; entmnt; TV; 25% statics; dogs €4.60; Eng spkn; adv bkg rec; quiet; ccard acc; tennis 3km; bike hire; archery; trout fishing; games rm; CKE/CCI. "Beautiful, well-run site in grnds of old mill; welcoming, friendly family owners; clean, dated san facs; vg rest; site rds narr, not suitable v lge o'fits; gd touring base; excel; poor maintenance (2015)." ♦ 13 May-16 Sep. € 30.00   2015*

VILLEFRANCHE SUR CHER *4G3* (8km SE Rural) *47.26917, 1.86265* **FFCC Camp Municipal Val Rose, Rue du Val Rose, 41320 Mennetou-sur-Cher [02 54 98 11 02 or 02 54 98 01 19 (Mairie); mairie. mennetou@wanadoo.fr; http://mennetou.fr/ tourisme/se-loger-restauration/camping-municipal]** Site sp fr D976/D2076 fr Villefranche (sm white sp); site on R in SW side of vill of Mennetou. To avoid narr bdge in town fr N76 onto A20, just outside town, turn imm R, site sp after L turn. Sm, pt shd, wc (htd); chem disp; shwrs inc; EHU (4A); lndry; shop nr; rest nr; playgrnd; dogs €0.20; Eng spkn; adv bkg acc; quiet. "Pleasant, well-kept site; friendly, helpful warden; excel, spotless san facs; excel lndry; pretty, walled town 5 mins walk along canal; mkt Thurs; htd pool adj; vg value; access for lge o'fits diff; excel NH." ♦ 13 May-18 Sep. € 13.00   2018*

VILLEFRANCHE SUR SAONE *9B2* (10km E Rural) *45.99104, 4.81802* **FFCC Camp Municipal le Bois de la Dame, 521 Chemin du Bois de la Dame, 01480 Ars-sur-Formans [04 74 00 77 23 or 04 74 00 71 84 (Mairie); camping.boisdeladame@orange.fr; www.ars-village.fr]** Exit A6 junc 31.1 or 31.2 onto D131/D44 E dir Villars-les-Dombes. Site 500m W of Ars-sur-Formans on lake, sp. Med, mkd, pt shd, pt sl, terr, wc cont; chem disp; shwrs inc; EHU (10-16A) €3-5; lndry; playgrnd; 60% statics; dogs €3; adv bkg rec; lake fishing; CKE/CCI. "Average site, but pretty & interesting vill; ltd facs LS; no twin axles; higher pitches have unguarded precipices." ♦ 1 Apr-30 Sep. € 16.00   2017*

VILLEFRANCHE SUR SAONE *9B2* (10km SE Rural) *45.93978, 4.76811* **Camping Kanopee (formerly Municipal La Petite Saône), Rue Robert Baltié, 01600 Trévoux [04 74 08 44 83; contact@ kanopee-village.com; www.kanopee-village.com]** Fr Villefranche take D306 S to Anse. Turn L onto D39/D6 for Trévoux, site sp in town, on bank of Rv Saône. Lge, pt shd, wc; shwrs; EHU (6A) inc; shop nr; playgrnd; sw nr; entmnt; 75% statics; dogs; adv bkg req; quiet; rv fishing adj; CKE/CCI. "Spacious rvside site nr vill; helpful staff; well maintained; access poss diff lge o'fits due statics; gd cycling rtes nrby; Trévoux interesting history; m'van o'night area at ent; excel shwr blocks; Aire at ent to camp; vg." ♦ 1 Apr-30 Sep. € 28.00   2018*

VILLEFRANCHE SUR SAONE *9B2* (5km SE Rural) *45.97243, 4.75637* **Camp Municipal La Plage Plan d'Eau, 2788 Route de Riottier, 69400 Villefranche-sur-Saône [04 74 65 33 48; fax 04 74 60 68 18; campingvillefranche@voila.fr; www.villefranche.net]** Exit A6 junc 31.2 Villefranche. Fr N turn R at rndabt, cross over a'route & str over next rndabt; cont to site on R bef Rv Saône. Or fr S turn R at rndabt & cont to site as above. Look for sp on rndabt. Med, shd, wc; chem disp; mv service pnt; shwrs inc; EHU (10A); gas; lndry; shop nr; snacks; bar; sw nr; wifi; 10% statics; adv bkg acc; quiet; ccard acc; fishing; CKE/CCI. "Busy site in gd position; easy access & nr m'way but quiet; a bit run down; gd rvside walking; NH only; san facs clean (2015); card ent sys." ♦ 1 May-30 Sep. € 22.00   2015*

> **"There aren't many sites open at this time of year"**
>
> If you're travelling outside peak season remember to call ahead to check site opening dates – even if the entry says 'open all year'.

VILLEFRANCHE SUR SAONE *9B2* (5km S Rural) *45.94050, 4.72680* **Camping Les Portes du Beaujolais, 495 Ave Jean Vacher, 69480 Anse [04 74 67 12 87; fax 04 74 09 90 97; campingbeaujolais@ wanadoo.fr; www.camping-beaujolais.com]** Exit A6 junc 31.2 at Villefranche & foll D306 S to Anse (foll sp Champion supmkt). Site well sp off D39, on banks of Rvs Saône & L'Azergues. Lge, mkd, hdg, hdstg, pt shd, wc (htd); chem disp; mv service pnt; shwrs inc; EHU (10A) €5.50; lndry; shop; snacks; bar; playgrnd; pool; paddling pool; sw; wifi; TV; 20% statics; dogs €2; phone; Eng spkn; adv bkg acc; bike hire; CKE/CCI. "Pleasant, friendly site; pitches poss tired end of ssn; some pitches sm, uneven & diff lge o'fits; ltd facs LS & poss stretched high ssn; shwrs sometimes cold (2011); pool poss overcrowded; poss muddy when wet; lge field avail at rear but no shd; rvside walking; rd noise fr A6 nrby & some rwly noise; Anse 10 min walk - bus to Lyons; narr gauge rlwy adj; lge o'night area; conv NH." ♦ 1 Mar-31 Oct. € 37.50   2013*

Site report forms at back of guide   *Last year of report

VILLENEUVE SUR LOT

VILLENEUVE SUR LOT 7D3 (8km E Urban) 44.39576, 0.80491 **Camping Les Berges du Lot, Place de la Mairie, 47140 St Sylvestre-sur-Lot [05 53 41 22 23 or 05 53 41 24 58 (Mairie)]** Exit Villeneuve-sur-Lot on D911 sp Cahors. Site in cent of St Sylvestre-sur-Lot. Foll Camping sp to rear of La Mairie (Town Hall) & supmkt; site accessed via car park to R of main rd. Sm, mkd, pt shd, wc; chem disp; shwrs inc; EHU (6A) €3.30 (poss long lead req); shop nr; rest nr; bar nr; pool; Eng spkn; quiet; boating; fishing. "Popular, comfortable, scenic site; clean facs; helpful staff; adv bkg rec; 2 pin cont el conn; many long term residents, inc British; mkt Wed & Sun am, when access diff; rec; cramped; untidy; birdwatching; not suitable for large o'fits." ♦ 15 May-30 Sep. € 11.50   2014*

"That's changed – Should I let the Club know?"

If you find something on site that's different from the site entry, fill in a report and let us know. See camc.com/europereport.

VILLENEUVE SUR LOT 7D3 (3km S Urban) 44.39483, 0.68680 **Camping Lot et Bastides, Allée de Malbentre, 47300 Pujols [05 53 36 86 79 or 06 14 13 78 93 (mob); fax 09 70 63 28 07; contact@ camping-lot-et-bastides.fr; www.camping-lot-et-bastides.fr]** Fr Villeneuve Sur Lot on D911 take L onto D118. At rndabt take 1st exit onto D911. Turn L onto Rue du General. Site on the R. Med, hdg, pt shd, wc; chem disp; mv service pnt; shwrs inc; EHU (16A); lndry; shop; snacks; bar; bbq; playgrnd; pool; twin axles; entmnt; wifi; 25% statics; dogs €2; bus adj; adv bkg acc; quiet; ccard acc; games area; CCI. "New site 2012; neat and clean; views of Pujols, most beautiful vill in France; lots to see & do in area; v scenic; friendly staff; bike hire." ♦ 1 Apr-30 Sep. € 31.00   2014*

See advertisement above

VILLEREAL 7D3 (2km N Rural) 44.65723, 0.72820 **Camping Château de Fonrives, 47210 Rives, Villeréal [05 53 36 63 38; contact@ campingchateaufonrives.com; www.camping chateaufonrives.com]** Fr Bergerac take N21 S for 8km, turn L onto D14 thro Issigeac; site is just outside vill of Rives in grnds of chateau. Med, pt shd, pt sl, wc; fam bthrm; shwrs inc; EHU (6A) inc; gas; lndry; shop; rest; bar; playgrnd; pool (covrd, htd); sw; entmnt; 10% statics; dogs €6; Eng spkn; adv bkg acc; quiet; ccard acc; fishing; golf; bike hire; games rm; waterslide; CKE/CCI. "Spacious site; gd, 3 pools; van poss manhandled on some shady pitches; easier access pitches without shd; some noise fr weekly disco; friendly owners; B&B avail; interesting town; mkt Sat; huge pitches nr pool/bar; poss noisy." ♦ 7 Jun-7 Sep. € 47.00   2013*

See advertisement opposite

VILLEREAL 7D3 (7km NE Rural) 44.65331, 0.80953 **Camping Le Moulin de Mandassagne, 47210 Parranquet [05 53 36 04 02; isabelle.pimouguet@ orange.fr; www.haut-agenais-perigord.com]** Fr D104/D2 bet Villeréal & Monpazier turn N sp Parranquet, site sp. Sm, mkd, pt shd, wc; chem disp; shwrs inc; EHU (6A) inc; gas; lndry; snacks; playgrnd; pool; entmnt; TV; Eng spkn; adv bkg acc; quiet; fishing; tennis. "Lovely countryside; v relaxing; slightly bohemian site; friendly owners." ♦ 1 Apr-1 Oct. € 15.00   2014*

VILLEREAL 7D3 (9km SE Rural) 44.61426, 0.81889 **Camping Fontaine du Roc, Les Moulaties, 47210 Dévillac [05 53 36 08 16; fax 05 53 61 60 23; reception@fontaineduroc.com; www.fontaineduroc. com]** Fr Villeréal take D255 sp Dévillac, just beyond Dévillac at x-rds turn L & L again sp Estrade; site on L in 500m. Med, mkd, hdstg, hdg, pt shd, wc; chem disp; shwrs inc; EHU (5-10A) €3.50-4.50 gas; lndry; rest; snacks; bar; bbq; playgrnd; pool; paddling pool; red long stay; wifi; TV; 2% statics; dogs €3.50; phone; Eng spkn; adv bkg acc; quiet; fishing 500m; bike hire; games rm; CKE/CCI. "Peaceful, well-cared for site; helpful owner; lge pitches; ACSI acc (LS); excel." 1 Apr-15 Oct. € 15.00   2016*

VIMOUTIERS

Yelloh Village Château de Fonrives F-47210 RIVES. FRANCE. Tel. +33 (0)5 53 36 63 38
www.campingchateaufonrives.com
contact@campingchateaufonrives.com

France

VILLEREAL *7D3* (3km NW Rural) *44.65253, 0.72375*
Camping de Bergougne, 47210 Rives [05 53 36 01 30; info@camping-de-bergougne.com; www.camping-de-bergougne.com/camping/]
Fr Villeréal, take D207 NW sp Issigeac/Bergerac. In 1km turn L onto D250 W sp Doudrac. Foll sm green sp to site. Med, mkd, hdg, pt shd, pt sl, terr, wc; chem disp; fam bthrm; shwrs inc; EHU (6A) inc; gas; lndry; shop nr; rest; snacks; bar; bbq (sep area); playgrnd; pool (htd); paddling pool; entmnt; TV; 15% statics; dogs; Eng spkn; adv bkg acc; quiet; ccard acc; games rm; fishing; games area; CKE/CCI. "Vg site; small café; bread del in Jul & Aug; friendly welcoming new owners; occasional events in bar/rest; v peaceful rustic ambience; vg." ♦ 1 May-30 Sep. € 24.00   2018*

VILLERSEXEL *6G2* (1km N Rural) *47.55763, 6.43628*
Camping Le Chapeau Chinois, 92 Rue du Chapeau Chinois, 70110 Villersexel [03 84 63 40 60; contact@camping-villersexel.eu; camping-villersexel.eu]
Leave vill on D468 N, site on R immed after rv bdge. Med, hdg, mkd, pt shd, wc; chem disp; mv service pnt; fam bthrm; shwrs; EHU (10A) €3.30; lndry; shop nr; bar nr; bbq; playgrnd; sw; wifi; 5% statics; dogs; Eng spkn; adv bkg acc; quiet; games area; CKE/CCI. "Vg." ♦ 1 Apr-6 Oct. € 19.00   2016*

⊞ **VILLEVAUDE** *3D3* (2km E Rural) *48.91258, 2.67025* **Camping Le Parc de Paris,** Rue Adèle Claret, Montjay-la-Tour, 77410 Villevaudé [01 60 26 20 79; fax 01 60 27 02 75; info@campingleparc.fr; www.campingleparc.fr] Fr N, A1 twds Paris, then A104 to Marne-la-Vallée, exit at junc 6B (Paris Bobigny), then D105 to Villevaudé, then to Montjay & site sp. Fr S exit A104 at junc 8 to Meaux & Villevaudé. Lge, mkd, hdg, pt shd, pt sl, serviced pitches; wc (htd); chem disp; mv service pnt; fam bthrm; shwrs inc; EHU (10A) €5; lndry; shop nr; rest; snacks; bar; playgrnd; sw nr; entmnt; wifi; TV; 50% statics; dogs €6; phone; Eng spkn; adv bkg acc; ccard acc; games rm; tennis 200m; games area; CKE/CCI. "Conv Disneyland, Paris, Parc Astérix (Disney tickets fr recep); gd san facs; twin axles acc if adv bkg; drive to local stn (10mins) & park free; shuttle service to Disneyland; gd sh stay; san facs tired, pitches sm and uneven." ♦ € 28.00   2013*

⊞ **VILLIERS SUR ORGE** *4E3* (1km SE Urban) *48.65527, 2.30409* **Camping Le Beau Village,** 1 Voie des Prés, 91700 Villiers-sur-Orge [01 60 16 17 86; fax 01 60 16 31 46; contact@campingaparis.com; www.campingaparis.com] Fr S on N20 turn off onto D35 heading E twrds Villiers sur Orge. Cont strt on to traff lts & sm Renault g'ge, turn R alongside rv. Turn just bef St Genieve des Bois. Med, hdg, pt shd, wc (htd); chem disp; mv service pnt; shwrs inc; EHU (10A) (poss rev pol); gas; lndry; shop nr; bar; bbq; playgrnd; wifi; dogs €2; phone; train 700m; quiet; games rm; kayaking; fishing. "Pleasant, well-run site; conv Paris; some statics/chalets; ltd space for lge o'fits; helpful staff." € 22.00   2017*

> "I like to fill in the reports as I travel from site to site"
>
> You'll find report forms at the back of this guide, or you can fill them in online at camc.com/europereport.

VIMOUTIERS *3D1* (1km N Urban) *48.93236, 0.19646*
Camp Municipal La Campière, Ave Dr Dentu, 61120 Vimoutiers [02 33 39 18 86 (Mairie); fax 02 33 36 51 43; campingmunicipalvimoutiers@wanadoo.fr; www.vimoutiers.fr] App Vimoutiers fr N on on D579/D979/D916, site on R 300m after passing junc with D16; turn R at flag poles (200m after Avia petrol stn). Or appr fr Gacé on D979 turn L at flag poles (on D916 just bef junc with D16). Site nr stadium & not well sp. Sm, hdg, pt shd, wc (htd); chem disp; shwrs inc; EHU (6A) €2.85; lndry; shop nr; rest nr; playgrnd; sw nr; 10% statics; dogs €1.50; adv bkg acc; tennis; bike hire; rv fishing 2km; CKE/CCI. "Excel, well-maintained, pretty site at cent of Camembert cheese industry; helpful, friendly warden; sports facs 2km; vg, clean san facs; noise fr nrby factory; boating 2km; unrel opening dates - phone ahead LS; attractive town; gd value." ♦ 1 Apr-31 Oct. € 13.00   2018*

VIRIEU LE GRAND

VIRIEU LE GRAND 9B3 (5km NE Rural) 45.87483, 5.68428 **Camping Le Vaugrais, Chemin de Vaugrais, 01510 Artemare [04 79 87 37 34; fax 04 79 87 37 46; contact@camping-le-vaugrais.fr; www.camping-savoie-levaugrais.com]** N fr Belley on D1504 then D904 to Artemare; sp in vill. Well sp fr D904 on rvside. Sm, hdg, pt shd, wc; chem disp; mv service pnt; fam bthrm; shwrs inc; EHU (10A); lndry; shop nr; rest nr; snacks; bar; bbq; playgrnd; pool; wifi; 10% statics; dogs €1; Eng spkn; adv bkg acc; quiet; fishing; CKE/CCI. "Charming site in gd location; some lge pitches with views; friendly owners; clean san facs, poss inadequate high ssn; nice pool; Artemare within walking dist; gd food at hotel in town; vg local walks; excel; app over narr bdge; gd views; highly rec." ♦ 1 Mar-1 Dec. € 25.00   2016*

> "We must tell the Club about that great site we found"
>
> Get your site reports in by mid-August and we'll do our best to get your updates into the next edition.

VITRE 2F4 (14km N Rural) 48.23090, -1.18087 **Camp Municipal du Lac, 35210 Châtillon-en-Vendelais [02 99 76 06 32 or 02 99 76 06 22 (Mairie); fax 02 99 76 12 39]** Take D178 fr Vitré to Fougères. In 11km branch L onto D108, sp Châtillon-en-Vendelais. Foll sp thro vill & turn R immed after level x-ing & bef bdge; site in 1km. Med, hdg, pt shd, pt sl, wc; shwrs inc; EHU (6A) €3.10 (poss rev pol); lndry; shop; playgrnd; 10% statics; quiet; fishing; tennis; CKE/CCI. "Pleasant site; clean san facs; warden on site 0900-1000 only; levelling blocks req most pitches; lake adj; quiet; gd walks; nature reserve (birds) nr." 15 May-30 Sep. € 11.50   2012*

VITRY LE FRANCOIS 6E1 (6km SE Rural) 48.69673, 4.63039 **Aire Naturelle Camping Nature (Scherschell), 13 Rue de l'Evangile, 51300 Luxémont-et-Villotte [03 26 72 61 14 or 06 83 42 83 53 (mob); eric.scherschell@wanadoo.fr; www.camping-nature.net]** Fr N44 ar rndabt take N4 sp St Dizier. Take exit sp Luxemont. At rndabt take 1st exit D396, at next rndabt take 4th exit sp Luxemont (D316). After 2.1km turn R, site on L in 100km. Sm, hdstg, shd, pt sl, wc; chem disp; mv service pnt; shwrs inc; EHU (6A) inc (poss rev pol & long lead req); bbq; playgrnd; sw nr; dogs €1; Eng spkn; adv bkg acc; quiet; fishing; CKE/CCI. "Delightful, CL-type site; well-kept & immac; helpful, friendly owners; gd, clean unisex san facs; nr canal & cycle paths; interesting area to visit; excel; poss mosquitoes." 1 May-15 Oct. € 14.40   2017*

VITRY LE FRANCOIS 6E1 (2km W Urban) 48.73020, 4.58114 **Camp Municipal La Peupleraie, 6 Esplanade de Tauberbischofsheim, Quai des Fontaines, 51300 Vitry-le-François [03 26 74 20 47 or 03 26 74 20 47 (Mairie); fax 03 26 41 22 88; camping@vitry-le-francois.net; www.vitry-le-francois.net]** Fr N on N44 turn R onto N4 at island with lge stone triumphal arch (sp Paris) & cont on dual c'way for 300m; then immed after sharp L bend turn R thro lge parking area. Fr Nancy on N4 turn R past Hotel d'Ville round rndabt into rue de Glaciers. Past lge arch (Port du Point) after sharp bend L, site on R, sp. Med, hdg, pt shd, wc; shwrs inc; EHU (5A) inc; gas; shop nr; rest nr; bar nr; dogs €1.55; quiet. "Delightful, lovely site; tight ent poss diff lge o'fits, no twin axles; lge pitches; san facs dated & poss tired end of ssn (2011); interesting town in walking dist; vg NH; park nearer rv to avoid traff noise; poss mosquitoes." 1 May-15 Oct. € 14.00   2015*

VIVONNE 7A2 (1km E Rural) 46.42511, 0.26409 **Camp Municipal, Chemin de Prairie, 86370 Vivonne [05 49 43 25 95 or 05 49 43 41 05 (Mairie); fax 05 49 43 34 87; vivonne@cg86.fr]** Exit N10 where it by-passes Vivonne & ent town. Site in municipal park to E of town. Med, pt shd, wc; shwrs; EHU (10A) €2.35; lndry; playgrnd. "Welcoming, helpful resident warden; clean facs; sh walk to town cent; noise fr rlwy, quieter w/end; worth a visit; as gd as ever; ideal NH." ♦ May-Sep. € 17.00   2014*

VIZILLE 9C3 (1km N Urban) 45.08660, 5.76814 FFCC **Camping Le Bois de Cornage, Chemin du Camping, 38220 Vizille [04 76 68 12 39; campingvizille@wanadoo.fr; www.campingvizille.com]** Site sp at x-rds of Rte Napoléon, N85 & Rte de Briançon D1091. Site on N o'skirts of town. Well sp. Med, mkd, hdg, shd, pt sl, terr, wc; chem disp; mv service pnt; fam bthrm; shwrs inc; EHU (10-16A) €4.50-5.50 (long lead poss req); lndry; shop nr; rest; snacks; bar; playgrnd; pool (htd); red long stay; 10% statics; dogs €0.80; bus; Eng spkn; adv bkg rec; quiet; CKE/CCI. "Helpful owner; excel clean facs; gd cycling & climbing nrby; mkd walks nrby; no vans over 5m acc; poss mosquitoes; frequent buses to Grenoble & Bourg-d'Oisans; vg." 24 Apr-10 Oct. € 16.00   2013*

⊞ **VOLLORE-VILLE** 9B1 (1km NE Rural) 45.79199, 3.60583 **Camping Des Plaines, Le Grun de Chignore, Les Plaines, 63120 Vollore-Ville [04 73 53 73 37; jenny-loisel@orange.fr; www.campingauvergne.fr]** Leave A89/E70 at junc 29 onto D906 S to Courpiere. Fr Courpiere take D7 to Vollore-Ville. Site on R at turning to Chabrier. Sm, mkd, hdg, pt shd, wc; mv service pnt; fam bthrm; shwrs inc; gas; lndry; shop nr; rest; snacks; bar; bbq; playgrnd; pool; twin axles; wifi; 20% statics; adv bkg acc; quiet; ccard acc; CKE/CCI. "Excel, well-kept little site; friendly owners; pleasant vill; conv for A89/E70." ♦ € 15.00   2014*

VOLVIC *9B1* (1km E Urban) *45.87208, 3.04591* **Camp Municipal Pierre et Sources, Rue de Chancelas, 63530 Volvic [04 73 33 50 16; fax 04 73 33 54 98; camping@ville-volvic.fr; www.ville-volvic.fr]** Exit Riom on D986: foll sp for Pontgibaud & Volvic. Site sp to R on app to town. Sm, shd, wc (htd); chem disp; mv service pnt; shwrs inc; EHU (12A) €3.50; lndry; shop; 10% statics; dogs €1.50; Eng spkn; adv bkg acc; quiet. "Pleasant, tidy site with lovely views; welcoming & helpful; excel, cleans san facs; access some pitches poss diff, particularly for lge o'fits; conv Volvic factory tour; no access for new arrivals when off is clsd." 1 May-30 Sep. € 20.00   2015*

VONNAS *9A2* (0km NW Rural) *46.22152, 4.98805* **Camp Municipal Le Renom, 240 Ave des Sports, 01540 Vonnas [04 74 50 02 75; campingvonnas@ wanadoo.fr; www.camping-renom.com/fr/ accueil-p1]** Fr Bourg-en-Bresse take D1079 W sp Mâcon. In 15km take D26 or D47 S to Vonnas; turn R in town cent (ignore sp on o'skts of town) & site on R in 300m by leisure cent. Med, hdg, mkd, pt shd, wc; chem disp; fam bthrm; shwrs inc; EHU (10A) €4.50; lndry; shop nr; bbq; wifi; 30% statics; dogs €1; quiet; tennis adj; rv fishing. "Warm welcome; interesting town- 10min walk; mkt Thurs; htd pool adj; gd site, but expensive; extremely well kept." ♦ 2 Apr-2 Oct. € 23.00   2013*

VOREY *9C1* (0km SW Rural) *45.18576, 3.90679* **Camping Les Moulettes, Chemin de Félines, 43800 Vorey-sur-Arzon [04 71 03 70 48 or 04 71 03 79 49; fax 04 71 03 72 06; contact@camping-les-moulettes.fr; www.camping-les-moulettes.fr]** Fr Le Puy take D103 sp Vorey. Site sp in vill; L in main sq. Sm, hdg, pt shd, wc; shwrs inc; EHU (10A) €3.50; lndry; shop nr; rest; snacks; bar; playgrnd; pool; paddling pool; wifi; 10% statics; dogs €1.50; Eng spkn; adv bkg acc; quiet; fishing adj; waterslide; games area. "Peaceful site by rv; gd sized pitched, many on rv bank; friendly owners; gd quality rest acc rv." ♦ May-Sep. € 23.50   2015*

VOUECOURT *6E1* (0km E Rural) *48.26774, 5.13671* **Camp Municipal Rives de Marne, Rue de Verdun 52320 Vouécourt [06 78 52 50 54 or 03 25 02 44 46 46; commune.vouecourt@bbox.fr; www. campingvouecourt.sopixi.fr]** N fr Chaumont on N67; sp to site in 17km; thro vill by Rv Marne; site on L bef main rv bdge, almost opp Mairie; well sp. Sm, mkd, pt shd, wc; chem disp; shwrs inc; EHU (10A) €2.50 (poss rev pol); gas; lndry; shop nr; rest nr; playgrnd; wifi; dogs; adv bkg acc; ccard acc; fishing; CKE/CCI. "Lovely, peaceful, rvside site; gd sized pitches; friendly warden calls pm; clean; rv poss floods in winter; forest walks & cycling; popular NH; new excel san facs (2015); crowded; excel." ♦ 29 Apr-30 Sep. € 15.00   2017*

VOULTE SUR RHONE, LA *9D2* (5km N Rural) *44.82663, 4.76171* **Camping La Garenne, Quartier La Garenne, 07800 St Laurent-du-Pape [04 75 62 24 62; info@lagarenne.org; www.campinglagarenne-ardeche.fr]** Well sp fr La Voulte. Fr Valence S on D86 La Voulte, approx 15km turn W onto D120; 300m after St Laurent-du-Pape cent, turn R bef PO. Med, pt shd, terr, wc; chem disp; shwrs inc; EHU (6A) inc (poss rev pol); gas; lndry; shop; rest; snacks; bar; playgrnd; pool; red long stay; entmnt; wifi; dogs €2.50; Eng spkn; adv bkg acc; quiet; bike hire; CKE/CCI. "Popular site; friendly, helpful Dutch owners; views fr terr pitches; gd clean san facs; sh walk to vill; vg; in cycling dist of the Dolce Via rte." ♦ 1 Apr-1 Oct. € 37.00   2015*

⊞ **VRAIGNES EN VERMANDOIS** *3C4* (0km N Rural) *49.88538, 3.06623* **Camping des Hortensias, 22 Rue Basse, 80240 Vraignes-en-Vermandois [03 22 85 64 68; campinghortensias@free.fr; www. campinghortensias.com]** Fr N on A1/E15 take exit 13 onto D1029 sp St Quentin; strt rd 16km until rndabt, take D15 (Vraignes) exit; site sp 1st on R in vill. Or fr S & A26, take junc 10 onto D1029 sp Péronne; after 15km at rndabt take D15 as bef. Sm, hdg, hdstg, pt shd, wc (htd); chem disp; shwrs; EHU (4-8A) €2.50-4.50 (poss long lead req); lndry; shop nr; bar nr; bbq; red long stay; wifi; 10% statics; dogs €2; quiet; CKE/CCI. "Lovely farm site; sm pitches, poss muddy when wet; helpful, friendly owners; vg, clean san facs; conv for Somme battlefields & m'way; excel; rec torch." € 13.00   2016*

WASSELONNE *6E3* (1km W Urban) *48.63739, 7.43209* **FFCC Camp Municipal, Rue des Sapins, 67310 Wasselonne [03 88 87 00 08; camping-wasselonne@ wanadoo.fr; www.suisse-alsace.com]** Fr D1004 take D244 to site. Med, mkd, pt shd, terr, wc; mv service pnt; shwrs inc; EHU (5-10A) €2.30-3.70; gas; lndry; shop; rest; snacks; bar; playgrnd; pool (covrd, htd); 30% statics; dogs €0.60; quiet; CKE/CCI. "Pleasant, pretty town; facs excel; cycle rte & bus (adj) to Strasbourg; gd NH." 15 Apr-15 Oct. € 17.00   2017*

WATTEN *3A3* (1km N Urban) *50.83521, 2.21047* **Camping Le Val Joly (Le Val Joli), Rue de Aa, 59143 Watten [03 21 88 23 26 or 03 21 88 24 75; www. campings-nord.com]** NW fr St Omer on D943; N of Tilques turn N onto D300; in 5km at rndabt turn R onto D207 sp Watten; at T-junc turn L onto D213; cross rv brdg & turn L in 500m at camping sp. Med, mkd, pt shd, wc; chem disp; shwrs; EHU (10A) €2.20-3.10; lndry; shop nr; playgrnd; 90% statics; dogs €1.55; adv bkg acc; fishing. "Spacious, attractive, well-kept site; conv NH for ferries; welcoming, friendly, helpful owner; basic, clean san facs; secure gates, locked 2200-0700, but off rd parking; cycling along rv/ canal; no site lighting (2010); few touring pitches - arr early or phone ahead high ssn; access to rv walk; glass works at Arques; vet nr; vg." 1 Apr-31 Oct. € 12.00   2018*

France

WIMEREUX *3A2* (1km S Coastal) *50.76131, 1.60769* Camp Municipal L'Olympic, 49 Rue de la Libération, 62930 Wimereux [03 21 32 45 63; fax 03 21 83 68 94; camping.wimereux@orange.fr; www.ville-wimereux.fr] A16 exit 32 & foll sp Wimereux Sud to vill; turn R at rndabt to site. Or N fr Boulogne on D940, at vill sp Wimereux & rndabt, turn R. Med, hdg, mkd, unshd, pt sl, wc; chem disp; fam bthrm; shwrs inc; EHU (6A) €4; lndry; shop nr; rest; bbq; playgrnd; beach 800m; 80% statics; dogs €2; Eng spkn; ccard acc; sailing; fishing; CKE/CCI. "Conv Boulogne; basic facs, stretched high ssn & poss irreg cleaning LS (2010); hot water runs out early; poss waterlogging after rain; gd vet in attractive seaside town; poor security, take care thieves at night (2009); useful NH only; pool 4km; off clsd 1300-1500." 16 Mar-18 Oct. € 18.00   2014*

⊞ **WIMEREUX** *3A2* (2km S Coastal) *50.75277, 1.60722* Caravaning L'Eté Indien, Hameau de Honvault, 62930 Wimereux [03 21 30 23 50; fax 03 2191 20 46; ete.indien@wanadoo.fr; www.eteindien-wimereux.com] Fr Calais on A16 exit junc 32 sp Wimereux Sud. Thro Terlincthun R after x-ing rlwy, site in 700m on R (do not enter 1st site, correct site is the 2nd one clearly sp above gate with site name) - narr, v rough rd. Med, unshd, pt sl, terr, serviced pitches; wc; chem disp; mv service pnt; fam bthrm; shwrs inc; EHU (10A) inc; gas; lndry; shop; snacks; bar; bbq (gas); playgrnd; pool (htd); paddling pool; beach sand 1.5km; red long stay; entmnt; wifi; 90% statics; dogs €3; phone; Eng spkn; adv bkg acc; games area; games rm. "Conv A16, Calais ferries; rec LS phone to check site open; ltd touring pitches & poss steep; muddy & unpleasant in winter; rlwy runs along one side of site; NH only if desperate!; new sw pool and MV area; gd clean facs (2012); poor facs for waste water." ♦ € 28.00   2014*

> "I need an on-site restaurant"
>
> We do our best to make sure site information is correct, but it is always best to check any must-have facilities are still available or will be open during your visit.

WINGEN SUR MODER *5D3* (1km S Rural) *48.91565, 7.36934* Camp Municipal/Aire Naturelle, Rue de Zittersheim, 67290 Wingen-sur-Moder [03 88 89 71 27 (Mairie); fax 03 88 89 86 99; mairie@wingensurmoder.fr; www.wingensurmoder.fr] W fr Haguenau on D919 to W end Wingen-sur-Moder. Site sp by rlwy arch. Sm, mkd, pt shd, terr, wc; chem disp; shwrs inc; EHU (13A); shop nr; rest nr; Eng spkn; adv bkg acc; quiet; CKE/CCI. "Excel, peaceful site but adj sports field poss used by youth groups/motorbikers high ssn; clean facs; warden calls am & pm; gd walking/cycling; pitch layout plan at the gate." 1 May-30 Sep. € 11.50   2015*

WISSANT *3A2* (8km NE Coastal) *50.91226, 1.72054* Camping Les Erables, 17 Rue du Château d'Eau, 62179 Escalles [03 21 85 25 36; boutroy.les-erables@wanadoo.fr; www.camping-les-erables.fr] Fr A16 take exit 40 onto D243 thro Peuplingues. Site sp to L on ent Escalles (on sharp R bend). Steep ent. Don't be put off by No Entry sp - 1-way system for c'vans on app rd. Sm, hdstg, mkd, pt shd, terr, wc (htd); chem disp; mv service pnt; shwrs; EHU (6-10A) €3.50-€4.50; lndry; shop nr; rest nr; bbq; beach sand 2km; wifi; dogs; phone; Eng spkn; adv bkg rec; CKE/CCI. "Lovely, well-kept open site with great views; family owned; spacious pitches but poss haphazard pitching; immac, modern facs; gates open 0800-2200; 2 pitches for disabled visitors with san facs; coast walks; sh walk to vill; private san facs extra; conv tunnel & ferries; gd site with view of Channel; excel grass pitch site; friendly, welcoming, helpful owners; popular site; ideal NH." ♦ 1 Apr-11 Nov. € 19.00   2017*

WISSANT *3A2* (4km E Rural) *50.88290, 1.70938* Camping La Vallée, 901 Rue Principale, 62179 Hervelinghen [03 21 36 73 96 or 03 21 85 15 43; www.campingdelavallee.net] Fr Calais exit A16 onto D244 & foll sp St Inglevert. Site on L at end Hervelinghen vill. Med, mkd, hdg, pt shd, wc (htd); chem disp; shwrs; EHU (6A) €3.60 (poss rev pol); lndry; rest; snacks; bar; bbq; playgrnd; beach shgl 3km; wifi; 75% statics; dogs €1; Eng spkn; quiet; games area; CKE/CCI. "Family-run site; clean san facs; conv Calais, Cité Europe; gd walking in area." ♦ 1 Apr-31 Oct. € 14.50   2013*

YCHOUX *7D1* (10km E Rural) *44.33060, -0.97975* Camp Municipal du Lac des Forges, 40160 Ychoux [05 58 82 35 57 or 05 58 82 30 01 (Mairie); fax 05 58 82 35 46] Fr Bordeaux take N10 S & turn onto D43 at Liposthey W twd Parentis-en-Born. Site in 8km on R, past vill of Ychoux. Sm, pt shd, pt sl, wc; chem disp; mv service pnt; shwrs; EHU (5-10A) €3.50 (rev pol); lndry; shop nr; rest; bar; playgrnd; pool €1.50; quiet; fishing; sailing. "Levelling blocks poss req; lake adj; pitches nr rd poss noisy." 15 Jun-10 Sep. € 14.00   2013*

YPORT *3C1* (1km SE Rural) *49.73221, 0.32098* Camp Municipal La Chenaie, Rue Henri-Simon, 76111 Yport [02 35 27 33 56; www.camping-normandie-yport.com] Take D940 fr Fécamp SW, D211 to Yport to site. Med, pt shd, wc; shwrs; EHU (10A); shop nr; beach shgl 1km; 80% statics; quiet. "Conv Le Havre." 31 Mar-30 Sep. € 33.00   2018*

YPORT *3C1* (0km SW Coastal) *49.73746, 0.30959* Camping Le Rivage, Rue Hottières, 76111 Yport [02 35 27 33 78; contact@camping-lerivage.com; www.camping-lerivage.com] Fr D940 bet Etretat & Fécamp take D11 2km NE of Les Loges, meeting up with D211 & head twd Yport. Site on D211. Or foll sp fr Yport. Med, hdstg, unshd, pt sl, terr, wc; chem disp; shwrs; EHU (6A) inc (poss long lead req); lndry; shop nr; snacks; bar; bbq; beach shgl 300m; TV; phone; adv bkg acc; quiet; games rm. "Well-situated, o'looking sea; steep descent to beach; san facs inadequate high ssn & long walk fr most pitches; rec stop at top of site & walk to recep bef pitching, as turning poss diff lge o'fits." 25 Mar-30 Sep. € 17.50   2012*

CORSICA

GHISONACCIA *10H2* (4km E Coastal) *41.99850, 9.44220* **Camping Arinella Bianca, Route de la Mer, Bruschetto, 20240 Ghisonaccia [04 95 56 04 78; fax 04 95 56 12 54; arinella@arinellabianca.com; www.arinellabianca.com]** S fr Bastia on N193/N198 approx 70km to Ghisonaccia. At Ghisonaccia foll sp opp pharmacy to beach (plage) & Rte de la Mer. In 3km turn R at rndabt & site well sp. NB When towing keep to main, coastal rds. Lge, mkd, hdg, shd, wc; chem disp; mv service pnt; fam bthrm; shwrs inc; EHU (6A) €5.50 (poss rev pol); gas; lndry; shop; rest; snacks; bar; bbq; playgrnd; pool (htd); paddling pool; beach sand adj; entmnt; wifi; TV; 45% statics; dogs €6; Eng spkn; adv bkg acc; ccard acc; games area; horseriding adj; games rm; bike hire; fishing; watersports; tennis; CKE/CCI. "Clean, well-run site; attractive lake in cent; trees make access to pitches diff; helpful owner & staff." ♦ 16 Apr-30 Sep. € 38.00   2016*

See advertisement

PIANOTTOLI CALDARELLO *10H2* (4km SE Coastal) *41.47272, 9.04327* **Camping Kevano Plage, Route du bord de mer 20131 Pianottoli-Caldarello [04 95 71 83 22; fax 04 95 71 83 83; campingkevano@gmail.com; www.campingkevano.com]** Turn off N196 in Pianottoli at x-rds onto D122 for 1km. Turn R in Caldarello, site on L in 2km. Med, mkd, pt shd, pt sl, terr, wc; chem disp; mv service pnt; shwrs inc; EHU (4-6A) €2.50; lndry; shop; rest; snacks; bar; playgrnd; beach sand 400m; entmnt; TV; 10% statics; dogs €1; phone; Eng spkn; adv bkg rec; quiet; ccard acc; CKE/CCI. "Beautiful, family-run site in macchia amongst huge boulders; san facs tired but clean; no dogs on beach Jul/Aug." ♦ 27 Apr-30 Sep. € 42.00   2013*

PIETRACORBARA *10G2* (4km SE Coastal) *42.83908, 9.4736* **Camping La Pietra, Marine de Pietracorbara, 20233 Pietracorbara [04 95 35 27 49; fax 04 95 35 28 57; lapietra@wanadoo.fr; www.la-pietra.com]** Fr Bastia on D80 N. In 20km ent vill & turn L onto D232. Site on R in 1km at marina beach. Well sp. Med, mkd, hdg, shd, wc (htd); mv service pnt; fam bthrm; shwrs inc; EHU (20A) €3.60; lndry; shop; rest; bar; bbq; playgrnd; pool; beach sand 600m; wifi; TV; dogs €3.50; bus nr; Eng spkn; ccard acc; lake fishing; tennis; CKE/CCI. "Generous pitches; helpful owners; excel facs; beautiful pool; gd beach rest." ♦ 20 Mar-4 Nov. € 29.80   2017*

PORTO VECCHIO *10H2* (5km NE Coastal) *41.62273, 9.2997* **Camping Les Ilots d'Or, Ste Trinité, Route de Marina di Fiori, 20137 Porto-Vecchio [04 95 70 01 30; info@campinglesilotsdor.com; www.campinglesilotsdor.com]** Turn E off N198 5km N of Porto-Vecchio at Ste Trinité twd San Ciprianu. In 1km fork R, site in 300m on L. Med, shd, pt sl, terr, wc cont; shwrs inc; EHU (6A) €3.5; gas; lndry; shop; rest; snacks; bar; beach sand adj; quiet. "Well-organised site; helpful family owners; many vg beaches in easy reach." 2 May-30 Sep. € 22.00   2013*

PORTO VECCHIO *10H2* (14km W Rural) *41.61788, 9.21236* **Campsite U Furu (Naturist), Route de Muratello, 20137 Porto-Vecchio [04 95 70 10 83; fax 04 95 70 63 47; contact@u-furu.com; www.u-furu.com]** Fr N on N198 turn R at rndabt sp Muratello. Foll sp to U-Furu. Sm, mkd, pt shd, terr, wc; chem disp; shwrs inc; EHU (6A); gas; lndry; shop; rest; snacks; bar; pool; sw nr; twin axles; entmnt; 10% statics; Eng spkn; adv bkg acc; quiet; games area; CCI. "Site on beautiful sm rv with rock pools and waterfalls; fabulous beaches within 40 mins; easy access to Ospedale area & Bavella Pass." 15 May-15 Oct. € 37.40   2014*

ST FLORENT

ST FLORENT *10G2* (1km SW Coastal) *42.67394, 9.29205* **Camping U Pezzo, Route de la Roya, 20217 St Florent [04 95 37 01 65; contact@ upezzo.com; www.upezzo.com]** Exit St Florent for L'Ile-Rousse on D81 then N199 Route de la Plage. After 2km sharp R immed after x-ing bdge. Med, pt shd, terr, wc; mv service pnt; fam bthrm; shwrs inc; EHU (10A) €4; lndry; shop; rest; snacks; bar; beach sand adj; dogs €3.50; adv bkg acc; quiet; horseriding; sailing; windsurfing; waterslide; fishing; CKE/CCI. "Pleasant site; mini farm for children." 1 Apr-15 Oct. € 19.00   2013*

SOLENZARA *10H2* (12km W Rural) *41.83495, 9.32144* **Camping U Ponte Grossu, Route de Bavella, 20145 Sari-Solenzara [04 95 48 26 61 or 06 14 79 80 46 (mob); info@upontegrossu.com; www.upontegrossu.com]** Fr N198, take D268 to U Ponte Grossu. Sm, mkd, pt shd, terr, wc; chem disp; mv service pnt; shwrs inc; EHU (6A); rest; snacks; bar; dogs; adv bkg acc; CCI. "Site alongside rv; rv adj; canyoning; rafting; access to fab mountain areas; vg." ♦ 1 May-20 Sep. € 25.00   2014*

ILE DE RE

ARS EN RE *7A1* (0km S Coastal) *46.20395, -1.52014* **FFCC Camping du Soleil, 57 Route de la Grange, 17590 Ars-en-Ré [05 46 29 40 62; fax 05 46 29 41 74; contact@campdusoleil.com; www.campdusoleil. com]** On ent Ars-en-Ré on D735, pass Citroën g'ge & in 700m take 3rd L dir Plage de la Grange. Site sp. Med, mkd, hdg, pt shd, wc; chem disp; mv service pnt; fam bthrm; shwrs inc; EHU (4-10A) €3.70-4.90; lndry; shop; rest; snacks; bar; bbq (elec, gas); playgrnd; pool (htd); paddling pool; beach sand 400m; wifi; TV; 35% statics; dogs €3.20; phone; adv bkg acc; games area; bike hire; tennis; CKE/CCI. "Pleasant, pretty site with pines & bamboo; helpful, friendly staff; gd pool; gd cycling & walking; sm pitches tight." ♦ 1 Apr-1 Oct. € 48.00   2017*

ARS EN RE *7A1* (2km SW Coastal) *46.20282, -1.52733* **Camping Essi, 15 Route de la Pointe de Grignon, 17590 Ars-en-Ré [05 46 29 44 73 or 05 46 29 46 09 (LS); fax 05 46 37 57 78; camping.essi@wanadoo.fr; www.campingessi.com]** D735 to Ars-en-Ré; do not enter town; turn L at supmkt. Site sp. Med, hdg, pt shd, wc (htd); chem disp; mv service pnt; fam bthrm; shwrs inc; EHU (5-10A) €3.95-5.60; lndry; shop; snacks; bar; bbq; playgrnd; pool; 20% statics; dogs €2.10; phone; Eng spkn; adv bkg acc; quiet; bike hire; watersports; CKE/CCI. "Attractive waterfront town; excel beaches 2km; gd cycling; gd oysters; vg; well run & clean facs."
♦ 1 Apr-31 Oct. € 28.50   2015*

ARS EN RE *7A1* (0km NW Coastal) *46.21130, -1.53017* **Camping Le Cormoran, Route de Radia, 17590 Ars-en-Ré [05 46 29 46 04; fax 05 46 29 29 36; info@cormoran.com; www.cormoran.com]** Fr La Rochelle take D735 onto Ile-de-Ré, site sp fr Ars-en-Ré. Med, hdg, mkd, hdstg, pt shd, wc; chem disp; mv service pnt; fam bthrm; shwrs inc; EHU (10A) €6; lndry; shop nr; rest; snacks; bar; playgrnd; pool (htd); beach 500m; entmnt; 10% statics; dogs €5.00; Eng spkn; adv bkg acc; quiet; ccard acc; games rm; sauna; golf 10km; bike hire; tennis; games area; CKE/CCI. "Delightful vill; vg site." ♦
1 Apr-30 Sep. € 49.00   2012*

See advertisement

COUARDE SUR MER, LA *7A1* (5km SE Coastal) *46.17405, -1.37865* **Sunêlia Parc Club Interlude, 8 Route de Gros Jonc, 17580 Le Bois-Plage-en-Ré [05 46 09 18 22; fax 05 46 09 23 38; infos@interlude. fr; www.interlude.fr]** Fr toll bdge at La Rochelle foll D201 to Gros-Jonc. Turn L at rndabt at site sp. Site 400m on L. Lge, hdg, hdstg, mkd, pt shd, serviced pitches; wc (htd); chem disp; mv service pnt; fam bthrm; shwrs inc; EHU (10A) inc; gas; lndry; shop; rest; snacks; bar; bbq; playgrnd; pool (covrd, htd); beach sand; wifi; TV; 45% statics; dogs €8; Eng spkn; adv bkg req; quiet; bike hire; watersports; fitness rm; boat hire; solarium; sauna; tennis nr; games area; jacuzzi. "Excel, well-run, clean, relaxing site; busy but not noisy; vg facs; some sm, sandy pitches - extra for lger; gd rest; nrby beaches excel; o'night m'vans area; walk to great beach; gd atmosphere, entmnt and shop." ♦ 11 Apr-20 Sep. € 50.00   2016*

Route de Radia 17590 ARS EN RÉ
Tel. 05 46 29 46 04
info@cormoran.com – www.cormoran.com

CAMPING ★★★★★ ILE DE RÉ

500m from the sea, at the border of a forest and 800m from the picturesque village Ars en Ré ; campsite Le Cormoran is a true paradise for young and old. Heated aquatic park (from april to September) with one pool, a children's pool and a spa, the «serenity space» with hammam, sauna and tisanerie, and high standard toilet blocks with air conditioning (renovated in 2015).

STE MARIE DE RE

COUARDE SUR MER, LA 7A1 (1km W Urban/Coastal) 46.19348, -1.43427 **Camp Municipal Le Remondeau, 12 Route Petite Noue, 17670 La Couarde-sur-Mer [05 46 29 84 27; fax 05 46 29 67 35; campingleremondeau@wanadoo.fr; www.leremondeau.fr]** Fr toll bdge foll D735 to rndabt on W side of La Couarde-sur-Mer & take D201. Foll sp to site. Lge, pt shd, pt sl, wc (htd); chem disp; mv service pnt; fam bthrm; shwrs inc; EHU (10A) €4.70; lndry; bbq; playgrnd; beach sand adj; red long stay; wifi; 10% statics; dogs €3; Eng spkn; quiet; CKE/CCI. "Vg site; great cycling base." ♦ 15 Mar-7 Nov. € 25.00 2018*

> **"Satellite navigation makes touring much easier"**
>
> Remember most sat navs don't know if you're towing or in a larger vehicle – always use yours alongside maps and site directions.

COUARDE SUR MER, LA 7A1 (2km NW Coastal) 46.20473, -1.44470 **Camping La Tour des Prises, Route d'Ars D735, 17670 La Couarde-sur-Mer [05 46 29 84 82; fax 05 46 29 88 99; camping@lesprises.com; www.lesprises.com]** Fr toll bdge foll D735 or D201 to La Couarde, then Rte d'Ars for 1.8km to R turn; site sp & 200m on R. Med, hdg, mkd, pt shd, wc (htd); chem disp; mv service pnt; fam bthrm; shwrs inc; EHU (16A) €5.50; lndry; shop; snacks; playgrnd; pool (covrd, htd); beach 600m; wifi; 30% statics; dogs €4; Eng spkn; adv bkg acc; quiet; ccard acc; bike hire; sailing school; games rm; CKE/CCI. "Excel, well-managed, clean site; lge individual pitches, mixed sizes; helpful owner & staff; excel pool; many cycle/walking tracks; beach 10 mins walk; ideal for families; lge o'fits drive cautiously, no one way; v busy; v friendly staff; cent located on Isle de Re; acc to cycle paths fr site gate." ♦ 5 Apr-28 Sep. € 47.00 2014*

COUARDE SUR MER, LA 7A1 (4km NW Coastal) 46.20408, -1.46740 **Camping de l'Océan, 50 Route d'Ars, 17670 La Couarde-sur-Mer [05 46 29 87 70; fax 05 46 29 92 13; info@campingocean.com; www.campingocean.com]** Fr La Rochelle take D735 over bdge to Ile de Ré. Past St Martin-de-Re & La Couarde twd Ars-en-Ré. Site on R, 2.5km after La Couarde. Lge, mkd, hdg, shd, wc (htd); chem disp; mv service pnt; fam bthrm; shwrs inc; EHU (10A) €5.50; lndry; shop; rest; snacks; bar; playgrnd; pool (htd); paddling pool; beach sand adj; entmnt; wifi; 40% statics; dogs €5; phone; Eng spkn; adv bkg acc; ccard acc; bike hire; games area; golf 6km; tennis; watersports; horseriding 1.5km; CKE/CCI. "Popular site in superb location; some sm pitches with diff access; site rds & ent to pitches narr; rd noisy; gd, clean san facs; friendly staff; twin axles not rec; recep clsd 1230-1400, if clsd, park in yard facing recep; gd walking & cycling; excel; toll fee to island €16." ♦ 16 Apr-18 Sep. € 39.00 2015*

ST CLEMENT DES BALEINES 7A1 (1km E Rural/Coastal) 46.24041, -1.56070 **Camping Les Baleines, Chemin Devaude, 17590 St. Clement-des-Baleines [05 46 29 40 76; fax 05 46 29 67 12; camping.lesbaleines@wanadoo.fr; www.camping-lesbaleines.com]** Fr bdge foll sp for Phare De Baleines. Sp 500m bef lighthouse. Do not foll sat nav. Narr vill rds. Lge, mkd, hdg, pt shd, wc; chem disp; mv service pnt; fam bthrm; shwrs; EHU (10A) €5-6; lndry; shop nr; rest nr; bar nr; bbq; playgrnd; beach sand adj; twin axles; wifi; 10% statics; dogs €2.10-3.10; phone; bus 200m; Eng spkn; ccard acc; games area; games rm; CKE/CCI. "Vg, quiet site in natural surroundings; helpful staff; clean modern shwrs; direct access to beach; bar 500m; 5mins walk to lighthouse." ♦ 22 Apr-20 Sep. € 48.00 2014*

ST CLEMENT DES BALEINES 7A1 (1km S Coastal) 46.22567, -1.54424 **FFCC Camping La Côte Sauvage, 336 Rue de la Forêt, 17590 St Clément-Des-Baleines [05 46 29 46 63; fax 04 73 77 05 06; contact@lesbalconsverts.com; www.lesbalconsverts.com]** Fr cent of vill, foll sp to site at edge of forest. Lge, mkd, pt shd, pt sl, wc; chem disp; mv service pnt; fam bthrm; shwrs inc; EHU (10A) €4 (poss long lead req); shop nr; snacks; beach shgl adj; swr; wifi; dogs €3; phone; Eng spkn; quiet; CKE/CCI. "Gd location; some pitches uneven; gd modern san facs; poss unrel opening dates; cycle rtes adj; gd." ♦ 6 Apr-29 Sep. € 29.00 2013*

STE MARIE DE RE 7A1 (1km S Coastal) 46.14504, -1.31509 **Camp Municipal La Côte Sauvage, La Basse Benée 17740 Ste Marie-de-Ré [05 46 30 21 74 or 05 46 30 21 24 (LS); fax 05 46 30 15 64; camping.stemarie@orange.fr; www.mairie-sainte-marie-de-re.fr]** Site sp fr main rd. V narr rds thro town. Med, mkd, pt shd, wc; chem disp; mv service pnt; shwrs inc; EHU (16A) €3.50; shop; snacks; bar; playgrnd; beach sand adj; quiet; ccard acc; fishing; CKE/CCI. "Excel location but poss windy; helpful owners; gd value snack bar; free parking for m'vans adj; highly rec." 1 Apr-19 Oct. € 15.00 2013*

⊞ **STE MARIE DE RE** 7A1 (4km NW Coastal) 46.16112, -1.35428 **Camping Les Grenettes, Route De L'Ermitage, 17740 Ste Marie De Re [05 46 30 22 47; fax 05 46 30 24 64; contact@hotel-les-grenettes.com; www.campinglesgrenettes.com]** Foll sp for D201 'Itinéraire Sud' after toll bdge in the dir of Le Bois-de-Plage; after approx 2km turn L. Med, mkd, pt shd, wc; chem disp; mv service pnt; fam bthrm; shwrs inc; EHU (6A) €4.50; gas; shop; rest; bbq; playgrnd; pool; paddling pool; beach 200m; entmnt; wifi; TV; dogs €4; Eng spkn; adv bkg acc; ccard acc; tennis; fishing; waterslide; bike hire. "Nice site close to sea; vg rest; many facs, but stretched in high ssn." € 44.00 2016*

ST MARTIN DE RE

ST MARTIN DE RE *7A1* (4km E Urban/Coastal) *46.18194, -1.33110* **Flower Camping de Bel Air,** Route de la Noué, 17630 La Flotte-en-Ré [05 46 09 63 10; camping.bel-air@flowercampings.com; www.bel-air-camping.com] Fr toll bdge take D735 to La Flotte. Turn R at rndabt to town into Route de la Noué, site sp. Lge, hdg, mkd, pt shd, wc; chem disp; mv service pnt; shwrs inc; EHU (6A) €3.84; lndry; rest; snacks; bar; playgrnd; beach 800m; entmnt; wifi; phone; adv bkg acc; quiet; games rm; tennis. "Walk to shops, harbour, beach etc; gd; friendly staff; toll bdge €8 winter ssn, €16 summer ssn." ♦ 30 Mar-3 Nov. € 29.00 2015*

ST MARTIN DE RE *7A1* (5km SE Rural) *46.18740, -1.34390* **Camping La Grainetière,** Route St Martin, 17630 La Flotte-en-Ré [05 46 09 68 86; fax 05 46 09 53 13; la-grainetiere@orange.fr; www.la-grainetiere.com] 10km W fr toll bdge, site sp on La Flotte ring rd. Med, pt shd, wc; chem disp; mv service pnt; fam bthrm; shwrs inc; EHU (10A) €4.50; gas; lndry; shop; playgrnd; pool (htd); beach sand 3km; wifi; TV; 70% statics; dogs €4.50; Eng spkn; adv bkg acc; bike hire; CKE/CCI. "Beautiful, clean, wooded site; haphazard pitching; helpful owners; gd san facs; gd pool; daily mkt; vg." ♦ 2 Apr-30 Sep. € 23.00 2013*

ST MARTIN DE RE *7A1* (1km S Urban) *46.19913, -1.36682* **Camp Municipal Les Remparts,** Rue Les Remparts, 17410 St Martin-de-Ré [05 46 09 21 96; fax 05 46 09 94 18; camping.stmartindere@wanadoo.fr; www.saint-martin-de-re.fr] Foll D735 fr toll bdge to St Martin; sp in town fr both ends. Med, mkd, hdg, pt shd, pt sl, wc; chem disp; mv service pnt; shwrs inc; EHU (10A) €3.70; lndry; shop; snacks; bbq; playgrnd; beach sand 1.3km; dogs €2; Eng spkn; adv bkg acc; ccard acc; CKE/CCI. "Busy site in brilliant location; san facs dated but clean; gd basic rest; poss children's groups mid-ssn; some pitches boggy when wet; gd cycling; site poss unkempt end ssn; vg mkt; beautiful situation on o'skirts of a lovely town, gd size pitches; pool 3km; superb position." ♦ 12 Mar-18 Nov. € 25.00 2017*

ILE D'OLERON

BREE LES BAINS, LA *7A1* (1km NW Coastal) *46.01861, -1.35446* **Camp Municipal Le Planginot,** Allée du Gai Séjour, 17840 La Brée-les-Bains [05 46 47 82 18; fax 05 46 75 90 74; camping.planginot@orange.fr; www.labreelesbains.com] N fr St Pierre d'Oléron on D734, turn R for La Brée on D273, site sp (if sp diff to see - foll 'plage' sp). Lge, mkd, pt shd, wc (htd); chem disp; mv service pnt; shwrs inc; EHU (10A) €3.60; lndry; rest; snacks; playgrnd; beach adj; 15% statics; dogs €2; Eng spkn; adv bkg acc; quiet. "Well-kept site in quiet location; friendly, helpful staff; gd cycling; daily mkt nrby; gd." ♦ 15 Mar-15 Oct. € 15.00 2015*

> "There aren't many sites open at this time of year"
>
> If you're travelling outside peak season remember to call ahead to check site opening dates – even if the entry says 'open all year'.

CHATEAU D'OLERON, LE *7B1* (3km NW Coastal) *45.90415, -1.21525* **Camping La Brande,** Route des Huîtres, 17480 Le Château-d'Oléron [05 46 47 62 37; fax 05 46 47 71 70; info@camping-labrande.com; www.camping-labrande.com or www.campings-oleron.com] Cross bdge on D26, turn R & go thro Le Château-d'Oléron. Foll Rte des Huîtres to La Gaconnière to site. Lge, shd, wc; mv service pnt; fam bthrm; shwrs inc; EHU (6-10A) €4-6; gas; lndry; shop; rest; snacks; bar; bbq; playgrnd; pool (covrd, htd); beach sand 300m; entmnt; wifi; TV; 60% statics; dogs €3; Eng spkn; adv bkg acc; ccard acc; tennis; golf 6km; games area; sep car park; bike hire; waterslide; CKE/CCI. "Pleasant owners; pitches at far end adj oyster farm - some noise fr pumps & poss mosquitoes; sauna; steam rm; 10 min cycle ride into town; vg." ♦ 1 Apr-5 Nov. € 44.00 2017*

See advertisement

Route des Huîtres
17480 Le Château d'Oléron
Tel. : +33 (0)5 46 47 62 37
www.camping-labrande.com

ST TROJAN LES BAINS

ST GEORGES D'OLERON *7A1 (7km E Coastal)*
45.96820, -1.24183 **Camp Atlantique Signol, Ave des Albatros, Boyardville, 17190 St Georges-d'Oléron [02 51 20 41 94; contact@signol.com; signol.camp-atlantique.co.uk/en]** Cross bdge onto Ile d'Oléron & cont on main rd twd St Pierre-d'Oléron. Turn R at Dolus-d'Oléron for Boyardville & foll sp in vill. Lge, mkd, hdg, pt shd, pt sl, wc; chem disp; mv service pnt; fam bthrm; shwrs inc; EHU (6A); gas; lndry; shop; rest; snacks; bar; playgrnd; pool (htd, indoor); paddling pool; beach sand 800m; entmnt; 70% statics; dogs (1 dog per pitch €4); Eng spkn; adv bkg acc. "Size of pitches variable; san facs stretched in high ssn; impressive pool complex; narr site rds; gd site & facs; vg activities for kids; low overhanging branches." ♦ 3 Apr-20 Sep. € 22.00   2017*

ST GEORGES D'OLERON *7A1 (2km SE Rural)*
45.96796, -1.31874 **Camping Le Domaine d'Oléron, La Jousselinière, 17190 St Georges-d'Oléron [05 46 76 54 97 or 02 51 33 05 05 (LS); fax 02 51 33 94 04; info@chadotel.com; www.chadotel.com]** After x-ing Viaduct (bdge) onto island foll sp dir St Pierre d'Oléron & St Georges-d'Oléron on D734; turn R on rndabt immed see Leclerc supmkt on R; at next rndabt turn L sp 'Le Bois Fleury'; pass airfield 'Bois 'Fleury' on R; take next R & then immed L. Site on L in 500m. Lge, hdg, mkd, pt shd, terr, wc; chem disp; mv service pnt; fam bthrm; shwrs inc; EHU (6A) inc; gas; lndry; shop; snacks; bar; bbq (gas, sep area); playgrnd; pool; paddling pool; beach sand 3km; red long stay; entmnt; wifi; TV; 40% statics; dogs €3.20; Eng spkn; adv bkg rec; quiet; ccard acc; bike hire; games area; games rm; waterslide; CKE/CCI. "Popular, well-organised, clean site; friendly, helpful staff; lovely pool; no o'fits over 8m high ssn; cycle paths; fair." ♦ 1 Apr-30 Sep. € 35.00   2017*

⊞ **ST GEORGES D'OLERON** *7A1 (6km SW Coastal)*
45.95386, -1.37932 **Camping Les Gros Joncs, Les Sables Vigniers, 17190 St Georges-d'Oléron [05 46 76 52 29; fax 05 46 76 67 74; info@camping-les-gros-joncs.com; www.camping-les-gros-joncs.com]** Fr bdge foll D734 to St Pierre, at 2nd traff lts (police stn) turn L to La Cotinière 4km, at x-rds turn R dir Domino (Ave De Pins) for 5km. Site on L past Le Suroit. V lge, pt shd, wc; shwrs; EHU (10A) €3; lndry; shop; rest; snacks; bar; playgrnd; pool (htd); paddling pool; beach shgl 200m; TV; 10% statics; dogs €3; adv bkg acc; quiet; games area; jacuzzi. "Excel pool; beach sand 1km; hydrotherapy sprays; great location; clean facs; rec." ♦ € 50.00   2016*

ST GEORGES D'OLERON *7A1 (7km SW Coastal)*
45.94756, -1.37386 **Camping Le Suroit, L'Ileau de la Grande Côte, 17190 St Georges-d'Oléron [05 46 47 07 25 or 06 80 10 93 18 (mob); fax 05 46 75 04 24; camping@lesuroit.fr; www.camping-lesuroit.com]** Fr Domino cent foll sp for beach, turn L for L'Ileau. Strt at x-rds. Fork L for La Cotinière, site on R in 150m. Lge, mkd, shd, wc (htd); fam bthrm; shwrs inc; EHU (10A) €4.50; gas; lndry; shop; rest; snacks; bar; bbq; playgrnd; pool (covrd, htd); beach sand adj; entmnt; TV; 10% statics; dogs €5; adv bkg acc; quiet; ccard acc; bike hire; games area; tennis; CKE/CCI. "Excel, well-organised site." ♦ 1 Apr-33 Sep. € 35.00   2015*

ST PIERRE D'OLERON *7B1 (4km SW Coastal)*
45.92315, -1.34130 **Camping Le Sous Bois, avenue des Pins, 17310 Saint Pierre d'Oleron [05 46 47 22 46; resa.lesousbois@orange.fr; www.camping-lesousbois-oleron.com]** Fr St Pierre take D274 to La Cotiniere. In La Cotiniere foll dir L'Ileau, turn R onto Ave des Pins. Campsite 500m out of town on R. Med, mkd, hdg, pt shd, wc; chem disp; fam bthrm; shwrs; EHU (3A, 6A-10A) €5-7; lndry; shop nr; bar nr; entmnt; wifi; dogs €4; Eng spkn; adv bkg acc; sauna; games area; beac 200m. "Gd cycle tracks; sailing school; jet ski; equestrian ctr in Cotiniere; conv location; bar 20m; vg." ♦ 1 Apr-31 Oct. € 33.50   2016*

ST PIERRE D'OLERON *7B1 (4km W Coastal)*
45.92394, -1.34273 **FFCC Camp Municipal La Fauche Prère, Ave des Pins, La Cotinière, 17310 St Pierre d'Oléron [05 46 47 10 53; fax 05 46 75 23 44; camping@saintpierreoleron.com; www.saintpierreoleron.com]** Fr bdge foll D734 N to St Pierre-d'Oléron. Turn L onto D274 for La Cotinière, site bef vill on L, sp. Med, mkd, shd, pt sl, wc; chem disp; mv service pnt; fam bthrm; shwrs; EHU (12A) €4.10; lndry; shop; playgrnd; beach sand adj; dogs €2; CKE/CCI. "Direct access to beach; most pitches sandy; gd; lovely site amongst pine trees; new san facs (2017); quiet." 1 Apr-30 Sep. € 22.00   2017*

ST TROJAN LES BAINS *7B1 (2km SW Rural)*
45.82947, -1.21632 **Flower Camping St-Tro'Park (formerly Camping La Combinette), 36 Ave des Bris, 17370 St Trojan-les-Bains [05 46 76 00 47; info@st-tro-park.com; www.st-tro-park.com]** Fr toll bdge stay on D26 for 1km, L onto D275 & L onto D126 to St Trojan-les-Bains. Strt ahead at rndabt with figure sculpture, then R at next rndabt sp Campings. In 1km turn L at rd fork, site on R in 1km. Lge, shd, wc; fam bthrm; shwrs inc; EHU (5-10A) (poss rev pol); gas; lndry; shop; rest; snacks; playgrnd; pool; beach 2km; entmnt; wifi; dogs; quiet; games area; bike hire. "Gd touring base; some super pitches; poss flooding in heavy rain; lovely site amongst pine trees; sauna; spa; gym; new san facs (2017); vg." ♦ 15 Apr-15 Oct. € 35.00   2017*

France

Sites in Andorra

⊞ **ANDORRA LA VELLA (ANDORRA)** *8G3* (1km S Urban) *42.50166, 1.51527* **Camping Valira, Ave de Salou, AD500 Andorra-la-Vella [722 384; campvalira@andorra.ad; www.campvalira.com]** Site on E site of main rd S fr Andorra-la-Vella; behind sports stadium; clearly sp. Lge, mkd, hdstg, pt shd, terr, wc (htd); chem disp; mv service pnt; shwrs inc; EHU (3-10A) €3.50-6 (no earth); gas; lndry; shop; rest; snacks; bar; playgrnd; pool (covrd, htd); paddling pool; wifi; dogs €2.10; Eng spkn; adv bkg acc; quiet; CKE/CCI. "Conv NH for shopping; 25mins walk to main shops; excel immac facs; vg rest; beware of sudden storms blowing up." ♦ € 25.00   2012*

⊞ **CANILLO (ANDORRA)** *8G3* (0km ENE Urban) *42.56740, 1.60235* **Camping Pla, Ctra General s/n, AD100 Canillo [601 283; fax 851 280; www.facebook.com/paco.cristina]** App Canillo fr S, pass Tarrado petrol stn on R; take 1st exit at 1st rndabt opp lge hotel, over bdge & turn L to site. Med, mkd, pt shd, wc (htd); chem disp; fam bthrm; shwrs inc; EHU (5-10A) €3; gas; lndry; rest nr; bar; playgrnd; 75% statics; dogs; bus adj; Eng spkn; adv bkg acc. "Excel location for skiing but poss unkempt/untidy LS; htd covrd pool in town; sports facs in town; ski lift 100m." € 14.00   2016*

MASSANA, LA (ANDORRA) *8G3* (2km N Rural) *42.56601, 1.52448* **Camping Borda d'Ansalonga, Ctra General del Serrat, AD300 Ordino [850 374; fax 735 400; www.campingbordaansalonga.com]** Fr Andorra-la-Vella foll sp La Massana & Ordino. Turn L twd El Serrat, site on R, well sp. Lge, pt shd, wc (htd); chem disp; fam bthrm; shwrs inc; EHU (10A) €5.60; gas; lndry; shop; rest; bar; bbq; playgrnd; pool; dogs; phone; Eng spkn; quiet; games rm; CKE/CCI. "Statics moved to storage area in summer; winter statics for skiers; quieter than sites on main thro rte." 17 Oct-25 Apr & 15 Jun-15 Sep. € 24.00   2016*

> **"That's changed – Should I let the Club know?"**
>
> If you find something on site that's different from the site entry, fill in a report and let us know. See camc.com/europereport.

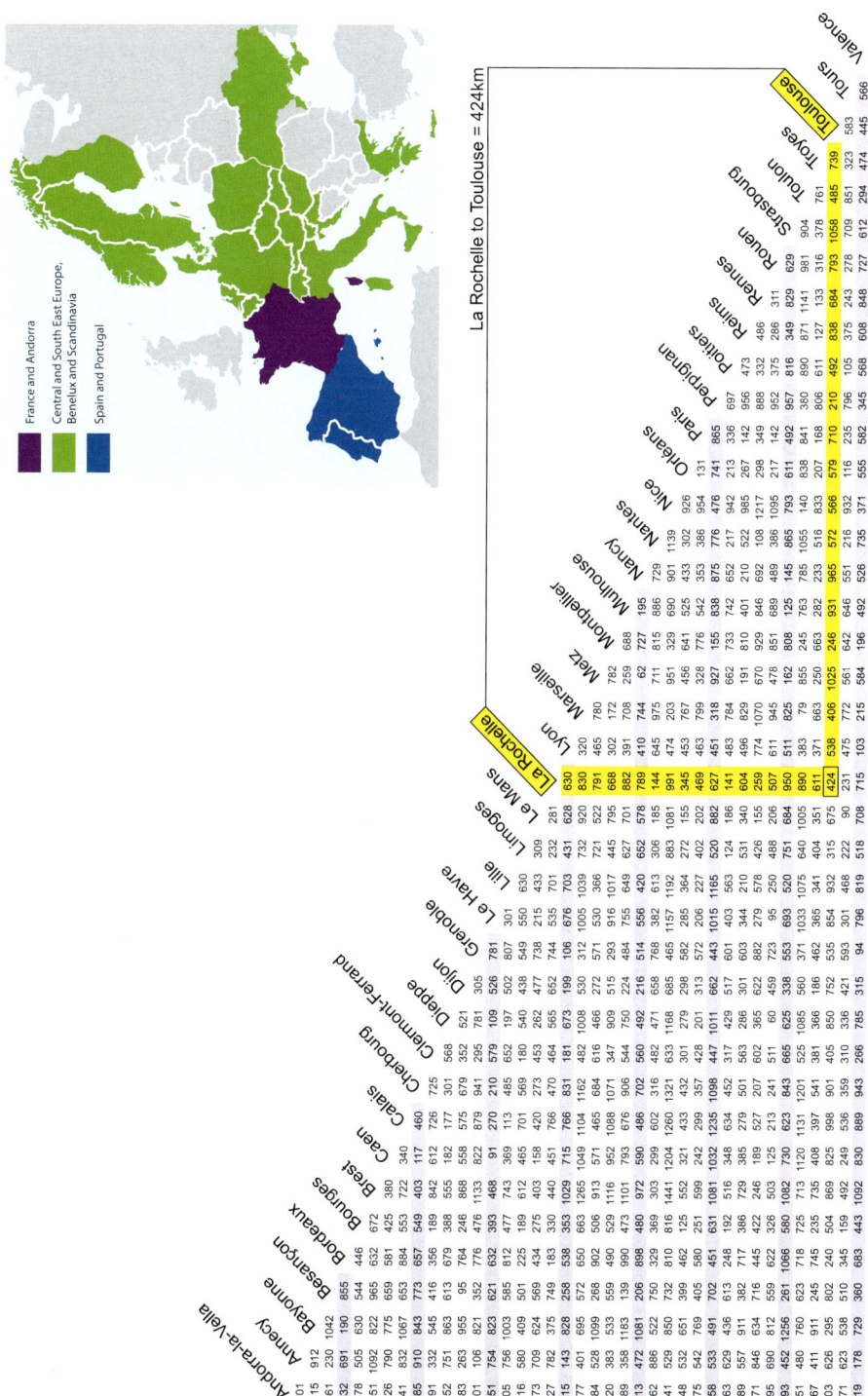

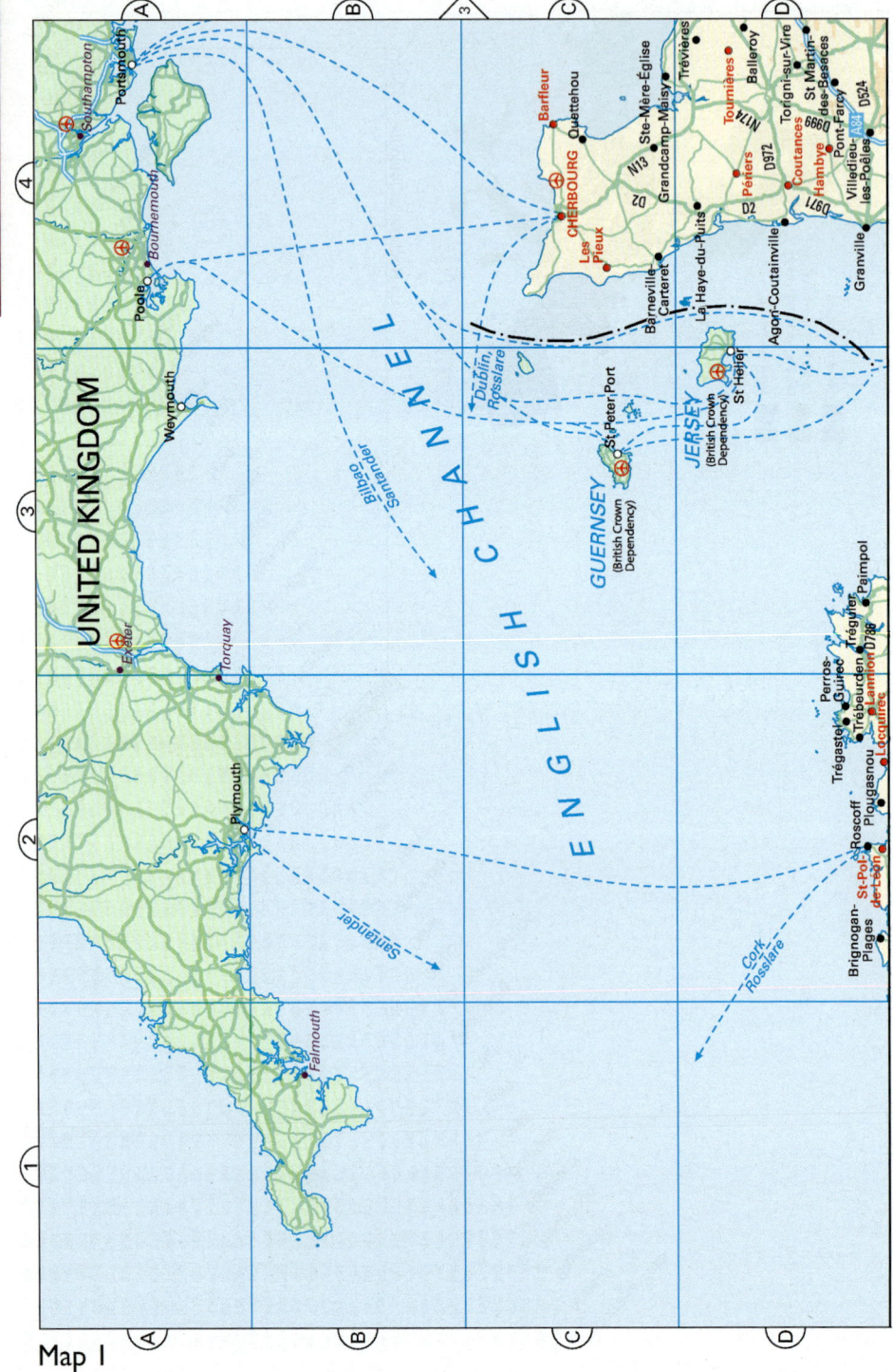

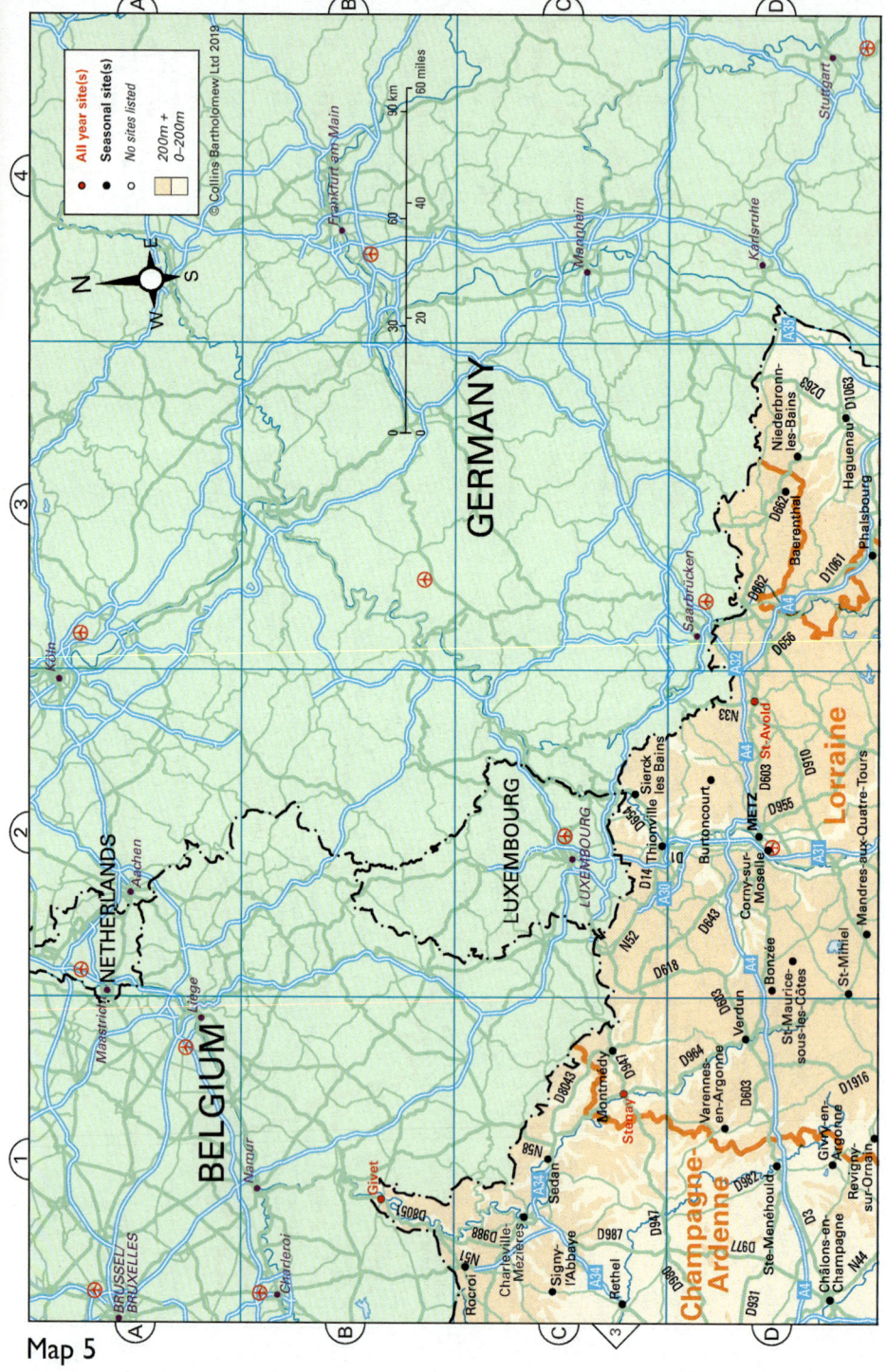

Map 5

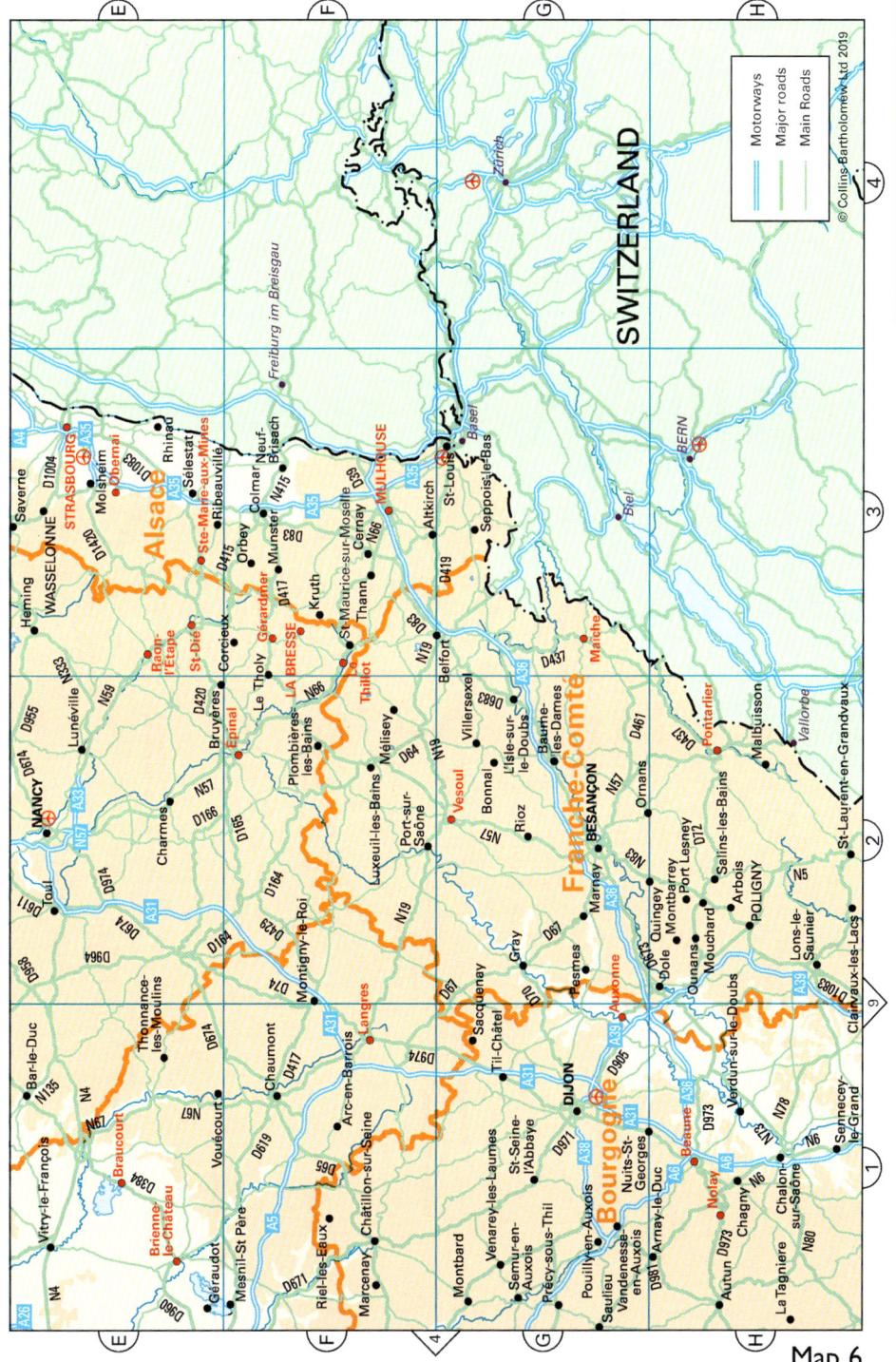

Map 7

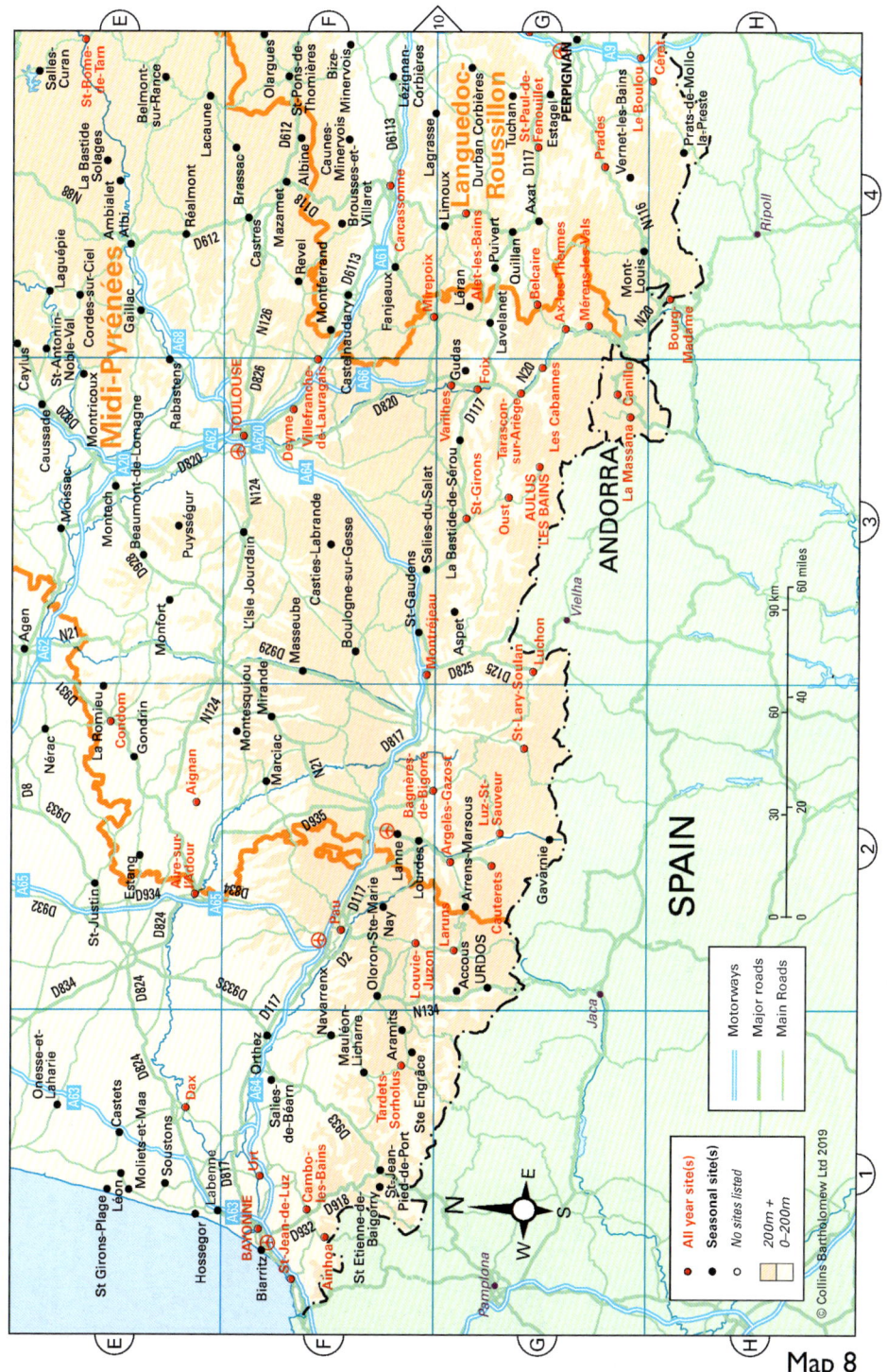

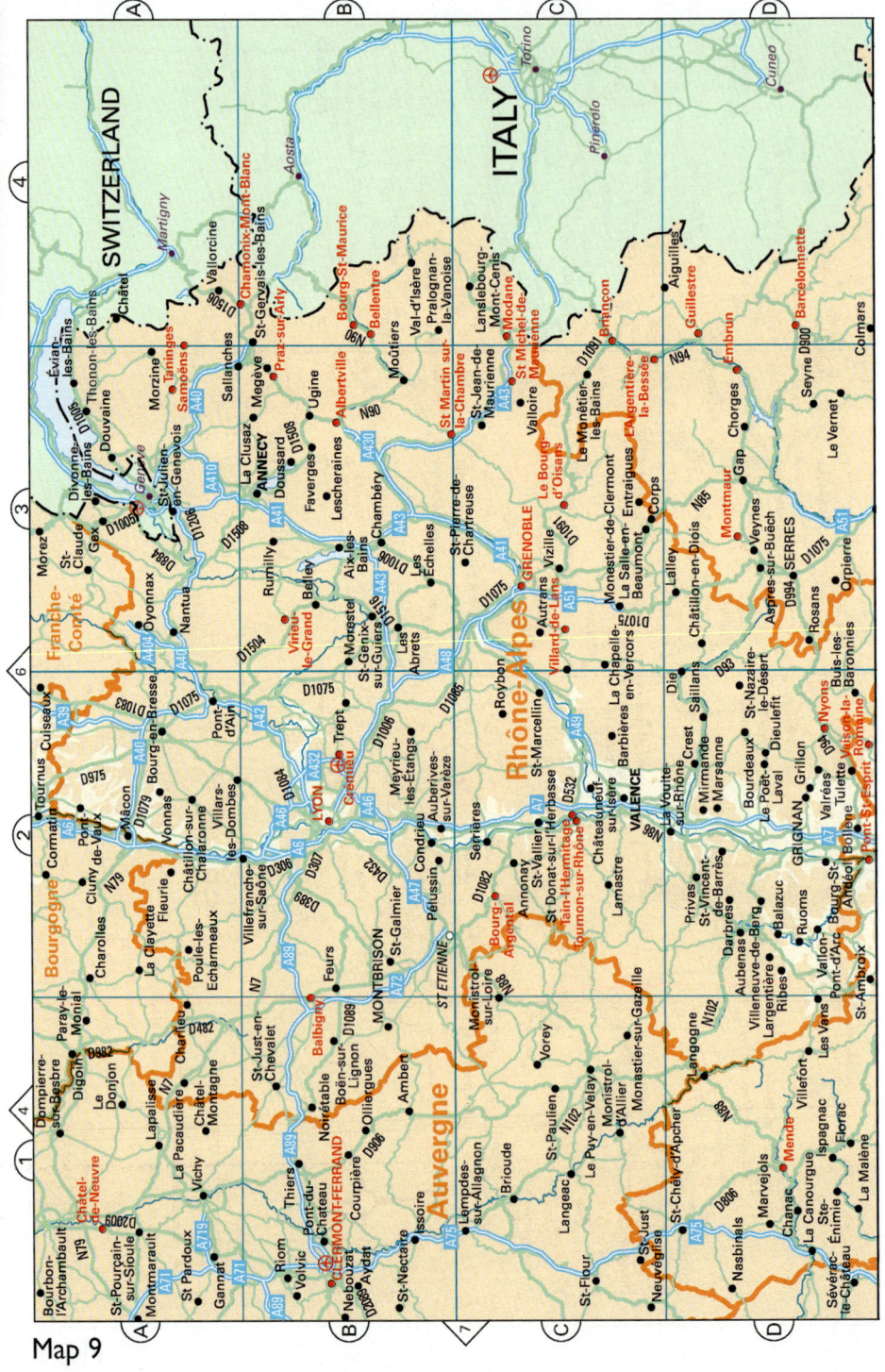

Map 9

France
Regions and Departments

Please note the first two digits of a French postal code refer to the department in which it is located.

Departmental numbers are listed below.

Alsace
67 Bas-Rhin
68 Haut-Rhin
Aquitaine
24 Dordogne
33 Gironde
40 Landes
47 Lot-et-Garonne
64 Pyrénées-Atlantiques
Auvergne
03 Allier
15 Cantal
43 Haute-Loire
63 Puy-de-Dôme
Burgundy
21 Côte-d'Or
58 Nièvre
71 Saône-et-Loire
89 Yonne
Brittany
22 Côtes-d'Armor
29 Finistère
35 Ille-et-Vilaine
56 Morbihan
Centre
18 Cher
28 Eure-et-Loir
36 Indre
37 Indre-et-Loire
41 Loir-et-Cher
45 Loiret
Champagne-Ardenne
08 Ardennes
10 Aube
51 Marne
52 Haute-Marne
Corsica
02A Corse-du-Sud
02B Haute-Corse
Cote d'Azur
06 Alpes-Maritimes
Franche-Comté
25 Doubs
39 Jura
70 Haute-Saône
90 Territoire-de-Belfort

Languedoc-Roussillon
11 Aude
30 Gard
34 Hérault
48 Lozère
66 Pyrénées-Orientales
Limousin
19 Corréze
23 Creuse
87 Haute-Vienne
Lorraine
54 Meurthe-et-Moselle
55 Meuse
57 Moselle
88 Vosges
Midi-Pyrénées
09 Ariège
12 Aveyron
31 Haute-Garonne
32 Gers
46 Lot
65 Hautes-Pyrénées
81 Tarn
82 Tarn-et-Garonne

Nord Pas-De-Calais
59 Nord
62 Pas-de-Calais
Normandy
14 Calvados
27 Eure
50 Manche
61 Orne
76 Seine-Maritime
Paris-Île-de-France
75 Paris
77 Seine-et-Marne
78 Yvelines
91 Essonne
92 Haut-de-Seine
93 Seine-St-Denis
94 Val-de-Marne
95 Val-d'Oise
Pays de la Loire
44 Loire-Atlantique
49 Maine-et-Loire
53 Mayenne
72 Sarthe
85 Vendée

Picardy
02 Aisne
60 Oise
80 Somme
Poitou-Charentes
16 Charente
17 Charente-Maritime
79 Deux-Sèvres
86 Vienne
Provence
04 Alpes-de-Haute-Provence
05 Hautes-Alpes
13 Bouches-du-Rhône
83 Var
84 Vaucluse
Rhône-Alps
01 Ain
07 Ardèche
26 Drôme
38 Isère
42 Loire
69 Rhône
73 Savoie
74 Haute-Savoie

Site Report Form

If campsite is already listed, complete only those sections of the form where changes apply or alternatively use the Abbreviated Site Report form on the following pages.

Sites not reported on for 5 years may be deleted from the guide

Year of guide used	20..........	Is site listed?	Listed on page no............	Unlisted	Date of visit	......../........../........

A – CAMPSITE NAME AND LOCATION

Country		Name of town/village site listed under *(see Sites Location Maps)*				
Distance & direction from centre of town site is listed under *(in a straight line)*	....................km	eg N, NE, S, SW		Urban	Rural	Coastal
Site open all year?	Y / N	Period site is open *(if not all year)*	................/................	to	................/................	
Site name					Naturist site	Y / N
Site address						
Telephone				Fax		
E-mail				Website		

B – CAMPSITE CHARGES

Charge for outfit + 2 adults in local currency	PRICE		

C – DIRECTIONS

Brief, specific directions to site (in km) *To convert miles to kilometres multiply by 8 and divide by 5 or use Conversion Table in guide*	
GPS	Latitude..(eg 12.34567) Longitude..(eg 1.23456 or -1.23456)

D – SITE INFORMATION

Dogs allowed	DOGS	Y / N	Price per night .... (if allowed)	
Facilities for disabled	♦			
Public Transport within 5km	BUS / TRAM / TRAIN	Adj		Nearby
Reduction long stay	RED LONG STAY	Credit Card accepted		CCARD ACC
Advance bookings accepted/recommended/required		ADV BKG ACC / REC / REQ		
Camping Key Europe or Camping Card International accepted in lieu of passport				CKE/CCI

E – SITE DESCRIPTION

SITE size ie number of pitches	Small Max 50	SM	Medium 51-150	MED	Large 151-500	LGE	Very large 500+	V LGE	Unchanged
Pitch features if **NOT** open-plan/grassy		HDG PITCH	Hedged	HDG PITCH	Marked or numbered	MKD PITCH	Hardstanding or gravel	HDSTG	Unchanged
If site is **NOT** level, is it		PT SL	Part sloping	PT SL	Sloping	SL	Terraced	TERR	Unchanged
Is site shaded?		SHD	Shaded	SHD	Part shaded	PT SHD	Unshaded	UNSHD	Unchanged
ELECTRIC HOOK UP *if not included in price above*		EL PNTS			Price..........................			Amps......................	
% Static caravans / mobile homes / chalets / cottages / fixed tents on site								............% STATICS	
Serviced Pitched			Y / N		Twin axles caravans allowed?			TWIN AXLES Y / N	

You can also complete forms online: camc.com/europereport

E – SITE DESCRIPTION CONTINUED...

Phone on site	PHONE			Wifi Internet		WIFI	
Television	TV RM		TV CAB / SAT	Playground		PLAYGRND	
Entertainment in high season	ENTMNT			English spoken		ENG SPKN	
Motorhome Service Point	Y / N						

F – CATERING

Bar	BAR	On site	or	Within 2km		
Restaurant	REST	On site	or	Within 2km		
Shop(s)	SHOP(S)	On site	or	Within 2km		
Snack bar / take-away	SNACKS	On site	Y / N			
Cooking facilities	COOKING FACS	On site	Y / N			
Supplies of bottled gas on site	GAS	Y / N				
Barbecue allowed	BBQ	Charcoal	Gas	Elec	Sep area	

G – SANITARY FACILITIES

WC		Heated	HTD WC	Continental	CONT	Own San recommended	OWN SAN REC
Chemical disposal point			CHEM DISP				
Hot shower(s)		SHWR(S)	Inc in site fee?		Y / N		
Child / baby facilities *(bathroom)*			FAM BTHRM			Launderette / Washing Machine	LNDRY

H – OTHER INFORMATION

Swimming pool	POOL	HEATED	COVERED	INDOOR	PADDLING POOL	
Beach	BEACH	Adj	or ....km	Sand	Shingle	
Alternative swimming *(lake)*	SW	Adj	or ....km	Sand	Shingle	
Games /sports area / Games room	GAMES AREA		GAMES ROOM			

I – ADDITIONAL REMARKS AND/OR ITEMS OF INTEREST

Tourist attractions, unusual features or other facilities, eg waterslide, tennis, cycle hire, watersports, horseriding, separate car park, walking distance to shops etc	YOUR OPINION OF THE SITE:	
	EXCEL	
	VERY GOOD	
	GOOD	
	FAIR	POOR
	NIGHT HALT ONLY	
Your comments & opinions may be used in future editions of the guide, if you do not wish them to be used please tick		

J – MEMBER DETAILS

ARE YOU A:	Caravanner		Motorhomer		Trailer-tenter?	
NAME:			MEMBERSHIP NO:			
			POST CODE:			
DO YOU NEED MORE BLANK SITE REPORT FORMS?		YES			NO	

Please use a separate form for each campsite and do not send receipts. Owing to the large number of site reports received, it is not possible to enter into correspondence. Please return completed form to:

**The Editor, Overseas Touring Guides, East Grinstead House
East Grinstead, West Sussex RH19 1UA**

Please note that due to changes in the rules regarding freepost we are no longer able to provide a freepost address for the return of Site Report Forms. You can still supply your site reports free online by visiting camc.com/europereport. We apologise for any inconvenience this may cause.

Site Report Form

If campsite is already listed, complete only those sections of the form where changes apply or alternatively use the Abbreviated Site Report form on the following pages.

Sites not reported on for 5 years may be deleted from the guide

Year of guide used	20..........	Is site listed?	Listed on page no............	Unlisted	Date of visit	........./........./.........

A – CAMPSITE NAME AND LOCATION

Country		Name of town/village site listed under *(see Sites Location Maps)*				
Distance & direction from centre of town site is listed under *(in a straight line)*		....................km	eg N, NE, S, SW	Urban	Rural	Coastal
Site open all year?	Y / N	Period site is open *(if not all year)*	................../.................. to ..../..................			
Site name					Naturist site	Y / N
Site address						
Telephone				Fax		
E-mail				Website		

B – CAMPSITE CHARGES

Charge for outfit + 2 adults in local currency	PRICE		

C – DIRECTIONS

Brief, specific directions to site (in km) *To convert miles to kilometres multiply by 8 and divide by 5 or use Conversion Table in guide*	
GPS	Latitude...(eg 12.34567) Longitude...(eg 1.23456 or -1.23456)

D – SITE INFORMATION

Dogs allowed	DOGS	Y / N	Price per night .... (if allowed)	
Facilities for disabled	♦			
Public Transport within 5km	BUS / TRAM / TRAIN	Adj		Nearby
Reduction long stay	RED LONG STAY	Credit Card accepted		CCARD ACC
Advance bookings accepted/recommended/required		ADV BKG ACC / REC / REQ		
Camping Key Europe or Camping Card International accepted in lieu of passport				CKE/CCI

E – SITE DESCRIPTION

SITE size ie number of pitches	Small Max 50	SM	Medium 51-150	MED	Large 151-500	LGE	Very large 500+	V LGE	Unchanged
Pitch features if **NOT** open-plan/grassy		HDG PITCH	Hedged	HDG PITCH	Marked or numbered	MKD PITCH	Hardstanding or gravel	HDSTG	Unchanged
If site is **NOT** level, is it		PT SL	Part sloping	PT SL	Sloping	SL	Terraced	TERR	Unchanged
Is site shaded?		SHD	Shaded	SHD	Part shaded	PT SHD	Unshaded	UNSHD	Unchanged
ELECTRIC HOOK UP *if not included in price above*		EL PNTS			Price..			Amps........................	
% Static caravans / mobile homes / chalets / cottages / fixed tents on site								.................% STATICS	
Serviced Pitched			Y / N		Twin axles caravans allowed?			TWIN AXLES Y / N	

You can also complete forms online: camc.com/europereport

E – SITE DESCRIPTION CONTINUED...

Phone on site	PHONE		Wifi Internet	WIFI
Television	TV RM	TV CAB / SAT	Playground	PLAYGRND
Entertainment in high season	ENTMNT		English spoken	ENG SPKN
Motorhome Service Point	Y / N			

F – CATERING

Bar	BAR	On site		or		Within 2km	
Restaurant	REST	On site		or		Within 2km	
Shop(s)	SHOP(S)	On site		or		Within 2km	
Snack bar / take-away	SNACKS	On site		Y / N			
Cooking facilities	COOKING FACS	On site		Y / N			
Supplies of bottled gas on site	GAS	Y / N					
Barbecue allowed	BBQ	Charcoal		Gas		Elec	Sep area

G – SANITARY FACILITIES

WC		Heated	HTD WC	Continental	CONT	Own San recommended	OWN SAN REC
Chemical disposal point			CHEM DISP				
Hot shower(s)		SHWR(S)	Inc in site fee?	Y / N			
Child / baby facilities *(bathroom)*			FAM BTHRM		Launderette / Washing Machine		LNDRY

H – OTHER INFORMATION

Swimming pool	POOL	HEATED		COVERED	INDOOR		PADDLING POOL
Beach	BEACH	Adj		or ....km	Sand		Shingle
Alternative swimming *(lake)*	SW	Adj		or ....km	Sand		Shingle
Games /sports area / Games room	GAMES AREA			GAMES ROOM			

I – ADDITIONAL REMARKS AND/OR ITEMS OF INTEREST

Tourist attractions, unusual features or other facilities, eg waterslide, tennis, cycle hire, watersports, horseriding, separate car park, walking distance to shops etc	YOUR OPINION OF THE SITE:	
	EXCEL	
	VERY GOOD	
	GOOD	
	FAIR	POOR
	NIGHT HALT ONLY	
Your comments & opinions may be used in future editions of the guide, if you do not wish them to be used please tick		

J – MEMBER DETAILS

ARE YOU A:	Caravanner		Motorhomer		Trailer-tenter?	
NAME:			MEMBERSHIP NO:			
			POST CODE:			
DO YOU NEED MORE BLANK SITE REPORT FORMS?		YES			NO	

Please use a separate form for each campsite and do not send receipts. Owing to the large number of site reports received, it is not possible to enter into correspondence. Please return completed form to:

The Editor, Overseas Touring Guides, East Grinstead House
East Grinstead, West Sussex RH19 1UA

Please note that due to changes in the rules regarding freepost we are no longer able to provide a freepost address for the return of Site Report Forms. You can still supply your site reports free online by visiting camc.com/europereport. We apologise for any inconvenience this may cause.

Site Report Form

If campsite is already listed, complete only those sections of the form where changes apply
or alternatively use the Abbreviated Site Report form on the following pages.

Sites not reported on for 5 years may be deleted from the guide

Year of guide used	20..........	Is site listed?	Listed on page no............	Unlisted	Date of visit	........./........./.........

A – CAMPSITE NAME AND LOCATION

Country		Name of town/village site listed under (see Sites Location Maps)				
Distance & direction from centre of town site is listed under (in a straight line)		..................km	eg N, NE, S, SW	Urban	Rural	Coastal
Site open all year?	Y / N	Period site is open (if not all year)	................./................. to ..../.................			
Site name					Naturist site	Y / N
Site address						
Telephone			Fax			
E-mail			Website			

B – CAMPSITE CHARGES

Charge for outfit + 2 adults in local currency	PRICE	

C – DIRECTIONS

Brief, specific directions to site (in km) To convert miles to kilometres multiply by 8 and divide by 5 or use Conversion Table in guide	
GPS	Latitude..(eg 12.34567) Longitude...(eg 1.23456 or -1.23456)

D – SITE INFORMATION

Dogs allowed	DOGS	Y / N	Price per night .... (if allowed)	
Facilities for disabled	♦			
Public Transport within 5km	BUS / TRAM / TRAIN	Adj		Nearby
Reduction long stay	RED LONG STAY	Credit Card accepted		CCARD ACC
Advance bookings accepted/recommended/required		ADV BKG ACC / REC / REQ		
Camping Key Europe or Camping Card International accepted in lieu of passport				CKE/CCI

E – SITE DESCRIPTION

SITE size ie number of pitches	Small Max 50	SM	Medium 51-150	MED	Large 151-500	LGE	Very large 500+	V LGE	Unchanged
Pitch features if NOT open-plan/grassy		HDG PITCH	Hedged	HDG PITCH	Marked or numbered	MKD PITCH	Hardstanding or gravel	HDSTG	Unchanged
If site is NOT level, is it		PT SL	Part sloping	PT SL	Sloping	SL	Terraced	TERR	Unchanged
Is site shaded?		SHD	Shaded	SHD	Part shaded	PT SHD	Unshaded	UNSHD	Unchanged
ELECTRIC HOOK UP if not included in price above		EL PNTS			Price..			Amps........................	
% Static caravans / mobile homes / chalets / cottages / fixed tents on site								................% STATICS	
Serviced Pitched			Y / N		Twin axles caravans allowed?			TWIN AXLES	Y / N

You can also complete forms online: camc.com/europereport

E – SITE DESCRIPTION CONTINUED…

Phone on site	PHONE			Wifi Internet	WIFI
Television	TV RM		TV CAB / SAT	Playground	PLAYGRND
Entertainment in high season	ENTMNT			English spoken	ENG SPKN
Motorhome Service Point	Y / N				

F – CATERING

Bar	BAR	On site	or	Within 2km	
Restaurant	REST	On site	or	Within 2km	
Shop(s)	SHOP(S)	On site	or	Within 2km	
Snack bar / take-away	SNACKS	On site	Y / N		
Cooking facilities	COOKING FACS	On site	Y / N		
Supplies of bottled gas on site	GAS	Y / N			
Barbecue allowed	BBQ	Charcoal	Gas	Elec	Sep area

G – SANITARY FACILITIES

WC		Heated	HTD WC	Continental	CONT	Own San recommended	OWN SAN REC
Chemical disposal point			CHEM DISP				
Hot shower(s)		SHWR(S)	Inc in site fee?	Y / N			
Child / baby facilities *(bathroom)*			FAM BTHRM			Launderette / Washing Machine	LNDRY

H – OTHER INFORMATION

Swimming pool	POOL	HEATED	COVERED	INDOOR		PADDLING POOL	
Beach	BEACH	Adj	or ……….km		Sand	Shingle	
Alternative swimming *(lake)*	SW	Adj	or ……….km		Sand	Shingle	
Games /sports area / Games room	GAMES AREA		GAMES ROOM				

I – ADDITIONAL REMARKS AND/OR ITEMS OF INTEREST

Tourist attractions, unusual features or other facilities, eg waterslide, tennis, cycle hire, watersports, horseriding, separate car park, walking distance to shops etc	YOUR OPINION OF THE SITE:	
	EXCEL	
	VERY GOOD	
	GOOD	
	FAIR	POOR
	NIGHT HALT ONLY	
Your comments & opinions may be used in future editions of the guide, if you do not wish them to be used please tick ………		

J – MEMBER DETAILS

ARE YOU A:	Caravanner		Motorhomer		Trailer-tenter?	
NAME:			MEMBERSHIP NO:			
			POST CODE:			
DO YOU NEED MORE BLANK SITE REPORT FORMS?		YES			NO	

Please use a separate form for each campsite and do not send receipts. Owing to the large number of site reports received, it is not possible to enter into correspondence. Please return completed form to:
The Editor, Overseas Touring Guides, East Grinstead House
East Grinstead, West Sussex RH19 1UA

Please note that due to changes in the rules regarding freepost we are no longer able to provide a freepost address for the return of Site Report Forms. You can still supply your site reports free online by visiting camc.com/europereport. We apologise for any inconvenience this may cause.

Abbreviated Site Report Form

Use this abbreviated Site Report Form if you have visited a number of sites and there are no changes (or only small changes) to their entries in the guide. If reporting on a new site, or reporting several changes, please use the full version of the report form. **If advising prices,** these should be for an outfit, and 2 adults for one night's stay. **Please indicate high or low season prices and whether electricity is included.**

Remember, if you don't tell us about sites you have visited, they may eventually be deleted from the guide.

Year of guide used	20..........	Page No.	....	Name of town/village site listed under	
Site Name				Date of visit	......./......./.......
GPS	Latitude...(eg 12.34567) Longitude..(eg 1.23456 or -1.23456)				
Site is in: Andorra / Austria / Belgium / Croatia / Czech Republic / Denmark / Finland / France / Germany / Greece / Hungary / Italy / Luxembourg / Netherlands / Norway / Poland / Portugal / Slovakia / Slovenia / Spain / Sweden / Switzerland					
Comments:					
Charge for outfit + 2 adults in local currency	High Season	Low Season	Elec inc in price?	Y / N	..............amps
			Price of elec (if not inc)		..............amps

Year of guide used	20..........	Page No.	....	Name of town/village site listed under	
Site Name				Date of visit	......./......./.......
GPS	Latitude...(eg 12.34567) Longitude..(eg 1.23456 or -1.23456)				
Site is in: Andorra / Austria / Belgium / Croatia / Czech Republic / Denmark / Finland / France / Germany / Greece / Hungary / Italy / Luxembourg / Netherlands / Norway / Poland / Portugal / Slovakia / Slovenia / Spain / Sweden / Switzerland					
Comments:					
Charge for outfit + 2 adults in local currency	High Season	Low Season	Elec inc in price?	Y / N	..............amps
			Price of elec (if not inc)		..............amps

Year of guide used	20..........	Page No.	....	Name of town/village site listed under	
Site Name				Date of visit	......./......./.......
GPS	Latitude...(eg 12.34567) Longitude..(eg 1.23456 or -1.23456)				
Site is in: Andorra / Austria / Belgium / Croatia / Czech Republic / Denmark / Finland / France / Germany / Greece / Hungary / Italy / Luxembourg / Netherlands / Norway / Poland / Portugal / Slovakia / Slovenia / Spain / Sweden / Switzerland					
Comments:					
Charge for car, caravan & 2 adults in local currency	High Season	Low Season	Elec inc in price?	Y / N	..............amps
			Price of elec (if not inc)		..............amps

Please fill in your details and send to the address on the reverse of this form.
You can also complete forms online: camc.com/europereport

CUT ALONG DOTTED LINE

Abbreviated Site Report Form

Year of guide used	20..........	Page No.	....	Name of town/village site listed under			
Site Name					Date of visit	......./......./.......	
GPS	Latitude..(eg 12.34567) Longitude...(eg 1.23456 or -1.23456)						
Site is in: Andorra / Austria / Belgium / Croatia / Czech Republic / Denmark / Finland / France / Germany / Greece / Hungary / Italy / Luxembourg / Netherlands / Norway / Poland / Portugal / Slovakia / Slovenia / Spain / Sweden / Switzerland							
Comments:							
Charge for outfit + 2 adults in local currency		High Season	Low Season	Elec inc in price?	Y / N	..............amps	
				Price of elec (if not inc)		..............amps	

Year of guide used	20..........	Page No.	....	Name of town/village site listed under			
Site Name					Date of visit	......./......./.......	
GPS	Latitude..(eg 12.34567) Longitude...(eg 1.23456 or -1.23456)						
Site is in: Andorra / Austria / Belgium / Croatia / Czech Republic / Denmark / Finland / France / Germany / Greece / Hungary / Italy / Luxembourg / Netherlands / Norway / Poland / Portugal / Slovakia / Slovenia / Spain / Sweden / Switzerland							
Comments:							
Charge for outfit + 2 adults in local currency		High Season	Low Season	Elec inc in price?	Y / N	..............amps	
				Price of elec (if not inc)		..............amps	

Year of guide used	20..........	Page No.	....	Name of town/village site listed under			
Site Name					Date of visit	......./......./.......	
GPS	Latitude..(eg 12.34567) Longitude...(eg 1.23456 or -1.23456)						
Site is in: Andorra / Austria / Belgium / Croatia / Czech Republic / Denmark / Finland / France / Germany / Greece / Hungary / Italy / Luxembourg / Netherlands / Norway / Poland / Portugal / Slovakia / Slovenia / Spain / Sweden / Switzerland							
Comments:							
Charge for outfit + 2 adults in local currency		High Season	Low Season	Elec inc in price?	Y / N	..............amps	
				Price of elec (if not inc)		..............amps	

Your comments & opinions may be used in future editions of the guide, if you do not wish them to be used please tick ....

Name ....

Membership No. ....

Post Code ....

Are you a Caravanner / Motorhomer / Trailer-Tenter?

Do you need more blank Site Report forms?   YES / NO

Please return completed forms to:
The Editor – Overseas Touring Guides
East Grinstead House
East Grinstead
West Sussex
RH19 1FH

Please note that due to changes in the rules regarding freepost we are no longer able to provide a freepost address for the return of Site Report Forms. You can still supply your site reports free online by visiting camc.com/europereport. We apologise for any inconvenience this may cause.

You can also complete forms online: camc.com/europereport

Abbreviated Site Report Form

Use this abbreviated Site Report Form if you have visited a number of sites and there are no changes (or only small changes) to their entries in the guide. If reporting on a new site, or reporting several changes, please use the full version of the report form. **If advising prices,** these should be for an outfit, and 2 adults for one night's stay. **Please indicate high or low season prices and whether electricity is included.**

Remember, if you don't tell us about sites you have visited, they may eventually be deleted from the guide.

Year of guide used	20..........	Page No.	....	Name of town/village site listed under	
Site Name				Date of visit	......./......./.......
GPS	Latitude..............................(eg 12.34567) Longitude...........................(eg 1.23456 or -1.23456)				
Site is in: Andorra / Austria / Belgium / Croatia / Czech Republic / Denmark / Finland / France / Germany / Greece / Hungary / Italy / Luxembourg / Netherlands / Norway / Poland / Portugal / Slovakia / Slovenia / Spain / Sweden / Switzerland					
Comments:					
Charge for outfit + 2 adults in local currency	High Season	Low Season	Elec inc in price?	Y / N	............amps
			Price of elec (if not inc)		............amps

Year of guide used	20..........	Page No.	....	Name of town/village site listed under	
Site Name				Date of visit	......./......./.......
GPS	Latitude..............................(eg 12.34567) Longitude...........................(eg 1.23456 or -1.23456)				
Site is in: Andorra / Austria / Belgium / Croatia / Czech Republic / Denmark / Finland / France / Germany / Greece / Hungary / Italy / Luxembourg / Netherlands / Norway / Poland / Portugal / Slovakia / Slovenia / Spain / Sweden / Switzerland					
Comments:					
Charge for outfit + 2 adults in local currency	High Season	Low Season	Elec inc in price?	Y / N	............amps
			Price of elec (if not inc)		............amps

Year of guide used	20..........	Page No.	....	Name of town/village site listed under	
Site Name				Date of visit	......./......./.......
GPS	Latitude..............................(eg 12.34567) Longitude...........................(eg 1.23456 or -1.23456)				
Site is in: Andorra / Austria / Belgium / Croatia / Czech Republic / Denmark / Finland / France / Germany / Greece / Hungary / Italy / Luxembourg / Netherlands / Norway / Poland / Portugal / Slovakia / Slovenia / Spain / Sweden / Switzerland					
Comments:					
Charge for car, caravan & 2 adults in local currency	High Season	Low Season	Elec inc in price?	Y / N	............amps
			Price of elec (if not inc)		............amps

Please fill in your details and send to the address on the reverse of this form.
You can also complete forms online: camc.com/europereport

CUT ALONG DOTTED LINE

Abbreviated Site Report Form

Year of guide used	20.........	Page No.	....	Name of town/village site listed under			
Site Name					Date of visit		....../....../......
GPS	Latitude...(eg 12.34567) Longitude...(eg 1.23456 or -1.23456)						
Site is in: Andorra / Austria / Belgium / Croatia / Czech Republic / Denmark / Finland / France / Germany / Greece / Hungary / Italy / Luxembourg / Netherlands / Norway / Poland / Portugal / Slovakia / Slovenia / Spain / Sweden / Switzerland							
Comments:							
Charge for outfit + 2 adults in local currency		High Season	Low Season	Elec inc in price?		Y / N	............amps
				Price of elec (if not inc)			............amps

Year of guide used	20.........	Page No.	....	Name of town/village site listed under			
Site Name					Date of visit		....../....../......
GPS	Latitude...(eg 12.34567) Longitude...(eg 1.23456 or -1.23456)						
Site is in: Andorra / Austria / Belgium / Croatia / Czech Republic / Denmark / Finland / France / Germany / Greece / Hungary / Italy / Luxembourg / Netherlands / Norway / Poland / Portugal / Slovakia / Slovenia / Spain / Sweden / Switzerland							
Comments:							
Charge for outfit + 2 adults in local currency		High Season	Low Season	Elec inc in price?		Y / N	............amps
				Price of elec (if not inc)			............amps

Year of guide used	20.........	Page No.	....	Name of town/village site listed under			
Site Name					Date of visit		....../....../......
GPS	Latitude...(eg 12.34567) Longitude...(eg 1.23456 or -1.23456)						
Site is in: Andorra / Austria / Belgium / Croatia / Czech Republic / Denmark / Finland / France / Germany / Greece / Hungary / Italy / Luxembourg / Netherlands / Norway / Poland / Portugal / Slovakia / Slovenia / Spain / Sweden / Switzerland							
Comments:							
Charge for outfit + 2 adults in local currency		High Season	Low Season	Elec inc in price?		Y / N	............amps
				Price of elec (if not inc)			............amps

Your comments & opinions may be used in future editions of the guide, if you do not wish them to be used please tick ....

Name ....
Membership No. ....
Post Code ....

Are you a Caravanner / Motorhomer / Trailer-Tenter?
Do you need more blank Site Report forms?   YES / NO

Please return completed forms to:
The Editor – Overseas Touring Guides
East Grinstead House
East Grinstead
West Sussex
RH19 1FH
Please note that due to changes in the rules regarding freepost we are no longer able to provide a freepost address for the return of Site Report Forms. You can still supply your site reports free online by visiting camc.com/europereport. We apologise for any inconvenience this may cause.

You can also complete forms online: camc.com/europereport

Index

A

Abbreviated Site Report Forms	Back of guide
Abbreviations	11
Abbreviations (mountain passes & tunnels)	49
Accessing the Internet	63
Accidents and Emergencies	31 & 67
Acknowledgements	9
Alcohol	31
ANDORRA	432

B

Beaches (Safety)	74
Breakdown Service	32
Booking a Campsite	80
Booking your Ferry	26
British Consular Services Abroad	78
British & Irish Embassy Contacts	79

C

Camping Card Schemes	14
Campsite Entries (explanation)	6
Campsite Fees	7 & 84
Camping Key Europe	14
Campsite Safety	74
Caravan Spares	43
Caravan Storage Abroad	81
Car Spare Kits	43
Channel Tunnel	27
Club Sites Near Ports	28
Club Together	64
Complaints	85
Contact Details - Sites	Individual Site Entries
Converting Gradients	49
CORSICA	427
Country Information	86
Credit and Debit Cards	25
CRIS document	17
Currency	21 & 86
Customs Allowances	21
Customs Regulations	21
Cycling	88

D

Distance Chart	433
Documents	14
Driving in France	31
Driving Licence	14
Dynamic Currency Conversion	25

E

E10 Petrol	33
Electrical Connections	70
Electricity	70
Emergency Cash	25
Emergency Services	86
Essential Equipment	40
European Accident Statement	18
European Health Insurance Card (EHIC)	66
Explanation of a Campsite Entry	10

F

Facilities and Site Description	81
Ferry routes and Operators	29
Final Checks (motoring)	30
Finding a Campsite	82
Fire Extinguisher	40
First Aid	67
Food (Customs)	23
Foreign Currency Bank Accounts	24
FRANCE	86
Fuel	33

G

Gas	72
Gas on Ferries and Eurotunnel	27
General Advice (campsites)	85
Global SIM Cards	62

H

Hands-free	63
Hazard Warning Lights	41
Headlight flashing	41
Hired or Borrowed Vehicles	17
HMRC Advice Service	23
Hooking up to the Mains	71

I

ILE DE RE	428
ILE D'OLERON	430
Insurance:	18
– Car, Motorhome & Caravan	18
– Holiday	19 & 67
– Home	20
International direct dial calls	62
Internet access	63

L

Lakes (Safety)	74
Legal Costs Abroad	19
Lights	40
Liquified Petroleum Gas (LPG)	33
Local Currency	24
Low Emission Zones	33
Lyme disease	68

M

Medical Services	66
Medicines (Customs)	23
Mobile Internet	63
Mobile Phones	62
Money	24
Money Security	77
MOT Certificate	15
Motorhomes Towing Cars	33
Motorway Service Areas	33
Motorway Tolls	34
Motorways	33
Mountain Passes & Tunnels	48
Mountain Pass and Tunnel Maps	54
Mountain Pass Information	49
Municipal Campsites	82

Index

N
Nationality Plate 41
Naturist Campsites 82

O
On the Ferry 26
On the Road Safety 76
Opening Hours .... 83 & 86
Overnight Stops 82
Overseas Site Night Vouchers 81
Overseas Travel Service 80
Overtaking 34

P
Parking 34
Passport 15
Pedestrian Crossings 36
Personal Possessions (Customs) 23
Personal Security 77
Pets on Campsites 83
Pets on Ferries and Eurotunnel 27
Pet Travel Scheme 16
Phone Cards 62
Plants (Customs) 23
Preparing for your Journey 30
Prices 84
Priority 35
Public Holidays 86
Public Transport 35
Punctures 43

R
Radar Detectors 38
Radio and Television 64
Recently Qualified Drivers 37
Reflective Jackets/Waistcoats 41
Registering on Arrival 84
Returning Home (Medical Advice) 69
Reversed Polarity 72
Rivers (Safety) 74
Roads 36
Road Signs and Markings 36
Route Planning 42
Route Planning Maps 46

S
Safety and Security 74
Sanitary Facilities 81
Satellite Navigation/GPS .... 7 & 42
Satellite Television 65
Schengen agreement 16
Seat Belts 42
Shaver Sockets 72
Site Hooking up Adaptor 72
Site Location Maps 434
Site Opening Dates .... Individual Site Entries
Site Prices .... Individual Site Entries
Site Report Forms .... 8 & 445
Spare Wheel 43
Spares 43
Speed Limits 37
Sun Protection 68

T
Telephones and Calling 62
Television 64
Tick-Borne Encephalitis 68
Touring 87
Towbar 43
Traffic Jams 38
Traffic Lights 39
Travelling with Children 17
Travel Money Cards 24
Tyre Pressure 43
Tyres 43

V
Vehicle Tax 17
Vehicle Registration Certificate (V5C) 17
Vehicles left behind abroad 19
Violation of Traffic Regulations 39
Visas 17

W
Warning Triangles 44
Water 69
Weight Limits 30
Winter Driving 44
Winter Sports 78